SERGEY PROKOFIEV
DIARIES 1924–1933
PRODIGAL SON

In the field of music administration and management, Anthony Phillips worked with leading Soviet-era musicians, orchestras, opera and ballet ensembles, becoming General Manager of London's Royal Festival Hall concert hall complex, a position cut short by the dissolution of the halls' then owners, the GLC, in 1986. Since then he has worked as International Operations Director of an opera and ballet touring management company in the USA and Europe, continuing to develop, in the immediate post-Soviet environment, his relationships with Russian musicians and organisations. More recently he has concentrated on translations and annotations of memoirs and letters by Russian writers and composers, including *Story of a Friendship*: Shostakovich's letters to his friend Isaak Glikman (Faber, 2000), *Anton Chekhov: A Life in Letters* (with Rosamund Bartlett) (Penguin Classics, 2004), the *Diaries* of Sergey Prokofiev in three volumes (Faber, 2006, 2008, 2012) and *Svetik: A Family Portrait of Sviatoslav Richter* (Toccata Press, 2015).

Further praise for this volume:

'Should appeal well beyond Prokofiev's immediate fan base to readers intrigued by the siren song of Christian Science and / or a sympathetic outsider's take on the Diaghilev set.' David Gutman, *Gramophone*

'Unsurprisingly, there's a somewhat breathless air about these fascinating diaries. Prokofiev is constantly moving between rented houses, always on a train for the next concert date, bumping into famous people in restaurants . . . Editor Anthony Phillips has once again lavished endless care on the translation and the footnotes.' Ivan Hewett, *Daily Telegraph*

by the same author

SERGEY PROKOFIEV DIARIES 1907–1914
Prodigious Youth
Translated and Annotated by Anthony Phillips

SERGEY PROKOFIEV DIARIES 1915–1923
Behind the Mask
Translated and Annotated by Anthony Phillips

STORY OF A FRIENDSHIP
The Letters of Dmitry Shostakovich to Isaak Glikman
with a commentary by Isaak Glikman
Translated by Anthony Phillips

Sergey Prokofiev
Diaries

1924–1933
PRODIGAL SON

TRANSLATED AND ANNOTATED BY
Anthony Phillips

faber

First published in 2012
by Faber & Faber Limited
Bloomsbury House
74–77 Great Russell Street
London WC1B 3DA

This paperback edition first published in 2022

Typeset by Agnesi Text, Hadleigh
Printed and bound by CPI Group (UK) Ltd, Croydon, CR0 4YY

All rights reserved
© The Sergey Prokofiev Estate, 2002
This translation © Anthony Phillips, 2012

The right of Anthony Phillips to be identified as translator
of this work has been asserted in accordance with
Section 77 of the Copyright, Design and Patents Act 1988

*This book is sold subject to the condition that it shall not, by way of
trade or otherwise, be lent, resold, hired out or otherwise circulated
without the publisher's prior consent in any form of binding or cover
other than that in which it is published and without a similar condition
including this condition being imposed on the subsequent purchaser*

A CIP record for this book
is available from the British Library

ISBN 978-0-571-38090-9

Printed and bound in the UK on FSC paper in line with our continuing
commitment to ethical business practices, sustainability and the environment.
For further information see faber.co.uk/environmental-policy

2 4 6 8 10 9 7 5 3 1

To the memory of Noëlle Mann
11 July 1946 – 23 October 2010

Contents

List of Plates, ix

Introduction, xi

Acknowledgements, xix

A Note on Text, Transliteration, Dates, Forms of Address
and Other Conventions, xxi

THE DIARIES

1924, 1

1925, 119

1926, 241

1927, 401

1928, 683

1929, 761

1930, 895

1932, 989

1933, 1041

Appendix
Mark Twain's experience of Christian Science medical treatment, 1075

Bibliography, 1077

Index, 1085

Plates

1. Portrait of Sergey Prokofiev by Anna Ostroumova-Lebedeva, Paris 1927
   © The Serge Prokofiev Estate
2. Portrait of Lina Prokofiev by Anna Ostroumova-Lebedeva, Paris 1927
   © The Serge Prokofiev Estate
3. Maria Grigorievna Prokofiev with her son, daughter-in-law and grandson
   © The Serge Prokofiev Estate
4. Olga Nemysskaya Codina with her daughter Carolina
   © The Serge Prokofiev Estate
5. Juan Codina y Llubera with his grandsons Svyatoslav and Oleg Prokofiev
   © The Serge Prokofiev Estate
6. The Prokofiev and Koussevitzky families
   from left Lina Prokofiev, Svyatoslav (on her lap), unidentified, Serge Koussevitzky, Natalya Koussevitzky, Sergey Prokofiev © The Serge Prokofiev Estate
7. Svyatoslav Prokofiev in his 'tasi' being pushed by his father
   © The Serge Prokofiev Estate
8. Visitors to Culoz: *from left* Lina Prokofiev, Fyodor Stravinsky, Sergey Prokofiev, Svyatoslav Prokofiev, Igor Stravinsky
   © The Serge Prokofiev Estate
9. Château de la Flechère at Culoz
   Courtesy The Serge Prokofiev Estate
10. On the Beach at St Gilles, July 1924
    © The Serge Prokofiev Estate
11. The Ballot motor car: *from left* Vladimir Sofronitsky, Sergey Prokofiev, Vladimir Dukelsky, Lina Prokofiev
    © The Serge Prokofiev Estate
12. *from left* Serge Koussevitzky, Gabriel Paichadze, Igor Stravinsky, Sergey Prokofiev
    © The Serge Prokofiev Estate
13. In the Swiss Alps: *from left* Lina Prokofiev, Boris Asafyev, Pavel Lamm
    © The Serge Prokofiev Estate
14. The Walking Tour: *from left* the 'coffee boy', Serge Koussevitzky, Gabriel Paichadze, Sergey Prokofiev
    © The Serge Prokofiev Estate
15. Vladimir Dukelsky
    Courtesy The Serge Prokofiev Estate
16. Group Portrait of 'Les Six' with Jean Cocteau at the piano
    standing from left Darius Milhaud, Georges Auric, Arthur Honegger, Germaine Taillefer, Francis Poulenc, Louis Durey; *at the piano* Jean Cocteau
    Private Collection/Roger-Viollet, Paris/The Bridgeman Art Library
17. Portrait of Ida Rubinstein as Salome by Valentin Serov
    State Russian Museum, St Petersburg,/The Bridgeman Art Library

18 Georges Rouault
    © The Serge Prokofiev Estate
19 Serge Diaghilev and Igor Stravinsky
    RIA Novosti/Lebrecht Music & Arts
20 Lyubov Chernichova and Serge Lifar wielding hammers in *Le pas d'acier*
    photo Sasha/Getty Images
21 Portrait of Gyorgy Yakulov by Pyotr Konchalovsky
    Tretyakov Gallery, Moscow/The Bridgeman Art Library
22 Georges Rouault's backcloth for *The Prodigal Son*
    Courtesy The Serge Prokofiev Estate
23 Lina Prokofiev and Serge Lifar
    © The Serge Prokofiev Estate
24 *from left* Sergey Prokofiev, Igor Stravinsky, Ernest Ansermet, Pyotr Suvchinsky
    © The Serge Prokofiev Estate
25 Maria Yudina in Tbilisi, 1926
    Courtesy The David King Collection
26 Alexander Borovsky
    Courtesy The Serge Prokofiev Estate
27 Sergey Prokofiev playing the score of Lt Kijé in the Belgoskino Studios, Leningrad, 1934
    © The Serge Prokofiev Estate
28 *from left* Nikolay Golovanov, Antonina Nezhdanova, Sergey Prokofiev, Moscow 1927
    © The Serge Prokofiev Estate
29 Yekaterina Peshkova
30 Anatoly Lunacharsky and Natalya Rozenel
    Courtesy The David King Collection
31 Vladimir Mayakovsky
    www.v-mayakovsky.com
32 Olga Kameneva in her apartment in the Kremlin
    Courtesy The David King Collection
33 *from left* Vsevolod Meyerhold, Sergey Prokofiev, Sergey Radlov
    © The Serge Prokofiev Estate
34 Vladimir Dranishnikov, Sergey Prokofiev and Sergey Radlov with the cast of the Mariinsky Theatre production of *The Love for Three Oranges*, Leningrad 1927
    © The Serge Prokofiev Estate
35 Portrait of Sergey Prokofiev by Wasserman of Paris, 1933
    © The Serge Prokofiev Estate
36 Lina Prokofiev with the year-old Svyatoslav, Paris 1925
    © The Serge Prokofiev Estate
37 *from left* Boris Asafyev, Nikolay Myaskovsky, Sergey Prokofiev, Moscow 1927
38 Lina Prokofiev with her two children about to board the train to Moscow, Paris 1933
    Photo by Sergey Prokofiev © The Serge Prokofiev Estate
39 Sergey and Lina Prokofiev, Moscow 1933
    © The Serge Prokofiev Estate

Every effort has been made to contact the copyright holders of images reproduced in this book. The publishers would be pleased to rectify any omissions or errors brought to their notice at the earliest opportunity.

Introduction

> Our departure for Russia is fast approaching. Whatever triumphs are destined for me there, it is still a journey into an unknown kingdom, from which much terror and violence has recently emerged.
> Diary entry for 28 December 1926, Paris

Russia. Russian speech, Russian friends, Russian food, Russian winter, Russian spring, Russian music, the Russian land. In Paris in 1933, the last year in which he wrote anything in the diaries he had been keeping for the past twenty-six years, Prokofiev unburdens his soul to Serge Moreux, composer manqué, writer, critic, trusted friend and putative biographer of the composer:

> Foreign air does not suit my inspiration, because I am Russian, that is to say the least suited of men to be an exile, to live in a psychological climate that is not of my race. My compatriots and I carry our country about with us. Not all of it, to be sure, but a little bit, just enough for it to be mildly painful at first, then increasingly so until at last it breaks us down completely. You cannot understand, because you do not know my native soil, but look at my fellow countrymen who live abroad. They are drugged with the air of their country. Nothing can be done about it. They will never eliminate it from their systems.

Fifteen years earlier Prokofiev had left his homeland with the words of his Petrograd friend Boris Demchinsky ringing in his ears:

> You are running away from history, and history will not forgive you. When you return to Russia you will not be understood because you will not have suffered what Russia has suffered, and the language you speak will not be Russia's language.

Feelings of dislocation from the Motherland were, of course, the norm among the many hundreds of Prokofiev's compatriots, creative spirits who found themselves living in Paris during the 1920s and 1930s, the period of the third and last volume of his Diaries (1924–33). Many of them populate these pages: Stravinsky, Diaghilev, Koussevitzky, Rachmaninoff, Glazunov, Tcherepnin, Suvchinsky, Grechaninov, Borovsky, Balmont, Obukhov, Tsvetayeva,

Bunin, Yakovlev, Kuprin, Merezhkovsky, Gippius, Benois, Dukelsky, Larionov, Goncharova, Karsavin – a long list, and an illustrious one. Generally they lived and worked in a cultural and domestic Russian cocoon, and this was true of Prokofiev as well, except that Lina's non-Russian background and cast of mind made their home life less claustrophobically Russian than most. Nor did the posturing antics of the Monarchist wing of the émigré community hold any appeal. Nevertheless, in page after page his diaries reveal a preoccupation with Russia, the fate of friends and family left there, the social, professional and financial implications of becoming again a Russian composer rather than a European composer with an international reputation and a Russian hinterland. Thoughts of Russia are a constant counterpoint to the intense, omnipresent compulsion to compose music and to secure performances of it; the distant longing was skilfully played on by those in Moscow who saw his return to the Soviet fold as a tempting prize, whether as a pure propaganda coup or, as was the case in some instances, for more honourable personal or artistic reasons. Invitations to Embassy receptions, seductive offers of well-paid and long-term commissions, a comfortable home in Moscow, five-star education for the children, the all-important guarantee of foreign travel, all appeared on cue as bait. Eventually, after several lucrative visits, beginning with the triumphant homecoming of winter 1927 in which Prokofiev and Lina were given royal treatment, the jaws of the trap began to close. It was made clear that for the relationship to continue a deeper commitment was required than that of the regular distinguished visitor. He would have to give it all up or become a citizen of the Soviet Union.

Other influences were also in play. An important one, kept private from all except Lina (who was in fact attracted by it before her husband), his secretary Gyorgy Gorchakov (already an adherent, the main reason he got the job) and a handful of his most intimate friends, was his growing absorption in the American religious sect Christian Science. According to its teachings only the divine spirit is truly real while so-called material reality, including all manifestations of evil and suffering, is no more than an illusion to be confronted not with reason or material means but by prayer. Failings of the body and the 'unreal' material circumstances of life can be corrected by the power of the Christian Scientist's trained mind. The lure of such a faith for someone continually debating with himself the wisdom of a step into the unknown is understandable, likewise the nebulous coupling of belief in the ultimate perfectability of man with ceaseless Soviet and Comintern propaganda heralding an allegedly inexorable march towards the New Society.

Professional life in the West did indeed leave much to be desired, as its success tracked up and down according to the fluctuating commitment of sponsors. Of these Diaghilev the impresario and Koussevitzky the conductor and publisher were the most loyal, but still prone to what the often bewildered composer could not help seeing as lapses of judgement and affiliation. All in all, despite Prokofiev's celebrity the West never provided him with the secure platform he needed. The punishing schedule of the touring virtuoso offered a shaky financial flywheel, but increasingly he resented it as a distraction from the main calling. In the good times there was enough money to buy a car, but never a home.

All professional paths were strewn with obstacles. Diaghilev's restless pursuit of novelty drew the Ballets Russes away from Russian exoticism to the gentler sophistications of Les Six's cabaret-inspired ballets, leading to the temporary dumping of his 'second son'. His face was in any case firmly set against opera. Did the mighty figure of Stravinsky really secretly intrigue against his interests in the political quagmire of the Ballets Russes? Prokofiev certainly thought so, and confides his suspicions to his diary. As for Koussevitzky, his priority as a conductor both in Boston and in Paris was the presentation of an uninterrupted stream of novelties, an approach that militated against Prokofiev's œuvre gaining an unassailable place in the repertoire. A similar eclecticism also held sway over Koussevitzky's publishing house; Prokofiev's new scores were often slow to be printed and less vigorously promoted than he wished, so that important opportunities were lost. On the concert platform Rachmaninoff continued to hold in his enormous hands adoring managers and public on both sides of the Atlantic, his crowd-pleasing programmes not only pushing the puritanical Prokofiev firmly into second place (or even third once Stravinsky had practised industriously enough to perform his own works) among Russian composer-pianists but sometimes reducing him to a frenzy of disgust.

Opera was the cornerstone of Prokofiev's ambitions. True, *The Love for Three Oranges* was at last establishing itself in Europe and in the Soviet Union with productions in Cologne, Leningrad, Moscow and the Berlin Staatsoper, although a promised home-grown production at the Paris Opéra in 1932 was rejected by its Director using the unconvincing argument that the work was now *vieux jeu*. *The Gambler* and *The Fiery Angel*, however, both needed radical recasting and orchestration to be knocked into performable shape. Untold hours of effort led to disappointment and frustration, with only two performances of a 'painstaking' (the composer's own judgement) but generally uninspired production of *The Gambler* in Brussels in the spring of 1929. More upsetting still were the rejection of *Fiery Angel*, first by Bruno Walter for the Berlin Opera (on dubious grounds of late delivery of the orchestral material) and later by Prokofiev's old adversary Giulio Gatti-Casazza, the conservatively inclined General Director of the Metropolitan Opera in New York. Prokofiev needed all his hard-won Christian Scientist philosophical defences to come to terms with these final reverses, after justifiably high expectations, for the work on which he had spent a total of eight years:

> At first when I read [his Paris publisher] Paichadze's communication I was upset and even angry, but with the help of Christian Science soon calmed down and my anger dissipated. It is simply the case that *Fiery Angel*, laden as it is with devilry, is not smiled on by fortune .. I had had to summon up all my strength to drag it to the top of the mountain, and now Berlin has delivered the coup de grâce. But how much music has been squandered!

Disappointment over *The Gambler* and *Fiery Angel*, after the hard slog of completing and rewriting what had, particularly in the latter case, always been intrinsically intractable operatic material, was exacerbated by doubts about the moral value of both operas, misgivings the composer had earlier confided to his diary:

> The year it [Dostoyevsky's novella, on which *The Gambler* is based] was written coincided with the birth of Christian Science. To think that at the very moment when in America this great doctrine was in process of being created our Russian genius was lurching between a mad woman and the gaming table, and then dashed off at white heat his autobiographical novella about both of them! Whatever the case, *The Gambler* and *Fiery Angel* both belong to that period of my life from which I have moved away. My plan now is to bring both works to a state of completion and then to finish with this dark world.

Thus was crystallised a mental, emotional and spiritual process that had been going on since the disastrous first performance of the densely Modernist Second Symphony at a Koussevitzky concert on 6 June 1925. A month or so later, Prokofiev acknowledged the problems with the 'dark work' in a letter to Myaskovsky:

> When I finally finished the Symphony, I was intending to write to you about it but Kouskin [Koussevitzky] wanted to perform it immediately, so I thought I would wait to write until after I had heard it. However, when I did so I was myself unable to work out just what sort of creature I had spawned, and from embarrassment decided to keep my counsel until things had settled themselves in my mind. And this was not only my reaction; everyone who heard the Symphony greeted it with blank incomprehension. So complicated was it that if even I, listening to the performance, was not able to see through to the heart of it, how could others be expected to do so? Well, *Schluss* – it will be a long time before I embark on another thing of such intricacy and complexity.

It was time to take stock, to exploit and recast the wealth of material in the back catalogue (resulting in the Third and Fourth Symphonies; the *Divertimento*, Op. 43; a completely new version of the 1909 *Sinfonietta*; a

Suite from *The Gambler*). Things looked up when Diaghilev, tiring of the perfumed suavities being turned out by his stable of Paris composers, turned again to Prokofiev for a 'Bolshevik' ballet intended to exemplify a Parisian view of the feverish construction symbolising the new life of the Soviet Union. The machine-age music and settings of *The Steel Step* (*Le Pas d'acier*) and Massine's choreography excited Paris and London but raised hackles in Moscow when Prokofiev tried them out on radicalised proletarian members of the Bolshoy Theatre company. Next came the lovely, limpid *Prodigal Son*, the last ballet Prokofiev wrote for Diaghilev, indeed the last ballet created for the Ballets Russes before the impresario's death. In these new ballets, in instrumental and orchestral works such as the two 'philosophical' piano pieces *Things in Themselves*, Op. 45; the String Quartet commissioned by the Library of Congress in Washington, DC, and the left-hand Piano Concerto commissioned (but never performed during either his own or the composer's lifetime) by Paul Wittgenstein, Prokofiev pursued the more transparent textures and consonant harmonies he envisaged for his 'new simplicity'. It was an artistic path, but at the same time one directed at the task he imagined would confront a composer writing for a Soviet audience.

The twenty-six-year-long chronicle of Prokofiev's Diaries comes to an end at the beginning of June 1933, three years before the composer and his family finally moved from Paris to Moscow. But well before that it has already become noticeably more patchy, with longer gaps between entries and more frequent instances of rough notes, aides-memoires that the author left without amplifying them into a full record. The eighteen months between New Year's Eve 1930 and May 1932 are a blank, and another gap occurs later that summer after a short holiday in the Channel Islands. The diary takes up again only at the onset of the composer's postponed third USSR visit on 20 November. Thereafter only a few notes cover the week at home in Paris before leaving for a tour of America – which is itself similarly unreported. The final year of the diaries, 1933, is confined to the two months from 8 April until 6 June, which Prokofiev, later joined by Lina, spent in the USSR. The diaries have become primarily a record of experiences in Russia. No more *tours gastronomiques* in the Beloved Ballot motor car, bought with the proceeds of the first Russian visit and sadly written off two years later (after a succession of lesser but still for the passengers hair-raising mishaps) on the way back to Paris from a happy summer holiday in Culoz, in the Rhône-Alpes midway between the Massif Central and the Swiss border. No more accounts of walking tours in the Swiss Alps, or baiting those annoyingly intrusive upstarts in the Diaghilev entourage Boris Kokhno and Igor Markevich. No more sardonic dismissing of bêtes noires such as the frivolities of Poulenc's *Les Biches* (however agreeable he obviously found the French composer's company). Russia, her hopes and fears, has moved centre stage.

As he moved steadily closer to reincarnation as a favoured Soviet-based composer with an international reach – the ultimate deception that was to be visited on him and his family with frightening speed once the die was finally cast in 1936 – Prokofiev set out his stall to his new public in a series of public statements and newspaper articles. He laid stress on the misty socio-political impulses underlying his new aesthetic credo. He would strive for simplicity, for his music to be enjoyed and valued by a mass, musically untutored, audience while maintaining standards of originality and craft consistent with his own ambitions and the output of his peers. Now it might read like empty rhetoric, but it was not. When we consider Prokofiev's Soviet-era music today, and keep in mind the moral and spiritual elements of the mix the diaries tell us were just as important to him, we must conclude that time and time again he achieved the impossible goal with a sureness, inspiration and sheer musical genius far beyond the imaginings of the mean-minded, frightened politicians and functionaries who wielded executive power not merely over art, literature and music but over life and death in the Soviet Union of the 1930s, 1940s and early 1950s.

For all Prokofiev's idealistic notions of the place of art in the building of the new society and the contribution he sincerely believed he could make to it, for all he might have convinced himself he understood the nature of the new Russia when the arbitrary harshness of its regime brushed the lives of family, friends and colleagues, the truth is that he was always going to be a fish out of water – a cosseted, precociously gifted and fêted child of pre-Revolutionary Silver Age St Petersburg who had immediately left to spend the best part of the next two decades as a cosmopolitan Western European artistic celebrity, with a foreign wife. His background denied him the instincts of a native, which would have helped him live more easily in the arcane, shifting mores of Soviet society.

In May 1933 Prokofiev and Lina were on a concert tour of the Caucasus, comfortably aboard an International Company sleeping-car.

> We were still asleep when we passed through Kharkov. At Lozova and succeeding stations we were brought face to face with the famine in the Ukraine. People were asking for bread, and we saw pitiful, emaciated faces. But the restaurant-car in our train, with its supplies from Moscow, fed us well. The train had a 'Culture and Rest Carriage', similar to the observation-cars on American trains, with comfortable chairs and chessboards (I won two games), a platform at the rear and a cinema. The film that was showing, however, was rubbish, a piece of naive propaganda.

The image of the luxurious, well-supplied train travelling like an insulated projectile through the horrors of the famine, the result of the unimaginable brutality of forced collectivisation, dispossession and (for millions of farmers and their families) deportation, starvation and death, is a metaphor for the couple's neutralised reality. How could either of them have known in their bones the Russia of the Gulag, the paranoid hysteria of the show trials, the systematic starvation of the peasantry, the lying sloganising propaganda, the destruction of the pre-war military leadership, the persecution of the intelligentsia, the crass straitjacket of Socialist Realism, the vast landscape of human misery entailed in the forging of New Soviet Man? To contemplate, to read and hear partial, coded accounts from a distance was one thing, to have been living through it quite another. Hindsight allows us to see in the diaries the faint shadow of what was to come. Their author did not have that privilege. Demchinsky's warning was more prophetic than even he could have dreamed. And yet, the operas and ballets of the years following the ceasing of the diaries, the Fifth, Sixth and Seventh Symphonies, the later piano sonatas, the Symphony Concerto for cello, the two great film scores, yes and the patriotic cantatas – these are, whatever the terrible cost to the composer, our inheritance.

Ten years ago Svyatoslav Prokofiev and his son Serge junior, the composer's grandson, completed in Paris their great work of transcribing the composer's diaries from the original notebooks, and published their scrupulously precise Russian edition under the sprkfv imprint. I began work annotating and translating them into English in 2004; Faber and Faber published the first volume in 2006 and the second in 2008. It is difficult to convey in this short Introduction to the third and final volume the sense of excitement and revelation that has accompanied my now eight years of discovery. The diaries themselves, their graphic, free-wheeling, playful, serious, intensely personal chronicle of people, places, ideas and events both private and public, have been an endless source of pleasure and interest. But most thrilling of all has been the gradual peeling away of myths, prejudices and half-truths, which for almost half a century after the composer's death resisted the best efforts of even the most long-sighted biographers and commentators both in Russia and the West to expose the true face and heart of a remarkable man unwaveringly dedicated to the task of sharing his prodigious talent with the world. It has been a privilege.

ANTHONY PHILLIPS
London, February 2012

Acknowledgements

As before, I thank the people who severally and collectively, in Paris and London, are the Serge Prokofiev Foundation. Since the publication of the second volume of Prokofiev's Diaries in English we have lost two irreplaceable figures. Had it not been for the first, no word of Prokofiev's reflections on himself, his art and his world would ever have reached a single reader in any language. Had it not been for the second there would have been almost no freely available source material, certainly none accessible to Anglophone readers, to enlighten those countless lovers of Prokofiev's music, scholars and amateurs alike, who wish to know more about the man who created it. Svyatoslav Prokofiev was the man responsible for extracting from the State Archive of Literature and Art in Moscow, where they had been effectively entombed for over forty years since his father's death, the contents of the notebooks in which Prokofiev wrote his Diaries. The result of Svyatoslav's work, assisted by his son Serge Prokofiev Jr., meticulously transcribing and then publishing the Diaries constitutes the primary source material for my version. Svyatoslav's death on 7 December 2010, at the age of eighty-six, broke the last personal family link with the composer.

The following day, such can sometimes be the melancholy conjunctions of chronology, a memorial concert took place in London's Queen Elizabeth Hall for Noëlle Mann, who had died in the spring after a long fight with cancer. A native of France from the Midi-Pyrénées, Noëlle became in 1994 the first Curator of the Prokofiev Archive with a brief to create a working, accessible resource from the extensive cache of private papers deposited a decade earlier by Lina Prokofiev, the composer's first wife. Noëlle set herself the task not merely of curating the uniquely valuable collection and greatly expanding its scope, but of widening access to it. This she achieved not only *in situ* at Goldsmiths College but, supported by the Prokofiev Foundation, by establishing the biennial journal *Three Oranges* devoted to Prokofiev scholarship. Its twenty-two (at the last count) published editions have become in themselves an internationally recognised resource. Both the Archive and the Journal in their present form are Noëlle's creations, and she herself was a walking encyclopaedia of Prokofiev lore. I and many, many others drew exhaustively on all three. This final volume of the Diaries in English is dedicated to her memory.

The composer's grandson Serge Prokofiev, sprkfv jr. or Sergey *mladshy* depending on your linguistic affiliations, has continued to be an unfailing source of moral and practical support, not to mention the family insights to which he now almost alone is heir. Fiona McKnight, who took over the job of Archivist on Noëlle Mann's retirement in 2006, was exceptionally generous as well as enlightening in sharing her knowledge whenever (which was often) I appealed.

The last entry in Prokofiev's *Diaries* relates to 8 May 1933, the day on which the composer and his wife arrived home to Paris after another temporary stay in the Soviet Union. Another three years were to pass before the Prokofiev family as a whole made the final break with the West, moved to Moscow, became Soviet citizens, and the composer finally entered into the third distinct phase of his personal and creative life. The silence of the three-year hiatus presaged the transformation from a fiercely individual, candid chronicler of himself and his times into a private person subject to the scrutiny of the collective environment in which he now lived. It is not surprising that for the next six, pre-Glasnost, decades little information besides officially sanctioned and generally tendentious commentary emerged about Prokofiev. The opening of the archives brought about a sea-change, signalled in Prokofiev studies by Simon Morrison's 2008 account of Prokofiev's Soviet years *The People's Artist*. I should like to record my gratitude to Professor Morrison (now Chairman of the Serge Prokofiev Foundation) for his readiness to elucidate and share information often critically important for annotations to entries from Prokofiev's later years in the West, a period during which many Diary references make sense only if explained in the light of subsequent developments which have recently come to light.

As with the two previous volumes I repeatedly badgered my long-suffering wife Karine Georgian, and her cousin Irina Anastasieva of the Gnesin Russian Academy of Music in Moscow, with musical and linguistic queries. David King generously opened his pictorial archive of Soviet-era imagery. Belinda Matthews at Faber never wavered from her first encouragement of the project almost eight years ago. I cannot imagine a more supportive editor or counsellor, and the same is true of the whole Faber editorial and production team. Kirsty Petre was an invaluable accomplice in the long, ungrateful haul of preparing an index which, since Prokofiev did so much, had so many interests and knew so many people, is a long one.

A book like the present one cannot be done without advice and ideas from many more people than I have mentioned. They should know how grateful I am to them all. But since the point of it has always been to present to the interested reader a remarkable self-portrait of a remarkable creative genius, I should like to end these Acknowledgements with the most heartfelt one of all: to the honesty, intelligence, self-knowledge, passion for his art and expressive imagination of the man who wrote the Diaries of Sergey Prokofiev.

A. P.

A Note on Text, Transliteration, Dates, Forms of Address and Other Conventions

The manuscript of Prokofiev's *Diaries* is preserved in a series of handwritten notebooks now in the Russian State Archive of Literature and Art in Moscow (RGALI). They are not just handwritten but employ a vowel-less shorthand script of the author's own devising, paralleled by the shorthand he developed for the laborious process of writing out orchestral scores. The Herculean task of deciphering, transcribing and editing more than three quarters of a million words was carried out by the composer's son and grandson, and the text I have translated and annotated is that published by them under the sprkfv imprint.

Russian orthography can be transliterated into Latin script in a bewildering variety of ways. The surname Vasiliev can appear as Vasiliev, Wassilev, Vasil'ev or Wassiljew. My guiding principle in rendering the hundreds of Russian names and proper nouns that appear in the text has been to make them as easy on the eye and phonetically plausible as possible to the English-speaking reader, largely consistent with the system adopted by the *New Grove Dictionary of Music and Musicians* (Macmillan, London 1980) but with modifications aimed at making the results look less alarming than strict adherence sometimes makes them. Names of people and places already familiar to English readers have retained their commonly accepted forms when they depart from the system, hence Alexander, Tchaikovsky, Steinberg, Diaghilev, Koussevitzky. (Strictly, the composer's own name ought to be written Prokof'ev). Sergey Rachmaninoff specifically requested that his surname be written thus in English, rather than the 'correct' Rakhmaninov. In bibliographical references, however, I have adhered to the *Grove* system. Where I have included citations from other writers I have preserved their spellings.

In place of the standard Russian formal way of referring to a person – the first name followed by the patronymic (Alexander Konstantinovich), roughly corresponding to the English Mr, Mrs, Miss followed by the surname – I have generally resorted to the English custom of first name followed by surname (Alexander Glazunov) when the reference is to an individual appearing in the narrative, but I have maintained the Russian style when the author either directly addresses an interlocutor or enjoys a long-running or close personal relationship with the person concerned. Where it seems appropriate, but not invariably, I have followed the Russian custom of attaching feminine endings to women's surnames. I have also kept precisely as written the innumerable diminutives and affectionate nicknames to which Prokofiev, as Russians generally, was addicted.

The Soviet Union formally made the change from the Julian to the Gregorian calendar, thirteen days later, on 31 January 1918. The day after the change was therefore 14 February. Wherever confusion may arise I have noted whether the date in question is OS (Old Style, i.e. Russian Julian) or NS (New Style, Western Gregorian).

A. P.

1924

The second volume of Prokofiev's Diaries *concludes on 9 September 1923 with a routine scolding, for his pathological indolence, of Prokofiev's friend, partner in chess and tennis marathons, the Sunday poet Boris Bashkirov, who was still living with Prokofiev, his now ailing mother and Lina Codina in the rented Villa Christophorus in Ettal, Bavaria. Lina was also not well but this was mainly because she was pregnant, a circumstance that led on 29 September to a civil marriage arranged with the help of a friendly retired colonel who piloted the couple through the otherwise impenetrable complexities and delays of German officialdom. In Paris on 18 October 1923 Sergey Koussevitzky had put the indispensable services of his orchestra, his prestige, his wife's money and his eighteen-year-old leader Marcel Darrieux at Prokofiev's disposal to give the premiere of the First Violin Concerto in an elite concert at the Opéra. Paris must clearly henceforth be the centre of operations, but Prokofiev's mother's health would not survive the upheaval of moving to yet another rented house in a different country, so she remained in Bavaria in the care of Boris Bashkirov while the newlyweds found somewhere temporary to live in Sèvres, on the outskirts of the capital.*

1 January

Ptashka[1] and I saw in the New Year at Samoilenkos.[2] Borovsky and I drank to our *Bruderschaft*.[3] We all had a little too much to drink, and eventually Ptashka and Frou-frou[4] had to go and lie down. Went back to Sèvres in the car. Got up next morning with a sore head. In the afternoon I learnt the Fifth Sonata[5] by heart.

2 January

A letter from B.N.[6] Mama is very weak, and will not be able to travel. The money is running out. I am puzzled and upset. What is to be done?

Went into town with Ptashka. At Le Boeuf's[7] suggestion I checked with the Society of Authors and found a great muddle with many inaccuracies.

---

1   Prokofiev's nickname for his wife, Carolina (Lina) Codina. It means 'little bird'.
2   Boris Nikolayevich Samoilenko, a former White Army officer, and his Azerbaijani wife Fatma Hanum, were friends from New York who had now moved to Paris, where Fatma Hanum was establishing a business as a fashionable milliner. See *Diaries*, vol. 2 *passim*.
3   The Russian custom, symbolised by drinking a mutual toast, whereby friendship is officially sealed and the intimate second person singular is henceforth used instead of the normal polite second person plural, as in the French *tutoyer* or the German *dutzen*.
4   Nickname for Prokofiev's friend Maria Baranovskaya, née Sila-Nowicki, now the wife of the pianist Alexander Borovsky. See *Diaries*, vol. 2 *passim*.
5   Piano Sonata No. 5 in C, Op. 38 (1923). Prokofiev had started work on it in Ettal during the interlude of calm domesticity during the summer of 1923, but had been interrupted by the need to complete the revision of the Second Piano Concerto. The sonata was, however, finished by the end of the year.
6   Boris Nikolayevich Bashkirov, aka Verin, who had been one of Prokofiev's most intimate friends in St Petersburg, now lotus-eating in Europe and increasingly reliant on Prokofiev for board, lodging, emotional and practical support of all kinds. Having been a long-stay guest of the Prokofievs in Ettal, when the owners of the Villa Christophorus sold up forcing the ménage to find other accommodation in Oberammergau he had gone with them, but was now staying on to help look after Maria Grigorievna Prokofieva. See *Diaries*, vols. 1 and 2 *passim*.
7   Henry Le Boeuf (1874–1935), banker, philanthropist, critic (writing under the pen-name of Henry Lesbroussart), and guiding spirit of the Société des Concerts Populaires in Brussels, which he had more or less single-handedly reconstituted after the ravages of the First World War. His money underwrote the beautiful Victor Horta-designed concert hall of the Palais des Beaux-Arts and he was also responsible for the formation of the Société Philharmonique, appointing the conductor Frans Rühlmann to oversee an ambitious programme of new music by Bartók, Webern, Schoenberg, Stravinsky, Ravel, Roussel, Prokofiev (see *Diaries*, vol. 2 pp. 699, 700, 709, for the Belgian premiere of the *Scythian Suite*), etc.

Pointed them out. They promised to reimburse me. Dined with Stahls,[1] *bliny*[2] with caviar. One of Janacopoulos's students sang the whole of Op. 35,[3] the first time I had heard some of the songs.

In the Russian restaurant where we were having dinner we were shown to our table by Grunau,[4] whom I failed to recognise. Embarrassed that I had just tipped him, I was exaggeratedly friendly.

3 January

A quiet day, spent peacefully at Sèvres. Learnt the Fifth Sonata. I now know almost all of it by heart. Waited for a telephone call from Idka.[5] Read *Journey to Tibet*,[6] exceptionally interesting if rather slow.

4 January

A very quiet day. Again learnt the Fifth Sonata and waited for Idka to ring. Also spent a good deal of time on a letter to Myaskovsky[7] I started yesterday

---

1 Alexey Stahl, formerly Public Prosecutor of the Provisional Government of Russia, and his wife the Greek-Brazilian soprano Vera Janacopoulos. They had become close friends of the composer in New York and, like the Samoilenkos, had now moved to Paris. See *Diaries*, vol. 2 *passim*.
2 A kind of pancake.
3 *Five Songs Without Words*, Op. 35, composed for Nina Koshetz in 1920.
4 An acquaintance from Russia.
5 Ida Rubinstein (1885–1960), dancer, choreographer, ballet impresario and patroness, and a celebrated beauty, having modelled nude in 1910 for one of Valentin Serov's most striking paintings. She was bisexual and more than ready to remove all her clothes on stage, for instance as Salomé in the production of Oscar Wilde's play she commissioned from Fokine. Having absorbed some of Diaghilev's tricks from her time as a dancer in the Ballets Russes, she formed several ballet companies of her own, commissioning artists in all genres to create repertoire for her dancers and for her own idiosyncratic talents. Composers she commissioned included Ravel (*Boléro* and *La Valse*, Diaghilev having rejected the latter), Honegger (*Les Noces d'Amour et de Psyché* and orchestrations of Bach), and Debussy (*Le Martyre de Saint Sébastien*, to a libretto by D'Annunzio). This last provoked a splenetic outburst from the Catholic Archbishop of Paris, who found it intolerable that St Sebastian should be portrayed by a Jewish woman. During the First World War Ida Rubinstein had distinguished herself by not only remaining in Paris throughout, but putting her entire fortune at the disposal of those tending to wounded and mutilated servicemen, establishing a hospital for the purpose and herself tirelessly nursing in it. See Vicki Woolf, *Dancing in the Vortex: The Story of Ida Rubinstein*, Harwood Academic Publishers, Amsterdam, 2000.
6 *In Unknown Thibetan Lands: Diary of a Journey across Tibet* by Capt. Hamilton Bower of the Seventeenth Bengal Cavalry, Macmillan & Co., New York, 1894. 'Quietly and modestly written by an English officer who has pluck and endurance,' said the *New York Times*.
7 Nikolay Myaskovsky (1881–1950), prolific composer and from their first encounter at the St Petersburg Conservatoire in 1907 Prokofiev's closest and most enduring musical confidant. Throughout Prokofiev's years in the West he never ceased to seek out and promote whenever possible opportunities for Myaskovsky's music to become better known. See *Diaries*, vols. 1 and 2 *passim*.

evening, getting deeply absorbed in it. Naturally any letter is a responsibility, but it is important to drag Myaskovsky out of his plodding ways and his old-fashioned, ungainly patterns, otherwise no one will listen to him.

5 January

Another quiet day. I am longing to get on with composing something, to say nothing of the financial situation, which is why a telephone call from Idka would be more than welcome. I remembered that I had not yet made a fair copy of the cadenza of the Second Piano Concerto, and embarked on that task. Read Sabaneyev's pamphlet on Scriabin.[1] What a terrible, utter madman! But suppose he was right? Suppose his madness was real – but also that at the same time somewhere in the beyond of the other world, there also the battle was raging, and from the heat and dust of that battle an invisible arrow really did fly out to pierce him?! All the same, Scriabin is remote from me now, I am much closer to full-blooded Stravinsky, with his fabulous technical mastery. The eternal question: what is the true path for the artist – to penetrate ever deeper into his own mastery or ever wider into the expanse of the cosmos? Scriabin or Stravinsky? Both, united in one!

6 January

The fourth quiet day in a row, even slightly monotonous, since there is no really urgent work to do. I wrote out and polished the cadenza. A letter from B.N. from Oberammergau: Mama is now so weak there can be no question of bringing her here. This makes everything very complicated: it is difficult and expensive for me to go there, and all to no real purpose. Yet not to go, when one's own mother is near death, cannot be right. I torture myself thinking what is best to do.

---

[1] Leonid Sabaneyev (1881–1968), mathematician, scientist, composer, pianist, biographer (Taneyev and Scriabin) and critic, initially deeply hostile to modernism in the shape of Prokofiev and Stravinsky, whom he considered unfit to be considered composers alongside his idol Scriabin. Prokofiev had been overjoyed at the chance to damage Sabaneyev's reputation after the latter reviewed (unfavourably, naturally) a performance by Koussevitzky of the *Scythian Suite* in December 1916 that in fact never took place; obviously Sabaneyev had not attended the performance. Sabaneyev's monograph *Scriabin* was published in Moscow in 1916; *Reminiscences of Scriabin* was to follow in 1925. See *Diaries*, vol. 1, p. 234, and *passim*; vol. 2, pp. 172, 693, and below p. 306.

7 January

Was in Paris, my mood fairly glum. Wrote to Demasy[1] expressing scepticism about how much reality there is in the Rubinstein enterprise.

8 January

Demasy telephoned to say that Rubinstein would receive me on the 10th. At long last the matter will be decided one way or the other. If I had only myself to worry about, the financial situation would not have be causing me much concern, but now that I have people dependent on me at both the dawn and the sunset of their lives, this question weighs heavily on me. However this may be, I do have a few little ideas for the *Biblical Suite* up my sleeve.

I can now play the Fifth Sonata by heart.

9 January

Had a headache, so did very little. We visited Shakhovskaya;[2] in her generally poverty-stricken state she has preserved some interesting documents: the diary of the Tsarevich Alexey and some letters by the Tsar's daughters to her parents, mostly from the time of their imprisonment in Yekaterinburg and Tobolsk. There is no doubt of their authenticity; many of them are still in their envelopes with addresses and stamps. The actual content is quite thin, a string of inconsequentialities. This may be because their circumstances did not allow them to write anything important, so they had to make do with generalities.

10 January

Went to see Ida: long, beautiful arms bare to the shoulder, her voice filled with graceful, captivating tones, the face beginning to age and the make-up round her eyes four thick straight lines so that when she screws up her eyes the lines are all you can see. She was very polite, respectful even. I told her the sort of music I was planning to compose; she found it very inspiring. She will present the play, but not before December, so there is plenty of time. I let her understand that although I was free at the moment, I could not guarantee

---

1 Paul Demasy, pen-name of the Belgian playwright Léopold-Benoît-Joseph Paulus (1884–1974), known for his unorthodox treatments of subjects from biblical and classical sources: *Jésus de Nazareth, Panurge, Dalila, La Tragédie d'Alexandre*. His plays were in vogue in 1920s Paris.
2 Princess Dagmara Shakhovskaya (1893–1967), whom Prokofiev had met through the poet Konstantin Balmont. One of Balmont's numerous lovers, she bore him two children.

being so later. She promised to write within a few days, presumably with business terms and conditions. On the subject of Demasy she said that he possessed a quality of suffering only a Jew can know rather than a Frenchman; about Bakst[1] that he had long dreamt of 'Juditha' as a subject; about me, that I alone would be capable of composing sufficiently profound music. Conclusion – I must be the only Jewish composer!

11 January

Thus it seems that the financial side of things may fall into place. I should like to compose a nonet for wind instruments with double-bass, to join battle with Stravinsky and his Octet, but it would be a big piece and I would not manage to complete it in between working on something else. If only someone would commission it from me!

In the meantime I played through Rimsky-Korsakov's *Sheherazade* in order to condense it into a seven-minute piano roll for Duo-Art. Perhaps they will send me an advance in gratitude.

12 January

Got on with *Sheherazade*, also a voice-and-piano version of Renata's aria[2] which I had orchestrated in the summer.

Stahl rang up to summon us to Paris for dinner and entertained us to the most sumptuous meal at Prunier's.[3] His affairs are flourishing. The Diva[4] recently appeared together with Stravinsky in Antwerp. Stravinsky conducted and was beside himself with agitation. He has apparently finished his piano Concerto and is learning to play it, trying to make some money as a pianist.

---

1 Léon Bakst (Lev Rosenberg) (1866–1924), artist and theatre designer, founder along with Benois and Diaghilev of the *World of Art* (*Mir Isskustva*) group and the Ballets Russes that grew out of it. More than any other designer his voluptuous and exotic settings and costumes in productions such as *The Firebird*, *L'Après-midi d'un faune* and *Sheherazade* were the touchstone for the Ballets Russes' impact on all the senses. In 1919 Bakst, much taken with *The Love for Three Oranges*, had tried, unsuccessfully, to interest both Diaghilev and the Metropolitan Opera in mounting productions of the opera. See *Diaries*, vol. 1, p. 598; vol. 2, pp. 434, 452.
2 From *The Fiery Angel*.
3 Emile Prunier had recently opened in the avenue Victor Hugo what was to become one of the most famous fish restaurants in the world.
4 Vera Janacopoulos.

13 January

After yesterday's dinner and vintage Rhône wine we slept badly, in addition to which I developed a streaming cold. Lunched with Hambourg[1] and played through Pizzetti's violin sonata[2] with him. It has some clever things, but there is no such thing as an Italian capable of avoiding lapses into cloying sweetness.

Today is the Russian New Year, but we spent it peacefully at home.

Pressed on with *Sheherazade*: I have to pick bits out of it to make up seven or eight minutes and stitch them ingeniously together.

14 January

Almost all day in Paris. The Borovskys[3] have found a three-room apartment and are pressing us to move into it (on a shared basis) since Borovsky will be frequently away on tour and Maria Viktorovna will be on her own.

Oeberg[4] presented his accounts for sales of my works. Very interesting to see how much, what and where. I am due about two thousand francs. Very timely. Received from Myaskovsky his Seventh Symphony. It begins in F major and progresses to B major. This is already progress from his Fifth!

Borovsky's concert in the evening. The third of three excerpts from *Petrushka*, phenomenally 'orchestrated' for piano,[5] was despatched in a colossal blaze of brilliance. What a huge leap forward from the fireworks of

---

1   Jan (Ivan) Hambourg (1882–1947), Russian-born violinist originally from Voronezh, studied in Europe with Otakar Ševčik and Eugène Ysaÿe. Brother of the cellist Boris and (the most famous member of the family) the pianist Mark, he was a member of the Hambourg Trio but also spent much time in Canada teaching in the Conservatory founded in Toronto by his father, Michael.

2   Ildebrando Pizzetti (1880–1968), Italian composer. The second of his two violin sonatas, in A major, was published in 1920 and was a favourite of the young Yehudi Menuhin.

3   Alexander Borovsky (1889–1968), pianist, and his wife Maria Viktorovna Baranovskaya (nicknamed Frou-frou by Prokofiev). Prokofiev and Borovsky had been friends since student days at the St Petersburg Conservatoire, and Prokofiev admired Borovsky as musician and pianist. Baranovskaya, independently a close friend, had at one time proposed marriage to Prokofiev. See *Diaries*, vol. 1 *passim*; vol. 2, pp. 664–5, 682–3, and *passim*.

4   Ernest Oeberg (d. 1925), Estonian-born managing director of Koussevitzky's publishing firms Russian Musical Editions and Editions Gutheil. He had taken over this responsibility on the sudden death in an accident of the original managing director, Nikolay Struve, in 1920.

5   Stravinsky openly admitted that in attempting to capture Arthur Rubinstein's interest in the piano solo version of *Petrushka* he made for him in 1921 he had made it as pianistically challenging as possible. The three dances are not transcriptions, the composer declared, and the intention was not to reproduce the sound of the orchestra but to exploit new possibilities of keyboard technique without losing musical values. The writing therefore calls for wrists like steel springs and includes enormous leaps, complex polyrhythms, dizzyingly fast scales, glissandos and tremolos.

old man Liszt! It seems there is nothing more the piano can do. But the form is unsatisfactory: the temperature cools at the end and the final glissando is coarse. I liked the first movement of Ravel's *Sonatine*.

Zederbaum[1] informed me that he had succeeded in interesting Rouché[2] in *Three Oranges*. (Rouché: 'I should like to present a Russian opera, for instance *Tsar Saltan*.'[3] Zederbaum: 'One of Rimsky-Korsakov's worst operas; you would do better to stage something more lively such as Prokofiev's *Three Oranges*. You would be able to get the scenery from America, where it is no longer needed.') Rouché expressed interest and wished me to play it to him. This is all very unexpected, although I take leave to doubt that the antediluvian Opéra will find it easy to swing into *Three Oranges*!

15 January

Carried on transcribing Renata's aria. Stahl came to visit, and we walked in beautiful weather to St Cloud. An elderly Canadian we met showed us a version of patience for two players called Russian Bank, and I remembered that I used to play it when I was six years old. I could even remember the way in which the packs of cards were laid out.

Shakhovskaya came to see us. Balmont[4] is very worried about Mirka,[5] who is in love and wants to get married. Balmont is the sole recipient of her confidences, to unburden herself of which she closets herself with him in the bathroom. Mirka is terrible trash, and although only sixteen I am sure is not a virgin, since before her present hero she had already encountered – as she put it – a 'fateful man'.

---

1   Vladimir Zederbaum, originally a doctor by training, had started working for Koussevitzky as his secretary and personal assistant in his publishing business, but had had a falling-out with Mme Koussevitzky, the domineering and extremely wealthy Natalya Konstantinovna. Zederbaum was now acting in a promotional and public relations role for Koussevitzky's various activities in Europe, thus by extension the composers published by Russian Musical Editions.
2   Jacques Rouché (1862–1957), director and major financial backer (married to the heiress of the Piver perfume empire) of the Paris Grand Opéra and Opéra-Comique from 1915 until the end of the German Occupation during the Second World War, a perhaps unfairly compromised end to a career that subsequently brought about his retirement from public life. Rouché was also an influential publisher, owning and editing *La Grande Revue*.
3   *The Tale of Tsar Saltan*, opera (1900) by Rimsky-Korsakov.
4   Konstantin Balmont (1867–1942), Russian Symbolist poet and translator. Prokofiev had been inspired by his poetry as early as 1910, and continued to set poems and translations, including the ancient Akkadian incantation *Seven, They Are Seven* in 1917. Their friendship had deepened in the Caucasus in 1917, where both artists had removed themselves from the turmoil of war and revolution, and still more in the summer of 1921 when they were holidaying near one another on the Atlantic coast of France near the mouth of the Loire. See *Diaries*, vol. 2 *passim*.
5   Balmont's daughter, Mirra. See *Diaries*, vol. 2, p. 219.

16 January

Thought about Scriabin's Second Sonata,[1] which Borovsky played yesterday. The first movement with its inadequate, démodé emotionalism is no good at all. The finale is conceptually interesting though: sharp, stabbing thrusts in the bass against a relentlessly rushing (if unpleasantly Chopinesque) right hand, out of which emerges a lovely theme, highly individual in its air of renunciation and abandon.[2]

17 January

In our new abode (which we like very much), we slept in late. Pleyel[3] sent a piano. I have no desire to leave the apartment to go anywhere. Ptashka talked to Frou-frou about her condition (eight months), which seemingly no one except Stahl has noticed until now. In the evening I corrected the proofs of the Third Piano Concerto and set out patience.

18 January

Went to a rehearsal of a new symphonic orchestral society, Cora,[4] where I met the conductor, Wolff,[5] whom as a matter of fact I had met before in New

---

1 Sonata No. 2 in G sharp minor (*Sonata-Fantasy*), 1897.
2 'Abandon' is written in English.
3 The firm of Pleyel et Cie was established in Paris as early as 1907 and its pianos rose to fame as the favoured instrument of Chopin. By the end of the nineteenth century Pleyel had (later than most manufacturers) reluctantly abandoned the straight stringing and direct, single-escapement action that had so pleased Chopin and was competing with the other major French, German and English makers. Like their rivals, Pleyel had a policy of signing up important performers who would use and endorse the instruments in return for having them provided for practice, performance and sometimes promotion. By the early 1920s Pleyel, as well as being a manufacturer, was one of the main concert managements of Paris with, among other assets, its own concert hall, and Prokofiev had agreed to be represented by the firm on this basis.
4 The Orchestre des Concerts Straram, founded in 1923 by Walther Straram (1876–1933), born in London as Walther Marrast, who made an anagram of his surname for professional use. His policy was to concentrate on contemporary scores, in contrast to the senior established formations in Paris. With money provided by Ganna Walska (see *Diaries*, vol. 2, pp. 582, 679), he was in a position to hire excellent musicians, and conductors when he himself was not on the podium.
5 Albert Wolff (1884–1970), composer and conductor who had served for a short while as head of French repertoire at the Metropolitan Opera in New York but was now Music Director of the Paris Opéra-Comique. In 1919 Prokofiev had played excerpts from *The Love for Three Oranges* and *The Fiery Angel* to a panel headed by the Met's intimidating General Director Giulio Gatti-Casazza (1869–1940) and including Wolff. The only listener brave enough to say a good word for what they were hearing, he was described by Gatti-Casazza as 'an anarchist'. See *Diaries*, vol. 2, pp. 402, 464, 492–3.

York when I played my opera to Gatti-Casazza. I sparked his interest in Myaskovsky's symphonies and will tomorrow show them to him. Practised the First Piano Concerto, and it went smoothly.

The 'ménage en trois'[1] is proceeding very pleasantly, except that the two 'barishny',[2] as I call Ptashka and Frou-frou, never stop complaining about their problems expecting the next generation.

19 January

Played Myaskovsky's Fifth Symphony[3] to Wolff, cunningly omitting most of the tedious second movement and leaving out the finale altogether. The Symphony found favour with the Frenchman,[4] because having been composed during the war (when the composer was actually serving at the front) it was based on Galician themes. Wolff will perform it on the 28th March. I was as pleased as if it had been my own work.

20 January

Left at noon for the concert in London, without much enthusiasm since the London critics delight in persecuting me and although I have now appeared there four times with orchestra, no other city in England pays any attention. The crossing was easy and the sea calm, and there was no trouble with passports.[5] I arrived in London precisely four hours before the start of a strike on the railways. How am I going to get back, I wonder? On Tcherepnin's[6] recommendation I stayed at the Craven Hotel but it proved to be a poor place and

---

1   *Sic*, written in French.
2   A *barishnya* was a well-brought-up genteel young lady from the landowning class before the Revolution.
3   Symphony No. 5 in D major, Op. 18. See *Diaries*, vol. 2, p. 267.
4   Wolff was actually Dutch although he never lived in the Netherlands and was a French citizen.
5   Prokofiev never renounced his Soviet citizenship, and for the nineteen years he spent in the West travelled with international identity papers for stateless refugees provided by the League of Nations. After 1922 these were formalised as Nansen passports; although they were honoured by most governments, one could never be sure that crossing international borders with a Nansen passport would be trouble-free.
6   Nikolay Tcherepnin (1873–1929), composer and conductor. After a rocky start as Prokofiev's conducting professor at the St Petersburg Conservatoire, Tcherepnin had become a friend and one of Prokofiev's most stalwart supporters. Following a post-Revolution spell as Director of the Conservatoire in Tbilisi, Georgia, Tcherepnin had made his way to Paris, where he was chiefly engaged in endeavouring (unsuccessfully) to rekindle Diaghilev's interest in him from the early years of the Ballets Russes as composer and conductor. See *Diaries*, vols. 1 and 2 *passim*.

not at all cheap. Spent the evening with the Tseitlins,[1] who had come into London on the same train as I. Their view of Merezhkovsky and Gippius[2] was that they are completely unmusical. So much for Myaskovsky's 'Zinka'![3]

21 January

Rehearsal at 10.30 with Goossens,[4] who accompanied very well given that he had never heard the Concerto before, and we fitted together admirably. The Concerto was my No. 1, a shame that it was not the Second, but it will take all my time to learn that for Koussevitzky in the spring.

Went to Victoria Station to find out about trains. Despite the strike the station was not completely dead; some trains are running and I was told that my train would be leaving tomorrow. I then dropped in to the London branch of the Aeolian Company, and it was a good time to do so as they had just received instructions from New York to agree a new recording contract with me, not for five years but for five seasons, i.e. for my next five visits to New York. This time it was proposed that I make three rolls a season, not five as before. Obviously my stock is not high enough in America to maintain the previous level, and since I can derive no benefit from the new agreement while I am in Europe, I requested that negotiations be postponed until my next visit to New York. In the meantime, however, I took advantage of the meeting to inform them that I had transcribed *Sheherazade* (even though I have not finished it) and to ask for an advance payment based on the still unexploited final year of the previous agreement. Mead, the director in London, said that there would probably not be a problem with the advance,

---

1   Tseitlin was a rich amateur poet friend of Balmont in Paris; he and his wife among other things helped arrange benefit concerts for the impoverished writer. Prokofiev variously spells the name Tsetlin or Tseitlin. See *Diaries*, vol. 2, pp. 610–11. There seems to be no connection with Lev Tseitlin, the violinist and leader of the Persimfans Orchestra in Moscow who was later to be an important contact for Prokofiev on his first return to Soviet Russia in 1927.
2   Dmitry Merezhkovsky (1865–1941), Symbolist writer and religious philosopher; Zinaida Gippius (or Hippius – there is no letter 'H' in the Russian alphabet) (1869–1945), married to Merezhkovsky despite her unconcealed lesbian inclinations. She was the central figure in an influential St Petersburg coterie of Silver Age writers dedicated to overturning conventions; one of her poems, 'The Grey Dress', was set by Prokofiev in his Op. 23 collection of 1915. The couple emigrated to Paris after the Revolution, becoming passionate and outspoken opponents of the Bolshevik regime and even (Merezhkovsky especially) flirting intellectually with Fascism.
3   Slighting reference to Myaskovsky's predilection for Gippius's poetry. Before the Revolution he made several settings of her verse: *On the Border*, 18 songs, Op. 4; *Derived from Z. Gippius*, 3 Pieces for voice and piano, Op. 5; *Premonitions*, 6 Sketches for voice and piano to texts by Z. Gippius, Op. 16.
4   Eugene Goossens (1893–1962, knighted 1955), composer and conductor, the third generation of musicians to bear the name Eugene Goossens. In 1921 he had conducted the British premiere of *The Rite of Spring* at the Queen's Hall in the presence of the composer.

but he would have to put in a preliminary request to New York. This is splendid: an extra six thousand francs into the budget![1]

The concert was at eight o'clock. As I went on stage and sat down at the piano, a button jumped off the waistcoat of my tails and dropped on to my knee. Goossens pulled a face at me, cheering me up no end. I played the Concerto pretty well, only smudging a few notes at the beginning. It was a good success, as on the previous occasion, but less so than in Geneva. I was called out four times. Nobody came to see me in the Green Room, and nobody paid me any money.

22 January

Got up early and hurried off to claim my cheque and exchange it for cash. Bought a new hat at Locks.[2] Because of the strike it was not known whether my train would be going or not. But the Continental train did run, and by two o'clock I was already in France, glad to be away from expensive, strike-bound and indifferent (to me) London. Sitting in the train, I pondered the fate and future of opera. Diaghilev and Stravinsky fulminate that we have had enough of declamation in opera and it is time to revert to the old forms of numbers, arias and ensembles. I am absolutely clear that this is as wrong as can be. The way to compose an opera is to make sure that, in contrast to legitimate theatre, the music always enhances the effect on the audience. The libretto must be created in such a way as to eliminate any need for routinely functional music, hence Musorgsky's *The Marriage*[3] is not on the right lines. It does not matter whether the chosen style consists of arias or some form of *recitativo* speech; what matters is that arias or ensembles are called for by the action on stage and not for any other reason, and that the dialogue needs music to make its full effect. Because of my failure always to take clear account of this principle I have missed many such opportunities in the operas I have composed so far, but I believe that I have now straightened the matter out in my mind and henceforward will act accordingly. In *The Gambler* and in *The Fiery Angel* I was too dependent on the text. From now on I shall be guided exclusively by the idea of the subject and will develop it with much greater freedom, in accordance with the principles I enunciate today.

I was home by seven o'clock in the evening and found both *barishny* in good form, except for head colds.

---

1   In February 1919 Prokofiev had signed a five-year agreement with the Duo-Art mechanical reproducing piano company to record five piano rolls a year. See *Diaries*, vol 2, pp. 339–689 *passim*.
2   Lock & Co. has been building and selling hats in St James's, London, since 1676.
3   Opera (1868) by Musorgsky based on Gogol's eponymous play. Musorgsky completed only the first act, but a completed version by Mikhail Ippolit-Ivanov was published in 1934.

23 January

Played the piano, practising the cadenza of the Second Concerto and the Fifth Sonata. Had an appointment with Manukhin,[1] who found further improvements in my heart condition. He prescribed more of the phosphorous medication phytin[2] and glycerophosphate, because the main defect of my organism is a lack of phosphorus. I am definitely feeling better and lately have been able to sleep on my left side, also my heart pounds less violently when I am actively engaged in music-making.

We spent the evening sitting at the dining-room table writing letters and laying out patience.

24 January

Practised the cadenza. Went to the Russian Consulate for a passport for Ptashka, because the only one she still has is her Spanish one in her maiden name. There were all sorts of complications, but the Consul has a daughter at the Conservatoire, and on learning that I was 'that' Prokofiev, promised to arrange matters.

In the evening Frou-frou told us stories of the Provisional Government and Kerensky, who had married a cousin of hers. She said it was very wrong of him to allow his romantic adventures to interfere with the government of the country.

25 January

Oeberg told me that the Neighbourhood Playhouse, a small New York theatre of 400 seats, wanted to put on *Chout*[3] in March, making their own version for a reduced orchestra. I wrote to Diaghilev asking for permission, since he owns *Chout* for two and a half more years. It is hardly a prestigious

---

1. Dr Ivan Manukhin, specialist immuno-biologist in Paris, who had treated Prokofiev's mother for a suspected malignant tumour in 1922. See *Diaries*, vol. 2, p. 673.
2. Phytic acid is found in almost grains and plant fibres in the form of insoluble calcium and magnesium salts (known as phytins), which are believed to store organic phosphorus in plants. The outstanding feature of phytic acid is its powerful chelating function. Phytic acid has an important function in the body as the inhibitor of the production of hydroxyl radicals and as an antioxidant, acting to combat cancer. It is also thought to reduce blood clots, cholesterol and triglycerides, which circulate through the bloodstream and thus help prevent heart disease.
3. Ballet by Prokofiev to a libretto by the composer based on Afanasiev's *Russian Folk Tales*, first produced by Diaghilev's Ballets Russes in Paris in 1921 to choreography by Mikhail Larionov and Tadeusz Sławinsky with designs by Larionov.

proposal and no doubt will be a feeble production, but it could generate a few hundred dollars and thus put bread on the table.

I had been counting on receiving some money from the Society of Authors, but all they have come up with is 52 francs. This was because the period covered was the summer, during which there were few performances.

The evening was spent at Koussevitzky's. I had a joyous meeting with Balmont, who read his new story 'Peter the Peasant'. Very consistent as far as the language is concerned, but I had the impression it was not so successful in terms of the form. Balmont repeated that he would like to publish a little book of translations of Heredia sonnets by himself, myself and B.N.[1]

Worked in the morning. Went in the afternoon to Boulogne, to the clinic run by Plekhanov's widow,[2] to find out whether it would be possible to install Mama there when she makes the journey from Germany. Mme Plekhanova knew of me through my concerts and tried in every way to be nice to me, but it still costs forty francs a day.

The Tcherepnins called later in the afternoon. I played *Three Oranges* and the Fifth Piano Sonata for them.

28 January

They told me in the German Consulate that there is a new direct train connection Paris–Munich, which is very good news as it will greatly simplify my journey to Oberammergau.

A fight with Ptashka, mainly on account of my having to go to Riga at the end of February for concert engagements, immediately after she is expecting her *délivrance*. Her mother has been held up coming from America and she is nervous about being alone. On the other hand, it would be very difficult for me to let this concert series go, as money is very tight and I have a mountain of expenses to meet.

---

1   In April 1922, in Ettal, Prokofiev and Bashkirov had devised a competition in which they would each translate into Russian from the original French a series of formally strict sonnets by the Cuban-born poet José Maria Heredia y Giraud, the results to be judged by Balmont and another well-known poet (Igor Severyanin), the respective authorship not being revealed to the judges. The contest was abandoned halfway through, with a clear advantage to Prokofiev. See *Diaries*, vol. 2, p. 674.
2   Rosalia Plekhanova-Bograd (1856–1949) had trained as a doctor in St Petersburg before she married the Marxist philosopher and theoretician Gyorgy Plekhanov in 1878, joining him in exile in Switzerland two years later as a result of increasing persecution from the Tsarist authorities. Plekhanov and his wife returned to Russia immediately after the Revolution of February 1917 but left again soon after the October Revolution because of Plekhanov's profound disagreement with Lenin. After his death the following year in Finland his widow moved to France, where she worked tirelessly to perpetuate his memory and his ideas, eventually in 1928 donating his archive to the Russian National Library where it now forms the basis of a separate institution known as Plekhanov House in St Petersburg.

29 January

Took Myaskovsky's Seventh Symphony to show to Koussevitzky. He seems to regard the work benignly, will look at it and may perform it in the spring.

A tender reconciliation with Ptashka.

In the evening, carrying only a small suitcase, I went by Métro to the railway station for the 11.35 train. The Munich carriage was there as promised, but people have not found out about it yet so there were not many passengers and I slept wonderfully right through the night.

30 January

In the morning, Strasbourg and the border where I changed to third class, which is more expensive in Germany than second class in France. After travelling all day we arrived at Munich in the evening. The Germans spent the whole time cursing the French carriage, which was certainly very dirty. Nevertheless they were all trying to get into it rather than the German carriage, since ours had upholstered seats while the German carriage had only wooden ones.

31 January

Got up early and went to the French Consulate to see about a visa for B.N. and Mama. Saw a typewriter in a shop window attached to a zither: each letter key produces a sound. Intriguing!

At half past twelve Boris Nikolayevich met me at Oberammergau station. Dr Lang said: 'If you are able to get a through carriage, take your mother with you. She is a little stronger now, but I doubt whether she is ever going to make much of a recovery.' Mama was indeed sitting in a chair, but she looked terrible: her face yellowed and shrunken, and on top of that her eye was inflamed and very red. She was overjoyed by the idea of coming to Paris. But, my God, how are we going to manage with someone in so weak a condition?

In Dr Lang's flat, where I installed myself, I have a very nice, but cold, room. B.N. has taught everyone here to play chess. I undertook (for the first time in my life) a simultaneous match against seven opponents, and won all seven games.

B.N. has sold the incubator[1] for five times what we paid for it. That is of course excellent, but what is the point now when so much money has been spent!

---

1 'In the third week of June [1923] a new toy arrived in Ettal: an electric incubator for chicken eggs attached to a hen coop.' (D. Nice, *Prokofiev, From Russia to the West 1891–1935*, Yale University Press, Newhaven and London, 2003.) 'Sergey was like a little boy: he would go on to the balcony at night to see whether anything was happening. Finally the eggs hatched but the chicks were sickly, miserable things. One egg refused to hatch for the longest time, and in the end a little duckling emerged. Eventually we gave all the chicks and the duckling away.' (Lina Prokofiev, interview with Harvey Sachs, quoted by D. Nice, op. cit.)

1 February

In Oberammergau the sun is shining and there is snow, which makes it all generally very lovely, although I am not paying much attention to the beauty of the scenery since I am wholly concentrated on the forthcoming departure. I made some sort of order out of my old correspondence from several years back, of which there is an enormous pile, enough to fill an entire trunk.

The problem of how to transport Mama greatly exercises me and B.N. Will we be able to manage it? And are we – that is to say I – doing the right thing in even trying? However this may be, she is delighted.

I went into Garmisch in order to obtain a police permit to leave the country. I was afraid there might be difficulties (the police always create difficulties in all countries!) but all went smoothly: they relieved me of sixty francs and issued me with the permit.

Generally I find it very hard to understand what is going on in Germany: compared with France living is terribly expensive, yet the Germans themselves seem to have plenty of money, but yet again as a country they do not seem able to pay reparations.

The train timetable is idiotic: I finished my business with the police at half past eleven, but the earliest I could get home, a distance of ten kilometres, would be seven o'clock in the evening. To kill time I wrote some philosophical reflections on 'Why I do not believe in the church', an exercise I enjoyed very much. On my return to Oberammergau I read it over to B.N., who commented, 'That's what I think too.' He approved my work with a few cavils at my manner of expressing some of the propositions, which I can easily leave out.

3 February

Sledged over to Ettal and spent three hours disembowelling my trunk, which I had left with the Mayor. This trunk is so heavy it is out of the question to drag it back to France, so I took out just the things I needed, and the scores. Loaded everything up on the sledge and, very tired, hauled it back to Oberammergau. B.N., who had woken up, came to meet me at the top of the staircase and offered to help. The idea of coming over to Ettal to help me had not, of course, occurred to him. I was angry and sent him off with a flea in his ear.

4 February

Today is the day we had planned to leave, but Mama has taken a turn for the worse, her legs have swollen and her pulse is very weak. She very much wants to leave, but is scarcely able to raise herself from the pillow, bursting into tears at the suggestion that she might have to stay here. In the evening I had a long discussion with B.N. about how to proceed. I stood firm that despite everything we should go, but B.N. said it was unthinkable in her present state – she could die en route. It was decided that I should go back alone (I could not stay longer because of the concerts and because of Linette's[1] condition) while he would stay and, if Mama's condition improved, bring her in two weeks' time.

A letter from Linette, in which she says that the doctor will soon let her know if it will be a boy or girl.[2] An absorbing thought! Hurry up, birth!

5 February

Practised the Second Piano Concerto. Went in to see Mama. She is very depressed at having to stay longer in Oberammergau. She is a little better today, but still keeping to her bed. How could she possibly travel with so weak a pulse and with legs still swollen?!

6 February

Mama is worse again, extremely weak and having difficulty speaking, barely able to raise herself from the pillow. It does not look as though it will ever be possible to get her to Paris. However, the pulse is no worse and the swelling in the legs is going down. Lang considers her condition grave but not immediately dangerous.

I have been thinking of leaving tomorrow, because I do not want to leave Linette on her own in her present state. It is hard to know what to do. I cannot divide myself in two.

7 February

This morning Mama called me and B.N. in to her and said she was dying. Indeed she looked very bad, the voice feeble, and yet through the awful weakness there was a gleam of arrogance. Lang said there was no doubt she had significantly deteriorated, and the weakness was now throughout the body. If she were able to fight it she might be able to hold on, but if not, then the end could not be far off. I explained the situation with Linette. He advised waiting another two days – by then it would be clear in which direction things were heading. I therefore sent a telegram to Ptashka saying that I would have to stay longer, and asking how she was.

1 'Linette' is how Prokofiev referred to Lina at the start of their relationship, until the adoption of the private, somewhat teasing pet name of 'Ptashka'.
2 In English.

8 February

Mama is worse, semi-conscious from the weakness. I asked her if she was feeling bad, and she replied, 'No, I am all right, only I overslept.' This made me cry out in anguish. She said she could smell a pleasant aroma of smoke. The doctor said it was a matter of a couple of days. B.N. and I went to consult the Catholic priest, since it was clear we had to make plans for the funeral. In the event he told us he was not authorised, and advised us to send for a Russian priest from Munich. Lang says death in such circumstances would be better than the alternative threat of dying from dropsy.

9 February

Mama is better. This morning she washed herself, lost her temper with the nurse and tried to slap her face. She is still very weak, however. The doctor's verdict: 'Die russische Dame kann ich nicht verstehen!'[1] He recommended that I go back to my wife, because Mama's present state could last a week, or even two. This evening I decided I would go. I went in to say goodbye to Mama, telling her that I was going to Paris for a few days to give a concert. There was little if any reaction. Boris Nikolayevich was charged with summoning me by telegram if any immediate danger should develop. By eleven o'clock in the evening I was in Munich, where I stayed the night.

10 February

Got up at half past six and continued my journey at eight. Railway travel has become appallingly expensive in Germany, twice as much as in France. I travelled in third and fourth class, but slept so badly that today I virtually bankrupted myself moving up to second class. It was not too long a journey; I read a book in English about Chinese legends, a present from Leona Spitzer.[2] I was worried that at the border they would rifle through the mass of scores and papers I had brought, but the only thing they took was a pack of cards. At seven o'clock in the evening Strasbourg, after which I lay down to sleep until we arrived in Paris.

11 February

Got up at five, and at ten to six the train was already in Paris. Everything was fine at home, and Ptashka was feeling better than I had expected. It was a

---

1 'This Russian woman is beyond my comprehension!'
2 Unidentified.

very joyful meeting. Borovsky had left the previous evening, only a few hours before my arrival. It's really unacceptable: first there is one husband, then the other, but never the two of them. In my absence he had been learning the March from *Three Oranges*, and now even the cook was singing it.

12 February

Life is back on its uneventful tracks. The only concern is not knowing what it holds in store in Oberammergau. Oeberg confirms that Stokowski[1] has put in a request for the *Scythian Suite*[2] in America.

Practised the Second Piano Concerto and started making a transcription for a second piano part. Put together a shortened libretto of *Three Oranges* which Ptashka translated into English: Mme Koussevitzky will be in London in March and wants to have it to do some promotion for *Oranges* there. Borovsky telephoned in the evening from Bordeaux. He played Prokofiev and Stravinsky there, but there was so much guffawing and noise from the audience that he hardly managed to get to the end.

13 February

I have purchased a portable Underwood typewriter – I am in thrall to it because I have in any case such a soft spot for machinery. It cost 52 dollars, but as B.N. sold my old one for forty-three I have spent only nine. I hear there exist such things as stenographic machines. In time I shall have to buy one.

14 February

Went with Ptashka to her doctor, Bouffe de Saint-Blaise, a very well-known specialist.[3] He found everything to be well, delivery anticipated between 22nd February and 5th March, with an 80 per cent probability of a boy, 40 per cent of a girl.

---

1   Leopold Stokowski (1882–1977), conductor, Music Director of the Philadelphia Orchestra until 1936, in tandem with Eugene Ormandy for the next four years, absent altogether for twenty years but making a triumphant comeback in the 1960s. He had originally invited Prokofiev to conduct the *Scythian Suite* himself. See *Diaries*, vol. 2, pp. 337–8, 343, 363, 367.
2   Four-movement *Scythian Suite*, Op. 20 (1915), using material from the discarded ballet *Ala and Lolli*. See *Diaries*, vol. 2, pp. 73–4, 103–4, 641–3, and *passim*.
3   Dr Gabriel Bouffe de Saint-Blaise was indeed a very well-known gynaecologist and obstetrician. His study *Les Auto-Intoxications de la grossesse*, published in Paris in 1899, was a standard work on some of the unexpected effects experienced by women during pregnancy, including, apparently, a strong tendency to kleptomania.

15 February

Stahl paid a visit. The Diva is in New York and he is missing her, so stayed with us from five o'clock in the evening until one o'clock in the morning. We played three-hand patience – very festive.

16 February

I attended a meeting of the Russian colony, where there were talks by Bunin (dry and academic; I really do not like him),[1] Merezhkovsky (more interesting, but he has such a reedy voice and trouble with his 'r's), Kartashov,[2] and some others. They all inveighed against the Bolsheviks, wept for trampled-upon Russia and in the name of Christ called for hatred. I heard them with interest, while trying not to take sides myself. I have been told that Pythagoras (or perhaps it was Archimedes), when his city was being taken by storm, sat by himself in his garden drawing theorems in the sand. Thus engaged, he was killed. A man truly in love with his learning!

17 February

Stahl is anxious that I should write some songs for the Diva with string quartet accompaniment. It is something he has been talking about for a long time. Today I composed a little along these lines, and even had a ferocious altercation with Maria Viktorovna when she came into the room to go through accounts with the cook.

---

1 Ivan Bunin (1870–1953), novelist, poet and short-story writer, one of the leading literary figures in emigration having left Russia in 1920 and settled in Paris where he remained an unwavering and outspoken scourge of Bolshevism. See *Diaries*, vol. 2, p. 533.
2 Anton Kartashov (1875–1960), theologian and historian of the Russian Orthodox Church. As Ober-prokuror (Chief Procurator) of the Holy Synod – the Church's supreme governing body – during the Provisional Government in which he also served as a minister, he had presided over the Synod's decision on 4 November 1917 to liquidate itself and devolve its responsibilities to the All-Russian Council of Churches ('Pomestny Sobor'). Kartashov emigrated in 1919 and came, via Finland, to Paris, where he served on many committees of ROCOR, the Russian Orthodox Church Outside of Russia, which by unilateral separation from the Moscow Patriarchate after the Bolshevik Revolution existed as a separate entity. This lasted until May 2007, at which time the eighty-year schism was officially brought to an end by the Act of Canonical Communion with Moscow. The reconciliation continues to be contentious among ROCOR's 400 parishes and approximately 400,000 members worldwide.

A letter from Demchinsky[1] critical of the *Fiery Angel* libretto for its turgidness, and promising to send some suggested alterations. These could be of the greatest interest.

Balmont came in the evening and read some poems, but not very persuasively.

18 February

This morning Ptashka was frightened by the suspicion that her waters were breaking. I telephoned her obstetrician, who said that she should go to the clinic. Just in case, I also telephoned a very famous Russian obstetrician, Proskuryakov, who delayed making an appearance until the evening and when he did, said that the birth process was under way. I then telephoned the clinic, who immediately sent an ambulance in which Ptashka and I went there together. I left her in reasonably good spirits.[2]

19 February

Was at the clinic to see Ptashka three times today, but there were no developments. It seems we may have come too early. Her friend Consuelo lay there in the same state for three days and then went home again. But Ptashka's doctor Bouffe de Saint-Blaise advises that she should not even get out of bed much.

Played the piano for a while, but on the whole have not occupied myself much with music these two days.

20 February

No change with Ptashka. Went twice to see her.

In the afternoon I made changes to the first-movement cadenza of the Second Piano Concerto, because of a clumsy link to the orchestral entry for the end of the movement. Oeberg, whom I went to see in order to discuss dates for my forthcoming recital, told me that next season he is planning to

---

1 Boris Demchinsky (1877–1942), philologist and writer. As early as 1908 Prokofiev had met and been greatly impressed by Demchinsky's powerful intellect, wide cultural horizons and literary skills. He had contributed significantly to the libretto of *The Gambler*. Remaining in St Petersburg after the Revolution, Demchinsky clearly suffered from the barbarity of the new regime, and was destined eventually to die wretchedly in the famine of the German blockade of Leningrad. See *Diaries*, vols. 1 and 2 *passim*.
2 In English.

support an opera company, and in that connection is interested in my operas. *Fiery Angel*? With this in mind I wrote to Demchinsky, urging him to get on with the changes to the libretto. How splendid, except I have to go to New York to cut the rolls!

21 February

An advance of $400 from Duo-Art, nothing to do with the new contract but for the final year of the old one. The money will restore the financial situation to something like balance.

Ptashka has moved to a new room, but apart from that there is no change. Much the same applies to Mama, according to Bashkirov's letter.

Dinner at Prunières',[1] who is always very nice to me. I played the Fifth Sonata. He liked it very much, as did Schloezer[2] and Le Boeuf. It went down much better than it had had when I played it to Borovsky and Koussevitzky, but I was now playing it pretty well whereas then I was no more than scratching the surface. The man in charge of the Amsterdam concert organisation where Mengelberg[3] conducts was very offended when I told him that when I played Mengelberg my compositions in America, he had not understood them at all.

22 February

No change with Ptashka. Checked the *Oranges* translation with her. Evening at Tseitlins', where there were also Milyukov,[4] Bunin, Merezhkovsky,

---

1 Henry (sic) Prunières (1886–1942), philosopher, musicologist, avid proponent of all aspects of contemporary art, founder (1920) and editor of the *Revue Musicale*. See *Diaries*, vol. 2, pp. 591–2.
2 Boris de Schloezer (originally Schloetser) (1881–1969), philosopher, music critic of the *Nouvelle Revue Française* and the *Revue Musicale*, expert on (and brother-in-law of) Scriabin. See *Diaries*, vol. 2, p. 530.
3 Willem Mengelberg (1871–1851), Musical Director of the Concertgebouw Orchestra in Amsterdam continuously from 1985 until 1945, interspersed with resident appointments with other international orchestra. See *Diaries*, vol. 1, pp. 295, 572, and vol. 2, p. 622.
4 Pavel Milyukov (1859–1943), historian and politician. Founder of the Russian Constitutional Democratic Party ('Kadets' from the acronym KD), Milyukov was Foreign Minister in the First Provisional Government following the February 1917 Revolution, and as such was the author of 'Milyukov's Note' to the Allied Governments guaranteeing Russia's continuing participation in the First World War. A close connection and ally of Prokofiev's friend, the journalist Iosif Gessen, who emigrated to Berlin where he published the influential émigré newspaper *Rul'*, Milyukov came to Paris after the Civil War, where he founded and edited the sister newspaper *Poslednye Novosti* (*Latest News*).

Kuprin,[1] Shmelyov,[2] Remizov,[3] Larionov[4] and others. The most fantastic figures were Shmelyov and Remizov, the latter having recently moved from Berlin to Paris. I asked him how he was liking Paris. He replied that he found the sound of the street traders crying their wares in the early morning very beautiful. Kuprin was gentle and rather drunk, Bunin dry and disagreeable. Merezhkovsky and I spoke of Knossos and Cretan culture, about which he is writing a novel.[5] Later on Stahl said: 'Tomorrow your son will be born, we must drink to his health', and dragged me to a night-club in Montmartre. We drank champagne and it was four o'clock before I tore myself away to go home.

1 Alexander Kuprin (1870–1938), short-story writer. Hailed by Tolstoy as the true successor to Chekhov, he wrote almost nothing during his long post-Revolutionary exile in Paris. He returned to Soviet Russia in 1937, the year after Prokofiev, but died a year later. See *Diaries*, vol. 2, pp. 533–4.
2 Ivan Shmelyov (1873–1950), novelist, short-story writer and (before the Revolution) publisher, who in 1912 established the Moscow Writers' Publishing House, which published among other leading writers Bunin. An enthusiastic supporter of both the 1905 and the February 1917 Revolutions, Shmelyov nevertheless rejected the Bolshevik regime and went south to the White-held Crimea of General Wrangel, whose overriding belief in the spiritual and social values of the old Russian intelligentsia he shared. When in 1920 Wrangel accepted defeat and went into exile, Shmelyov and his son Sergey, an officer in Wrangel's army, declined to follow him, Sergey having faith in the amnesty offered to serving members of the White Army. This did not protect him from being arrested and shot without trial by Bela Kun's Revolutionary Committee, after which an appalled and despairing Shmelyov yielded to Bunin's persuasion to follow him into exile. In the early years of the twentieth century Shmelyov was one of Russia's most prominent writers, but in emigration his lyrical, traditionalist style was seen as old-fashioned and out of touch. For all that, *Solntse myortvykh* (*The Sun of the Dead*), written in 1923, is a fine, moving and deeply personal account of the fate of the intelligentsia marooned in the Crimea awaiting their inevitable fate.
3 Alexey Remizov (1877–1957), Modernist writer with a taste for the exotic, the fantastic and the bizarre, notably in the context of the more luridly Gothic imaginings of Russian folk tales and peasant culture. An associate of Nikolay Roerich at Princess Maria Tenisheva's Talashkino estate, which had seen the genesis of Stravinsky's *Rite of Spring*, Remizov's demonically inspired fantasies became a cult among the émigré community in Paris. Prokofiev had seriously contemplated writing first a ballet and later an opera based on Remizov's pagan fable of the spirit world, *Alaley and Leila*, but had been dissuaded by the negative reaction of Demchinsky, Suvchinsky and Asafyev, with whom he had discussed the project. See *Diaries*, vol. 2, pp. 144–5, 185, 197, 648.
4 Mikhail Larionov (1881–1964) and his wife Natalya Goncharova (1881–1962) were prime movers in the pre-Revolutionary avant-garde of painting and sculpture, and were also members of the *Blaue Reiter* group in Munich. There they inaugurated the abstract school known as Rayonism, incorporating into their work elements of Cubism, Fauvism and Futurism. Husband and wife both designed settings for Diaghilev's Ballets Russes, Larionov also taking responsibility, with mixed success, for the choreography of the Ballets Russes production in Paris and London of Prokofiev's *Chout* in 1921. See *Diaries*, vol. 2 *passim*.
5 *The Birth of the Gods: Tutankhamen in Crete* (1925). To describe this as a novel is stretching the idea of the genre rather far. It is a discursive, amorphous and highly personal collection of researches into ancient history, Hellenic, Egyptian and Judaic. 'Many people think I am a historical novelist, which is a misguided view. What I do in the Past is only search for the Future. The Present is a kind of exile to me. My true home is the Past/Future, which is where I belong.' (Article in *Zveno* (*The Link*), 16 March 1925.)

23 February

Slept from half past four until half past eight, upon which I dashed to the hospital thinking that Stahl's prediction might have come true. But no, all was as it had been. Ptashka had been moved to a third room, enormous, sunny and quiet. Twice, at five o'clock and eleven o'clock at night, I went to the station to meet Ptashka's mother, but she did not come.

After yesterday's debauch I desperately wanted to sleep.

24 February

Maria Viktorovna had Slavina[1] to lunch, our celebrity prima donna from the Mariinsky Theatre. When the production of *The Gambler* was being planned she considered the part of Babulenka, and was going to sing it, but when it came to the point was not particularly impressed. Her attitude now, however, is quite the reverse: she was full of praise for my music. Ptashka's mother arrived at six o'clock, and naturally her first question was: how is Linette? I took her to the hotel where a room had been reserved for her, and then on to Ptashka. It was quite a meeting.

25 February

Olga Vladislavovna[2] is very anxious and determined not to be any trouble to anyone, nor to spend so much as a copeck of anyone else's money. She spends all the time at the hospital with Ptashka, whose condition is still unchanged.

M.V.[3] is off to Madrid to join Borovsky, and is running about after visas and passports.

I am practising the Second Piano Concerto. Schloezer came to listen once more and to praise the Fifth Sonata. He was in ecstasy over the Second Concerto, deeming it better than the Third.

26 February

Went in the evening to Ptashka, intending just to spend a few minutes with her. It looked as though things were coming to a head. However, the pains were not very severe and in between we played cards. I remained all evening,

---

1 Maria Slavina (1858–1951), dramatic soprano, in every respect an operatic *grande dame* (in private life Baroness Medem) the first interpreter of Carmen in Russia. See *Diaries*, vol. 2, p. 143.
2 Olga Vladislavovna Codina, née Nemysskaya (?–1947), Lina Prokofieva's mother. She had come over from America for her daughter's confinement.
3 Maria Viktorovna Borovskaya, formerly Baranovskaya, the third member of the 'ménage à trois'.

and at midnight Ptashka asked me to stay longer. I lay on the couch and dozed. Ptashka was groaning, but several times in between the pains went to sleep. At one o'clock the pains increased in severity. The nurse came in every hour, and at three o'clock sent me off to sleep in an unoccupied room.

27 February

At the entrance to the hospital I ran into Olga Vladislavovna. The doctor had already been in, chased her away and told her to come back in half an hour. We wandered about the neighbouring streets, O.V. extremely agitated and I trying to keep her spirits up. Then while O.V. remained outside on the street I went into the hospital and approached the door of Ptashka's room, but it was closed and all inside was quiet. Suddenly the sister appeared and announced that it was all over, everything had gone well, my son had been born and I could go in. The doctor, putting on his coat, congratulated me.

Ptashka was lying there, terribly flat, with no belly. She was still half asleep, but smiled when I came up to her. The baby was in a cradle, purple and hideous. The sister hurried out into the street to summon O.V. The birth, which had taken place at 8.45 a.m., had been exceptionally straightforward.

My feeling for the child is one of warmth, if only he doesn't cry too much. Ptashka very much wanted a son. I had no strong feelings either way. We decided to adopt my suggestion of calling him Svyatoslav. I would have liked Askold,[1] but probably no priest would baptise him with that name.

28 February

Ptashka is feeling well, lying in bed not stirring. Svyatoslav looks a little more presentable and has lost his purple tint. Generally he resembles me more than he does Ptashka.

I have been turning over in my mind a new form of 'musical drama', which could develop from the genre of recitation accompanied by music. This recitation must be delivered rhythmically and could be notated by means of *kryuks*,[2] so that it can be accurately co-ordinated with the music. In

---

1 No doubt inspired by the ghostly presence in *Askold's Tomb*, the opera by Alexey Verstovsky first staged in Moscow in 1835 and thus pre-dating Glinka's *A Life for the Tsar*, which is usually considered the first Russian opera. The opera was a great favourite of Chaliapin, and centres around mysterious events at the Tomb of Askold, still to be seen in Kiev. Verstovky's opera is based on the novel by M. N. Zagoskin dealing with the legend of Askold. As related in the monk Nestor's *Primary Chronicle of Kievan Rus'*, Askold was one of two heirs to Rurik murdered by Oleg of Novgorod in ninth-century Kiev so as to secure the throne and take power over the empire of Rus.

2 The *kryuk* (literally 'hook') was the form of musical notation used in Russian hymnody from the twelfth century. It derived and was adapted from the neum of Early Byzantine intonational chant used for the reading of sacred texts. When transplanted to Russia, neum/*kryuk* notation

fact the co-ordination would not have to be absolutely precise, so long as the strong accents of the bar were in time (otherwise the speech could become over-constrained). Additionally it would be possible to indicate the raising and lowering of the vocal intonation without in any sense relating it to pitch, by writing it on three lines. In this way all the drama would be firmly bound to the music. The main difficulty would be the unattractive combination of the human speaking voice against a background of music, but here, I believe, techniques of orchestration could be learnt much as orchestrating piano Concertos is a technique that has to be learnt. In a piano Concerto it is all too easy to give rise to disagreeable combinations of sonorities. I must give this idea more thought and try to bring it to fruition.

29 February

The day that comes only once every four years. Svyatoslav's birthday should really have been today.

A letter from Riga, from which it is clear the concerts will not take place. This is regrettable from the financial point of view, but inertia was making me reluctant to travel there in any case. As a result of crossing out Riga, I settled on 9th March for my Paris recital. M.V. has departed for Madrid at the 'invitation' of Borovsky, who is giving concerts all over Spain.

1 March

Did some work, wrote some letters, typed out the abridged libretto of *Oranges* translated by Ptashka, went in to see Ptashka, visited the Russian Consulate to get my new passport. Spent the evening with Stahl, the Diva's sister and her husband Volkovyssky. Adrienna wants to do my bust.

2 March

Fell out with Ptashka over the need to redo the English translation of *Oranges*, to the accompaniment of Svyatoslav bellowing like one possessed.

3 March

Ptashka and I worked together on the *Three Oranges* translation.

---

acquired some of the characteristics of the Russian land and the Russian character, replacing the angular agitation of Early Byzantine chant with the spacious serenity of Russian hymnody as exemplified by its most famous manifestation, Znamenny chant.

This time Svyatoslav did not cry. He stops while he is being fed, and won't let go of the breast until you squash his nose right into it. Then he cannot breathe, and so has to let go. Delightful!

4 March

In the afternoon practised for the concert. In the evening was at Merezhkovsky's and made the acquaintance of Gippius. It was the first time I had been there, but Andrey Bely[1] in his reminiscences of Blok[2] has described their domestic life so well that I felt as though I was entering an already familiar household. I liked Gippius very much indeed, in spite of her obnoxious Petersburg habit of drawling her vowels. I engaged her in conversation about Mayakovsky[3] in an attempt to establish whether, politics aside, she recognised any talent in him, but she refused categorically to do so. Merezhkovsky showed me his new novel drawn from the life of ancient Crete, and there was talk of the possibility of my writing an opera based on the novel. Both [Gippius and Merezhkovsky] acknowledged that they knew nothing about music, but Gippius was aware that I had written a song to her poem 'The Grey Dress'.[4]

5 March

Gippius presented me with a book of her verse written over the past ten years. Those from before the war are good (very good!) but the ones during the war and the time of the Bolsheviks are worse. But oh dear, 'The Grey Dress'! I have everywhere the *greyish* dress, because that was how

1 Andrey Bely (pen-name of Boris Bugayev) (1880–1934), one of the main theoretical and spiritual progenitors of Russian Symbolism as an aesthetic movement. Inspired by the mystical-poetical philosophy of Vladimir Solovyov, Bely categorised his first published work, the prose poem *Second Symphony: Dramatic,* as a 'poetic Symphony'. The idea is that Joycean techniques of rhythm and structure derived from music symbolically amalgamate mathematics, philosophy, music, aesthetics and mysticism into a universal principle of Sofia, the Divine Feminine.
2 *Reminiscences of Blok* (*Vospominaniya o Bloke*), 1923. Blok and Bely had had a stormy up-and-down relationship not helped by Bely's love affair with Blok's wife Lyubov Mendeleyeva. At one point challenges were even issued to a duel.
3 Vladimir Mayakovsky (1893–1930), the poetic face of Bolshevism and Agitprop, came first to public attention in 1912 with his poems in the Futurist publication *A Slap in the Face of Public Taste.* His status was confirmed with *A Cloud in Trousers* (1915) and Vsevolod Meyerhold's production, seminal for the direction Soviet theatre was to take, of *Misteria-Bouffe* in 1918. Prokofiev had met him first at his (Prokofiev's) recital in Moscow in February 1917, and had fallen under the spell (evoking a parallel response from the poet) of the ferocious power of his demotic language and imagery. This was not the first time Prokofiev had carried the torch for Mayakovsky in unpromising contexts: he had done the same with Stravinsky and Diaghilev in Berlin in 1922. See *Diaries,* vol. 2, pp. 141, 171, 195, 262, 697–81, and *passim.*
4 *Five Poems for Voice and Piano,* Op. 23 No. 2. Gippius's poem was written in 1913.

Derzhanovsky gave me the text, whereas it should be just *grey*. But nothing can be done about it now, there is no way it can be changed.¹

Today I again felt something amiss with my heart.

In the evening I was with Fatma Hanum² and did not manage to get to Balmont's reading, which I had planned to attend.

6 March

All this time O.V. has been frantically looking for a flat, as in view of her imminent child M.V. is delicately, or rather not too delicately, intent on chucking us out. Today, via a Russian broker to whom I had to pay 800(!) francs – although he swears that he has to pay the concierge 500 of these – I found one. The apartment has four small rooms, all of them with a sunny aspect, with a scrap of a view of the Seine. The furniture is nothing special, but it will do.³

7 March

Called on Mme Koussevitzky, who is on her own and suffering from a cold. The maestro has gone to London. Natalya Konstantinovna loves playing patience, as I do. We had a good talk. Incidentally, Lourié⁴ has been chased

---

1 The title of Gippius's poem, and of Prokofiev's setting, is 'Seroe plat'itse' ('The little grey dress'). But Derzhanovsky, when giving Prokofiev the actual text of the lyric, had mistakenly written '*seren'koe* plat'itse', which is not only one of those diminutives of which Russians are so fond and are practically impossible to render in another language, but can also carry an even stronger overtone of drabness then the plain adjective. 'Devochka v serom plat'itse' ('The girl in the grey dress') is a kind of refrain in the poem, repeated five times. The redundant extra syllable, of course, has been reflected in the musical setting, hence Prokofiev's unhappiness at not being able to put the mistake right. See p. 413, n. 3, for information about Derzhanovsky.
2 Boris Samoilenko's wife.
3 No. 5, rue Charles Dickens, in Passy.
4 Arthur-Vincent (Artur Sergeyevich) Lourié (1892–1966), progressive Futurist composer and sometime head of the music division of Lunacharsky's Commissariat of Popular Enlightenment ('Narkompros'). In 1921 he defected, rather than emigrated, while on an official visit to Berlin, and came to Paris where he became intimate with Stravinsky's circle, acquiring, however, a dubious reputation as an intellectual opportunist and eventually falling out with the Stravinskys. By this time he had already lost for ever the good opinion of Prokofiev because of his failure, while he was a figure of authority in post-Revolutionary Petrograd, to do anything about his promise to take care of the papers and possessions left in the Prokofievs' abandoned apartment. 'That restless musician whose biography is almost more interesting than his compositions. An exquisite aesthete, a highly cultivated and extremely clever man, he possesses that quality of "moral anarchism" which in Russia so often overtakes even men of standing. We see this petty Cagliostro swept by the Revolutionary tempests into high places: Lourié, musical kommissar of the new Russian Republic, reducing to order and organising its cultural life [. . .] always with the same bored air of a man who knows everything in the world and therefore finds nothing interesting.' (L. Sabaneyev, 'Three Russian Composers', *Musical Times*, vol. 68 no. 1016 (October 1927) pp. 882–3.) See *Diaries*, vol. 2, pp. 89, 682, 691, 694.

out of Paris: somebody denounced him as a commissar. Suspicion falls on Yakobson – likewise a composer, and likewise a swine.

8 March

A gentleman from Lyon called to invite me to play in his city on the 30th. He is paying pennies: a thousand francs, but they have already performed my works on four occasions. I therefore agreed.

Went to see the apartment, which I did not like very much, but in Paris beggars can't be choosers.

9 March

Recital at three o'clock: my second in Paris this season and the first performance of the Fifth Sonata. The audience was small, Oeberg had not done a good job in publicising it, but so much the worse for him. All the same, it is not pleasant to play for such a small public. My performance was well, but undemonstratively, received, inhibitions being relaxed only towards the end. Present were Poulenc,[1] Auric,[2] Schloezer, otherwise few notable people. Afterwards we had tea at Samoilenkos', to which Oeberg came, and then I went to see Ptashka.

10 March

Overall, I am not completely happy with the way yesterday's concert was organised. But at least I don't have to spend any more time on the programme.

11 March

M.V. has returned. I was intending to be rather cool with her: after all, she is edging us out of the flat. But she talked so engagingly and entertainingly of Spain, and the stories she told were so interesting, that any frigidity soon melted. I practised the Second Concerto. The orchestral parts of the Third Concerto have arrived for proofing. They are being printed in Paris, but have

---

1 Francis Poulenc (1899–1963), French composer.
2 Georges Auric (1899–1983), for a time a favoured composer of Diaghilev, composing a ballet a year for him (*Les Fâcheux* 1924, *Les Matelots* 1925, *La Pastorale* 1926). Like Poulenc Auric was a member of Les Six; his exceptional fluency produced a mass of work in many genres but posterity, especially in Anglophone countries, knows him mainly as a prolific composer of film scores, notably Ealing comedies (*The Lavender Hill Mob, The Ladykillers*, etc.).

been done in white on such a bright blue background that I would soon go blind if I had to proof-read all of them. I shall have to send them back.

12 March

Practised, and started packing things for the move to the new flat. I outlined to M.V. my plan for a new form of 'musical drama' – after all, she had worked with Meyerhold[1] and even lectured on theatre – but she did not have anything very interesting to say.

In the evening called on Koussevitzky. He does not want Stokowski to have the material of the *Scythian Suite* for Philadelphia as he plans to perform it there himself, as well as in Boston and New York. Not only that, but Cortot[2] will play the Third Concerto in Boston, and the orchestra's leader will play the Violin Concerto there also. Very good.

13 March

After loading up a mountain of trunks and a stack of music a metre high, O.V. and I made the move to the new apartment at No. 5, rue Charles Dickens. It is nicer than I had first thought, and very sunny. Ptashka comes tomorrow.

The French Parliament has voted in favour of the union of Bessarabia with Romania.[3] The Russian press is ranting and fulminating against it and

---

1. Vsevolod Meyerhold (1874–1940), outstanding actor and theatre director, who began his career under Nemirovich-Danchenko in the Moscow Art Theatre. By the time he met Prokofiev, Meyerhold had moved on from the Stanislavskian ideals of the Art Theatre and was developing experimental approaches to theatre derived from Symbolism and *commedia dell'arte*. An enthusiastic supporter of the October Revolution, Meyerhold joined the Communist Party but his free-wheeling avant-gardism and ill-concealed contempt for the dead hand of Socialist Realism inevitably brought him into conflict with the rigid and authoritarian cultural regime of the 1930s. Earlier, in 1918, he had virtually single-handedly set Soviet theatre on a radical new path with its first great theatre production, Mayakovsky's *Misteria-Bouffe*, to be followed by a string of seminal Constructivist productions for his own Meyerhold Theatre, and successfully infected Prokofiev with his love of *commedia dell'arte* in the shape of his own treatment of Carlo Gozzi's *The Love for Three Oranges*. The authorities finally closed his theatre in 1938; in June the following year, in the midst of preparations for Prokofiev's opera *Semyon Kotko*, which Meyerhold was staging, he was arrested and a month later his wife, the actress Zinaïda Raikh was brutally beaten to death in their apartment. On 1 February 1940 one of Russian theatre's greatest and most imaginative directors was executed by firing squad.
2. Alfred Cortot (1877–1962), French pianist, probably more celebrated for Chopin and Schumann than for Prokofiev, but this is a reminder that he had a wider repertoire than the staple Romantic composers.
3. Bessarabia is what Imperial Russia called the eastern half of what was then the Russian principality of Moldavia, ceded by the Ottoman Empire after the Russo-Turkish War of 1806–12 and bounded by the Dniester River on the east and the Prut River on the west. Later, the western part of Moldavia united with Wallachia to become the Kingdom of Romania. In 1918, just before the end of the First World War, Bessarabia declared its independence from Russia and eventually united with Romania. Give or take the vicissitudes of the Second World War and a few subsequent border adjustments with Ukraine, what was formerly Bessarabia is now Moldova.

of course they are right. But my reasoning is as follows: the only thing that matters in French politics is the relationship with Germany. Consequently while Russia amounts to not very much, it is politic for France to strengthen even by a little her lesser friends. But as soon as Russia regains her old self and takes back Bessarabia, this self-same French Parliament will cheerfully, with a clear conscience, vote for reunification of Bessarabia with Russia!

14 March

Collected Ptashka and the little one and brought them back. Ptashka approved of the flat. The piano was brought in today, a grand, they could hardly get it in. We have particularly unappealing neighbours: below us lives a girl who keeps on bashing out the most terrible rubbish on the piano from six o'clock in the evening until half past ten. I am in despair, especially if this is going to go on for three months. I hammered on the floor with my heels, very loudly, her response to which was to shriek indignantly. The walls in this building are made of cardboard.

15 March

Sold some dollars because the franc, which had recently fallen to as much as twenty-eight or even twenty-nine to the dollar, has now risen to twenty-one. Practised the Concerto, which is beginning to show signs of coming together. Altogether it is a colossal contraption and I'll never write anything like it again. I must do a really small Fourth Concerto! In the evening Stahl telephoned to invite me out first to the cinema and then to an extremely smart place where we should have been in full evening dress, in tails, but were wearing jackets. We drank champagne and ate *shashlik*, because the establishment had Russian origins.

16 March

At nine o'clock the wretched female on the floor below began strumming on the piano, and as the night before I had gone to bed at four, I did not get enough sleep. Ptashka commissioned O.V. to buy some wax plugs for me to stop up my ears, on account both of the girl and of Svyatoslav. It is just as well that I have no plans to compose this spring! In June we will go somewhere by the sea, and then . . .!

17 March

Went to sit for Adriana.[1] She does not model as quickly as Deryuzhinsky,[2] but has some interesting pieces. Also, she is more progressive as an artist than he is.

19 March

In the evening accompanied Stahl to *King David*, an oratorio by Honegger[3] which incidentally incorporates readings, and some musically accompanied recitations. This latter concept is of the greatest interest to me. The success was colossal, and certainly some passages are achieved with unusual brilliance and invention. The recitation to a background of keening women (reminiscent of Rachmaninoff) is wonderful. The nasal-sounding phrase in the Jewish march, first heard low down on the bassoons and in the second movement high up on the violins, is quite stunning. But alongside these are moments of dreadful vulgarity and banality. Honegger's melodic gifts are weak. He is a sort of latter-day Richard Strauss, with Straussian inventiveness and Straussian sparkle brought right up to date, albeit lacking Strauss's gift for melody. One way and another it was a stimulating experience to hear, and the work does have something from which young composers (and not only young ones) could learn.

Someone, by the way, told me it was an early work. When I went to the Green Room afterwards to shake his hand, Honegger told me this was not at all the case. Had it been the lapses would have been understandable, but in a mature context they are positively alarming!

20 March

Still needing to sleep longer, I left in the morning to give a concert in Marseilles. Twelve and a half hours in a *rapide* – an excellent and very fast train – but how tiring! On the way I read Merezhkovsky's *Babylon*[4] and was

---

1   Adriana Volkovysskaya née Janocopulos (1897–?), Vera's sculptress sister.
2   Gleb Deryuzhinsky (1888–1975), sculptor whose early success in Petrograd with portraits of such notables as Kerensky could not be expected to survive the Bolshevik Revolution, and who escaped from the Crimea in 1919 by signing on as a deckhand on a boat going to New York. He made a bust of Prokofiev in New York in 1920. See *Diaries*, vol. 2, pp. 479–80, 483, and *passim*.
3   Arthur Honegger (1892–1955), another member of Les Six, Swiss by nationality but born, musically trained and active in France. *Le Roi David* was originally written in 1921 as incidental music to the play of that name by René Morax, but Honegger later (1923) recast it as a 'symphonic psalm' by combining Morax's narrative with his music and turning it into the oratorio form in which it is known today.
4   *Tayna tryokh: Yegipet i Vavilon* (*The Triple Secret: Egypt and Babylon*), Paris, 1923, an attempt to find explanations for the apocalyptic catastrophe (as he saw it) that had befallen Russian civilisation with the Bolshevik Revolution and the Civil War in the fate of these ancient civilisations.

absorbed in the myth of Gilgamesh. That would be a subject for an oratorio like Honegger's – and how much more interesting! But without the interruptions of spoken texts, only accompanied recitations! This could be a commercial proposition, and I shall return to the thought.[1]

21 March

When I had been in Marseilles before to meet Mama[2] I had hardly paid any attention to it. Now that I looked more closely at it I saw that it is a splendid city something like Paris. Most of all, of course, I wanted to gaze on the Mediterranean, but it was drizzling rain and there was not much in the way of colour.

The concert took place at half past five in a small auditorium, but the audience was attentive (apparently this concert society has no more than 400 members). The work that had the most success was my Sonata No. 2.

22 March

Next morning, the *rapide* back to Paris. The weather was sunny today, and the Mediterranean sea, along the shores of which the track from Marseilles at first goes, was a deep blue. The peach trees and *genêts*[3] were all in flower.

Arrived back in Paris, very tired in the evening. Ptashka and the 'oyster' are in good shape. There was a letter from B.N.: Mama is better and is able to walk a little, but the doctor still will not let her travel.

23 March

Spent the day at home, learning the Second Piano Concerto. Apparently they did present *Chout* in New York at the tiny Neighbourhood Playhouse Theatre, with a reduced orchestra concocted by someone or other from my piano score. It was probably very bad, and would certainly have borne no resemblance to what I would have done. Only one question remains: shall I be able to extract some dollars from the exercise?!

---

1 Bohuslav Martinů composed his symphonic cantata-oratorio *The Epic of Gilgamesh* in 1955.
2 In June 1920, when Maria Grigorievna Prokofieva arrived in Marseilles on the steamer *Souirah* from Constantinople. See *Diaries*, vol. 2, pp. 530–1.
3 Prokofiev wrote this word as *jeunets*, in French, but at least in a horticultural context it does not seem to exist. As before, when he first noticed and was attracted by the yellow-flowering broom bush at Les Rochelets in the spring of 1921, it seems likely that he confused it with the homonym *genêt*. See *Diaries*, vol. 2, p. 593.

24 March

Borovsky is back from Spain but goes to Germany tomorrow. M.V. is feeling guilty about me, and therefore made use of her husband's return to come to see us. Borovsky was very nice, and had much to tell about Spain. Stravinsky conducted a concert in Barcelona and had a tremendous success – even the Queen attended – but his programme consisted of *The Firebird* and *Pulcinella*, that is to say his most popular things.

Oeberg came, and we jointly wrote a letter to the Neighbourhood Playhouse as from the publishers asking for payment for *Chout*.

I went to a Balmont evening,[1] in which I could not participate this year owing to my agreement with Oeberg. Tobuk-Cherkass[2] sang, boringly and inappropriately, although Tobuk (who in principle sings well) performed various songs to Balmont's words: Stravinsky, Tcherepnin, and some of mine. Balmont read a garland of sonnets, which he called *The Golden Hoop*,[3] an admirable thing although few people had any understanding of the virtuosity required to produce a collection of sonnets. The atmosphere of the whole evening was a little chilly. This is sad, but I was not myself much taken with it.

25 March

Ptashka received 3,000 francs from Mrs Garvin[4] to cover the expenses of the confinement and birth. She was surprised and embarrassed to get this money, but such a sum is very timely indeed for us. Stahl came in the evening and we played two-hand patience. He told us what was happening to the Diva in America, and I told him of my plans for *Gilgamesh*. Stahl's advice was to make settings of five poems by Tseitlin, in gratitude for which he would underwrite the composition of *Gilgamesh*. I added: 'and then we could publish the songs as *Songs Without Words*!'

26 March

Consulted Polack[5] about my eyes. The left eye has not altered very much, but the right eye is catching it up and has deteriorated. He changed the

---

1 Balmont, being in straitened circumstances, arranged – or rather his wealthy friends the Tseitlins arranged for him – benefit appearances in Paris. Prokofiev took part in the first of these in June 1921 and again somewhat unsatisfactorily in May 1923; he may have done likewise in 1922 but there is no mention of it in the *Diaries*. See *Diaries*, vol. 2, pp. 610–11, 710.
2 Maria Tobuk-Cherkass, soprano, sang principal roles at the St Petersburg Musical-Historical Society and the Hermitage Theatre before emigrating to Paris after the Revolution.
3 A linked sequence of fifteen sonnets.
4 A rich American friend.
5 Paris eye-surgeon, who had operated on Prokofiev's mother's eyes soon after she arrived in France. See *Diaries*, vol. 2, p. 572.

prescription for my glasses. How curious that I suffer neuralgia in the left eye but it is the right one that is getting worse.

Larionov came with a proposal that I write a short, fifteen-minute puppet ballet to be presented in Monte Carlo at the end of April and subsequently in Paris. Alas, no time!

27 March

Continued to practise the Second Concerto. Every morning I sit down at the piano straight away after coffee. I don't remember a time when my practising had to be so assiduous.

Zederbaum brought the French translation of *Seven, They Are Seven* done by Laloy.[1] I had not expected it to be done with such skill, but even so there are holes and I asked Zederbaum to arrange a rendezvous for me with Laloy so that we could talk about them.

28 March

M.V. asked us to dinner, as Borovsky is back from Germany for two days, we declined on the grounds that Ptashka is not yet going out. As a result Borovsky came to us and I played him the Fifth Sonata, to which his attitude is now one of enthusiastic admiration.

Schloezer also came to talk about the same ballet project as Larionov, but I again explained that two or three weeks was not enough for me to dash off fifteen minutes of music, especially seeing that I had to carry on learning the Second Concerto.

29 March

Went to Lyons for my concert there. A journey of seven hours is not in itself so exhausting, but the train was an hour and half late, and on this date all over France the clocks went forward an hour, so that I arrived very late at night, landed up in a hotel with cardboard walls and slept badly, owing to the presence next door of an amorous couple (quite a production) and then, at four o'clock, the hotel's night caretaker decided to sweep the floors very noisily.

---

1   Louis Laloy (1874–1944), music critic, translator, scholarly and perceptive writer on Debussy, Ravel and Stravinsky. At various times Laloy was administrator of the Monte Carlo Opera and head of the public relations department of the Paris Grand Opéra. In his autobiography, Jean Cocteau attributes the opium habit with which he struggled all his life to the influence of Laloy in Monte Carlo.

30 March

Lyons is built on a long, narrow peninsula formed by the confluence of the rivers Rhône and Saône. One bank is high and beautifully constructed, but the town itself is boring, the houses ugly and uniform. I understand that life here is insular and locked in the previous century.

The concert took place in a beautiful hall, and each piece was preceded by a short introduction by the Director. I played well, better than in Marseilles and Paris, and the audience was particularly attentive and discerning. The concert was a great success and the organisers were pleased.

Was entertained to dinner by a local musician, Mme de Lestang, who sang my Op. 35 songs[1] to me.

31 March

Having transferred to another, quieter hotel, I slept splendidly and at 11.30 the next morning set off back to Paris, arriving home at eight o'clock where I found all well.

1 April

Zederbaum and I went to see Laloy to discuss changes to *Seven, They Are Seven*. Laloy is head of the press office of the Grand Opéra and has an office in the theatre building. He is a very nervous gentleman, making me think he might be a narcotics addict, and our conversation proceeded in a stormy fashion, sometimes almost bordering on a quarrel. However, he is talented, and suggested several excellent improvements. We parted peaceably.

In the evening I was at Tseitlin's, where there was a gathering of all our writers: Bunin, Merezhkovsky, Gippius, Kuprin, Remizov, and also some of the *Latest News*[2] staff. It was piquant to see Osorgin,[3] who has recently caused a stir with his appeal to Russian youth to return immediately to Russia, playing chess with Milyukov. Milyukov had set up a good defence and played

---

1 *Five Songs Without Words*, Op 35 (1920).
2 *Poslednye Novosti*, the newspaper edited by Pavel Milyukov.
3 Mikhail Osorgin, pen-name of Mikhail Ilyin (1878–1942), novelist and journalist. In 1922 Osorgin had been one of the seventy or so leading artists, philosophers and thinkers rounded up by OGPU (see below, p. 439, n.1) on the orders of Lenin to be deported as potentially disruptive to the intellectual docility of the Bolshevik totalitarian state, and threatened with execution should they attempt to return. As Lesley Chamberlain puts it in her account of this extraordinary and intellectually significant episode, *The Philosophy Steamer: Lenin and the Exile of the Intelligentsia* (Atlantic Books, London, 2006): 'These thinkers clashed with Lenin and in an instant lost their homeland, because they were convinced that a new Russia would go astray if it did not enshrine religious moral values in its programme of social reform.'

cautiously, but lost. I then sat down with Osorgin and crushed him with a pawn sacrifice. I wanted to talk to Merezhkovsky about *Gilgamesh*, but he was so deep in conversation with Bunin about the mission of the Russian émigré community that I could not get a word in.

2 April

Apart from the Concerto, I am busying myself writing out all three translations of the Akhmatova songs.[1] At long last these translations have been finished and the work can now be reprinted in four languages. These songs are among my most 'accessible', yet no one knows them.

I went to a general rehearsal by the Romantic Ballet, which is headed by Romanov,[2] the same who was going to stage *Ala and Lolli* had that ballet ever come to fruition. But I did not like their production and Metzl's[3] music was unbearable.

3 April

I must take a grip on myself preparing for the Second Concerto; the need for accuracy is terrifying. I am not permitting myself a single doubtful note. If I keep this up I shall be able to match Rachmaninoff for impeccability.[4]

4 April

Schloezer sent along a singer called Gonich so that I could hear her in my songs. She proved to be a young, beautiful woman, and she sang not badly although her vocal control is not flawless. She has recently come from Moscow, and it seems plans to return there.

---

1   *Five Poems of Anna Akhmatova*, Op. 27 (1916).
2   Boris Romanov (1891–1957), choreographer. As a young balletmaster at the Mariinsky Theatre he had staged two ballets and one opera for Diaghilev: Florent Schmitt's *La Tragédie de Salomé* in 1913, Richard Strauss's *Josephslegende* (1914) and Stravinsky's *Le Rossignol* (1914: the later ballet *Le Chant du rossignol* was staged by Massine). Diaghilev had suggested Romanov as an appropriate choreographer for the ballet *Ala and Lolli*, a commission he had given Prokofiev in 1914 but rejected when at the beginning of 1915 in Milan Prokofiev finally played him work in progress on the score. Romanov called his Berlin-based company 'The Russian Romantic Ballet. See *Diaries*, vol. 1, pp. 757, 766–70, 784, 786–7; vol. 2, pp. 22–4, 52.
3   Vladimir Metzl (1882–?), Moscow-born composer who after studies with Taneyev emigrated in his twenties to Berlin where he presumably met the choreographer Boris Romanov. The sole work of his that seems to have met with success in both London (London Symphony Orchestra conducted by Safonov on 13 May 1907) and New York was the tone-poem *Die versunkene Glocke*, scored for a gigantic orchestra, based on a macabre fairy-play by Hauptmann. After this Metzl seems to have disappeared from view.
4   See *Diaries*, vol. 2, pp. 532–3.

Later, an evening was held for Remizov, which in contrast to the Balmont occasion was very lively. Remizov himself is such a picturesque figure, a sort of vampire. He reads delightfully, phrasing his 'little words' most adroitly and reverting from time to time to an affecting simplicity. The evening was a great success.

5 April

Even though my main activity at this time is piano practice, I still do not play for more than an hour and a half or two hours a day. My heart is still not in completely sound order and gets very tired if I do too much energetic playing.

I took Ptashka out for a walk and to the hairdresser, because the lift in our building has been out of order for a week. She is not allowed to use the stairs for the time being and so has not been out of the house at all. When we reached the main entrance, she felt giddy.

In the evening Stahl and I went to *R.U.R.*,[1] the Czech play about the life of robots (artificial people). I was fascinated, Stahl less so.

6 April

Invited to Prunières' for the evening. This was Ptashka's first foray into the world, although she was tired after yesterday's excursion. A mass of composers were there: Ravel,[2] Poulenc, Auric, Honegger, Roussel.[3] Ravel buttonholed Schloezer on the subject of Tchaikovsky, saying something to the effect that 'you peoples of the Byzantine culture will never understand us Westerners . . .' at which I butted in: 'especially as Schloezer is Belgian . . .' Auric and Poulenc, who are no friends of Ravel, burst out laughing hysterically. At the same party I met the Director of Universal Editions in Vienna, who was keen to know whether he could publish my compositions, even the operas. He promised to facilitate performances in Vienna if I would give him the rights. I had to tell him that I was bound to Koussevitzky's publishing house and recommended him to speak personally to Koussevitzky, who would be coming back to Paris from London in two days' time.

---

1 *Rossum's Universal Robots*, the play by Karel Čapek first produced in Prague in 1921. The play introduced the word 'robot', which although it did not mean quite what it means today has displaced older words such as 'automaton' or 'android' in virtually all languages (Karel Čapek identified his brother Josef as the true inventor of the word). In the original Czech, *robota* means work (*rabota* in Russian). The name *Rossum* is an allusion to the Czech word *rozum*, meaning 'reason', 'intellect' or 'common sense' (in Russian, *razum*).
2 Maurice Ravel (1875–1937), French composer.
3 Albert Roussel (1869–1937), French composer much influenced by the impressionism of Ravel and Debussy but with strong tendencies towards classicism.

7 April

A new contract from Duo-Art. They have agreed my conditions, that is to say three recording sessions a year each with three pieces, at $479 a piece. It means I shall have to go to New York next February.

Saw Manukhin, who finds my heart is normal, not enlarged. The pulse, however, is irregular. He prescribed a continuation of the phosphor medication and the temporary addition of valerian with lily of the valley. He said, 'If you were just a copyist, I would let you do whatever you want and go wherever you like, but since you are a composer, and a remarkable one to boot, we must keep you in good shape with the phosphor.'

In the evening I went to a concert of Bach, which had a very refreshing effect, even though the performance dragged at times.

8 April

Practised the Concerto. I incorporated some corrections I had made to the score into the orchestral parts. In the evening Ptashka and I were at the Samoilenkos and played four-hand patience. The tension was so nail-biting that we howled from excitement and cursed our partners.

9 April

Made a few sketches for pieces for a string quartet. The one I had begun to rough out in Borovsky's apartment is no good.

Very loving relations with Ptashka. It is six weeks since Svyatoslav was born. In the evening I called on Koussevitzky, who is back from London and leaving for Warsaw tomorrow. At the moment he and I are on excellent terms.

His publishing firm is entering into an agreement with the Oxford Press,[1] which has representation in all British colonies, and this in turn means

---

1 The man at the helm of Oxford University Press for most of the twentieth century until the end of the Second World War was Humphrey S. Milford. The Press had occasionally published music, notably the first edition of the English Hymnal edited by Percy Dearmer and a young Ralph Vaughan Williams, but it was no more than a sideline to the core business of academic book publishing. In 1921 Milford appointed Hubert J. Foss who, it later emerged, was not particularly interested in academic or educational publishing but was passionate, well informed and perceptive about music, originally as an assistant to the manager of the Educational Department. Foss took the ball he had accidentally been offered and ran with it. A fiftieth-anniversary pamphlet published by the Music Department in 1973 states that OUP 'had no knowledge of the music trade, no representative to sell to music shops, and – it seems – no awareness that sheet music was in any way a different commodity from books'. However, intentionally or intuitively, Milford took three steps that launched OUP on a major operation. He bought the Anglo-French Music Company and all its facilities, connections, and resources. He engaged a full-time sales manager for music. Finally, in 1923 he established the new Music Department with its own offices in Amen House and with Foss as first Musical Editor. The link with Koussevitzky's Russian

that my compositions will be brought out in Tasmania and Singapore and everywhere else. Koussevitzky told me that there had been a request from Scotland for 500 copies of the March from *Three Oranges* – this is splendid, the first time for an order of such a size. Needless to say, the publishers did not have this quantity in stock, and so they are printing a second edition especially to meet the order.

From Koussevitzky I went on to a concert at which Villa-Lobos's[1] Trio for oboe, clarinet and bassoon was performed. He has an excellent knowledge of these instruments and deploys a mass of interesting ideas in rhythm, sonorities, etc., but he lacks a sense of flow and I am not sure how worthwhile the actual material is. If he were twenty-two, I would say without hesitation that he has the makings of a significant composer, but as he is already thirty-two all one can do is hold back from too harsh a judgement on the less successful passages while awaiting further compositions. Stahl gave a dinner after the concert, at which I found Milhaud[2] an attractive personality, not having much liked him hitherto. He surprised me very much by telling me that when he is orchestrating he takes himself off to a sanatorium where there is complete quiet, and works from nine o'clock in the morning until eleven o'clock at night, completing as many as thirty-two pages a day. If this is true, it is quite incredible. The most I have ever been able to do is nine to fifteen pages, and the norm is four or five.

Musical Editions was an early example of the expansionist philosophy espoused, from different standpoints, by both Foss and Milford. Foss's ambition was to establish the largest possible list in the shortest possible time; from the off he was adding titles at the rate of over 200 a year so that by the end of the 1930s there were 1750 titles in the catalogue.

1 Heitor Villa-Lobos (1887–1959), prolific Brazilian composer championed by European musicians including Arthur Rubinstein, Andrés Segovia and Darius Milhaud. Although Villa-Lobos drew heavily on various strands of indigenous Brazilian music, embracing Portuguese, American Indian and African elements, he was also concerned to integrate them into, or at least cross-illuminate them from, Western classical, romantic and Modernist streams. He had been deeply impressed by the Ballets Russes tour of Brazil in 1917.

2 Darius Milhaud (1892–1974), a member of Les Six, a group of composers, studied with Charles-Marie Widor and Vincent d'Indy. As a young man, visiting Brazil (as secretary to Paul Claudel, the poet and playwright who was serving as French Ambassador at the time) and America had a profound and life-long effect on his musical horizons, extending them to embrace Latin American rhythms and sonorities, especially the Brazilian *choros*, and jazz, which he heard in Harlem. By 1924 he had already produced several of his most popular works, including the ballets *Le Boeuf sur le toit* (*The Ox on the Roof*), with a scenario by Cocteau and designs by Dufy, after which a famous cabaret-bar much frequented by Cocteau and Co. was named, and the jazz-inspired *La Création du monde* (the ubiquitously heard *Scaramouche* was later, 1937). The Nazi threat (Milhaud was Jewish) caused the composer to emigrate to America in 1939, where as well as continuing to compose prolifically he embarked on a remarkable teaching career, which after the war he combined with a post at the Paris Conservatoire. The long, and eclectic, list of his students contains such names as Burt Bacharach, William Bolcom, Dave Brubeck, György Kurtág, Steve Reich, Philip Glass, Karlheinz Stockhausen (not for long, though), Morton Subotnick and Iannis Xenakis.

10 April

Practised the Concerto. Adriana, who is completing my bust, congratulated me on my appearance. She told me that over the last ten days my cheeks had filled out, and she needed to add clay. In the evening I caught up with my diary.

11 April

Balmont and Shakhovskaya came to call, with their son (an intolerable child who crawls everywhere and tugs at everything but as a 'specimen' is admirable: plump and strong). Balmont is soon going away to the seaside, but will come back for the performance of *Seven, They Are Seven*. He admired Svyatoslav. Svyatoslav smiled at him. Balmont was delighted with the smile, and exclaimed, 'He likes me!'

12 April

Stahl and Janacopoulos in the evening. She thinks d'Harcourt's translation of the Akhmatova songs is hopeless.

16 April

Invited to lunch by Mme Dubost,[1] the first time I have been to her house. Among the other guests were Tailleferre[2] and Florent Schmitt.[3] The latter at first did not recognise me, but then became exceedingly friendly, told me how much he admired *Chout* and the *Scythian Suite*, and asked me to call on him.

---

1   Dubost was among the most stylish salon hostesses in Paris, and was in the habit of organising soirées at which prominent composers and visiting musicians performed. She also ran a ballet school for children. In the spring of 1927 she dismantled her fan and presented a leaf from it to each of ten composers of her acquaintance, asking them to write a little dance for her students. (The ten composers were Roussel, Auric, Delannoy, Ferroud, Ibert, Milhaud, Poulenc, Ravel, Roland-Manuel and Schmitt.) The result was the collaborative ballet entitled, appropriately, *Jeanne's Fan* (*L'Éventail de Jeanne*), some numbers from which, notably Poulenc's *Pastourelle* and Ravel's *Fanfare*, survived as independent pieces.
2   Germaine Tailleferre (1892–1983), French composer, the only female member of Les Six.
3   Florent Schmitt (1870–1958), prolific French composer whose 1907 ballet *La Tragédie de Salomé* Stravinsky initially acknowledged (although he later denied it) as an influence on the composition of *The Rite of Spring* for its polyrhythms, stabbing percussive chords and use of bitonality.

17 April

Sat for Volkovysskaya. Since I am getting seriously bored with this, today she had asked a photographer to come, who took photographs from all angles, and she will finish the work without me.

The Concerto is making progress and is at last beginning to come together.

18 April

Went to the dress rehearsal of Demasy's *Jesus of Nazareth*. Since Demasy is first and foremost a Jew and his writing treats exclusively biblical subjects, I was very interested to see what he would make of Christ. But I was unable to reach any conclusion about this as I had to leave halfway through – the rehearsal dragged on interminably. Demasy is not very original, but he does have some well-thought-out moments. The music, of which there was a lot, was very tiring to listen to: each of the eight scenes was preceded by an overture or similar piece by Wagner or Franck. A particularly crass idea was the overture to *Lohengrin*, which is all about the Middle Ages – but when the curtain rises, you find yourself in Judaea!

In the evening was at Natalya Koussevitzky's, who had also invited Stahl so that we could work on Koussevitzky's article (he was away in Warsaw) attacking Schloezer. The two are conducting a war through the columns of a newspaper. The reason I had been invited was so that I could add some venomous phrases to the article. Naturally I am on Koussevitzky's side in this polemic, although I cannot wholly share Koussevitzky's determination to see in Schloezer nothing but an infinitely malignant excrescence.

19 April

Zederbaum has made a fair copy of yesterday's article and brought it round to read to me. Natalya Konstantinovna is so consumed by this polemic that she came too. I continued to make suggestions and invent still more poisonous formulations, although in the present instance I am acting as a pure mercenary, less from any desire to annihilate Schloezer than from sheer love of the fray.[1]

---

1 This recalls an episode in Prokofiev's student days when he enthusiastically entered into his friend Eleonora Damskaya's on-off relationship with a determined suitor: 'I composed for her another letter to her Sergusya. He is still determined to marry her, knowing that she likes him, but she is "playing a game of chess" with him, a game to which for love of the art I am interested in contributing.' Largely owing to Prokofiev's disinterested urging, Damskaya finally rejected her suitor, who was shortly afterwards killed in the war, leaving her his enormous fortune. See *Diaries*, vol. 1, pp. 759–88.

Lunched with Maria Viktorovna, where was also present a relation of hers, my first harmony teacher, Pomerantsev.[1] He showed us a good version of patience, but his reflections on music were narrow-minded and out of date. When I got home I learnt that the Zakharovs, Boris and Cecilia, had called to see us.[2] They have just returned from America; on learning that I was out they started to write a letter but then, anxious to see what sort of a wife I had got myself, burst in on Ptashka in the bedroom. I am not overly pleased with this.

21 April

Went to see the Zakharovs in their hotel. Celia blushed, which is very becoming in her. Zakharov has changed very little, but is beginning to look quite old. We had a very good time together.

I then called on Janacopoulos and chose songs for her to sing in my concert on 12th May. She badly wanted to be invited to sing in this concert, but now she is trying to put in as many old numbers as possible in order not to have learn new ones.

22 April

Dined with Natalya Konstantinovna, Oeberg also there. We finally agreed on a contract, because there had been all sorts of outstanding minor details, as a result of which they have been publishing my works without a signed agreement.

23 April

Received 411 francs at the Society of Authors for the term (for concert performances of my works). It's not much, but a substantial increase on

---

1   Yury Pomerantsev (1878–1933) was an exceptionally cultivated musician who had studied composition with Taneyev, piano with Scriabin and conducting (perhaps his most enduring contribution to music with nearly a decade of conducting at the Bolshoy Theatre) with Nikisch. A friend of a friend of a relation of Prokofiev's mother, in 1901 when still a student at the Moscow Conservatoire, from which he would later graduate with the Silver Medal, he heard the ten-year-old boy brought to Moscow to meet him by his proud mother, and seeing the potential recommended him to his own teacher Taneyev. Taneyev in turn suggested more lessons while still in the capital with Pomerantsev, although recommending Reinhold Glière for more extensive holiday coaching at home in the Ukraine. Pomerantsev was also the music consultant to Boris Romanov's Russian Romantic Ballet company, for whom Prokofiev composed the ballet *Trapèze*, the music for which was later reincarnated as the Quintet, Op. 39.
2   Boris Zakharov (1887–1942) and his violinist wife Cecilia Hansen (1897–1989) had been friends of Prokofiev (particularly Zakharov, who was for some years his closest companion) since they were all students at the St Petersburg Conservatoire. Zakharov had some success as a pianist in Russia and in Europe, but was overshadowed by the greater fame of his wife, who was often referred to as 'Queen of the violin'. See *Diaries*, vol. 1, pp. 4, 157, and *passim*; vol. 2 *passim*.

previous amounts. Ptashka was given a present of 2000 dollars by Garvin in America for Svyatoslav and the costs of his nanny, as well as a promise to send more in the future. All this, apparently, because she heard that I want him to be taken care of somewhere else for the summer so that his presence doesn't bother me. Would be a great pity to jeopardise this source of funds.

In the afternoon I called on the Zakharovs and took Cecilia flowers, as she is suffering from angina. In the evening Boris came to us on his own, and was joined by the Borovskys. I remembered that today I turned thirty-three ('What's that noise I can hear from the next room?' 'That's the sound of me turning thirty-three.') Boris was very taken with Ptashka.

24 April

Got a letter from Janacopoulos with the programme: only three new songs, she has sung all the others before. If I don't like it, she wrote, she can cancel. I replied saying that she can sing whatever she likes, but will she please inform me who is going to accompany her (by which I was letting her know I declined to accompany her in a programme that holds no interest for me). The response came in the evening, this time from Stahl, and very rude it was too: Jan will not sing. This is a really shabby trick! Who was it who kept on urging that she be included in the concert? Stahl. And now she is cancelling, and very churlishly to boot!

25 April

Slept badly, turning over in my mind how to reply. In the morning I wrote my response, which was polite but pointed out the shabbiness of their action. I expected an explosion from Stahl in the afternoon, and decided that were he to appear I would exit through the back door and leave word that I had gone out of town to look for a dacha. But Stahl did not show up.

In the evening I was at N.K.'s, who was very sympathetic and said she would help find another singer. From her I went on to hear Stravinsky's *Soldier's Tale*, which was on at the Champs-Elysées. I found it less effective than the concert performance I had heard in the autumn. The staging kept getting in the way of the music, while the music slowed up the action. The passage where the devil declaims rhythmically to the music is marvellous. This is exactly what I have been thinking of. When I met Stravinsky we kissed, and I told him I would like very much to see him to chat about things and show him the Fifth Sonata. He said, 'With pleasure, I'm very fond of you, please telephone me in a couple of days.' He was very proud of having got several engagements to perform his Concerto. He was with Sudeikina,[1] whom for some reason I can never recognise.

26 April

Practised a great deal, and thought about how to reconstruct the recital programme in the event there is no singer. Hébertot[2] did not seem to mind very much that Janacopoulos had cancelled.

Evening at the Borovskys, together with the Zakharovs and N.K. Tomorrow is the Russian Easter and at twelve midnight we all embraced one another with the triple kiss. N.K. told us the touching story of Medtner coming from Germany and Rachmaninoff from America to Italy so that they could be together. Delicious!

27 April

Russian Easter.

Dinner at N.K.'s: Borovskys, Zakharovs, Ptashka and I. N.K. had planned to invite the Stahls, but knowing of our quarrel had put off their invitation. The dinner was wonderful, a particularly fine salmon the like of which I had never eaten, not even in Russia. When I said that *Seven, They Are Seven* lasted only seven minutes, Zakharov said, 'That's one minute for each one of us here!'

Zakharov related how once in Riga he had taken home an inebriated Glazunov[3] from the party they had both attended. 'And how did you get on with our host?' asked Zakharov, for something to say. Hardly able to get his

---

1 Stravinsky met Vera Sudeikina, then married (probably bigamously, according to Stephen Walsh) to the designer Sergey Sudeikin, at Nikita Baliev's cabaret Théâtre de la Chauve-Souris in 1921. Sudeikin had designed sets for the Chauve-Souris. (That year he also acted as the ambitious young Boris Kokhno's mentor, one might uncharitably say pander, in stage-managing his meeting with Diaghilev, which was to have such far-reaching consequences.) By 1924 (Vera having given Sudeikin his marching orders in the middle of 1922) the affair was widely known and although the Stravinskys never separated formally and Stravinsky did not marry Vera until after Katya Stravinsky's death, there was little if any attempt to conceal the relationship. See S. Walsh, *Igor Stravinsky: A Creative Spring*, Jonathan Cape, London, 2000, pp. 324, 343–5, 350–51.
2 Jacques Hébertot (pen-name of André Daviel) (1886–1970), playwright and theatrical manager. Since 1920 Hébertot had been the Director of the Théâtre des Champs-Elysées, the magnificent theatre founded by the spectacular but wayward impresario Gabriel Astruc.
3 Alexander Glazunov (1835–1936), composer and teacher, the first and, along with Rimsky-Korsakov, the most prominent, prolific and gifted member of the Belyayev Circle. Glazunov had been appointed Director of the St Petersburg Conservatoire in the wake of the student and general political unrest of 1905, continuing to serve in that capacity through both Revolutions of 1917 and until 1922, finally emigrating only in 1928 although nominally not relinquishing his directorship of the Conservatoire until much later. Prokofiev's *Diaries* make no secret of his disdain for Glazunov as a man and, latterly at least, as a composer, but there are many accounts of his enlightened humanity and generosity to generations of students – notably an impoverished young Shostakovich, whose music cannot have been any more congenial to Glazunov's innate conservatism than Prokofiev's – that go a long way to counterbalance the unflattering portrait

tongue round the words, Glazunov replied, 'Decent enough fellow, but what a terrible drunk!'

That morning I had received from Mangeot, one of Hébertot's associates, a letter recommending to me a singer called Yurevskaya. I made some enquiries. N.K. and Boris were both very complimentary, and the latter said that he knew her well personally, so we immediately set out to go to see her. She had recently arrived in Paris and was very happy to appear in my concert. The situation was thus speedily resolved.

It turned out that I had known her twelve years ago at the Conservatoire, when I was having a mild flirtation with Lena Klingman.[1] I had completely forgotten about it, but when it came back to me I realized that this Yurevskaya was at that time known as Zinka Lenkina,[2] but Max Schmidthof[3] and I always deliberately mangled her name into Lenka Zinkina. Since then she has transformed herself into a good singer, appearing at the Mariinsky Theatre and the Berlin Staatsoper.

28 April

Ptashka has a fearful cold and is in bed. Yurevskaya came and we made a selection of my songs. She is taking it upon herself to learn eight songs in two weeks, almost none of which have been sung in Paris. So much for the Janacopoulos attitude. A very nice letter from Balmont with suggestions for seaside dachas. After the contretemps with Stahl such kindness is very welcome.

Haensel[4] has informed me that I am engaged to play in Boston (with Koussevitzky). He also reminded me what I owe him.

29 April

Borovsky has scrupulously learnt the second piano part of the Second Concerto and today we went together to Pleyel's shop to rehearse it. In places

---

that emerges from the *Diaries*. Prokofiev never forgot or forgave Glazunov for walking out of the first performance of the *Scythian Suite* in 1916. See *Diaries*, vols. 1 and 2 *passim*.
1   See *Diaries*, vol. 1, pp. 249–637 *passim*.
2   Ibid., pp. 290, 308–9. The soprano known as Zinaida Yurevskaya was born Zinaida (Zinka) Lenkina in 1892 in a town in Estonia called at that time Yurev, from which she took her stage name in 1918 on graduating from the Petrograd Conservatoire. Because of her marriage to an Estonian, Georg von Bremer, whose brother had fought with the Volunteer Army in the Civil War, she was arrested and imprisoned in 1920, rescued by the personal intervention of Glazunov, who persuaded the authorities that he needed an Estonian interpreter and musical assistant to accompany him on a tour to that country, whence she had subsequently proceeded quickly to develop a successful European career singing roles such as Jenufa at the Berlin Opera, Sophie in *Rosenkavalier* in Amsterdam and other principal roles in German opera houses.
3   Maximilian Schmidthof (189?–1913), Prokofiev's most intimate companion, the person he regarded as his alter ego during his years at the St Petersburg Conservatoire until Max's shocking suicide in 1913. Ibid., *passim*.
4   Fitzhugh W. Haensel, of the agency Haensel and Jones, Prokofiev's American managers.

it was comic, because the second piano threw me off course and I could not manage my part, especially in the Intermezzo and the beginning of the Finale.

30 April

Yurevskaya came and sang the songs she had chosen. So far, of course, they are only in rough. She has a nice lyric timbre, but is practically inaudible when singing *piano*. She had much to tell me about her time at the Mariinsky Theatre during the Bolshevik regime, mentioning many familiar names. Marusya Pavlova had also been in the Mariinsky company, but was not singing leading roles.

1 May

Rehearsed with Borovsky at Pleyel. It's going better. He is enthralled by the Concerto. On account of its being the first of May there were no taxis, and as a result it was pleasant to be in Paris: nobody tries to run you down as you cross the street.

2 May

Koussevitzky has returned from Poland, where he conducted six concerts. Borovsky and I dined with him and played him the Second Concerto right through, although it was not an easy task on a single piano. Koussevitzky was delighted. He wants to include *Seven, They Are Seven* twice in the same concert and play it twice to promote better understanding of the work. The soloist and chorusmaster already have their copies and are said to be very happy with the work. This is important for good preparation.

3 May

Played the Second Concerto to Koussevitzky. As we entered the Pleyel shop we encountered Stravinsky, jacketless and unbuttoned shirt, rehearsing his Concerto with Jean Wiéner.[1] We were in time to hear only the concluding

---

1 Jean Wiéner (1896–1982), composer and pianist. A student of Yves Nat, as with a subsequent Nat student Jacques Loussier he discovered the delights of American jazz. His partnership with Clément Doucet became a celebrated piano duo, mixing jazz with the classics. Wiéner, often to be seen and heard playing in Milhaud's night-club Le Boeuf sur le toit, was an equally passionate adherent and promoter of all forms of new music, having successfully tapped the Princesse de Polignac for funds to establish an imaginative new-music concert series in Paris. Wiéner and Stravinsky were rehearsing for a private play-through of the new Concerto to be given on two pianos in the Princesse's salon in ten days' time, in advance of the public Koussevitzky premiere. Wiéner was clearly an exceptional pianist: he gave the first performance of Stravinsky's *Three Movements from Petrushka* as part of a special Stravinsky Christmas concert in December 1922. Later in life he had a prolific career as a composer of movie scores.

bars, which came over very well, dramatically effective even in the technically bravura passages where Stravinsky rose to the occasion, throwing himself with abandon into the octaves. He proudly showed us his biceps. Where can he have got those from?

4 May

Koussevitzky came to us after lunch to go through the Second Concerto: I played while he followed with the score and conducted. This was a useful exercise for me, and he convincingly pointed up some nuances. Yesterday he and Stahl had been together at Honegger's *King David*, which is receiving its fourth colossally successful performance this season. Stahl had had too much to drink, and shouted 'encore!' at such lunatic volume that he had to be hushed. I imagine he was partly doing so to spite me.

5 May

The first rehearsal with orchestra, in the foyer of the Grand Opéra which is so boomy it is hard to understand anything. Koussevitzky simply read through it, without me, in order to familiarise the orchestra with the material and to iron out some mistakes in the parts.

After the rehearsal we went together to a shop he had recommended for me to choose an overcoat. We chose a Scottish one in black and white.

6 May

For safety's sake Borovsky and I went through the Concerto once more on two pianos. He has been very kind in rehearsing so much with me even though he has a concert of his own tomorrow.

I hear that a 'Janacopoulos Festival' has been announced for the 17th May in the Champs-Elysées. Quite incredible! Before the rehearsal with Borovsky I called in on Koussevitzky to collect the music. He is not well and was lying in bed studying the score of *Khovanshchina*,[1] which he is due to conduct at the Opéra. Extraordinary how poorly *Khovanshchina* has been orchestrated; hard to believe it is a Rimsky-Korsakov score! When I called again on the

---

1   Opera by Musorgsky, first performed (in Rimsky-Korsakov's version and orchestration) in St Petersburg in 1886. At Diaghilev's request Stravinsky provided a new ending, which was included in the production Diaghilev mounted in his 1913 Paris season with Chaliapin as Dosifei. Prokofiev saw a performance although he does not seem to have realised Stravinsky's contribution. In 1960 a revised version orchestrated by Shostakovich from Pavel Lamm's reconstruction of Musorgsky's own vocal score was produced at the Kirov Theatre in St Petersburg. The version most often produced today is Lamm–Shostakovich incorporating the Stravinsky finale.

way back to return the score of the Second Concerto, I ran into Stravinsky complaining that he had damaged his fingers practising his Concerto. I recommended to him the Rachmaninoff treatment of bandaging with cotton-wool.[1] We left together, and Stravinsky said that he had always loved playing the piano since childhood, and was determined to perform his Concerto as a pianist, not as a composer who can earn a pat on the back for a brave try. 'See the smoke from that chimney creeping about the ground?' he said. 'That means there is a change in the weather and that's why the skin on my fingers is cracking open.'

7 May

The second rehearsal with orchestra. We went through two movements of the Concerto: the scherzo and the finale, but the circumstances were not propitious, the orchestra was down in the orchestra pit while I was up on the forestage playing on a miserable upright piano. I could not see Koussevitzky nor could he hear me. Only tomorrow will we have a proper rehearsal.

In the afternoon I went to Pleyel to try pianos. Coincidentally there was a rehearsal going on there at the same time of the *Overture on Hebrew Themes*,[2] which is to be played in a week's time and which for some curious reason has been called in the programme *Jewish Rhapsody*.

8 May

General rehearsal. I felt vigorous and in control. We rehearsed with great diligence, but of course we really need another rehearsal, especially bearing in mind that Koussevitzky is not a particularly good accompanist. Honegger's *Pacific*[3] is also having its first performance in the same concert, a marvellously orchestrated piece and a prime example of how something interesting can be made without any actual music.

In the afternoon I felt good (I had been worrying about my heart and my nerves). In the evening, Koussevitzky and I both drank some Kola Astier[4] to

---

1 See *Diaries*, vol. 2, p. 353.
2 Op. 34, composed in 1919 in New York.
3 *Pacific 231*, mouvement symphonique, first performed in 1923.
4 Dr Astier's Kola Nut Remedy (alas, no longer available at Boots the Chemist even under prescription) appears to have been a popular preparation to combat flagging energy. The kola nut is a caffeinated nut from the evergreen Cola nitida tree native to West Africa that can grow up to eighty-two feet high. The website www.nativeremedies.com states: 'Herbal remedy kola nut fights signs of fatigue & weakness and helps protect human tissue from damage', and further advises, 'We Use Kola Nut in the Following Products: Ikawe for Men, Promotes strong erections, sexual arousal and energy, plus systemic balance in the reproductive system.'

keep up our strength. *Pacific* was on before my Concerto and was greeted with noisy acclamation: some people wanted it encored; others booed. *King David* has made Honegger *the* fashionable composer and the public adores him. A year ago *Pacific* would have been booed off the stage. Either what musical material there is in it has simply passed me by, or there is actually none, but its absence is concealed by much inventive use of orchestration and sonority. This 'locomotive' with its famous whistle will now go round the world, treading on the necks of many composers, but when other composers try to make use of its discoveries, mistaking it for real music, the engine will be sent for scrap. Surely it cannot just be a failure on my part that I cannot detect any music in it!

My performance of the Concerto was almost good. I kept myself continually in check, and the enormous lengths I had gone to to prepare it securely paid off. I got very tired in the cadenza, but the scherzo probably went the best it has ever done. The orchestra went awry in the finale. The audience demanded one or even two bows from me after each movement, but the applause at the end was relatively modest, which may partly be explained by the unusual length of the first half of the concert, my Concerto coming at the end and wearing the listeners out. Whatever the reason its success was considerably less than the success of *Pacific*. There were a lot of visitors to the Green Room in the interval. Honegger and I congratulated each other on our respective successes. Stravinsky said he had remembered something of the Concerto from Italy in 1915, and that he liked the third movement best. In spite of Honegger's colossal success, Stravinsky was reluctant to come down from his pedestal, and in answer to my enquiry what he thought of *Pacific*, replied, 'Very, very nice.'

Damrosch[1] came in to shake Koussevitzky by the hand, but I pretended not to see him and he reciprocated, unless it was that he did not recognise me.

The Stahls sat with Bodanzky[2] in the third row and applauded discreetly. There was a supper party after the concert: Koussevitzky, ourselves, the Borovskys, Oeberg and Zederbaum.

---

1   Walter Damrosch (1862–1950), composer and conductor, Music Director of the New York Symphony Orchestra founded by his father Leopold, one half of which subsequently, in 1928, was to be reconstituted as the New York Philharmonic. Prokofiev had played the *Classical Symphony* and *First Piano Concerto* to him in New York in 1918 but Damrosch had not responded with enough enthusiasm to do anything about performing any of his music, and had not endeared himself to the young composer by comparing the Symphony with that of Kalinnikov in the evident belief that this would be welcomed as a compliment. See *Diaries*, vol. 2, pp. 330, 332, 334.
2   Artur Bodanzky (1877–1939), Austrian-born conductor. As head of the German repertory at the Metropolitan Opera he had been a member of the Met's audition panel for *The Love for Three Oranges* when Prokofiev played it for them in March 1920. Bodanzky had not much liked it. See *Diaries*, vol. 2, pp. 474, 487, 492, 523.

9 May

Spent the day relaxing. Although I have a recital coming up in three days, after yesterday my fingers are shattered, and I must rest at least until tomorrow. However, I did rehearse a little with Yurevskaya. I thought more about *Pacific*: a good lesson to learn, and I must really buckle down to instrumentation and inventiveness!

10 May

Settled down to serious work on the recital I am to play on the 12th. Thought more about *Pacific*. All right, granted there is very little musical material in it, but God knows there is not much more music in *Seven, They Are Seven*! But I am very deeply affected by *Seven*. Evidently *Pacific* does have something in it that I overlooked, and that something is a head of steam, the very power that drives that locomotive onwards with such impetuosity.

11 May

More intensive preparation. Yurevskaya came to rehearse. She has a good voice, superior to the Diva's, and has learnt the songs thoroughly although she has not yet sung herself into them with complete security. Went to Borovsky's concert in the evening: a Russian programme. He began with Tchaikovsky's Sonata No. 1, just the first movement. It is probably the only way this sonata can be performed. He played my Prelude and Toccata,[1] the latter with great élan. He ended with Stravinsky's *Petrushka*, the composer making an appearance for the last piece and sitting with Sudeikina in the box next to ours.

12 May

Polished up the Toccata in order to make a no less convincing job of it than Borovsky. My concert took place in the evening. There was a bigger audience than on the previous occasion, but still not many for such a big hall. My playing was poised and clean; my two months of work at the piano preparing for the appearance with Koussevitzky had made me a professional pianist, and Borovsky thought that I played very well.

Yurevskaya sang not at all badly, but on catching sight of Koussevitzky took fright and went wrong in 'I light the fire'.[2] After the concert Yurevskaya, her husband, Borovsky and I had tea together.

---

1 Prelude, from *Ten Pieces for Piano*, Op. 12 No. 7; Toccata, Op. 11.
2 'Ya svet zazhgu' ('I light the fire along this dark river bank'), *Five Poems of Konstantin Balmont*, Op. 36 No. 1: 'An Incantation of Water and of Fire'.

13 May

Early in the morning, before I had really had enough sleep, I was on a train going in search of a dacha near where Balmont was staying at the seaside. At six o'clock in the evening I was at Châtelaillon with Balmont, Yelena[1] and Mirra who, incidentally, has grown from a little girl into a young lady. The Balmonts were all for having a good time, but I said that before any of that I must look for a dacha, and went on the hunt with a local agent until ten o'clock at night. To begin with everyone came with me, but one by one they dropped out. Châtelaillon is a fairly drab little place, the beach is not up to much and the worst of it is that it is bounded by an ugly stone reinforcing wall. Finally there was not one dacha standing in its own grounds, all of them were huddled up with other buildings. At ten o'clock we all had supper, Balmont treating us to delicious langoustines accompanied by a bottle of white wine. Their dacha, which is small though nice, is right on the beach by the sea. I had a room to myself, in which I sank into the sleep of the dead.

14 May

The agent turned up at nine o'clock in the morning and we embarked once again on the search. Mirra leapt up to come with me. I embraced a still half-asleep Balmont. We found one extremely modest dacha, which we might take as a last resort. With Mirra and the agent we went by car to the next village of Angoulin, but the beach there was squalid. I then bought a guide-book, and on discovering that there are other beaches, chose one of them for investigation, at St Gilles, took a train and, after innumerable changes finally towards evening arrived there.

15 May

The little town of St Gilles-sur-Vie lies about 80 kilometres south of St Brévin.[2] You approach it through the wonderful surrounding French countryside, but after a few kilometres it becomes more arid because of the nearness of the ocean. The beach is magnificent. I found a very comfortable house for rent at a cost of 4,200 francs until the 1st November, the only disadvantage of which was that there was no garden. But I lost my heart to the beach, and since we had been dreaming of the sea the beach was the number one priority. I paid a deposit and at four o'clock started my journey back to Paris.

---

1 Balmont's third wife, Yelena Konstantinovna Balmont (1880–1943). Mirra was their daughter.
2 Prokofiev's seaside retreat during the summer of 1921 had been near St Brévin at Plage des Rochelets. The Balmonts had coincidentally been holidaying nearby.

16 May

Slept indifferently, even though I was alone in a 2nd-class carriage. Getting back to Paris at six in the morning, I immediately tackled the job of proof-reading the orchestral parts of *Seven, They Are Seven* in preparation for the forthcoming performance.

17 May

Met Hébertot. Next season he is presenting opera, and has it in mind to audition *The Fiery Angel*. The conductor would be Wolff, the producer Komissarzhevsky,[1] whom I knew slightly (he had introduced himself to me the previous autumn). As the audition is to take place in a week's time, I wrote to Komissarzhevsky suggesting that I read the libretto to him.

Received a letter from Mama advising me to place Svyatoslav with suitable people to bring him up. I replied that I had been talking along these lines for some time. This reduced Ptashka to tears, and was the cause of a quarrel.

18 May

Began to proof-read the score of the Third Concerto, which has been lying around for more than a month. In the evening I went to Pavlova's[2] performance: a monumental gala occasion, the gate amounting to 80,000 francs. She dances wonderfully, but to such vile music it sickens the ears. Met Diaghilev with two boys. Diaghilev was majestically affable, I playfully urbane.

19 May

Continued proofing the Third Concerto. Made peace with Ptashka. Went to a chamber concert in the evening in which the *Hebrew Overture* was

---

1 Fyodor Komissarzhevsky (1882–1954), theatre and opera director and educator, brother of Vera Komissarzhevskaya the famous actor, director and founder of the theatre bearing her name in St Petersburg. Fyodor Komissarzhevsky directed a number of productions in his sister's theatre, some in collaboration with Meyerhold, as well as other theatres in St Petersburg and Moscow including Nezlobin's Theatre and the Zimin Private Opera Company. Initially influenced by Meyerhold's Symbolist theories, he later developed his own approach to the 'transformation of reality'. After emigrating in 1919 Komissarzhevsky based himself in London, where he taught at the Royal Academy of Dramatic Art and enjoyed a successful career as a guest director in Europe and America. Eventually, just before the Second World War, he moved to America, where he continued to work as a director, taught at Yale University and founded his own acting studio.
2 Anna Pavlova, the ballerina (1881–1931). Pavlova had danced with Nijinsky in Diaghilev's first Ballets Russes seasons in Paris, but then embarked on almost continuous world tours with a company she formed specifically to showcase her unique gifts.

performed. It was well done and well received, although by a small audience. For some reason the clarinettist considered himself the soloist and during the applause came out to take a bow on his own. Koussevitzky came to the concert and liked the overture very much.

20 May

We went to a concert by Damrosch, who is giving a series of six Beethoven programmes. The French do not take him seriously, and indeed the old man conducts miserably. Still, owing to the participation of the Irish tenor McCormack[1] the hall was full and the audience prinked to the height of fashion.

21 May

Went to hear Stravinsky rehearsing his Concerto,[2] playing with orchestra for the first time in his life. He was extremely nervous, made mistakes, had memory lapses and buried his nose in the score, which he had put up on the desk in front of him. The Concerto itself is a fusion of two influences: Bach and American ragtime. The first influence I disapprove of; the second I approve, very much! He has served up music à la Bach before, in the finale of the Octet, and I took an instant dislike to it then as being so obviously fake (I have nothing against Bach's music, only against counterfeiting it). As the mainspring of its vitality the Concerto does boast a certain sturdy severity, deriving in part from the lack of strings in the orchestration. Up to a point I liked this asceticism, but only up to a point as I found myself missing the mezzo-tints and softenings that come with the strings. Here and there the brass was simply crude, blaring so as to drown the piano.

22 May

At the concert I was sharing a box with N.K.[3] and Borovsky. We were on tenterhooks for Stravinsky: suppose he got completely lost? 'He's like a girl about to lose her virginity,' I observed. His entrance on to the stage showed how much he was on edge, but the ovation he received gave him courage. He had a copy of the score beside him on the piano stool in case of an emergency, but he played well, with élan and without obviously coming off

---

1 John McCormack, Irish tenor (1884–1945), after the death of Caruso considered by many to be the greatest tenor of his day. The title of Papal Count, among a host of other honours and awards, was bestowed on him in 1928 by Pope Pius XI in recognition of his work for Catholic charities.
2 Evidently the dress rehearsal.
3 Natalya Konstantinovna [Koussevitzky].

the rails. The success was tremendous, as well it might be, a forty-year-old composer unexpectedly debuting as a pianist, and such a dashing one too. It was as if I were to appear playing a solo on the bassoon! The Concerto is certainly not easy to play, even if it does have passages of no great interest pianistically speaking. But I do not care for the imitative style of the music with its plethora of pilferings, even if they are from the ancients.[1]

23 May

Chorus rehearsal for *Seven, They Are Seven*. Apparently this is the sixth rehearsal the chorus has had but the first to which the composer has been invited. However, when I got there it transpired that the rehearsal had been postponed until tomorrow because today's rehearsal was devoted to Chaliapin, who was working with Koussevitzky on *Godunov*. Chaliapin had come over from America and was touring round several places. I did not mind too much, since it was fascinating to watch Chaliapin take charge of the rehearsal, not merely singing but generally stage-managing it to the extent of encroaching into Koussevitzky's conducting, a procedure that exasperated the latter no little given that the interventions, couched though they were in the most affectionate terms ('Seryozha, my dear friend ...') were hardly expressed in the most tactful manner. (Chaliapin to Koussevitzky: 'Serge, why do you fling your arms about like that: you don't give yourself time to finish the gesture,' or: 'Serge, please make sure you leave a decent pause here. Pauses, after all, are part of the music!'

I talked to him after the rehearsal; he was a real 'charmeur',[2] and immediately proposed that I make a setting of a text that had caught his fancy about a king and a jester. There and then he declaimed the verses with great refinement. Afterwards I came back with Koussevitzky, who spent the whole

---

1   'Stravinsky's Piano Concerto has been fashioned out of Bach and Handel, and I do not much like this. Nevertheless it has been cleverly and confidently stitched together. It sounds severe, mainly because of the brass accompaniment – there are no strings except for double-bass, and the woodwind has a less prominent role than the brass. Here and there appear contemporary dance-syncopated rhythms which greatly enliven the scratchy-sounding Bach. (A caveat: I love old man Sebastian but do not like imitations of him.) Stravinsky himself was the soloist and not at all bad; he was mortally nervous and put the score beside him on the piano stool. But there were no disasters.' (Letter to Myaskovsky of 1 June 1924.) Asafyev's considered opinion was perhaps more penetrating: 'My first impression of the work was that its composer had lost his way and become becalmed in a sea of stylisation. But after having given closer attention to the style of Handel and other Italian sources which might have served as models for Stravinsky, I became persuaded that the initial impression was in fact false. Though there is, of course, a superficial similarity of intonations, rhythms, and general procedure, Stravinsky's syntax and rhetoric are deeply contemporary.' (B. Asafyev, *A Book About Stravinsky*, trans. R. F. French, University of Michigan Research Press, Ann Arbor, 1982, quoted in S. Walsh, op. cit.)
2   In French.

journey in a very bad temper, complaining that Chaliapin had upset him by interfering in his conducting, now he was feeling ill and for two pins would withdraw from conducting the concert.

24 May

Accompanied Olga Vladislavovna to the station to see her off back to America. She has been the greatest possible help to us in all sorts of housekeeping ways, her visit far from being any sort of holiday having consisted of working round the clock.

In the afternoon, the chorus rehearsal of *Seven, They Are Seven* took place. The choir knows the work very well and sings it better than I had expected, in places with real passion. Especially impressive was 'Be ye exorcised! Be ye exorcised!' just before the timpani solo. On the other hand, the chorus glissandi sound less effective than I had expected.

25 May

Price[1] and his daughter took us in their car to Sèvres to have tea. It was the first time Svyatoslav had been left completely on his own in the apartment, but on our return he was perfectly all right, although exhausted from crying.

Price was at one time on the point of dying from heart disease, and when his doctor told him there was nothing more he could do for him, a Christian Scientist practitioner began to work with him, and completely cured him. This story made a profound impression on me.

26 May

First orchestral rehearsal of *Seven, They Are Seven*, in the foyer, which made everything sound absolutely deafening, although not particularly clear. I listened with a mixture of interest and emotional agitation. A few minor details need revising, but not many.

In the evening, the opening of the Diaghilev season: a glittering assembly of the *beau monde*. I was most interested to hear Poulenc's ballet *Les Biches*,[2]

---

1 An acquaintance made through Prokofiev's growing interest in Christian Science.
2 *Les Biches* (*The Hinds*), ballet by Poulenc, choreography by Bronislava Nijinskaya, designs by Marie Laurencin. Diaghilev had originally asked Poulenc for a ballet based on Glazunov's version of *Les Sylphides*, but Poulenc came up with other ideas derived from Watteau's painting *Le Parc aux biches*. 'A contemporary drawing-room party suffused with an atmosphere of wantonness which you immediately sense if you are corrupted, but which if you are an innocent girl you would not be conscious of,' as the composer himself described the feeling he wished to convey. Diaghilev immediately saw the potential.

but was not so much disappointed as dismayed. The material is danceable in a barrel-organish sort of way, but naive. As for the musical material, good luck to him, far be it from me to cross swords with him; obviously he resorts to it because he thinks it reflects the times we live in. So be it. But the truth is he doesn't make particularly good use of it, it all lacks form (the whole thing consists of four-bar phrases tacked on to other four-bar phrases to which they bear no relationship), there is no development, and the instrumentation, though attractive, is in the last analysis a zero.[1]

Biches was followed by *Les Noces*,[2] which I was hearing for the first time. This is the work of a master, with an intensity approaching that of *The Rite of Spring*. A marvellous work. I went to congratulate Stravinsky; we kissed, but when I voiced my criticisms of *Biches* I was astonished to hear him leap to Poulenc's defence. I said: 'I simply can't believe you like it.' Stravinsky (offended): 'What reason do you have to doubt my sincerity? You and I simply look at this from different perspectives.' I really do not understand this at all, and would like to have a serious conversation with Stravinsky about it. I had nothing to say to Poulenc, and I imagine he was disconcerted by my attitude. But it has also upset me, as I had thought him a real composer.

27 May

A good rehearsal under the direction of Koussevitzky who was naturally increasing his grip on his players, although he himself was not completely secure in his tempi, sometimes hurrying and sometimes dragging.

---

1 The orchestration does have at least one surprise: the addition of a hidden chorus to the orchestra in the pit.
2 *Les Noces* (in Russian *Svadebka*), dance cantata by Stravinsky, choreography by Bronislava Nijinskaya, first produced in Paris in 1923. The version heard by Prokofiev was the latest in a series of orchestral habiliments reflecting Stravinsky's move from the extreme opulence of *The Rite of Spring* to the frugality of *The Soldier's Tale* and the Piano Concerto, as well as his interest in mechanical forms he considered fitting for the representation of Russian peasant and village music-making. Stravinsky's first 'mechanical' inspiration was for a pianola, two cimbaloms, a harmonium and percussion, but cimbalom players being in short supply, Pleyel agreed to construct a mechanical cimbalom-playing machine known as a luthéal. But the instruments were not ready by the time of the premiere production scheduled by Diaghilev in 1923, so Stravinsky produced the instrumental guise in which the work is known today, consisting of four pianos and percussion. See the website of the Pianola Institute at www.pianola.org/history/history_stravinsky.cfm, whose information is gratefully acknowledged, for an absorbing and detailed account of Stravinsky's works for pianola. At the first performance Diaghilev decreed that the four keyboards, which were in fact two Pleyel double pianos (in effect two grand pianos enclosed in a single rectangular case with a keyboard at either end, a combined soundboard and lid to project the sound towards the audience) should be on either side of the stage rather than in the pit, thus forming part of the decor and the action. The four pianists were Georges Auric, Edouard Flament, Hélène Léon and Marcelle Meyer.

In the evening I went again to Damrosch's concert, where Hofmann[1] played Beethoven's Fourth Piano Concerto. It was surprising that Hofmann, who is so enormously successful in America and in Russia, was performing for the first time in Paris. He played with simplicity and refinement, and had a boisterous reception.

28 May

General rehearsal of *Seven, They Are Seven*, the only rehearsal involving both choir and orchestra. It began problematically, as the tenor had not realised it was due to start at ten o'clock and was extremely put out that nobody had informed him. In short, a huge to-do ensued. He wanted to cancel, and it fell to me to persuade him otherwise, a tremendous argument at an extremely inauspicious moment. He has a piercing little voice, not particularly beautiful, but he is a good musician. *Seven, They Are Seven* in a big hall sounded less menacing than I thought it would. The chorus of eighty to ninety people really needed to be a hundred and fifty. The tam-tam player was dreadful. I was a prey to terrible nerves because it had got off to such a rocky start, but Koussevitzky made a great effort and by the end had everything under control. By the time I returned home I was utterly exhausted.

In the evening I went to Szigeti's concert. He is the first violinist to have become a dedicated admirer of my Violin Concerto, and will play it in Prague in a few days' time.[2] He is a meticulously correct violinist, chaste in his artistic

---

[1] Josef Hofmann (1876–1957), Polish pianist, whom Prokofiev had met in New York. He was among other things Dagmar Godowsky's uncle. See *Diaries*, vol. 2, pp. 473–4.

[2] Josef Szigeti (1892–1973), Hungarian violinist, distinguished by his intellectually discriminating approach to new music and in particular that of his fellow countryman Bartók. Szigeti had been in the audience for the first performance of Prokofiev's Violin Concerto in October (in a version for violin and piano played by Nathan Milstein and Horowitz) the previous year, and by the time of this meeting had already given the first performance of the work in Russia, in Leningrad, earlier in the year. See *Diaries*, vol. 2, p. 712. Szigeti's beautiful recording of the Concerto with Beecham and the London Philharmonic Orchestra has recently been expertly remastered and reissued by Pristine Audio as PASC074. The sleeve notes accompanying the album in which Columbia's original 78 rpm shellac discs were issued draw attention to the Prague performance: 'The vogue of the work dates from the memorable Prague International Festival of Contemporary Music when Szigeti's playing of it resulted in invitations from almost every conductor in Europe to introduce it in his particular series. Szigeti played it under Furtwängler, Bruno Walter, Malko, Ansermet, Fritz Reiner, and many other conductors in virtually every capital in Europe. Russia first heard it from Szigeti and it had to be encored in all performances in Leningrad, Moscow, Kharkov. Szigeti also played it in the United States with the New York Philharmonic, the Philadelphia and Boston Symphony Orchestras, and introduced it in Tokyo, Shanghai, Sydney and Melbourne. Carl Flesch, in his encyclopaedic work *The Art of Violin Playing*, maintains that future generations will always identify the names of Prokofiev and Szigeti when speaking of the Concerto in D; they will see the work through his eyes and will consider his performance a standard difficult to equal, impossible to surpass.'

manners, and a good musician. I asked him about Moscow and Myaskovsky's Sixth Symphony, which he had recently heard. Szigeti had made nine appearances in Moscow; life was very expensive, audiences very attentive. He had not much liked Myaskovsky's Sixth: in his opinion it lacked unity and was not especially well realised.

29 May

The day began well with a letter from Szenkár,[1] the conductor of the Cologne Opera, expressing in the most flattering terms his desire to stage *Three Oranges*. This was followed by Szigeti's arrival to play to me the Violin Concerto. He played well, but I found it hard to think deeply about it, preoccupied as I was by the imminent performance of *The Seven*. In the evening, Ptashka and I were in Koussevitzky's box, as were the Borovskys, Debussy's widow,[2] and later on Ravel. I was very nervous and could hardly bring myself to listen to the preceding works on the programme. It was unfortunate that the piece immediately before mine was an extremely noisy work by Florent Schmitt. My agitation increased during the playing of *Seven*, but it was a good performance and had a great success. I was called out, and came to the rail at the front of the box to acknowledge the applause. Stravinsky then performed his Piano Concerto, but to less acclaim than on the previous occasion. In the interval I saw Bakst, Tcherepnin and Milyukov, all of whom were unstinting in their praise for my piece. They were followed by a whole *pléiade* of elegant ladies: Fatma,[3] Tamara and others. In the next box was Ida Rubinstein whom, accompanied by Bakst, we went in to see. With her was Rouché. Ida was saying to Demasy, who also came in with me: 'Here is the musician you need for your thing,' and followed this up by saying that she would invite me in a few days' time for discussions.

The second half of the concert included Debussy's *Nocturnes*, after which *Seven, They Are Seven* received a second airing. This time I was able to listen more calmly but the reception was cooler than it had been the first time and I was not invited to take a bow. The evening concluded with the dances from

1   Eugen Szenkar (Jenö Szenkár) (1891–1977), Hungarian-born conductor, less well known than his pre- and early post-war career would suggest (Budapest, Cologne, Berlin, Prague, Moscow, America, Israel, Brazil) since he had an intense dislike of recording and apparently never realised the importance of recordings to the building of a wide reputation. While at Cologne he conducted the 1926 premiere of Bartók's ballet *The Miraculous Mandarin* with Hans Strohbach as producer, which caused such outrage, as much for the perceived viciousness and eroticism of the subject as for the music, that performances were banned by the then city Mayor, one Konrad Adenauer. Other productions during Bartók's lifetime were distressingly few and far between.
2   Emma Bardac (1862–1934), the singer for whom Fauré composed the cycle *La Bonne Chanson* and for her daughter the *Dolly Suite*, later Debussy's second wife and mother of Claude-Emma (Chou-Chou), inspiration for the *Children's Corner* suite.
3   Hanum, Boris Samoilenko's wife. Tamara Hanum was her sister.

Prince Igor[1] complete with chorus. Ravel came for the second half only. He praised *Seven*, saying that I had demonstrated powerful expressive means and new sonorities. Mme Debussy told Ptashka that she approved of the independence of my music. 'You understand what I mean,' she added, and given that the preceding work had been her husband's *Nocturnes*, which she had heard with tears in her eyes, and before that Stravinsky's performance of his Concerto the opening bars of which were lifted straight out of his own *Nightingale*,[2] one can only imagine that the implied criticism was aimed at him.

30 May

An enjoyable feeling of relaxation, satisfaction and idleness, as if in the aftermath of a struggle. Nevertheless I sat down to proof-reading the score and parts of the Third Piano Concerto, which have been with me for so long they are going stale. Oeberg came and together we wrote a reply to Szenkár. Oeberg recounted how he had met Medtner, who was in Paris incognito, at Koussevitzky's previous concert before last night's. Medtner was indignant at Stravinsky's Concerto, saying that it was music that should be played with the feet. Medtner: 'Why does your publishing house not publish my compositions?' Oeberg: 'We can't afford to.' Medtner: 'Well, you publish Stravinsky.' Oeberg: 'N.K. pays to publish Stravinsky's works from her own pocket.' Medtner: 'And what about Prokofiev?' Oeberg: 'Likewise.'

Medtner is spending the summer in France by the sea and will then go to America, where Rachmaninoff has contrived to get him a contract.

31 May

Komissarzhevsky has at last answered my letter about *Fiery Angel* and requested a meeting. Reviews of *Seven, They Are Seven* have begun to appear, on the whole favourable although their content is hardly profound.

Ptashka and I went to the Vienna Opera in the evening, in Paris to perform Mozart. The production was *Die Entführung aus dem Serail*. It is a wonderful company, and the conductor, Schalk,[3] was highly entertaining. I had

---

1   *Prince Igor*, unfinished opera by Borodin, completed by Rimsky-Korsakov and Glazunov, first performed in 1890.
2   *Le Rossignol*, opera (Act 1, composed 1908; Acts 2 and 3, 1913–14), by Stravinsky. Prokofiev had seen and heard the ballet *Le Chant du rossignol*, choreographed for Diaghilev by Massine in Paris in 1920 from the symphonic poem Stravinsky fashioned from Acts 2 and 3 of the opera.
3   Franz Schalk (1863–1931), Music Director of the Vienna Staatsoper from 1919 to 1924, a position he shared with Richard Strauss. As a symphonic conductor, Schalk was best known for performing the symphonies of his teacher, Bruckner, notably the Fifth Symphony, in versions heavily revised by himself. Schalk's elder brother Josef performed a parallel and more lasting, perhaps also even more intrusive, service for the final (1890) version of Bruckner's last completed Symphony, the Eighth.

not heard *Die Entführung* before. It has dated rather, but much of it is very nice.

1 June

A relatively quiet day. I wrote a long letter to Myaskovsky. At lunchtime Ptashka drank some Chianti I had bought, and got a little tight.

In the evening, the Vienna Opera again, this time for *Figaro*, once again marvellously well done. Although less so than *Die Entführung*, it is also old-fashioned, the subject more than the music. One cannot get too excited about what they all get so steamed up about. Mme Newman was with us.[1] Diaghilev came up, complaining of expiring from boredom. The reason for his approach was not in fact to talk to us but to Mrs Newman, because back in London she has a husband who is an acid-tongued but influential critic, and when the Paris season finishes Diaghilev wants to take his troupe to London. With me he was friendly but remote. When he addressed Mme Newman in English, I exclaimed, 'Oho, you've really come on!' 'Yes,' he smiled, 'the boy's developing well.'

2 June

Suvchinsky[2] came, having meant to be in Paris to hear my Concerto and Stravinsky's, and for *The Seven*, but was too late and missed them all. We had a euphoric reunion, hardly knowing where to begin with our conversation. 'Where shall we start?' asked Suvchinsky. I played him the Fifth Sonata. He had come on Eurasianist[3] business; he has become increasingly caught up in

---

1   Mrs Ernest Newman, the wife of the *Sunday Times* music critic, writer on opera generally and on Wagner in particular.
2   Pyotr Suvchinsky (after emigration via Bulgaria and Berlin to Paris in 1922 known as Pierre Souvtchinsky) (1892–1985), one of the most knowledgeable and widely cultivated figures in the entire Russian émigré community. Heir to a huge sugar fortune in the Ukraine, he had come into Prokofiev's orbit in Petrograd in connection with the new music magazine *Muzykal'nyi Sovremennik* (*Musical Contemporary*) he founded and edited with Andrey Rimsky-Korsakov, the son of the composer, and its associated concert series. In Paris, Suvchinsky's circle of friends, correspondents and associates embraced the gamut of Russian and European intellectual, literary and artistic life: among many others Stravinsky, Cocteau, Satie, Artaud, Jean-Louis Barrault, Pasternak, Schoenberg, Yudina, Meyerhold, Gorky, Tsvetayeva, Boulez, Stockhausen, Karsavina (his second wife was Karsavina's daughter Marianna), Claude Rostand. An early admirer of Messiaen and Boulez, Suvchinsky in 1953 was one of the three co-founders with Boulez and Barrault of the Domaine Musicale. Although never a performer or creative artist (aside from perceptive essays on writers such as Rozanov, Remizov and Blok), Suvchinsky was a good enough pianist to give private lessons to Géza Anda. See *Diaries*, vol. 1, p. 773; vol. 2 *passim*.
3   Along with Princes Nikolai Trubetskoy and D. S. Mirsky, and P. N. Savitsky, P. Arapov and S. Efron, Suvchinsky was one of the leading figures in the Eurasianist movement (*Yevraziistvo*; its adherents were known as *Yevraziitsi*) that had currency in Russian émigré communities in the

this movement. He says their activities are growing, and announced that 'our aim is to baptise the Bolsheviks'. I introduced him to Ptashka, explaining that I had not previously told him anything about my marriage because he had not mentioned his to me, and therefore I thought he would be more comfortable in this way. Ptashka liked him.

At this point Romanov appeared, the same Romanov who in 1914 should have been staging *Ala and Lolli*. He wants to commission a ballet from me for a tiny ensemble of about six musicians. This chimes with my own desire to compose something for a small group. He hoped to secure my agreement in principle, and proposes to enter into firm commitments in a week or two.

In the evening Ptashka and I were again at the Vienna Opera for *Don Giovanni*. This is by far Mozart's best opera both from the musical and the dramatic point of view, and has lost none of its original freshness. The ball scene, with its three orchestras in three configurations, brought back vividly the time I, in full-fig evening dress, conducted on the stage of the Conservatoire.[1] How daring, alive and inventive Mozart was! But if one is to be super-critical, the trick does not quite come off as the ear cannot pick out the three different rhythms, which can only be seen from the score.

---

early 1920s. The basic notion was that – drawing on earlier nineteenth-century Slavophil ideas – the Russian character and culture owed considerably more to their Asiatic heritage than to Western civilisation, and the Bolshevik Revolution was in part an inevitable and not necessarily catastrophic counterbalance to the increasing Westernisation of Russian society. The worst excesses of the October Revolution – the mindless violence, the militant atheism, the obsession with the urban proletariat – should in time soften and evolve into a harmonious non-European society under the beneficent aegis of the Eastern Orthodox Christian Church (as opposed either to Roman Catholicism or Communism) with appropriate governing institutions. This comparatively undoctrinaire and optimistic view was completely at odds with the prevailing anti-Bolshevik, militaristic and/or monarchist attitude of the majority of the White Russian community. By the end of the 1920s *Yevraziistvo* ceased to have much influence among émigrés, having been fatally damaged by a successful Soviet scam known as TREST, a deliberately fabricated organisation expressly designed to split the Russian community abroad by inveigling the more gullible *Yevraziitsi* leaders (not Suvchinsky, however) into participating in bogus meetings inside Russia, and the movement gradually faded away. But in post-Soviet Russia the ideas have not died completely, because a neo-Eurasianist movement based (with modifications) on 1920s Eurasianism found expression in 2002 in a new political party, the Eurasia party (*Yevraziya*). Under its founder and leader Alexandr Dugin the party campaigns on a largely anti-Western, specifically anti-American platform. That the ancient tension between East and West is still very much alive under the surface has recently found expression in an important recent study of contemporary Russian and Chinese foreign policy by Bobo Lo (*Axis of Convenience: Moscow, Beijing, and the New Geopolitics*, Brookings Institute Press, Washington, DC, 2008).

1 The implication is that it was *Don Giovanni*, but it wasn't, it was *The Marriage of Figaro*. See *Diaries*, vol. 1, pp. 571–630 *passim*.

3 June

Komissarzhevsky came: having promised to be here at two o'clock, he came at three. He looked tired, indolent, his face clean-shaven and very intelligent, his head bald. His whole demeanour was somehow strange, but behind this strangeness I felt a certain rapport with him. I read him the libretto of *Fiery Angel*, remembering Demchinsky's strictures and asking him to point out any lacunae he noticed. However, he found the libretto entirely cogent dramatically, and only in three places suggested minor interpolations with the object of better stitching together the separate acts. These suggestions I immediately adopted. He asked me to let him know when I was proposing to play the score through to Wolff, so that he would be able to exert influence on him in my favour.

In the evening I heard a concert in which Heifetz[1] played the Beethoven Concerto, very good, impersonal. The audience went wild.

Blois[2] tells me that Damrosch is planning to perform *Seven, They Are Seven*.

4 June

Suvchinsky lunched with us, devouring with relish a cutlet set before him by Ptashka. He expatiated on the subject of idleness, and as I am continually criticising B.N. for his indolence and parasitical attitude, Suvchinsky's theories were very interesting to me. While he naturally disapproves of people who never do anything, he does consider that people who elevate work into a cult fall into error. 'Look at present-day Germany or America,' he said. 'The consequence of these countries having developed technology to such a pitch is that millions of people do nothing but work without ceasing for the whole of their lives. In the end they themselves turn into machines, because they have no time to think. But those who allow themselves occasional periods of idleness are often very good people.'

After lunch we went to the Opéra, where Chaliapin should have been rehearsing *Khovanshchina*, but we were too late and met Chaliapin leaving at the end of the rehearsal. We had a short conversation, after which Suvchinsky said, 'Apart from anything else, I love Chaliapin simply as a thing. He is magnificent purely as a piece of meat!'

---

1 Jascha Heifetz (1901–1987), Lithuanian-born violinist, a student of Leopold Auer at the St Petersburg Conservatoire where Prokofiev had first encountered him at the age of thirteen, playing Glazunov's Violin Concerto. See *Diaries*, vol. 1, p. 584; vol. 2, pp. 394, 511.
2 Pierre Blois, music critic and arts administrator. He also held a management position with Maison Pleyel, the Paris piano-manufacturing company and concert agency.

In the evening, Ptashka, Suvchinsky and I were at the Diaghilev premiere of Auric's *Les Fâcheux*,¹ P.P.² wearing my top hat. He greatly admired the sets, but had nothing particular to say about the music. As for myself I could not go so far as to say I liked the music, but at least it did not enrage me as Poulenc's had done. It may not be very talented, but in any case it was not as scandalously bad as *Biches*. Diaghilev ignored me (and Suvchinsky), the first time he has pulled a weird stunt like that.

5 June

The day went fairly quietly. I went out to buy tutors for the French horn, the trumpet and other wind instruments, to ensure that my scores are conveniently and effectively written for the instruments. Unfortunately these tutors are all very old editions and often out of date in terms of contemporary technique.

6 June

Mrs Wake came to see us. When we were at Sèvres she was living in the same *pension* as we were, and told us amazing things about Christian Science. Price, the very nice elderly man who was also living there, and who was barely clinging to life from heart disease when we knew him at the time, was cured absolutely after a few treatments.

7 June

Hébertot, whom I had alerted to the fact that I would be leaving Paris on the 10th and who had promised that before that time there would be an audition of *Fiery Angel*, sent a letter saying that Wolff was terribly busy and it would not be possible to arrange a time to hear it. However, if an opportunity to present my opera should present itself, he would get in touch with me during the summer. I inferred from this letter the obvious conclusion that *Fiery Angel* was not going to get a production in the immediate future. It is a pity, but it may be for the best: I shall compose a Symphony, because it is some time since I wrote any new music, if you do not count the Fifth Sonata. All my 'novelties' that were heard for the first time in Paris this season were essentially not new pieces.

---

1 *Les Fâcheux* (*The Bores*), ballet by Georges Auric, libretto by Boris Kokhno after the Molière–Beauchamp comedy-ballet, choreography by Bronislava Nijinska, scenery and costumes by Braque.
2 Pyotr Petrovich (Suvchinsky).

Was at the Borovskys. He played my Third Piano Concerto through to me, which he had learnt in three weeks. It was interesting to hear it in someone else's interpretation.

Thought about Christian Science. One simply cannot pass over such astonishing results without wishing to know more about it.

8 June

As Ptashka has still not fully recovered from post-partum complications, she wants to consult a Christian Science practitioner. I support her in this, and may go myself because of my heart and my neuralgia. We thought of going today, because I hate to procrastinate, and the practitioner lives very near by, but were prevented by a constant stream of people visiting.

Suvchinsky dropped in to say that he been to see Stravinsky, and had had a very friendly lunch with him. Stravinsky had even telephoned Wiéner especially to ask him to come round so that Suvchinsky could hear the Concerto. Of me, Stravinsky said, 'What is bad about Prokofiev is that he still wants to go on being a Modernist.' Presumably this was after hearing *Seven, They Are Seven*. And then, suddenly: 'It's terrible that Prokofiev is still setting Balmont's verse.' Well, what about Stravinsky setting Diaghilev's boy Kokhno?!'[1]

9 June

As it appears that the Christian Science practitioner who was living near us is no longer there, Ptashka and I went today to another one, Mrs Getty. But today is a holiday and she was not there. In the afternoon we attended a christening; Ptashka is godmother. The ceremony was conducted by the Abbé Petit, a sprightly former musician who was very anxious to meet me. I talked to him at length about modern French music. He is acquainted personally with Poulenc, Auric and Tailleferre. When I told him I how I happened to have been in a box with Tailleferre at the performance of *Biches*, and how I thought she had been offended by my criticisms of Poulenc, the Abbé responded, 'I have never found Tailleferre at all averse to hearing her colleagues criticised!'

---

1 Boris Kokhno (1904–1990), librettist and choreographer, assistant to Diaghilev and after his death mainly responsible for the struggle to keep the Ballets Russes alive. See *Diaries*, vol. 2, pp. 595, 599, 607. Prokofiev is referring to *Mavra*, the short *opera buffa* originally conceived as a curtain-raiser to *The Sleeping Beauty* and first performed in a production by Diaghilev on 3 June 1922. Kokhno wrote the libretto based on Pushkin's short story 'Domik v Kolomne' ('The Little House at Kolomna'). Writing to Kokhno in January 1922 Stravinsky expressed his opinion that 'it is the best thing I have done'. See S. Campbell, 'The Mavras of Pushkin, Kochno and Stravinsky', *Music and Letters*, vol. 58 no. 3, July 1977.

10 June

We had been planning on leaving for the country today but Mama and B.N. are still far from being in a position to dig themselves out of Oberammergau, neither have my affairs yet resolved themselves. We managed to extend our lease of the apartment by a little and therefore will stay put for a while. It looks as though the most promising of the various propositions that have been in the offing for me is the most unexpected: the ballet for Romanov.

Damrosch is giving a Beethoven cycle in the Champs-Elysées Theatre. The Parisians scoff at him but they still go to the concerts because he gives the proceeds to retired French musicians – the only effective gesture this particular conductor is capable of making, as the common gibe goes. Blois, who dances attendance on him, took my scores to show him, and has now come back with the news that Damrosch wants urgently to perform *The Seven* in New York, and asks me to call on him tomorrow morning.

11 June

Ptashka went to see Mrs Getty. She was very kindly received, and Mrs Getty after speaking to her for some time said, 'Now I will make you a treatment.'[1] She covered her eyes with her hand and remained in a state of concentration for about ten minutes. Then she said, 'You will be well.'

While this was going on I went to see Damrosch. The old man was courteous, and said among other things, 'I am too old to dissemble, and I must tell you straight out that I do not like your Third Piano Concerto, but *Seven, They Are Seven* is a splendid thing and I wish to perform it in New York.' I already knew that he had not in fact attended the performance, but his daughters had and were ecstatic about the work. The reason the old man was so enthusiastic was that he had not heard it. We left it that Oeberg would come to see him to discuss the hire of the material.

In the afternoon I had a severe headache. I took a powder, but this will be the last time as tomorrow I am going to consult Mrs Getty, following which my head should no longer ache, but if it does then I must keep faith and not resort to medicine.[2] My headache cleared up and in the evening I once again attended Diaghilev's production of *Biches*. This time the tunes lodged themselves in my ears and were hummable, but this does not demonstrate true melodic invention: he has simply taken now-forgotten but once-fashionable

---

1 In English.
2 It is a fundamental tenet of the First Church of Christ, Scientist, founded by Mary Baker Eddy in Boston in 1879, that since all of God's creation including mankind is spiritual and the material world merely an illusion, sickness is also an illusion resulting from fear, ignorance and sin. Using the power of the mind to correct these errors with will cause the sickness to vanish.

tangos languishing on the shelf on account of their intrinsic meretriciousness and vacuity. Met Szymanowski.[1] He had been at a music festival in Prague where, according to him, the greatest success had been enjoyed by two violin Concertos, his and mine. In answer to my question how he, as a visitor to the city, was enjoying the musical novelties being offered in Paris, he replied, 'I don't understand them, but Milhaud's "Salades",[2] which is on at the Pigalle, is even worse.' Picasso observed amiably, 'I always answer questions like that by saying "oh, very nice".'

After *Biches* I did not return to the auditorium for the *Igor* Dances[3] but stayed outside talking to the Spanish painter Sert.[4] Sert is quite well known and has good connections with the court of the Spanish royal family. Diaghilev sneers at him but from time to time, because of his connections, commissions designs from him. Sert is married to Mme Edwards, a great benefactor of Diaghilev and a woman I do not like. When I revealed to Sert my opinion of *Biches*, he said, 'Ravel, who was sitting next to me at the performance, is of exactly the same opinion.' Later in the conversation he said, 'There is no such thing as up-to-date or out-of-date in art; there is only talented and untalented.'

We were speaking very openly, from the heart, and as we said goodbye he said he hoped we would meet more frequently next season. The moral for me was an unexpected one: it is that the company of conservatively minded people is more congenial to me. Surely I couldn't be emulating the evolutionary path of, say, Medtner, an innovator at twenty and a fossilised academic at thirty or thirty-five. Could I?

12 June

Rose early and went to Mrs Getty in order to be one of the first there. I waited half an hour for her to arrive, and was in a state of some agitation. Mrs Getty

---

1   Karol Szymanowski (1887–1832), Polish composer and poet. Prokofiev had first met Szymanowski as early as 1915 in Kiev, and admired his compositions, especially for the violin. The friendship between the two composers grew when they were staying near one another in New York in early 1922. See *Diaries*, vol. 2, pp. 33, 109, 665–6.
2   In 1919 Milhaud, back in Paris after two years in Brazil, wrote a set of twelve piano pieces, later arranged for orchestra, which were published as *Saudades do Brazil*. 'Saudades' is of course not the Portuguese word for salad, but for longing, or nostalgia.
3   The *Polovtsian Dances* from Act 2 of Borodin's opera *Prince Igor*.
4   Jose-Maria Sert (1876–1945), Spanish painter, mural artist and scenic designer, at this time the third (and most deeply loved) husband of the Paris hostess and artistic patron Misia Godebska/Edwards/Sert. When Prokofiev had played his Second Piano Concerto to Diaghilev on the occasion of their first meeting in London in 1914, Sert, who was also present and who had not realised Prokofiev understood French, exclaimed, 'Mais c'est une bête féroce!', a remark that seems to have delighted both Prokofiev and Diaghilev. See *Diaries*, vol. 1, p. 706.

has an 'office'¹ in a very good American-style business building. In person she is a very pleasant lady of about forty to fifty years of age, quite ordinary-looking at first glance. She sat me down facing her in an armchair by the window. I said that my wife had been to see her yesterday and now I was here myself; I had been suffering from neuralgia for the past ten years, episodes occurring with surprising regularity three times a month, and I also had some heart trouble. Although the last condition was better than it had been, it had still not completely stabilised. She asked me what I knew of Christian Science, and I answered that while I had had occasion to witness some remarkable manifestations (meaning Price), the knowledge of its essential elements I had gleaned from others (Mrs Wake) was unfortunately not solid enough to allow me to form a proper understanding of its true nature. She then said, 'Maintenant je vais vous faire un traitement,'² and put into my hands a copy of *Science and Health*,³ telling me, 'Read this.' I started to read, she covered her eyes with her hands and withdrew into herself. I read for quite a long time, at first finding it hard to concentrate but then, supposing that she would ask me questions on what I had read, forcing myself to construct a clear account of my new understanding. After some time she said that she hoped I and my wife would be well and would not need any further assistance. I said that from what I had read I understood that man was a reflection of God and as such should not be subject to suffering; it is forgetting this fact that brings suffering in its train. Pleased with this, she replied that I had understood correctly. I had been informed that the cost of one visit was twenty francs, but as I had thirty in my pocket I offered them all to her; Mrs Getty, however, insisted on giving ten back. I said goodbye, kissed her hand, and left. On the way home I found myself involuntarily experimenting to see what effect rapid walking would have on my heart, but then told myself to focus on the moral, rather than the medical, aspect of the treatment.⁴

In the evening I called on Koussevitzky to tell him about my notion of composing a Symphony. He approved wholeheartedly of the intention and said that the moment it was written he would perform it in America. He

---

1 In English.
2 'Now I am going to give you a treatment.'
3 *Science and Health with Key to the Scriptures*, a primary text for adherents of Christian Science, was published by the founder of the First Church of Christ Scientist, Mrs Mary Baker Eddy, in 1875. 'It is the first time since the dawn-days of Creation that a Voice has gone crashing through space with such placid and complacent confidence and command,' commented Mark Twain in Book I of *Christian Science*, his lengthy and devastating 1907 demolition job on the book, the claims of Christian Science and the personality of its self-styled Discoverer.
4 A very different initial experience of Christian Science treatment from that of Mark Twain, who out walking one day in the Tyrolean Alps fell and 'broke a few arms and legs and things'. See Appendix 1.

advised me to be sure to make one of the movements a theme and variations, and this appealed to me.

13 June

A letter from Hébertot: Wolff has made some free time and will listen to *Fiery Angel*. It is extraordinary how all this is panning out: I should have left Paris this morning, but delayed my departure because Mama had not arrived and various matters needing attention had not been resolved. The train on which I had intended to travel left at 8.40 a.m., and Hébertot's letter was delivered at nine o'clock. Are Wolff's intentions serious, or is this merely a tactic? Whatever the true situation, I shall treat the invitation as a serious one and put faith in Wolff and in Komissarzhevsky. I set off to call on Wolff, who was genial and friendly, showing me a long and already printed list of operas that they are announcing for the forthcoming year, but adding, 'Don't be alarmed, we are not going to present all of them, and some of those that have been announced will be replaced by others.' *Fiery Angel* audition is set for the day after tomorrow.

In the evening Ptashka, I, Suvchinsky and his sister-in-law Apukhtina were at the theatre for Diaghilev's latest production. This was of some operetta or other by Chabrier, originally with spoken dialogue subsequently turned into recitative with music provided by Milhaud.[1] The result was a long, vacuous and insipid production without a shred of wit or animation. Diaghilev had put it on in pursuance of some unfathomable ordinances forming part and parcel of his present evolution. The audience was unimpressed: as the performance wound on sounds of hissing, booing and whistling emanated from the gallery in attempts to unsettle the actors, alternating with noisy and inappropriate applause intended to drown out the music. In short, the action in the auditorium was a lot more interesting than what was taking place on stage. Stravinsky, sitting in a box not far away from us, was visibly enraged by the behaviour of the audience, occasionally booing back in the direction of the gallery. I do not exclude the possibility that it was Stravinsky who had persuaded Diaghilev to put the thing on in the first place.

At the end, Suvchinsky said to Stravinsky, 'I see that there could be reasons for presenting this sort of stuff, but the choice of this one seems to me to have been an unfortunate one. Why pick something as tedious as this? *The Barber of Seville* is in a similar vein but vastly more entertaining.' Stravinsky got hot under the collar, and muttering, 'You're all savages', turned on his heel and left.

1   *Une Éducation manquée* (*An Incomplete Education*), one-act operetta composed by Chabrier in 1879. Diaghilev asked Milhaud to replace the original spoken dialogue with recitative, and Milhaud also composed an extra aria for the heroine, Hélène, taking for the purpose a melody he had found among Chabrier's unpublished manuscripts. Sets were by Juan Gris.

The last piece in the programme was *The Rite of Spring*. This I listened to with great absorption, and once again decided that I liked it better in a staged than a concert performance. Heard in concert *Sacre* is formless, but when it is staged this very formlessness is its own justification. It is just the other way round with *Les Noces*: there I find the staging unnecessary, seeming to have been tacked on. That work I should very much like to hear in concert form. After *Sacre* I ran into Stravinsky in the corridor, and going up to him clapped him on the shoulder and said, 'Bravo, well done, old man!' I meant 'old man' in the affectionate way the French use 'mon vieux', but Stravinsky flared up at once: 'As if you weren't an old man yourself!' he snapped, and rushed off without saying goodbye, leaving the bystanders in a state of amused astonishment.

14 June

Was at Wolff's. I went through the libretto with him, which he judged to be somewhat confused, but interesting. I then played him Renata's hysterical scene and her narrative; as the latter has already been orchestrated he followed it with the score, and expressed his approval. His wife then appeared, a very interesting woman but whose intrusive intervention into the matter in hand I did not appreciate. But she soon took off her husband to lunch, and the audition will be continued tomorrow.

In the afternoon Ptashka and I went to have our photographs taken by Lipnitzky,[1] at his invitation for no fee. He is a most entertaining individual, with a continual stream of patter through which he manages to take your photograph when you are least expecting it.

15 June

Went with Suvchinsky to the Kokhánskis. Kokhánski[2] is learning my Concerto to perform it in America next season. At last. I wanted to consult

---

1   Boris Lipnitzky (1887–1971), photographer. Studio Lipnitzky in the rue du Colisée produced memorable portraits of a great number of artistic celebrities, including Picasso, Ravel, Brigitte Bardot, and perhaps his most famous image, Albert Dieudonné in the role of Napoleon in Abel Gance's epic film.
2   Paweł Kokhánski (1887–1934), outstanding Polish violinist whose technical and interpretative gifts encouraged many composers besides Prokofiev to turn to him as a valued collaborator. Among them were Szymanowski, who dedicated his First Violin Concerto to him, and Stravinsky, who wrote for him the five-movement arrangement for violin and piano of the *Pulcinella* Suite. It was Kokhánski who, having been denied the opportunity to give the planned premiere of Prokofiev's D major Violin Concerto in Petrograd because of the October 1917 Revolution, made his own edition of the solo violin part and brought it out with him when he left Russia in 1921 for the United States, where he became Professor of Music at the Juilliard School of Music in New York. See *Diaries*, vol. 2, pp. 33, 230, 292, 536, 588, 614, 621, 665–6.

him on various effects which can be produced on the violin, in which field he is a master. Dukelsky[1] was there also, a young composer I had met in America. Mme Kokhanskaya whispered to me that he was a great admirer of my music, but he seemed to me a rather detestable young man, and I purposely paid him no attention. Arthur Rubinstein[2] also came in, comporting himself with rather more discretion than in America. He is working on the piano transcription of *Petrushka* which he will include in his concert next week. 'Only to think', he exclaimed tragically, 'that I showed Stravinsky the way to do all those passages when he was writing the piece, and now I have to torture myself learning to play them!' Apparently in the making of the two-hand piano version of *Petrushka* he genuinely had played an important and technically valuable part.

16 June

Played Wolff more of *Fiery Angel*, not straight through but those parts I judged most suitable for his attention, approximately half. Wolff then took me to lunch, after which I played him the rest. Wolff was impressed. 'Well,' he said, 'we must certainly put it on. I will speak to Hébertot.' I asked him to do this before my departure.

17 June

I don't know what will happen with *Fiery Angel*, but as far as Romanov is concerned things are working out. The next move is up to me, since I do not

1 Vladimir Dukelsky, aka Vernon Duke (1903–1969), composer with a double life comparable to Kurt Weill or Gershwin. The classically trained Dukelsky enjoyed the serious consideration and respect of, *inter alia*, Prokofiev, Diaghilev and Koussevitzky, while as Vernon Duke (a rebranding suggested by the already successfully rebranded George Gershwin) he became a prolific and successful producer of Broadway scores and popular songs: 'April in Paris', 'Autumn in New York', 'Walk a Little Faster'. His dual personality lasted until 1955, after which he credited his compositions in all genres to Vernon Duke. He was also a good writer of both Russian and English; his autobiography *Passport to Paris*, long out of print, would merit republishing. Dukelsky had first encountered Prokofiev before either of them went to America, in 1916 at a piano recital Prokofiev gave in Kiev, an occasion colourfully described in *Passport to Paris*. They had met occasionally in New York, but the friendship, after the somewhat unpromising start described in this diary entry, was now to develop and deepen in Europe. See *Diaries*, vol. 2, pp. 152, 282.
2 Arthur (the 'h' seems to come and go almost at will) Rubinstein (1887–1982), outstanding Polish pianist, a man of extraordinarily wide culture equipped to read and communicate fluently in eight languages, an enthusiastic and discriminating proponent of new music, especially by French, Spanish and South American composers, as well as displaying a special affinity with the music of his compatriot Szymanowski. His two books of memoirs (*My Young Years*, published in 1973, and *My Many Years* in 1980), both published by Alfred A. Knopf, are irresistible if disingenuous accounts of his life, times, performances, travels and liaisons. He and Prokofiev had become friends from their first meeting in New York. See *Diaries*, vol. 2, pp. 330, 386, and *passim*.

want to commit myself before the situation with *Angel* becomes clearer. Romanov is prepared to pay me 10,000 francs. I think it will take me about six weeks to complete the work.

During this time we had from the agency a succession of possible nannies for Svyatoslav: Danish girls, Swedes, Norwegians. Mrs Garvin has generously undertaken to bear the costs. Today, finally, a Norwegian girl, Miss Mack, appeared, pleasant-mannered, clean and modest.

18 June

Ptashka bought a copy of the book *Science and Health*, the primary Christian Science text. We are reading it.

Suvchinsky came in the evening, bringing Dukelsky with him. He played his Piano Concerto. Not bad at all. It shows some influence from me. Suvchinsky has to cut short his stay in Paris and go to his mother in Nice; today will be his last visit to us. It is very sad that we have to part again.

19 June

At two o'clock I went to meet Mama and B.N., arriving from Oberammergau, but they did not appear until five o'clock, by the next train. I was anxious, as I did not know what kind of state Mama would be in; the last time I had seen her, in February, she had been near death. But Mama now seemed in good form, walking briskly when I took her arm. This was little short of miraculous, given that she had been near death all winter. Mama was fascinated by her grandson. I found for B.N. a room in a hotel which he did not scruple to deprecate as inadequately luxurious, and relieved me of 3,000 francs. Ptashka made a delicious dinner with wine, which to the travellers accustomed to German cuisine was all the more appetising.

20 June

In the evening Ptashka and I attended the premiere of Milhaud's *Le Train bleu*,[1] a deliberate essay at vulgar material orchestrated in a vulgar style. But it is all of a piece with these 'new' directions, the point of which escapes me.

---

1   The ballet, with its sharp libretto by Cocteau and witty score by Milhaud, is a skit on the life and amusements of the metropolitan *beau monde* conveyed in the first-class-only Calais–Méditerranée Express sleeper from Calais to the Riviera. Described by Cocteau as a 'danced operetta' rather than a ballet, it was choreographed by Bronislava Nijinska and starred Diaghilev's latest discovery, the twenty-year-old Anton Dolin, in a role created to show off his gymnastic skills. As Diaghilev's programme note warned the audience: 'The point about *Le Train bleu* is that there no blue train to be seen. This being the age of speed, the train has already reached its destination and disembarked its passengers.' Choreography was by Bronislava

As we were going in I met Koka Benois,[1] who not long ago arrived in Paris from St Petersburg. He is my great aficionado, and I have been very interested in him as to me he was showing signs of becoming a promising artist. He has now turned into a most interesting young man, and to cap it all announced that he has got married, slyly adding, 'to a very good friend of yours'. In the interval I was quite stunned to see him with ... none other than Marusya Pavlova![2] Ever tactful, I immediately blurted out: 'Marusya, but you're so much older than he is!'

She was looking as pretty as ever, especially the eyes, but very slightly ravaged, no doubt by life in St Petersburg. She had been singing at the Mariinsky, but not in leading roles. All four of us lamented that Ptashka and I were going away in two days and thus would have no opportunity to see one another and talk about old times.

21 June

Hébertot categorically refused to pay me any money at all for *Fiery Angel*, even as an advance on future performance fees. He agreed that the opera would be presented next season, but stopped short of giving any guarantee. In short, it was all looking very shaky. He was very keen that next season Koussevitzky should be at the Champs-Elysées rather than at the Opéra. I proposed an introduction to Koussevitzky, hinting that Koussevitzky might come up with some money to pay me to orchestrate *Fiery Angel* if Hébertot would guarantee a production.

Nijinska, who also danced the role of the Tennis Champion (modelled on Suzanne Lenglen). Cocteau's libretto, backed by Milhaud's witty music-hall score, pressed into service as many modish characters and pastimes as possible: flappers, gigolos, cocktails, tennis, golf, aeroplanes, photography. Coco Chanel designed the costumes, Henri Laurens the sets. Picasso created the fabulous front curtain, seen in all its gigantic glory (34 feet by 38 feet) in the copy made by the scene-painter Prince Alexander Shervashidze and authenticated by Picasso, at the Victoria and Albert Museum's Diaghilev exhibition in August 2010. Prokofiev's censorious reaction was not widely shared: the ballet was tremendously popular, but when Dolin left the company the following year it evidently proved impossible for another dancer to re-create his particular blend of athleticism with classical style, and it vanished from the repertoire for the next six decades.
1   Nikolay (Koka) Benois (1901–88), painter and theatre designer, the son of Alexander Benois. He had left Russia in 1923 and was immediately absorbed by Diaghilev into the Ballets Russes domain, for which he provided several settings. He and his father later moved to Italy, where Nikolay became one of the leading designers for La Scala, collaborating with Visconti notably on the re-creation of period jewellery and costumes.
2   Maria (Marusya) Pavlova, soprano, had been a singing student at the St Petersburg Conservatoire when Prokofiev first fell for her vivacious charms in 1911 and danced attendance on and off for several years. Later, Boris Zakharov also came under her spell, which caused some tension between the two – among others, one understands – admirers. See *Diaries*, vol. 1, pp. 200–201, 377, 404–5, and *passim*; vol. 2, pp. 57–198 *passim*.

We therefore went together to see Koussevitzky and Hébertot immediately undertook to present Fiery *Angel* in the autumn of 1925 (i.e. the season after next). Koussevitzky in turn promised to provide him with the orchestral material and a vocal score with a French translation of the libretto. Both sides agreed a forfeit of 10,000 francs should the agreement fail to be honoured. The discussion then turned to the possibility of Koussevitzky giving concerts at the Champs-Elysées Theatre. Koussevitzky said he would consider the possibility, and Hébertot then left, after proposing that Oeberg call on him to draw up an agreement on what had been discussed. The deal thus seems to be in the bag, and I am very grateful to Koussevitzky. Concerning the money, Koussevitzky confided to me, away from Hébertot's hearing, that he would simply subsidise me to the extent of the 10,000 francs independently of the *Fiery Angel* agreement. This money would be a loan, which I should repay when it was convenient to do so. Koussevitzky's action demonstrated not only what a gentleman but what a friend he is. The flowering of our friendly relations was no doubt helped by the fact that some days previously I had told him that were I to write a Symphony it would be for him, and I would dedicate it to him.

In the afternoon B.N. brought in Nikita Magalov,[1] whose piano playing is immaculately clean and whose compositions equally so but without a shred of personality. True, he is still so very young that it is impossible to predict what will become of him. I have noticed that with child composers the critical age is thirteen to fourteen, that is to say the age of puberty. This is the point at which talent either withers in the face of other interests, or establishes itself on a solid footing.

Nikita is a very prepossessing boy, but has been so spoiled by the ladies in America, and above all his Mamasha, that he has turned into a revolting little poseur.

22 June

The day before our departure, consequently a day of madness.

I signed a contract with Romanov: 10,000 francs, and an easy and pleasant job to fulfil. After that, since *Fiery Angel* is evidently well on track, I asked

---

1 Nikita Magalov (1912–1992) was Boris Bashkirov's nephew, the son of his sister the Princess Varvara Magalova and her husband Prince Magalov (originally Magalashvili, as he was a Georgian aristocrat). Prokofiev had known him as a two-year-old when engaged to give piano lessons to his mother. The family emigrated to America immediately after the Revolution, and the six-year-old boy, already showing extraordinary talent as a pianist, eventually studied with Isidor Philipp at the Paris Conservatoire, graduating with the premier prix. He was particularly admired by Ravel, and formed a close association with Szigeti, whose daughter he later married. Renowned also as a teacher, he was chosen in 1949 to take over Dinu Lipatti's class at the Geneva Conservatoire when the great Romanian pianist had become too ill to continue teaching. See *Diaries*, vol. 1, p. 251; vol. 2, pp. 136, 138–9.

Komarov[1] to visit me with a view to his making a French translation (he is translating *Kitezh*[2] very well), and a copyist.

In the afternoon, guests: Marnold,[3] (critic of the *Mercure de France*), a passionate aficionado of mine, and Downes[4] (the critic of the *New York Times*), as yet less committed but still extremely interested in my music, which is saying a lot for an American critic. I played them the Fifth Sonata and some other things. Concurrently appeared Mme Chevillier, a violinist and rather piquant lady who had learnt my Violin Concerto. One of the reasons she had travelled from Strasbourg was to play it to me. A whole group of people arrived at the same time: B.N., Dr Polack, Oeberg. The last-named had been to see Hébertot, but he was away from his office. This seemed strange to me, and when the last of the guests had gone we went together to find Hébertot, upon which I was told that he was unwell and had not been seen in the theatre that day. This struck me as a bad sign. I very much wanted to have the terms of the contract signed before I left Paris, because I was not confident either of Hébertot's real commitment or of Oeberg's competence in the matter, he is such a dilatory and at the same time rapacious individual. In the evening I once again telephoned the theatre while the performance was in progress, and asked Oeberg to go there as well. I enquired from the managers and staff on duty what the situation was with Hébertot, but they confirmed the story. It was clear that I would have to put further matters in the hands of Oeberg, as I could not put off my departure any more: the tickets were booked, our things virtually all packed, our lease of the apartment would be up the following morning, in short we already had one foot beyond the perimeter of Paris.

23 June

Got up at six; had it not been for Miss Mack we would never have managed. As it was we were on the train at 8.40: Mama, Ptashka, Svyatoslav, Mack, myself, seven suitcases in the luggage van and fifteen in the compartment. We changed trains three times; during one of them the porter dropped and

---

1 Anatoly Komarov, a translator from Russian into French.
2 *The Legend of the Invisible City of Kitezh and the Maiden Fevronia*, opera (1904, first produced 1907) by Rimsky-Korsakov.
3 Jean Marnold, pen-name of Jean Morland (1859–1935), a much respected critic, perceptive supporter of Ravel in his difficult early years, and co-founder with Louis Laloy of *Le Mercure musical*.
4 Olin (Edwin) Downes (1886–1955), the often choleric music critic – especially where music of the Second Viennese School was concerned – of the *New York Times* between 1924 and 1955. He was by no means hostile to all new music, however, championing the works of Prokofiev, Shostakovich, Stravinsky and above all Sibelius, with whom he established a personal relationship and whose biography he wrote.

smashed my typewriter. We reached St Gilles at eight o'clock in the evening. From the outside the dacha did not look very impressive, sticking up rather like a sore thumb, but inside it was comfortable. We got ready to go to bed, but not before Ptashka and I made a preliminary sortie to the sea.

24 June

Mainly rested today. We went down to the sea, which is still too cold for swimming. The beach when the tide is out is stupendous: smooth, sandy and boundless. It is the chief delight of St Gilles.

25 June

Proof-read the orchestral parts of the Third Concerto. Stravinsky is right when he says that printed parts must always be corrected by the composer, since after all the orchestra plays from the parts, not from the score, and all the flavour is in the orchestra. But my God, what a chore!

Svyatoslav slept for two days after the journey!

26 June

A strong wind blows from the sea, and I have caught a cold. Our room is upstairs, a large room with many cupboards, a big table and a comfortable couch. The balcony has a view of the ocean. Next to ours at the back is Svyatoslav's and Miss Mack's room. On the ground floor below us there is a large room for Mama, and below Svyatoslav's is the dining room and kitchen. That is all.

27 June

The piano was brought in, sent by Pleyel very quickly and free of charge from Paris. It was impossible to get it upstairs into our room, so it was put into Mama's. I can start work tomorrow.

A letter from Demasy: he is the opinion that Rubinstein[1] will write to me in a few days with an official invitation to compose the music for *Juditha*. I had already more or less washed my hands of it, but I had already composed a few thematic ideas.

---

1   Ida, not Arthur.

28 June

We get up (or rather start getting up) at seven, drink coffee at eight, so at half past eight I am ready to sit down to make a start on the ballet for Romanov, which I have finally decided to write for a quintet, and even to keep in mind as I compose not merely ballet music but a concert piece for quintet. I composed the first theme in Paris before leaving, as I walked along the street, and wrote it down by the light of a street lamp. Now I settled down to develop it, worked for an hour, and then set it aside. I then carried on with proofing the Third Concerto.

29 June

Although my cold was threatening to get the better of me, I continued composing and got on quite well with the third movement.

Had a headache in the afternoon: a neuralgic pain, which after Mrs Getty's treatment ought not to be happening. I read the Christian Science book and did some more proof-reading, although not much. By evening the headache had disappeared, a rare event.

30 June

Composed in the morning and completed the first variation. It progresses easily.

I then went for a walk by the sea and thought out a second subject for my Symphony. The main theme I shall take from my notebooks: I composed it some time ago when I was in Rochelets,[1] and I am very attached to it.

1 July

Composed: took a theme for the second movement I had composed in Paris shortly before we left, and developed it. I think the Quintet will turn out extremely well.

A pram arrived for Svyatoslav, sent from Paris, so we took him out for a walk. In one way this was delightful, but from another point of view it was rather embarrassing to be seen out in such a role.

---

1 In the summer of 1921.

2 July

Worked a little, not much, on the third movement. Even so, the pace of progress is not bad. I might be able to finish the whole thing in four or five weeks.

I have been reading some recently published excerpts from Chekhov's notebooks: material that he did not manage to make use of. All his jottings and thoughts are full of utterly enchanting observation, humour, freshness. I derive more pleasure from reading them than from the finished productions of other writers.

3 July

Worked on the Quintet, and achieved the second variation of the first movement. The weather is cold, windy and wet. In the afternoon I experienced a sharp attack of rheumatism in my right hand. My rheumatism has its origin in the scarlet fever I once had,[1] when I suffered from it in both hands. There were two repeat episodes of it in Ettal, each time for a single day. Today's attack was very painful, and I hardly knew what to do with myself. When it subsided I read Christian Science, and by evening it passed off completely.

4 July

My hand is better. However, I did not compose today: I decided to have a break after working for a whole week. In the afternoon I checked the translations of some of my songs into French and English, done by Laloy and Burness. Marnold's review in the *Mercure de France* of Koussevitzky's concerts extols me and lambasts Stravinsky.

5 July

A sore head (but not a neuralgia pain), consequently did not compose much but went for a long walk which successfully walked off the tension. Even so I managed to complete the outline of the second movement of the Quintet. A disappointing letter from Oeberg: Hébertot continues to drag his heels and has not concluded the agreement for *Fiery Angel*.

6 July

Played through against the clock the complete music of the Quintet: it came out at seven minutes. Not much! I thought I would have got up to ten, and

---

1 In America in the summer of 1919. See *Diaries*, vol. 2, pp. 406–7.

altogether it needs to be fourteen or fifteen. I've been composing a link passage into a serious Adagio: as to the quality of the music, it may not be as high as the first three movements, but as it seems to have caught the mood right off, I think I could keep it.

A letter from B.N.: some catastrophe or other seems to have occurred and he asks me to let him have 1,000 francs. It made me angry, he's always asking for money. But I do feel sorry for him, and therefore decided to send him 700.

7 July

Worked on the fifth movement of the Quintet: the link. Is it coming out too serious? But I always bear in mind that Chopin originally wrote his Funeral March on the death of his dog.

Parcelled up the proof of the Third Piano Concerto and took it to the post.

Thought through the first movement of the Suite from *Three Oranges*. I have been turning this suite over in my mind for a long time, but never quite got into the right mood to realise it. Of course, it will be a poor relation compared to the Suites from *Chout* and *The Fiery Angel*.

In the evening, went for a solitary walk along the seashore. One of the glories of the place we are in is that within ten minutes one can walk to the beach, quite removed from civilisation, with no villas, fences, no traces whatsoever of humankind, the sea, the sandy beach and the shallow dunes securely sheltering a continent. I wandered and thought: this beach was here a thousand years ago, and ten thousand years ago, and people came here to gaze upon the selfsame illimitable ocean.

8 July

Finished the fifth movement. Began work on the fourth, taking the theme from one of my notebooks. In the afternoon orchestrated the *Three Oranges* Suite (first movement). I'm a little nervous about the Trio.

9 July

Worked again on the fourth movement. In the afternoon a dramatic letter arrived from Oeberg: Hébertot has not moved a muscle about *Fiery Angel* and has not signed the contract; but not only that, they have sent from America $272, that is to say 5,000 francs, for the production of *Chout*, and I was not expecting more than 1,000.[1]

---

1   From the Neighbourhood Theatre production. See above, entry for 25 January and *passim*.

Next, there was a letter from Gauk,[1] saying that the Mariinsky wants to produce *The Gambler* and *Chout*. I do not know whether anything will in fact come of this, but whatever the case it is pleasant to think that St Petersburg is once again showing an interest in me. I wrote a long reply.

11 July

Finished the fourth movement, working in the morning and the afternoon.

Today was the first warm weather we have had, even though the cold wind still threatened to give both Ptashka and me a cold. I read Cocteau[2] and Leonid Andreyev.[3] Wrote letters.

12 July

Read in the local guidebook that St Gilles has existed from times immemorial and was in all likelihood a Phoenician or Carthaginian colony.

13 July

Worked on the second variation of the first movement and nearly finished it in all its details. In the afternoon orchestrated two pages of the Eccentrics from the *Three Oranges* Suite.

A very nice letter from Szenkár, a panegyric to the masterpiece that is *Three Oranges*. He promises to produce it without fail next winter in Cologne.

---

1 Alexander Gauk (1893–1963), one of the Soviet Union's leading conductors, holding a range of distinguished musical directorships including the USSR State Symphony Orchestra and the inaugural leadership of the Moscow Bolshoy Radio Symphony Orchestra. Also an outstanding teacher, he numbered among his pupils Yevgeny Mravinsky, Alexander Melik-Pashayev and Yevgeny Svetlanov. Prokofiev had established friendly relations with Gauk when they were fellow members of Tcherepnin's conducting class at the St Petersburg Conservatoire; the relationship would be resumed and strengthened when Prokofiev began increasingly frequent return visits to Russia in 1927 and after his final move back in 1936.

2 Jean Cocteau (1889–1963), French novelist, playwright, librettist, actor, Surrealist, illustrator, filmmaker, seminal influence on the gamut of artistic life of Paris throughout the 1920s and 1930s, self-described *Prince frivole*. Despite his almost limitless range of talents, interests and friendships, he regarded himself first and foremost as a poet.

3 Leonid Andreyev (1871–1919), novelist, playwright and short-story writer, a leading exponent of Expressionism in literature, protégé of Gorky, and between the 1905 and 1917 Revolutions one of the best-known writers in Russia. Appalled by the failures and excesses of the Bolshevik Revolution, he emigrated and died in poverty in Finland – not, however, before issuing a stream of vitriolic anti-Bolshevik manifestos, which demonstrate all too clearly his increasingly anguished and unstable mental state.

14 July

Decided to put the sixth movement aside for a while, as ideas have dried up, and instead to concentrate on polishing the first five, which will take as long as their composition. In the afternoon I had a migraine (but not the neuralgia pain). Read Christian Science. By evening the headache had almost gone.

15 July

Did no work in the morning, as my head was still a little sore. However, it soon cleared up altogether and I wrote a heap of letters.

Today for the first time Ptashka, Miss Mack and I went for a swim, shrieking like anything as we entered the water which, on this first attempt, felt horribly cold, although in truth it was not. The bottom ought to have been just sand, but because of the tempestuous nature of the previous few days a mass of little pebbles had been dragged up, very uncomfortable for inexperienced bare feet.

16 July

Worked in the morning and in the afternoon, and made a fair copy of the third movement, the most difficult one, as well as revising much of the second. If the final detailed work goes as quickly for all the movements as it did for this one, I shall be able to finish the ballet by the end of the month.

Read and thought about Christian Science. Not everything is easy to accept, but then I have not yet read a great deal and have not fully grasped everything I have read. One thought-provoking notion (if I have understood it aright) that insinuates itself repeatedly is that men are partly sons of God and partly sons of Adam. The thought had already struck me that those who believe in immortality are themselves immortal; those who do not are mortal, while those who have not made up their minds will have to be born once again. To this last category, in all probability, belong those unbelievers for whom the spiritual life nevertheless takes precedence over the material.

17 July

Completed the detailed working out of the second movement.

18 July

Put more flesh on the fourth movement (the Quintet will have five) and played through the fifth. I thought I wanted to make changes in the oboe parts, but in the end they proved to be better left as they were.

An exciting letter from Berlin. A manager there, Meri (not Mary) Bran is proposing thirty(!) concerts throughout Germany, Poland and the Baltic countries, and wants to know my terms. Naturally, the prospect of devoting my labour to these far-flung border territories, especially at a time when I am so anxious to get on with composing, is hardly the most seductive, but in the first place it might earn a decent amount of money, and in the second it is undoubtedly flattering to be asked to fulfil thirty concert engagements (the first time!). In the third place it would be interesting to see somewhere new. Best of all would be if they would also engage Ptashka to sing my songs. Her voice is sounding better, and it would be a good experience for her, while for me it would be jollier to travel with her.

19 July

Worked on the detail of the first movement, but did not quite finish it. The most difficult task is to get the opening absolutely right.

Sent my power of attorney to Zagorsky[1] to raise an action against the International Bank (a piquant detail is that this will involve action against Vyshnegradsky!).[2] Mama and I had some accounts with this bank; my information is that the bank had succeeded in bringing its documents and statements out of Russia and therefore it might be possible to extract something from them. In the meantime, the lawyer's bill is 500 francs.

20 July

Decided to compose a sixth movement. At first nothing would come together, but later it did. In the afternoon I checked the English translations of the Op. 9 songs.[3]

Went for a long walk by the sea.

21 July

More composition of the sixth movement, but it goes more slowly than the others. In the afternoon finished the Eccentrics for the *Three Oranges* Suite.

1　Alexander Zagorsky, a lawyer in Paris.
2　Alexander Vyshnegradsky (1867–1925) had before the Revolution been head of the bank in question, the Petrograd International Bank, and was subsequently imprisoned by the Bolshevik regime in the Peter and Paul Fortress. A composer as well as a banker, he managed to complete a fourth Symphony during his incarceration. On his release he emigrated, first to New York and later to Paris. Flattered that Prokofiev treated him as a composer rather than as a banker, he had been a generous supporter, helping to finance Prokofiev's New York appearances in 1918 and advancing funds when needed in France. See *Diaries*, vol. 2, pp. 348–50, 421, 538, 540, 614.
3　*Two Poems for Voice and Piano*, Op. 9: No. 1 'There Are Other Planets', words by Balmont; No. 2 'The Boat Cast Off', words by Alexei Apukhtin.

Bathed, the first time we had done so when the tide was going out. The beach was magnificent. It was very enjoyable.

22 July

Schloezer has written an article summarising the whole season. He says many of the recently unveiled works mark a shift in musical aesthetics that has plunged musicians and composers into a state of bemused anguish. Schloezer is an idiot of course, probably the last person to understand what is actually going on, but somehow the article reawakened in me all the feelings, not exactly of dismay but of bewilderment, I had experienced at Diaghilev's recent productions. But what precisely is it that gnaws at me? When all is said and done the most that Poulenc, Milhaud, Auric, etc., can be judged guilty of is trying to make something out of low-quality material. On the other hand what Stravinsky is doing does not trouble me in the least. So what is the problem for me? I think it must come down to the close association Stravinsky has formed with Poulenc and Auric, something I cannot understand for the life of me. And the same goes for Diaghilev, hanging on to the coat-tails of these youngsters and suddenly not wanting to know me. Try as I may I cannot fathom the aesthetics involved. I do not like what they are doing and so have placed myself into a position of open hostility to them. But what I keep asking in my heart is why, given the undoubted prominence of these people, do I find what they do so baffling?

23 July

Yesterday evening, under the shadow of all these musical reflections, I composed little as I felt very dissatisfied with myself. But things went better today. One more small push and the Quintet will be finished. The orchestration – if one can call it that, in fact it is more a matter of writing out the parts – will be a quick and easy job, although making the piano score will be harder.

Began orchestrating the fifth movement of the *Three Oranges* Suite: the Prince and Princess.

24 July

Worked on the sixth movement. In the afternoon did a page of the Prince and Princess. I must get a move on, as I also have to make a start on the score of the Quintet, and then start composing the Symphony. I do not want to run out of time.

All the letters I have to write are suffocating me. Whatever I do I shall never manage to answer all of them.

25 July

Just a few more bars and the Quintet will be finished. I patched one or two places in the first movement and could have started orchestrating it, but decided I needed a break and would be better making a fresh start on a new day. We are not sleeping well: wine, the sea and the wind – it is very windy here. The house is rented until November, but I have heard that the owners would like to move back in during the autumn. Perhaps we should restore their house to them in October and ourselves move somewhere more restful. The only problem with that is the fuss and bother of moving with all the baby impedimenta.

26 July

Settled down to the score. It is pure pleasure, since everything has essentially already been completely thought out. I get the same kind of satisfaction as a child colouring in a picture. I managed four pages.

27 July

My head was aching, therefore I achieved only one page of score. I walked for a long time ('running away from my headache'). Ptashka was also coming apart at the seams, probably from bathing in the cold sea. In the afternoon we read Christian Science and wrote to Mrs Getty, requesting a remote healing treatment for Ptashka. Towards evening my bad head almost passed off, which practically never used to happen in the old days.

A letter from Gottlieb with a highly laudatory review of a performance of my Violin Concerto in Prague. By a coincidence I found amazing, the review was from the *Christian Science Monitor*.[1]

28 July

Achieved a deal of orchestrating today, and at the same time started on the two-hand piano transcription. If the first is enjoyable, the second is often dispiriting, since the point of it is to dispense with the score. Ptashka is finding it a hard struggle to keep going, perhaps because she has been doing gymnastics, which she probably ought not to have done. Read Christian

---

1 Ephraim Gottlieb, a loyal and devoted admirer from Chicago who had consistently provided support and useful staff work for Prokofiev since the stressful negotiations with the management of the Chicago Opera over *The Love for Three Oranges* in January 1920. See *Diaries*, vol. 2, pp. 460, 547–8, and *passim*. See above p. 59 on the subject of the performance in Prague.

Science. It destroys not only all earthly concerns but also much that is abstract – philosophy, science – consequently reading it often brings on feelings of perplexity.

29 July

Finished the first movement and began orchestrating the second. The piano score lags but nevertheless inches forward laboriously. I orchestrate in the mornings and work on the piano score in the afternoons.

B.N. is once again asking for money. He wants to sell diamonds, that is to say an easy (and completely useless) method of making a lot of money, but so far nobody seems inclined to buy any from him. The result is that I pay for him.

30 July

Ptashka has a reply from Getty: 'Do not think about pain, and it will not think about you,' and directed her to certain pages in the book. We both read these pages, and I realised that Christian Science and Kant have much in common: both believe that the world we find all around us is no more than a representation and in all probability an invalid one; ideas lie at the root of everything and Kant denies the feasibility of perceiving them truthfully through the five senses and reason. Christian Science's route to perception is through the Divine Spirit.

Did some work.

31 July

Orchestrated the third movement. Made a start on the first movement of the piano score.

A reply from Bran. The terms she is offering are considerably better than I had been expecting, and she has agreed to engage Ptashka. In one way it is depressing but in another rather attractive to be appearing in Vilnius, Kaunas[1] and such places. Revel[2] is a long way away, but what makes it an attractive prospect is that it is only two steps from Petersburg! The overall financial position is thereby much improved: the auguries are good for next year to avoid the worries and insecurities of last.

---

1 Vilnius is the capital of Lithuania, Kaunas the second largest city.
2 Revel was the Russian name for Tallinn, capital of Estonia, when the country formed part of the Russian Empire.

1 August

The third movement has a great deal of colour in it, but transferring this into the score takes an inordinate amount of time!

At long last the weather has warmed, and the sea as well: 21°! Ptashka feels a little better.

2 August

Finished orchestrating the third movement and carried on with the piano transcription of the second. I must hurry up and finish, I want to get on with the Symphony.

3 August

If Christian Science through healing of the sick demonstrates the truth of God's existence and hence converts people, is it not the case that those who are thus converted are less deserving than unbelievers who nevertheless strive to do good for the sake of it? In the first case a man will loan money to another against a pledge for its restitution; in the second he offers the money without expecting it to be returned. This is the way the mind of man works: without proof of God's existence he is reluctant to believe, but faced with the possibility of such proof, he is concerned that for him to enter on the path of belief is less meritorious than the path chosen by others who do not believe at all.

Did no actual orchestration today, but undertook considerable conceptual revision of the instrumentation. The third movement turns out to be particularly resistant to transcription for the piano, and I must make another orchestral version to make it more accessible.

4 August

Christian Science rejects much of the Old Testament, but does accept the account of the creation of the world. Does this mean that it also rejects scientists' theories on the origin of species and the geological record, and similar evidence? In my opinion, it does not. It does not follow from the fact that God created the lion that the lion sprang into existence fully formed. The genesis of the idea of the lion was followed by millions of years during which it developed from the primeval mollusc to its ultimate state. The composer creates his Symphony, it may already be notated, but still it exists solely for the author. It has before it several stages, taking perhaps many months or years, through which it must pass before it can be presented to the listener:

first it must be written out as separate parts, then these parts must be learnt by musicians.

Finished the piano score of the third movement and began on the now required simplified orchestral version. I worked long and hard.

5 August

Finally finished off the third movement and scratched out the mistakes I had marked on the margins. Began orchestrating the Adagio.

In the evening went for a long walk.

6 August

Sent off the first three movements to the copyist. Finished the fourth movement.

7 August

Am reading a book (in French) *Beasts, Men and Gods*. The author, fleeing the Bolsheviks, spent several months in the forests and then wandered on foot through Mongolia. An extraordinarily interesting story.[1]

9 August

The Borovskys have a daughter, Natasha. Borovsky, swooning with rapture, is sure she resembles him. We sent a telegram: 'Hurrah for Natashka, Mamochka, Papashka!'

---

1 *Beasts, Men and Gods* by Ferdinand Antoni Ossendowski (1878–1945), a Polish Revolutionary, writer, journalist, scientist, explorer, jailbird, soldier and spy who wrote in Russian, English and Polish, was originally written in English and first published in New York by E. P. Dutton in 1921. It was an account of his attempt to reach India from Siberia via Mongolia after the Red Army had defeated Admiral Kolchak's White Army in 1920 – a campaign in which Ossendowski had served as a White intelligence officer and liaison officer with the abortive American Intervention Corps. The account details Ossendowski's close encounters on reaching Mongolia with the incredible Lt-General Baron Roman Fyodorovich von Ungern-Sternberg, aka the Bloody Baron, a sobriquet that reflects the atrocious cruelty of his guerilla warfare and his short-lived regime of terror as self-described Dictator of Mongolia and reincarnation of Genghis Khan. In effect one of the bloodthirsty warlords that roamed over Siberia and Mongolia in the aftermath of the Civil War (he had for a time been Grigori Semyonov's right-hand man), Sternberg's lunatic ambition to restore the Qing dynasty to the Chinese throne ended with his capture and summary execution by the Red Army in 1921. Ossendowski meanwhile got himself to New York and thence back to Poland, where he continued to live, writing and lecturing to great public acclaim, until the German Occupation of the Second World War during which, characteristically, he was an active member of the Resistance. In post-war Communist Poland his books were banned as anti-Soviet, and were not seen in print again until 1989.

10 August

Complete the orchestration of the Quintet. There remains only the piano score to do.

12 August

Worked very hard, but progress on the transcription is slow. It is hard, also I feel exhausted.

13 August

Christian Science teaches that the material world is unreal and that sin (error) is likewise unreal, for God is all-encompassing and can have created nothing that is not good. Therefore only good is real, error and the material world are equally unreal. However, nowhere could I find an explanation as to what could then be the source of these unreal objects? What was their point of departure and what was it that moved them from that point? I thought about this and came to the following conclusion: for man to be not merely a shadow but a fully existent being equipped with reason and individuality, he was given free will. When free will manifests itself, it can lead in certain instances to error. Materialised error constitutes the essence of the material world, which is thus unreal by virtue of being in error.

14 August

The whole work is finished. There remain only a few mistakes to be scratched out and corrected, all previously noted in the margins. I had said in Paris that I would finish the Quintet not later than the 15th August, after which I would settle down to the Symphony.

Svyatoslav cried all day: some of the time because he was cutting teeth, and sometimes his belly was aching. Tending to him, Ptashka also cried. Altogether we both felt rather unsettled. By evening all was better. Svyatoslav is very loving towards me and whenever I come into the room he never takes his eyes off me.

15 August

Had a headache, which ruined most of the day. I corrected the mistakes, and now the score can be sent to the copyist.

17 August

Started thinking about the Symphony. I had decided some time ago that it would be in two movements: first a sonata-allegro, second a theme and variations. The main subject of the first movement and the theme for the variations had also been composed a long time ago: the first of them at Rochelets, the second as long ago as when I was in America. I now turned my attention to the second subjects, which will have something of a choral character.

18 August

Pondered the Symphony, but did not write anything. In some ways I do not know quite how to proceed.

In the afternoon I tried accompanying Ptashka in 'The Grey Dress', transposing it a tone higher.[1] Musorgsky I could transpose without difficulty, but my own music I could not do at all: the result was a complete mess, and when eventually I got it right it was still not my music at all. A strange phenomenon! The composer grows ever more inextricably intertwined with his tonalities.

19 August

Yesterday I received a letter from Boris Demchinsky which I interpreted as meaning that, as far as he himself is concerned, he is ready to work on revising the libretto of *Fiery Angel*. The only problem is that life is hard for them at the moment: a delicate hint that such work should be paid for, which is only reasonable. I wrote my answer.

The Symphony has not yet left the starting blocks, although I have been thinking about it. On the other hand I finished the fifth movement of the *Oranges* Suite. My work on the Suite is thus complete: the only remaining task is for the copyists to transcribe some sections of the existing opera score.

20 August

The Symphony still has not moved, which does not improve my mood.

Once upon a time Demchinsky told me Gogol's dictum: 'If you find the writing won't come, take a clean sheet of paper and write anything on it, even if it is only "Gogol, Gogol, Gogol" – and you'll see, it will suddenly start

---

1 *Five Poems for Voice and Piano*, Op. 23 No. 2, words by Zinaida Gippius. The original setting is in A minor and goes down to D above middle C. Middle C is normally considered the lower limit of the soprano tessitura, but evidently the D was uncomfortable for Lina.

of its own accord.' He is right, of course: if you force the issue there is a greater chance of putting something down on paper than if you simply sit with your arms folded, but there is also the risk that you will write something not very good that, because it is interleaved with something that is good, in the end has to be left.

22 August

The Symphony positively refuses to budge, even though each morning I brood on it or sit at the piano. I decided that for the time being I would put the first movement on one side and concentrate on the variations: they are easier to get into the swing of.

Read some Christian Science. When Christians first began to preach the immortality of the soul, the Romans objected that since man comes into being through birth he is inevitably bound to die, for something that is finite at one end cannot be infinite at the other. In answer to this Christian Science states that it is not the case that man (in the shape of his soul) comes into being through birth, and will not die. But if I was never born, that is to say I always existed but with no memory of my previous existence, how can I be sure that this present existence is mine and not that of some other being? After all, if my birth into this world entails the removal of all my memory of the past, for me the past does not exist. In that case the future cannot exist for me either, for by cutting off my memory death also cuts me off, in the same way as birth brought me in. Christian Science's explanation is therefore not clear to me. Generally speaking there are fewer difficulties believing in the mortality of man than in his immortality. On the other hand, it is also easier to conceive of oneself as a being created by God than as a wholly godless creature of nature. It follows from this that for man the most natural understanding of the world is that expressed by Wells, whose theory I found so attractive a year ago:[1] God exists but man is mortal. Wells believes that man is no more than a stage in the divine creation, one link in the biological chain extending from the primeval slime that first appeared on the surface of the not yet cooled waters of the infant planet, to the superhuman being into which we will one day develop and which, perhaps, will then be deserving of immortality. In the meantime the role of mankind is to play his part in this onward movement during his lifespan and then to die, that is to say to vanish and become a *quantité négligeable*,[2] in the same way as half-completed sketches and drafts are discarded along the way. Even though Christian

---

1 When staying in Les Rochelets in the summer of 1921 Prokofiev every evening read aloud a chapter of H. G. Wells's *The Outline of History* to his mother and Boris Bashkirov. See *Diaries*, vol. 2, pp. 610, 703.
2 In French.

Science regards this theory as erroneous, it cannot entirely condemn it because at its heart lies humility, while its elements conform to almost all the Beatitudes of the Sermon on the Mount. Christian Science's teaching is more optimistic but it is essential, before accepting it, to understand and clarify with much greater precision what this teaching consists of.

23 August

Ptashka and I went to Sables-d'Olonne, thirty kilometres from St Gilles, in an enormous and very comfortable omnibus, which no doubt had formerly done service taking curious Parisian sightseers to the battlefields. Sables-d'Olonne is a seaside spa resort, not chic enough to be actively nasty.

On our return I found letters from Cologne: although the management is not guaranteeing to produce *Three Oranges*, it does promise to attend to them in terms proper to the most loving of parents. As I have no choice, I must content myself with these expressions of affectionate concern.

24 August

Sat down to the first variation. Managed to compose a bit.

25 August

Second variation. It turns out that the theme is not especially well adapted to variation. Invention is very difficult, nose-diving into stupidity all too easy.

In the evenings I play patience.

26 August

Finished Kuzmin's novel *Travellers by Sea and Land*.[1] Kuzmin is a good writer, so why did he write such rubbish? The novel's homoerotic tendencies are so banal as to do a disservice to the ideal of pederasty so hymned by Kuzmin. And on top of that, what is the point of so much empty verbiage?

---

1   Mikhail Kuzmin (1872–1936) was the first openly homosexual writer in Russian literature, achieving enormous success with his 'coming out' novel *Wings* in 1907. A gifted musician who had studied with Rimsky-Korsakov at the St Petersburg Conservatoire, he wrote the music for Meyerhold's seminal production of Alexander Blok's play *The Fairground Showman*. Veering away from music towards literature, he could still often be heard at the Stray Dog café singing his own songs, which he characteristically described as 'only little music, but it has some poison in it'. His was an important voice in the Symbolist and later Acmeist movements of Silver Age poetry, and at various times was closely associated with Akhmatova, Mandelshtam, Blok, Vyacheslav Ivanov and Bryusov, as well as Diaghilev's *World of Art* circle. The novel *Travellers by Sea and Land* (*Plavayushchie Puteshestvuyuschie*) was published in 1915.

28 August

Five variations are conceived in outline, and two are sketched almost completely. I have been composing better these last few days.

29 August

We got up at six and at half past seven were on quite a large motor-boat heading towards the Île d'Yeu.[1] On the boat were twenty of us trippers and the crew of two. Two hours later we tied up at the island, which is quite small (six kilometres long by three broad) and stony, but pleasing in its remoteness from the world. Some of its inhabitants have never left their native island. We toured it on horseback. Vegetation is sparse owing to the continual winds and the stony soil, these winds being the chief drawback to life on the island. We visited the ruins of an old castle, in which at one time an old duke lived and ruled the island. Beside the main landing-stage is a neat little town, where we had an excellent meal.

We made the return voyage not with the engine but under sail, as the owner wanted to economise on petrol. The sea was quite rough and the pitching and rolling of the boat made some of the passengers seasick. I felt a bit sick myself. We were issued with lifebelts 'to make it more comfortable to sit'. We were glad to get back on dry land, all the more so because sailing added an hour to the voyage, making it three hours instead of two.

30 August

Composed a little. Went back to the first movement and came up with an opening.

31 August

Composed nothing whatsoever today, all I succeeded in doing was splinter my nerves. Gave up and wrote letters.

---

1 L'Île d'Yeu is a small island off the Atlantic coast of France. Its Vieux-château is a strikingly rugged fourteenth-century construction later enclosed by towered curtain walls built by Italian engineers during the Renaissance. It was demolished by Louis XIV at the end of the seventeenth century because he was afraid its virtual impregnability and island location could make it too useful to an invader. Admirers of Hergé's *Adventures of Tintin* books may recognise it as the inspiration for the castle in *The Black Island*.

1 September

The work went better, and I got somewhere with the first movement.

2 September

Svyatoslav smiles at me continually and generally loves me, I believe mainly on account of my red striped jacket and my spectacles. *Par contre*[1] he detests the white-coated chemist to whom he is taken every day to be weighed. If I divest myself of my jacket to revel my white tennis shirt, he starts to cry bitterly, as he obviously thinks I am the chemist.

3 September

Finished a book about Mikula Buyanovich,[2] which I read with great pleasure. The Symphony is making better progress.

4 September

Worked on the second subject, which incidentally I had composed earlier, some weeks ago. I work on the Symphony from nine o'clock until eleven, and sometimes again from five o'clock to six. It is a pity there is no proof-reading to be done, as I have time for it at the moment, and later on, when there will be no time, I shall be drowning under it from Germany and from Paris.

---

1   In French: 'in contrast'.
2   This must have been Gyorgy Grebenshchikov's trilogy *The Byliny of Mikula Buyanovich*, whose eponymous hero is a mythical *bogatyr* (medieval hero or knight-errant of Kievan Rus; the word comes from *baghatur*, the ancient Altaic word for a warrior or hero). An English translation was published in 1949 by the Alatas Publishing Company in America under the title *The Turbulent Giant*. A *bylina* is a rhythmic free-verse epic narrative dealing with allegedly real events (from *byl'*, a fact or true story, something that truly was, as distinct from fiction). The oral *bylina* tradition persisted for many centuries throughout Russia and Ukraine to be drawn on and imitated by many later poets. Grebenshchikov (1882–1964) was the son of an illiterate peasant in the Altai region of Southern Siberia. He left school and home at the age of twelve and his writings soon attracted the attention of such masters as Gorky and Kuprin. Emigrating to Paris after the Revolution he became a close friend of Nikolay Roerich, Konstantin Balmont and other artists who were attracted to the mythology of ancient Russia, and as such would have been known to Prokofiev. Moving to America in 1924 he founded together with Ilya Tolstoy, the son of the novelist, and Roerich an idealistic émigré Russian artistic and spiritual colony in Southbury, Connecticut, called Churayevka, which became a place of pilgrimage for many leading Russian artists such as Rachmaninoff and Chaliapin who found themselves in the largely alien environment of twentieth-century America. Grebenshchikov eventually moved to Florida, where he became Professor of Creative Writing at Southern College, Lakeland.

5 September

Did a little more on the second subject. The Symphony moves slowly, but at least it is moving. The sketches are very rough, not finished at all, but the main thing is to get the skeleton constructed.

We had an excellent bathe today. July and August had dreadful weather, but it looks as though September will be good!

6 September

Composed the concluding material. I did not work much, as a headache was threatening. But it failed to develop.

In the afternoon a photographer came to take our pictures. Svyatoslav was the star.

8 September

A letter from Bran about the tour. All in all her proposals are definitely worth considering. But I don't like the thought of going without Ptashka, and must try hard to persuade Meri Bran to engage her.

13 September

The proofs arrived of the *Songs*, Op. 27,[1] a new edition in four languages.

A row with Ptashka about her singing.

14 September

It was cold all summer, but the weather now is beautifully warm. The sea is also warm. Swimming is intensifying.

15 September

The proof of the Violin Concerto has arrived, which will be quite a lot of work. But thank God for that, it is high time this Concerto appeared in print. Szigeti writes from Moscow that he performed it there and encored the scherzo.

---

1 *Five Poems of Anna Akhmatova*, Op. 27 (1916).

18 September

Sensational news: I read in the newspapers that in Bellevue, near Paris, there is a huge winter dacha to let for 1,200 francs, that is the same as we have been paying for the cramped flat on the avenue Charles Dickens. In a month's time we were going to have to move back to Paris and torment ourselves with the search for a new apartment, probably uncomfortable and not big enough: the prospect was already poisoning our life. I have always preferred to be in the country rather than in the town: the air is better and it is better for working. But here was one for the same price, and what a spacious expanse it was offering! In short, a family council was held and we dispatched a long telegram to B.N. asking him to investigate the dacha and, if it proved satisfactory (he knows what we like) to reserve it.

No composing today, although usually I do some every morning.

19 September

Finished the sketches for the first movement of the Symphony. A letter from Gauk, my erstwhile fellow student in the conducting class. A sweet-as-sugar fellow, careerist, good friends with one and all. He is now at the Mariinsky Theatre and writes that there is a possibility of putting on *The Gambler*[1] there. This is very exciting! I sent a long letter to Oeberg asking under what financial conditions he could provide the performing material once the score has been revised.

20 September

Work was interrupted by a telegram from B.N. and led to further discussions and cogitations about the dacha.

Svyatoslav utters the word 'da'[2] very clearly, and occasionally 'nn-da'. The remainder of his conversation is obscure, although his Mamasha and Grandma assert otherwise.

21 September

Composed a slow variation (it will be the fourth or fifth). It worked well. In the afternoon I spent a good deal of time on the proofs of the Violin Concerto.

---

1 *The Gambler* (*Igrok*) opera (1916) based on Dostoevsky's novella. The 1917 Mariinsky Theatre production planned to be by Meyerhold, designed by Golovin and conducted by Albert Coates was abandoned because of the October Revolution. See *Diaries*, vol. 2 *passim*.
2 'Yes'.

I had a curious dream. The beginning was extremely real: I was sitting in some kind of theatre foyer when Hébertot appeared, and noticing that my attitude to him was somewhat hostile, hastened to tell me that he was not planning any new productions this year. I thereupon decided to put in a word for Koshetz,[1] recommending her for his company as a singer. Smallens,[2] who for some unknown reason was also there, supported me. Hébertot then made for the exit, followed by Smallens, with me bringing up the rear. However, at that moment I noticed that through an inner door had come Rimsky-Korsakov, who halted ten paces from me. He looked very much as I remembered seeing him in the Conservatoire, although a little younger, and wearing a blue suit. Fully aware that Rimsky-Korsakov had died some years ago, I called out to Smallens, 'But this is not real!', and with these words ran up to Rimsky-Korsakov. However, scarcely had I got near enough to touch him when he immediately took himself off into the room next door from which he had emerged. I dashed after him, and found that it was a large hall, something like a dining-room in a big hotel. Rimsky was standing about twenty paces away from me; I ran up to him and seized his hand. This time he did not move, and I realised, to my extreme astonishment, that his hand was perfectly tangible and indeed warm to the touch. I kissed it, but Rimsky-Korsakov did not move, looking to one side with a half-smile on his face. I kissed his beard, and then somewhat unceremoniously took his face in my hands, turned his head towards mine and kissed him several times on the lips. Thoughts of Christian Science flashed through my mind. Rimsky-Korsakov then disappeared – how I do not remember – and I turned towards the exit, but could not find my hat. I looked for it underneath the table, then went back into the big hall, but it was nowhere to be found and its disappearance seemed in some mysterious way to be connected with Rimsky-Korsakov. Seeing all the people seated in the dining-room, I thought: surely my behaviour and all that had happened must have created some surprise? But they paid no attention and carried on as if nothing had happened, snatches of their conversations reaching my ears from time to time. At that point I woke up.

1   Nina Koshetz (1894–1965), outstanding soprano celebrated for her beauty as much as for her artistry. Prokofiev wrote the *Akhmatova Songs*, Op. 27, and the *Five Songs Without Words*, Op. 35, for her, although the former has no formal dedication (see below, p. 207). Serially involved romantically with both Rachmaninoff and Prokofiev, at least to judge from Prokofiev's *Diaries*, the latter was instrumental in arranging her emigration to America in 1921. Nina Koshetz was the original Fata Morgana in *The Love for Three Oranges* when it was premiered at the Chicago Opera in December 1921. See *Diaries*, vol. 2 *passim*.
2   Alexander Smallens (1889–1972), Russian-born conductor whose musical training and career was in America and who became known for his association with Gershwin's *Porgy and Bess*, the premiere of which he conducted in 1935. He had worked with Prokofiev on the Chicago Opera production of *The Love for Three Oranges* and conducted the opera's second performance on 5 January 1922. See *Diaries*, vol. 2, pp. 435, 617–81 *passim*.

22 September

Continued the slow variation (the fourth). The composing was going well. In the afternoon did a lot of proof-reading. But there is still no definite answer from B.N. about the dacha.

23 September

An answer from B.N. advising us that the owner had gone away, leading us to fear that the dacha is already taken. This is not surprising, in view of the enviable description in the advertisement. We cursed B.N. for his inefficiency; Mama did her best to defend him, but was also embarrassed by his long silence. I finished the fourth variation.

24 September

Began a new variation, a quick one. Finally received a contract from Bran, but alas without including Ptashka. Wrote a long letter to Boris Nikolayevich giving him a good telling-off and demanding more energetic action over the dacha, instead of which all he had done was offer a description of it.

25 September

Continued the quick variation begun yesterday. Composition went well.

26 September

Am having some palpable success grasping the essence of Christian Science, reading it with great concentration and attention. Wrote a lengthy answer to Gauk, which took me four hours to compile. Went on composing the scherzo variation. Played patience.

28 September

Composed. Read proofs. Since receiving the proofs of the Violin Concerto I have not had a moment's free time.

29 September

Sent a telegram to B.N. as on waking in the morning it had occurred to me that while nothing has happened about the dacha, I had sent him 500 francs for the deposit nine days ago. Suppose he had decided to gamble with it, had lost the money, and that was the reason for his silence?

Five of the variations are now completed in sketch form.

30 September

Pondered the best way of concluding the Symphony: compose a third movement, a finale, but how? An idea: to develop the last variation and incorporate into it themes recalled from the first movement.

A telegram from B.N. to the effect that today (i.e. yesterday) he would finally speak to the owner. Hard words were said about B.N. being a 'regular scoundrel' and quite right too: the dacha could have been rented two weeks ago and he still has not managed to rouse himself to talk to the owner.

1 October

Decided to compose a large-scale variation incorporating themes from the first movement and to conclude the Symphony with a repeat of the calm theme on which the variations are based, in short much as I had originally envisaged it. I made a start on composing this variation.

Finished proof-reading the second movement of the Concerto; I have not yet received the third movement. Also began proof-reading the Fifth Sonata, which has been extremely well engraved by Breitkopf, particularly when compared with the wretched engraving one gets on Capdeville tracing paper.

2 October

A telegram from B.N. asking for a further deposit on the dacha, this time for 1,000 francs. After discussion we decided to send the money.

Had a headache and therefore did not compose. Attempted to combat it with Christian Science.

It has become essential to settle the Vyshnegradsky business. I have engaged a lawyer, Zagorsky, to take action against the International Bank, originally of Petersburg but now with a branch in Paris, in an attempt to obtain interest on securities Mama had deposited there before the Revolution. Now, when the point has arrived at which I have to sign affidavits, it transpires that the action will be against Vyshnegradsky, the President of the bank, and this is embarrassing since in America he had given me money ($450) to arrange my first recital.

4 October

I have done no composing for two days, but today managed a fair amount in the sixth variation, albeit still in and around the opening bars.

A telegram from B.N.: the dacha is ours! Great excitement, heated discussions and even a general mood of elation: after all, to a certain extent this will determine the shape of our lives for the whole winter. B.N. would not have risked renting the dacha if it were no good.

5 October

No chance of work today: packing, paying bills, urgent letters to the bank and other places about our change of address, and so on and so forth.

It had been our intention to stay on here for another three weeks, but the Bellevue dacha is rented from today; accordingly we would be better off moving there straight away. It gives us much more space; we are already in October and it is beginning to get dark; it is windy, the sea is cold and blustery, at times positively menacing. There is a wild beauty here but one could hardly describe it as snug.

7 October

Today saw the move from St Gilles to Bellevue. We got up at 5.30, which because of the clocks going forward in France was really 4.30. Miss Mack, our Norwegian maid, was indispensable in helping us pack; we would not have managed without her. The transfer was accomplished in generally good order, grandma and grandson both conducting themselves well. We arrived in Paris at 6.20 in the evening. B.N., attired in morning coat and bowler hat, met us at the station. He has altered a lot, has lost weight and changed his hairstyle: formerly it had a parting but now it is brushed straight back *à l'embusqué-loin du front*,[1] as is the fashion in Paris. All these little touches somehow smacked of something mildly repellent. He seems to be earning the wherewithal to live, not by playing at the gaming tables – he does not have the money for that – but simply by being around them, in some manner I have yet to discover. All his conversation and anecdotes revolve around the subject of cards. After St Gilles, the sea, the Symphony and reading Christian Science, this produced a strangely depressing effect, a sort of slimy ooze.

We struggled over to another platform in the same station and transferred to a desperately overcrowded suburban train, scarcely able to get our fifteen pieces of luggage on board, and embarked with B.N. on the fifteen-minute

---

1 In French: from the forehead to the back of the head.

journey to Bellevue. Our carriage was at the end of a long train and stopped beyond the end of the platform, which made it very difficult for us to get our bags and baggage out. B.N. went to find someone on the railway staff, who got a trolley for the luggage while we went on foot to the house. The garden is glorious, full of flowers, which in St Gilles were conspicuous by their absence. The house itself produced an unexpected impression. Some of the rooms are fine, others very small, with narrow staircases and steps everywhere, and a multitude of rooms disposed in the most unorthodox way. This is because the house actually consists of three houses which have been joined piecemeal into one. B.N. was probably right when he first cabled us that he had 'mixed feelings' about it, a phrase that had so irritated us at the time. Mama seems to like it. I like the garden. B.N. soon went off to the club and we went to bed. Back in St Gilles, when we read about the number of rooms this house had, we had thought of offering one or two rooms to B.N., but his present attitude, the things he talks about and his general demeanour have so disturbed us that we are uncertain what to do. In Ettal[1] we had grown used to regarding him as one of the family, but now it was clear he would strike a discordant note.

8 October

In the morning, I walked round the garden, which is varied and interesting, with urns and sarcophagi standing about in it. The owner told B.N. that one of them was worth more than the house. But I don't like them much, especially given that the back of the house is in a kind of medieval style while the front has all these urns. All the same, one of them I did find more attractive because it reminded me of a Scythian vessel I once saw, where I don't remember. I think I must have Asiatic blood in me: Asian antiquities attract me whereas those of Greece and Rome (the birth of Europe) do not.

I went into Paris but did not find Zagorsky at home. I did glimpse Vyshnegradsky, to whom I was going next, on the street but did not approach him as I did not think it appropriate to conduct a delicate conversation in the midst of a crowd of people. Oeberg is in London.

I then went in search of Blois, to ask him to send an instrument out to Bellevue. Blois was full of all kinds of news, among which was the story of the collapse of Hébertot's operatic enterprise. This was a quite incredible story: it seems that the attractive woman I had seen with Wolff was not only his mistress but also that of a rich American banker. She undertook to get hold

---

1 For eighteen months from April 1922 until the autumn of 1923 Prokofiev, his mother Maria Grigorievna, Lina Codina and Boris Bashkirov had all lived together in the Villa Christophorus in Ettal, Bavaria.

of a large sum of money for Hébertot's opera company in order for Wolff to become its Director. She herself, apparently, was to sing in the company. Everything was going well until the banker caught her in bed with Wolff, following which everything disintegrated and Wolff even had to leave France as he had signed a number of contracts he was no longer in a position to fulfil. The signature on the remaining agreements was that of Hébertot, who thereupon invited the artists in question to visit him, bringing their contracts with them, at which point he announced that he needed to take the contracts back in order to add a supplementary point, offering financial compensation in exchange. Since the compensation appeared more important than the supplementary contractual detail, the artists willingly complied, handing back their contracts. Hébertot promptly threw the lot on the fire, and in this manner was liquidated the enterprise on which depended the fate of my *Fiery Angel*. And I – I was speechless with rage!

Finishing his tale, Blois put me into his little car and drove me to Bellevue, touching 80 kilometres an hour in the Bois de Boulogne. When we reached the barrier at the edge of the Bois, two policemen appeared, one on either side of the car, and demanded Blois's papers for having exceeded the speed limit. It transpired that, just like a scene from a movie, we had been careering along at 80 k.p.h. while the two policemen had been vainly trying to catch up with us on their motorcycles. Blois boasted that he had connections, and would be able to escape any punishment.

Today is my name-day. We had invited B.N. and bought a bottle of fine port, but he sent a telegram to say he was not well. We were not sure whether to believe this: probably he had to be at the club.

9 October

In the morning I settled down to proof-reading and then walked in our garden. Excellent! There are no neighbours, no intrusive noise, the garden is interesting from a botanical point of view with a variety of plants and a good greenhouse. Above all there is no wind, while in St Gilles the wind used literally to blow us out of our scrawny garden.

Went into Paris to clarify with B.N. our precise relationship with the owner of the house, since we had already been there three days and not a soul had appeared to make an inventory of its contents. When he had made the agreement to rent the place, B.N. had of course blurted out that he was doing so on his own behalf but would be coming and going, not staying there permanently, while 'his friend, the well-known composer Prokofiev' would be living in the house. This information, however, made no impression on the owner. B.N. gave me the owner's telephone number and I rang him up. He was uncommonly civil and bowed and scraped, having in the meantime found out who I was. His surname is Lapin, but as this has unflattering connotations in French,[1] he changed it to Lapinà. A Jew who had taken French nationality, a rich but slovenly man, he is the director of a large engraving business that had made a lot of money during the war producing pictures of half-naked women.

As for B.N., he so graphically described the heart condition that had prevented him from attending yesterday's celebration that I felt quite sorry for him. He had only just woken up when I came to see him at four o'clock in the afternoon, but got dressed and came out in fine fettle with me for a walk. On the way we spoke about the club: what was I worrying about, it was merely the struggle for existence. I: 'An unworthy struggle.' He: 'No more unworthy than playing the stock exchange, and any trade of itself involves squeezing money out of people.' I: 'You might as well open a brothel.' He: 'No, that is trading in blood.' I: 'The trade in a gambling saloon is in nerves and bile.' All these disputatious debating points produced a disagreeable impression. Next, he tried to take 1,000 francs off me ('there is no risk to you, they won't leave my wallet, but it's important when I open my wallet that the notes should be seen there'), but I did not give him any, reminding him that he still had 300 francs from the money I had sent him to pay the deposit on the dacha.

I saw Zagorsky and explained the difficulty in which I found myself over Vyshnegradsky. He agreed that the thing to do was for me to go to see him.

When I returned to Bellevue, Blois's efforts had resulted in Pleyel sending an upright piano, but I was so tired I did not even try it over.

10 October

Another trip into Paris, this time to see Vyshnegradsky in his bank. I was conducted into a splendid salon. Involuntarily the thought flashed through my mind: what if they refuse to hand over the securities?

Vyshnegradsky was good-humoured and friendly and sat on a chair tucking his foot underneath him. For his age he seems remarkably young: he has a son born at the same time as my Svyatoslav and as his own grandson. But when I explained to him that I was in concert with others involved in a claim against the International Bank for the return of securities, his face darkened (evidently this whole affair is a sore subject with him) and he immediately rose from his seat saying, 'All right, then, we shall have to settle this in court.' I began to explain that this was all most distasteful to me personally, that I retained the clearest memory of how he had helped me in the past, and finally that if he resented my involvement I would desist. 'No,' he replied, 'one person more or less attached to the parties makes no

---

1   It is the French word for 'rabbit'.

difference to us.' With that he bowed and left the room. In this way, although formally I had received his blessing, I went away with an unpleasant taste in my mouth.

Returning to Bellevue, I worked intensively reading the proofs of the Violin Concerto.

11 October

Thank God I do not have to go to Paris today. In the morning I settled down to the Symphony and composed the final variation. This went well. More proof-reading in the afternoon.

What a blessing that we are not in Paris but out here in the quiet and green of the country.

12 October

Composed the Symphony and did more proof-reading.

The tenor Alexandrovich took up a good deal of time: he is the Director of the newly formed Russian National Conservatoire in Paris.[1] He is extremely insistent that I teach orchestration. But for me teaching is an utter waste of time, and so whatever he proposed I rejected, the more so as although the Conservatoire has not yet opened its doors it is already facing controversy on several fronts: a Jewish lobby, a Russian lobby, some people wanting serious professors and others mainly concerned with how to get positions for their relations, etc. I consented to play a nominal part in the opening concert of the Conservatoire, but only on condition that Hébertot would give permission (which I was perfectly certain he would not).

In the evening the dacha owners came round. In appearance he is a boorish Jew, but he was excessively polite and since he 'knows with whom he is dealing' there will be time enough for the inventory.

13 October

Composed. The Symphony is moving. The complete form of the skeleton is now visible, even though today also involved a complete rearrangement of the furniture, the beds, the piano, which caused considerable interruption to my working. I did not do much proof-reading, although I did finish the Fifth Sonata.

---

1   See below pp. 110, 136, 139, 1000 n.1.

The Ranvids[1] came to call: a colonel with a limp and an elderly but energetic wife, with whom Mama had struck up a friendship when they were on the Princes' Islands.[2] Now she is joining our household to take care of the domestic management and to cook. He will also live with us, although he is not fit for work, having only one leg. He is a very handsome old man.

15 October

We went into Paris: I had to go with Zagorsky to the Palais de Justice to affix my signature to the complaint against the bank. It was rather horrible seeing the lawyers in their medieval robes swarming all over the Palais. The individual whose presence Zagorsky had arranged to witness my signature and that of another plaintiff, a woman, turned out to have been living in St Gilles over the summer. On learning that I was a composer he was very friendly to me.

I then went to see Oeberg in the publishing firm's new premises. Oeberg told me it was likely a production of *Oranges* could be arranged in London, although the fees would not be large and the publishers would take at least half of them. I protested angrily: they had been very critical of Salter,[3] but here were they behaving worse than a dozen Salters. Returned home very tired. How wonderful to be in Bellevue!

16 October

Composed more of the Symphony and proof-read a good portion of the Violin Concerto.

17 October

Finished the sketches of the Symphony. But how much work is still to do! First it all has to be worked out in detail, then orchestrated. Went into Paris, to the Society of Authors, where I got 940 francs. This was an unexpected bonus, as I

---

1 Marianne Ranvid and her husband, friends of Maria Grigorievna Prokofieva.
2 A chain of nine small islands off Istanbul in the Sea of Marmara, the largest of which is Büyükada (in Greek Prinkipo, meaning 'Prince'). After many trials and tribulations Maria Grigorievna had succeeded in getting away from Novorossiisk, the last Crimean stronghold of General Wrangel's White Army, in the spring of 1920, to land in Prinkipo along with thousands of refugees, many of whom found temporary sanctuary there. Prinkipo also provided an initial safe haven for Trotsky when Stalin exiled him from Soviet Russia in 1929; during his four years there he wrote his *History of the Russian Revolution*.
3 Norbert Salter, one of Germany's best-known impresarios. In 1922 he had proposed to Prokofiev a deal whereby he, Salter, would buy the rights to produce *The Love for Three Oranges* in Germany and other European countries (but not France or America) for a percentage of the receipts. Prokofiev entered into an agreement with Salter, but nothing came of the arrangement. Koussevitzky was among those who warned Prokofiev of Salter's business probity. See *Diaries*, vol 2, pp. 678, 681, 685.

had been expecting 300. I then went to see Oeberg in the new shop, where we fell out over London. Oeberg is an awkward character and tricky to have dealings with. But he said, 'The publishing company must have the means to exist, and you don't know whether or not, in the future, the Koussevitzkys will bequeath the business to a rich merchant.' I take this to be a hint that the more there might be to leave, the more the composers themselves might ultimately benefit.

18 October

Finished reading the proofs of the score and parts of the Violin Concerto. Koshetz came to see us, with Schubert and Marochka.[1] She has just returned from South America and is now going to seek her fortune in Europe. In the Americas she had some success, but not enough to amount to a career. Today was the first time she and Linette had met. Linette decided at first glance that Koshetz was probably Jewish. Koshetz said to me that I had grown fatter and younger. Marochka is twelve, a fairly unbearable little girl, but it cannot be expected that she could be well brought up in such a crazy family.

19 October

Made a start on working out the details of the Symphony. This will be a huge amount of work, since in places the skeleton is not very substantial. Today I began at the very beginning, the first bar. If I keep firmly to the schedule (until eleven o'clock each morning – I cannot do more, my brain loses its edge) I think I will finish this stage of the work in a month.

We had guests again in the afternoon; Sunday afternoon is generally considered the time to pay and receive calls. Today there were Consuelo (a friend of Ptashka's), B.N. and Oeberg. We had the idea of leading them through the suite of rooms one by one: they were impressed, and tried to guess how much the rent would be. I resolved to settle with Oeberg the question of *Oranges* in London: seeing that it was going to be an expensive proposition for the publishers, we would split the fees fifty-fifty. B.N.'s sole conversation was of the club and cards. He has so far departed from his old ways that I do not even know if anything has come of his Bryusov[2] project,

---

1 Nina Koshetz's husband was the artist Alexander von Schubert; Maria (Marochka) was their daughter.
2 Valery Bryusov (1873–1924), leading Symbolist poet and novelist with a pronounced taste for the macabre, the esoteric and the supernatural. His strangely compelling roman à clef (as it turned out to be) about demonic possession in sixteenth-century Germany formed the basis for Prokofiev's opera *The Fiery Angel*. An ardent supporter of Bolshevism, Bryusov remained in Russia after the Revolution, accepted a position in Lunacharsky's Cultural Ministry and later played a dubious role in the State's hounding of poets such as Mandelshtam.

but he assures me that his present way of life has no effect upon him. Incidentally, there was an amusing incident: Oeberg also sometimes gambles in the same club, sometimes staying until five o'clock in the morning. Meeting B.N. at my house, he frowned and asked me in a low voice, 'Tell me, what is that gentleman's occupation?' It seems Oeberg is not too pleased that I have discovered his little weakness, and still worse, that I might be inclined to spread the information around.

20 October

In the morning, worked as usual on the Symphony.

Thank God, there are no proofs to be read, but there is a mass of correspondence to attend to. Romanov confirms that he will be sending the money for the ballet within a few days. Not before time: he has paid only 2,000, since when not a sausage.

Yesterday and today I have been nursing a cold, but after some work with Christian Science by this evening it has all but disappeared. This is significant: a cold with me usually lasts a week.

21 October

Not much progress made with the Symphony: I am stuck with the 'provisional' second subject. It is Ptashka's birthday, and so once again we are entertaining guests: Tamara Hanum,[1] the Samoilenkos. B.N. promised to come, but did not turn up. Last time he got my old overcoat, but now there is nothing for him. I expect he is aware of our disapproving attitude to him: he does like to be praised and admired. However hard we are on him we do love him – after all, he lived with us for two years in Ettal. He also says that we are his only family. Apart from his mother he does not feel a close connection with any of his own family, and he has some justification for this.

24 October

The day went by with no work done because of a headache. A letter from Suvchinsky: he may come to France in December and if he does will stay in Bellevue. This makes Ptashka and me very happy. Perhaps we should rent out to him part of our composite Bellevue property? That would upset B.N. . . .

Diaghilev has commissioned a ballet from Dukelsky. Dukelsky is a capable and extremely likeable young man, but whether or not he will prove to be

---

1 Fatma Hanum's sister. See *Diaries*, vol. 2, pp. 553, 609.

Diaghilev's great new discovery is hard to predict. The real mystery is why Diaghilev has suddenly turned away from me!

25 October

Worked on the Symphony, and worked well. In the afternoon busied myself with the second proof of the score and parts of the Third Concerto. The second proof consists of my checking that the corrections made to the first proof have in fact been made. Heaps of them have not been done – Nielle is a scoundrel. That is the result of having cheap engraving done on tracing paper!

26 October

Did little work as I was afraid of a headache coming on. But I did finish the exposition. In fact the incipient headache began to wear off, and to make completely sure of its disappearance I went off to Chaville to see Tcherepnin. I got lost on the way, although it is not very far. At Tcherepnin's there was a whole collection of people; among other professors from Petersburg were Lyapunov[1] and Handschin.[2] Greeting the latter, I said, 'Here is the man who made me fall out of love with the organ.' Handschin, thinking he must have misheard me, asked me what I meant, but the fact is that in the ninety minutes my lessons with him lasted he never once told me anything about the beauties of which the organ is capable but confined his attention exclusively to training my fingers to play legato and co-ordinating my left hand with my right foot. And to think that there once was a time when I wanted to compose an organ sonata. Now, however, seeing that my remark had offended him, I changed the subject in a less objectionable direction.

Handschin was actually nice and displayed quite an interest in contemporary music. He now lives in Zurich and misses Petersburg. He invited me to stay if ever I found myself in Zurich. Tcherepnin played me his new ballet, the one I had been asked to compose in May,[3] but after I declined had been offered to him. There were some good passages in it, but overall it is a weak piece and, strange to relate, shows the influence of Stravinsky, whom he so loves to disparage.

---

1 Sergey Lyapunov (1859–1924), composer, conductor and fine, powerful pianist. See *Diaries*, vol. 1, pp. 343, 532–664 *passim*; vol. 2, p. 115.
2 Jacques Handschin (1886–1955), organist and musicologist. Prokofiev had studied the organ with him at the St Petersburg Conservatoire, mainly in order to avoid military call-up. See *Diaries*, vol. 1, p. 784; vol. 2, pp. 77–8, 86–130 *passim*.
3 Actually in March. The ballet was a commission for Anna Pavlova's touring company, *The Romance of the Mummy*, based on a short story by Théophile Gautier. See p. 36, above.

Mme Tcherepnin is, as ever, in love with Ptashka and was exceptionally affectionate towards her. She was highly disapproving of Marusya Pavlova (now Benois: Koka Benois is Mme Tcherepnin's cousin),[1] considering her middle class and bourgeois. Ptashka was interested in her voice. According to Sasha Tcherepnin[2] her voice is strong but not particularly even.

27 October

Began working out the development. Oeberg rang up from Paris: there has been a telegram from Koussevitzky about the success of the *Scythian Suite* in America. Went into Paris in the afternoon and ordered myself new concert tails: the old ones were getting tight and Olga Vladislavovna[3] had had to let out the waistcoat in the spring. In any case, after six years I think I deserve one. Discussed my agreement with Oeberg: they have printed a whole heap of compositions but there is still no signed contract. Oeberg is demanding 50 per cent royalties from mechanical reproduction. I do not agree – it's too much. Oeberg says that on the other hand the publisher would keep an eye on this aspect and protect me.

28 October

Continued working on the development section. After lunch read proofs of Op. 9,[4] which is appearing in four languages. The wretched Laloy is keeping silent and not making any of the changes I wanted in the French translation. He is talented, but there are still places I am not happy with.

In the evening I attended a lecture on Christian Science in Paris. The atmosphere was relaxed and joyful.

29 October

Worked on the Symphony and checked the Op. 9 proofs. How pleasant not to have to go anywhere today. A letter from Hébertot very kindly offering to release me from my agreement with him. But this is not at all to my advantage, as according to it there should be ten concerts over two seasons,

---

1 Tcherepnin's wife was Maria Albertovna Benois, whose father Albert Benois was the elder brother of the *Mir Isskustva* painter and Ballets Russes designer Alexander Benois. Nikolay Alexandrovich (Koka) was Alexander's son and thus first cousin to Maria Benois.
2 Alexander Tcherepnin (1899–1977), the son of Nikolay and father of Ivan Tcherepnin, thus the middle one of three generations of composers. Alexander was a prolific composer with a substantial output of operas, ballets, symphonies, Concertos, choral and instrumental music. See *Diaries*, vol. 2, pp. 91–2.
3 Lina Prokofieva's mother.
4 *Two Poems for Voice and Piano* (1910–11).

that is to say 20,000 francs. But suppose he goes out of business altogether? Then I would have no concerts and no money. Perhaps it would be better to strike a compromise before it is too late.

30 October

Went into Paris to negotiate with Oeberg over the 50 per cent mechanical reproduction royalties. The mechanisation of music is advancing at such a rapid rate that it may even become the dominant source of income. But Oeberg adamantly refuses to yield an inch. 'Don't quarrel with Koussevitzky,' he advises. 'I assure you that in time the publishing rights will come back to the composers.' I dined with Rühlmann,[1] a Belgian conductor. I played him the Third Piano Concerto and *Chout*, both of which he plans to conduct in Brussels where two years ago he dazzled audiences with the *Scythian Suite*.[2] Bought a copy of Myaskovsky's 'Circles',[3] an enchantingly melancholy song. I played it to Ptashka; we both love it very much. Ptashka wants to learn it.

31 October

The opening of the Russian National Conservatoire, which consisted of a gala occasion with a separate concert section. The Conservatoire has forty students and forty-two professors, but it enjoys the financial support of Maison Pleyel, who paid for the event. Lyapunov had transcribed the Overture to *Ruslan and Lyudmila* for two pianos, and in the morning we rehearsed it together to play as the opening number, Lyapunov on piano one and I on piano two. During the applause I made him step forward to take a bow as the author, and the old man beamed as though he himself had been the composer of *Ruslan and Lyudmila*. I had a conversation with Blois about Hébertot. He told me that Pleyel also has dealings with him, and they are pretty well informed about his present situation: in January he will go bankrupt. His advice was to try to squeeze at least two or three concerts out of him before the New Year, at least that would be something.

1 November

A headache, so did little work. Nielle sent back a stack of proofs of the orchestral parts of the Third Piano Concerto, once again with a mass of uncorrected mistakes. Romanov has not sent any money. I sent him a

---

1 François Rühlmann (1868–1948), conductor having a long association with the Paris Opéra. An early visitor to the recording studio, he made a series of fine recordings for Pathé.
2 On 13 January 1923. See *Diaries*, vol. 2, pp. 699–700.
3 The third song in Myaskovky's cycle *Three Poems of Zinaida Gippius*, Op. 5 (1905–8)

telegram. Hébertot has gone bankrupt. What a joy! Thanks for that, although Blois did say yesterday evening that he would try to arrange a commission for me from a Swedish ballet company.

2 November

More detailed work on the Symphony. It being Sunday we were expecting guests, but nobody came. I typed out some reviews in connection with the Meri Bran tour. Svyatoslav cut his first tooth. His nanny, Miss Mack, has left us. In the spring she had been very nice and useful, but of late she had become too acclimatised and grumbled all the time.

3 November

Worked. Received some interesting letters from Myaskovsky giving a detailed account of his impressions of my Violin Concerto when it was performed in Moscow (Szigeti). Evidently the orchestra did not excel, but the piece was encored because of the violinist!

4 November

In the afternoon I went into Paris to have it out with Nielle. Dined with Oeberg. He was telling me about B.N., whom he comes across in the club. In July B.N. lost 8,000 francs. Whose, pray? He cannot have had that much money himself. His ring perhaps, the diamond one with a ruby that is no longer on his finger? This may be what lay behind the letter in which he referred to a 'catastrophic misfortune'. According to Oeberg, he no longer gambles although from time to time he plays cards not on his own account, fortunately, but on someone else's, and if he wins gets something from his sponsor. Or he loans money to people who have lost at the tables against the surety of gold watches. People generally look askance on him; Oeberg speaks contemptuously of him, and certainly there is a great decline from the heights of Ettal. He would be better sweeping the streets.

The concert of music by Sasha Tcherepnin is evidently his first. As compositions they are pleasant to listen to but the material is not very interesting. The chatter all around is that he is totally influenced by me. At the concert I saw an affectionate Alexander Benois,[1] also Koka and Marusya. She is thinner

---

1   Alexander Benois (1870–1960) artist, designer, critic, historian, conservationist, founder member with Diaghilev and Bakst of *Mir Isskustva* and first editor of its journal. Benois designed many of the earlier Ballets Russes productions, also at the Moscow Arts Theatre. Prokofiev had come into his orbit on Easter Sunday 1914 at the home of the journalist, editor

than she was and has lost some of her good looks, although she was elegantly dressed in Parisian style. In the old days there was a hint of half-maidenly coquettishness about her that was rather affecting. But on this occasion I saw her only in passing and had no time to do more than tease that she was not very skilful at putting on lipstick. She complained to Ptashka of feeling lonely in Paris. Koka is very good-looking, but I saw him only for a moment. Sashenka came on stage looking sheepish, but he played well, although as a composer who can play rather than as a pianist. This was as a matter of fact what appealed to me about his playing. Nikolay Nikolayevich[1] was very keyed up about his son, and had clearly had a bit too much to drink, as is usually the case with him these days.

5 November

Because of getting home late last night, I did not get as much work done today. In the evening Kolya Kedrov came round; he is the son of Kedrov[2] (of the Kedrov Quartet) and Gladkaya, both of whom taught at the St Petersburg Conservatoire and are now professors at the Paris establishment that opened yesterday. The son had come to pick up my songs for his mother. He is a very nice, modest and well-mannered young man of nineteen. One hears so often that Bolshevism has ruined everything in Russia: the upbringing of the young, morals, the general outlook on life, everything. But if the family is firmly integrated, then you end up with a pleasant and straightforward young man like this one. The Kedrovs have been out of Russia only a few months, having lived through the whole Revolution. Kolya studied at the St Petersburg Conservatoire, and I was very interested in what he had to say in answer to my questions about the institution in which I had myself spent ten years, all my youth. He says the building has not changed at all either outside or inside; the only thing is that the pianos are even worse than they used to be. The male students often wear leather jackets, and sometimes even felt boots. The girls take more trouble over their clothes, and therefore look much as they used to, but some among their number are dedicated communists, tremendously self-confident. On the whole life drags on in its accustomed way, so that even Kolya was reluctant to part with the Conservatoire, even though he is glad now to be living abroad.

---

and Constitutional Democrat Iosif Gessen, and the two formed an immediate friendship which revived when they were both living in Paris.

1 Tcherepnin.
2 Nikolay Kedrov (1871–1940), baritone, founder of the celebrated Kedrov Vocal Quartet, which was toured by Diaghilev and recorded with Chaliapin. His wife was the lyric soprano Olga Gladkaya (1875–1965), who had made her debut at the Mariinsky Theatre as Marguérite in Gounod's *Faust*.

6 November

Did more detailed work on the Symphony. The end of the first movement is in sight. Read proofs.

7 November

Bad headache. For some reason I am getting them quite often nowadays, although I try to regard them as a delusion as Christian Science teaches. I read Christian Science texts meticulously every day and am certainly making progress.

Was in Paris on various matters, including making another attempt to sort out with Nielle the uncorrected mistakes in the proofs. I should really have given him a telling-off, but confronted with this respectable old man sitting there, speaking in a quiet voice and suffering from asthma to boot, my hand was stayed. Meanwhile the work continues to be done slowly and not very well, and above all never on time.

A letter from Zederbaum giving details of the great success being enjoyed by the *Scythian Suite* in America. When I first went to America in 1918 this great republic was too stupid to appreciate me, but over the intervening six years the intelligence quotient has visibly improved. I am glad of this, because in other respects I like America very much, and it was the birthplace of Christian Science.

My head ached until the evening, but at ten o'clock suddenly vanished.

8 November

Blois communicated to me the findings of Maison Pleyel's lawyer on the position vis-à-vis Hébertot. On the basis of what he told me I spent all morning writing to him. Romanov has sent no money. Hébertot has vanished into thin air; not long ago my budget was satisfactorily balanced, but now 18,000 francs on which I had been counting is looking distinctly parlous. Meanwhile Ptashka has just ordered new clothes to the value of three to four thousand francs!

15 November

The premiere of the *Chout* Suite at the Concerts Populaires in Brussels. I played the Third Piano Concerto and had a success.

16 November

Repeat of yesterday's concert.

19 November

A letter from Koussevitzky, a long one and very gracious in tone. Plainly we are a very famous person but inclined to benevolence.

A disagreeable communication from the Palais de Justice: I have been summonsed in connection with the Argus affair, but the notice having meandered interminably round our previous addresses the date has already passed. I thought I had managed to extricate myself from Argus, but no, here I am in court. It is very unpleasant to be the subject of legal action, although it is not certain whether Argus will win their claim for 250 francs.[1]

20 November

Started working out the second movement and in particular the theme of the variations. Romanov has sent me a reassuring letter to the effect that he will be sending the money.

A very nice letter from Dukelsky in the Riviera about my *Ballade*.[2]

21 November

Did not compose in the morning but practised for tomorrow's recital in Brussels. Spent the afternoon on visa and proof corrections business, and also went to the arbitration court. I had prepared a lengthy explanation as to why I had not presented myself in answer to the summons and the reasons why there had been such a delay in my receiving it, but my somnolent young lady interlocutor explained that I had been asked to appear for purposes of conciliation, and it did not matter that I had not been there. Were I to receive another notice, I would have definitely have to respond to that one. I consulted Zagorsky, who roared with laughter: I was not 'in court' at all, merely the subject of an enquiry such as happens to millions of people without in any way staining their reputations.

A letter from Zederbaum about Brennan,[3] the manager of the Boston orchestra. He is agreeable to taking over as my manager and even to paying

---

1 This dispute has not been identified, but has something to do with an insurance policy.
2 *Ballade* for cello and piano, Op. 15 (1912).
3 W. H. Brennan, one of the best-known orchestra managers in America, had been appointed Assistant Manager of the Boston Symphony Orchestra in 1909. In March 1918, by that time in the top job, Brennan was responsible for publicly accepting the resignation of Karl Muck because the orchestra's revered Music Director was under arrest as an enemy alien, languishing in gaol in Fort Oglethorpe, Georgia, until the end of the war before being deported to his native Germany. Muck apparently chose this relatively civilised procedure over the more draconian penalties for an offence under the 1910 Mann Act (primarily intended to address prostitution, immorality, and human trafficking) allegedly for refusing to conduct *The Star-Spangled Banner*.

Haensel $1,000 in part settlement of my indebtedness to him. Oho, this is serious stuff. America is really falling into line.

22 November

Went through my programme and at eleven o'clock set off for Brussels, arriving there at five o'clock. After going for a stroll I read some Christian Science and meditated intensively on the complex problem of my commitment to it. I came to the conclusion that in renouncing the use of medicines but continuing to wear glasses I am guilty of inconsistency and bad faith. I determined to stop wearing glasses. Mine are not very strong and I can do without them relatively easily. Yet doctors in prescribing them tell me that if I do not wear them my eyes will soon deteriorate. Nevertheless, after a heated discussion with myself, I decided that if I truly believe in Christian Science I must discard them, and that Christian Science will ensure that my eyes improve. In this manner the question was resolved and I took them off. The concert was at half past eight and the hall was not quite full, about two-thirds. I played quite well, the greatest success coming near the end, when the audience applauded very vociferously. In the Green Room during the interval, who should appear but . . . Liana Collini.[1] Six and a half years ago, at the time of our dramatic parting in Rostov, she had said that if, in future, she ever saw my name on a concert programme or in the newspapers, she would come to meet me in whatever town I was appearing. Now the town in question was Brussels. She did not seem to have grown any older, although when I recollected how she had been, it did appear to me that the years had left their mark on her. She is married now, to a Yugoslav, and has a child. I proudly informed her that I also had a wife and son. She was impressed that Ptashka is Spanish – is this the loyalty of southern women? 'I regretted not going with you,' she said. 'I was stuck for a long time in Rostov and then in Odessa.' In Romania she had managed to trace her family's assets, but that was as far as her fortune had gone.

We conversed very animatedly and with great warmth on both sides. Needless to say I have long ceased to harbour any feelings towards her, but seeing her brought back a vanished epoch, and lifted a curtain behind which lay concealed a picturesque chapter of my former life. The encounter left me with a deep impression.

1 The Italian-Romanian woman to whom Prokofiev had become romantically attached when staying in Kislovodsk in 1917–18 before (in response to Collini's original suggestion) deciding to try to leave Russia for America. En route, however, the withdrawal of Romania from the Central Powers alliance prompted Signora Collini to abandon her intention to go to New York with Prokofiev in favour of a new plan to return to her now-neutral native country in the company of a dubious compatriot, an entrepreneur called Sarovich. See *Diaries*, vol. 2, pp. 232–58 *passim*, 297.

After the concert a certain Piron took me to drink wine at the house of some rich man called Maier, who told me he knew Stravinsky very well, and that Stravinsky had been to his house on his last visit to Brussels. According to him Stravinsky had roundly criticised Milhaud and been very complimentary about me.

23 November

Went to bed at one, got up at half past six, left to return to Paris and was home in Bellevue at two o'clock. On the journey I read Koshetz's book, in which she notes down various sayings, poems, fables, some of her own and some dictated to her through spiritualist means. Much of the book consists of Christian generalities, but there are some good tales, like the one about life and death, and some happy turns of phrase, for example: 'He stretched out his arms to embrace Life, but they were seized by Death', or: 'One should not regard the salt of one's tears as the salt of life.'

Hardly had I entered the house when guests arrived. It was somewhat of a gala occasion with twelve guests, among them Auric, with whom a rapprochement is taking shape. He is completing a second ballet for Diaghilev (*Les Matelots*)[1] and plans to write an opera next. 'But Diaghilev will kill you!' I said. 'Don't forget, he thinks opera is an outmoded form.' Auric just laughed. I asked him about Dukelsky, sketches for whose ballet for Diaghilev Auric had seen. He thinks they are well done, but of course not the work of a genius.

24 November

Did not compose because of a bad headache. Went into Paris, taking with me the corrected proofs of the score and parts of the Violin Concerto which will now be given to the printers, overtaking the material for the Third Piano Concerto. At the publishers they were saying that the news from America is that Medtner has had a colossal success with his New York debut. That is a surprise! Of course as a pianist he is out of the top drawer, but his music is boring for American audiences.

---

1 *Les Matelots*, ballet in five scenes, libretto by Boris Kokhno (with more than a nod to the plot of *Così fan tutte*), choreography by Léonide Massine, designs by the Barcelonean artist Pedro Pruna, premiered at the Gaîeté-Lyrique in June 1925, danced by Serge Lifar, Taddeus Sławinski, Leon Woizikowski, Vera Nemtchinova and Lydia Sokolova. Auric's music consisted of a suite of hornpipes for winds and brass drawn from sea-shanties.

25 November

A great joy to be at home all day. Polished the Symphony's first variation. Then wrote letters, a great pile of which has accumulated. Sent out complimentary passes to my recital on 5th December, which I have after all managed to wrest back from Hébertot. Altogether I posted forty-one packets. Am doing without wearing glasses.

5 December

Recital in the Champs-Elysées Theatre. A thin audience. I was paid my money. Ira Ruzskaya[1] chattered away in the interval. We have not seen one another for ten years.

12 December

Mama died, in my arms, at 12.15 in the morning of 13th December.

---

1 Irina Ruzskaya, daughter of Prokofiev's friend and early patron and dedicatee of the *Ballade*, Op. 15, the amateur cellist Nikolay Ruzsky. Prokofiev had been close to the Ruzsky family in St Petersburg, but had always had an edgy relationship with the two daughters Irina and Tatyana. Ruzsky had brought his family out of Russia to Paris in 1920. See *Diaries*, vol. 1 *passim*; vol. 2, pp. 44, 61, 68, 71, 76, 82, 120, 535.

1925

1 January

We had planned a different kind of New Year celebration this year, with Benois and Tcherepnin, but in the event the Tcherepnins changed their plans and went to Vyshnegradsky (we just can't refuse, Sergey Sergeyevich, it's a tradition, we're such old friends). We contemplated sending Tcherepnin a card with a quotation from *The Snow Maiden*: 'His love and caresses he reserves for the rich, but for the shepherd naught but thank you and goodbye.'[1] So we had a domestic celebration all by ourselves at Bellevue, except that we had an unexpected visit from B. N. Bashkirov. Half an hour before the New Year hour struck we opened a bottle of fizzy wine, because the last train back to Paris left at 12.30 a.m.

My head ached the next morning, as it does every year: another tradition but a very unwelcome one. Zederbaum, Koussevitzky's secretary, called after lunch, having gone with him to America but finding Natalya Konstantinovna insupportable having come back to Europe after a quarrel.[2] He is very well disposed towards me, and told me he thought there were good prospects of an American tour for me which were it to be well organised could net me as much as $10,000. Oho! Maybe in a year's time I shall be able to buy a house with a garden and a small-holding and raise some cattle! A vision of pastoral bliss . . .

2 January

Orchestrated the Symphony. I am nervous about it, but I'm getting one or two pages, occasionally three, done each day.

Was visited by a young composer from Odessa with a very Jewish name I cannot remember. His score is well put together, very much so, but seems like a throwback to the last century. It appears that to this day nothing new is to be heard in Odessa, except the Second Symphony of Scriabin. Little is known there about me except my name; for some reason I am regarded as a 'proletarian composer' and am even the subject of fierce controversy. The young composer had now come to pay his respects and to introduce himself.

---

1 *The Snow Maiden*, pantheistic opera (1880–81) by Rimsky-Korsakov.
2 See *Diaries*, vol. 2, p. 684.

4 January

Was visited by one Chernetskaya (Inna Samuilovna), who had approached me a few days ago at the theatre and asked permission to call on me. She is a dancer and producer who has recently arrived from Moscow, where she danced with the Bolshoy Ballet and had staged a version of my *Sarcasms*[1] (some time ago I had indeed seen a photograph of it in a magazine). She assured me that she had developed something quite new in dance technique and had even demonstrated to Diaghilev in what a dead end he was now immured.[2] She was in search of a new ballet, and said that if I would compose one for her it would be pounced upon joyfully in Moscow. She had much of interest to tell me about Moscow. Rachmaninoff is no longer in favour there and is all but forgotten. Can this really be so? The Bolshoy Theatre audience is extremely receptive and discerning: not everything from the old days has perished; there are students and a communist intelligentsia. She will come again to hear *Chout*, which I promised to play for her.

5–8 January

Preparing to go to Poland. Complications with Meri Bran, who is refusing to pay me an advance.

9 January

Departure. To travel through the night sitting up in second class followed by a whole day's journey is rather tiring, so I took first class as far as Cologne and was alone in my compartment. Ptashka and Tanya Kalashnikova[3] saw me off. I was not allowed to get any sleep all night: first it was French passport control, then Belgian, then Belgian Customs, then ticket inspection by the Belgian guard, then German Customs: 'bitte Ihre Pass', 'die Fahrkarte, bitte'[4] and so on and on. Once every half-hour someone would come into the compartment, with the result that I got properly off to sleep only just before morning and woke up when the train was already standing in Cologne station.

---

1   *Sarcasms, Five Pieces for Piano*, Op. 17 (1912–14).
2   Inna Chernetskaya was one of the leading exponents of the free-dance movement exemplified by Isadora Duncan still in Russia. Herself a former Isadora Duncan pupil, apart from her activities in the Bolshoy, in 1923 she had established her own experimental Studio of Synthetic Dance in Moscow's Choreological Laboratory, where she pursued her ideal of abstracting dance movements into machine-like poses. Her studio became known as a centre for experimentation in free-dance techniques such as those espoused by Duncan, Dalcroze and Rudolf Steiner. See below, pp. 438, 450, 473–4.
3   An acquaintance.
4   'Your passport please'; 'Tickets please'.

10 January

The moment I awoke I jumped up and made a dash for the second-class carriages, where I got a seat next to the window. I then washed (even shaved without cutting myself) and drank coffee in the Speisewagen.[1] Café-complet and two pieces of cheese cost 13 francs – not French prices! The weather was good, with no snow, but the scenery monotonous. France is more beautiful.

Arrived in Berlin at five o'clock and disembarked at the Charlottenburg station where I was met by Suvchinsky and Gessen.[2] Suvchinsky looks extremely fit and plans to move to Bellevue in a month's time. We went together to Gessen's house, where I am staying. Hardly had we got there when Bran was on the telephone, but they told her I had gone out to send a telegram. It appears that Gessen had not told her I was arriving at Charlottenburg and she had rushed off to meet me at the Friedrichstrasse Bahnhof, taking Weber from my publishers[3] along with her. At this point there occurred a confusing coincidence: Gessen was combining coming to meet me with seeing off Gzovskaya,[4] who took my seat in the train for its onward journey to Warsaw. The next stop after Charlottenburg was, as it happened, Friedrichstrasse, where Bran instead of me found Gzovskaya, who told her that Prokofiev had already gone to Gessen's house.

11 January

I slept the sleep of the dead. At seven o'clock in the morning there was a telegram from Fitelberg[5] telling me that my visa would be waiting for me to collect at the Polish Consulate in Berlin. Gessen came with me to Yurevskaya's, where we rehearsed my songs together: she will sing 'Birdsong', 'The Butterfly' and 'Remember Me'.[6] Yurevskaya told me the story of Salter having been caught perpetrating a swindle: his firm had been closed down and no longer exists. Every half an hour there was a telephone call from Bran, but I spoke to her only once, to ask her to come tomorrow morning to sort things out. In the meantime

---

1 Restaurant car.
2 Iosif Gessen (1886–1943), lawyer, journalist (publisher of *Rech* (*Speech*) in St Petersburg and later, having emigrated to Berlin, the émigré newspaper *Rul'* (*The Helm*)). Gessen had been an influential supporter of the Constitutional Democrat Party before the Revolution and close ally of its leader Pavel Milyukov. See *Diaries*, vol. 1, pp. 612, 616, 634, 711, 713, 715; vol. 2, pp. 74, 156, and *passim*.
3 Fyodor Weber, Berlin chief of Russian Music Editions.
4 Tatyana Gzovskaya, dancer, choreographer and costume designer.
5 Grzegorz Fitelberg (1879–53), Polish conductor and composer who in 1935 founded the Polish National Radio Symphony Orchestra. He conducted the first performance of Stravinsky's *Mavra* for the Ballets Russes in June 1922. He had conducted Prokofiev in the First Piano Concerto in the summer season at Pavlovsk as early as 1915, and repeated it two years later. See *Diaries*, vol 2 pp. 55–6.
6 *Five Songs of Konstantin Balmont*, Op. 36 (1921), Nos. 2, 3 and 4.

I must make contact with a Serbian pianist who, according to Suvchinsky, has $1,000 available to arrange a concert, and wants to put on this concert with me.

At five o'clock I took part in a concert at the offices of the *Vossische Zeitung* newspaper.[1] The audience was almost exclusively Jewish. Suvchinsky said his attempt to identify at least five Christians had not been successful. I played well and Suvchinsky, who had not heard me play since Russian times, complimented me on my pianism. Yurevskaya sang well, although she did not hold the final notes of 'Butterfly' and 'Remember Me' quite long enough. Ranchev (a Bulgarian tenor with a nice, sweet voice) had not learnt any of my songs and so sang some by Rimsky-Korsakov, which was justified to the audience by the explanation that Rimsky had been my teacher. Photographs were taken and cartoonists made drawings of us. I left the building with Suvchinsky, and as we walked along we talked about theology. When I cautiously broached the subject of Christian Science, he brushed it aside: 'Well, that is a pretty rum do, is it not? What's that all about?' But I fancy all he has heard about Christian Science will have been no more than vague rumours.

We dined at the Fürstenhof,[2] the same place as two years ago. The Serb came and we discussed an orchestral concert: he wants to play my Third Piano Concerto with me conducting. The remainder of the programme would consist of my works.

12 January

Meri Bran came in the morning. She is small, like Tanya, but not so pretty and narrower across the shoulders. She cuts a comical figure, like a boy whose beard has not yet grown, and this boyishness extends over her whole person. She wears her hair with a parting, and is dressed in a suit and man's tie. She is about twenty-five years old. Despite her best efforts to smooth things over, even to the extent of agreeing to pay me an advance (in Poland and, presumably, out of my earnings from the Polish leg of the tour), I informed her that I considered her in categorical breach of our agreement. She was most upset by this, and almost burst into tears as we went out into the street together.

---

1   Originally (at its inception in the seventeenth century) called the *Königlich Privilegierte Berlinische Zeitung von Staats- und Gelehrten Sachen*, when it recast its masthead a century later to the somewhat snappier title reflecting its then owner C. F. Voss, the *Vossische Zeitung* was not only one of Germany's oldest national newspapers but the one commonly regarded as the stately paper of record, akin to *The Times*. Doubtless for this reason it was often referred to, in a pre-echo of the BBC, as 'Tante Vossin'. The paper's overtly liberal editorial stance was not appreciated by Hitler's National Socialist Party, which in 1934 closed it down and replaced it with its own more strident organ, the *Völkische Beobachtung*. This survived as long as its sponsors but no longer.
2   A Russian restaurant near the Tiergarten. Prokofiev had been in Berlin in October 1922, where he had spent a good deal of time in the company of Diaghilev, Stravinsky, Mayakovsky and Suvchinsky. The Fürstenhof seems to have been a natural watering-hole for such a group of *bon vivants*.

I went to the Polish Consulate, but there is no visa yet. Strohbach[1] came to see me, the producer and designer for *Oranges*. He is has been given leave of absence from Berlin to work on this production in Cologne. He is thirty-four, Szenkár thirty-two and I am thirty-three, so the combined ages are ninety-nine. Strohbach is wildly enthusiastic about *Oranges*, and says that dramatically it is the most interesting opera he knows. '*So lustig!*'[2] He has thought up a mass of devices and will start rehearsing the chorus on the 1st February. He showed me some sketches of the scenery: they seemed faintly ridiculous, Cubist fantasies, but it was hard to get a true impression from his pencil sketches. He has a few criticisms of the German text of the libretto.

13 January

A second telegram from the Philharmonia that the visa has been sent. I went once more to the Consulate, killing two hours in the process, going round everybody from the secretary to the Consul-General, but no authorisation could be found and without it nothing could be done. They sent me to the Ambassador, where his secretary told me the visa had just that moment been received. These delightful *pans*[3] and their idiotic rules and regulations completely wore me out.

Today is the Russian New Year and Suvchinsky invited me to join him at Professor Karsavin's,[4] a very nice man, but I was tired. Bran telephoned again. She was so upset by our contretemps that she had been taken ill in the evening, but was now proposing new terms and conditions for April, this time to include Ptashka.

1 Hans Strohbach (1891–1949), radically inclined designer and producer, designer at the Volksbühne in Berlin, one of the most innovative theatres of Germany dominated throughout the 1920s by Erwin Piscator. Strohbach was well known throughout Europe between the wars, and was put in charge of the productions of J. A. Westrup's Oxford University Opera Club from 1931 to 1933.
2 'So jolly.'
3 A *pan* is a Polish gentleman.
4 Lev Karsavin (1882–1950), historian, philosopher and theologian, Professor of Medieval History at the University of St Petersburg, thereafter at Berlin, was the brother of the prima ballerina Tamara Karsavina and also (at the time) Suvchinsky's father-in-law. Karsavin had been one of the two hundred or so leading academics, thinkers and artists deported by Lenin in 1922 as inimical to the ideals of the Bolshevik Revolution – an initiative that proved to be a long-term disaster for the intellectual health of the new society, as movingly documented in Lesley Chamberlain's *The Philosophy Steamer* (Atlantic Books, 2006). Karsavin's tragedy did not end with his deportation, however, because in 1928 he accepted chairs first at the Universities of Kaunas then of Vilnius, in Lithuania, which was at the time an independent country. But in 1940 Lithuania suffered occupation first by the USSR and then by Nazi Germany, only to become once again part of the Soviet Union at the end of the Second World War. At that time Karsavin unsurprisingly found himself once again an object of interest to the NKVD, not least because of his presumed association during the years of enforced emigration in the 1920s with the *Yevraziist* preoccupations of his father-in-law Suvchinsky. Nine years of Chekist persecution followed, culminating in his dismissal from his university post, arrest and in 1949 a sentence of ten years' hard labour in the camps at Vologda, where he died the following year.

I read Christian Science in the evenings. My eyes do not seem to be improving.

14 January

Suvchinsky lives in Süd-Ende, a kind of Berlin version of Bellevue, and today he asked me out to lunch there. He has a very beautiful sitting room and a small, long and narrow bedroom. His wife is a pleasant but colourless woman. With us was Mlle Guchkova, the daughter of the author of 'Order No. 1'.[1] She is also Ziloti's[2] niece and related to

1   See *Diaries*, vol. 2, pp. 183–4 for Prokofiev's encounter with 'Order No. 1'. Alexander Guchkov (1862–1936) was the leader of the bourgeois 'Oktyabristi' faction and served as Minister of War in the Fourth State Duma. Together with the leader of the Nationalist/Monarchist faction Vasily Shulgin, and General Nikolay Ruzsky (ibid., p. 234, and vol. 1, p. 734) representing the Imperial armed forces, Guchkov had been the third member of the delegation to whom the Tsar personally give his signed manifesto abdicating in favour of his brother Grand Duke Michael. In fact although as War Minister he did sign the order, Guchkov was reluctant to do so and was neither responsible for nor supported the catastrophically demoralising provisions of the Petrograd Soviet's Order No. 1 to the troops, which removed the normal observances of the chain of command and designated the Petrograd Soviet itself as the ultimate authority in place of the existing military High Command. At a stroke not merely the Petrograd garrison but the entire Russian military machine was effectively destroyed as a disciplined fighting force. Guchkov's subsequent memoir, published in exile in Paris (*Latest News*, 23 September 1936) makes his ambivalence clear: 'To this day I find it hard to say whether I acted correctly or not. Of course I could have instituted a complete rupture with the Petrograd Soviet, but in the first place it is doubtful whether such a step would have enjoyed the support of my colleagues in the Provisional Government, and secondly, at this early stage of revolution when the Petrograd garrison was resisting subordinating itself to the Provisional Government, a break with the Soviet could have led to anarchy and civil war.' Far from Guchkov himself being the author of Order No. 1, the document was the result of a spuriously engineered rumour that the officers of the Petrograd Garrison were demanding the disarming of rebellious rank-and-file soldiers. The actual drafting, seen as an exercise in calming damage-limitation, was remitted to members of a specially appointed delegation of the Soviet's Executive Committee, assisted (and clearly influenced) by ordinary soldiers. Prominent among the drafters was the Social Democrat N. D. Sokolov, taking his instructions from the assorted gaggle of mainly Bolshevik-inclined soldiers' and workers' deputies. The provisionally finished draft was hastily typeset in the offices of *Izvestia* newspaper, which had conveniently a few days earlier been taken over by the Bolshevik journalist Vladimir Bonch-Bruyevich, who it is reasonable to assume will have done whatever may have been necessary to edit the text (the original of which has disappeared) to suit Bolshevik ambitions. The *Izvestia*-typeset version was delivered about 4 a.m. to the War Committee of the Duma where Guchkov, as explained, felt after much soul-searching that he had no option but to sign it and issue it as a proclamation, to the horror of the military authorities and most people who were well enough informed to have some inkling of its likely consequences. A piquant detail in Guchkov's subsequent career after resigning as War Minister was his chairmanship of a Provisional Government committee charged with re-igniting Russia's paralysed economic and industrial base, members of which included not only the scion of the giant Putilov engineering concern but also two tycoon figures whose biographies touched Prokofiev's: Alexey Meshchersky (*Diaries*, vol. 1 *passim*; vol. 2, pp. 39–43, 508), the father of his adolescent love Nina Mescherskaya; and the banker Alexander Vyshnegradsky (*Diaries*, vol. 1, p. 725n; vol. 2, pp. 348, 350, 359, 421, 538, 540, 614, and above pp. 83, 99, 101, 103–4).
2   Alexander Ziloti (1863–1945). To quote the late Michael Steinberg's review of Charles Barber's biography of Ziloti, *Lost in the Stars*: 'To most people who listen to and read about classical music,

Rachmaninoff.[1] Aged eighteen, she sometimes acts as Suvchinsky's secretary. After lunch Suvchinsky and I returned to Berlin, to Gessen's, where we found Meri Bran waiting for me with a new contract. This, however, was of course very poorly written and I insisted that she do it again. She will send a fair copy for me to sign in Warsaw. The three of us then went to the station, where I failed to find any sleeping-car berths. I departed in ordinary second class, but at the border (where incidentally we had to wait three hours) I transferred to an empty first-class compartment, where I slept not badly. I had no trouble at the border, but one Russian woman who had something amiss with her documents was thrown off the train.

15 January

Warsaw at nine o'clock in the morning. A beaming Fitelberg met me at the station, attired in a superb fur coat. We embraced, and he told me that he had had to leave Warsaw for a few days, which was the reason for the muddle with the visa. He also said that I would be staying, not in a hotel, but with a Mme Grossman, a half-Russian, half-Polish woman. In Petrograd she had been the owner of a large piano firm called German & Grossman, and between 1904 and 1908 I had had one of their pianos, which was not at all bad, quite a powerful instrument.[2] Her apartment was huge and elegant, with two maids and a footman. My room is very comfortable. My hostess is about forty to forty-five, very pleasant, and speaks excellent Russian. She told me not to stand on ceremony and to treat staying with her 'as if it were a hotel'. There was already a rehearsal with the orchestra at ten o'clock, wholly devoted to my Third Piano Concerto. Fitel had made great efforts to learn the piece thoroughly, but I was very tired.

After the rehearsal Fitelberg took me out to a restaurant for an enormous lunch (*flaczki*[3] *à la polonaise*), after which I went to sleep. At five o'clock I

Ziloti is at best a name in a footnote to a programme note about his cousin Rachmaninoff. But an immense public force and presence in his great years, Ziloti was a remarkable musician – pianist, conductor, composer, teacher, editor, impresario – whose life path intersected with a multitude of characters from Liszt to Eugene Istomin by way of Tchaikovsky, all three piano-playing Rubinsteins, Elgar, Scriabin, Schoenberg, Stravinsky, Prokofiev, Ysaÿe, and Casals, to list just a few of the most famous' (C. Barber, *Lost in the Stars: The Forgotten Musical Life of Alexander Siloti*, Scarecrow Press, Lanham, Maryland, 2002). Ziloti's initial reaction to the young Prokofiev in St Petersburg had been dismissive, but he quickly revised his opinion to become one of his most influential and effective supporters. Ziloti left Russia in 1919, finally settling in New York where he lived until his death. See *Diaries*, vol. 1, p. 79, and *passim*; vol. 2 *passim*.

1 Her mother was Ziloti's sister.
2 See *Diaries*, vol. 1, p. 38. Having 'recently given unmistakable signs of giving up the ghost' the German & Grossman was traded in for 275 roubles for a new Ratke costing 900 roubles.
3 A Polish national dish, a kind of thick soup made from tripe, beef marrowbone stock, vegetables and cream.

went for a walk round Warsaw, which reminded me of Moscow and Petrograd: the domestic architecture has something in common, with the house numbers in transparent yellow lettering on triangular blue illuminated signs. There were a lot of people out and about in fur coats, and old women in shawls.

My concert was in the evening. The hall is very good, a good-sized audience but not full. In the first half I played the Third Concerto to great acclaim. In the second half I played a selection of solo pieces, including 'Suggestion diabolique'[1] (in Polish 'Zmora'), which had a tremendous success. I gave three encores, and could have given another three, because the audience surged down to the stage shouting for 'March'[2] or 'Fairy Tale'[3]! Apparently both these pieces had been performed here by Orlov,[4] Borovsky, Artur Rubinstein and two Polish pianists, and the public wanted to hear how the composer would play them. The general opinion was that my success was greater than that enjoyed by Stravinsky, who had appeared at the start of the season in his Concerto. In the evening there was a dinner at Mme Grossman's: Fitelberg, the Directors of the Conservatoire and the Philharmonia, the secretary of the President of the Republic, and some others. The President's secretary was nice and said that he would be glad to arrange a visa for me on the spot whenever I might need one.

16 January

Spent the morning practising for my recital, then lunched with Fitelberg. His wife is in Berlin and he lives with his sister in a modest flat. I have caught Bran out in a lie: in Berlin she had told me that the reason the concert in Łódź was cancelled was because when the city had learnt I had no visa they had given the hall to another artist. When I mentioned this to the Director of the Warsaw Philharmonia, he exclaimed that this could not possibly be the case; he knows his Łódź colleague personally and he would not act in such a way. He had sent a telegram and just today received an embarrassed reply contradicting Bran's account. I have this telegram safely in my pocket.

In the evening I attended the premiere of *Siegfried* in the box of the Director of the Conservatoire. The theatre is not particularly big and the sets were bad, the singers mediocre, but some of the acting was not bad and the audience well dressed. The Polish language, with all its hissing, buzzing consonants, is quite expressive in dramatic and comic scenes (Mime), but

---

1 'Suggestion diabolique', *Four Pieces for Piano*, Op. 4 No. 4.
2 Perhaps from *The Love for Three Oranges* but in context more likely Op. 3 No. 2.
3 'Skazka', *Four Pieces for Piano*, Op. 3 No. 1.
4 Nikolay Orlov (1892–1964), pianist, pupil of Konstantin Igumnov in Moscow and after his emigration a successful performer in the West specialising in Chopin. See *Diaries*, vol. 1, p. 325.

less effective in lyrical passages. After the performance a whole group of us including the prima ballerina – a very pretty woman – went to dine in a night club, the Oasis, with dancing and entertainment, where we stayed until three o'clock. The ballerina's fiancé paid the whole bill and would not let any of us make a contribution.

17 January

Since the audience is well acquainted with my piano works I must not disgrace myself, and therefore practised diligently. My hostess was kind enough to suggest bringing in a Steinway, but I declined the offer. All manner of celebrities have stayed with her in the past: Rachmaninoff, Safonov,[1] Casals.[2] I had lunch with the Meyers, wealthy Warsaw residents at whose home Stravinsky had practised when he was in the city. They told me that Stravinsky was very rude about Schloezer, who is always very deferential to him in his articles and sideswipes me. Stravinsky is wont to say: 'This Schloezer, he is always writing about me, but of what he writes, he knows nothing.' After this, Fitya (as they call him hereabouts) and I went to call on the ballerina, who was holding a farewell tea-party before leaving for Bucharest. A gentleman present said, 'I have a cousin who is also quite a good pianist.' 'Oh yes,' I responded in an offhand way, 'and who might that be?' 'Hofmann,' he replied. Somewhat unexpected! I then went to the offices of the Russian-language newspaper published here, which is edited by Filosofov.[3] Ten years ago he had rounded on me for writing music to such a stupid text as 'The Wizard'.[4] Yesterday evening, seeing me at *Siegfried*, he

---

1 Vasily Safonov (1852–1918), pianist, conductor and famously combative teacher, Rector of the Moscow Conservatoire in which capacity he quarrelled with Ziloti. From 1906 to 1909 he was Chief Conductor of the New York Philharmonic Orchestra. Prokofiev had met him first as a Conservatoire student on holiday in the Caucasus in 1914. See *Diaries*, vol. 1, pp. 725–6, 729–30, 732; vol. 2, pp. 234, 236, 254–5.
2 Pablo Casals (1876–1973), noted Catalan cellist and conductor, credited with the rediscovery in 1890 (in a second-hand copy of Grützmacher's edition), and eventual rehabilitation as important concert works, of J. S. Bach's suites for solo cello.
3 Dmitry Filosofov (1872–1940), writer and literary critic, was Diaghilev's cousin. Together with Alexander Benois the trio founded in St Petersburg in 1899 the artistic and literary movement *World of Art (Mir Isskustva)* embodying the highest standards in art, writing, performance, culture and Art nouveau principles of individual expression contrasted with academic conformity. The group's influence, deeply embedded in Diaghilev's original Ballets Russes seasons in Paris among other outlets, spread throughout Europe. Filosofov, who lived in an amicable ménage à trois with Dmitri Merezhkovsky and his wife Zinaida Gippius, the various sexual permutations of which have lost none of their fascination, was editor of and frequent contributor to the group's influential journal, also entitled *Mir Isskustva*. After the Revolution Filosofov chose a different émigré destination from his cousin and other colleagues, ending up in Warsaw, where he founded and edited the anti-Bolshevik newspaper *Svoboda (Freedom)*.
4 'Kudesnik', No. 5 of *Five Poems for Voice and Piano*, Op. 23, words by Nikolay Agnitsev (1915).

declared he was glad to meet in me 'a genuinely great master', and went on to say that he wished his newspaper to celebrate my visit to Warsaw and the success I had enjoyed there, whereby he could underline the significance of Russian culture. For this reason I went along to 'answer a few questions' for the article in question. In the office I met Artsybushev,[1] who also has something to do with the newspaper. The former hymner of 'pneumatic breasts'[2] and sturdy young men violating beautiful young girls is now almost completely deaf, but we did have one thing in common: he is a passionate chess-player. In the evening I was invited by the Director of the Conservatoire to play bridge: he, I, the Director of the Philharmonia, Mme Grossman and the Secretary to the President of the Republic, the same who had promised me help with visas. I thought that since my days of bridge glory in America I would have forgotten how to play, but all went well and I emerged with honour and fifteen francs richer.

18 January

Practised in the morning, and afterwards played bridge with Spiess. Dined in the evening with rich Jews, friends of the Director of the Conservatoire, who stuffed me with food to the gills. Some young people who were also there played me my March and *Visions Fugitives*,[3] pretty decently. But enough, enough! I have had my fill of going out and being entertained, although it is gratifying that Warsaw has received me with such eagerness.

19 January

Practised and read the newspapers, which contain an entire literature about Stravinsky and me. It was very entertaining, although there were some mistakes (concerning Debussy, the sonatas, and so on). My hostess has an interesting autograph album dating back to the time of her business

---

1 Nikolai Artsybushev (1858–1937), by profession a lawyer, as a member (with Lyadov and Glazunov) of the conservatively inclined three-man Belyayev Concerts selection committee in the early years of the twentieth century, occupied a position of influence far in excess of his gifts as a musician and composer. (Ossovky's view was that 'he composed featureless music in small forms in a competent manner'.) Nevertheless, as an ambitious administrator he was eventually to become overall head of the Belyayev Publishing House. Hardly surprisingly he had been antipathetic to the point of obstruction to the iconoclastic young Prokofiev during his years of struggle for recognition in St Petersburg, although eventually (in his other position as chairman of the Petersburg branch of the Russian Musical Society) Artsybushev relented enough to sanction performances in that august environment of the First and Second Piano Concertos, in 1917 and 1914 respectively. See *Diaries*, vol. 1, pp. 57, 122–3, 749–50.
2 The Russian word is 'uprugy' – 'springy', 'elastic', but the pre-echo of *Brave New World* (1931) seemed too apt to let pass.
3 *Visions Fugitives* (*Mimolyotnosti*), 20 pieces for piano, Op. 22 (1915–17).

activities; there were Liszt, Gounod, Boito, Puccini, Rachmaninoff, etc. Stravinsky had drawn the outline of his hand in pencil – proud pianist as he has recently become. When my hostess requested my autograph I added a note below it: 'When I reach forty and shall have acquired a modest skill on the bassoon I will draw you a picture of my lungs.'

20 January

M.V.[1] came: 'I simply couldn't not come to your recital.' Her family has an estate in Poland, part of which belongs to her, and she is spending the winter there. She had lunch with us and told me how Borovsky, who is at the moment in New York, had been to see Rachmaninoff and played him some contemporary music including Stravinsky and Prokofiev. Needless to say Rachmaninoff was very critical, but about my music had this to say: 'Prokofiev is talented when he wants to shock, but when he wants to be serious he is no better than the others.'

The recital was in the same hall in the Philharmonia as the concert had been, but the audience was slightly smaller, as was the success. But I was not completely in the mood, and was also a little tired, so was stingy with the encores, playing only two.

21 January

I got $500 in nice American banknotes, and also a sleeper berth even though I had been told there were none left. I left hospitable Warsaw seen off by Maria Viktorovna, for whom I felt very sorry as once again her kidneys are giving trouble and she was feeling rotten, and by Fitel, who appeared in a magnificent fur coat.

Constant salutations to right and left, because a great many fashionable people were travelling on the Paris express and so there was a great crowd of well-wishers. In view of his demonstrable affection for me I proposed to Fitelberg that we move to 'ty'[2] without drinking the usual toast, to which he cordially assented.

22 January

Crossed the German border at six o'clock. I was a little worried, because one is not supposed to take more than $100 out of the country, but there were no

---

1 Maria Viktorovna Borovskaya, née Baranovskaya ('Frou-frou').
2 The intimate, second-person-singular form of address, reserved for family, intimate friends, also children and inferiors such as servants.

difficulties. At noon arrived in Berlin, where I left the train and went back to stay at Gessen's, where I played the piano in the afternoon.

23 January

Mme Wolff, directress of one of the biggest German concert agencies,[1] asked me to call. I went, but she was not there. I left, disgruntled. Meri Bran came in the afternoon. She agrees to everything and will prepare a new contract incorporating all my conditions; she also undertook to pay my fee tomorrow before the concert. I insisted that she bring the fee at four o'clock 'so that I am not unnecessarily obliged to put on evening dress'. Agreed. At Gessen's there was a young organist from the Petersburg Conservatoire, who started asking me all sorts of questions. I obliged, oracularly. But when I asserted that nowadays Stravinsky had taken to claiming Bach as his father, he set me right. 'Does he really come from Bach? Is it not rather a secondary line from his predecessor Vivaldi?' I replied: 'The difference is not so important. What matters is the descent from the epoch crowned by Bach.'

24 January

In the afternoon Suvchinsky took me to meet Mme Guchkova, Ziloti's sister and the mother of Mlle Guchkova whom I had met at his house. Here there was a gathering of *Yevraziisti*: Professor Frank, Professor Trubetskoy, Professor Ilyin[2] – who asked me a series of extremely complicated questions

---

1 'As directress of Wolff and Sachs, Germany's most powerful concert agency, Louise Wolff's stable of artists included many of the top performers not only of that day but of the entire century. They included (to name only a few of the hundreds) Edwin Fischer, Adolf Busch, Sigrid Onegin, Georg Kulenkampf, Karl Muck, Felix Weingartner, Teresa and Artur Schnabel, Emmi Leisner, Karin Branzell, Jascha and Tossy Spivakovsky, Claire Dux, and Carl Flesch. The newspaper advertisements heralding performances of her clients were usually the largest in the Sunday editions and were set off with a thick black border running around all four sides. Louise Wolff was known as Queen Louise in musical circles throughout Europe, and more respect than sarcasm attended her title. She had taken over the successful agency founded by her husband Hermann after he died in 1902 and made it grow in prosperity by holding on to established talents while nurturing promising new ones.' (Note taken with grateful acknowledgement from Sam H. Shirakawa, *The Devil's Music Master: The Controversial Life and Career of Wilhelm Furtwängler*, Oxford University Press, 1992).
2 The religious philosopher Semyon Frank (1877–1950) was born a Jew but converted to Orthodox Christianity. Linguist and philosopher Prince Nikolay Trubetskoy (1890–1938), whose father was Rector of Moscow University, was one of the main thinkers and proponents of the Eurasianist movement, although his seminal contributions to comparative linguistics, phonology and the origins of language are now regarded as more significant. He and Suvchinsky met in Sophia, where Trubetskoy's *Europe and Humankind* was published in 1920. Lev Karsavin's admission that he had read this book was a crucial cause of his conviction, likewise Trubetskoy's 1925 study *The Legacy of Tchingis-khan: A Look at Russian History Not*

about music – and a certain visitor from Moscow who embarked on a clamorous eulogy of Roslavets[1] and Myaskovsky. A prominent element in these protestations was Muscovite patriotism which had evidently grown mightily: see what fine fellows we are now! When I began to add my own measure of praise for Myaskovsky and it became clear that I knew even more about him and loved him even more dearly than my interlocutor, he immediately abandoned his rodomontade and became very obliging. Later Suvchinsky whispered in my ear that this man was important in the Red hierarchy, but was sympathetic to the *Yevraziist* point of view and was here incognito.[2] It was a pity I did not know this before, otherwise I would have paid more attention to him. Suvchinsky himself sat quietly in a corner with Mlle Guchkova, the pair of them billing and cooing to one another like a pair of turtle-doves.

I returned home to Gessen's around four o'clock, but there was no sign either of Bran or of the money. I lay down to rest before the concert, but at five o'clock there was still nothing. Finally there appeared a gentleman with a martyred air who announced that everything was in order, the concert would take place as planned and the money would be paid. I responded that I found it hard to place any confidence in this information since the primary condition, i.e. the delivery of the fee by four o'clock, had not been fulfilled. He embarked on more protestations, but I cut him short by saying that I had no intention of putting on my concert clothes until the money was safely in my pocket. The gentleman departed, and we sat down to eat. By a quarter to eight (the concert was due to begin at eight) of Meri Bran there was neither hide nor hair. I decided nevertheless to put on my concert tails, and the Gessens also got ready to go to the performance. We all sat around in the drawing-room, as if waiting for New Year. Gessen said, 'I can't understand this – after all, the audience will be in its seats by now!'

From the West But From the East, which must have been written shortly after this meeting. The religious philosopher Ivan Ilyin (1883–1954), like Karsavin and Frank, had been among those expelled on the 'Philosophy Steamer'. An unrepentant Monarchist and more vehement opponent of the Bolshevik regime than his colleagues, he was eventually threatened by the rise of Nazism and in 1938 was helped financially by Rachmaninoff to escape from Germany to the safety of Switzerland. This little group in a Berlin drawing-room thus constituted a uniquely influential concentration of Eurasianist thought and ideology, and one cannot help wondering where the true sympathies and motives of the musical enthusiast visiting from Moscow lay.

1 Nikolay Roslavets (1881–1944), avant-garde composer influenced by the mystic chord theories of Scriabin. Associated initially with such icons of Futurism as Malevich, Meyerhold and Lourié, in the bitter struggle for musical supremacy in the 1920s Roslavets unluckily picked the wrong horse (the Association for Contemporary Music over the rival Russian Association of Proletarian Musicians), and by the end of the decade was vilified as a counter-revolutionary, decadent, formalist, bourgeois artist and Trotskyite saboteur, and ejected from the Composers' Union. The new elite of the Composers' Union did not take prisoners; poverty and relentless persecution brought on a disabling stroke in 1939, and Roslavets died in 1944.
2 He might well have been an OGPU (see below p. 439) plant from TREST.

Finally at twenty past eight there was a telephone call from the same suffering individual on behalf of Meri Bran: 'Please hurry up, there is a large audience waiting and Bran will hand you your fee as soon as you arrive at the hall.' We procured a car and set off: Gessen, his wife and two sons, and I. I joked that with such protection I felt safe from any attacks Meri Bran might launch in my direction. But in the event the Gessens proved to have no stomach for the encounter, because the moment we got near the hall and saw Meri Bran and the afflicted gentleman standing at the entrance, the whole family tumbled out, turned tail and fled, while I lurked alone in the depths of the car. The afflicted one came up to me and politely began urging me to reconsider, but I declined to emerge until I received the agreed payment, and furthermore said if I did not receive it I would leave forthwith. At this Meri Bran herself entered the fray in a climax of agitation, sobbing, crying, threatening, pleading, and generally turning in a creditable paroxysm worthy of Renata in the first act of *Fiery Angel*. She pleaded that she would pay me as soon as the concert was over and would give me now whatever written undertakings I wanted. She finished by sobbing that if I refused she would be bankrupted and even risked being sent to gaol. At this point she ran off, her place being taken by her German partner, a quite respectable young man. However, Meri Bran herself returned in such a frenzy of excitement that I was afraid she was going to hit me. I surreptitiously adopted a boxer's guard whereby I could deflect the expected punch with my left hand while pushing her away from the car with my right.

By this time her vociferous exclamations had risen to such a pitch that they were attracting the attention of passers-by, who were beginning to cluster round the car. It was clear we were moving towards some sort of resolution: either I had to leave, or I should go on and play. I reasoned thus: I was obviously not going to get any money, and the feasibility of appearing at any further concerts under the lady's auspices had obviously gone straight down the drain. The easiest thing would be to leave. However, the audience – not to mention the critics – was already in place; not only that but the woman was so stupid that, who knows, she might actually end up in prison. I decided to shift the locus of the dispute from the car to the Green Room, and try to extract from her at least the promised written guarantee. I therefore got out of the taxi and paid the driver, after which we entered the building by the main entrance and navigated along the side corridor to the Green Room.

The party now consisted of myself, Bran's German colleague and Gessen, who had reappeared from wherever he had been hiding. Bran herself had vanished. It was now about nine o'clock, the concert having been timed to start at eight, and some disgruntled members of the audience had begun to leave. One lady, identifying me as the artist, flung over her shoulder: 'So young and so insolent!' A critic said angrily to me as he passed: 'Wir sind nicht gewöhnt dazu!' I replied: 'Ich auch!',[1] meaning that I was not used to not being paid. That stopped the German in his amazed tracks, after which he continued towards the exit while I went to the Green Room. There was no sign of Bran there; her colleague went in search of her but could not find her. When I asked him, 'What exactly is your role in this affair?', he replied that his relationship with Bran was quite fortuitous: he had his own concert bureau through which Bran had booked the hall and printed the posters and tickets. He was now acutely embarrassed at having had anything to do with her.

Gessen advised sending her to hell and going on stage to do the concert. I opened the door and peeped out into the hall: it was about three-quarters full and that decided the outcome of the evening. It was simply not possible in the face of such a crowd to turn on my heel and depart. The German impresario had a suggestion: 'Would you like me to go out and make an announcement that Bran has swindled you and that is the reason for the delay?' Not for the first time in my life I was stupid enough to play at *noblesse oblige*, so I said, 'She's not worth finishing off; she's in enough trouble as it is,' and with that went out half expecting to be greeted by whistles and catcalls, but in fact being quite warmly applauded. I bowed and sat down to play the Second Sonata. This evidently was another error of judgement: I ought to have apologised in German for the delay in starting. Had I done so the press notices would have been less savage than they in fact were.

In the first movement of the Sonata I had not quite recovered my equilibrium after all the excitement, and had to watch a bit too carefully what I was doing. But after the scherzo things settled down and the rest of the concert went well, to great acclaim. Needless to say, no one came to me after the concert with either money or a promissory note.

25 January

Next morning, after going out for a while and coming back, yesterday's abject-faced man was waiting for me at the Gessens' entrance. He handed me a proposal from Bran to proceed to an arbitration court. I replied that this was not a matter for an arbitration court: I would be suing for the sum of $1,000 for breach of contract (our agreement genuinely did contain such a penalty clause). The little chap muttered something or other, then after humming and hawing for a while bowed and took his leave.

My train was due to leave at eight o'clock in the evening, but the Gessens were leaving to go somewhere in the afternoon, so I packed my things and at

---

[1] 'We're not used to this kind of thing!' 'Neither am I!'

four o'clock went with them to their station, after which I strolled about Berlin. Meri Bran might, I reasoned, be lying in wait for me at the station I was leaving from, but since Berlin is well endowed with railway stations and my train would be passing through several of them, I chose one from which she would never expect me to leave, and indeed met no one there.

26 January

Cologne early next morning, and Paris at five o'clock to a loving reunion with Ptashka, who had come in to the station to meet me. We made our way out to Bellevue.

27–31 January

Got on with the orchestration of the Symphony: the second subjects. This has to be my main activity at the moment, otherwise I will never finish in time for anything. It has to be done for Koussevitzky's Paris season of concerts in May. A letter from Liana Collini: she is in Paris and would like to see me. Decided with Ptashka's agreement to invite her to come to us on Sunday, when we are generally At Home.

Blois tells me that the Russian Conservatoire which has opened in Paris is on the point of collapse, and should it be minded to appeal for support from Maison Pleyel the latter would insist that it be completely reorganised. The Director, Aleksandrovich, who has managed to get on bad terms with everyone, will have to be replaced by someone with a name, like, for example, me. I replied that I loathe and detest administrative responsibilities and suggested Tcherepnin:[1] he loves that sort of thing and moreover was formerly Director of the Conservatoire in Tiflis.

On the subject of Christian Science. Observing from the perspective of Christian Science the objects that surround us it is difficult to believe that matter is real. But this is not the point of view from which we usually do observe them. If one looks at the material world from the perspective of eternity, where a day is no more than a fleeting moment, a year is but a moment, a million years but a moment (for in eternity these million years will pass as a single second in a man's life), then naturally everything that flares into brief existence and then as instantaneously disappears cannot partake of much reality. Only unshakeable truths are real, those truths that exist outside time.

---

1 Tcherepnin was indeed appointed and served as Director of the Paris Russian Conservatoire from 1925 to 1929 and again from 1938 until shortly before his death in 1945.

1 February

Intensive work on the Symphony. I manage two to three pages of orchestration a day, to do more is hard. Very occasionally I can manage four pages, but sometimes only one page of three bars. But I am keeping at it doggedly and unswervingly.

2 February

Went with Schubert to the Grand Opéra for a performance of *Boris Godunov*, Koshetz in the part of Marina. An appalling production – Paris should be ashamed of an institution like this! It was limp, incoherent, the scenery ancient, in short a disgrace. Nor was Nina Pavlovna herself up to much: the role is too low for her, and she has put on weight to an embarrassing extent. All the same, she is having great success in Paris and neighbouring countries, and has eclipsed Janacopulos. Schubert jokes that if she is called 'Zhena-copulos' then Stahl ought to be called 'Muzha-copulos'.[1] We laughed heartily at this, and at the idea of the great Stahl being transformed into a mere muzhacopulos.

3 February

Headache. Treated it through Christian Science, and it passed off in the afternoon. This was the first time I have had such a positive and definitive result.[2]

Christian Science is undoubtedly having a noticeable effect on our domestic life. It softens our characters and smooths over stupid quarrels, sometimes to the point of eradicating them altogether.

6 February

Oeberg gave Laloy my song with the textual corrections I had made. He refused to do any more but agreed that I could commission whomever I wished to continue with it.

7 February

Three Oranges has been postponed from the 21st February until the 14th March: most aggravating.

---

1   Untranslatable pun. 'Jana' sounds like 'zhená', which is the Russian for 'wife'. 'Muzh' is the Russian for husband.
2   Christian Science also achieved excellent headache results for me on the 12th and 16th February. The attack I suffered on the 22nd was less successful: although I worked on it with Christian Science I could not dispel it entirely. By evening it was better, but still there. [Subsequent note by author.]

8 February

Shakhovskaya came to see us. She is pregnant with her second child – but Balmont is now with Shoshana Avivit.¹

9 February

The Fifth Sonata has come out in print and looks very good; I am pleased with its design.

Schloezer, the idiot, writes that I am merely marking time not developing. This set me thinking about how opinions change: time was when people used to complain about anything new, but now everyone is so accustomed to endless novelty that the composer is censured if his latest compositions fail, compared to previous works, to display the most advanced discoveries. History, however, teaches us that composers, once their style has evolved, maintain it for the rest of their lives, and this was considered an admirable trait betokening an individual personality, a unique voice. Such were Haydn, Schumann, Chopin.

16 February

An evening of Balmont and Shoshana Avivit, the first time Balmont and I have met since he boycotted the performance of *Seven, They Are Seven*.² He is very happy to reconnect, but alas! although I will always defend him, in truth Balmont has to some extent become remote and foreign to me. I was irritated by the sapphires and emeralds he is so addicted to wearing. Shoshana was more lively, a pale woman with pinkish eye-shadow, lending her an emaciated look. She read from Isaiah in the ancient Hebrew. It was a frenzied, overwrought reading, with I thought a touch of the infernal about it – shaking one's fist in rage at the heavens. I had meant my praise of it to Balmont to be ironic, but he took it seriously, and (as I later heard) went around saying that Prokofiev had been ecstatic – the fist had made the heavens tremble. What I should really

---

1   Shoshana Avivit had been a leading actor in the Jewish Habimah Theatre founded in Moscow in 1917 with the active support of Stanislavsky, who recommended his student Yevgeny Vakhtangov as its first Artistic Director. The theatre's productions were spoken in Hebrew, not Yiddish. By 1925 the Habimah company was already beginning to disintegrate, with most of its stars having left the Soviet Union, but after some years of peregrination in America and Europe it began a new lease of life in Tel Aviv, becoming recognised as the national theatre of Israel in 1958. Shoshana Avivit was also a writer, contributing regularly to the newly re-established Parisian Jewish periodical *Rassvet* (*Dawn*).
2   In May the previous year. Balmont had evidently not bothered to come up to Paris from his holiday retreat.

liked to have heard her read was some Balmont, and this was in the programme, but instead she read some Hamsun!¹ What vulgarity. I was most indignant.

Letters from Fitelberg, Szigeti and Szymanowski about the huge success my Violin Concerto has enjoyed in Warsaw. Who could have expected Warsaw to take me to its heart in this way?

17 February

Zak called – the Secretary of the Russian Conservatoire in Paris, sounding out the ground about my becoming its Director. He was terribly flattering – or perhaps he is a true admirer? – and spent so long spinning out his compliments that he missed the last train and had to stay the night. He went away early the next morning, taking a book which he has not returned.

19 February

Szigeti's concert. An idea: some *Songs Without Words*? I ought to compose some small pieces for violin.

Chernetsky's[2] complaints about Blois. Very excited at the prospect of my being the next Director.

21 February

Borovsky's concert with Koshetz. Her success – not entirely deserved, since every now and then she resorts to vulgarity. But she is now more famous than she ever was in Moscow, and has become very rich.

As for Borovsky, his performance of *Sarcasms*[3] was the first I had heard for seven years (except for No. 3 when it was reprinted in America). B.N.[4] sat beside me and breathed noisily throughout. The pieces were played so fast as to be incomprehensible. The Toccata[5] was also played at a ridiculous tempo, so inevitably the piece suffered but the pianist gained a victory. My heart had palpitations.

The applause had scarcely died down when I ran into Balmont. He handed me a letter from Avivit, referring to Balmont practically in terms of his dominating the entire cultural life of Palestine. I was put off by the letter's excessively solemn tone, and said, 'Well, why don't you both come and see me tomorrow?' 'I think it is your place to call on the lady.' In my opinion, if

---

1   The reading was from Knut Hamsun's novel *Victoria* (1898). [Note by author.]
2   A musician and teacher at the Paris Russian Conservatoire of Music.
3   *Sarcasms, Five Pieces for Piano*, Op. 17 (1912–14).
4   Boris Nikolayevich Bashkirov.
5   Toccata in C, Op. 11 (1912).

someone is wanting something of the maestro he or she should pay the call, not the other way round. Nevertheless, of course I would have gone, had it not been for the Hamsun . . . 'Prokofiev! There are limits to good manners and decency, and you are overstepping them!' Oeberg, B.N. and a whole crowd standing around.

Koshetz, a packed hall, flushed with excitement, flowers. In 'There Are Other Planets'[1] she went wrong, the first time she has done so. Generally it was very good, but she dragged out the song: it needs less bel canto and to get on with the story.

They asked me to stay for dinner afterwards, but I had to catch my train.

22 February

Avivit's plans are explained to Tcherepnin.

23 February

To a lecture on Christian Science – very interesting, a magnificent voice. Where does evil come from, seeing that God created man in his own image and can create only good? (A question I have always asked myself.) The immediate answer is that Christian Science is so dedicated to the creation of good that it has no time to pursue such enquiries, especially since evil is not part of reality. For example, when a child has a nightmare and cries out, 'Mama, Mama, I'm being eaten by a wild animal!', what the mother must do is to waken him and calm his unfounded terror, not enquire into what sort of beast the child has seen in his dream.

On the other hand, if one really wants to know where evil comes from, the lecturer suggested referring to the Book of Job – probably the only example of humour in the Bible: regarding Satan and so forth. That is to say, evil is an illusion, an error, not something that comes from anywhere.

The lecture prompted good deal of thought and my reflections were as follows: if good is a manifestation of the *positive* and evil of the *negative*, it is a mistake to conceive of positive and negative as their commonly understood mathematical indicators. In mathematics, negative numbers can produce results identical to positive ones simply by reversing the symbols. Evil, however, being a negative concept, negates everything, and in so doing ends up by negating even itself. What is the result? God created good and denies evil, while evil denies itself. The equal sign as described in Christian Science is thus made manifest: evil equals illusion.

1   *Two Poems for Voice and Piano*, Op. 9 No. 1 (words by Balmont) (1910).

24 February

With Blois, discussing the directorship: there must be a complete purge, including Zak[1] and, it is to be hoped, his mistress. About Chernetsky, it appears that he is under investigation by the police and there are warnings about him from Berlin.

27 February

Mrs Cobbe, Christian Science. We are delighted. We can trust her absolutely; she has twenty-five years' experience dealing with children. She took Svyatoslav straight away into the kitchen wearing just his shirt, with the stove hot and the window open, but we were not worried at all.

1 March

Piano Concerto performance (No. 3) with the Paris Conservatoire, a colossal success in the packed small hall. This seems to have been the first time without any untoward incidents. The previous day there was a public general rehearsal, but with fewer people. My Violin Concerto was simultaneously being performed in another hall but I was unaware of this as no one had told me. Afterwards we entertained at home: the Borovsky couple, Samoilenko and ourselves, all crammed into a taxi out to Bellevue, later joined by Schubert (Koshetz is in Spain), B.N., Kolya Kedrov, Roblin,[2] Tanya.[3] Five bottles of champagne and eighty-five pasties. It was very nice.

2 March

Conius[4] on slurs and bowings in the *Classical* Symphony – some interesting suggestions, for instance three in one bow, followed by one, then three again. Or divisi in chords, of two notes and of four.

---

1 B. A. Zak, piano professor and Secretary of the Paris Russian Conservatoire of Music.
2 Louise Roblin, Prokofiev's childhood governess. See *Diaries*, vol. 1, pp. 9–11, 317, and *passim*.
3 Rayevskaya, the widow of Prokofiev's cousin Andrey Rayevsky.
4 Yuly Conius (known in France as Julius Conus) (1869–1942), one of three brothers in a gifted and cosmopolitan family of French extraction at the centre of Moscow musical life in the late nineteenth and early twentieth centuries. Yuly had close links to composers including Tchaikovsky (with whom he studied composition), Glazunov, Scriabin, Medtner and Rachmaninoff, with whom he formed (with Anatoly Brandukov) the trio for whom Rachmaninoff wrote his two *Trios elégiaques*. Yuly led the Bolshoy Orchestra, was professor of violin at the Moscow Conservatoire, and also gave (with Taneyev and Brandukov) the first performances of Tchaikovsky's Trio. His own melodious Violin Concerto in E minor was a staple repertoire work in Russia and was later championed by Kreisler and Heifetz in America. Conius and his pianist brother Lev had come to Paris in 1919 and were teaching at the Russian

3 March

Borovsky's concert with the Scriabin 9th Sonata. It is a long time since I heard any Scriabin, and my last impressions had been of how alien he had become, hence my great interest in now putting these feelings to the test. In the first place, the work was marvellously played (and Borovsky was note perfect). Secondly, it portrays a fascinating image of a certain mystical striving mixed with eroticism and a kind of shadowy, dark power, a striving that at times erupts in convulsive spasms followed by the melancholy of impotence and a dreamy, exhausted, resignation – the consequence alike of eroticism and a neurotically insistent mysticism. Thirdly, I came back to my paradoxical assertion that it is Scriabin, not Stravinsky, who is the national composer, because Scriabin with his passion for theosophy interwoven with eroticism, his soaring eruptions, his refinement and his enervation, reflects the Russian epoch in its entirety. But Stravinsky? His use of folk tunes hardly makes him a national composer. The very fact that he is more loved abroad than at home is a great grief[1] to his nationalist aspirations. And leaving this question aside, the threat will always hang over him that he is not a true Russian, but the facsimile of a Russian the French have wanted to construct for themselves!

The first movement of the Symphony is finished.

Blois introduced me to a new manager, Boquel, mainly on account of Ptashka.

Monteux[2] is taking the *Chout* Suite to Russia. He telephoned me – a reconciliation. (In the event nothing happened: the French welcomed the

---

Conservatoire, but with the growing Nazi threat Lev emigrated to America in 1935 while Yuly returned to Moscow in 1939, remaining there until his death. Yuly's younger son Boris married Rachmaninoff's daughter Tatiana in 1932; their son Alexander is the present head of the Rachmaninoff Foundation and occupant of the villa Rachmaninoff built in Switzerland at Senar.

1   Prokofiev uses the English word.
2   Pierre Monteux (1865–1974) had begun life as a violinist, distinguished enough to share the First Prize at the Paris Conservatoire at his graduation in 1896 with Jacques Thibaud. His position as Principal Conductor of the Ballets Russes from 1911 involved him in such notable first performances as *Petrushka*, *The Rite of Spring* with its celebrated scandal, *Jeux* and *Daphnis et Chloé*. By 1918, when Prokofiev first came to New York, Monteux was in charge of the French repertoire at the Metropolitan Opera, and the following year he began his lifelong association with the Boston Symphony Orchestra, although after 1924, the same year as he embarked on a ten-year stint as the oddly named 'eerste dirigent' of the Concertgebouw Orchestra alongside Willem Mengelberg as Chief Conductor, he yielded to Koussevitzky the Boston Principal Conductor position. Later in his long life, which never ceased to be filled with music-making at the highest level, Monteux accepted at the age of eighty-six the Principal Conductorship of the London Symphony Orchestra, insisting on a contractual condition stipulating that the contract run for twenty-five years with an option to renew for a further twenty-five. In conversation with Hans Keller's wife, the artist Milein Cosman, Monteux once observed that the main job of conductors 'is to keep the orchestra together and carry out the composer's instructions, not to be sartorial models, cause dowagers to swoon, or distract audiences by our "interpretation"'. In

plan but at the last moment the Soviets would not grant visas. Rumour has it that this was because of intrigues by German conductors.)

8 March

Ptashka got on with packing, while I made adjustments to the first movement of the *Classical* Symphony according to Conius's suggestions. The second subject proved particularly troublesome with its two-octave leaps. Conius's suggestions need to be treated with caution: when it is simply a matter of bowings they are all well and good (although even here he sometimes descends into unnecessary refinements that are not actually playable at a fast tempo), but when, for example, he wants to change the distribution of the chords he immediately falls over. Sometimes the simplest chord can be divided imaginatively, but Conius is inclined to alter chords that do not need it and the result is vulgar.

Koka and Maria Benois came by, and Blois. We watched a film.

9 March

Rose at half past five, left Bellevue at forty-seven minutes past six, and Paris at ten past eight. The Brichants[1] met us at Liège. Cologne at 6 p.m. Mme Nobel (widow of old man Nobel in Kislovodsk). Her plush house, interesting in its archetypal German-ness, into which she welcomed us with extraordinary warmth, arranging a car every day to take us to rehearsal.

Szenkár in the evening: young, extremely courteous, his wife diminutive with enormous eyes, also very friendly but one feels she could turn into a termagant. Both are passionate about *Oranges*.

10 March

Piano rehearsal. When I entered I was presented to the cast, who all rose to their feet, and I bowed acknowledgement. They sing with great vigour, and the chorus punch out their rhythms with admirably accentuated precision. Here and there I did not agree with Szenkár's tempi, and cautiously made some observations on this, but he revealed a streak of obstinacy. At this I

---

the *Diaries* some of Prokofiev's earlier, New York encounters with Monteux elicited less admiring comments, possibly from disappointment that Monteux had not invited him to appear as soloist in Boston the moment he got the job there. See *Diaries*, vol. 1, p. 707; vol. 2, pp. 351, 423.

1 Sonia Brichant, married to a Belgian, was Prokofiev's second cousin and had been especially supportive over arranging the composer's mother's permission to come to France from her exile in Princes' Islands. See *Diaries*, vol. 2, pp. 488–538 *passim*.

gave way, because I do not in principle like interfering in an artist's interpretation provided he means it and it is the result of thorough consideration.

During this rehearsal a scenery and lighting rehearsal was proceeding on stage. The sets are less opulent than Anisfeld's, but they are wittier. I would add that they are also more schematic, in order to cut down on the time for scene changes: there is only one interval, after Act Two, thus dividing the opera exactly into two halves of fifty minutes each.

11 March

First rehearsal with everything together, in the settings and partly costumed. The stage is modern and up to date. I was particularly struck by the carefully worked-out staging of the chorus. As directed by Coini[1] they did not act at all, and the principals acted according to their own inclinations and talents, not as an ensemble. Here the hand of a director who loves his craft is evident throughout.[2] As for the quality of the voices, the women were on the whole middling and the men pretty good, some of them – like King Chelio, excellent.

12 March

Semi-general rehearsal.

13 March

Public full dress rehearsal. Scene two very demoniacal, Chelio and Fata beautifully lit. The Prologue was stylised, there ought to be more of a fight. The Monsters' Battle was not very good and neither, because of Fata Morgana, was the penultimate scene. But overall it raced along far better than Chicago, where Coini's stupid obstinacy spoiled everything.

14 March

Oeberg came. Nothing much happened in the afternoon; the premiere was in the evening. Quite a lot of English people in the audience. Red uniforms and the Emptyheads, hardly any slip-ups in the performance. Ptashka and I were in a box, but for the second act I moved to another box above the orchestra, having in mind the need to take a bow in the only interval, at the end of the second act.

---

1 Jacques Coini, producer of the Chicago Opera premiere of *The Love for Three Oranges*. Prokofiev had had an acrimonious relationship with him during the rehearsals and was dissatisfied with many aspects of the production. *Diaries*, vol. 2, pp. 618–62 *passim*.
2 Hans Strohbach.

But the response was not over-enthusiastic, and I was a little disconcerted. However, old hands told me that the audience here is apt to be taken aback by something they do not know, and are uncertain how they should react. They all talk about it and compare notes during the interval, and by the end it will be a success. This prediction proved accurate. We were perhaps a little too brisk taking our curtain calls, which according to one critic amounted to twenty.

I did not read much Christian Science, but I did read some, and thought deeply about certain aspects of it, trying to penetrate to its essence. If God created man, then there must necessarily have been a time when man did not exist. But Christian Science disputes this conclusion, asserting that mankind has always existed. And it is true that, if mankind had a beginning then it must also have an end, which is to say that man cannot be immortal, since nothing that is eternal can be finite at one end. Thus the assertion by Christian Science that man is eternal in the future as he is in the past conflicts with the first proposition, that there was an instant in time when God created man, before which there was no man. Similarly, this proposition is contradicted by the following conclusion: if it is so that there was a moment when God, who is eternal, created man, then eternity must have existed before this moment and after it, which suggests that there must be two eternities, each limited at one end. This is demonstrably absurd, since eternity – illimitableness – that is finite at one end is a contradiction in terms. To reconcile these contradictions it is necessary to conclude that our understanding of eternity as one hour succeeding another and so on without end is incorrect, and that beyond the confines of our own world the laws of time (and therefore doubtless of space as well) are quite other.[1] In all probability our death is the route our consciousness takes to exit from the limits of time and space. But if this is so, that is to say our conception of time is no more than a local conception, then by the same token we

---

[1] Einstein had published his *General Theory of Relativity* in 1916, having been working on it since 1905. With his omnivorously questioning mind, Prokofiev would no doubt have been aware of it and at least the outline of its startlingly counter-intuitive implications. Einstein's Field Equations, incorporated in the *General Theory*, are non-linear differential equations which define gravity as a property of space and time, and depart significantly from the assumptions of classical physics – not to mention conventional human understanding – notably in respect of the passage of time. As a limerick current at the time had it: 'There once was a lady called Bright/Who could travel faster than light/She went out one day/In a relative way/And came back the previous night.' At the time of writing, two separate groups of physicists, one named 'Opera' and the other 'Icarus', at the Gran Sasso laboratory in Italy engaged in analysing the velocity of neutrinos sent there from CERN in Switzerland are in dispute about whether this particular transmission did or did not exceed the speed of light. If it can be demonstrated that superluminal particles are indeed theoretically possible, Einstein's equations must be re-evaluated and along with them many of the commonly accepted laws of physics. At the present time the onus is on 'Opera' to demonstrate the verifiability of their findings beyond doubt, but so far they have not been able to do so in such a way as to convince those who doubt the possibility.

are incapable of approaching the question of the creation of mankind. We cannot even pose the question: was there a time (in eternity, which does not contain time) when man did not exist? For this reason, it is impossible to answer yes or no to my first question. In the same way the question asked by some people who, when they contemplate the idea of immortality, become so frightened that they cannot decide which is more terrifying, mortality or immortality, should be *hors de combat*. Such questioners must likewise have it explained to them that in eternity the concept of time cannot exist.

15 March

An automobile trip, in which we touched 90 kilometres an hour. We saw another car overturned, with its wheels in the air. Bonn, and drinking tea on the banks of the Rhine.

16 March

Departure, although somewhat delayed. Evening with the Brichants. Andryusha's[1] fiancée.

17 March

Left around eleven, home by dinnertime.

Op. 27[2] has come out in a new edition, which I had touched up a little from the first one. For protection against being reprinted in America the new edition states: 'ed. Spalding', although of course all the alterations are by me, not by Spalding, on whom I have never clapped eyes.

18 March

Wonderful press notices from Berlin.

19 March

Lunch at Dubost's.[3] Prunières told a story about a woman with a trumpet[4] at Stravinsky's concert in Geneva. Guest of honour at the lunch was

---

1   Sonya Brichant's twenty-four-year-old son Andrey (Andryusha). See *Diaries*, vol. 2, p. 538.
2   *Five Poems of Anna Akhmatova for Voice and Piano* (1916).
3   Mme Jeanne Dubost. See above, p. 42.
4   'Truba' in Russian could be either a pipe (smoker's) or a trumpet. The context does not make it clear which is meant.

Weiss,[1] who expressed a desire to visit me. He did so, spent the whole day and stayed to dinner, listening to the Third Piano Concerto and *Chout*. He promised to propagandise my symphonic works among German conductors and my operas in Berlin. I laid stress particularly on *Fiery Angel*.

20 March

Busy following up Conius's suggestions in the second and third movements of the *Classical* Symphony.

22 March

Got up at 6.30 to go with Ptashka to Monte Carlo. Going south we were lightly dressed, and so shivered with cold. Left Paris at nine o'clock on a splendid *rapide*, one of the fastest trains in France, and at 9.30 in the evening arrived in Marseilles, where we stayed overnight. We strolled about the streets for a while, eyeing the colourful population of the port: sailors, Africans, tarts and so on.

23 March

Next morning we continued our journey and at two o'clock were in Monte Carlo, en route flashing through Cannes, Nice, Beaulieu and Monaco. We savoured looking out of the window and the feeling of being in the south, even though the weather was chilly and drizzling rain. We put up at the Hôtel National: a nice room on the top floor with a wonderful view of the sea, which was a deep blue despite the greyness of the weather. After going for a stroll we sat in the foyer of the Casino and watched the people running in and out of the gaming hall, trying to guess from their faces whether they had won or lost. It was a dispiriting impression: many people came out of the hall as if in a trance, shuffling their feet and seeing nothing. The old women were terrible . . .

24 March

Rehearsal. The orchestral accompaniment was fairly limp, but as it is Monte Carlo I am not too concerned. While I was rehearsing, Kokhno and Dukelsky

---

1   Adolf Weissmann (1873–1929), Berlin-based critic and writer on music, who rose to prominence in 1911 with a magisterial survey of the capital's importance as a musical centre, *Berlin als Musikstadt seit 1740*. This magnum opus was followed by biographies of Bizet, Chopin, Puccini and Vladimir de Pachmann. A survey of virtuosity, *Der Virtuose: Die Musik in der Weltkrise* (1922), published by Dent in London in 1925 as *The Problems of Modern Music*, was an influential analysis.

came up to Ptashka, Dukelsky ostentatiously applauding me. We all went off together afterwards. Dukelsky is finishing off the orchestration of his ballet for Diaghilev. Kokhno enquired about the ballet I had composed for Romanov. I replied that the work was not primarily composed as a ballet but as a quintet for concert performance, but in view of the fact that Romanov had paid me money for it, he had the right to produce a ballet based on it. I asked about Auric, Milhaud and Poulenc. Auric is writing a new ballet for Diaghilev, Milhaud is getting married to a fat but rich cousin. Poulenc, according to Kokhno, is turning out trifles 'which suit him better'. Since whatever comes out of Kokhno's mouth is an expression of Diaghilev's opinions, it is interesting to observe the change from last spring.

In the evening we went to the new opera *L'Enfant et les sortilèges*.[1] The very beginning is rather painful, also the coffeepot,[2] but when the armchairs get going it is very good, in fact there is much that is excellent, like the cats' duet and the attack on the arithmetic teacher by the harp and the numbers, the lamb, and many other places where Ravel has contrived a mass of inventive effects. Alongside these delights must be set the melancholy appearance of the book, the highly dubious taste of the ballet and a good many other failings: in short the production was very uneven. But the orchestration is enchanting. I heard that Auric – who detests and despises Ravel – was given the job of reviewing the opera by some newspaper or other, and did not know how to extricate himself from the situation. All the same, Auric should count himself lucky if he could orchestrate half as well as Ravel.

Dukelsky was waiting for us after *L'Enfant* to play us his ballet,[3] so we proceeded into a rehearsal room where we were joined by Kokhno. Dukelsky described the ballet as 'classical with a whiff of Russian', a description I did not much care for. And certainly the first number, which was lively and not at all bad, answered to the description. But I already liked the theme of the second number, and the rest of the piece, especially the superb theme and variations (even though the theme itself was in some ways derivative and stylised). The penultimate number I liked less. All in all, though, this was an evening that happens all too rarely: having before one a genuinely important composer. I do not think I am mistaken. I congratulated Dukelsky most sincerely and returned home with the ballet ringing in my ears. Dukelsky was visibly delighted with my praise.

---

1 Opera by Ravel, libretto by Colette, first produced Monte Carlo Théâtre du Casino, 21 March 1925.
2 It is in fact a teapot.
3 *Zéphyr et Flore*.

25 March

Letters from Ziloti and Myaskovsky, both on the subject of the Fifth Sonata. Ziloti had not liked it at all, while Myaskovsky's praise was nevertheless tempered with some reservations.

The concert was at three o'clock. When Ptashka had been with Getty, Getty in reference to her 'nerves' had told her, 'Sing as if you are singing for God.' I thought of this today. It is good advice. I played well and was not nervous. The old man accompanied reasonably accurately, and the orchestra was better than at rehearsal, although not as good as the Paris orchestra. The hall was not full, but the Prince of Monaco was in the royal box. The ruling Monegasque dynasty is the Grimaldi family, but since this name is also shared with a whole race of antediluvian people, one gets the impression that the Grimaldi dynasty is so ancient as to have come from before the Flood.[1]

Diaghilev appeared backstage after the performance, having just arrived from Paris. Kissing me, he said that the Prince had expressed a desire for me to be presented to him. Diaghilev then invited us to supper that evening. Following this, Ptashka and I went to see Sasha Tcherepnin for tea. He lives with an elderly and very rich American lady, which astonished us no little. Presumably he had foreseen our embarrassment and so, to ameliorate it, had sent a laurel wreath to the concert, attaching a visiting card from himself and from her. I love Sasha very much (not as a composer, however) and did my best to repress suspicions of mercenary intent in this cohabitation, but what led this twenty-five-year-old to set up with a fifty-year-old woman, not especially attractive to boot, remains a mystery to me.

I talked to Dukelsky. He said, 'Thank goodness Stravinsky has gone to America, because with him everything was a matter of rule. This you can love, this you cannot. At the time when everyone was uniting against you, I was the only one to stick up for you.'

In the evening we went to the Diaghilev performance, all old productions. In the interval Dukelsky and I were invited to the Prince's box, where were his daughter, the young Polignac, and the old Princess Polignac.[2] I talked mainly to her, about an evening of my works at her house in Paris.

---

1 Not quite pre-Noah, but still venerable, the dynasty dates back to Grimaldo, Consul of Genoa in 1133. The Prince in the royal box at the concert was Louis Grimaldi II (d. 1949), father of Prince Rainier Grimaldi III, who died in 2005, to be succeeded by his son, the present Prince, Albert II.
2 Princesse Edmond de Polignac (1865–1943, née Winnaretta Singer, the sewing-machine heiress) was Paris's richest, most influential and most imaginative artistic patron and salon hostess. As well as munificently supporting the Ballets Russes and hosting inconceivably glamorous evenings in the gigantic music room of her mansion on avenue Henri-Martin, she distributed her considerable largesse with great intelligence and discernment to such composers and writers as Ravel, Debussy, Stravinsky, Cocteau, Satie, Proust, Ethel Smyth, Falla, Colette and Nadia Boulanger. See *Diaries*, vol. 2, pp. 507, 512.

Then, supper with Diaghilev at the Café de Paris: the two of us, Dukelsky, Kokhno and a few others. Ptashka, the only female, was looking extremely attractive; she danced with Dukelsky which amused Diaghilev: 'Mon cher, vous voilà cocu!¹ Dukelsky is better-looking than you.' He was very interested in my ballet for Romanov (I told him that I had not in fact written a ballet but a quintet, but seeing that Romanov had paid me money for it, he had acquired the rights to stage it as a ballet). Diaghilev started to talk about a new ballet, to which I responded vaguely. He came up with a few barbs: 'Like Noah, I have three sons: Stravinsky, Prokofiev and Dukelsky. You, Serge, will have to forgive me, but you are my second son!' – a sly hint at Ham. I said, 'Just wait, when you get drunk, I'll have the last laugh on you!'

26 March

Sasha Tcherepnin and his lady collected us in their car and drove us up into the hills. I have always wanted to know what the hinterland of the Côte d'Azur was like.

27 March

Nice, in the rain; Mme Suvchinskaya; a farewell call on Diaghilev, then a dash to Cannes. Dukelsky running about looking for cufflinks. He came with us to the station at five o'clock to see us off, and we kissed.

28 March

Travelled all night and at four o'clock in the afternoon were back, tired but happy to be home.

29 March

Began orchestrating the second movement of the Symphony. I had composed the theme in January 1919, contemporaneously with the first act of *Oranges*. Now it underwent considerable revision.

31 March

General rehearsal of *The Idiot*.² An appalling dramatisation. I don't much care for Ida Rubinstein – she princessises too much for me.

---

1 'My dear, you're being cuckolded!'
2 A stage adaptation of Dostoevsky's novel by Vladimir Bienstock and Fernand Nozière, with sets and costumes by Alexandre Benois, directed by Armand Bour. Ida Rubinstein produced and starred in the production, but it was not one of her successes.

2 April

Nouvel[1] informed me that he is arranging a visa for Suvchinsky.

3 April

1,600 francs for the first production of *Oranges*: not a great sum, I had been expecting 3,000. Oeberg tells me that there is interest in *Oranges* from Vienna, where they are perusing the vocal score.

4 April

Went to see Ida Rubinstein about writing music for *Juditha*. Now it is she who wants it, but I am not so sure: after the Symphony I am not drawn to any more orchestral works. Moreover, if Diaghilev gets up a head of steam about a commission I shall have to compose a ballet for him.

5 April

Derzhanovsky: the success of the Third Piano Concerto in Moscow, and my delight at this news. On Sunday we had the Borovskys, Koka and Marusya Benois, and showed them a film that had been shot in our garden. In consequence of our lack of skill and poor light most of it was no good, but there were some very amusing bits. Marusya on the subject of Zakharov's imminent arrival, there's a little affair going on there I think. For some reason Marusya is annoyed with him.[2]

I played Borovsky some of the Quintet. Despite an awful version for piano, which I played very badly, he was very enthusiastic about it.

6 April

Borovsky's concert. A Sonatina by Auric was rubbish.

---

1 Walter Nouvel (1871–1971), writer and music critic who, as one of the original 'Nevsky Pickwickians' group of St Petersburg aesthetes had been along with Diaghilev and Benois a leading figure in the *Mir Isskustva* movement that gave rise not only to the *Mir Isskustva* journal, for which Nouvel wrote music criticism, but the Ballets Russes. Nouvel and his friend Alfred Nurok had been among the first to recognise and promote Prokofiev in St Petersburg in the years before the First World War, through the 'Evenings of Contemporary Music' concert society they had founded. Nouvel had remained a member of Diaghilev's inner circle after emigrating to Paris in 1919 and was later to ghost-write Stravinsky's only attempt at autobiography, *Chroniques de ma vie*, which appeared in French in two volumes in 1935 and 1936. See *Diaries*, vol. 1 *passim*; vol. 2, pp. 45, 75, 160, 593–5.
2 Marusya 'en veut' written in French. See above, p. 74, n.2.

7 April

[Théâtre des] Champs-Elysées, which has been turned into a music-hall. This is offensive, like knowing personally a previously respectable woman who has turned into a tart.[1] And the music-hall is boring, very slow.

Koshetz is singing everywhere and getting 18,000 for two weeks (16 performances) but I am very displeased with her: she is not singing any of my music anywhere, even with so many appearances. Little liar!

8 April

Gallié:[2] accept 2,000, otherwise you will not even get that. From 18,000 down to 4,000, and from 4,000 down to 2,000.

9 April

Another Borovsky concert, including among other things works by Szymanowski and Honegger, the latter having of late become extremely well known, especially within France. But the music itself, it must be admitted, is negligible.

10 April

The artist Zak,[3] known now as Léon Zack, came to see me accompanied by two friends, also artists. They came to listen to the Quintet, since Zack will be doing the designs for the ballet production. Even though I played disgracefully badly, they found the music very interesting and animatedly discussed the production, which, alas, will not be before the autumn.

---

1 The impresario Gabriel Astruc's superb new theatre on avenue Montaigne, designed by Auguste Perret with a magnificent Art Deco frieze by Emile-Antoine Bourdelle depicting Apollo and the nine Muses on its main front elevation, opened in 1913 with the Ballets Russes season that included the scandalous first night of *The Rite of Spring*. The theatre had almost immediately run into financial problems, and Astruc himself resigned soon afterwards, but it continued to host opera, ballet and concerts until some years after the First World War. In 1987 it was fully restored to its original Art Deco splendour, and now is home to the Orchestre National de France and the Orchestre Lamoureux. See *Diaries*, vol. 1, pp. 426–7, 428–9.
2 A manager in Paris. The project referred to has not been identified.
3 Lev Zak (Léon Zack) (1892–1980), painter, sculptor, illustrator and stage designer. Left Russia in 1920 via the Crimea–Constantinople route, and after some time in Rome and Florence came to Berlin in 1922, where he became chief designer to Romanov's Russian Romantic Ballet Theatre. He moved to Paris in 1923, later concentrating on abstract canvases.

11 April

A letter from Princesse de Polignac. Where has all this sudden interest come from? Previously it was all Stravinsky. The Zakharovs telephoned; they have arrived from America.

12 April

The French Easter. Being Sunday, our customary At Home day, there was a mass of visitors: the Zakharovs, Samoilenkos (four of them), the Borovskys. Everything is in bloom in the garden. Altogether, with the onset of spring, Bellevue is getting to be a wonderful neck of the woods to be in.

13 April

Did not work, as a bad headache.

Went for a long walk with Ptashka, as far as Chaville (4 kilometres), to the Tcherepnins. They were delighted to see us. N.N.,[1] as refined as ever, now seems to have lost his way and leads a nugatory existence like a first-class railway carriage that has left the rails and been shunted into a siding. Because he is not getting any significant commissions he is writing music for the cinema, hopelessly meretricious and woolly stuff.

14 April

Called on Nouvel to discuss a visa for Suvchinsky's wife, and met there Sirota,[2] an entrepreneur from Berlin. Last spring he did not want to see me at all, now he wants me to give him my German representation and is promising to get me a series of orchestral engagements.

16 April

Went to see Ida Rubinstein at her invitation. About *Juditha* she did not give a straight answer yes or no, but the implication was towards yes. I hear that Honegger is writing an oratorio on the subject of Judith,[3] so there will be competition! But today's conversation was on other lines: Benois was present, and I played through the *Scythian Suite*. Ida wants to put this on as

---

1 Nikolay Nikolayevich Tcherepnin.
2 Peter Sirota, a Berlin manager.
3 Honegger's opera seria *Juditha* was completed in 1925, but was recast two years later as an oratorio, in which form it enjoyed more success.

a ballet. A long time ago I suggested this to Diaghilev, but it went in one ear and out of the other.

17 April

B.N.B.¹ has suffered a severe attack of abdominal pain. He collapsed in the club and fell to the floor unconscious, and had to be taken to hospital. The cause appears to be either kidney stones or a kink in the intestines.

18 April

Russian Passion Saturday. A barn in Meudon² has been turned into a little church and a service of Prime was held there at half past eight. Ptashka and I attended. It was a touching occasion; the choir sang with feeling even though rather all over the place. We met the painter Petrov-Vodkin³ – a runty little peasant whom I was very pleased to see again. We dragged him home with us to eat painted eggs⁴ and drink wine.

A letter from Popa.⁵ How on earth did they know I was a Christian Scientist?

19 April

Russian Easter, and a letter from Demchinsky, fairly cool in tone (no wonder, from a Christian with such an un-Christian malevolent smile!) but business-like. He is prepared, for a fee, to work on the libretto of *Fiery Angel*. This is wonderful news: at last I have got what I was after. Even so, he played hard to get for two years, worse than any operetta heroine.

---

1 Boris Nikolayevich Bashkirov.
2 A small town south-west of Paris, about one kilometre from Bellevue. Prokofiev's mother was buried there.
3 Kuzma Petrov-Vodkin (1878–1939), one of the most original and controversial St Petersburg artists in the early years of the twentieth century. A protégé of Alexander Benois, Petrov-Vodkin introduced a wide and superficially incompatible variety of influences into his pictures, ranging from icons and nineteenth-century Russian landscape painters to Munich Secession painters, Gauguin and Matisse. See *Diaries*, vol. 2, pp. 100, 111.
4 Decorating eggs is a Russian custom at Easter time.
5 Gyorgy Popa-Gorchakov (1903–1995) was later to become Prokofiev's secretary, and a family friend even after his secretarial duties were taken over by Mikhail Astrov in 1929. Gorchakov's own life story, marked by his own ambitions as a composer, his life-long dedication to Prokofiev, and his unswerving adherence to a religious instinct compounded of Christian Science, Islam and the contemplative life, which caused him to end his days in Tunisia, is a fascinating one in its own right, as detailed by Noëlle Mann, Serge Moreux and Serge's son Bernard in *Three Oranges*, no. 11 (May 2006).

As it was Sunday we were At Home to the Zakharovs, B.N.B.[1] and Tcherepnin. It was very nice. Tcherepnin got slightly drunk, but entertainingly so. B.N. recited some poetry, but stammered and forgot his lines. He is on a diet, eating nothing but dairy products. For this reason he consumed the whole *paskha*[2] all by himself.

20 April

A letter from Aunt Katya.[3] I have not yet told her of Mama's death. She writes about Shurik. What sort of illness can it be? Paralysis? Mental disorder? It's very sad to see how the family is disintegrating.[4]

21 April

The forest around Meudon is a blaze of green. Glorious weather. Went walking. The 'Hermitage'.[5] Coffee. Marvellous.

22 April

Ptashka, speaking of Cobbe, says that she sees everything through the prism of Christian Science with perfect clarity. She answers all questions without

---

1   Boris Bashkirov.
2   A sweet dish made of cream cheese, eaten only at Easter.
3   Yekaterina Rayevskaya, née Zhitkova (Aunt Katya) was Prokofiev's mother's elder sister. She had married Alexander Rayevsky (Uncle Sasha), a prominent and well-connected civil servant in St Petersburg. Their children, Prokofiev's first cousins, were Andrey (Andryusha), Alexander (Shurik) and Yekaterina (Cousin Katya). See *Diaries*, vols. 1 and 2 *passim*. During the years Prokofiev and his mother lived in St Petersburg he had been very close to his uncle and aunt and cousins. Aunt Katya and her daughter (Cousin Katya) had left Moscow and were living in Penza, in the south-east of Russia.
4   Prokofiev had not at first grasped the significance of the euphemism, necessary to evade the censor, whereby arrest and imprisonment were commonly expressed as 'illness'. Details are hard to come by, but it seems that Alexander Rayevsky, as a former student of the upper-class Alexandrovsky Lycée in St Petersburg had been, in common with approximately a hundred and fifty of his former schoolfellows, arrested on the night of 15 February 1925 as part of an OGPU (see below, p. 439) swoop on alumni. The charges were the usual ones of violating Statute 58 of the Soviet Penal Code, mostly Articles 10 and 11 relating to membership of counter-revolutionary and Monarchist organisations. OGPU's 'incontrovertible proof' of guilt rested on three planks: attendance at reunions of former students held annually on 19 October; the existence of a mutual-fund savings bank; and attendance at memorial services for deceased alumni, at which members of the former Imperial family might be present. At least thirty of the accused were shot immediately on conviction, the remainder were given prison sentences of varying lengths in the camps. Most perished there; Shurik was one of the lucky few who survived. See below, p. 361.
5   L'Hermitage de Villebon at Meudon is an old hotel and restaurant set in idyllic woodland surroundings.

needing to reflect. The case in point: whence comes evil? Seneca[1] says: 'If All-Directing Reason did not know that evil would arise, it follows that He cannot be all-knowing; if He knew but could not eliminate it, then He cannot be all-powerful; if He knew and could avert it but chose not to, then He cannot be all-loving.'

Ptashka posed this question to Miss Cobbe. She countered with the old reply: evil is error. But her illustration of it was interesting: a child goes to school and is taught that 2 + 2 = 4. When the child comes home, the mother asks: well, what does 2 + 2 make? The child answers: 5. Where did the mistake come from? After all, nobody can have taught it to the child.

Evidently error is a thing in itself, self-generating, as the Bible says: 'The devil is lies and the father of lies.'[2] From this I return to my theory: Man was created so as to be the living reflection of God, not an automaton without will. It was necessary that man should have been given free will, that is to say the ability to choose between acting thus or thus. Here is to be found the source of error or the Fall, and man's consequent long ordeal, during which on the one hand error multiplied and on the other began to be understood. After enduring all this travail and finally grasping the essence of error, man is at last returning to the bosom of his origins, still possessed of free will but already beginning to be insured against the possibility of error.

23 April

I am thirty-four years old today. In the old days I used to shriek: What! Twenty-five already? Already thirty? How old I am! But now, thanks to Christian Science, the years somehow no longer matter. The passing years, and time in general, are merely constructs invented to serve the convenience of mortal life; in eternal life there can be no concept of time, and it makes no sense to try to parcel up eternity into little bits!

In the evening we were at the Samoilenkos, taking B.N. there with us for the first time. He dedicated a sonnet to me recalling Ettal – the time of his most golden memories.[3] The sonnet was not bad, except that two of its lines had extra syllables, with which I publicly challenged him.

---

1 Seneca (Lucius Annaeus Seneca, c. 4BC–65), as a Stoic philosopher, subscribed to the view that the universe is governed for the best by a rational providence.
2 'Ye are of your father the devil, and the lusts of your father ye will do. He was a murderer from the beginning, and abode not in the truth, because there is no truth in him. When he speaketh a lie, he speaketh of his own: for he is a liar, and the father of it.' John 8:44.
3 Boris Bashkirov had lived in the Prokofiev household in Bavaria from April 1922 until February 1924. Among the two friends' leisure occupations had been a sonnet-translating competition. See *Diaries*, vol. 2, pp. 671–713 *passim*.

From Liège I received a contract for a concert by Ptashka and myself – this will be her first appearance after a two-year interval. She is preparing for it with immense seriousness and zeal. Personally I would not rush to go to Liège for a fee of 1,000 francs, but it is very good for Ptashka to start off in a provincial city, so we are going.

25 April

Continued writing an exceptionally long letter to Demchinsky, on which I have spent four days now.

Natalya Konstantinovna[1] has not fixed me up with a manager for America, and this is a serious blow to the chances of a future 'momentous' visit. Thank God, I now feel myself on reasonably solid ground in Europe.

26 April

Am chasing about hither and yon in search of a copyist in order to get everything ready for Koussevitzky's concert.

27 April

A telegram from Koussevitzky about the success of the Violin Concerto in Boston.

Got the first proof of the *Classical* Symphony, but no time to go through it.

28 April

The trunk from Ettal finally arrived,[2] an enormous, heavy thing but full of junk. We went through the contents, occasioning some venomous remarks from Ptashka about pictures of my former romantic liaisons.

A letter from Prunières about a concert of international music. The Suite from *Chout* is too long, they can allow only eight minutes.

Auric has settled in Bellevue so as to be able to work undisturbed on orchestrating his new ballet *Matelots* for Diaghilev.[3] After doing ten pages a

---

1 Koussevitzky.
2 The trunk with remaining possessions that had not been brought to Paris with Prokofiev's mother and Boris Bashkirov when they left Bavaria in February 1924 had been left for safekeeping with the Mayor of Ettal. See above, p. 17.
3 Auric's second ballet for Diaghilev, a lighthearted *Così fan tutte*-like frolic choreographed by Massine and starring Serge Lifar.

day he comes round to me to relax and chat. His comment on Prunières was that he is a 'perpetual troublemaker'.

29 April

Koshetz has not shown her face for two months, ever since she embarked on the giddy whirl of Parisian celebrity.

A proposal from N. K. Koussevitzky for a performance of *Fiery Angel*, but only one act. Is it worth it? I'm seizing the opportunity to do some plotting, via the Borovskys.

In the evening I went to see Ida Rubinstein, to continue playing her the *Scythian Suite* for a possible ballet version. The arrangement had been made two weeks ago, but there was no one at home, so rushing there was a complete waste of time. I left a note: 'Disappointed by my reception. I shall not call again.'

2 May

Through the Borovskys I was invited to visit the Paris Observatory.[1] I was irritated that the Borovskys had assembled a heterogeneous mob of people to come along, who made things worse by being late. We were welcomed by two astronomers, each of whom was in charge of a tower with a telescope. One of them, Fatou,[2] proved to be a great admirer of my music and was exceptionally pleased that I was there, which astonished and flattered me in equal measure. The other astronomer, no doubt because of his colleague, was equally amiable. His name was Jacobi, and he looks as if he drinks, but he is the discoverer of seven comets and has thus immortalised his name: in five hundred, or perhaps a thousand, years people will observe the return of Jacobi's Comet. The moon displayed marvellous dark blue reflections, and Saturn its rings. They showed us a double star (Gamma Leo), whose separation could be seen quite clearly, but whose colours (each one is a different colour) I could not make out.[3] Apparently astronomers sometimes cannot themselves distinguish the different colours. Afterwards we went to Mrs Barbara's to drink wine, where

---

1   First opened in 1671, the Paris Observatory at Meudon is France's leading astronomical institution and one of the world's largest. Towards the end of the nineteenth century its then Director, Amédée Mouchez, had instigated the ambitious but ultimately only partially successful attempt known as the Carte du Ciel, involving twenty major observatories worldwide, to use the new technology of photography to catalogue and map millions of stars as faint as the eleventh or twelfth magnitude.
2   Pierre Joseph Louis Fatou (1878–1929), mathematician and astronomer, with distinguished contributions in both fields.
3   Gamma Leo, also called Algieba ('the lion's mane') is a star in the constellation Leo, which through a powerful telescope can be distinguished as consisting of two separate bodies: one orange-red and the other yellow.

the astronomers asked me to play, which I was most willing to do; they were delighted.

Wrote to Aunt Katya and Cousin Katya. What is this with Shurik? Paralysis, some sort of mental illness? About help for Sasha Rayevsky:[1] this is a difficult ethical problem. I decided for the time being I would decline, but meanwhile I would let Aunt Katya know I would be sending some money to her.

Ptashka went to see Miss Olmsted, whom she has consulted quite frequently of late, because she is still feeling insecure about her forthcoming concert, also about my eyes. Today Miss Olmsted said that she had achieved a degree of concentration and lucidity that had been rare in her experience, and therefore was sure that from today my eyes would recover fully.

3 May

These past few days I have been firming up the final variation. When I was composing the Symphony in the autumn, I ran out of steam towards the end, but the character of this variation demands especial tautness. Now I was seriously worried: would I be able to bring it off or not, particularly as time is short: the whole Symphony has got to be finished during the month of May. But in fact the work went well: even though the sketches I had made in the autumn were not very coherent, they contained plenty of material there and it did not take me too long to get the variation on its feet and fill in all the details. After this it will need orchestrating, forty or so thickly covered pages.

It being Sunday, Koshetz and Schubert put in an appearance. The cunning plan I had instigated worked out with almost mathematical precision. Koshetz was nice, ebullient, assured me that she had been singing, and would continue to sing, my music everywhere, and asked me to make a version with orchestra of *The Ugly Duckling*[2] – something I ought to do in any case. Very cautiously and obliquely she asked about a concert with Koussevitzky. On this subject I was impenetrable, partly because of not being sure myself and partly to punish her. So she went away empty-handed.

4–5 May

Working hard on the Symphony: this is the main object of my time and attention. For relaxation I walk to the Forest of Meudon; it is divinely beautiful there and each time a little greener and better. The smell of the growing grass and the trees. Sometimes you cannot see the flowers, because they also are green, but the fragrance is amazing.

1 The son of Prokofiev's deceased cousin Andrey and his wife Tanya.
2 *The Ugly Duckling* (*Gadky Utyonok*), Op. 18, fairy tale for voice and piano after Hans Christian Andersen. As well as this orchestration, Prokofiev made a second one, for his wife, Lina Codina, in 1932.

Balmont, with whom relations were broken off after the Shoshana incident, is once again holidaying by the sea, having chosen this time our St Gilles, and none other than our Béthanie.

6 May

At eleven o'clock in the morning Ptashka and I set off for Liège for her first concert appearance in two years, for which she has been preparing assiduously. I have been rehearsing with her and coaching her. The town was well chosen: the fee is only 1,000 francs, but it is for Ptashka. We arrived in Liège at six in the evening and went to Sonya's.[1] Headache; early to bed; the bed too narrow and we did not sleep well.

7 May

Next morning we went to the hall, which is a picture gallery; the concert will therefore take place against the background of the exhibition (by coincidence I am playing *Pictures from an Exhibition*!). There was not a single soft object in the room, so without an audience it was colossally reverberant. All the better for Ptashka, as it takes away any worry about whether or not her voice will sound. The concert was in the evening: a large audience, partly because the tickets were not expensive. I was generally fairly unconcerned; Ptashka was nervous and did not reach all her high notes in her first group (my songs) but sang quite well in her second, which was Russian songs and had a great success, not less than my own. After the concert Lyolya Brichant[2] produced a bottle of 1911 champagne (a stellar year for wine) in our honour.

8 May

We left at eleven and were back home by evening. N. K. Koussevitzky had sent copies of the reviews of the Boston performances of the Violin Concerto – they are brilliant. How fickle and mysterious are the wellsprings of success: London was hostile and critical, whereas Boston – despite a less good violinist[3] – was exceptionally loud in its praises.

A telegram from Bashkirov appealing for help, as things are bad with him. I don't know how he survives, altogether.

---

1 Brichant.
2 Sonya Brichant's husband. Lyolya is usually a girl's name.
3 Richard Burgin (1892–1981), the orchestra's leader, gave the US premiere of Prokofiev's First Violin Concerto on 24 April 1925. See also below pp. 259–60.

9 May

Ptashka got excellent notices, better than mine. Evidently the Liègeois were not wild about my music even though they discussed it in respectful terms.

Natalya Koussevitzky has arrived back in Paris, himself having travelled straight on to London for concerts there. I went to see her. To my great surprise she did not say yes or no about performing the Symphony, because Koussevitzky does not have much rehearsal time and in any case would prefer to premiere the Symphony in Boston. A reprimand I was not expecting! She was insistent that I go to America next year: Koussevitzky has already proposed seven concerts for me – true, for a mere $3,000.

I also saw Haensel, who was passing through Paris. He said not a word about my plan to leave him and go over to Brennan: either he has not realised or did not think it worth talking about. His attitude was very friendly, but things are very difficult in America, because domestic radio has seriously undermined the concert business. He said he would cable Parmelee[1] instructing him to take all possible measures. I dangled out a line for Ptashka, showing him her reviews.

10 May

Romanov, who has returned to Paris, came to call. Smirnova[2] is still ill, nevertheless Romanov hopes to present the ballet at the end of June. He already has the promise of a four-month tour of Germany next year. I played him the ballet. He was thrilled with it, and we embraced, but still would like some sections of it changed. Well, fair enough, but it is a pity: I worked according to the requirements of the plan he himself created, and I found it not by any means easy to write the concluding section in conformity with it. And now, if you please, it has to be altered. But the concert form of the music, the Quintet, will stay as it is, because of the tonality.[3]

Auric dropped by, in a foul mood. He is working like a madman, producing sometimes thirteen pages a day, and as a result is not only

---

1 Assistant and publicity representative of Haensel & Jones. See *Diaries*, vol. 2, p. 542.
2 Elena Smirnova (1888–1934) prima ballerina of Boris Romanov's Russian Theatre Ballet Company, also Romanov's wife. At this time she was recuperating from a major operation, but never fully recovered her health.
3 Not for the last time in his career Prokofiev did not appreciate a choreographer's wish to play about with the internal integrity of his score, especially one that had from the outset been specifically conceived with a view to independent existence on the concert platform. A little later, when Romanov wrote politely requesting a minor cut to suit the requirements of the dancing, Prokofiev replied, '"Make yourself at home with my insides", as the patient lying on the operating table said to the surgeon. I feel like saying the same about your bloodthirsty intention.' (Letter of 2 October 1925.)

exhausted but, as it seems to me, not entirely happy with the result. I can manage two, three, four and rarely five pages in a day; of course it is impossible to orchestrate as many as eight to thirteen pages and maintain any inventiveness or imagination!

12 May

In the evening I was invited by Dukelsky, just back from Monte Carlo where according to him the dress rehearsal of his ballet had enjoyed a tremendous success – the premiere will be in Paris – to visit him along with Auric and Poulenc. 'Auric fine, but please can Poulenc be left at home.' 'That's not possible, they are both with me at the moment.' Well, to hell with it, let him come. Apparently Poulenc himself was very embarrassed and on the way to Dukelsky's wanted to turn back. But since I had 'sanctioned' his presence, I had to be polite to him. Poulenc likewise outdid himself with *politesses*, and so harmony was restored. Auric looked tired out, and sat slumped like a sack. Dukelsky turned on the charm and chattered away nineteen to the dozen, mildly irritating Ptashka by his tendency to boast which, however, he restrained in front of me. His story about the monocle in the soup. He has borrowed wholesale a job lot of expressions from Diaghilev. About the midinettes. He asked Ptashka if she could fix him up with an introduction to an attractive woman, preferably single. My guess is that he was deliberately drawing attention to his desires because of rumours about the nature of Diaghilev's interest in him.

14 May

A witty letter from Meyer[1] about getting any money from Bran. It seems it will be very difficult.

Svyatoslav is not very well, he has some stomach problems. Mrs Cobbe is treating him with Christian Science methods, and is giving him unboiled water to drink. Svyatoslav is a bit lethargic and miserable, but is bearing up like a brave little boy.

15 May

We asked B.N. to dine as it was his birthday. Varvara[2] is at the moment travelling from China across the Indian Ocean and is expected in Paris soon, an event that should improve matters for Boris. He behaved himself, and did

---

1 An acquaintance in Warsaw. See above, p. 129.
2 Princess Varvara Magalova, Boris Bashkirov's sister.

not ask me to lend him any money. Ptashka and he do not get on well, although they are friendly enough on the surface. On the whole he tries to ignore her, but she finds his perpetual sponging, cadging and snide comments about other people intensely annoying. Neither of them seems to take any account of the fact that their skirmishing upsets me very much.

17 May

Worked as usual in the morning, trying my utmost to get the Symphony finished. Guests in the afternoon. Dukelsky and Mrs Barbara, a quite attractive, rich American divorcee who flirted assiduously with him. He tried to impress her by playing foxtrots, which he adores but which I find nauseatingly banal. He then played his Concerto to Borovsky and me, and also the first number and the theme and variations from *Zéphyr*.[1] I listened to the ballet with undisguised enjoyment. The Concerto begins well, but afterwards deteriorates. At Dukelsky's request I played my Fifth Sonata and some of the Quintet. He was enthusiastic about much of what he heard, particularly the fugue from the Quintet, but regretted that I had moved away from the diatonicism of the Third Piano Concerto. I agreed with him, and said that I had done so only for the sake of variety, but of course would soon revert.

In the evening I was at Koussevitzky's, who had just come back to Paris from London. I played through the Symphony, very roughly and cursorily. He said he found it the most powerful of anything I had written, but was aghast at its complexity, suggesting that it would better to postpone performing it until America, where it would be possible to have as many as ten rehearsals. I was in despair at this; composers like Stravinsky, Honegger, Auric, Dukelsky always present themselves in Paris with new works, whereas I seem to be everlastingly condemned to stale goods like the *Scythian Suite*, the Second Piano Concerto, the *Classical* Symphony. He promised to have a talk with the manager of the orchestra with a view to seeing whether an extra couple of rehearsals could be arranged.

18 May

Again called on Koussevitzky, but the rehearsal situation is still not clear. I recommended Dukelsky to him for publication, and by way of illustration played him the theme and variations from the ballet. Koussevitzky laughed: 'In America Rachmaninoff heaps praise right and left on Medtner because Medtner writes like Rachmaninoff. As soon Medtner arrives, he starts

---

1 *Zéphyr et Flore* (1924), Vladimir Dukelsky's first ballet for Diaghilev, choreographed by Massine and designed by Braque.

evangelising Rachmaninoff. Now it's the same thing all over again: Dukelsky composes in your shadow and you can't say enough about him.'

19 May

The Symphony is finished: two easy pages left and it's done. Two hundred and twelve pages and nine months' work. When I started on it I thought it would take three! I feel like a gymnast who has got through a gruelling test. It was the time that Suvchinsky was due to arrive back in Paris, so I went in and met him at the station, from where we returned to Bellevue by taxi. He is now staying with us. Miss Olmsted was paying her first call on Ptashka. I was amazed to learn from Ptashka that she was no more than thirty-five years of age; she looks forty-five, with wrinkles around the eyes. However, she radiates health and serenity, with a special kind of stillness. Knowing that she is active in music I made that the subject of my conversation with her, and then thanked her for her 'help' (she does not refer to it as 'treatment'), and told her that although I was not sure that my eyesight was fully restored (it is not as good as it is with spectacles) I was no longer suffering tension in my forehead at the intersection of the optic nerves. We did not have long to talk, since at this point Suvchinsky made his appearance, and I had to rush off to see Koussevitzky to discover the Symphony's fate. Miss Olmsted proffered her assurance that all would be well with me, and later told Ptashka what a good impression I had made on her.

At Koussevitzky's I learnt that the extra rehearsals had been agreed, and the Symphony would go ahead – hurrah! There will be four extra doublebasses, making fourteen in all. To Koussevitzky I enlarged on the difference between a work dedicated subsequently and a work 'written for'.

20 May

Frantic dashing around to copyists, of which there are eight, all in different outlying parts of Paris.

Suvchinsky talked about the other Gospels besides those we all know: these four were chosen from a whole series of accounts. But the others do not add a great deal of substance. Suvchinsky spoke against neglect of the body: man will be resurrected in the flesh after death, and after his Resurrection Jesus Christ suffered his disciples to touch his body.

21 May

Suvchinsky said that in Berlin he had seen Sasha Rayevsky. True, he had only glimpsed the back of his head, but he had been struck by its similarity to my own. Sasha is lazy in his studies, lively and popular in society, and a good dancer.

22 May

Dukelsky came at my invitation to play his ballet to Suvchinsky. As usual I enjoyed listening to it. According to Suvchinsky there was not a drop of Stravinsky but a healthy dollop of Prokofiev plus a dash of Chopin and Schumann. Suvchinsky then dragged me off for half an hour to see Lev Shestov,[1] after which Dukelsky dragged us to a night-club adorned by half-naked girls of more or less repellent appearance draped over the furniture. They took us into a separate room for a demonstration of 'live cinema'. When in preparation for this entertainment they started to wash themselves I found it so horrible that I left, pursued by a furious Dukelsky disconcerted by my 'abandonment midstream' and a chortling Suvchinsky, who said that the most enjoyable part of the evening had been watching Dukelsky. We then repaired to a more respectable café and Dukelsky regaled us with an account of how he had lost his virginity a year previously, and various other intimate details of his life. His shamelessness borders on the naive; nevertheless Suvchinsky and I decided that he is at heart a good fellow.

23 May

Since I started making rough drafts, I have long lost what skill I had in writing on to the page.

Koussevitzky's concert, with the first performance of Honegger's Concerto for Piano. It was nice, pleasant orchestral effects from modest forces, and some attractive tunes. But it was an extremely boring work for the pianist, and technically elementary. I said it would be a good new Concerto for Stravinsky to add to his repertoire. Suvchinsky liked the work, but Dukelsky was very critical. It was followed by Scriabin's *Extase*, which I have not heard for a long time and which, apart from a few passages, I now listened to with

---

[1] Lev Shestov (Yehuda Leyb Schwarzmann, 1866–1938), Ukrainian-born existentialist philosopher and literary critic, an archetypal religious thinker whose initial associates in Russia included Berdyayev, Merezhkovsky and Rozanov. Lacking sympathy with the Bolsheviks, he settled in Paris in 1921, where he gave courses of lectures at the Sorbonne, his reputation greatly helped by the advocacy of Boris de Schloezer who also translated his works into French. The essence of Shestov's philosophy, the very antithesis of rationalism developed into a system of thought, is concerned with the fundamental inability of reason to deliver answers to the paradoxical and incomprehensible mysteries of human existence. Albert Camus was one writer deeply influenced by Shestov's magnum opus *Athens and Jerusalem*, the summation of a lifetime's thought, published in Russian the year before his death with parallel editions in French and German (but not in English until 1966, which partly accounts for his relative neglect).

some enjoyment. I shall doubtless be stoned for this admission, since these days hardly anyone has a good word for Scriabin. But I believe this to be a temporary phenomenon.

24 May

Today was our last At Home day since our lease is ending and the landlord is evicting us from Bellevue. Our guests included several female American and Italian friends of Ptashka's, Mme Koussevitzky and Dukelsky. Svyatoslav was the centre of attention, and Mme Koussevitsky teased me that the son is better looking than his father. Svyatoslav has just begun more or less to totter about on his own two feet, although his forwards gait is that of a paralytic. When he hears the sound of an aeroplane he lifts up his head and looks for it in the sky.

Dukelsky could not contain his excitement at a thrilling message Diaghilev had asked him to pass on to me just as he – Diaghilev – was leaving for America: would I write a ballet for him for next season? Dukelsky is very anxious that good relations should be restored between me and Diaghilev, as he thinks that I would be a good support for his own connection. I responded guardedly – yes, I would compose a ballet, but I needed to know about the money. If it was niggardly, then no. Diaghilev is due to return on the 7th of May. I asked Dukelsky to write and tell him that my Symphony would be performed on the 6th, and I should like Diaghilev to hear it.

In the evening Ptashka, Dukelsky and I set off for the Borovskys, where we were to be joined by Suvchinsky, Zakharov, B.N., and the Samoilenkos. It was very interesting to have a gathering of all my friends. The Samoilenkos had never met Dukelsky or Suvchinsky. Suvchinsky discreetly kept to one side and scarcely entered into the conversation, although whenever he did say something it was cogent and everyone listened with respect. Dukelsky played his ballet, but people did not pay enough attention. The Samoilenkos did not take to him much; B.N. was also horrified and could not understand how such an unprepossessing youth could be a remarkable composer. B.N. himself looked terrible, he had had another attack of his kidney – or possible bowel – problems and was short of money. Varvara[1] had not returned, or if she had returned was keeping out of sight and incognito, not wishing to see any of her relatives. Boris clung to me all the time, relating *sotto voce* his ailments, while I wanted to bring Suvchinsky and the Samoilenkos together. They said to Suvchinsky: 'We so much want to get to know you, because whenever we tell Sergey Sergeyevich about something we are particularly proud of, he replies, "But I have Suvchinsky."'

---

1 Boris Bashkirov's sister, the Princess Magalova.

26 May

During the night and the next day there came into my head an idea for a ballet (partly against the possibility that Diaghilev really would commission one, and partly for fear that if he did he would saddle me with a libretto by Kokhno).

The ballet would be called *The Violin Clef and the Sardine-Tin Key*.[1] Enter the Treble Clef with a group of Semiquavers whom he tries to position on five lines. Enter a group of Rests. The Semiquavers ought in theory to obey the Treble Clef because their meaningful existence depends entirely on him, but for the Rests the Clef has no importance. The Clef frantically rushes about getting his Semiquavers arranged on their five lines; calm at last descends when they are all finally in position. At this point, enter a tin of Sardines. The Key of the sardine-tin, capering about and turning somersaults, opens the tin, releasing six Sardines. They worship the Key who has restored to them their freedom, and form up in a group on the other side of the stage from the Semiquavers. The Clef and the Key now take notice of one another, ceremonially advance and meet. The Key praises the submissiveness of his Sardines, while the Clef bewails the unmanageability of the Rests. Both groups now approach one another, the Rests continually misbehaving and being rude to the Key. But the lumpen Sardines are so overwhelmed by the unearthly beauty and grace of the artistic symbols that they are ready to expire from ecstasy. However, an embarrassing situation develops: the Rests and the Semiquavers become aware of the smell of the olive oil enveloping the Sardines. They are sickened and fall ill, as does the Treble Clef, and to the bewilderment of the Sardines a panic-stricken flight ensues. In their ears still linger the sweet sounds of the dance of the Semiquavers and the Rests. The Key sorrowfully packs them back in their tin and closes the lid. Curtain.

27–29 May

Copyists for the Symphony. Packing up the huge house we have been living in. Search for a flat or a *pension* in Paris.

Miss Olmsted visited us on the 28th. We were bemoaning the fact that we had nowhere to lay our heads. She said that we should not worry, all would be well. The next day I found splendid rooms in a good *pension*.

---

1 The pun on the Russian word ключ (*klyuch*), whose primary meaning is a key or a spanner, would also work in French, but does not work at all in English. Musically, the English 'key' refers to tonality (in Russian 'tonal'nost'), whereas the symbol denoting the pitch at which notes written on the stave are to be played is 'clef' – in Russian 'klyuch', the same word as the key that opens the door or, if you like, rolls back the lid of the tin of sardines. The violin clef (G) is the familiar treble clef.

30 May

The second of Koussevitzky's concerts, including a piano Concerto by Tailleferre. At first it seemed an attractive piece, light and Mozartian. But not for long: later on it turned into a derivative bore. From the point of view of a pianist playing this Concerto it was very feeble. It is no easy matter to compose a Concerto that is interesting for a pianist to play. Time was when Ziloti was very critical of my First Piano Concerto in this respect: it was insufficiently pianistic. Well, this one was far less so, and to make matters worse she[1] was barely audible.

The other novelty was a long piece by the American Taylor.[2] Dreadful. There was catcalling from the gallery, in which I joined.

Afterwards I took tea at the Kokhánskis. He will play my Violin Concerto in New York in December. Stravinsky is making a violin arrangement of *Pulcinella* for him.

31 May

Played the Symphony to Koussevitzky: not before time, as tomorrow is the first rehearsal. Naturally, after only two play-throughs, he does not know much about it, and tomorrow I will start the rehearsal off from the podium.

When I got home Svyatoslav was bawling, but when I sat down to play the piano he stopped, under the impression that this was being done to pacify him. However, he was offended by the fact that I continued playing and paid no attention to him, and once again set to screaming.

In the evening I went again to see Koussevitzky, who was not at home. I sat on my own to receive the copyists (four of them) who had brought the copies of the string parts.

---

1 Presumably in this first performance the composer was the soloist.
2 Deems Taylor (1885–1966), a prolific and successful if essentially Sunday composer. In 1919, when the work in question, *Suite Through the Looking-Glass, Four Musical Portraits Based on Lewis Carroll* was composed, his day job was supervising the editorial page of *Collier's Magazine*); he later became editor of *Musical America* and President of ASCAP. A witty man in person and on the page, he was a leading member of the Algonquin Round Table and a close friend of such humorists as Robert Benchley. Not content with this, he had another and even more prominent career as a radio presenter for the New York Philharmonic's broadcasts, and, being a good friend both of Leopold Stokowski and of Walt Disney, as the on-screen MC of *Fantasia*. At one point he dated Dorothy Parker, from which one may infer that he must also have had nerves of steel. None of these distinguished and varied achievements appears to have cut much ice with Prokofiev's opinion of his music.

1 June

We should have moved from Bellevue today, but because of today's rehearsal have put it off until tomorrow. It was a two-part rehearsal: two hours of strings, and two of wind. At Koussevitzky's request I started it off, while he sat with the score to acquaint himself with it. I have not conducted for almost five years, moreover I have done hardly any work on my Symphony from the perspective of the conductor, and there are some very tricky places in it, for example a 6/4 and a 3/2 in the first movement recapitulation. It was extremely hard work rehearsing, and I was very glad when Koussevitzky finally chased me off the podium and took charge himself. I could then look at the score in peace and quiet myself. After two hours the string players departed, to be replaced by the wind players, and again I worked with them first, followed by Koussevitzky. I find it hard to say precisely what my impression was: on the whole it was not favourable, but this is usually the way when a new work is being split up into sections. The orchestra read the notes not too badly and generally behaved fairly decently to the music and to me.

Back at home I had a short rest and then helped Ptashka with clearing up the house.

2 June

The morning saw the most colossal packing session, and around noon we left in a lorry laden with twenty-five trunks. No. 32, rue Cassette was where we installed ourselves: we have a very good large room, Svyatoslav and Mrs Cobbe a smaller one. The food is excellent.

Ptashka dreams of an apartment in Paris so as to have a permanent nest; this constant moving about is agony. What I should love is to have a plot of land near Paris, say 3,000 square metres, on which to build a small house. But I could only possibly have the money to buy this after a good success in America.

3 June

Second rehearsal, a full one this time in the theatre foyer, which meant that everything was very loud. Some things sounded well, but most of it was unsatisfactory.

Koussevitzky does not know the tempi, neither am I absolutely sure of them. The result was more annoying than pleasurable. I shall not rush to embark on another piece as dense and unwieldy as this one: Dukelsky is right, one must write more simply and diatonically.

Mrs Cobbe has left us; it has been in her mind for some time to go to Italy with her friend. We parted the best of friends. Ptashka is in despair at the thought of having to cope with Svyatoslav on her own, but it will not be easy to find another treasure like Mrs Cobbe.

In the evening to the dress rehearsal of Demasy's play *Cavalière Elsa*.[1] He has talent; some of his scenes and characters engrave themselves on the memory.

4 June

A letter from Asafyev:[2] the Mariinsky Theatre has serious plans to stage *Three Oranges*. This gave rise to a conversation with Oeberg, in which I tried to forestall any obstacles being put in the way by the publishers. But Oeberg is demanding a high fee and substantial guarantees, while I maintain that such sums cannot be demanded from impoverished Russia. On this point there is no meeting of minds whatsoever.

Another letter was from Mme Lapina, protesting furiously about the mess in which the house had been left.

The third Symphony rehearsal was similar to yesterday's.

---

1   *La Cavalière Elsa*, adaptation by Paul Demasy of the eponymous novel by Pierre Mac Orlan, the *chansonnier* and chronicler of urban lowlife in numerous very popular novels. The star of this particular production was the black artist's model from Martinique Aïcha Goblet, known as the Miss Africa of Montparnasse, who sat frequently for Soutine and Modigliani. Like her younger rival Joséphine Baker, Aïcha was a music-hall dancer and singer as well as a model, but with a sufficiently different reputation (as G. Fuss-Amoré and M. Desormiaux remark in their book *Montparnasse*, published in 1925: 'She holds fast to the old principles . . . Any coarse male who would come too close would face a wild cat') to command a much lower rating on the celebrity scale.

2   Boris Asafyev (1884–1949), composer and critic who wrote under the pen-name of Igor Glebov. In St Petersburg he had been one of the earliest and staunchest propagandists for Prokofiev's music, leading the composer to dedicate his first Symphony, the *Classical*, to him. He was also a prolific composer and three of his twenty-eight ballets are still in the repertory: *The Fountains of Bakhchisarai*, *The Flames of Paris* and *The Stone Guest*. Once the Bolshevik regime was firmly entrenched, never taking his eye off the need to stay on the right side of the shifting cultural politics of the regime, he concentrated mainly on the relatively safe area of music for children, and was eventually humiliatingly forced into joining the 'Zhdanovshchina' chorus denouncing Shostakovich, Prokofiev and Myaskovsky, of whom he had formerly been an unswerving supporter. Myaskovsky never reconciled himself to the betrayal but Shostakovich and Prokofiev were more forgiving. Prokofiev, as Simon Morrison has pointed out (*The People's Artist: Prokofiev's Soviet Years*, OUP, New York, 2009), was more upset by Asafyev's blatant plagiarising, in the ballet *The Flames of Paris*, of French melodies Prokofiev had collected for him. Asafyev never moved away from his native city and survived the 900 days of the Leningrad blockade by the Nazis. He died in January 1949, his death undoubtedly hastened by guilt over his betrayal of friends and colleagues, whom he sincerely understood and admired, in the horrible events of the previous year.

5 June

General rehearsal. Not everything is as it should be. Suvchinsky, Dukelsky and Obukhov[1] sat with their heads buried in the score. Dukelsky said that the material is excellent and magnificently worked out, but why does the texture have to be so overloaded? This is not the way to write. Neither Suvchinsky nor Obukhov said anything.

6 June

Concert. The first movement went almost ideally, the variations less so. The horns were particularly weak, even though there were five of them: one in reserve to allow the others to take a breather. Despite this, they did not stand out in the passages where they are needed. Also, the acoustic in the Opéra is hopeless.

The work had a moderate success, not as good as *Seven, They Are Seven* last year. There were calls for the composer, and I stood up to take a bow from the box once I was satisfied that the applause was insistent enough. One or two people had a go at booing. Once upon a time this was a fashionable way simply of signalling a piece in the modern style; nowadays it is plainly stupid.

After the Symphony Cecilia Hansen[2] was the soloist in a Mozart Concerto, then came the interval, in the course of which a mass of people I know came to shake my hand. I could see the bewilderment written all over many of the faces. Princesse Polignac was first into the box to congratulate me: a very

---

1 Nikolay Obukhov (Nicolas Obouhow) (1892–1952), composer much influenced by Scriabinesque mysticism and embryonic dodecaphonic techniques, in the use of which he was an early pioneer and invented for the purpose a system of notation that ignored the distinction between, for example, G sharp and A flat, thereby eliminating the possibility of enharmonic subtleties. Prokofiev had come across his music at a 'Musical Contemporaries' evening in St Petersburg in 1916, describing it in his diary entry as 'interesting harmonic invention but thematically dull – routine even, fragmented and sterile. All this I can forgive, but the last-named is particularly dispiriting.' Obukhov had come to Paris in 1918 and had attracted the benevolent attention of Ravel. See *Diaries*, vol. 2, pp. 76, 103–4, 109, 121, 156.
2 Cecilia Hansen (1897–1989), known as 'the Queen of the Violin' (and by Yehudi Menuhin as 'an angel'), was one of the outstanding generation of violinists (Mischa Elman, Jascha Heifetz, Efrem Zimbalist among them) trained by Leopold Auer at the St Petersburg Conservatoire. She had an exceptionally long and successful career specialising in the Romantic repertoire, although Pyotr Suvchinsky, on hearing her perform Prokofiev's First Violin Concerto in Berlin in 1922, caustically commented that she was pure *chair à violon*, violin made flesh, suggesting that intellectual depth was not her strongest point. Cecilia Hansen was the wife of Prokofiev's close friend the pianist Boris Zakharov, whose international career was overshadowed by his wife's fame. She ended her life in London and was still playing the violin at the age of ninety. See *Diaries*, vol. 1 *passim*; vol. 2, pp. 3, 51, 91, 107, 109, 132, 136, 155, 670.

elegant gesture on her part. Obukhov and Demasy were full of praise. Tcherepnin prattled nonsense, Koshetz likewise. Suvchinsky mumbled something or other.

When Stravinsky showed up, I said to him, 'Well, now let me have your brickbats.' He began a long peroration about how I should know how much he loves and admires me, but this was not at all what he had been expecting since hearing that Prokofiev was composing a Symphony. I replied that this was pure music, hence music deriving from polyphony, which was to a great extent our common heritage – so wherein lay the disagreement? Stravinsky: 'We must have a long talk about this at home in private.' I: 'I should like nothing better. When?' Stravinsky: 'I'm very busy just now, but in a few weeks I shall be free, and then we must meet and talk.' Hypocrite! If he truly 'loves and admires' my music, he has no business putting off our discussion for a month.[1]

Others who were there were Coates,[2] Fitelberg, Cooper,[3] Steinberg[4] and Grechaninov[5] (the last two newly arrived from Russia) but I did not see them to speak to.

In the evening Ptashka, Cecilia, Zakharov and I all went to the Casino de Paris, then out to dinner and got agreeably tipsy. In other words we went on the binge to celebrate my premiere and her debut in Paris.

1 In a later letter to Myaskovsky, dated 28 October, Prokofiev remarks that Stravinsky had been at the performance of the Symphony but had 'understood not a single note of it'.
2 Albert Coates (1882–1953), the St Petersburg-born English conductor who from 1914 to 1919 was Principal Conductor of the Mariinsky Theatre. At the same time he was enjoying a growing reputation in Europe and America, becoming Beecham's associate at Covent Garden and taking over the London Symphony Orchestra from 1919 to 1922. Coates had consistently championed Prokofiev's music and had been the main driving force behind the Mariinsky Theatre's decision to produce *The Gambler* in 1917, the production that had to be cancelled because of the October Revolution. See *Diaries*, vol. 1, pp. 655–6, 677; vol. 2 *passim*.
3 Emil Cooper (1877–1960), Russian conductor. He became known in the West through Diaghilev's seasons in Paris and London. As Musical Director of the Bolshoy Theatre he was one of the most prominent conductors in Moscow until his emigration to North America in 1923, where he conducted the Chicago Lyric Opera and became Music Director of the Montreal Opera Guild. See *Diaries*, vol. 1, pp. 181, 193, 209, 211, 435; vol. 2, pp. 157–8, 171–3.
4 Maximilian Steinberg (1883–1946), composer and teacher, pupil and son-in-law of Rimsky-Korsakov, and chief guardian of the flame. At the St Petersburg Conservatoire, although never officially one of Prokofiev's teachers, he had maintained a polite but guarded attitude towards the young iconoclast's achievements. A later student, who invariably paid tribute to the knowledge and experience he passed on to him, was Shostakovich. See *Diaries*, vol. 1, pp. 44, 120, 156, 263, 362, 366, 644, 663–4, 764; vol. 2, pp. 73, 80.
5 Alexander Grechaninov (1864–1956), composer in the Romantic tradition much influenced by his teacher Rimsky-Korsakov. At this time he had recently arrived in Paris, where he remained until just before the Second World War when he emigrated again to America. Although Grechaninov is best remembered today for his liturgical compositions for the Russian Orthodox Church, he wrote prolifically in other genres, completing five symphonies, several operas, song-cycles and chamber music including four string quartets.

7 June

The Symphony has come and gone, leaving me, however, with a sense of dissatisfaction as much from the reaction of the public and the musical community as from the actual performance. But it could hardly have been otherwise with a work of such complexity that had taken me nine hard months to complete, and then only just! Leafing through the score I saw a few places that should be altered, but not very many, and was once again persuaded that much of it had not been realised in the performance.

I took Svyatoslav to the Zakharovs for tea. Natalya Konstantinovna was there, and for some reason had clearly set out to badger me, which she proceeded ceaselessly to do, no doubt because of the confrontation with Oeberg (at which she had been present), over the score and parts for the Mariinsky, and also over the inordinate time and trouble the maestro had taken over the Symphony, while himself probably being disappointed that it had fallen short of a brilliant success. But this offends me: I dedicate the Symphony to him, and my reward is to be taunted with gibes. A swinish trick!

8 June

Called on the Ruzskys, and then to the orchestral rehearsal of Dukelsky's ballet.[1] It turned out he had come round to invite me to it, but was late and had missed me.

Dukelsky said that he had liked my Symphony much more on second hearing. Poulenc had apparently praised it, also Nouvel. I was surprised and pleased to hear this. Nouvel, who when Diaghilev had cold-shouldered me last spring had followed suit by turning his back on me, was now vowing eternal friendship. Nice chap, isn't he?

In the evening I went to an orchestral concert of contemporary music conducted by Straram.[2] Delage,[3] Casella,[4] Ravel's *Valses nobles* – all deeply

---

1   *Zéphyr et Flore*.
2   Walther Straram (1876–1933) anagrammed the name under which he was born in London, Walter Marrast, to reincarnate himself as prqbably the leading French conductor and promoter of new music in the Paris of the mid-1920s. In 1925 he established the series of concerts known as the *Concerts Straram*, with an orchestra especially formed for the purpose. The concert on 8 June 1925 would have been the first presented by the organisation later responsible for introducing to Parisian audiences, along with premiere performances of the Paris avant-garde such as Milhaud and Roussel, the works of Berg, Webern, Weill and Hindemith, as well as the early orchestral works of Messiaen. The Straram orchestra was of a high enough quality to be chosen by Stravinsky for his first recording of *The Rite of Spring* in 1929 and by Toscanini for his Paris debut in 1934.
3   Maurice Delage (1879–1961) had studied with Ravel and was a member of the group known as 'Les Apaches', which also included M. D. Calvocoressi, Ravel, Florent Schmitt, Tristan Klingsor,

soporific. There was more life about the Italian Rieti,[1] whose piece had much charm and wit; but no Italian can resist the temptation from time to time to lapse into a special kind of Italian vulgarity – a pity!

9 June

Marnold is transported with delight by my Symphony and came round to pick up the score so that he could study it in detail. The other press reviews are hostile although most of them, as I predicted, with some circumspection.

In the evening, Borovsky's concert, in which the first work was my Second Sonata. The first three movements were so-so, not done as well as I play them, but the finale was quite brilliant. The success was lukewarm.

B.N. says his sister has returned. However, a crisis is brewing: relations with her husband are rocky, the result of a mixture of debts and romantic liaisons.[2] B.N. himself has so far received 850 francs and had his hotel bill paid. He complains of stomach pains, believes he has a duodenal ulcer and thinks he is not long for this world.

10 June

A letter this evening from Aunt Katya, who still does not know of Mama's death. A month ago I wrote and told her that I would be sending her 25 roubles, but what with all the rushing about and our recent lack of money I still have not sent it. I therefore ran to the bank and dispatched the money.

In the evening Cecilia's concert, which included the scherzo from my Violin Concerto and the second *Song Without Words*, which I had no

---

Manuel de Falla, Stravinsky and the pianist Ricardo Viñes. Particularly drawn to exotic timbres and techniques of non-Western musical cultures, especially Indian, Delage's best-known works are *Quatre Poèmes hindous* for piano or string trio and singer, and *Ragamalika*, which is unusual in calling specifically for a prepared piano to imitate the sound of the tabla.

4 Alfredo Casella (1882–1947), Italian composer and pianist who spent his formative years, musically speaking, in Paris, where he studied at the Conservatoire under Gabriel Fauré.

1 Vittorio Rieti (1898–1994) in the course of a long life wrote more than a dozen ballets, seven operas, five symphonies, several Concertos, chamber music for a wide variety of instrumental combinations, songs and choral works. His style and outlook were formed in the Paris of the 1920s, notably by Les Six and Stravinsky. Moving to America at the outbreak of the Second World War, his music moved still further in the direction of the neo-classical, in which vein he composed several ballets for Balanchine. As to the gaiety and liveliness Prokofiev heard in this work, Rieti's compatriot and mentor Casella once observed, 'Rieti's oeuvre stands apart in its specific clarity, gaiety and sophistication of a kind only he possesses, yet it hides a good deal of melancholia.'

2 Princess Varvara Magalova's husband was the Georgian Prince Dmitry Magalashvili (russified to Magalov), with whom Prokofiev had quarrelled quite violently over a game of cards.

difficulty in transcribing for violin. It turned out very nicely and was much liked by the audience. I stood up to take a bow.

I rather enjoyed talking to Cooper and Steinberg, the latter passing on an official invitation from the Leningrad Philharmonia for next season. But I said that I would not risk going without a guarantee that I could leave the country to return.

Saw Anna Grigorievna Zherebtsova.[1] She has put on a lot of weight, begun to sag and looks older.

11 June

Suvchinsky dropped by when I was out. He is not going to London but will stay in Paris, because the Eurasianist congress has been moved from London to Paris.

Dukelsky called, just for a chat. He says Stravinsky has been honouring him with many marks of attention. But there is a conflict: Stravinsky was praising Honegger, whom Dukelsky cannot stand.

After him came B.N. with Nikita and his sister, and also the head of her husband's Shanghai business empire, the last two attending at B.N.'s request 'as specimens of the menagerie'. But he seems to have plans, not to mention a new grey suit of indifferent quality. Nikita has not been doing well; his playing lacks masculinity.

We talked about talent. The question that interests me is: since talent is a gift from God, how does it happen that talent is often bestowed on bad people?[2]

Miss Olmsted came to dine. She liked the Symphony, although she admitted that she did not understand all of it. What is the connection between the divine gift and the perfectibility of man? And does the recipient of the gift thereby have a greater responsibility before God? I did not understand her answers to these questions, mainly because she spoke in English.

Afterwards all three of us went to the third of Straram's concerts. The young German Kurt Weill is inventive, but somehow passionless, dead. Two of Schoenberg's *Five Orchestral Pieces* were strange, unearthly, interesting; the others terminally boring.

---

1 Anna Grigorievna Zherebtsova-Andreyeva (1868–1944), mezzo-soprano, widow of Prokofiev's St Petersburg friend the tenor Nikolay Andreyev. In Petersburg Prokofiev had been a close friend of both husband and wife, but later there had been a falling-out. Anna Zherebtsova had given the first performance of Prokofiev's fairy-tale *The Ugly Duckling* in January 1915. See *Diaries*, vol. 1 *passim*; vol. 2, pp. 5, 38, 56, 78, 80, 100, 109, 115, 142, 145, 511.
2 'PISHCHIK: Most enchanting Charlotta Ivanovna . . . I'm simply in love! CHARLOTTA: You, in love? (*Shrugs.*) Are you really capable of love? Guter Mensch aber schlechter Musikant.' (Chekhov, *The Cherry Orchard*, Act 4.)

12 June

The general rehearsal for Koussevitzky's final concert of the series, devoted to Stravinsky. However, it was all old stuff! There's fashion for you. In fact for me there was one old novelty: *Ragtime*, composed six years ago but I had never heard it. Ten instruments, conducted by Stravinsky (who is getting much better at conducting: he did not conduct *Ragtime* so much as dance it). Not that interesting a piece. Koussevitzky, after an obligatory preamble about how much he loves my music and will always tell me the truth, confessed that although he found my Second Symphony basically good and liked the main subject, the second movement theme and all the variations, he did not like the first movement's second subject. If he were I, said he, he would not hesitate to revise it radically by composing completely new material for the second subject. I replied that this was inconceivable: it would entail throwing out half of the exposition, all the development and half of the recapitulation. All that would be left would be the opening statement of the main subject, and the concluding material. A radical rewrite on this scale was not a realistic proposition: if it is the case that the second subject is inadequate, the only comparison one could make would be a situation where cancer of the liver has spread so far that its removal would result in the loss not only of the liver but of its owner.

It is very hot. Heat and distraction is preventing me from working. And I ought to be getting on with the proofs of the *Classical* Symphony.

13 June

The final Koussevitzky concert, consisting of works by Stravinsky. I listened with great pleasure to *Petrushka* and *The Rite*, although both works, when done without staging, tend to come across as formless and fragmented (except the first movement of *Petrushka*). Stravinsky has made strides not only as a conductor[1] but as a pianist, and rattles through his Concerto with great vigour, even though he has a tendency to bang the keyboard unpleasantly. He had a great success, and the audience was more numerous than at the previous concert. But as before I do not find the Concerto congenial, except for a few splendid places. Dukelsky loved it, and I said to him: 'Oho, now you've well and truly put your foot in it!' Some musicians (Gaubert,[2]

---

[1] In this concert Stravinsky not only played the solo part in the Piano Concerto but also conducted the Paris premiere of the orchestral version of *Ragtime*.
[2] Philippe Gaubert (1879–1941), composer and flautist, one of the most influential musicians in Paris by virtue of the positions he held: he was Principal Conductor of the Paris Opéra and Musical Director of the Société des Concerts du Conservatoire.

Marnold, Casadesus,[1] Szymanowski, made a great show of praising my music and criticising Stravinsky's.

15th June

In the afternoon I went to the rehearsal of *Zéphyr*, alerted by Dukelsky, but as matters turned out *Zéphyr* had been rehearsed in the morning and I had happened along to bits and pieces and tidying up of problems in Auric's *Matelots*. Diaghilev appeared, embraced me, and after wandering up and down for a while came to sit beside me. 'Revolting music,' he smiled at one of Auric's melodies, 'supremely tasteless vulgarity', but said with a certain indulgence towards the music. After a while, he said, 'Well now, Serge, you and I have to come up with a ballet, do we not?' 'Indeed we do,' I replied, 'but first we have to settle what sort of music it has to have. This sort of thing (meaning the Auric we had just heard) I cannot write.' Diaghilev: 'Every composer composes in his own way. You cannot dictate to a composer who has formed his own style.' And that, for the present, was how matters were left.

The evening saw the opening of Diaghilev's season and the premiere of *Zéphyr*. It was preceded by *Pulcinella*, which I heard with great pleasure – most skilfully and charmingly done. Then *Zéphyr*, and with it some disappointment: wan and often clumsy orchestration, not nearly as effective as it sounded on the piano. Braque's settings were flabby, and Kokhno's libretto pointless. Only in the finale, when the nymphs fan out lying on their backs around Boreas and invite him to give himself to them, did the audience get much in the way of pleasure. The success was lukewarm. Dukelsky came out once to take a bow, anxiety written endearingly on his brow. To sum up, it was rather a disappointment. Nevertheless, the ballet could be re-orchestrated and the settings re-designed, because purely as music it is one of the most significant events of the season.

---

[1] It is difficult to be sure to which member of the Casadesus dynasty this refers: perhaps the celebrated pianist Robert Casadesus (1899–1972), or perhaps the violinist Marius, one of Robert's two uncles, who gave the first performance of Ravel's *Tzigane*. One characteristic shared by all the Casadesus was a fondness for musical hoaxes: the Société des instruments anciens, founded by the other uncle Henri with the enthusiastic collaboration of Saint-Saëns, specialised in performances of rediscovered works by dead composers such as J. C. Bach and Handel, most of which were written, à la Kreisler, by either Henri or Marius. Marius was responsible for the most successful hoax of all: the so-called Adélaïde Violin Concerto, supposedly composed by the ten-year-old Mozart for the daughter of Louis XV and 'realised' by Marius, deceived many scholars including the eminent musicologist Friedrich Blume, and was recorded by Yehudi Menuhin. Only in 1977, as a result of a copyright dispute, did Marius Casadesus admit to the authorship.

16 June

Called on Marnold, who had also invited Straram for the purpose of persuading him to perform my Symphony. I played it, and Straram lavished praise upon it. It was decided that next season, in the course of which Straram will give no fewer than twelve concerts, both my symphonies will be played, and *Seven, They Are Seven*! Very good news.

Straram is not much of a conductor, but can allow himself as many rehearsals as he needs since, according to the latest gossip, he lives with Ganna Walska.[1]

Returning home and feeling tired, I went to bed for a nap, but was burst in on by Dukelsky and Auric, the former unable to accept the general consensus that his ballet was poorly orchestrated. 'But it's what I intended. I *wanted* a "chamber-music" orchestration, we've had quite enough Rimsky-Korsakovian fireworks.' I said that chamber-music orchestration was one thing, clumsy orchestration quite another. Auric and I joined forces to tease Dukelsky with his plain inability to orchestrate his own ballet, which drove him completely out of his mind.

17 June

A letter from Terpis,[2] Balletmaster of the Berlin Staatsoper, about a ballet for Berlin. I do not plan to compose one, but it could come in useful as a bargaining chip with Diaghilev.

Went to see Blois. He had some suggestions for cheap but good dachas in the Dordogne, and also confirmed that he had succeeded in arranging a performance of the Suite from *Chout* with the Pasdeloup Orchestra.[3]

To Diaghilev's season again yesterday. The first item was *Le Chant du rossignol*[4] – slow and boring. There followed the premiere of *Matelots*. These

---

1   The flamboyant Polish chansonnière with a dubious past, with whom the inconceivably wealthy Chicago industrialist Harold McCormick, principal financial backer of the Chicago Opera, had become infatuated four years previously. McCormick, determined to repackage her as an opera diva, was widely perceived as the real-life model for Citizen Kane's similarly doomed enterprise. See *Diaries*, vol. 2, pp. 582, 679.
2   Max Terpis (1889–1958), dancer and choreographer. The probable reason he was in Paris at the time of the *Pulcinella* revival was that he had recently choreographed a production of the ballet, conducted by Erich Kleiber, for the Berlin Staatsoper, of whose ballet company he was Balletmaster from 1923 until 1930.
3   Established in 1861 by Jules Pasdeloup to give popular, low-priced Sunday afternoon concerts to the masses at the Cirque d'hiver, somewhat along the lines of August Manns's Saturday afternoon Crystal Palace concerts in London, which had begun six years earlier in 1855, the Orchestre des Concerts Pasdeloup is today France's oldest Symphony orchestra, although its musicians have never been under contract.
4   The ballet choreographed by Massine and designed by Matisse, made up of material from the second and third acts – the 1913–14 material – of Stravinsky's opera *Le Rossignol*. Prokofiev had been at the first performance in May 1920, when he seems to have thought the designer was Picasso. See *Diaries*, vol. 2, p. 509.

sailors are delineated in the simplest outline, and it is obvious that Auric was in a terrible rush when composing the score. The music is 'nautical', which is to say rollicking but *à la française*, which is further to say that it is gay and tuneful in a chansonnier sort of way. Some of the material is quite attractive but some of it is unbearable, for instance the tune we had been discussing at the rehearsal the day before yesterday. The settings, by the young artist Pruna,[1] a follower of Picasso, are simple and pleasing. Massine's staging of the ballet was ebullient and good-humoured; in general freshness and good humour were the dominant qualities both of the music and of the whole production, and account for its vociferous success. These very qualities were in sharp contrast to the viscid turgidity of the *Nightingale*, which had it followed *Matelots* would have been completely unlistenable to in spite of all Auric's deplorable lapses of taste. 'Whenever I hear this, I get a stomach ache,' Diaghilev once commented about one of the *Nightingale* themes.

After *Matelots* came *Les Biches*, which Poulenc claims to have completely revised and re-orchestrated. In fact it is just as it was before: a bit of tango, a little something filched from Beethoven, a slice of *Life for the Tsar*. A dilettante – that is the definition of Poulenc, and his ballet was thrown into stark relief alongside *Matelots*, which is the work of a master and succeeded in sinking its companion without trace. One image, only one, of *Les Biches* will remain, and that is the seductive silhouette of Nemchinova.[2]

18 June

One jolly little tune from *Matelots* we liked very much; we sing it to Svyatoslav and it makes him laugh. When I asked Auric if it was some kind of folk song, he candidly revealed that he had taken the rhythm from a Tchaikovsky tune

---

1 Pedro Pruna O'Cerans (1907–1944), Catalan painter who on moving to Paris in 1921 became a youthful disciple of Picasso and was championed by Diaghilev, who commissioned him to paint a full-length portrait in oils of his (Diaghilev's) adored protégé Serge Lifar, 'the Adonis who swam in the Lido under Diaghilev's jealous eye' according to Lynn Garafola (*Dance Magazine*, October 1984). 'Mon dieu,' wrote Roger Fry to his long-term partner Helen Anrep, referring to the spectacular rise of Pruna, 'the arrivism, the mercantilism, of the art world here! It has fallen very low and it seems to me all the young are given over to the determination to arrive and to attract attention.' (Quoted in Garafola, op. cit., p. 258). Diaghilev was kinder: 'Pruna is simple, and therein lies his complexity. His painting is sweet but at the same time saltier than salt, yet even so it leaves one with a pleasant aftertaste of sugar' (letter to Kokhno, 21 July 1924, quoted in R. Buckle, *Diaghilev*, Weidenfeld and Nicolson, London, 1979).
2 Vera Nemchinova (1899–1984) was by this time effectively Diaghilev's prima ballerina, having previously created roles in Massine's ballets *La Boutique fantasque* and *Pulcinella* (Pimpinella). It was her account of the Girl in Blue in *Matelots*, however, that set the seal on her stardom. Her post-Ballets Russes career included establishing her own companies, first with Anton Dolin and later, in New York, where she based herself for the remainder of her life, the Ballets Russes de Vera Nemchinova, for whom Balanchine created *Aubade*.

he particularly liked and fitted a new melody to it. There and then he played the Tchaikovsky melody to us, which incidentally was completely dissimilar to his own. Auric is a nice lad, a bit of a daft bumpkin, but with his heart in the right place.

Dukelsky came after lunch and sat with me for a long time. In strict secrecy he unveiled to me a conversation he had had with Stravinsky about my Second Symphony, but expressed in such woolly and diffuse terms I found it hard to understand its drift. Apparently Stravinsky is critical of me for failing to break free of Musorgskian pathos and Korsakovian Russianism, and for continuing to write florid melodies whereas what one must do is move to a purer classicism. What, like Bach? – whose face Stravinsky disfigures like smallpox![1] Stravinsky's comment on seeing somewhere or other the title page of my First Symphony with the heading 'Classical', had been: 'What a fool the man is! Only Prokofiev could have given it a title like that.'

Dukelsky then gave me the outline of an article he had written on the influence of ragtime on the new direction of contemporary music. The article was supposed to have been published in America last year, but had not been. The idea was developed with intriguing and paradoxical subtleties, but I cannot now recall it coherently: when I have a chance I shall ask him to repeat it. In the meantime I told him of the proposal I had received to compose a ballet for Berlin. Dukelsky said he would mention it to Diaghilev, to which I replied, 'Please do tell him about it, because I must give some sort of answer to Berlin, but make sure you present it to Diaghilev so that it comes out as a piece of provocation.' Dukelsky: 'Don't worry, I'll handle it very carefully.'

I had a bad headache. Miss Olmsted, who has recently moved into our *pension* (she has struck up a close friendship with Ptashka) is treating me. She told me that every morning on waking, while still in bed, I should study a lesson from the Bible and from *Science and Health*, or at least part of a lesson. There are special booklets for each Sunday containing texts from the Bible alongside appropriate passages from *Science and Health*, and the Sunday services attended by Christian Scientists consist of readings from them. During the week preceding each Sunday Scientists read these texts, and the fact that everyone has been reading the same material has a unifying effect on them. Miss Olmsted advised me to begin following the same practice each morning, saying that it was a good pledge for the whole of the coming day. I resolved to make a start tomorrow.

1   Writing to Myaskovsky in August, Prokofiev describes Stravinsky's recently premiered Piano Sonata as 'a frightful piano sonata, which he himself plays, not without chic. But as music it's a sort of pockmarked Bach.' (Quoted in S. Walsh, *Igor Stravinsky, A Creative Spring*, Jonathan Cape, London, 1999.)

In the evening there was a tribute to Koussevitzky at the Comédia[1] to celebrate his appointment to the *Légion d'honneur*, which he had received before leaving for America last year.[2] Casadesus, who organised the occasion, asked me to write a short *pièce d'occasion*, saying that a whole group of composers had written pieces for the most unlikely combinations of instruments. I had therefore, a few days ago, written a fragment for pianola: it begins simply but later on inflates into passages where it appears that twelve hands are playing the piano. This was recorded into the pianola to be performed in the evening, after all the speeches, along with some things by other composers – Honegger, Tansman,[3] Roussel, I think Ravel. Casadesus played out a little comedy saying that Prokofiev had become *très timide* and was too nervous to play in public, so as soon as I had come out on stage the curtain was lowered and the pianola began to play. As long as the music stayed conventionally simple nothing much happened, but when it grew to twelve hands the effect was very funny. Koussevitzky himself was not particularly friendly, having been recently infected by an enhanced sense of his own importance.

My headache is better. It did not pass off entirely but was not bad enough to spoil the evening.

19 June

Started on the Christian Science lessons. The lesson for each week is divided into six parts. I did two.

Anxiety about the summer and money: nothing has been agreed with Diaghilev, the *Juditha* project with Rubinstein is hanging fire, and half the

---

1 The theatre in the Boulevard de Strasbourg that had begun life as the Eldorado Café Concert, propelling into legend such stars as Yvette Guilbert, Mistinguett and Maurice Chevalier. Only in 1918 had it transformed itself into a more conventional venue for music-hall and operetta.
2 Koussevitzky was made a Chevalier of the *Légion d'honneur* in 1924 before taking up his appointment as Chief Conductor and Music Director of the Boston Symphony Orchestra, where he would remain for twenty-five years.
3 Alexandre Tansman (1897–1986), prolific Polish-born composer and pianist who lived and worked in Paris for most of his career except for a period during the Second World War spent in Hollywood. In Paris, although he maintained friendly contact with composers such as Poulenc, Milhaud and Honegger, he declined their invitation to join Les Six, wanting to leave undisturbed his predominantly neo-classical style with a distinct traditional Polish tinge. Perhaps more significant was his close friendship with Stravinsky, whom he later encountered in Los Angeles, resulting in an unusually balanced and informative biography, probably the most authoritative until the two-volume surveys respectively by Richard Taruskin and Stephen Walsh, of the famously fugitive composer. The book was published in 1948 in French as *Vie et oeuvres d'Igor Stravinsky* and the following year in a translation by Charles and Thérèse Bleefield as *Igor Stravinsky: The Man and his Music*. As a composer, Tansman is today most remembered for some guitar pieces commissioned from him by Segovia.

summer has already gone with no money to hand. Wrote to Rubinstein, but in guarded terms.

To Diaghilev's programme in the evening, for the second performance of *Zéphyr* – impression much the same as before. After Dukelsky's splendid performance on the piano the orchestral version sounds somehow slack, in addition to which the music lacks an overall sense of colour and personality. This is a defect of form and the way the musical material is distributed. The success was moderate. At Straram's invitation we sat in Ganna Walska's box. He is completely under her thumb; as for her, the beauty is already beginning to fade and the corners of her mouth display lines of malice and bitterness. Indeed!

Met Diaghilev in the interval. He said, 'Don't even think of writing anything for Germany!' Evidently Dukelsky has spoken to him. 'For myself, I have no desire to,' I replied, 'but in that case please let us have a serious talk, you and I.' Diaghilev asked me to telephone him in two days' time to set up a rendezvous.

Suvchinsky put in an appearance, having disappeared from view for two weeks: he has been very occupied with Eurasianist affairs (or perhaps with Mlle Guchkova, who was on his arm?). 'Well, are you or are you not going to write a ballet for next season?' he asked in a decisive tone of voice. I: 'This is still not settled.' Suvchinsky: 'That's what I'm hearing from conversations hereabouts.' The manoeuvrings of the Diaghilev entourage are altogether mysterious to me: just as the reason for the decision last spring to cast me into outer darkness remains obscure, so is the impulse now to bring me back to life. After all, I haven't changed! And what caused me such worry and heartache last spring was precisely this, that I remained as I was while they abandoned me like rats fleeing a sinking ship. But now we see the other side of the coin: here I stand, the same as ever I was, while the more they fall over themselves to come back to me, the more I feel a sense of superiority since the truth is plain for anyone to see: it is they who have been rushing hither and yon while I have stood firmly in my place.

Clearly, not the least role in all this Diaghilev toing and froing has been played by Stravinsky. Sometime during the winter of last year his attitude to me, hitherto favourable, was transformed into opposition. What exactly brought this about is hard to say, but with Stravinsky it was ever thus: this one must love, that one must not. The change went in parallel with Diaghilev's elevation of the French group – Poulenc, Auric, Milhaud. Stravinsky backed Poulenc and disparaged me – why is incomprehensible, but so it was. Now that Poulenc and Milhaud have failed to cut the mustard with Diaghilev, because Diaghilev is after all enough of a musician to understand that Poulenc is simply not up to it, and Auric scrapes through with seven out of ten, a white knight has appeared in the form of Dukelsky, ballyhooed with as much hyperbole as anyone could be. The ballyhooers were right in principle, but failed to take into consideration his youth and inexperience, and this season Dukelsky has been swaggering about with a swelled head of fantastic proportions (true, he was underestimated before). Meanwhile Stravinsky has taken the bait of pure music and has abandoned the theatre, hence presumably Diaghilev as well. So the net result of this season is the following: Dukelsky is not a sensation; the only Frenchman left is Auric; there are no new names; Stravinsky has absented himself from active service; that being the position the principal persecutor of Prokofiev has left the field. And this is what lies behind Diaghilev's rapprochement to me.

20 June

The young conductor Désormière[1] came to see me to go through the Third Piano Concerto, after which we went together to rehearse at Princesse Polignac's with a reduced orchestra of thirty-two players. What this actually meant was that the strings were cut down, but the Princesse proudly proclaimed that for her I had especially arranged the Concerto for a small ensemble. She has a gigantic mansion – a palace, of which I should not like to be the owner. The huge corps of footmen was on its own enough to make one feel queasy. Désormière had made great efforts to get to grips with the orchestration of the Concerto. Listening to the rehearsal in a corner of the hall was a group of rather ordinarily dressed ladies, whose presence irritated me. Later the hostess appeared and presented me to them. Every single one of them was a duchess.

In the evening, the concluding performance of Diaghilev's season. Nowadays no one has a good word to say for *Le Train bleu*,[2] but I remember that last season there were several similar offerings that earned many plaudits. To this day I can recall the beaming countenance of Roland-Manuel.[3]

---

1 Roger Désormière (1898–1963) conductor and flautist, a favoured conductor of Diaghilev in the later seasons of the Ballets Russes. In 1941, with the Germans already occupying Paris, he was to conduct the first complete recording of Debussy's *Pelléas et Mélisande* with Jacques Jansen and Irène Joachim, an enterprise of iconic patriotic and artistic resonance as against all the odds it preserved the unbroken line of the performance tradition to which this cast of singers were heirs. In 1945 he was appointed Music Director of the Paris Opéra and two years later Chief Conductor of the Orchestre National de France. Désormière was also noted for his scrupulous reconstruction of works by French baroque composers including Couperin, Rameau and Delalande. In 1952, however, at the age of fifty-four, he suffered a massively disabling stroke, which denied him any further activity for the remainder of his life.
2 Its indispensable star Anton Dolin left the Ballets Russes at the end of the season.
3 Alexis Roland-Manuel (1891–1966), critic and composer, a composition student of d'Indy and Roussel. Ravel, whose acolyte and biographer Roland-Manuel became, was a subsequent mentor. In 1939–40 he collaborated with Suvchinsky and Stravinsky on the preparation of the six Charles Eliot Norton lectures the latter delivered (in French) at Harvard University, later published as *The Poetics of Music*.

After the performance the Serts[1] held a dinner in honour of Diaghilev to which Ptashka and I were invited, so once again I am back in the Diaghilev circle. However, there was nothing very interesting about the dinner.

21 June

Called on the Koussevitzkys in the afternoon as they were due to leave Paris to go to Germany. However, it transpired that they are not going just yet. I then wanted to find out from Brennan the dates of my American concert appearances, but Brennan was not yet in a position to tell me. Ravel, who was also there, was very critical of Dukelsky. I stuck up for him.

In the evening there was the concert at Polignac's. Incredible pomp, the air thick with titles. But there were also some musicians (Diaghilev, Stravinsky, Dukelsky, Arthur Rubinstein, Borovsky, Kokhánski, Szymanowski) so I had to take myself sharply in hand. They listened very well. I was told that when Stravinsky played his Sonata, they talked throughout, and Baron Rothschild walked about shuffling his feet. The performance was a great success, which was quite remarkable seeing how standoffish this audience was. Among the innumerable luminaries we were introduced to, the Duchess of Marlborough[2] was particularly charming: she is one of the richest and most distinguished women in England. She invited us to call when we are in London.

Diaghilev and I went off into a corner and had our first serious talk about the projected ballet. The question of the subject was raised, and I tentatively hinted my concept involving characters based on notes and rests. Diaghilev threw out the suggestion at once. 'In ballet, at the end of the day,' he said, 'the most beautiful object is the human body, and I do not want anything with symbolic figures or constructivist costumes.' Further discussion was postponed until tomorrow.

22 June

A letter from Asafyev and Dranishnikov,[3] incorporating an agreement to pay the fee I had requested for the production of *Oranges*, but over two seasons

---

1 The Spanish painter José Sert and his wife Misia, née Godebska, formerly Mme Edwards.
2 Alexandra Mary Cadogan, daughter of Viscount Chelsea and wife of the 10th Duke of Marlborough.
3 Vladimir Dranishnikov (1893–1939) was by now a leading Soviet conductor of opera and ballet, at this time serving as Music Director of the Kirov Theatre in Leningrad and later at the Shevchenko Theatre in Kiev. A friend and supporter of Prokofiev at the St Petersburg Conservatoire, he had played the second piano for the composer's Rubinstein Prize-winning graduation performance of his First Piano Concerto in 1914. In Petrograd/Leningrad during the 1920s Dranishnikov was responsible for many first performances in the Soviet Union, among them Prokofiev's *Love for Three Oranges* (1926), Berg's *Wozzeck* (1927), Strauss's *Rosenkavalier* (1928), as well as the first Soviet production of *Boris Godunov* (1928). See *Diaries*, vol. 1, pp. 636–64; vol. 2, pp. 34, 85, 145, 692.

rather than one. The consequence of this would be that the sum demanded by the publishers would stay the same, but mine would be cut in half. At first this infuriated me but then I thought of a plan: to haggle with the publishers rather than with the Mariinsky Theatre.

In the afternoon the Borovskys held a grand reception with a crowd of guests. Koshetz sang one of my *Songs Without Words*, followed by some songs by Grechaninov – an enticing combination! I saw Oeberg and successfully advanced my stratagem, a telegram of agreement was sent to Leningrad. From there I went on to Ida Rubinstein's. She was splendid and displayed the most elaborate friendliness. We talked about a ballet, either a new work or a staging of the *Scythian Suite*, and also about *Juditha*, but not a word of anything concrete was said.

After that it was Diaghilev – the third production to be discussed in a single day! – who said, 'If I want a foreign ballet, I have Auric; nobody has any interest in another Russian ballet on an Afanasiev folk tale or on the life of Ivan the Terrible. What we need from you, Seryozha, is a *contemporary* Russian ballet.' 'A Bolshevik ballet?' 'Yes.' I must confess that this was a long way from what I had had in mind, although I could immediately see that something might be done with it. But this whole area is an extremely delicate one, as Diaghilev himself appreciated. I decided that the first thing I should do was consult Suvchinsky, and indeed even thought of suggesting to Diaghilev that he be brought in straight away, for Suvchinsky not only knows his theatre and his music, but is also extremely well informed about everything that is going on in Russia. There was one other reason why I thought it politic to introduce Suvchinsky into the plan, and that was that for the past three years every time there was any question of a libretto Diaghilev would immediately thrust under one's nose his young man Kokhno (now demoted from his former status[1] to that of merely a colleague on the aesthetic front, but strange to tell still possessed of enormous influence over Diaghilev). Kokhno had provided librettos for Stravinsky, Auric and Dukelsky. Worst of all, the posters for these ballets always proclaimed at the top a ballet by Kokhno, below that music by so-and-so, then scenery by so-and-so and then choreography by so-and-so. Whenever I caught sight of any of these posters they always brought on an outburst of voluble cursing, and now there was talk of my composing a ballet I resolved to fight to the death in order not to have to write music for anything of his. Crucially important factors often have a way of coinciding with trivialities, and so it was now: the moment Diaghilev came up with his surprising proposal for a Bolshevik ballet I quickly weighed up in my mind the pluses and minuses and at once calculated that to put forward Suvchinsky would effectively unseat Kokhno from

---

1 As a lover.

the saddle, as being obviously out of his depth in such territory. Diaghilev, who knows and likes Suvchinsky, said he would be glad to discuss the matter with him, and since Suvchinsky was away in London and Diaghilev was going there the day after tomorrow, it was agreed that I should immediately write to Suvchinsky asking him to call on Diaghilev at the Savoy Hotel.

The conversation then turned to money. I reminded Diaghilev that I had been paid 30,000 francs for *Chout*. Diaghilev responded that he could not hear of such a sum: he had paid Auric 5,000 and Dukelsky the same, but since I was older he would pay me 10,000. I said that 10,000 was not serious money at all, and again the discussion was postponed until the morrow. Privately I had been counting on 20,000; 10,000 is really very little.

23 June

Today's meeting with Diaghilev was fairly inconclusive: Auric, Pruna, I and some others were all present, and Diaghilev picked us off one by one to sit with him on a sofa in the corner. I joked that it was like a doctor's appointment. Diaghilev and I argued about the length: twenty or twenty-five minutes. I said I had no powder for more than twenty, to which Diaghilev retorted that a ballet lasting less than twenty-five minutes is not a proper ballet. On the matter of the fee, we agreed on 15,000: five to be paid on signing the contract, five on production of the piano score and five on production of the full score of the ballet. We then proceeded to seal the bargain by striking hands, Diaghilev inviting Auric, who was standing near by, to separate our now joined hands. Auric did so by striking each of our hands in turn. Diaghilev then struck hands with Auric (a ballet to a Kokhno concept about a movie being shot in a village) and I did the separation.[1] 'Well,' exclaimed Diaghilev, 'we have two new ballets!' He will be back from London on the 15th July, at which time we will conclude our discussion about the subject of the ballet.

After this I went to a concert of Polish music: Szymanowski's Concerto performed by Kokhánski. Not bad, in fact well done, although verging on the boring and, despite all its complex sophistication, somehow provincial: Szymanowski just adores luxuriating in yesterday's effects. Arthur Rubinstein played a Chopin Concerto, and I fail to understand why a pianist as abreast as he is of contemporary developments should play Chopin with such a serious mien. In my opinion Chopin is a composer it is simply not possible to hear nowadays: it would have been a different matter fifty years ago, and will be fifty years hence, when it will be possible to apprehend him as one does Mozart.

---

1 A traditional Russian way of sealing a bargain.

24 June

A telegram from Weber: *Oranges* has been accepted for the Staatsoper in Berlin. This is a tremendous development: if it does well in Berlin, the rest of Germany will follow. In today's world only productions in Vienna and Scala can compete.

25 June

Went to see Casella, who is passing through Paris and with whom I have been in correspondence over my participation in his Rome concerts, and possibly in New York, where he is to conduct a series of concerts next January. Then on to Ida, where I found A. N. Benois, to talk over a ballet version of the *Scythian Suite*. I played it from the score. Benois has to think up a concept. It goes without saying that Ida's role will have to be the apotheosis.

Had a headache, and talked to Miss Olmsted, who now lives in our *pension*. She explained to me something that up till now I had not been completely clear about, namely that there is a technique of prayer about healing. She told me that the way to pray about healing was to have a clear understanding that evil does not come from God, that it is an error, that illness is a projection of human reasoning which is neutralised by the action of Higher Reason, Truth and Love. I outlined to her my theory that the origins of sin lay in the consequences of the free will that had been given to man but that through inexperience had been misused by him. She replied that this was a man-made theory:[1] an idea emanating not from God but from a human mind. The search for the origins of evil is a pointless activity, akin to the attempt to work out the patterns left on the sand by the waves on the seashore. We must remember that God knows no evil, truth exists outside evil, therefore all researches in this field are doomed to miss the target and are accordingly vain.

26 June

Lunched with Romanov at Neuilly and played the Quintet through to him. I can now play it more fluently, and he listened very attentively. He is generally very fired up with the idea of this ballet although the plot is still not fully worked out and is constantly undergoing changes. Altogether he is not a quick-witted person. The production will debut in the autumn, and already there is a confirmed four-month tour of Germany.

---

1 Written in English.

Diaghilev has left. I saw Kokhno, who promised to sing me some *chastushki*[1] from the early days of the Revolution. He was quick to mention that he had a concept for the ballet, and in point of fact had been saving up these very *chastushki* for that purpose. I had no interest whatsoever in his concept and only wanted him to sing the *chastushki* so as to get an idea of the sort of thing that was in the air and being sung in Russia at the start of the Bolshevik era; the point was not to write them down and make use of them. Kokhno has a good memory for this kind of thing and sang me a dozen or so. There were some quite lovely rural ones, the urban ones, however, mostly sentimental rubbish. The new regime brought a new vocabulary, but not new tunes.

Suvchinsky has given me a book, *The Legacy of Tchinghis Khan*, a view of Russian history from an Eastern rather than a Western perspective. The author was not acknowledged – could it have been Suvchinsky himself?[2] It was a fascinating glimpse into the way our history developed.

27 June

Demasy came to read me his *Juditha*. Ida told me yesterday that the production had been definitely decided upon, and that Golovin[3] who, Bakst having died, had been engaged to design the production, would be coming from Leningrad. Since Demasy was going south in two days' time the reading had been arranged for today with a view to deciding where music would be needed. Much of *Juditha* is very good: the combination of high tragedy with everyday life appeals to me. But the ending is less good – patriotic and naive. I had hoped that Demasy would maintain the lofty tone and climax in some kind of dramatically compelling situation, instead of jingoistic patriotism.

---

1 The *chastushka* (from the slang verb *chastit'* meaning to speak very rapidly – imagine a limerick performed by a rap artist) is a popular, short – usually four-line – piece of rhyming doggerel, not unlike the limerick in its aptitude for delivering the satirical, irreverent, black, often obscene comments of the Russian soldiery, peasantry and proletariat about their masters and on life in general. *Chastushki* are more often than not lewd, scatological, devastating to norms of taste, decorum, social and (especially in Soviet times) political propriety. They can be strung together in stanzas like ballads to make up a kind of narrative or commentary, and those who have a wide repertoire (there are thousands) or are gifted improvisers in the genre are rightly prized as virtuosi. Conventionally *chastushki* were sung to the accompaniment of a balalaika or an accordion.
2 The author was in fact Prince Nikolay Trubetskoy. See note on p. 62, n. 3 above.
3 Alexander Golovin (1863–1930), artist and theatre designer with a characteristic blend of Symbolism and Modernism, known for his sets and costumes for the Ballets Russes, the Moscow Arts Theatre and Meyerhold's theatre among others. There is a famous portrait of Meyerhold featuring the fez that he affected – see p. 565 below. His magnificent front curtain for the Mariinsky Theatre, created in 1914, still has the power to awe visitors, although the dark red of its original colour scheme was changed in 1952 to blue.

Kokhno came while Demasy was reading and interrupted the session. The purpose of his visit was not entirely clear: Diaghilev had telephoned him from London to report that he had seen Suvchinsky but Suvchinsky had not added anything new to the discussion. Kokhno revealed that he has a complete ballet scenario already worked out which incorporates *chastushki*. It is a ballet about a janitor-cum-caretaker and therefore, in his opinion, absolutely right for Diaghilev's conception (but surely, there are no longer any janitors in Russia, and if there are they are former generals!). Although this ballet has already been earmarked for another composer, it could easily be taken away from him and another commission substituted. In short, it was perfectly obvious what the real point of his visit was, but I played deaf and dumb and was more concerned to hear the details of the conversation between Diaghilev and Suvchinsky. I soon excused myself on the grounds that Demasy was waiting to continue his reading of *Juditha*.

28 June

Nothing much happened today. The normal constituency of Paris is beginning to dissolve into its summer vacation state, but we are once again marooned in the city, partly because so many things are still unresolved and partly because we have not yet decided where we should go. But given that our *pension* is comfortable, pleasant and not too expensive, our rooms are huge, and Mrs Cobbe has taken Svyatoslav for two weeks, we decided to stay here until the 15th July, awaiting the return of Diaghilev and the final resolution of the ballet question.

Went to the Borovskys in the evening and talked about Koussevitzky, whose nose this year is stuck high in the air and who has become less pleasant company. The publishing company has accepted Dukelsky into its list, partly as a result of my intriguing and partly because Diaghilev commissioned a ballet from him – and now all of a sudden they have decided not to print *Zéphyr*. This is because it was not a success and attracted a lot of criticism, and also because the firm does not have enough money.

29 June

Called on Oeberg. He is in a state of frenzy over the Koussevitzkys: 'They interfere constantly in the running of the business and are not putting any money into it.' Between ourselves, it is no bad thing that they do interfere in the business activities of such a dithery old mumbler as Oeberg ('the old red corpuscles don't stay on the boil as they used to,' he says, tapping his forehead), but starving the firm of money is a disgrace. They have plenty of money, and it would only take peanuts to eliminate the blockage in the printing of my compositions and get going on Dukelsky's.

Dukelsky himself came to see me soon after, terribly agitated having heard from Oeberg that *Zéphyr* is not to be printed. Almost exploding, he said that Engel[1] would take the work immediately and pay a higher fee, but as it happened I already knew from Auric that following the tepid reaction to *Zéphyr* Engel had cooled towards the idea of publishing it. My advice to Dukelsky was as follows: 'Don't talk either to Engel or to Oeberg, go direct to Koussevitzky. You must understand that Oeberg's refusal is not based on principle but on purely material factors – Koussevitzky has cut off his money supply. If you talk to Koussevitzky it may be that money is after all found and all will be well. Go and see him tomorrow at noon: I know that Oeberg has an appointment with him then and you will catch them both together.'

At this point who should happen by but Tcherepnin, to whom I introduced Dukelsky and made him listen to *Zéphyr*. This encounter was not without its piquant side, since Dukelsky and Tcherepnin's son[2] had recently had some blazing rows. But Papa Tcherepnin rose nobly to the occasion and (apparently with perfect sincerity) was full of praise for *Zéphyr*.

Ptashka and I then got dressed up and went to Princesse Polignac, who was holding a farewell soirée,[3] a glittering, and very boring, occasion. Arthur Rubinstein played, but there were fewer people than at mine, and the evening itself lacked sparkle. The season was coming to an end, and people were beginning to leave Paris.

30 June

We were at Baronne de Brimont's;[4] there is such a writer. She read me her play about Indian life drawn from documents provided by her friend, the Russian scholar and archeologist Golubev,[5] who even now is immured in

---

1 Carl Engel (1883–1944), French-born composer, musicologist and managing editor of the music publishing division of G. Schirmer in New York. A frequent contributor to *The Musical Quarterly*, he was also head of the Music Division of the Library of Congress.
2 Alexander (Sasha).
3 For the end of the season.
4 Mme la Baronne Renée de Brimont was a dilettante poet whose elegiac, discreetly erotic but sexually ambivalent musings had their admirers in the salons of the Faubourg. Her collection *Mirages* had caught the ear of the ageing Fauré, who set four of the poems for his eponymous valedictory cycle in 1919.
5 Viktor Golubev (1878–1945), Russian-born Orientalist and archaeologist, was not one of the wave of Russian landowners, generals and merchants who descended on Paris after the Revolution, having moved there in the early years of the century to pursue at the École française d'Extrême-Orient his passion for the history and culture of the Far East. He became one of the EFEO's most distinguished scholars, spending almost a lifetime in Cambodia and Vietnam studying and recording in photographs and monographs the then virtually unknown monuments of Khmer culture, notably the great jungle city of Angkor-Wat. He eventually died in Hanoi.

Indo-China. The play is stupendously inept. I am being asked to write music for it. I excused myself with all manner of sophisms and left, taking the play with me.

A. N. Benois dined with us, an enchanting man. After dinner I played the *Scythian Suite* to him and together we roughed out a scenario for Ida. Later Ptashka and I went to the Kedrovs, where the old guard was assembled: Zherebtsova-Andreyeva (older and fatter, speaking rather sourly of her adored B.N.), Cooper, Steinberg. The last-named handed me with an air of triumph the official invitation from the Leningrad Philharmonia, but I told him that until I had an absolute guarantee of free passage out of Russia I would not even enter into negotiations. All the same I am most anxious that neither Ossovsky[1] nor the Philharmonia should personally be offended by my refusal; it is in no way directed at them but at the passport system.[2] Cooper was friendly, although he is in general not a nice man – a rather good conductor, however. He is currently conducting in Spain and enjoying great success there. He proposed coming to visit me to hear my compositions.

1 July

Was at Kokhánski's, and we took a good look at Opus 35,[3] transcribing it for violin. I have been meaning for some time now to write a work for violin and piano, especially after the success of the Violin Concerto, and had indeed decided to get on with it this August. But Cecilia[4] somehow got hold of the second of the *Songs Without Words* and we found it went beautifully for violin. It was at that point that I decided to make a version of the whole opus, but to collaborate not with the naive Cecilia but with Kokhánski, whose skills in this respect are fabulous. Kokhánski was delighted to fall in with the plan, and it so happened that he had recently been working with Stravinsky

---

1 Alexander Ossovsky (1871–1957), critic, editor, musicologist and professor at the St Petersburg Conservatoire, had studied with Rimsky-Korsakov. An early and committed admirer of Prokofiev's talent, he had been extremely helpful to the young composer in his student days, particularly in the matter of persuading both the Moscow publisher Jurgenson and the Petersburg conductor and concert organiser Ziloti to take his music seriously. Ossovsky was a survivor and at this juncture was serving a two-year spell as Director of the Leningrad Philharmonia, to which he returned in the 1930s as Artistic Director. His wife Varvara was a professor of piano at the Conservatoire.
2 Prokofiev never renounced Soviet citizenship and therefore had never been in a position to apply for the nationality of another country. His travel permits within Europe and to the United States were accordingly always a source of potential bureaucratic harassment. By the same token, he would not have the same protection as a foreign national could theoretically call upon were he to enter the USSR.
3 The *Five Songs Without Words*, written for Nina Koshetz in 1920.
4 Hansen.

on a version of *Pulcinella*.¹ Accordingly today I set for Kokhánski's, armed with preliminary sketches, particularly of No. 5 where I planned substantial modifications to the middle section. We worked for two hours and recast practically the whole opus. Kokhánski is marvellously gifted and imaginative, qualities in him that are indeed universally recognised. The final version of the transcription will be left until his return from London. He was very taken with the songs, I believe (and hope) genuinely.

Dukelsky appeared for dinner beaming with satisfaction: he had been to see Koussevitzky, catching him together with Oeberg, and played them his variations. Koussevitzky's reaction was that they were splendid but that when he had first heard them in their orchestral form he had not understood at all what they were about. Certainly they would be printed, moreover Dukelsky would receive 6,000 francs.

After dinner we were planning to go to the Exhibition,² where we were to be joined by the Zakharovs and the Samoilenkos. During dinner at the *pension* (where everyone eats together) Dukelsky caught sight of a young American Jewess, an acquaintance of Miss Olmsted, who had just arrived from the States. From the first moment he could not take his eyes off her, and started asking in a whisper if we could take her along with us. We did not know her at all, but wishing not to deny Dukelsky his heart's desire had a word with Miss Olmsted, and the result was that they both came with us. Dukelsky took the girl by the arm and did not let go of it all evening; I must say she gave no sign of not welcoming the attention. Our little company was greatly amused by this, not least by the figure Dukelsky cut in his exaggeratedly wide-trousered grey suit, which he assured us was the very latest fashion and had been custom-made for him by a superb London tailor.³ I started a rumour that Suvchinsky had passed on an old suit, and this was the reason for its excessive width.

---

1   Stravinsky made altogether three arrangements of the material from *Pulcinella* for a string instrument with piano: the first, referred to here, for Kokhánski in 1924, the second (for cello and piano, entitled *Suite Italienne*) in collaboration with Piatigorsky in 1927, and the third, once again a violin suite but a version of the cello compilation, also called *Suite Italienne*, with Samuel Dushkin in 1934.
2   The Paris Exhibition of 1925, the *Exposition Internationale des Arts Décoratifs et Industriels Modernes*, the gigantic post-war boost to consumerism that marked the high point of Art Deco. Sixteen million visitors passed along the brilliantly illuminated avenues separating the thousands of pavilions celebrating the style, inventiveness and general pre-eminence of French manufacturing and taste. The rides in the fairground presumably demonstrated a state of the art comparable to the lavish exuberance of the goods on display.
3   In 1924 Oxford University proctors banned the wearing of knickerbockers, i.e. loose-fitting knee-length trousers gathered at the knee, at lectures. Defiant undergraduates (or their High Street tailors) soon came up with an even baggier trouser that could be slipped over the proscribed knickers and as easily doffed once the lecture was over. Oxford Bags were born and soon swept the world of fashion.

We rode on the roller-coaster: the slopes on these ones are quite unbelievably steep. The little cars get up to speeds of 11 versts an hour[1] descending almost vertically, then climb up again, followed by an equally precipitous descent, and so four times without a moment in between to recover one's senses. So strong is the force trying to make them jump off you can feel the wheels knocking against the rails, and the effect is so powerful that when you finally climb out of the car you feel as though you have just downed a large glass of champagne in one go. Dukelsky was so terrified before the ride that he deliberately hung back and did not get on to the first train that all the rest of our group was in. Three more trains went by, and only from the fourth did I meet him emerging with his girl. 'How was it?' I asked. 'It wasn't so frightening. I wasn't scared at all,' he replied, white as a sheet. The American girl told us how on the downward trajectory he covered his face with his hands and bent double with his head between his knees. However, going up he started making a pass at her, but then the car tipped over to start the descent again, the head went back into the knees, and so on for all four stages. We laughed until we cried.

2 July

Worked on Op. 35, putting in order what Kokhánski and I planned out yesterday. It is time I got down to some work. It was good being out in the country, but I have decided to wait until Diaghilev gets back, and things are still undecided with Ida – great heavens, this has been dragging on for almost two years! The pity is that our nice *pension* is closing, and once again we shall have to move.

B.N. has sent me a begging letter for 100 francs, this time in a more confident tone: 'I shall be able to return them to you in a few days.' Even so the letter annoyed me: of late B.N. has been treating me like a thoroughgoing *intéressé*.[2] He never even put in an appearance at my Symphony, neither the rehearsal nor the performance, even though I sent him a ticket by post. Only when he needs money do I ever hear anything from him. Two, three, four weeks of complete silence go by, and then a letter or a visit: 'Serge, if it's no trouble, could you manage a hundred?' This time, instead of sending money I drafted an angry letter, but then felt sorry for him and eventually sent nothing, neither letter nor money. Since then he has gone to ground. At the same time he has a sister with millions and a brother with thousands, while he himself has no desire to work: the sum product of a year is a few feeble sonnets, not to mention no real attempt actually to earn his bread.

---

1 The verst is just over a kilometre in length.
2 Prokofiev uses a Russian version of the French word, meaning someone whose only interest is to take advantage.

I have been reflecting on time, in connection with a thought that struck me earlier: that in that other life, in eternity, there is no conception of time, and consequently time is connected uniquely with our life on earth. This was followed by another thought: that time, as we know it, has only one dimension, and indeed a sub-dimension, in that within this one dimension we can move in only one of its two directions, not both. Even though at first glance it may appear that with the aid of memory we are able to move backwards, this is not in fact so: memory can help us to catch hold of a few fragments of time which lie behind us, but any movement we may make within this fragment can only be forwards. For example, if we recall yesterday's automobile excursion, we cannot induce our memory to act in such a way that the car retraces its journey back to the place it started from. Is it impossible to conceive of a condition in that 'other' world in which time possesses more than one dimension – three, like space, or even where both time and space have four?!

In an attempt to use imagination to go beyond mere scholastic speculation, I started to think what two additional dimensions, width and thickness, could consist of. It is known that the flow of time sometimes leaves no trace: looking back into the past it is hard to say what period has elapsed, a week or a month. And sometimes the opposite is true: a particular hour may contain so many impressions that it would take a whole year to recall them. Is it not legitimate to regard this as a symbol of the greater or lesser thickness of time? And if such a symbolic representation is allowed, then it becomes possible to conceive of moving through time in that dimension. A third dimension of time – width – may be defined as omnipresence, ubiquity. In speaking of omnipresence I am not here confusing time with space, for ubiquity must be understood not only as the ability to be simultaneously in different places in space, but as the ability simultaneously to assimilate multiple different thoughts (God assimilates contemporaneously the prayers of millions of people). I do not insist that the additional dimensions of time must be those I have suggested, they may be quite other, I submit them merely as examples of the way in which it is possible to imagine time possessing other dimensions.

None of this, needless to say, provides an answer to the question of eternity from the perspective of the infinity of time, just as extending the number of dimensions in space fails to resolve the conundrum of its illimitability. But admitting at least the possibility of three-dimensional time, offering the consequent possibility of moving through it in different dimensions, brings with it the obligation to pose many questions in a form not possible heretofore.

3 July

Since Romanov has commissioned me to recast the Schubert Waltzes for two pianos so that they can be used in the context of a ballet, and also wants me to compose an Introduction to the Quintet as it will be used for the ballet (this will naturally not form part of the concert Quintet) and will pay 5,000 francs for it, and since I am free at the moment, I sat down at the piano to play the Waltzes and scattered some decorative flourishes through them, taking all morning over it and enjoying myself very much in the process. When I made a version of the Schubert Waltzes for two hands, I was terribly strict and did my best not to change anything Schubert had written, my aim being solely to select and compile in order to make up a suite. Now, by contrast, the aim was to embellish and in so doing to produce a toothsome morsel for two pianos.

Dukelsky barged in while I was absorbed in the work, which I found very aggravating while I was at white heat, so I said to him, 'Go away, please go away, my dear fellow, I am working and am terribly busy.' But when I realised that Dukelsky was not hurrying to take his departure but was likely to stay as long as he pleased in the next room ogling the American girl, I yelled out, 'Ptashka, please take Dukelsky away.' Ptashka indeed moved quite promptly but kindly to escort him out, at which a chagrined Dukelsky babbled, 'I only came because I am so very fond of Sergey Sergeyevich, I appreciate that he is working but I don't see why it is necessary to be so peremptory about it . . .' In short, he took offence, and then went to London and temporarily disappeared over the horizon.

In the afternoon Ptashka and I went to the film studio where Benois was working as art director of a huge film on the life of Napoleon.[1] It was the first

---

1 Abel Gance's silent epic *Napoléon* was a gigantic account of the rise of Napoleon, playing in its original form for five and a half hours. It starred Albert Dieudonné as Bonaparte and was crammed full of ground-breaking techniques and effects including vast crowd scenes, hand-held cameras and a triptych finale showing on three screens simultaneously. Premiered at the Paris Opéra in April 1927, even at five and a half hours' running time it covers only Napoleon's early achievements and represents barely one-sixth of Gance's projected epic in its entirety. After Metro-Goldwyn-Mayer bought the rights soon after its initial run, it was drastically reduced in length and scale, so effectively butchered (especially as the talkies made their appearance about this time) that it virtually dropped out of sight for half a century until the film historian Kevin Brownlow made it his life's work to reconstruct the original. Brownlow's first attempt in 1981 stunned audiences at Radio City Music Hall with the beauty and imagination of the photography, the sweep and visual poetry of Gance's direction. Later researches produced still more of the original, culminating in a version shown at the Royal Festival Hall in 2000 which must be as near to Gance's vision as will ever be achieved. Showings, however, continue to be rare partly because of the technical problems of the final Polyvision scenes, and partly because of an unresolved dispute over the rights, notably the provision of the live orchestral score by Carl Davis. Aside from strictly cinematographic talent, Gance recruited exceptionally distinguished artistic consultants, with Honegger retained to produce the accompanying score and Benois to head the art direction team. Honegger's score suffered from Gance's incessant re-writes and re-edits, as a result of which the final score, reduced to a mish-mash of self-borrowings and folk material, could not be made to hang together in any convincing way, and most of it has been lost with only some fragments remaining.

time I had been on a movie set, and I found it most interesting. A set had been erected inside an enormous barn, or hall, representing a room in Corsica. A very insignificant scene was being filmed, but this did not prevent it having to be started over again from the beginning five times. Three cameras were being used, the director yelled through a megaphone, but the main thing was the incredibly blinding illumination from a whole battery of lights focused on the acting area. I was amazed that the actors could tolerate such an intensity of radiation: I was standing in shadow, but the lights still made my eyes water. I was told that it is much more interesting when they are filming crowd scenes with three hundred people.

4 July

Spoke by telephone to Count San Martino,[1] who at the Princesse Polignac's soirée had proposed that I undertake a tour of Italy. It is not the first time this idea has been raised, but this time it seems a serious proposition.

Lunched with Romanov. Zak has come up with three different sketches for the design of my Quintet ballet; they look very good. Romanov still has not formulated any scene titles.

5 July

Continued retouching the waltzes for two pianos. At three o'clock went to see Kokhánski, who is passing through Paris on his way from London to the South of France, and we made final adjustments to Op. 35. I wanted to state in the published edition 'transcribed by Kokhánski and the composer', but he declined and was very happy when I dedicated three of the songs to him. One (the one she played) was dedicated to Cecilia, and one to Szigeti for being the player who really launched my Concerto while Kokhánski was still timidly vacillating, but to be candid Cecilia understood nothing whatsoever about the piece.

7 July

We have had to bid a sad farewell to our lovely *pension* because it is closing, and have moved to the Hotel Terminus opposite the Gare Montparnasse. It is expensive, cramped and noisy. Went with Benois to see Rubinstein, and

---

1 Count San Martino was President of the Augusteo Orchestra in Rome; Prokofiev had met him ten years ago when Diaghilev had first launched him on the Italian public with his Second Piano Concerto. 'A merry old gent married to a delightful young woman', as Prokofiev had noted in his diary for February 1915 after dining with the Count in his palace. See *Diaries*, vol. 2, pp. 21, 23.

once again played through my *Scythian Suite*, while Benois pondered a scenario. I asked Ida what the latest situation was with *Juditha*. She said that Golovin, who is to design the production, has now been granted a visa and would come from Leningrad to Paris in about three weeks' time. She invited me to come again in three days' time to come to a final agreement about terms. About time too, we have been talking about it for two years.

8 July

Since Romanov plans to rehearse my ballet during the summer (or rather two ballets if one counts the Schubert Waltzes), and since there are still loose ends in Paris that obstinately decline to be tied up, we decided to look for a dacha not far from the city, a couple of hours away, and today Ptashka and I got up early and headed off in a northerly direction. Following Blois's recommendation we got out at Vernon, a small town surrounded by beautiful countryside, with forests and rivers. The agency gave us several addresses, so we took a car and toured round the localities where there were houses available. One was charming and comfortable and in its own grounds, but had no garden. We then went further afield, to Les Andélis, but found nothing suitable there. It was pleasant to be travelling around in the open after the city, but we got very tired and it was late by the time we returned home.

10 July

Next morning we went to Sèvres for a meeting with the inspector of taxes, who had slapped on me a residence tax of 900 francs for our stay in the Lapin dacha. When I objected that during 1924 I had lived in this dacha for less than three months, he explained that even if I had not taken up residence until the 31st December, I would still have been due a whole year's tax. But if I had started living there on the 2nd January and quitted the place on the 31st December, I would not have had to pay anything. It follows that the fateful date in the French tax system is January 1st. I fear there is no way out of paying this sum of 900 francs, although they do allow six months' grace. I had intended to visit Mama's grave, but did not manage to as the train timetable prevented it.

In the afternoon I called on Ida to sort out the agreement of *Juditha*, but although it was she who had made the arrangement the wretched woman has gone off somewhere. Disgusting behaviour.

We have moved out of the Terminus Hotel into the Victoria Palace, because the Terminus would not allow me to bring a piano in. The room we were given at the Victoria happened to be that previously occupied by the Stahls, and I had stayed there myself on several occasions. The Samoilenkos told me they seen Stahl not long ago, and he had enquired, 'How is my son?' – meaning me. 'I love him as much as I ever did.' Nice to hear, but why then did he treat me so shabbily?

11 July

Since we had not found a suitable dacha to the north of Paris, we headed south, in the region of Fontainebleau because we wanted to be in a forested area, moreover Ptashka's singing teacher, to whose lessons she is devoted, is spending the summer round about there. We consulted the Fontainebleau estate agent and saw several dachas near by (God preserve us from Fontainebleau itself); and then went on further south, to Moret. But we could not find anything there either and eventually, although we were dog-tired, continued still further, to Montigny. Here, at a place called Marlotte, we saw three dachas which we found acceptable, and one of them, clean and newly renovated, whose owner had not yet moved in to it at all, quite took our fancy. We decided to think about it, and if we really liked it to telegraph our agreement.

12 July

Lunched with Suvchinsky, who had dropped out of sight for some time. Naturally, we spent all the time talking about the 'Bolshevik ballet'. Suvchinsky said he had been giving it some thought, and while not revealing any cards had spoken to several knowledgeable people who had recently been visiting from Russia, among them the artist Rabinovich,[1] and also Ehrenburg.[2] Suvchinsky does not much care for the latter, but considers him an intelligent

---

1 Isaak Rabinovich (1894–1961), Ukrainian-Jewish painter, graphic artist and stage designer. His main career was in Moscow, at the State Jewish Theatre, and with the Vakhtangov and Nemirovich-Danchenko companies. He would later design *The Love for Three Oranges* at the Bolshoy Theatre. See below pp. 437, 468, 507.

2 Ilya Ehrenburg (1891–1967), prominent Soviet poet, journalist and novelist. By the time of this encounter, Ehrenburg already had an ambiguous past, having as an Old Bolshevik been exiled in 1908 to Paris, where he knocked about with Lenin, at the same time as entering fully into the avant-garde artistic milieu of Picasso, Diego Rivera, Apollinaire, Léger and Modigliani. Returning to Russia after the Revolution he became a committed propagandist for the Soviet regime, while maintaining the privileged existence of a sanctioned go-between for Russia and the European intellectual fraternity, allowed to spend a good deal of time abroad. His 1954 novel *The Thaw* was widely seen as encapsulating the atmosphere of Krushchev's moderation of Stalinist excesses; for this book, and perhaps for his opposition to the orthodoxy of Socialist Realism and other less widely known examples of courage in support of persecuted fellow writers such as Pasternak, history will probably judge Ehrenburg to have been a flawed but basically estimable fighter on the side of the angels. See *Diaries*, vol. 2, pp. 685, 695, for Prokofiev's admiration for Ehrenburg's first novel, the Gospel parody *The Extraordinary Adventures of Julia Jurenito and his Disciples*, and for his distillation of experiences as a First World War correspondent, *The Face of War*.

and interesting person if unattractive both as a man and as a thinker. The general upshot of the conversations was that a ballet of this nature was hardly a feasible proposition. The present situation is so acutely contentious that there would be no chance of creating a neutral work; it would have to be either a White ballet or a Red ballet. White would be out of the question, since a Russian composer could not contemplate representing the Russia of today through the monocle of Western Europe; in any case, what would be the purpose of my severing all ties with Russia at the moment, just when there is such interest in my music there? Neither would a straightforward Red ballet be an option, because it would simply be a calamity with the bourgeois Parisian public. Finally, it would be impossible to find a neutral standpoint acceptable to both sides, since the Russia of today is dominated by precisely the struggle of the Red faction against the White, from which it follows that any attempt to represent an objective approach would not accurately reflect the moment. 'Whoever is not with us is against us';[1] consequently a neutral point of view would be rebuffed from here and from there.

As we emerged from the café we ran into Ehrenburg, to whom Suvchinsky introduced Ptashka and me. He has an interesting face, but spattered as it was with tobacco ash, his teeth rotting,[2] cheeks unshaven and hair dried out and untended, he reminded me of a tree stump in the forest. He was more than willing to talk, but something in his manner created a disagreeable impression. I felt that this person had been schooled in some kind of Revolutionary training of which I knew nothing. He had many interesting things to say, and it seemed as if there was much one would find attractive in today's Moscow. On the subject of the ballet he said much the same as Suvchinsky.

We said goodbye to him and to Suvchinsky, and to the latter I added that tomorrow or the next day Diaghilev would be returning from London and there would be a chance to have conclusive discussions about the ballet. But Suvchinsky said that he had already expressed himself fully on the subject, and declined further involvement. Consummately fastidious Pontius Pilate! No doubt the reason Pilate washed his hands was fear of picking up microbes from the Jewish mob – at least that would probably be his defence if his soul is called upon to answer.

13 July

We decided to take the dacha at Marlotte and sent our telegram, getting a telegraphed reply that the dacha was ours. I cannot be sure that it was a wise

---

1 'For he that is not against us is on our part' – Luke 9:40.
2 Ehrenburg as a seventeen-year-old youth had been badly beaten up by the Tsarist Okhrana after the 1905 Revolution, many of his teeth knocked out or severely damaged.

choice, but at least it is clean and we are not in a position to be too fussy looking for a holiday home in the middle of the summer. It is a good feeling that the house is rented and is awaiting our arrival.

There has been no apology, nor indeed any other sign of life from Idka Rubinstein after her boorish behaviour. In view of the fact that so many complications have arisen over the subject of the ballet for Diaghilev, I made up my mind to have one more go at coming to an agreement with her and therefore sent a telegram today telling her that I would be going away from Paris in a few days' time and would like to know her terms before I did so.

I had expected Diaghilev to be returning to Paris from London this evening, and went to make enquiries at the Grand Hôtel. There I was told that other people had been asking for him, but he had not appeared.

14 July

Today was a national holiday, and there was a mass of people out on the streets dancing on the pavements outside the café. Instead of a telegram from Rubinstein there was one from her companion, Mme Regnée: Ida has gone to Italy but will soon be returning. What a bitch! It becomes imperative to sort matters out with Diaghilev, otherwise everything will go to the devil.

Romanov dined with us. I played him the Introduction to his ballet which at his request I had composed over the last few days.

15 July

A very nice, conciliatory letter from Balmont, but somehow I seem to have grown away from him. Just imagine: he is in St Gilles, and has moved into the house we had last year! Went round once again to the Grand Hôtel, but Diaghilev has still not arrived and has not even booked a room for the next days. I cabled him: When? Our dacha is rented, it is time I got to work, but nothing is settled in any direction.

16 July

Marnold was here to give me back the score of the Second Symphony, on which he has done a complete analysis for a huge article he is writing. He is ecstatic. He seems to be the sole admirer of my Symphony, and the most amazing thing is that this is a man over sixty years of age. Romanov also came with the pianist who is going to accompany rehearsals of my ballet (the Quintet). I therefore twice played through for them the Quintet and the added Introduction. Marnold was equally ecstatic over the Quintet. Romanov wants me to compose one more number – a '*Matelote*',[1] and outside in the hallway we discussed the fee: 2,000 francs. I shall accept of course: for the time being Romanov is the only source of firm commissions.

A telegram from Diaghilev: he is coming back tomorrow. Since he is coming from London, it will be evening before he is here.

17 July

Early in the evening I went to the Grand Hôtel – still no Diaghilev. I called on Nouvel, and it appears that he will arrive around eleven o'clock and is not staying at the Grand Hôtel but at the Vouillemont.[2] This is so that he can avoid being importuned by people hę does not want to see, especially those who might demand money from him.

18 July

At last Diaghilev is here and today we had lunch with him: he, I, Kokhno, Lifar (a name constructed according to the same principles as svinar, zvonar, etc.),[3]

---

1 Sailor's Dance. From Prokofiev's original piano score it looks like a sort of hornpipe. The Overture and the *Matelote* were not bundled into the Quintet score, because they are so stylistically different, but Prokofiev used them in a revised and fully orchestrated form as the first and third movements of the *Divertimento*, Op. 43. (Diaghilev requested that the Overture be incorporated into the score for the 'Soviet' ballet but Prokofiev refused.) For a full discussion of the history of *Trapèze* and the music composed for it, see *Three Oranges*, no. 4 (November 2002), article by Noëlle Mann.
2 The Hôtel Vouillemont in the rue Boissy d'Anglas is now the Hôtel Sofitel Paris Le Faubourg.
3 In Russian the ending *ar'* – with a palatised soft sign following the *r* – generally denotes a practitioner of the activity indicated by the preceding syllable, hence *svinar'*, from *svin'ya* – a pig, is a swineherd, while *zvonar'*, from *zvon*, the sound of a bell, is a bellringer and by extension a rumour-monger. Prokofiev's morphological analogies suggest a reaction to his new acquaintance that falls short of adoration. Serge Lifar (1905–1986) had been introduced to Diaghilev by Nijinsky's sister Bronislava, and joined the Ballets Russes in 1923. Talented, creative, egotistical, clearly identified by Diaghilev as star material but short on classical training, he was despatched by the impresario to study with Enrico Cecchetti and Nicolay Legat. One reason Prokofiev may not have warmed to him was the iconoclastic view he was already promulgating, that what mattered in dance was neither music nor decor but solely choreography, which has its own meaning independent of musical or visual context, an approach that soon brought him close to Balanchine. The concept was exemplified in Lifar's 1935 ballet *Icare*, conceived without music but with a rhythmic pulse transferred for performance purposes to a subsequently composed percussion score by Honegger. After Diaghilev's death Lifar joined the Paris Opéra Ballet as *premier danseur*, later Artistic Director, in which capacity he served throughout the Second World War, attracting some obloquy for suspected collaboration with the Nazi occupation, an accusation he consistently denied.

Nouvel and 'Pashka',[1] an enchanting old man, a cousin of Diaghilev. I asked Diaghilev, 'Are you absolutely insisting on a Bolshevik ballet?' Diaghilev: 'Absolutely. Before leaving London I had a word with Rakovsky, our ambassador there.'[2] '*Our* ambassador?' Diaghilev smiled. 'Yes, well, you know what I mean, Russian.' Thereupon I outlined Suvchinsky's point of view, saying that I found it entirely reasonable. But for Diaghilev it went in one ear and out of the other. 'In Russia today,' he exclaimed, 'there are twenty million young people, who ...' (an unprintable expression related to the climax of sexual desire). 'They live, they laugh, and they dance. And they do all these things quite differently from how they are done here. And this is typical of Russia today. We don't have to have anything to do with politics!' I cited Ehrenburg's opinion. 'Very good,' said Diaghilev, 'we'll try to meet Ehrenburg and talk to him.' He then mentioned the artist Yakulov,[3] recently arrived from Russia where he had lived through the whole Revolutionary era. A range of models of his Moscow theatre settings had formed part of the Russian section of the Great Exhibition, as had a project commissioned from him for a memorial to some revolutionaries who had perished in Baku. I had myself been to this part of the Exhibition and had seen his work. Both the Constructivist scenery and the memorial (an enormous tower, spiralling upwards several storeys high) had impressed me very much, and so I was not at all averse to meeting Yakulov. It was decided that after lunch Kokhno and I would go in search of both Ehrenburg and Yakulov, neither of whose addresses did we know, and try to get everyone together with Diaghilev at five o'clock.

In order to track down Ehrenburg I suggested going to the café where I had first met him, as he had told me he was always there around two or three

---

1 *Sic*. Pavel Koribut-Kubitovich, Diaghilev's much loved cousin and faithful factotum for most of his nomadic life with the Ballets Russes, universally known as Pavka, not Pashka.
2 Khristian Rakovsky (Christiu Stanchev, 1873–1941), Bulgarian-born journalist, Soviet politician and diplomat, had been part of Trotsky's entourage during the unilateral peace talks that led to the Treaty of Brest-Litovsk. In 1923 he was appointed Foreign Minister of Ukraine shortly before being appointed USSR plenipotentiary to London. Firmly in the Trotsky camp as regards world revolution, he had been active in the Second International and a founder member of the Comintern. Already marginalised within the Party as a member of the Left Opposition, his postings as Ambassador first to London and then to Paris were preludes to the inevitable recall in the autumn of 1927, expulsion from the Party at the Fifteenth Congress and internal exile to Astrakhan. Here he languished until arrest and inclusion in the 1938 Show Trial of the Twenty-One, following which he received a prison sentence of twenty years and was executed in 1941.
3 Georgy Yakulov (1884–1928), Armenian-born painter and stage designer. In Moscow Yakulov's restless desire for innovation and experimentation had given him a reputation as something of a wild man even among artists. Affiliations with Futurism and Constructivism soon led from the canvas to three-dimensional installations and design; in the early years of the twentieth century he was already collaborating with the young Meyerhold on interiors for the 'Pittoresque' and 'Pegasus's Stall' artists' cafés. By 1925 Yakulov had become one of the most prominent stage designers of Moscow theatrical productions.

o'clock in the afternoon. Although there was hardly anyone in the café, there indeed was Ehrenburg, and so after a brief conversation during which he agreed to rendezvous with Diaghilev at five and told us where Yakulov was staying, we continued on our way to the latter. However, he was not at home so we left a note and went to see Suvchinsky, whom we did find. Kokhno waxed philosophical about the importance of the libretto in ballet, causing us much private amusement, nevertheless we did arrive at an important conclusion, namely that Kokhno himself confessed his lack of competence to create a libretto based on contemporary life in Russia – probably feeling the time had come to absent himself from the field of battle. In this way the threat of my having to collaborate with him evaporated. Kokhno then left us, while Suvchinsky and I began making our way to Diaghilev, as by now it was almost five o'clock. Ehrenburg arrived soon after, and we sat for quite a long time in the bright and spacious salon of the Hôtel Vouillemont waiting for Diaghilev to appear, which he eventually did. The discussion began inauspiciously before settling into a debate between Diaghilev and Ehrenburg while Suvchinsky maintained a dogged silence, interjecting no more than a couple of minor observations. I also sat and listened. There were a good many digressions from the main topic, for instance a fairly lengthy argument about what exactly Constructivism consisted of. For the most part Diaghilev was asking about Russia and Ehrenburg expounded. Nothing concrete was achieved on this day, and by eight o'clock it was time to go. Diaghilev wrote down Ehrenburg's address and promised to contact him over the next few days. To me he said that tomorrow we must set up another meeting, this time with Yakulov.

19 July

Next morning we again foregathered in the Hôtel Vouillemont salon but this time the group consisted of Yakulov, myself, Diaghilev, Lifar and Kokhno. Yakulov is a man of about forty, with pronounced Armenian features and a startling violet waistcoat. He had brought with him a whole portfolio of drawings and sketches of his Moscow productions as well as the project for the Baku tower. He showed all of this to us, but mainly to Diaghilev, accompanying his exposition with copious and involved explanations. The general impression was of someone desperately anxious to arouse Diaghilev's interest, but unsure of where exactly this interest might lie, all the time probing the ground, showing first one style and the another, inundating Diaghilev the while with a stream of confusing explications. In answer to the latter's enquiry whether it was feasible to create a ballet on the subject of contemporary life in Russia he replied that it unquestionably was. His response to the question whether or not it was necessary to collaborate with

Ehrenburg was equivocal because it was obvious that he was not sure what relations existed between Diaghilev and Ehrenburg, but still managing to leave the impression that should it be necessary it would be perfectly feasible to bypass the latter. The upshot of the discussion was that Diaghilev seemed pleased with Yakulov, but we had not settled on the actual subject of the ballet. It was decided that I would today pack up and leave Paris and go to Marlotte, but would return for another session with Diaghilev in two days' time. In the meantime Diaghilev would have further talks with Yakulov, and Yakulov would give some thought to a subject.

At 4.22 Ptashka, I, Svyatoslav and a young Swedish woman (our new nanny, a very nice girl) departed from the Gare de Lyon en route for Marlotte. Even though one trunk had been sent on by American Express and we left two boxes at the publisher's, we still had twenty-five pieces of luggage with us.

The journey to Bourron, where we had to disembark, took two hours. We had left Paris under clear skies, but it was now pouring with rain. Ready to take us the kilometre and a half to the house was a van we had ordered in advance by telegram, and when we arrived the owner was waiting with an umbrella, a kind thought. He was very nice and helped us carry in the luggage – a great contrast with pig-face Lapin. I handed over 1,800 francs for half our rent, and he proceeded with the inventory, everything clean and new, spick and span as a new pin, after which he mounted his bicycle and rode away. A charming Frenchman. We slept the sleep of the dead, savouring the stillness.

20 July

Our house has turned out to be much better than it had seemed to us before. There are hardly any neighbours: on the other side of the street is a school which is empty during the summer, and the mayor's office. A farmer's wife lives in a detached house in the other street, and that is all. No wonder it is so quiet, with nobody singing, no out-of-tune pianos, no gramophones. The country immediately round about is open, pleasant French fields dotted with single trees, but a hundred paces away is the edge of the forest of Fontainebleau which stretches for tens of kilometres. We have a mass of places to walk: in the forest, across the fields, and along the river. Our property also boasts a garden, quite small but full of flowers. The house itself has a bathroom, electricity, and a comfortable armchair in my study – in a word we are all delighted. I settled down to work, but since as yet there is no piano, nor any agreement with Diaghilev, I concentrated on putting the final touches to Op. 35bis.[1]

---

1   The version for violin and piano of the *Five Songs Without Words*.

21 July

Went to Paris to meet Diaghilev. It is quite a long way: more than two hours' journey. Once again we met in the same hotel: Diaghilev, Yakulov and I. While I was away Yakulov had presented Diaghilev with an outline scenario for the ballet. His idea was that it should consist of three elements, representing three different aspects of Bolshevik life: the first being Sukharevsky Square,[1] complete with bagmen,[2] commissars, the bustle of the market, sailors with bracelets; the second would be the world of NEP,[3] a comic number about dubious get-rich-quick speculators; and the third a scene in a factory or showing life on a collective farm (Russia is starting to rebuild herself). Diaghilev and I generally approved the plan, but Diaghilev was unhappy about the second strand, the NEP, saying that essentially this was poking fun at the nouveaux-riches, which would not be much of a novelty in Paris where countless numbers of people had flourished in exactly this way after the war. Yakulov stuck up for his scenario, but soon conceded defeat on the second element. The whole ballet he envisaged graphically as three discs, presented in a row, the outer two of which would encroach on the middle one, annexing part of it. In this way the central component, the NEP section, would be quite short although aspects of it should be introduced towards the end of the first section and at the beginning of the last. Diaghilev did not object to this, but I said I did not see how I was going to represent NEP musically. Yakulov replied, 'It has to be a scherzo.'

After this Diaghilev excused himself on the grounds of having other business to attend to, telling Kokhno to take us to lunch. Because Kokhno had

---

1 Sukharevsky Square is on Moscow's Garden Ring Road, more or less due north of Red Square, and in the sixteenth century was the area in which the *streltsy* (the musketeers who formed the backbone of the Russian army until the military reforms of Peter the Great) had their barracks. According to legend the famous Sukharev Tower, one of the architectural landmarks of Moscow until its barbaric destruction by Stalin in 1934, was erected by Peter in gratitude for the actions during the August 1689 uprising against him and his stepsister of one *strelets* commander, Lavrenty Sukharev, who alone among his peers committed his regiment to the defence of the young Tsar, effectively saving his life and his reign. The square was also the location of one of Moscow's busiest and most colourful markets.
2 During the years of War Communism that immediately followed the Revolution and Civil War, the famine in the cities, brought about largely by Lenin's insistence on the complete abolition of private commerce (the *prodrazvyorstka*), was so extreme that an entire black-market culture of 'bagmen' had grown up in which bag-carrying entrepreneurs would hitch rides on freight trains (there were virtually no passenger trains anyhow), go into the villages and buy or steal produce from the peasants which they would bring back to sell in street markets such as the one in Sukharevsky Square. A similar situation prevailed in Germany, as is well described in Erich Maria Remarque's 1931 novel *The Way Back* (*Der Weg Zurück*). See also *Diaries*, vol. 2, p. 400n.
3 The New Economic Policy promulgated by Lenin in 1921 in recognition of the overwhelming need to salvage something from the collapsing Russian economy by mitigating the stringency of its predecessor, the *prodrazvyorstka*, allowing a limited amount of private enterprise.

again started his old trick of interfering in the discussion about the subject of the ballet, I decided to put him in his place. As soon as we had parted from Diaghilev and were out on the street I went on the attack over his unshaven chin, which I declared made him an impossible companion for respectable people to go to lunch with. Kokhno, who is extremely good-looking and extremely vain, went over to look in a mirror in a shop window, and agreed that his toilet left something to be desired.

'Please, go and have a shave,' I said.

'After lunch.'

'No, before lunch. You quite spoil my appetite.'

'All the barbers are closed at the moment.'

'No, it is already two o'clock and they will just have opened.'

'Sergey Sergeyevich, I trust you are not serious . . .'

'I am perfectly serious. It is out of the question to have lunch sitting opposite a pug-face. Off you go; we will reserve a table in the restaurant and wait for you.'

Kokhno shrugged his shoulders and went off to be shaved. Yakulov and I, still talking about the ballet, went to the restaurant, where we were joined twenty minutes later by Kokhno.

'What a pleasant sight a good-looking man is,' I said as he took his place on the other side of the table.

'Certainly more pleasant than the sight of a pernickety fusspot,' Kokhno parried, but thereafter conducted himself with decorum.

Yakulov recounted how in his youth he been very interested in music and had even contemplated making a career in it but had soon abandoned the idea. He had spent the entire war at the front, had been wounded and decorated. As a result, when there was shooting in Moscow during the Revolution he had been able calmly to carry on painting. He had continued to live permanently in Russia afterwards, and had completely grown into the new regime. A faintly ludicrous figure, there is also something about him that is slightly repellent, as there is with anyone who has survived the rise of Bolshevism in Russia and found even a partial accommodation with it.

When we returned to Diaghilev, he thought that Yakulov's schema was acceptable in general terms but needed fleshing out in details. Yakulov said that he had plenty of material and ideas. Diaghilev said that he was postponing his departure yet again, and since we did not yet have a subject solid enough to stand on its own two feet I would need to come for another meeting as soon as Yakulov had fully worked out his ideas. Yakulov promised to come back with some sketches for the settings and costumes, and on that note we parted. Obviously there are going to have to be more visits to Paris.

On my return home I found the upright piano had been delivered. There was also a letter from Szigeti in which he asked me if I could come to Paris to see him and to meet a certain Krasin,[1] a representative from the Russian Philharmonia, who apparently had some business with me. Krasin was also the Ambassador's brother.[2] Moving in anti-Bolshevik circles as I do all the time, I have become accustomed to not having anything to do with Bolsheviks for fear of 'taint by association'. But I knew from Myaskovsky's letters that this Krasin was a decent fellow, and besides I was curious to know what the business might be that he wanted to discuss with me. Lastly, I had good reasons for wanting to see Szigeti, which is why I replied to him that I would be in Paris in two days' time and would call on him in order to present him with the piece dedicated to him.

Here I was referring to the transcription of Op. 35: three of the pieces I had dedicated to Kokhánski; one (the one she played) to Cecilia; and one to Szigeti as the chief exponent of my Violin Concerto. In practice if not on paper all the original songs were dedicated to Koshetz, but she rarely sings them and then only one of them, and in any case surely a different version may be dedicated anew! But Koshetz will be beside herself!

22 July

Made the final revisions to Op. 35, and will send them to Kokhánski for a last check-over.

A letter from Magdeburg: they are interested in the possibility of producing *Chout*. Nice to think that even small cities are beginning to take an interest in me.

23 July

Started on an orchestral overture for Romanov's ballet. The work is going smoothly.

---

1 Boris Krasin (1884–1936) had been involved in left-wing cultural movements since before the 1905 Revolution, and soon after the October Revolution of 1917 was appointed Director of the music section of the Moscow branch of Proletkult, the ambitious proletarian cultural movement that attracted many adherents from the artistic avant-garde, so much so that by late 1920 Lenin saw dangers in its radical iconoclasm and its bid for autonomy from the iron discipline of the Party, and took steps to clip its wings. Krasin prudently stepped sideways to the less controversial environment of the Russian Philharmonia, the nationwide orchestral and concert organisation.
2 Leonid Krasin (1870–1926) had a long history of involvement in Bolshevik terrorism, having been (with Maxim Litvinov and Stalin) one of the co-conspirators in the 1907 Tiflis Bank Robbery. After a successful career in the West as an electrical engineer, during which he made a great deal of money, he returned to the new Soviet Union to be appointed Commissar of Trade with a seat in the Central Committee. He became the USSR's first plenipotentiary to Paris, appointed immediately France recognised the nation in 1924. The following year he was in London negotiating Great Britain's formal recognition of the Bolshevik government but was taken ill and died while there. He was cremated at Golders Green Crematorium and the ashes transported to the Kremlin Wall Necropolis in Moscow.

A letter from Lapin's wife, an exceedingly unpleasant one, presenting a bill for 1,500 francs for *dégats*.[1] We were upset and angry, and discussed what to do. Damn them! They are so rich anyhow.

24 July

Back to Paris. Yakulov had brought a stack of very interesting sketches for costumes (a commissar, a sailor), also of sets, all steel-grey in colour and with platforms of varying heights. Diaghilev admired them, and this surprised me greatly as always before he had aimed at settings that would be as portable as possible so that they could be easily shipped. How on earth he thought he was going to be able to tour these complicated structures about I could not imagine.[2] At all events the visual side of the ballet's plot was now somewhat clearer, even if the subject itself had not fully revealed itself. Yakulov had promised by today to fill out his concept of the three 'spheres', but his exegesis was so confused and woolly that Diaghilev did not hide his exasperated concern: 'We're simply going to have to commission someone or other to produce a scenario, otherwise we're never going to get anywhere. It's not so difficult to think up a subject, but we cannot afford to take an ordinary Western European plot to Soviet Russia. In the Russia of today people think, and love, and enjoy themselves differently, and so our only solution is to ask a Soviet author to write the libretto.'

But who? We thought and thought, but nobody in Paris came to mind. We reverted to Ehrenburg. Yakulov and I wrinkled our brows – only as a last resort. But Diaghilev disagreed: Ehrenburg had made a very favourable impression on him. Disagreeable personality he might be, but he was clever and observant. We yielded, but argued for bringing Ehrenburg in as a consultant, in other words not to end up with a specifically Ehrenburg libretto but merely to pay him for his advice and his sources of information while we would develop the final libretto ourselves, in short to squeeze everything we could out of him and then send him on his way. On this we parted, with a request to return to Paris in two days' time.

I went round to call on Szigeti. He was away on tour, so at home were only his wife and B. B. Krasin, who seems to be staying with them. Krasin is tall, with prominent cheekbones, coarse-featured but pleasant in manner, with a faint air of the seminary about him. He speaks simply, but at the same with a conscious effort to use language well, which causes him to wrinkle his nose. With him was a young Jew, a good-looking youth, very calm and self-possessed. I could not rid myself of the thought that Krasin was not a true

---

1 Damages (Prokofiev uses the French word).
2 See below, pp. 652–3.

Communist whereas the young man was there in the capacity of the true believer, the ears and eyes of Moscow.

'Well, Sergey Sergeyevich,' began Krasin, 'it really is time you came to Moscow!'

I said I thought it was too.

'I've brought you an offer from the Central Executive Committee.'[1]

He extended a document to me and unfolded it. I instinctively put out my hand to take it, but he turned the document round in such a way as to allow both of us to read it. He did not give me the paper, but started to read it out loud. I aborted my gesture in mid-stream, concluding that his orders did not extend to letting me have the document.

Krasin then read through a proposal from the Committee that I should compose a 'cinema symphony' (!) in celebration of the twentieth anniversary of the 1905 Revolution. 'If it is difficult for you to tailor the music precisely to events in the film, you can simply write an overture and some separate numbers. The jubilee event itself will consist of a gala concert in the Bolshoy Theatre attended by representatives from all over Russia.'

He added, 'I told them, Prokofiev won't come cheap. But the answer was, that's all right, we'll pay.'

But it was obvious to me that this was not a proposal I could possibly accept. Saying yes would mean signing up to Bolshevism, and goodbye to any career in bourgeois countries! Not to mention my dislike of any political involvement whatsoever. However, I felt it was important not to offend Krasin, and so I enquired, 'And when would this have to be delivered?'

'By the New Year.'

'Oh dear, I am afraid that this commission has come too late: I have just accepted a commission from Diaghilev. I should not be able to fulfil both, and it is impossible for me to turn down Diaghilev at this stage.'

'Well, think about it, Sergey Sergeyevich,' said Krasin, 'and then give me your final answer.'

Saying this he laid the document on the table, but I hesitated to touch it, and he then went on to talk about a concert tour of Russia he would like to invite me to make, on behalf of the State Philharmonia. As by this time I was in a great hurry to get to Diaghilev, we left it that on my next visit to Paris I would once again call on Szigeti and we would talk further about the concerts.

---

1   The Central Executive Committee (Tsentral'nyi Ispolnitel'nyi Komitet or TSIK) of the USSR was the supreme executive organ of the Government between 1922 and 1938 when it was replaced by the Supreme Soviet, as distinct from the Central Committee (Tsentral'nyi Komitet or TSK) of the Communist Party. Its principal Chairman was Mikhail Kalinin (representing the Russian Federation) although theoretically the chairmanship rotated to allow representation from other republics of the Soviet Union.

Incidentally, he promised to find out the address of Ekskuzovich,[1] who had just arrived in Paris. When I said that I very much wanted to speak to Ekskuzovich about the forthcoming production of *Oranges*, Krasin replied, 'And Ekskuzovich very much wants to talk to you.'

I went back to Diaghilev, but nothing new had transpired. It was decided that tomorrow he would see Ehrenburg and squeeze him dry. Then after two more days I would come again to Paris. When Yakulov accompanied me to the station, I said to him, 'You are always saying that you have lots of material for the subject of the ballet, but when it comes to the point you wander off the point into a maze of obscurity.' Yakulov then embarked on a recital of the scene: here we would have cigarette-sellers, here ladies wearing lampshades transformed into hats, here some hoodlums escaping from the commissars by swinging on ropes attached to the grid from one platform to another, here factory workers with hammers (I really liked this! You could have the hammers as percussion instruments on the stage!), here someone making a speech from a book attached to him with a rubber band so that when he throws the book away it comes straight back to him. Suddenly before my eyes was a complete picture of a Bolshevik ballet. I said to Yakulov, 'It's true, you really do have a mass of ideas; all we need to do is pull them into shape, and we have our ballet, there's no need for any Ehrenburg.' 'That's just what I've been saying,' rejoined Yakulov. But what he lacked was the ability to weld it into a coherent whole.

25 July

How good it was to be in the country!

I am finishing off the overture to Romanov's ballet.

26 July

Made a piano version of the Overture.

---

1 Ivan Ekskuzovich (1882–1942). Following the October Revolution Ekskuzovich had replaced Telyakovsky as head of the Petrograd State Theatres, including the Mariinsky, but by now (after 1923) had risen to take control of all the principal theatres of the Russian Federation which meant that he was also responsible for the Bolshoy Theatre in Moscow. At the time in 1918 when *The Gambler* was still going to be produced in the Mariinsky Theatre, Prokofiev was still trying to extract an agreement from Ekskuzovich in the last days before leaving the country with his exit permission from Lunacharsky. Eventually Prokofiev, without having a face-to-face meeting with Ekskuzovich, had to depart with no agreement, leaving Suvchinsky with power of attorney to sign any contract that was eventually offered. None was. Bearing in mind the circumstances Ekskuzovich was naturally not to blame for the fact that the production never took place as planned, but the arguments about the contract, the delay in concluding it and the consequent non-payment of the provisionally agreed down payment of 6,000 roubles had soured relations at the time.

27 July

Paris again. I left at seven in the morning and got back at eleven at night. I dropped into the publishers, and as there was still time before I was due to meet Diaghilev I called on Suvchinsky, whom I found just getting out of bed. I gave him an account of how things were going with the ballet, to which his reaction was: 'I still don't see how you are going to make a ballet of it.' He then told me about Vera Guchkova, who is related to Rachmaninoff and has been staying with him for a few days. Rachmaninoff has married his daughter off to a high-society Prince Volkonsky, and because the Prince is studying painting in Paris Rachmaninoff decided to spend the summer in detestable France, detestable because everyone laughs at his music here. He is renting a splendid castle near Versailles, and Medtner has settled into a more modest dacha in the vicinity. They spend a lot of time together. Soon after Guchkova had arrived, Medtner appeared and Rachmaninoff laughingly said, 'Now, Nikolay Karlovich, I've long been looking forward to the moment of you two getting together. Vera Alexandrovna is a great admirer of Stravinsky and Prokofiev, neither of whom you can stand.' Medtner lost his temper: 'You just find it amusing, but I lie awake at nights trying to work out what makes them tick!' Poor old Medtner!

I continued on to Diaghilev. He had seen Ehrenburg, but I had the impression that on this occasion Diaghilev had not so much squeezed anything out of Ehrenburg as Ehrenburg had eaten Diaghilev alive. According to Diaghilev he had tried his best to explain to Ehrenburg that his role was to be not the author of the libretto but an adviser. Diaghilev: 'I even told him that Prokofiev always writes his own librettos, and he is a horrible person who cannot bear anyone collaborating with him.' But Ehrenburg retorted in no uncertain terms that the idea of participating as an adviser did not appeal at all. But if Diaghilev wanted to commission a libretto he was ready to get to work. He would set the first scene not in a market but at a railway station, because in the early stages of Bolshevism railway stations were archetypal places for trade and the haggling that went on between bagmen and starving city-dwellers.

Diaghilev was inclining towards commissioning Ehrenburg, and when the latter appeared Diaghilev took him off into a neighbouring room to discuss terms and conditions, eventually emerging in a very bad temper. Shortly afterwards Ehrenburg took his leave, with Diaghilev promising to write to him within a few days. After Ehrenburg had left, Diaghilev exclaimed angrily, 'Imagine that! Here's a man without so much as a pair of trousers to call his own, and as soon as you suggest working together, he tries to sting you for five million!' It emerged that Ehrenburg had asked Diaghilev for 5,000 francs, giving him to understand at the same time that although he was willing to write a libretto, it was not a project of any great interest to him. Apparently it was this last aspect that had so particularly enraged Diaghilev.

I decided the time was right to strike, so I said, 'Sergey Pavlovich, my feeling is that Yakulov's rambling presentations made you think that he does not have much in the way of material, but after our last meeting, when he and I were in a taxi going to the station, I managed to worm out of him a great store of fascinating ideas and plot outlines, so much so that there suddenly opened before me a complete picture of Bolshevik life and of our ballet. The only thing Yakulov lacks is the organisational impetus to pull all this material together into a coherent whole, but that I can supply. Now you have had a tiff with Ehrenburg, and that is all to the good. I suggest that tomorrow Yakulov comes out to me in the country and in one day we will be able to create the libretto. If you approve what we come up with, that will settle the matter, but if not, Ehrenburg won't be going anywhere for a couple of days.'

Diaghilev's response to this tirade was considerably more welcoming that I had expected: evidently Ehrenburg had succeeded in thoroughly offending him. It was decided that Yakulov would come down to Marlotte the day after tomorrow, after which we would all get together once again.

Today also saw the signing of my contract with Diaghilev, who had evidently heard of my negotiations with Krasin and my planned meeting with Ekskuzovich. The signing of the contract was preceded by lively haggling, mainly about the timetable (when the score must be delivered, how long Diaghilev would have the rights to the ballet, and so on). Most things I conceded; Diaghilev gave way only on a few minor points.

After this I went back to Szigeti's apartment, and Krasin. Szigeti appeared fleetingly and then disappeared again. I talked to Krasin and the young Jew, Tutelman by name.[1] They offered me a tour of ten concerts, one with orchestra apiece in Moscow and Leningrad, and two recitals apiece in Moscow, Leningrad, Kharkov and Rostov. They asked about my fee. Because I judged that in the present circumstances good relations were more important than a few hundred extra dollars, and in any case I had no desire to fleece an already bankrupt Russia, I said, 'I don't wish to make a fortune out of you, so please tell me what you would consider appropriate in the circumstances.' Clearly this produced a most favourable impression; they even went so far as to look rather sheepish and had to confer privately. Eventually

---

1 When Prokofiev made his first return visit to the Soviet Union eighteen months later he found that Tutelman had been dismissed in dubious circumstances from the All-Russian Philharmonia (Rosphil) but had found another position as a representative of the Ukrainian State Theatres, in which capacity he proposed a concert tour of the Ukraine and Georgia, which after some hesitation Prokofiev accepted. See below, pp. 465–562 *passim*.

Tutelman proposed two possibilities: either they would pay $200 per concert, or $150 plus 25 per cent (I think it was) of the net takings. They considered that the second proposal would be the fairer, and assuming success, of which they were not in doubt, would be more advantageous for me as well. I said that the most important thing for me would be a cast-iron guarantee that I would be free to leave the country and travel abroad again, and that we could revert to the subject of the fee since it was unlikely I would be able to come next season, which was already fully accounted for as far as I was concerned; the earliest would be the autumn of next year. Krasin asked, 'May we take it that your attitude to such a visit is basically favourable, and can we announce to the press that you are intending to come?' I: 'Oh yes, certainly.' Tutelman, whose initial demeanour had been rather cool and suspicious, was now much mollified and clapped me on the knee.[1]

Incidentally, they had also been to see Medtner, who told them that he had rented his house near Paris for a whole year and intended to work there all the time, but after that he would happily return to Russia not merely for a visit but permanently. They had attempted to see Rachmaninoff, but he had declined to meet them, saying, 'I know they will try to get me back to Russia, but I have given my solemn pledge that I am not going to go, so there is nothing to discuss.' Krasin then gave me Ekskuzovich's telephone number, saying he (Ekskuzovich) was very anxious to meet me, and also handed me the paper he had held on to at our last meeting, asking me to reply in writing so that he would have something to show on his return to Moscow. With that we parted.

28 July

Composition of Romanov's *Matelote*.

29 July

Carried on with the *Matelote*. Yakulov arrived at two o'clock. For a while we engaged in small talk with Ptashka, mostly about Russia, and then felt it was

---

1 At some point during the next few weeks Prokofiev received a letter from Nadezhda Bryusova, a member of the Arts Department of the State Academic Council, delegated by Lunacharsky to offer specific guarantees to certain prominent Russian artists living abroad. The letter stated: 'The People's Commissar for Enlightenment Anatoly Vasilievich Lunacharsky instructs me to convey the following to you: "The government agrees to your return to Russia. It agrees to grant you full amnesty for all prior offences, if any such occurred. It stands to reason that the government cannot grant such amnesty for counter-revolutionary activities in the future. It likewise guarantees complete freedom of travel into and out of the USSR as you desire." I am certain that the entire musical world of our Union will sincerely welcome your return.'

time to get to work. As it was a lovely day we decided to discuss the scenario while going for a walk. Hardly noticing where we were going we got as far as Grez, a village on the banks of the river Loing,[1] which is particularly picturesque hereabouts, with its old bridge, fast-flowing stream and overhanging trees. Just by the bridge, right down on the waterside, we espied a garden with some tables in it. This turned out to be a hotel, 'La Poule d'eau'.[2] We went inside, and ordering coffee, set to work on the libretto. Yakulov laid out his material, and I tried to fashion it into something convincing. First of all I decreed that the opening scene should be not Sukharevsky Square but a railway station – the sole useful contribution we had gleaned from Ehrenburg. Inspiration thereupon descended on me, and the first act speedily took shape, very much as it has remained. At first we got stuck on Act Two, but then again a ray of light burst in, and the act assumed the following form: the scene changes, we are in a factory working at full stretch, machinery revolves, hammers hammer. After a while a separate episode unfolds on the forestage: an orator castigates the regime and departs with his suitcases to go abroad, to the satirical accompaniment of a young female worker and a sailor. Work carries on in the factory. But suddenly the managing director enters and announces that because of a shortage of raw materials and funds the factory will have to close. Account books are produced, but the workers indignantly chase the managing director away. Facts, nevertheless, are facts; they cannot be so easily ignored, and the factory ceases work. An unhappy meeting of the hands discusses what to do. At this moment, to the noisy accompaniment of side-drums and capering somersaults, a children's procession passes by (Yakulov says this is a typical event in present-day Moscow), joined by the young female worker and the sailor. The procession passes on, but the sailor stays to persuade the workers that instead of yielding to despair they should engage in gymnastic exercises, because the health of the body is the most valuable asset of all. The ballet ends with vigorous PT.

---

1   Grez-sur-Loing is best known to music-lovers as the home of Delius from 1897 until his death in 1934. The house in Grez actually belonged to the German artist Jelka Rosen, who was Delius's lover and – from 1903 – wife.
2   'The Water Hen'. 'By the summer of 1897 all concerned [Delius and his then lover Jelka Rosen] were established in the *Poule d'eau* under the wing of the good Mme Chevillon, who for many years had mothered her big family of artists, Swedish, English, Japanese, French, Danish, American, not knowing at the time that under her roof were men and women who were destined to be widely known: August Strindberg, Robert Louis Stevenson, Carl Larson, with frequent visits from others such as Rosa Bonheur, Rodin, Corot, Oscar Wilde, Cézanne and Alfred Sisley. Everything in the hotel was done in the simplest fashion, Mme C. and her daughters doing all the work. The food was brought into the room and put on to a side table and everyone helped himself. In this way the price could be kept at a figure that even the smallest purse could manage.' (Philip T. Oyler, 'Delius at Grez', *Musical Times*, vol. 113 no. 1551 (May 1972), pp. 444–7.)

I was happy with the ambiguity of the subject: no one would be able to say whether it was pro- or anti-Bolshevik, and in that sense it was exactly what was required. Yakulov agreed, although he still had some reservations that Moscow might find it offensive, and after all it was to Moscow that he himself would be returning. In any case, we left 'La Poule d'eau' and went home, after which Yakulov returned to Paris, while I planned to go to Paris by the first train next morning in order to submit the scenario to Diaghilev. Yakulov also came up with a clever title for the ballet: *Ursignol*, based on the acronym for the official name of the Soviet Union.[1] This immediately appealed to me as suggesting half-jokingly but without giving offence both a little bear[2] and a punning caricature of Stravinsky's *Rossignol*.

30 July

By nine o'clock I was at Diaghilev's hotel, but Yakulov overslept. I outlined the plot of our scenario, which met with Diaghilev's approval. He made two observations: he wanted more development of the individual characters' sub-plots, and he did not want the ballet to end with the gymnastics but with the factory going at full blast with plenty of hammering on stage. I: 'But you yourself said that all those Komsomol gymnastic displays are so typical of contemporary Russia and that it would be a good idea to end the ballet on that note!' Diaghilev, however, could not be budged from his factory conclusion with the hammering, judging that it would be a more balletically effective ending, and I agreed with him except that it meant completely rejigging from scratch the second scene. This was to be our last meeting, because Diaghilev was leaving that evening for a month's holiday in Italy. We decided that I should have one more session with Yakulov at the 'Poule d'eau' and then, having refined and written it out, would send the complete scenario to Diaghilev in Venice.

Upon this I was given a cheque for 5,000 francs – the first advance of my fee. Yakulov, who had by this time made an appearance, then had to have his five minutes of discussion with Diaghilev about his own financial agreement, a situation gleefully exploited by Diaghilev who crowed, 'You ought to have been here earlier!' After this I took myself off to lunch, and from there to Ekskuzovich, whom I was meeting for the first time.

I had not actually met Ekskuzovich before. Shortly before I had left Petrograd, at which time he had just been appointed Director[3] and the

---

1 In French, l'Union des Républiques Socialistes Soviétiques–l'URSS.
2 In French, *ours*. The bear, as a symbol of the warrior (Old English 'beorn', Scandinavian 'bjørn', Slav languages 'med'ved' – honey-eater), lives on as the universally recognised national personification of Russia.
3 Of the Mariinsky Theatre.

question of a production of *The Gambler* had once again reared its head, he telephoned me to announce that unfortunately it would not be possible to make a decision before my departure. 'Where can you be contacted by telegraph?' he enquired. Irritated, I replied, 'In Buenos Aires, *poste restante*.' Now, Ekskuzovich proved to be a very courteous and amenable individual, and when I expressed not only my satisfaction at the prospect of a production of *Oranges* at the Mariinsky Theatre but also my readiness to accommodate him in any way I could, he blossomed. It emerged that *Oranges* would definitely be produced, possibly in Moscow as well; that they were interested in staging *Chout* and also *The Gambler*. Should I insist on revising the latter, they would be prepared to let me have the score[1] on condition that I promised them the premiere. Next, Ekskuzovich proposed that I conduct the opening performance of *Oranges*, an invitation I declined on the grounds that I was out of practice as a conductor. The whole conversation proceeded in an atmosphere of the friendliest undertakings, and when we parted I felt extremely happy with the way it had gone.

That evening I returned to Marlotte.

31 July

Finished the composition of the *Matelote*.

All in all, the month of July had been marked by an unexpected flowering of relations with Russia: now there was a real chance of going there, and of my works being produced. Hitherto there had been a complete breach.

1 August

Started orchestrating the *Matelote*.

2 August

Finished orchestrating the *Matelote*.

3 August

Made a piano score of the *Matelote*.

I am reading Leonov's *The Badgers*,[2] a new novel just published in Russia. Very interesting, astringent, and highly concentrated. Daily life in Soviet

---

1 Which Prokofiev had left in the Mariinsky Theatre library when he left Russia.
2 Leonid Leonov (1899–1994), novelist and playwright, worked as a reporter during the Civil War. His 1924 novel *The Badgers* deals with the way in which the Revolution impacted on rural

Russia is absorbing to me, especially now when I am about to start work on the ballet and have spent the last several days in close contact with people from there.

5 August

I had made a promise to Diaghilev to start working on the ballet from the 1st August, and have received my first advance. The first four days of the month I had in fact devoted to Romanov's bits and pieces, but everything is now completed and the signals are set to go. I thought about the ballet's form.

An idea occurred to me of how I might bring in 'Yablochko':[1] I should compose a theme whose contours and rhythm would be related to 'Yablochko', and then through symphonic development would gradually transform itself into the actual 'Yablochko', whereupon it would immediately revert to its former self. I then settled to composing some themes, and without difficulty came up with four. I don't know how many of them will survive.

The afternoon saw two incidents: Svyatoslav banged himself against the floor and started bawling because he had bumped his head and his leg, and snivelled until late at night. The next thing that happened was that they had lit the boiler when there was not enough water in it, so that the small amount there was boiled and spewed out brown boiling water, in counterpoint with Svyatoslav's crying.

Read more of *The Badgers* in the evening. The first time I have come across this author – a true child of Soviet Russia. It is splendid stuff. I'm absorbed in it, even though it is not easy to read because of being so dense.

August–September

Began work on *Ursignol*, starting with the themes. As a reaction to the Symphony, which no one seems to have understood (and no more do I

---

life and employs the classic trope of two brothers on opposite side of the war. Later books and plays that consolidated his reputation as a stylist and a profound dissecter both of human personality and of the issues arising from the cataclysmic formation of a new society include the play *Untilovsk*, about a remote Siberian community, and the novels *The Thief* and *Skutarevsky*. The latter 'explores the psychological problems of an eminent scientist working in a socialist state and, in what is undoubtedly an autobiographical statement, traces his development from a sceptical critic of the new order into an enthusiastic supporter' (Edward James Brown, *Russian Literature Since the Revolution*, Harvard UP, 1982). In 1934 Leonov was together with Gorky to be one of the founders of the Union of Soviet Writers.

1   'Yablochko' was one of the most popular *chastushki* of the Civil War, the words and meaning endlessly adapted (one of the great virtues of the genre) by both Reds and Whites from a traditional Moldavian and Ukrainian song: 'Hey, little apple, where do you think you're going? Into my mouth, that's where, never to return.' As in a football crowd chant, you need only to change a couple of words to turn the enemy's war cry into your own and vice versa.

understand whether it came off well or not) I have decided to write diatonic and melodious music. The composition went easily. The score was completed in rough in three weeks, by the end of August. I then recomposed, revised and polished it; this took up all of September, but alongside, in breaks from the work, I also orchestrated *The Duckling*.

Yakulov visited several times. We went out to the 'Poule d'eau' hotel in Grez and worked on the libretto there on the banks of the Loing. He was delighted with the music sketches I played him, saying they did reflect the atmosphere of contemporary Russia.

I read the whole of *The Beavers*, with much enjoyment, and also profit in respect of *Ursignol*.

The time passed very productively and pleasantly. I was overburdened with correspondence, although I must admit I sometimes indulge myself in my replies.

We did not have many visitors: Oeberg, and on one occasion the Zakharovs and the Borovskys. In September the Koussevitzkys came back from Germany and we met before they left again for America. The reasons for the meeting were the publication of Asafyev's book, and my complaints about the reluctant progress of the publishing company (as if doling out alms in the workhouse) on getting my music into print. On the latter subject the answer was that no publishing house is able to print beyond its resources, and if I am so prolific a composer, then I should have two or more publishers. To this I replied that I had no intention of leaving them, because I wanted to remain with a Russian publisher, but decent alternatives in Russian publishing houses did not exist, and foreign publishers would inevitably defraud me. Apparently this produced a favourable impression, as Koussevitzky then unveiled a new thesis, that the publishers were actually printing non-stop and producing all that was required of them. In the end we parted on good terms until our next meeting, which would be in America. I think the outcome of our talk may well be beneficial and they will be motivated to get on a bit faster with the printing. All the same, I shall not forget the implied suggestion that I move, even in part, to another publishing house.

5 October

Finished orchestrating *The Duckling*. We await the arrival of Olga Vladislavovna.[1]

---

1 Lina's mother.

6 October

Olga Vladislavovna arrived.

7 October

Telegram from Diaghilev. Paris, a three-hour wait, then I play the ballet through twice. Nine numbers (out of twelve) were approved. Length of the interval. Nouvel also liked it.

8 October

Name-days: duck, Asti. Letters. Made some revisions to the Symphony.

9 October

A bit of a headache, so did not do very much. Thought up some alterations to *Ursignol*. My strange mistake about the length of the interval.

10 October

More revisions to the Symphony. Excellent news from Gaubert:[1] *Three Oranges*. *Three Oranges* also *Chout* in Cologne.

11 October

Went with Ptashka to Paris. Leya Lyuboshitz[2] played my Violin Concerto, Wolff conducting. We were in a box: Ptashka, Maria Viktorovna,[3] Fatma Hanum and I. The performance was really rather good; I listened with the closest attention. Of course, the opening of the Concerto can still not be heard, and the passage with a tremolo background hangs in the air, with nothing to support it in the bass. The tremolo lower voices need to be much stronger. The performance enjoyed a great success. There was an attempt to call me out, but I concealed myself behind the box. After this we went to a

---

1 In his capacity as Musical Director of the Paris Conservatoire Concerts Society.
2 Leya Lyuboshitz (1885–1965), Odessa-born violinist, a student of Mlynarsky in Odessa and Ivan Grzhimaly (Jan Hřímalí, the great Czech violinist and teacher, close associate of Tchaikovsky and Arensky) in Moscow. Leya Lyuboshitz emigrated to Paris in 1924 and then to America, where she pursued a solo and chamber music career (with her pianist brother and cellist sister), and taught at the Curtis Institute in Philadelphia.
3 Borovskaya, née Baranovskaya.

rehearsal of *Trapèze*,¹ and then made our way to the Borovskys, where we were staying the night.

12 October

Rehearsed the Second Piano Concerto with Zakharov on second piano, because the way I am playing it now is like a well-brought-up young lady and I keep losing the place. Then I had all sorts of things to do and was exhausted by the time I got home in the evening. The money has arrived from Russia – I have joined the ranks of the comfortably-off. Bought a copy of *Eugene Onegin* and read it with enjoyment. B.N.B.² has vanished from the face of the earth for three months, but a week ago Oeberg saw him, alas at his old habits in the club! Rachmaninoff is off to America, for a mere twenty-five concerts at a fee of 4,000 a time, as well as 50,000 for making gramophone recordings and another 50,000 for something or other. But he is suffering terribly from neuralgia, and his eye is all swollen up.

13 October

Revised the Symphony and wrote a great many letters; corrected the second proofs of the *Classical* Symphony parts.

15 October

More of the Symphony. In fact I have now been right through the score and made changes, with the exception of the first page where I am still in two minds. But now I have to carry over all these revisions into the orchestra parts!

16 October

Paris. First orchestra read-through of the Suite from *Oranges*; it sounded horrible, as first rehearsals always do. The copyist is one Lieutenant-General Voyevodsky. I ordered two new suits, having received a cheque for $1,200 from Oeberg, with whom I lunched at the club and saw B.N. In a week's time Boris is taking a test to become a taxi-driver, and showed me a list of streets he must memorise. It is a whole new world of one-way streets. Meeting with Yakulov, who had a clutch of interesting sketches.

1 The name Romanov had, with Prokofiev's agreement, been given to the ballet the score of which now consisted of the Quintet movements with the additional Overture and *Matelote* numbers.
2 Boris Bashkirov.

Diaghilev, where I met Larionov and Kokhno, both of whom were very enthusiastic about the ballet. Judging by his mood, I seem to have impressed Diaghilev as well. The main discussion was between Diaghilev and Yakulov about whether there should be beauty in the depiction of contemporary life in Russia. As I took my leave Diaghilev was keeping up appearances, bestowing a tender smile on me without interrupting the flow of his conversation. Ptashka is annoyed that Bashkirov comes to see us and that, of course, I give him some money. We even had a quarrel on the subject.

17 October

Received the proofs of Op. 35bis[1] and went through them all. There were interesting letters from Derzhanovsky in Moscow, Haensel in New York and Casella in Rome. I get a lot of letters and I write a lot myself, but the sheer quantity of correspondence oppresses me.

18 October

A headache made work difficult, but I still managed to do quite a lot on correcting the proofs of the *Classical* Symphony parts.

19 October

Dealt with correspondence. Finished the *Classical* Symphony proofs. Began thinking about the orchestration of *Ursignol*. Evidently the trick is to think everything out to the last detail and make notes, then it is quick to write out.

21 October

The end of my period of sustained work. Commenced packing up to leave.

22 October

Departure. Landlord very nice. We parted on good terms, with mutual exchange of compliments. Dragged ourselves and our million impedimenta back to the city. Olga Vladislavovna. Svyatoslav and his Nanny went to a *pension* in St Cloud, Ptashka and I for one night to a small hotel, but tomorrow we shall have a room in the Victoria Palace, one of the few hotels that allow one to bring in a piano.

---

1   The *Five Songs Without Words* in their version for violin and piano.

23 October

From early morning, a mass of business affairs. Went to Diaghilev about a further cheque and to find out by when the piano score must be delivered. Diaghilev was affable but busy and our conversation was inconsequential. Dukelsky is ecstatic at the prospect of seeing me, but how sincere is he really? He dropped in for a moment at our hotel in the evening, was vicious about Moscow composers, at which I grew angry and responded in kind about Poulenc and Auric, charging them with lack of both taste and technique. Dukelsky said it was impossible to talk to me, that I adamantly refused to give any thought to the direction in which music should be going while he, in contrast, had been thinking seriously about it, was quite clear about what he should be doing and was firmly establishing himself accordingly. His determination impressed me, but I remain unconvinced by the merits of Auric. We could not finish our discussion, as he had to hurry off to another appointment.

24 October

Rehearsal of *The Ugly Duckling*, sung by Koshetz and conducted by Bâton.[1] The circumstances were dreadful, since Bâton did not know the piece at all and the orchestral parts were full of mistakes. The wretched copyist had transposed the clarinet parts down three semitones instead of up three semitones, so that they were in E flat rather than A. In the afternoon I buckled down and rewrote the clarinet parts myself. Transposing up a diminished fourth is very difficult. Luckily I hit on the idea of writing them in B flat, so that they could simply be transposed up a fourth. I barely finished in time for the concert.

The *Duckling* went quite well and sounded good, but had only a moderate success partly because in the printed programme the text was poorly set out in Russian and without a translation.

In the evening I played *Ursignol* to Dukelsky and to Balanchivadze,[2] at Diaghilev's request, as he was contemplating asking the latter to

---

1 René-Emmanuel Bâton (1879–1940), Breton composer and conductor who took the pen-name of Rhené-Bâton. He had conducted for Diaghilev in the London and South American seasons of the Ballets Russes in 1912–13, and served as Principal Conductor of the Pasdeloup Concerts from 1919, the year of their revival after a lapse of thirteen years, until 1933. During his tenure he was responsible for the first performances of many notable new works, including Debussy's *Printemps* and the orchestral versions of Ravel's *Alborada del gracioso* and *Le Tombeau de Couperin*. The Orchestre Pasdeloup was and still is a self-governing organisation administered by a committee rather than under the direction of a chief executive.

2 Georgii Melitonis dze Balanchivadze (George Balanchine) (1904–1983), one of the most musical and inventive choreographers of the twentieth century. After graduating from both the Petrograd

choreograph it. Dukelsky was completely absorbed in listening, and apart from occasionally uttering cries of euphoria did not say a word. At the end his comment was that he found the (lyrical) theme of the sailor exceptional in its freshness, and the second subject of the opening number also very good; for the rest it was good, strong material, but for him personally antipathetic.

Dukelsky told me about going to see Stravinsky in Nice, where he lives in a heavily Russian-style household. He went out of his way to be kind to Dukelsky, much vodka was drunk and many colourful obscenities expressed revolving around the comparison of music with a woman. He is composing a *Serenade* which, according to his own description, is 'nasty, evil music'.[1] *En passant* he delivered a few sideswipes in my direction.

26 October

Rehearsed the Second Piano Concerto on two pianos with Dukelsky, in preparation for my forthcoming performance in Stockholm. He is a good sight-reader. He was particularly taken with the most unexpected passages, for example the transition to the solo cadenza in the first movement. After this I agreed to his request to accompany him in his Concerto, which is at present in proof.

Spent much time chasing about over visas, dentists, etc. What a life!

Our material situation has improved, consequently I have two new suits and Ptashka new dresses and so on.

Conservatoire and the Petrograd Theatre Ballet School (the post-Revolution name of the old Imperial Ballet School in which Balanchine had originally enrolled) he had defected to the West while on tour in Germany in 1924. Gravitating inevitably to Paris and the Ballets Russes, by 1925 and reincarnated as George Balanchine by Diaghilev, he was rapidly becoming a new 'favourite son' of the impresario, who appointed him, at the age of twenty-one, Balletmaster of the company in succession to Bronislava Nijinska. In all Balanchine made eleven ballets for Diaghilev including a reworking of Massine's *Le Chant du rossignol* to Stravinsky's music, and in 1927 Prokofiev's *Prodigal Son*, but *Ursignol* or, as it later became, *Le Pas d'acier*, was not one of them.

[1] The *Serenade in A* (1925), for piano. The four movements (*Hymn, Romanza, Rondoletto, Cadenza Finale*) are all short, having been conceived for phonograph recording and therefore having to fit on to one side of a 78 rpm disc. For what it is worth, in his 1936 autobiography, *Chroniques de ma vie*, Stravinsky – or rather his ghostwriter Walter Nouvel – has this to say about the compositional impulse behind this work: 'Whereas these compositions [eighteenth-century serenades] had been written for ensembles of greater or less importance, I wanted to condense mine into a smaller number of movements for one polyphonic instrument. In these pieces I represented some of the most typical moments of this kind of fête. I began with a solemn entry, a sort of hymn; this I followed by a solo of ceremonial homage paid by the artist to the guests; the third part, rhythmical and sustained, took the place of the various kinds of dance music intercalated in . . . serenades and suites of the period; and I ended with a sort of epilogue which was tantamount to an ornate signature with numerous carefully inscribed flourishes.'

28 October

Got my tickets for Stockholm. I am to receive 1,000 crowns minus 150 to the managers, which means that I actually get 5,000 francs, while the travel there and back for two comes to 4,500!

Checked the final proof of the orchestral material of the *Classical* Symphony. It is now ready for printing.

29 October

Marnold asked me to play through to him and some friends the Second Symphony. He was enthralled, and took the opportunity of berating Stravinsky.

To Meudon to visit my mother's grave. Discussed transferring it from the thirty-five-year category to perpetuity.

30 October

Met Stravinsky at the publishers. We kissed and talked for twenty minutes with the utmost cordiality. He was very interested in learning where I would be touring this winter and how much I would be paid.

Packing for the trip with Ptashka until late at night. Svyatoslav and Olga Vladislavovna are going to stay on at Clamart. We shall go there too for about three weeks when we get back from Sweden; Olga Vladislavovna will try to find a room for us near by, which I am very happy about as living in the hurly-burly of Paris is sheer torture.

31 October

Rose at six, and at ten past eight left Paris for Stockholm. Saw the Brichands in Liège. Andryusha has got married. Met, and were invited to dinner with, Szenkár in Cologne. The opera company will produce *Chout* this year. They definitely want to produce *The Fiery Angel*, and whereas when I had raised it with him during the *Oranges* run Szenkár's response had been provisional, he now wanted to make it a firm commitment. I did not say either yes or no, putting the blame for my indecision on the publishers, as if to say I was dependent on them. But should I in fact not let Berlin have it?

1 November

Slept very well in our *Schlafwagen*, Ptashka less well, the first time we have shared a sleeper.

Berlin next morning, where we saw Weber[1] and Kurtz.[2] Changed trains to excellent Swedish rolling stock.

The four-hour ferry crossing of the gulf, with the train on board, was quite rough, not quite enough to make one sick but enough to make the gorge rise. By nightfall we were in Sweden, with a comfortable sleeping car. The previous night, in Malmö, there had been a bad rail crash, in which sleeping cars had been derailed and overturned, and had it not been for our training in Christian Science we would have been very unpleasantly nervous.

2 November

Stockholm at 9 a.m.; Mme Nobel was there to greet us on the platform. She is a friend of Samoilenkos and two months ago had invited us to stay with her. Her husband is a descendant of the famous Nobel, instigator of the Prize.[3]

Rehearsal at eleven o'clock, conducted by Dobrowen.[4] A swarthy, animated, nicely mannered and extremely attentive individual, he accompanies well, better than Koussevitzky.

---

1   Fyodor Weber, Berlin manager of Russian Musical Editions.
2   Efrem Kurtz (1900–1995), St Petersburg-born conductor who had studied with Tcherepnin and Glazunov, and later with Nikisch. Noted as a ballet conductor (he was chosen by Anna Pavlova to conduct her numerous tours), he was Chief Conductor of the Ballet Russe de Monte Carlo from 1932 until 1942, subsequently holding a number of important Symphony orchestra posts in America and Britain. A year before this meeting he had been appointed Principal Conductor of the Stuttgart Philharmonic.
3   The Mme Nobel in question seems to have been Mary Landzert Nobel, the wife of Alfred Nobel's nephew Carl and sister-in-law of Emmanuel Nobel, president of the giant Branobel oil empire and the man chiefly responsible for insisting (against vocal family opposition) that the terms of his uncle's will bequeathing the bulk of his fortune to the establishment of the Nobel Foundation and the Nobel Prizes be scrupulously adhered to.
4   Issay Dobrowen (born Itzhok Zorakhovich Barabeichik) (1891–1953), multi-talented Russian-born conductor, pianist, conductor and opera producer who eventually took Norwegian nationality after emigrating, initially to Dresden, from Russia in 1922 in response to the ominous non-renewal of his contract as Musical Director of the Bolshoy Theatre. Ironically for someone who in later life was an outspoken critic of the Bolshevik regime, Dobrowen is today chiefly remembered in his native land as the pianist who entranced Lenin with a performance of Beethoven's *Appassionata* Sonata in 1920 while staying with Maxim Gorky, a close personal friend. An enviable career as guest conductor with some of Europe's and America's most famous orchestras was curtailed when he had to leave Nazi Germany for Scandinavia in the 1930s. After the war Dobrowen became one of Walter Legge's stable of conductors for his newly founded Philharmonia Orchestra, and many of the superb HMV recordings that resulted are still in the catalogue. As for composition, an activity to which he devoted progressively less attention as his conducting and opera-producing career demanded more and more time, Dobrowen produced about twenty works mostly for piano, of which a piano Concerto and a second sonata show clear influences of Rachmaninoff, Scriabin and Medtner, and could well sustain wider recognition.

3 November

Slept round the clock from nine until nine. We find the spacious, peaceful, dimly lit flat very relaxing after the frenzy of Paris. Our hostess is very charming, critical of Sweden and full of affectionate memories of Russia. The second rehearsal also went well. Stockholm is an attractively laid out and pleasant town. I am orchestrating *Ursignol*, that is to say not writing out a full score but noting instrumentation on to the sketches.

4 November

Another rehearsal in the morning, although we could have managed without it. The concert in the evening was in the Auditorium, a large, ugly, circular hall resembling a circus. People joke that it was formerly a huge oil tank. There was a big audience. The piano was a Steinway, a good make but stiff to play. Used to the light action of the Pleyel, I misjudged the attack, and technically the cadenza was not very good, however the scherzo was. In the main subject of the finale I was too occupied in listening to the orchestra and went wrong in my part, but Dobrowen showed his mettle and caught me with great skill. The performance was a success, and I was called back three times. Dobrowen's subsequent performance of Tchaikovsky's Sixth Symphony was met with a clamorous ovation; it is a long time since I heard the Sixth and therefore was able to approach it with fresh ears: the first movement is a magnificent construction, the second the direct opposite, badly done and poor material. The Scherzo is superbly put together and mostly very beautiful, except for the end, which is bad. The conclusion of the fourth movement is astoundingly beautiful (and what a sound!), but the remainder of it is debatable.

There was a post-concert reception at the Nobels', during which I talked a lot to Dobrowen whom I liked very much and who had many entertaining things to say. We recalled the incident when, after Scriabin's death, Rachmaninoff had performed his, Scriabin's, Fifth Sonata, after which I had commented, to Rachmaninoff's great vexation, 'Well, Sergey Vasilievich, in spite of everything you played the Sonata very well.' But Dobrowen told me that there had been a far worse fracas with Alchevsky[1] when Rachmaninoff

---

1 Ivan Alchevsky (1878–1917), Ukrainian tenor, soloist at the Mariinsky and Bolshoy Theatres, guest principal also at the Paris Grand Opéra. Among his most celebrated roles were Herman in *The Queen of Spades* and Don Juan in Dargomyzhsky's *The Stone Guest*, directed by Meyerhold at the Mariinsky in 1917. Prokofiev admired him greatly as an artist and had chosen him for the role of Alexey in the Mariinsky production of *The Gambler* in 1917, but even had the production gone ahead it would have been without Alchevsky, whose sudden death from meningitis when appearing in Baku (two days after appearing in *Aida* to great acclaim) occurred in April that year. See *Diaries*, vol. 2, pp. 66, 101, 103, 109, 112, 125, 141, 146, and *passim*.

repeated his performance of the same piece in Moscow. Alchevsky, who worshipped Scriabin, was so incensed that he had to be held down by the coat-tails, but at the end of the performance he broke free, rushed up to Rachmaninoff and declared, 'How glad I am, Sergey Vasilievich, that I'm not a composer, in case when I die some ass might mangle my music just as you have done.' He was dragged away by his friends to avoid a scandal.

5 November

We were in bed by three but it was six o'clock before we fell asleep, and as a result Ptashka was exhausted from lack of sleep. Ever since leaving Paris she has been suffering from a slight hoarseness, and her concert is tomorrow. She was therefore in a very bad mood all day, and at night I was sent to sleep in another room (this apartment has plenty of bedrooms) in order that nothing should prevent the singer from having a good night. In short, our focus is now on her performances, not mine.

Our hostess translated lengthy reviews from the Swedish (there were six): neither particularly intelligent nor egregiously stupid, but needless to say my Concerto was seen as lacking depth while the Violin Concerto, which Szigeti had played here eighteen months ago, was considered the superior work. In other words, the critics fell into all the usual traps, having failed to penetrate the depths of the Second Piano Concerto and preferring the Violin Concerto purely because of its greater accessibility.

6 November

The local impresario telephoned in the morning wanting to know if the afternoon's chamber recital should be postponed because so few tickets had been sold. Postponed? But till when? The prospect of waiting around in Sweden lacked allure. We decided against postponement.

It emerged that today was the anniversary of the death of Gustavus Adolphus,[1] so the whole world would be going to a glittering gala performance at the Opera. The hall where we were performing, which was quite a large one, contained about fifty people, or perhaps fewer. The acoustic was terrible anyhow, and with the room empty practically nothing could be heard. I decided to shrug my shoulders and performed my part of the programme without bothering too much about it. But Ptashka, worried about her hoarseness, was nervous, sang badly, and was greeted with very little applause, which upset her very much.

---

1 King Gustavus Adolphus of Sweden (1594–1632), 'The Lion of the North' and de facto founder of the Swedish Empire, was killed leading a cavalry charge at the Battle of Lützen, in the Thirty Years War, on 16 November (in the Gregorian calendar) 1632.

Strangely, despite the small number of public in the hall, the impresario suggested an extra orchestral appearance in a week's time, which I declined. What could have been the reason for this invitation? Probably the local conductor (Dobrowen was a guest) had faith in me and had managed to raise some money to pay for a concert with me.[1]

7 November

Mme Nobel drove us round the countryside surrounding Stockholm. It was beautiful, but very cold.

Ptashka is most upset by her lack of success yesterday. I advised her not to pay any attention to it; it had been caused by a combination of unfavourable circumstances.

8 November

My second orchestral appearance with the Second Concerto. I played better than the first time. It was also more of a success: on this occasion, Dobrowen, conducting Borodin's Symphony, did not eclipse me. All the same, I had better polish the Concerto meticulously so that in future it goes irreproachably.

9 November

Mme Nobel brought in the reviews, which acknowledged that this time I had made a better fist of the Concerto. Then packing for departure. In the evening we left to return home, by the same train as Dobrowen.

10 November

On the steamer crossing with the Dobrowens, I was struck by the thought that I should introduce him to Diaghilev with a view to his conducting my ballet. Hamburg in the evening: M. Rein.[2]

11 November

Paris–Clamart. Our two rooms, cold.

---

1 The Stockholm Concert Society (later to be called the Royal Stockholm Philharmonic Orchestra) was in fact experiencing an interregnum in 1925. The Finnish conductor Georg Schnéevoigt was Principal Conductor from 1915 until 1924, to be succeeded by Václav Talich, but not until 1926.
2 Maria Rein, a relation of the composer.

12 November

Efforts to get some warmth into the place; the stove. I busied myself with the second proof of the *Classical* Symphony, which had hundreds of uncorrected errors.

14 November

Finished the proof and took it to the copyist.
Met Suvchinsky, who by coincidence is staying almost exactly opposite.

15 November

Began orchestrating the ballet, a very pleasant task.

16 November

Orchestrated a lot.

19 November

American visa; one of the secretaries is a Russian woman. They were friendly and gave me the visa straight away.

20 November

Went in for the rehearsal of *Oranges*, but Gaubert has postponed it; a great to-do, eventually scheduled for the 29th. A letter from S. Esche, very nice to hear from her.[1]

21 November

Koshetz's concert, a 'dog's breakfast' to quote Fatma Hanum. Koshetz sang 'For the Shores of Your Distant Homeland'.[2] The programme as a whole was vulgar. End of the concert. Suvchinsky introduced his new wife;[3] I congratulated him on a splendid choice. We travelled home together.

---

1 Sofia Esche, a romantic interest of Prokofiev at the St Petersburg Conservatoire. See *Diaries*, vol. 1 *passim*; vol. 2, p. 57.
2 Setting (1888) by Borodin of a famous elegiac lyric by Pushkin.
3 Suvchinsky had married Vera Guchkova, having divorced his former wife, the daughter of Lev Karsavin.

22 November

Thought about wherein lies the enchantment of 'For the Shores of Your Distant Homeland'. The melody, after all, is not striking; even within its limitations it could have been made more interesting. There is not a hint of counterpoint. Could it be just the harmony, and the 'feeling'? Something in music that resists analysis?!

23 November

Did more orchestration. I must get a move on, I have so much travelling coming up. When shall I ever get time to complete the ballet?

A letter from Dranishnikov. *Oranges* has gone into rehearsal in Leningrad. Ten years ago, when I first started going to the Mariinsky Theatre, what feelings of awe it inspired, the house itself with those pale blue seats! And now, when my opera will at last be seen there, I am at the other end of the world. A great shame.

27 November

Met Suvchinsky. He looks incredibly youthful and is even better looking, from happiness. Although we live across the street we hardly see one another, as we are both so busy. But I have a bone to pick with him over *Ursignol* and over Asafyev's book; in both cases I turned to him as a friend and both times he weaselled away. I felt badly let down.

28 November

General rehearsal of the *Oranges* Suite at the Conservatoire, conducted by Gaubert. Called for Suvchinsky, as he had said he would like to come. It was an open rehearsal; both the playing and the acoustic were mediocre. I am under no illusions, this is of course not one of my more important pieces, but even so it did not sound good today. I could not help thinking: did I simply write rubbish? Suvchinsky evidently did not like it much either; he said nothing.

29 November

The concert performance of the Suite. Ptashka and I were given disgustingly bad seats, in the back row of someone's box, from where I could not see the conductor at all. I was angry – typical French! The Germans would never think of putting the composer in such a position. But today they played very well indeed, the sound was fine, and the success was immediate. The March was encored. There were calls for the composer at the end, but as I had been placed out in the sticks nobody could see me and I did not have to take a bow, which suited me very well.

Later in the evening we went out to Benois at Versailles. I love him very much. Koka and Marusya were there; Marusya is staggered at Ptashka's fluency in English and Italian. She cannot understand how such a thing is possible. Koka is going up in the world: he has been engaged by La Scala to design *Khovanshchina* and is off to Milan. Marusya has fallen on her feet in society and is also putting herself about! I asked Benois casually about Idka, but he contrived to change the subject. Of course, things are different now, and I could not care less about her project. All the same, what happened with the old she-devil?

1 December

All this fuss I'm having with Demchinsky and his equivocations over *Fiery Angel*! My best hope is now Eleonora,[1] and I can see I shall have to woo her, a real marriage of convenience. I have another letter from her: she needs strings, a handbag, gloves, a scarf, all these must be offerings on the altar of *Fiery Angel*, since she promised to 'arrange matters' with Demchinsky.

I wonder how this slip of a girl can have such influence over Demchinsky? I suppose it must be something to do with the piano,[2] her misery at my anger,

---

1   Eleonora Damskaya, harpist friend of Prokofiev from Conservatoire days, for whom the original version of the piano Prelude in C, Op. 12 No. 7, was written. Her over-intrusive affection for Prokofiev and demands for intimacy had eventually got on his nerves although he frequently turned to her for help and practical advice (she had unexpectedly inherited a large fortune) in several contexts, notably interceding with Kerensky for an exemption to military call-up and with Lunacharsky for a foreign travel visa, and after he left Russia the rescue of his piano and other effects from the abandoned St Petersburg apartment. See *Diaries*, vol. 1 *passim*; vol. 2, pp. 3, 95, 95, 139, 204–12 *passim*, 260–61, 691–4, and *passim*, and above, p. 43, n. 1.
2   Prokofiev, from a safe distance, had gone to great efforts to protect the contents of the St Petersburg apartment, including the precious Rubinstein Prize piano, enlisting the help of his friends still in the city, in particular Damskaya, Suvchinsky, Asafyev and the composer Arthur Lourié, who was temporarily in an influential position as head of the music division of Lunacharsky's Commissariat of Popular Enlightenment. Damskaya did manage to do something about the piano, as the entry below for 21 February 1927, when Prokofiev visited his old Conservatoire and found the piano in Asafyev's classroom, makes clear, but on 16 December 1922 he received a letter from Damskaya admitting that all efforts to recover the other effects, including precious diaries, manuscripts and photographs, had failed. This had enraged Prokofiev. His diary entry for that day reads: 'When I first read the letter I was in a rage: at Asafyev for not having rescued and preserved the papers in time; at that scoundrel Lourié for not giving him permission to do so when he, Lourié, had the power; and at Suvchinsky, who installed his "loyal building supervisor" in my apartment, a man who then disappeared without trace and abandoned my apartment to the four winds.' See *Diaries*, vol. 1, pp. 291-4, and below, p. 522.

his indignation and promise to teach me a lesson, and in parallel with this the way she runs after Demchinsky and procures the material necessaries of life for him. That is the key to Eleonora, if I read her aright.

3 December

Left with Ptashka for Strasbourg at ten in the morning, for a concert in a small town with a small fee. But mainly it is for her sake, and it is good experience for her. We arrived in the evening, and Chevillier[1] invited us to dinner.

4 December

Practised in the afternoon for the concert: I was nervous about the Fifth Sonata, which I had completely forgotten. Some Russian students came to see me; even in a place like this you find refugees from Russia turning up. I enjoyed playing: the small hall was packed and the audience, thanks to Chevillier's efforts, knew something about new music and listened attentively. Chevillier opened the proceedings by giving a short talk (based on what I had told him) about contemporary Russian music, and spoke about Stravinsky, me and Myaskovsky. Ptashka sang quite well and in this room her voice sounded better than in the awful Stockholm hall. She got four curtain calls and Stravinsky's 'Rosyanka'[2] was encored. Personally, I had a great success with the Toccata and the Gavottes.

5 December

Return journey.

6 December

Looked out documents, clothes, various things and got them in order as I am going to Holland and will have only one night in Clamart before going to America.

7 December

Chasing around after visas and a host of other urgent matters, and a pile of business letters to write.

---

1 Acquaintance in Strasbourg who had organised the concert.
2 'Sundew', the second of two early (1908) settings of poems by Gorodetsky.

8 December

More running around in Paris. Ptashka and I went to have our portraits taken by Shumov,[1] at his invitation. At Oeberg's ran into Stravinsky; we embraced, he told me he was learning to drive a car, and I told him of the success Ptashka had enjoyed singing his songs. In the evening, dog-tired, I finished off the letters I had to write. Ptashka has not been feeling at all well, and went to see Olmsted, but found that she also was in an enfeebled state, ill and confined to her armchair. She said some odd things: one must not abuse one's body but take care of it, not get too tired, and so on. This plunged us into confusion. Were Miss Olmsted's low spirits due to illness? Or perhaps the presence of non-Christian Science relatives who were staying with her?

9 December

Left to go to Holland. Ptashka is staying for another six days for lessons, her toilette and packing (we have somehow to get all our possessions into three trunks, two chests and a countless number of suitcases. Lord, when shall we ever have a place to call our own?). In the train, I felt a pain in my heart. All summer it had given no trouble, but in October, when we were leaving Bellevue and I had to carry the suitcases, it had been bad again. I tried to control it with Christian Science. It seems to have worked; I experienced some relief! It was evening by the time we got into Holland. I could see nothing through the window, and therefore my impressions were limited to two: (a) the train was going extremely fast; (b) everything costs a great deal of money. In the same restaurant car in French territory dinner cost fifteen francs, here it was thirty-five. Nobody met me, and I took myself straight to the Amstel Hotel, where I had a room booked and where they told me that Monteux had telephoned to say that the rehearsal would be at nine o'clock in the morning.

I was stunned by the newspaper reports of Yurevskaya's suicide in Switzerland: she was said to have taken morphine, had cut her throat (and what a throat!) and had thrown herself from the Devil's Bridge into the torrent below[2] – veritably into the arms of the Devil. What can possibly have induced her to do this? What part had been played by her husband? The

---

1 Pyotr Shumov (1872–1936), Paris photographer best known for his studies of Rodin's sculptures.
2 The bridge over the Schöllenen Gorge leading to the St Gotthard Pass over the River Reuss is one of many designated as *Teufelbrücke*; this is the one crossed by Alexander Suvorov in his 1799 rearguard action to save the doomed Russian army from annihilation by the French by traversing the Alps. See *Diaries*, vol. 1, pp. 458–9.

Dutch papers were also carrying stories about her, which I translated with the help of the hotel concierge, a music-lover who had known Yurevskaya personally as she had stayed at the hotel. The Dutch papers were full of speculations that the case might be a hoax, as the body had not been found.[1]

10 December

The rehearsal began with the *Scythian Suite* (but they had already had two rehearsals before my arrival). Then Schmuller[2] in the Violin Concerto. Finally we read through No. 3 [Piano Concerto] with me as soloist, an excellent first reading. Monteux is very conscientious, precisely carries out everything I tell him and has an attentive ear for all mistakes. Schmuller is also very meticulous, takes slow tempi and plays every note. After the rehearsal I lunched with him. He had been back to Russia two years ago and therefore we had much to talk about. Essentially it was through Schmuller that I was engaged here. He is a great admirer of mine, but caustic about Stravinsky. Stravinsky had a great success here last year but had been rude to everyone and made a lot of enemies.

11 December

Once again almost the whole rehearsal was devoted to me: *Scythian Suite* and the Third Concerto. I listened to the Scythians with pleasure, imagining how people will take to it in Moscow, where it is to have three performances this winter. As for the Third Concerto, despite my 'technique, facility and rhythm' which is so written up and talked about, I am still not playing it with immaculate correctness, although I am gradually mastering it.

The Amstel is an appallingly expensive hotel. In view of Ptashka's imminent arrival I enquired about the cost of a double room – 17 florins, which is terrible by comparison with France. While in search of alternative accommodation I happened on the *pension* where Monteux is staying and the proprietors are very nice. I got two decent rooms there.

12 December

One more rehearsal. We went once through *Scythians* and once through the Third Concerto, although this was a luxury and we could have managed

---

1   The body was not found until the following April when the ice melted. There was also a suicide note, posted to her husband the morning of her death, asking for the cause of death to be reported as apoplexy in order to minimise the suffering of her family. Von Bremer, however, was forced eventually to publish the letter to still the continuing speculation.
2   Alexander Schmuller (1880–1933), Russian-born violinist and conductor who settled in Holland and would later, in 1928, become Principal Conductor of the Rotterdam Philharmonic Orchestra.

without it. I moved to the Museum *pension*, where the local Pleyel representative had already sent in a piano. Lunched with Monteux. He lives with a very pleasant American woman. In February he is going to Moscow and Leningrad, and will among other things perform *Chout*. We discussed his Moscow programme. I recommended omitting Chausson and Rabaud,[1] in neither of whom could anyone in Moscow conceivably be interested. I drew his attention to Myaskovsky's symphonies.

In the evening, the concert in The Hague. The whole orchestra, conductor and soloist were transported there by special train. The Concertgebouw generally does things in style: we were taken to the train by car, installed in first class for the journey to The Hague, and then by car to the hall where sandwiches, tea and wine were laid out in the Artists' Room, all paid for by the Concertgebouw. The hall is not as good as the one in Amsterdam, but it is large and was well filled. Amsterdam is more of a centre for music, but The Hague is an international diplomatic city. I played the first two movements well, but got tired and lost my way in a few places in the finale, so it was not as good. It was a great success, however, and I got three curtain calls, which for standoffish The Hague was said to be good going. People came round to congratulate me. Then the journey back, the cars and the special train.

13 December

The anniversary of Mama's death. I thought of her. What a shame she did not live to see the elimination of her concern so often expressed: 'But we're in a tight spot with money!'

In the afternoon *Scythians* and the Third Concerto in Amsterdam, the main event of my Dutch tour. To begin a programme with *Scythians*, having its first performance in the country, is quite something. It had a good reception, if a little restrained. After that I played the Third Concerto, better than yesterday, without getting lost, and even whipped up the tempo. Its success was exceptional, the hall (three-quarters full) rose to its feet and gave me a standing ovation. Some of the orchestra also stood, the first time in my life this has ever happened, and I was overwhelmed. Afterwards I we took tea at Schmuller's place, and spent the evening at home in the *pension*.

14 December

In the morning I went through the Concerto putting to rights what had been amiss yesterday and the day before. A letter from Ptashka, for which I have been waiting several days. She is probably arriving tomorrow.

---

1 Henri Rabaud (1873–1949), composer of conservative inclinations. He had been appointed Director of the Paris Conservatoire on the retirement of Fauré in 1922.

In the evening we travelled to Rotterdam in the same way as we had gone to The Hague the day before yesterday, except that it is a little further away. The hall in Rotterdam is smaller, and generally this performance was of lesser importance. It is the first time I have ever performed three days in a row, and I felt sleepy from fatigue. I took slightly slower tempi and played cleanly, but in the slow variation almost went fully off to sleep and made a dangerous mistake, landing in the wrong place. All the same the success was colossal: not only the whole audience but the entire orchestra rose to its feet (and what an orchestra! One of the best in Europe!). This produced a profound impression on me. Afterwards, the hour and a half journey by special train back to Amsterdam.

15 December

Ptashka arrived from Paris in the evening, to a tender reunion. But she is tired and her nerves are bad: she has been worrying herself over her dresses for America, and also is not feeling well.

16 December

A telegram: Oeberg has died suddenly. What can have happened? Can it have been his kidneys? I always had the feeling, whenever I looked at him, that he was not going to live long. The news has distressed me very much. He treated me as a friend, and the fact that he had the interests of the publishing house, to which he was devoted, close to his heart was touching. What effect will his death have on the firm? Ernest Alexandrovich had his faults – sluggishness and obstinacy – and it is a toss-up whether after him things will be better or worse. Worse for sure, in the short term.

17–18 December

Made a piano reduction of *Ursignol* for Diaghilev. Ptashka is not well and her voice is not sounding, as a consequence of which the atmosphere at home is one of gloom.

19 December

As Ptashka's voice is not in good shape we decided it would be better for her not to sing. The Concertgebouw is a premier organisation and it would be a pity not to do oneself justice here. Instead, I decided to add the Sonata No. 2. The administration behaved in the most gentlemanly fashion, understood the situation and reacted calmly. They made no deduction from the fee and even managed to produce a new printed programme. The orchestra itself was performing in The Hague today with Thibaud as soloist, but he also was indisposed, so the administration had to divide itself into several pieces cutting and pasting programmes. My evening concert was in the Small Hall of the Concertgebouw, which was three-quarters full. It was a very good success, and afterwards we were entertained to supper. Ptashka did not come to the concert, which was awkward, but they went round to fetch her and brought her to the supper.

20 December

The *Scythian Suite* was in the programme for an open concert.[1] I heard it from a box behind the orchestra. This to some extent made the sound less homogeneous: individual instruments stood out with greater clarity, but the ensemble did not sound as good. The success was great and I was called out to take a bow.

21 December

Ptashka left early in the morning, disgruntled and dissatisfied with herself, although she acknowledged that she had done the right thing in not singing. In the evening the orchestra, conductor and soloist were once again loaded on to the special train to go to Arnhem for the fourth performance of the Concerto. Once again it was a tremendous success, the audience and orchestra stood to applaud and I was presented with a laurel wreath by the local concert organisation. It was after midnight by the time I got home, and I had to pack.

22 December

Left early in the morning by the same train as Ptashka had taken. By coincidence a fellow passenger in my compartment was Alyokhin,[2] and we talked non-stop all the way, mainly about the recently concluded Moscow tournament, which Alyokhin had decided not to attend for fear of the Bolsheviks. B.N.,[3] meeting Alyokhin in Paris, had borrowed 100 francs from him and

---

1 That is, not included in the subscription series.
2 Alexander Alyokhin (Alyekhine) (1892–1934), chess Grandmaster, whom Prokofiev had first encountered at the St Petersburg International Tournament of April 1914, at which Tsar Nicholas II issued an ukase formally conferring for the first time the title of Grandmaster on Alekhine and his four other co-finalists, Emanuel Lasker, Raúl Capablanca, Siegbert Tarrasch and Frank Marshall. See *Diaries*, vol. 1, pp. 584, 640–42, and *passim*; vol. 2, p. 192.
3 Boris Bashkirov.

then insisted on luring him into his club, where Alyokhin thinks he gets money for bringing gamblers in. It had all made a very unpleasant impression on Alyokhin. When we got to Paris Alyokhin was met by his wife, a heavily made-up woman ten or fifteen years older than he.

I did not get home to Clamart until eight o'clock in the evening. Ptashka, Olga Vladislavovna and I spent all the rest of the evening sorting out which of our belongings were to stay, which to go into store, and which to go to America.

23 December

Rose while it was still dark, finished off the packing, worried whether the car would come (it was late). At nine o'clock we set off for America. Svyatoslav, in Olga Vladislavovna's arms, started to cry, and this set Ptashka off too. At the Gare St Lazare there was a good crowd to see us off: the Borovskys, Olmsted, the copyists, Conius and Paichadze.[1]

Paichadze told us something about the last days of Oeberg. His blind gut had inosculated[2] into his liver. The perforation had happened while he was lunching with Stravinsky. Because of the terrible pain and Ernest Alexandrovich's semi-conscious condition, a decision was taken by his sister, Stravinsky and Paichadze to agree to an operation, but this did not improve his prospects. At five the next morning his heart began to give out and half an hour later he was dead.

The train departed at eleven o'clock in the morning. We met Lankow,[3] a bass from the Chicago Opera, a splendid fellow but a bit of a blockhead. At four o'clock in Le Havre we boarded the *De Grasse*,[4] a new and very clean French liner. We put out to sea in a pretty cold wind, but as we were heading through the Channel it was not too rough. But that evening there was a storm that even damaged the roof at Clamart.

---

1 Gavriil Paichadze had been appointed Director of the Paris branch of Koussevitzky's publishing company Russian Musical Editions on the death of Oeberg.
2 Meaning that an opening had occurred between the gut and the liver and the one was bleeding into the other.
3 Edward Lankow (1883–1940), bass, had a distinguished career in the Boston, Metropolitan, New York and Chicago Operas, where he was a fine Arkel in *Pelléas et Mélisande*. During the First World War he served as a specialist in lung hygiene, devising deep-breathing exercises to wounded men, and wrote a book called *How to Breathe Right*, published by E. J. Clode in 1918, which is still in print.
4 The *De Grasse* had recently been built at the Cammell-Laird shipyards in Birkenhead and sailed on the Le Havre–New York line until 1940, when she was seized by the Germans, only to be sunk by the Allies in 1944. Raised and refitted the following year, she continued in service until bought by Canadian Pacific for their South American run in 1953 and renamed *Empress of Australia*. Her ultimate incarnation was as the *Venezuela*, owned by the Italian Grimaldi Siosa Lines, but she was lost off Cannes in 1962.

23 December–1 January 1926

Ocean voyage. It was bearable as long as we were still coming out of the Channel, but the moment day dawned the boat began rolling. We and Thibaud, who was also on board, were invited to the Captain's table, which was very flattering but *à la longue*[1] turned out to be a bore, because lunch and dinner were both served more slowly and more ceremoniously than at other tables, so that each meal lasted more than an hour. For the first few days the rolling did not make me feel sick but did make me sleepy and morose, so I ate on deck. After three days or so I got used to it and managed everything fine.

I did a bit of work transcribing *Ursignol* and answering correspondence. I took part in a chess competition and took first prize as I won all my matches; my opponents were weak. Ptashka reacted well to the rolling. All the men tried to flirt with her, including the Captain; he was very nice.

We did not greet the New Year as the following morning we were due in New York and the previous evening there had been a ball and we were very late to bed. Ptashka and I had a tiff; she had tired herself out with all the packing of the trunks, said she wished she was not coming to America at all and would definitely not come to California. The ball was fancy dress, with prizes, but we did not participate. The best part of it was coming out on deck and contrasting the bright lights, music and glittering costumes inside with the snowstorm outside. The rolling of the ship added to the entertainment value of the dancing.

---

1 In French: 'eventually'.

1926

1 January

On the morning of the 1st January we made our approach into New York on the *De Grasse*. It was a lovely day, clear and cold, and all the passengers poured out on deck. New York, at least its silhouette as you near it, is very beautiful. I would say more: I don't recall any other city as beautiful in its approach. Like good Russians of any stamp, despised émigrés, we experienced a flutter of alarm at American passport control, but everything passed off smoothly. Only in Customs, where I was foolish enough to declare that I was bringing in music, did they fleece me of six dollars' import duty. Then it was a taxi, the hideous streets round the harbour, and the Great Northern Hotel, nowadays the fashionable stopping place for musicians,[1] where we had reserved a suite of two rooms with bath and where the piano already delivered by Steinway was in situ. This was very pleasing: for Pleyel you wait two weeks.

It was already beginning to get dark, and we sallied forth into the city to stroll around and have dinner. We found ourselves right in Times Square on Broadway, with incredible crowds on account of the holiday. Coming from Europe one cannot help being struck by the overabundance, the prosperity and the tastelessness. Ptashka, a real expert on fashion who had been thirsting to return to New York, was especially put off by the vulgarity of the women. We dined in a rotisserie that I had often patronised in the past. Then we were visited by Mme Schmitz,[2] who discussed the details of the Pro Musica tour with which my activities in America were to begin. It emerged that Ptashka's travel expenses were also to be covered, although not for every city, and it was therefore clear

---

1 The Great Northern Hotel was on West 57th Street, to this day the preferred location for musicians' managers to have their offices.
2 The wife of E. Robert Schmitz (1889–1942), French-born pianist, voice coach, writer, impresario, physiologist and indefatigable promoter of new music. Prokofiev had first met him with the critic Michel Calvocoressi in Paris on his first visit there in 1913, and had played him his First and Second Piano Concertos. Schmitz had one of the most varied lives in music one can imagine. In Paris, as well as coaching in collaboration with the composer singers such as Maggie Teyte for her role as Mélisande, he founded and directed the Association Moderne et Artistique, which became one of the leading vehicles for new music before the era of Les Six. Moving to America after the First World War, Schmitz continued to perform as a pianist and also founded the International Franco-American Society, later known as Pro Musica. This fearless organisation brought to America for the first time such figures as Ravel and Bartók, and also exported American composers to Europe.

that she would be taking part in some of the concerts. As she had not been certain of this beforehand she was well pleased, and I am also pleased for her even though it means that there will be many more difficulties on the tour and the mood of everything will depend on how her voice is sounding.

2 January

Went to see Haensel in the morning. He is nice, lethargic, but at least is not demanding payment of what I owe him which, it seems, now amounts to $1,300. Thence to Duo-Art. Managing Director Schaad[1] is likewise a remarkably nice man, in fact both these gentlemen are exceptionally attractive representatives of the American male. It was agreed that I should cut eight rolls: five for the final year of the previous contract, under which I had already received in Europe two-thirds of the fee as an advance, and three for the first year of a new contract. In all I stand to get $1,600.

In the afternoon Zakharov appeared; a most happy meeting, and we went together to Fifth Avenue to partake of an American concoction: chocolate, milk and egg all beaten up together.

Vladimir Bashkirov[2] telephoned, tentative at first, fearing that I would shout at him, but seeing that I was quite relaxed professed undying love for me and told me that I was one of his closest friends. He soon came round to see us, nervously twisting in his hands a cheque, admittedly not yet written out, for the outstanding amount ($100) of the cost of the ticket I had bought for B.N. to get from New York to Europe. He asked about his brother. Needless to say I did not enlarge on the precise nature of B.N.'s occupation, although I did say that he was prone to hanging around the club. Damrosch's daughter also called: she is very anxious that her father should perform *Seven, They Are Seven*. She invited us to a concert he is about to conduct.

Ptashka is not feeling well and has decided to consult a Christian Science practitioner, America being the birthplace of Christian Science. She went off to the Aeolian Building, where there is a Christian Science reading room, and asked for a recommendation to a practitioner. But it is against their rules to give preference to any one individual over another, and so they gave her a complete list of all of them in the building – apparently there are twelve. Ptashka had no idea whom to choose, but alighted at random on one Warren Klein. She says he was quite different from the women we know in Paris: very forthright and cogent. I should also like to consult him.

---

1 Hermann Schaad, Managing Director of Duo-Art New York, had been trained as a conductor. He was generally known as 'Baby', which probably did not get his conducting career off to a flying start.
2 Brother of Boris Bashkirov. See *Diaries*, vols. 1 and 2 *passim*.

3 January

Practised in the morning, finishing the polishing of *Sheherazade* for Duo-Art, while Ptashka sang. Lunch at the Zakharovs', very nice and jolly. Celia has one admirable characteristic: the more famous she becomes, the more simply she behaves. Her renown in America is now very great, and rightly so: she plays wonderfully, looks good especially on stage, and among female violinists has no rivals worthy of the name. At lunch also was Boris's brother Vasily, whom Boris has brought over to America and who is earning not bad money as a cellist in a big movie orchestra. I was very glad to see him.[1] Afterwards we went to Damrosch's concert, but were late and caught only a snatch of Gershwin's Concerto, performed by the composer. Gershwin has made a big name for himself in jazz and is now branching out into serious, or to be precise 'half-breed', music, composing jazz concertos. America has jumped at this, and indeed I do believe that this may be the way forward to a national American music. I must admit that there is much that is attractive in his Concerto; it is inventive and full of energy as far as rhythm is concerned, but the material is thin and that is, after all, the main thing. I was left with the impression that here was not a real composer but a precursor of another, later, composer who using these means would compose real music.

Damrosch has aged. His whole body seemed to cry aloud that he will either die soon, or at least will cease to conduct. I felt sorry for him and resolved not to pick a fight with him. He wants *Seven, They Are Seven* for next year, but I do not know whether Koussevitzky, who also had it in mind to perform, will agree. Damrosch then said that he was generally on the lookout for new works, and it was on the tip of my tongue to suggest my Second Symphony. But then I took fright: Damrosch would certainly wreck it, and in any case it was too soon to offer such a morsel to America; it would be suicidal. I therefore said I would think about it and write to him.

In the evening we were at Charles Crane's,[2] a great figure in America and a friend of Russians. I had heard of him even before my first trip to America,

---

1 Prokofiev will have remembered him from the many times in his Conservatoire years he stayed with the extended Zakharov family at their large dacha in Terijoki on the (then) Finnish coast of the Gulf of Finland.
2 Charles Crane (1858–1939) inherited great wealth from his Chicago industrialist father and used it to further business, political and cultural interests in Eastern Europe, especially Czechoslovakia, and the Middle East. He had been a member of President Wilson's Special Diplomatic Commission (the Root Commission) to Russia in 1917, aimed (unsuccessfully) at keeping the new regime in the First World War on the side of the Allies, and of the post-war Paris Peace Conference. In 1920–21 he had served as American Ambassador to China, and also helped finance the first oil explorations in Saudi Arabia and Yemen, being largely responsible for the American oil concessions in those countries.

from Safonov in Kislovodsk. Later he had come with Milyukov[1] to a rehearsal of *Oranges* in Chicago. Now at his house we met L. L. Tolstoy,[2] the son of the writer, and a Russian woman whom I liked but Ptashka did not. Tolstoy, of course, benefited from the aureole of his father, but from B.N. I knew that at the Bashkirovs' he had lost heavily at cards, a fact which he concealed from his wife. Crane is intimate with Roerich, and showed me several of his latest pictures, painted in India. Roerich himself had been commanded by his spiritual teacher to take himself to Tibet for his final initiation. With his wife and son he had crossed the Himalayas in autumn, suffering great hardships, but upon arrival at the frontier the Tibetan authorities would not let him go any further. To return was now impossible, winter having set in and the roads having become impassable. A sympathetic inhabitant of those parts did, however, manage to get back to India, and from the first town he came to wired off a lengthy telegram to Crane begging him to petition Washington to put pressure on Peking to secure permission for Roerich to pass through Tibet to Peking. Crane did what he could, but the response from Washington was that China was in the middle of a revolution and that if Roerich did in fact get permission to travel through Tibet he would undoubtedly be killed. Therefore the best thing was to stay put where he had fetched up, and that is where he still is, in the wilds of nowhere.[3]

1 Pavel Milyukov (1859–1943), historian and politician. The founder of the Constitutional Democratic Party ('Kadets', from the acronym KD), Milyukov became Foreign Minister in the First Provisional Government following the February 1917 Revolution, and as such was the author of 'Milyukov's Note' to the Allied countries guaranteeing Russia's continuing involvement in the First World War. Fleeing Russia for Paris after the October Revolution and Civil War, Milyukov published and edited there the émigré newspaper *Latest News* (*Poslednye Novosti*). With his friend and fellow Kadet newspaper editor Iosif Gessen, Milyukov was an admirer of Prokofiev's music and had several times attended performances. See *Diaries*, vol. 2, pp. 84–5, 100, 187, 530, 647, 679.
2 L. L. (Lev L'vovich) Tolstoy (1869–1945) was one of the more talented children of the great writer. Having married a Swedish woman in 1896 (altogether they produced ten children) he emigrated to Sweden soon after the Revolution. Long before that time he had dissociated himself from his father's moral and political teachings and become outspoken in his dissent. A belletrist of some reputation as well as a painter and sculptor, he studied for some time with Rodin.
3 Nikolay (Nicholas) Roerich had long ago expanded his initial ethnographic interests in pagan Russian ritual, which gained early expression in his Talashkino-inspired designs for Diaghilev's 1913 production of *The Rite of Spring*, to an all-encompassing search for eternal truth through such various avenues as botany, linguistics, ethnography, archaeology, the study of ancient Eastern religions, spiritualism and – under the influence of Mme Blavatsky – theosophy. Obeying the astrally transmitted instructions of his mysterious Teacher (who fulfilled this role also for Mme Blavatsky) Mahatma Morya, aka Ahazhulama, the Blue Teacher, the Chohan of the First Ray, a claimed Buddhist Ascended Master whom neither Roerich nor anyone else seems ever to have actually met in person and whose corporeal existence therefore is open to speculation, Roerich, his wife Helena and his son Gyorgy (George) arrived in Mumbai to start their epic trek through the uncharted Himalayan regions of Northern India, Chinese Turkestan, Altai, Mongolia and Tibet. The incident Charles Crane relayed to Prokofiev is

4 January

Ptashka has paid a second visit to Klein. She alerted him to the prospect of her husband's also coming to him, and today I did so. The immediate cause was fleabites on my hands, which had suddenly erupted in huge red marks, most untimely in view of forthcoming concerts at which everyone will be looking at my hands, and of the receptions at which one has to shake hands.[1] However, while I was sitting waiting my turn in Klein's waiting room I noticed some improvement in my hands, so when I went in I decided to add to the hands problem the neuralgia I suffer in my temples, which comes on two or three times a month and has been doing so for the past almost thirteen years. He told me this was all due to apprehension. Klein is a small man, fresh-complexioned but with grey hair, I suppose about forty-five years

---

described in the book Roerich wrote of their astounding five-year-long pilgrimage on foot and yak (they were later joined by the Roerichs' second son Svyatoslav), which among other achievements produced no fewer than five hundred paintings Roerich somehow executed en route. The book, *Heart of Asia*, first published in Russian in New York in 1929 as *Сердце Азии*, is an exhilarating compendium of travel adventures, triumphs and disasters, emotional and spiritual insights, all shot through with Roerich's unquenchable belief that obstacles of any kind were there only to be conquered, and in the ultimate benevolence of the divine spirit:

'The main route of the Expedition widely encircled Central Asia. The chief points to be mentioned were the following: Darjeeling, the monasteries of Sikkim, Benares, Sarnath, Northern Punjab, Rawalpindi, Kashmir, Ladakh, Karakorum, Khotan, Yarkend, Kashgar, Aksu, Kuchar, Karashahr, Toksun, the Turfan region, Urumchi, T'ien-Shan, Kozeun, Zaisan, Irtysh, Novonikolaevsk, Biisk, Altai, Oirotia, Verkhneudinsk, Buriatya, Troitskosavsk, Altyn-Bulak, Urga, Yum-Beise, Anhsi-chou, Shih-pao ch'eng, Nanshan, Sharagolji, Tsaidam, Neiji, Marco Polo range, Kokushili, Dungbure, Nagchu, Shentsa-Dzong, Tingri-Dzong, Shekar-Dzong, Kampa-Dzong, Sepo La, Gangtok, and back to Darjeeling.

'We crossed the following mountain passes. We have a list of thirty-five passes from fourteen to twenty-one thousand feet: Zoji La, Khardong La, Karaul Davan, Sasser Pass, Dabzang Pass, Karakorum Pass, Suget Pass, Sanju Pass, Urtu-Kashkariym Daban, Ulan Daban, Chakharin Daban, Khentu Pass, Neiji La, Kokushili Pass, Dungbure Pass, Thang La, Kam-rong La, Ta-sang La, Lamsi Pass, Naptra La, Tamaker Pass, Shentsa Pass, Laptse-Nagri, Tsang La, Lam-Ling Pass, Pong-chen La, Dong-chen La, Sang-mo La, Kyegong La, Tsug-chung La, Gya La, Urang La, Sharu La, Gulung La and Sepo La.

'While speaking of the crossing of the passes, it may be mentioned that during the entire journey with its many passes, except on the Thang La, no one suffered seriously. In the case of the Thang La, the conditions were exceptional. There was a feeling of nervousness in the Expedition over the uncertain negotiations with the Tibetans. The conditions of the pass itself are also most exacting. George had such an exhausting heart attack there that he almost fell from his horse. Our doctor administered large doses of digitalis and ammonia and, expressing anxiety for George's life, restored the blood circulation by massage. Lama Malonov also fell from his horse there and was found lying unconscious on the ground. Also, three more members of the caravan had serious attacks of "Soor", or mountain sickness, which is evident in headache, poor blood circulation, sickness, and general fatigue. In any case, such weakness, in a varying degree, is characteristic during the crossing of the mountain passes. On the passes bleeding often sets in, first from the nose and later from other less protected organs.'

1 'Shake hands' is written in English.

of age. He discourses with great energy, expression and conviction, occasionally reinforced by banging his hand on the table and raising his voice. 'You must understand God not as a person to whom you make requests, but as a principle, as a law – and not only that but as being in Himself the essence of love.' He went on to say that while the old theology taught that we are sinners suffocated by our sins, and some day in some way it might please God to release us from them, this is not the case. Man is a son of God and his sins are forgotten the moment he puts himself on the true path and approaches God. Klein had much more to say, and every one of the truths that came out of his mouth struck me with force, although later I found I could not reconstruct everything he told me. The secret of why this should be so escaped me, so much was I straining all my attention to listen to him. In conclusion he gave me a treatment for my nerves, which he judged to be the root cause of everything, and then obliged me to repeat after him that I had no fear, I had no pain, I had no rash on my hands, and 'I know this to be true'. I left him in a very elevated mood, and walking along Fifth Avenue reflected that New York contains not only industry, houses and dollars, but also true ideas.

Played for Duo-Art the seven- or eight-minute transcription of *Sheherazade* I had made specially for them (and for which I had received the advance payment they sent to Europe) and four of Myaskovsky's *Caprices*.[1]

5 January

Strummed through the Third Sonata and the Andante from the Fifth. Stokowski is performing Myaskovsky's Symphony No. 5 today, using orchestral parts I sent a year ago to Ziloti, who was responsible for arranging this performance. I had asked Ziloti the day before yesterday to get me a ticket; he prevaricated, saying Stokowski's concerts were always sold out, and in short it appeared today that there was no ticket. Although V. Bashkirov had invited us to dinner at the Russian Restaurant opposite Carnegie Hall (he brought along a very pretty but slightly vulgar Jewish girl) I excused myself halfway through to catch the interval of the concert, hoping to find some way of getting in. But there was a crowd of about a hundred people all desperate for access, pushing and shoving, and at the artists' entrance it was the same story. For half an hour I elbowed my way through, apologising, cursing and sweating, until I finally managed to grab the coat-tails of the assistant manager, who was trying to hide from his assailants on every side. To him I spluttered out, 'I am just off the boat from Europe and at Myaskovsky's express request must hear his Symphony. It was I who provided the material you are using for the performance.' He understood

---

1 *Caprices* (*Prichudy*), Six Pieces for Piano, Op. 27.

not a word, but something in what I said made an impression on him, and he asked what my name was. I identified myself, not imagining for one moment that it would mean anything to this wretched institution, which had never performed any of my music. But the assistant manager smiled: 'Oh, we have been wanting to perform your Violin Concerto. Come this way, although you will probably have to stand.' Ptashka and I were let through, and found ourselves among a crowd of people standing, including Ziloti, Casella and Szigeti. What an uncivilised organisation! If all the tickets have been sold, things must be going well, and if they are going so well then why could they not allow themselves the luxury of keeping a couple of boxes aside for visiting musicians? The orchestra[1] is genuinely superb: Stokowski conducted well, from memory. When I had looked at the score it seemed to me there were a few places where not everything would be heard, but with this orchestra everything did sound. Szigeti commented, 'This orchestra sounds so marvellous it makes no difference what they play.' The Symphony itself is not Myaskovsky's best. It has too many Glazunovian devices, which come across as simply 'prentice pieces, and there are longueurs. I was not very pleased with it. Nevertheless, it had a decent reception and some parts of the hall applauded loud and long.

Ptashka was almost jostled off her feet, but then Mme Schmitz gave up her place to her and she ended up in the third row next to Ganna Walska. As soon as the Symphony was over we rushed away to get our trunks packed for tomorrow's departure.

6 January

Getting up at seven o'clock, by 8.45 we were on the train to Chicago. It was Ptashka's first time in an American sleeping car. How solid and comfortable everything is! And lovely views of the Hudson.

Bought the American papers; the Myaskovsky got very good reviews, better than any I ever got. I wrote a letter to him.

7 January

Despite our arriving in Chicago at seven o'clock in the morning, Gottlieb was there to meet us at the station, very well dressed – his prospects have improved and he makes 6,000 dollars a year. He took us to a wealthy acquaintance, where we stayed until evening. Dr Schmidt[2] laid on an

---

1 The Philadelphia Orchestra.
2 A rich German acquaintance in Chicago, who had entertained Prokofiev over the period of the premiere of *The Love for Three Oranges* at the Chicago Opera in December 1921.

elaborate lunch in my honour, and as I could not think of a way of getting out of it, I had to make a speech in English, about music in Russia, and about what I had been doing in my four years' absence from America. I was placed in the presidential seat between Carpenter[1] and Morris,[2] the former American Ambassador to Sweden. In the evening we left for St Paul, seen off at the station by Gottlieb.

8 January

St Paul is a city celebrated for its total absence of beauty. Pro Musica, the society that has engaged me, has as its aim the promotion of new music. It has many branches in provincial cities, and this is the department of it under whose auspices we are now travelling. Its affairs are mainly directed by the ladies of the society, and most of the concerts are restricted to members of the society.

In the afternoon we rehearsed in the apartment of the local president, who put the apartment at our disposal and then left us alone. The concert in the evening took place in a private house, with about 150 people present, very stylishly turned out. Ptashka had been tired and not in good voice all day, but sang not badly in the evening. Neither of us was at all nervous. Could this be Klein's doing?

The concert was a great success, and afterwards there was a reception in our honour.

9 January

Lunch in our honour in a club, with about twenty people. As I had no wish to make a speech, there was a question-and-answer session: questions included one about the provenance of dissonance (I explained the theory of overtones), one about *Seven, They Are Seven*, and so on. Ptashka says I explained things quite well. We left again at six o'clock, Ptashka so tired that

---

1 John Alden Carpenter (1876–1951), composer who had studied with Elgar and, like Charles Ives, combined composition with a career in business. One of the first American composers to use material derived from jazz and Tin Pan Alley, his ballet *Skyscrapers* had been rejected by Diaghilev but was produced to great acclaim by the Metropolitan Opera in 1926 and made the composer a household name in America. 'A procession from the banal to the ephemeral, often easy on the ear but always nugatory,' as Prokofiev described it in his *Diaries* in May 1920. Carpenter and his wife had been influential supporters of Prokofiev in 1920 at the time of his struggle with the management of the Chicago Opera over the contract to produce *The Love for Three Oranges*. See *Diaries*, vol. 2, pp. 432–662 *passim*.
2 Ira Nelson Morris (1876–1942), scion of a prominent Chicago packing family, served as US Ambassador to Sweden from 1914 to 1923.

she quickly collapsed into sleep, while I on my upper bunk read a Russian newspaper published in Paris.

Before leaving St Paul I sent Diaghilev the piano reduction of numbers six to nine inclusive of *Ursignol*, a transcription I had made in New York and during the liner crossing.

10 January

Omaha early in the morning. Ptashka, who is rather hard to please at the moment, was grumbling at having to get up so early. And certainly the schedule is idiotic, because arriving at seven o'clock in the morning we have to wait until two o'clock in the afternoon to get our next train. On the other hand, as we approached Omaha we crossed over the Missouri and could feast our eyes on the river at sunrise. It was very beautiful, with cherry-red going to dark-blue clouds, which made the sky appear not blue but green. The Missouri is a wide, beautiful river but Omaha with its smoking chimneys spoils the countryside. The weather was cold and the town hideous. I got down to orchestrating *Ursignol* (up to now I have done only two and a half numbers, and of course will nowhere near finish on schedule). Some of the orchestration I did in the hotel where we drank coffee, and some at the station, and completed five pages. At two o'clock we set off again on our journey. Observation car. Snow. Flat landscape and the single track of the railway, barely discernible in the snow.

11 January

Denver at seven o'clock the next morning, snowbound because it is a mile above sea level. At the Hotel Metropole, where we are staying, the lady organiser appeared almost immediately. Once again lunch in a club, about fifteen people, but at least I did not have to speak. We were then taken on a car tour of Denver, but sadly the mountains surrounding the city were not visible because of the misty weather. An upright piano had been brought into our hotel room, so we were able to practise. There was another evening reception in our honour, American-style, which means that we were positioned against the wall while the guests (a hundred or hundred and fifty of them) filed past to shake hands with us. They are paying $300 for both of us, and for that money they want not only to hear us play but to shake our hands! We were entertained by a local composer and singer, and light refreshments. Both one and the other were bad. All the same, one must give credit to the fact that these societies exist for the specific purpose of acquainting people with new music, and for that reason I am received with respect and they do their best to celebrate what I do without snide grins or complaints that I am not playing

Chopin, as happened on my previous tours of America when I was playing not for Pro Musica but appearing in ordinary concert series.

12 January

Because we were performing in the evening we categorically refused all lunches and receptions, all the more so as there was a piano in the room and we could work. I orchestrated three more pages and got quite a lot of practising done.

The concert took place in a small hall with three to four hundred seats, of which about two hundred were filled. Once again, I was not at all nervous, and Ptashka only very slightly. Can it really be that Klein has lifted this burden from us?! When you are not nervous, what possibilities there are for creative inspirations while performing! Ptashka sang not badly, especially taking into consideration how tired she is, that she is not feeling well and that her voice was not sounding at all this morning. The audience was attentive and well disposed, trying hard to understand the music, but only at the end, after the Toccata, was there serious applause. Another post-concert reception, very tedious.

13 January

At one o'clock I left for Portland. Portland and San Francisco had not wanted to pay the fare for Ptashka, so I went alone while Ptashka remained in Denver in the care of one of the Pro Musica ladies. It was a wonderful sunny day, from the observation car at first there was a view of a mountain range on the horizon and then the flat steppe and the marvellous air, reminding me of Sontsovka.[1]

Caught up on my diary.

14 January

Another sunny day in the observation car, but now the steppe was hilly, sometimes mountainous and blanketed by snow, which the train covered by a white cloud in its wake. I did a lot of work thinking out and making notes for the instrumentation of *Ursignol*. I have a new system for doing this work while on the road: I work out how many bars there will be on a page of full score, then mark in detail the orchestration, making a note of which instruments are to be scored, in other words how many staves will be required for that particular page of score. In this way, when the time comes to write out

---

1 The small rural estate in the Ukraine where Prokofiev was born and spent his childhood.

the actual score, it comes down to purely mechanical work, not very different from that done by a copyist.

I thought of a new opening for the Second Symphony, significantly different from the first version, which had never satisfied me. I had tried to recompose it in the summer, but unsuccessfully; perhaps it will work out this time.

15 January

Portland next morning. The view is quite different from yesterday's. Here are rocky mountains covered with pine forests, mosses, dotted with green grass, elsewhere dried-out ferns. The views were beautiful and smiling, the line twisted and turned, and the air was warm, reminiscent of early spring. At the station in Portland I was met by a Pro Musica representative, Mrs Jesse, a diminutive teacher. Then two interviews, followed by a lunch for approximately fifteen people with me in the place of honour, and speeches. This is an indispensable aspect of demonstrating the activities of the Society, and to raise awareness of a young enterprise. The local conductor was present, van Hoogstraten,[1] and one Hodgkinson, I think a piano professor from Sydney. The latter thrilled me by telling me that my music is very well known in Australia and he hoped I would soon be invited to go there. I have always been interested in travelling to Australia and New Zealand. This time I had to speak, and touched on the state of music in contemporary Russia, on the conductorless orchestra,[2] on composers – which gave me an opportunity

---

1   Willem van Hoogstraten (1884–1964), violinist and conductor, had recently been plucked from his position as Associate Conductor of the New York Philharmonic to take over the Oregon Symphony on the sudden death of the previous incumbent, Theodore Spiering. He stayed there, combining the post with summer seasons by the New York Philharmonic at Lewisohn Stadium, until 1938, when he returned to Europe to become Director of the Salzburg Mozarteum, a position he retained until 1945, thus causing post-war speculation about his Nazi affiliations especially as his former wife was the distinguished but outspokenly pro-Nazi German pianist Elly Ney.
2   The Persimfans Orchestra with which Prokofiev would make his debut appearance on his return visit to the USSR in 1927 is an abbreviation of Perviy Simfonicheskiy Ansambl' bez Dirizhora (First Conductorless Symphonic Ensemble). It was established in 1922 by the violinist Lev Tseitlin, inspired by the Bolshevik mantra of 'collective labour'. As is traditional for a chamber music ensemble, questions of tempo, dynamics, style, sonic balance, rhythm and interpretation were settled collectively in rehearsal. Surprising as it may seem to Western audiences inured to the dominance of the maestro, the orchestra achieved extraordinary heights of virtuosity and musicianship in a wide and enlightened repertoire, and its regular weekly appearances in the Great Hall of the Moscow Conservatoire were highlights of the Moscow musical scene. Inevitably, so a cynic would say, it could not last and by the end of the 1920s internal discord had so fractured the orchestra's monolithic artistic integrity that in 1932 it disbanded – not, however, before its members had successfully fertilised the ground for the formation of the Large Symphony Orchestra of All-Union Radio in 1930 and the USSR State Symphony Orchestra, both of which went on to achieve enviable national and international reputations.

to do some propaganda for Myaskovsky, in which I was so effective that they asked me to add some of his pieces to my programme. In the afternoon I was taken round the beautiful surrounding countryside, after which I had a chance to do some work before the concert in the evening. The audience was small, about a hundred (the total membership of the Portland branch of Pro Musica is only seventy) but very attentive.

A tragicomic incident occurred: in the same building, two storeys higher up, a ball was in progress, the thumping of the drums and the wail of the saxophones carried through into our hall and disrupted both playing and listening. Negotiations ensued, as a result of which the interest of the drummer was aroused and he came in to listen to me, while the saxophonists agreed to play more quietly.

The audience was receptive,[1] and the journalists who had interviewed me wrote that I was the greatest living composer. Could I ever have expected this in America?! However, no doubt this accolade was essential for the prestige of Portland.

16 January

After last night's concert and a light supper I packed my things and went to sit (or rather lie down) in the train. Today's journey south, to San Francisco, is a very pleasant one. The railway line literally winds itself between low hillsides covered with pine trees. Even though by evening we had gone a fair way south the weather grew colder and it began to snow. That's California for you! During the day I did a lot of work, using the time whenever the train halted to put notes into the score, but towards evening my head felt heavy and I stopped work.

17 January

In the morning the train reached Oakland, and I had to take the ferry across the Bay to reach San Francisco on the other side. On the crossing I recalled my first arrival in the United States and my unexpected visit to Angel Island.[2] Schmitz met me on the jetty and took me to the Hotel Clift, where he himself is staying. Unfortunately I had begun to develop a headache; I thought Klein had cured me once and for all of these attacks from which I had suffered for fifteen years. Schmitz told me that today's concert was

---

1 Written in English.
2 See *Diaries*, vol. 2, pp. 316–21, for Prokofiev's hilarious account of his interrogation and brief incarceration in the immigration centre of Angel Island in August 1918.

the first to be presented by the San Francisco branch of Pro Musica. There would be no programme, it was informal. As well as my own compositions it would be a good idea to play some Myaskovsky and perhaps some Musorgsky. I therefore stayed in Schmitz's room and went through them. Schmitz himself plays a great deal of modern music and is also learning Myaskovsky's *Caprices*. Curiously enough, from the six pieces he had chosen the same four as I had.

One of Schmitz's friends drove me in his car round the environs of San Francisco. I saw the Golden Gate, the green parks and San Francisco itself from the top of a mountain, laid out as if on the palm of a hand. The day was warm, sunny, and all the colours were bright.

During the afternoon my headache gradually eased: I worked hard to promote this direction. I dined with Hertz,[1] the local conductor, a heavy, courteous, reserved man. The concert was in a club, with an audience of about a hundred and fifty. Schmitz delivered a speech inaugurating the branch of the Society and introducing me. He spoke in a monotonous, dreary voice, thank God only for fifteen minutes. After that I played. The audience listened attentively and applauded. The Gavottes and other small pieces elicited cries of 'Oh!' There was a modest supper in the same place afterwards. Various ladies came up to me and said, 'We met here four years ago', or 'five years ago in New York'. I was embarrassed at my failure to remember any of them.

18 January

Next morning I packed my things, rehearsed the Third Concerto in Schmitz's room and wrote postcards. San Francisco is one place from which it is essential to send postcards to Europe, as everyone there knows that San Francisco is somewhere at the ends of the earth. At one o'clock I set out on my journey back East, once more crossing the Bay on the ferry to Oakland, where I boarded the train.

A new trial to plague me: my front tooth has begun to hurt.

---

1 Alfred Hertz (1872–1942), a fine conductor of the old school. Born and trained in Germany, crippled by a childhood attack of infantile paralysis that left him lame for life, he had come to America to head the Metropolitan Opera's German opera department, which he continued to do until 1915 when he accepted the post of Music Director of the then four-year-old San Francisco Symphony Orchestra, a post he held for the next fifteen years. A noted Wagnerian, he had conducted the American premieres of *Parsifal* and of Strauss's *Salome*, and made an early (1913) recording with the Berlin Philharmonic of the Suite from *Parsifal*. Prokofiev had met him when playing recitals in the San Francisco area in 1918 and had got on well with him; they had played bridge together. See *Diaries*, vol. 2, pp. 557–8.

19 January

This afternoon we crossed Salt Lake. The weather is snowy, grey and cold; the view over the lake empty and unwelcoming. Only as we approached Ogden did some watercoloury tints creep into the scene. The sky cleared, the lake turned a delicate pale blue and the snow on the mountains was rose-tinged in the setting sun, while the shady slopes of the mountains became a deep-dyed blue. The pain in my tooth subsided. I occupied myself with the proofs of Op. 23[1] – a new edition in four languages, which I had been sent in December, but had not been able to bring myself to attend to. Proof-reading is the ideal occupation for a train journey.

20 January

My train passes through Denver, where I had left Ptashka, reaching there just before noon. Ptashka was looking green about the gills and worn out: she had reacted badly to the altitude in Denver (1.5 kilometres) and the attentions of the ladies, which had, far from confining themselves to assuring her peace and comfort, consisted rather in dragging her to a succession of lunches and dinners. Only in the last days of her stay, by which time Ptashka was almost collapsing in a faint, did this round of entertaining cease.

I carried on with my proof-reading.

21 January

Kansas in the morning. We were met at the station and taken to our hotel where two good rooms had been reserved for us – needless to say at our expense, hence the two. The fees are modest, but the hotel reservations are costly. Haensel had forwarded a packet of letters from Europe – very welcome. Particularly so was a letter from Derzhanovsky about the exceptional success my music was enjoying in Moscow. Next on the agenda was an interview, after which we were taken by car round the town, which is actually rather pleasant, especially if you come in summer. After this excursion we asked not to be disturbed, and were left on our own. As a piano had been sent in we were able to practise. But the domestic atmosphere was far from easy, since Ptashka's voice was not in good shape. She was feeling tired after Denver, in fact seems to have been so since November.

---

1 *Five Poems for Voice and Piano*, words by Goryansky, Gippius, Boris Verin (pen-name of Boris Bashkirov), Balmont and Agnitsev (1915).

22 January

The concert was in a club, a very good one, membership of which costs $1,000. The building has twenty-two floors and the hall is on the twenty-second, but lacks an Artists' Room. To begin with we were accommodated on the fourth floor, but then we were taken higher up and found space not far from the piano, behind a screen. The lady president delivered a speech about me and Ptashka (the hall seated about four hundred) but mainly about the ambitions of the Society. It is a new one, less than a year in existence. Before the first concert they had no more than 160, after the first concert it went up to 175, then 190, and now it stands at 240. This is impressive, especially taking into consideration that the aim of the society is to extend knowledge of new music. I played well. Ptashka sang not badly, better than in Denver and in any case much better than I was expecting from her morning exercises.

After the concert we were carefully positioned on the stage, and of the four hundred people present at least three hundred came up to shake hands. Some proffered a limp macaroni, others gripped the fingers so hard they crunched. As they did so, most of them uttered, 'I am so glad, I am sure.'[1] This 'I am sure' intrigued me very much: it was as though, not being entirely convinced, they were anxious to assure both themselves and us.

We changed into day clothes there and then in the club and were taken to the station to catch our train. Kansas City is famous for the vast size of its railway station. There are no stations like this in old Europe: there they built huge cathedrals, here train stations: each culture has its ideals!

23 January

All day we travelled in the direction of New York. I read proofs.

24 January

We were supposed to get to New York at half past one, but during the morning it became clear that we were running three hours late. For this reason the engine-driver put on speed and drove the train as hard as he could. Suddenly the train was enveloped in a thick layer of steam like a cloud, so thick that nothing could be seen, except that water was coming out of the cloud and gushing down the windows. Obviously something had happened. The train slowed and finally stopped. People ran up, and it was discovered that the boiler had burst. A new engine was summoned, which turned up quite quickly, half an hour later. The wounded engine was shunted onto a

---

1 In English.

siding; the boiler was indeed smashed just below the driver's compartment. Apparently we had been very lucky, as we could have been derailed.

We arrived in New York some time before six in the evening. We put up at the Laurelton, where Haensel lives, and where I had myself stayed for two weeks in September 1919.

25 January

I took the cheques I had earned during the tour to the bank. Practised at Steinways: we are in New York for only two days and it was not worth having one sent to the hotel. We dined with the Zakharovs, who were very nice.

26 January

Today Ptashka has no voice at all, and we therefore decided it would be better if she did not sing at all this evening. The concert (a Pro Musica one) was in a private apartment; we had been told there were three interconnected halls, but in the event it proved to be three average-sized rooms. The public consisted of about thirty people, mostly female, so that when I sat down to play I felt almost stupid, especially since in the absence of Ptashka I was not even sure whether I would be paid all of the promised $200. I played well, and when I finished the programme it turned out that the auditorium had doubled in size and some musicians had come as well. Zakharov and Cecilia were especially complimentary about my playing, and this flattered me very much, since Zakharov has always adopted a moderately sceptical attitude towards my piano-playing. The money was also paid in full, and flowers were sent to Ptashka. In the evening we left for Boston, where tomorrow morning there is a rehearsal with Koussevitzky. We had reserved a compartment to ourselves, an extremely comfortable arrangement here, much more so than in Europe, but Ptashka still did not sleep.

27 January

Boston at seven in the morning. We stayed at the Lenox Hotel. Boston reminded me of England, and the thawing snow of St Petersburg. Ptashka went to bed and I went to the rehearsal. Koussya welcomed me very tenderly, Natalya Konstantinovna also came to the rehearsal and was extremely friendly, although during the summer our relations had become rather cool. The orchestra, needless to say, read through the Concerto well, and I was also complimented on my playing. It is true that I had no nerves or anxiety whatsoever, and in consequence achieved greater accuracy and more opportunities to give rein to my imagination during the performance. Not to suffer from nerves in provincial recitals is hardly a great event, but if the same could be true of orchestral appearances in Boston and New York it would constitute a great victory, an immense result from my visit to Klein. And a tremendous relief as well! For what tortures were occasioned by these anxieties!

After the rehearsal we went to collect Ptashka and on to lunch with the Koussevitzkys, who live quite far out from the centre in a delightful detached house. They have a Russian cook and we had a delicious lunch with delicious wine, which despite Prohibition they get from Canada. The replacement for Oeberg, evidently, is going to be Paichadze, who has already been his assistant for six months. He is more businesslike and flexible than Oeberg was, and a gentleman. Oeberg ran the whole operation out of a notebook, and left the business in such a neglected state that now Paichadze is trying to disentangle everything but cannot even determine whether the publishing company is in funds or is in debt. Paichadze is forty-five years old, a Georgian, knows several languages, a calm and courteous person, and is married to an old friend of the Koussevitzkys.

28 January

Second rehearsal. The orchestra plays well, although not all the passages are completely clean. The leader is Burgin,[1] from the St Petersburg Conservatoire. He it was, fifteen years ago or so, who seduced Katyusha Borshch,[2] my inamorata at the time, whom I was attempting rather unsuccessfully to court. They were together for ten years, I think they married, and eventually

1 Richard Burgin (1892–1981), violinist and concertmaster. Born in Warsaw, before entering the St Petersburg Conservatoire to study with Leopold Auer he had studied with Joachim in Berlin. Brought by Monteux to Boston in 1920 at the start of his chief conductorship, Burgin occupied the concertmaster's chair for the next forty-two years, also serving as Assistant Conductor. In this role, with his phenomenal memory and impeccable schooling, he was Koussevitzky's indispensable right-hand man. A touching curiosity is the posthumous biography written in verse by his daughter, the writer Diana Lewis Burgin (by his second wife the pianist Ruth Posselt), Professor of Russian at the University of Massachusetts. The biography is composed entirely (in English) in stanzas modelled precisely on those of Pushkin's *Eugene Onegin* (*Richard Burgin, A Life in Verse*, Slavica Publishers, Bloomington, 1989).
2 Yekaterina Borshch, at the time a student in Maria Barinova's class at the St Petersburg Conservatoire, was certainly of great romantic interest to Prokofiev and there are references to her throughout the *Diaries* between 1909 and 1914 but, as he himself says, he did not get anywhere with her. No doubt Richard Burgin was the reason: in a faintly wistful diary reference for October 1918, referring to the Conservatoire's Quinquennial Competition for recent female piano graduates, in which Katya Borshch was competing, Prokofiev writes, 'Afterwards I mixed with the hopefuls awaiting the awarding of the prize, my old flame Katya Borshch among them. She has regained her former beauty, flirted very amiably with me (and I with her) and asked me to give her my Concerto. Most willingly. She is married now and lives in Helsingfors.' See *Diaries*, vol. 1, p. 760. Away from Russia, Katya performed under the name Henrietta Borshch.

ended up in America, where the Persian Consul fell in love with her and carried her off to Persia. Burgin came to the Boston Orchestra, and last year, at Koussevitzky's suggestion, learnt and performed my Violin Concerto.

Today Koussevitzky was also rehearsing Scriabin's Third Symphony. I cannot understand why in Paris today, urged on by Stravinsky and Diaghilev, Scriabin is so disregarded that any interest in him is considered as in poor taste. Granted Scriabin is often incoherent, granted his predilection for programme music and philosophising often lends his works an alien quality, nevertheless I still consider that wholesale rejection of him is equally a purely fashionable response. Scriabin possesses a wonderful melodic gift and great flair for counterpoint, a raft of beautiful harmonies (but not when he becomes a slave to his own harmonic invention); put all of this together and he is a great composer deserving of greater respect than Stravinsky pays him. Today it was with extreme pleasure that I heard the *Divine Poem*.[1]

In the afternoon I orchestrated more of *Ursignol*.

29 January

In the afternoon took place my first concert with the Boston Symphony. The hall was completely sold out. Ptashka was seated next to Natalya Konstantinovna, taking Slonimsky's[2] seat. Slonimsky had to stand in the wings. I was not at all nervous, thanks to Klein. What a relief! And how much better I played! It is all the more remarkable, because I had gone to see Klein for something completely different – my headache and the rash on my hands, and the simple desire to learn something from him, but he told me that all these symptoms were due to anxiety, and he really seems to have cured me of it. Koussevitzky noticed the improvement in my playing. He was very generous: brought me out on stage as though to present me to the audience,

---

1 Scriabin's Symphony No. 3 in C minor, Op. 43 (1904).
2 Nicolas Slonimsky (1894–1995), self-described *diaskeuast* ('reviser or interpolator'), added to his encyclopaedic knowledge of music and musicians of all ages a highly developed sense of humour and a taste for the offbeat, as evidenced by his *Lectionary of Music* ('An Entertaining Reference and Reader's Companion') and *Lexicon of Musical Invective*, a compendium of critical assaults on composers since Beethoven's time. The index, or rather 'invecticon' of this book is a minor masterpiece, with entries such as 'tortured mistuned cackling' and 'topsy-turviest doggerel of sounds' allowing the reader to turn instantly to the maliciously cited critiques of works that subsequently entered the acknowledged canon. Slonimsky's *Thesaurus of Scales and Melodic Patterns* was a seminal influence on many jazz and avant-garde American musicians such as John Coltrane, John Adams and Frank Zappa. *Baker's Dictionary of Musicians*, of which he was editor-in-chief from 1958 to 1992, is still a consulted work of reference. Slonimsky had worked as a rehearsal pianist for Koussevitzky in Paris, and came to be his assistant at the Boston Symphony in 1925. His autobiography *Perfect Pitch* (OUP, Oxford, 1988) contains personal insights and anecdotes about Koussevitzky, Stravinsky, Cowell, Ives and a host of other major figures in twentieth-century music.

and applauded me after each movement and at the end. The orchestra did likewise, and I had five curtain calls, which in the opinion of Koussevitzky was the greatest success of any soloist this season. But for me the main thing was that I was able to play so calmly. After the concert we went to the Koussevitzky home, where we dined and spent the rest of the evening. I spoke to Natalya Konstantinovna about publishing Asafyev's book, and to Sergey Alexandrovich about performing Myaskovsky's Symphony. I tried to get agreement on the engraving of my next score, but no more engraving is to be done until May, by which time Oeberg's chaotic legacy should be disentangled. Thank God work is proceeding on the score and parts of the Suite from *Oranges*, and on the new edition of the Op. 23 songs.

Koussevitzky and I discussed the possibility of making cuts in the *Divine Poem*, as the piece is unconscionably long. I proposed removing the tumour in the first movement between the end of the reprise and the coda, also several long-drawn-out passages in the finale, because there are plenty of longueurs in the second movement, in spite of the cuts Koussevitzky has already made.

Did some more orchestration in the afternoon, but not much. In the evening yesterday's concert was repeated with the same programme. It went with no less calmness and success; the applause may have been even warmer than yesterday's, but there were only four curtain calls instead of five. Afterwards we had dinner at the Koussevitzkys.

The Christian Science church, the first to be established in America, is situated right near the concert hall. At night its cupola is illuminated all the way round by floodlights placed on the surrounding buildings; this is very beautiful.

The cuts we made yesterday in the *Divine Poem* seemed to me successful, but the bass drum I had suggested adding to the conclusion of the theme of the Introduction for some reason did not sound right after all.

31 January

We visited Ptashka's father.[1] Ptashka had already been to see him over the previous few days and he had come to the concert, which he had greatly enjoyed. He is sixty years old but could pass for forty or forty-five. I formed a very good impression of him even though both his French and Russian are pretty bad.

1   Juan Codina (1866–?1935), tenor, Prokofiev's father-in-law. Don Juan Codina y Llubera (his daughter used the name Lina Llubera as a stage name) came from Barcelona and was proud of his Catalan roots. Completing his vocal studies at the school attached to La Scala in Milan he had met there another singing student, Olga Vladislavovna Nemysskaya, and in spite of the great disparity in origins, culture and religion they married.

At five we left to return to New York, arriving at ten o'clock at night, and stayed at the Laurelton where we have a good room with bath and will be staying a whole month.

1 February

Gottlieb presented himself in the morning; he has come to New York for the whole duration of my stay. He tried to give me $100, which I declined, but politely. Ptashka was offended that he should offer me money, but I explained that though perhaps tactless this was from pure kindheartedness.

In the evening we went to Szigeti's concert, but I did not much care for the way he played.

2 February

Lunched with the Zakharovs, and then did some orchestration.

3 February

Natalya Konstantinovna has come to New York bringing with her material for a 'Carmen Suite'. The Moscow Art Theatre has chopped up *Carmen* and redone Bizet's music. The result is a heightened dramatic intensity, with some of the recitatives being replaced by dialogue.[1] It revived in me thoughts of a piece to be constructed on the basis of rhythmic melodic declamation. But for that I would have to be in Russia, because anything of that ilk would be intimately bound up with the language, and if I were to compose something of the kind it could only be in Russian. Not only that, but for a first attempt it would be essential to find an appropriate subject.

After the performance, which I found uncommonly interesting, Salzédo,[2] upset at the manipulation of Bizet's score, flew at me and was even rude to me.

---

1 Not to be confused with the two orchestral suites created by Fritz Hoffmann from Bizet's opera score soon after the composer's untimely death, nor obviously the *Carmen-Suite* Rodion Shchedrin devised as a showcase for his wife, the Bolshoy Theatre ballerina assoluta Maya Plisetskaya, in 1967. It was probably drawn from the 'manipulated' musical accompaniment to Nemirovich-Danchenko's adaptation for the Music Studio of the Moscow Art Theatre of Bizet's *Carmen*, entitled *Carmencita and the Soldier*, which had been a sensation on the company's first American tour in 1923. See the *New York Times*, 16 August 1925.
2 Carlos Salzédo (1885–1961), French-born composer and harpist. Salzédo had moved to America in 1909 at the invitation of Toscanini to join the Metropolitan Opera Orchestra, and lived there for the rest of his life except for the period of the First World War when he was drafted into the French Army as a cook in an infantry regiment. Back in America he became the unquestioned doyen of harpists and a seminal influence on the teaching of the instrument and the way in which contemporary composers treated it.

4 February

In the evening my New York appearance with the Boston Symphony, the central event of my American stay. For an artist New York is the most abominable city there is: overstuffed, hearing all the best performers, carping, almost totally ignorant of new music but at the same time feeling equipped to decide the fate of an artist for the whole country; in sum the parvenu who has bought an ancient castle. Just before dinner I did experience a tremor of nerves, but by the evening it had vanished. I played well. The hall was full. When I went out on stage and sat down at the piano it felt as though everything was trembling: it turned out this was the subway running underneath.

The success was actually greater than in Boston. I was called out three times and then a final fourth, and then went back to the Green Room, but after a little while I was sent for and told that I must take another bow as the audience was still clapping. I went out a fifth time, to be greeted by a huge ovation. Into the Artists' Room came Klemperer,[1] the German conductor who is making a big name for himself in Russia, Gieseking,[2] Tailleferre, and others. They all congratulated me. After the concert we went out to supper: the Zakharovs, ourselves, Burgin and Saminsky.[3]

5 February

A most elegant (and delicious) lunch at Steinways: Toscanini,[4] the Rachmaninoffs,[5] the Koussevitzkys, Auer,[6] the last-named spry and jolly in

---

1   Otto Klemperer (1885–1973), German-Jewish conductor and composer, regarded as one of Europe's greatest conducting talents and in his youth a sterling champion of contemporary music, although by the time he was 'rediscovered' by Walter Legge and in 1959 placed at the head of the newly created Philharmonia Orchestra he was concentrating almost exclusively on the works of the great German composers.
2   Walter Gieseking (1895–1956), outstanding German pianist whose main reputation, despite an exceptionally wide repertoire, rests on his performances of French music, in particular Debussy.
3   Lazar Saminsky (1882–1959), composer, conductor (mainly choral) and musicologist, chiefly of Jewish music. He had been a fellow student of Prokofiev in Tcherepnin's conducting class at the St Petersburg Conservatoire. See *Diaries*, vol. 1, pp. 4–66 *passim*, 132, 159, 398, 529, 677, 685.
4   Arturo Toscanini (1867–1957), most celebrated of all Italian conductors, was already a star in America from his Metropolitan Opera appearances in the first two decades of the century. When he brought his own orchestra of La Scala, Milan, on a concert tour in the 1920–21 season, the stage was set for his later iconic status as the man for whom the NBC Symphony Orchestra was created in 1937.
5   Sergey Rachmaninoff's wife was his first cousin, Natalya Alexandrovna Satina.
6   Leopold Auer (1845–1930), distinguished violinist and teacher whose pupils at the St Petersburg Conservatoire included Mischa Elman, Jascha Heifetz, Efrem Zimbalist and Cecilia Hansen. As a violinist, Auer is perhaps most remembered for declining to give the first performance of Tchaikovsky's Violin Concerto, deeming it unplayable (although he later changed his mind and performed it frequently).

spite of his eighty-two years. As soon as Rachmaninoff had greeted me he withdrew to another room, and then at lunch was seated at the other end of the table from me, but before we parted I asked him about his concerts and about Medtner, and Ptashka asked about his granddaughter, all of which topics were pleasant to him. Toscanini is incredibly short-sighted, almost blind, but his most attractive feature is his eyes. I did not get much chance to talk to him, but he and Koussevitzky contrived to have a conversation about new works, in the course of which Koussevitzky recommended the *Classical Symphony*, which Toscanini said he would conduct in May in Milan. Ptashka conversed in Italian with him and with his wife, a stout and somewhat primitive Italian woman, and they invited us to visit them when we were in Italy.[1]

There was barely time, once we got home, to have a rest, get changed into evening dress and go out to Koussevitzky's, with whom I set out for Brooklyn. Our wives were tired and remained at home. We did the Concerto well, but it was less lively than the night before in New York, because we ourselves had lost a bit of nervous energy. There were three or four curtain calls. Among the audience was Klein, to whom I had sent a ticket. To see me in the Artists' Room came the Anisfelds and Gottlieb, with his brother and sister. The Anisfelds have recently been through a bad patch of neglect and lack of success, but things are once again looking up for them.[2]

A telegram from Weber saying that without benefit of any acquaintance with the music *The Fiery Angel* has been accepted by the Berlin Opera.

6 February

In the afternoon the second New York performance, which went as well as the first. Green Room visitors included a now grey-haired Aslanov,[3] whom I have not seen for eight years, and Lucy Khodzhayeva, by marriage Davydova although she is now divorced.[4] Lucy has changed: I remember her as a young

---

1 Toscanini's wife was Carla de Martini, thus the mother of Wanda who was to marry Horowitz. The Toscaninis had been married since 1897, when Carla was nineteen. Toscanini had a reputation as a womaniser, but the couple stayed married until Carla's death in 1951.
2 Boris Anisfeld (1878–1973), painter and theatre designer, associated with the *Mir Isskustva* group and responsible for several productions for the Ballets Russes. Anisfeld had designed the scenery and costumes for the premiere production of *The Love for Three Oranges* in Chicago in 1921–22. Ibid., pp. 337, 411, 413, 639–55 *passim*. Anisfeld was at this time on the brink of being appointed a professor at the School of the Chicago Art Institute, a post in which his talents, experience and dedication found full expression. Among the many students who passed through his hands were Red Grooms, Leon Golub and Claes Oldenburg.
3 The conductor Alexander Aslanov (1874–1960) had been the Artistic Director of the summer seasons of concerts in Pavlovsk, near St Petersburg, and had been an active promoter of Prokofiev's music, including the *succès de scandale* of the premiere of the Second Piano Concerto.
4 Lucy Khodzhayeva was the elder of two daughters of a family with whom Prokofiev had been friendly in Kislovodsk in 1918 before setting out on the journey that eventually brought him to

lady, almost a girl; now her face has an attractive intensity but looks worn. How early for this to happen! We did not have much of a chance to speak. Her parents and Liza are in Kislovodsk.

In the evening we went with the Koussevitzkys to the conductor Schelling,[1] where there was a mob of celebrities: Toscanini, Gabrilowitsch,[2] Olga Samarova[3] and others.

In Brooklyn yesterday, while I was waiting to go out on stage, a new solution occurred to me of the old 'eternal' question of the source of evil. Man is

---

America. Prokofiev and Lucy met again in Paris in June 1921, by which time Lucy had married one Davydov, with whom she had fled the Revolution and ended up in Paris virtually destitute. Davydov got a job as an actor in the Russian-nostalgia cabaret at the Théâtre de la Chauve-Souris, and Prokofiev was heavily involved with his future wife Lina Codina, but this seems not to have prevented either of them from enjoying at least one romantic encounter. See *Diaries*, vol. 2, pp. 611–12.

[1] Ernest Schelling (1876–1939), pianist, composer and conductor. Two years before, Schelling had become the first conductor of the New York Philharmonic's immensely popular Young People's Concerts, designed to foster an interest in music in children. Schelling had studied at the Paris Conservatoire and his largely forgotten works have a European flavour, although the *Suite fantastique* for piano and orchestra is an attractive Moszkowskyesque confection of American themes, good enough to be included in Hyperion Records' survey of the Romantic Piano Concerto.

[2] Ossip Gabrilowitsch (in the German transliteration he adopted in the West) (1878–1936) studied piano and composition at the St Petersburg Conservatoire, and subsequently with Leschetitsky in Vienna. He left Russia well before the Revolution and settled in America, where in 1918 he was appointed Music Director of the newly created Detroit Symphony Orchestra, a position he held until his premature death in 1936. A condition of his acceptance was that a complete new auditorium be built for the orchestra, and this was accomplished in the space of four months and twenty-three days, a remarkable example of can-do. In 1922 the Detroit Orchestra under Gabrilowitsch with Schnabel as soloist gave the world's first radio broadcast of a symphony concert. In 1909 Gabrilowitsch had married Mark Twain's daughter, an occasion that prompted the following exchange between Twain and a journalist: 'The marriage pleases you, Mr Clemens?' 'Yes, fully as much as any marriage could please me or perhaps any other father. There are two or three tragically solemn things in this life, and a happy marriage is one of them, for the terrors of life are all to come . . . I am glad of this marriage, and Mrs Clemens would be glad, for she always had a warm affection for Gabrilowitsch, but all the same it is a tragedy, since it is a happy marriage with its future before it, loaded to the Plimsoll line with uncertainties.'

[3] *Sic*. Olga Samaroff (1880–1948), née Lucy Mary Agnes Hickenlooper of Texas, wisely invented her professional name in order to be taken seriously as a pianist, and in 1905 set about promoting herself by renting Carnegie Hall, Walter Damrosch and the New York Philharmonic in order to perform the Tchaikovsky Piano Concerto. No Florence Foster Jenkins, she made a genuine impression and enjoyed a major career as a pianist and educator, making her considerably more famous than the young church organist Leopold Stokowski she discovered and lobbied furiously to get appointed to the Philadelphia Orchestra in 1912. By the time of the meeting with Prokofiev Olga Samaroff had suffered two major setbacks: Stokowski had left her for Greta Garbo, and an awkward fall had broken her shoulder and obliged her to give up performing. Nothing daunted, she concentrated on her teaching positions at the Philadelphia Conservatory and the Juilliard School of Music in New York, where she mentored an astonishing roster of talents including William Kapell, Richard Farrell, Bruce Hungerford, Raymond Lewenthal, Eugene List, Vincent Persichetti, Thomas Schippers, Rosalyn Tureck and Alexis Weissenberg.

made in the image of God; a man is an individual being possessed of an individuality that is preserved for ever. According to Christian Science this individuality never perishes, is never absorbed into other entities, and does not dissolve into the deity. Whenever a man is created, that is to say whenever an individual being is created, into each individual must be inserted a consciousness of his own individuality. It follows that each individual must be aware that he differs from his brother, and therefore he is not his brother. Herein lies the origin of self-love: this is I, not he. Could it be that the immature individual being needs a certain amount of self-love to avoid being swallowed up by other beings? For without the individual's love for himself there is a tendency towards amalgamation: imagine a man who loves another more than himself; he begins to take on the beloved's characteristics and gradually loses his own. But the moment we accept the birth of self-love, by the same token we accept the birth of evil, for evil arises from loving oneself more than others. The conclusion is that evil is an unavoidable element in the process of creating an individual. God did not create evil, God created individual beings in order to become fully Himself. Christian Science regards evil as illusory because evil is a manifestation of the temporal; in eternity, where there is no time, everything that is temporal is an illusion. It is a fleeting instant of this world bearing no relation to eternity. For how long will evil persist? Until such time as individual beings grow strong enough to resist the pull of attraction to other beings resulting in amalgamation and dissolution. From this it follows that when man turns towards good and rejects evil, it is a symptom of his individuality maturing.

7 February

The critics after each of the three concerts were divided: half of them were good and half terrible. The good ones were looking over their shoulders, the bad ones were simply arrogant. Most intelligent of them all was the elderly Henderson:[1] although he did not understand much, he advised a careful and serious approach to my music. That would have been good advice for the above-mentioned pups, who are too stupid to see how stupid they are. How glad I am that I do not depend, as so many unfortunates have to, on these dregs of society: in three weeks' time I shall be leaving the country, and if I

---

1 W. J. Henderson (1855–1927), the critic of the New York *Sun*. The author of several books, including a novel entitled *The Soul of a Tenor*, he also lectured on the history of music in the New York College of Music. He was evidently more reverential towards Prokofiev than he was subsequently to be towards Shostakovich, whom he described as 'without doubt the foremost composer of pornographic music in the history of art.'

return it will be because there are conductors who will invite me irrespective of the critics (which is not the case in the American provinces), but on the basis of the respect paid to me in Europe.

8 February

The following period in New York has been reconstructed from very abbreviated notes, therefore it is not documented in full.

9 February

Called on the publisher Knopf.[1] Last summer the Koussevitzkys themselves had mentioned in passing that they would be interested in publishing books by Asafyev. When in this connection I wrote to Asafyev he replied with great feeling expressing his dream of writing a book about style in Russian opera. At this the Koussevitzkys went back on their word, and so I found myself in an embarrassing position with regard to Asafyev. For this reason I was always badgering them about it, saying that somehow or other the situation must be resolved. In New York the Koussevitzkys had become friendly with Knopf, a young and wealthy publisher and an admirer of theirs, and had now recommended me to lay the position before him. Knopf was friendly, and presented me with an English translation of Rimsky-Korsakov's autobiography, beautifully produced by his firm, but said that Asafyev's book would not have much of a market, and that if he did publish it, it could only be 'for sentimental reasons'. In other words, he is prepared to take the book, but the fee would be negligible. As I thought I should go in search of a better offer, I decided to let the matter rest for the time being.

In the evening old man Nelson, who had entertained me to supper after the first night of *Oranges* in Chicago,[2] invited us to dinner at the Plaza and then to the theatre to see the play *The Patsy*,[3] except that in his half-witted way he thought the play's title was *The Taxi*. Everything would have been fine but for the fact that he had also invited an incurably dense woman who ruined the whole evening for me and so irritated me that by the end I relapsed into an outrageous sulk.

---

1   Alfred A. Knopf senior (1892–1984) founded the publishing house that bears his name in 1915, mainly to fill what he saw as a gap in the market, that of European and Russian literature. Knopf was not shy of expressing his opinions; his comment on *Doctor Zhivago* is worth noting: 'If Khrushchev had banned it for *dullness*, he would have been in the clear.'
2   See *Diaries*, vol. 2, pp. 656, 661.
3   Comedy by Barry Connors, about a Cinderella character (Pat, the Patsy of the title), hopelessly overshadowed by her prettier and more favoured sister, who nevertheless gets her man. It was later made into a successful film by King Vidor, starring Marion Davies.

10 February

In the afternoon I boarded a very nice and comfortable American-style saloon coach to go to Boston. Ptashka came to the station to see me off.

11 February

In the morning I went to the rehearsal, because Koussevitzky had promised to play my Quintet with the same expanded forces as he performed it in New York in the autumn. The players had naturally forgotten the Quintet (well, probably they had never learnt it thoroughly in the first place), while Koussevitzky was miles away from being able to conduct the third movement and had to leave it out. In consequence the Quintet sounded like nothing on earth and the whole impression was painful. I was upset, but when I got home and looked at the score I found that in fact it was all well constructed and should have sounded good, except that it needs to be learnt by heart and, of course, played without doubling the instrumentation.

In the evening I drove out with the Koussevitzkys through colossal snow-drifts to Cambridge, a town which is really part of Boston and where the programme was repeated for the sixth time. It went well, although a little more somnolent than in New York, not to mention that the Steinway supplied for the provincial concert was disgraceful.

Afterwards I had supper with the Koussevitzkys, who were in their most unpretentious and amiable mode, and insisted that I take a bottle of genuine Portuguese port back for Ptashka, a most generous present in 'dry' America. I energetically pursued my scheme to have Myaskovsky's Symphony No. 7 performed in Paris in the spring. Koussevitzky said all right, it's agreed.

12 February

Return journey. Just as the train was leaving on jumped Szigeti. We sat together in the restaurant car and chatted. For two full years he has been playing my Violin Concerto all over Europe, and it would be hard to say whether he made a career for the Concerto or the other way round. But now that he has come to America something has caused him to take fright, and although he was asked to play the Concerto in Boston and Philadelphia, he preferred to play the Brahms. Not clever. With my Concerto he could have made a real impact, but it goes without saying that the Brahms is played better by Heifetz, Kreisler and others. Today Szigeti was saying that America is a strange place: if an artist makes a success then hundreds of cities invite him to play concerts, but if not then it is as if there is a stone wall round him, and despite the huge number of possible engagements he simply has to leave the country, otherwise he will starve to death.

Damrosch had asked me to telephone him, saying that he wanted to discuss performing my music. Today Ptashka called him at my request, but now it appears that he is too busy and cannot tell me anything definite at this time. In short he has twisted it to make it seem as though it was not he who asked me, but I who was importuning him.

13 February

An evening of contemporary music, with a dull quartet by Casella and Stravinsky's *Les Noces*. The interest in the hall was palpable; a lot of musicians were present. Stokowski conducted, but he had not thoroughly studied the score, and got away with it only because the four pianos were in reliable hands: Casella, Tailleferre, Enesco[1] and Salzedo.

It went pretty well, and it was very enjoyable to listen to *Les Noces*. When all is said and done it is Stravinsky's best work. It was a huge success. The programme opened with *Les Noces*, then Casella's piece (worthless and boring) and then *Les Noces* was repeated. Sitting in one of the front rows was Rachmaninoff. As soon as he saw that the musicians were taking their places to play *Les Noces* again, he rushed headlong out of the hall, knocking over chairs and treading on the toes of all who were in his path.

15 February

In the morning I went to see Klein, who was full of praise for my Concerto which he had heard me play ten days ago in Brooklyn. Today's session was less successful than the first, because it was constantly interrupted by telephone calls, some of them about the new apartment to which he is shortly moving. Klein, however, has an amazing ability to concentrate immediately and take up the thread again once the call has ended. Incidentally, Klein spoke of the simplicity of how God should be perceived, saying that God is not somewhere remote, aloft in metaphysical heights, but here and now, by our side, a ready help in any difficulty, for God is not an abstract concept but the principle of

---

1 Georges Enesco (1881–1955), Romanian violinist, pianist, conductor and composer, and probably the most outstandingly gifted musician of his time. Described by Pablo Casals without conscious hyberbole as 'the most amazing musician since Mozart', he was as inspired and selfless as a teacher as he was at every other aspect of his musicianship: few if any other pedagogues can ever have claimed students of the calibre of the violinist Yehudi Menuhin *and* the pianist Dinu Lipatti. In America at this time he was becoming known as a great conductor, having made his debut with the Philadelphia Orchestra in 1923, and so luminous was his reputation that he was actively considered as a successor to Toscanini when in 1936 the latter stepped down from the New York Philharmonic.

Good, in fact Good itself, so that any good deed manifests the presence of God. I told him of my struggle with toothache and how, although the acute pain has subsided, from time to time the tooth still today lets me know of its existence. I also told him of the marvellous result of having conquered my anxiety during concert performances, and that only once this month had I suffered neuralgia, and that mildly. After this Klein gave me 'help'[1] and then made me repeat that there was no neuralgia, there was no 'dental low',[2] there were no evil representations, there were no representations of illness. He wished me success in Providence, and asked me to come again.

Based on the past month with its single instance of mild neuralgia, I thought I was finally cured of this companion who has dogged my steps for thirty years, but in the afternoon for no reason at all I was subjected to an acute attack which ruined the rest of the day and ceased only at night. Patience!

16 February

Travelled to Providence, a pleasant journey of four hours in a comfortable Pullman car in the sunshine. Caught up on my diary.

The concert (seventh and last with Koussevitzky) went well and was probably the best performance of the seven. Koussevitzky told me that I could not be engaged again next year by the Boston Symphony, which never offers engagements two years consecutively, but the following year he would arrange an even more extensive tour.

I spent the night in Providence in a very comfortable hotel, but slept badly on account of very noisy plumbing. So much for the elaborate facilities – but no thought of their clients' rest.

17 February

Return from Providence to New York.

18 February

In the afternoon I attended the general rehearsal of Carpenter's *Skyscrapers*. The history of this ballet is as follows: Diaghilev, dining with Carpenter, had once said to him, 'Why is it that you Americans have never written a genuinely American ballet?' and started improvising, dreaming up skyscrapers,

---

1 Written in English.
2 Written in English.

machines and so on. Carpenter took the bait and, his imagination fired, composed a ballet along these lines, and a year later presented himself to Diaghilev in Paris with these words: 'I have composed the ballet you were speaking about, and have come specially from Chicago to play it to you. I shall be going back to America in a few days.' Diaghilev was sufficiently discombobulated at someone having come over from Chicago in order to play a ballet through to him to make some encouraging noises during the performance. Carpenter thus went away confident that his ballet was accepted, but Diaghilev stuffed the score into a trunk and forgot all about it. A year went by, or longer, at which point an emissary from Carpenter presented himself to Diaghilev and enquired whether or not he was going to stage the ballet, and if not please to return the score, as in that case it would be presented in America. Diaghilev retrieved the score and commissioned Dukelsky to look through it. Dukelsky's verdict was that as a ballet, notwithstanding the Carpenters had been very kind to him, and not to mention that he, Dukelsky, had made a pass at their daughter when he was living in New York, *Skyscrapers* was a lemon. Diaghilev thereupon gave back the score. In this way it had beached at the Metropolitan and was now about to experience the glare of the footlights.

Dukelsky, as it happens, was quite right. The scenery looked nice but the dancing was feeble, more running about than dancing. The music was Modernistic and admirably orchestrated, but empty, with snatches of *Petrushka* and of the French composers.[1]

In the evening I visited the Ingermans.[2] Aslanov was there as well. His wife gives singing lessons and he plays accompaniments for her students.

19 February

Worked. Despite all the distractions, the orchestration of the ballet is coming along.

Evening at the Anisfelds. After several years in which he flourished, the most dazzling of which was the year of the *Oranges* production, Anisfeld and America ceased to take much interest in one another and he endured a very thin period. But now he has risen again, at least materially, he has work somewhere or other and has taken out American citizenship. When I took

---

1 Presumably Les Six and their adherents. See *Diaries*, vol. 2, p. 516, for Prokofiev's own reaction to the score in Paris in May 1920: 'a procession from the banal to the ephemeral'.
2 Drs Sergius and Anna Ingerman, husband and wife doctors in New York who had treated Prokofiev with exemplary care for scarlet fever in 1919. Prokofiev credited Anna Ingerman with probably having saved him from deafness as a result of abscesses in the region of the ear drums. The Ingermans had subsequently become friends.

him to task for betraying Russia, he replied, 'Look, I was a Bessarabian and now that means I would be a Romanian: better to be an American.'¹

21 February

In my previous American sojourns the critic of the most influential of the New York evening newspapers, the *Evening Post*, was a certain Finck, the most conservative conservative of all.² But times have changed, and now sitting in his chair is Mme Olga Samaroff, a contemporary pianist, divorced wife of Stokowski, an American who had assumed a Russian stage name. She invited me to call on her today and I gave her an interview, my first proper interview in America. The questions she asked were serious, to the point, and many of them forced me to think before replying. Hooray, America is making progress! At Samaroff's I heard a new young violinist, Weisbord, a young Russian Jew from the Baltic.³ He seemed to me an absolutely wonderful violinist. It was a pity that he was accompanied by an appalling papa, somewhat like Elman's,⁴ who continually intervenes in conversations and talks up his son at the most inopportune moments.

1   One cannot but have some sympathy with Boris Anisfeld's position. Bessarabia was that melting-pot surrounded by Ukraine, Moldavia, Romania and Russia, bounded by the Dniester river to the east and the Prut river to the west. Until just before the end of the First World War Bessarabia was a province of Imperial Russia, but at that time declared independence from Russia and three months later united with Romania. It then remained part of Romania until the Molotov–Ribbentrop Pact in 1940 effectively gave it back to the Soviet Union. After the confusion of the Second World War, during which it changed hands several times, the 1940 Soviet annexation was formally recognised and what was Bessarabia became part of the Moldavian Soviet Socialist Republic (now the Republic of Moldova), since 1991 officially independent again.
2   Henry Theophilus Finck (1854–1926) had recently retired from the New York *Evening Post* through ill-health and was to die later in the year. The prolific author of several full-length books on Wagner, Massenet, Grieg, Chopin and Anton Seidl, he had been the newspaper's music critic since 1881.
3   From the National Film Board of Canada's publicity about a 1996 documentary by David Vaisbord: 'Mischa Weisbord. The name was once legendary to music lovers throughout Europe. He played for kings, was hailed as "the new Paganini", and performed in Carnegie Hall and the most prestigious theaters of Europe. Yet when he died in 1991, alone and impoverished in a Brooklyn apartment, his body lay undiscovered for days. He had not performed for decades, and his neighbors knew nothing of his past as a wunderkind violinist, the toast of London and Paris. Who was Mischa Weisbord and why did he die in such obscurity? Director David Vaisbord, Mischa's nephew, takes us on a personal journey from Russia, through Europe and Israel, to New York City. Through conversations with friends, family and admirers, the mystery of his uncle Mischa is unravelled over time and distance. David explores the phenomenon of the child prodigy, and the complexities of the musical world. As the journey to discover Mischa unfolds, the director pays bittersweet homage to his memory, and reflects on his own childhood in the dark, yet brilliant, shadow of his uncle.'
4   Mischa Elman (1891–1967), famous violinist from Odessa who settled in America and left a very large recorded legacy on HMV. Prokofiev had come across him in New York in 1918 and was happy to have beaten him at chess, in which Elman had the reputation of excelling. See *Diaries*, vol. 2, pp. 289, 338–9, 402.

Went to a concert given by Klemperer, who has been enjoying a furious success in Soviet Russia. He did not make much of an impression on me. Here, he is being beaten into second place by his compatriot Furtwängler.[1]

22 February

Worked in the afternoon. In the evening was with Edward Lasker, the chess player and namesake of the champion.[2] He it was who had placed my chess games on record in the American press. Also there were the elder Piastro[3] with his wife Berezovskaya,[4] who had been a fleeting attachment of mine twenty years ago at the Conservatoire (oho! what times my life has already seen!), and Mischa Elman, who to my astonishment now has a quite passable wife. Needless to say, he and I immediately sat down to the chess board – an old *rivalité*! This time he lost in fairly short order. He opened with quite a good *Giuoco piano*,[5]

---

1 Wilhelm Furtwängler (1886–1954), the great German conductor, had been invited to guest-conduct the New York Philharmonic the previous year, and such was his success that he was invited again for the two succeeding seasons.
2 The champion was Emanuel Lasker (1868–1941), Grandmaster and world chess champion, whom Prokofiev had got to know at the St Petersburg International Tournament in 1914, in which Lasker narrowly prevailed against Capablanca. See *Diaries*, vol. 1, pp. 640–79 *passim*. The engineer and inventor Edward Lasker (1885–1981), German-born but living in America since before the First World War, was not as a chess player quite in the class of his namesake, to whom it transpired he was distantly related; nevertheless he won five US Open Championships. With Emanuel a willing collaborator Edward also became fascinated by the Oriental board game of Go, which originated in China 2,500 years ago, and after initial scepticism grew to consider it a genuine rival to chess in its intellectual and strategic complexity. The game is played with black and white pieces, identical except for their opposing colours, on a grid formed by 19 x 19 intersecting lines. The object is for your colour to control the board by capturing and removing unprotected opposing pieces, and the strategic problems arise from the tension between the tactical urgency of protection through fortress groupings and the strategic planning of widespread influence. In his book *Go and Go-Moku: The Oriental Board Games*, published in 1960 and still widely regarded as the best introduction to the game for Westerners, Edward Lasker wrote, 'While the Baroque rules of Chess could only have been created by humans, the rules of Go are so elegant, organic, and rigorously logical that if intelligent life forms exist elsewhere in the universe, they almost certainly play Go.' It can be played by a four-year-old, but when the two Laskers played, in consultation with each other and with a nine-piece handicap, against a visiting Japanese mathematician they were beaten effortlessly.
3 Tosya Piastro, violinist, brother of the better-known Mikhail (Misha) Piastro with whom Prokofiev had associated in Japan during his 1918 sojourn. Both were fellow students of Prokofiev at the St Petersburg Conservatoire, where Tosya's evident charms successfully put paid to more than one of Prokofiev's numerous romantic inclinations, including with Elfrieda Hansen, pianist sister of Cecilia. See *Diaries*, vol. 1, pp. 152, 158, 162.
4 Nyura Berezovskaya, 'extremely beautiful but terminally dull. This phrase sums up her entire personality' was at one time ranked No. 6 in Prokofiev's meticulously documented ladder of Conservatoire female interests. Ibid., pp. 114–58 *passim*.
5 The 'quiet game', said to be the oldest recorded chess opening, attributed to the seventeenth-century Italian chess player Gioacchino Greco, although known to have existed for at least a hundred years before him. It is aimed at rapid development and occupation of the centre.

but then weakly lost his position and I won with a rather pretty sacrifice. 'What's the matter with you?' I asked, to which he replied, 'I can't concentrate, you see I am expecting a child!' I asked if he knew Weisbord. He said, 'Yes, he is a good violinist but his career is being wrecked by a dreadful papa.' A rich observation to hear from the mouth of Elman, notorious for his own monstrous papasha.

24 February

Koussevitzky has been made an honorary doctor of Brown University, which has made him very happy, and today is the day of his coronation. I sent him a congratulatory telegram.

25 February

Went to Furtwängler's concert. He is enjoying the most tremendous success here. I was interested to hear what a German would make of a piece like Tchaikovsky's Sixth Symphony: it was a little restrained and all the passage-work played with punctilious accuracy. Although I was not acquainted with him personally, I decided to go round after the concert and shake his hand – after all, plenty of conductors I don't know have done the same to me! Furtwängler asked how I had found the Sixth Symphony. I told him: 'Very interesting, a little too classical.' In an offended tone of voice, Furtwängler asked, 'What do you mean by too classical?' I started to explain to him, but stumbled with my German. Just then various ladies came up to him and occupied his attention to such an extent that I took my leave and departed, with a sense of having gone in intending to shake his hand but having in fact said something disagreeable.

26 February

Left to go to Syracuse for the last concert of my tour, for which incidentally I am being paid two copecks. The city of Syracuse is remarkable for the fact that the train runs right along the street, almost brushing the cars parked by the kerb. In the hotel I found the conductor Savich,[1] and we went through the tempi of my Third Piano Concerto.

---

1 Vladimir Savich (1888–1947), conductor born and educated in Russia but now resident in America. He would later conduct the premiere of the Suite from *Le Pas d'acier* at the Bolshoy Theatre in Moscow, in a performance described by Prokofiev in private correspondence as 'second-rate'.

27 February

Morning rehearsal. The orchestra is provincial, but tries hard. We are doing only the first movement of the Third Concerto. Everything was very difficult, and in any case the programme had to be kept short. I am glad of this; for a $250 fee even one movement is plenty. The concert immediately followed the rehearsal, at noon. I had a success, but a much greater success greeted the local whistler. The programme also included Respighi's *Pines of Rome*, which incorporates the sound of nightingales usually conveyed by a gramophone recording of the real sound of a nightingale.[1] But in this performance instead of a gramophone they had invited a local Miss whose whistling was superior to that of the gramophone. And since Miss was the daughter of a local celebrity, the audience greeted her performance with an ovation. At the end, while she was standing with her bouquet of roses, I asked her if her lips were not liable to freeze from nerves. She laughed and said that no, her lips did not freeze up, but it had been very frightening. The last item on the programme was Liszt's *Les Préludes*. It is long since I heard this work, and now I listened with interest. It is good, but much of it is contrived and cold.

There was a lunch after the concert and then I got the train back to New York. I arrived late in the evening, very tired, but Ptashka had gone to a Fokine[2] performance and afterwards gone with the Fokines and Mme Rachmaninoff to have supper, not getting home until three in the morning. I was very angry. Rachmaninoff had also been at the theatre, sitting in the box with Ptashka, and was nice to her, but did not go on to supper.

28 February

Haensel and his wife invited us to dine in a Swedish restaurant, where there was such a mass of hors d'oeuvres that I had no appetite for the main dish.

1 March

I am correcting the Duo-Art rolls. I sit for several hours a day to the point of stupefaction, but it has to be finished before I leave. The editor with whom I am doing it worked with Medtner last year: he says Medtner is an excellent musician and it was interesting working with him.

---

1 The third movement, 'The Pines of the Janiculum', ends with the recorded sound of a nightingale forming a bridge to the final movement 'The Pines of the Appian Way'.
2 Mikhail Fokine (1880–1942), the choreographer whose insistence on naturalism and symbolism had unlocked the aesthetics of dance from 'the currant smiles of the ballerinas . . . and the vegetable obedience of the *corps de ballet*' – Osip Mandelshtam, *The Egyptian Stamp*. See *Diaries*, vol. 2, pp. 443, 591.

A concert in the evening at which a symphony of Milhaud's was played, his sixth I believe, for small ensemble of voice and several instruments. Interestingly conceived as to its sonority, but poor music.

2 March

Continued correcting Duo-Art. Dined with V. Bashkirov in Brooklyn; his mother made a delicious Russian dinner. With him was a pretty girl, whom he unofficially presents as his fiancée. She writes verses, and Vladimir Nikolayevich is planning to publish them. Poor B.N., if only he knew![1] A.D.[2] was hospitable and polite, but her demeanour was reserved. I expect she blames me for abandoning Boris Nikolayevich to his fate in Paris, but after all I cannot be expected to breast-feed him for ever!

3 March

Furtwängler invited me to lunch to try to clarify what I was getting at with my remark about 'too classical an interpretation'. We talked of music and of Stravinsky, and Furtwängler said he plans to perform my music in Germany.

4 March

Duo-Art. I am working as hard as I can possibly can. In the evening we were at Klemperer's, who also expressed interest in my compositions and wanted to know if he could have the rights to premieres – specifically premieres, not just performances – in America and Germany. He does not know much about my works, and loves Stravinsky.

We paid some farewell calls, among them to Steinway and to Ziloti. With Ziloti it was a combined farewell visit and introduction to him of Ptashka, because although we had been in America for two months, with all the coming and going we had never found a moment to go and see him. Ziloti had evidently taken offence, and on the pretext that he had a student with him declined to receive us. Later he rang me up and we discussed how to extract a fee from the Philadelphia Orchestra for the orchestral parts of Myaskovsky's Fifth Symphony.

---

1   Boris Bashkirov, Vladimir's brother and Prokofiev's intimate friend from St Petersburg days, was an ambitious but incorrigibly dilettante poet. See *Diaries*, vols. 1 and 2 *passim*.
2   Initials of the Christian name and patronymic of Vladimir Bashkirov's mother.

5 March

Olga Samaroff passed on to me an invitation to lunch with Mrs Otto Kahn.[1] She seems to be making active propaganda on my behalf. Mrs Kahn was interested to know whether *Fiery Angel* was going to be produced in Berlin. If it was, and the production was to be this spring, she would send Gatti-Casazza over to hear it (a fat lot of good that would do!). I answered that the score still needed finishing off and orchestrating, and therefore if it were to be produced, it would be next season.

6 March

We sailed back to Europe on the *France*, until recently the pride of the French line, but now outdone by the more elegant and bigger *Paris*.[2] We had an excellent stateroom. No one came to see us off.

The net profit from my American tour amounted to approximately $2,000, but as well as this I had paid off several old debts totalling about $1,000 (Haensel, Hussa,[3] newspaper advertising, etc.).

12 March

Early in the morning the English coast came into view. Before noon we sailed into Plymouth and by evening we were at Le Havre, although so that people did not have then to travel to Paris at two o'clock in the morning we were allowed to sleep on board. We went to bed early, but had almost no sleep because of the noise made by drunken passengers until one o'clock, while

---

1 Mrs Kahn was the wife of the stupendously wealthy Otto Kahn (1867–1934), builder of the second-largest private house ever built in America, on Long Island, the exterior of which was used by Orson Welles for *Citizen Kane*. He was also one of the most generous patrons of the arts America has ever known – 'I must atone for my wealth' – and held among other positions the chairmanship of the Board of the Metropolitan Opera. Mrs Kahn being, in the way of American elite wives, almost as powerful as her husband, Prokofiev had via Ernest Urchs, then Head of the Concert and Artists Department of Steinway & Sons, cultivated acquaintance with both Mr and Mrs Kahn in 1919 in hopes of getting *The Gambler* accepted by the Met. Although Kahn had been sympathetic to the idea it foundered on the hostile rocks of the autocratic and conservative General Director, Giulio Gatti-Casazza. See *Diaries*, vol. 2, pp. 401–2, 404, 465, 492, 496, 588.
2 Although the *France* had yielded flagship status to the *Paris* in the Compagnie Générale Transatlantique's fleet in 1921, the Versailles-like opulence of her interior caused her to remain the liner of choice for many of the super-rich until the Depression cut a swathe through their ranks. In 1932 she finally steamed under her own power to the scrapyard.
3 Dr Philip Hussa, who had been Prokofiev's dentist on his previous stays in New York. Ibid., pp 385–6, 395–6, 405–6, 589, 699.

unloading of the ship commenced at half past four. When the ship is under way noise does not penetrate so much into the cabins, but when she is anchored one realises the walls are made of cardboard.

At night I pondered the libretto, thought up a new plan and worked out the final scene in some detail.

21 March

One day in America, when I was on the train, I had an idea of how I should revise the first eight bars of the Second Symphony. Now I finally implemented these changes, orchestrated them and pasted them into the score, ready for the performance by Straram on the 6th May.

Have been reading the book I was sent from Moscow: Sabaneyev's biography of Scriabin.[1] It was fascinating to read about the indignation with which Scriabin reacted to my music. Sabaneyev himself has recently come to Paris; I am indifferent to him, but Myaskovsky very much takes to heart his criticisms of his, Myaskovsky's, music and seems to want me to support him if ever I should come across Sabaneyev here.

22 March

Almost the whole day went on getting visas for my forthcoming trips. In the evening Dukelsky unexpectedly appeared. He is just in from London, where he has spent the winter composing operettas and revues and earning tidy sums of money. For some operetta or other he now earns a 'pension' of £15 a week. New suits, ties and erotic adventures, which he recounts to me with naive brazenness. He also played me the beginning of his new, 'serious' ballet. It was interesting. It defeats my understanding how he can combine composing foxtrots with real music, and good music at that!

23 March

Diaghilev has come from Monte Carlo. No rehearsals of *Ursignol* have yet taken place. Diaghilev sent a telegram to Yakulov asking him to invite Meyerhold to stage the ballet, but Yakulov replied that Meyerhold was busy until June and suggested Taïrov,[2] whom Diaghilev could not accept because

---

1 Sabaneyev's monograph *Scriabin* was published in Moscow in 1916; *Reminiscences of Scriabin* was to follow in 1925. See note above on p. 5.
2 Alexander Taïrov (pseudonym of Kornblit) (1885–1950) was, theatrically speaking, a child of Meyerhold having worked under him at the Kommissarzhevskaya Theatre in St Petersburg in the early years of the century. Moving to Moscow in 1913 he soon established the Taïrov Chamber Theatre (Kamerny Teatr), which became a nodal point of creativity for

Taïrov had been to Paris and Paris had not warmed to him.[1] Diaghilev was not against the idea of postponing the production to next year, as that year would be the twentieth anniversary of his, as he put it, 'glorious activities', and he wished to present an exclusively Russian season (Stravinsky – Prokofiev – Dukelsky). But the key point is that at the moment he has no money. 'Find me 800 francs and I'll start rehearsals of your ballet tomorrow.' Naturally, everything may change in either direction, depending on a whole series of circumstances. But I personally am inclined to the view that once again I've written a good piece that is destined to be put away in the pickle store for the duration.

We had lunch and dinner as a threesome, Ptashka, Dukelsky and I, and went together to the Samoilenkos, where Dukelsky made eyes at Fatma, and Tamara and Milya.[2] He agreed with me that Stravinsky's *Serenade*, which has just come out in print, contains melodic turns of phrase derived from Rachmaninoff and sonorities that sound like Medtner. Ha ha!

24 March

Next morning I left for Frankfurt-am-Main for my first appearance with orchestra in Germany. The journey was enjoyable. I was not asked for my visa, and arrived in Frankfurt at ten o'clock in the evening. A large, fine German city. There were hardly any motor cars on the streets. I strolled about and then went to bed.

---

experimentally inclined actors, artists, writers and musicians. In 1937 Prokofiev was to collaborate with Taïrov providing incidental music for a staged enactment of *Eugene Onegin* to an iconoclastic re-working of the text by Sigizmond Krzhizhanovsky intended to form part of the centenary Pushkin celebrations, but aborted at a late stage by the All-Union Committee on Arts Affairs. Earlier, in 1933–4, before taking up permanent residence in the Soviet Union, Prokofiev had composed a total of forty-four numbers for Taïrov's 'Cleopatra' montage of excerpts from Pushkin, G. B. Shaw and Shakespeare entitled *Egyptian Nights*. The production was premiered on 14 December 1934, two weeks after the murder of Sergey Kirov, which prompted a seismic escalation of repression throughout Soviet society. A week later the Suite drawn from the incidental music was broadcast on Moscow Radio. Initially, the concept and the production were well received, the latter running for over a hundred performances, and Taïrov was awarded the accolade of People's Artist. The political climate changed, however, and in the 1930s Taïrov's theatre company was exiled to Siberia although he himself was permitted to keep a residence permit in Moscow. Nothing, however, could prevent its complete demise after the Zhdanov cultural purges in 1948 and the company was officially disbanded the following year. Taïrov died of brain cancer a year later.
1   The Moscow Chamber Theatre (Moskovsky Kamerny Teatr) had brought Charles Lecocq's 1890s' opera-bouffe *Giroflé-Girofla* to Paris in 1923, with Taïrov's wife Alisa Koonen starring as the sister playing the double role of herself and her twin.
2   Tamara and Milya Hanum were sisters of Fatma Hanum, Samoilenko's wife.

25 March

It transpires that I had been summoned here a day earlier than I need have been, as there is no rehearsal until tomorrow. The conductor Krauss[1] is a man of about my age, good-looking, with attractively greying hair and resembling the Toreador in *Carmen*. Someone told me he was the illegitimate son of an Austrian archduke.[2] In the afternoon I wrote letters and responded to news of the production of *Oranges* in Leningrad. I walked around Frankfurt on a wonderful spring day.

26 March

Rehearsal from ten until eleven o'clock, and then at eleven a paying audience entered the hall for what was therefore a public rehearsal. Krauss accompanied very well. After this a lady connected to the organisation took me off to her house for lunch. She was Dutch, married to a German, and Szigeti had stayed with her. Her house was a large mansion, and she had sweet daughters, particularly one of about fifteen who is at school in Switzerland. The lady's name was Roediger. In the afternoon I slept, and when I woke up I realised it had been raining and outside there was the most glorious spring air. I went out into the square, redolent with the scent of everything bursting into bud, and the moist earth. Ah, when shall I ever again be able to greet the spring in the countryside?!

The concert was at seven o'clock in the evening, a glittering affair, one of the subscription concerts with an audience as rich as it was bored. But the Concerto was a success and I got three curtain calls. Afterwards there was supper in a club with about fifteen people. I was told that someone in the hall had been displeased by the castanets striking up in the second subject of the first movement. 'What's the point of that?' he asked. His neighbour, who obviously knew a little of my biography, explained: 'He has a Spanish wife.' Terrific!

---

1   Clemens Krauss (1893–1954), front-rank Austrian conductor, had been appointed Intendant of the Frankfurt Opera in 1924 and also of the city's Museum concerts. Later he would become Musical Director of the Vienna Staatsoper together with the Vienna Philharmonic, and later still of the Berlin Opera. A close friend of Richard Strauss, he conducted the premieres of *Arabella*, *Friedenstag* and *Die Liebe der Danae*, and wrote the libretto for *Capriccio*.
2   Not quite. He was actually born on the wrong side of the blanket to a fifteen-year-old dancer in the Vienna Imperial Opera Ballet, his father being a rich Greek banker in Vienna. But the banker's sister Eleni, Krauss's aunt, was married to Baron Albin Vetsera, a diplomat in foreign service at the Austrian court, and their daughter, Krauss's cousin, was Marie Vetsera, the mistress of the Crown Prince Rudolph and the female half of the mysterious double tragedy that had taken place in 1889 in the Emperor Franz Joseph's hunting lodge, known to history and the theatre as the Mayerling Affair.

27 March

Wrote letters. I was tempted to orchestrate *Ursignol*, but decided I had better get on with my correspondence. Went for a walk along the banks of the Main. Dined with Krauss, who has a splendid apartment. He was full of praise for my compositions, which he likes far more than Stravinsky's, but this is not so much of a compliment since Krauss loves above all his Viennese compatriot Richard Strauss.[1] That said, he is promising to perform next season a series of my orchestral works and is interested in my operas, since he also conducts at the Frankfurt Opera.

Once again I have red blotches in my eyes. I worked with Christian Science yesterday and today, and today they are better.

28 March

On the Friday there was another subscription concert for a very stiff-necked audience, and today at eleven in the morning a popular one. This time the hall was filled mainly with young people and they were extremely warm. I played very well and Krauss accompanied well. There was loud applause from the whole audience, with four curtain calls. When we emerged onto the street and got into our car, some young girls were standing and waiting for us to come out. They stood absolutely immobile with faces utterly devoid of expression, exactly as if they were at a funeral. As soon as we got into the car they dispersed. At twenty-seven minutes past three I left for the return journey to Paris, taking with me the most pleasant impression of Frankfurt.

1 April

Rose at 6.15 because our train left at 8.10, and we travelled the whole day until half past eight in the evening when we got to Modana, on the Italian border, where we stopped to stay the night in order not to have to continue through the night. We had not been able to obtain sleeper berths as they had all been sold; everyone is going to Italy for Easter. Modana is at an elevation of 2,000 metres and is hemmed in by mountains, and just below our window was a mountain stream. It is a very nice place, but only for a short stay.

---

1 Strauss was not, of course, Viennese, but since 1919 he had been joint Director of the Vienna Staatsoper and his family was living there.

2 April

We walked around for a bit in the morning, but the light was so strong my eyes watered. Then I orchestrated some more of *Ursignol*, which I have been neglecting since my spirit-lowering conversation with Diaghilev. But whatever happens, whether he puts it on this season or next, the score needs to be finished, and only when it is can I get down to *Fiery Angel*. I gave more thought to a theme for the main subject of the skyscraper Overture, the composition of which I had begun in Paris. At noon the evening train from Paris arrived and we boarded it, paying extra for first class as the train was crammed full. At five o'clock we came to Turin, where we had to change trains, and had some time to walk around the city. We were not very taken with Turin, but it was extremely pleasant sitting in the park above the Po with the enchanting scents of spring in the air, the view of the river and across it to the far side, and a great number of boats out on the river. At eight o'clock in the evening we departed in a sleeping car to Rome.

3 April

Approaching Rome, we caught a glimpse of the sea and of bright green fields. We arrived in the city at 9.25 a.m. Our trunk has not yet come but we went to the hotel where a room had been reserved in advance. The Hôtel des Princes is, after American hotels, a fairly antique establishment, the room not up to much and the price double what it would have been in Paris, but one can hardly complain since tomorrow is Easter Day and Rome is stuffed to the gills. We ran into Borovsky, much rejoicing. Apparently he had been on the same train as us, and tomorrow is going on to Naples to perform there. Together we set out to explore the city. Rome makes a powerful and inspiring impression: round every corner one encounters buildings new-minted in their antiquity. Borovsky then had lunch with us, after which we went to collect our trunk. A Customs official attempted to extort money from us, illegally, and when I asked for a receipt he shouted angrily, 'Rome has existed for two thousand years! I don't need your money!' This is the general rule here, they try and get money out of you everywhere you go, sometimes sharp practice and sometimes downright fraudulent, and therefore one's feelings about Rome are mixed: exaltation tempered with irritation.

4 April

Borovsky had managed to unearth Muratov, a writer and journalist with a comprehensive knowledge of Rome and a great willingness to show it to people. All morning he led us along ancient streets, past palaces and up to the top of a hill where the Spanish Academy is situated, and an enchanting small church in a courtyard where legend has it the Apostle Peter was crucified. From here one can see the whole city and count the seven hills on which Rome was built.[1] Then we walked to the Cathedral of St Peter with its overwhelmingly vast interior, said to be able to hold up to thirty-five thousand people. Again it induces contradictory feelings: on the one hand the grandeur of the Cathedral and awe at the power of Catholicism as an institution; on the other the rottenness at the heart of this same institution when to the left of the altar Muratov showed us a pope's tomb on the pedestal of which there is a sculpture of a naked woman, the model chosen by the sculptor being the pope's mistress. Neither did I much like the baroque altar with a sort of hellish flame coiling round papal figures. Muratov advanced the theory that the strength of Catholicism lies in the celibacy of the clergy. It is not important that some priests sin, what matters is that they do not have families, so there are no ties, the priest senses himself to be a soldier, the agent of a famous mission.

My concert has been postponed to the 7th April because of a performance today of Honegger's *King David*, which in turn had been rescheduled because the government had requisitioned the hall for some demonstration or other. Today's was the second performance of *David*, and on account of its runaway success the first time, my concert was sacrificed to it and moved from a holiday day to a weekday. Not only that, but Molinari, the Principal Conductor, with whom I had performed eleven years ago,[2] was so busy with *David* that he had deputed the youngster Rossi[3] to conduct me. Altogether a disgusting way to treat me. We were sent tickets for tonight's performance of *David* but decided not to go.

Yesterday we got so tired with all the walking that today we decided to take things a little easier. Also, I had to work, to answer letters and to play the Concerto through to the conductor. Rossi (twenty-four years old) proved to be a good musician, he knew the score thoroughly and had even managed to ferret out some mistakes.

---

1 The Janiculum, named after Janus, the two-faced god of beginnings, is the highest eminence in the centre of Rome and commands a breathtaking view over the city. The Church of San Pietro in Montorio is said to have been built on the site where St Peter was put to death. The Janiculum, however, is not itself one of the Seven Hills of Rome.
2 Bernardino Molinari (1880–1952), Principal Conductor of the Augusteo Orchestra. Prokofiev had been quite complimentary about him when he conducted the Second Piano Concerto in February 1915. See *Diaries*, vol. 2, pp. 20–22.
3 Mario Rossi (1902–1992) had been appointed Assistant Conductor the previous year. Subsequently he would become the Resident Conductor of the Maggio Musicale Fiorentino in Florence, and after the Second World War Chief Conductor of the RAI Orchestra in Turin.

6 April

Rehearsal with orchestra. When Rossi, as is the custom, introduced me to the orchestra, they rose to their feet in response to my bow – a courtesy not generally accorded by other orchestras: normally their acknowledgement of the soloist's bow is to sit flaunting their bellies and tapping their bows against the violins or stands. But during the rehearsal they sneezed and chattered, perhaps because they cared not a brass farthing for Rossi. He was very polite to the orchestra, but had not much idea how practically to manage a rehearsal. In the afternoon I went through her songs with Ptashka, who still cannot master her nerves. There was another rehearsal with the orchestra in the evening, at which we played quite smoothly through the whole Concerto from start to finish.

The secretary of the concert society handed us letters addressed to the Monsignor in charge of arranging papal receptions, telling us that we could obtain an audience. It had not entered our heads that we could do this, not realising it was such a simple procedure, but we were very interested to take advantage of it.

7 April

In the morning I went to the Vatican bearing the letter from the academy requesting an audience with the Pope. I was greeted by a Swiss Guard dressed in medieval costume created, so I later was informed, according to designs made by Raphael. He showed me the way to the Monsignor's office. There sat twenty or so individuals of all different sorts and conditions – nuns, Englishmen; I had to wait for half an hour before I could approach the desk of the secretary, an energetic and courteous monk. He asked on which day I should like an audience, and I replied, 'Tomorrow.' He said, 'Tomorrow morning we will send you an invitation.' I thanked him and took my leave. When I got back to the hotel I learned that while I had been sitting in the Vatican some old woman had taken a pot shot at Mussolini and shot away part of his nose, and as a result all Rome was in an uproar. The vital issue was that apparently the woman was Russian. So much for today's concert! They will either hiss me off the stage or throw something at me, or worse, shoot me – or perhaps cancel the concert altogether and with it the entire Italian tour! My mood was black.

The two o'clock papers revealed that the nationality of the gunwoman had not been established, but apparently she was of Slav extraction. This was a relief, since there was no concrete evidence that she was Russian. At five o'clock we made our way to the concert hall and there learned from San

Martino that she was not even a Slav but an Irishwoman.[1] The mood lightened altogether, except that the heads of the audience were full of things other than the music, and in any case there were not many of them: about a thousand, which meant that the hall was a quarter full. The Concerto went reasonably well, but Rossi allowed the orchestra to drown me. The reception was only moderate: I was called back once, and even then the applause did not last until I reached the door leading out of the stage. The programme was stupidly put together, provincial, probably reflecting Rossi's limitations as a conductor: Mendelssohn's *Hebrides* Overture and the *Polovtsian Dances* from *Prince Igor*[2] – so much for the capital city of Italy!

8 April

At eight o'clock there was a knock on the door: the tickets for the audience with the Pope. The instructions written on the tickets stated that men must wear evening-dress and white tie, ladies black and veiled. There was an illustration of a very pretty woman in a black dress down to her ankles, although nowadays the fashion goes down only to the knee. This caused consternation, as Ptashka possesses nothing of the sort, nor was any other modern woman likely to have anything. Eventually she got a black dress from Casella's mother, I arrayed myself in evening-dress and we set off. I was uncertain whether I should wear a black or a white waistcoat, so I put on white and took a black one with me, rolled up in a tube which I put in the pocket of my overcoat. Our costume gave us cause for some hilarity, as if it were fancy dress, but on the way we asked each other such questions as: if the Pope asks us, 'What is your faith?', what should we answer? 'Do you have children?' 'Yes, a son.' 'Is he baptised?' What do we say to that? 'Do you believe in my infallibility?' To this I proposed answering that, 'We have profound respect for the concept.' I said that as a matter of fact I thought it unlikely he would ask ticklish questions of this sort; more probably there would be a throng of people and we would not have any conversation at all. As we neared the Bronze Doors,[3] the main entrance to the Vatican to the

---

1   The would-be assassin was Violet Gibson, the fifty-year-old daughter of the former Lord Chancellor of Ireland, Edward Gibson, created Baron Ashbourne. As there seemed no plausible reason, and no co-conspirators, for the attempt on the Duce's life, it was decided that she must be insane. She was deported and spent the rest of her life in a mental hospital in Northampton, where she died in 1956.

2   From Act 2 of Borodin's opera *Prince Igor*, composed between 1899 and the composer's death in 1887, first performed in the version completed and realised by Rimsky-Korsakov and Glazunov in 1890.

3   The doors, the main visitors' entrance to the papal reception rooms, are made from wood and bronze taken from ancient Roman temples. They were designed and installed at the north-west end of the colonnade by Bernini, the architect of the colonnade surrounding St Peter's Square, in 1663. In October 2007 they were restored after a two-year absence.

right of St Peter's, we saw several carriages from which were emerging women in black veils, but there were not many men in evening-dress, most were wearing black jackets and a few, oh horror, tuxedos. We entered the building where the office is and after ascending through several floors came out into a courtyard much higher up than St Peter's Square (the Vatican stands on a hill). When we got here a Swiss Guard showed us another entrance, and along with other visitors we walked up several flights of a beautiful marble staircase. Here we were invited to take off our overcoats and render our tickets. Several of the ladies preferred to keep their coats on, probably because they were not wearing black dresses underneath. At this point we were already inside the palace, and we were shown where to go by footmen wearing short caftans. Through several huge, empty rooms with extremely beautiful marble walls and floors we were led into the long throne room with chairs lining the walls and at the end a throne with a baldaquin. Along the walls, forming a kind of spread-out circle, stood about three hundred people all dressed in black, awaiting their audience. Hardly had we taken up a position near the door by which we had come in but from where we could see the throne, when a footman came up to us and asked us and some of the other visitors to follow him. Moving forward we were apprehensive lest we were the first to be taken up to the Pope, and what were we supposed to do? Fall to our knees? On one knee? Or two? Kiss his ring or his shoe? And what should we say? As a matter of fact we had been advised in advance that it was not done to kiss the shoe but his hand when he extends it to kiss the ring. I decided the reason we had been chosen was that we were standing to one side and I was wearing tails. There were three or four other men in tails, but they were in the midst of the throng. Leading us through a suite of other, smaller, rooms (in one of which I much admired the green marble on the walls), they took us into a new hall, against all four walls of which were standing yet another party of black-clad visitors, about sixty or seventy of them. We joined the queue, and since it was going to be quite a long time before the Pope appeared, we all sat down on the benches that ran along the walls. Some of the footmen scrutinised the women whose throats were bare, and asked them to pin a scarf round them. An American woman sitting next to Ptashka, who had previously been received, told us that the Pope did not usually ask any questions.

Eventually there was a stirring in the ranks of the footmen, several Monsignors came into the room. We visitors rose to our feet and then dropped to our knees. In came the Pope accompanied by two black-clad Monsignors wearing purple cloaks. Although it was later explained to me that they were from extremely aristocratic families, they looked pretty rough to me. The Pope himself is a small man, clean-shaven and bespectacled, with insignificant features but a benevolent expression, much more so than appears in photographs. He was dressed in a simple, full-length garment with a cream-coloured cape and a purple cap on his head. Entering, he stopped, uttered a few words of prayer, and then began to circle the kneeling visitors forming three sides of a square round the room. He walked slowly, stopping and extending his right hand with the ring, for people to kiss. Preparing myself to do this, I tried to make my imagination comprehend that I was really about to kiss the ring of the representative of Peter; to kiss, if I may so put it, the idea. However, I did not succeed in this, because the nearer the Pope came the more closely I found myself observing the formal aspects of the matter. He held out a limp hand with the fingers pointing downwards, the kisser thrust his own fingers behind the Pope's hand in order to give it support and then kissed the ring. The ring consisted of an elongated, but not particularly large, emerald surrounded by diamonds, although Ptashka thought they were pearls. I did not actually manage to kiss, I merely brushed my lips against the ring, but with Ptashka, whose overcoat was all puffed out from kneeling on the floor, the Pope probably assumed she was pregnant and so allowed his hand to linger a little longer.

When he had completed his circuit of everyone, the Pope turned to face those present, pronounced a prayer and a blessing and then continued on his way, no doubt to those who were still in the other room. We all got back on our feet and gradually made our way out through the suite of rooms we had come in by. Many people lingered by the windows, from where there was a splendid view over Rome. We went out into the street, tired, but were unable to find a cab since they had all been grabbed by the visitors.

In the afternoon we rehearsed Ptashka's songs, and at five set out to visit Vyacheslav Ivanov.[1] He has apparently been living in Rome for two years now, in a meagre, cramped flat with his son and daughter. His former red hair has turned to grey, but it seemed to suit him; you could take him for a German scientist. He has not written any poetry recently, confining himself to scholarly work. He had some perceptive things to say about my Concerto. All the same there was an air of decline in the atmosphere, of something having been needlessly thrown overboard. His daughter, a somewhat plain blonde of about twenty-eight, is studying the theory of composition with Respighi at the Rome Conservatoire and will graduate this year. She played

---

1 Vyacheslav Ivanov (1866–1949), Symbolist poet. Before he moved from St Petersburg to Moscow in 1913 he was regarded as the most important of the Petersburg Silver Age Symbolists, and his apartment (known as 'The Tower') was effectively the crucible of the movement. Ivanov's poetry is elaborately declamatory, erudite and stuffed with classical allusions, although the later *Winter Sonnets*, written in 1920 and describing the hardships suffered by the poet during the Civil War, are touching in their direct humanity. Ivanov defected from the Soviet Union in 1924 on a cultural exchange visit to Italy, and remained there until his death, surviving mainly by teaching classics at universities.

me her compositions, her father plainly giving off the while signs of anxiety. She has ability, I really liked a prelude and fugue, but I fear that her father's influence is not helpful: he constantly imports literary associations into the music and her resultant attempts to grasp at large concepts and express the elemental are apt to descend into insipid or plain bad passages. The son is a very splendid young man of about thirteen, but during the journey the fingers of his right hand were cut off. I left them with feelings of sadness.

9 April

Rehearsed with Ptashka in the morning, for the afternoon concert in Santa Cecilia. At the beginning there seemed to be hardly anyone there, but this is a place with a fashionable public which likes to turn up late, and by the end of the concert the hall was three-quarters full. The programme was roughly the same as in the American provinces, but the reception was fairly cool, even though afterwards San Martino, Casella and others tried to assure us that for Roman audiences this was a resounding success. Ptashka was not in good voice, but was complimented by Rieti and Casella, even receiving from the latter an inscribed copy of his songs. Besides the above-mentioned, Vyacheslav Ivanov also came to the Artists' Room, his head drawing glances from all those present. I introduced him to San Martino and to Casella, which visibly pleased him as such acquaintances could be useful for his daughter. I received cash in hand 3,000 lire for my concerts in Rome, and very much wanted to give one of those thousands to Ivanov but did not know how to do it. I kept trying to bring the conversation round to the subject, but each time I did so someone came up and interrupted. I decided to postpone the idea and ask Muratov's advice tomorrow.

After the concert Casella entertained us to dinner in a small but exceptionally delicious restaurant, the Alfredo. This was the first time anyone had shown us any hospitality in Rome. Casella praised my Toccata,[1] saying that there was something inhuman in it: listening to it he felt he was going in a train. He thought Honegger's ultra-fashionable *Pacific* must have been derived from it. After dinner Casella took us to see Respighi, who rents an apartment in one of the old palaces of Rome – one sees quite a number of these astonishing buildings in the city. Respighi was very gracious to me, and despite the fact that he had a number of guests spent most of the time sitting with me. I had the distinct impression that before me was the Italian Glazunov.

---

1 Toccata for Piano in C, Op. 11 (1912).

10 April

Spent the morning packing – one of the tedious aspects of any travel – and then left for Siena. When I went to say goodbye to Muratov I asked him about Vyacheslav Ivanov. Muratov said that of course Ivanov was living in straitened circumstances, but he was not currently under any urgent necessity as he receives a salary from Baku as a professor of the university there.[1] The worst of it was that he was soon going to have to go back to Baku, he did not want to take the children with him, and so was facing the misery of separation. It would not be appropriate to offer him 1,000 lire; better would be to write music to his verses and offer to pay him as an author.[2]

We enjoyed the lovely journey to Siena, the fields beautifully cultivated, the vineyards and gardens all resplendent in their April bloom. Arrived at Siena in the evening; nobody met us and we did not know in which hotel rooms had been reserved for us. We tried the Grand Hotel, and as it turned out, that was indeed the right one. Siena is an old town, whose development stopped in the sixteenth century. No cars or vehicles are allowed on the main street.

11 April

Today's concert is to take place in the castle of Count Chigi, a very ancient building dating, apparently, back to the thirteenth century.[3] Out of love for music the Count organises every year a concert series and pays the artists, the proceeds from ticket sales devoted to charitable purposes. The superintendent of the castle did not come to see us so we had to find our own way to the castle. When we got there he apologised in an offhand sort of way, but did not greet us. I adopted a frigid, even curt tone with him. It was a holiday, and through the streets were going religious processions in elaborate vestments, with banners and music. Looking through the windows of the castle which overlooked the main thoroughfare we could see one of the

---

1. Ivanov held the chair of Classical Philology at the University of Baku. He did not return to it after leaving the USSR and settling in Rome in 1924.
2. No such plan seems to have been realised.
3. When Count Guido Chigi Saracini inherited the magnificent Palazzo Chigi-Saracini, one of the medieval palaces lining the Via Città in Siena, he determined to make it a centre for music and art and began by establishing in 1923 a prestigious series of concerts in the palace's rococo Sala dei Concerti, entirely at his own expense. To this he added and extended the family's already extensive art collection, a vast literary and music library and a collection of historic musical instruments. In 1932, with the help of Casella, he founded the Accademia Musicale Chigiana, designed as an international centre for advanced musical studies. In 1961, four years before his death, the Count made over his entire estate to the Fondazione Accademia Chigiani, which today continues the work of one of the most notable advanced music-training institutions in the world.

processions winding its way through the narrow street, producing an effect straight out of the Middle Ages. Such a sight could well have met the eyes of Ruprecht[1] in the sixteenth century during his Italian wanderings.

In Rome we had been told that the concert would take place in the afternoon, but they had made a mistake as the announcements stated that it would be in the evening. We, however, had brought only daytime concert clothes, so we had to appear in them and excuse ourselves to the audience. We were received without warmth: the impression given was that they did not understand much. Ptashka sang a little better than she had in Rome. The Count himself put in an appearance only towards the end of the programme; he had come from the country, a clean-shaven man of about forty-five, very gracious but not sufficiently so to dispel the wall in which he appeared to have encased himself. I had never been in such a luxurious Artists' Room as the one here: one of the drawing rooms of the castle, furnished and decorated in the height of antique opulence, with red-silk furniture and wall-coverings of the same material.

12 April

Went to bed at midnight and got up at six to take the train at eight for Genoa, where we were due to perform that evening. We changed trains in Pisa, so had lunch there and looked round the town. Pisa is not a beautiful place, especially after Siena, but the main square is quite fascinating with its Cathedral, the Leaning Tower and the Baptistery. I had heard about the Tower in childhood, ever since I overheard someone saying about someone else: 'He has a nose like the Leaning Tower of Pisa.' But more than anything I was interested in the Baptistery: its unusual architecture outside, and inside its acoustic properties. When a note is sounded, as soon as it decays it can still be heard sounding clearly for several more seconds in the dome. There must be a whole system of small reflections that coalesce so as to give the effect of a continuous sound. If you sing an arpeggio loudly and clearly the whole chord will sound in the dome, and what is particularly remarkable is that singing the chord from top to bottom sounds better than singing from bottom to top. Clapping one's hands together several times makes the dome resound with the sound of applause.

We arrived in Genoa at six and the concert was due to start at nine in the theatre, which was reasonably well filled with the audience. Tired from the journey, Ptashka had almost no voice at all, and we decided that she should not sing. Instead of her group of songs I would play the Second

---

1 The leading male character of the opera *The Fiery Angel*.

Sonata, which incidentally I had not touched for three months. It was announced to the audience that she was indisposed. The success was moderate, as in Rome.

13 April

Genoa is a lovely and very friendly town.

I did some more of the orchestration, and changed my Italian fees into dollars, by way of a New York cheque which I shall pay into my American bank account when I am back in Paris. I was paid in full for last night's concert. We had our photos taken by a local Russian photographer, at his invitation.

15 April

For some unknown reason, perhaps because of the root of the name being Flora, I had always thought of Florence as a haven of flowers. In fact it is just the opposite: a hot, dusty city without a single tree. But that is not in any case what we were supposed to be directing our gaze towards: we set off dutifully in the direction of the Pitti Palace art gallery.

17 April

The Florence concert took place in the hall of the Pitti Palace, in the same building as the art gallery. It was the first real success I had in Italy. Ptashka was only moderately in voice, but was also well received: the audience demanded an encore after the Myaskovsky songs, and she was presented with an enormous basket of five dozen roses.

18 April

Travelled from Florence to Naples, where an extra concert had been inserted into the schedule. Through the window we looked at the lovely Italian countryside, especially between Rome and Naples. Celentano met us at the station, the local representative of the Society for Contemporary Music which had engaged me. A hotel room had been booked for us by a third party, not on the Embankment but right in the centre of the city. The Embankment is where the English and Americans, foreigners in general, stay, and it is therefore clean and comfortable, whereas we were right in the middle of local people, therefore dirty and uncomfortable. Ptashka has a cold and does not know whether she should sing or not. The organisers of the concert are relaxed about this and have given us carte blanche.

19 April

In pursuit of a better hotel we found ourselves on the Embankment. Here is a completely different matter: sun, blue sky, comfort – but, of course, much more expensive. We dined in the town centre in a little restaurant where the Italian diners demanded to be brought live fish, from whom they made their choice with gusto. Into the restaurant came a man with the face of a murderer, who cried out in a terrible voice, 'Oysters, fresh oysters!'

Chose the piano. We were introduced to a Catalan monk, a great patriot and music-lover. He was very interested to learn that Ptashka's forebears came from Catalonia and that she could speak the language.

20 April

Concert in the afternoon. I played solo. The success was real this time, a great reception. An elderly artist came to me in the interval, begging. I gave him 50 lire. In return the old man took me to one side, showed me porcelain receptacle and said, 'This is in case the signor should wish to do a Number One.'

At the end of the concert Gorky's son came round to say that Gorky[1] was in the hall and hoped very much that I would come to dinner with him. We went out front to meet him and left together. Gorky hailed a taxi and he, Ptashka, the son and I all drove to Gorky's rented dacha on the shores of the Gulf, far out on the very edge of Naples or perhaps even in the suburbs. The dacha was a large house with enormous, somewhat

---

1   Maxim Gorky (pseudonym of Alexey Peshkov, 1868–1936) lived on the island of Capri from 1906 until 1913, partly for health reasons and partly because the atmosphere in Tsarist Russia was hardly conducive to a politically and socially free-thinking writer. He returned to Russia in 1913 under the auspices of an amnesty granted to celebrate the 300th anniversary of the founding of the Romanov dynasty, and stayed through the Revolution supporting with his pen and his iconic personality Lenin and the Bolsheviks, although far from uncritically. The arrest and murder of Nikolay Gumilyov, the husband of Anna Akhmatova in 1921, despite Gorky's personal plea to Lenin, set the seal on his long-gestating disgust with Bolshevik distortions and brutality, and along with recurrent ill-health prompted a further period of living abroad, mainly in Sorrento, until 1929, after which in a scenario that bears uncanny parallels with Prokofiev's he made increasingly frequent visits to the Soviet Union before yielding in 1932 to Stalin's blandishments to return permanently. It bore all the marks of a great propaganda coup. As with Prokofiev, the relations of an independently minded great artist with a repressive totalitarian regime could not be easy; in 1934 Gorky was placed under effective house arrest, the next year his son Maxim Peshkov died suddenly and the year after the writer himself, in mysterious circumstances that are never likely to dispel speculation that it was on Stalin's orders. To the young Prokofiev in 1917 St Petersburg Gorky had been a generous older friend and champion, interceding with Kerensky to secure Prokofiev's exemption from military service. On countless occasions throughout the Revolutionary and Civil War period and the later repression of the 1930s he similarly helped and backed up people in whom, irrespective of their political affiliations or class backgrounds, he believed. With few exceptions Gorky was a man who stood by his friends and his beliefs. The admiration was mutual. See *Diaries*, vol. 2, pp. 173, 187–8, 202–14 *passim*, 245n, 684.

forbiddingly bare rooms. The son is married to a young and exceedingly beautiful woman who runs the household. Needless to say, from the start conversation centred around Russia. Gorky at first reacted negatively to my plans to visit there: 'What about your past history? What about military service?' but later told me to let him know if I was going so that he could write to Rykov, who as Prime Minister is of course all-powerful there.[1] Gorky gets a mass of letters, manuscripts and books from Russia and keeps up assiduously with contemporary literature, finding much of interest in it. Among writers he cited Pasternak,[2] Tynyanov,[3] Olga Forsh,[4]

---

1   Alexei Rykov (1881–1938), appointed Prime Minister (formally Chairman of the Council of People's Commissars, or Sovnarkom) of the Russian Federation and of the Soviet Union two weeks after the death of Lenin in 1924, survived in the posts until respectively 1929 and 1930. Although he had supported Stalin against the so-called 'leftist' United Opposition of Trotsky, Kamenev and Zinoviev, this did not save him from Stalin's subsequent moves against the 'Rightist Opposition'. The serial loss of the prime ministerial positions at the end of the 1930s signalled the inevitable slide of removal from the Central Committee and the Politburo culminating in arrest for treason and conviction at the Show Trial of the Twenty-One on 13 March 1938. Two days later Rykov was executed.
2   Boris Pasternak (1890–1960), poet and novelist, son of the painter Leonid Pasternak and the pianist Rosa Kaufman. Pasternak, influenced by Scriabin, had originally intended to be a composer and spent several years at the Moscow Conservatoire, but changed path to poetry via philosophy. Known primarily in the West as the author of the novel *Doctor Zhivago*, published abroad in 1957 but not in the Soviet Union until 1988, in Russia he is more celebrated as a great poet, and above all for the collections of verse published in the early 1920s – *My Sister Life, Themes and Variations, Sublime Malady, The Childhood of Lyuvers*. At the time of Gorky's recommendation to Prokofiev, Pasternak was deeply engaged in a famous three-way multi-lingual correspondence with Marina Tsvetayeva and Rainer Maria Rilke, which for many people epitomises what John Bayley, reviewing in the *New York Review of Books* the correspondence in the English translation by Margaret Wettlin and Walter Arndt, calls 'the high-minded cosmopolitanism ... of a vanished age of European culture'. Following the Western publication of *Doctor Zhivago*, Boris Pasternak was awarded the Nobel Prize for Literature in 1958 but under intense pressure from the Soviet authorities declined it.
3   Yury Tynyanov (1894–1943), novelist, scholar, translator and literary theoretician. He was an established authority on Pushkin, Tyutchev and Griboyedov, and his book *Theses on Language*, co-authored with the linguist Roman Jakobson, is regarded as an important precursor of Structuralism, laying stress on the study of structure and artistic devices rather than of social or ideological content – classic Formalism, in fact. As a creative writer Tynyanov concentrated on historical novels; in 1933 Prokofiev was to collaborate with him on Faintsimmer's film of Tynyanov's satirical novella *Lieutenant Kijé* (*Podporuchik Kizhe*) in which the author combined his linguistic preoccupations with his knowledge of the reign of Tsar Paul I and a Gogolian black humour. Tynyanov wrote the screenplay for the film, which a viewing on Youtube will reveal to be a fine period example of sharply satirical Soviet acting and cinematography, and Prokofiev, of course, composed the music.
4   Olga Forsh, pen-name of Olga Komarova (1873–1961), historical novelist. An orphan, Forsh was a late developer, and at this stage had just published her first big success, the first of her historical novels called *Dressed in Stone* (*Odety kamnem*), to be succeeded by several more including a trilogy on the eighteenth-century radical Alexander Radishchev. An orphan, Forsh had been for two years in the early 1920s a resident in the 'House of Art' ('Dom isskustva') in Petrograd, the hostel for homeless writers and artists established by Gorky in the former

Kaverin[1] and Nikulin,[2] all of whom he recommended me to read. He also had praise for Leonid Leonov.[3]

We sat down to dinner. At the meal we drank French wine, which Gorky loves – why, one wonders, when there is so much good Italian wine in Italy? He is a heavy smoker and coughs continuously, a short, dry cough, disagreeable and even frightening to hear like a dog barking, a continual reminder that he has only a quarter of his lungs left. He talked of the settlement for homeless children named after him somewhere in the south of Russia, and about how important it is for them to be treated with tenderness and affection.[4] We stayed for quite long time, and then Gorky's son accompanied us to the tram, telling us about the amazing countryside everywhere around: wherever one turns over the ground one finds relics of the ancient past. Ptashka completely fell in love with Gorky.

21 April

We completed an ascent of Vesuvius. First we went on a little train, and then on a funicular railway. Getting out of the funicular we found ourselves on the bare sides of the mountain, extraordinarily forbidding and unpleasant. The slopes are just bare and jagged, destitute of vegetation. We climbed up to the crater by a narrow path covered in a grey powder. Normally one thinks of a crater as a big hole, about the size of a swimming pool, or at the most large enough to accommodate a house. Nothing of the kind: the circumference of this crater is three kilometres and is nowhere less than 100 metres deep, a bit like a round bathtub except that the base is rough and craggy and in the middle of it there is a cone-shaped pimple from which erupt puffs of steam that blaze up in a dark crimson colour and eject particles of stone. From time to time one hears a sound like heavy banging, which if one

---

Yeliseyev Palace in which most of the artistic elite including such characters as Zoshchenko, Gumilyov, Mandelshtam, Zamyatin, Tynyanov, Kaverin and other members of the group called the Serapion Brothers, seems to have lived at some stage or other and which became a perpetual cauldron of intellectual debate and criticism. Forsh's fictionalised memoir *Ship of Fools* (*Sumasshedsky Korabl'*) describes this extraordinary cultural hothouse.

1   Venyamin Kaverin, pen-name of Venyamin Zilber (1902–1989), writer, was Yury Tynyanov's brother-in-law. His best known novel is *The Two Captains* (*Dva Kapitana*) whose subject is Russian polar explorers before and after the Revolution.
2   Lev Nikulin, pen-name of Lev Olkonitsky (1891–1967), novelist and journalist. His is a less familiar name today; his chosen genre was adventure stories of the Revolutionary and Civil War period.
3   See note above, pp. 216–7, n. 2.
4   The Revolution and the Civil War, like many another cataclysmic social upheaval, had spawned an army of orphaned children who had lost home, family and any kind of roots in society, and who roamed in feral gangs robbing and killing at will. (See below, pp. 551–2.) In 1928 Gorky and the renowned educationalist Anton Makarenko had together established a sort of humane and (from a Communist perspective, naturally) profoundly idealistic boot-camp near Poltava for the rescue and re-education of these outcasts.

descends to the bottom of the crater where it reverberates against the steep walls is very loud. The cone is, of course, not really so small, it is perhaps fifty metres high, but from the rim of the crater it seems like just an average-sized pimple. Our guide proposed to take us down, at a price, and show us the molten lava. Although the way down was steep, like the price demanded by the guide, we decided that as we were actually on the edge of the crater we really ought to see the lava, and so with his help we went down. Once on the bottom it was a scramble to move about: once upon a time it had all been boiling lava, and lava, once it cools, goes into sharp spikes that tear your shoes and even stockings. As we drew nearer to the erupting cone the effect of the thunder-like noise grew to a pitch of real menace. The lava flows quite some distance from the cone, a slow-moving mass of fire that was so hot one could not go anywhere near it, but almost immediately subsides into dark grey ash. Round about were standing some citizens desirous of earning money who took our coins and baked them in the molten lava in return for coins extracted from us of a rather larger denomination.

Exhausted from the unfamiliar terrain we had been walking across, we made our way back to the funicular and descending from the mountain stopped off to have lunch. We drank some marvellous red wine from vines growing on the slopes of Vesuvius, called Lacrimi Christi – the tears of Christ, a somewhat blasphemous appellation no doubt bestowed by a drunken viniculturist in a fit of ecstasy at the splendour of the wine he had produced. After lunch we continued our way down and Ptashka wanted to go on further to Pompeii, but I was tired and also it was getting late, there would not be time to examine it in detail, and a cursory look was not worth the trouble. The result of this was a furious argument during which we said a whole lot of stupid things to one another, all completely unnecessary.

22 April

At two o'clock we left for Paris. We had wanted a train *de luxe*, but there were no tickets left. I do not usually like paying extra for luxury, not from parsimony but because I find the idea of disgorging money just to save a few hours and to travel with the appearance of chic repellent . . . But we were tired, and the Naples concert was a supernumerary one which we had accepted only for the pleasure of the trip. And so, not having secured *de luxe*, we took an ordinary train to Rome and there changed to a sleeping car for Turin.

23 April

Arrived at Turin in the morning and changed trains. We saw very beautiful views as we approached the frontier, mountainous scenery carpeted with flowers. After crossing the frontier we stayed the night at Chambéry in order not to have another night on the train. Unexpectedly Chambéry proved to be a most charming town with a fine castle.

Read an article about Doctor Coué,[1] who has just died. I had heard about him on several occasions. His treatment consists in obliging his patients to think and say, 'Every day, in every way, I am feeling better and better.' A great many people have been helped by this. Well, I'm sure they have! Knowing Christian Science as I do, it is entirely understandable. In this respect Coué was closer to Christian Science than most doctors. But here I was struck by an imaginary dialogue I conceived taking place between Coué and a Scientist. The Scientist says, 'Yes, you are right, illness is an illusion and, through affirmation of the God-given truth that man is perfect and immaterial, the illusory representation of illness will disappear.' Coué responds, 'You may console yourself as much as you please with your divine truths, they interest me very little; I simply state that if a man repeats to himself every hour that he is feeling better, then his organism will come to subject itself to the idea.' Doctor Coué really needs to have his error pointed out to him, but how to do this? At first a challenge struck me as a particularly difficult proposition, because Coué would not listen. True, one does not have to go far to find examples: all manner of ailments have been cured by Christian Science, even the most hopeless cases, many of them immediately in a manner incomprehensible to a medical doctor. Coué, on the other hand, cures only a limited range of diseases, and those not only gradually but to a limited extent. This, the advantage of Christian Science over Coué's system, is precisely what would have to be pointed out in the imagined debate and only then, once Coué had accepted that the system advanced by the Scientist could justifiably claim more impressive results, would it be possible to explain to him the limitations of his own.

Coué was not an old man when he died. 'Every day I feel better and better' had not helped him.

---

[1] Emile Coué (1857–1926) developed a procedure he called 'optimistic autosuggestion', a precursor of the contemporary psychiatric treatment known as Cognitive Behavioural Therapy. From clinical observation, Coué noted that patients taking medication whom he had successfully persuaded of its efficacy showed better results than patients to whom he had not said anything. Departing from the usual belief that the power of the conscious will is the engine of success, Coué believed that the unconscious could be manipulated to do the job better: repeating a mantra such as his formulation '*Tous les jours à tous points de vue je vais de mieux en mieux*' would eventually stimulate the unconscious to absorb the message and in turn would assist the organism to produce the desired result both psychologically and, Coué claimed, organically.

24 April

After a good sleep we wandered round Chambéry and at noon proceeded to Paris.

Yesterday was my thirty-fifth birthday, but with the travelling it passed unremarked. We arrived in Paris in the evening and put up at the Victoria Palace, which with my improved finances has become my habitual hotel. It was a delight to be back in Paris, whose charm never fails. Even approaching the city provokes feelings of pleasurable excitement.

25 April

The moment I was back I settled down to orchestrating the ballet. We went out to Clarmart to see Olga Vladislavovna and Svyatoslav. Avi[1] came. He is swarthy, pleasant and more or less insignificant. As if to punish him for his insignificance, his wife and daughter put him down the whole time, which he tolerates with amazing forbearance.

26 April

Went to the Guaranty Trust, where there was a pile of correspondence awaiting me. Many of the letters were from Russia, also reviews, very good ones, of the production of *Oranges* at the Mariinsky Theatre.[2]

From the Guaranty Trust I went on to the publishers. Paichadze is an exceptionally congenial and charming man for whom I have great affection. He will be a lot easier to deal with than the late Oeberg, who although a dear fellow was 'not without a maverick streak', as Tcherepnin put it. Paichadze gave me the proof copy of the Suite from *Oranges*.

27 April

Got down to some correspondence. There was a telegram from Koussevitzky about the exceptional success enjoyed by *Seven, They Are Seven* in America. Hooray for America!

---

1 Juan Codina, Lina Prokofieva's father. 'Prokofiev addressed Juan as Avi in the Spanish style and Olga as Mémé' (Serge Prokofiev junior, article about his great-grandparents in *Three Oranges*, no. 15 (May 2008)).
2 This had taken place on 18 February, conducted by Vladimir Dranishnikov with designs by Vladimir Dmitriev. The production was by Sergey Radlov, whose aim had been to avoid technically complex and cumbersome stage machinery and 'to create a certain fairy-tale mood and lightness . . . I tried to make the whole scenic action dynamic' (quoted in D. Nice, *Prokofiev: From Russia to the West*, Yale UP, New Haven and London, 2003, p. 237). Radlov's description comes from an article he wrote for *Rabochy i Teatr* (*The Working Man and Theatre*), the eventual hardline successor journal to *Zhizn' isskustva* (*Life of Art*), on 15 February 1926.)

29 April

Went in search of a dacha, setting out at half past seven in the morning and getting back at half past eleven at night not having found a thing and exhausted from having ceaselessly chased about all day. We were looking for a dacha not too far from Paris so that if various needs arose we could maintain contact. Since Ptashka's favourite singing teacher lives in Fontainebleau, we concentrated our search in that area. I had nothing against this, as Fontainebleau is surrounded by forests and rivers and fields, a lovely landscape. Last year we had stayed in the area and liked it.

30 April

Straram started rehearsals of the Second Symphony. He is not much of a conductor and the orchestra does not respect him, but he does have a sack full of money at his back and in addition is not a bad musician. One way or another he has made an effort seriously to get to grips with the Symphony: today's rehearsal was a sectional rehearsal devoted exclusively to the violins. Splendid! At the beginning he asked the players how many of them had played the Symphony the previous year with Koussevitzky. More than half raised their hands. Then the swotting began.

Afternoon reception at Mme Dubost's, at which a wind quintet by Schoenberg was performed. I listened with great attention, but could not derive any pleasure from it and longed for it to end. Had a long conversation with Gil-Marchex,[1] a French pianist who has recently returned from a tour of Russia. He reported favourably on the *Oranges* production and told me that in Russia I was basking in 'unheard-of popularity'.[2]

Towards the end of Dubost's reception Stahl appeared. We exchanged glances from afar, upon which he went off with my 'enemy' Schloezer into a corner, where they embarked on a long and heated conversation. Once he said to the Samoilenkos: 'There goes Prokofiev, I love him very much but now when he encounters Vera Grigorievna,[3] he doesn't even acknowledge her.'

---

1 Henri Gil-Marchex (1894–1970), French pianist and writer on Japanese music; also on Liszt and Ravel, of whom he was a friend and colleague.
2 'Popularité inouïe'.
3 Stahl's wife, the soprano Vera Janacopulos. See *Diaries*, vol. 2 *passim*.

1 May

Straram's second rehearsal was given over to the violas, cellos and basses (that's the way we do things round here!). I decided I could give it a miss, so Ptashka and I went off again in search of a dacha. Last time we had seen one in Samoreau, a very attractive one buried deep in the forest but a little expensive at seven and a half thousand – although we are not likely to find anything cheaper.

Today we thought we should look at it again. Our second survey yielded a positive result and we took it without being absolutely sure we had made the right choice. But today is the 1st of May and tomorrow is Sunday: if we don't watch out the last remaining decent dachas will have been snapped up, so we felt we had to come to a decision. The house is quite old, but it has electricity, a bathroom and plumbing. Round about is green and full of flowers. I have an excellent room to work in, large and cool.

By two o'clock we were back in Paris and I settled down to the proofs of the Suite from *Oranges*.

2 May

Third rehearsal of the Symphony. Yesterday's rehearsal of the violas, cellos and basses had been productive, and now they were united with the violins as the full string quintet. This is excellent, exactly the right way to get this Symphony set on its feet.

Lunch with Borovsky, who has had a successful tour of England. In the evening, a concert of works by Auric and Poulenc. The hall was full, and there was warm applause. But my God, what music! It consists entirely of barrel-organ trifles, facile and vulgar doodles in which it is hard to detect any composition at all. And yet unlike the work of some provincial Kapellmeister there is an element of contrivance behind it: it pays lip-service to the peculiar, snobbish style currently fashionable in Paris at the moment, a style that needless to say will tomorrow wither away. Someone said, 'Well, yes, but of course it's just *musique d'occasion*; Auric was commissioned to write it for some theatre or other . . .'

Boris and Cecilia Zakharov were at the concert. They have just come back from America, where Cecilia's success continues to grow. She played my Violin Concerto in Chicago. The little girl is really growing up: in Berlin in 1922 she understood nothing whatsoever about the piece, but now look what a success she is having with it. Gottlieb was dancing attendance on her in Chicago and took her to see Dr Schmidt. He has been saying that relations between him and me had cooled. Although he promised to send me the reviews he has not done so.

3 May

Today's rehearsal was wind alone, always a torture for the composer: it sounds harsh, bare, coarse without the strings to soften and lubricate it. In a few places I caught myself thinking: did I really write such awful stuff? – and guiltily intercepted looks from the musicians who, it seemed to me, were quite indignant at what they were having to play.

In the evening I went to hear a Polish pianist, a very nice man whom I had met when I was giving concerts in Warsaw. He was the first pianist to perform my D flat Concerto[1] in Warsaw and in Riga. I went today out of politeness – and how I suffered for my courteous act! He played appallingly, and my Toccata was just beyond words. This was the precise moment chosen by his impresario, ginger-haired de Valmalète,[2] to bustle up to me shrieking, 'What a pianist! How thrilled you must be!' before disappearing. I was so taken aback I could find no words to reply. Just then Labunsky came up and asked if it was true I was looking for a secretary. In fact I have been looking for one, as I am overburdened with all the letters I have to write: last summer they gobbled up several hours every day. Also, while I was in America and orchestrating my ballet on the train, I had hit on a new system whereby the donkey-work of orchestrating could be devolved to a secretary. The shaking of the train made it impossible to notate, because there was no way I could be sure of getting on to the right position on the stave. Therefore, sitting there in the carriage I thought out and marked up the entire orchestration, but complete and in such detail that when I got to my hotel it was a quick and almost mechanical job to transcribe it on to a page of full score. This mechanical work I could train a secretary to do, provided he was something of a composer and could interpret my abbreviated instructions. But whom could I engage, and whom would I let into my house? To whom would I entrust my correspondence? It would have to be someone efficient, a gentleman, and discreet, not a gossip. And then, a few days ago, Schubert, Koshetz's husband, had said to me, 'Look, Nina Pavlovna has a secretary, a very decent and sensible Pole, and she doesn't have any need for him over the summer. Would you like me to ask him?' Certainly I would. And so, here is Labunsky, citing Schubert, approaching me. He looks all right, a solid citizen, somewhat lethargic in manner, although at first glance not terribly prepossessing, enormously tall and tow-haired.

---

1 Piano Concerto No. 1 in D flat, Op. 12.
2 Marcel de Valmalète, founder of the Paris concert agency that still bears his name.

4 May

Fifth rehearsal, the first with the whole orchestra. The result was reasonably together and not too messy, better than at the rehearsals with Koussevitzky last year. Koussevitzky made a great show of authority and grand gestures but did not actually know the score, consequently the general outline was not too bad but the details were a shambles. Straram was just the opposite: he had studied the score with great conscientiousness, even putting in some bowings for the strings, and it was pleasant to see how much attention he was lavishing on the nuances. But would he have a line for the 'big picture'? Marnold, most cantankerous of the French critics and my greatest supporter, came to the rehearsal. It was he who had prompted Straram to programme the Symphony, and now he was taking the rehearsal very close to his heart, occasionally shouting things out to Straram from the hall, so that I had to grab his arm to keep him quiet.

In the evening I went to Godowsky's concert. His playing is clean, but inhibited and boring. In the Green Room afterwards I saw Borovsky, the Zakharovs, Weissmann and Coini, who had so disastrously directed the production of *Oranges* in Chicago. The moment I saw him I shied like a horse and executed a sidestep to mingle with the crowd. Labunsky made himself very agreeable to Ptashka, hoping to make her like him. Maria Viktorovna[1] told me about Dagmar Godowsky, how she has begun to lose her looks, grown coarse and fat.[2]

5 May

Sixth rehearsal. Not at all bad, although of course with time this Symphony will be much better played. I must rethink the transition from the second subject to the concluding reprise of the first movement, also the sixth variation in the second movement. Savich, the conductor from Syracuse, was at the rehearsal and very interested in the Symphony. Reviews of *Seven, They Are Seven* have come in from Boston, and are very good. They say that in this piece I have succeeded in conveying the most extreme terror. But after all, according to Christian Science, there should be no such thing as terror. Oh yes, my Third Symphony will be all sweetness and light. This Second Symphony with its 40th opus number will conclude my dark period.[3]

---

1 Borovskaya.
2 See *Diaries*, vol. 2, pp. 560–78 *passim*.
3 Not quite, because Prokofiev had not at this juncture contemplated taking material from *The Fiery Angel* and transforming it into a symphony (Symphony No. 3, Op. 44, 1928). Symphony No. 4, Op. 47 (1929–30) uses material from the ballet *Prodigal Son* and is certainly lighter in texture, while the next symphonic opus, the *Symphonic Song*, Op. 57 (1933), does end radiantly but still failed to please the Paris critics.

Saw Tarnovsky,[1] a student of Yesipova[2] who graduated as a pianist some years before my time. He has been teaching in the Kiev Conservatoire, from where he has recently arrived. He says my music is much loved there and indeed recalled four student concerts entirely devoted to my compositions.

Borovsky met the Stahls, as we are all (that is to say the Borovskys, the Stahls and ourselves) staying in the same hotel, the Victoria Palace. 'And how is our revered friend?' asked Stahl. Borovsky told him what he knew. 'All the same, how he does exploit people,' Stahl continued. 'Schmitz organises an entire tour of America for him, and now he can't even be bothered to go to his concert!'

6 May

General rehearsal of the Symphony, better than yesterday's. Two American conductors were there, Reiner[3] and Savich. Reiner is very keen to perform the Symphony in Cincinnati and New York, but is he up to it? He would do better to start with another piece. The concert was in the evening. Usually Straram does not draw much of a crowd, but today was in the nature of a gala occasion and there was a big audience, in part because of me and in part because of Horowitz. Straram was nervous and did not do as well as in the morning. Nerves had somehow stiffened his arms and he whirled like a windmill. The first movement was greeted with a smattering of applause but the second was much more successful than I expected; I rose twice from my seat to acknowledge the applause. Prunières and Roland-Manuel, who had shamefully avoided me after last year's performance, now said that they understood and acclaimed it. Honegger and Roussel were courteous and

1 Sergey Tarnovsky (1882–1976), pianist and teacher, whose students at the Kiev Conservatoire had included Vladimir Horowitz. However the chemistry between the two was anything but cordial, causing Horowitz controversially to shake the dust of Kiev and his former teacher from his feet and move to St Petersburg and Felix Blumenfeld. When both men later found themselves in America, Horowitz with a glittering virtuoso career and Tarnovsky with a more struggling pedagogic position in Los Angeles, Horowitz went out of his way to deny any connection with Tarnovsky, thus depriving the latter of what would have been an impregnable reputation as a teacher.
2 Anna Yesipova (Essipova) (1851–1914), brilliant pianist and revered teacher at the St Petersburg Conservatoire, had been a favoured student of Leschetitsky, whom she subsequently married. In 1909 Prokofiev had set his heart on becoming Yesipova's student, which entailed considerable diplomatic manoeuvring not only to secure her agreement but also the acquiescence of his current teacher, Alexander Winckler. Winckler was obviously disappointed but in gentlemanly fashion did not stand in Prokofiev's way, in recognition of which Prokofiev dedicated to his former teacher his *Four Etudes*, Op. 2. See *Diaries*, vol. 1 *passim*.
3 Frederick 'Fritz' Reiner (1888–1963), eminent Hungarian-born conductor who in 1922 abandoned a promising career in Germany as Principal Conductor of the Royal Opera in Dresden to come to America, where he moved through a trajectory starting with the Cincinnati Symphony through the Curtis Institute in Philadelphia, the Pittsburgh Symphony, five years at the helm of the Metropolitan Opera to, in 1953, the position with which he is most indelibly associated and that he held until shortly before his death, the Chicago Symphony.

congratulated me affably. Tcherepnins father and son were there but papa was gabbling inconsequential rubbish and it was obvious that the Symphony was not to his taste. Bodanzky put in a fleeting appearance; well, he would be most unlikely to have thought much of it. Horowitz, who is much talked about of late, then played a Liszt concerto, Prunières goes so far as to say that he is the greatest pianist since Anton Rubinstein. 'Did you ever hear Anton?' 'No,' conceded Prunières, somewhat embarrassed. Horowitz's performance had brilliance and interest, but was effeminate. Borovsky listened jealously. Afterwards Borovsky, the Zakharovs and I all went to a café.

7 May

Yesterday's emotions took their toll and I had a bad headache. I looked through the symphony and made a note of the corrections and revisions that are necessary. Svyatoslav saw the score and said: 'That's Papa's zizik.' We had lunch in the hotel restaurant: the Borovskys and ourselves with Svyatoslav. This entailed going shoulder to shoulder past the table where the Stahls were sitting. 'Bear up!' Borovsky whispered to me.

In the afternoon we went to Sasha-Yasha's[1] exhibition. He had been a member of the Citroën expedition across Africa[2] and had produced a great

---

1   Alexander Yakovlev (1887–1938), painter, graphic artist and scenic designer. Yakovlev had always been interested in Oriental and African motifs and after the Revolution went first to China and then to Paris where, except for two years during which he taught at the School of Fine Arts in Boston, he lived for the remainder of his life. See *Diaries*, vol. 2, pp. 81, 100, 290, 519–20, 609.
2   In 1923 the great automotive engineer and innovator André Citroën had pulled off the first of what would be a series of spectacular publicity and marketing stunts by despatching an expedition headed by Georges-Marie Haardt and Louis Audouin-Dubreuil, respectively the firm's managing director and a well-known explorer, to accomplish the first crossing of the Sahara Desert by an engine-driven vehicle, using half-track trucks powered by Citroën's new B2 engine. The expedition left Algiers in December 1922 and arrived safely in Timbuktu in February 1923. Between October 1924 and July 1925 Haardt and Audouin-Dubreuil led an even more ambitious convoy, known as the *Croisière noire*, of sixteen men and eight half-tracks across Africa from Algeria to Madagascar. Two years later, Haardt and Audouin-Dubreuil published their account of the trip (*La Croisière noire: Expédition Citroën Centre-Afrique*, Librairie Plon, Paris, 1927). 'This time it was not a question of carrying out a rapid and, as it were, a sporting attempt, but of making a collection of important artistic, scientific and economic data, and of fulfilling the different missions which had been entrusted to the expedition by the Minister of the Colonies, the Under-Secretary of State for Aeronautics, the National Museum of Natural History, and the Geographical Society of France... The ethnographical studies were entrusted to Alexandre Iacovleff, a great traveller in Asia, China, and Japan, an accomplished painter and indefatigable worker, who in the course of the expedition made over a hundred paintings, designs and sketches.' Finally, in 1931–2 the dauntless pair accomplished the hat-trick with the *Croisière jaune*, 30,000 km through Central Asia along the Silk Road from Beirut to Beijing, intended to demonstrate how men, and above all their invention of the automobile, could 'abolish geographical, cultural and political frontiers throughout the world'. This final challenge ended in triumph with the expedition's successful arrival in Beijing, but also in tragedy as Haardt's health had suffered from exposure to the Chinese winter and he died of pneumonia in Hong Kong before being able to reach his goal.

pile of sketches from which after much furious work he had assembled a most singular exhibition of African characters and landscapes. It was all very interesting, but the profusion of black faces and bodies with, as Prince Volkonsky[1] described it, a 'frenzy of nipples', eventually turned into a species of nightmare.

8 May

Proof-read the Suite from *Oranges*. Bought the newspapers, but there are still no reviews of the symphony.

9 May

Went to the cinema with Borovsky to see the film of the Citroën African expedition, the one that had inspired Yakovlev's exhibition. There was much to enjoy in it: the trucks with their caterpillar tracks, the sandy deserts, the bones in the desert, then the impenetrable forests, elephants, Negroes, half-naked Negresses dancing (presented in slow motion on purpose to annoy the French), and Sasha-Yasha himself shooting hippopotami in the water, etc.

When we emerged from the cinema and were sitting in a café, a young boy handed me a note handwritten in pencil. It proved to be from Bashkirov, who was waiting round the corner and was asking me to come out to see him. I was astonished. Some time in the autumn, still owing some unpaid bill or other, he had disappeared from sight and I had not set eyes on him for half a year. But why all this secrecy? I went out to him. He was wearing my Mama's old overcoat, that is to say mine from 1915 which Mama then wore, and I had donated it to Bashkirov when she died, but at least he had a clean shirt on. The creases in his cheeks were deeper than they had been, and a

---

1 Not Prince Pyotr Grigorievich Volkonsky, the artist husband of Rachmaninoff's daughter Irina, who had died suddenly at the age of twenty-eight the previous year. This was another Prince Volkonsky, Sergey Mikhailovich (1860–1937), scion of a Decembrist family, who in the early years of the twentieth century had a stormy two years as a trail-blazing Director of the Imperial Theatres in which capacity he appointed the young Diaghilev to a senior post and gave work to many who were to become leading figures in *Mir Isskustva* and the Ballets Russes, such as Bakst, Benois, Korovin and the choreographers Fokine and Gorsky. Later he became a passionate adherent of the system of calisthenics combined with singing, declamation and dancing created by François Delsarte to develop bodily grace, and Jacques Dalcroze's eurhythmics concept of experiencing musical concepts through movement, to the promotion of both of which he dedicated much of his subsequent life in theatrical and educational environments and through a continual stream of articles in literary and cultural journals. In Paris, where he lived after leaving Russia in 1921, he was a commanding and ubiquitous figure in émigré cultural, rather than political, circles, a professor at the Russian Conservatoire from its inception in 1923 and its Director from 1932. In 1936, having married the daughter of an American diplomat, he moved again to America but died there shortly afterwards.

faint smell of wine hung about him. Spotting me sitting in the café he was very anxious to see me but was reluctant to approach me in company, dressed as he was and his mood not feeling up to it. He reproached me for not having kept in touch. We chatted for a while and then I left him, promising to telephone. Ptashka and the Borovskys were surprised and upset that he had not come in.

10 May

Finished the proof of the full score of the Suite from *Oranges* and got on with the orchestral parts. Lunching at the Du Guesclin restaurant[1] I bumped into Suvchinsky, whom I have not seen for a hundred years (since last year's contretemps over *Ursignol* I had tended towards a slight cooling of relations. After some slight embarrassment we kissed and embarked on a conversation characterised by a mild edginess. I: 'Why were you not at the performance of my Symphony?'

Suvchinsky: 'Why didn't you let me know about it? I didn't know it was happening.'

I: 'My dear fellow, I can't let everyone in the world know.'

Suvchinsky: 'That's just the point, I don't mean everyone.'

I: 'Anyhow, tant pis pour vous.'[2]

Suvchinsky: 'No, I think it's the worse for you.'

(This is all, in point of fact, nonsense as the event was well reported in the newspapers.)

Yavorsky[3] is in Paris and has been for ten days. Suvchinsky says they have met quite frequently and talked, among other things about me. He gave me the address where Yavorsky is staying and added that he very much wants to see me. This is a turn-up for the books, since I had particularly wanted Yavorsky to hear the Symphony.

---

1   Named after the famous Breton general in the Hundred Years War and Constable of France Bertrand du Guesclin.
2   'So much the worse for you.'
3   Boleslav Yavorsky (1877–1942), musicologist and teacher, a student of Taneyev at the Moscow Conservatoire. An extremely erudite musician, his theories about the underlying structure of music based not only on tonality but rhythm and pitch were influential in Russian musical circles and had a considerable influence on the young Shostakovich, to whom he acted for some years as a mentor. See B. L. Yavorsky, ed. S. V. Protopopov, *The Elements of the Structure of Musical Speech*, 1931. Sadly, the exhaustive two-volume treatise of Yavorsky's compositional theory of combining what he termed modal speech rhythm with the unstable harmonic implications of the tritone and a scale of up to seventy-two microtones was dismissed by a Congress of the Composers' Union shortly after its publication as not serving the needs of the Revolution. Protopopov's book was translated with a commentary by G. D. McQuere as a Ph.D. thesis for the University of Iowa in 1978. See also G. D. McQuere, 'The Theories of Boleslav Yavorsky' in *Russian Theoretical Musical Thought*, ed. G. D. McQuere, University of Rochester Press, 2009.

In the evening Ptashka and I went to Schmitz's concert (in order that Stahl should not calumniate me). As it happened, Schmitz played Myaskovsky's *Caprices*, but not very well and quite differently from my interpretation. Borovsky was sharing the concert with him. Coming in during the interval, I sat down next to Zakharov, who said, 'Don't you recognise her? This is Kuznetsova, our classmate when we were studying with Yesipova.'[1] And indeed I then saw, sitting in the next seat to Zakharov, Kuznetsova – a small girl with a large head but quite attractive, a southern type from the Caucasus. After fifteen years she was still the little girl she had been then. I greeted her very cordially as an old comrade, asked if she had been in Paris long, was she playing concerts, and so on. But at that moment who should brush past me, heading for the exit, but Yavorsky, who either did not notice me or made as if he had not noticed me. I rushed after him and caught him up. 'What's all this about? How came you to be here but no one hears anything of you?' Yavorsky stammered something to the effect that he had been meaning to ring me up, that he had been at the Symphony but had not come backstage as he wanted to hear it as an independent listener, and that he would be glad to have lunch with me tomorrow.

Saying goodbye to Yavorsky I re-entered the hall to hear Borovsky give a splendid account of the piano transcription of Stravinsky's *Petrushka*. Afterwards we, with the Borovskys and the Zakharovs, repaired to a café to share our impressions. As we approached the café we saw Kuznetsova sitting at one of the tables outside. I gave her my hand and was about to pass on, but she called me back, and indicating the man sitting next to her, said, 'Allow me to introduce to you my husband.' 'Oh, very pleased,' I said, and extended my hand. As I did so I became aware that the face was vaguely familiar. Surely it couldn't be Sabaneyev, thought I, but he had already seized my hand with both of his sweating ones and was saying, 'Once upon a time there was a misunderstanding between us,[2] but it is time to put that behind us . . .

---

1   See *Diaries*, vol. 1, pp. 161, 216.
2   Before the Revolution Sabaneyev's passionate admiration of Scriabin's music had tended to prevent him forming an objective assessment of the merits of the new generation of St Petersburg composers including Stravinsky, Myaskovsky and Prokofiev. In December 1916 in Moscow a performance of the *Scythian Suite* failed to take place as announced because too many musicians in Koussevitzky's orchestra had been called up for military service. Nevertheless, the *Novosti Sezona* (*News of the Season*) newspaper printed the following day a venomous review of the work by Sabaneyev. Prokofiev never forgot, or forgave. In his 1941 'Short Autobiography' he writes: 'He had written the review in advance, had not troubled himself to go to the concert and therefore did not know about the changed programme . . . Now the enemy had dug his own grave! The odd thing is that although Sabaneyev had not heard the *Suite* or even seen the score, he could have had at his disposal any amount of detailed information about it and no doubt would have not altered a single word in his article if he had in fact heard the music. The fiasco resulted in his having to resign from several newspapers and the damage to his reputation as a critic lasted a long time.' See *Diaries*, vol. 2, pp. 172, 693, and above p. 5, n. 1.

and as you will see, I am not as bad as all that . . . after all you are a classmate of my wife . . .' I scarcely knew where to put myself and could only mutter something like 'Yes, yes, of course' as I tried desperately to extricate my hand from his grip. When I eventually managed to make my way inside the café, where our group was already ensconced at a table, I was greeted by gales of laughter: 'Well old boy, had a nice chat with Sabaneyev?' I rounded on Zakharov: 'What do you mean by that, you bald-headed devil, not telling me that Kuznetsova was married to Sabaneyev? Introducing her as Kuznetsova!' Defending himself, Zakharov protested, 'My dear fellow, it never occurred to me that you didn't know . . .'

11 May

I invited Yavorsky to lunch at the Du Guesclin, where the conversation with Suvchinsky had taken place the day before. Although Yavorsky is a descendant of the Lithuanian royal family (a fact of which, apparently, he is secretly very proud) he is now a rather important official in the Commissariat of Popular Enlightenment[1] in the Soviet government. In any case he has the power to dismiss professors from their jobs in the Conservatoire. His is a suspicious nature, at least as far as other people are concerned, and one cannot rely on him, but I have known him for twenty years and was glad enough to see him to treat him to lobster with Chablis and chicken. Seeing that I was being straightforward with him, Yavorsky also opened up. He said, 'In Moscow you are now as popular with the public at large as Tchaikovsky was in the last years of his life.' My Symphony not only could but must be performed in Russia, where it would be understood and appreciated. His personal favourites among my compositions were the Fifth Piano Sonata and the Balmont Songs.[2] He told me he believed I ought to go to Russia, and went so far as to admit that he had been given a specific mission to sound out my reaction to the idea and under what conditions I would be prepared to undertake the visit. I replied that I was not particularly exercised about the financial conditions of the offer, as I considered it inappropriate at the present time to try to squeeze too much out of starving Russia. If I were to visit Russia it would be with a view to meeting Russian musicians, to see what they were doing and to show them what I was doing. My greatest concern was to have an absolute guarantee of free passage into and out of the country, since I knew of so many completely non-political people who had encountered obstacles

---

1 From 1922, following the defection abroad of Arthur Lourié, until 1930 Yavorsky was head of the music division of Lunacharsky's Narkompros, the Commissariat of Popular Enlightenment, effectively the Ministry of Culture.
2 *Five Poems of Konstantin Balmont*, Op. 36.

when attempting to leave that one could no longer be secure in the knowledge that, on entering the country, one would be able to leave. I wanted to know that I could enter and leave the country precisely on schedule, down to the minute. Yavorsky assured me that there was no cause for concern whatsoever on this point; I could be given any guarantee I considered necessary that no artist entering the country of his own free will would be detained against his will. Finally, he told me that he had been authorised to propose to Russian artists living abroad the following compact: the Soviet government is willing for them to live abroad for eleven months in the year provided that they agree to spend the twelfth in Russia. In this way Russia would see at least something, even if not very much, of all her artists, while the artists would have the benefit of knowing that they could come to Russia without fear of being kept there. Krasin,[1] to whom I had talked last summer, had now left Rosphil,[2] which was currently undergoing reorganisation.

When I asked Yavorsky about Myaskovsky, he told me that he was enjoying great popularity and that he had mellowed. He was playing an important role in the State Publishing House. 'But he is such a soft person,' I objected. Yavorsky corrected me: '*Speaks* softly, more like.' French artists touring Russia, such as Monteux, Milhaud, Wiéner, Marchex, had not been a particular success with the public, and had not generated high box-office sales as there were only a limited number of fellow musicians who were interested in them. We left it that we would have another lunch the day after tomorrow, this time with Borovsky, and parted for the time being.

In the afternoon I called on Shoshana Avivit, the Jewish reciter, with whom in the past I had crossed swords on the subject of Knut Hamsun and had consequently provoked a quarrel with Balmont.[3] I met her again recently, I think at the performance of my Symphony, and she had asked me to call on her to discuss a project she had in mind. Recalling last year's confrontation I resolved to do the decent thing and went to see her. Avivit is a tragic actress, and carries the 'burden of the world's sorrows' into her private life, or at least tries hard to do so. The project she had in mind amounted to her desiring to commission me to write music for some biblical excerpt or other, one of the Psalms or a passage from the prophet Isaiah. Among the composers writing for her are Honegger and someone else, but I am 'the only composer capable of writing a biblical work'. Well, nothing new about that: after all I am the only true Jewish composer![4] Fortunately, in this case the situation was easily

1 See above, p. 207.
2 Abbreviation of the Russian Philharmonia, (Rossiiskaya Filarmonia) the countrywide orchestral and concert organisation.
3 See above, p. 139.
4 See above, p. 7.

resolved: the piece would be needed by the end of June, and I am up to the ears in work, accordingly there was no question that the project had to be buried. What I found curious was the texts she had chosen from the Bible: they were either the vengeance of the Jewish people, or implacable Sabaoth sallying forth to wreak bloodshed among people.[1] I was appalled, not having realised that such dreadful things were contained within the pages of the Bible!

12 May

The Koussevitzkys returned from America yesterday, looking flourishing and contented with life. They related the unprecedented success of *Seven, They Are Seven* in Boston (it has not yet been performed in New York, owing to the need to transport the whole chorus there). They predict a triumphant return to America for me the season after next – he does not have the right to invite soloists two years running. Even so, in his forthcoming Paris season the only piece of mine included will be a Suite from *Chout*, and only a few numbers from it at that. He has backed down on Myaskovsky, despite the promise he made to me in Boston that he would perform his Seventh Symphony. Based on what he told me I had in turn made a promise to Myaskovsky, so once again Koussevitzky has put me in a stupid situation, just as he did over Asafyev's book.

An interesting letter from Dranishnikov about the *Oranges* production at the Mariinsky Theatre, including some photographs of the sets and a report of a *chastushka*[2] composed on the subject of my opera – is this not incontrovertible evidence of popularity?!

I had another encounter with Sabaneyev. He came to see Borovsky at the Victoria Palace, and I happened to come down to get something from the lobby just when he was there. Sabaneyev bowed in greeting, came up to me and as before enfolded my hand in his clammy ones, stammeringly protesting that he had changed his mind about me and was even engaged in writing a book about me. But what the devil does he mean by 'changed his mind'? What about his readers? For ten years now he has been hammering on in the same vein, and presumably his readers have got the message by now. So up he comes with a winning smile and says he has changed his mind and is

---

1 Jehovah, Lord God of Sabaoth – the 'Lord of Hosts'. The cognomen occurs 270 times in the Old Testament but significantly not in the Pentateuch. The implication of this is that the title carries more of a universal metaphorical meaning: the hosts of heaven, rather than the earlier, more primitive, connotation of a warrior God at the head of Israel's armies in their all too physical struggle against their enemies. The subject remains a matter of debate among rabbinical scholars and theologians of all denominations.
2 See above, p. 188.

going to say the reverse of what he said before – but what of the public? Will they be persuaded? Sabaneyev invited me to call on him: 'After all, you are a friend of my wife's, so do let's meet.' Altogether it was rather pathetic. I thought of Scriabin who, according to this selfsame Sabaneyev, was invariably polite to those who bored him, but still contrived to keep them at a distance. This was how I now behaved to Sabaneyev.

Dined with B.N. in a Russian restaurant, a quite chic and expensive one. Needless to say, I paid the bill. B.N. went out of his way to keep telling me how dearly he loved me, saying that now he knew for certain that I was the only person he truly loved and that his relation[1] was divine retribution on him. He is now making a living driving a taxi at night.

13 May

In the morning I read more proofs and then it was time for another lunch in the same restaurant: Yavorsky, the Borovskys husband and wife, and I (Ptashka was in a bad temper and did not join us). Borovsky's conversation immediately took a more businesslike turn than I had done, and he began to ask concrete questions such as: how much would he be paid; what financial guarantees would be offered; in which currency; what would happen about passports; with whom would he be dealing; and so on.[2]

After lunch we all went to see Koussevitzky. On the way Yavorsky told the story of the occasion when the famous conflict between Scriabin and Koussevitzky had erupted but had not yet reached its terminal stage. Scriabin, on seeing Natalya Konstantinovna at a concert, had gone up to her and bowed, but Natalya Konstantinovna had turned her back on him and withdrawn her hand, which Scriabin had been about to kiss. Yavorsky said that every time he remembered this incident he boiled over with anger at Natalya Konstantinovna.

Nevertheless, the meeting with Yavorsky and the Koussevitzkys passed off very well. I played them the new Diaghilev ballet and the Fifth Sonata. Both Koussevitzky and Yavorsky took every opportunity to show their admiration of me, as if I had really become a great celebrity!

When I got home I again buried myself in the proofs and got a lot done. These blue sheets make my eyes pop out of my head after a while.[3]

---

1 Presumably his brother Vladimir.
2 I learned later that this emphasis on practicalities had not been well received. [Author's subsequent note.]
3 The proofs came from the printers printed in white reversed out of a blue background. See above, pp. 30–1.

14 May

Today I felt unwell, with a temperature and a headache that was all over my scalp. I had to take to my bed, something I have not done for five years. I commenced working intensively on myself through Christian Science. Maria Viktorovna came to see me and recommended taking some aspirin straight away, to knock the illness in the head. By six o'clock my temperature had gone even higher and my face was lobster-red, but later in the evening I was over it and quite well again. A remarkable demonstration![1] The most interesting thing was Maria Viktorovna got ill in my stead.

Ptashka and I quarrelled as she felt insulted that Bashkirov had wanted to have dinner with me the day before yesterday without saying a word about her coming, and even so I had gone. But my feeling so ill had brought about a reconciliation, which I was very pleased about and which greatly helped my efforts with Christian Science.

15 May

Fully restored to health – a quite remarkable cure. Maria Viktorovna is still in bed and had to call a doctor. Today I went to visit her.

Tomorrow is B.N.'s name-day and he has invited me to dinner at his club, which occasioned yet another blazing confrontation with Ptashka. However, with the help of Christian Science we managed to damp down the flames of the row, which undoubtedly represents a victory in terms of my work on myself.

16 May

Went out to Clamart to see Svyatoslav and his grandparents. Svyatoslav has a cold and his eyes are all red, like a rabbit's.

Dined with B.N. at the club, where I had previously been with the late Oeberg. B.N. was exceptionally nice and was intelligent enough not merely to enquire about Ptashka but to suggest that he should call on her. I should be so happy if this question could be resolved. The endless altercations with Ptashka on the subject of B.N. are extremely tiring. I have no intention of giving up seeing him because she does not like him, since at the end of the day my friendship with him is a matter for me, not for her. B.N. reminisced about Ettal and my Mama. Life in Ettal was the happiest memory of his life, since before it had been Bolshevism and after it his struggles in Paris, but

---

[1] 'Demonstration' written in French.

there in Ettal he had enjoyed a life of carefree indolence, in the bosom of me and my family. Nowadays he spends every night driving his taxi. But there are some pluses: he looks a good deal healthier, spending so much time in the open air.

17 May

Went to a gala Satie memorial concert in the afternoon, it being the anniversary of his death, proceeds towards the erection of a statue. It was all I could do to last the first half, so hopelessly tedious and limp it was. In life Satie did have some pretensions to be a composer, and had written articles that landed a good few telling blows on some colleagues. But any topical relevance they once might have had had now evaporated and nothing at all remained beneath it.

Met Milhaud, recently back from Russia and looking more handsome as a result. He had seen *Oranges* in Leningrad, praised the production and told me of the incredible popularity of the March. Even on the streets 'on le sifflote'.[1] He had also met Asafyev there, 'c'est un homme charmant'.[2]

18 May

Today the publishers were visited by the three leading composers: Rachmaninoff, Stravinsky and me – but at different times.

The new Diaghilev season had its opening performance this evening, without my ballet, however. To think how I had slaved over it last summer! A surpassingly elegant audience filled the theatre to capacity. The first number was *Pulcinella*, which I heard with the greatest pleasure. How masterfully it is done! The second number was a novelty: *Romeo and Juliet*, by the young Englishman Constant Lambert.[3] During the interval preceding

---

1 'People are whistling it.'
2 'A charming man.'
3 The prodigiously gifted Constant Lambert (1905–1951) was variously composer, conductor, pianist, timpanist, jazz fan, critic, broadcaster and provocatively progressive writer on music (*Music Ho: A Study of Music in Decline*, published in 1934, still has the capacity to start arguments); 'a marvellous musician and companion whose conversation was like a display of fireworks', according to Sir Thomas Armstrong. *Romeo and Juliet* was the accidental result of an attempt by William Walton, who was an indifferent pianist, to interest Diaghilev in a ballet commission by playing through to him his overture *Portsmouth Point*. Diaghilev was bored to tears by it. But Dukelsky and Walton's friend Constant Lambert were also present, and Lambert played his 'suite dansée' *Adam and Eve*. In the account Dukelsky writes of the encounter, a 'beatific smile' crossed Diaghilev's face. 'Diaghilev said: "I like your little ballet. I'm going to produce it, but not with that silly title." He took a big red pencil, crossed out "Adam and Eve" and wrote "Romeo and Juliet" over it. Constant burst into uncontrollable tears' (V. Duke, *Passport to Paris*, Little, Brown & Co., Boston, 1955). So it was that at the age of twenty Lambert

this ballet, however, it became known that there was to be a demonstration. Evidently there exists a group of Surrealist artists opposed to any kind of utilitarianism in art, and in this context art includes theatrical decor, especially when it has been paid for with good money. Diaghilev, apprised of this, had shrewdly engaged two leaders of the Surrealist movement, Max Ernst and Joan Miró, to create the sets for *Romeo*. The disgruntled group thereupon resolved to organise a scandal at the premiere, and to give them credit did so with such panache that I could not imagine a more effective way of achieving the desired result. Our seats were in the balcony near the gangway. Almost as soon as the performance began some young people appeared and began blowing whistles, shouting and hurling proclamations down into the stalls. There were quite a lot of them, fifty or so, and the noise and whistling were deafening. Diaghilev, who had excellent sources of information on what was in the wind, had in turn briefed the dancers and the orchestra and instructed them to keep the show going whatever was happening in the auditorium. Thus the orchestra was playing something (but what could not be heard at all), the dancers on the stage were dancing something (but nobody was paying any attention to them as everyone was watching the demonstrators), while the house resounded with piercing whistles countered by ostentatious clapping and insults from those who wanted to hear the performance. Naturally I was among those who were clapping in support of the performance. Poulenc, sitting alongside me in the box, thrust out his hand to one of the yelling disrupters and said, 'Let me have a leaflet.' The man looked at him, realised who it was and shouted, 'Give you one? Not on your life!' The thing was, this demonstration also had something of a proletarian side to it, protesting against the misappropriation of art by the rich, and Poulenc is certainly not poor. The most curious aspect of the affair was that the biggest

---

became the first English composer to receive a Ballets Russes commission. Diaghilev cast no lesser stars than Karsavina and Lifar in the title roles and engaged Bronislava Nijinska as choreographer, but Lambert was disappointed that despite his plea for Christopher Wood, his friend and fellow member of the intellectually superior Sitwell-dominated literary and artistic world in which he moved, to design the sets, the Surrealists Max Ernst and Joan Miró had been engaged – perhaps, as Prokofiev suggests, in an attempt to pre-empt the expected pro-Surrealist demonstration. Nevertheless the prestige of the Ballets Russes helped greatly to establish Lambert as a seminal influence in English ballet. Indeed with his musical directorship of the Vic–Wells Ballet from its creation in 1931 until 1947 he is, along with Frederick Ashton and Ninette de Valois, one of its founding fathers; it is certainly his most enduring legacy. Rather than *Romeo and Juliet*, Prokofiev might have had more enjoyment from *Prize Fight*, Lambert's short 1924 ballet lampooning the topical confections of such as Poulenc, Milhaud and Satie, in which the boxing ring occupied by fighters (one of whom is black) too apathetic to land punches on one another despite infusions of Bovril and magnums of champagne, collapses under the weight of an invasion by angry punters and the police. (Information from Stephen Lloyd's liner notes for the 2004 Hyperion recording CDA 67545 of Lambert's *Romeo and Juliet* and other works is gratefully acknowledged.)

reaction against the demonstration came from the gallery, which had of course bought its tickets with its own hard-earned money and did not take kindly to having its pleasure spoilt.

Before long the police arrived, briefed in advance by Diaghilev, and set about ejecting the demonstrators from the theatre. Meanwhile the performance continued, and this was mainly the achievement of the conductor, because had the demonstrators succeeded in knocking him off his perch the show would have foundered. They had evidently worked this out for themselves because they tried hard to surge forward through the stalls. But this in turn provoked an unexpected reaction: since it was a premiere of an English work there was a large number of Englishmen present, magnificent gentlemen in full evening-dress complete with monocles. They, entirely ignorant of what the demonstration was actually about, jumped to the conclusion that it must be an anti-English protest against the staging of a ballet by an English composer, and therefore felt impelled to stand up for themselves. From my balcony vantage-point I witnessed these superb tail-coated specimens deploying classic techniques of the noble art and landing fearsome blows on the unfortunate demonstrators. One of them, reeling from an uppercut to his cheekbone, cowered to the floor and buried his face in his hands while a lady in full *décolleté* pummelled him with her programme.

Eventually the police succeeded in clearing the hall, and the audience called for the ballet to be performed again from the beginning. It became clear at this point that the actual music was rubbish, a feeble sort of sub-*Pulcinella*. The sets were attractive, but did not strike me as particularly interesting. Essentially, therefore, the production had not justified the demonstration.

During the interval a group of Soviet Jews could be observed giggling happily under the impression that the demonstration had been a Bolshevik inspiration.

The third number was Auric's *Matelots*, which despite a few exuberant moments seemed to have lost some of the vigour of its run the previous year.

Home again. After all the emotional upheaval I slept badly at night.

20 May

Was at the Pro Musica concert. Now 'the greatly respected one' (Stahl) has lost all claim to credibility for his malicious innuendoes. The boredom level was terminal, and we hastened to relocate to the other hall, where a concert of compositions by N. Tcherepnin was going on to celebrate his birthday. The programme included excerpts from his new opera *The Matchmaker*, which he had played me some time before when I happened to call on him.[1]

---

1 *The Matchmaker* (*Svat*) (1930), based on a comedy by Ostrovsky.

He told me at the time that he had discovered a new method of composing an opera, but it appears to boil down to no more than a way of having recitatives accompanied by wishy-washy motions in the orchestra. No, the way to compose an opera is to make sure that interest does not flag either in the drama or in the music *qua* music: to be specific, to achieve a result that is not only a coherent musical form considered from the purely musical perspective, but at the same time a faultless dramatic entity. This union is the ideal, but is very difficult to achieve, starting with the construction of the libretto.

The jubilee was a warm and touching affair with speeches, the Kedrov Quartet, hugs all round, but there was at the same time something melancholy about it, a sense that in the last analysis Nikolay Nikolayevich was a failure. Needless to say we had forgotten to send flowers, and remembered only when we saw that others had done so. Shameful.

21 May

Am completing the proof-reading of the Suite from *Oranges*. It has taken too long, and the dark-blue print makes my eyes swim. It is annoying: the time would have been much better spent composing something new. But now that the *grande saison* is under way life is so full of distractions that it is hard to concentrate on anything more creative.

22 May

The first of Koussevitsky's concerts. As usual we were in a box with Natalya Konstantinovna. There was a work by Copland, one of Koussevitzky's American protégés. Malicious rumours have it that his name is really Kaplan, and that he had changed it to Copland on emigrating to the United States.[1] There are some, but not many, arresting moments in his work; at first glance the thematic material is unimpressive and the whole piece somehow lacks formal integrity.[2] Very pleasant it was after a long time to hear once again

---

1 Aaron Copland (1900–1990), American composer and pianist who succeeded in forging a genuinely new synthesis of the calls for an authentic American music reflecting the landscape and character of the New World, with the traditions of the *vieux continent*. Copland was of Lithuanian Jewish descent; according to Howard Pollack's biography of the composer, it was his father who anglicised the name from Kaplan to Copland before emigrating. Copland himself was born in Brooklyn, in the family apartment above his father's department store.
2 Koussevitzky had become a strong advocate of Copland after hearing his *Symphony for Organ and Orchestra* (1924) and continued to premiere and perform his works throughout his tenure at the Boston Symphony. The piece Prokofiev heard in Paris was probably either the *Dance Symphony*, a reworking of the Dracula-inspired ballet *Grohg*, or *Music for the Theatre*, written the previous year (H. Pollack, *Aaron Copland: The Life and Work of an Uncommon Man*, Henry Holt, New York, 1999, pp. 114, 121–4).

Strauss's *Till Eulenspiegel*, a dashing piece very well done by Koussya. The programme ended with Respighi's *Pines of Rome*. This is a very fashionable piece today, consisting of little but opulent and skilful machinations, but the conductor relished wallowing in the sea of sonorities, and the audience also approved. In the evening Koussya telephoned me to ask my impressions of the concert, the first time such an honour has been bestowed upon me.

23 May

The proof of the *Oranges* Suite is finished, but alas this is only the first proof; the second is yet to come. But I correct everything the first time, so the second is just an extra, a check to see that all the misprints have indeed been amended. I settled down to further orchestration of *Ursignol*, which still has about thirty pages of score to do, as well as revising my original sketch of the final dance. But I am doing only a little at a time; there is no hurry as it will not in any case be produced before next year.

Went to see Tcherepnin in the afternoon. He is about to go to Riga to conduct some summer concerts there and will include my Classical Symphony; he wanted me to show him some of the tempi and also to ask the publishers to hire him the orchestral material at a cheap rate. Somehow I felt sorry for him. I then went to Koussevitzky, to play him the Suite from *Chout*. We chose four numbers, no more as we did not want to exceed the allotted ten minutes. Met at his house a young Romanian composer, Filip Lazar.[1] Koussevitzky was full of praise for him and said that he was planning soon to perform his *Scherzo*. I had a look at some of his piano pieces, but found them anaemic. Koussevitzky would do better to play Myaskovsky's Symphony, which he had promised he would do in America but now, you see, there is no space for it.

Ptashka and I dined with the Zakharovs, and afterwards visited a sort of fair where we did some target-shooting. We got tickets for a lottery the draw for which will be in a month, and we might win a Peugeot car.

25 May

Was at the publishers. Had a long conversation with Paichadze about all manner of musical matters. He was friendly, and said, 'Our aim is to enrich, not the publishing house, but our composers.' He compares very favourably with Oeberg, who although he also was a nice man was, as Tcherepnin used to say, 'eccentric'.

---

1 Filip Lazar (1894–1936), Romanian-Jewish composer and pianist.

In the evening, back to the Diaghilev season. Following the scandal with the Surrealists there had been such a frenzied run at the box office that those who had complimentary tickets were not being let in. We sneaked in through the stage door; this was not difficult since if one was stopped one only had to say, 'I'm with the company.' And if this still did not work, one said, 'I'm from the management', which usually gained admittance because the local custodians had no idea who was in the company or from the management. But we still had no seats. 'I've already got twenty people in my box!' screamed Diaghilev. Kokhno simply slithered away. We had to stand. Rieti, whose ballet *Barabau*[1] was receiving its Paris premiere this evening, did have seats but gave them up to someone or other, and got a *strapontin*[2] instead, which he offered to Ptashka. At first she refused – how could she accept, he was the composer! – but eventually sat down while Rieti and I stood in the passageway. When he appeared I had a real set-to with Nouvel, whom Diaghilev has put in charge of distributing the invitations, and at the opening chords of *Barabau* we cordially sent one another to the devil. The music is pleasant, jolly and easy on the ear, a little Rossiniesque, as though nowadays one is not allowed to compose anything that is not someone-or-other-esque. There are glimpses of some attractive tunes; others strike the listener as more random. The counterpoint is clear and unpretentious. Sets were by Utrillo,[3] an artist who has descended into the pit of poverty and drink. Now that he has become completely mad people are showing interest in him and it is considered chic to present work in his settings. But as a matter of fact, what sort of

1   *Barabau*, the first new production by Balanchine for the Ballets Russes (he had previously cut his teeth on a revival of *Le Chant du rossignol*) was a no-holds-barred farce based on an old Italian nursery rhyme. The dancers, who included Woizikowsky, Lifar, Sokolova (aka Hilda Munnings, whose entertaining memoir *Dancing for Diaghilev*, John Murray, London, 1960, details the stages through which she passed from Munnings to Munningsova to Lydia Sokolova just before the company's first American tour in 1916 – 'Please forget from now on that you have ever been anything but Russian'), Danilova and Tamara Geva, wore peasant costumes, false noses and padded rumps. '*Barabau*', wrote Bernard Taper (*Balanchine, a Biography with a New Epilogue*, University of California Press, Berkeley & Los Angeles, 1996) 'brought a breath of fresh garlic to the ballet stage.' It had opened in London, where Cyril Beaumont was not amused: 'Merely vulgar and rather tedious ... as a whole *Barabau* filled me with misgivings as to the wisdom of Diaghilev's choice of Balanchine as a choreographer.' The Parisians, as Prokofiev sourly notes, liked it much better.
2   Folding chair.
3   Maurice Utrillo (1883–1955), was the illegitimate son of a disputed father (possibly Renoir) and Suzanne Valadon, who had learned her own very considerable artistic skill by modelling and, in some cases, becoming the mistress of such masters as Renoir, Berthe Morisot, Toulouse-Lautrec and Degas. Utrillo suffered from mental instability from an early age, leading to many long periods of confinement in institutions and ultimately to religious mania. He was also a lifelong victim of alcoholism; nevertheless nothing, not even confinement, was ever able to quench his passion for painting, and his innumerable poignantly characteristic views of ordinary Montmartre streets, many made from memory and from postcards, and his still lifes have made him one of the most enduring and most loved of all French artists.

settings are they? Utrillo is no longer capable of producing anything himself, so his paintings have simply been commandeered and copied on to the scenery. Together with the costumes this produced an effect of pretty, juicy splashes of colour. The choreography was 'grotesque', to use the current maddeningly modish expression, with much clumsy jerking of the legs and backward movements. I didn't care for it, but the audience guffawed heartily.

26 May

Going into the publishers I encountered Stravinsky, our meeting provoking another extravagant demonstration of affection such as is the fashion nowadays. In truth this time it was probably more genuine, on my side at least, since having recently seen just how insignificant are the pygmy composers currently swarming all over the place, I experienced a sudden rush of tenderness towards him. We talked long about this and that, partly about music and partly about other things like taxes and the French obsession with levying them on earnings from abroad. In France, working till you drop won't earn you more than two copecks, but the moment you bring them into the country from somewhere else they make you pay tax on them!

Next I went to a reception for Schmitz. Several young French composers – the generation after Les Six – complimented me on my Second Symphony.

In the evening, having dinner in a restaurant, I met Somov[1] and Ostroumova,[2] the latter recently over from Leningrad. Ten years or so ago Dobychina,[3] visiting our flat on Pervaya Rota Street, had been dismayed at the pictures hanging on

---

1 Konstantin Somov (1869–1939), artist, graphic and theatre designer, a prominent founder member of the *Mir Isskustva* group, contributed frequently to its eponymous journal. A fine portraitist, notably of Silver Age personalities such as Blok, Vyacheslav Ivanov, Kuzmin, Rachmaninoff, his images are clearly under the spell of Watteau and Fragonard but with an underlying tension and irony that markedly differentiates them from their eighteenth-century predecessors. After the Revolution Somov emigrated first to America, which he found deeply uncongenial, then to Paris.
2 Anna Ostroumova-Lebedeva (1871–1955), engraver and watercolourist, founder member of the *Mir Isskustva* Group. ('Lebedeva' was added to her name following her marriage to the celebrated chemist Sergey Lebedev.) Like Somov, Ostroumova had studied in Paris at the end of the nineteenth century, where they both associated with Benois, the catalyst for their *Mir Isskustva* involvement, but apart from several trips abroad in the 1920s she remained in Petrograd/Leningrad, establishing herself particularly in the admiration and affections of her fellow citizens by continuing to work and exhibit throughout the blockade. She deployed her chosen media of engraving, woodcuts and watercolours to striking effect in her representations of her city.
3 Nadezhda Dobychina (1884–1949), St Petersburg gallery owner, artist agent and organiser of exhibitions, musical and literary soirées; also an imaginative concert impresario. The Dobychina agency existed from 1911 until 1929 as an influential and discriminating backer of artists such as Marc Chagall. Dobychina herself had been a friend and supporter of Prokofiev in his St Petersburg days, and after the February Revolution in 1917 had urged him (unsuccessfully) to compose a new National Anthem to replace 'God Save the Tsar'. See *Diaries*, vol. 1, p. 656; vol. 2, pp. 41, 173, 180, 186.

the walls. Mama understood nothing about painting and merely bought objects within gold frames to fill up blank walls. Two days later she sent me a small picture by Ostroumova-Lebedeva, a gifted artist from the *Mir Isskustva* group, and another a little while later as a birthday present. Somov, who before our arrival had evidently been discussing with Ostroumova who might be good subjects for her art during her stay in Paris, exclaimed, 'Now there's somebody whose portrait you should do!' 'Would you like me to?' asked Ostroumova. I said I would, very much, and it was agreed that the day after tomorrow I should visit her to pose, but on condition that I be punctual.

27 May

At Zakharov's request I listened to a piano concerto by a young composer called Vinogradova, who has recently arrived from Revel.[1] It was played to the accompaniment of a second piano. But my God, what provincialism, what extinct language such as one could have perhaps employed last century but not today. There were some nice moments, but overall it was unbearably tedious and irrelevant. When it was over I had to rack my brains as obviously I had to find something to say. Merely to utter a few vague phrases or bitter-sweet compliments would only throw dust in the composer's eyes and could actually be harmful. I decided to eschew diplomatic pusillanimity in favour of explaining to her honestly that what she was doing was of no use to anyone, that she had spent too long living in the provinces, that she must make an effort to write in a completely different way and then, just possibly, something might come of it. Vinogradova burst into tears and through her sobs thanked me.

In the afternoon Milhaud gave a reception in honour of Meyerhold. Milhaud and I now address each other as 'cher ami' – a new friendship based on explicit mutual rejection of one another's music. An interview with him has appeared in the French newspapers about his impressions of Russia, very interesting although they do not correspond precisely with what he has been saying in private, for example about me, and about Rosphil,[2] etc.

[1] Until 1918 the capital of Estonia, then still a province of Imperial Russia, was known as Revel. After 1918 it became and has remained Tallinn.
[2] Very likely a reference to the birth of jazz in Russia. Rosphil was the state concert agency, whose antennae had picked up news of a revue called *Chocolate Kiddies* being put together to tour authentic all-African-American Harlem jazz to Europe. *Chocolate Kiddies* featured singers such as Adelaide Hall, Sam Wooding's eleven-piece band, and some new numbers specially written by a young Duke Ellington: 'Jo Trent came running up to me on Broadway. He had an urgency in his voice. "Tonight we have to write the music for a show. Tonight!" Being dumb and not knowing better I sat down that evening and wrote a show . . . How was I to know composers had to go up to the mountain or the seashore and commune with the muses to write a show?' *Chocolate Kiddies* opened in Berlin in May 2005 and was an immediate sensation, staying on the road throughout Europe for the next two years. In 1926 Rosphil succeeded, with some difficulty, in enticing the production to Leningrad and put it on in a circus tent with a specially built stage. As everywhere

Among those who showed up was Cocteau. In his time he had been one of the prime inspirations, if not the founder, of Les Six. Because of his relentless attempts to generate noise around second-rate composers I had always found him an annoying figure, and had ignored him. This encounter was the first we had had on private ground; Cocteau set out to dazzle, doubtless aiming to add my scalp to his collection, and in fact was genuinely interesting. I was very taken with his story of how Diaghilev, bewitched by Lifar, still could not reconcile himself to his nose and resolved to transform it into a classical Greek profile with the help of subcutaneous injections of paraffin. A little later Lifar went to witness a house on fire, when the heat caused the paraffin to leak downwards and form big bumps all round his chin. Another story concerned Diaghilev's plan to commission designs from Braque for one of Tchaikovsky's ballets, but Braque was demanding too high a fee. However, in the course of one of their negotiations Braque had made a few indications on paper showing Diaghilev how he proposed to tackle the job (apparently it was a dark sky with stars), and Diaghilev kept the paper. When the negotiations with Braque ended in failure, Diaghilev summoned one of his minor artists and ordered him to produce a set with a dark sky and stars based on the sketch and announced in the programme that the ballet was 'designed by Braque') An incandescent Braque took him to court, but Diaghilev was able to prove that the designs were in fact based on Braque's sketch, enlisting his friend Picasso to support his argument. Cocteau had several other interesting tidbits.

At this point Meyerhold himself appeared. When I had known him before he was slim and full of energy, but since then he had put on weight and walked in with a scowl on his face. Later on he became his old, charming self, and told me how much he loved me. I looked at him and was glad to see him, but could not rid myself of the thought that he is an atheist. He was with his wife, an actress, formerly married to Yesenin, repellent but at the same time beautiful to look at.[1] The most remarkable thing is how determinedly she

---

else it went, the show sparked tremendous interest and a direct consequence was to motivate Gyorgy Landsberg to establish his Jazz-Capella, the prime laboratory of Soviet jazz. Landsberg himself was arrested and murdered at the height of the Terror in 1938, at the age of thirty-four.

[1] Zinaïda Raikh (1894–1939), actor. Her unhappy marriage to the poet Sergey Esenin from 1917 until 1929 had produced a daughter and a son, who were adopted by Meyerhold when they married the year after her divorce. She was a beauty and a personality rather than a born actress, but Meyerhold nevertheless made her a star member of his company and had recently controversially cast her as one of the two female leads in his ground-breaking 1926 production of Gogol's *Government Inspector*. In the midst of final rehearsals for Prokofiev's opera *Semyon Kotko* in June 1939 Meyerhold was arrested, tortured and finally executed – the culmination of the great director's progressive fall from grace under the combined threats of Stalin's Terror and the deadening blanket of Socialist Realism that by then dominated every aspect of Soviet culture. A month later, on 15 July, Zinaïda Raikh was the victim of an atrociously sadistic murder by multiple stabbings in their Moscow apartment. Neighbours who heard her screams said they thought she had been 'rehearsing'.

keeps him to heel. As soon as Meyerhold and I met he embraced me and began to urge me to visit Russia. Gradually other guests arrived: Poulenc, Auric, Sauguet,[1] Jakob.[2] Since Milhaud had been so enraptured by Meyerhold's productions every appearance by him was eagerly awaited and people turned up just to gawp at him, but Meyerhold speaks not a word of any acceptable language and as a result the reception was not terribly productive. From time to time I made attempts to translate. Milhaud showed him photographs of scenery from some production or other, and Meyerhold muttered something in response.

In the evening the second of Koussevitzky's concerts took place, again with no works by a Russian composer. Bully for the Russian conductor! Well, I can see that if he were, for instance, a Swede with no music worth speaking of by a compatriot to perform – but for a Russian, it is simply crass. Tansman gave the first performance of his new Piano Concerto. He is no pianist, but seeing how easy it was for Stravinsky to do it, all composers now take to the platform however well or badly they perform. Some bits of the Concerto showed my influence, but overall it was second-rate stuff. It was followed by Brahms's Fourth Symphony, a work so hideous in its content and so ineptly put together that it utterly spoiled my mood. At the end of the concert I asked Natalya Konstantinovna what was to be done about Asafyev's book on opera, to which she replied that she had no time at the present to attend to it. I said, 'You never seem to have time to deal with matters you promised to.' N.K.: 'You are becoming disagreeable. I must bid you goodbye.' I: 'And you become disagreeable when you oblige me to lie to others.'

Of course, N.K. was out of order, but in this case there was another culprit as well: that stupid symphony of Brahms.

---

1   Henri Sauguet (pen-name of Henri Poupard) (1901–1989), French composer. Initially a collaborator and fellow collector with Joseph Canteloube – with whom he had studied composition – on the lusciously harmonised and ever popular arrangements for soprano and orchestra of folk songs in the Occitan dialect from the Auvergne, Sauguet is now mainly remembered for his ballets, starting with the Ballets Russes commission of La Chatte in 1927, choreographed by Balanchine. The most enduring of Sauguet's ballets is the 1945 Les Forains (The Strolling Players) for Roland Petit, to a libretto by Boris Kokhno.
2   Maxime Jakob (1906–1977), composer and organist, in his subsequent incarnation as a Benedictine monk (having converted from Judaism to Catholicism) being known as Dom Clément Jacob. He was a friend of Sauguet and both were leading figures in the group 'L'Ecole d'Arcueil', formed by Satie and named after the working-class district in which he lived, after his rupture with the composers of Les Six. Satie's mentoring style of his young acolytes was distinguished by such specific guidance as: 'Marchez seuls. Faîtes le contraire de moi. N'écoutez personne.' Maxime/Don Clément Jacob is not to be confused with Max Jacob, the poet, painter and friend of Picasso who was also born Jewish, converted to Catholicism and was a close associate of Satie and his group, but who died in a Gestapo concentration camp awaiting deportation in 1944.

28 May

Wrote to Asafyev: with N.K. dragging her feet like this I had to offer some explanation. In the afternoon I sat for two hours for Ostroumova. She is staying in a very modest little *pension* with a window opening on to a quiet square – such incredible places there are in Paris!

Anna Petrovna Ostroumova is a most pleasant lady and the two hours passed easily in conversation. She has the gift of engaging the interest of her subject while working on a portrait. She has a very interesting portrait of Andrey Bely, done last year in the Crimea, in which he is tanned to a crisp and with bright blue eyes. Also intriguing was a portrait of Maximilian Voloshin,[1] angled up and foreshortened from below. But I don't know Voloshin, whereas I still love Bely for his 'First Encounter'.[2] In the evening, an invitation to Prunières', a whole crowd of people. Lazarus[3] played his opera. A young French-Jewish composer, he is married to Ariadna Scriabin, the composer's daughter and thus, incidentally, a relation of Schloezer. All these connections have sucked him into a world of mysticism that informs his opera. I had the feeling that it was alien to the general climate of interest currently preoccupying fashionable Paris. A few passages had been lifted from my 'Pillars'.[4]

---

1. Maximilian Voloshin (1877–1932), poet, watercolourist, critic and superb translator from French into Russian. Having led a cosmopolitan life before the Revolution, he returned to Russia to live in a small town in the Crimea, where he remained all through the Revolution, the Civil War and for the rest of his life. His reputation as a humanist of integrity and a philosophically insightful commentator on the horrors of the Civil War miraculously preserved his life but little else: none of his poetry was published between 1928 and 1961, and he is generally considered fortunate to have died before the worst of the Terror.
2. Bely's long autobiographical poem *First Encounter*, published in 1921 soon after Bely left Russia, is a requiem for the vanished intellectual, artistic and spiritual life of Russia in the Silver Age. The poem had a profound effect on Prokofiev; he and Boris Bashkirov spent evenings reading it to one another when they were living in Ettal in December 1922 (see *Diaries*, vol. 2, pp. 670, 681, 690). Such was the pull of the motherland, however, and so disenchanted was Bely by the West, that he had returned to Russia in 1923. Prokofiev met him in Berlin shortly before he returned to the Soviet Union: ibid., p. 681.
3. Daniel Lazarus (1898–1964), pianist and composer, sometimes drafted in as a seventh member of Les Six in the Consultative Committee of the combined Opéra and Opéra-Comique. Lazarus was himself Artistic Director of the Opéra-Comique from 1936 until 1939. He was a prolific composer of ballets and other works for the stage; the opera Prokofiev heard was *Trumpeldor*, a three-acter to his own libretto about a Russian-Jewish political activist and pioneer of the Zionist movement. Ariadna Scriabina, poet and daughter of the composer, had married Lazarus soon after her arrival in Paris in 1924; she was later to marry two other men, the second of whom was the émigré Russian-Jewish poet David Fiksman, who wrote under the name Dovid Knut. Ariadna herself became an active member of the Resistance during the war and was to perish in Toulouse in 1944 at the hands of the Gestapo while carrying out a clandestine operation.
4. The fifth of Prokofiev's *Five Songs on Verses of Konstantin Balmont*, Op. 36.

Present at the evening was the conductor Kurtz, who has recently completed a tour with Romanov's ballet company. It seems that *Trapèze*[1] was seen in a whole series of German cities including Munich, and then had nearly ten performances in Turin, with the March from *Three Oranges* being played as a curtain-raiser. Kurtz promised to send me the press notices. But from Romanov himself not a word, despite the fact that not long ago he had himself been in Paris! No doubt this is because he owes me at least 4,000 francs, perhaps even more.

From Prunières we went on to a soirée at the Princesse de Polignac's where I endured a sleep-inducing programme of music: some glutinous Chausson and from the younger generation the insignificant Jakob. Baron Rothschild (Robert, not the head of the family)[2] drove us home and talked about Ptashka and me performing at one of his evenings. He asked if it would be possible to have some chamber music by me? I suggested Op. 35 in the arrangement for violin and piano, with Celia as violinist. He immediately began to negotiate, saying that a violinist would probably be expensive and he would not be able to afford it ... We returned home at three in the morning.

29 May

Even though I was very late to bed I got up early as I had promised Meyerhold I would call for him so that we could go together to the Diaghilev rehearsal. Although I had assured him that Diaghilev would be delighted to see him, Meyerhold was still nervous about going alone. He was staying somewhere out of the centre, in a small hotel. As I arrived I saw him running out after the milkman. 'Just wait a moment,' he shouted, 'I'm only going for some milk!' Fifteen minutes or so later we all set off for the rehearsal: he, his wife, another man, an eminently dislikeable Bolshevik of some sort who was acting as his interpreter, and I. When we came into the theatre through the stage door Meyerhold was seized by diffidence, saying that Diaghilev had not replied to the two last letters he had sent him. The rehearsal had already started, but Diaghilev was not there. When he did come into the auditorium, I went up and told him that Meyerhold was here, at which Diaghilev became very agitated and rushed over to him. They kissed, and Diaghilev at once

---

1 *Trapèze* is the title under which Romanov toured the ballet fashioned to Prokofiev's Quintet.
2 Baron Robert de Rothschild, fourth generation in the banking family, was a partner in the bank of de Rothschild Frères in the rue Lafitte. His wife was Nelly Beer, a great-great niece of Meyerbeer, and their younger son was Baron Elie de Rothschild, later famous as the man who resurrected the fortunes of the premier cru vineyard at Château Lafite-Rothschild in Pauillac after the Second World War. The de Rothschilds' Paris residence was a grand establishment at 23 avenue de Marigny.

began to apologise for not having replied to his letter. 'You understand, I am so insanely busy at the moment with all the premieres ... as now, for instance, the show is tonight but nothing is yet sorted out ... But I have your letters with me in my pocket all the time so that I can answer them ...' and promptly fished out from his pocket all manner of letters and papers, but as luck would have it Meyerhold's letters were not among them. All this while the rehearsal was still going on, Diaghilev kept being called away and soon disappeared altogether, but not before he had invited Meyerhold to his box for all the performances. With me he exchanged not a word.

I sat through the remainder of the rehearsal with Meyerhold, and after a while we were joined by Milhaud and Auric. The next piece to be rehearsed was Auric's new ballet *Pastorale*.[1] Devil take him, Auric gets a commission for a new ballet every year! A trifle shame-faced, he half jokingly whispered in my ear that this was not a serious thing, just simply ... And in truth the music did have a strong whiff of the circus about it. It had something of *Matelotes*, but without any particularly striking tunes, except one, in the penultimate number, that was splendidly catchy even if not from the top drawer as far as quality is concerned. All the same, it is a tune capable of carrying the ballet. The sets by Pruna are very nice. The production contained much that was indecent, but Balanchine has really done well. Lifar was always late to the music with his jumps, as Meyerhold observed. My facetious explanation for this was that the nerves emanating from his ears were too long. Meyerhold laughed at this and said, 'Oh, I must remember that one.' He thought that there was no relationship between the groupings on the stage and the scenery, that the lighting was terrible and that altogether there was no ensemble, just like an amateur production. We spoke further about Moscow, about how essential it was for me to go there, and about *The Gambler*,[2] which he is very anxious to produce, and said that if I was nervous about moving about in Moscow he would arrange for me to have a bodyguard of two Communists who were even more devoted to the theatre than they were to the Commune and would see that I came to no harm.

Another visitor to the rehearsal was Picasso, who very gracefully said to me, 'After all, we are almost compatriots,' referring obliquely to our wives.

In the afternoon I had my second sitting with Ostroumova, again spent in very agreeable conversation although I did get pretty tired. 'This is nothing,' commented Anna Petrovna. 'When I was young and living in Paris and

---

1 Libretto by Kokhno, choreographed by Bronislava Nijinska with an entr'acte by Balanchine, sets and costumes by Pruna.
2 In February 1917 *The Gambler* had been accepted for production by the Mariinsky Theatre, to be produced by Meyerhold with Golovin as designer. Orchestral rehearsals conducted by Coates had begun, and Prokofiev had heard the first two acts, but by April, following the February Revolution, everything had changed and the production had to be abandoned.

Somov was painting my portrait, a very famous portrait too, I had to sit for him seventy-three times!'

30 May

Third sitting for A.P. This time she had many colourful stories to tell about Valery Bryusov. He has an evil, tigerish mouth and exceptionally long eyelashes which even at the age of fifty-five he still enjoyed fluttering, and whenever he had his portrait painted something always befell the pictures: some malign fate always lay in wait for them. Several were destroyed by their authors before completion. Renata was based on a real woman who is apparently still alive and living in Paris. Bryusov (Rupprecht) was in love with her while she in turn was in love with her Heinrich. The most piquant aspect of it all was that this Heinrich was none other than . . . Andrey Bely, whom Bryusov went so far as to challenge to a duel. The duel never took place, but I recall its being mentioned in Bely's reminiscences of Blok, although the duel itself has always been shrouded in a dense fog of literary disputes. When Bryusov was asked if it was true that he dabbled in magic and if so had he done so for *Fiery Angel*, or that *Fiery Angel* itself was the result of magical practices, he replied that his practice of magic was for its own sake but that *Fiery Angel* was indeed to some extent the result of his activities. Not long before his death Bryusov took up with a woman and lived with her. When he fell ill, she was not allowed to go to see him. She sat on a bench near the house and wept. Someone asked the dying Bryusov if he wished to see her. 'She can go to the devil' was Bryusov's reply. When he died, his body was subjected to a post-mortem examination, and his skull was also trepanned. The brain was removed, but when it was time to close up the skull again it was necessary to fill the space with something, and nothing else could be found to hand except some sheets of *Pravda* which were torn into scraps and stuffed into the head cavity. Thus he was buried with a Bolshevik newspaper instead of his own brains – fate's revenge for his defection to Communism, undertaken not out of conviction but out of calculated advantage. Bryusov's memory is encrusted with macabre legends of this sort – just like Agrippa of Nettesheim!'[1]

---

1   When Prokofiev started work on *The Fiery Angel* early in 1921, and for many years afterwards in fact until this revelation from Ostroumova, he had no idea that Bryusov's occult, demonic novel was in fact a *roman à clef* dealing with real events and personalities, the three main protagonists being Bryusov himself (Rupprecht), his rival and imagined nemesis Andrey Bely (Count Heinrich/Madiel) and Nina Petrovskaya (Renata), the woman with whom they were both obsessively in love. Prokofiev met Bely, whose poetry he loved and admired, in Berlin in November the following year, at which time Bely was in a deep depression occasioned partly by the failure of his main mission in coming to the West – to reconnect with Rudolf Steiner's anthroposophy community in Dornach – and partly by the reappearance in his life of the by

Attended the Diaghilev season in the evening, and heard a repeat performance of *Barabau*, which had noticeably lost much of its attraction since the first hearing. By contrast it was as enjoyable as ever to hear *Les Noces*. Poulenc, Auric and Rieti were at three of the pianos, and the fourth ought to have been Dukelsky, but he did not return in time from London and his place was taken by Marcelle Meyer.[1] The hall was again full. When Poulenc asked Diaghilev for a seat in the house, Diaghilev answered, 'I don't understand what you want: don't you have a perfectly good seat in front of the piano?' This was such a marvellous riposte Poulenc did not know whether to be angry or amused.

31 May

Called on the publishers with a whole series of trivial matters to raise. Met there Rachmaninoff, who announced with some embarrassment, 'My wife sent a letter to your wife today.' This concerned Aunt Katya, who had written to us about some relations of Rachmaninoff's wife who were struggling with great poverty in Penza, and Aunt Katya wanted to know the Rachmaninoffs' address. To save time, I suggested Ptashka write direct to his wife, but this had happened some time ago and there had been no reply; it was this silence that had elicited Rachmaninoff's announcement.

At seven o'clock I presented myself at Baron Rothschild's, who had asked me to call to discuss his forthcoming musical evening. He is a tall man, nearing fifty years of age, quite handsome with clean-shaven features. His wife, most untypically for a Jewess, has not a trace of refinement about her; she may well not even be Jewish. His house, despite being right in the middle

---

now almost completely deranged Nina Petrovskaya (she eventually committed suicide in Paris in February 1928). Bryusov had died of pleurisy in Moscow in October 1924. Disillusioned with the West, Bely had returned to the Soviet Union in 1923 and was still there, remaining until his death in 1934. Heinrich Cornelius Agrippa von Nettesheim (1486–1535), scholar of the occult and ancient wisdom, author of one of the most comprehensive surveys of occult knowledge ever compiled, *De occulta philosophia libri tres*, thought to be himself an accomplished sorcerer, continues to perplex students of his vast learning by having produced an equally magnificent denunciation of *all* fields of human intellectual achievement, rational and non-rational alike, including his own, *De incertitudine et vanitate scientiarum et artium*. Agrippa makes an important appearance in Bryusov's novel and Prokofiev's opera.

1   Marcelle Meyer (1897–1958), remarkable French pianist admired equally by such disparate personalities as Diaghilev, Ravel, Satie, Stravinsky, Cortot and Les Six. An occasion to which one would have rushed to accept an invitation was when Ravel chose Meyer to play through with him his two-piano version of *La Valse* to an audience consisting of Diaghilev, Stravinsky and Poulenc. In later years, having married an Italian lawyer, she lived in Rome and became an effective advocate for the music of composers such as Casella, Dallapiccola and Petrassi. Many of her recordings of French music from Rameau to Ravel, many made for Les Discophiles Françaises in the 1940s, are repeatedly reissued today as touchstones for an unmatched tradition of grace, style and musicality, notably the seventeen-CD set by EMI Classics.

of Paris, has an enormous and beautiful garden. Rothschild would like Ptashka to sing and me to accompany her. We agreed that she should sing some of my songs and some Spanish ones by Falla. At Yakovlev's recent exhibition he had bought a whole lot of African pictures[1] which we looked at, with great pleasure on my part.

In the evening I went to Kurtz's cello recital.[2] It was deeply uninteresting but I went on account of his brother the conductor, who had promised to give me the programme and press notices of *Trapèze* and also to give me some notes on which parts of my score had not worked and why. Conius informed me that Rachmaninoff had not only completed his Fourth Concerto but had played it to him, Conius. 'Well, what is it like? Is it interesting?' Conius launched into a panegyric, but then added, 'I didn't understand all of it. But then, when Pyotr Ilyich[3] played me his Sixth, I didn't understand any of that either . . .' Marvellous!

1 June

A telegram from Demchinsky: 'Plan despatched.' Well, well! Can it really be that I have at least succeeded in winkling out of him a *coup de main*[4] with *Fiery Angel*? At quite some cost, however. Went to practise at a friend of Ptashka's, because we still do not have a piano in our room and the friend is out all day, so her flat is empty. Sat for Ostroumova. As Ptashka would very much like a portrait of herself (Goncharova and Yakulov both tried, but unsuccessfully) I have been sounding out the ground with A.P. At first she said that usually her female portraits are of ugly women, but gradually I got out of her that her fee for a portrait is 100 roubles. Eventually I brought the subject round to Ptashka, and Ostroumova agreed. I returned home very pleased, but then began to have second thoughts: Ostroumova may indeed be a fine artist, but is she not perhaps rather *vieux jeu*? Not necessarily the right image for a modern composer commissioning portraits of himself and his family!

---

1   See above, pp. 303–4.
2   Edmund Kurtz (1908–2004), cellist brother of the conductor Efrem Kurtz. The family left Russia after the Revolution, and after study with Julius Klengel, Pablo Casals and Diran Alexanian, Edmund joined his brother in the Pavlova entourage, later reflecting that he must have played the *Dying Swan*, the Saint-Saëns number accompanying Fokine's *pièce d'occasion* that became the ballerina's most celebrated performance, countless times. (Pavlova is believed to have performed it more than four thousand times.) Kurtz moved to America in the 1930s and had a distinguished career there as soloist, cellist of the Spivakovsky Trio and for a time principal cellist of the Chicago Symphony.
3   Tchaikovsky.
4   Assistance.

Telephoned Yavorsky, because he is still in Paris and no one is taking any notice of him, but it turns out he has unexpectedly been called back to Moscow and is leaving tomorrow. I invited him to dine with me and he was happy to accept. There was not a table to be had in the hotel; however much fuss I created with the maître d'hôtel nothing could be done. We therefore went to the restaurant Du Guesclin where we had lunched on the first occasion. We were joined by Ptashka, to whom Yavorsky behaved with extreme courtesy and gallantry, scattering compliments and saying that everyone in Moscow was so interested in knowing about my wife, especially with her being Spanish. He had only just had a letter from Moscow 'from the high-ups' expressing satisfaction at his fruitful account of the meeting that had taken place between us, and also at the answers I had given, in particular my emphatic disclaiming of a financial incentive. He was being called back to Moscow in connection with the restructuring of Rosphil after B. Krasin had been dismissed from his post. I thought Yavorsky was dropping hints that he might himself be appointed Director of Rosphil, and this could explain today's sunny mood of contented affability, not to mention candour. We agreed that in the event I were to receive a proposal from Russia I would consult Yavorsky before responding, in order to acquaint myself with the ins and outs of institutions who might engage me. I said again that the most vital thing for me was a cast-iron guarantee of being able freely to enter and leave the country: only under such conditions would I be prepared to consider travelling. After saying goodbye to Yavorsky (to whom Ptashka had greatly taken) we went on to the Diaghilev season, where we saw and heard *Pastorale*, which was very boring. Auric's star is fading.

2 June

Went to Koussevitzky's rehearsal but was too late to hear *Chout*, which had already been played. Natalya Konstantinovna was very pleasant and herself raised the question of Asafyev's book. The publishing house has decided henceforth to confine itself to printing sheet music, to the exclusion of books about music. However, they will try to find another outlet for Asafyev, and even have something in mind.

When I got there they were rehearsing the Prologue to Obukhov's *Book of Life*.[1] This crazy composer had already frightened everyone in St Petersburg

---

1 Nikolay Obukhov's magnum opus *La Livre de vie*, whose Prologue Koussevitzky included in this programme, features a Theremin-type electronic instrument producing sounds by means of heterodyne oscillators, a sort of precursor of the Ondes Martenot. Obukhov, who had himself devised the instrument in collaboration with Pierre Duvalier, called it a *croix sonore*. In deference to the composer's mystical and religious fervour, the circuitry and oscillators were built into a 44cm diameter brass orb and the antennae disguised by a large 175cm-high crucifix adorned with

before the Revolution. Subsequently he had embarked on a Great Work – the *Book of Life*, which had occupied not just several years but the whole of his life. It is a sort of nightmarish oratorio in which figure Jesus Christ, Judas, Tsar Nicholas II and Nikolay the Ecstatic, the last-named being none other than Obukhov himself.[1] Those who have already heard this work have whipped up interest in something that purports to be altogether exceptional. The first bars I heard gave me an impression of something curious, with some interesting harmonies and a feeling for orchestral colour, more notable for being the composer's first essay in writing for orchestra, before he had spent much time on his orchestration studies with Ravel. But in the rare moments when it actually appears the melodic line is of doubtful quality and not completely free from a tendency towards vulgarity. The compositional plan appears to be something like this: separate episodes of three to five bars in slow tempo, followed by a general pause. At first this produces an impression of gravitas, but *à la longue* simply succeeds in irritating. Nevertheless, I congratulated Obukhov on the work when I met him during the interval, in response to which to my surprise Obukhov, who is normally quite unaware of anyone and anything besides himself, said that praise from me was adequate compensation for all the sniggering and sneering he usually heard from all sides.

Sat for Anna Petrovna. Ptashka came too, to talk about her portrait and to view mine. I was a little disappointed with mine, and so was Ptashka. Ostroumova acknowledged that she was not completely happy with it either.

3 June

Koussevitzky's general rehearsal. He is performing only four numbers from *Chout*, but they are in my opinion the most effective. The tempi were a little on the slow side, but everything was clear. Then *The Book of Life* (*The Book*

---

a central star. 'Inspired by Vladimir Solovyov's notion of "*sobornost*" (collective spiritual or artistic experience), Obukhov sought to abolish the traditional performer–audience polarity in favour of a merging of these previously mutually exclusive groups into one of participants.' (Simon Shaw-Miller, *Skriabin and Obukhov:* Mysterium *&* La livre de vie *The concept of artistic synthesis*, in *Consciousness, Literature and the Arts.* Archive. vol. 1, no. 3, December 2000 (http://blackboard.lincoln.ac.uk/bbcswebdav/users/dmeyerdinkgrafe/archive/skria.html).

1 Among Obukhov's other eccentricities was his habit of referring to himself as 'Nicolas l'illuminé' and 'Nicolas l'extasié'. 'He appears to be the author of a new system (only I fear it is a very old one) of notation without sharps and flats (but on the other hand with little crosses), and an adherent of the method of twelve-note harmonies. Their viscid, amorphous mass undergoes a sort of arithmetical, unorganised shifting, which reminds one of the wanderings of plasmodium or similar amoebiform bodies, undifferentiated and unorganised. Obukhov's "mystery" has a political purpose – the restoration of the throne to the last Russian Emperor, who is supposed to be alive and well, but in hiding.' (L. Sabaneyev, 'Three Russian Composers', op. cit., p. 883.)

of the Belly, as it was in old Church Slavonic).¹ Sitting beside me, Suvchinsky whispered, 'Koussevitzky must be a real devotee to try to get this juggernaut of a thing off the ground!' And in truth, *The Book* is such a lumbering great beast as to be virtually unmanageable. The orchestra includes two grand pianos, one of which was being played by Obukhov with fistfuls of wrong notes. Koussevitzky was beside himself and yelled at him, 'If you cannot play your own music, however do you expect anyone else to play it properly?' The normally spectrally pale Obukhov went bright red to the roots of his ears and tried to justify himself. I was angry at Koussevitzky for shouting at the composer: all praise to him for taking on such a difficult work, but that is no reason to jump down the composer's throat ... Suvchinsky told me that Obukhov heard voices during the night and would immediately leap out of bed to write down what he heard. This was how *The Book* was composed.² If there had indeed been voices, they cannot have come from above but from below, not from heaven but from the nether regions. In fact, malign forces had even wormed their way into the performance: after the rehearsal Obukhov explained that he had lost his place in his piano part today because he was so worried about his wife. The day before, hurrying to get to the rehearsal, she had been hit by a car, had been knocked unconscious and for a long time was unable to tell anyone who she was. Obukhov therefore knew nothing of what had happened. She is still in hospital.

Coming out of the rehearsal we spied Ravel, also on his way down to the street. Suvchinsky and the others, knowing of Ravel's great interest in Obukhov, that he was giving him lessons in orchestration and had even gone to the trouble of obtaining a small pension for him, wanted to quiz him on his impressions of *The Book*. I accosted Ravel, and the others crowded round to hear. Ravel said, 'He is a genius, and also a madman.'

In the afternoon I was again with Ostroumova. Since I last saw her she had done a lot of work on the portrait, and it is now much better than it was. She rubbed out the mouth yesterday and painted it afresh. A few more brush strokes and the portrait will be finished.

1 In Old Church Slavonic, the original Slavic language codified in AD 862–3 by the missionary saints Cyril and Methodius, there are two words, *zhizn'* and *zhivot*, both having 'life' as their primary meaning and clearly sharing a common etymology. The secondary meaning of *zhivot* is 'stomach'. In modern Russian, however, *zhizn'* means 'life' while *zhivot* means 'stomach' or 'belly'. Since Obukhov employs Church Slavonic for much of the text of *The Book of Life* (*Kniga Zhizni*), Prokofiev is able to make his linguistically perfectly correct but conversationally slightly ludicrous observation.
2 'Obukhov did not consider himself the composer of this work; instead, he saw himself as the person permitted, by divine forces, to "show" it. Parts of the score, one version of which is nearly two thousand pages in length, are marked in the composer's blood. The music is preceded by a lengthy exposition in archaic Russian, while the work concludes with one section the score of which unfolds into the form of a cross and another, taking the shape of a circle, which is fixed onto a golden and silver box decorated with rubies and red silk.' (Simon Shaw-Miller, op. cit.)

In the evening, Koussevitzky's concert. The first item on the programme was Stravinsky's *Feu d'artifice*, a rather listless performance. The Suite from *Chout* was very well played and was a great success. I twice had to stand up in Koussevitzky's box to take a bow. Then *The Book of Life* commenced. Obukhov's wife had managed to hobble to the concert and sat beside Ptashka. Ptashka said that Mme Obukhova was in such a state of nerves that she infected even her. *The Book* is, first and foremost, a bore: its habit of stopping and starting every few bars soon becomes unbearable. If the whole work had lasted five to eight minutes the public would have been able to stand it, but twenty-five minutes was beyond its power to endure. The audience grew restless and laughter started to be heard. There was, however, little point in either laughing or hissing, since as part of their dramatic text the artists on stage were themselves required to do both those things. Some of the audience thereupon began making use of the lengthy pauses to applaud ironically, the noise of which naturally interrupted the performance. An opposing faction started to boo the sarcastic applauders, and battle was joined. For the last five minutes of the piece nobody could hear anything, and this was a pity, since it was by far the most interesting part of the work. The end was greeted by noisy jeers, and some feeble applause by way of protest. Ravel stood right in the front of his box clapping as loudly as he could; I stood alongside and also clapped. A lot of musicians were present: Stravinsky, Rachmaninoff with all his family, Mary Garden. 'The most splendid box in the whole theatre!' said Fatma Hanum of the Rachmaninoff box. Mary Garden came rushing up to me in the interval, pumped my hand and showered me with compliments. Afterwards we went to a café with the Zakharovs and the younger members of the Benois family. Stravinsky sat at another table with his entourage. He said how much he admired *Chout*, and how he had always considered it my most successful work.

4 June

Our dacha is rented from the 1st June, but it will be at least two weeks before we can get there and so we decided in the meantime to transport Svyatoslav and his grandma and grandpa thither, as they will be more comfortable there than at Clamart (Clamart is now so full of Russians that Suvchinsky, who incidentally has moved out there himself, calls them Clamarinsky Peasants, punning on the Kamarinsky Peasant of the folk song.)[1] So today we all went

---

1 The Kamarinskaya is one of the most popular of all Russian folk songs, celebrating the archetypal Russian peasant. The first two lines go: 'Oh you son of a bitch, Kamarinsky peasant/ Put your feet up and lie on the stove.'

down *en famille* to Samoreau. Svyatoslav behaved perfectly, did not cry at all and spent the whole journey looking out of the window. Our impression of the dacha we have taken is as follows: it has a lovely garden, screened from people looking in, with a quantity of rosebushes that sadly are now beginning to fade; the house itself is rather cramped and does not seem too clean. Olga Vladislavovna[1] undertook to give it a comprehensive clean-up. The surrounding countryside is delightful. Ptashka and I left the older and younger generations in Samoreau and returned to Paris the same evening.

5 June

Dukelsky burst into our hotel the next morning, having spent the whole season in London. He sports dazzling new suits, expensive shirts and gorgeous ties but apparently very little in the way of new compositions – a few pages of a second ballet (this made me laugh: dedicated to Diaghilev and no more than two bars of music!), and three songs, part of which he had played to us some time before. Espying a young American woman in our hotel, Dukelsky immediately took out his monocle and subjected her to a detailed examination. We appealed to him not to ruin our reputation in the hotel. Romanov, of whom we had not heard a word since last autumn, was also there. *Trapèze* had been performed in Stuttgart and other German cities before going to Turin. I do not think it should be presented any longer in its present form; it is riding for a fall. It should be orchestrated for a normal orchestra, it should have another number added to it formed from the material of the Overture and one of the Quintet movements, and the libretto should be completely revised. Romanov has now been invited to become the Balletmaster[2] of La Scala and wants to stage *Chout* there. Kurtz, his conductor, has a few corrections he advises me to make in the Quintet as regards orchestration. To my surprise there are not many of them and they are quite small.

To the Diaghilev presentation in the evening: *Zéphyr et Flore*. Dukelsky sat with us and held his head in his hands on account of the dreadful performance. Of late it has been Diaghilev's practice not to allow much time to rehearse the music. This evening's performance was so bad it was impossible to tell whether the changes Dukelsky had made to the score were any good or not. But whatever the case I am inclined to think that even in a good performance Dukelsky's orchestration will sound like a poor man's Brahms, and this ballet actually sounds much better on the piano. To the production from last year Braque has added two new sets, but I did not care much for either of them. While during the interval we were perambulating with Dukelsky, he in

1 Lina's mother.
2 That is, chief choreographer.

full evening-dress with top hat, white gloves and cane, Milhaud, who had turned up in a jacket and a crumpled shirt, took the seat behind Dukelsky from where he chortled at him like a lunatic. When I happened to turn round Milhaud, embarrassed, dried up completely. Ptashka chatted to Pruna and his wife; she secretly hopes Pruna will paint her portrait. He has done a most successful one of Mme Milhaud.

6 June

A. P. Ostroumova came so that Ptashka could choose a dress in which to have her portrait painted, and then stayed to lunch. In the afternoon Blois took us in his fast sports car to Versailles to see Alexander Benois, who is soon bound for Leningrad. He is not particularly keen to go, but feels he must: the Hermitage is there, also his apartment, and they are pressing him to be there. Koka and Marusya were also present, and Sasha Tcherepnin[1] with a young black woman, a pianist. All of a sudden Lyolya, Benois's daughter, beckoned me into the next room and confided, 'You know, this Negress, she and Sashenka are engaged.'

I lost my temper: 'What do you mean? Do you take me for a complete idiot?'

But all she said was: 'You'll soon see.'

When we came back into the drawing room, Lyolya said, 'Sasha, wouldn't your fiancée like to play us something?'

Sasha replied that she was too tired. I went back into the other room, followed by Benois *père*, who announced with comically exaggerated astonishment, 'What the devil is that all about!', folding his hands over his stomach and rolling his eyes behind his spectacles.

We took our leave not long after with Blois, discussing and dissecting the sensational news the whole way back. He cannot be serious! But how dare he hoodwink the old man like that, and in his own home to boot![2] Ptashka was even more taken aback than we were by the news.

7 June

At eleven o'clock the next morning we went to the Rothschilds to rehearse for Ptashka's performance. She sang well. When we returned home for lunch Dukelsky appeared, complaining that his shirts had been stolen in the hotel, shirts moreover from the best London shop, and now he had not a single one

---

1 Nikolay Tcherepnin's son.
2 Alexander's mother Maria Tcherepnin was the niece of Alexander Benois.

to his name. After lunch we went with him to his hotel where he had it out with the landlady, but needless to say to no avail. Dukelsky conducted himself impeccably, in patrician style. In his place, of course, I would have created a scandal and called them all a pack of thieves. After this, since he had nothing better to do, we went together round a series of house agents, because Ptashka and I had decided that we must try to find an unfurnished apartment in order to set ourselves up in our own little permanent corner of Paris. Ptashka particularly wants to do this, because the business of packing up all our goods and chattels five times a year is literally driving her into an early grave. However, it is no easy matter to find an unfurnished apartment in Paris.

In the evening I attended a concert by Burgin, who was playing three violin concertos, one of them mine. He does not have a particularly beautiful tone and his high notes do not sound; he also went wrong in a couple of places but managed to extricate himself. Nevertheless he had a success, although I did not get called out as composer. Since I do not like going to concerts on my own, and had a spare ticket, on the way I had called in at the club where I found Boris Nikolayevich dining (but was that all he was doing there?). He was delighted to come with me. Dukelsky was also at the concert; he had been dining with the Koussevitzkys and came with Natalya Konstantinovna. Somewhat unexpectedly he praised my Concerto, especially the second and third movements. I was certain that neither he nor the circles whose opinions he reflects would care for the Concerto at all.

I have received Demchinsky's scenario for *The Fiery Angel*. Well, well, at long last! I dived into it straight away, although at first it was hard to grasp. There are some interesting details in it, but I had been expecting something more.

8 June

Played through *Chout* to Romanov. True Russian that he is he was an hour and a half late and then never stopped apologising. He was delighted with *Chout* and wants very much to stage it in La Scala, the problem being that although they want a Russian ballet they do not want one drawn from Russian life. Strange notions these people have! Lunch: Suvchinsky, Dukelsky, Romanov, Ptashka and I. We had the jolliest of meals. Dukelsky told some scandalous stories about the Serbian pianist who had proposed appearing with me in Berlin, but disappeared into thin air only to turn up as accompanist to the Diaghilev troupe. Romanov listened with incredulity to Dukelsky's stories, snorting into his napkin. Suvchinsky and I then led Dukelsky to the piano and he played some excerpts from his new ballet. He has not composed very much – only two pages more than he played us in March, no more than five minutes' music for the whole of the winter, moreover the character of the music in no way represents progress, rather the reverse in relation to *Zéphyr*, even though it does contain some extremely nice passages. Suvchinsky and I chastised him severely.

In the evening I was supposed to have been performing at some sort of Russian cultural event intended to demonstrate to Parisians that the Soviet Revolution has not yet entirely destroyed Russian culture. Suvchinsky, however, blew up: 'You don't know what you are doing! Russian culture today is wholly sustained by Stravinsky's compositions and yours, while inside Soviet Russia there are some writers who still, despite everything, produce wonderful work. But here you have some émigré scum cobbling together a farrago which is not something you should have anything to do with.' Impressed, I sent a telegram to the effect that unforeseen circumstances, etc. . . .

9 June

In the morning Vyshnegradsky[1] came to show his piece, written in quarter-tones. It was performed on two pianos, tuned with one a quarter-tone higher than the other, so that a quarter-tone theme wanders from one piano to the other and then back again. I am not particularly interested in quarter-tones, considering that much still remains to be done with semitones, but I was certainly interested to hear Vyshnegradsky's experiment. As a composer he lacks talent, and his work must be considered not from the perspective of music but as an example of the inherent possibilities thus demonstrated, much as one would listen for instance to a clarinettist showing what can be done with exercises from a clarinet 'school'. I enjoyed hearing how the melody could slide up and down in quarter-tones, and some of the resulting chords were unusually sonorous, creeping into one's ear like a brush!

---

1   Not the banker and Sunday composer Alexander Vyshnegradsky but his son Ivan (1893–1979), whom Prokofiev had encountered in St Petersburg when he conducted an early (non-microtonal) *Andante* for orchestra by Vyshnegradsky in Tcherepnin's conducting class. At that stage Vyshnegradsky was strongly influenced by Scriabin, but after emigrating to Paris he became a staunch adherent of the most avant-garde techniques including the use of quarter-tones. Experiments constructing keyboard instruments tuned in quarter-tones, first with Pleyel, later with Grotrian-Steinweg, then a harmonium made by Otto Pape in Berlin and finally a three-manual instrument by the German maker Förster, all eventually proved impractical and Vyshnegradsky settled for the expedient of two pianos tuned a quarter-tone apart – this at least had the advantage of allowing the separate piano parts to be notated so that they *looked* and could be played like conventional scores instead of needing a completely new system of notation. Around this time Sabaneyev felt able to write, referring to Vyshnegradsky's 'fanatical devotion' to his absolute form of ultrachromaticism, that 'his harmonies are not merely new passing notes between old academical resonances – he devotes himself *con amore* to the quest of some specific thing, he seeks for new sensations . . . many of the harmonies discovered by him are very effective, very subtle and ingenious . . . Vyshnegradsky affirms that he has entirely retuned his musical thought to this new world.' The piece he played for Prokofiev may have been the *Prélude et danse* for two pianos, Op. 16, composed in spring 1926.

After this I played some excerpts of *Chout* to Bolm,[1] who is now Balletmaster at the Chicago Opera and would like to produce the ballet there, if circumstances prove to be propitious.

In the evening we had the concert and reception at the Rothschilds'. Ptashka sang reasonably well, better than in Italy. There was a good reaction from the audience, although without especial enthusiasm. Maybe they are all too well groomed and too solicitous of their delicate palms. Among musicians present were Poulenc, Tailleferre and Rieti. Marcelle Meyer played a piece by Rieti, indescribably bad. Rieti skulked about with an offended air, but truthfully nobody has any right to perpetrate such rubbish! Sasha-Yasha[2] was also among the guests, he and I had a nice talk, and he pointed out to me some of the more remarkable paintings in the Rothschild collection.

10 June

Had a bad headache, which made for an unproductive day. However, by evening it was better and eventually passed off altogether.

We went to the Samoilenkos, who are mightily impressed that I plan to engage a secretary. Sasha-Yasha was also there. Fatma Hanum said, 'I like Stravinsky, I love ugly, pock-marked faces like his.' Yakovlev, who was sitting on the carpet at her feet, simpered and said, 'Fatma Hanum, you'd be much better off with me. I assure you, je sais très bien faire ma petite besogne!'[3]

11 June

Went to the Koussevitzky rehearsal in the morning, to hear a work by Ernest Bloch.[4] I used to think him not at all a bad composer, but this piece is

1   Adolph Bolm (1884–1951), dancer and choreographer, had been a premier danseur in Diaghilev's first Ballets Russes season in Paris in 1909. When the company toured America for the second time in 1916, Bolm was placed in charge of recruiting and directing the troupe, following which he remained in New York to direct opera and ballet productions at the Met, and also to form his own ballet company Ballet Intime with Ruth Page as prima ballerina. Bolm and his wife had become close friends of Prokofiev during the composer's first stay in New York in 1918; at the Brooklyn Museum soon after Prokofiev's arrival dancer and composer-as-pianist had shared a platform, Bolm having choreographed a suite of solo dances to *Visions fugitives*, in what was in fact Prokofiev's American debut appearance. Bolm was originally engaged to choreograph the dances for *The Love for Three Oranges* at the Chicago Opera in 1919, but this production was acrimoniously abandoned owing to the sudden death of the Opera's Director, Campanini, and when it finally reached the stage through the good offices of Mary Garden in December 1921, Bolm was not involved. See *Diaries*, vol. 2, pp. 330, 348, 413, and *passim*.
2   The painter Alexander Yakovlev.
3   'I do my little tasks very well!'
4   Ernest Bloch (1880–1959), Swiss-born composer who became an American citizen in 1924. His music is strongly influenced by Jewish liturgical and folk music, notably *Schelomo* for cello and orchestra and the *Israel* Symphony, both written in 1916. Prokofiev had met him in America in 1918. See *Diaries*, vol. 2, p. 353.

hopelessly uninteresting and inept, even in poor taste. His idea was to have a little joke by deploying technically sophisticated means to write very simple music, the result being a piece of pomposity that might deceive people in America, but not in Paris.[1]

I spent all day thinking about the libretto for *Fiery Angel*. I sat in my room surrounded by Demchinsky's plan, my old libretto and Bryusov's novel. I thought the whole thing out from end to end and seem to have had some good ideas: the new libretto will be a modest construction, neither Demchinsky's nor my original one, but something new. My conception covers not just alterations, combinations and additions but answers to Demchinsky's objections: why this way and not another? It had been a very useful exercise, for with an unseen devil's advocate to joust with I had continually to subject my invention to criticism. Demchinsky had not in essence provided me with much material, but there is no doubt that he had injected a new vitality into the first two acts. The thing I had been most in need of was a push to jolt me out of my stone-like inertia over the text. The actual quality of Demchinsky's suggestions did not matter: if it was good, so much the better, but if not (as was in fact the case) at least criticising it gave me ideas.

We dined with Koka and Marusya Benois and had a very good time, followed by a visit to the Palais. Marusya is losing her provincialism, and Koka is exceptionally nice.

12 June

Viewed the unfinished portrait of Ptashka. Some parts of it are very good (eyes, mouth, even though the eyes have a very sad expression), but somehow the whole ensemble is not quite right, as to do her justice Ostroumova herself acknowledges. In the afternoon we attended Koussevitzky's final concert. Hindemith's Concerto for Orchestra eschews beauty and charm, but is not bad in its rough-hewn way and contains many brilliant inspirations and interesting sonorities. Honegger's *Pacific* is not short of energy and diversion, but I am not convinced that it has any real musical qualities. Saw Mary Garden: she was charming and full of praise for the *Chout* excerpts she had heard at the previous concert. I could not get any news from the Koussevitzkys about Asafyev's book or about publishing my recent scores. 'We' are so frightfully busy these days. Generally Koussevitzky is in one of his

---

1 The work was Bloch's Concerto Grosso No. 1, which had already had considerable success in America, having been performed in Chicago (with Stock), Philadelphia (Stokowski), San Francisco (composer) and Boston (Koussevitzky). This performance in the Paris Opéra was the work's European premiere.

disagreeable phases, which usually come over him during his Paris season when he is tired and being torn in different directions at once.

13 June

Spent all day writing to Demchinsky, commenting on his *Fiery Angel* scenario.

14 June

Called at the publishers to collect various manuscripts of mine, which for reasons of safety I generally do not like to keep at the hotel but deposited with the publishers. As I did not succeed in getting an audience with the Koussevitzkys I charged the amiable Paichadze with speaking to them when a suitable occasion presented itself. First of all I want the Second Symphony printed. And something has finally to be decided about Asafyev's book.

16 June

Because of the franc's volatility on the Stock Exchange, the change of ministers and discussions about a possible tax on capital, we transferred $2,000 to America. This was not a simple matter to arrange and we managed it only by being able to prove that we were not permanent residents in France and that it was only a few months since we had brought these $2,000 to Paris from New York.

Anna Petrovna has completed Ptashka's portrait, which she has altered considerably since we last saw it. It is now an attractive picture and a good likeness. We paid her $50. Anna Petrovna said that apparently 'Renata'[1] is still alive and living in Paris. When she goes back to Russia she will find out from Voloshin everything she can about this woman and write to me.

Fiedler[2] took us to see a flat but we were not able to view it because the concierge would not let us in. Even though Fiedler is the managing agent he is new, and the concierge did not know him. The building is in an excellent location, near the Invalides, but from the outside looks old. Fiedler, however, is enthusiastic about the flat. We left matters as they are, because we still have time: the flat is due to have repairs done and to be generally renovated.

This was followed by packing and departure to Samoreau. Boris Nikolayevich accompanied us to the station, looking longingly at our

---

1 The hysterical woman at the centre of the plot of *The Fiery Angel*. The reference is to Nina Petrovskaya, the real woman with whom Bely and Brysuov had both been in love. See above pp. 325–6, n. 1.
2 Architect and estate agent in Paris.

first-class tickets (we had taken them only because with such a mass of luggage we were afraid of the crowds.) We arrived at Samoreau in the evening. It was raining, but quiet and the air is wonderful. The garden is still full of roses.

17 June

Samoreau is three kilometres from Fontainebleau, on the other side of the Seine, and lies between two forests: the Forest of Fontainebleau and the Bois de Valence. Olga Vladislavovna has thoroughly cleaned the house and now it does not look bad at all; the garden is lovely and enclosed within a fence so that the neighbours can be neither seen nor heard. My workroom is large and comfortable, but the other rooms are on the small side. Svyatoslav gives us great joy. He has really come on, chatters away in both French and Russian and is making quite successful efforts to pronounce the letter 'r'. When he enters the house he wipes his feet and when he goes out he closes the door behind him. These are great achievements for a two-and-a-half-year-old.

I went early in the morning into Fontainebleau to get the upright piano Pleyel had sent down for me, and to buy a table to work on, a kitchen table since the one in the house was falling to pieces. There is a tram that goes from where we are to Fontainebleau, but I walked there along a beautiful road – generally there are delightful walks all around. I got caught in the rain, but did everything I needed to and came back in the lorry with the piano and the table.

In the afternoon I continued writing my response to Demchinsky, which I had begun in Paris, getting up to sixteen fairly densely written pages. All in all Demchinsky had not contributed much, but he had contributed something, and I needed in my letter to engage in all kinds of diplomatic and obsequious circumlocutions in order that he would not be tempted to remove anything that was good nor, indeed, to abandon the project altogether.

18 June

In the morning, composed the conclusion of *Ursignol*, my first draft never having satisfied me. Spent the afternoon typing out my letter to Demchinsky, but from being out of practice typing and its being so many pages my fingers were all thumbs and I did not finish it.

Our quiet little corner is ideal for working, and I have a lot of plans: over the summer I want to finish composing *Fiery Angel* and orchestrate two acts; I must finish orchestrating *Ursignol* (there is not much to do) and make a piano score of it. I have already completed about a quarter of this. I have to write a five-minute Overture for Duo-Art; I must revise the *Sinfonietta*;[1] make final corrections to the Second Symphony and to the Quintet so that they are ready for publication; and there will be proof-reading to do. I think that will be enough to keep me busy!

19 July

Worked on *Ursignol*, composing the end of the final number, doing the orchestration, scratching out and correcting mistakes. Finished typing out the letter to Demchinsky and posted it. The rain that has with a few intervals lasted for two months finally ceased. I get up at eight and go to bed at ten. How quiet it is here after Paris!

20 June

Carried on working on *Ursignol*. I discover that I began the orchestration without using bass clarinets and completed three numbers like that. But when I resumed work on the score in America I added bass clarinets and now set about including them in the first three numbers.

The weather is warm and sunny. Thank God for summer!

21 June

Orchestrating the end of *Ursignol*. Looked through the *Sinfonietta*, an attractive piece, fresh and not at all badly composed. I now find its four-squareness and predictable sequentiality annoying, however. I shall make some changes, but not so as to violate the style.

22 June

Put the finishing touches to the composition of the finale of *Ursignol*.

An extensive postbag from Moscow: Myaskovsky has sent me *Autumnal*, on which I have not set eyes for ten years[2] and which I have partly forgotten. From Persimfans an enquiry as to whether I would be prepared to come to Moscow to appear with them. Dianov[3] sent some cuttings from Moscow newspapers.

---

1 The *Sinfonietta*, Op. 5, Prokofiev's first mature composition for orchestra, was written in 1909 and had already been revised once, in 1914.
2 This piece, Op. 8, one of a pair of tone-poems for orchestra, the other being *Dreams*, Op. 6, was composed in 1910 and revised in 1915.
3 Anton Dianov (1882–1939), composer mainly of piano and chamber works, and a large output of songs.

Autumnal stands in less need of revision than the *Sinfonietta* but is also more resistant to tinkering. There is something sentimental in the basic conception of the piece. Nevertheless I have very warm feelings towards it, even though I cannot quite see where it is likely to be performed: it would certainly be a failure in Paris being too far removed from Parisian sensibilities, while it is too soon to think of its being performed in Russia, where they expect different things of me, and in America it would sink without trace as lacking brilliance . . .

23 June

Finishing off the final pages of the orchestration of *Ursignol*; it crawls along, giving me a lot of trouble on the way. In the afternoon I wrote to Yavorsky and also some other letters. Did nothing in the evening although I should have practised the piano: in Russia they know all my sonatas and concertos by heart and therefore, if I am to go there, I will have to play them really well. But by evening I am tired and have no desire to sit down at the piano. In Ettal Boris Nikolayevich and I used to play chess, an absorbing activity but havoc-wreaking on the organism: the next day the brain was not as fresh for work as it could be and if, God forbid, I lost the game, my mood would be terrible.

Made a simplified version of the March from *Oranges* as a crowd-pleaser for the Russian public. The process of denuding for the sake of simplicity is highly disagreeable.

24 June

My secretary, Labunsky, came. Back in Conservatoire days I had known or heard something of his brother,[1] a piano student of Nikolayev.[2] Labunsky is a Pole who lived in Russia and studied at the Polytechnic Institute in St Petersburg before deciding to concentrate on music. He then studied

---

1. Prokofiev's new secretary was Felix Labunsky. His younger brother was Viktor Labunsky, who as well as studying piano was a composition student of the Latvian Jazeps Vitol and Stravinsky's first teacher Vasily Kalafati. Returning to his native Poland he taught piano at the Krakow Conservatoire before in 1928 migrating to America, where he continued his teaching career and produced a number of compositions including a symphony, piano concertos and solo piano pieces including several transcriptions of Bach's organ works. Felix, three years older, also settled in America but not until 1936, and likewise taught and produced a range of orchestral and concerted works, piano sonatas, cantatas for voice and orchestra, and a string quartet.
2. Leonid Nikolayev (1878–1942), influential pianist and teacher at the St Petersburg, later Leningrad, Conservatoire. Prokofiev had known and admired him while studying at the Conservatoire with Anna Yesipova, and the respect was mutual. Nikolayev was later to be the much loved piano teacher of Shostakovich. See *Diaries*, vol. 1 *passim*.

counterpoint and fugue,[1] but his grasp of orchestration is problematical. He is tall, blond, withdrawn, correct, and moves slowly.

Ptashka's father and mother have gone to the seaside. One of the reasons for this is a conflict of views between Ptashka and her parents over the upbringing of Svyatoslav. There is no doubt that Olga Vladislavovna has been indulging him.

Because Labunsky needs to play the piano for two hours a day and I don't want any more music than necessary in the house, I promised to find him somewhere near by where we could rent a piano for him. We visited one of the other dachas where, as we had been told, there might be a piano, and the lady of the household asked whether he was a serious musician or merely an amateur. Labunsky replied that he was a composer. When the lady asked why he did not play the piano in our house, Labunsky said, indicating me, 'Monsieur est aussi compositeur.' Thus it is that my secretary is the composer, while I am 'also a composer'. Nevertheless, the lady did not give him permission to play her piano.

25 June

Continued working. I asked Labunsky to tidy up and copy out my simplified arrangement of the March from *Oranges* and then to score those pages in the finale of *Ursignol* that are identical to the equivalent passages in the first number. It was immediately apparent that he is a slow worker. As I had a bad head, I went for a long walk and went as far as Bas-Samois, a charming spot on the banks of the Seine three kilometres from us; I had coffee in the tennis club there on the river bank. Incidentally, Labunsky is a prize-winning tennis-player, but for our part we have given up the sport, and anyhow were never any good at it.

26 June

Finished orchestrating *Ursignol*. I put the date of 26–6–26, but this opus is still not finished as I have to make a piano reduction. Only three numbers have been done properly, the remainder only sketchily, but at least I must have something to send to Diaghilev.

Labunsky worked all day recopying the necessary pages of *Ursignol*, making a handsome number of mistakes in the process. My lynx eyes caught them immediately.

---

1   By 'fugue' in this context Prokofiev means the general academic study of baroque and classical polyphony as taught in conservatoires rather than the strict deployment in composition of fugues as such.

27 June

Made some alterations to the *Sinfonietta*. As it was Sunday Labunsky had a day off. Pleyel sent a good grand piano in place of the rotten upright. With it came also the boxes and trunks I had deposited with Pleyel, containing scores, summer clothes and old things.

28 June

I am ready to get down to serious work, but Demchinsky is dragging his feet with *Fiery Angel* and Straram has not sent the score of the Symphony, in which I need to make some final changes (among them quite significant ones in the reprise of the second subject and in the final variation). I therefore got on with the *Sinfonietta*, which I need to do a little bit of work on, and tidied up a few things in the Quintet. I asked Labunsky to divide the long bars in the third movement of the Quintet into three. He is awfully slow, and the letters I asked him to type for me were very badly done.

1 July

The Second Symphony has finally been sent, score and parts, to be collected from the neighbouring station of Vulaine. I took Svyatoslav's pram with me to get them, otherwise I would not have been able to carry them. Then I unearthed the list of revisions I wanted to make, which I had compiled after Straram's last performance, and set to work.

2 July

Made changes to the Symphony, mostly small ones. Our servant has left, so the household is in chaos as far as lunch and dinner and so on is concerned. Boris Nikolayevich came round in the evening, and I was very glad to see him. We had a lot to talk about. He is appalled at the idea that I plan to go to Russia in January. What will people say? Surely I cannot be ready to shake hands with 'those murderers'? I replied that I was not going for money but to connect with musicians in Russia. The easiest way to shut the mouths of those who would criticise me for so doing is to ask them: 'And what about you? If you had the opportunity to go to Russia, to see again the places of your native land, to see your friends, just to stroll round Moscow and St Petersburg, and then freely to come back here again, would you really not want to go?'

3 July

Today was thundery, the atmosphere oppressive and not conducive to any kind of work. I did almost nothing. All the same, a few ideas for improvements to the reprise of the Symphony did come into my mind. I proof-read the second proof of the Suite from *Oranges* Boris Nikolayevich had brought with him the previous day. Labunsky is a slow but reasonably methodical worker: his main problem is lack of experience. Today he got through everything he was asked to, and I even let him go home before evening.

4 July

Today at last I clarified my thoughts on how to reorganise the reprise, the problem having been that some of the joins were not smooth enough and were not feeding effectively into the succeeding passage. I worked on it all day and got very tired, but was happy with the results.

Blois came in the evening.

5 July

Ptashka and I went together into Paris. We had not been there for three weeks; the time had flown past without our being aware of it. We looked at a flat in the Lowendal *quartier* that had been recommended to us by the Koussevitzkys' architect. It was hard to judge the apartment itself because it was in such an extraordinarily dirty state, but Fiedler promised to bring it up so that it glistened. The location is excellent, but the flat itself rather small. Fiedler said we could think about it for a month.

Was at the publishers, whence I took away with me part of the second proof of the Suite from *Oranges*. Paichadze told me that in ten days' time, when he returned from Berlin, he would be able to issue the Quintet. As for the Second Symphony, he had spoken to Koussevitzky, and Koussevitzky, while he had given him *carte blanche* to do whatever he decided, had expressed reservations as to whether it was advisable to rush immediately into print with such a substantial and expensive work. Paichadze's suggestion was that the score should be engraved, but that only a second handwritten set of parts be prepared. This seems to me quite an elegant solution.

Visited the Banque des Pays du Nord, which turns out to be a Bolshevik bank, and was presented with $120 representing royalties from Russia, which I immediately transferred to New York in order to avoid paying tax in France. The Jew who handed me the cheque recognised my name and fawned all over me.

At eight o'clock in the evening we went back to Samoreau.

6 July

Did more work on the Symphony and this time stitched it all together anew, going right through the reprise from the exposition to the concluding section. I think now it will all hang together smoothly and will sound well. I then disgorged all this work on to Labunsky for him to incorporate the new material into the orchestral parts: to patch it all in will take him four days or so. Composed some of the 'Overture for Seventeen' – can I really call it that?[1] – but did not get very far with it.

Svyatoslav, sent to call me into dinner while I was playing the piano, said, 'Papa, nyum-nyum, that's enough boom-boom.'

7 July

Read Bunin's *Mitya in Love*, one of his most recent things, which is much talked of in émigré circles.[2] I don't like Bunin much, in fact not at all, but Gorky had particularly praised *Mitya in Love* when I asked him about it in Naples. It is easy and enjoyable to read, and is calculated to awaken pleasurable memories of youth in anyone. But that is all one can say about it. From the point of view of style it is smooth and bland.

8 July

A telegram in reply from Demchinsky, or rather from his wife: 'Lettre reçu. Barbe[3] Demtchinsky.' No doubt 'himself' is away and Varya is answering on his behalf. But anyone familiar with French *argot* could read it like this: 'Letter received, what a pain' – on account of my having once again completely altered the scenario. In any case it is really monstrously, unforgivably inconsiderate behaviour when the fellow gave me his word I would have the first and second acts by the first of June. It is all to the good that I am smoothing out the awkward places in the Symphony but what I really need to be getting on with is *Fiery Angel* – the Symphony can always be fixed up in the gaps.

---

1 The 'Overture for Seventeen Performers', commissioned by Duo-Art. It is usually known as the *American Overture* in its versions for large ensemble (Op. 42) and for orchestra (Op. 42bis).
2 This novella, written in 1924, is a lyrical, *Werther*-like account of the sorrows and illusions of first love, contrasting life in Moscow with life in the depths of the Russian countryside. It is generally considered to be one of Bunin's masterpieces.
3 Demchinsky's wife was Varvara, usually known as Varya (Barbara). 'Quelle barbe!' is indeed an idiomatic exclamation meaning 'What a nuisance', or a rather stronger expression of discontent. But in this case, 'Barbe Demtchinsky' (written in Latin script), almost certainly refers to Demchinsky's wife's name.

9 July

Labunsky asked for leave to go into town today. It was pleasant not to have an outsider around. I opened up *Fiery Angel*, corrected a few passages in the vocal parts, made some notes about orchestration and other things I am not happy with in preparation for the revision. But it is impossible to get down to serious work on it until I have a final text, at least for one act. To be honest I am not expecting much more from Demchinsky... but somewhere buried deep inside I still hear a voice saying: but what if?! Demchinsky may be a barren vine, but he is still capable of producing the occasional shoot and I need to catch hold of any that do appear.

While Labunsky is in the house I cannot train myself to sit at the piano and compose. Today, profiting from his absence, I settled down to the 'Overture for Seventeen' and worked on the second subject. At first it seemed that I had forgotten how to compose and had no idea how to begin, but eventually I did succeed in writing some material for the second subject.

Sent a second telegram to Demchinsky (in fact, counting from the beginning, the sixth or seventh) asking him whatever happens to let me know when I could expect Act One. To think of how much money is being squandered on all these quite unnecessary telegrams – what a strange man he is.

10 July

Did more work on the Symphony, and developed the second subject of the Overture. Despite everything it seems to be turning out quite well. I have no desire to write a sonata-allegro but want something more akin to a rondo form *à la* Schumann with more material and less development (I have had quite enough development after the Symphony). For the third theme I can take the tune I sketched out on the train during my Italian tour.

Ptashka is moping.

A cable from B.N. asking for three hundred and fifty. It's starting again.

Mayevsky[1] called. It took me some time to realise who he was, but it transpired that he was in fact one Shmayevsky, whom I had not seen for fifteen

---

1 Yury Mayevsky, pianist and composer/arranger. Mayevsky had left Russia for Finland in 1922 and then migrated to Latvia, but subsequently returned to the Soviet Union where he taught piano at the Leningrad Conservatoire and earned a reputation as an arranger of traditional and popular material for piano duet, for which he earned the title of Honoured Artist of the Russian Federation.

years but who in the meantime had contrived in the interests of euphony to lose the initial consonants of his surname. He and I had studied in Yesipova's class at the same time but had not had much contact. Now, however, he was professing undying affection and friendship, and promised to help arrange concerts for me in Riga, where he now runs a music school. He was most taken with Svyatoslav. He is married, but has no children.

11 July

In the morning composed more of the Overture and made some changes to the Symphony, all drawn from the list I had made the other day after the performance by Straram. In the afternoon Ptashka and went into Fontainebleau to do some shopping. It was hot and noisy and crowded with Americans. We are much better off in the depths of the country.

12 July

Developed further the third theme. Labunsky's presence no longer stops me working. The first step is the hardest.

Since Labunsky had had a day off on Friday he was working today, slowly patching the changes I had made to the score of the Symphony into the orchestral parts. Even though he is studying fugue and his name appears in the list of Polish composers in the *Revue musicale*, he makes all kinds of mistakes in the transposing instruments and I have to check his work and send it back for him to erase and correct them. Tanya, who copied these parts last year, did all the transpositions with no errors; she had not studied fugue, merely paid attention to what she was doing.

13 July

Got on rather well with the Overture and composed a presto figure linking two B flats. But during the afternoon felt heavy and lethargic and did very little, even to the extent of snatching a clandestine hour's snooze behind Labunsky's back as he sat there patching amendments into the parts. In the evening, as it was the eve of the 14th July, there were processions with lanterns and out-of-tune though deafeningly loud trumpets. We got no sleep until one o'clock in the morning, having gone to bed at ten. The only one who got any sleep was Svyatoslav, but what a fall from grace from the 14th July two years ago! Then he was not a grown-up person of two years and four and a half months old, only four and a half months, but at ten o'clock at night he was given a pacifier to suck, and gazed in fascination at the fireworks. Now he slept right through the most ear-splitting fanfares.

14 July

Sat down with great enthusiasm to continue the bustling passage I started yesterday between the two B flats. Today, however, it seemed rather pointless and not very robust. I gave the orchestration some thought, and then it seemed more acceptable, especially when I added a few touches to it. In the afternoon I worked on the Symphony and polished up the Quintet for its engraving, and also dictated some letters to Labunsky. Today we had the first warm weather.

15 July

What am I to do with Demchinsky? I really must get to work on *Fiery Angel*. Today I looked through all the music I have written and found that that Demchinsky's new version will not work in the scene between the Hostess, the Workman[1] and Ruprecht, so I revised it and cleaned it up (changed some of the harmonies and a few things in the vocal parts), and since it was now scribbled all over with my alterations, gave it to Labunsky to make a new fair copy. I then set about marking up the orchestration. I do this with as much detail as possible, from the ground up so to speak, in order that Labunsky can copy it into the staves of the full score. This is my new system and the principal reason why I engaged Labunsky. If it is successful, I shall be relieved of the chore of transcribing five hundred pages of *Fiery Angel* score.

16 July

The experiment has proved more or less a success: Labunsky spent about three hours on one page, but he did transcribe into it all the instrumentation as I had indicated it. True, there were dozens of mistakes, but this is because in the first place it was the first attempt, and in the second either he is temperamentally unable to concentrate his attention or is simply not used to having to do so.

Today I put aside the Overture, Op. 42, and bent all my attention to *Fiery Angel*, continuing the work I had begun yesterday. The music for the rape scene was frankly bad, but I had some ideas of how to do it differently, and better.

This evening, as I sat writing my diary, I spied through the open window a cat creeping up the tree towards a nest. A silly bird had made her nest two paces away from the house at about the height of a man. True, the nest was

---

[1] This character disappeared from Prokofiev's later revisions.

fairly well camouflaged and the trunk of the tree was entwined with thorny rosebushes, but even so as soon as the cat appeared it was a poor look-out for the nest. Now we were particularly fond of three little fledglings with enormous open mouths. Shrieking, I hurled myself at the cat, which fled. We then racked our brains as to how to protect the nest, but there seemed to be nothing to hand with which to achieve this. On one side of the tree I stretched out a hammock, and on the other placed some garden furniture on a very wobbly base, so that if the cat were to jump up on the chairs they would overturn and scare off the cat. Hardly had we got back up to the bedroom when the cat was back. I chased her away once more and strengthened the defences. Until two o'clock I slept fitfully, thinking all the time that the cat was crawling up. But then I closed the window – what good could I do, after all? – and went soundly off to sleep.

17 July

An enquiry from the Leningrad Philharmonia: what would be my fee be for four concerts? The letter was signed by Klimov,[1] short and dry and typed on an atrocious typewriter with the letters so uneven that trying to read it crossed one's eyes. I know Klimov; he was in the conducting class but a long time before me, an amiable, smiling moon-face. Deeply respectful of Glazunov, he was anything but a great brain, but methodical. How such a person could in Revolutionary Russia rise to become head of the Philharmonia is a mystery. I replied to his letter myself, rather than diverting Labunsky from his work on the score, on which he spent the whole day.

During the night the cat succeeded in gobbling up the chicks. The chair she jumped on did overturn, but did not frighten her away.

18 July

I had a headache, not a very bad one but enough to stop me working. I went for a long walk, as far as Héricy where I took a boat and crossed the Seine and walked back along the other bank. I have made this excursion twice now. The weather was very oppressive during the evening, even heavier at night until finally there was a thunderstorm which afterwards brought a delightful freshness.

---

1   Mikhail Klimov (1881–1937), choral conductor, studied conducting at the St Petersburg Conservatoire under Nikolay Tcherepnin. He was Principal Conductor of the Leningrad Capella, which he made into an internationally respected ensemble, from 1917 until 1935. From 1925 until 1927 he served as Director of the Leningrad Philharmonia, the principal music-performance administration of the city.

19 July

After yesterday's thunderstorm today was sunny, not too hot and altogether very pleasant. The work went well. I revised a good part of Act One, as I feel in its present form it is well suited to the changes Demchinsky has made. This strange gentleman is staying mum and not replying to my telegram. I sent another one. Labunsky is transcribing my orchestration into the score, working slowly and of course omitting the sharps. Ptashka's parents have departed: she and her mother love one another very much, but absolutely cannot live together.

20 July

Herriot[1] has formed a new cabinet, and as a result the dollar has soared to 48 francs. Nothing but gloom is predicted for France. In one way it is an excellent time to buy furniture for a flat; on the other hand with such an uncertain atmosphere in the country is it a good idea to acquire an apartment and settle permanently?

Worked a great deal on *Fiery Angel*. It is going well. I worked out orchestration and noted down detailed instructions for specific passages for Labunsky to copy. Of course while working like this I can get through ten pages of the eventual score in a day, but this is a joke as Labunsky, when he gets to it, will manage only two or three! After all, it is not he who is orchestrating, but if one put it like that, merely taking orchestral dictation.

21 July

As *Fiery Angel* has made such good progress in the last few days, Labunsky will need a week to catch up, so I decided to revert to the 'Overture for Seventeen Instruments' and today concentrated on it. However, it was not very successful and I did not achieve much. In the afternoon I thought more about the *Fiery Angel* orchestration.

My days are divided up as follows: I wake up between seven thirty and eight o'clock, rouse Labunsky and then go into the bathroom to wash. Living in the country I shave only every other day, and depending on this go downstairs a quarter of an hour or half an hour later. I have coffee, open the shutters and sit down to work before ten. At ten they bring the post, which

---

1 Edouard Herriot (1872–1957), left-wing Radical who was three times Prime Minister of France and long-serving President of the Chamber of Deputies. In his first ministry he was a prime mover in France's recognition of the USSR. This, the second of Herriot's ministries, lasted precisely three days. Herriot was also a respected literary critic and the biographer of Madame Récamier.

interrupts work. If there are not many letters I soon resume work and continue until half past eleven. After that I allow Ptashka in to sing while I go out for a walk, sometimes taking Svyatoslav in his three-wheeled carriage which he calls his 'tasi', a mangled version of the English 'taxi'. Sometimes I do a little more work when I get back from my walk. Lunch is at a quarter to one. After lunch I dictate one or two letters to Labunsky if they are needed. I do not work as intensively in the afternoon as I do in the morning, that is to say I rarely compose in the afternoon although from time to time I do some revising. However, I do read proofs, or work on alterations to the Symphony, or think about orchestration. At four o'clock, tea, and at half past five I go for a long walk of five or six kilometres, sometimes as far as Champagne, taking the train back to be home for dinner at half past seven.

I spend some time in the evening playing the piano (Second Concerto, Fourth Sonata) and write my diary, either new entries from the recent days or filling out notes made from earlier entries. We go to bed at ten.

22 July

Worked on the Overture. It has plenty of material, and is good, but somehow does not hang together very well. Meanwhile from Demchinsky there is still no reply to the telegram I sent him three days ago. I decided to wait a further couple of days and then to send him an ultimatum. But before taking this step and risking a final break with Demchinsky, I thought carefully about whether I would myself be able to finish the work from my own resources. The result of this cogitation was that, yes, if necessary I could. Demchinsky was admirable as a critic, but when it came to producing material himself, the scenario he had provided was inferior to mine. Certainly he had given me a much-needed prod, I had emerged from a state of paralysis, had reshaped the libretto, and now, so far as I could see, the opera has a coherent form, which is the most important thing. What more has he to offer me? A few elegant conceits, the sort of thing I always expected from him? These, perhaps, he could and would provide. But he might not, given that he is a spent force. It is important to me to make use of the summer in order that the music I compose should be what is needed, and in particular so that the opera should be ready for production in Berlin. There is no time to lose. These thoughts impelled me to send my ultimatum, the more so as his attitude to the work was clearly not a responsible one.

23 July

Worked on the Overture, which despite everything is making progress, and in the afternoon on *Fiery Angel*. At the very least I do not need to wait for

Demchinsky to revise the beginning of Act One. Today Labunsky managed five pages and is working better: he is gaining experience.

24 July

Wrote to Demchinsky along the lines I had determined the day before yesterday. I tried to be firm without being unnecessarily harsh. I am gearing myself up to finish the libretto without his help: sending the letter I must guard against being taken completely unawares by a final rift.

25 July

Labunsky took his day off and went to Paris to see Koshetz to report to her on the dacha he has found for her a kilometre from us – there's friendship for you. We were left *en famille*: Ptashka, Svyatoslav and I. It was very nice.

26 July

Labunsky is back. Koshetz has had second thoughts and is not taking the dacha. In a word, the danger is over.[1] Ptashka went into town today, and brought back with her the proofs (the score, not the parts) of the Suite from *Oranges* and a letter from Klein – he is in Paris! – as well as other bits and pieces of news. I walked in the pouring rain to meet her at the station and humped back the package of proofs under my umbrella, protecting it rather than myself as the engraving is done on tracing paper and if it gets wet the whole thing is ruined. Paichadze told her that *Three Oranges* has been requested for Kharkov, Kiev, Odessa and Zagreb. Wonderful news! *Oranges* making inroads into the provinces.

28 July

The day before yesterday Ptashka brought back with her, at my request, Stravinsky's *Serenade*.[2] I played it through. A strange piece ... but it is dangerous to dismiss it altogether, as so often this composer has invented tricks that reveal themselves to the understanding only years later. The music is deliberately unpleasant. It is difficult to understand what was in Stravinsky's mind and what aims he was pursuing when he developed this language. But

---

1 Lina had by no means conquered her feelings of jealousy over Nina Koshetz, very likely fuelled by the *Five Songs Without Words*, Op. 35, Prokofiev had written for her in 1920.
2 The *Serenade in A* for piano, composed the previous year. Editions Russes had just published the work. See above, p. 223.

one thing above all strikes one: the hideousness of the melodic line. Another most peculiar aspect is the occasionally encountered Medtnerish turn of phrase. Stravinsky influenced by Medtner – a truly absurd idea!

29 July

Felt myself exceptionally motivated to work today. I lined up everything still needed for the Overture so that the skeleton is complete. Now what remains is to finish the composition and to devise three variations for the thrice-repeated B flats. In addition I worked on *Fiery Angel*, and in the evening caught up on my diary.

30 July

Revised Renata's hysterical scene in Act One but could not get deeply involved in it. Christian Science has completely alienated me from this subject, and I no longer feel drawn to manifestations of delirium or demonic possession. Earlier I had thoughts of how much easier it would be to abandon altogether a subject from which I had so far distanced myself . . . but it would a pity to lose the music. And now the time is approaching when I shall be concentrating on the music rather than the scenario, and perhaps this is all to the good.

I did little work today. Ptashka and Svyatoslav and I took a long walk to Champagne and came back by train. It is the first time this summer that I have managed to drag Ptashka out for a walk.

31 July

Put *Fiery Angel*, which has taken a great leap forward, to one side and worked on refinements to the B flat episodes in the Overture. Did not achieve much.

B.N. has repaid the money he borrowed the last time. First time in history.

1 August

Work went well today: I revised the whole of Renata's hysteria scene and recomposed Rupprecht's prayer.

Went walking with Ptashka and Svyatoslav. The latter distinguished himself today: he loaded all his bears into his little carriage and set off with it out of the garden on to the main road – looking for the steamers he saw yesterday on the Seine. Along the road he attracted the attention of some little boys who started to poke about looking at his bears, at which Svyatoslav set up a roar. Ptashka saw him out of the window on the upper floor – he was already quite a long way down the road – and hurtled desperately to the rescue, after which he was brought home and subjected to the severest possible reprimand. The main bear he calls 'Khmee', the initial letter being a consonant of his own devising which he enunciates by expelling air through his nose and wrinkling it at the same time.

2 August

The morning was cold, with a heavy mist coming off the Seine. It felt really autumnal. But as the day went on it became bright and warm. In between bouts of work I walked a good deal with Svyatoslav and Ptashka; we must have covered about fourteen kilometres. I have grown accustomed to carting Svyatoslav about with me in his little carriage, I am sure this was also the source of my childhood love of pulling 'trains' after me everywhere I went, a passion that stayed with me almost until I entered the Conservatoire.

Fine-tuned what I had composed yesterday.

Received an airmail letter from Klimov (it took three days, the first time I have got anything so quickly). He proposes twenty concerts from Leningrad to Tiflis,[1] including two engagements to conduct *Oranges* at the Mariinsky Theatre, for a fee of 9,000 roubles plus hotel and travel costs. This represents a solid proposal. But I must have a preliminary check with Yavorsky.

4 August

In the morning, worked on the B flat episodes in the Overture and then went for a long walk to Vulaines and Héricy. At three o'clock Klein and his friend Barton, whom we had been expecting, arrived by car. It was not long before the conversation turned naturally to the subject of Christian Science, which then occupied all the remaining time. Barton, an actor from New York, is also a Scientist. I liked him, mainly because of the conviction with which he stated: 'I know there is no such thing as death; it is only those who remain behind after someone has died who have created the idea of death.' He has sharp features and penetrating eyes, but Christian Science has made him uncommonly gentle. He evidently has powerful gifts as a medium: tables turn for him and his hand writes independently of his consciousness, but this neither interests him nor worries him. 'How naive it is to imagine that this is communication with the other world,' he says, 'in these days when there is a wireless telegraph in every American home. It is quite natural to

---

1 Now Tbilisi, the capital of Georgia.

think of such a capability as a receptor of other people's will, thoughts and desires. A medium is an apparatus analogous to a wireless telegraph – nothing more or less than that.' Klein was, as always, a wonderful person. He was very taken with Svyatoslav, who happened to be on his best behaviour and, after the guests' departure, talked about the 'gentil monsieur'. Klein said it is an error to believe that at the present time we are far away from perfect enlightenment, that we need time before this can be achieved, that at present we only dimly reflect the image and likeness of our Father. This is not the case: we are indeed even now, this very moment, the reflection of the Father, and it is essential that we know this. Not tomorrow, not at some time in the future, but now.

I asked whether this was not perhaps because in eternity there is no concept of time, therefore for the purpose of the present discussion there is no yesterday, no tomorrow, but only the present. He said this was a very good answer. We had tea, and all the way through talked of Christian Science (Labunsky, thank God, had taken the day off and gone to Paris), and left after two hours leaving behind the most heartwarming impression. They plan in two days' time to drive to Geneva, then go to England and after that to return to America.

After they had gone Ptashka and I went for a long walk and shared our impressions, to find on our return that Kokhno had turned up on an unexpected visit. It was evidently a diplomatic mission. Diaghilev has left recently for a holiday in Venice, and Kokhno is to follow him in a few days' time. Diaghilev definitely wants to present *Ursignol* next season, and obviously wants to sound out the ground about my feelings on this score, and incidentally to get from me the libretto and some excerpts from the piano score he had contrived to mislay somewhere. Kokhno was overflowing with friendliness, I responded in kind and promised within the next few weeks to complete the piano reduction of the numbers I have not yet done. (Before, in America, I had sent Diaghilev only the most approximate piano score; sooner or later I shall have in any case to make a proper version and so I will get on with it in the intervals of doing other things.) At Kokhno's request I played him some passages from my new Overture, but he did not much like the beginning, preferring the theme in three-four time, although he did immediately qualify this opinion by saying that he had no right to sit in judgement. Dukelsky is staying somewhere just outside Paris but not it seems doing much work as he is much preoccupied with the daughter of the concierge of the pension where he is staying. Since Kokhno will be seeing him tomorrow, I asked him to pass on the message that he, Dukelsky, had behaved like a pig in the spring by leaving without saying goodbye, and that it would be no bad thing if he were to come down and see us.

5 August

Did a lot of work. In the morning polished up the Overture's A flat theme in three-four time. In the afternoon started on the piano score of *Ursignol* and wrote letters. Almost before I noticed it, the day had flown by.

The franc has risen in value, and as a result the French are more polite. When the franc was falling, the level of French politeness fell with it.

6 August

More fine-tuning of the Overture's three-four subject. In the afternoon turned to *Fiery Angel* and thought about the libretto for the conclusion of the act: the scene with the fortune-teller. I shall have to write it myself. There is not much hope of anything from the prophet of invention – Demchinsky.

In general I am overwhelmed with work, and now on top of it all there is the piano score of *Ursignol*.

7 August

Finished the three-four section of the Overture. I think all the music is now composed, and it is time to get down to orchestrating it. This will be quite an unfamiliar job, given the composition of the ensemble I have opted for.[1] I strolled round the garden and thought about the instrumentation of the B flat section. My head started to hurt in the afternoon, and after dictating two letters to Labunsky I abandoned work. I must say that although I do continue to have headaches I do not suffer from them as often as I used to do, and they are in any case less severe. I walked for quite a long time.

I have received proposals for concerts in London and Lyons. I should need to take a lot of money off them in London, because the critics always savage me there. I can put up with that if the money is worthwhile. In Lyons, by contrast, I must agree because of Ptashka. It is a rich town, but the French are greedy.

A Vera Prokofieva has surfaced, having the same surname as mine and using the same bank as I do as a correspondence address, in consequence of which some letters destined for me end up by an oversight with her. She writes very kindly, but not very grammatically, in French, having forgotten all her Russian: 'We both possess this common name, which has been made famous by you.' I had better keep on good terms with her, so that she will pass on any of my letters she gets . . .

---

1 The seventeen instruments are: flute, oboe, two clarinets, bassoon, two trumpets, trombone, percussion, celesta, two harps, two pianos, cello, and two double-basses.

8 August

The tortoise-like Labunsky has nevertheless managed to catch me up in the orchestration of *Fiery Angel*. I will have to take another chunk that I am not likely to change much even if Demchinsky does send me his revised libretto, a prospect that now seems very unlikely. I accordingly took the first scene of Act Three, and spent the morning burnishing it, making a few minor changes and thinking about the orchestration. Generally ploughed more than a full furrow.

Paichadze writes that Tcherepnin has twice performed the *Classical Symphony* in Riga, and Cooper is going to perform the Suite from *Oranges*.

9 August

Started on orchestrating the Overture. Because of the unorthodox combination it is not easy, especially as the piece begins with a sonorous tutti. But I got on quite well and orchestrated two pages of score. In the afternoon, went on thinking about and correcting Act Three of *Fiery Angel*. There is so much to do. Ptashka very much wants to go for a week to the seaside, to the Zakharovs who are at Royan, but I simply do not think it is possible for me to tear myself away from my work. Basically I have become a slave to my occupation. This is not good. And the main point is, there is no real need for it.

Ptashka's parents went back to America today, having spent the three or four days before their departure with us. Parting was emotional, but there is a feeling that part of their reason for going is that mother and daughter are unable to bring their different characters into line, and the recognition of this fact brings great sadness to both of them. Olga Vladislavovna promises to come back in January to look after Svyatoslav if we go to Russia. They do not have a great deal of money, but they travel simply, in third class.

10 August

Did two more pages of orchestration in the morning, and felt very tired afterwards. However, I did mange more work in the afternoon and made some corrections to Renata's narrative. Ptashka's advice was: 'Stop working if you are tired, it will not be any good.' Around ten o'clock, tired out, we went to bed angry with Labunsky who had gone off somewhere which meant that we could not lock the door, when suddenly there was a knocking at the gate and the sound of the bell. To my enquiry 'who's there?' an embarrassed voice came out of the darkness: 'It's me, Dukelsky.' He explained that he had left Paris at five o'clock but Kokhno had given him misleading directions on how to get to us, and had only just found us. He was tired and had not eaten. While Ptashka made him an omelette he lost no time in regaling us with an account of his latest adventure. This concerned a young Irishwoman who had come to him in London and with whom a passionate affair developed, culminating in the threatened advent of a small Dukelsky. At this the senior Dukelsky made the rounds of various doctors, none of whom would have anything to do with his pleas, saying that for such activities people were sent to gaol in England. There was nothing for it but to bring his inamorata to Paris, where yesterday the hoped-for outcome was successfully brought about, 'and she woke up in bed surrounded by flowers'. Shortly the delectable Irish girl will return to London, deeply grateful to Dukelsky for the care he has lavished on her and for the chance to see something of Paris; none the less the exercise has relieved him of 10,000 francs, and were it not for two new operettas he has been commissioned to write he would be in a gravely parlous financial condition, but if the operettas are successful he will be pulling in £80 a week.

We put him to bed in the parents' room, and because clean sheets were needed he slept on a clean and ironed linen bag for storing fur coats.

11 August

While Dukelsky slept I got another page of orchestration done. Then I played him the Overture, which he liked, all except for the opening theme. In his opinion my best work is the Third Piano Concerto and that is the style in which I should write; my least good work is the Fifth Piano Sonata, which is dry and boring. He played me his new ballet, to which he has added two more numbers. Some of it is nice, but not notably so: stylised ballet music in the Russian-Italian manner. By far the best bit is the opening. We then joined together in condemning Stravinsky's *Serenade*, but he did succeed in showing me some most attractive places in *Mavra*,[1] although even here one can trace some of the stylisation back to Dargomyzhsky.[2] In a week's time he is off to Venice to see Diaghilev, who he says (Dukelsky is prone to exaggerate) has decided to put on his new ballet next season. After lunch Dukelsky took himself back to Paris and I settled down to polishing Act Three of *Fiery Angel* and thinking about its orchestration.

While Ptashka and I were working on some songs by Casella, the vibrations caused a pile consisting of a year's worth of press reviews and programmes Ptashka had been sorting in preparation for sticking into a

---

1 Opéra bouffe in one act to a libretto by Kokhno after Pushkin, composed in 1921–2.
2 Even so I proved to him that in the *Serenade* there are several passages drawn from Medtner. [Author's note.]

scrapbook to fall down from a shelf. Now they were all muddled up, and Ptashka will have the job of sorting them all over again. Casella's songs are not much good, certainly not so good as to justify this catastrophe.

18 August

I have not been writing my diary for the past few days as I have been expending tremendous effort on the orchestration of the *American Overture*, calculating that not much time remains for this task, especially in view of the extra difficulty – far more than I had expected – caused by the unusual combination of instruments. Also I had to finish orchestrating the section of *Fiery Angel* I must give to the copyist, who had set aside time for this purpose. In short, those evening hours I normally devoted to playing the piano and writing my diary have had to be consecrated to orchestration, and this accounts for the blank pages in the diary.

The exchange of correspondence with the Leningrad Philharmonia is progressing satisfactorily. Thanks to airmail, letters from there 'fly' here in three days. They regret that I have declined to conduct *Oranges*, which is to be presented both at the Mariinsky and at the Bolshoy Theatre in Moscow, and in Kharkov. Think of that – 'Could he ever have dreamed of such happiness?' to quote *The Ugly Duckling*! But Yavorsky, with whom I am also corresponding, is wary of giving specific advice. He is a devious person, and were it not for my personal respect for him as a musician rather than Suvchinsky's assertions that Yavorsky is a man one can trust, I would be having doubts. There is one particular phrase: 'The photograph of your wife is creating such a sensation that I seriously advise you to leave her behind in Paris.' A dyed-in-the-wool émigré would, of course, regard this is a warning and say I should not take her; she might be kept back as a hostage. But I believe it is no more than an elegant pleasantry.

19 August

Orchestrating the Overture is beginning to wear me out. The weather was rather oppressive today and everyone was going about in a bad mood. All the same, I completed three pages, and the end is in sight. We sprayed with fixative the pages of *Fiery Angel* score written out by Labunsky in pencil to send to Jasmine, the copyist: sixty-nine pages. But there are almost as many again in which only a few corrections remain to be made (in Renata's narrative, which I orchestrated as long ago as when we were in Ettal), and once that is done they can also go to Jasmine.

Today Svyatoslav uttered the words 'Svyatoslav Prokofiev'. So he has at last learnt to say his own name, although he is quite reluctant to do so.

Whenever he used to be asked: 'Baby Svyatoslav?' he would reply 'Baby obyezan'.[1] And a little later, instead of 'Svyatoslav Prokofiev' he used to say: 'Tra-ta-ta Prokofiev'.

21 August

From early morning I had a bad head and therefore did no work but tried to walk it off. All day it alternated between being painful and easing, but towards evening I began to feel quite unwell. I did no work on the Overture, all I managed was a few changes to *Fiery Angel*.

We were expecting Dukelsky at five o'clock, but as is his wont he appeared when we were already putting up the shutters to go to bed. At first I received him frigidly – what a louse he is, after all! – but this provoked a torrent of excuses and accounts of extraordinary occurrences. At lunch he had choked on a bone, which had to be removed in hospital with the aid of pincers and two mirrors. This is why he was late. Then, he had brought sketches of the new ballet to show me, on which he has made substantial progress, but he had put them on the luggage rack in the train, and the top page got caught by the wind and flew out of the open window into the field.

22 August

Dukelsky's conversation had dispelled my headache, and this morning I announced that I intended to work, as the Overture needed to be finally despatched. Dukelsky slept in and it was eleven o'clock before he had shaved and come down. Having completed two pages of score I set out on my customary walk, and Dukelsky sat down at the piano to try to reconstruct the page of the ballet that had disappeared out of the window. After lunch I carried on orchestrating in the sitting room, while Dukelsky did the same in the dining room with his Concerto. Incidentally, I do not like his score: he does not really know how to orchestrate. At four o'clock he, I, Ptashka and Svyatoslav went out to Samois and had tea in the garden of a large hotel on the banks of the Seine. Dukelsky was very nice to Svyatoslav and paid him a lot of attention. He told us stories about another Svyatoslav, Roerich's son, who is the same age as he, about life in New York, about his (Dukelsky's) affair with Valentina Bolm, who suffered from split personality, and about the incredible drama and scandal that erupted when it was discovered that he and Svyatoslav Roerich had sent her an indecent object as a gift about which she, in tears, had complained to Roerich *père*.

1 'Obezyan' is an ape or monkey.

Dukelsky dined with us and afterwards we played to each other our compositions: he liked mine very much, and I also liked his new ballet more than I had done the last time he played it. Eventually he missed his train and had to spend a second night with us. The remainder of the evening was spent in a furious row brought about by my criticising him for composing operettas, which I said consisted of nothing but reach-me-down commonplaces. He defended his position with equal fervour, saying that operetta music existed on such a different plane that it could have no possible effect on his serious composition. I retorted that the influence most certainly did make itself felt, moreover in a way of which he was not himself conscious. One fine day he would find real musicians beginning to distance themselves from his music and he himself descending to the status of a second-rate composer. At that point he would abandon serious music altogether and would confine himself to operettas. We were separated by Ptashka, who suggested that the neighbours, hearing our raised voices, would say that 'les monsieurs russes ont trop bu'.[1]

A strange letter from Nadya Rayevskaya.[2] Some time ago Aunt Katya had written that Shurik was ill and was in a sanatorium. I was concerned that this meant he was mentally ill. But now suddenly all was clear: 'illness' and 'sanatorium' were coded references to prison, to which Shurik had been condemned as a former pupil at the Lycée. So that is our dear Russia – not so dear these days!

24 August

Today, thank God, I completed the Overture. It was high time to finish it off, otherwise it would have finished me off. Labunsky is copying those pages which repeat material previously notated, and is correcting the mistakes I had spotted, while I proof-read everything he has transcribed.

I pondered the question of 'the divine trial': 'God sends these things to try us.' I think this expression is misleading. One could imagine God reasoning thus: 'Let us see whether man can survive this ordeal. If he can he will be strengthened and will move forward. If not, regrettably against all hopes he will perish.' But this is absurd. God knows in advance the outcome of the ordeal, and if the result of the trial is known in advance, it is not a proper trial. The only true way to consider it is therefore this: God sends man only such trials as a man has it in his power to withstand; as a result of such trials

---

1 'The Russian gentlemen have had too much to drink.'
2 Nadezhda (Nadya) Rayevskaya née Meindorf, who had married Prokofiev's first cousin Alexander (Shurik) Rayevsky in 1912. Prokofiev's Aunt Katya (Yekaterina Rayevskaya) was thus her mother-in-law.

man either becomes stronger or atones for sins, or both. The kind of 'trial by ordeal' that a man is unable to withstand is not in fact a trial sent by God at all, but simply a concatenation of random circumstances emanating from the world of human imaginings. It has nothing to do with divine reality (Christian Science). Even so, in the latter case it is still necessary to fight on to the end, in order not to succumb to the blind power of circumstance, bearing in mind that circumstance is a sign of the non-divine world, the world of unreality.

25 August

The Overture is finished, but I still today checked the pages Labunsky has transcribed, inevitably finding in them a mass of errors. These I fished out until my head burst, as Oeberg used to say, but still managed to complete the job and the Overture went to the copyist. I spent some time thinking about orchestration, but generally was very tired.

26 August

Today I got to the end of Renata's narrative, while Labunsky transcribed the score according to my notes from yesterday.

The weather was gloriously sunny and we took Svyatoslav into the forest, where we found a small lake. As we were passing by a chained-up dog, who lunged at us barking furiously even though every bark ended in a strangled yelp as the chain constricted his throat, Svyatoslav observed calmly, 'That's enough, good dog, silly dog.' Tomorrow he will be exactly two and a half years old.

27 August

Thought a great deal about the orchestration of *Fiery Angel*, and composed a little of the end of Act Three. I also gave some thought to the second scene of this act, since there is no point in counting on anything more from Demchinsky.

At five o'clock, tired, went with Svyatoslav into Fontainebleau for a break and to meet Ptashka, who had been having a singing lesson there. Bought a big ball for Svyatoslav. I had my hair cut, since it was curling over my ears.

29 August

Labunsky had a day off and I practised the piano. The day was hot. We were expecting Koshetz, but only Schubert and Marochka came; Koshetz had not returned from her concert in Vichy. Marochka has only just turned fourteen, but already looks like a grown-up girl. 'C'est bien rond'[1] as the local priest used to say of the girls in Ettal. Schubert is a nice man. He has made a pledge to give up drinking wine for a certain length of time in aid of a theosophy-derived programme to improve the health of Koshetz's brother. When we went out for a walk the country air made his head spin. He tried smoking a cigarette, to no avail. At home he asked secretly for some wine so as to come back to himself, but to conceal it from Marochka as he did not want to lose face in front of his daughter. At dinner I asked him if he would like some syrup with water. 'Yes, please,' he said. 'May I have some of that yellow stuff?' I understood that he wanted wine, so I went to the cupboard, poured some vermouth into a glass and came back to the table, holding the glass of wine in one hand and in the other a bottle of yellow lemon syrup. 'Try the syrup first without any water,' I said. Schubert drank down the vermouth with evident pleasure and said, 'Delicious.' Then I poured some syrup into his glass and diluted it with water. Neither Ptashka nor Marochka noticed anything. At nine o'clock they went back to Paris.

30 August

Because I have to go to Paris tomorrow, I spent today catching up on the orchestration so that Labunsky would have something to do tomorrow. While she was doing her Christian Science lesson a thought struck Ptashka: a good person to be my secretary would be Popa-Gorchakov from Kishinyov.[2] He writes me enthusiastic letters and plays my music, is a Scientist, which means he is a good person, dedicated and 'one of us'. I tried to remember

---

1 'It's quite rounded.'
2 Gyorgy Popa-Gorchakov (?1902–1995) was the intense young man, a polyglot linguist and fellow Christian Scientist, who arrived from Kishinyov to Paris to work as Prokofiev's personal and musical secretary. He remained in this position as a member of the household until May 1928, mainly occupied in transcribing into full score Prokofiev's detailed notes on the orchestration of *Fiery Angel*, and in typing out from dictation the diary of the composer's first return visit to the Soviet Union in January to March 1927. Despite moments of exasperation Prokofiev and the family became fond of the young man with his ambitions to become a composer, and an affectionate relationship continued after he left Prokofiev's employ, for a time finding humble work at Prokofiev's publishers Edition Russe de Musique. He remained devoted to Prokofiev as a man and as a composer and for many years planned to write a biography but, as he himself confessed being – *hélas!* – neither a musicologist nor a sociologist nor a novelist nor a poet, after completing three versions found the task beyond him. Nevertheless, the final 638-page manuscript, a copy of which is in the Prokofiev Archive at Goldsmiths College in London, contains many invaluable insights into the composer's chronology, domestic and creative life. Volunteering as a merchant seaman during the Second World War, Gorchakov was recruited to monitor enemy communications by the French Résidence in Tunis, where following the Axis occupation and subsequent liberation by the British he lived for the remainder of his life. See *Three Oranges*, no. 11 (May 2006), pp. 2–13.

when I last heard from him; apparently it was in April. In his letter he wrote that around the 1st November he would be finishing his military service. It all fits, and I wrote a few lines to him immediately asking him how he was and what plans he had on finishing his military service. Perhaps he would like to come to Paris?

31 August

Went into Paris in order to cast a final eye over the Suite from *Oranges*, score and parts, before it goes off to the printers. Lunched with Paichadze, who told me that the bosses were back from Switzerland and had been asking after me, so it would be a good idea to go and see them. I, however, recalling how busy they had been in the spring, said I was reluctant to disturb them. They had recently been into the publishing house and Paichadze had given them a two-hour-long report on the current state of affairs. At the end of it Koussevitzky expressed his gratitude that the enterprise had never before been in such brilliantly good shape. There was pleasant news that *Oranges* has also been accepted for Mainz, something I had not heard about previously. I must look up on the map where this excellent city is located.

Spent three and a half hours reading proofs. Everything I had last time asked Labunsky to check I had to check all over again, as needless to say the great booby had let through a quarter of the errors. I rang up Fiedler, who told me that he had his eye on a splendid flat for us near the Champ de Mars, and that he would be sending us a telegram about it in a few days' time. I was delighted to hear this, and Ptashka even more so when I told her about it on my return. I tried to telephone B.N. but could not get through. By half past eight I was back again in the quiet of Samoreau.

1 September

Yesterday, while I was away, Labunsky worked all day and produced seven pages, which is a respectable amount, but with an even larger quota of mistakes than usual. The day therefore began with me spending a solid hour on picking them out and noting them in the margin, while Labunsky stood beside me, his ears pink. I then thought about orchestration and wrote some letters. A sensational letter from Weber: the premiere of *Oranges* in Berlin is scheduled for the 30th September. So soon! I thought it would be in November. I had planned to attend with Ptashka, but what would we do about the baby?

Ptashka and I have had no rows recently, and relations between us are very good. Christian Science has played a big part in this.

2 September

Did a lot of work. B.N. appeared at half past five. He is a reformed character, writing sonnets and articles for French newspapers, and earning 2,800 francs a month from driving his taxi. He is even working in the evenings on an essay demonstrating that if man has evolved from the apes up to the present time, in future he will so far develop as to attain divinity. This evolution will consist of the shedding of animal elements in parallel to the expansion of spiritual ones.

'What correlation do you envisage between these ideas and religion?' I enquired.

He replied, 'For me, the Christian religion remains inviolable.'

'But in that case, how is Christ supposed to act towards you when you have died as a link in the chain so far removed from divinity as we presently are?'

I had immediately put my finger on a weak spot: it appears that the connection with the Christian religion depends on hints to be found here and there in the Gospels about a new birth for mankind. It was not at all my purpose to demolish his ideas: thank God he has settled down to work on something! What a blessing is Christian Science, which offers such a well-proportioned edifice of faith and so harmoniously unites religion and science! And how jarringly incongruous I found this phrase of B.N.'s: 'You see, Serge, in my work I do not want to be diverted by abstract questions, I want to stay strictly within the realm of science.'(!)

3 September

Recomposed the end of the first scene of Act Three. This went well.

There was quite a large post. The owner of the dacha, who has not fulfilled a single one of the undertakings she gave us, and to whom to teach her a lesson I am delaying paying the rent, is threatening to take us to court. I am countering with a threat to do the same on the grounds that the electric pump was supposed to be in working order but in fact is broken, as a result of which we have had to rely on drawing water from the well for a whole month. A long and touching letter from Katya Ignatieva:[1] she parted from her husband twelve years ago but they have now resumed contact by letter,

---

1   Yekaterina (Katya) Ignatieva née Rayevskaya, Prokofiev's first cousin, sister of Andrey (Andryusha) and Alexander (Shurik), had married Pavel (Palya) Ignatiev, a captain in the Guards Engineer Regiment, in January 1908. It was a high-society wedding and the seventeen-year-old Prokofiev had been the number-two best man. The marriage had been unhappy because of Ignatiev's profligacy and arrogance and had ended in divorce after three years. After the revolution Cousin Katya and her mother (Aunt Katya) had moved from Petrograd to Moscow thence to Penza, where they were now living. See *Diaries*, vol. 1, p. 37, and *passim*.

she in Penza and he in Serbia, on different sides of the frontier the Revolution had brought about. Suvchinsky wrote a short letter in which he says he has seen Zoya Lodi,[1] recently in from Moscow. According to her, when she sings my songs in Russia, the mere mention of my name sends an electric thrill round the audience. 'Good for Russia and for you,' adds Suvchinsky in an edifying aside. If I am so close to my native soil, it is no wonder I feel so alienated from those who have severed their links with it.

4 September

Orchestrated what I had done yesterday. It was a lot of work, and I got tired. It is impossible, I am becoming a slave to my profession.

A very nice letter from Persimfans. It seems there are stronger and stronger reasons for me to go to Moscow, and when I board the train I shall do so not with fear in my breast so much as pleasurable anticipation in my heart. Mme Liebmann[2] has been ill all summer and although she is recovering will not be back in Berlin until the middle of October. Everything is conspiring to prevent Ptashka accompanying me to the premiere of *Oranges* in Berlin: Liebmann, who had invited us to stay with her, will not be there; there is no solution as to where to arrrange for Svyatoslav to be; we still have nowhere to live in Paris; matters are still not sorted out with the dacha. But psychologically the summer already feels over, and the mists coming from the Seine roll over us all day.

6 September

My head ached, not badly but enough to stop me doing much work. I managed a little revision, but no more. B.N. has produced a new sonnet – 'Beethoven' – quite good but not particularly memorable. While I was thinking about Beethoven, the thought occurred to me that he is a remarkable example of what Christian Science teaches, namely that the only way we can possibly know reality, the truth, is through the spirit, not through the sense organs. Beethoven composed music of genius and performed it to his contemporaries. They, possessed of excellent hearing, were unable to understand what this deaf madman was playing to them and assumed that because he could not hear it, it made no sense. But what was really happening? It was that the deaf man was hearing beauty not with his ears but

---

1 Zoya Lodi (1886–1957), lyric soprano and teacher at both the Moscow and Leningrad Conservatoires who had been a pupil of Prokofiev's former friend and first performer of *The Ugly Duckling*, Anna Zherebtsova-Andreyeva. See *Diaries*, vol. 1, p. 781.
2 Acquaintance who had offered accommodation to the Prokofievs if and when they visited Berlin.

with his mind, while those with perfectly functioning ears were unable to hear it at all . . .

I was not working because of my headache, and Labunsky cleverly managed to squash his finger in the door, like a nut. What a star! This meant that for half a day he could do no work either. In the evening he got very excited and wanted a warm compress to put on his finger. 'Why don't you stick it in your mouth for the night?' I offered. I think Labunsky may have been offended by this suggestion.

7 September

During the night my headache passed off and today I finished the first scene of Act Three, and began to revise and orchestrate the entr'acte. In the afternoon I got on with replying to the Leningrad Philharmonia letter, not wishing to involve Labunsky in this correspondence. He is still nursing his finger and cannot write. I suggested that he take today off instead of Sunday, but Ptashka later objected that one should not make concessions like this, because illness creates a problem for the boss, not for the worker. Well, yes, if the worker in question is a real worker rather than someone who can barely put one foot in front of the other.

Ptashka had a letter from Natalya Koussevitzky with an invitation to her name-day and wedding anniversary tomorrow and, since we live out in the country, to stay the night. She hopes that 'S.S. has got over the offence he took and will also come.' We decided to go. It will be fun.

8 September

In the morning, orchestrated the entr'acte. It was not really working, but I forced myself to go as far as the point where I had begun to revise the music. Ptashka went early into Paris for various reasons: mostly to go the hairdresser, as her hair had grown long over the summer in the depths of the country and now was a perfect time to cut it. I set off later, at four o'clock, we met and had a light dinner, bought flowers and went around nine o'clock with our overnight suitcase to the Koussevitzkys. What was our amazement to discover an enormous table spread for dinner with everyone already seated and waiting for us. Among the guests were Borovsky, just back from the Riviera; Dukelsky, who has still not left to go to Italy to see Diaghilev; Tansman madly clinging to Koussevitzky's coat-tails and leaving no stone unturned to persuade the latter's wife of the attractions of his compositions; Copland; Paichadze; Fiedler, etc., etc. It was a gay party, I particularly enjoyed Dukelsky's venomous spitting about Tansman, for Dukelsky has never been able to reconcile himself to Koussevitzky's 'support of the untalented'. In fact this is not really such a serious issue: Koussevitzky is perfectly well aware that Tansman is, in the most charitable analysis, a star of second-order magnitude, but Tansman flatters Koussevitzky in every conceivable way, Kousssevitzky enjoys this and in gratitude occasionally performs a work by him. Towards me Koussevitzky displayed every mark of friendship: my celebrity in Russia has reached Paris, apparently, via the many people who come here from there, and the welter of flattering comments I now hear are the direct reflection of my success in Moscow. One way or another, this winter Koussevitzky in America will perform the Suite from *Chout* (in its abbreviated form), the Suite from *Oranges*, the *Classical* Symphony and *Seven, They Are Seven*. He says that when I get to America I shall be carried shoulder high through the streets. 'Better still if he could go in his own car,' observed Paichadze. Ptashka and I both liked Mme Paichadze very much. Koussevitzky said that he would also definitely perform Myaskovsky's Seventh Symphony in America. Later on Koussevitzky played wonderfully some things on the double-bass, marvellous full sound from those thick strings. At two o'clock the guests dispersed, we went to bed at half past two, I fell asleep at three, Ptashka not until five.

9 September

As usual I woke at eight, and immersed myself in the splendid Koussevitzky bathtub. Then a cousin of Fiedler's appeared and took us to look at flats suggested by a sympathetic estate agency of some sort. But everything we saw was depressingly bad, despite the fact that for one of them 45,000 francs key money was being asked. The price of flats has greatly increased, but what is even worse is that in France income tax (especially for those whose occupations are in the private sector) is assessed on the basis of the cost of accommodation and rises in proportion. Accordingly, the more expensive the flat, the higher one's income tax rockets skywards.

The Koussevitzkys were very loving and insisted that we come back for lunch, after which we renewed the apartment hunt. At six in the evening, discouraged by the fruits of our labour, we returned to Samoreau where we found everything in good order and Labunsky, whose finger had healed, had transcribed in the space of two days thirteen pages of score. Would it be a better idea than renting in Paris to take one of the new houses Fiedler has built in Boulogne?

At home there was a letter from Ekskuzovich: *Oranges* is officially confirmed to be presented in the Bolshoy Theatre in Moscow, and Ekskuzovich awaits a contract. The fee will be $1,200! The hire of the material has yielded a fat bonus. But might it not be better to go with the recommendation of the Moscow Society of Authors and opt for a percentage?

Ekskuzovich is also asking my advice on repertoire for the Academic Theatres.¹ This is also a serious request.

10 September

Composed a quantity of revised material in the entr'acte, a part of the score that was previously not good (the transition to the lyrical theme).

In the afternoon I dictated and wrote letters (six, three of which were engendered by Ekskuzovich's one) and got tired. But it is good news that *Oranges* is to be put on at the Bolshoy Theatre, and it had also been most gratifying that my success in Russia had had its effect on the attitude of Koussevitzky, Paichadze and others to me yesterday.

11 September

Corrected Labunsky's work and started orchestrating the revised passage from yesterday. In the afternoon wrote a long letter to Persimfans that I had not wanted to make Labunsky privy to. I may have a secretary, but still sometimes the number of letters I have to write oppresses me.

12 September

Orchestrated the whole passage I produced the day before yesterday. It being Sunday I gave Labunsky the day off, saying that I would absorb the time lost on his squashed finger on my account.

13 September

In the morning I tried to make detailed notes of as much as I could of the orchestration so as to give it to Labunsky to work on, and at two o'clock Ptashka and I went back to Paris to renew the hunt for an apartment. Taking advantage of Koussevitzky's invitation we went straight to their house, where we had previously alerted Fiedler to wait for us. He drove us out to look at the house he had built in Boulogne² and which he was proposing we might rent. He was obviously very keen for us to do this, because he suggested additionally knocking through a wall and making a door into a room in the

---

1   After the Revolution the principal theatres were dignified by the addition of 'academic' to their titles, presumably in order to replace the previous 'imperial' designation. Thus, for example, the Mariinsky Theatre became the Gosudarstvenny Akademichesky Teatr Opery i Baleta (GATOB, the State Academic Theatre of Opera and Ballet, later to be renamed the Kirov Theatre), and the Bolshoy became the Gosudarstvenny Akademichesky Bolshoy Teatr (GABT, the State Academic Bolshoy Theatre). The same principle was applied to the major drama theatres, and orchestras.
2   Boulogne-Billancourt, a suburb of Paris, not the seaside town of Boulogne-sur-mer.

next-door apartment; in short he is ready to do anything we might want. The house itself is nice, but it would be stupid to live in a place like that. If one wants to live in Paris then let it be Paris, but if not then let us have some green. Where we were is neither one thing nor the other. Fiedler agreed to give us until the end of the week to make up our minds.

Ptashka spent the evening with the Koussevitzkys and the Tansmans (who hang round the Koussevitzkys every day) at the cinema. I strolled about Paris and thought: how many houses there are in this city, why ever should we go and bury ourselves in some stupid suburb?

14 September

In the morning we had made arrangements with Fiedler's cousin to go round the town looking at yet more flats, this time from a list supplied by another agency, not the first one. We rushed about the whole day, getting through hundreds of francs in taxi fares, and at last – the only useful outcome – saw a magnificently lordly apartment off the Champs-Elysées, for which we would have to pay what is known hereabouts as a 'pas de porte' (i.e. a 'step through the door' or 'key money') of 50,000 francs. We do not have enough money for that, but the flat itself was superb. If only we could find a smaller one, with a lower 'pas de porte' premium, *cela ferait notre affaire*.[1] Returning after our trip to the Wolff agency, the first one, we discovered that there is an excellent apartment on avenue Kléber, certainly more expensive than we had bargained for, but very good all the same.

By rights we should have returned to Samoreau, where Svyatoslav was in the care of the cook, and where Labunsky had no doubt finished transcribing the pages I had prepared for him, and to boot the Koussevitzkys were leaving the following morning for America, so it was certainly time for us to say thank you and goodbye, but the Koussevitzkys were so pressing in their readiness for us to stay, saying that we were in no way inconveniencing them, that in the end we decided to stay an extra night, to see them off on their journey, and to inspect the avenue Kléber.

At dinner were the Tansmans, Fiedler, and Paichadze. We drank champagne to wish our hosts *bon voyage*.

Before going to bed, Koussevitzky asked me with great gentleness, 'I think you are not very impressed by Tansman's music?' Seeing their close friendship I mumbled something inaudible and then added, 'He is not to be compared with Dukelsky.' Koussevitzky hastened to agree. So Dukelsky, who had been so upset by Koussevitzky's friendship with Tansman, can rest easy.

1 'That would suit us just fine.'

15 September

We got up early and went to the station to see the Koussevitzkys off. Only a small number of other well-wishers had done the same. I took a few snapshots. Borovsky drew me to one side and asked to borrow $70, for which I promised to send him a cheque. He almost fainted when he saw Koussevitzky kissing not only me but also Ptashka. Koussevitzky considers that he has reached the age when it is permissible to kiss young ladies.

From the station we took ourselves to the avenue Kléber. The flat is really good, large and comfortable. We decided to take it. It is a little expensive for us, but there is no doubt it is worth more. I asked the servant, 'Are any of the neighbours musicians?' She replied, 'Yes, the conductor Straram lives upstairs.' Now there's a coincidence! I remembered that just a few days ago I had sent a letter to him at this address. I decided to go up and see Straram, to find out how many pianos he had and which rooms they were in. Himself was away but I spoke to his wife, and immediately the conversation took an unexpected turn. 'Are you planning to rent the flat downstairs? The thing is, we are also looking for a flat for our daughter who is getting married, and it would be ideal for us.' I saw that our scheme was running into difficulties, so started to invent some confusing story about us likewise having to wrest the flat away from some other people, but if we were successful we would somehow manage to come to an agreement with the Strarams(!) The situation was eased when it became clear that without her husband Mme Straram was not in a position to make any decisions.

Baron Wolff, on hearing what had transpired, was appalled and said that I had ruined the whole transaction. He would not be able to negotiate with the Russian owner before the morrow, while we could not stay another night in Paris, so there was nothing for it but for us to go back to Samoreau. I decided to approach the matter in a Christian Science manner: if higher powers have decreed that the flat be ours then there is no cause for worry; ours it will be. If we do not get it, it simply means that we have not yet found our flat.

20 September

The general view is that we cannot slacken our intensive search for a flat because as autumn comes on more and more people gravitate to Paris, and the later it gets the more difficult it is to find somewhere. For that reason we set off again on our search. An agency we had not tried before, Ognev by name, run by Prince Trukhanov, had very nice people in it. Yet another, Dietrich, were swines: they immediately took 300 francs from us for expenses, promising to return the sum if they did not succeed in finding us anything.

However, we have little faith in them doing so and suspect that we have achieved nothing except to subject ourselves to anger and disappointment.

We lunched with Paichadze and dined with the Borovskys, who have fixed themselves up in a furnished apartment in the same building as they were last year and seem very relieved to have done so. We spent the night in the empty Koussevitzky house, where Ksyusha, the cook, had had instructions to receive us.

21 September

From early morning we embarked again on the hullabaloo of the flat hunt. This time, however, we did see some good ones. There was one we hesitated about, but the moment the hesitation began to incline to the positive it emerged that the owner's son had indicated he might want it, therefore it was not clear whether it would be available. To sum up, once again we went away empty-handed except for reliance on the Ognev agency, where they had sniffed out who I am and evidently decided to *nous caser*[1] no matter what it took to do so.

Got home at ten o'clock in the evening. Svyatoslav was vociferous in his joy at our return.

22 September

After two days' absence I had a lot of work to do: I finished orchestrating the entr'acte (which has begun to bore me) and moved the second scene forward, changing a few things and recomposing some passages. This took up most of the day. In this new version of the scene, which I thought out walking in the fields round Samoreau, there are considerable divergences from Bryusov; on the other hand it is stronger and more dramatic than the first version and in this respect conforms more closely to Bryusov.

23 September

Getting up in the morning I learnt that at six o'clock in the morning there had been a terrible accident at our little railway station of Vulaines-Samoreau: the express from Lyons had ploughed into three carriages which had been uncoupled from a Swiss train that had passed through in the same direction fifteen minutes earlier. Labunsky and I immediately hurried to the scene of the accident.

Did little work today.

1   'fix us up'.

24 September

A letter from Razumovsky,[1] clarifying my author's rights in the event of *Oranges* being produced in Moscow. Consequent on this I dictated to Labunsky letters to Weber and Ekskuzovich outlining my conditions.

Did more work on the second scene of Act Three. Received the proofs of the score of the Quintet. It has been engraved in Paris(!) but not too badly. Usually engraving in France is much inferior to Germany, but it is now so expensive in Germany that it is out of the question to have it done there.

25 September

Worked on the second scene, wrote and dictated letters.

The weather has turned cold: grey mists roll right up to the clouds. Towards evening I received a telegram from the lettings agency that there is a good flat, and asking me to telephone to Paris at eight o'clock in the evening. But the telephone exchange packs up at six o'clock, so I took the tram into Fontainebleau to telephone from there. Missed the last tram back, so had to walk the whole way in total darkness.

26 September

Worked.

A letter from Klimov. He is taking advantage of my expansive gesture and settling my fee at 500 roubles. Had I bargained I could probably have got more. As against this, he now signs himself 'most respectfully' whereas before it was simply 'Klimov'.

In the afternoon we took Svyatoslav and went to look at the apartment I was told about yesterday evening. It belongs to a Russian called Trachtenberg who is making himself a fortune in Paris from his big night-club restaurant.[2] It is a typical bachelor apartment, splendidly done up but too small for us. He entertained us to tea, after which we returned home still with nothing to show for our efforts.

Svyatoslav, however, was in ecstasy from the trip: the tram, the 'tasi' and the chuff-chuff.

---

1 Sergey Razumovsky (1864–1942), playwright and critic, author of an unpublished autobiography (1927), was the representative of MODPiK (Moskovskoye Obyedinenie Dramaticheskikh Pisatelyei i Kompozitorov, the Moscow Association of Dramatic Writers and Composers) which also functioned as a publishing house. See below pp. 474–5, 507.
2 This was the Bar Kazbek, a favourite haunt of émigré Russians with a superior roster of cabaret acts aimed, like Nikita Baliyev's 'Théâtre de la Chauve-Souris', at Russians pining for a nostalgic taste of the songs, scenes and dishes of their vanished homeland.

27 September

Some interesting letters. Popa agrees. Ostroumova has come up with information about the personalities about whom *Fiery Angel*, the novel, was written. 'Renata' apparently is still living in Paris. But the most intriguing detail of all is that 'Madiel' is none other than Andrey Bely. How marvellous!

For the past few days something has been not right with my heart. I seem to have carried too heavy a suitcase on one of our trips to Paris. It is very annoying: for almost a year now I have had almost no trouble with my heart.

28 September

Out for a walk today I posed myself a direct question: given that the subject of *Fiery Angel* is in direct opposition to Christian Science, why am I still working on it? Either I have not fully thought this through, or I am not being honest with myself. If I seriously accept Christian Science then I should not be devoting day after day to its adversary. I tried to think out this conundrum from its root, succeeding only in overheating my brain. The solution can only be that *Fiery Angel* must be consigned to the flames. Was it not a mark of greatness in Gogol to take this step with the second part of *Dead Souls*? That is, is it not the case that so radiant are his other works, and so strong and finely tuned his own critical awareness, that he was right not to shrink from destroying anything, however precious, that fell below his standards?[1]

At home I told Ptashka what had been going through my mind, although stopping short of actually announcing my intention of burning the work. In this I had the advantage over Gogol: I would be able to recast the musical material into a symphonic work. It was the *subject* from which I felt I must disentangle myself. Ptashka, however, advised me not to take any irrevocable decisions: for better or worse I had chosen the subject some time ago, since when to all intents and purposes I had finished with it and was now concentrating on the music, having comparatively little to do with the subject. Such

---

1 Gogol published the first part of *Dead Souls* in 1842. It was quite reasonably perceived by contemporary readers as a grotesque but hilariously biting satire on the absurdities and hypocrisies of feudal Russia, but Gogol himself had a wider vision based on Dante's *Divine Comedy*, in which the first part corresponded to the Inferno while the second part, the Purgatorio, would depict the purification and ultimate redemption of the morally barren antihero Chichikov. Over the next ten years Gogol wrote most if not all of Part Two, but influenced by a priest who had convinced him of the immorality of imaginative literature in general, he burned his unpublished manuscripts shortly before dying from a combination of depression and malnutrition at the age of forty-three.

a quantity of music should not be squandered. The task now is to complete it while giving a wide berth to such material in the future. Needless to say this was a much less painful resolution than rising to Gogolian heights of madness, and I adopted it.

29 September

We both went into Paris, I to get my visas for the trip to Berlin, Ptashka for some things she needed to do and both of us to continue looking for a flat. We had lunch with Paichadze and Stravinsky, whom I ran into at the publishers. He was nice and showered praise on me, saying that of all composers today I was closest to him, that while of course not everything I wrote was to his taste there was always something to like in every work. When he was visiting the engraver and they gave him an engraved page to look at as a sample, although it was just an oboe part he could see at once that it was by Prokofiev. In short, however sincere all this may or may not have been, he evidently felt it necessary to give me a pat on the head. And it was all the more unexpected, since not long ago Dukelsky was telling me how Stravinsky, hearing a performance of my Third Piano Concerto at the Princesse de Polignac's, had stormed out into the next room and said, 'This is not to be borne! A sort of Russian-style pseudo-classicism, a musical Vasnetsov!'[1] Today, Stravinsky delivered himself of somewhat guarded opinions about Dukelsky's music: pleasant, accomplished, but lacks individuality. At the mention of Milhaud and Casella he foamed at the mouth, a reaction I wholeheartedly endorsed. Auric and Poulenc he regards as second-rate composers, Poulenc, however, the more honest of the two. Himself he is composing a major work; precisely what is a secret.[2] Lunch proceeded most enjoyably.

After lunch Ptashka and I set off on another round of flat-hunting. One overlooked a garden and had a sunny aspect but the woman letting it demanded 45,000 francs for the horrible furniture she insisted on palming us off with along with the apartment. Negotiations collapsed. We then saw another, on the rue Davion, not so sunny but spacious and comfortable, at

---

1 Viktor Vasnetsov (1848–1926), Russian Revivalist painter of historical, mythological and folk-legend subjects associated with the socially conscious anti-aestheticist Realist group known as the *Peredvizhniki* ('Itinerants' or 'Wanderers'). In common with his Slavophile colleagues Repin, Surikov and others, Vasnetsov idealised the life of the Russian countryside and peasantry. At least for a time in his immediately post-Rimsky-Korsakov years, Stravinsky might have tolerated Vasnetsov's fairy-tale and religious subjects, but not the genre paintings he produced in the 1870s and early 1880s.
2 Not from Paichadze, however, since Stravinsky had signed a contract for *Oedipus Rex* with Editions Russes Musicales in June (S. Walsh, op. cit. pp. 439, 646).

which we jumped. Ognev undertook to negotiate immediately with the people responsible. Altogether we are exhausted with all the running about. We called in for an hour or two to the Samoilenkos and then went back to sleep at the empty Koussevitzky house.

1 October

Worked very hard and finished orchestrating Act Three. I then composed the unfinished beginning of the act, up to the words 'Rupprecht, he is here', partly revising the old version and partly recomposing it afresh. The most successful bit was the short episode in which Rupprecht sings: 'Forget the knockings and the ghosts: they are all fraudulent manifestations of delirium.' Could this success be a sign that I am justified in continuing to compose *Fiery Angel*?

Another telegram from Weber: the premiere of *Oranges* having been 'definitely' fixed for the 8th, it has now been moved to the 9th. An odd thing to do, to move by a single day. Meanwhile we have all kinds of domestic problems to resolve: should we move to town now, into a hotel, or wait until I get back from Berlin? Ptashka also very much wants to come to Berlin for the premiere, but what are we to do with Svyatoslav?

My heart has settled down and is behaving itself.

2 October

Again worked hard and orchestrated everything that I had composed yesterday. Sent Labunsky into Paris to change my sleeping-car reservation from 4th October to 6th. Ptashka went to the post office and tried endlessly to ring up Blois to find out when Pleyel could send a lorry for the piano and our belongings, for on this depends when we remove from the country. She struggled for over an hour but did not succeed on getting through to him.

Svyatoslav called the soup we were having 'tyompenky' instead of 'tyoplenky'.[1] A lovely word.

3 October

After two days' energetic striving I had a headache today and therefore did less work, although I am anxious to press on before the interruption that will inevitably occur with my journey to Berlin and our move to the city and the

---

1 Meaning 'warm'; Svyatoslav's coining has no meaning but sounds nice.

as yet non-existent apartment. Made a piano reduction of quite a lot of the third act.

A very welcome letter from Schaad: the Overture[1] reached America in good order and the money has been transferred to my account. Each second of music has earned me three dollars.

4 October

Carried on revising Act Three. Put right Labunsky's mistakes in the score. Fulfilled a lot of administrative chores and dictated letters prior to leaving for Berlin.

5 October

A very good letter from Persimfans: for my arrival in Moscow they are arranging five symphony concerts of my compositions. This is incredible: for a comparable honour one would have to look back to Beethoven, on the centenary of his death. But that is Moscow for you! During our stay in the USSR Ptashka and I will be issued with 'travel documents' and so will not have to get involved with the business of Soviet passports. I shall be able to exchange these travel documents for my customary League of Nations passport[2] when I leave the USSR. They will not, however, issue me with an exit visa in advance of my departure, even though they assure me there will be no attempt to impede me at that point.

My mood today has been generally not of the best and I have little desire to go to Berlin even though I know it will be interesting. My heart is playing up and affecting my breathing, despite my attempts to counteract this through Christian Science. At six o'clock Ptashka and I left for Paris so as to employ the following morning in the search for a flat. We again spent the night in the empty Koussevitzky house.

---

1   The *American Overture*, commissioned by Duo-Art. Schaad was the manager of the Aeolian Company, owners of Duo-Art.
2   The 'Nansen Passport', conceived and introduced by the Norwegian scientist, explorer and diplomat Fridtjof Nansen when he was serving as the League's High Commissioner for Refugees after the First World War. There could have been a problem for Prokofiev in that the Nansen passport, although indefinitely renewable once it had been issued, should by rights have become invalid if the holder returned to the country from which, as a condition of qualifying for the passport, he or she was defined as a refugee. This was why it was important that he should *not* be issued with a Soviet passport. During his years of residence abroad, Prokofiev never seems to have considered giving up citizenship of his country of origin to seek another nationality, preferring the relative inconveniences of the Nansen travel papers and their presumption of refugee status.

6 October

Went looking for flats through the Ognev agency and Baron Wolff. We saw one nice one with a bedroom and a big garden, but the apartment was too small for us; another was also not bad but surrounded by four smoking factory chimneys and opposite some waste ground on which they are going to build a house, which means noise and dust for a year. The upshot was that once again we did not find anything. Lunched with Paichadze. The orchestral material for the Suite from *Oranges* has just come off the press and Paichadze slipped me a copy for Berlin, where they want to perform the Suite in concerts which will be broadcast on the wireless (Telefunken).

The Nord Express, on which I had booked myself a ticket, turned out to be the most luxurious train: new, dark blue carriages picked out with copper stripes. Ptashka was most chagrined not to be coming with me to Berlin, and I was also sad to be parting from her. An unexpected appearance was Dukelsky, recently back from Italy where he had been to see Diaghilev. But Diaghilev is not doing anything about my ballet at the moment, preparing instead a ballet by Berners[1] that the latter has, apparently, only half written. Incredible man, Diaghilev! Auric has changed direction and is now writing operettas.

The train moved off and Dukelsky took Ptashka to the Samoilenkos. I had a compartment to myself, very comfortable, but I still did not sleep well: the moment I had drifted off I was woken up by 'deutsche Zoll'.[2] The train went very fast, but the weight of the carriages is such that there was little rocking about and one was scarcely aware of the speed.

---

1   Gerald Hugh Tyrwhitt-Wilson, Lord Berners (1883–1950), archetypal English eccentric famous for having installed a specially built clavichord in his Rolls-Royce, dying the pigeons on his estate a dazzling variety of unsuitable colours, and inviting a giraffe to tea. He had first encountered Diaghilev and his circle while serving as a member of the British diplomatic corps in the plum postings of Paris and Rome, and rapidly became attuned to the most up-to-date artistic currents, including the astringent harmonic languages of Stravinsky and Satie and the world of Dada Surrealism. *The Triumph of Neptune* has a nonsensical harlequinade scenario by Sacheverell Sitwell inspired by the penny-plain tuppence-coloured toy-theatre prints beloved of Victorian children, which also provided the basis for the sets and costumes. Choreography was by Balanchine. Among its delights are a parody of 'The Last Rose of Summer' sung by a resonant baritone in his bath, and a spectacular number entitled 'The Frozen Forest', which Ronald Crichton, in his note reproduced in the Chester Novello score, tells us was known to the Lyceum stage hands who had to struggle with it in the London production, as 'Wigan by Night'. Not everyone was amused or seduced by the whimsy: the eminent Russian-born critic André Levinson sniffed about its very English flavour representing 'the puerile romanticism of a race of grown-up, laughing children'. But it is hard not to like a man who could produce verses such as: 'Uncle Fred and Aunty Mabel/Fainted at the breakfast table./Isn't that an awful warning/Not to do it in the morning?'
2   German Customs.

7 October

Arrived in Berlin at nine o'clock in the morning to be met by Weber, who had booked me a room at the Hotel Fürstenhof, a good place where I had several times had lunch with Suvchinsky on my previous visits. The rehearsal began at eleven. The Staatsoper theatre itself is undergoing reconstruction, so performances currently take place in another theatre attractively situated in the leafy surroundings of the Tiergarten. The conductor, Blech,[1] informed me that he had made a few changes, here and there repeating bars in common time in order to assist with scene changes, making small cuts in two places, with which I was glad to agree, but there were two instances where the changes were more substantial. The passage in which the Prince spits had been cut out, on the grounds that it was too coarse, and inevitably the final scene with its haring about the stage had defeated the producer, so that had also been cut. In its place the March was repeated before the final curtain. There was little point in arguing; for that I would have had to be there before the last rehearsal, but I did enter a protest, albeit a mild one, about the spitting scene.[2]

The rehearsal began with all the tempi being unnecessarily slow. However, the orchestra did play all the notes accurately. On stage, the Prologue proceeded pretty confusingly, with a lot of pointless rushing about, but vocally it was noticeably superior to the Cologne production. Cologne, though, was much more interesting from the scenic point of view, largely because the producer there had been the youthful and fiery 'sehr lustig' Strohbach,[3] whereas here the producer is the elderly timeserver Holy, clearly a close relation of Chicago's Coini. I made notes of all the mistakes and other shortcomings and passed them to the conductor and the producer. The sets for the first act were mediocre, but the Act Two celebration was good, the

---

1. Leo Blech (1871–1958), composer and conductor. Having studied composition with, among others, Humperdinck, he launched his conducting career in his native Aachen before in 1906 being appointed Chief Conductor of the Königliches Schauspielhaus in Berlin, later renamed the Staatsoper, where so rapidly did his reputation grow that Richard Strauss insisted on Blech conducting the Berlin premiere of *Elektra* in February 1909. In spite of being Jewish, Leo Blech survived at the Staatsoper until 1937, and after spending the war years in Latvia and then Sweden, returned triumphantly to the Städtische Oper (the Staatsoper being by then in East Berlin in the GDR), where he remained until his death.
2. This had also created a problem in the opera's first production in Chicago, leading to a furious row between Prokofiev and the producer, Jacques Coini, during which composer informed producer that after the former's death the latter would be free to mangle the opera as he wished, but not until. Prokofiev eventually gave way and permitted the substitution of a sneeze, but the incident rankled. See *Diaries*, vol. 2, p. 641.
3. A month after this diary entry, Strohbach would be responsible for the scandalous production, also in Cologne, of Bartók's *The Miraculous Mandarin*. See above, p. 60, n. 1.

Act Three desert reminiscent of that in Cologne but better, while Creonte's castle was altogether splendid with its *trompe l'œil* perspective. But by comparison with Cologne, there was less love for three oranges.

After the rehearsal I invited Weber to lunch with me at my hotel, then took a nap and in the evening went to see the Gessens. I was curious to see how the friendly editor of a conservative Russian newspaper would react to my forthcoming visit to Russia. He said, 'Of course you must go. In your place I would do the same.'

8 October

General rehearsal, attended by the public but only by invitation. Before it started I got hold of Blech and once again asked him to step up the tempi as much as possible. I think this irritated him, as he has an enormously high opinion of himself, but I still feel I have to do it so that my wishes at least take up a position in his brain. The difference between Blech and Holy consists in this: when I express my wishes to the former, he replies, 'At this stage nothing further can be done,' but then covertly does something about them. With the latter, when I make a suggestion, he invariably exclaims, 'I've been thinking just the same myself!', but everything stays exactly as it was. The tempi were a little livelier, but not enough. On stage most of my requirements were not met, so once again I put them down on paper and spent an hour after the rehearsal going through them with the producer. The Prologue went more smoothly, there was some evidence of planning and control on stage, but what was truly bad was the Prince. This was no sixteen-year-old spoilt boy but a superannuated Siegfried; no wonder this singer has specialised in Wagner. He sounded most unconvincingly amused in his laughter scene (although some people in the audience laughed); the love scene was more like Act Two of *Tristan* than a delicate aquarelle. The Cook was very good; in fact there was much that I liked about the performance. There were applause and curtain calls at the end of the rehearsal, and I was told that in undemonstrative Berlin this counted as a great success. However, that was not how it struck me and I did not go on stage to take a bow, for which I was later criticised.

Spent the evening at Weber's.

9 October

Slept badly. Spent the afternoon on various errands: return train ticket, visas for the journey back, money, and a visit to the publishers where Weber and I discussed current business.

The premiere took place in the evening. I sat in the stalls for the first two acts with Weber and Borovsky, who happened to have shown up, but for the third act I went into the wings. Terpis,[1] the balletmaster, is evidently well disposed towards me and says he has plans to stage my ballet.[2] He advised me to pay some attention to the singers and actors, and thank them for their efforts. I took the hint and went round shaking hands right and left. This is fine in an opera like *Tristan*, in which after two people you have amply fulfilled your obligations, but in *Oranges* there are millions and I was run off my feet. Some were delighted with my expressions of gratitude, some acknowledged with scrupulous correctness, but there were others like the Prince, to whom no doubt the producer had transmitted more than one of my observations, who would barely shake my hand before scuttling away. There was an amusing incident just before the start of the performance, when I was leaving the wings to go into the auditorium. I met the trombonist, who has to come out on stage with the Herald in the Prologue. I imagine he has spent his entire life conscientiously playing his part tucked away in the orchestra pit, and now suddenly he has been dressed up in a clown's costume, make-up slapped on his face, and a red bow tied onto his trombone. There he stood, angrily fingering his instrument. When I stopped in front of him to give him a cheery smile, he said, 'Think of all that good German money they've spent on the sets and costumes, but what will the takings amount to?'

And so I ran around shaking hands, and meanwhile the performance went on its way more or less as it had done at yesterday's general rehearsal. Holy agitatedly shrieked instructions from the wings, but none of the suggestions I had made was translated into action. The entry of the Cook was most effectively done. Aravantinos,[3] the designer (a Greek) had created for this scene an amazingly ingenious perspective, the effect of which was to make the back of the stage seem five versts distant, so that when the Cook made her appearance from there she seemed so gigantic it was as though a colossal sun was coming up.

The performance came to an end, the curtain calls began to the accompaniment of reasonably, although not excessively, loud applause. Blech came up

---

1   Max Terpis (stage name of Max Pfister (1898–1958), Swiss-born choreographer. He had been appointed by the Staatsoper Director, Max von Schillings, to the position of Chief Choreographer in 1923 and held the position until 1929, producing in that time no fewer than nineteen ballets, all by Modernist composers, but his predilection for the austerely Expressionist-Constructivist never made him a favourite with the public and his reign was to end abruptly in 1929 with the arrival of the new Music Director Otto Klemperer, who found his art completely lacking in musicality.
2   The following year, 1927, Terpis did produce a ballet to Prokofiev's music: the *Scythian Suite*, to which he added 'some scenes from Dante with demonic forces, tormented souls and an angel sent to relieve them from their sufferings'. See below, p. 583.
3   Panos Aravantinos (1886–1930), Greek painter and designer. A year before, he had designed a particularly successful production of Stravinsky's *Renard*, also staged by Franz Hörth and conducted by Erich Kleiber.

from the orchestra pit. I tried to go up to him, but he, muttering something, slipped past me evidently in an inimical frame of mind, and went out to take his bow. The Intendant, Hörth, then appeared and led me out on stage. I went out and bowed several times. Blech then vanished, while I for form's sake thanked old man Holy for his work. My gratitude not having been marked by much in the way of praise, Hörth over-compensated by the fulsomeness of his. Afterwards Borovsky, Weber and I went to a big new café for supper.

10 October

With Weber went to the Städtische Oper[1] for a meeting with Bruno Walter[2] about the forthcoming production of *Fiery Angel*. Weber explained that this theatre was much less afflicted with red tape than the Staatsoper, and there was no doubt that their staging of *Fiery Angel* would be superior to that of *Oranges*.

Walter is a most impressive gentleman. The Intendant of the theatre was also present, by name something like Titian, and he is destined in a short time to take up the post of overall head of all the theatres in Prussia. We talked about casting, about the decor, and I played some excerpts from Act One. It made very little sense to them, not surprisingly as there is as yet no German version of the libretto. For this reason we confined ourselves mainly to technical questions. When they asked in what style I envisaged the production, I told them that when I had been in Antwerp the Plantin House Museum[3] had made a great impression on me, and this was the kind of setting in which I saw *Fiery Angel* being staged. Titian put in: 'I know this museum.' In general he said little, and in a quiet tone of voice, but with authority. As we parted, Bruno Walter said that if I come up in time with the score and material the premiere could be expected to take place around the 1st April.

1 The Municipal Opera House, formerly the Deutsche Opernhaus in Charlottenburg, today the Deutsche Oper Berlin.
2 Bruno Walter (1876–1972), one of the most admired conductors of the twentieth century. Having worked closely with Mahler as his assistant and protégé, he accepted the composer's widow's invitation to conduct the premieres of both *Das Lied von der Erde* and the Ninth Symphony, in both of which works he stands to this day as most nearly representing the authentic voice of their creator. Walter had been appointed General Music Director of the Städtische Oper the previous year.
3 The museum is in a sixteenth-century house that originally belonged to one of the founders of printing in Holland, Christoffel Plantin (1520–1589). Plantin's printing house 'De Gulden Passer', established in 1555, published a great number of books on anatomy, botany, geography and theology; it was a centre of humanist learning. Its most famous achievement was the *Biblia Polyglotta*, a typographical masterpiece in five languages. 'A true, living museum of old books, manuscripts and drawings, all housed in an environment created at exactly the time when Rupprecht lived . . . a perfect illustration of the ambience in which the story of *Fiery Angel* unfolds.' See *Diaries*, vol. 2, pp. 709–10.

From the Städtische Oper I made my way to Gessen's for dinner. There I was greeted by acclamation for *Oranges*. Four newspaper reviews are already out, two good and two bad.

Gessen has a wireless telegraph apparatus,[1] and as my March and Scherzo from *Three Oranges* was to be broadcast today, at the appointed hour we huddled round the apparatus and heard first Weissmann[2] giving a lecture (which made me imagine how silly he must look speaking so earnestly to an empty room), and then the March and the Scherzo. It was not bad, quite entertaining, the huge orchestra transformed into a tiny little ball. The timbres of the instruments sounded odd; it was just about possible to work out which of them were playing although perhaps only if one knew the score. Of course, the apparatuses of today will certainly improve and the timbres will in future be reproduced with greater fidelity.

At nine o'clock in the evening I left to go back to Paris.

11 October

Was obliged to change trains in Cologne at an unearthly hour of the morning. Since the Paris train left three hours later, I shaved, drank coffee and went for a walk. Thinking of the crude and loveless Berlin production of *Oranges*, I recalled how they had done it in Cologne and was seized by a desire to write some warm words to Szenkár, which I did. Relations with him have, however, cooled: it seems he was offended that I did not react to the idea of *Fiery Angel* being produced in Cologne, even though that is the city in which the action of the opera takes place and in that respect it would have been an appropriate location for the world-premiere production. But the Cologne public had had enough trouble digesting *Oranges* – what on earth would they have made of *Angel*?

Paris at five o'clock in the evening. Ptashka met me, and so did Dukelsky, who had heard from the publishers that I was returning then. It was amusing that Ptashka and Dukelsky had seen me off and now were welcoming me back. We spent the night in the Koussevitzky house.

12 October

Looked at a whole range of flats, quite a number of which were not bad, but one was dark, another available only from the 15th January. At last a third on the rue Michel-Ange we liked very much and decided to make a serious effort to get, even though the agent who showed it to us was a pretty rough character. But it was far from plain sailing: bribes must be paid to the letting

---

1 A wireless set, a radio.
2 See above p. 147.

manager, to the concierge, and to the agent, and to yet another agent who tipped our agent off about it; in short heaps of cash were extracted from us in the most underhand manner. However, it is well known that in Paris today there is no other way to get hold of an apartment. We spent so much time running about the city that I did not even manage to buy the German newspapers with articles about *Oranges*.

13 October

There is no rest here either. We were woken at 7 a.m. by the lorry from Pleyel to take away the piano. They set out yesterday evening and spent the night somewhere in order to be here at first light. We were thrown into panic because not only were they supposed to take the piano but also our trunks, but we were expecting them tomorrow and had not yet done anything about packing. Then it emerged that not only had they got the wrong day, they had also brought the wrong cover for the piano: the one they had was for an upright whereas it should have been for a grand. The grand piano could not possibly fit into a cover for an upright, and the instrument could not be transported without a cover because it was an open lorry and it was raining. So they went away empty-handed, and will come back tomorrow.

I reclothed Act Three in piano dress[1] while Ptashka did the packing. My heart is worrying me again.

15 October

We were afraid we were going to be harried over the inventory, but the hand-over proceeded auspiciously, very auspiciously in fact, as we were billed only 16 francs for damage we had caused. We made our way to Paris, and as has become our tradition tried to stay at the Victoria Palace, but there was no room to be had there and so we repaired temporarily to the Koussevitzkys' house, where we were warmly welcomed by Ksyusha.

16 October – 25 November

We stayed for four days chez Koussevitzky, but then decided we must move out as to stay longer would be embarrassing. We went to a small hotel nearby, the Hôtel Beauséjour in rue Ranelagh. Our dealings with the flat on the rue Michel-Ange stretched out interminably: first, someone had to pursue the delicate negotiations about a bribe to the letting manager (this gentleman apparently controls almost seventy apartments and has a huge office

---

1 That is, prepared the vocal score.

dedicated to this activity), then the letting manager has to negotiate with the owner of the property but he is away at present, and so on, and so forth. To cut a long story short, initially the backhanders were going to amount in all to about 15,000 francs and the annual rent would be 14,000. Then we were told that actually the rent would be 19,000 but could be reduced to 13,000 (because of the tax rules it is important to have the rent nominally as low as possible) but to achieve this it would not only be necessary to pay the difference over the three years, that is to say 3 x 6,000 francs = 18,000, all at once in advance, but also to offer a further 15,000 in bribes. It meant that in all we would be immediately shelling out to these criminals 33,000 francs. We shed tears, complained bitterly, but we liked the flat, it had six rooms, two of them large, there was plenty of green around, and in a word we agreed. Some time later we were eventually invited to sign a contract, but at this point it emerged that a further 11,000 would be due for repairs. At this point we had had enough, told them all to go to hell and walked away from the deal, having frittered away on the whole business about 2,000 francs on stamps, deposits and suchlike. To furnish the apartment would have cost another 90,000 or so, which would have effectively put us on the rocks financially. In any case we found all this unscrupulous exploitation deeply repellent.

We decided that for this winter we would have to take a furnished apartment, but this also proved far from easy. Paris was full to the gills and the price of everything had risen tremendously just over the past few months. When the value of the franc had gone to blazes during the summer the French had had a rush of blood to the head and put their prices up, but even when the franc recovered its former stability prices remained at the dizzy heights to which they had ascended. All the fun and games we had had trying to find an apartment had played havoc with our nerves and we had even begun to quarrel, although thank God this had not been a problem during the summer months. But even though we were currently in a nice, comfortable room, it was very inconvenient sharing it with Svyatoslav, and Svyatoslav himself, taking his cue from his overwrought parents, also took to behaving fractiously. We took him to spend time with Ksyusha, and with Maria Viktorovna, but from Ksyusha's daughter he learnt appalling manners while the atmosphere at Maria Viktorovna's was also charged with electricity because Borovsky's mother had recently died in Leningrad and he had heard the news in the middle of a concert tour. Maria Viktorovna worried about him, and on top of everything the concerts were not going well: in Poland he had not received the whole of his fee, he was experiencing difficulty getting a visa for Riga, and so on.

What with the search for a flat, at first I was little inclined to work, but after a while I started doing something little by little, either at the Borovskys' or at the home of a friend of Ptashka's called Franciz who was always out during the day. I set about revising Act Four, and this went easily because this particular act had been better done than the others so the revisions were not so major. Having finished this I turned to the orchestration, preparing the ground for Gorchakov, whose arrival from Kishinyov we were awaiting, by means of the abbreviation technique I had developed in the summer. My heart was not behaving perfectly: sometimes it was fine and nothing was amiss, at others I felt as though my throat was suffocating.

At long last, through friends and not through any one of the four agencies who were working on our behalf, we found a furnished flat on the rue Troyon near the Etoile. The flat was right at the top of the house, a mansard flat, with six small rooms and a roof terrace. The building itself was good, but the street disreputable, full of brothels, and in the evening the girls would clutch at your sleeve. The flat was cheaply furnished but it had a few fabrics and carpets, a touch of the *vie de bohème*, and this was at least better than the usual furnished apartment clichés. We decided to take it, changed our minds, then after another week's fruitless searching decided in favour again – and took it. I was glad finally to have my desk, a piano and somewhere to work, but Ptashka suffers more keenly than I do about where we live. She was cast down that once again we were reduced to camping out with no permanent nest of our own, the rue Troyon flat seemed an awful place to her (even though we had decided on it jointly!) and she was unhappy there. Certainly, every morning we were woken up by the noise of cars coming out of a garage somewhere down below us in the street, but at seven o'clock some kind of electric device emitted such a regular pulsing sound and that was the moment I actually waited for because after it all the car horns ceased and I went back soundly to sleep. Ptashka, however, could not bear this noise. Although I agreed that we did need to find our own place, and this was the time to do it as we had accumulated some money, I am not as drawn to the city as Ptashka is. If I have a successful tour of America, what I should like to do is buy a villa outside Paris but within reach of the city, and to have a bachelor *pied à terre* which we could use for the days, weeks or even months when we need to stay in town.

One day Bashkirov happened to mention his cherished dream of giving up driving his taxi and buying a farm. He had already identified a partner with whom to join in making the purchase and had some hopes of getting money from his sister Varvara even if this meant the property would be in her name. He had gone down to inspect the farm, which was near Versailles and thus quite accessible. I am most sympathetic to the notion and interested in his plans: life is better in the countryside than in the town. I would have taken a share in the enterprise myself except that B.N. is an impossible person with whom to have business dealings: he expects all his associates to do everything while he himself will not lift a finger.

We made the move to the apartment on rue Troyon on the 30th November, and on the same day Popa-Gorchakov arrived from Kishinyov. The bizarre conjunction of these two surnames had come about in the following manner. His family, being natives of Bessarabia, were called Popa but his father, a singer, was a member of the Bolshoy Theatre company under the stage-name of Gorchakov. In order to rid himself of what he considered an unattractive family name, he made an official application to the authorities to change it to Gorchakov. The application was granted, but when Bessarabia became part of Romania,[1] the Romanian authorities did not accept the change, and thus some of the papers of my future secretary referred to Popa and others to Gorchakov. He is twenty-three, dark, holds himself somewhat stiffly and self-consciously, like a soldier, having only just finished his military service. He wears two George Crosses[2] on his chest, which he had won during Kornilov's campaign:[3] as a boy of fifteen he had run away to join the Volunteer Army opposing the Bolsheviks, and had found himself embroiled in the severest part of the 'Ice Campaign'.[4] In life, three things interest him: Christian Science, music and the Boy Scout movement. He has been a follower of Christian Science since the age of six, was cured of gangrene and a host of minor ailments, and at one time spent several hours a day studying *Science and Health* very intensively. He is a serious person, firm in his convictions although in some ways rather strange, preferring to remain silent on a number of questions. He does not smoke or drink, and probably has no knowledge of women. If he really does know Christian Science so well and has such firm beliefs, it will be valuable to be in close contact with him.

As soon as we were settled in rue Troyon work on Act Four rushed ahead at a great pace: there were several days when I succeeded in orchestrating no fewer than fifteen pages of score. Gorchakov put up at a hotel but came every

---

1 In 1918. See above, pp. 31–2, n. 3, 271–2.
2 The Order of St George was established by Catherine the Great in 1769, its four classes intended to recognise varying categories of military valour. Originally restricted to officers, by 1913 its scope had been extended to encompass all ranks of the Imperial Army. The Order was abolished by decree after the October Revolution in 1917 but survived, until their eventual defeat, in the various elements of the White Armies during the Civil War.
3 See *Diaries*, vol. 2, pp. 226–7 for an account of General Kornilov's ill-fated march on Petrograd to support (as he believed) Kerensky's Provisional Government, the failure of which impelled Kornilov willy-nilly into leadership of the White counter-revolutionary forces.
4 The 'Ice Campaign' is how the first Kuban Campaign of March 1918, undertaken by the Volunteer Army led by General Kornilov and after his death by General Denikin, came to be known. Its purpose was to unite the Army with the White-supporting Cossacks of the Kuban. The weather turned unexpectedly cold, with temperatures dropping below 20° Centigrade, so that greatcoats froze on the backs of the troops already exhausted from long marches across the frozen black earth of the Kuban steppe, and the wounded had to be prised from their ice-clad wagons each evening with the aid of bayonets. The fighting was also savage, the Volunteer Army suffering over 400 killed and 1,500 wounded in the unsuccessful attempt to capture the capital city of the Kuban, Yekaterinodar. On 31 March (O.S.) Kornilov himself was killed and it fell to his successor, Denikin, somehow to extricate his stricken forces from what by that time was almost complete encirclement. This he achieved, and led them to safety.

morning to get to work on the Act Four score. He works slowly but makes few mistakes when compared with the half-witted Labunsky. I completed the orchestration of the act on the 25th November, but Gorchakov lagged behind on account of my arrow-like progress.

On the 24th November we had a house-warming party to which came the two Samoilenkos, the two Paichadzes and Maria Viktorovna (Borovsky being away on his travels). Champagne was served and we had a convivial evening. A. N. Benois was also there, recently successfully back from Russia where he had encountered none of the alarming experiences he had anticipated when leaving Paris. Charming as ever, he told me many interesting things, and said, 'Of course you must go; nobody will lay a finger on you there.'

Among other events I should mention some lectures given by Karsavin on Euroasianism, which were extremely interesting. We attended several of them at Suvchinsky's invitation. At them I met Marina Tsvetaeva,[1] but our conversation did not extend beyond a few words. Twice we visited the home of Prince Bassiano,[2] a feeble composer but a very nice man, married to a rich American woman. They have a wonderful villa near Versailles, and each time

---

1 In 1925 Marina Tsvetaeva (1892–1941), one of the most inspired and inspiring poets in any language of her generation as well as one of the most emotionally fragile, accompanied by her husband Sergey Efron, their son Gyorgy ('Mur') and the surviving one of their two daughters Ariadna (Alya), had settled in Paris seeking sanctuary from penury and marital misery in Prague. Tsvetaeva and her son were to stay in Paris for the next fourteen years, largely ostracised by émigré circles because of her husband's and her daughter's increasingly open support for the Bolshevik regime and her own ambivalence, needless to say stemming from emotional and cultural rather than political sympathies. Tsvetaeva and Mur returned despairingly to the USSR in 1939, preceded by Efron and Alya. Efron was executed in 1941, Alya served eight years in the Gulag, Tsvetaeva as a compromised 'cosmopolitan' with criminal relatives was denied any meaningful work and even subsistence-level means of support. She committed suicide in Yelabuga, to which she had been unwillingly evacuated, in August 1941. Mur survived, to be killed in July 1944 fighting with the Red Army against the Germans near Vitebsk, now in Belarus.

2 Roffredo Caetani, Prince of Bassiano and 17th Duke of Sermoneta (1871–1961), a colourful, exquisitely mannered and cultivated scion of one of the most ancient princely families of Rome, had been a godson of Liszt and, as a boy, befriended by Liszt's daughter Cosima, who had become Wagner's wife shortly before Caetani's birth. His American heiress wife, Marguerite Chapin, was if anything even more interesting: she sat for portraits by Vuillard and Bonnard; the literary journal she founded in 1924, *Commerce*, had Paul Valéry as one of its three editorial directors; its first number included excerpts from Joyce's *Ulysses*, T. S. Eliot's 'The Hollow Men' (Eliot was her cousin), prose and poems by Hardy, Edith Sitwell, Virgina Woolf, William Faulkner, Roy Campbell, all in the original English with French translations. The Caetanis oscillated between the Palazzo Caetani in Roma and the Villa Romaine in Versailles, their legendary but unthreateningly Bohemian hospitality embracing virtually *le tout Paris artistique* from Sylvia Beach's Shakespeare & Co. bookshop clientele (not excepting its owner) to Stravinsky, Cocteau, Picasso, Ezra Pound, Rilke, Hofmannsthal, George Antheil, Gertrude Stein, etc., etc. Roffredo may have had limited talents as a composer, but his opera *L'isola del sole*, to his own libretto, opened astonishingly in Rome in 1943 at the height of Mussolini's dictatorship, its anti-Fascist message cunningly concealed behind the novelettish surface story of lovers finding happiness on the Isle of Capri.

they send a car to collect us. I do not much like going out into the 'beau monde', but these people are so exceptionally kind and welcoming, give us such splendid lunches, bring us there and take us home again, that it is always a real pleasure to visit them. Not only that, but this time Suvchinsky, Karsavin and other Eurasianists were also there.

26 November

Diaghilev has twice recently been in to see Paichadze at the publishers, and even paid them some money for something or other – an extremely rare event with him. Paichadze asked him, 'What is happening with Prokofiev's new ballet?' Diaghilev replied that he would be presenting it next spring, but that it would need a completely new scenario as Bolsheviks were no longer *à la mode*.

Fabulous lack of ceremony! Perhaps internecine strife in China might be a more fashionable subject at the moment, and our dear Sergey Pavlovich has plans to hack it into shape to fit my music? Incidentally Suvchinsky enquired what the ballet was called, and I told him I did not know for certain, but Yakulov and I had named it *Ursignol*; Diaghilev, however, found this vulgar. Suvchinsky said that, on the contrary, he liked it very much.

27 November

Set to work on Act Five. There is much more to do than there was in Act Four. Much of it had been only very approximately sketched, and now it was in need of virtually comprehensive recomposition. It is beginning to look as though the opera will not be finished by January and therefore the production scheduled for March must be postponed until next autumn.

B.N. appeared, unshaven and gaunt, asking for money 'just until Varya[1] gets here'. She is due here from China in a week's time, bringing large sums of money with her. I gave him 200 francs.

I have received the programmes and press reviews from Boston. What on earth is going on in America? The tone of them is not so much laudatory as positively reverential. The fact that the birthplace of my American success is Boston is symptomatic! On the other hand, the charming English stay true to their unmusical tradition: a week ago Bruno Walter performed the Suite from *Oranges* there, to be greeted by an exemplary scourging in the press.

---

1 Boris Bashkirov's sister, Princess Varvara Magalova.

29 November

Went to the bank, where I found many letters that for some reason had not been forwarded to me. Among them was a letter from Morolyov.[1] There's life in the old dog yet! Many times I had sent numerous postcards to Nikopol but never had a reply, and I was sure he had perished at some point during the Revolution. I am very glad indeed of his resurrection even though in all probability we would not find we had much in common nowadays.

Called on Prunières and spent a whole hour consulting him about books Asafyev has asked me to obtain and send to him.

30 November

We went to a Christian Science lecture. I liked it less than the one we had attended last Tuesday, finding it primitive. The lecturer, from San Francisco, spoke in a squeaky voice and took an age to expound the most commonplace truths. One of them, while still no doubt a commonplace, did nevertheless strike me as very important: if you are experiencing pain somewhere in your body and wish to relieve it, you must remember that it is not you who are hurting but that God, who is omnipresent, is there in that very place which seems to you to be the source of the pain. As for the pain, it is not you, nor even a part of you, but an intruder from somewhere outside of you. If you can think of it in this way, you are on the way to recovery.

2 December

B.N. came, in a state of great agitation. There was a fine he had been unable to pay, and his vehicle had been impounded. He appealed to me to come to his rescue. At first I refused: I cannot take on my shoulders his protestations of friendship that invariably express themselves in appeals for a loan. But then I felt sorry for him and gave him the money. He gave me his word of honour that he would bring it back to me tomorrow.

3 December

Had dinner with Borovsky, who is in Paris for two days en route from Finland to England. We had pancakes. Borovsky had played my Fourth

---

1   Vasily Morolyov (1880–1949), the former veterinary surgeon from Nikopol near Sontsovka, where Prokofiev spent his childhood. Morolyov had a virtually ungovernable passion both for music and for chess, and soon became the young pianist's and composer's most ardent supporter and friend. Morolyov it was who christened the piano pieces Prokofiev was writing in 1907 'doggies' because of their bite, a name that soon passed into the private language of Prokofiev and Myaskovsky in their correspondence. The First Piano Concerto was dedicated to him. See *Diaries*, vol. 1, pp. 180–81, 235, and *passim*; vol. 2, p. 53.

Sonata in Leipzig, where the critical response was that composers of such music should be severely punished for their irresponsibility in producing work of such paralysing tedium. I played Borovsky the Fifth Sonata, to which in my own playing I have begun to take a new, more highly coloured, approach. Russia is getting nearer by the day, and I am spending longer at the keyboard as I must be sure to be in decent form there.

B. N. let me down and did not bring the money. I don't need the money so much as honesty.

5 December

Svyatoslav orchestrated a fine concert at night, as a result of which we rose late and heavy-headed. I went walking in the Bois, and then worked hard until four o'clock, making real progress with Act Five. To a great extent I am recomposing it. Some scraps of material survive from the old version, and the general plan of the act. Essentially it falls into three parts: the first calm, until the entry of the Grand Inquisitor; the second semi-stormy, culminating in the expulsion of the spirits from the young nuns; and the third a full-blown tempest with Renata and the others in the grip of devilish possession. Today I completed the second part. Before me lies the third, the most difficult and demanding.

10 December

We were at the Benois'. Koka and Marusya are living with his parents. I spent some time talking about cars to Lyolya's[1] new husband, who has something to do with automobile business. Nobody recommends the small Peugeot – it is a very different animal from the big Peugeot. Braslavsky's opinion is that the best marque is the Renault, and one can find bargains in slightly used second-hand models.

12 December

Once Act Five had been, if not finally composed, at least firmly set within its frame, its orchestration proceeded quickly and easily. I am only afraid that I have not much time to devote to it, since I must extend my piano practice in the light of Russia, and even before that my performance in two weeks' time of the Second Piano Concerto with the Pasdeloup orchestra. The concerts are fairly low-grade affairs and there is no fee, but it will be a rehearsal in the provinces before the appearance in the metropolis – Moscow.

---

1 Alexander Benois's daughter, Yelena. She had recently married Alexander Braslavsky, a poet whose day job, evidently, was in the car business.

13 December

Today was the day of my first driving lesson with the Versigny School, the same institution as taught Stravinsky. With the instructor we headed out into the Bois de Boulogne, where he explained the function of all the various levers. To my dismay there were far more of these than I had expected. All the declutching, changing gears and so on completely addled my brains, and then when the car was actually moving I was terrified of hitting something. Altogether the lesson proceeded in an atmosphere of extreme tension, and I returned home overwhelmed with the complexity of the science, mildly comforted only by the thought that one often finds nineteen-year-old idiots past-masters at the art of driving a car. If they can do it, so can I!

14 December

We went to the Opéra to hear Horowitz. He is still a young man, but his gifts as a pianist come straight from God. He was at his best in the Sonata by Liszt: this piece is close to his heart and he genuinely feels every bar of it. Horowitz's technical apparatus is staggering, even if he could do with a touch more power. In Bach he is too lightweight: he is not yet old enough. We were in Maria Viktorovna's box; she never relaxed for a moment during the performance, and was very critical of Horowitz.

15 December

My second driving lesson, and – oh, horrors! – we had to come out of the Bois and go into Paris! When you still do not know how you are supposed to speed up and slow down, it is quite an alarming experience to cross the avenue du Bois!

Sabaneyev, whom I met at the publishers, had an amusing story to tell about Yavorsky. It seems that in 1920, when robberies were happening every day in Moscow, Yavorsky called on Sabaneyev. The door was opened by Sabaneyev's elderly mother who, on seeing someone she did not recognise, asked, shaking with fright, 'Who are you?' Her consternation transmitted itself to Yavorsky, who stammeringly attempted to pronounce his name: 'Ya... vor... Ya... vor...' The old woman in panic slammed the door in his face.[1]

Fate has punished Sabaneyev for all the mud he has flung at composers: having no other wherewithal to earn money he is reduced to copying music

---

[1] 'Ya' in Russian is the first person pronoun 'I', and 'vor' means 'thief'.

for our publishers, and has to sit there slaving away over manuscripts by Grechaninov.

16 December

America is certainly an inordinately talented youth and is developing at an exemplary pace. Stokowski has given concerts in Philadelphia and New York consisting entirely of Myaskovsky's Sixth Symphony and my *Scythian Suite*. Not only did audience and critics listen to it all, they absorbed it and apparently even liked it. Which pleased them more, Myaskovsky's Symphony or my *Suite*, is hard to say. Probably the Symphony, as it will have seemed a more substantial work. In any case I am sincerely happy for Myaskun. New York still wants to take a piece out of my leg, but it will not be long before America yields to me, and then so much the worse for the biters.

Miss Crain came to tea with us, the practitioner whom Ptashka consulted on several occasions last spring when she was not feeling well. At first glance Miss Crain does not make a particularly appealing impression, but this is only at first. I raised with her the subject of repentance. Hitherto, no doubt influenced by my Orthodox upbringing, I thought I knew that repentance and self-reproach for acts committed are good and necessary things, but Miss Crain says that such a state of self-abnegation is inappropriate for a being who is a reflection of God, and does nothing to advance us. What one must do is condemn one's bad deeds, avoid repeating them and in this way draw a line underneath them. Learning that I do not attend the Christian Science Church on Sundays, she extracted from me a promise that I would go. The reason I have not been going is that it has always seemed to me that I concentrate my attention better in solitude than in a crowd of people.

17 December

The third driving lesson. Picking up speed in second gear, I was intending to move the gear lever up to third, but by mistake went into first instead. Something shuddered below my feet and in a panic I stamped on the wrong pedal. The instructor, sitting behind the dual wheel, quickly brought the car to a halt and upbraided me severely and at length. I understood nothing of what he was saying, and my only thought was: have I or have I not wrecked the car? Seeing my crestfallen expression, he relented and said, 'Well, let's continue!'

I have evidently been spotted hurtling about the Bois de Boulogne. In the Métro one day Gorchakov overheard the following conversation: 'Things can't be going too well for Prokofiev – he's learning to drive a taxi!' Gorchakov said he nearly died laughing.

18 December

To Gorchakov I expressed the thought that memory of the past is an indispensable constituent element of immortality, because in this life we are cut off from the past when we have lost memory of it. Gorchakov replied that this is an un-Scientific thought because there can be no concept of time in immortality. I objected that it is an error to confuse 'time' with 'the chronological sequence of events'. If there is no time in eternity, this does not mean that there is no chronology of events; if this were so then chaos would ensue. The characteristic feature of time as we are bound by it in our present existence is its ability to move only in one direction. But it is possible that in eternity the disappearance of our present concept of time may manifest itself precisely in our new-found ability to move in time on both directions, and moreover at any speed we choose. This hypothesis would confirm my proposition that memory is an inseparable part of immortality (equals our own eternal existence) precisely because memory would have the ability to move in either direction and at any velocity.

19 December

Fulfilling my promise to Miss Crain, I went to the Christian Science church. They have two services on a Sunday, first in French and then in English. I attended the English one. I caught myself thinking that a lot of people would recognise me, would stare at me and talk about me. Tried to dispel this feeling as one of egocentricity. Only by succeeding in this endeavour can one become truly absorbed when coming to church, otherwise there is really no point. The church itself is in a large hall with soft lighting and comfortable chairs. There is a wonderful moment when you sense everyone present engrossed in the paternoster and mindful of the spiritual interpretation of it given to us by Christian Science. Several psalms are sung, to text and music composed by various people especially for Christian Science services. The psalms are quite pleasant, but not when they are sung solo from behind a curtain by a female singer with a wavering, unfocused voice, and the music is terrible. This destroyed my concentration and I had to struggle with myself by asking myself the question: can I be so sure that my own taste, if seen from the heights above, is infallible? The core of the service was the sermon. I went away afterwards with mixed feelings. The service would be much closer to my heart if the musical element could be omitted.

22 December

In the morning I played through the Second Piano Concerto to Bâton in the Pleyel showroom, with Borovsky playing the second piano part. A contretemps arose before we started as Bâton was expostulating that the publishers were asking 300 francs for the hire of the orchestral parts, an unheard-of demand in France. It was not at all certain that the Committee of the Concerts Pasdeloup would agree to pay. Devil take these French skinflints: I play for them *gratis* and they still want to haggle about 300 francs! I declared that the publishers would not yield by so much as a centime: if France has not yet got round to expecting to have to pay to hire material it is time it did, as do all other countries, and if the Committee has still not decided whether or not it is going to pay then today's rehearsal will be postponed until such time as it does. Whereupon I put on my scarf and hat. Bâton became somewhat agitated and said there was no need to put the issue as sharply as I had done, while Blois intervened to say that if the Committee would not pay, Maison Pleyel would. At this the rehearsal got under way.

When it was over Borovsky and I went with Ptashka to the Soviet Consulate. The Consulate is like all consulates: there was a map on the wall displaying the manifold natural riches of Russia, and a large portrait of Lenin. If you stand in front of it you immediately become aware of warmth being radiated, just like in one of those openings in the ground through which heat escapes – what the French call a 'bouche de chaleur'. 'Citizens Borovsky and Prokofiev!' came the summons. First we were taken to the Assistant Consul, and then to the man himself, the Comrade Consul. He has a fine office and a fine fur coat. Ptashka noticed that he had a severe look about him, Borovsky that he had beautiful hands. To me he appeared a straightforward, intelligent man. The Consul informed us that our visas were waiting for us and we would be able to obtain travel documents whenever we needed them, but in that connection he felt it necessary to advise us that we would be allowed to leave Russia only as Soviet citizens and would have to apply for exit permits in Moscow under generally applicable regulations. 'Now if you had taken the same citizenship as your wife,' he added, 'it would have been much easier for you to go to Russia.' It would certainly be an interesting situation if I were to turn up in Moscow as a Spaniard!

For the present, the prospect of having to obtain a Soviet passport is anything but appealing as far as future visits are concerned. The Persimfans people have been writing to me insisting that everything has been perfectly arranged, and now all of a sudden here are these unexpected hindrances. The Consul and I decided that I would contact Moscow once again: there is still time, although God knows not much, so I trust they will not hold matters up too much there.

23 December

The first rehearsal of the Second Concerto with the Pasdeloup orchestra: Bâton read through it with the orchestra while I stood beside him.

Two telegrams from different ends of the earth on the subject of *Oranges*: one from Reiner in Cincinnati asking what the rights for the opera would cost overall. What exactly does 'overall' mean? The other one was from Ekskuzovich: why are the publishers holding up their response about a production in Moscow? Well, I never! Here was I thinking that Moscow had gone to sleep on the possibility of staging *Oranges*. Needless to say, the publishers are not responsible for the delay, but clearly there has been a misunderstanding somewhere.

In the evening I went to Borovsky's concert of music by Bach. The audience was small, but he played very well and I enjoyed listening to Bach.

24 December

Second and final rehearsal with Bâton. The orchestra's playing was mediocre. Bâton is a poor conductor, and deaf to boot. The rotten French horn-players cannot be heard at all in the *fortes*.

We took Svyatoslav to see the Borovskys' Christmas tree and stayed to have dinner with them. They gave us cold sturgeon in aspic, a treat Russian émigrés have long forgotten.

A letter from Weber containing an explanation of yesterday's telegram from Ekskuzovich. It seems that Ekskuzovich wants to produce *Oranges* in Moscow on the same conditions as in Leningrad. But this is no longer advantageous to me, in view of the success the work is having, with such good box-office takings and frequently repeated performances.

25 December

A very funny conversation between Svyatoslav and Paichadze on the telephone.

Decided to cable Ekskuzovich pointing out that the Leningrad conditions are no longer equitable, so that in Russia I should not be criticised for appearing to bargain with them.

26 December

Attended the Christian Science church for the second time. Again, those moments were good when all silently immersed themselves in the Lord's

Prayer, in Christian Science's adaptation,[1] and during the sermon, but as before I found the greatest difficulty in reconciling myself to the solo singing in that quavering voice, and above all to the horrible music (doubtless written by an American). The psalms, in contrast, were very nice, one of them characterised by strange voids caused by the absence of thirds in the chords. Apparently the music was originally by Haydn, and later adapted to fit the Christian Science words. I left the church in the best of spirits.

The concert began at five o'clock, my piece was at six. When I arrived at the hall I found that there was no Artists' Room and I had to fold up my overcoat and leave it on a chair backstage. I played reasonably well, better than two years ago with Koussevitzky. But in every work there comes a time when it begins to play itself, and this moment has not yet arrived with the Second Concerto. For the Third Concerto it came just a year ago in America. This time there were moments when I was nervous, but I fought them with Christian Science and kept reminding myself that one time I had succeeded in overcoming my nerves, and had no intention of letting them take over again. Bâton's conducting was, of course, not very good, and in the introduction to the third movement he set off at such a fast tempo that I could scarcely make my entry. I did what I could to slow him down, and to give Bâton his due he did follow me, but this had cost me such an effort that altogether the performance was rough-hewn with an axe rather than a considered interpretation. I had a good success and was called back about four times. Later I learnt that Ptashka and her friends had had great difficulty getting into the performance even though the day before I had been assured she would be given a box. Damn them to hell! I am playing for them for no fee, and they cannot even arrange a box for my wife, even though several were unoccupied. I was terribly angry and said that the only possible justification for dealing with beggars was if they were at least polite. Since at that moment there was nobody present from the Pasdeloup Concerts administration, my ire was vented on Blois – quite groundlessly, of course. I think he was most offended.

---

1 'PRAYER. A brief and good one is furnished in the book of By-laws. The Scientist is required to pray it every day. 'THE LORD'S PRAYER–AMENDED. This is not in the By-laws, it is in the first chapter of *Science and Health*, edition of 1902. I do not find it in the edition of 1884. It is probable that it had not at that time been handed down. Science and Health's (latest) rendering of its "spiritual sense" is as follows: "Our Father-Mother God, all-harmonious, adorable One. Thy kingdom is within us, Thou art ever-present. Enable us to know – as in heaven, so on earth – God is supreme. Give us grace for today; feed the famished affections. And infinite Love is reflected in love. And Love leadeth us not into temptation, but delivereth from sin, disease, and death. For God is now and for ever all Life, Truth, and Love."' M. Twain, *Christian Science*, op. cit.

Dined with Fortier,[1] and ate snails for the first time in my life. Spent the evening at Prunières'.

27 December

We slept late after yesterday's exertions. I made a start on practising the Third Concerto. The Second is dealt with now, after yesterday, but I must get on with the remainder of my programme. Had a driving lesson, and learnt the three-point turn, that is to say a manoeuvre to turn round and face the other direction. In the evening we went to some silly play or other, invited by Fortier.

28 December

Although the passport business is still not settled, our departure for Russia is fast approaching. Whatever triumphs are destined for me there, it is still a journey into an unknown kingdom from which much terror and violence has recently emerged.

All the more interesting, therefore, was the letter I received from Maria Kilshtedt,[2] my former librettist for *Undina*. Today she is in her seventies, the widow of a general, and still writing for *New Times*,[3] and what praise she has for the youth of today, with whom she has kept in contact, and how buoyant her regard for the literary figures still writing in Russia!

With our departure growing ever closer there is a host of new matters to deal with, and I also have to step up my piano practice. Work on *Fiery Angel* has therefore begun to dry up. I shall not succeed in finishing the orchestration of the now fully composed fifth act.

---

1   The French Canadians Mr and Mrs Fortier had been Prokofiev's solicitous hosts in Montreal during his tour in January 1920. See *Diaries*, vol. 2, pp. 466–9.
2   Maria Kilshtedt was an aristocratic literary friend of Prokofiev's Aunt Katya Rayevskaya in St Petersburg and in 1904 had invited the then thirteen-year-old composer to set her libretto based on a translation by Zhukovsky into Russian hexameters of Friedrich de la Motte Fouqué's fairy tale *Undine*, in its day a much admired touchstone of German Romanticism. Prokofiev worked away at it for a couple of years, but finally abandoned the project in 1908. Two acts survive in manuscript. See *Diaries*, vol. 1, p. 58.
3   *New Times* (*Novoye Vremya*) was the leading St Petersburg newspaper published from 1868 until 1917, reaching its apogee under the inspired if reactionary editorship until his death in 1912 of A. S. Suvorin, the close friend and supporter of Chekhov. Lenin closed the paper on the 26 October 1917 (O. S.), the day after the Bolshevik October Revolution, categorising it as the 'very emblem of a corrupt and venal newspaper'; 'New Timesism' ('Novovremenstvo') rapidly became a useful portmanteau term of abuse embracing everything from apostasy and revisionism to grovelling sycophancy. Suvorin's son revived the paper in emigration in Belgrade, continuing to produce it until the mid-1930s.

29 December

Practised the piano, had a lesson driving the car, and ordered a warm overcoat for Russia. The instructor says I need several more lessons before taking the test, which can often be tricky. Tansman, for example, failed three times.

Labunsky came to see me: he has been invited to write a weekly Paris column for *Musical America*, for which he will be paid 1,000 francs a month. I am his first interviewee. This is very good of him, but the amazement in this most venal of scandal-sheets will be great: why on earth start with Prokofiev?

31 December

In view of the mountain of things we have to do, and my wish to get as many of them as I can completed before we go, we decided to go out as little as possible, even not to celebrate the New Year at all. But after talking to the Samoilenkos we said we would go there without ceremony. Boris Nikolayevich[1] was running a temperature and we persuaded him to stay in his dressing-gown. We welcomed the New Year first at ten o'clock, that is Moscow time, until someone protested that he did not want to celebrate it like a Bolshevik. We deferred it then until eleven, Berlin time, and than finally at midnight in Paris. It was very nice, and unpretentious.

---

1 Samoilenko, not Bashkirov.

1927

1 January

Spent the first day of the New Year working.

2 January

Went to Meudon to my mother's grave. I have not been for a long time. The grave is rather overgrown; I gave orders for it to be tidied up and for gravel to be spread on it.

A telegram from Malko[1] replying to the one I had sent him on the 23rd December. My entry and exit permits will be arranged and appropriate instructions passed to the Soviet Consulate in Paris. This sounds much more promising than what the Consul had told me when I went to see him.

Mlle de Saussine,[2] a violinist, came to see me on the recommendation of Blois. She wants to appear in concert with me. But playing my Violin Concerto today she went astray several times. I advised her to learn the work thoroughly and to postpone any further discussion of the subject until such time as she had accomplished this.

3 January

During December my heart seemed to have been better, but in recent days has begun to bring on feelings of suffocation in my throat. I went to

---

1 Nikolay Malko (1883–1961), Russian conductor with a distinguished international career. Prokofiev had had an uneasy relationship with him in St Petersburg/Petrograd days, notably over the preparation of vocal scores of *The Gambler*. In 1916, when the opera had been accepted for production at the Mariinsky Theatre, Malko occupied not only a senior conducting position (he would be appointed Chief Conductor shortly before the Revolution) but was also as part of his duties in charge of the copying department. Following the Revolution Malko retained his position and also became Principal Conductor of the Leningrad Philharmonic Orchestra, in which capacity he directed the first performances of Shostakovich's First Symphony and Myaskovky's Fifth, until his defection from the USSR in 1928. Once in the West he guest-conducted in major European musical centres including Vienna, London, Prague and Copenhagen, before in the 1940s embarking on a less eminent career in America. From 1956 until his death he was Principal Conductor of the Sydney Symphony Orchestra in Australia. See *Diaries*, vol. 1, pp. 24, 27, 54, 70, 765; vol. 2, pp. 35, 109–10, 116–19, 137–41, 165, 692.
2 Renée de Saussine (1897–?) had a modest career as a violinist, but became better known as a biographer of Paganini. Her *Paganini le magicien* was published by Gallimard in 1938 and appeared in an English version by Marjorie Laurie, published by McGraw-Hill in New York in 1954.

Miss Crain and told her that I had tried to work on the condition myself but had not succeeded in getting any result. She was very pleased that I had gone to her: 'I myself was cured of a heart condition, and I know that you will be also.' She expressed one other interesting thought, almost a play on words: 'We are accustomed to think of the heart as the motor ("the motive") of the organism, and therefore it is important to control those elements ("the motives") that act upon the heart.'[1] She gave me a treatment. In connection with yesterday's visit to my mother's grave I asked her if praying for the deceased brought any benefit to them. She replied in the negative: the dead continue to develop in the life beyond the grave, but it is inappropriate for us to intervene in this development. At home, I asked the same question of Gorchakov: he, with his accustomed air of certainty, replied, 'Of course not.' But there is still something here I do not understand.

5 January

I took my test for the 'carte-rose' today, that is to say to acquire a driving licence. I was afraid I would not pass, because the truth is I have only just learned to drive a car and was understandably not confident; hence if all were to go smoothly I might have a good chance of passing, but the slightest unforeseen circumstance or nervousness could fluster me and make me do something stupid.

On my way to the test I reviewed it in my mind according to the principles of Christian Science: what exactly was I afraid of? A hostile examiner? But I ought to keep in mind that he also is a reflection of God, just as I am, and therefore there was no reason to fear him. And the moment I lose my fear of him I shall drive no worse than I did during my most recent lessons, and consequently I should pass. If, nevertheless, I do fail, it simply means that I am not yet a good enough driver, and God should be thanked that as such I am not allowed out on the busy Paris streets.

As it turned out, the examiner was quite a pleasant man. We started in one of the side streets off the avenue de la Grande Armée, and the first test was a rather hard one: I had to carry out a hill start and make a difficult turn, but while I was trying to do it another car appeared at speed and I had to give way to it. The examiner was most annoyed, but not at me, rather at the other car, who ought to have given way to me.

I executed a few more manoeuvres, answered three questions, and then bearing my coveted pink sheet went home beaming from ear to ear.

---

1 Prokofiev writes 'motive' both times in English.

6–12 January

At first my visit to Miss Crain yielded remarkable results and I started to feel much better as far as my heart was concerned. After a little while, however, I felt that the improvement had ceased; indeed I was feeling worse again, and went to see her a second and a third time. She asked me if there was anything else that made me feel unwell, and I mentioned my headaches. Miss Crain gave me the definition of God in *Science and Health* and said that there was no use in skimming through it quickly; I must meditate for several minutes on each word, mulling it over until I had fully comprehended each and every aspect of the definition. Then something enormous would gradually take shape before my eyes. And I must never forget that we are reflections of the divinity.

Our departure to Russia grows ever closer.

13 January[1]

Today is the day we leave for Russia. Not only that, but we are moving out of the flat on the rue Troyon and this means cleaning, checking the inventory, packing and general bustle, so that we worried that we would not manage to get everything done before the train left. One suitcase, newly purchased, turned out to be lacking its keys. Gorchakov, despite having been a Boy Scout, proved not to have the faintest idea how to tie up a single parcel even though he claimed to have been a specialist in knots in his scouting days. By the end we were well and truly in a rush. On the way to the station we collected various items we had previously left at the publishers': more

---

1 For the period of his first return visit to Russia, from 13 January to 25 March 1927, Prokofiev kept a fuller and more detailed diary than usual. As his son Oleg remarks in the Preface to the English-language edition of this part of his father's *Diaries* he published in collaboration with Christopher Palmer (*Sergei Prokofiev, Soviet Diary 1927 and Other Writings*, Faber and Faber, London, 1991): 'This [the entry for 25 February] indicates it was Prokofiev's intention to keep an unusually detailed diary right from the beginning of his visit to the Soviet Union, as if he considered this particular journey to be special and in a totally different category from his everyday itinerant life in the West. It seems more than likely that when he returned to Paris he sat down at his desk as soon as he could and began to type it in the very form in which it has come down to us after more than sixty years (with only a few corrections made in his own handwriting) . . . It seems he kept this diary separately from all the others, because when after his death all his papers were sent back to the USSR this was not among them.' Its existence came to light when Oleg Prokofiev discovered the manuscript of the *Soviet Diary* among the papers of his mother, Lina Prokofieva, after her death in London in January 1989. It was first published in Russian in 1990 by the Russian-language publishing firm Syntaxis and a year later by Sovietskii Kompozitor in Moscow, the same year as the Faber English edition. Oleg's supposition (he had not at that time had access to the notebooks of the complete *Diaries* in the RGALI State Archive in Moscow) that his father collated and himself typed out his notes immediately on return to Paris in March 1927 turns out not to have been correct: see below, pp. 657–8.

suitcases, pictures and so on, eventually getting to the station only ten minutes before the train was due to leave. Quite a lot of people were already there: the Borovskys, the Samoilenkos, Paichadze, etc. Our train was tremendously elegant, blue with gold decorations. It was one I had chosen on purpose, a gesture: no one must think of us as poor fugitives scuttling off to the land of the Bolsheviks. If we were going to the proletarians it must be aboard nothing less than the Nord-Express. Chocolates, delicious ones, were liberally proffered and we departed in high spirits.

Ptashka and had separate compartments with a connecting door between them. We would have slept very well if we had not been woken up at midnight at the German border. There was only a cursory examination of our belongings and passports, but when I mentioned that we also had a large trunk in the baggage car, the German official said there was no such object there, despite my having a clear memory of seeing it being loaded in. Events later proved that the good German was mistaken, but his information had a bad effect on our mood and on our sleep.

14 January

Berlin in the morning, with Weber and Tanya Rayevskaya[1] at the station. Sashka again failed to put in an appearance, but this time with the reasonable excuse of the 'flu, assuming he was not lying. Our first job was to order up keys for the suitcase we had bought in too much of a rush to check that it had any; otherwise we would not have been able to leave it safely in the left-luggage office, even allowing for German probity. Then the four of us had coffee in a big café on Unter den Linden, after which we went shopping, mainly for presents to take to Russia or for things we had been asked to bring – in short, everything we had not had time to obtain in Paris. I invited everyone plus Weber's wife to lunch at the Hotel Fürstenhof, then went to the publishing-house office to settle a slew of minor matters. My accounts for the year 1926 were not yet ready but there is apparently little prospect of them having improved significantly on the previous year. The kind of sevenfold leap I had in 1924–5 is obviously not going to be a pattern for every year. Stravinsky's sales have dropped, but this was to some extent balanced by bonus performance fees. From the publishers' office Ptashka went to the Webers' flat to practise, while I went to buy a fountain pen for Kucheryavy.[2]

---

1 Tatyana Rayevskaya was the widow of Prokofiev's cousin Andrey (Andryusha) Rayevsky, who had died of typhoid in 1920. Alexander (Sashka) was their son. Tanya and Sashka had escaped by ship across the Black Sea from Novorossiisk in southern Russia to the refugee island of Prinkipo (Princes' Island) in Turkey together with Prokofiev's mother in 1919. See *Diaries*, vol. 2, p. 494.
2 Nikolay Kucheryavy, Russian businessman who had befriended a penniless Prokofiev in New York and who had returned to live in the USSR. Ibid, pp. 351–582 *passim*.

At twenty to seven we left Berlin for Riga, accompanied to the station by the Webers. After dinner in the restaurant car we promptly retired to bed, tired out by all the rushing about we had done in Berlin, and probably by what had preceded it in Paris.

15 January

By morning we were in Eydtkuhnen, the former border town between Russia and Germany and now with Lithuania.[1] Here we changed from a luxury carriage into an ordinary one, cold and cheerless. One of the things I had managed to do in the rush before leaving Paris was have a new overcoat made, not – to the consternation of all – a fur, but since I had never worn fur coats when I lived in Russia I saw no reason why I should change the practice now.

Lithuanians are calm, courteous people who speak Russian as though their country was Russia, not Lithuania. The train crawled along; in the old days it was very different on this line. I was spotted in the restaurant car by Piotrovsky,[2] a tenor who had once been a fellow student of mine at the Conservatoire. He turns out to be actually a Lithuanian, and because of that country's generally impoverished level of musical life has become its leading musician. As a matter of fact he sings quite well and for a tenor is very musical. He formed an opera company in Kovno, where there had been none previously, and his fame spread not only all over Lithuania but as far as other provincial capitals such as Riga and Revel.[3] Now on his way to Riga he was friendly and enjoyed reminiscing about his time in Russia. He has been invited back to Leningrad but is fearful of going: the Lithuanian government is moving politically to the right and recently rearrested several Bolsheviks, consequently prominent Lithuanians are being advised not to enter Russia in case they are taken as hostages.

The day dragged slowly on, the train moving as sluggishly as ever through the white, snowbound landscape. I asked Piotrovsky why our train was so

---

1   The town is now called Chernyshevskoye, having been incorporated into the Soviet Union as a result of the implementation of the Oder–Neisse line following the Second World War. As it is the end of the old Prussian Eastern Railway, the gauge changes at this point from the European narrow gauge to the Russian wide gauge, necessitating a change of trains.
2   Kipras Piotrovsky (Petrauskas) (1885–1968), Lithuanian-born lyric-dramatic tenor, one of the founders of the Lithuanian State Opera Theatre in Vilnius. After the Second World War, when Lithuania became part of the Soviet Union, Piotrovsky was made a People's Artist of the USSR. When *The Gambler* was being considered for production by the Mariinsky Theatre in 1916, the conductor Albert Coates had suggested Piotrovsky for the role of Alexey, but Prokofiev preferred Ivan Alchevsky. The planned production, of course, did not take place, a casualty of the Revolution. See *Diaries*, vol. 2, p. 112.
3   Now Tallinn, capital of Estonia.

snail-like, and his philosophical explanation was: 'Well, you see, it's a small country. The slower we travel across it, the bigger it seems.' On top of this the train decided to be about two hours late, so by the time we eventually arrived in Riga it was half past eleven at night. Mayevsky[1] was there at the station to meet us along with the two concert managers who had engaged me. It was a great pleasure to sit in a sleigh; I cannot remember the last time I did so. Mayevsky affected to be my dearest friend and evidently saw himself as my host, since it was through his efforts I had come to Riga. His two manager associates proved to be amiable Latvians who gave us supper and treated us to vodka out of a teapot – because spirits are forbidden in Latvia on Saturdays, to discourage people being drunk on Sundays.

16 January

In the morning I gave interviews to three journalists, two Latvian and one Russian. Towards the end of the session Ptashka emerged looking most attractive in a light blue dress, and she also answered questions. Then we had our photos taken against the background of the Riga Opera House and in front of the poster advertising our concert, Ptashka's leopard-skin coat standing out in a splendid splash of colour. Shubert, my former classmate in Anna Yesipova's class,[2] turned up. It seems he is a Latvian national, and today the foremost figure in the world of Latvian music, much more important than Piotrovsky by virtue of Lithuania being beside Latvia a mere smudge on the landscape. Shubert managed to get himself appointed a director of the Riga Opera and is now Inspector of the Conservatoire. I could not stop laughing when I looked at him: Pavlusha Shubert, whose main pleasure in life was playing chemin-de-fer, boozing in restaurants and other indulgences, whom no one would dream of taking seriously, now an Inspector of irreproachable respectability in a magnificent morning-coat, the solidest of citizens and not a little conscious of his position. He responded with grave formality to my cackling, but later showed that at heart he had remained a good fellow.

We went for a walk round the town which, if short of the grandeur befitting a capital city, is still not a bad place. It was cold, and the air carried the scent of cold snow sometimes with the admixture of dung, since there are no cars here and all traffic is horse-drawn. This mixture of smells brought back from the distant past pleasant memories of winter in St Petersburg. I have a good memory for smells, and sometimes they can conjure up entire pictures for me.

At two o'clock we went to Mayevsky's for lunch. His sense of himself as the hero of the hour and my special friend from the cradle onwards was unabated,

1   See above pp. 346–7.
2   Pavel Shubert, pianist. See *Diaries*, vol. 1, pp. 113, 151–2, 157, 162, 186, 224.

even though we met infrequently at the Conservatoire and not at all thereafter. As well as Shubert Kreisler also came, a good fellow with whom I had always got on well; we had addressed each other in the intimate second person singular since we were in the conducting class together.[1] Having fled Russia, where apparently he left behind a substantial fortune, it took him a long time to get on his feet and even once wrote to me in Ettal to ask my advice and help, but at the time I could do nothing for him. The situation was not helped by my recollection that he was as bad a conductor as he was nice as a person. He is now married to a woman much older than himself and seems more or less settled materially, but not artistically or indeed domestically. After the meal Ptashka and I went to rehearse for our programme.

In Mayevsky's house I saw a portrait of Myaskovsky. Myaskovsky always disliked being photographed and I had only ever seen one portrait of him before, an impromptu snapshot by Derzhanovsky subsequently enlarged, which was in fact a very good likeness. The picture Mayevsky now showed me was probably only the second ever taken in his life. I was astonished by the change in him: a bored expression, a heaviness about the eyes, and instead of a jacket he was wearing a sort of tunic buttoned up to the chin. I hoped it was one of those photographs taken at the wrong moment.

In the evening I was invited to *May Night*[2] at the Opera. It was curious to hear the no more than half-remembered music sung in Latvian. I was overcome by a rush of youthful memories of the production of the opera when I was at the Conservatoire, especially during the enchanting first act. Act Three, however, is silly and boring: the denouement of the plot was beyond the powers of the librettist at the time.[3] Still, it was not a bad production and the big chorus scenes were enjoyably spirited. The reason for this is that many fine singers have left Russia, and this has raised the general level of the local theatre. The Director, Reuter, came to greet me during the interval: he had at one time been a student of our conducting class, but he is evidently younger than I and I barely remember him. Nowadays, like Shubert, he takes great pains with his dress and is obviously well primed for the role of guardian of the future of Latvian music.

17 January

Ptashka did not feel well during the night, she slept badly and kept me awake. In the morning we booked our tickets for Moscow. After lunch we rehearsed

---

1 See *Diaries*, vol. 1, pp. 515–795 *passim*; vol. 2, pp. 34–5.
2 Opera by Rimsky-Korsakov, full of folk melodies. It was first performed at the Mariinsky Theatre in January 1880 and featured Stravinsky's father Fyodor in the bass role of the Village Headman.
3 Rimsky wrote his own libretto, based on the source, a short story by Gogol.

and tried to be avoid being side-tracked into the kind of social activities that had taken up much of yesterday. Our concert took place in the theatre where I had been the previous night. In the opinion of the managers it was a good house: 1,400 people, although they immediately added that about three hundred complimentary tickets had been distributed.

My performance was a little nervous. What has happened to my American detachment, which I had thought to be a permanent acquisition? The response to the Fifth Sonata was muted, to say the least, but I had not expected it to go down particularly well with the Rigans and had included it in the programme as a try-out before Moscow. The last part of the programme consisted of my short pieces including the March from *Oranges*, gavottes and other palatable morsels. These were vociferously received, with curtain calls and encores. Ptashka sang two groups of songs, but her voice did not sound strong because she was not feeling strong in herself. They were greeted with no more than polite, but decent, applause.

After the concert there was quite a crowd in the Artists' Room.

18 January

Next morning I was given my fee and changed it into roubles. Then I had a visit from a Jew who was passing through on his way from Moscow to America where he has various commissions to fulfil on behalf of organisations to set up connections in the music business. This at any rate is what he says. Other people say he is not telling the truth and just uses his cultural contacts as a cover to pursue his own little schemes. But he intrigued me: going as I am to Russia I wanted to know what sort of types are coming out of her. And this one was a quite remarkable specimen. He began by pulling out all his papers and laying them out in front of me so that I should know who he was. Could this be because he was, in fact, lying? What he wanted from me was a card of introduction to Vitol, the Director of the Conservatoire,[1] in gratitude for which he would undertake to fix things with the Soviet Consul, since I needed to be insured against any unpleasantnesses I might encounter at the border. According to him, the Consul was offended that I had not approached him myself.

In the evening Ptashka and I called on Anna Grigorievna Zherebtsova-Andreyeva, who was delighted with our visit and talked without stopping. She complimented Ptashka on her singing the previous evening, which raised the latter's spirits a little. After seeing her we returned to the hotel,

---

1 Jazeps Vitol (1863–1948), prolific composer, teacher and critic of distinctly conservative leanings, with whom (as Iosif Wihtol, the Russianised version of his name) Prokofiev had studied Theory at the St Petersburg Conservatoire. See *Diaries*, vol. 1, 61, 66, 68, 91, 149, 421, 592.

collected our things and went to the station, to enter Bolshevizia. Thoughts kept coming: should we perhaps forget about it and simply stay put? We could not be certain whether or not we would be allowed to return. And here we have a whole series of potential concert engagements, which in themselves would justify the trip to Latvia. However, such cowardly reflections were brushed aside and we arrived at the station, from which the train was due to depart at half past twelve at night. It was pleasant to see Russian carriages, although they were all third class and their interiors very dimly illuminated. Soviet Russia has no such thing as first class, in fact no classes at all; the only difference is between 'hard' and 'soft' coaches. The hard-class coaches retained the green livery of the old third class, while the second- and first-class carriages, designed as 'soft', had been painted yellow.

We boarded our soft coach. It was forbiddingly cold and gloomy, no carpets on the floor, and the washbasin in our compartment was boarded up. Our three managers turned up (they run the concert agency as a triumvirate), and despite the lateness of the hour had come to see us off. I had told all our other friends not to bother coming. The train jerked into motion and we got into our bunks in a slightly sombre mood. The Russian guard had put sheets on the beds but they were rough and the bunks themselves unyielding.

19 January

We did not get much sleep as we crossed the border early in the morning, first the Latvian side and then the Russian. Since our own basin was boarded up we had to resort to the communal toilet to wash, but the water in it was so icy our fingers froze. Customs at the Latvian border did not look at anything, and we had some coffee at the station. The thought returned: this was positively our last chance before it would be too late to turn back. Yes, it would have been humiliating, but if it had been a matter of life or death we could have accepted it.

While we were thus reflecting a tiny shunting engine was being attached to our train. It was a glorious, sunny day, without a cloud in the sky, and the thermometer standing at minus 12 Réamur.[1]

With such thoughts still in our minds we settled into the train and proceeded into the dread USSR. Crossing from the Latvian border to the Russian took about an hour. We passed the post marking the Latvian border, then a snow-filled ditch, the actual frontier, and then the train passed under

---

1 Minus 15° Celsius.

an arch with the words 'Proletarians of All Lands, Unite!' inscribed upon it. Beside the track stood a Russian soldier in a cloth helmet and a long greatcoat down to his heels. The train stopped to let him come on board and a moment later he was in our compartment taking away our passports.

Soon we arrived at Sebezh, the Russian Customs post, where a porter appeared and took our luggage. With our belongings piled high on the Customs table I enquired if a telegram had been received about the Prokofievs entering the country. It had, it was produced, and shed an agreeable light over the inspection, which was superficial, merely leafing over a few pages of some French books on music which I was bringing for Asafyev. The big trunk and the bag of reeds for Persimfans were to go straight to Moscow. I still had to sign a document stating how many items of luggage we were taking with us. They were at a loss to understand what pyjamas were and what Ptashka's nightdress could be. But on the whole they behaved politely, even to a Jewish woman near us from whom they confiscated many items. Another lady had some children's shoes taken from her. This upset Ptashka and made her think of Svyatoslav. Once the inspection was over the porter brought our belongings back to our coach. On the wall was a notice stating that 25 copecks should be paid for each piece of luggage carried. Ptashka wanted to add a tip, but I loyally objected that in a Communist country, if a rate has been established, it would be wrong to give a tip, so I did not offer one.

It was noon and as there was an hour to wait until the train left again we went to have lunch in the station buffet. We studied with interest the people who came in, apparently station and Customs staff who wanted staff meals. Everyone looked healthy and relaxed, with an air of confident courtesy. Many of the visibly working-class customers took pains with their table manners and refrained from stupid chatter. After the meal I tried to buy some chocolate, but it was five times the pre-war cost and nothing like the quality. It may well be that they fleece you at a station on the border. We got back to our compartment and the train started.

All around, as far as the eye could see, was a blanket of snow, looking like delicious whipped cream up near the track. There was no restaurant car on the train, so whenever it stopped we made a dash to the buffet and bought sandwiches. We also bought a pile of Moscow newspapers; even though they were not particularly important stations the news stands had all the musical and arts journals. I looked to see if anything was being written about my arrival. Not much: the papers were mostly full of speeches by political leaders. But there was one reference to the organisation of a Prokofiev welcoming committee, including Asafyev as the Leningrad representative. Officialdom is my greatest dread, but it would be good if Asafyev were there: at least he will keep me right about how I should behave.

20 January

We woke early. Outside it was dark, inside too because the gas lamp was broken. We hardly noticed the approach to Moscow, but I believe we came in to the Alexandrovsky Station, which was wearing a somewhat homespun aspect. At half past seven the train, already well behind schedule, unexpectedly drew up at a wooden platform, and while we were calling out for a porter, of whom there was clearly a shortage, Tseitlin[1] and Tsukker[2] came into the carriage and behind them Derzhanovsky.[3] Tseitlin is the representative of Persimfans and its guiding spirit; he was formerly the leader of Koussevitzky's orchestra in Moscow. Tsukker, as I later learned, is an active and committed Communist. In his youth he had had ambitions to be a singer, and this had brought him into contact with music. He had taken a militant role in the Soviet Revolution, and is now some sort of secretary in the All-Union Executive Committee, which gives him access to all the members of the government. He is the only individual in the Persimfans organisation who is not a playing member of the orchestra; his responsibilities extend to planning programmes, giving radio talks

---

1   Lev Tseitlin (1881–1952), violinist, architect and leader of Persimfans, the conductorless Moscow orchestra that existed from 1922 until 1932. See p. 253.
2   Arnold Tsukker, party activist and administrator of Persimfans. Little is known about Tsukker's career before or after the less than flattering account given of him by Prokofiev on his first Soviet visit, except that he must have suffered the fate of so many true believers in the terrible years of the 1930s and 1940s because he fortuitously turns up in a prison memoir written by Dr Henry-Ralph Levenstein-Johnston, son of an American father who had been working before the Revolution in the Ukraine, and a Russian mother. In September 1941 Levenstein, by this time a qualified doctor, had been sentenced under the catch-all anti-Soviet articles of the RSFSR Penal Code Statute 58 to a total of seven years' imprisonment, during which he worked as a camp hospital doctor in the forced labour (mostly timber-felling) camps dotted about the remote Mari El Republic in the Russian Central European Plain. Among the prisoners he encountered was Arnold Tsukker, whom he describes as a frightened man avoiding personal contacts wherever possible and concerned only to keep out of trouble, serve his sentence and emerge alive, in which he appears to have succeeded. All this, of course, lay far in the future for the depressingly conformist zealot under whose watchful eye Prokofiev passed the two months of his first homecoming, but Levenstein's character sketch rings true. Levenstein himself was released at the end of his sentence in 1948 but exiled for life to the Mari-El Republic where he was eventually allowed to live in the capital city of Yoshkar-Ola. His fascinating memoir is one of an archive of 1,517 testimonies written by Gulag prisoners in the Andrey Sakharov Museum and Public Centre in Moscow.
3   Vladimir Derzhanovsky (1881–1942), music critic, editor, journalist and impresario, one of Prokofiev's earliest and most loyal supporters in Russia. He was behind the young composer's first appearance in Moscow, played an active part in persuading him to return for the 1927 visit, pressed for productions at the Bolshoy Theatre and generally stage-managed his engagements in Moscow. Derzhanovsky was a leading light in the Western-orientated Association for Contemporary Music (Assotsiatsiya Sovremmenoy Musyki, ASM), which eventually lost the battle for influence in contemporary music against the militantly populist Russian Association of Proletarian Musicians (RAPM). See *Diaries*, vol. 1, pp. 212, 522, 553–4, 587–90, and *passim*; vol. 2, pp. 34, 155, 157, 690, 695.

during concert broadcasts and, naturally, steering every aspect of the Persimfans agenda through government channels. Derzhanovsky does not seem to have altered much except that he has lost weight and is smaller. He was wearing felt boots, in fact all three of them were dressed in the strange hats and sheepskin coats that so alarm foreigners.

Greetings and exclamations – 'how unbelievable for Prokofiev to be here in Moscow!' – and then, having walked through the shabby little station, we tumbled into a taxi, of which there are not many but some at least in Moscow. The car windows were completely frozen over so we could not see much of the city as we went through it. Tse-Tse (Tseitlin and Tsukker) could not wait to tell us of the innumerable problems, hopes, fears and excitements created by our coming. They were falling over each other in their excitement to get the words out. Tsukker told us that Litvinov, no less, had given special authorisation for us to be issued with Soviet papers without our Nansen passports being confiscated. Naturally I wouldn't be arrested, but it would be advisable not to show the Nansen documents more than absolutely necessary.

We arrived at the Metropole. At the very beginning of the Soviet Revolution this hotel had been requisitioned for living accommodation for the staff of various Soviet institutions, but the decision had recently been taken that it would be more economical to transfer them elsewhere and to convert the building back into a hotel. However, it was proving difficult to decant all the personnel simultaneously into overcrowded Moscow, so for the time being only one floor has been cleaned up and restored to its original function, and this floor has been let to Germans to operate as a hotel. The upper floors were still inhabited by the organisations' staff members, in consequence of which everywhere was a frightful mess with the exception of our corridor, which has an excellent carpet, a good hairdressing salon and is generally clean. Our room had a spectacular view directly out onto Theatre Square, today known as Sverdlov Square.[1]

The room itself was spotlessly clean and spacious, with unusually high ceilings. The beds were in niches separated from the rest of the room by green plush curtains reaching almost to the ceiling. But there was no bathroom, and the water was in jugs. I ordered coffee for everyone and it was brought in glasses with silver holders. There was much to talk about, but the important thing was to get straight down to business, since the first

---

1 Since 1991 known as Theatre Square – Teatral'naya Ploshchad. The Metropole Hotel is situated on the square, one side of which is occupied by the Bolshoy Theatre. The pre-Revolutionary career of Yakov Sverdlov (1885–1919) included a long period of exile in Siberia alongside Stalin. Appointed Chairman of the Central Committee of the Russian Communist Party soon after the October Revolution, he played a major role in the murder of the Tsar and his family in Yekaterinburg, subsequently – until 1991 – named Sverdlovsk.

orchestral rehearsal is tomorrow morning. First of all I needed a piano in the room: I wanted to be in form for my first appearance in Moscow. There is a dearth of instruments in Russia: very few, if any, new ones are manufactured and it is impossible to get a licence to import one from abroad. Derzhanovsky suggested going to 'Kniga',[1] a shop selling printed music and books on music of which he is the Director; he thought I might get hold of a piano there.

Coffee over, we set out to go there. There were quite a lot of people out on the street. On the one hand there seemed to be plenty of fur collars, but on the other there were also plenty of women in headscarves. Reams have been written about how shocked visitors from abroad are by the poverty of people's clothing, but I cannot say that it shocked me, perhaps because so much noise has been made about it, or perhaps because there have always been large numbers both of headscarves and of sheepskin coats on Russian streets and therefore they were no surprise to me. Heading towards us we saw enormous omnibuses – the pride of Moscow. They are not only very big but very beautiful; although manufactured in England they have much better lines than London buses.

The 'Kniga' piano was no good as it was worn out. I met Lyolya[2] there; she now works as Derzhanovsky's secretary. And now for the first time I was brought up sharp against the length of time I have spent outside Russia: Lyolya had stayed in my memory as a plump thirteen-year-old girl, but here she is a tall young lady. It was lovely to see her again.

We continued to another shop, apparently the former Diederichs, which since nationalisation has become a state enterprise.[3] There was a quite new upright with a fairly stiff action, just what I need. I settled on it at once and it was delivered during the afternoon. Out on the street again it was cold and frosty, the crowds placid and benign. Can these really be the ravening beasts that have so terrified the world?

It was past one o'clock and we were hungry. Tse-Tse pointed us in the direction of the recently refurbished Bolshoy Moskovsky Hotel, and we went in to have lunch there while the others went on about their own affairs. The dining room was an enormous hall with hundreds of tables. It was noticeable that everything about the place has been done up new: clean but crude. We were practically the only people in this huge space, nobody in Moscow eats at two o'clock in the afternoon as they come in later, around three or four o'clock, but it is mainly in the evening that the room is full. Russia is the

---

1 Literally 'Book'.
2 Lyolya (Yelena) Zvyagintseva was the younger half-sister of Derzhanovsky's wife, the singer Yekaterina Koposova-Derzhanovskaya. See *Diaries*, vol. 1, pp. 589–90, 603, 637, 733; vol. 2, pp. 34, 172.
3 Prokofiev had had friendly contact with Andrey Diederichs of the piano manufacturers Diederichs Gebrüder before the Revolution. See *Diaries*, vol. 2, pp. 56, 224, 234, 271.

kingdom of caviar, but not here: the prices for fresh caviar in this restaurant were so huge that after studying the menu we thought better of it and passed on the caviar, the *à la carte* prices being no lower than in America. The *prix fixe* menu is available only later in the day. The waiters were civil and did accept tips. When the maître d'hôtel, resplendent in a dinner-jacket, put his hand on the table his fingernails were so glossily manicured the gleam from them lit up the whole table.

Coming out of the restaurant we decided we would like to walk round Moscow a little. While we had been rushing about in search of a piano Tse-Tse and Derzhanovsky had never let up on their merciless chatter, but now we found it interesting to saunter on our own about Moscow, this much feared city. We went on to Tverskaya Street, bought some pastries as we were expecting guests in the evening, and then went back to the Metropole. We did not want to walk for too long, because for someone as out of practice as we were it was very cold. Not long after we got in, Tseitlin arrived with a journalist and a photographer to interview me. While the journalist was still asking his questions, guests began to arrive. Every one of them was someone I very much wanted to see, but Tseitlin's journalist never drew breath and the situation became utterly ludicrous: I would be answering one of his questions when there would be a knock at the door which I would dash to open – hugs, cries of greeting, then back into the room to another question from the interviewer which I would have to think about in order not to say something stupid; then another knock at the door, and so on and so on. Asafyev appeared, looking a little fatter and in better health. Under his jacket, instead of a waistcoat, shirt and collar, he was wearing a brown knitted pullover with a collar right up to his chin, so no having to bother about a clean collar. He was followed by Myaskovsky, who all things considered had changed very little. It did not feel as though I had not seen him for ten years, and the photographer in Riga had either done a bad job or it had been an unfortunate moment. Myaskovsky was as refined as ever, and with the same charm. Perhaps there were a few more wrinkles on the face, barely noticeable except when he is tired, but when he is out in the fresh air they disappear. Evidently he found me much more changed than I him, for at first he simply looked at me for a long time, smiling, no doubt astonished at how fat and bald I have become.

Next Saradzhev came in, a little greyer but still a handsome presence and with an even closer resemblance to Nikisch than before. Besides Saradzhev there were also our companions from the morning, Derzhanovsky and Tsukker. The interview, thank God, finally came to an end and we asked the photographer to take a group picture of everyone present. Since film is expensive in Russia and he had been commissioned only to photograph the guest from abroad, at first he hesitated and was reluctant to accommodate us, but when Tsukker rounded on him and explained that gathered together in this one room were all the musical celebrities of Moscow he agreed, and his picture indeed served the needs of several newspapers.

General conversation proved to be sticky as everyone was simultaneously excited and ill at ease. Myaskovsky, Asafyev and Saradzhev buried themselves in my new scores: the Second Symphony, the Quintet and the *Overture for Seventeen Instruments*. 'But it's not so complicated after all!' exclaimed Saradzhev as he perused the score of the Second Symphony. He, rather than Persimfans, would dearly like to be given the opportunity to perform it,

Most of the party left soon afterwards, they were all busy people with things to do who had torn themselves away for a few moments to see me. Asafyev and Tsukker stayed the longest, but Asafyev, who had an engagement elsewhere, could not stay to join us for dinner, and when he had gone Tsukker took us to a restaurant on Prechistensky Boulevard, where he said the food was simpler, tastier and cheaper than in the Bolshoy Moskovsky.

Tsukker is an active and very devoted Communist. All the way there he regaled us with enthusiastic descriptions of the bountiful achievements of his party. It was indeed an interesting account and on an astronomical scale. I was fascinated to see the giant Comintern building, a sort of huge jar full of microbes waiting to be dispensed to the whole world.

The restaurant to which he took us was in a detached wooden building right in the middle of the Boulevard. Apparently in summer the tables sneak outside, and then it is sheer delight. Tsukker told us that the restaurant is run by 'former people' from rich merchant and aristocratic circles, and certainly we were served by charming, well-educated ladies. From the conversations between the cashier and the barmaid, and the instructions called down to the chefs toiling below in the basement, we could tell that that these were not common folk. The meal was uncommonly delicious: hazel-grouse, fabulous whipped cream, and altogether a whole selection of superb, virtually forgotten Russian delicacies. Tsukker would not hear of us paying.

After dinner we parted from him, got into a sleigh and were whirled home through the frost. As we got into bed we noticed that the sheets were of exceptionally fine linen such as we had never come across in any European or American hotel. The pillow-slips and towels were likewise top quality. We feel completely overwhelmed by Moscow, but I cannot get out of my head the extreme lengths I have been told the Bolsheviks go to in order to show off to foreign visitors. We shared our impressions in a whisper, not that we necessarily believed the stories repeated in émigré circles of microphones under the beds, but between our room and the one next door was a locked door behind which anyone who needed to could easily be listening. We fell asleep dog-tired.

21 January

We got up at half past seven. Tsukker called for us in a taxicab to go to the rehearsal in the Great Hall of the Conservatoire. Even though there are not a great number of cabs in Moscow, there are always some waiting in the square where our hotel is. They are all Renaults, evidently bought as a job lot in France.

As we came into the stage door of the Conservatoire I almost slipped and fell on the ice that was covering the whole floor of the vestibule. Tsukker said, 'See, Raisky[1] has been crying for joy at your arrival, and these are his tears that have frozen.' Raisky is in charge of the Bolshoy Zal and Director of Rosphil, the semi-governmental symphony organisation that is locked in deadly rivalry with Persimfans.

As we went up the staircase to the hall, Tsukker asked, 'Can you hear? They're playing a bit of *Three Oranges*.' I thought we must be late for the rehearsal and quickened my pace, at the same time informing Tsukker that the tempo was too slow and I would have to tell them to increase it. But then I realised that it was a sort of fanfare: the orchestra had been tipped off that I was arriving and was accompanying my entrance into the hall with the work of mine that had provided them with their greatest success.

At the conclusion of the March the orchestra applauded. I went up on to the stage. Tseitlin made a welcome speech about the joyful occasion of my being here in Moscow. Speeches always throw me into a panic, because I know I have to reply, but this time I plunged in head first and said what a joy it was for me to be in Moscow once again, especially in the presence of the orchestra I consider one of the best in the world. Applause, bows in all directions, and then we launched straight into a rehearsal of the Third Piano Concerto. Now it was not I who was nervous but the orchestra, as was obvious from their inability to maintain a steady tempo.

'Don't rush, comrades,' shouts Tseitlin. 'What are you worrying about?'

Tseitlin is more or less in charge of the rehearsal. On his first violin desk is not the first violin part but the full score, into which his neighbours also peer. Every now and again the second trombone will stand up, or the third horn, and say, 'Comrades, this bit ought to go like so . . .'

---

[1] Nazary Raisky (1875–1958), tenor, at this time Director of the Great Hall of the Moscow Conservatoire and of Rosphil (the Russian Philharmonic Society). Raisky had been a distinguished singer in his day, an outstanding Lensky for the Zimin Opera and partnered in recitals by such as Goldenweiser, Igumnov and Goedicke. He became an equally distinguished teacher at the Conservatoire, among his pupils being Lemeshev. He was also a good writer, publishing memoirs of Taneyev and Rachmaninoff.

Despite this the rehearsal proceeds productively and pleasantly. The orchestra has played the work twice before, once with Feinberg[1] as the soloist and on the other occasion a very young pianist, Oborin.[2] But this was a disadvantage, because both of them had adopted tempi very different from mine. Oborin's were actually not so very different, but Feinberg's playing was so neurotic and hysterical much of the piece was turned inside out. Where does he find hysteria in my Third Piano Concerto, I should like to know?

It takes longer, obviously, for an orchestra without a conductor to get to grips with a work than it would do with a conductor, but there are places where only a conductor can work out particular passages or make the voices clear by harrying the players. Here, by contrast, the players are conscientious enough to play the notes honestly as written; they faithfully observe all nuances as marked and do not waste rehearsal time learning their parts; if they are difficult to play they take them away and study them at home. But when you have, for instance, a *ritardando* which with a conductor would happen almost automatically, twenty minutes can be spent getting it right because everyone slows down at their own pace. An example of this was the transition from the end of the last variation to the recapitulation of the theme, in which the orchestra simply could not keep time with me. The problem was compounded by the fact that Feinberg had introduced a *ritardando* at this point which is not in the score, while I wanted an *accelerando*, which is not in the score either. Apparently this *rit.* had been the cause of an argument between Feinberg and Myaskovsky. When I later said to Myaskovsky that there was no case whatever for a *rit.* here, he was very pleased and exclaimed, 'I must tell Feinberg so!' But when I thought I would make him even happier by adding that I actually make an *accelerando* here, the pedantic Myaskovsky was indignant. 'I think that's rather excessive,' he said.

At the end of the rehearsal Ptashka, Tseitlin and I repaired to the Persimfans office, which is in the Conservatoire, one floor below where we

---

1 Samuel Feinberg (1890–1962), pianist and composer, having studied with Alexander Goldenweiser and Nikolay Zhilyayev respectively. Better known during his lifetime as a pianist, he nevertheless produced a substantial number of compositions including seven piano sonatas and two piano concertos. An interest in experimental and serial techniques was abruptly curtailed with the arrest and execution of his mentor Zhilyayev in 1932, after which he concentrated mainly on teaching.

2 Lev Oborin (1907–1974), pianist with a fine international reputation, notably in chamber music as the long-time sonata partner of David Oistrakh and trio partner of Oistrakh and the cellist Svyatoslav Knushevitsky. He was also a commanding solo performer, and later in 1927 was to win the Gold Medal at the 1927 Chopin Competition, in which Shostakovich was also a finalist. Oistrakh and Oborin gave the first performance of Prokofiev's Violin Sonata No. 1 in F minor in 1946, the first and third movements of which were played by Oistrakh with Feinberg at Prokofiev's funeral. (S. Morrison, *The People's Artist: Prokofiev's Soviet Years*, Oxford University Press, 2009, p. 278.)

were. 'Persimfans Office' sounds impressive, but in fact it is nothing more than a small room which also serves as living quarters for Tseitlin and his wife, who bed down behind a curtain. A million people crowded into it, with its two chairs and two tables piled high with papers and a constantly ringing telephone in the midst of the uproar – it was a madhouse. As soon as we had settled a few minor current problems we escaped with Tseitlin to the same restaurant on Prechistensky Boulevard as Tsukker had taken us to yesterday.

After lunch we strolled together to Okhotny Ryad, where he showed us shops in which we could buy caviar, cheese and butter. There were tons of caviar, at different prices, and the shops were full of people, so much so that we would not have had time to get to the end of the queue. We could not understand this at all: where was starving Moscow, then? True, today there were many more people out shopping than usual because it was a holiday – the anniversary of Lenin's death – and a Sunday.

'See how good life is here!' said Tseitlin triumphantly. 'Thank God you got out of Paris. All the papers are full of the shortage of coffins there.'

I was staggered. 'Coffins? What coffins?'

'Oh, come now. Anyone would think you hadn't just come from Paris. What about the influenza? The papers are saying there are so many deaths every day they don't know how they are going to bury them all.'

It was clear that in Moscow the lies about Paris are as inventive as those in Paris are about Moscow.

Taking us back to the Metropole, Tseitlin continued to expatiate: 'See the Bolshoy Theatre, there. Not long ago the front had to be refaced. They were so concerned about the aesthetic effect of the work that they wouldn't use new stone, which would have been out of keeping with the age of the building. The structural engineers went to a cemetery and found headstones of the right date, and now look at how well it has turned out. It's true, every word,' he went on, seeing the dumbstruck look of utter unbelief on my face.

Saying goodbye to Tseitlin we sat quietly in our room for a while, resting and marvelling at life in Moscow. Then, seeing that we were expecting some Persimfans people in the evening, we went out once more to buy some things: ham, pastries, and so on, from the huge co-operative store next to the Bolshoy Theatre. It was full of customers, but good order prevailed. There were lots of delicacies out on the counters which the assistants wrapped up for us in excellent paper, not stinting on the amount.

The entire Persimfans management team came in the evening – five people. We talked and drank tea with a few bites to eat, although they were terribly well behaved and ate hardly anything, I suppose out of shyness. We discussed tempi for *Chout* and the Suite from *Oranges*. We also had to decide the days on which I can go to Leningrad. Persimfans, needless to say, has grabbed all the best dates for itself, and as a result it will be two weeks before

I can go to Leningrad. They will be very offended. But Tse-Tse insisted that Khais,[1] in their opinion a contemptible character who is nevertheless very powerful in the Leningrad establishment, has shamefully exploited my reluctance to talk about my fee by setting it much lower than it ought to be. What is even worse, he has been rubbing a lot of people's noses in it by boasting about what a clever trick he has pulled. This brought us to the subject of my still unconfirmed conditions for working with Persimfans, but we did not get very far because it was getting late. Nor did we get round to some of the other propositions I am receiving, from the provinces. In any case it is too soon to be talking about the provinces.

22 January

Next morning Tsukker again called for us and we set off for the rehearsal, which was a learning session for *Chout*. They are proposing to play almost the whole suite, omitting only two of the numbers. For my taste this is already too long, but Tseitlin is very persistent and would really like to play all ten. The orchestra has good, well-balanced sound; the relationship of the instrumental sonorities is just what I want it to be, and if the initial pass does not produce exactly what is required then a single observation from me puts it right. Persimfans's critics claim that not having a conductor means they are unable to play a single chord together; chords are invariably arpeggiated as if played by a drunken hussar. That may be so, but at least each musician in the orchestra plays his notes scrupulously and as a result everything is played, and sounds, just as the composer intended. It is quite a different matter when you are saddled with those dreadful freelance extra players, who merely pretend to be playing their instruments but in fact leave out half their notes, bothering to play only when they have a passage that is absolutely obvious and they have no choice but to play it. The moment they accompany or play an inner part that might be heard or not as the case might be, they are all over the place. Inevitably the piece starts to sound much worse and the orchestration ends up being nothing like what the composer intended.

Feinberg attended the rehearsal. As I know that he plays my Third Concerto and that he would have come to listen with jealous ears to how I do it, I was a little ill at ease rehearsing this work.

The rehearsal over, Ptashka and I accompanied by Tse-Tse made our way to the usual restaurant on Prechistenki but on account of the holiday it was closed, so we retraced our steps and went back to our hotel. The Metropole does not yet have a restaurant, they serve only tea and coffee, but we had

---

1 Director of the Leningrad Philharmonia in succession to Klimov.

some tidbits in our room and were able to organise a light lunch in the course of which we discussed my Leningrad dates and how to dovetail them with the timetable for Moscow. While this was going on Lunacharsky[1] telephoned to greet my arrival and asked me to call on him at seven o'clock. Thanking him for the invitation, I said that I was due to dine with friends at five o'clock and therefore would not be able to come until eight. Lunacharsky said that would be quite convenient, and with that the conversation came to an end.

Soon afterwards Asafyev came round again and we went together to Myaskovsky's flat in Denezhny Lane. He lives in a large building overlooking a small garden or courtyard and therefore quiet. The flat had evidently been a good one in its day but now, as is the case with all apartments in Moscow, it is home to several families. Myaskovsky himself has just one room, and his sister Valentina Yakovlevna is in the adjoining one with her daughter. Myaskovsky's room is long and narrow, quite large but so stuffed with furniture that what with the bed, the washbasin, the grand piano, a large writing desk, several cupboards and shelves full of music, it is a problem even to turn round! Myaskovsky said that if he moves the piano the chair in front of the keyboard pushes up against the desk, and if he moves the desk the chair jams up against the piano. The only solution is to rearrange the furniture according to the specific needs of the moment.

We happened on Myaskovsky when he was correcting the proofs of his Seventh Symphony. Needless to say I was passionately interested to know what had happened to my trunk full of manuscript scores, letters and diaries that while the Revolution was going on I had given into Koussevitzky's safekeeping, whence it found its way into Muzsektor and eventually (at,

---

1 Anatoly Lunacharsky (1875–1933), the Soviet Union's first People's Commissar of Enlightenment (Narodnyi Kommissar Prosveshcheniya or Narkompros) responsible for all aspects of education and culture from 1918 until 1929. This was a portfolio in which he achieved extraordinary success, in particular a huge increase in literacy. Lunacharsky was that rare thing, an educated and civilised senior Soviet politician with a genuine appreciation of, and desire to support, the living traditions of Russian art. He was also a good writer, and his *Revolutionary Silhouettes* (*Revolyutsionnye Siluety*), pen-portraits originally written in 1919 of Lenin, Trotsky, Zinoviev, Plekhanov et al., but pointedly omitting any reference to Stalin, are still a pleasure to read. In 1918 Lunacharsky had been characteristically sympathetic to Prokofiev's request to leave the country for an implicitly assumed temporary absence, had arranged the necessary permission and had attended out of genuine interest a rehearsal of the *Classical* Symphony. See *Diaries*, vol. 2, pp. 260, 266–7, 270–72. Such a man and such a record could not be expected to survive Stalin's purges for ever; Lunacharsky was removed from his post in 1929. Although he survived the first wave of purges of Old Bolsheviks, he was demoted to the chairmanship of the USSR Science Council. He also worked as an editor on the *Soviet Encyclopaedia of Literature* and served as Soviet representative at the League of Nations, an organisation Stalin regarded with considerable suspicion. Later he was appointed Soviet Ambassador to Spain, often the prelude to recall, arrest and execution, but in December 1933 died in France on the way to taking up the post.

presumably, some personal risk) into Myaskovsky's own safekeeping.¹ From the letters he and I had exchanged I could not work out if this case had ever been unsealed and subjected to inspection, and was very afraid it might have been disembowelled at some point. To my great joy it was in perfect order and even the sealed packets of documents had not been opened. After all, during the Revolution, searches and inventories of possessions could and did happen to everyone.

I asked Myaskovsky what he thought I ought to do about Jurgenson. The point is that all Jurgenson's publishing assets have been nationalised, but this of course has force only within the borders of Russia. There was therefore the possibility that if he were prepared to sell back to me the rights for sales abroad, all those works I had originally ceded to him could be assigned to Gutheil.² Myaskovsky replied that this was a very delicate matter, since were it to become known that Jurgenson was trading in foreign rights he would be sent to prison, therefore arrangements could be made only in secret and only if Jurgenson were prepared to enter into discussions on a strictly confidential basis.

The three of us went outside and walked to Derzhanovsky's flat, not far away, where we had all been invited to dinner at five o'clock. I told them about Suvchinsky, how he spent his time, whom he had married, what sort of thing he was engaged upon, what Eurasianism was all about, but because this is a proscribed subject dropping my voice whenever passers-by were within earshot. Asafyev, moreover, observed that letters to and from Suvchinsky do go missing. The side streets along which we were walking, however, were fairly deserted and so we were able to talk freely.

When I paused for breath, Myaskovsky looked at me critically and said: 'Well, that's good, at least you don't seem to have forgotten your Russian.'

---

1   See *Diaries*, vol. 2, p. 225. Myaskovsky's day job was as an editor at Muzgiz (Gosudarstvennoye Muzykal'noye Izdatel'stvo), the State Music Publishing House that incorporated Prokofiev's former publishers P. Jurgenson following Lenin's decree on nationalisation of all private enterprises. Thereafter the firm was initially known by the acronym Gosmuzizdat, becoming Gosizdat Muzsektor (Music Division of the State Publishing Company) in 1922, and Muzgiz in 1930. From 1964 to 2006 it was known as Muzyka. In addition to the Moscow facility, branch offices operated in other Soviet cities, notably Leningrad and Kiev. From 1918 until the 1930s, the State enterprise frequently reprinted items that had been issued originally by Russian publishers Jurgenson, Belaieff, Gutheil and others, often retaining the original plate numbers. In 1956, due to the heavy production schedule at Muzgiz, whose resources were then directed towards the complete editions of Tchaikovsky, Glinka, Rimsky-Korsakov and numerous folk-music projects, the Soviet Composers' Union established its own publishing enterprise, Sovietski Kompozitor, to publish new works. Sovietski Kompozitor was later incorporated into Muzgiz as part of the 1964 reorganisation, but regained its semi-independence three years later because of continuing delays. In 2004 Musgiz was privatised and reverted to the name of P. Jurgenson.
2   See, for the history of Prokofiev's not always harmonious relations with the publishing house of Jurgenson, *Diaries*, vol. 2, pp. 31–2, 33–4, 55, 66, 72, 74, 75, 92.

This touched a raw nerve and I reacted with some heat: 'And what on earth makes you think I might have forgotten it?'

Myaskovsky: 'Well, when I was in Vienna I met Sashenka Tcherepnin, and what he said was so larded with Gallicisms I could hardly understand a word' – and to illustrate his point Myaskovsky produced some examples which I must admit were rather amusing. After that I paid more attention to how I spoke and this of course made my speech stumble.

We found Ptashka at Derzhanovsky's. Our host had gone to collect her himself and was clearly begining to flirt with her. Hardly had we finished the meal when Tsukker appeared and took her off to the Bolshoy for the performance of *Sadko*. I promised to come later if I was not kept too long by the Commissar of Enlightenment. I made the acquaintance of Lyolya's husband, a rather pleasant, quiet young man, smaller than his wife and to all appearances thoroughly under her thumb.

After dinner, therefore, well after seven o'clock, Myaskovsky, Asafyev and I walked together along the same silent, frozen streets as we had come, back to Myaskovsky's apartment at No. 7, Denezhny Lane. Lunacharsky's house was a few houses further on, and Asafyev, who had visited him there before, volunteered to take me not just to the building but right to Lunacharsky's door. It was a large house, and clearly at one time had been very grand, but now the staircase we climbed to reach the upper floor was disgustingly dirty. The lift was out of order.

I rang the bell, and Asafyev went back down the stairs. The door was opened by a fat cook who asked my name and then went to announce me. She then asked me to wait in the sitting room, an enormous, reasonably comfortably furnished chamber. The door into the dining room next door was ajar, and through it I could hear someone reading poetry. After a few minutes the fat cook came back and asked me to go into the dining room. Lunacharsky came to greet me, affable as ever, but a little less trim than he had been in 1918.

About fifteen people were sitting round a small table. Some of them got up to greet me, but the poetry reading was not yet at an end and Lunacharsky gestured for silence and for me to sit down, asking the poet to continue.

The poet's name was Utkin,[1] and he went on reading for some considerable time. Having just arrived in the USSR and now, moreover, present at a gathering hosted by no less a personage than the Commissar of Enlightenment,

---

1 Iosif Utkin (1903–1944), poet and journalist (mainly for *Komsomolskaya Pravda*). He had served as a partisan during the Kolchak era in his home town of Irkutsk and later as a volunteer in the Far East front, and much of his verse had a military flavour and was popular with soldiers. In the Second World War he immediately volunteered for the front and was badly wounded but insisted on going back. He was killed in 1944 when the aircraft in which he was returning from the front crashed.

I naturally expected the poetry being read to contain above all Revolutionary fervour, but this was conceptually and in subject-matter quite innocuous stuff, tending more towards decadence than joyful celebration of proletarian values. Finally Utkin stopped, and I was introduced to all those present, among whom were some half-remembered faces from the pre-Revolutionary arts world. Lunacharsky's wife, rather the most recent of his wives, is a beautiful woman, at least when seen from the front; her predatory-looking profile rather less so. She is an actress whose name is Rozenel.[1]

We repaired to the sitting room, where several young people came up to me and showered me with compliments. Lunacharsky does most of the talking, seldom allowing his interlocutor to get a word in edgeways. He had some pleasant news for me: next spring an international competition has been proposed in Paris between theatre companies of different lands. Four countries have already signed up, including the USSR, and their secret weapon could be *The Love for Three Oranges*. The choice has not yet been finally decided, but the wheels are in motion. I was surrounded by several young poets and musicians who wanted to talk about my compositions and asked me to play. I sat down at a somewhat indifferent piano and played the March from *Oranges*. Lunacharsky then invited one of the pianists present to play the finale from my Second Sonata, which he, Lunacharsky, declared was his favourite piece of music. The pianist complied, and played it rather badly. After this we moved to yet another, smaller, room, quite comfortably furnished. Lunacharsky produced the first issue of a new journal published by Mayakovsky, *LEF*,[2] which title he explained stood for 'Left Front', adding that Mayakovsky regarded me as an exemplar of *LEF*'s standpoint. 'So,' he

---

1   Natalya Rozenel (1900–1962), actress in the Maly Theatre and in silent films. In 1962 she published a very good memoir, *Memory of the Heart* (*Pamyat Serdtsa*) about her life in Soviet theatre and the many literary and theatrical leading lights she encountered, among them Bryusov, Mayakovsky, Mardzhanov, Yuzhin, Brecht and many others.
2   It was in fact *Novy LEF*. The original *LEF*, the journal of the *Levy Front Isskustv* ('Left Front of the Arts'), began publication in 1923 and was edited by Mayakovsky and Osip Brik with cover designs by Rodchenko. The magazine's declared aim was 'to abandon individualism and increase the value of art for developing communism'. It ceased publication in 1925 after seven issues, riven by internal criticism from its own extreme radical wing of the 'literary trash, trapped in the cage of the old, everyday, banal, life' allegedly favoured by its editors and many of its writers including Isaak Babel, Yury Tynyanov and the Formalist critic Viktor Shklovsky. In 1927 Mayakovsky had another go, reviving the magazine as *Novy LEF* ('New LEF'), his co-editor now being the playwright, screenwriter and photographer Sergey Tretyakov. Led by Tretyakov, *Novy LEF* had a new, utilitarian cultural synthesis to promote: 'Factography', the notion of 'Production Art', art that rather than aiming for realism actively tries to intervene and transform reality. 'If facts destroy theory, so much the better for theory,' said Shklovsky. *Novy LEF* was, sadly, to be no longer lived than its predecessor, foundering on the implacable rocks of Socialist Realism and ceasing publication in 1929. Mayakovsky tried one last time to establish *REF* ('Revolutionary Front') but the tide had, for the time being, turned and it was stillborn. The short lives of *LEF* and *Novy LEF* had a profound influence on design, film and architecture, an influence that still resonates today.

went on, 'it would be very salutary for you to read Mayakovsky's Address, which appears in this issue.' He then proceeded to read, with considerable skill and passion, Mayakovsky's letter in verse addressed to Gorky. This is certainly not lacking in bite, and some turns of phrase are truly choice. The message is: why, Alexey Maximovich, are you still living in Italy when there is so much to be done in Russia? The application to myself could hardly be clearer, and when Lunacharsky finished the reading he laughingly recommended me to take the poem to heart. I asked him what status Mayakovsky currently enjoys in literary circles. Lunacharsky replied that it stood very high, although there are some who like the thought of rattling *LEF*'s cage and holding it up to ridicule.

I then had some more conversation with Rozenel, and at nine o'clock excused myself, saying that I still wanted to catch some of the performance at the Bolshoy Theatre. Everyone came out with me into the hall, and one of Yavorsky's young students took me to the theatre in a hired sleigh. 'We are jealous of the world outside Russia having you,' he said as we drove through the side streets. But the frost outside was terrible, and although I tried to say something in reply, I in my Parisian coat without a fur collar was more worried about protecting my ears from frostbite.

In the Bolshoy Theatre I was conducted to a box in the dress circle occupied by Ptashka and Tsukker. This is the box next to the Tsar's in the middle of the circle, and is usually reserved for the management. The theatre was full, although the audience seemed for the most part to be drably dressed. I thoroughly enjoyed the scene in which Sadko pushes out from the shore in his boat; the music is so extraordinarily beautiful, but a lot of the staging was inept. Some parts of the underwater fantasy, which in their day probably seemed revelatory, are in any case now stale and represent little but boring expanses too seldom relieved by any real music.

During the interval, also from time to time during the action, the Bolshoy's conductors came into the box: Golovanov,[1] followed by Pazovsky.[2] They

---

[1] Nikolay Golovanov (1881–1953), conductor, had been conducting at the Bolshoy Theatre since 1915 and was appointed Principal Conductor in 1919, a position he held until 1928 contemporaneously with the Music Directorship of the Moscow Philharmonic Orchestra and a conducting class at the Moscow Conservatoire. He continued to conduct some performances at the Bolshoy, and in 1937 was offered the position of Principal Conductor and Artistic Director of the Bolshoy (i.e. 'large', not the eponymous theatre) All-Union Radio Symphony Orchestra, returning to his old job at the Bolshoy Theatre from 1948 until his death in 1953. His wife was the outstanding lyric coloratura soprano Antonina Nezhdanova, and being a fine pianist he often accompanied her recitals.

[2] Ari Pazovsky (1887–1953), violinist and opera conductor, honed his conducting skills with the Zimin Private Opera Company in Moscow and came to the Bolshoy Theatre in 1925 for a three-year spell before taking Artistic Director posts at the opera houses of Kiev, Kharkov, Baku, Sverdlovsk and eventually in 1936 the Kirov Theatre in Leningrad, returning to the Bolshoy as Principal Conductor and Artistic Director in 1943.

wanted to talk about the production of *Oranges* which, evidently, is planned for the end of the season. Golovanov is to conduct it, and he asked me if, as soon as my initial concerts are over and done with, perhaps in a week's time, I would play the opera through to him so that I could indicate my tempi and other preferences. Talking later to Pazovsky, I could not get out of my head the memory of a phrase once written by Kankarovich[1] nearly fifteen years ago when, as a newly fledged critic, he was inveighing against my First Piano Concerto. In support of his views he quoted the comment of a conductor, one Pazovsky, who was, so he said, sitting beside him at the performance: 'Reminds me of a cretin[2] chasing about.' Who precisely this conductor Pazovsky was I had not known until today, but now that he was talking ever so ingratiatingly to me this 'cretin dashing about' kept reverberating in my head.

23 January

The whole morning went on rehearsal, in the course of which I stopped the orchestra quite often to give instructions on tempi and orchestral balance.

Glière[3] came to listen, my old teacher. We still keep up our conversational conventions of twenty-five years ago when I was a child: I call him 'you' and address him as 'Reinhold Moritsevich', he calls me 'thou' and 'Seryozha'. Glière has grown stout and middle-aged, with the glossy air of a well-nourished cat. Although he must be nearing sixty, he talked a lot about his

---

1 Anatoly Kankarovich (1885–1956), violinist and conductor, had been a fellow conducting student of Prokofiev in Tcherepnin's class at the St Petersburg Conservatoire and had helped him to master some basic techniques. His postgraduate studies were with Nikisch in Leipzig and Mengelberg in Amsterdam. Kankarovich's professional career never quite rose to the expected heights and he never occupied a prominent music director position but as well as writing music criticism for various journals he worked consistently in the second-string houses of the capital and a number of provincial theatres such as Voronezh and Simferopol. See *Diaries*, vol. 1, pp. 5–159 *passim*, 127–8, 208, 436.
2 The word Pazovsky actually used was 'Durashkin'. Durashkin is a real surname, perhaps an unfortunate one as 'durak' in Russian means a fool. The inference is quite clear, however: the silent-comedy films of the French-born actor André Deed were extremely popular in Russia in the early years of the twentieth century. Most were made in Italy and featured the misadventures of the hero (Deed himself), who went by the name of Cretinetti. In England he was known as 'Foolshead', in Russia 'Glupyshkin' ('stupid fellow') or 'Durashkin'.
3 Reinhold Glière (1875–1956), prolific composer and educator of, among others – at the suggestion of Taneyev – the very young Prokofiev, over two extended summer visits to the family home in Sontsovka, Ukraine. As is clear from the composer's two autobiographical essays and from later references in the *Diaries* (which began after the time with Glière), Prokofiev absorbed much valuable training and also enjoyed his senior colleague's company, but increasingly began to see the limitations of his musical horizons. Glière was, nevertheless, an extremely successful composer and during the Soviet era many of his works were core repertoire, notably the programme symphony *Ilya Muromets* and the ballet *The Red Poppy*.

piano practising and about having discovered a wonderful new system for identifying the specific muscles in the back that affect the fingers, which he insisted on demonstrating on my back. It has enabled him, he says, to make great progress. He has toured all over Russia with a singer, accompanying her by heart in full-length programmes of his own songs, an idea he would like to extend to Germany. In which case, pity the poor Germans, not to mention poor Glière. I talked to him about Dukelsky, another of his pupils, and told him that sometimes when we were out walking we amused ourselves by humming the themes from his First and Second Symphonies, recalling our youth.

At this point I was needed on stage, as the main task for today was to learn the Variations and Finale of the Third Piano Concerto. Then in the afternoon I needed a rest from all the demands of life in Moscow, which are beginning to exhaust me even though I know we have hardly started yet.

After my rest I went to look at a Bechstein piano for tomorrow's concert. Despite the general dearth of decent instruments in Soviet Russia this proved to be a superb Bechstein, but to get hold of it Tseitlin had to engage in a war to the death with the administration of the Conservatoire, to whom it belongs and who jealously guard it as the apple of their eye. Raisky and Igumnov were against letting it be used. For Raisky this is understandable, but surely Igumnov is one of my admirers? In the end Tseitlin contrived to get round their objections and they agreed to let us have it, for fifty roubles a concert, apparently.

Ptashka and I went to Nadya Rayevskaya[1] at No. 5, Arbat. As Shurik is in prison for 'political unreliability', our visit felt like an illegal act. Suppose we had a detective on our tail, following us in another cab? Or perhaps there would be a policeman keeping watch on their door, aware that these are my relatives and wanting to see whether I am making contact with counter-revolutionary elements? Just in case, we stopped the cab some distance away from the actual building and swiftly sneaked in through the gates, conveniently ignoring the fact that Ptashka's leopard-skin coat was such an eyeful that, once seen, no one was likely to forget it. Our friends could recall only one other remotely similar in Moscow, and that belongs to Nezhdanova.

The Rayevsky family occupies an apartment on the courtyard consisting of four ground-floor rooms gained through an inevitably filthy entrance.

---

1 Nadezhda Rayevskaya, née Meindorf (Nadya) was the wife of Prokofiev's cousin Alexander (Shurik) Rayevsky. In 1929 she herself would be sent to the Belomor Canal labour concentration camp – the first major project constructed in the Soviet Union using forced labour, in which an estimated 100,000 prisoners died – and not released until 1933, two years after Shurik was finally released.

There we met Katyusha Uvarova,¹ whom I remember as a pretty fifteen-year-old girl but who is now a solidly built, coarse-grained woman coming up to thirty. She greeted me with joy, but when I introduced her to Ptashka she assumed that she would not understand Russian, extended her hand and said, 'Charmée.' I almost burst out laughing, thinking of the Babulenka in *The Gambler*, and had to explain that my wife speaks Russian like a native. Nadya was not in, but her three daughters appeared, aged between three and twelve, nice girls but rather sickly-looking and not particularly pretty, distinctly undersized for their age.² I hastily explained to Katya Uvarova in an undertone that because we were in a rush we would not be able to wait for Nadya to come back, but that I very much wanted to arrange permission for Aunt Katya and Katya Ignatieva to travel from Penza and that I could pay for this. Furthermore, I said, provided I maintain good relations with the authorities I intended to take steps to secure Shurik's release, but this is not something that can be hurried. In short, I did my best to blurt out everything relevant to the family and bring them completely up to date, seeing that it was probably inadvisable for us to be visiting them too often.

As we said goodbye and were on our way out we bumped into Nadya. She seemed extravagantly pleased to see us, but at the time her joy struck me as slightly forced. Years of hardship have left their mark on her, and she bore an uncanny resemblance to the Empress Alexandra Fyodorovna. Shurik is manfully serving his ten-year prison sentence, which has been reduced by one-third. All kinds of people are in gaol, both criminals and political prisoners, the latter being mainly people of a similar background to Shurik's, and they stick together in prison. Shurik works in the cobbler's shop and also plays the piano for film shows. I started to explain to Nadya what I had already told Katya Uvarova, but stopped when a man came into the flat, dressed like a *muzhik* in felt boots and a hat with ear-flaps. This garb was sharply at odds with his refined, handsome features and the tinge of grey in his beard. Seeing my discomfiture Nadya said, 'It's fine, this is my sister's husband, Lopukhin. You can say anything in front of him.'

We soon made our farewells and made a second exit, as we were in a hurry to get to Derzhanovsky's where Mme Derzhanovskaya³ is today celebrating her fiftieth birthday. This is a bold step for a woman to take, even though unkind tongues say that the only reason she is doing it is that otherwise everyone would take her for sixty.

---

1 A family friend of the Rayevskys.
2 Katya, Alyona and Sonya.
3 The singer Yekaterina Koposova-Derzhanovskaya.

At the party were Myaskovsky, Asafyev, Alexandrov,[1] Feinberg, Polovinkin,[2] Knipper,[3] Kryukov,[4] Mosolov[5] and a few others. Almost all of them had studied with Myaskovsky and naturally were under his spell. I worked out which was Feinberg straight away – his face is quite unlike anyone else's – but I had no recollection whatever of the quiet, unremarkable-looking Alexandrov. The

1 Anatoly Alexandrov (1888–1982), pianist, composer and teacher. He studied composition with Zhilyayev and Taneyev, and piano with Igumnov at the Moscow Conservatoire. He wrote two symphonies, several string quartets and a piano concerto, but his fourteen piano sonatas, showing the clear influence of Scriabin and Medtner, are his major contribution to the repertoire. Not to be confused with Alexander Alexandrov, founder of the Alexandrov Ensemble (later the Red Army Song and Dance Ensemble) and composer of the Soviet National Anthem.
2 Leonid Polovinkin (1894–1949), composer who studied with Myaskovsky and in the 1920s was in the forefront of the avant-garde with Mosolov, the pre-emigration Lourié and Vyshnegradsky, etc. Later he simplified his style and shortly after this encounter joined Natalya Sats's Moscow Central Children's Theatre as its Music Director. The children's pieces he refers to seem to be *Six Pieces for Piano* (1927–9). Polovinkin continued to compose music for children as did, of course, Prokofiev, most notably *Peter and the Wolf* for Natalya Sats's theatre company and the twelve pieces of *Music for Children* (*Detskaya Muzyka*), Op. 65, of 1934.
3 Lev Knipper (1898–1974), from a talented family whose members have a more than usually persistent whiff of compromise about them, beginning with his aunt, the Moscow Arts Theatre actress Olga Knipper-Chekhova, widow of Anton, whose devotion to her dying husband is seen by biographers perhaps unfairly as less than unimpeachable. Lev's elder sister, also Olga, sometime wife of the actor and director Mikhail (Michael) Chekhov and therefore also Olga Chekhova, is revealed by Antony Beevor in *The Mystery of Olga Chekhova* (Penguin, London, 2004) as a Soviet spy at the court of Hitler and Goebbels, while Lev himself was a rehabilitated White Guardist, recruited by OGPU while in exile with Baron Wrangel's defeated White Army in 1922 and turned into an active agent for OGPU and the NKVD. A student of Glière, as a composer (rather like his teacher) he was extremely prolific, turning out five operas, twenty symphonies and a quantity of smaller works. He wrote at least one memorable hit tune, from the Fourth Symphony of 1934: 'Polyushko-Pole', which became virtually the anthem of General Alexandrov's Red Army Choir and entertained audiences all over the world with its swaying ranks of bemedalled, barrel-chested singers quietly intoning its lilting march. Lev Knipper and his wife Masha were later to be close friends of Prokofiev's second wife, Mira Mendelson.
4 Vladimir Kryukov (1902–1960), composer who graduated from Myaskovsky's class in 1925. He also worked as a music producer for the radio. His younger brother Nikolay was likewise a composer who doubled as a sound engineer.
5 Alexander Mosolov (1900–1973), composer and pianist, studied piano with Igumnov and composition with Glière and with Myaskovsky, and on graduation from the Moscow Conservatoire was accepted into membership of the ASM. His early works were striking in their use of dissonance, polytonality, extreme chromaticism and thickly layered ostinati creating a machine-like effect, most famously in *Iron Foundry* (*Zavod*, meaning 'Factory'), projected as the first movement of a ballet to be entitled *Steel*, which the ASM were to premiere at the end of 1927. (It is uncanny that Prokofiev, slightly earlier but in the different world of cosmopolitan Paris, should himself have been prompted by Diaghilev to address the same subject in the ballet which became *Le Pas d'acier* (*The Steel Step*) although its original, rejected, title was the less industrial literary in-joke *Ursignol*.) Initially praised for his 'mighty hymn to machine work', Mosolov's aesthetic as early as 1929 began to founder on the rocks of the rising doctrine of Socialist Realism and by 1932 he was reduced to writing a forlornly intemperate personal plea to Stalin to allow him to compose and publish: 'Either put pressure on the troglodytes in the Russian Association of Proletarian Musicians to end their persecution of me, which has been going on for a year now, and allow me to work in the USSR, or permit me to go abroad, where through my music I can be of greater service to the USSR than I can be here where

most talented of the younger ones seems to be Mosolov, whose compositions are said to be complex. He is quite handsome, not so his wife, who appears to be older than he is. She is, nevertheless, regarded as a notable pianist, although this reputation is based on a recital she gave of contemporary sonatas – but *what* sonatas! Myaskovsky's, one of mine, her husband's, some late Scriabin, and some other edifices of equally convoluted construction.

A little later Feinberg was asked to play, in response to which he gave us his *Improvisations*, a set of complicated but essentially empty pieces. The way he plays is unbelievable: he displays every emotion, breathes stertorously through his nose and bends right over the keyboard, so painful is the effort to draw every note out of himself. He doesn't so much play as suffer. His listeners were made to feel positively uncomfortable at having forced him to undergo such torture. Then I was asked to play, and of course I played the Fifth Sonata. If I could not play it here, where would I be able to? My listeners were silent and very attentive, but no one had an opinion to express. Another request followed, and I played the Third Sonata, after which I went into the next room where Asafyev was sitting. He observed that I had played it quite differently from the way I used to before leaving Russia for America in 1918. Thanks to this he had lost a bet with someone because my current tempo was very far from what he had been insisting it would be. He also reminded me that formerly I had played the transition to the second subject in a way he liked better, introducing a pause in the bass before the theme begins. I agreed with him and promised to restore the pause in future.

Lyolya and Mme Derzhanovskaya were laying the table for supper while we were out of the way in the room referred to as 'Tsekubu', which stands for 'Tsentral'ny Komitet Uluchsheniya Byta Uchonykh', the 'Central Committee for the Improvement of Scholars' Living Conditions'. This was Derzhanovsky's ruse whereby he had managed to secure the whole flat for himself and his family (except for one room which was given over to the cook). As for the actual Tsekubu room it had proved, not surprisingly, to be redundant, and by rights someone ought to have moved into it, but Derzhanovsky appealed to the aforesaid Central Committee for the Improvement of Scholars' Living Conditions and managed to convince them that he needed a separate study in order to pursue his academic music work.

I am harried and persecuted and not permitted to display my powers or test myself.' Early in 1936 Mosolov was expelled from the Union of Composers, two years later arrested and convicted of counter-revolutionary activities and sentenced to eight years in the Gulag. Glière and Myaskovsky courageously interceded on his behalf, laying stress on his 'reform from previous errors' and got the sentence commuted to five years' exile from residence in capital cities, following which Mosolov's experience was a test case of the Soviet Union's progressive crushing of experimental avant-garde Modernism across the spectrum of the arts from the late 1920s on. See L. Sitsky, *Music of the Repressed Russian Avant-garde 1920–29*, Greenwood Press, Westport CT, 1994, pp. 60–83.

When we sat down to supper I found myself between Myaskovsky and Asafyev. In this household Myaskovsky has a permanent chair next to the hostess which no one else has the right to occupy. I was thunderstruck to hear him addressing Lyolya in the intimate second person singular, and asked her, 'Whatever did you do to seduce Kolechka?' I truly believe she is the first woman with whom he has even been on such terms.

To a man the young composers to a man paid court to Ptashka in every way they could, but Derzhanovsky outdid them all in persistence. Later in the meal champagne even appeared, a rare object indeed in Soviet Russia, but we escaped before the end of the evening because tomorrow is the general rehearsal and my first Moscow concert.

24 January

Even so we had been quite late getting home. Nevertheless, we had to get up at eight because the general rehearsal was due to start at nine. Golovanov was there, sitting with the score of *Chout* and pencilling into it the directions he heard me making to Persimfans. The Persimfantsy, who do not regard him as a friend, gossip maliciously that he has no idea how to conduct *Chout* and therefore has to write down how every bar goes. When it was time to rehearse the Third Piano Concerto the hall filled up with quite a lot of people who vanished again the moment I finished. The two Suites, from *Chout* and *Oranges*, went well, although an extra rehearsal would have done no harm.

In the afternoon we drove out with Tseitlin to the Customs depot because my trunk, the one that had not been examined at the border, had been detained by Customs in Moscow along with the bag of reeds for the Persinfans wind instruments. All the players are waiting anxiously for these reeds, since their old ones are completely worn out and goodness only knows what they have to blow into at present, because new ones are unobtainable in Russia. Tseitlin had, of course, taken care to arm himself with all the necessary authorisations and clearances, so in the event hardly any inspection took place, they merely opened the trunk and untied the bag as a formality. Nevertheless, when they spotted a silk skirt so old that Ptashka no longer wears it, that we had brought to give as a present to poor relatives, they immediately showed interest and began to give us a hard time, but eventually, seeing how ancient it was, relented and let us keep it.

We had lunch on our own at three o'clock in the Bolshaya Moskovskaya, although I hardly know whether it was lunch or dinner as all mealtimes hereabouts are mixed up and many people in Moscow eat their main repast in the middle of the afternoon, perhaps running two meals into one for the sake of economy. Meckler, a local impresario who had already left a couple of notes for me, was at the next table, with Polyakin,[1] a violinist who in his day had been a wunderkind in Auer's class at the same time as a very young Cecilia Hansen, but his lustre had gradually faded, ultimately to be eclipsed by the brilliance of her success. He had managed to get a foothold in America and to acquire American citizenship, but success having eluded him there, Meckler was now touring him round Russia. They made an immediate dive to come over and sit at our table, and Meckler went straight into the attack with a string of propositions. Sensing, however, my general lack of enthusiasm for the provinces and my reluctance to respond to his blandishments, he switched to Ptashka, thinking to dazzle her with his tales of all sorts of concert opportunities for her as a singer. In support of his credentials he name-dropped the 'world-renowned artist' Marchex whom he had also been touring in Russia and proposed to do so again. We guffawed at this and explained that Marchex was frankly a third-class pianist. But Meckler stuck to his guns and said, 'But, pardon me, you must admit that he is a real gentleman.' I said, 'It may well be he tries to present himself as an aristocrat, but in Paris he's a down-and-out.' Polyakin suddenly burst out laughing and exclaimed, 'A bum!' but then glanced at Ptashka, and lapsed into silence, abashed.

We finished our lunch before they did and were just going out down the staircase when who should pop up beside us but Meckler, offering to arrange concerts in the provinces at 350 roubles a time. By the time we were in the foyer of the hotel his offer had risen to 500, and when I emerged on to the street he was saying 1,500 a concert in Moscow and even 3,000 for two. I must admit that this last figure quite embarrassed me, but I could not help feeling some sympathy for such a sorry specimen as Meckler was showing himself to be, so as I said goodbye I asked him to telephone me in about a week's time, once the excitement of my first concerts had subsided.

Back at the hotel we rested before the concert. Seryozha Sebryakov[2] telephoned. Ptashka, not knowing who he was, rebuffed him, saying I would not take any calls before a concert. When she told me about it she said he seemed very upset at my refusal to speak to him, so I had to ring him back and ask him to come in before the concert, telling him we would take him in with us.

After resting we got dressed and went to the Great Hall of the Conservatoire for the concert. It was full and there were even some people standing although

---

1   Miron Polyakin (1895–1941). He had made his debut in St Petersburg at the age of fourteen, and launched a spectacular international career between 1917 and 1926, making his New York debut in 1922. He had returned to the USSR in 1926 and became a professor first at the Leningrad and later the Moscow Conservatoires.
2   Sergey (Seryozha) Sebryakov was the son of Dr Sebryakova-Zhitkova, cousin to Prokofiev's mother, who had been in practice in St Petersburg and Petrograd before the Revolution. He was therefore the composer's first cousin once removed.

this is against fire regulations. In the Green Room, waiting to greet me was none other than Morolyov, whom I was delighted to see – but how he has changed over these fifteen years! Yes, it really is fifteen years, quite a stretch. He is now quite grey, and although one could not call him an old man he is well past the prime of life.

The concert began with the Suite from *Chout*, which was quite long as they played ten numbers. I could hear it perfectly from the Artists' Room, which is separated from the stage only by a thin partition wall with gaps in it. The Persimfans played the Suite with great precision and clarity, expressivity and obvious enjoyment. The end of the Suite was greeted with applause and cries of 'Composer!' but I had previously agreed with Tse-Tse that I would not react to any such demands in order not to anticipate my entrance on stage to perform the Concerto. Tseitlin, however, was in such a lather of excitement when he burst into the room that he was all for abandoning our pact and suggested I go out after all. But we talked more about it as the applause continued, and decided that on balance it would be better not to.

Before my Concerto performance I began to suffer from nerves, but worked on myself and managed to calm myself down. All the same, I am on the point of appearing in Moscow, where everyone has been waiting for me and where, worst of all, they know every bar of my Concerto. This is a serious matter and my performance must be beyond reproach.

At last in came Tabakov,[1] the principal trumpet (a superlative player) to tell me the players were settled and in their places, and it was time for me make my entrance. As I did so the orchestra played a fanfare and then stood to applaud me. The combined ovation of the audience and the orchestra was not only huge but extraordinarily long. I stood for a long time bowing in all directions and wondering what I should do. At last I sat down but the applause continued and I had to stand up again and start bowing, still not knowing quite what to do. It was ten years since I had been in Moscow, I desperately wanted to concentrate in order to play as I knew I should, but these emotions were the complete opposite of what I needed to become absorbed in the music. Eventually I lost patience and sat down at the piano with a deliberate show of firmness. Tseitlin, whose chair was immediately behind my back, whispered to me that I should sit quietly for a couple of minutes to let myself, the orchestra and the audience calm down and come to ourselves. I tried not to catch anyone's eye but to lose myself in the piano. After perhaps three minutes we began.

1   Mikhail Tabakov (1877–1956), in addition to occupying the principal trumpet chair in the Bolshoy Theatre orchestra for more than forty years, was also Koussevitzky's solo trumpet until the conductor emigrated in 1917. Tabakov played a leading role in the establishment of Persimfans, and also had a long career as professor at the Moscow Conservatoire, where among his star pupils was Timofey Dokshitzer.

My playing was hardly unruffled, but it was reasonably good. There was only one awkward moment: in the third variation I somehow went wrong, I don't remember exactly where, but disaster was avoided and we immediately got back on track. At the end of the Concerto the hall erupted. Nowhere, ever, had I had a reception to match it. There was no end to my curtain calls. As an encore I played first the Gavotte from the *Classical* Symphony and then the Toccata, both of which came off well. Finally I escaped to the solitude of the Green Room while the orchestra played the Suite from *Oranges*. As has become traditional the March was encored, and then at the end of the programme there were more calls for me and I went out to take more bows. One of the first visitors to the Green Room was Litvinov, who in the absence of Chicherin[1] abroad is currently serving as Foreign Minister. Running a little to fat, clean-shaven, thin-lipped and with an intelligent expression, he resembles nothing so much as a middle-ranking pharmacist. His comfortable embonpoint sits strangely with the desperate reputation that still clings to him as a result of his involvement in the Tiflis Bank Robbery.[2] But Litvinov

---

1   Gyorgy Chicherin (1872–1936), the USSR's first Commissar of Foreign Affairs. A man of phenomenal intellectual abilities, he was a genuinely polyglot linguist said to have a faultless command of all major European languages, as well as Hindi, Arabic, Latin and Hebrew, such that he was equipped to sign the 1922 Treaty of Rapallo between the Weimar Republic and the Soviet Union without even requesting a Russian translation of the German document. He is unquestionably the only Soviet leader to have published a book about Mozart: 'the greatest friend and closest comrade of my life ... for me there has only been the Revolution and Mozart. Mozart was a foretaste of future joys; the Revolution is now.' But he was also a solitary and repressed individual who had (literally) no other home than a room in the Foreign Ministry, and was probably inclined to homosexuality. As such he was distrusted and disliked by most of his colleagues, not least by his deputy, Maxim Litvinov, who conducted what was in effect a continuing internal political and personal war with his chief. Chicherin, a fervent believer in world revolution and a principal architect of the Comintern, and Litvinov were also increasingly at odds with each other over the growing Stalin-dominated consensus in the Politburo in favour of 'Communism in one country'. When Chicherin fell ill with diabetes and nephritis it was therefore convenient to pack him off to Germany for long-term treatment. He would not be officially pensioned off and replaced as People's Commissar by Litvinov until 1930, but the functions had in fact long been discharged by Litvinov.
2   In 1907 a plot was hatched by leading Bolsheviks including Lenin, Stalin, Litvinov, Bogdanov, Krasin and the eventual front man of the actual heist, Simon Ter-Petrossian (known as 'Kamo'), to hijack a stagecoach carrying over 300,000 roubles in cash (roughly $3.5 million today) between the Tiflis (Tbilisi) Post Office and the Imperial State Bank on 26 June 1907. Litvinov and Stalin were the two members with the most practical experience in international gun-running, and the Party was badly in need of money to acquire more arms. Stalin did most of the planning for the robbery, including obtaining inside intelligence from bank employees and arming Kamo's gang. The coach was duly attacked with guns and bombs even though the police (very likely tipped off by Stalin through his Okhrana contacts) were well informed and lying in wait. The overkill of the explosives killed altogether around forty people including the coach drivers and bank guards and bystanders, and many more were injured. Despite the police tip-off none of the conspirators was caught at the time and Kamo himself successfully escaped with almost all the money, which, by a variety of clandestine routes, eventually got to Lenin in Finland, which was at the time part of Russia. The bulk of the cash was in 500-rouble notes, the serial numbers of which were easily traceable in Russia, so the main objective was to get it abroad where it could in theory be more

is an important figure for me, because it was through him that all the passports, concessions and arrangements of convenience connected with my visit to the USSR were made. He came up himself to make my acquaintance and then introduced me to his wife, who is an Englishwoman.¹ I was immediately appropriated by other visitors: Myaskovsky, Asafyev, Morolyov, the

---

readily exchangeable. Lenin farmed the notes out to several colleagues, including twelve – i.e. 60,000 roubles – to Litvinov who, under a variant of his Polish-Jewish birth name Meir Wallach, was arrested trying to cash them in Paris. The French authorities declined to extradite him to Russia and instead deported him to England, which remained his base as the Party's principal armaments procurer until the Revolution. Kamo was similarly arrested trying to cash notes in Berlin but successfully feigned insanity, in which spurious condition he was extradited to Tiflis for long-term confinement in a psychiatric institution. From this he escaped by the classic device of sawing through the bars of his cell, met up with Lenin and Krupskaya in Paris and was in the final stages of planning another bank robbery when he was caught again, returned to Russia and this time sentenced to death on four separate counts. Astonishingly the sentence was commuted to imprisonment for life as part of an amnesty offered during the tricentennial celebrations of the founding of the Romanov dynasty in 1913. Kamo was, naturally, released from prison soon after the Bolshevik Revolution, but evidently still preferring to live dangerously was riding his bicycle in Tiflis in 1922 when he was run over and killed by a wayward lorry.

1 Eva Valterovna Litvinova was born Ivy Lowe (1889–1977), the daughter of Walter Low, in his day a well-known writer and a close friend of H. G. Wells. In 1916 Ivy, herself a promising and slightly scandalous young writer, had married Maxim Litvinov, then a Bolshevik agent stationed in England for clandestine political and financial activities. After the October Revolution kicked such scandalous escapades as the Tiflis Bank Robbery into the long grass Litvinov was able to operate diplomatically in the open and soon returned to the USSR to work in the Ministry of Foreign Affairs (Narkomindel). Here his abilities and background made him rise swiftly through the ranks; by the mid-1920s he was already influential and, having backed Stalin over Trotsky, by 1930 became Foreign Minister, in which capacity he was responsible in 1933 for negotiating the recognition of the USSR by America in the new Roosevelt administration. As a Jew he was obviously unsuitable to remain in the post during the years of the Molotov–Ribbentrop pact and was dismissed in the spring of 1939. But two years later, following the Nazi Operation Barbarossa, Litvinov was restored to favour as Soviet Ambassador to Washington. According to Isaiah Berlin Ivy was 'a typically emancipated "new woman" of her time, bold, headstrong, deliberately irreverent, *revoltée* and heterodox on principle, passionate, warm-hearted, observant, amusing, tactless, giving herself recklessly to people and to causes, neither obsessed nor egomaniacal. Her love was not politics but literature.' Given all that it was surprising, to say the least, that she survived in Stalin's Soviet Union to which she stubbornly clung after her husband's death (uncharacteristically for discarded Old Bolsheviks, in his own bed) in 1951 for another twenty years before a final, productive, half-decade in Hove. In the Introduction to his moving biography of Ivy Litvinov, the historian John Carswell, whose mother was one of Ivy's closest friends and who himself knew her in the last decade of her life when she finally moved back to England, gives a perceptive pen-portrait: 'No woman could have loved her children and grandchildren more, or have given more of herself to them. She was unforgettable, overwhelming in her affection. She was unfaithful almost on principle, and inconsiderate almost as a habit. For her the idea of guilt did not exist. Her heart went out with sudden enthusiasms to unlikely recipients and was often bruised as a result. So there was the side I have called delinquent, which developed as she grew older into moods of misanthropy and combativeness. Guilt she repudiated: but she was riddled with shame. In all perplexities her recourse was literature. She read and wrote as some people eat and drink, with a passion and persistence that overrode all other considerations.' Prokofiev notes on several occasions her interest in speaking English: some time later this was to become a life-changing passion (one of her 'sudden enthusiasms to unlikely recipients') when she conceived the necessity of teaching Basic English as a

current Director of the Conservatoire, Goldenweiser,[1] with whom I exchanged a few phrases not, as a matter of fact, about music but about chess; Glière, Feinberg, Alexandrov and others. Extricating myself from them I felt obliged to go over to Litvinov, who was sitting on one of the sofas. As I neared him he stood up: pharmacist he may be but he is still a diplomat, and not a bad one. I thanked him for his help to me and introduced Ptashka to him and to his wife, who was thrilled to find someone with whom to speak English. But then I was dragged away by yet another group: Golovanov, Dikiy[2] and Rabinovich[3] – respectively conductor, producer and designer responsible for the Bolshoy Theatre production of *Oranges*. I was very glad to meet Rabinovich, of whom I had good reports from Suvchinsky. At one stage when the *Ursignol* project was being developed, Diaghilev was hesitating between Yakulov and Rabinovich.

---

universal language to Russians, and sentenced herself to several years of voluntary exile in Sverdlovsk devising courses and coaching students in this far more practical alternative, as she saw it, to Esperanto. She returned to Moscow and the bosom of her family only when Maxim, as a Jew, was abruptly removed by Stalin from his Foreign Minister position in favour of Molotov in the run-up to the Molotov–Ribbentrop Pact. He had, needless to say, every expectation of being speedily arrested and executed, but the collapse of the pact and the Nazi invasion unexpectedly brought him back into favour as Soviet Ambassador to America with the task of persuading Roosevelt to join the Allies. (J. Carswell, *The Exile: A Life of Ivy Litvinov*, Faber and Faber, London, 1983.)

1 Alexander Goldenweiser (1875–1961), pianist, composer and teacher. A link to the glory days of Moscow pianism as exemplified by Zverev's students Rachmaninoff and Scriabin (Goldenweiser's debut on the concert platform was as the duet partner of Rachmaninoff, who later dedicated to him his Second Suite for Two Pianos and joined him in its first performance), and also to Medtner, Goldenweiser was generally unsympathetic to Modernist tendencies in music and seems to have had less difficulty than most in endorsing the proscriptions of the Stalin/Zhdanov 1948 Decree against the 'anti-Soviet formalism' for which Prokofiev, Shostakovich, Khachaturian and many others were condemned. Goldenweiser was a front-rank pianist, however, as his surviving recordings (the earliest of which date from when he was already over seventy) and his illustrious roster of students demonstrate. Among the latter are Lazar Berman, Samuil Feinberg, Dmitry Kabalevsky, Tatiana Nikolayeva and Nikolai Kapustin, though his favourite was Grigory Ginzburg with whom he made a memorable recording of the Rachmaninoff Second Suite, still in the catalogue. He twice was appointed Director of the Moscow Conservatoire, from 1922 to 1924 and again from 1939 to 1942. As a young man he was a close friend of Tolstoy, often visiting Yasnaya Polyana and noting down the sage's sayings which he subsequently published as a memoir *Vblizi Tolstogo* (*Close to Tolstoy*).

2 Alexey Dikiy (1889–1955), stage and screen actor and theatrical director, already a celebrated Moscow Art Theatre actor, later to establish in 1931 and direct his own studio. In 1936 the Dikiy Studio was closed down and its director sent to the camps for four years, his taste for the grotesque in comedy and the savage edge of satire not being appreciated by the ascendant cultural hierarchy in the Party. Dikiy was, however, subsequently allowed to resume his career and was eventually chosen, reportedly at Stalin's request, to play the role of the Generalissimus in three films, notably *The Battle for Stalingrad*.

3 Isaak Rabinovich (1894–1961), artist and designer. He designed productions for the Moscow Art Theatre Opera Studio and the Vakhtangov Theatre, as well as large-scale public art installations such as Metro stations and the Palace of the Soviets in the Kremlin. He also designed for the movies, having as a young man assisted Alexandra Exter on the remarkable Constructivist Martian sets and costumes for one of the very first Soviet science-fiction films, *Aelita, Queen of Mars* (1924).

Among the people mingling with the crowd in the Green Room was Chernetskaya, the dancer who had come to our house once when we were living in Bellevue.¹ Now she was taken up with wonderful plans for a new ballet, which she could realise only with me, her conceptions being such as would revolutionise the entire world of ballet. She was all set there and then to expound these ideas, but I was already being torn in pieces by people besieging me on all sides, so thankfully the overturning of ballet as we know it had to be postponed. Gradually as the Green Room emptied I began to relax, and eventually, by evening, we were able to emerge on to the street. Tse-Tse, both of them jabbering exuberantly, accompanied Ptashka and me back to the Metropole.

25 January

As it was the first morning with no rehearsal we were able to rest on our laurels and did not have to rush anywhere. Lunching with us at the restaurant on Prechistensky Boulevard, Asafyev was full of his summer trip to the Far North where, he says, many remnants of the past are still to be found and where the Soviet influence, although it has penetrated to some extent, has stayed mostly on the surface. Ptashka was delighted with Asafyev. When she asked him about the currently existing marriage code he stated his view that while, of course, it was unsatisfactory it was arguably the best way to do something to protect women following the dissolute conditions prevailing in times of war and revolution. In amplification of his words he went on to say that that these days there was a perceptible sense of policies being tightened.²

---

1 See above, p. 122.
2 The year 1926 was, from the conventional Western perspective of the sanctity of marriage, perhaps the lowest point of the Soviet rejection of marriage as a divinely ordained bond to be dissolved only under strictly defined and limited circumstances. The 1918 Code of Laws applicable to the marriage and divorce of Soviet citizens began by stating *tout court* that 'the State will in future recognise only civil marriages; religious marriages solemnised concurrently with the obligatory civil marriage are now a purely private concern of the parties'. The Code went on to legislate that grounds were no longer needed for divorce: in cases of mutual consent a mere declaration to that effect would suffice, and if contested a unilateral submission could be made to the courts, which would then have jurisdiction to determine. But even these provisions were eventually deemed inadequate for the radical new society being constructed, and in 1926 a new Code was enacted abolishing the obligation to register a marriage at all, cohabitation being considered in every way equivalent to a registered marriage. The requirement for a court hearing to determine a contested divorce was similarly abolished, all that was now needed being a declaration to the appropriate official by either party. If contested the declaration still had to be formally approved by a court, but the court was specifically prohibited from withholding approval. The consequence was that Soviet law henceforward regarded a marriage or cohabitation arrangement as fully terminable at the will of either party. It is hard to see how Asafyev could argue that the new regulations added to the protection of women. It is also interesting, and unconsciously prophetic, that Lina Prokofieva should, at this early stage in her

After parting from Asafyev I met Tsukker and went with him to apply for a passport to travel abroad. Since the procedure to obtain such a document can take a month or more, Tse-Tse's advice was to lose no time in taking steps to guarantee my permission to leave the country. The passport section is physically housed in a department of the Ministry of Foreign Affairs, but Tsukker explained that in fact it is controlled by the GPU.[1] I entered the GPU premises with not a little curiosity. We were seen by Comrade Girin, a brisk, auburn-haired, elegantly dressed young man, resembling a Lycée student who has just got his first job as a civil servant. Tsukker did the talking while I stood back. By way of emphasising my privileged position, Tsukker opened by referring to Litvinov as being the person who had arranged my entry to the Soviet Union. But Girin merely smiled: 'It was not necessary for you to involve Comrade Litvinov. You could have come straight to us.'

He then took the questionnaire I had already filled in and asked me to pay six copecks. I was amazed at the modesty of the defrayment, but Tsukker put me right by explaining that the actual passports would each cost $100 unless we could wangle some species of fictitious business trip,[2] in which case the fee payable would be reduced by three-quarters. The six copecks were a preliminary payment for the cost of the document we had submitted. The whole business was completed promptly and efficiently. As he escorted us out Girin told me he had been interested to hear my concert on the radio yesterday. Reciprocating, I said how impressed I had been by the good order in his office, which I compared favourably with the chaos of the Paris

---

experience of life in the Soviet Union, be voicing a concern about the new laws, since the issue of the legality in the Soviet Union of the Prokofievs' own marriage – which had been solemnised and registered in Germany – was to become a contentious issue when Prokofiev wanted a divorce in 1948. At that time the courts decided that the marriage had always been invalid and Lina, a foreign national, accordingly lost whatever protection she had enjoyed as the wife of a Soviet citizen, with fateful results.

1   OGPU (1922–34), the USSR's secret police. The intials stand for the innocuous-sounding Ob'yedinnyonoye Gosudarstvennoye Politicheskoye Upravlenia – Unified State Political Directorate. The organisation, successor to the Tsarist Okhrana ('Protection') and the initial Bolshevik Cheka (Vserossiiskaya Chrezvychaynaya Kommissiya po Bor'be s Kontrrevolyutsiyei i Sabotazhem – All-Russian Emergency Committee for the Struggle against Counter-Revolution and Sabotage) was hierarchically speaking a department of the NKVD (Natsional'nyi Kommissariat Vnutrennykh Del' – National Commissariat of Internal Affairs) headed by Felix Dzerzhinsky. With some name changes – 'Political Directorate' being replaced by 'State Security' (Gosudarstvennoi Bezopasnosti, which gives the GB of the eventual KGB) – the organisation continued to be part of the Internal Affairs Ministry (Commissars and Commisariats became Ministers and Ministries in 1946) until 1954, following the death of Stalin and the purging of the universally unmourned Lavrenty Beria. The KGB continued as an independent force until Boris Yeltsin dissolved it in 1991. Its functions are now carried out by the FSB (Federal'naya Sluzhba Bezopasnosti – Federal Security Service). Before becoming President, Vladimir Putin – himself a KGB veteran – was Director of the FSB, appointed by Yeltsin in 1998.
2   Obviously *from*, not *to*, the USSR.

Préfecture, where one has to sprinkle bribes right and left to have any chance of obtaining a passport in good time. Girin was pleased and asked me to come back and see him in due course.

In the evening the violinist Konstantin Mostras[1] and his wife, both of whom are directors of Persimfans, hosted a small reception on behalf of the Persimfans management. Tse-Tse and Yampolsky[2] were there as well. In their day the Mostrases had been well off and they still lived in their former splendid apartment with enormous, high-ceilinged rooms. With the advent of Bolshevism, however, other residents were settled into the apartment and the original owners were left with only one room, the largest. This room was then judged to be too big, so was divided in half and then in half again, resulting in something like a long, narrow corridor with a disproportionately high ceiling and a single window. The food to go with the Tokay was delicious: caviar and a stupendous white salmon. I was presented with a series of hand-made models of characters from *Chout*, including the Buffoon himself, the Merchant, the Goat and some others. Tsukker had brought along his camera and wanted to take a photograph of us all. The camera was equipped with a magnesium flash, and each time when the shutter was open and he had lit the fuse for the magnesium flare, Tsukker would dash round to include himself in the picture. This produced a farcical mix-up because Tsukker was desperate to stand next to Ptashka but his colleagues, anticipating his intention, made it their business to ensure he could not do so. Tsukker, frustrated and flustered, would try again with another photograph.

26 January

We both woke up feeling out of sorts. Either we are exhausted or we are coming down with a cold, so we must concentrate our efforts on working on ourselves.

Derzhanovsky appeared in his felt boots, looking undernourished and peering foxily out from behind his wobbly pince-nez. He wanted me to go

---

1 Konstantin Mostras (1886–1965), violinist, was a member of one of the first Soviet string quartets, the Lenin Quartet, and in addition to playing in the Persimfans Orchestra and participating in its management, was a professor of violin at the Moscow Conservatoire, rising to be head of the department and numbering among his pupils Ivan Galamian. He also collaborated with David Oistrakh on a new edition of Tchaikovsky's Violin Concerto.
2 Abram Yampolsky (1890–1956), violinist and one of the most celebrated pedagogues in the Soviet school of violin playing. From the assistant leader's desk of the Bolshoy Theatre Orchestra he had transferred to the newly formed Persimfans Orchestra and also taught classes both at the Moscow Conservatoire and the Gnesin Institute. This enabled him to nurture young violin talents from an early age through to maturity, and his world-class pupils included Leonid Kogan, Yulian Sitkovetsky, Igor Bezrodny, Mikhail Fichtengolts, Boris Goldstein and many others.

with him to choose a piano for this evening, but I was lazy and left the choice in his experienced hands.

Tse-Tse called in the afternoon to discuss at long last our financial arrangements, which there had not been time to do before. They were scathing about the head of the Leningrad Philharmonia, Khais, who had not only tried to get away with offering me the least advantageous terms possible but then boasted openly about it. As for Persimfans, each member of the orchestra gets the same fee, 20 roubles a concert, and if there is any residual profit it goes into the orchestra's funds. They did not want to exploit me and would have been happy for any profit, less a small management deduction, to go to me. However, they are obliged to account for any agreement they make with a foreign artist, and such a formula would not be acceptable for this purpose: all fees have to be agreed in accordance with predetermined norms. To sum up, they proposed that my fee should be set at not too exaggerated a level, but they would also bear the costs of my travel, my hotel accommodation, my subsistence and any other appropriate expenses that could be thought of.

Back in Paris Yavorsky had told me that it would be very important to give a concert for charity, and as soon as Tsukker mentioned something along these lines I seized the opportunity to announce that I should like to dedicate one of my recital appearances for the benefit of the homeless, an idea that immediately elicited an enthusiastic response from Tse-Tse.

After they went I was still feeling well below par and dozed off three times. In the evening Derzhanovsky came to take me to the private recital for the Association of Contemporary Music, of which he is the head. It was a private occasion in that it was restricted to 'musicians and people working in the arts', as Derzhanovsky had explained to me in correspondence while I was still in Paris. He had also wanted Ptashka to sing, but at the time she had said neither yes nor no and since we had been besieged by so many people and obligations in Moscow her voice was not in the best shape, so we decided it would be better for her not to sing than to fall short of expectations through tiredness.

Derzhanovsky was in a great state of anxiety because, as he explained: 'The hall seats three hundred but there are at least fifteen hundred people who want to come, the telephone is ringing off the hook, there will be screams of protest from all those who can't get in and I shall end up with nothing but enemies.'

Arrived at the concert and I met many people I knew, including Shura Sezhenskaya, my second cousin once removed, whom I remembered as an unruly little girl and who is now a lady with hair on the way to turning grey, also Kostya Sezhensky, her cousin and my second cousin, although we are not in fact related by blood since he was adopted. Kostya is rising twenty, a clumsy, ill-favoured youth who is studying at the Conservatoire and seems stunned to discover that he has a famous uncle.

I told Asafyev about the machinations of Khais. 'As a patriotic son of my city I find this disgraceful. I must speak to him about it.'

Derzhanovsky told me I could go and sit in the hall, as the programme would begin with the *Overture on Hebrew Themes*, to be followed by a singer, and only then would I be on to play.

The hall was not large, but packed to the gunwales. As I walked through it everyone applauded, and when I eventually sat down in the only vacant seat in the house, left for me in the front row, Saradzhev came out on stage and pronounced a welcome speech. This made me nervous, but not so much so that I omitted to notice a mistake in a quotation he dragged in about Hans Sachs. The speech was greeted by another ovation, after which we finally got down to the *Jewish Overture*, in which Igumnov, the Director of the Conservatoire, took the piano part. Sitting where I was, in the front row, the balance sounded anything but blended, and I derived no pleasure from the performance. Igumnov then quitted the stage to come into the body of the hall, there was a general shuffling round of seating and he took the now vacant seat next to mine.

Igumnov is quite an amusing character, tall and thin and clean-shaven, with the remains of teeth sticking out of his mouth. I was interested to see him, because it was about twenty years, when I was staying with the Smetskys at Sukhum,[1] since I had heard anything of him. The singer then took the stage to sing three of my songs; she was nervous and sang the first two badly and the third somewhat idiosyncratically.

Then it was my turn. I clambered on to the stage and played Sonatas Nos. 2 and 3 and the Toccata. The piano was clangy, not at all good; Derzhanovsky's choice had not been a distinguished one. I was reasonably relaxed and for some extraordinary reason went off into a daydream in the Third Sonata and came to a halt. I immediately pulled myself together, however, and there were no more lapses after that. After the applause I played the Gavotte from Op. 32.[2] When I had finished I came back down from the stage to be surrounded by an incredible hubbub with everyone coming up to me at once. There was Igumnov, and the Administrative Director of the Conservatoire, who presented me with a book containing an article about me, and old man Jurgenson,[3] once the Zeus-like figure whose

---

1 Nikolay and Olga Smetsky had been well-off and generous friends of Prokofiev's parents, with whom Prokofiev and his mother had sometimes stayed on holiday. See *Diaries*, vol. 1, pp. 53–5, 105, 371.
2 From the *Four Pieces for Piano*, composed in 1918 in America.
3 Boris Petrovich Jurgenson, the son of the founder of the music publishing company. See *Diaries*, vol. 1, p. 70.

thunderbolts used to rock the world of music publishing but now a minor official in Muzsektor, which now lords it over the very building that was formerly his property. Under cover of the general buzz of conversation he managed to tell me he would telephone me to make an appointment to meet. The matter which Myaskovsky had regarded as almost too delicate to handle thus seems to be on the way to being resolved.

Boris Krasin[1] was there too; he had previously rung me up but Tseitlin, who happened to pick up the telephone, told him I was not in. Krasin is connected to Rosphil, an organisation opposed to Persimfans, so Tse-Tse do all they can to keep them at arm's length from me. Bearing this in mind and remembering how eighteen months ago in Paris Krasin had gone out of his way to be kind to me, I made use of the present occasion to be extra civil to him. Kostya and Shura Sezhensky turned up again. Ptashka finds Kostya rather touching but dislikes Shura. Shura, however, mentioned that she still had in her possession some photographs belonging to my parents and this intrigued Ptashka. Since all the family photographs belonging to me had been lost in the St Petersburg flat, Ptashka made it her business to try to assemble from my surviving friends and relations whatever had been preserved in their photo albums. I asked Shura what had become of my other Moscow nephews and nieces. My father's sister, my aunt, had produced four daughters who are therefore my cousins, and all of them in turn produced countless progeny, male and female cousins of this Shura. But Shura said they had scattered widely and she had lost sight of most of them, which distresses me less than it should, since with few exceptions they are a dull collection of people. My most interesting niece is probably Nadya Faleyeva, who became an actress and tours provincial theatres somewhere.

The public began to drift away as we were due to go on somewhere else for supper. After changing we went to a nearby club 'for the improvement of the living conditions of scholars', i.e. the very Tsekubu courtesy of which Derzhanovsky was enabled to keep his precious room. This club proved to be in an enormous detached house whose former sole owner and occupant had been the widow of a general, but she had died about the time the Bolsheviks took power. Tsukker could not let the opportunity pass to point out that in the old days this monstrous pile had been home to one old woman who probably could not even get herself from one room to another, whereas today it was the property of writers and academics who could use it to do honour to Prokofiev.

A whole series of long tables had been laid for supper in the huge hall of the house. I sat between Asafyev and Yekaterina Koposova-Derzhanovskaya.

1   See above, pp. 207–13, 308, 328.

Ptashka was put next to Myaskovsky. Our table also had some of the Persimfans people, Yavorsky, and a few of the young composers. Toasts were drunk and photographs taken, Derzhanovsky doing his best to be pictured near Lina Ivanovna.[1] He, Mosolov and the youngsters were all paying court to her as hard as they could.

After a few toasts, hints began to be dropped that I ought to say something. I tried to evade it, but eventually there was no way out and I rose to my feet. A hush immediately spread over the hall, broken only by the exhalation of a satisfied 'aaahh!' Clearly, much was expected of me. But to whom and to what should I invite everyone to raise their glasses? Inspiration came in the nick of time and I toasted musical Moscow, which I explained I had come to value even more after my peregrinations round the world. I drank, and there was applause for what I said even though they were clearly hoping for something rather more elaborate and florid. A little later I migrated to another table where the young composers had congregated, joined already by Myaskovsky, Asafyev and Belyaev.[2] A group photo was taken of us all together in which I appear looking like an incredible orang-utang. Generally I felt quite overwhelmed by so much adulation. I was told that the first review of my concert had appeared in *Evening Moscow*, which is a measure of the political importance attached to my visit. At one o'clock in the morning I was suddenly overcome by tiredness and although the feasting was clearly set to continue for some time Ptashka and I decided we should call it a day. We made our way out accompanied by the entire gathering clapping us. Kostya Sezhensky caught up with me at the bottom of the stairs; he had apparently also been at the supper but was sitting somewhere far away from the top table, behind a palm-tree, so I had not seen him. He seemed intoxicated by the acclamation being heaped upon his uncle, perhaps also by the wine, and in grotesquely ecstatic tones begged me to autograph a copy of the Third Sonata.

27 January

Our room is quiet and peaceful and after the pomp of yesterday we slept well and long. Tseitlin rang up to say that they had begun rehearsing the second programme including the *Overture for Seventeen Instruments*, but I decided to get more sleep, give the rehearsal a miss and let them make a start on working it out without my presence. When I asked what sort of an impression the

---

1 Lina Prokofieva. Her father was the Spanish Juan Codina, so for Russians she was Lina Ivanovna.
2 Viktor Belyayev (1888–1934), critic and musicologist, a former pupil of Jazeps Vitol. He was a leading figure in the ASM. See *Diaries*, vol. 1, p. 607; vol. 2, p. 174.

Overture was making, Tseitlin gulped a little and began extolling other works. Probably they have not yet got the measure of the piece, or they are not used to the new sonorities, or it may just be that Tseitlin, as a violinist, does not find it particularly interesting.[1]

I used the remainder of the morning and part of the afternoon to do some serious piano practice. At a time like this it is vital to be on top playing form, and yet there seems to be time for everything else that people want me to do but none for the piano. The weather has improved and it is mild and pleasant out of doors. Ptashka and I had lunch *à deux*, and observed with astonishment that the imperial eagles were still in their place on the Iversky Gates. We were informed that it had proved impossible to remove them without wrecking the building, and in any case, 'Soviet power is such that it will not be shaken by a few eagles, even if they have got crowns on their heads.'

I gave an interview to a journalist, and in the evening Ptashka and I went to Myaskovsky's. Asafyev was also there. Since the next-door room is occupied by Myaskovsky's sister Valentina, an absolutely delightful woman, I asked his permission for Ptashka to come with me so that she could pay a call on Valentina. Besides ourselves and Asafyev we were joined by Myaskovsky's other sister Vera and her husband V. V. Yakovlev, but her personality is not as refined as Valentina's and she has a much less sensitive understanding of Myaskovsky. Valentina's sixteen-year-old daughter was also there; she made a somewhat disagreeable impression on me with her round, puffy face and disagreeable manners. Her features reminded me strangely of her father, whom I had seen only once or twice at Myaskovsky's house many years ago, probably before this girl was born. Once when I had called on Myaskovsky at home I found him in a greatly upset state and everybody in the house speaking in whispers. The cause, Myaskovsky explained, was that Valentina's husband had just shot himself. I asked why. Myaskovsky replied, 'He had got himself mixed up in dubious financial transactions.'

This evening went very pleasantly, the men together in Myaskovsky's room while the womenfolk congregated at Valentina's. We talked inconsequentially of this and that, not going deeply into any subjects.

We went home on foot in the mild weather, I in front with the Yakovlevs, Ptashka following on behind with Asafyev. After the skyscrapers of America and the apartments of Paris all plonked down one on top of another, it was pleasant to be in these Moscow side streets, some of which consisted entirely of large mansions, quiet and comfortable-looking. I commented on this to Yakovlev, who said in reply, 'Yes, that may well be how they were in the past. But nowadays they are crammed impossibly full of separate households, and

---

1 The original version of this work is scored without violins.

while there are a lot of rooms in these houses they only have one kitchen. This kitchen is usually where all the conflicts blow up between the families.' And, indeed, one can imagine the hell that must be created in the kitchen when the eighteen families now living in this tranquil mansion are trying to cook eighteen suppers on eighteen primus stoves.

When Ptashka and I were on our own again she relayed to me the interesting events that had taken place in the female territory while I had been in the male preserve. It seems that Valentina's daughter is a fervent Komsomol member chock-a-block with Communist slogans, who creates a living hell for her mother and never lets her open her mouth without interrupting: 'Well, that's just typical of your bourgeois ideas.' Her crude observations on everything had completely spoiled Ptashka's evening, even though Ptashka had been careful not to get involved in discussions of this kind more than she could possibly help. On top of this the young lady lives entirely at her mother's expense, goes for expensive manicures and is given to disappearing no one knows where. As they walked along through the quiet streets Asafyev told Ptashka that not only did the girl drive Valentina to distraction but Myaskovsky as well, sometimes bringing him to the point of screaming at her and stamping his foot. Try as I may, to construct a mental picture of Myaskovsky screaming and stamping his feet is beyond my powers. But this is what Asafyev said, and no doubt his information came from Myaskovsky himself, so it must be true. Back in the safety of the Metropole Ptashka and I gave rein to our indignation and secretly longed for the moon-faced niece to run off with a Komsomol youth as soon as possible and clear the air for everyone else.

28 January

A photographer came in the morning, and then for most of the afternoon I kept away from people because that evening I was to give my first piano recital and needed time to concentrate and bring my abilities up to full strength. I managed quite a bit of practice. *Izvestia* is carrying my portrait, a distinction that has at least as much political significance as it does musical.

The recital in the evening, in true, admirable Russian style, started half an hour late. The audience was clearly accustomed to this convention and did not hurry to take its seats, filling the hall only slowly. But by the time I came on to play the whole Great Hall was packed.

The first item was the Third Sonata – it was Suvchinsky who had at one time recommended that I should always begin with this piece – and I followed it with ten of the *Visions fugitives*. Both works were accorded a good, if not overwhelming reception. Next, the Fifth Sonata, which was received with some reserve although a group of perhaps fifty people clapped relentlessly and kept shouting for me to take another bow. Real success came with the March from *Three Oranges*, which had to be repeated because of the instant roar of approval from the audience. This set the pattern for the rest of the recital, the second half of which consisted of smaller pieces concluding with the Toccata. It provoked a screaming and a roaring the like of which I had never in my life heard before. As encores I played the second of the *Tales of an Old Grandmother*, the Gavotte from the *Classical* Symphony and finally Myaskovsky's *Caprice* No. 5.[1] So that this last piece should not be mistaken for my own work, I announced the title and the composer to the audience, as I thought reasonably loudly and clearly, but I was told later that half of the audience had not heard me. Knowing that Myaskovsky was in the audience, and knowing also of old that he was invariably dissatisfied by performances of his music, I was extremely nervous in the *Caprice* and unforgivably in the first half smudged some notes and went wrong, but pulled myself together for the slow middle section and finished it quite respectably. Even so the screaming and shouting showed no signs of abating, and after the *Caprice*, which despite my efforts the majority of those present thought I had written, I still had to come out for several more bows although I played no more encores.

The Green Room once again filled with people, including Mme Litvinova who conversed with Ptashka in English. The great chemist himself was not there. One person who did come was Yurovsky,[2] the head of the State Music Publishing House. Having introduced himself he announced that it was imperative that we meet in order to regularise my relations with the State Publishing House, which is printing and selling my compositions. Yurovsky is a tall gentleman not without a certain elegance in his demeanour; not only is his face shaved clean but so is his head. With great courtesy he said that as soon as I had the time he would come to see me, or he would be happy for me to call on him at the Publishing House.

Back at the hotel I was angry with myself for having again been a prey to nerves. It is after all stupid and pointless to be so affected, especially after having worked so hard on myself before and during the concert. Last winter,

---

1 Myaskovsky, *Caprices* (*Prichudy*), Six Sketches for piano, Op. 25 (1922–7). No. 5 is marked *Allegro vivace*.
2 Alexander Yurovsky (1882–1952), pianist and professor of piano at the Moscow Conservatoire, Director of the State Music Publishing House from 1922 until 1944. Brother of the economist Leonid Yurovsky, Alexander Yurovsky narrowly escaped being deported along with Berdyayev, Zamyatin, Frank, Karsavin and other intellectuals categorised as 'anti-Soviet' on Lenin's 'Philosophy Steamer', as recounted by Lesley Chamberlain in her book of that title (L. Chamberlain, *The Philosophy Steamer: Lenin and the Exile of the Intelligentsia*, Atlantic Books, London, 2006). The original list drawn up by Kamenev and Unschlicht includes Yurovsky's name but states that resulting from the representations of one Comrade Vladimirov he was not selected for exile.

while I was so calm during my American concert tour, I thought this was a spectre I had finally rid myself of for ever.

29 January

We had lunch with Seryozha Sebryakov in the Bolshaya Moskovskaya restaurant. I wanted to quiz him about the details of Shurik's arrest in order to equip myself as effectively as possible in my attempts to get him released from prison. But I did not learn much that I did not already know. Seryozha confirmed that he had not been found guilty of any illegal political activity, but had associated with the wrong sort of people, and had not helped himself by refusing to give the names of anyone he thought might be implicated by such a step.

An extraordinary person, this Seryozha Sebryakov. As a student in the distant past he had been the Reddest of Reds and even long before the 1905 Revolution was continually sounding the alarm about the impending collapse of society. Now at the age of fifty he has lost none of his scaremongering tendencies, and now here he was, sitting in the Bolshaya Moskovskaya restaurant questioning us in a conspiratorial manner about an alleged English plot to bomb Moscow from the air with so many gas-filled missiles that the entire population would be instantly suffocated, and whether there was any truth in the rumour that the English had decided to sacrifice the city's population of two million in order to poison the leaders in the Kremlin. By the end we were relieved when the lunch was over, because even though he was talking nonsense his cloak-and-dagger air and his whispering must have made it look as if we really were collaborating in the fiendish plots of the English.

In the afternoon we had a visit from Shurik's eldest daughter, Alyona, who brought with her a letter from her mother. She is a very nice girl, thirteen years old but you would be hard put to it to think she was more than ten. Nadya has clearly been concerned about what I might be able to do to secure Shurik's release, and although I have been reluctant to get involved prematurely before having a chance fully to absorb all the details and establish the best people to approach, I decided to test the water with Tsukker. He is after all a secretary in the Party Central Committee, and ought to be able to look into the matter quite easily and without spending too much time on it. It so happened that he came round at seven o'clock to fill in some forms connected with the foreign passport. One of the questions concerned my relatives and this neatly opened the door to a mention of Shurik, so I took the opportunity of asking him if there was anything he could do about getting my cousin released from prison. Tsukker was at first embarrassed, then advised me to find out from Nadya exactly all about the sentence of the court: when it had been pronounced, what precisely the offence was, the term of imprisonment and so on.

Following our talk Ptashka, Tsukker and I went to the Moscow Art Theatre No. 2.[1] They were presenting Leskov's *The Flea* adapted by Zamyatin and produced by Dikiy. *The Flea* is one of the most sensational productions to be seen, and we had already heard about it in Riga. We were shepherded into the Director's box, which is right beside the stage. Someone was already installed in it, but the luckless individual was immediately liquidated and packed off to the stalls. The first act opened with a caricature of Alexander I and his imperial court, but done with such crude slapstick that Ptashka and I could only exchange glances with a wild surmise. 'Marvellous, isn't it?' gasped Tsukker in an ecstasy of admiration. We concurred as far as the bounds of delicacy and moderation permitted, and had to admit that the characters of some of the chamberlains were quite well drawn. The nub of the matter was that this was the first time we were witnessing a Soviet theatre production, and we could not altogether suppress the thought that kept rearing its head: surely they're not all going to be like this? However, the

---

1 The origins of Moscow Art Theatre 2 are complex, reflecting the sharply differing artistic ambitions, ideologies and techniques of its leading protagonists. It grew out of the original MKHAT Studio One (the inevitable Russian acronym, MXT, is usually rendered MKHAT in English), created in 1912 by Stanislavsky's partner and co-director Nemirovich-Danchenko, with Stanislavsky's approval since the creative ideas of the two co-founders had by this time so far diverged as to threaten the collapse of the parent Moscow Art Theatre itself. MKHAT Studio One's principal directors were, besides Nemirovich-Danchenko, Mikhail Chekhov (Anton Chekhov's nephew) and Yevgeny Vakhtangov, and between them they nurtured a generation of outstanding actors, among them Alexey Dikiy. After the October Revolution the Studio continued the MKHAT tradition of psychological Method acting initiated by Stanislavsky, but with an increasing emphasis on theatricality, anti-realism and expressionism. From 1922 Mikhail Chekhov was the dominant figure, but the creative tensions between the powerful and passionate individual talents seemed to call for a new structure in which they could operate productively without wishing to murder one another. This was provided yet again by Nemirovich-Danchenko, who created a new ensemble called MKHAT-2, in which for a brief period he served as Administrative Director and secured premises for it at the old Alkazar Theatre on Triumfalnaya Square. MKHAT-2 gave Dikiy his first opportunities to direct, and one of the group's most celebrated productions was his of Leskov's *The Flea*, dramatised by Zamyatin. Conflict between Chekhov and the group (including Dikiy) that wanted a harder ideological line came to a head later in 1927, and the group left MKHAT-2 in a body, several of them, Dikiy among them, to set up their own companies, thus ending the theatre's most distinguished and productive period. Mikhail Chekhov, deeply disillusioned, left the Soviet Union altogether in 1928 and after ten years acting, directing and teaching in Europe, including establishing an acting studio at Dartington Hall in Devon, went to America and ultimately Hollywood. Here his teaching was to inspire a generation of famous actors including Gary Cooper, Marilyn Monroe, Gregory Peck, Patricia Neal, Clint Eastwood, Anthony Quinn, Ingrid Bergman, Jack Palance, Jack Nicholson, Lloyd Bridges, Anthony Hopkins and Yul Brynner, the last-named contributing a preface to Chekhov's book on acting, *To the Actor*. MKHAT-2 continued until February 1936 when, in the fall-out from the Stalin-inspired *Pravda* attack on Shostakovich's *Lady Macbeth of Mtsensk*, the theatre was closed without warning and its acting company dispersed.

opening of the second act with its *chastushki* from Tula immediately lifted our spirits. The *chastushki* themselves were a delight, the sound of the Cossacks approaching from afar was rendered with uncommon inventiveness, and generally from this moment on the production was superb. The London scene was especially good.

Tea, sandwiches and cakes were served during the interval in the little retiring room next to the box. Dikiy came in; as well as directing the play he was playing the role of the ataman Platov. We talked about my impressions of the production of *The Flea*, and also the forthcoming production of *Oranges* at the Bolshoy Theatre, which Dikiy is to direct. I was presented with a letter of welcome from the MKHAT management, so in every way was accorded a warm and appreciative reception, especially considering that this was not the musical but the theatrical world.

30 January

In the morning I ran through the programme for this afternoon's recital at half past one in the Great Hall of the Conservatoire, a repeat of what I had played the first time. The hall was full. This time I felt quite relaxed because I am getting used to the Russian public and therefore played with no mishaps. The reaction was similar, with the success coming at the same places as the day before yesterday. Despite the fantastic screaming at the end I made them close the lid of the piano after the second encore, but even that did not stop the noise, which went on for some while after. In the Green Room today were, among others, Meyerhold, Yavorsky, Lunacharsky with his wife, and Chernetskaya, who still insists that her ballet projects need immediate discussion. When the crowd dispersed Yavorsky took us off to his place to dine.

We travelled to Zamoskvorechie[1] in two sleighs through wonderful frosty weather, Ptashka and Yavorsky in the first and I with Protopopov[2] in the second. Yavorsky lives with Protopopov and addresses him as 'Mussenkin'. As we crossed the Moscow river I called across to Ptashka to look back at the Kremlin, which lit by the sun was looking stunningly beautiful. Our sleigh caught up with theirs and I asked Yavorsky to point out to me Suvchinsky's old house: his is a name best not shouted out too loudly in these parts.

Yavorsky and Protopopov with tremendous gallantry refused to let us pay for the sleighs. Their flat is small, its three rooms crammed to bursting with

---

1 The mainly residential quarter of 'old Moscow' tucked in to the south of the big bend in the River Moskva just south of the Moskva where it flows past the south walls of the Kremlin.
2 Sergey Protopopov (1893–1954), pianist, composer, musicologist and disciple of Yavorsky. See above, p. 305, n. 3.

furniture, including two grand pianos. Yavorsky treated us to a phenomenal meal, probably the most delicious we have had yet during our stay in the USSR. Hors d'oeuvres, fabulous *bliny* and incredible *pirozhki*,[1] so that halfway through the meal I was unable to eat another mouthful. Also at the table were the singer Derzhinskaya[2] with her husband, and Protopopov's mother.

After the meal I thought it would be only polite to ask to be shown Protopopov's compositions since I know how Yavorsky goes into ecstasy over them, although I know with equal certainty how terminally boring they would be. Such a delicious dinner demands, however, a certain sacrifice. Hardly were the words out of my mouth when Yavorsky was seated at the piano playing from manuscript a Sonata (No. 2, apparently) by Protopopov. The piano was ear-splittingly loud, the rooms tiny, the celebrated pianist Yavorsky never for one moment took his foot off the pedal, the music thundered up and down the gamut of the keyboard, the strings jangled and the windows rattled. Concluding the performance, Yavorsky apologised for having split some of the notes and for having failed to bring out clearly enough all seven voices of a seven-part canon with extension and inversion. In order to find something to praise I showed interest in the canon, which did indeed seem have been very skilfully done. Yavorsky and Protopopov then sat down at the two pianos and played the latter's 'Gudochek',[3] an unpardonably extended song approximately four times the length of my 'Ugly Duckling', composed to a dismal folk melody recently collected from the north of Russia. This opus has already been published. Yavorsky using one copy played the complicated accompaniment while Protopopov at the other piano took the voice part. He went wrong several times, at which Yavorsky became very angry and shouted at the composer. The song wound on at a funereal tempo for about forty minutes.

On the grounds that dinner had now been amply paid for we permitted ourselves to return to the dining room for coffee. I decided that to allude to

1   *Bliny* are little pancakes, often served with caviar; *pirozhki* small patties filled either with meat or with vegetables, usually brassica.
2   Ksenia Derzhinskaya (1889–1951), coloratura soprano less well known than perhaps she deserves to be on account of having, despite repeated offers, accepted only one engagement to sing away from the stage of the Bolshoy Theatre where she took innumerable leading roles between her debut in 1915 and her retiring in 1948: that of Fevronia in Rimsky-Korsakov's *The Invisible City of Kitezh* at the Paris Opéra in 1926 under Emil Cooper. Neither did she cross over to the gramophone-friendly repertoire of songs and romances, or even much in the way of live recitals. Her milieu was the Russian opera stage, and principally the core Russian repertoire.
3   A *gudók* is usually a factory siren or steam whistle or car horn – anything that makes a hooting noise. A *gudóchek* is a little *gudók*. But the word also refers to an ancient instrument having three strings stretched over an asymmetric bridge and played with a bow, of which archaeologists have found examples in Novgorod dating back to the tenth century.

the terrible tedium of 'Gudochek' and its distressing habit of resorting to Scriabinesque harmonies would spoil the pleasant atmosphere and so refrained. But I could not help asking myself how, if Yavorsky, as I have so often been told, has devised a system of genius to identify and exploit modes, a system that Protopopov has omnivorously adopted and indeed employs to annotate and analyse every half-dozen bars of his own compositions, does it come about that he always ends up with one of Scriabin's augmented ninths?

In the meantime the conversation had moved on to other subjects. Derzhinskaya, a charming woman, spoke of the colossal demand for tickets at all the Moscow theatres despite the high prices. People do not have enough to eat but still want to go to the theatre. Yavorsky told me how last May, after he had returned from Paris, the authorities already knew the details of our conversations,[1] because during our lunch – either accidentally or on purpose – there had been a man sitting at a nearby table writing down all that was said and then reporting it back. His story flowed naturally into a general discussion about surveillance in Moscow, particularly of anyone coming from abroad. Yavorsky described the special noise that can be heard on the telephone when an official eavesdropper is connected to the line. We had sometimes noticed this noise ourselves, and although we we had not said anything compromising over the telephone it is as well to be aware of the practice. All today's conversations led us to one rather surprising conclusion: however bitterly Muscovites criticise what their city has become, they are morbidly anxious to hear it praised.

When we left together with Derzhinskaya, Yavorsky and Protopopov came with us to the tram, which was so crowded we could get on board only with great difficulty.

31 January

The morning rehearsal was devoted to freshening up the programme played at the last orchestra concert, which is to be repeated this evening.

In the afternoon I visited Nadya Rayevskaya and asked her to prepare for me a note spelling out the details of Shurik's case. I gave her 100 roubles to send to Aunt Katya's in Penza, and another 50 roubles for herself.

I received an anonymous letter from someone calling herself 'A Russian Woman'. It contained some advice for me: as soon as the adoring multitudes cease wafting incense over me and leave me time for tranquil reflection, I must recognise that my true calling is not composition but peforming Beethoven, with all this passion and titanic power. If I do this the world will fall at my feet. This is all I need. Thank you, Russian Woman.

---

1 See above, pp. 307–8.

The evening's orchestral concert took place in the Great Hall of the Conservatoire with a repeat of the previous programme. Once again the hall was full. From the Government only Lunacharsky was present, but he did not come to the Green Room afterwards. The orchestra's performance of the Suite from *Chout* was admirable. My entrance was prefaced, at Lunacharsky's request, by an announcement from the stage by Tsukker that a pianist from Moscow, Oborin, had been awarded first prize in the recent International Piano Competition held in Warsaw. Oborin is young, nineteen years of age I believe, and before my arrival had played my Third Piano Concerto with Persimfans. He is also said to be a composer and would like to study with me.

The Third Piano Concerto, in fact, went less well today than on the previous occasion, but this was the fault of the orchestra not of the soloist, since I was almost completely relaxed and played well, if a shade slower than before. The orchestra, by contrast, has suffered thirty-three misfortunes:[1] the principal double-bass had a heart attack, the first flute developed pneumonia and the principal viola broke his leg, and without their section leaders they were all at sea. In the third variation the double-basses lost their way at the tricky place for them where I have syncopated accents off the beat while they have to play firmly on the beat a quaver later. My accents threw them out, they got lost and as a result I was thrown off course as well. But eventually I caught the rhythm again and we got through the passage in reasonable order. The end of the Concerto was greeted with roars of applause and demands for encores. In the Suite from *Three Oranges* that concluded the programme, by what has now become tradition the March had to be repeated.

1 February

Got up at eight for the start of the rehearsal for the *Overture for Seventeen Instruments* at nine. However, the orchestra was late assembling and I was the first to arrive. The tempo they chose was too slow, which made the *Overture* sound flabby and boring; now I understood why the orchestra had not taken to it at their first rehearsal. When I made them quicken the tempo and put in some accents it sounded much better. After the *Overture* they made a start on the Second Piano Concerto, the working out of which seemed to go on for ever. The orchestra obviously likes the work and the players clapped loudly after each movement, but I still found the rehearsal a great strain because most of it consisted of me sitting at the piano and getting the difficult Concerto into some kind of shape.

---

1 Cf. Yepikhodov in Chekhov's *The Cherry Orchard*, whose nickname is 'Twenty-two Misfortunes' because 'every day some misfortune or other befalls me. But I don't grumble about it, I'm used to it and even smile at it.'

As a result I felt tired afterwards and rested at the hotel in the afternoon. To tell the truth I have felt tired ever since coming to Moscow, and indeed never got on top of it the whole two months I was there.

Golovanov came round at five o'clock to take us out to his home in Srednyaya Kiselyovka to play through *Three Oranges* and generally talk about it. After a series of complicated twists and turns we eventually got to his flat, a large and quite luxuriously furnished apartment. Golovanov is probably younger than I am and lives with Nezhdanova, who is the wrong side of fifty. But she it was who brought him out into the world and as a result he now occupies a position rather more elevated than his talent. He is a nice enough fellow, however, and evidently seriously interested in staging *Oranges*, the piano score of which he knew pretty thoroughly. Also present were the proposed team of producer Dikiy (not a stage name, by the way, but his real one)[1] and the designer Rabinovich. About the latter Suvchinsky used to say very good things both professionally and personally, and indeed he proved to be someone of great charm.

We got down to work straight away: I sat at the piano, Golovanov and Dikiy stood behind me pencils at the ready. I played and expounded and referenced the good and bad points of previous productions of the opera. Dikiy scribbled in his notebook while Golovanov immediately, as if it was the easiest thing in the world to do, converted my tempi into metronome indications which he then wrote into the score. I found it incredible that anyone should be able to ascribe a precise metronome speed simply by ear, and kept looking suspiciously at his marks in the score. But at the same time I remembered Tcherepnin saying that Rimsky-Korsakov also had this ability; he was very proud of it and would declare that he possessed 'not just perfect pitch but perfect rhythm'. I must say that all three were uncommonly energised by the forthcoming production: no matter what it might cost they wanted to outdo the Leningrad one. Rabinovich had already gone to Leningrad 'to see how not do do it'. Dikiy took the opposite view: he decided it would be better not to go, indeed to pay no attention, but to keep himself free of any outside influences. Golovanov worried that the season was already so advanced that he could not envisage the opera being staged before May.

Between Acts One and Two we took a break for something to eat. Golovanov outshone himself with the dinner, with all kinds of antipasti and a vintage Polish vodka to which he recommended we pay particular attention. I had only one sip, but Dikiy downed glass after glass with evident relish.

Then an Angora cat appeared on the scene, and a special kind of camera with an extremely light-sensitive lens, which allows photographs to be taken even under lamplight with a comparatively short exposure time, at least less

---

1 'Dikiy' in Russian means 'wild'.

painfully long than is usually the case. The photograph later appeared in the newspapers; Ptashka was not in it because Tsukker had by this time come to take her to the Stanislavsky Opera Studio for a performance of *The Tsar's Bride*. We returned to *Three Oranges* and went through Act Two.

The idea had been that when we had finished the second act I would also go to *The Tsar's Bride* performance, and there were even several telephone calls from the theatre asking if I would soon be there, but we did not finish our work until half past ten, by which time I was very tired and it seemed hardly worthwhile to struggle over just for the last act, so I went home instead. However, it turned out that I ought to have gone because they had been waiting for me and left instructions that I should be admitted to the auditorium even while the performance was in progress, and had even laid on some sort of welcome reception. Ptashka did not get back until half past twelve because the show itself was very long and there was such a crush of people afterwards she had taken an age to get her coat. I was angry and spoke sharply to her, complaining that her gadding about had prevented me from getting to sleep at a proper hour when I had to start work early in the morning. The result was a quarrel at bedtime.

2 February

Made it up with Ptashka. Yesterday's performance of *The Tsar's Bride* had impressed her very much. The standard of the singing and the orchestral playing may not have been on the very highest level, but the director's concept and the refinement of the singers' gestures were what had interested her. She had said to Tsukker yesterday: 'This is the kind of theatre I should like to work in.' Tsukker: 'Splendid. If you like, we can sign a contract tomorrow.'

This is enough to make Ptashka ready to move altogether from Paris to Moscow.

Kucheryavy rang up: I had written him a note because there had been no sign of him. Everything seems to be going well with him, although I did notice that the triumphant tone of his earlier letters, exhorting everyone to return to the USSR and work for the reconstruction of the country, was now more muted.

I practised the piano and worked on the programme for my second recital, then made my way to the Great Hall of the Conservatoire where I was due to rehearse the two-piano version of the Schubert Waltzes with Feinberg. I waited for ever for him, and when at length he appeared his first words were something like: 'Don't for a moment imagine it's my fault for being late.' It seems some unforeseen problems had cropped up, or his watch was slow, but the result was it was now too late to rehearse in the Great Hall and therefore we went to Lamm's flat, which is near by and has two pianos. This was the same Lamm¹ who had accompanied Myaskovsky's pieces when I was playing in my first Moscow concerts, organised by Derzhanovsky.

This was my first opportunity to hear my transcription of the Schubert Waltzes in this form, except that I could not really listen to them as I was preoccupied with ensemble problems and the attempt to play the right notes, since of course I had not properly learnt my part. While we were playing Myaskovsky came in with Lamm himself, and we had tea. Myaskovsky was critical of Persimfans, whose accompaniment to the Third Piano Concerto on the last occasion had, he said, been disgraceful.

'But they did have some excuse,' I demurred, 'as they were missing three key players.'

Myaskovsky: 'That's just what I mean! The lack of front-desk woodwind and string musicians made the brass completely lose the rhythm.'

He had warm words for Oborin as a composer. Not everything he writes is attractive, but all of it shows clear signs of talent.

The score of Myaskovsky's Seventh Symphony has just come out in print. Universal has made a most beautiful job of it: the printing of our publishers is markedly inferior.

In the evening we did not go out as we did not feel like tearing off anywhere. In any case I needed to practise, as the Fourth Sonata, for instance, was by no means fully prepared.

3 February

In the morning I went through the recital programme, mainly the Fourth Sonata. There was a letter from Gorchakov with a scrawl from Svyatoslav: 'Baby is gooboy.'

In the afternoon I looked in at the Persimfans office. There I found an ominous telegram from one Vorobyov in Kharkov, an official in the Ukrainian Ministry of National Education, stating that were I to contemplate appearing in the Ukraine under any auspices other than the Ukrainian State Theatres, my concerts would be proscribed. This made me see red and my immediate reaction was to say that if such were to be the case then I

---

1   Pavel Lamm (1882–1951), pianist and musicologist. Today he is probably best known in the West for his performing editions of Musorgsky's original scores for *Boris Godunov* and *Khovanshchina*, Borodin's *Prince Igor* and Tchaikovsky's *Voevoda*. After Prokofiev's return to the USSR he became a trusted friend and collaborator, transcribing and preparing full scores from the composer's shorthand scores of *Semyon Kotko*, *Cinderella* and *War and Peace*. Prokofiev's many detailed and revealing letters to Lamm, edited and annotated by Irina Medvedeva, may be seen in the collection *Sergey Prokofev: Reminiscences, Letters, Articles*, Deka-BC Publishers, Moscow, 2004, pp. 274–317. Prokofiev had first met Lamm at a concert promoted by Derzhanovsky in Moscow in January 1914, at which Lamm accompanied the cellist Yevsey Beloúsov in Myaskovsky's Cello Sonata No. 1. See *Diaries*, vol. 1, p. 589.

would appear not for the State Theatres but for a private impresario and would devote all proceeds from the concerts to the homeless. Let's see if they dare to put a spoke in that particular wheel. Tseitlin, however, laughed the whole thing off, saying that no threats coming from Kharkov mean anything since they have no rights in such matters.

I rehearsed the Schubert Waltzes with Feinberg on two pianos. They sounded good. However, I was informed that tickets are not selling well for tomorrow, possibly because the posters do not make it clear that this is a new programme, so the public probably thinks that what I am going to play is a rehash of what I have already offered them.

I spent the evening at home in the hotel, since the programme has not yet been brought up to the necessary level and needs more practice.

We had tea with Morolyov, with whom it was nice to chat. He grumbles about his life, although there really seems no need for his discontent; others are much worse off. His main salary may be only a hundred roubles but he has another job as well, for which he gets another hundred. On top of this his eldest daughter has just started work and gets about a hundred roubles, and finally his private practice brings in about another hundred. Four hundred a month seems quite acceptable to me.

4 February

I had a rehearsal with the orchestra this morning, which was filmed. This process ended up consuming a quarter of the rehearsal time, because first they filmed me with the whole Persimfans Orchestra, during which we made some dreadful mistakes. Then they filmed me on my own, and now I was surrounded by so many blinding lights that not only could I not see anything, I was boiling hot while being asked to play 'oh, anything where we can see your hands leaping about'. To this end I chose the finale of the Fourth Sonata, the passage in which scales are swapped between the two hands and, distracted by the hissing of the lights and the cameraman cranking his machine, needless to say made a desperate mess of it. Afterwards I thought: suppose this footage is preserved for posterity[1] and someone who would like to know how the composer played his own works can view it projected in slow motion. Then the full horror will be plain for all to see!

When the rehearsal was over Ptashka – wearing her leopard-skin coat – and I were taken to the foyer of the hall and there, seated side by side, required to converse with one another. All the time tears were running down

---

1 It was. But it is a short clip (silent, of course; *The Jazz Singer* would not be seen even on American screens until October 1927) and even following with the score does not show up any egregious errors.

my cheeks from the lights, so if the film is ever shown this scene can be entitled 'A Tearful Scene in the Prokofiev Family'.

This over, Tseitlin and I went to the Foreign Passports Department where Comrade Girin was again his courteous and urbane self. In the course of the interview he said, 'We have been obliged to make representations on your behalf,' and explained that a report had appeared in the *Evening Red Paper*[1] to the effect that Prokofiev had applied to have his Soviet citizenship restored and that the application had been granted. I had already seen this report and had been very displeased by it. It had obviously emanated from the fact that I had asked for a passport to leave the country and go abroad. I told Girin that I had even given an interview to a reporter who had asked me this very question about my having applied for Soviet citizenship, and that I had said in reply, 'This quote is untrue. I have no need to make any such application, since when I left the country in 1918 I did so with Soviet papers and they are those with which I have now returned. What then would be the purpose of my application?'

'Perfectly correct,' said Girin. 'We ourselves sent a correction to the newspaper.' (But I never saw any such correction printed.) As far as today's formalities for obtaining foreign passports were concerned some additional documents were needed, which Tseitlin undertook to provide. Girin also suggested my approaching the People's Commisariat for Education to see whether there might be some way of avoiding payment of the 400-rouble fees.

Back at the hotel I prepared for the evening's recital but still did not manage get fully on top of the Fourth Sonata. The Great Hall of the Conservatoire was once again full. I was told that a lot of tickets had been bought at the last moment, although it may be that the Persimfans management had distributed unsold tickets to the general public. Tseitlin was evasive on the subject, either so as not make a bad impression on me or because he did not want me to accuse him of having crammed in too many concerts one after the other.

The programme began with the Second Sonata, which went well, followed by *Tales of an Old Grandmother*. I went wrong in the third of these pieces, that is to say for two bars I forgot what the right hand should be doing and carried on with the left hand alone. Afterwards I flung my arm round Myaskovsky's neck wailing, 'What a horrible mess I made of the third *Tale!*', at which he smiled slyly and said, 'Yes, and it was quite noticeable. But it really didn't matter at all. At least you didn't play any wrong notes.'

Apart from this mishap I played the *Tales* well, 'with feeling and atmosphere' as the critical cliché has it. The reaction was much more enthusiastic than it had

---

[1] *Vechernyaya Krasnaya Gazeta*.

been for the first recital programme, especially so after the *Tales*. I asked that no one be admitted to the Green Room during the interval, so only Tsukker was there, delighted with the success of the *Tales*. 'That's exactly the kind of music we should be giving the public,' he said. I reacted indignantly to this, saying that on the contrary the public must be educated to appreciate more complex and meaningful works, and it was depressing to find him, whom I had believed shared my views, advocating pandering to the taste of the crowd.

After the interval came the Fourth Sonata, which I did not play very well. The first movement now strikes me as tedious and I did not enjoy performing it; the second movement was better although I had an attack of nerves about going wrong in the easiest part of all, the middle section. The finale was, as I confessed to Myaskovsky afterwards, more 'decorative' than accurate, but was, nevertheless, a great success.

After this the lid of the second piano was opened and Feinberg and I played the Waltzes which went, I thought, very well indeed and elicited applause on a level comparable to the two previous recitals. I played one encore from the Op. 12 set and then declined to play any more, asking the staff to close the piano, but Yavorsky ran in clamouring for the Waltzes to be repeated. At his command the two pianos were opened again and Yavorsky dashed on to the stage in front of us with the music, announcing that he would turn the pages. Feinberg and I reluctantly followed him and encored the Waltzes, to the great delight of the audience but considerably less so at least for me, whose piano had by this time been pushed right to the edge of the stage meaning that I had to play with a mass of people pushed up close where they drank in every movement of my hands and feet.

In the Green Room Yavorsky's students presented Ptashka with a bouquet of flowers.

5 February

Another orchestra rehearsal in the morning. This time the *Overture* was better. Tsukker suggested reseating the seventeen players and even drew a plan of where they should go. Previously they had sat in their normal orchestra positions and were too far away from one another, giving the impression of an orchestra playing rather gloomily at half-strength. Now the seventeen players sat in a group, and according to Tsukker's plan the harps were in a place they had never expected to be, at the front. This produced a situation in which it soon became delightfully apparent that all the time they had been sitting comfortably at the back they had been playing their difficult parts extremely approximately, whereas now, in full view at the front, I twice caught them playing passages full of wrong notes. They blushed with embarrassment and promised to take their parts home and learn them properly. Overall the

Overture had pulled itself together, but the Second Piano Concerto, on which the bulk of the rehearsal was spent, was still limping along.

In the afternoon I rested and then practised the piano. Yesterday I had received another anonymous letter, from a different Russian woman, but this one was signed 'Pava' and was considerably less edifying in character, in fact downright erotic not to say diabolical in its suggestiveness. A telephone number was attached, with an invitation to phone. Ptashka and I amused ourselves by fantasising that she, Ptashka, would make the call and pretend to be my private secretary. Before passing the letter on to me she would like please to have more precise details of the pleasures and entertainment Pava planned to offer me. But we had to abandon this ruse because at that moment Derzhanovsky, Jurgenson and Kucheryavy all arrived. We did get a phone call with an impatient female voice demanding to speak to me, but I declined.

Jurgenson appears to have aged, but that is hardly surprising since I have not seen him for twelve years. He spoke in a slow, convoluted manner, frequently getting off the point, which made the conversation tediously protracted. He now occupies a lowly position in Muzsektor and therefore works in the very shop of which in former times he was the proprietor. We kept our voices low, because we did not know who might be listening on the other side of the locked door separating us from the adjoining room.

The gist of what he had to say was the following: when the publishing rights in Russia formerly owned by his firm were nationalised, he had transferred all the foreign rights to his friend Forberg, who on the strength of this had reprinted and was selling abroad a whole series of compositions, including all of mine that had previously been published by Jurgenson, with the exception of the First Piano Concerto. In return for this he from time to time transfers to Jurgenson certain sums of money, although not very often and not very accurately accounted for. Not that there can be any question of accurate accounts, seeing that the whole enterprise is at best semi-legal.

The essence of the conversation from my side was to see how an arrangement could be made whereby the rights could be diverted from Forberg to our publishing house, with a view to dividing the royalties accruing to me from sales equally between me and Jurgenson, that is to say each of us receiving 12.5 per cent of the value of the sale. The non-commercial ethos of our publishers would guarantee Jurgenson an accurate proportion of the receipts. Jurgenson was most willing to agree to the proposal, but the difficulty would be to make Forberg cede his rights to our publishers. Although 'Brutus is an honourable man' it is still the case that the reprinting of the works has cost him money and therefore he might try in all sorts of ways to steer clear of doing what we propose.

Jurgenson would write to him, but it would be impossible to do this openly because the letter might be intercepted by the censors. Communication would have to be by some circuitous route, perhaps through some contact in the German Embassy.

Kucheryavy had put on weight since I knew him in America. I gave him the fountain pen and propelling pencil he had asked me to bring him from abroad. The buoyant mood of his first letters after arriving back in Soviet Russia, where he had had taken up a post as director of a glue-boiling factory in Moscow, had declined sharply. It was impossible to work properly, he said, on account of the universal laziness, bureaucracy and red tape. Private enterprise was an indispensable principle; without it business simply ground to a halt, not to mention the torture of being obliged to maintain good relations with the Communists, who control everything and spy on you to boot. Switching to English and dropping his voice he added, 'And here every sixth person you meet is a spy.'

Tsukker called for us in the evening because we had been invited to visit Kameneva, Trotsky's sister and the wife of the Soviet Ambassador in Rome. Kameneva herself is head of cultural relations with foreign countries, which means on the one hand representing Soviet Russia's cultural assets abroad and on the other inviting to Russia whatever from the foreign cultural sphere is, from a Soviet perspective, considered valuable.[1] Since she lives inside the

---

1   Olga Kameneva née Bronstein (1883–1941) was Trotsky's sister and the first wife of Lev Kamenev, whom she had married around 1905. Both were close to Lenin in Paris and edited the main Bolshevik expatriate magazine *Proletarii*, Kamenev and his fellow Marxist Revolutionary Bogdanov being Lenin's two closest associates at that time. After the October Revolution Kameneva was initially put in charge of the Theatre Division of the Education Commissariat, working with Meyerhold, but was subsequently moved sideways by Lunacharsky to various essentially propaganda projects. She was still an influential figure, however, and from 1926 to 1928, that is to say at the time of this meeting, was Chairman of VOKS, the USSR Society for Cultural Relations with Foreign Countries, and thus the figurehead for contact with the leading Western artists and intellectuals who visited the Soviet Union in such numbers. By this time her marriage to Kamenev, who with Zinoviev had already been expelled from the Politburo and sent out of harm's way to be Soviet Ambassador to Italy, had come to an end although it is clear from this reference that this fact was not common knowledge. But at the XVth Bolshevik Party Conference later in the year all the signs were that the so-called United Opposition (that is to say Trotsky, with whom Kamenev and Zinoviev were now aligned) had failed and it would henceforth be all downhill for the principals and anyone associated with them. The beginning of the end came for Olga Kameneva in 1935 when she was banned from Moscow and Leningrad for five years, and after her former husband's trial and execution at the first of the Moscow Show Trials in 1936 she was arrested, to languish in the camps for four years until her trial in 1941. At first, Zinoviev and Kamenev had held out against confession, but after especially brutal torture and threats against their families they both agreed to sign confessions on condition of a guarantee from the Politburo that their lives and those of their families and followers would be spared. This plea was accepted, but when they were taken to the supposed Politburo meeting to be provided with the guarantee, only Stalin, Voroshilov and Yezhov were present, claiming that that they were the troika commission appointed by the Politburo to give the promised assurances. Kamenev and Zinoviev duly confessed, but after the trial Stalin not only broke his promise to spare their lives, he had most of their relatives arrested and shot. The Kamenevs' two sons were shot in 1938 and 1939, their mother in September 1941.

Kremlin we were issued with special passes and this journey into the Kremlin was in itself not devoid of interest. We went there on foot, and as we neared the Kremlin gates showed our passes at a little guichet. After some formalities, exactly what I do not know since Tsukker took care of them while I jigged about from foot to foot because of the terrible cold, we passed through the gates guarded by soldiers with rifles whose glittering bayonets sparkled iridescent from the frost. It was a strange feeling to penetrate actually into the Red Kremlin, that union of the ancient with the seat of Revolutionary new ambition to reconstruct the whole world.

Tsukker walked along beside us spluttering with excitement as he pointed out celebrities: 'Look, there's so-and-so, he is the Minister of Something-or-Other, this is the spot where Lenin did thus-and-such, and that building is where Demyan Bedny[1] lives. 'Good heavens,' I exclaimed. 'Fancy him being so important that he lives in the Kremlin!' 'Well,' explained Tsukker, 'he is an Old Communist. But it is not very convenient to live inside the Kremlin: if he wants anyone to visit him there are endless complications with passes.'

After passing through a series of long corridors in one of the huge ministerial-type Kremlin buildings we found ourselves outside Kameneva's door. First we were admitted to a rather nonsensical entrance hall, and thence to an enormous room comfortably furnished with magnificent armchairs and sofas and a multitude of bookcases and open shelves with more books on them. We were ceremoniously led in to an atmosphere redolent of deference which left us in no doubt that we were in an exalted domain.

Olga Davidovna herself seemed to me a lively and pleasant lady, mildly Americanised. Ptashka did not feel the same way at all, finding her neither pleasant nor American. Also present was Karakhan,[2] and before long Litvinov

---

1 Demian Bedny (pen-name of Yefim Pridvorov, 1883–1945; 'bedny' means 'poor'), poet and satirist. His poems, particularly those attacking religion, were much favoured by both Lenin and Stalin in the 1920s. But even ideologically irreproachable artists were never immune from censure, and ripples from Bedny's fall from grace in the 1930s were to extend to Taïrov's Kamerny Teatr over a revival of Borodin's problematical comic opera *Bogatyri* (*Russian Knight-Heroes*) for which Bedny had written a libretto criticised for 'contradicting history and being thoroughly false in its political tendency', and beyond that for the Pushkin centenary production of a dramatic realisation of *Eugene Onegin* (to a text by Sigizmond Krzhizhanovsky with incidental music by Prokofiev) which by decree of the Committee on Arts Affairs was abandoned before being performed. The tortuous reasoning of the Committee on Arts Affairs and their Chairman Platon Kerzhentsev is comprehensively laid bare in *Power and the Creative Intelligentsia: Documents of the Communist Party and the Cheka/OGPU/NKVD about Cultural Policy 1917–53*, International Democracy Foundation, Moscow, 1999, also by K. Clark, E. A. Dobrenko, eds., *Soviet Culture and Power: A History in Documents 1917–53*, Yale University Press, 2007.

2 Lev Karakhan (1889–1937), politician and diplomat. He had served as secretary to Trotsky's delegation at Brest-Litovsk and after various diplomatic posts was appointed Deputy Commissar for Foreign Affairs (i.e. Litvinov's deputy) in 1926. He held this position until 1934 when he was despatched to Turkey as Soviet Ambassador, having in the meantime married the ballerina Marina Semyonova. In May 1937 he was abruptly recalled to Moscow, arrested and

and his wife arrived on the scene. Both Ministers are very fond of music and know something about it; Karakhan for example told me that when he was in China[1] he had a Duo-Art player-piano with several rolls recorded by me, which he enjoyed listening to in the evenings when resting from official duties. I found this terribly touching: Karakhan, in the midst of sowing the seeds for revolution in China, drawing relaxation and renewed strength from the sound of music I had composed.

Tsukker sidled cautiously over in my direction to nudge me into what he considered a good move: to play something. I was quite ready to do so as it seemed that all those present genuinely liked my music. I played mostly smaller pieces, and in between went to chat to Litvinov and Karakhan. They asked me about my impressions of the USSR and other countries I had visited. I responded by concentrating, of course, on the arts, criticising the less favourable aspects of Western countries while laying stress on what I found good in the USSR. In this way it could be seen that we were all more or less of one mind.

After this our hostess invited us to go in to supper, in the dining room. The table was spread neither lavishly nor meagrely, but seemed to have been prepared without much thought. The napkins were embroidered with the initials A III.[2] We were served by a chambermaid, addressed

---

tried by the Military College of the Supreme Court for counter-revolutionary activities, sentenced on 20 September 1937 and shot later the same day. Karakhan was thus one of the 40,000 or so victims of the special execution lists drawn up by Stalin, signed by himself, Voroshilov, Kaganovich, Zhdanov and Molotov and transmitted by the NKVD to the Military College for summary implementation in accordance with the 'simplified procedure' laid down by the Act of 1 December 1934. The provisions of this Act were indeed simple: proceedings to be heard in secret before three judges drawn from the membership of the College; no witnesses to be called. Trials lasted an average of five to ten minutes, exceptionally up to half an hour. Within this time-frame the three judges were charged with the following duties: to read the accused his or her rights; to enunciate the charge(s); to clarify the essence of the alleged offence; to establish the connection of the accused to the offence; to hear the testimony of the accused; to withdraw to a separate room for consultation and to put the sentence in writing; to return to the court and pronounce the verdict. Death sentences (the norm) were not generally announced at this time; the first intimation the victim would have was to be taken to the execution chamber. Even after Stalin's death his successors were in no hurry to repeal this legislation: it remained on the statute books until April 1956 and in an irony that provides, if not actual pleasure, at least some sort of grim satisfaction, was employed to the letter for the trial of Lavrenty Beria in December 1953. It was also the procedure under which Lina Prokofiev would be tried and convicted for anti-Soviet activities in 1948.

1 From 1923 until 1926, during which period he was responsible for negotiating the important Sino-Russian Agreement for joint administration of the Chinese Eastern Railway, the line that shortcuts Chita in Siberia to Vladivostok without having to loop northwards through Khabarovsk (as the Trans-Siberian Railway still does, in order to stay throughout on Russian territory), and (via a southern spur from Harbin known as the South Manchuria Railway) to Changchun and eventually Beijing.
2 Tsar Alexander III, father of the last Tsar of Russia, Nicholas II.

with formal courtesy by her first name and patronymic. Several other people besides Litvinov and Karakhan were also dining, none of whom made much impression. Among them was Kameneva's son, a very young man with an even younger wife who looked about fifteen but must I suppose have been older. She is studying ballet and was very interested in my music, so it was a pity that she was late getting home today and so had not heard me play.

After supper Kameneva asked me to play especially for the girl, but I decided that this was an occasion when I must stand on my dignity so I replied that it was getting late, and in any case I was tired. The girl made a face at this, so I observed somewhat waspishly, 'You should have come home in time.' But it transpired that she had not been able to, as she had had to go somewhere to dance.

I said, 'In that case you will be able to hear me at one of my next concerts.' But this would not do either as she is always busy in the evenings, and Kameneva persisted in her efforts to get me to play for her. My patience was beginning to wear thin, and I answered, 'I shall also be busy tomorrow morning at rehearsal, and I need to have a clear head and strong fingers', and added, 'If you are really so anxious to hear me play then why could you not have managed to arrange matters so that you could? If not, then you cannot have been so very anxious after all, in which case it hardly seems worthwhile my playing to you now.'

On this note we began to make a move to depart. Evidently this is not the way one is supposed to talk to a princess of the blood, and my intransigence made a bad impression on Kameneva. But for my part I am happy to have put the child in her place.

However, it was not such a simple matter to leave, as it was already past midnight, the validity of our one-day passes had therefore expired and we would not be allowed to pass back through the gates with them. A call had to be put through to the Kremlin Commandant's office to obtain a freshly dated pass. Litvinov kindly offered to take us out in his car, as he lives outside the Kremlin. 'They won't ask you for your pass if you are with me,' he said.

We therefore had to go on drinking tea while waiting impatiently for Litvinov's car to be brought round. I was desperate to get to bed, as tomorrow's rehearsal starts early. At long last the message came that the car was ready for us; we said goodbye to Kameneva and walked back along the endless corridors. Mme Litvinova carried her boots in her hands as she did not want to soil the carpets in the corridors. We all piled into Litvinov's roomy limousine, he with his wife, I with Ptashka, Karakhan and Tsukker.

'How I love this quiet Kremlin,' said Mme Litvinova dreamily. Knowing what frenetic activity in fact goes on all the time in this quiet Kremlin, I found this a curiously naive observation.

When the car stopped at the Kremlin gates Litvinov, Tsukker and Karakhan took out their permanent passes while we sat hidden in the back. Then the car moved on and Litvinov drove us to the Metropole.

Safe in our room we shared our impression. Ptashka wanted to know who was the polite, swarthy gentleman who had so vigorously shaken her hand. I told her it was that very Karakhan who had so antagonised the entire Chinese nation. Ptashka was astonished to hear this, and then told me about the amusing conversation she had had with Litvinov's wife. 'You know,' the latter had observed, 'it's so difficult with taxi drivers in Paris – they're all white.' Ptashka was about to explain that there are not many black people in Paris altogether, only in New York does one expect to come across Negro taxi-drivers, when Mme Litvinova clarified her thoughts: 'Well, obviously, every third one is one of Wrangel's officers, and as soon as they realise where you want to go is the Soviet Embassy they not only refuse to take you there but are rude to you into the bargain!'

Mme Litvinova then urged Ptashka to be sure and call on her, presumably anticipating the pleasure of having someone with whom to converse in English.

6 February

The rehearsal started at 9 a.m. with orchestra and me getting to grips with the Second Concerto. The rehearsal over, I asked Tseitlin for his advice about the proposal Tutelman is making to me for six concerts in the Ukraine. Tutelman is the man who had come to Paris with Boris Krasin two years ago.[1] I had not liked him much then, and he has a dubious reputation in Moscow as well. A year ago he was removed from his post in Rosphil in something of a scandal, but being an adroit operator had found himself another billet with the Ukrainian State Theatres. Tseitlin said that Tutelman was unquestionably a shady character but since he is offering a contract with the Ukrainian State Theatres it must be sound, and if he offers a decent fee, payable in dollars, there is no reason why I should not accept.

When I returned to the Metropole I met a greatly agitated Meckler who does not want to lose me to Tutelman, of whose circling round me he must have got wind. In his excitable way Meckler offered me $1,000 for each appearance in the provinces, more in Moscow, and even pressed the same sum into my hand as a deposit, without asking for a receipt, purely to clinch the deal. In support of his claim to be an international manager he showed me a telegram from Gil-Marchex agreeing to twenty concerts at a fee of 120 roubles a concert. Poor Marchex, swaggering about Paris boasting of his colossal success in

---

1 See above, pp. 212–13.

Russia – 120 roubles, and with a semi-reputable impresario to boot! Of course, to the French this might seem a decent fee, at least it is something. But despite the international telegram and a fee ten times the size, I gave Meckler his $1,000 back and made my escape in a flurry of vague protestations.

When I went up to our room, the telephone was ringing. It was Tutelman. I did not feel up to weighing the various proposals and so prevaricated, asking Tutelman to put off any discussion until tomorrow. A decision will have to be taken tomorrow, however, as Tutelman is going back south while I am going north to Leningrad.

In the afternoon I rested: yesterday night we had got to bed at 2 a.m., this morning I rose at eight, rehearsed all morning, then sold myself to the Ukraine – result: exhaustion and the heaviest of heads.

At five o'clock I made my way to the Bolshoy Theatre, as I had received a note from the theatre directorate specifically asking me to come to a meeting to discuss the impending production of *Oranges*. The meeting took place in the Director's box, or to be precise in the retiring room attached to the large side box just above the orchestra pit which is reserved for the Director's use. The box was also often occupied by members of the government, and it was not unknown for them at the end of a performance to sequester themselves in the adjacent retiring room to decide affairs of state. The room was also used for meetings on theatre business.

When I came in the only people I knew were Golovanov, Rabinovich and Dikiy, and this being for the two last-named their debut production for the theatre they were both newcomers. As the meeting progressed I gradually worked out who was who. The Director of the Bolshoy, Burdukov, was an old Party man who knew nothing whatsoever about the theatre and in the present company appeared like a kind of alien thorn driven by the government into the side of the living organism of the theatre.[1] Apparently he was a former soldier, a not unhelpful background in that he knew how to take command and act decisively. In general he conducted himself decently, even

---

1 A. A. Burdukov, a classical Old Bolshevik and intimate Civil War comrade-in-arms of both Trotsky and Nikolay Muralov, had spent a long period of imprisonment in the Schlüsselberg Fortress outside Petrograd before the Revolution. According to the memoirs of the choreographer Igor Moiseyev, who knew him well, his long incarceration had caused him to lose all contact with the real life of the world outside, and the Bolshoy sinecure was his reward for durance vile. Immediately after the Revolution he had headed the Moscow Military Revolutionary Committee before being put out to grass in the Bolshoy, where he stayed until 1932 before being given another sinecure as Director of the Timiryazev Moscow State Agricultural Academy, whose operations included a notable House of Culture. But as with innumerable others who had the temerity or bad judgement to oppose Stalin in the post-Lenin power struggle of the mid-1920s the old association with Trotsky and the Left Opposition was not forgotten or forgiven, and in January 1937 Muralov was one of those accused in the second of the Moscow Show Trials, the so-called Trial of the Seventeen, found guilty and executed, Burdukov following not long after.

modestly, doing his best to reconcile the differences of opinion among his wild artistic colleagues; he made a favourable impression on me. I found Lossky,[1] the Chief Producer, a much less sympathetic character. It was obvious that he did not take kindly to the appearance of another producer on his stage in the shape of Dikiy, and in his quiet voice was continually putting spokes in Dikiy's wheel.

Besides the above-mentioned, there were present Avranek, the elderly chorusmaster,[2] and a few other representatives of the technical production staff, lighting designers, property masters, and so on.

The purpose of the meeting was to decide whether or not it would be feasible to stage *Oranges* in the course of the present season. Dikiy was asking for an impossible number of rehearsals, prompting Lossky to declare that with so many it was inconceivable that *Oranges* could be presented even as late as May. How many orchestra rehearsals Golovanov would need was also discussed. Rabinovich outlined what would be necessary for the construction of the scenery; Avranek did the same in respect of chorus rehearsals, the technical personnel for making the props and costumes, and so on. My presence was mainly passive, only occasionally did I vouchsafe an opinion in an undertone either to Dikiy or to Golovanov.

A major stumbling-block along the way was *The Red Poppy*, a ballet on a Revolutionary theme with music by Glière[3] scheduled to be presented

---

1 Vladimir Lossky (1874–1946), bass, combined his operatic singing career with production, having made his debut with Cui's *Prisoner of the Caucasus* at the Bolshoy in 1909.
2 Ulrich Avranek (1853–1937), Czech-born conductor, was appointed Chief Chorusmaster and Second Conductor of the Orchestra of the Bolshoy Opera in the 1880s, and it was under his leadership that the chorus attained an international reputation, engaged for example by Diaghilev for his first Paris season in 1908 for the productions of *Prince Igor* and *Boris Godunov*. Once at the Bolshoy Avranek never departed from it, and made an important contribution to the success of the theatre's premiere productions of Borodin's *Prince Igor*, Rimsky-Korsakov's *Christmas Eve* and *Mozart and Salieri*, and others.
3 Glière had been inspired to compose the ballet by the ballerina Yekaterina Geltzer towards the twilight of her career; she danced the role of the beautiful Tao-Hoa, sacrificing her life for principles amid the brutality of Kuomintang China in the 1920s. Apart from having a politically fireproof ideological background, the ballet contains at least one really good tune, or at least a successful orchestral treatment of a folk tune: 'Yablochko' ('Little Apple'), even better known as the 'Russian Sailor's Dance' (see above, p. 217). The premiere, choreographed by Lev Lashchilin (Acts 1 and 3; Vasily Tikhomirov – Geltzer's husband – was responsible for Act 2) took place in June 1927. Thirty years later, at a time when the Soviet Union was pouring billions of roubles in economic and military aid into Afghanistan, the Bolshoy's revival of *The Red Poppy* was renamed *The Red Flower* so as to avoid the unfortunate association with the interesting properties of the plant so lucratively cultivated there. Glière, nothing if not a competent composer and teacher, equally adept at steering a middle course between the competing factions of the Association for Contemporary Music and the Russian Association of Proletarian Musicians, was appointed to an important position in the Union of Composers on its establishment in 1938, and as a result enjoyed a longer, more comfortable and on the whole more productive career than most of his contemporaries.

before *Oranges*. Burdukov, however, had evidently received instructions from on high that *Oranges* should be inserted into the schedule at the earliest possible moment, so was insisting that my opera be staged before the 1st June. Was this, perhaps, why I found him such a likeable character? Another reason for Burdukov's impetuosity, of course, might have been his desire to eclipse the Leningrad production with his own theatre's, in the hope of its being chosen for the foreign tour in preference to the rival one from Leningrad. In any case the meeting ended happily for me, with the declared intention of sparing no effort to bring *Oranges* into the repertoire some time in May.

The meeting over, I went back to the hotel to collect Ptashka. We were joined by Rabinovich and together set out on foot to dine at Golovanov's. On the way Rabinovich enthusiastically expounded his great plan to repaint Moscow. 'Moscow looks so shabby at the moment it's quite repulsive,' he said. 'Hundreds of buildings have the paint peeling from them and they have been left so long they are in a bad state of repair. It will take a long time to bring them back into a reasonable condition. But if in the meantime they could at least be painted according to an agreed plan you would have at least an acceptable-looking city. Imagine a whole street painted blue, with one crossing painted in two different colours . . .'

I liked the sound of this project very much, but of course it is just an idea.

The company at Golovanov's was the same as before, except that this time Nezhdanova was also there. Ptashka was pleased by this as, knowing the fame of the Nezhdanova coloratura, she has been very much wanting to meet her. Nezhdanova is an exceedingly tall lady, of a certain age as they say, and very pleasant to meet. One hears that she is beginning to lose her voice, but Golovanov is keen that she should sing Ninetta. How on earth does he envisage such a substantial person fitting into an orange?

Today's dinner was as marvellous as the first time. Towards the end of the meal Derzhanovsky appeared to take Ptashka back to his house, as they have At Home gatherings on Sundays and he was most anxious that Ptashka should be there. It was a shame I could not be there as well, but the young composers would take good care of her.

After the meal I played through Acts 3 and 4 of *Oranges*, while Golovanov as last time impressed with his 'absolute rhythm', writing down the metronome marks from my playing. Dikiy noted down all my remarks in his notebook. By eleven o'clock we had at last completed the play-through of the whole opera, and I returned home tired out and with a headache. I fell asleep as if I had been poleaxed, but was woken up at one o'clock by the deafening ringing of the telephone. I sat on the edge of the bed for a long time unable even to think where I was. By the time I got to the phone nobody seemed to be at the other end.

7 February

I woke up tired and enervated, but gradually came to myself. Another rehearsal was beginning, but I did not get to it at the start. We spent most of the time on the Second Concerto, which is at last beginning to take shape in a clearer form. The rehearsals of the Second Concerto are no less useful to me than they are to the orchestra, since they have given me the opportunity to become fully secure in this exceptionally difficult piece and to integrate thoroughly with the orchestra. Next we went through the *Overture* one more time. Derzhanovsky and Golovanov sat in the hall to listen, and then Tutelman came with his contract, amended in accordance with the conditions I had made yesterday.

After the rehearsal I secreted myself with Tseitlin and, having read through the agremeent with him, signed it, thus committing myself in a month's time to six concerts in the Ukraine. Ukrainian State Theatres will, naturally, be making a profit out of me, but still they are offering a real fee, and in dollars, to be paid by cheque directly to my account abroad.

Back at the Metropole there was a telephone call from Khais, the Artful Dodger who had contrived to pay me for my Leningrad concerts half what Tutelman was paying for my provincial appearances. Khais, having just arrived from Leningrad, was anxious to pay his respects to me personally. On the pretext that I was too busy I said I could not receive him just now. It transpired, however, that he was already in the hotel and was telephoning me from the lobby, and was also the bearer of a letter to me from Asafyev. I told him that I was just on my way out, and if he cared to wait a few minutes I would be coming down. Five minutes or so later I went down to the lobby, exchanged a few official words with him, and then left again.

The programme for the evening concert was the second of my orchestral programmes. The Great Hall of the Conservatoire was completely sold out. First on the programme was the *Overture for Seventeen Instruments*, Op. 42. Although all seventeen musicians put their utmost into it the piece failed to come alight and was coolly received. It must be remembered that the *Overture* was designed for the Aeolian Hall in New York, which seats 250 people, and inevitably in a hall with ten times the capacity it can sound a little poverty-stricken.

The end of the Overture was followed by much rearranging of the orchestra seating before I could come out to play the Second Piano Concerto. I was nervous, and kept asking myself why this should be so? Pride, of course: what would people say if Prokofiev himself can't play it? I tried to convince myself of the fallibility of this train of thought: so what if I make mistakes? The Concerto is still the Concerto. This reasoning helped, and I went out to play in a fairly calm state. It did not last, however, through the most testing passages, for example in the cadenza where it is marked *colossale*. I also went wrong at the beginning of the third movement where the two hands have to leap over one another. Shameful. All the same, the rest of the time I played well and with elan. The end of the first movement was an immediate, palpable success. We took a short break at the end of the scherzo, during which there were cries of 'encore!', but of course there was no question of my being able to comply. The success at the end of the whole work was, indeed, colossal, and there was no doubt that it produces a much stronger impression than the Third Concerto. After I had come out a few times to take a bow, the orchestra still in place, Tseitlin whispered to me that it would be a good idea to repeat the scherzo. Although I still did not feel truly rested enough, the triumphant mood of the hall and even the orchestra imbued me with enough strength to try, so we repeated the scherzo. This time we pressed the tempo too much and lost a little of the precision.

Yavorsky gave me a tumultuous greeting in the Green Room, followed by Myaskovsky and Mme Litvinova. Nadya Rayevskaya was also there and it was strange to see the two women side by side: an Englishwoman given to carrying her boots in her hand, by some quirk of fate the wife of a minister, and an aristocrat with a husband in prison helpless to get him out. However, it would have been tactless to introduce them to one another, so I had to talk to them separately, one after the other. In any case I was pulled over to meet Sosnovsky,[1] an Important Communist whose articles in the press carry great weight and to whom Tsukker refers in reverential tones. Sosnovsky enquired whether I had read a Revolutionary poem some Komsomol members had sent me. I had some difficulty extricating myself from this interrogation, since a book of some kind had undoubtedly been addressed to me at the Persimfans office, but I had left it there without looking at it. Sosnovsky droned on relentlessly about the virtues of this Komsomol book and how enlightening I would find it if only I would give it my attention, leaving me wondering how the leaders of Communism and the books they recommend could possibly be so achingly boring.

Eventually the Green Room began to empty of people and Sosnovsky left me alone. The second half of the concert started with the March and the

---

1   Lev Sosnovsky (1886–1937), journalist, unequivocally associated with the Left Opposition, a former colleague of Larissa Reissner and Karl Radek. After the Revolution he had been a highly placed Party activist, heading its agitprop division and editing the peasants' and rank-and-file soldiers' newspaper *Poverty* (*Bednota*). In 1927 the clouds were already gathering over Sosnovsky: at the XVth Party Congress in December he would be expelled from the Party and the following year sent into exile. Arrest and five years' imprisonment followed, but after recanting membership of the Left Opposition Sosnovsky was allowed to return to Moscow in 1934 and to continue working as a journalist. Two years later, however, he was arrested again, tried and executed in July 1937, one more victim of the 'simplified procedure' of Stalin's Supreme Court Military College.

Scherzo from *Three Oranges*, in the category of 'Universal Popular Requests', and then the Suite from *Chout*. I stayed outside in the Green Room, from where I could hear perfectly through gaps in the thin partition wall. The Suite sounded good, and there were loud calls for the composer at the end. When I stepped out on to the stage there was a veritable uproar: the orchestra played a flourish and the entire audience rose to its feet, applauding and whooping deafeningly. When it was all over we still had to go to RABIS,[1] a club for people working in the arts, which had long been asking me to visit and play at least a few of my works. Apparently I had made a promise to look in after today's concert, a fact of which I was now energetically reminded. Ptashka, Tseitlin and I therefore made our way there. As it was not far, somewhere in one of the lanes near the Nikitsky Gates, we went on foot, surrounded by the audience streaming out of the concert that had just taken place and animatedly discussing what they had heard.

RABIS was populated by a strange assortment of people, including some youngsters still wet behind the ears, and some whose appearance did not suggest great intelligence. It seemed that a big congress was going on today, and this explained the colourful public. Somewhat impatiently I asked to be put on to play my pieces as quickly as possible so that I could go home. At this the crowds milling about all over the building piled into the hall, I played five short pieces and, ignoring the clapping and cries of 'encore!' rapidly made my escape and went home.

Tomorrow we are at last off to Leningrad. I already have letters and telegrams from there, and a comprehensive timetable of how our time is to be spent there, drawn up by Asafyev. It so happens that our visit coincides with a performance of Myaskovsky's Eighth Symphony, and today I asked Nyamochka[2] if he would be going to hear it. But it seems he is still having his teeth fixed and so will not be able to travel. I badly wanted to offer him money for the fare, as the stuff seems to be pouring into my hands willy-nilly, but cannot work out how to do this without giving offence.

8 February

Yesterday we performed the whole of the second programme and later today we are going to Leningrad, but there is still a rehearsal I have to go to. This is because the 14th of the month will mark the fifth year of Persimfans's

---

1 RABIS, acronym for Rabotniki Isskustv, 'workers in the arts', a combined society of a number of smaller unions of different professional artistic disciplines such as stage technicians, producers, artists, designers, orchestrators, etc.
2 Prokofiev's affectionate nickname for his strait-laced friend, made up of Myaskovsky's initials N Ya M plus one of the diminutives often added to an intimate's first name.

existence, so there is to be a gala concert at which only two works will be played, both Persimfans warhorses: the *Scythian Suite* and Scriabin's *Poème d'extase*.¹ So today I was asked most particularly to attend the *Scythian Suite* rehearsal so that I could check how the orchestra plays the work and to pass on any composer's injunctions. And indeed there were several tempi I felt needed correcting and accents to be added in the interests of bringing the lineaments of the work into sharper relief. This is how we rehearsed: while they played I walked round the hall stopping them whenever I saw the need. 'Oh, so that's the way to do it,' Tseitlin would exclaim with joy whenever I made a suggestion, and immediately passed on 'Sergey Sergeyevich's wishes' to the orchestra. Tabakov hit some fabulous B flats in the 'Sunrise' finale.

Ptashka and I had a long-standing invitation to lunch from Saradzhev, and although our time was so limited I did not feel we could possibly decline such a gesture from the first man to perform my compositions in Moscow,² especially since Saradzhev, who is already beginning to turn grey, has never despite his enormous gifts as a musician made it into the ranks of the great conductors. There hangs about him an understandable sense of resentment at the indifference of the musical world in which he lives. He lives in a huge room, like a large artist's studio, in the Philharmonia building. His daughters, who were little more than toddlers in those far-off days when Saradzhev premiered *Dreams*, are now very nice, slim young girls. I did not like to ask about Kotik, whom I remembered from those times as a nine-year-old³ with a whole album of extremely lively piano pieces to his credit. I had heard, not in Russia but abroad, troubling rumours that he suffered from epilepsy and was mentally deranged.⁴

---

1   'Divinely fouled up, all fire and air . . . like a bath of ice, cocaine and rainbows' – Henry Miller, *Nexus*.
2   Konstantin Saradzhev (Russianised form of his Armenian name Saradzhian) (1877–1954), violinist, conductor and dedicated advocate for new Russian music, whose many first performances included works by Prokofiev, Shostakovich, Myaskovsky, Stravinsky, Khachaturian. Apart from a private rehearsal by Hugo Wahrlich and the St Petersburg Court Orchestra of the early Symphony in E minor in 1909, Saradzhev was the first conductor to programme an orchestral work by Prokofiev: the symphonic tableau *Dreams*, in his 1911 summer season of concerts in Moscow's Sokolniki Park, and the following year the premiere of the First Piano Concerto. See *Diaries*, vol. 1, pp. 212, 234.
3   As Kotik (Konstantin Saradzhev junior) was born in 1900 and the year in question was 1911, he must have been a little older than this.
4   At the age of seven, Konstantin Konstantinovich Saradzhev (1900–1942) was so strongly affected by hearing a church bell that he fainted, and although he also studied the piano, he devoted his life to the music of the bells, in which he became recognised as the supreme authority, composing 'bell symphonies' that made use of the microtonal complexities of Russian bells. He found, alas, that he was unable to realise them to his satisfaction in Russia. From the *New Yorker*, 27 April 2009: 'He was known not just for his ringing but also for his superhuman aural acuity: between two adjacent whole tones, he perceived not just one half-tone but a half-tone flanked on either side by a hundred and twenty-one flats and a hundred and twenty-one sharps. Although a skilled pianist, he always referred to the piano as "that

Myaskovsky and Derzhanovsky were also at lunch, and immediately launched into an interminable debate about the significance of Persimfans. It seemed obvious to me that a conductor's house was not the right place for a discussions about an orchestra that has elected to do without a conductor, so I took little part in it apart from pointing out, in defence of Persimfans, the importance of playing the right notes, to which this ensemble devotes much attention, and the improved sonority that flows therefrom.

After a most delicious lunch (every lunch and dinner we have had in Moscow has been more delicious than the last one) we moved to the piano and Saradzhev asked me to demonstrate the tempi and my interpretative wishes for the *Classical* Symphony and the *Oranges* Suite. The reason for this was that, although Persimfans had almost entirely got their hands on me, Derzhanovsky had craftily secured the Moscow premiere of the *Classical* Symphony for the Association of Contemporary Music, and Saradzhev was to conduct it. Here Saradzhev impressed me with his musicianly eye: he pointed out a misprint in the printed score I had not spotted despite the care with which I had read the proofs.

At this point Kotik appeared, nowadays a young man sporting a beard, with a strange look in his eyes and a strange manner. I did not know how to talk to him, or what about, and his presence introduced a feeling of uneasiness into the gathering. In any case it was time to leave, because we were expecting a succession of visitors at the Metropole; also we had to pack our cases and leave for Piter.

My visitors had all been given an appointment like a dentist's waiting room, with half an hour allotted to each. But as is mandatory with Russians they were all late and formed a gaggle, later complaining that they had got in one another's way.

First in was Chernetskaya, the one whose ballet concept was projected to turn the whole world upside-down. She had got into the Green Room after

---

well-tempered nitwit": a piano can produce only twelve tones per octave, whereas Saradzhev perceived one thousand seven hundred and one. This sensitivity perhaps explains Saradzhev's intense delight in Russian bells, which are unparalleled in their microtonal complexity. Each bell sounds a unique cloud of untempered frequencies, producing intervals unplayable on any twelve-tone keyboard. By such acoustic fingerprints, Saradzhev could distinguish all four thousand of Moscow's church bells. He described his hearing as "true pitch" (by contrast with perfect pitch). The capacity for true pitch, he said, lay dormant in all humans, and would someday be awakened.' When in 1930 Harvard University invited Saradzhev to help install at Lowell House the original Danilov Monastery bells Charles R. Crane (see pp. 245–6 above) had bought for their value as scrap metal and shipped from Russia (they were restored to the reopened Danilov Monastery in 2008 and replicas made for Harvard), his entire luggage apparently consisted of four pairs of socks and two handkerchiefs. He is thought to have died in an insane asylum in 1941. In 1977 Anastasia Tsvetaeva, the sister of the poet, published a memoir about this gifted but tragically unorthodox musician.

several of my concerts and each time insisted on setting up a rendezvous so that she could explain her ideas to me. I have no confidence whatever in any of them, and the reports I had heard of her from other parties were far from encouraging, but Chernetskaya is not easy to deflect, there is something almost demonic about her, and there was also the fact that she had been Lunacharsky's lover. Not only that, but she had delayed her departure for a day in order to read me her manuscript; in short there was no way of preventing her coming to see me.

The plot of her ballet was quite complicated and as she set it out in minute detail it took at least forty minutes to read. The subject was an archetypal piece of Soviet saccharine involving noble workers, corrupt bankers, factory floors, luxurious bourgeois apartments – everything, in fact, that even the most bigoted Communist was by now sick to death of. The reading of the second half of the ballet proceeded in the most unfavourable circumstances imaginable for Chernetskaya, as I could see that it had no merit at all while at the same time the next phalanx of visitors was already coming into the room, the telephone never stopped ringing, Ptashka was busy telling someone who had come to interview me that he was too late – a reader's vision of hell yet Chernetskaya, bloodied but unbowed, desperately carried on while for politeness's sake I listened with one ear, marvelling at her heroism. As a matter of fact some individual moments were quite ingenious even if already out of date: the dance of the figures in the Stock Exchange elevating the bankers one minute and casting them down the next was not badly conceived,[1] but although she might not know it, Ravel's latest opera features numbers singing and dancing;[2] the factory gearing up to work in balletic idiom is also not a bad thought, but this is exactly what Yakulov and I did in my last ballet for Diaghilev,[3] which no doubt she did not know either ... When I explained all this to her she threw in the towel and, quite cast down, said, 'I did not know this; you are killing me.' But at least it was the *coup de grâce* for the whole project and no more was heard of it.

My next visitor was Razumovsky, the secretary of the Moscow Society of Authors, a charming gentleman with whom I had already been corresponding from abroad.

---

1 Prokofiev had already thought of something analogous and suggested it to Diaghilev, who had rejected it out of hand. See above, p. 167.
2 The finale of the first act of Ravel's *L'Enfant et les sortilèges*, first performed in Monte Carlo in March 1925 conducted by Victor de Sabata with choreography by Balanchine, has Le Vieillard Arithmétique assisted by a ballet of spiteful Numbers taking revenge on the naughty Child for neglecting his homework.
3 *Le Pas d'acier*.

There was a whole series of matters I needed to settle with him: preventing unauthorised reprints of my works in the Ukraine; receiving royalties for concert performances of my works; objecting to deductions imposed by the Society from the author's fees I earn directly from the Mariinsky Theatre not through the Society. Razumovsky informed me that receipts from the first two orchestral concerts were 2,500 roubles apiece, and from the recitals 3,500 roubles apiece. It looks as though my stay in the USSR will net me in excess of 1,000 roubles purely in royalties.

A few more people were seen in the twinkling of an eye, and then Tsukker arrived. I asked him what progress was being made in Shurik's case, and he said that the information I had given him was still on his desk and is constantly on his mind, but the person he needs to see about it is away and will not be back for another four days or so. I am beginning to have my doubts about Tsukker; I believe he wants to get out of what might turn into an awkward situation for him.

All this while Ptashka was getting on with packing our things as by now we are in a great rush and pother. The hotel bell-boy presented us with a bill for two roubles for pressing my trousers. I blew up and said it was sheer exploitation. 'That is the charge,' he replied.

I: 'There is no country in the world, not even America, where sums like that are charged. It takes ten minutes to iron a pair of trousers, so a tailor is going to earn twelve roubles an hour. In that case, why doesn't everyone in Moscow press trousers for a living?'

Tsukker intervened, but the bell-boy cheeked him. Tsukker is a Communist down to the marrow of his bones, a ramrod Jäger of His Royal Highnesses' Life-Guards, and drawing himself up to his full height he informed the bell-boy that his conduct would be reported to the appropriate Trade Union and a strip would duly be torn off him. I do not know how the affair ended, but I did not pay for the trousers and we departed in a taxi to the station, Tsukker in attendance.

At the former Nikolayevsky Station, now the Oktyabrsky, I saw Chernetskaya who is also on her way to Leningrad, evidently on something to do with the same ballet project, because she was telling me she had read the libretto to Lunacharsky and he had warmly recommended her to give it to Ekskuzovich.

When we got to the platform I examined with great interest the express train on which we were to travel. From our guidebook I already knew that it had kept up its pre-war speed, but the make-up of the carriages has altered greatly. In former days it was smart and immaculately maintained but now, although the first carriage we saw was an International Wagons-Lit sleeping car, all the others were a seemingly endless tail of third-class carriages, nowadays known as 'hard' class, with one second-class carriage somewhere far off in the distance.

Our small compartment was in the International Company carriage. Tsukker, standing at the entrance to the carriage, said, 'Ekskuzovich is travelling in this carriage as well.' 'Oh, how convenient,' I said. We said goodbye and the train began to move. As we went along the corridor to our compartment I greeted Ekskuzovich, but not very decisively as I was not absolutely sure it was he. Noticing the expression of surprise that crossed his face, I concluded I had saluted the wrong individual and we hurried past to our compartment. Fifteen minutes or so later I emerged again into the corridor to see Ekskuzovich standing there, and this time I was certain it was he. But he was deep in conversation with some other people and paid no attention to me, no doubt offended by the strangeness of my earlier greeting. Not only had he taken the decision to stage *Three Oranges* but had done so in spectacular style and now, if you please, here was the composer barely giving him the time of day and brushing straight past him! He carried on the conversation with his neighbours for ten minutes and then immediately turned to me with a civil phrase. At this moment Ptashka came out of our compartment and Ekskuzovich, the ultimate ladies' man, almost prostrated himself before her. After this we talked for a whole hour.

He confirmed that it was his firm intention to take *Oranges* to Paris and even asked my opinion on various technical details, such as ticket prices at the Grand Opéra and what sort of box-office gross he could expect, on which matters, needless to say, I was quite unable to advise him. He was very interested in my new Soviet ballet: did I think there was any prospect of winkling it away from Diaghilev for the forthcoming season, when the tenth anniversary of the October Revolution would be celebrated? He told me they had a wonderful new ballerina, still a young girl,[1] and they would have to go to great lengths to prevent Diaghilev spiriting her away abroad. The usual portrayal of Diaghilev here is as a rapacious bird of prey continually on the prowl to gobble up whatever takes his fancy.

It was about one o'clock before we finally separated to go to our own compartments, Ekskuzovich reminding me (which I already knew from Asafyev's letters) that there was to be a special performance of *Oranges* the day after tomorrow given in honour of my arrival. Ptashka was impressed by Ekskuzovich, finding him good company and not lacking in *chic*.

9 February

I leapt out of my bunk at eight o'clock to shave and look out of the window at the familiar outskirts of St Petersburg. However, beneath a thick blanket

---

[1] Presumably Galina Ulanova, who had just turned seventeen and would make her Mariinsky debut the following year.

of snow there was not much I could recognise, not even Sablino, my famous Zet hideaway.[1]

At ten o'clock, Leningrad! On the platform to meet us were Asafyev, Ossovsky, Shcherbachov,[2] Deshevov[3] and half-a-dozen other people representing various musical organisations. While a porter was extracting our luggage and I was embracing my friends, Ekskuzovich briskly made his farewells and departed bearing his little attaché case, but as we moved along the platform towards the exit, he was still there with a knot of people to whom he introduced me, saying, 'Here, Sergey Sergeyevich, are the Academic Theatres'[4] representatives, come to meet you.' I exchanged bows all round, after which we parted until tomorrow, for the performance of *Oranges*. Asafyev commented, 'A sly one, that Ekskuzovich! Of course they weren't there to meet you, they had come dutifully to make their reports to their boss, but he immediately turns it round to make it look like a welcome party for you.'

We dashed through the familiar station and were loaded into a car. Leningrad was blanketed with snow, and the bright, clear weather lent it a clean, crisp look. The behemoth-like statue of Alexander III has been left in place for the edification of his Communist heirs, to show what clumsy monsters the Tsars were. Driving along Nevsky Prospect I was filled with

---

1 In May 1917 Prokofiev had taken himself out of Petrograd to a remote rented farmhouse in Sablino, a village just outside the city, where away from the tensions of the build-up to the October Revolution and without a piano he could concentrate in seclusion on the composition of the *Classical* Symphony. To friends he referred to it as 'Zet' in order to prevent them finding out where he was. See *Diaries*, vol. 2, pp. 53–8, 193–230 *passim*, 370, 694.
2 Vladimir Shcherbachov (1889–1952), composer and teacher, a student of Maximilian Steinberg and of Lyadov. By training and instinct a composer of the old school, inimical to the iconoclasm of the young Turks, he nevertheless demonstrated great integrity and courage by abstaining from the infamous Composers' Union Resolution condemning Shostakovich for the crime of Formalism following the January 1936 *Pravda* editorial 'Muddle Instead of Music' despite explicit pressure from the Congress chairman. Prokofiev had conducted Shcherbachov's *Procession* ('so simple one could conduct it with the left foot') at the Conservatoire's Graduation Concert in May 1914 following his own triumph with the First Piano Concerto. See *Diaries*, vol. 1, pp. 664–9, 676–7.
3 Vladimir Deshevov (1889–1955), pianist and composer. He had been a friend at the St Petersburg Conservatoire and had provided moral support around the time of the scandalous first performance of the Second Piano Concerto at Pavlovsk in August 1913. Prokofiev dedicated to him the Scherzo, Op. 12 No. 10. See *Diaries*, vol. 1, pp. 446–7, 486–9, and *passim*.
4 After 1920, when the old imperial names of St Petersburg's principal theatres – Mariinsky, Alexandrinsky, etc. – were officially abandoned, the general designation became 'State Academic Theatre', hence the Mariinsky was the State Academic Theatre of Opera and Ballet, 'Akopera' for short or the even less lovely acronym GATOB, the Alexandrinsky Theatre 'Akdrama' and so on. This lasted until 1935 when the Mariinsky Theatre and its resident companies were given the name of the assassinated Leningrad Communist Party leader Sergey Kirov. The same principle was applied to the theatres of other capital cities, including Moscow, thus the Bolshoy Theatre in Moscow became the State Academic Bolshoy Theatre (Gosudarstvenniy Akademichiskii Bolshoy Teatr, or GABT).

excitement and joy. Catherine the Great's statue is still there, and the square with the Alexandrinsky Theatre is also very beautiful. It was a shock to the eyes to see so many boarded-up shop windows in Gostiny Dvor.[1] We turned into Mikhailovsky Street, now known as Lassalle Street,[2] and stopped at the Europa (Yevropeiskaya) Hotel. The taxi-driver demanded an exorbitant fare, but eventually had to be content with half the amount, given him by the hotel commissionaire at the door.

A spacious room had been reserved for us with a large bathroom and beds in a curtained-off recess. The room was considerably bigger than the one we had had in Moscow, but the latter was as clean as a new pin and had a sensational view from the windows. The Europa Hotel, by contrast, has a rather decrepit air compared with its former glory, although it still is, as it always was, the premier hotel in the city.

Asafyev had come in with us and we drank coffee together. He was in seventh heaven and went through yet again the schedule he had drawn up for my stay in Leningrad, taking special care to leave one day completely free so that we could spend it with him in Tsarskoe.[3] Ossovsky and Shcherbachov soon came back; I was extraordinarily happy to see Ossovsky who has remained the same gentle, courteous person he always was, only now with a few flecks of grey. I was surprised by Shcherbachov making so much of me: in former times at the Conservatoire we had not had much to do with one another, but Asafyev explained that he, Shcherbachov, is now his closest and most trusted assistant on musical matters.

Malko turned up, spruce and spry as ever, although looking older. Some faces seem to have changed little over the past ten years, while with others it is a very different story: when you compare them with the former images still clearly in your memory, you are suddenly aware of how much water has flowed under the bridge. Malko is now Director of the Leningrad Philharmonia, after having been deputy to the now-departed Klimov. In the

1   The fine, colonnaded department store on Nevsky Prospect.
2   Mikhailovsky Street runs between Nevsky Prospect and Mikhailovsky Square, where the Russian Museum is situated. After the Revolution it was renamed after Ferdinand Lassalle, the nineteenth-century German lawyer and socialist who corresponded (somewhat acrimoniously) with Marx and Engels and founded what was to become the Social Democratic Party. In 1940, presumably to avoid the German connotation, the street was once more given a new name, that of Isaak Brodsky, the painter who lived in the square (now also renamed Arts Square) at the end of the street. In 1991 Mikhailovsky Street reverted to its original name but the square is still known as Arts Square (Ploshchad Isskustv).
3   Tsarskoe Selo ('The Tsar's Village'), a residential district about fifteen miles to the south of the centre of St Petersburg grouped around the imperial residences: the baroque Catherine Palace and the neo-classical Alexander Palace. Inevitably its name changed after the Revolution to Detskoe Selo ('Children's Village') but this may have seemed too silly even for the Bolshevik Party and, probably with relief, the occasion of the centenary of Pushkin's death in 1937 was used to change the name of the whole area to Pushkin, which it still retains.

history of the way I had been taken advantage of over my fees, Malko thus had an unassailable position. 'What, me? I had nothing to do with it, it was my predecessor, and his financial estimates had already been passed.'

Malko did not stay long and departed after telling a few amusing stories in his deadpan voice. In his place came Dranishnikov, the one friend whom the passing of time seems not to have touched at all. He was just as youthful and merry as in the old days: the only results of the years of tragedy and hardship have been gains in maturity and the general attractiveness of his personality. He immediately started enthusing over *Oranges*, gleefully telling me of the changes and improvements he had made for the production. Most of them were quite trivial, but all of a sudden he was overcome with qualms and asked me not to be too critical when I came to listen tomorrow.

Since it was getting on for one o'clock I made everyone – Asafyev, Dranishnikov, Shcherbachov and Ossovsky – stay to lunch: Ossovsky ought to have gone back to the Conservatoire some time ago to pursue his administrative duties, but telephoned to say he would not be coming in. Lunch lasted until half past four, when we all weighed anchor, except Ptashka who was very tired and stayed behind to rest. But I was burning with impatience to see Petersburg and so went out with the rest of the group. We walked down to the end of Mikhailovsky Street and then turned right on Nevsky, heading towards the Admiralty. My posters were everywhere, in two versions: one advertising the two orchestral concerts and the other the two recitals.

Over my long years of wandering in foreign lands my memory of the true essence of Petersburg had blurred and I had somehow fallen for the myth that her beauty had been an imaginary graft arising from the patriotism of her residents, while the true heart of Russia lay, of course, in Moscow. I therefore expected to find that Petersburg's European attractions would now seem jejune before those of the real thing in the West, and that by contrast the Eurasian aspect of the Moscow lanes would possess a unique charm. Still in the grip of this mental cast I was utterly overwhelmed by the grandeur of Petersburg, so markedly more elegant and majestic than Moscow! The impression was enhanced by the whiteness of the snow and the sharp clarity of the air.

One by one Ossovsky, Dranishnikov and Asafyev peeled off to go about their separate affairs, but Shcherbachov elected to stay with me. We arrived at the Winter Palace, where I found some changes. The wrought-iron railings round the garden had been taken away and the garden itself opened to the public. This removal of the railings, however, has not spoiled the beautiful overall effect; on the contrary, the square now seems more spacious. Shcherbachov told me that the dramatically enlarged Hermitage Museum has encroached on the Winter Palace and scooped up more than half its rooms.

The General Staff Headquarters has been painted bright yellow with the columns picked out in white, whereas before it was dark red, like the Palace.

The latter has retained its deep tint, but has also been scheduled for repainting. Is this a good thing? I love that dark red colour. But Shcherbachov explained that originally the Palace was a different colour.

By the time we got to the Neva the sun was setting. It was a fantastic, rose-coloured sunset, and it turned river, snow and even the buildings pink. In this light the Neva and the Peter and Paul Fortress are fabulously beautiful. We walked along the Embankment and turned off at the Zimnyaya Kanavka.[1]

Shcherbachov, who now teaches Composition Theory at the Conservatoire, was agog to make me party to his new system of teaching and the still more ambitious plans for innovations the system would bring in its train. I still have in my mind's eye the old Conservatoire with its hallowed and inexorable sequence of harmony, then counterpoint, then fugue and form, and it was strange to me now to be hearing Shcherbachov's new theories according to which all the old progressions would be consigned to perdition to be replaced by entirely new principles, which he was now excitedly describing to me as someone in the vanguard of new music.

Shcherbachov accompanied me all the way back to the Europa Hotel where I collapsed into bed to get as much rest as I could before the evening, for which a bumper programme had already been set up for me. Sleep, however, was out of the question because a female singer was vocalising the other side of the wall. When I could stand it no longer I rushed downstairs to confront the hotel management, who explained to me that my neighbour was the tenor Smirnov.[2] 'That simply cannot be,' I screamed. 'I am quite capable of distinguishing a female voice from a male voice.' But it was explained to me that Mr Smirnov received female visitors who also sang. He would, however, be leaving in a few hours and after that all the annoyance would cease.

1 The 'Winter Canal', the canal constructed at the beginning of the eighteenth century to connect the Neva with the Moyka river, so called because it starts near the Winter Palace.
2 Dmitry Smirnov (1882–1944), lyric tenor. Much admired for his beauty of tone and impeccable vocal technique, while eschewing the *Helden* repertoire he had sung principal roles in the Bolshoy and Mariinsky Theatres until the Revolution, as well as regular invitations to the New York Met, Paris Opéra, Berlin, Drury Lane (for the Diaghilev–Beecham Russian Season in June 1914), etc. Leaving Russia after the Revolution he continued the career of a guest artist in great opera houses and making a large number of recordings. He was admitted to the USSR twice for short periods: in 1927 to teach and in 1929 for a concert tour, but unlike Prokofiev stayed domiciled in the West. He eventually settled in Riga, where he died at the end of the German occupation of Latvia in April 1944 just as Soviet forces were re-annexing the country. It is to be hoped that he remained unaware that he had thus unwittingly re-entered the USSR. (Lord Halifax, British Ambassador to Washington, had already revealed as far back as 1942, 'Mr Eden cannot incur the danger of antagonising Stalin, and the British War Cabinet have . . . agree[d] to negotiate a treaty with Stalin, which will recognise the 1940 frontiers of the Soviet Union.' And a year later, Roosevelt remarked, 'The European people will simply have to endure Russian domination, in the hope that in ten or twenty years they will be able to live well with the Russians.')

Lida Karneyeva[1] telephoned. It was a long time since I had had news of her, but it seems that everything has turned out reasonably well for them, and at ten o'clock in the evening she, Zoya and 'Grigorovich', as Zakharov always called Lida's husband, all came to see us. The girls were well dressed, and just as in the old days I could not stop thinking of them as young ladies even though Zoya is thirty-one and Lida thirty-three. Lida has begun to show her age but is still beautiful and has preserved the gentleness and charm she always had. The intervening ten years have left Zoya precisely as she was so that at thirty-one she is as radiant as she was at twenty-one. 'Grigorovich' is retired; I had worried that as a naval officer things might have gone badly for him, but he was not touched. Life was not so kind, however, to the girls' younger brother Lyova: the combination of the atmosphere of the Revolution and an unhappy first marriage affected him so badly he was on the point of losing his mind. But he feels all right now and is happy with his second wife. Lida suffered a nervous breakdown but recovered and now plays the piano in the cinema. The younger sisters are all well, and their Mama is still alive. We chatted for an hour and Ptashka liked them all immensely.

At eleven Asafyev, Dranishnikov and Shcherbachov reappeared to take both of us to the Literature-Arts Circle on the Fontanka, where as I knew from previous correspondence in Moscow an evening had been arranged in my honour. On the way we passed the Alexandrinsky Theatre, illuminated *à la* Grand Opéra by bright crimson lighting concealed behind the columns, so that against this background the white snow-covered trees and the statue of Catherine the Great looked extraordinarily beautiful.

At the Literature-Arts Circle there was a mass of people, among them many familiar faces I was glad to greet instantly. Yershov,[2] Lyonochka Nikolayev,[3] Deshevov (whom I had already seen in the morning), Berlin,[4] still lovely, and her husband, the Ossovskys and many others.

The actual concert programme started at the remarkably late hour of half past one, because the musicians had got delayed somewhere or other. First

---

1 Lidia Karneyeva, her sister Zoya and their younger brother Lev had all become friends of Prokofiev during the summer holidays he spent with Boris Zakharov in the Zakharov family dacha in Terijoki. See *Diaries*, vol. 1 *passim*; vol. 2, pp. 46, 49, 52–6, 92, 137, 158, 268.
2 Ivan Yershov (1867–1943), *Heldentenor*, with Leonid Sobinov the most famous Russian tenor of his generation, taking a total of fifty-five principal roles at the Mariinsky Theatre since his debut there in 1895. Yershov disliked the life of the international star singer and appeared very seldom outside Russia, singing all his roles in Russian. Prokofiev had cast him alongside Alchevsky as Alexey in *The Gambler* for the production that never took place in the Mariinsky Theatre in 1917, but he did take the role of Truffaldino in Sergey Radlov's production of *The Love for Three Oranges* in 1926. He was also a successful producer, and a renowed teacher at the Petrograd/Leningrad Conservatoire.
3 The pianist and teacher Leonid Nikolaev.
4 A fellow piano student at the St Petersburg Conservatoire. See *Diaries*, vol. 1, pp. 121, 161, 216, 224, 267, 367, 620, 658, 664, 674. She had been a rival contestant in the Rubinstein Competition.

was the 'Jewish Overture', which was played too slowly. Then a pianist called Druskin[1] who has recently graduated with a prize from the Conservatoire played my Sonata No. 4, not particularly well so that the work seemed to me tedious. Then four bassoonists emerged to play the Scherzo,[2] very well, with verve and cheek; this was a tremendous success and had to be repeated. After this it was intimated to me that it was my turn, so I complied and straight away played a series of small pieces that were greeted with loud applause.

Everyone then went out of the hall to allow tables to be brought in and laid for supper for this large collection of people. At our table sat the same people who had been at lunch, with several additions including the actor Yuriev,[3] who still contrives to strut his stuff flashing cufflinks emblazoned with Tsarist crowns. The food itself was dismal, but still apparently cost the diners more than could be afforded by Conservatoire pupils (they are all 'students' these days, however). They had therefore clubbed together and paid for a delegation of two, which I found very touching.

At the end of the meal Ossovsky, sitting next to me, got to his feet and delivered a long and literary speech, about which he was so nervous I could see his fingers, resting on the table to support him, trembling slightly. It was an address to me and dwelt on the importance of my return to Russia, the importance of my music and even the importance of my personality, which he characterised as exceptionally attractive. I began to tremble as well, from terror as it became increasingly clear to me that I would have to respond. After a little while I whispered to Ossovsky: 'Alexander Vyacheslavovich, should I say something in reply?' 'It's entirely up to you, Sergey Sergeyevich,' he mumbled sheepishly.

Obviously I did have to, and the sooner the better to get it over and done with. I therefore got to my feet and, recalling the speech I had made in Moscow, drank a toast this time to Leningrad and her musicians, and larded it with some species of inconsequential nonsense. Ptashka was very flattered when Ossovsky stood up once more and proposed a toast to her.

---

1 Mikhail Druskin (1905–1991), pianist, critic, musicologist and later a revered teacher at the Leningrad Conservatoire, author of many studies of contemporary composers including Stravinsky (M. S. Druskin, *Igor' Stravinskiy. Lichnost'. Tvorchestvo. Vzglyady*, Sovetskiy Kompozitor, Leningrad, 1962; trans. Martin Cooper, *Igor Stravinsky: His Personality, Works and Views*, Cambridge University Press, 1983).

2 'Humoresque Scherzo' for four bassoons, Op. 12a. This piece was later transcribed for solo piano as No. 9 of the *Ten Pieces for Piano* published as Op. 12. See *Diaries*, vol. 1, pp. 253, 274–5, 281, 288–9, 292, 316, 399, 505, 689.

3 Yury Yuriev (1872–1948), leading actor of the pre-Revolution Alexandrinsky Theatre in Petrograd, subsequently renamed the Puhskin Theatre. Yuriev devoted most of his career to this theatre, with a spell in Moscow from 1929 until 1935, first in the Maly Theatre and then in Meyerhold's company until its dissolution.

Then photographs were taken, and the moment it seemed possible I extricated myself to go home, my justification being the rehearsal the following morning. It was not a moment too soon, because we did not get back to the Europa until three thirty, but we heard that in our absence the supper party continued until five in the morning.

10 February

In the morning, the first rehearsal with Dranishnikov and the orchestra. I did not have far to go: the Assembly of the Nobility is just outside our window and all we had to do was cross the street.[1] How beautiful the Hall of Columns is; how many memories does it summon up extending right back to my childhood! What reverence was evoked by the sight of a full symphony orchestra extended right across the stage! Today's Philharmonic Orchestra, it must be admitted, is no longer first-class. Among the musicians are many younger ones, some of them former friends from the Conservatoire who were playing in the Conservatoire Orchestra when I conducted it – even though I could recognise only a few, and those with difficulty. But a good few elderly mushrooms still linger on inherited from the present orchestra's progenitor, the Court Orchestra, and to this day they have made no adjustment to new music, wincing from an unresolved second as they would from the bite of a flea. 'The day will surely come when I shall murder that principal cello,' said Dranishnikov to me in a fury during the interval.

He devoted the first half of the rehearsal to the Suite from *Chout*, applying himself to it with great zeal. He has developed into a first-rate conductor. During the break I was surrounded by my old Conservatoire colleagues, who plied me with questions about whether I was staying long, and if indeed I was planning to stay for good. 'Don't!' was their advice. 'If you're well set up there, stay permanently. Here is no good at all.'

After the break Dranishnikov concentrated on the Third Piano Concerto. I sat at the piano, and after so much time spent with Persimfans felt how easy things are when you play with a conductor. But even here I found Feinberg a great nuisance: he had played the Concerto here as well and adopted quite different tempi, causing some of the venerable mushrooms to take issue with Dranishnikov's directions: 'Last time you wanted us to play quite differently.'

---

1   Both Moscow and St Petersburg possessed an Assembly of the Nobility (Dvoryanskoe sobranie) dating from the eighteenth and nineteenth century respectively, magnificent buildings in the centre of town, each containing a large hall with columns (Kolonniy Zal). Soon after the Revolution the Moscow building was transferred to the Union of Trade Unions and became known officially as the House of Unions although the old name persisted. Petrograd's became the home of the city's Philharmonia, since 1975 the Shostakovich Philharmonia, and its Kolonniy Zal is now the Great Hall of the Philharmonia.

Among those listening to the rehearsal were Asafyev and Shcherbachov, and when it was over they plus Dranishnikov, Ptashka and me went off to lunch. On the way we dropped in at the Europa Hotel, and while Ptashka was up in the room and we were waiting in the lobby, who should appear but Katya Schmidthof,[1] all trace of whom I had lost since 1917. We kissed each other and then went into a quiet corner to talk. When I asked, 'Well, how are you getting on?', she pointed sadly to her right arm. She had lost it as long ago as 1922, falling from a tram. She had jumped out of the front car while it was still moving, had fallen, and the following car's wheels had trapped her arm, severing it. Just at this time she was beginning to make headway in the theatre but the catastrophe nipped her career in the bud. She – like Lidusya – had married a retired sailor, and has a son a little younger than Svyatoslav. She had been waiting a long time to see me and was happy to have caught me so early in my stay. But as the others were waiting we could not talk for long, and so I said goodbye, arranging that she would come to the next rehearsal of my concerto.

Now the group went off to find somewhere to have lunch. But Leningrad does not seem to have anywhere as nice as the restaurant on Prechistenki, and nobody had any suggestions where to go. In the end we fetched up in a strange establishment just opposite, where we had to wait for a long time to be served and were given bad, expensive food.

Afterwards it was time to go to the Hermitage, where today a viewing had been arranged especially for us to see various highlights of the collection. We walked there, taking the opportunity to show Ptashka something of Leningrad as we went. Asafyev and Dranishnikov left us to go about their own affairs while Shcherbachov took us, in our capacity as honoured guests, into the Hermitage through a special entrance to introduce us to his wife, who works there. The Director, Troinitsky,[2] came out to meet us, a most

---

1 Yekaterina Schmidthof was the sister of Max Schmidthof, Prokofiev's beloved friend at the Conservatoire, who had committed suicide in 1913. The Second Piano Concerto and the Second and Fourth Piano Sonatas are dedicated to Max's memory. In the light of his relationship with Max, Prokofiev had always felt a responsibility to Katya. See *Diaries*, vol. 1, pp. 251, 309, 381, 386, 392, 407, 410–12, 432, 447, 547, 555, 568, 588, 602–3, 637, 710, 728, 791–2 (Katya); 133–742 *passim* (Max); vol. 2, pp. 32, 46 (Katya); 8, 88, 127, 201, 272, 281–2, 291, 403, 425, 561, 563, 573, 692–3.
2 Sergey Troinitsky (1882–1948), an expert on heraldry and on jewellery who had held senior posts in both the Imperial and Provisional Governments, was appointed Director of the State Hermitage Museum in 1918, responsible for the cataloguing and photographing in 1922 of the Imperial Family's eye-watering collection of jewellery and precious stones. (Troinitsky's committee of experts included the son of Carl Fabergé.) The catalogue resulted in the publication in 1925 of a volume published, astonishingly enough, in Russian, French and English, entitled *Russia's Treasure of Diamonds and Stones*. This book is now extremely rare, because almost immediately it appeared in print Stalin ordered all copies in all languages, so far as possible, to be recovered and destroyed, because he had decided to sell off for hard cash as much as possible of the Tsarist legacy to Western collectors such as Calouste Gulbenkian and Armand Hammer who could be trusted to be discreet, retaining only the minimum needed to

interesting and stylish gentleman who despite his distinctly un-Bolshevik background as a former Lycée pupil had for many years been at the head of the Hermitage, a position he filled with uncommon expertise and understanding, despite the innumerable underwater reefs lying in wait for anyone who has to deal with the Communist government.

Troinitsky personally conducted us to see the most priceless part of the Hermitage – the jewellery collection. It is not easy for even the Director to gain access to this section of the museum, involving as it does prior signing of the register, running the gauntlet of the guards, and completing a whole range of formalities. It contains much that is of beauty and curiosity, although personally I am not much attracted to these incalculably valuable *objets*. There were tiaras encrusted with diamonds, snuff-boxes, ceremonial swords belonging to the Tsars, all of them lustrous with precious stones of every conceivable colour. Troinitsky showed us these objects with a nonchalant grace which belied the enormous pride in them he really takes, his brief explanations enlivened from time to time with a discreet pleasantry.

From the jewellery room, in which by the way we were locked for the duration of our inspection, we passed into the Scythian section, where Troinitsky left us after handing us over to another curator, an expert in this department. Here the most interesting items were those worked in soft gold.[1]

Next was the Persian section, and yet another specialist, but we had already been looking at things for some hours and were tired. We cantered through the picture galleries without stopping, for it was getting dark. All we could do was get a general impression, but even so we could see how huge was the proportion of the Winter Palace the Hermitage Museum had annexed.

Utterly exhausted, we eventually found ourselves out on the street again. Nevertheless, the Hermitage had welcomed us royally, with no less a person that its Director showing us its most secret part and arranging for two other experts to show us the rest. Leaving the museum we made our way to pay a call on Glazunov. While I was a student at the Conservatoire our relationship had never progressed beyond a wary tolerance, but since he is

---

preserve the credibility of the traditional heritage of a great power. See C. Morgan and I. Orlova, *Saving the Tsar's Palaces*, Polperro Press, Clifton-upon-Teme, 2005. Troinitsky, like many of his genuinely knowledgeable and dedicated colleagues, was purged at the end of the 1920s 'in Category One', meaning that he was no longer permitted to work in a government organisation, and was transferred to the dubious enterprise known as 'Antikvariat' which had the job of masterminding this sale of the family silver. No doubt he did what he could to mitigate the depredations, but in 1935 he was arrested as a socially undesirable element and exiled with his wife to Ufa. Fortunately for Russia's heritage, by the middle of the 1930s the officially sanctioned pillage was much reduced.

1 Gold is the most malleable and ductile of all metals. A single gram can be beaten into a sheet a metre square; an ounce into a sheet 300 feet square.

still an important figure in Leningrad even though musical life essentially now passes him by, I had resolved when I was still in Paris that I would do the correct thing and call on him.

I could not remember the number of his house, but I could remember what it looked like and found it without difficulty. But the main door to the street was shut tight: I knew that at the beginning of the Revolution it had been common practice to lock the main street doors of a building, but had not expected to find it still the case. We therefore went in by the back door, and found ourselves in an enormous courtyard full of trees – the well-to-do merchant family of the Glazunovs had built their residence expansively. Asking the concierge the way to the Glazunov apartment, we began to climb a somewhat dilapidated and grimy staircase until we came across a brass plate with engraved upon it the name Glazunov, shorn of first name or patronymic.

We rang the bell. No result. We rang again – still nothing. Then, in case the bell was not working, we knocked, but as there was still no answer we concluded no one was at home and fumbled in our pockets for a visiting card to leave in the letterbox. So keen was the frost, even inside on the stair, that our fingers froze as soon as we removed our gloves. Before leaving, however, we knocked one last time, a little harder, and now heard footsteps the other side of the door. When the door opened we saw two ladies, one quite young, the other clearly older but still quite youthful in appearance. They were mother and daughter, the former more attractive than the latter.

As long ago as 1918 when I was first in New York I had heard from Vyshnegradsky[1] that Glazunov had got married, but this had all the hallmarks of a joke and was indeed going the rounds in that form. The story was that his wife was a pupil at the Conservatoire and was still a young girl. Others pooh-poohed the idea on the grounds that Glazunov had never considered marriage. The most intriguing aspect of it was that even now, here in Petersburg, nobody seemed to know whether he was indeed married or not, and if he was, whether to the mother or the daughter. What was indisputable was that these two quite lively and attractive ladies had made their home with Glazunov and were looking after him. The elderly composer's domestic circumstances were certainly in need of a woman's hand, and no doubt it was very dull for him all alone in the huge apartment to enjoy, which, to give them due credit, the Bolsheviks had left him in sole occupancy.[2]

I explained to the ladies that I had come with my wife to pay my respects to Alexander Konstantinovich, and when the ladies had explained in their turn that he was not at home, they willingly invited us in. We were taken

---

1 Alexander Vyshnegradsky the banker, not his son Ivan, the composer.
2 See below, p. 708 n. 1 for an explanation of the relationship of the two ladies to the composer.

through the kitchen into a large room familiar to me from those far-off days when I had brought along to show Glazunov my E minor Symphony, now defunct except for the Andante which I had transcribed and incorporated into my Piano Sonata No. 4.[1]

We stayed for ten or fifteen minutes while the ladies complained about the regime, the problems of daily life in Soviet Leningrad, the constant surveillance both overt and covert. They knew one woman who had wanted to emigrate, but at the last moment the authorities sent someone round to visit her, then someone denounced her and instead of being sent abroad she was arrested, and so on and so on. We got up to say goodbye, the ladies happily escorted us to the door, and we hurried off home to try to snatch some rest before going to the performance of *Oranges*. There we found an invitation for us to sit in the Director's box and the offer of a further box for friends, but it was already too late to take advantage of this and we could make no use of the box. Perhaps we could have got on the telephone and started ringing round, but we preferred to sit quietly and recover our equilibrium.

Before long Asafyev arrived and we left together to go to the Mariinsky Theatre. Ptashka and Asafyev sat in the first sleigh and I was behind them in the second, urging on the driver as it was going to be a rush to get to the theatre on time. Familiar places flashed past: Kazanskaya Street, Vosnesensky, Offitserskaya. We passed the Conservatoire, and here at last was the Mariinsky, which has been repainted in a dark red shade like the Winter Palace was before. And although I used to love the Winter Palace in dark red, I am a little sad that the Mariinsky is no longer yellow.

Inside the theatre we went straight up to the office, where we were offered the choice between sitting in the side box of the dress circle, or in the stalls, which would have a better view. I opted for the stalls and a secretary took us down to seats in the fourth row next to the centre gangway. I rejoiced to see my beloved Mariinsky again and craned my neck to look round at it several times, but Dranishnikov was already on the podium and the performance was about to start. Ptashka pointed out the box on the left-hand side of the stage (looking from the auditorium): it was filled with the Tragicals, who appear in this production as reviewers. When the Comicals entered they occupied the forestage, but the Empty-heads now appeared in the box at the end of the dress circle on the *right* side, which produced a curious counterpoint, one voice in the right ear, the other in the left. When the Herald entered, he himself played the trombone – an effect Dranishnikov had told me about beforehand and of which he was particularly proud: 'Our singers are so talented they can even play the trombone.'

---

1 See *Diaries*, vol. 1, pp. 67–71, 79–85. The Fourth Sonata's Andante had also a later full-dress incarnation, re-orchestrated in 1934 for symphony orchestra as Op. 29bis.

Beside the Herald was a little boy who did not actually do anything, but was still very funny. All these unusually inventive little details won me over to the production from the start; clearly it had been devised in a spirit of love and talent.

There followed a whole series of gags, every one of which made me laugh: when Truffaldino was summoned from the hall he seemed to fly in from above the stage (a dummy figure instantaneously replaced by the live actor); an absolutely fantastic hell inflated to overwhelming proportions complete with puppets floating and writhing all over every level of the stage; and the magician Chelio most amusingly decked out as Father Christmas. The table that concealed Smeraldina ran after Leander so as to overhear his conversation with Clarissa. The casting of the spell with which the first act ends was a serious piece of theatre with mirrors reflecting lights of almost unbearable intensity on the necromancers, lending them a truly fantastical character.

For the second scene of Act Two, the festivities, trapezes had been hung from the flies for some of the characters to sit on. I had already heard two contradictory views on these trapezes: some thought them a marvellous idea enabling the whole vertical plane of the stage to be populated with characters; others found the actors so paralysed by fear of falling that they presented rather a sorry sight. For myself, I did not agree with this second view and very much liked the scene. The Monsters' fight, however, was no more successful than it has been in any of the previous productions. But when Truffaldino pushed Fata Morgana and she fell over with her legs in the air, one saw that she had an extra pair of artificial legs hidden under her skirt, and those were what she pulled up, to killingly funny effect. But the dimming of the lights that immediately follows Fata Morgana rising to her feet again had the effect of interrupting the action, and I resolved to eliminate it in future. During the casting of Fata Morgana's spell the Little Devils howled their imprecations through megaphones, just as I had suggested and as they had done earlier in the inferno scene, producing a satisfyingly terrifying effect.

In Act Three Chelio, having called up Farfarello, was himself frightened by him. Farfarello did not just sing but jigged about the whole time, another thing Dranishnikov pointed out to me with evident pride. When Chelio halted the Prince and Truffaldino on their way to find the Oranges he did so from a bridge thrown over from one side of the stage to the other, and so could talk down to them from an elevated vantage point, and it was from there he also threw them the red ribbon. The discussion between the Prince and Truffaldino in Creonta's castle, before the stealing of the Oranges, was staggeringly well done. Their duet, against a background of a chattering figure on the strings taken by Dranishnikov at an insanely fast tempo, was not only sung with total precision but acted with unforced naturalness on stage. The stealing of the

Oranges was likewise done in perfect time to the music. Leander addressed the final phrase of Act Three ('His orange has gone bad, and his Princess turned out black') directly to the audience, perhaps a shade too sarcastically.

In the last act Fata Morgana's fight with Father Christmas-Magician-Chelio was so vicious that she pulled his beard right off. She was locked up by the Eccentrics, not in one of their towers but in a cage dragged on to the stage for the purpose, and there she had to sit like an animal. The King summoned the guards for help in a terrified voice, and they fired on the rat from a cannon. The final chase had been staged with more care than in any other production I had seen. Acrobats had been added to the general mix, and this did make the movements of the crowds more lively but at the same time somehow lowered the general sense of urgency. Altogether the chase was nearly, but still not quite, well done. It has never been completely right anywhere.

At the end of the first interval, when the audience was already back in its seats but the curtain had not yet risen, Wolf-Israel appeared in front of it and, indicating my presence in the hall, pronounced a greeting to me. The audience gave me an ovation, although less warm then those I had received at my concerts. This is quite understandable, however: the public at the concerts had come specially to see me whereas here they had come primarily to the theatre and so were less excited by the prospect of glimpsing my person. For the second act I had moved from the stalls to the box and rose to bow from the front of the box. There were calls for the composer also in the second and third intervals, and I duly acknowledged them in a similar fashion.

This Wolf-Israel, by the way, is the same cellist in the Mariinsky Orchestra who had created the biggest scandal when my works were first being performed in the Ziloti[1] concerts, most notably at the first performance of the *Scythian Suite*. Ziloti, ever the consummate politician, managed to shut him up by offering him a solo appearance in the concert playing my *Ballade*

---

1 Ziloti had been actively hoping for a *succès de scandale* with the premiere of the raucously dissonant *Scythian Suite* conducted by the twenty-five-year-old composer, and was not disappointed by either the reaction of the players in the Mariinsky Orchestra (with a particularly disgruntled Wolf-Israel in the principal cello chair) or with the near-riot that greeted the actual premiere. Prokofiev's diary entry for 12 January 1916, written after one of the rehearsals, reads: 'In the interval I was surrounded by players from the orchestra, and one of them said to me that the constant extreme dissonances had affected his nerves so badly that he was becoming quite ill. He enquired why I should want to write in this way, surely it could not be from the heart so much as the fruit of a distorted imagination?' And the following day: 'When a number of people in the orchestra privately expressed their indignation at the appalling music they were being forced to play, Ziloti said to them: "Quite true, in your position I should not like to play it either, it sounds so awful when you are sitting in the orchestra. But I have been listening from the hall, and there it comes out magnificently."' See *Diaries*, vol 2, pp. 65–76.

for cello. But times have changed, and now this self-same Wolf-Israel[1] is publicly welcoming me.

During the next interval I was invited into the orchestra's dressing-room where Wolf-Israel delivered a short speech on behalf of the orchestra. In my reply I most sincerely congratulated the orchestra on their excellent standard of playing, and there followed kisses and conversations, all as it should be! Then, in the third interval, I was dragged up to the top floor of the theatre by the principal singers, to have my photograph taken with the singers grouped around me. Tea, pastries, hors-d'oeuvres and wine were served in the sitting room off the Director's box in the company of Ekskuzovich, Yershov, Malko, the conductors and producers on the staff of the Mariinsky – in a word, a full-scale reception. I was overwhelmed and enraptured by the quite out-of-the-ordinary inventiveness and sheer gusto of Radlov's[2] production, and flung my arms round my old chess partner. I also thanked the designer, Dmitriev,[3] but found difficulty in making my words carry enough conviction, since his scenery was in fact dull and generally the least successful aspect of the production.

After the performance Dranishnikov took us back to his house for tea; Asafyev and Radlov and their wives came with us. Whether Dranishnikov is married or not is not clear, but at all events a rather attractive woman, evidently a dancer in the Mariinsky Ballet, lives with him and did the honours as hostess. A chessboard made its appearance, but the crocodiles (Radlov and I) declined to play, our heads being too full of other matters, so Ptashka and Asafyev's wife tried their hands. It was hard to tell which of them was worse. Radlov mentioned Chudovsky,[4] who had been sentenced to be exiled

1   Yevgeny Wolf-Israel (1874–1956), cellist, principal cello of the Mariinsky Theatre Orchestra. See *Diaries*, vol. 2, pp. 69–75, 149, 154.
2   Sergey Radlov (1892–1958), theatre director and disciple of Meyerhold. Prokofiev had first encountered him and his younger brother Nikolay, an artist and cartoonist, at an exhibition in St Petersburg in 1913 and had enjoyed his company especially over the chessboard. See *Diaries*, vol. 1, p. 539. In the Kirov *Three Oranges* production, which had opened on 16 February 1926, Radlov's stated aim was to avoid technically complex and cumbersome stage machinery and 'to create a certain fairy-tale mood and lightness . . . I have tried to make the whole scenic action dynamic' (quoted in D. Nice, *Prokofiev: From Russia to the West*, Yale University Press, New Haven and London, 2003, p. 237). Radlov's description is quoted from an article he wrote for *Rabochy i Teatr* (*The Working Man and Theatre*), the hardline eventual successor to *Zhizn' Isskustva* (*Life of Art*) on 15 February 1926.
3   Vladimir Dmitriev (1900–1948), theatrical designer. His early training as a painter had been with Yelizaveta Zvantseva and Petrov-Vodkin and he had also worked in Meyerhold's experimental Theatre Studio in Petrograd. In 1941 he became Chief Designer of the Moscow Art Theatre, a post he held until his death.
4   Valerian Chudovsky (1882–1937), philologist, translator, writer and literary critic, on the staff of and a regular contributor to *Apollon* magazine. Prokofiev had met him at the first chess tournament in which he competed (to the displeasure of his mother) at the St Petersburg Chess Club in 1908, the same occasion on which he first met Boris Demchinsky. Chudovsky, Radlov and Sergey Makovsky, the editor of *Apollon* magazine, were collaborating on the publication of a Russian edition of the works of Stefan George; Chudovsky and Radlov were both at the exhibition

because of some political business with which as a matter of fact he had no connection at all. We got back at 2 a.m. Ptashka is in love with Leningrad.

11 February

In the midst of the madhouse of our Leningrad days (not to mention those in Moscow before we got here) today is a day off, because at our first meeting with Asafyev in Moscow he reserved the day for us to go to visit him in Detskoe Selo. Having got up in a more leisurely fashion than usual, we took a train from Tsarskoselsky Station at noon. The train, in former times such an elegant one, now consists solely of 'hard'-class carriages and is rather slower than it used to be. The passengers were a dowdy lot, but our smart clothes and Ptashka's leopard-skin coat did not raise any eyebrows.

A delighted Asafyev met us at Detskoe Selo Station and we set off on foot through the dazzlingly white snow to his house. He lives in a large, spacious wooden house not far from the station, on the edge of Detskoe Selo, thus on one side he has the town and on the other a wide expanse of uninterrupted snow. He occupies three huge rooms on the second floor,[1] part of a flat formerly belonging to a police officer. The whole setting is that of a provincial Russian town, and what with the brilliant sunshine and the expanse of snow stretching into the distance seemed to transport us into an entirely different world.

The first room was a dining room big enough easily to accommodate twenty people round the table. The second room was Asafyev's study, and the third the bedroom, which, however, we could not enter because it was currently housing two violently aggressive dogs. One of them, a bitch, Asafyev had found somewhere or other as a starving puppy suffering from a virulent subcutaneous eczema which he spent months anointing with a vile-smelling preparation. The dog recovered, but is now completely wild and

---

in St Petersburg and Chudovsky had introduced Prokofiev to his friend and colleague. See *Diaries*, vol. 1, pp. 60, 63, 524, 539, 550, 552–3. In the chilling directory in the *Book of Memory of Victims of Political Repression in the Republic of Bashkortostan* published between 1997 and 2001 (over 21,700 names are listed for this one small region of Russia, where so many found themselves in the camps of the Gulag) we find that Valerian Chudovsky was arrested on 25 August 1937, convicted of offences according to Statute 58 articles 10 and 11, and shot on 4 November. As this diary entry confirms, it was not the first time he had been caught up in the machinery of repression: he was arrested on 7 April 1925 in connection with the so-called Lycée Affair, in which hundreds of former pupils at the Alexandrovky Lycée in St Petersburg (including Prokofiev's cousin Alexander Rayevsky) were arrested for the anti-Soviet crimes of attending annual reunions, funeral services for deceased alumni, etc. In Chudovsky's case the crime had been punished by five years' exile to Nizhny Tagil in the Urals, with confiscation of property. It was a mild rap on the knuckles compared to what happened to him later. See above, p. 155, n. 4.

1 This would, in Britain, be the first floor.

has to be kept away from visitors. But as we were with Asafyev for the whole day there were two occasions when the dog had to be taken for a walk: her hair bristling, she growled and pawed at the ground with her claws. Asafyev told us how once, on just such a walk as this, she had attacked a goat. The goat, however, stood her ground and adopting a fighting position butted the dog, upon which a furious fight ensued. Seeing the owners of the goat approaching, Asafyev in a panic tried to pull off his dog by her hind legs. You have to know the studious, bookish Asafyev to be able to visualise the scene. Eventually he managed to drag the dog away and the pair of them darted into the nearby bushes before the goat's owners arrived on the scene.

We wanted to take advantage of the sunshine and have a walk before it got dark. Ptashka was tired from all our exertions so she and Mme Asafyeva went in a cab while Asafyev and I went on foot. How beautiful the green Elizabeth Palace[1] is! We feasted our eyes on it for some time. But one of the streets leading up to it has been renamed Beloborodov Street in honour of the Communist who had shot the Imperial Family.[2] This strikes me as verging on the tactless: even if it really was necessary to shoot both grown-ups and children, surely there is no call to swank about it, it is plainly stupid.

From the Elizabeth Palace Asafyev and I struggled knee-deep in snow round the former gardens of the Tsar. But soon it was time to go home: first of all it was very cold, and secondly we were starving hungry.

1 Usually known as the Catherine Palace after the first and the third of its three builders, respectively the Empresses Catherine I and Catherine II (Catherine the Great), the magnificent palace in Pushkin (when it was Tsarskoye Selo) owed its original existence to Catherine I, Peter the Great's mistress Martha Skavronskaya who became his second wife using the name she had taken on converting to the Orthodox Church. The younger of the two of their twelve children to survive into adulthood, Elizabeth, as Empress in her turn, considered her mother's modest, two-storeyed house quite inadequate as an imperial palace befitting the autocrat of a great empire, and she it was who commissioned Rastrelli to create the baroque masterpiece in blue with white pilasters. Her successor Catherine II and her architects, the Russians Yury Velten and Vasily Neyelov along with the Scot Charles Cameron, continued the tradition by greatly extending the already huge building, but to Catherine's credit she did not tamper with Rastrelli's central design. Prokofiev undoubtedly has a point in referring to it as the Elizabeth Palace.
2 Alexander Beloborodov (1891–1938) did not himself pull the trigger on any member of the Imperial Family. As Chairman of the Urals Regional Soviet he signed on 6 June 1918 the Soviet's order for the entire family to be executed. On 13 June 1918 the head of the Perm secret police, Gavriil Myasnikov, abducted and shot Grand Duke Michael, the Tsar's brother, who had effectively renounced the succession on Nicholas's abdication, and his English secretary, Nicholas Johnson, thus instigating what would end in the liquidation of the whole family. The Tsar himself and his family were killed in a basement room of the Ipatiev House in Yekaterinburg by an execution squad under the command of Yakov Yurovsky. Subsequently Beloborodov, having backed the wrong horse in the Trotsky–Kamenev Opposition in 1936, was arrested, subjected to torture by express order of Stalin, tried according to the special 'simplified procedures' of the Military Council and shot in the Lubyanka's execution chamber on 10 February 1938. But in 1927 he was still honoured by having a street named after him.

The lunch to which Asafyev entertained us was glorious; halfway through we had no space left for any more and had to leave the second half. Afterwards we settled down to write a letter to Ekskuzovich. After yesterday's performance his secretary had dropped a hint to me that it would be no bad thing to write him a few lines giving my impressions of the production. The hint was not really needed as I wanted to write in any case. Now was a convenient moment to avail myself of Asafyev's presence to compose the letter jointly.

Asafyev then showed me a leaflet he had produced about me in connection with the *Three Oranges* production and asked me to correct any mistakes I might find in it. We had also intended to look through the draft of a book about me Asafyev had prepared for our publishers, but spent so much time chatting there was no time for this. At ten o'clock we set out on the return journey. Vera Alpers,[1] on discovering that we were spending all day with Asafyev, had tried hard to inveigle her way in on the pretext of needing to ask me some questions, but Asafyev, jealously guarding his day with me, had declined to let her in. I learned about this only later.

Back at the Europa Hotel we found that Glazunov had left two visiting cards. With his gentlemanly manners he had returned our call the next day. I remembered the occasion, almost twenty years ago, when my mother had first taken me to see him. And with the same punctiliousness he returned the call to my Mama a few days later although, in all conscience, there can scarcely have been any need to go to such lengths for every Mama presenting her talented young hopeful to a celebrity. But had it been because this was the one time when Glazunov still hoped that I might turn into a proper composer?

As well as the Glazunov visiting cards there were two express letters from Moscow. A few days before, in Moscow, I had had a very touching, even tearful letter from a certain Givnin. He was, it seemed, an emerging talent, and found himself in dire straits, to assuage which he was seeking help. On the grounds that he might indeed be talented, before I left I wrote him a few lines enquiring what sort of help he had in mind, and to what extent. One of the letters now before me was from Givnin, full of extravagantly inflated gratitude for my consideration, and intimating that his expectations of help would start at 500 roubles and upwards. The second letter, far more intelligent and written in a better hand, warned me that Givnin was nothing but a dissolute wastrel always on the scrounge for a few coppers to squander in a night-club. That will teach me to try to help budding talents!

---

1 A friend from Conservatoire days. Prokofiev had been close to her and her family and engaged in a lively correspondence during the holidays, but gradually lost any romantic interest he once had although continuing to keep up the correspondence, a selection of which can be read in H. Robinson (ed. and trans.), *Selected Letters of Sergei Prokofiev*, Northeaster University Press, Boston, 1998. See *Diaries*, vol. 1 *passim*.

12 February

Morning rehearsal in the Philharmonic Hall. Dranishnikov had rehearsed yesterday as well while we were enjoying ourselves in Tsarskoe: they went through *Chout* and *Scythians*. Quite a lot of people had come into the hall to listen, but they were told to sit behind the columns and not to disturb the rehearsal. Dranishnikov began with the *Scythian Suite*, in which I proposed some alterations to tempi and sonorities. The Suite was followed by *Chout* and then the Third Piano Concerto, which went quite well.

Malko appeared, saying that the Philharmonia was prepared to settle accounts with my publishers for all the previous unauthorised performances of my works, that is to say performances based on manuscript rather than printed copies. Having brought with him such a pleasing tidbit, he pressed his advantage by asking me to be a little more friendly towards Khais, 'who is upset by your attitude to him'.

Katya Schmidthof, to whom I had given a pass to come into the rehearsal, sat next to Ptashka, who was flanked on her other side by Knipper, a young composer from Moscow in Leningrad for talks with Ekskuzovich about his ballet who was relentlessly paying court to Ptashka. After we had finished rehearsing the Concerto Tyulin[1] and a few other acquaintants came to me commenting on the remarkable change in my pianism.

We spent the remainder of the day quietly and peacefully. In view of my imminent concert I declined any appointments or meetings. Arriving in the Green Room I was greeted by Asafyev, who informed me that he had dropped a heavy hint to Malko about the inappropriately low fee I was being paid. Malko promised to consider the matter and, if possible, to improve the conditions.

There was an immense crowd in the hall, I could even describe it as a phenomenal crowd. In Moscow the fire authorities allow only a seated audience; standing is forbidden. But here in Leningrad Khais, who shows himself to be adept not merely at negotiating favourable fees for the Philharmonia but at manipulating the visible impact of concerts, had succeeded in getting permission to admit standing customers, and had used the concession to fill the hall to such effect that it was literally black with people in every corner.

---

1 Yury Tyulin (1893–1978), musicologist and composer, writer on music theory and biography, professor at the Petrograd/Leningrad Conservatoire and later at the Moscow Conservatoire and the Gnesin Institute, a chess-playing friend. Shortly before he died Tyulin wrote an interesting personal memoir about his friendship with the young Prokofiev, 'On the Path to Recognition', included in V. Blok (ed.), *Sergey Prokof'ev: materialy, stat'i, inter'viu* (*Sergey Prokofiev, Materials, Articles, Interviews*), Progress Publishers, Moscow, 1976; English trans., 1978. At one time Prokofiev believed that the score of *The Gambler* left at the Mariinsky Theatre when he left Russia was in Tyulin's possession. See *Diaries*, vol. 1, p. 791; vol. 2, pp. 69, 72, 95, 145 166, 187, 694.

The first item was *Chout*, after which there were calls for me to appear, but in a repeat of the ritual I had adopted in Moscow I declined to do so. Next came the Third Piano Concerto. As soon as the audience had quietened down after *Chout* the piano was wheeled on to the stage, and then I was called to the stage. As I entered Dranishnikov launched into the *Slava*,[1] at which a colossal ovation erupted, approximately the same as on my first appearance in Moscow. It is not worth describing again, except for an amusing incident that occurred when the *Slava* had already been played twice and Dranishnikov was beginning it for the third time: at this point some particularly loud instruments came in a bar late so that the whole piece the third time round was played as a canon. It was obviously impossible to end the salute there and then because the players did not finish together, so Dranishnikov had to play it a fourth time even though three is what by tradition it should be.

The Concerto went well; I was relatively relaxed although falling short of the wonderful calm on which I had so prided myself during my last American tour. There was no applause between the movements, but at the end the roar from the audience was comparable to Moscow's. I first came out to bow on my own, then several times with Dranishnikov. As encores I played the Gavotte and two of the *Visions fugitives*. I was presented with a basket of flowers, but not a very large one.

In the interval Ossovsky came in with a message from Glazunov: he had been present for the Concerto but now had to leave for a meeting to which Ossovsky was also going. Glazunov had thus found a clever way to get out of his predicament: on the one hand he had as decency demanded put in an appearance at the Concerto, but on the other he had found a plausible excuse to avoid having to meet me. Ossovsky's departure was followed by a group consisting of Steinberg,[2] Weisberg[3] and Andrey Rimsky-Korsakov,[4] the

---

1 The celebratory finale of Glinka's opera *A Life for the Tsar*, in which the people sing a chorus of praise glorifying Holy Russia and her new Tsar, Mikhail Romanov.
2 Maximilian Steinberg (1883–1946), conservatively inclined composer and teacher, beloved student and son-in-law of Rimsky-Korsakov, and guardian of the flame. His encyclopaedic knowledge of form and orchestration caused him to be respected even by those of his students who rejected tradition, such as Shostakovich. He was never one of Prokofiev's teachers, so direct confrontation did not arise. See *Diaries*, vol. 1, p. 44, and *passim*; vol. 2, p. 73.
3 Yulia Weisberg (1878–1942), composer, member of the editorial board of the journal *Muzykal'nyi Sovremennik* (*Contemporary Music*) together with Pyotr Suvchinsky and Andrey Rimsky-Korsakov, the son of the composer (who was her husband). Suvchinsky and Asafyev, who was also a member of the editorial board, had left the journal after a furious disagreement over the merits of the progressive new generation of composers: Stravinsky, Prokofiev and Myaskovsky. See *Diaries*, vol. 1, p. 362, and *passim*; vol. 2, pp. 87, 109, 174, 473.
4 Andrey Rimsky-Korsakov (1878–1940), musicologist, critic and writer on music, the son of the composer Nikolay Rimsky-Korsakov. In 1914, in collaboration with Suvchinsky, he had founded a journal in St Petersburg, and a concert series, both dedicated to new music and called *Musical*

musically conservative group even before the Revolution in opposition to new music ever since their fierce fight with Suvchinsky and Asafyev, the defenders of Stravinsky, Myaskovsky and Prokofiev.[1] Now, however, the group has come to terms with the situation and welcomed me with every sign of pleasure. Could this be because otherwise they have no one to adhere to?

Then there were the Karneyeva sisters, ornamental as ever, Ostroumova-Lebedeva, Borovsky's sisters, the Alpers brother and sister, looking surprisingly well although the brother is even more nervous and the sister more faded than before. From somewhere lost in the mists of time emerged Rudavskaya,[2] who was little changed, the features perhaps a shade coarser, but with the same lovely eyes.

The interval came to an end and Dranishnikov performed the *Scythian Suite*. The orchestra is much inferior to Persimfans but Dranishnikov conducted with fervour and did a wonderful job. At the end the success was if anything greater than at any of the previous concerts: the entire audience, especially those who were standing, exploded in a frenzy. I took a bow on my own, then with Dranishnikov, then alone once more, and so on times without number, while all the time the audience shouted its approval.

While I was shuttling back and forth between the stage and the Green Room, an interesting scene was being played out in the latter setting. Ekskuzovich stood there, flanked on one side by Asafyev and on the other by Dranishnikov, both of them at each new curtain call pumping into him the absolute imperative of staging *The Gambler* and *Chout*. Ekskuzovich, apparently far from displeased by this insistent pressure, sat down, was extremely pleasant to me and the acme of charm to Ptashka.

The Green Room began to fill up again with acquaintances. Eleonora Damskaya has put on weight and grown considerably less attractive. I was polite to her but not effusive, and almost immediately turned to someone else wanting my attention. But Eleonora was not to be deflected and got

---

Contemporary (*Muzykal'ny Sovremennik*). Initially Andrey had been very supportive of Stravinsky and indeed Prokofiev, but turned against the former after *Petrushka*, which, in his opinion, betrayed the legacy of his father to whose inspiration, support and guidance he believed Stravinsky owed unswerving loyalty. This developed into a generally conservative attitude to Modernist tendencies in new music. See *Diaries*, vol. 1, p. 773; vol. 2, pp. 87, 109, 379, 473.

1 Suvchinsky, whose money had been behind both the *Contemporary Music* journal and the series of concerts presented under its auspices, started with Asafyev and the critic Viktor Belyayev a rival magazine with a policy of supporting the new wave of composers. It was called *Melos*, but produced only two issues before the events of 1917 made all such ventures unsustainable and it folded, as did *Contemporary Music*. See *Diaries*, vol. 2, p. 174.

2 Antonina Rudavskaya, a Conservatoire student to whom Prokofiev had been seriously attracted but whose intellectual powers were eventually not strong enough to keep her in the running. See *Diaries*, vol. 1, pp. 165–80, 204–5, and *passim*.

Asafyev's wife to introduce her to Ptashka, telling her that she had preserved some photographs from the sack of our flat in Pervaya Rota Street. Ptashka added that she thought she had understood Eleonora to say that she had also retrieved some letters. That was really all I needed, that correspondence from my ransacked apartment should of all people have fallen into her hands. However, Ptashka could not be certain what had actually been said about the letters, but since she has a great weakness for photographs and avidly collects any that have survived from my youth, she was very civil to Eleonora.

After the concert we went, as previously arranged, to Radlov's. He has a splendid flat and a splendid tea was served with hors d'oeuvres. We met there the chess-player Professor Smirnov[1] and the poet Kuzmin. The latter read some of his poems while we were having tea, in a faltering, lisping voice but for all that very expressive. I sat off to one side and studied with fascination his skull, which is absolutely flat on top, as if it had been chopped off by a sabre. He was poorly dressed, and his overcoat had holes in it. As we were putting on our coats in the hall I felt ashamed of my Paris coat with its new silk lining, over which I saw his eyes sliding.

We all left together at three in the morning, into a frosty night. In terms of success for me, Leningrad has eclipsed Moscow.

13 February

A quieter day, for visitors to call. Weisberg (!) appeared, and Dobychina, whom I always remember as kind, straightforward and warm-hearted. Benois had told me that she is now extremely well connected in the Communist elite and therefore has it in her power to be very helpful or very unpleasant, according to her inclinations. Her aspect today was funereal and she spoke in hushed tones. The burden of her song was, as she had already hinted to me at yesterday's concert, that the Chamber Music Circle, of which she is President, is at its last gasp for lack of funds. They have no money to pay for premises, so if I do not extend a helping hand by giving a concert in aid of the Circle, it will expire. Yesterday at the concert I managed to deflect her assault, but today she turned up again accompanied by Weisberg and began applying her sotto-voce pressure. Not only did I have no desire to play another concert, preferring to go out to see Asafyev at Detskoe, I was also well aware that there exist several such organisations and if I play for one I shall have to play for the others. After twenty minutes of painful refusals I finally got the two ladies off my hands, because the next deputation was already waiting.

---

1 Alexander Smirnov (1883–1962), literary critic and translator, Romance languages philologist, expert on Shakespeare, chess-player and writer on chess.

This group of people was less tedious but represented even more danger. It also wanted a concert, but this time for the benefit of MOPR, an acronym standing for the International Society for Help to Revolutionaries. Were I to give such a concert and were the Communists to advertise it widely, I would never again get a visa to visit another state, because this is no Russian society, it is an international organisation dedicated to the cultivation and fermentation of microbes destined to infect the whole world. However, I managed to squash the idea in a frank and open manner by saying, 'You understand, I should dearly love to help you, but since I have to give a great many concerts abroad, and since it is important for Soviet Russia that I should do so, I have to be particularly careful not to become involved in such enterprises, lest my foreign concerts begin to attract opposition.'

My excuse was so plain and unequivocal that they immediately agreed with me and left me in peace to receive Balaev,[1] my old Russian-language teacher at the Conservatoire. Balaev, now an old man, is head of a High School somewhere. He also was soliciting my appearance in aid of something or other, but he was honest enough to admit that although he was obliged to transmit the request of the people who had sent him, he perfectly understood the hopelessness of the appeal. In this way the third of my supplicants was dealt with painlessly, and we parted with an affectionate embrace.

In the afternoon we were obliged to go to an open-to-all Philharmonic concert which Malko had particularly asked me to attend, extracting from me a promise that I would. We were taken to the place of honour in the former Tsar's box. The concert was preceded by a talk given by Karnovich, whose *Variations for Orchestra* I had conducted fifteen years ago at the Conservatoire's Graduation Concert, when he was graduating and I was a student in the conducting class.[2] Doubtless as pre-arranged by Malko he contrived at one point in his talk to refer to me, although none of my works was on the programme. This gave an opening to indicate my presence and point out from the stage where I was sitting in our box, and the audience started to clap, so I had to stand and bow to acknowledge the applause.

The programme included some songs by Rimsky-Korsakov in his own orchestration, the scores for which had only recently been excavated from the composer's archive and were thus being heard for the first time. The

1 Nikolay Balaev, Prokofiev's Russian teacher in the academic (non-music subjects) class at the St Petersburg Conservatoire. See *Diaries*, vol. 1, pp. 12–48 *passim*.
2 Nikolay Tcherepnin, Prokofiev's conducting teacher at the Conservatoire, suggested that Prokofiev should conduct the *Variations for Orchestra* by Karnovich, a composition student of Steinberg, at the Graduation Concert for 1913. It coincided with the aftermath of the suicide of Prokofiev's friend Max Schmidthof, and this may have coloured his mixed feelings for the work, but with some of the *Variations* cut he admitted that it was well made and 'on the whole very nice'. Evidently Karnovich had subsequently managed to get himself a position on the faculty of the Conservatoire. See *Diaries*, vol. 1, pp. 362–404 *passim*.

exercise seemed hardly worth it, as the orchestration was uninspired and not at all Korsakov-like.

Returning from the concert we packed our suitcases to go back to Moscow. We were intending to go for only a few days, and then come back to Leningrad. On our way by sleigh to the Nikolayevsky Station our driver pulled up alongside another sleigh, and the horses suddenly reared up on their hind legs. Perhaps ours was interested in the mare now beside him, or perhaps he was simply out of control; in any case he leapt and pranced about so violently that the shafts began to crack. The shaft of our sleigh then got itself entangled with one of the other's shafts, so that neither could move forward or backward. Ptashka, who was sitting on the side with the trapped shaft, shouted in a fright, 'Get out, get out quickly!' But this was not so easy, because the cover had been fastened down and was piled up with our cases. While I was trying to extricate myself from under it the horses managed to separate themselves and Ptashka realised that in the melee she had lost her handbag. We looked right and left, high and low for it, but then heard some shouts from about fifteen paces behind us. It transpired that the bag had fallen into the snow and had been picked up by an old woman, who ran off with it. However, she had been spotted by a drunk man, who took the bag off her and it was now returned to us. A crowd had gathered, voicing its indignation at the event. The drunk demanded a rouble for having saved the handbag; I would have been more than happy to give him something for his trouble had he made his request rather less emphatically than was the case. Eventually he made himself scarce, pursued by the imprecations of the crowd: 'You should be ashamed of yourself, citizen, trying to fleece him like that.'

We had the same compartment in the International Company sleeping car as we had had before. In the same carriage were Ekskuzovich and Asafyev, and in the next car Rapoport, Chief Producer of the Mariinsky, who bore a striking resemblance to Donner in *Rheingold*. Evidently the possibility of our meeting had been foreseen and was being taken advantage of so that we could discuss future productions of my works in the Mariinsky Theatre.

Soon after the train moved off they all gathered in our compartment. The main topic was the forthcoming production of *The Gambler*, and Ekskuzovich promised to let me have my original score back, which was still secreted in the bowels of the Mariinsky's library. I in turn promised that the premiere of the opera would be in the Mariinsky as, indeed, we had discussed two years ago in Paris. In addition to *The Gambler* a ballet programme was mooted, to consist of *Chout, Ala and Lolly*[1] and, if Diaghilev could be induced to give his consent, my new Soviet-themed ballet.

---

1 The ballet, to a libretto by the poet Sergey Gorodetsky that Diaghilev had rejected in Milan in 1915, the music from which Prokofiev made into the *Scythian Suite*.

When I cautiously enquired if Meyerhold would be acceptable as a producer for *The Gambler*, since he had been the designated producer for the aborted 1917 production, Ekskuzovich responded with enthusiastic agreement. Generally, everything Ekskuzovich said was interesting, even scintillating, and he went out of his way to be charming. Asafyev sat in a corner and for the most part said very little, while who or what Rapoport was remained a mystery to me. I was interested to know to what extent he was a Communist sympathiser, because at one point without preamble he raised the question of whether it might not be a good idea for me to compose something for the forthcoming tenth anniversary of the October Revolution. However, there was not much enthusiasm for this notion and it soon lapsed.

There was also some talk of *Three Oranges* and the possibility of their version being toured abroad, in which case certain inadequacies of the production would have to be addressed. 'Just you wait,' said Ekskuzovich 'until I abandon my role as director, which bores me, and become a producer on my own account. Then you'll see how I'll stage *Oranges*.'

The meeting came to an end and everyone dispersed to their compartments. Before Asafyev left I asked him if Ekskuzovich had been put out by my mention of Meyerhold. 'On the contrary,' replied Asafyev, 'he was very happy with it. Through you he might be able to secure Meyerhold's services, whereas it might not have been appropriate to make a direct approach. It could all work out very well.'

14 February

Moscow in the morning, and Tsukker at the station to meet us. We had the same room in the Metropole Hotel; it had not been let during our absence but kept for us at half-price.

The phone calls started almost immediately, all those I had put off until I returned from Leningrad. Before I left it had been so easy and convenient to ask people to ring on the day of my return, but now the chickens were coming home to roost. On top of that I had a headache, I felt tired and even slept a little in the afternoon.

In the evening, the grand gala celebration of the fifth anniversary of the founding of the Persimfans Orchestra. I made sure they knew I had come specially from Leningrad for this occasion and even my next concert in aid of the homeless had been scheduled to fit in. The programme for this evening's concert had only two quite short pieces in it: the *Poème de l'extase* and the *Scythian Suite*, Persimfans being particularly proud of its interpretation of the latter. In view of the importance of the occasion I wore a dinner-jacket for the first and last time, but this may have been inappropriate since in this company I stood out as an obviously foreign body somehow parachuted in from abroad. Hardly anyone wears evening-dress here, except perhaps a few artists who have toured successfully abroad and like to exhibit their privileged relationship to foreign lands. Among the people who were coming to my concerts dressed thus, I noticed only two: Saradzhev and Yavorsky.

We were seated in the eighth row, next to Tsukker's papa and a rugged Red Army soldier who was obviously bored by the *Poème de l'extase* but who, later on, gave quite a powerful speech as the representative of some organisation or other for whom Persimfans had once performed.

After *Extase* the stage was cleared and a large table was placed on the right side for the Committee of Honour presided over by Lunacharsky. Behind the table sat delegates from various institutions who one by one stepped forward to deliver congratulatory addresses. The Persimfans players sat on the left, Tseitlin at their head. A million speeches ensued, interesting at first but eventually a sheer endurance test to sit through, as clearly there was no question of leaving the room.

Lunacharsky's address was a very accomplished performance, although the Persimfansers were always saying that not once in the five years of their existence had he offered them any support whatsoever. This was strange, in view of the essentially communistic spirit of an orchestra without a conductor: to whom should one look for support unless the Communist Commissar of Enlightenment!

Sosnovsky also spoke, he who had bored on so crucifyingly in the interval of one of my concerts. But this time he was not too bad. A mass of other people said their pieces: people from the theatre, from the Conservatoire, workers' organisations and so on. Derzhanovsky also made a speech, but with his hoarse voice what he said could hardly be heard.

At last the interval came to an end and the chairs and music stands were replaced on the stage for the orchestra to perform the *Scythian Suite*. The 'Dance of the Evil Spirits' elicited thunderous applause; there were insistent calls for the composer but I did not rise as this was not my day. Even so, at the conclusion of the Suite there were renewed calls for me to appear, and Tseitlin himself was applauding from the stage. At this point I did stand up and went up to the platform to shake his hand. As I did so he thrust out his hand and pulled me up on to the stage with such force that we both nearly lost our balance and fell over. Before bowing to the audience I pumped Tseitlin's hand, congratulated him on the anniversary and we then publicly embraced one another. I felt it was necessary to make some display of approbation as until this point I had not offered my congratulations on the jubilee to anybody.

After the performance there was supper. I had a headache and wanted nothing so much as to go to bed, especially as I had a concert the next day, but it was impossible not to attend given that a number of important personalities who had been expected had cried off – the place cards at the top table for Lunacharsky and Litvinov had no occupants. The supper did not have the air of a successful event.

As always there were many toasts. Hints were dropped that I should make one, but I declined, saying that mine had already been made half an hour ago in the shape of the *Scythian Suite*. One of the critics sang a paean of praise to the industrialisation of the countryside and advanced the suggestion that music should increasingly reflect the machine age. I immediately felt impelled to get up and propose a toast to Hanon,[1] but was restrained by people tugging at my coat-tails on the grounds that it would be in poor taste.

Around one o'clock in the morning the atmosphere of the supper party was livening up as by then people had had enough, or perhaps too much, to drink (except me). The toasts, gradually becoming more and more incoherent, followed one another thick and fast, and judging it appropriate to remind Tsukker of my concert the next day I signalled to Ptashka that we should beat a retreat. However, where we were seated made it impossible to disappear inconspicuously; tables and chairs had to be moved out of the way. To the sound of yet another proposal that Prokofiev should make a speech, we made our escape.

15 February

My headache has gone, and I was able to practise for the concert, not having touched the instrument the previous day or, indeed, during our time in Leningrad.

We lunched with Asafyev at the Prechistenki restaurant. The day before yesterday, when we had all gathered in our compartment en route to Moscow, Asafyev, Ekskuzovich and Rapaport had all been on their way to an important meeting about theatre politics. This was the meeting that was supposed to determine the future direction of the theatrical repertoire as a whole. The meeting had taken place yesterday, and today at lunch Asafyev was eager to tell us what had happened at it.

There was a war between two opposing camps: on one side the Communists, who wanted theatres to function basically as propaganda workshops ('If they depend on the workers' money then they must work for the benefit of the workers') and on the other the theatre professionals, who wanted the theatres

---

1   Charles-Louis Hanon (1819–1900), author of *The Virtuoso Pianist in 60 Exercises*, published in 1873, a relentlessly technical volume of digital calisthenics, musically dispiriting but according to no less an authority than Rachmaninoff largely responsible for the great flowering of virtuoso pianists from Russian and Soviet Conservatoires in the late nineteenth and twentieth centuries. Shostakovich makes sardonic reference to Hanon in the finale of his Second Piano Concerto, written for his son Maxim who had clearly been suffering from them, as presumably had Prokofiev in his own Conservatoire piano studies.

to remain above all theatres and not arenas for political education ('If they depend on the workers' money they must produce what the workers find interesting'). It boiled down to the Communists, inevitably, insisting on the Communist point of view, while the theatre professionals were vulnerable to the charge of not supporting Communism, or even being anti-Communist, thus laying themselves open to the accusation of counter-revolutionary views. Accordingly they had to be very cautious and diplomatic in what they said.

The proceedings had begun with Ekskuzovich inviting Asafyev to read his report on the situation with opera. This, by Asafyev's own admission, failed to produce any effect on the assembled delegates beyond acute boredom, and he left out a good half of his report in order to get through it more quickly. Yavorsky, who is highly placed within musical officialdom, also read out something so obviously designed to sit on the fence and avoid offending either one side or the other that it was more or less incomprehensible.

Lunacharsky, in the chair for the session, preferred to keep his own counsel. His position naturally puts him in the Communist camp, but with tastes leaning to the aesthetic and the theatrical he had to manoeuvre very delicately. The weakness of his position was seized on by the Communists, who launched a coarse and brutal attack on the theatricals, showing no sympathy whatever for the art.

At this point Meyerhold took the floor. On the one hand he is a Communist and a decorated Red Army soldier; on the other a passionate believer in the art of the theatre. He began like this: 'Comrades, first of all I must ask you not to interrupt me while I am speaking. Because I am nervous I have just taken some valerian, and as a result I cannot answer for my actions. Some of you may remember what happened when I was interrupted last time.' (Asafyev could not tell us what had occurred last time as he was not there, but evidently it was something traumatic.)

'You, Communist comrades, probably have no conception of what our worker comrades actually want.' (Here Meyerhold rooted around in his pockets and pulled out a letter.) 'This is an appeal I received from the workers of such-and-such a factory where we performed.' (And he proceeded to read out a plea to produce dramas or comedies, anything indeed except edifying political tracts, which were not wanted under any circumstances.) 'So, therefore, comrade Communists, do you want us to put on the kind of plays that will stop working people coming to the theatre altogether? If the theatres are empty, the Communist government will simply have to increase the subsidy to them. And where do you think the money for this will come from? From the workers and peasants, that's where, and so the result is that the workers will be forced to pay for empty theatres instead of paying for full ones, that is to say for what they enjoy.'

Towards the end of his peroration Meyerhold was shouting so loudly that the meeting threatened to descend into scandal, and an interval was announced. Lunacharsky, giggling furtively into his moustache, muttered that his dream was to be able to leave his job at the Enlightenment Ministry. How the affair ended Asafyev did not know, because he left, but he did say that no one but Meyerhold would have been able to get away with delivering such a sensationally provocative speech, because he has nothing to fear. It would not be politic to send a decorated Red Army hero to prison, while he could hardly be exiled abroad since he would have no trouble setting himself up there and the only loser would be Moscow.

Asafyev's stories carried us all the way through lunch, and then we left the restaurant together. I had had a telegram from Diaghilev asking about Yakulov, and therefore wanted to telephone him. But Yakulov was in Tbilisi, and I first spoke to his wife and then to his brother, who promised to send him a telegram in Tbilisi. The inference is that Diaghilev has decided to stage my ballet and so it is now a serious proposition. Consequently, he will exercise his exclusive rights over the ballet for three years, and that means that the idea of including it as one of the items in a triple-bill at the Mariinsky Theatre must be abandoned. I consulted Asafyev as to what could replace it. It occurred to me I might take the Overture and *Matelote* dance from the ballet I had written for Romanov two years before,[1] add to them three or four numbers from the Quintet and compose one or two linking numbers using themes from both sources. If all this material was orchestrated and a libretto created to go with it, it might not be too difficult to fashion a new ballet.

In the evening I despatched Ptashka to the Bolshoy Theatre to see *Kitezh*,[2] while I went over to the Hall of Columns to play my concert in aid of homeless children. One sceptical view I overheard was that 'it was not really in aid of the homeless but in aid of bullets, since there is no other way of getting rid of them'.

It was a pleasure to play in the noble Hall of Columns, so much more beautiful than the Great Hall of the Moscow Conservatoire, and with a better sound as well. I played the same programme as I had on the 4th February, but better this time, even though I landed on wrong notes every time in the four passages of scales in alternating hands in the finale of the Fourth Sonata. The conclusion of the programme was a tremendous success; I played the March from *Oranges* and the Gavotte from the *Classical* Symphony as encores, and the whole place erupted.

Nadya Rayevskaya was at the concert and came backstage to see me accompanied by an attractive red-haired woman from the Vakhtangov Studio.[3]

---

1 See above, pp. 194–5, 200–1, 213.
2 The *Invisible City of Kitezh and the Maiden Fevronia*, opera by Rimsky-Korsakov, first performed in 1907.
3 The third incarnation of the Moscow Art Theatre Studio, formed in 1921 and in 1926 given the name of its guiding spirit, the actor and director Yevgeny Vakhtangov (born 1883) who had died of stomach cancer in 1922.

She was the wife of Nadya's brother-in-law Sheremetiev, whom I have already met, but I could not remember her name.[1] There then appeared to thank me a man and an ancient woman, representatives of the committee to abolish children's homelessness. I was very moved by what the lady said to me: 'If I die, do not forget the children who have no homes to go to. You see, we have a plan to eliminate this problem entirely within three years, and my colleagues are working tirelessly to implement it, but we shall not achieve our goal unless we have funds.' Then she thanked me once again for the concert I had given for their benefit. I replied, 'Eliminating homelessness of children is something we are both concerned about. I have given one hour to the cause but you devote all your time to it, therefore you should not be thanking me, it is I who should be thanking you.'

16 February

As early as ten o'clock we were invaded by Meyerhold and Asafyev. The decorated Red Army soldier is so important a personage that I was amazed at his modesty in coming to see me to signify his agreement to direct *The Gambler*. Could this unassuming behaviour be because in Paris I had likewise called on him early in the morning, to take him along to a Diaghilev rehearsal? This morning he lost no time in telling me that he would undertake the production with the greatest of pleasure, and so this matter is settled. And since the Mariinsky is making such an effort to secure a big fish like Meyerhold, the production is sure to be a spectacularly good one.

I told Meyerhold that before getting down to revising *The Gambler*, which I plan to do root and branch, I would like him to tell me any pointers he might like to give me for alterations to my old libretto. The part that most worried me was the last scene. Meyerhold said, 'We must certainly discuss all sorts of details the moment you return from your second visit to Leningrad, in about two weeks' time. Then you must come to dine with me, and I will try to get hold of Andrey Bely, if you have nothing against that idea.'

'On the contrary,' I said, 'I should be delighted as I like Bely very much. But is he an experienced man of the theatre?'

Meyerhold: 'Oh yes, he has a wonderful feeling for the stage, and is even now adapting one of his poems for me in a most interesting way.'

On this note we parted. Soon after, Myaskovsky came in to take me off to Muzsektor, which is housed in the old Jurgenson shop. Yurovsky was waiting for me there so that we could settle the question of their editions of my old

---

1 She was Cecilia Mansurova (1896–1976), a leading actress of the Vakhtangov Studio. Mansurova was her stage name, taken from the name of the street in which the studio was located. Her husband was Count Nikolay Sheremetiev. See below, p. 1070, n. 4.

compositions, formerly published by Jurgenson and Gutheil but since the Revolution transferred to Muzsektor. But Muzsektor had been established to expropriate merely the publishers, not to penalise the composers. Composers living abroad may have presented a murky problem in this respect but Myaskovsky, a person of great influence in Muzsektor, and his entourage had always insisted that I was not an émigré but someone who had gone abroad for an extended stay, quite legally and with a Soviet passport. My current presence in Moscow underlined this position, and therefore it was up to Muzsektor, in the form of its president, Yurovsky, to find a way of legalising their relationship with me. This could turn out to be a costly amusement for Muzsektor, because they would have to pay royalties on everything they had sold in the nine years since the Revolution as well as acquiring rights for a number of years in the future.

Muzsektor, following a scheme originally suggested by Myaskovsky, had adopted a system for calculating compensation for each composition which was based on counting the number of crotchets in a work multiplied by its scale (solo piano, ensemble, orchestral score, etc.) and then multiplied again by the reputation of the composer, who would then receive a royalty usually between 7 and 12 per cent of the retail price of the printed score.

My discussion with Yurovsky went on for about two hours. His initial proposal was a 12 per cent royalty, but observing the look of dissatisfaction on my face, immediately upped it to 15. This 15 per cent amounts in fact to more than the 25 per cent paid by Koussevitzky's publishing house, because Muzsektor's payments are based on the retail price of the publication whereas Koussevitzky's are based on the trade price at which the publisher sells them to the retailer, which represents a discount of almost 50 per cent.

I declined to sign a binding contract for an indefinite period, but suggested instead an agreement limited to three years as a trial period with the option to extend it. It was a compromise solution, but Yurovsky agreed, and then raised the subject of a work for the tenth anniversary of the Soviet Revolution, which would occur in six months' time. This was the most awkward part of our conversation because I could not possibly do anything but decline, but equally had to do so without giving offence and for plausible reasons. I replied that I would consider it wrong to compose something trivial and in haste, and because I was contracted to complete *Fiery Angel* by the end of the summer there would not be enough time for me to produce an appropriately serious piece by October. Yurovsky rejoined that for Muzsektor it was so important to have a work by me that they would not be baulked by a very substantial fee; money was no object for them. At this point I remembered my ballet for Diaghilev, and told him that I already had a new work on a Soviet theme. The problem was therefore not merely one of time but of my reluctance to contemplate writing a second piece before seeing how the first one turned out. In short I extricated myself from the situation so ingeniously that when Yurovsky and I had parted on the friendliest terms and I was leaving, his secretary ran after me and as I was putting on my coat in the other room said, 'You probably think Alexander Naumovich (Yurovsky) is a Communist. But it was only the responsibilities of his position that made him feel he had to ask you about the jubilee composition.'

I met Ptashka and we both went to see Rabinovich who was very anxious to show me his models of the sets for the *Three Oranges* production. We were tired when we reached him, partly because his place was almost impossible to find, but we were well rewarded because the models were truly stunning. *Oranges* has never had such superbly stylish settings. I especially liked the first scene with its perspective formed by mirrors extending right to the back. Rabinovich is a master at making his models, and therefore his conceptions are presented most effectively. He announced with pride that he was dedicating them to me.

We then had to race back because Razumovsky, the Secretary of the Society of Authors, was expecting me. I wanted to write a formal statement of protest to the Society about the 15 per cent it was proposing to levy on my performing-right fees for the Bolshoy Theatre production of *Oranges*. I don't mind if they take even 25 per cent from such minor activities as my concert appearances, because the sums involved are a few roubles, or even copecks. But when it is a mattter of substantial sums from the Bolshoy Theatre – which they do not even keep themselves but pass on to Koussevitzky via Kniga – 15 per cent is outright robbery. In France the Society of Authors takes around 2 per cent, or even less.

I set all this out to Razumovsky and together we drafted my statement. Razumovsky intimated that in all probability the Society would meet me halfway, because to enter into dispute with me at a time when I am having such a success would be against their best interests.

When Razumovsky had left we had to pack our cases again, because this evening we are due to go back to Leningrad. Tsukker came to wish me well and to accompany us to the station. I asked him what was happening about Shurik, but he only mumbled something about it being difficult, a very delicate situation, one had to tread very carefully in order not to make matters worse, the person he needed to approach about it had still not returned to Moscow, etc., etc. I could see that Tsukker did not want to get involved in the affair, and was concerned mainly to avoid getting himself into bad odour for any representations he might make.

We loaded our cases into the car, and accompanied by Tsukker left for the station. By a curious coincidence our compartment in the International sleeping-car was the same as on the last two trips, but this time Ekskuzovich was not with us. Asafyev, however, was, but as the surcharges for the

International cars are so steep, several times the price of an ordinary ticket, Asafyev on this occasion was economising and travelling in 'hard' class. As soon as the train started I went to find him. 'Hard' class is, needless to say, not terribly comfortable, but Asafyev had a separate bench on which he could lie down and some soft bedding, so he could get at least some sleep. We chatted for a while; I had just been given a packet of reviews by the Moscow press-cuttings bureau, and we looked through them.

I told Asafyev that on the way to see Yurovsky today I had offered some money to Myaskovsky so that he could come to Leningrad for the performance of his Eighth Symphony, but Nikolay Yakovlevich had refused, saying that he had no desire at all to go. But in my mind I was certain that this was simply because he did not want to accept a gift of money, and that if in fact he did have the money he would very much like to come. Asafyev agreed, and said he would write to him to drag him by hook or by crook up to Leningrad for the performance of the Symphony.

After a bit of discussion about my programme for this stay in Leningrad – which in fact had already in the main been settled during my last visit – we said good night and I made my way back to the comfort of my aristocratic sleeper, which no amount of disruptions and revolutions had been able to remove from circulation.

Later, Asafyev told me that his neighbours in the 'hard'-class carriage had recognised me and when I had gone were very respectful to him. Asafyev hates smoke fumes, and they refrained from smoking so as not to annoy him.

17 February

Leningrad at ten o'clock in the morning, and before it several glimpses through the window of the snow-covered outskirts. This time in spite of its white coverlet I was able to discern the familiar features of Sablino. We parted from Asafyev at the Nikolaevsky Station and made our own way to the Europa Hotel, where we were assigned a splendidly light and spacious suite consisting of a huge sitting room, a bedroom, bath and entrance hall, and even a hiding place for a lover, as I designated the big dark store-room next to the hall.

The first person to appear was Katya Schmidthof. She related how well her career in the theatre had been going before the catastrophic loss of her arm, and went on to say that now, although of course her career as an actress was finished, she could still train as a producer, a calling to which she felt very attracted. In short, could I give a concert for her benefit, which would enable her to take a two-year course of study as a route to re-entering the theatrical profession that had been so tragically closed to her. Her request was couched in the same sweet, unaffected simplicity that her brother used to adopt when touching me for money long ago.

And yet, seen from her point of view, did it not look such a simple matter? I could say yes, play another concert (when I am playing so many, what difference does an extra one make?), and lo! a new life opens up for her. But when I thought about it, I reasoned that the loss of an arm was too great a handicap for these studies to have a realistic propsect of a successful outcome. Moreover, it was not in fact such a simple matter to organise a concert. I therefore replied that for my visit to Leningrad I was wholly committed to the Philharmonia, and so there could be no question of a concert not under their auspices.

After this I left to go to the rehearsal of the orchestral concert, while Katya stayed behind with Ptashka and told her the story of her life. She was currently on her third marriage. Her first husband had been an actor whom she had married in 1917 or 1918, soon after my departure for America. This had been a marriage for love, and their journey together to Siberia, where he was performing, was despite the tribulations of the Civil War one of the happiest memories of her life. But their happiness lasted no more than a few months: her husband fell ill and died, leaving her in a calamitous situation and a mood of crushing dejection. In this mood of utter hopelessness she married a Communist whom she did not love but hoped that he would offer her some support. This Communist, an archetypal male chauvinist, was as cruel as he was jealous, and Katya was very unhappy with him. He would lock her in her room and came near to beating her physically. During one of these scenes a young man attempted to come to her aid, and in the ensuing fight he was killed by the Communist. Obviously the husband was jealous of the young man, although Katya insisted that he had no reason to be. The Communist was sent to prison but, after only a few months, released as a result of some manifesto or other, he turned up again. Katya recoiled from him in horror, but he continued to press his claim on her as his wife, saying, 'You won't find another man as good as me in a hurry.' Katya, however, would not go back to him and married a third time, to a naval officer by whom she has a child, and is reasonably happy although her husband is away much of the time, at sea in the far north. Katya smokes incessantly, and has become expert at striking matches with one hand.

Today's rehearsal was taken by Malko and was for a new programme, namely: the Suite from *Oranges*, the *Classical* Symphony, the new Overture, and the Second Piano Concerto. Malko was rehearsing today the *Oranges* Suite and the Symphony: pretty good results, serious and precise as always, but short on elan and conviction. When I went out on to the street I saw that there was an enormous queue for tickets; people recognised me and started clapping. What patience they must have – to stand in a queue for two hours and still want to clap!

Back at the Europa Hotel I observed to my chagrin that there was still no piano, although on my last visit I had agreed with Khais that one would be sent over to me from the Philharmonia this morning. I put through a testy phone call to the Philharmonia, which elicited the information that the piano had been held up but would be sent any moment. This was most irritating, since my first recital is tonight and it is essential for me to go through my programme, which I have not played for almost three weeks.

At four o'clock I was finally informed that the piano had arrived in the hotel. I opened the door, rearranged the furniture and waited, but after another half-hour had gone by there was still no sign of the piano. I went down into the lobby of the hotel where I found a huge piano indeed standing there, but nobody anywhere near it. It transpired that while the instrument was being manhandled into the hotel the horses who had drawn the conveyance in which it was transported had bolted and the coachmen were trying to catch them. Why this should take half an hour was not explained. I rang up the Philharmonia yet again and at long last, at half past five, the piano was heaved into my room on the backs of no fewer than nine hotel porters. It looked like a centipede. I sat down to practise my programme, but this ludicrous business with the piano had wrecked my whole day. I was able neither to rest after a night travelling, nor to practise as I needed to.

In the evening the Hall of Columns was filled to capacity. My performance was almost good apart from a few gaffes: the notorious ending of the first movement of the Fifth Sonata, slips here and there in *Visions fugitives*, and so on. The response conformed to what is now the custom: good after the Third Sonata, restrained after the Fifth, and explosive as soon as I played the March from *Oranges* and other bon-bons. After three or four encores the shrieking and roaring continued until the lights were doused, and even for some time after that.

Andrey Rimsky-Korsakov, who has already written one favourable review of the previous concert, cornered me about collaborating on a theatre piece to a text by Razumnik[1] with scenery by Petrov-Vodkin and to be directed by

---

1   Ivanov-Razumnik, the pen-name of Razumnik Ivanov (1878–1946), writer and critic, author of critical editions of Belinsky and Saltykov-Shchedrin, a *History of Russian Public Thought* and a particularly interesting memoir of writers who suffered exile and imprisonment (as he had done). In 1917 and 1918 he collaborated with Andrey Bely and Sergey Maslovsky-Mstislavsky on two important radical collections of writing in 1917 and 1918 entitled *Scythians*, the jackets of which were designed by Petrov-Vodkin. A little later Ivanov-Razumnik co-founded an association in Petersburg called the Free Philosophical Association (Vol'naya Filosofskaya Assotsiatsiya or Volfila) which had the support of Lunacharsky and whose distinguished membership of philosphers, poets and artists included besides Razumnik, Mstislavsky and Petrov-Vodkin such luminaries as Blok, Yesenin, Meyerhold, Karsavin, Lossky, Bely, Kluyev, Platonov, Radlov, Zoshchenko, Zamyatin – the flower of literary Petersburg in the early 1920s. Many of them chimed with the underlying philosophy of the Association, which was to

Meyerhold. This is not the sort of proposition I would normally agree to, but seeing that it came from Andrey Rimsky-Korsakov, until recently a sworn opponent but now an adherent displaying the zeal of the newly converted, I sidestepped with soft words about being overwhelmed with work until the end of the year, and suggesting it would be better to postpone discussion until my next visit.

Dobychina appeared and pursued me with quiet but importunate insistence. She is obviously after something, probably the concert in aid of the quartet society I thought I had managed to duck. While I was taking my curtain calls she waited behind the columns on the way out to the Artists' Room and said in a low voice, 'Look at them all shouting their heads off. Perhaps you think it shows their love for you? Not at all. Love does not express itself by shouting but by quiet understanding.'

I remembered that she is well connected to the Cheka and so heard her out. But just then the Karnevey girls were approaching and Lidusya could see from afar the boredom on my face. She came up to me and drew me to one side. 'Do you want me to rescue you from this old woman, Sergusya?' 'Oh yes, for God's sake please do, Lidusya – she'll poison my entire visit.'

We linked arms and behind the columns moved away from Dobychina. All of a sudden the applause, which had begun to subside, erupted again: as we were moving along behind the columns we had come into view by the public, which on spotting me renewed their clapping with redoubled energy. Embarrassed, we quickly fled the scene.

There were a lot of people in the Green Room, among them Asafyev, Dranishnikov, Ossovsky, Malko, Katya Schmidthof, the Alpers brother and sister, Rudavskaya, etc. The last-named had rung me up this morning because the last time we met I promised her a ticket for the concert. When I was telling her that a ticket would be left for her in an envelope at the desk in the hotel, I asked her, 'Antonina Alexandrovna, how many times have you been married?' This is quite a normal question to put to a pretty woman in Soviet Russia. But with her customary aplomb she stopped me at once by saying, 'Sergey Sergeyevich, these are not matters one should discuss on the telephone.'

Ptashka was very taken by the Karneyev girls and made an arrangement with Lidusya, who has retained her fashionable sense of style, to go to look at

---

welcome the Revolution but to argue at the same time that the formation of a new society also required a spiritual revolution. This was hardly to the taste of the developing proletarian cultural movement: a large part of the philosophical membership was deported abroad on Lenin's Philosophy Steamer, and Ivanov-Razumnik himself was repeatedly arrested and exiled for alleged 'narodnik' tendencies (the discredited efforts of intellectuals in the nineteenth century to go to the country in order to educate the peasants). In 1941, living in poverty in German-occupied country near Leningrad he was deported to a concentration camp in Prussia, and on release made his way (via Lithuania) to Munich, where he died soon after the war.

furs tomorrow. Furs are the one indispensable purchase everyone living abroad has to make when coming to Russia.

18 February

Second rehearsal for the same concert. The orchestra was behaving erratically – 'mischievously', as Malko apologetically put it. The musicians are not of the same calibre as those in the Persimfans Orchestra, although the Overture, Op. 42, which was being rehearsed today, went better with a conductor than it had done in Moscow. As well as the Overture we worked intensively on the Second Concerto.

After the rehearsal Khais and Malko asked me to come up to the administration offices of the Philharmonia, which are located in the same building. Malko informed me that the Philharmonia would pay my publishers for all 'illegal' performances of my scores for which handwritten parts had been used. Khais then asked where he should make payment of my fee. There was no mention of any additional payment, merely an anxious look as much to say: am I going to raise the matter?

At the same time he tried to haggle with me about the amount I was due for the expenses of my visit. This enraged me, although I did not show it. And then, when he brazenly starting talking about my giving concerts next year, I replied, 'I doubt if this will be possible. It's not worth my while to play concerts for the Leningrad State Philharmonia. It is better for me to go south, to Kharkov or to the Caucasus, where I am paid twice as much as here.'

Khais was rocked back on his heels. The effect of my statement far exceeded anything I had expected. Malko mumbled and hummed and hawed, repeating that he had only recently become Director and all the negotiations had been done in Klimov's day.[1] I said reassuringly that I was quite aware of this. Khais stammered something and Malko did his best to steer the conversation into calmer waters.

The result is to make it appear that I have no intention of entering into discussion with Khais about next season whereas I might perhaps come to an agreement with Malko. Khais leapt to his feet and declared that he would leave the room so as not to inhibit our discussion. We restrained him and he stayed, though going out after a short while under some pretext or other.

Malko was highly amused and obviously delighted with the turn of events as my actions have handed him a trump card against Khais in his power struggle over the management of the Philharmonia. He then turned to other topics and in connection with *Fiery Angel* told me a story about Bryusov. It seems that when he died, the authorities asked his widow for his unpublished

---

1 See above pp. 349, 373, 421, 478.

manuscripts. Either there weren't any, or not enough, so the widow suggested his diary, which he, proud of his great learning, had recently taken to writing in Ancient Greek. The proposal was avidly seized upon and a translation immediately commissioned, but at this point it was discovered that this most venerated of Communists had been savaging the Soviet system with unparalleled relish. No one, accordingly, knows what has now become of the diary.

Khais returned. After exchanging a few phrases with him I took my leave, affectionately with Malko and politely with Khais. But the fact remains that these admirable gentlemen added not a single copeck to what they were paying me, merely letting me know obliquely that there could be no question of exceeding the sum already agreed and that any revision of that amount would bring disagreeable consequences upon their heads from their superiors.

Back at the hotel I practised the Second Concerto and slept. Ptashka had gone out with Lidusya to look at sables. Katya Schmidthof came to tell me that she had found the perfect apartment for herself, but needed 250 roubles to secure it, which she does not have. It is clear that even if I don't give a concert to help her I have to do something; I promised to find half the money which I would send from Moscow, since I don't have enough with me here. The Philharmonia is transferring all my fees directly abroad in dollars.

Khais rang up to say what a painful effect today's conversation had had on him. He was not the guilty party, he claimed, the blame lay entirely with Klimov who was the Director at the time but was now in retirement. He is lying: he, Khais, is certainly in charge of all such matters. But now, on the telephone, I said merely, 'You are correct in what you say, since all the letters I received from the Philharmonia were signed not by you but by Klimov.'

This phrasing gave Khais little satisfaction, because while formally agreeing with his explanation I was still holding him responsible. In this way the conversation ended inconclusively.

A telegram from Yakulov in Tiflis. Apparently the discussions with Diaghilev's company about the staging of my ballet are going well. This prompted me to send letters and telegrams to Diaghilev in Paris and Yakulov in Tiflis.

Ptashka came back at seven o'clock with Lida and a sailor who lives with them in their flat, a polite but taciturn young man. We sat and chatted, and Lidusya and I reminisced about Terijoki and all the fun and games we had in those days.

We did not go out any where in the evening but stayed in and went to bed early.

19 February

Another orchestral rehearsal. The Overture is better prepared than with Persimfans. I played the Concerto well but the orchestra lacks discipline and exhibits a lack of seriousness about their work. I heard that when Klemperer came to conduct them he was so rude to the orchestra that they decided not to admit any members of the public to the rehearsals in order not to expose them to disgrace.

At the rehearsal I told Asafyev about yesterday's confrontation with Khais. As a 'patriot' of his city Asafyev was upset by the Philharmonia's attitude. Khais put in an appearance, but only to hand me some tickets for the concert in a coldly businesslike manner. For all that, he did give me the number I had asked for, ten or twelve, for friends and acquaintances.

During the afternoon I practised and slept. Through the wall there was singing and wailing of gypsy songs. The Revolution may have done away with the arrogance of the aristocracy and the debauchery of the merchant class, but threw in the towel before gypsydom!

The concert, conducted by Malko, took place in the evening. The programme began with the Overture, which for the greater edification of the public was played twice in succession. Even so, the success of the work was not much greater than in Moscow, which is to say no more than moderate. I played the Second Concerto freely and cleanly, the first time I had done so without any untoward incidents. Further memories of this evening are confused with other concerts, and there are no notes in my brief diary entries.

20 February

As Lunacharsky had come up to Leningrad for a few days, a performance of *Oranges* was arranged especially for him this afternoon. He has not yet seen the production on stage and it is up to him to decide whether this production or some other is the one to be sent to Paris.

The theatre management kindly sent me tickets for two complete boxes, of which I made full use, distributing all twelve seats including one to Maria Kilshtedt, the librettist of my adolescent opera *Undina*.

When Ptashka and I arrived for the performance, we met a gathering in the producer's office consisting of Lunacharsky, Rapaport and Ekskuzovich. Not surprisingly a lively although friendly bantering conversation was in full swing about the forthcoming despatch abroad of a Soviet theatre company.

'After all,' said Lunacharsky, 'if we do send your production of *Oranges*, the, er, Bolsheviks will make my life not worth living.' As he spoke the word 'Bolsheviks' he gave a little laugh, letting us know that he was making a play on words alluding to the Bolshoy Theatre production of *Oranges* which they are desperately rushing to get on to the stage, confident that Rabinovich's set designs will be more spectacular than those of the Leningrad show.

An assistant came into the office to ask if Dranishnikov could begin the performance. We were conducted into one of the boxes in the dress circle on the left side of the auditorium. We arranged the seating as follows: Lunacharsky, Ptashka and myself in the front row, Ekskuzovich and Lunacharsky's two companions in the row behind. Lunacharsky leaned over to me and said, just as if he were paying a compliment to a young lady, 'It is a great pleasure to be hearing this opera sitting next to you.' This was said so sweetly that I could find no words to reply.

On a second hearing, or perhaps I should say viewing, of *Oranges*, now that all the stunts were familiar and had lost their power to surprise, I began to notice some defects. I pointed out some of them in a whisper to Ekskuzovich, who was sitting behind me, and during the interval he seized on my critical cast of mind to ask me to note down all my observations and suggestions so that they could be considered and acted upon.

For the interval we removed into the Director's withdrawing room off the box beside the stage for tea and refreshments. At one point Glazunov shambled in; he was evidently not attending the performance but just happened to be passing. Lunacharsky at once asked him how he liked *Oranges*, but Glazunov only mumbled something incomprehensible in reply and thrust some tickets for a Beethoven concert into Lunacharsky's hand. Dranishnikov immediately improvised a variant of a well-known saying along the lines of 'understanding as much as Glazunov does of *Oranges*'.[1]

Ekskuzovich took me on one side and confided to me his idea of combining productions of *The Gambler* and *Chout* so that they could be performed in a single evening. I was appalled. The effect of one would destroy the other; also it would rule out any project for a full evening of my ballets. I protested energetically and at once passed the idea on to Asafyev, asking him to oppose it at the first opportunity.

Over tea Lunacharsky lavished praise on the *Scythian Suite*, commenting on its power and vitality. Someone asked, 'What would you say about *Oranges*?'

'*Oranges*', replied Lunacharsky, 'is a fizzing, foaming glass of champagne.'

We went back into our box and the performance continued. In one of the intervals there were calls for the composer and I took a bow from my seat in the box. At the end of the show I appeared with the artists in front of the curtain, but most of the other intervals I spent in the Director's withdrawing room.

In the passage in front of our box I was caught by Maria Grigorievna Kilshtedt, and then Natasha Goncharova,[2] whom I did not at first recognise and then could recall to mind only dimly. Barkov brought up his and Lidusya's daughter to meet me, a delightful ten-year-old. But all these

---

1 The saying is: 'He knows as much about that as a pig does about oranges.'
2 Not the painter wife of Mikhail Larionov but a former singing student at the St Petersburg Conservatoire to whom the young Prokofiev had been much attracted. See *Diaries*, vol. 1, pp. 248–431 *passim*, also below p. 645.

encounters were like a kaleidoscope of impressions and there were probably more of which I have no memory.

Afterwards we went with Asafyev to dine with Malko, while Lunacharsky said goodbye and asked if I would be going in the evening to Alexey Tolstoy's, whom I had met in Paris before he ostentatiously abandoned his émigré status to transform himself into a model Soviet citizen. Tolstoy had indeed telephoned me the previous day to invite me, but my evening is already committed first to Malko and then to Shcherbachov, and I was obliged to decline.

Malko lives quite near the Mariinsky Theatre, on Kryukov Canal, in the building where Ziloti used to live. While we were waiting for dinner to be prepared Malko talked to Asafyev and Ptashka talked to Malko's wife, a very pretty Jewish woman he had acquired somewhere in the south. I meanwhile sat at a desk with the vocal score of *Oranges* which I read through from first page to last making notes, as Ekskuzovich had requested, of all my observations on both the staging and the musical aspects of the performance.

The dinner was delicious, as have all the meals been to which we been entertained in Russia. Malko reeled off a string of anecdotes without stopping: he has a real gift for telling amusing stories about nothing in particular, and there were so many of them that by the end my head was about to burst. At nine o'clock we said farewell and went off to Shcherbachov, who had assembled in my honour all the young composers of Leningrad.

Shcherbachov lives on Nikolayevsky Street – which, as is the custom today, has a new, Revolutionary name[1] – not far from Lyadov's old home. We had to travel right across town by sledge in the most frightful frost, Ptashka and I in one sledge, Asafyev in another.

As we drew near to Shcherbachov's, I began to worry that I was in a rather stupid position. On the one hand all these young composers had gathered together to play me their compositions, but on the other I had no idea what was the prevailing *Zeitgeist* among them. I did not know if they considered me one of 'theirs' or not. And further, it's all very fine to be a famous composer, but whether or not he is ever in fact going to amount to anything every young composer automatically thinks of himself as a Columbus, and usually starts by looking with a jaundiced eye on an established maître.

Shcherbachov has a fine apartment, but as almost everywhere in Leningrad to get into it one has to come up by the back stairs. Because we got there fairly late everyone else was already there and all the chairs and sofas were taken. But the atmosphere was immediately much more pleasant and unpretentious than I had expected, because I was straight away surrounded by old

---

1 By this time the street had had two changes of name: under the Provisional Government it was the catchy Twenty-Seventh February Prospect, but after the October Revolution it became Marat Street (Ulitsa Marata).

friends: Deshevov, Tyulin, Shcherbachov. Deshevov has not altered at all: the same old lively, friendly fellow, full of enthusiasms. He must be nearly forty, and yet one still thinks of him as just setting out on a path that promises great things. But there was no time to waste: before us was a long list of compositions for me to hear, and so the music began at once.

First to play was Schillinger,[1] with a complicated piece that held little interest. If that was a sample of the whole evening, thank you kind sir. When he finished I did not know what to say, but Schillinger solved the problem by coming over to sit beside me and going through the score note by note, explaining the structure of the piece, which incorporated various Revolutionary melodies such as the Internationale, 'We Fell as Victims',[2] and so on. This was no help at all in elucidating the work, and I endeavoured to extricate myself from my predicament by asking a series of questions while refraining from expressing my opinion.

Second up was Shostakovich, quite a young man,[3] not only a composer but also a pianist. He played by heart and with panache, having passed me the score to peruse as I sat on the sofa. His Sonata[4] opened with a vigorous Bach-like two-voice counterpoint, and the second movement, which followed without a break, is written with supple harmonies surrounding an interior melody. It was pleasant, but diffuse and rather too long. The Andante

---

1   Joseph Schillinger (1895–1943), composer, music theorist and teacher. It is in the last of these fields that Schillinger's name is mainly known today, because of the substantial influence he exerted on American composers after emigrating there the year after this encounter. Musicians such as George Gershwin, Benny Goodman, Henry Cowell, Oscar Levant and many others, including Vladimir Dukelsky, acknowledged the debt they owed to Schillinger's strictly mathematics-based analysis. Among Schillinger's students was Glenn Miller, who revealed that the 'Miller Sound' was the result of working with Schillinger; *Moonlight Serenade* was apparently written as an exercise under Schillinger's guidance. Schillinger also collaborated with the inventor Léon Theremin and in 1929 wrote for Theremin's keyboardless oscillator-driven instrument the *First Airphonic Suite*. Schillinger taught at a number of educational institutions but the primary medium for disseminating his ideas was his postal tuition courses, which after his death was codified and developed into the *Schillinger System of Musical Composition*, published in two volumes compiled by Lyle Dowling and Arnold Shaw. Here is Dukelsky writing in 1947 about studying with Schillinger: 'The art of orchestration became a science with the advent of Joseph Schillinger. A score by a Schillinger pupil can be recognised not only because of its previously unexplored sonorities but also by reason of the peculiar lucidity of its texture and the effective economy of its orchestral language. These combined qualities present a truly integrated image to the listener's ear.' (V. Dukelsky, 'Gershwin, Schillinger and Dukelsky: Some Reminiscences', *Musical Quarterly*, vol. 33 no. 1 (January 1947), pp. 102–15.)
2   One of the two most widely sung Revolutionary anthems of the early years of the twentieth century – the other being Lenin's favourite, 'Tormented by Grievous Bondage' – often in the form of a funeral march to remember fallen comrades in the February and October Revolutions and the Civil War. One of the most famous occasions was at the execution of nineteen sailors who had at Bolshevik urging participated in the second Kronstadt Uprising in 1906 following the disastrous Russo-Japanese War. The words were by the nineteenth-century radical poet A. Arkhangelsky (real name Anton Amosov) and the tune was a popular song 'The Drum Did Not Sound'.
3   Shostakovich was twenty years old at the time.
4   Sonata No. 1, Op. 12.

leads into a quick-tempo finale, disproportionately short in relation to its predecessors. But it was altogether so much more lively and interesting than Schillinger's piece that I launched with joy into a paean of praise for Shostakovich. This amused Asafyev, who commented that the reason I had liked the first movement of the Sonata was because it showed my influence.

It was followed by a published collection containing works by five or six composers including Tyulin, perfectly nice but bloodless, slightly reminiscent of some of the *Visions fugitives*, and Shcherbachov, much more interesting that I had expected, remembering his *Procession* that I had once upon a time conducted at a Conservatoire Graduation Concert.

After an interval for tea the performance continued. Deshevov, whom Milhaud had so extravagantly praised when on a visit to Leningrad, came to the keyboard. His music is spirited and humorous, not overly dissonant, and so long as you accept that he has no pretensions to be regarded as a significant composer, pleasant to listen to. On the strength of some zestful pieces he was commissioned to write a ballet, but although individual numbers came off successfully the challenge of a large-scale work was too much for him. He was reluctant to yield his place at the piano, wanting to play first one thing and then another, transcriptions for two and four hands, but I was already keen to move on to other composers as it was getting late and my attention was beginning to lose its edge.

When Deshevov was eventually delicately prised away from the piano, his place was taken by Popov for his Octet and Nonet, composed for strange combinations of instruments and written in pencil, which made them difficult to read.[1] Amidst the generally close-woven contrapuntal texture there were occasional flashes of interest, and I would no doubt have detected many more had it not been for the crashing waves now undulating through my head as a result of all the music I had heard during the day.

Evidently alive to the dense contrapuntal texture of his piece, Popov had elected to give the listener some light relief by introducing an

---

1   Gavriil Popov (1904–1972), composer, student of Shcherbachov. In his 'Short Autobiography' prepared at the request of Kabalevsky, then General Editor of *Sovetskaya Muzyka*, Prokofiev refers to a Septet by Popov performed on this occasion (S. Shlifshteyn (ed.), *S. S. Prokof'ev Materialy, Dokumenty, Stat'i*, Gosmuzizdat, Moscow, 1956, p. 61). The catalogue of Popov's works does not include a Nonet, although there is an Octet, Op. 6, also composed in 1927, so the likelihood is that on this occasion Prokofiev heard work in progress on the Septet and the Octet. The Septet (subtitled 'Chamber Symphony') is scored for flute, trumpet, clarinet, bassoon, violin, cello and bass. The crashing waves in Prokofiev's head may have taken the edge of his appreciation but as with Shostakovich he had heard enough to take Popov seriously as a composer and to recommend him around in the West, an opinion shared by Asafyev. In 1948 Popov, along with his senior colleagues, was to be a victim of the Zhdanov onslaught, after which he considerably moderated his dissonant, Modernist style, a tendency that seems already to have begun by Prokofiev's visit in 1929, as can be inferred from several diary entries in this period (see below, pp. 871–2).

inconsequential little tune which, however, had the effect of irritating me because in his desire to create a contrast I thought he had overdone it. Drowning from fatigue I waited impatiently for the Nonet to end and then asked Shcherbachov if he would play some of his Sinfonietta, after which I thought I could decently go home. But he said it was essential to hear an organ piece by Kushnaryov,[1] a particularly interesting and well-written work, which the pianist Yudina[2] had just arrived especially to perform. There was nothing for it but to agree, so the composer and Yudina settled down to play it on the piano. The music was of a quite different sort to the rest of what we had heard, much more old-fashioned with some nods towards Rachmaninoff, but certainly well done.

But I had gone past the point of no return, and every note hammered into my brain like a red-hot nail. When Kushnaryov's work came to an end I felt I could not listen to another note. We said goodbye and left, although I was very sorry not to have heard Shcherbachov's Sinfonietta, as apparently he is an enormously touchy man and it was above all his work that I had not heard.

While the music had been going on the frost outside had tightened its grip still further and probably reached the lowest temperature of our stay in the USSR, at any rate the thermometer was showing minus 20° Réamur,[3] which in the absence of a fur hat and a fur collar is quite dangerous. As we dragged our way in the sledge back to the Europa Hotel, I constantly wiggled my fingers and toes so that the movement would warm those parts of the body that were liable to frostbite. On the credit side, the shock of the cold was useful in sweeping away all the sounds I had accumulated during the day.

1 Khristofor Kushnaryov (1890–1960), composer of Armenian extraction with a particular interest in Armenian traditional music and monody. He wrote extensively for organ. Prokofiev would come across both Kushnaryov and Yudina again in 1933 on his concert tour to Armenia and Georgia. See below, pp. 1060–2.
2 Maria Yudina (1899–1970), one of the greatest pianists of her time, distinguished by a fiercely independent musical, literary, philosophical and religious outlook. Her impeccable pedigree of studies with Yesipova, Nikolayev and Blumenfeld at the Petrograd Conservatoire was put at the service not only of Bach and the classical masters but the contemporary Russian avant-garde and the effectively banned leading figures of modern Western composition: Stravinsky, Medtner, Křenek, Bartók, Hindemith. While her uncompromising attitudes to music and virtually all aspects of life in Soviet society got her repeatedly into trouble and caused her to be dismissed from positions of influence, she somehow contrived a sort of immunity from the usual consequences of offending authority, as the innumerable well-attested stories of Stalin's admiration for her bear out. Svyatoslav Richter (in B. Monsaingeon, *Richter: Ecrits, Conversations*, Editions Van de Velde, 1998, pp. 78–9) tells a characteristic story about himself and Neuhaus going backstage to congratulate Yudina on a 'splendid' wartime performance of Bach's Forty-Eight Preludes and Fugues, puzzled only by a surprisingly fast and loud account of the B flat minor Prelude from the second book. Neuhaus: 'Maria Venyaminovna, but why did you play the B flat minor Prelude in such a dramatic fashion?' Yudina: 'Because WE ARE AT WAR!!'
3 Minus 25° Celsius.

21 February

Today was the day for the Conservatoire, about which Asafyev had written to me in Paris and settled the details in conversation in Moscow. After yesterday's musical excesses we slept in and got up in a leisurely fashion, dawdled over our coffee and, as a result, by the time a student came to collect us just before two o'clock, we had still not had lunch.

When the car with the student arrived at the Conservatoire I gazed with the keenest curiosity at the institution that had for ten years, from the ages of thirteen to twenty-three, been the centre of my life. It was a strange sensation to see the same building, every corridor and every stair of which was so familiar to me, peopled by entirely different people.

We were wheeled at a fast trot up to the Director's office, the selfsame room in which at the age of thirteen I had undergone my entrance examination. Several professors I knew were already there, and they were joined by others: Asafyev, Ossovsky, Nikolayev, Malko, Chernov,[1] Steinberg. Malko had already begun to tell the story about how Glazunov could not bear the portrait of Rubinstein not hanging straight, so the students, noticing one day Glazunov getting up to straighten it, now routinely tilt it slightly out of plumb before meetings in the Director's office (which are nowadays attended by representatives of the student body) and wait with bated breath until the moment when Glazunov gets up to put it right.

Meanwhile preparations were afoot in the Small Hall. Ossovsky, Asafyev and Malko were constantly going out and coming back in again, because tickets had been distributed to the students and they were up to all sorts of tricks with them, the Small Hall not being large enough to accommodate the whole student body at once. A week ago Ossovsky had asked me which room I would like to play in, and I without hesitation chose the Small Hall, which is an integral part of the teaching life of the Conservatoire and is much closer to my heart. It was there that I pursued all my orchestral studies and sat all my exams, whereas the Great Hall is less intimately bound up with the Conservatoire's activities and is usually hired out for concerts. It does not matter if the Small Hall is not big enough to for everyone to get in, since they can always squash in a bit more tightly; I remember this often happening at important events and adding to the enjoyment.

Eventually it was announced that all was ready in the Small Hall and we made our way in a body right through the Conservatoire: Ossovsky, Ptashka,

---

1 Mikhail Chernov (1879–1938), composer, musicologist, professor of orchestration and of composition theory. One of the first musicians to recognise Prokofiev's talent, he had given him some lessons in counterpoint and had been instrumental in bringing him to the attention of the Evenings of Contemporary Music in 1908. See *Diaries*, vol. 1, pp. 38, 41, 45.

I, Asafyev and a professorial group – in short, a ceremonial procession. I caught myself observing this procession as if from the outside, and remembered how during my time as a student, when some visiting foreign celebrity came, there would be a procession just like this one. The students would watch it with wide-eyed curiosity and then hurtle at breakneck speed to the Small Hall in order not to miss the beginning, and also to grab the seat next to whichever female student they were running after at the time.

As we came into the Hall applause broke out to welcome me. The student orchestra, directed by Malko, who now occupies the position held in his day by Tcherepnin as professor of orchestral classes, was in position on the stage. The orchestra began by playing the first movement of Beethoven's Seventh Symphony, the very movement I had had to struggle through in Tcherepnin's class. Could that have been why it was chosen today? I doubt it: surely nobody would have remembered. After the Seventh Symphony there followed a very lively account of the first and third movements of my *Classical Symphony*. It was a very nice touch that the Conservatoire orchestra should have prepared for my visit.

This concluded the first part of the Conservatoire's welcoming celebrations, and we returned to the Director's office because the orchestra now had to be cleared from the stage and the students had temporarily to vacate the hall. It would now be my turn to play. Of course my appearance was what the students had been so eagerly anticipating, and the reason why they had been getting up to mischief outside with the tickets.

This time we were met in the Director's office by Glazunov. As the host he did his best to be civil, but civility does not come naturally to him, in fact it comes very unnaturally, and he stammered away unintelligibly, as is his wont. Instead of the usual cigar he had a pipe stuck in his mouth, perhaps because these days it is difficult to get hold of cigars in Russia. At last, when the Small Hall had emptied and then filled up again, we were taken back through the Conservatoire, and now the hall was full to bursting, the stage itself was thick with people, and some people were even standing by the entrance to the Artists' Room.

Just as I was on the point of coming out of the Artists' Room to go on stage, I caught sight of Glazunov. I could not work out what he was doing there, but he is after all the Master of the House and can go wherever he pleases. Then, however, I saw that he was following me on to the stage as I came out to make my bow in acknowledgement of the ovation that greeted me. He addressed me as follows: 'Greatly esteemed Sergey Sergeyevich...' (See what has become of yours truly, formerly that degenerate reprobate!) The opening salutation was followed by a conventional speech of welcome, and then a delving into the past recalling 'the time when you, Sergey Sergeyevich, brought us the...' at this point the effort to find the right word, something like 'honour' or 'pleasure', proved too much and brought on an interruption to the flow. Glazunov could not quite make himself say 'honour', while 'pleasure' seemed inadequate to the solemnity of an occasion which had in any case been arranged by the Conservatoire rather than by any initiative of the Director personally. So he continued '... brought us the joy of your being a student in this very Conservatoire'.

A few more words concluded the speech of welcome, while I wondered whether I ought to reply to this quite unexpected peroration, and if so what sort of nonsense would be appropriate to spout. Good grief – 'the joy I brought him by my mere presence within the walls of the Conservatoire!' However, at this point Glazunov extended his hand to me, and before I had a chance to mumble any words of gratitude, left the stage. Now, as soon as the applause died down, I could happily sit down at the piano and get on with my short programme.

I played the Third Sonata, then the Second, and finally a selection of small pieces. These last had a resounding success, generating not so much applause as a sort of minor explosion. At the end of the concert Asafyev took us up and down staircases and along corridors crowded with departing students to his classroom, where stood the Schroeder piano, my Rubinstein Competition prize, with its silver plaque still on the fall. When Eleonora succeeded in rescuing it from my looted flat, after a whole series of adventures it had ended up in the Conservatoire. Asafyev had commandeered it for his classroom, which is on the ground floor near the street entrance to the stairs going up to the Small Hall. Here it is well protected from grubby fingers, because practically the only person who plays it is Asafyev himself, and then mainly to illustrate his lectures on musicology. At other times the room is locked. I touched the keys with a few chords and found it in much better shape than I expected, having thought that it would be no more than a shadow of its former self.

After sitting for a while in Asafyev's room we went to see Ossovsky, who is now installed in the flat formerly belonging to the late Inspector of the Conservatoire, Gabel.[1] This is within the Conservatoire itself, on the third floor. I was famished – we had had no lunch and I had expended a fair amount of energy – but no food was served for another hour. A lot of people had been invited, among them Malko, Nikolayev and Asafyev. The meal was delicious, and served with the expansive cordiality characteristic of the Ossovskys' hospitality in pre-Revolutionary times, as I made sure to mention to them. By the end of the meal I found my eyelids so heavy I was dozing off, and as I

---

1   Stanislav Gabel (1849–1924), operatic bass, was a professor of singing at the St Petersburg Conservatoire for a total of forty-four years and trained a large roster of famous singers including Ivan Yershov and Nikolay Kedrov. During Prokofiev's years he directed the Opera class and as such had a friendly relationship with his awkward young charge.

knew that the celebrations were by no means at an end I asked my hostess if I could find somewhere to lie down for half an hour, and we were conducted to the Ossovskys' bedroom where in darkness and on a comfortable bed I went to sleep as if dead while Ptashka merely dozed. The Ossovkys' flat is commodious and extremely conveniently arranged – when the Conservatoire was being built they really had an eye to the comfort of its senior staff.

Around nine o'clock I woke up refreshed and crawled back into the dining room, where some of the guests were still sitting at the table. Before us was still a concert of my music by Conservatoire students, so we removed into the Small Hall which was once again packed out. I felt very honoured that the students were devoting an entire programme to my compositions, but Ossovsky explained that the number of those wishing to take part in the evening was three times greater than the available opportunities, and a choice had had to be made.

In the programme were, among other items, the *Ballade* for cello, the First Piano Concerto (to the accompaniment of a second piano), the Third Piano Sonata and some smaller things. We were taken up to the front rows, but there was no specifically allocated seating and I was able to move around from place to place. Between two of the items, while the harp was being hoisted into place, I was talking to Professor Musina, and as the harpist started her performance noticed that my place in the third row was now occupied by someone else. I looked around for somewhere to sit, but the only empty chair was in the very front row. I sat down, only to find myself right under the player's feet. This proved fatal for her, because as soon as she saw me there she got hopelessly lost in the C major Prelude (thank goodness she did not attempt the harp number from *Visions fugitives*, which is more difficult than the C major piece!). In short, the performance turned into a kind of nightmare and though towards the end she slightly collected herself and earned some applause by way of encouragement, rather than taking a bow she not so much walked as ran from the stage. But this was the only untoward incident. All the other performers played well, some more tentatively than others. But the First Piano Concerto, which I have not heard for a very long time, gave me real pleasure and I caught hold of Asafyev's arm and asked him what he thought of it, just as if it were a work by someone else: 'I say, that could still be played in an orchestral concert, couldn't it?'

And Asafyev replied, 'I was thinking just the same while I was listening to it, and I really believe it could.'

There was a post-concert supper in the conference room, where thirteen years ago amid noisy scenes I had been awarded the prize on graduating from the Conservatoire. This time, however, Glazunov, the main cause of the protests then, was not present. No doubt the necessity of pronouncing a speech in honour of 'greatly esteemed Sergey Sergeyevich' had been too much for him.

In the long, narrow conference room the tables had been arranged in a T-shape, with a long bar running up and down the room and a short bar across the top. I sat between Asafyev and Nikolayev, and the other professors sat on either side of the cross-table, but I could not make out who was sitting at the long table. Ossovsky pronounced the first welcoming speech on behalf of the absent Glazunov, to which I immediately replied with a toast to our dear absent friend, the father of the Conservatoire, Alexander Konstantinovich Glazunov. There then followed a string of toasts, among them one from the Communist student who is the student representative to the professorial faculty. His speech was addressed to me and invited me, in the loftiest, most grandiloquent tones, to assume the leadership of Young Musical Communism. My heart's desire – come and be our leader! Asafyev, seeing the strange expression on my face, whispered, 'Pay no attention to his bombastic speeches; actually he loves Bach and adores the *Matthew Passion*. He is not so difficult to deal with over Conservatoire business; you just have to know what makes him tick.'

Another speech from Ossovsky: 'I was a witness of how hard it was for you to forge a path for your new ideas, so startling were they for those people charged with the direction of our music at that time, but now, Sergey Sergeyevich, your time has come, the levers of power in music are in the hands of your people, people who support you and agree with you.'

As a declaration this might be considered excessive, but it is true that in the years I have been away my friends have come to the fore, they have yoked themselves to my music and worked to make it accepted by the rest.

Musina-Ozarovskaya[1] embarked on a very involved speech. She is now a full professor, and following her divorce from Ozarovsky and his death has become plain Musina. Perhaps she had had a bit too much to drink, or perhaps the excitement of the occasion had tipped her over the edge, but her address declined into a series of such ecstatic ejaculations that the room dissolved into uncontrollable laughter and she was unable to finish.

There were more toasts to others present and to individual professors, and this gave me an opportunity to get to my feet once again and propose a toast to Asafyev 'to whose opinion Europe listens'.

One o'clock came and went and still the dinner was far from winding up, but I could last no longer. We made our farewells, thanked everyone, and went home. The Conservatoire had opened its doors to me for twelve hours on end,

---

1   Darya Musina-Pushkina (1873–1947), a true and indomitable survivor of Silver Age Petersburg, actress and singer at the Alexandrinsky Theatre, intimate friend of Chekhov, Chaliapin, Kommissarzhevskaya and Isadora Duncan. Her third husband (the producer Ozarovsky having been the second) was Major-General Vladimir Alushkin. In 1931 Alushkin was arrested and exiled to Vologda; Musina (her stage name) followed him into exile and established there a school so that she could continue teaching the free-movement techniques of François Delsarte she had imbibed from Isadora Duncan and had herself been teaching at the Conservatoire.

from two o'clock in the afternoon until two o'clock the next morning. In some ways (not in all, though) the Conservatoire has not changed. Many of its former distinctive characteristics are still in place: familiar faces among the professors, the corridors, the couples sitting on the windowsills, the Small Hall with its organ and its mirrors. But also how many changes there have been in these thirteen years! As we were saying goodbye Chernov caught up with me and handed me some fragments of *The Giant*.[1] It seems that a female student had been living on the same staircase as my old apartment and got to know that the people now in it were burning manuscripts to warm themselves in the cold. She managed to exchange some firewood logs for some of the manuscripts, but unfortunately got there too late to retrieve anything of much value except for the scraps of *The Giant*. The rest was either orchestral parts or copies of material I already have.

22 February

After yesterday's excesses, and in view of tonight's concert, it was essential to spend the day more quietly.

However, there was a telephone call from Eleonora.[2] She talked about her affairs, especially about how the salvaging of my piano had cost her a great deal in trouble and expense – approximately 12 English pounds at the rate of exchange then current. Moreover, she is in some financial difficulty at present, her mother is not well, and in a word she needs money. I told her that I would send her the £12 as soon as I get back to Moscow, but that she must give me in return the photographs she managed to save from my looted flat.

In the afternoon I dropped into the Philharmonia offices, where I was informed that my fees had already been transferred abroad in dollars, which is why I could not immediately settle with Eleonora. Khais, seeing that I had mellowed (after all, even I have to take a break from my sarcasm sometimes) asked me for a signed photograph, I expect so that whenever rumours surface about a rift with Prokofiev he can point to the photograph and say, 'See that, he even signed it for me.' 'With pleasure,' I replied. 'Next time I come.'

In the evening I played my second recital programme. Ptashka was packed off with Lidusya to the Mariinsky to see Rimsky's *Vera Sheloga*,[3] from which they should get back in time for the end of my concert.

---

1 Prokofiev's first opera (*Velikan*), composed when the composer was eight and performed by him with friends and family at his uncle's house near Sontsovka. Cousin Andrey played the piano part and the composer sang the title role. See Shlifshteyn, op. cit., pp. 10–11.
2 Damskaya.
3 *The Noblewoman Vera Sheloga*, one-act opera composed by Rimsky-Korsakov in 1898 to be used as Prologue to *The Maid of Pskov*, using music drawn from that originally intended for the full opera but omitted from the score. Rimsky wrote the libretto, which concerns a previous visitation to the city by Ivan the Terrible during which he seduced the wife of the boyar Ivan Sheloga, resulting in his unacknowledged child Olga being born.

I was, however, tired today and played sleepily. I had to shake myself awake during the Fourth Sonata, but by the end pulled myself together and played the finale perfectly, for the first time this trip. At Asafyev's suggestion I played the Schubert Waltzes with Kamensky,[1] a most gifted pianist, and they went better than they had done with Feinberg. The piece scored a tremendous success and had to be encored. The cries of approval and the clapping tonight were the equal of my first concert, when my homecoming was being greeted.

A great throng crowded into the Green Room and the passage from it to the stage. Mme Pototskaya told me about the fate of her daughter Nina, my childhood dancing partner.[2] Mme Pototskaya had herself arranged for her to obtain a residence permit for Petersburg, away from the quiet spot in which she was living, in the belief that she would be safe here from any threat of danger. But once in the city she was suspected of having contact with White counter-revolutionaries, for which she was tried, convicted and shot. The tragic story unfolded in snatches between my curtain calls on stage, and the amalgam of an audience roaring their approval and the images of trial and execution relayed by a mother barely able to hold back her tears mingled strangely in my mind.

Eleonora appeared and gave me the photographs which, however, were less interesting than I had expected, as most of them were ones I already had.

Ptashka and Lidusya returned just at the end of the concert because they had been detained at the Mariinsky Theatre. Tonya Rudavskaya and Zoya also came, Zoya succeeding in picking a quarrel with Lida just like old times.

Saying goodbye to the Karneyeva sisters we went next to the Artists' Club, from whom I had received a telegram sent to me in Moscow announcing the members' desire to hold a reception in my honour. A mass of people were there for supper and entertainment. The latter consisted of Shaporin's[3] music for the

---

1   Alexander Kamensky (1900–1952), pianist who studied piano with Nikolaev and Blumenfeld, and composition with Shcherbachov and Steinberg, at the St Petersburg Conservatoire, where he subsequently taught. A fine pianist and gifted all-round musician, like the poet Olga Berggolts he became a legend in his home city for his selfless determination to continue making music throughout the 900 days of the Leningrad blockade, playing on Leningrad Radio for half an hour between 10 p.m. and 10.30 p.m. every single evening, as well as constantly playing for units at the front and in reserve (taking care to take his own tuning fork with him). After the blockade, which he survived, he wrote his memoirs, excerpts from which are included in the memoir of his life written by his wife Alexandra Bushen, who had been a close friend (and doughty walking companion) of Prokofiev in their student days (A. Bushen, *Alexander Kamensky, Study of his Life and Work*, Soviektskii Kompozitor, Leningrad, 1982). Bushen also stayed in the city throughout the blockade, and survived.
2   The Pototsky family, friends of Prokofiev's Aunt Katya Rayevskaya, came from the top echelon of Petersburg society. Stepan Pototsky, a fashionable surgeon, was Chief Medical Officer of the Obukhov Hospital and the salon of their house was large enough to accommodate balls and dancing classes. Prokofiev participated in both, but by all accounts never became a natural mover on the dance floor. See *Diaries*, vol. 1, pp. 21, 138, 585.
3   Yury Shaporin (1887–1966), composer, studied with Nikolay Sokolov and Maximilian Steinberg. His magnum opus, the opera *The Decembrists*, begun in 1920, was not finished until 1953.

Leningrad production of *The Flea*,[1] using *chastushki* accompanied by a small orchestra with added accordions, which created some most interesting sonorities. This was followed by a scene from a Japanese tragedy staged by Radlov.

At our table were Dranishnikov, Asafyev, Radlov and Musina. Her daughter Tamara Glebova,[2] whom I have known for twenty years and used to engage in a war of words that reduced us both to stupefaction, flirted outrageously with me. When in conversation with someone or other I let slip a somewhat risqué phrase about Communism, Dranishnikov came over to whisper in my ear that I should be careful, because also sitting at our table was a Communist known to have a dangerously venomous tongue.

Although I had implored my hosts not to have any speeches during the evening, they were unable to restrain themselves. Among the speakers was Brender[3] from the Akopera management. Asafyev and Dranishnikov both told me this individual had done his best to wreck the theatre's production of *Oranges*. Now he was bent on expressing his delight at the success of the production into which so much effort and love had been poured. As he finished, Asafyev muttered sotto voce, 'To hear that from him, of all people!' Another speech was made by Weisberg, whose hair colour incidentally over the past couple of days has undergone a transformation from grey to black. Yes, yes, now I was being welcomed by Weisberg, one of my most implacable enemies during the whole of my career.

    Initially the libretto was by Aleksey Tolstoy, but the later versions were written by Vsevolod Rozhdestvensky. Together with Asafyev he was a leading member of the Leningrad branch of the ASM, of which he had been a founding member, until it was disbanded in 1930. Shaporin was appointed professor of composition at the Moscow Conservatoire in 1938; among his students was Rodion Shchedrin.

1 *The Flea* (*Blokha*) was a dramatic adaptation by Zamyatin (author of the seminal dystopic novel *We*) of a short story by Leskov, produced by Alexey Dikiy at the Moscow Art Theatre Studio Two, the production seen by Prokofiev at the end of January. Shaporin's incidental music, later turned into a concert suite, is indeed unusually scored: woodwind, horn, trumpet, sixteen domras, three baians (a type of accordion), piano, double-bass, flexatone, xylophone, timpani and other percussion. The flexatone is particularly prominent in the sonority that so appealed to Prokofiev, and it seems to have appealed to Khachaturian as well, in the slow movement of his Piano Concerto.

2 See *Diaries*, vol. 2, pp. 111, 269.

3 V. A. Brender was literary adviser to Akopera (the Kirov Theatre). Twenty years later, we learn from Mira Mendelson's memoirs, he was to play his part in the catastrophe that was the audition rehearsal of *Story of a Real Man*, the Soviet Realist opera for which Prokofiev and his second wife together wrote the libretto, based on the novel by Boris Polevoy. It was such a disaster that it ended all hopes of a production not only of this work but also of the still only partly produced *War and Peace*. Brender had called on Prokofiev and Mira the evening before and ominously talked about everything but the forthcoming performance. Obviously he was privy to the impending fiasco and doubtless had been party to it. M. A. Mendel'son-Prokof'eva, 'Vospominaniya (Fragment 1948–51)' in M. P. Rakhmanova (ed.), *Sergey Prokof'ev Vospominaniya, Pis'ma, Stat'i*, Deka-BC Publishers, Moscow, 2004, p. 120.

There was a tremendous desire on all sides to hear me speak, but today I was quite unable to squeeze out a single word, and in any case I had made it clear from the start that I would not say anything. To disappointed looks all around we were finally allowed to depart.

23 February

With yesterday's concert the official part of my stay in Leningrad came to an end. We had intended to go back to Moscow today, for the start of rehearsals for the orchestral concert, but there was a chance of grabbing a day back from the rehearsal schedule and Asafyev persuaded me to spend one more day at Detskoe Selo. This to me was a most appealing proposition and so we went out to visit him.

It was again a wonderful, sunny day with sparkling white snow. Dranishnikov came with us and we went together to the park. Ptashka and I took turns in taking pictures of the group with the little camera we had brought along, but unfortunately they did not turn out particularly well.

The Radlov couple and Shcherbachov joined us for lunch, the latter entertaining us with many stories of musical life, notably about Glazunov. When he was in England visiting some university or other (evidently in connection with the award of an honorary doctorate),[1] the director invited him to adjourn to his study in order to sign the distinguished visitors' book. When the book was opened at the appropriate page, it transpired that the new signature would be immediately below that of Richard Strauss. 'Although,' added the director, 'if you would prefer, you could sign on a fresh page.' 'If you would allow me, I should prefer that,' said Glazunov.

At this the director, himself not an admirer of Strauss, peeped out into the corridor to check that no one was inconveniently passing, closed the door of his office and taking from the cupboard a bottle of Madeira and two glasses, suggested, 'Let's have a drink.' Unanimity of minds thus established, the two proceeded to enjoy their unscheduled refreshment.

The day passed before we noticed it, and yet again Asafyev and I failed to devote any time to talking about the book he is writing about me. Dranishnikov was exceptionally good company and I was delighted at the advances he has been making in his career recently. As last time, the semi-wild dogs had to be let out from the locked bedroom and taken for a walk, growling and scratching

---

1   In 1907 Glazunov was at the height of his fame and following the success of Diaghilev's revelatory series of five 'Concerts russes historiques' in Paris, which Glazunov conducted, he was awarded honorary doctorates by both Oxford and Cambridge Universities. The Professor of Music at Oxford at the time was Sir Charles Hubert Hastings Parry Bt, his opposite number at Cambridge Sir Charles Villiers Stanford; it would be pleasant to think that the drinking session involved one or other of these distinguished musical knights.

the floor with their claws. They terrified Dranishnikov, who took care to keep out of their way.

It had been rumoured that Myaskovsky might nevertheless be coming to the rehearsal of his Eighth Symphony, and indeed during the evening Asafyev's wife was heard shrieking joyously, 'Nikolay Yakovlevich has arrived! He's really come!' Somehow or other he had managed to scrape up the money for his fare, without appealing to me.

Little by little the other guests dispersed until only we remained, chatting happily to Myaskovsky and Asafyev for the rest of the evening. Myaskovsky said that after my session with Yurovsky at Muzsektor several days had been spent exclusively on calculating how much money was due to me for works of mine they had sold, the rights for which I had assigned to them. His sister works at Muzsektor and has been engaged on this very task.

We returned to Leningrad at midnight in the company of Myaskovsky, agreeing as we parted to meet tomorrow at the rehearsal of his symphony.

24 February

As I left the hotel next morning to go to the rehearsal, whom should I run into on the stairs but Eleonora, clearly agitated lest my promise, expressed as she thought rather casually, to send her the money from Moscow, was merely a device to evade paying her. I did my best to reassure her, promising again to send it the moment I got back to Moscow. Then we exchanged a few more phrases in which Demchinsky was mentioned, and I said that although he had shown himself to be a brilliantly perceptive critic, he did not come up to expectations when it came to producing work of his own. Eleonora said nothing in response to this, and I rather wished I had kept off the subject. As I was in a hurry to get to the rehearsal I did not wish to prolong our discussion and began to say goodbye, but then I saw that she had some more photographs with her, so sent her up to our room, where Ptashka still was. Eleonora spent quite some time there, stunned by the size of our suite and looking at our Paris clothes with hungry eyes.

I got to the rehearsal just as they were beginning Myaskovsky's Eighth Symphony, which I found very interesting, more so than all his others except the Sixth, which I have not heard. But there are still too many four-bar phrases, sequences and movements of voices from the bass to the treble and vice versa. There are also needless longueurs, especially at the end of the Andante. The trumpet solo in the first movement was very good indeed. In the scherzo the first beat in the bar is not strongly enough marked, partly because of the way it has been orchestrated, but this is something that can probably be corrected in performance.

Today's rehearsal was the second, and although Malko was obviously trying as hard as he could, the orchestral playing was disgracefully bad. I sat next to Myaskovsky looking at his rough score. Whenever there were wrong notes Myaskovsky groaned and clutched his head in his hands, agonising over all the lapses. But by now one would think he would have got used to the fact that first rehearsals of new works always sound awful. Asafyev came at the end of the rehearsal; he and Myaskovsky went to talk to Malko at the end of the symphony while I returned to the hotel, having extracted from them a promise to come to lunch. While we were having it I took some snapshots as it was such a bright day.

Myaskovsky left us after lunch, and Asafyev and I went to the offices of the Academic Theatres administration for a meeting with Eksuzovich, Radlov and Dranishnikov on the subject of the proposed spring tour of *Three Oranges* to Paris. Eksuzovich announced that he was practically certain the tour would take place, and told us he had with him in his briefcase (here he slapped it encouragingly with his hand) a document to that effect. However, he cautioned, from bitter experience he would be certain of it only when they were all sitting in the train ready to depart. He wanted to be sure I had given Dranishnikov and Radlov my list of comments, and added that he supposed the main changes would concern the scenery. Entirely new sets might have to be built, perhaps in Paris where the materials are less expensive.

I was asked a great many questions, some of them so detailed that I lost the thread and did not know what to say. Then Ekskuzovich and I exchanged letters whereby I assigned to him the rights to the premiere production of *The Gambler* and he undertook to get the score to me in Moscow before I left the country.[1] He could not give it to me right away because they wanted to make fresh copies of some missing sections.

Parting with the company I returned to the hotel, where a great party had already gathered: Malko, Lidusya (who had been out with Ptashka collecting the furs), Katya Schmidthof, a flirtatious Tamara Glebova and a taciturn Alpers. At last I realised with a start that it was already getting late, and we had not even started to pack. 'Ladies and gentlemen, I implore you to leave us immediately otherwise we shall miss our train!' 'You show us the door so insistently that we cannot even take offence,' said a chagrined Tamara.

---

1 The original score had been deposited in the Mariinsky Theatre library in 1917, for orchestral and vocal parts to be copied in special chemical ink for lithographing and distribution. The work was proceeding very lackadaisically, much to the annoyance of the composer, and this gave rise to acrimonious discussions with Malko, whose responsibility it was at the time to oversee the work. See *Diaries*, vol. 2, pp. 137–41. Prokofiev left Russia before receiving a revised contract for the opera to be produced once the present disruption of the Revolution and the change of management had abated and repertoire planning could be resumed. All Prokofiev could do was give Suvchinsky power of attorney to conclude on his behalf any contract that was proposed but there the project, and the score, had rested. Ibid., pp. 273–4.

It was a near thing and we barely made it to the train. Shcherbachov and Miklashevsky came to see us off, the former purely from affection, the latter complaining that as he has so few career opportunities here he hoped to use our good offices to get a foothold abroad.

25 February

At this point my brief diary notes finished and the remainder of our stay in Moscow has been reconstructed from Ptashka's notes and other records, in consequence of which some facts may have been left out, although what remains is a true record.

Arriving back in Moscow from Leningrad we moved back into the same room at the Metropole Hotel as we had been in before. I went immediately to rehearsal, as from now on my appearances are the responsibility of the Association of Contemporary Music, the head of which is Derzhanovsky, rather than Persimfans. As an institution the ASM has fewer resources than Persimfans, therefore they had to be content with the leftovers from the Persimfans presentations. They were also paying less, but reflecting my long-standing friendship with Derzhanovsky I generously told them to pay me whatever they could afford. A skilled operator, Derzhanovsky had still managed to arrange two concerts with almost new programmes. The first was an orchestral concert conducted, needless to say, by Saradzhev, from whom Derzhanovsky continues to be inseparable. This was the rehearsal to which I was bound this morning.

Over the past ten years Saradzhev, so far from ascending the heights, has actually fallen back. He does not have enough grip of the orchestra, and wastes a lot of time in talking. This is not just my opinion; Myaskovsky concurs. It is a pity, because he is an excellent musician and still not at all a bad conductor.

Today we were rehearsing the *Classical* Symphony, which is receiving its Moscow premiere – one plum Derzhanovsky had succeeded in wresting from Persimfans. The Hall of Columns, where we were, was decorated with banners of red material hanging vertically beside the columns, and the combination of red stripes with the gleaming white of the columns made me think irresistibly of a red and white blancmange. I gazed at the hall and tried to decide which was the more beautiful: Moscow's or Leningrad's.

After the rehearsal Ptashka and I took Derzhanovsky and Saradzhev to the restaurant on Prechistenki for *bliny*. Then, after saying goodbye to them, we went to see Aunt Katya, who during our absence had finally got herself to Moscow from Penza and was staying with Nadya. Our reunion was very touching. Aunt Katya has turned into an old woman (hardly surprising at the age of sixty-nine) but despite her paralysed leg was in tremendously good form and has not lost any of her charm. My cousin Katya has grey hair now, and is so deaf that communication with her was very difficult. They both very much liked Ptashka, and she them.

As we had a free evening we decided to go to Medtner's concert. Medtner had arrived in the USSR a little after me, and had given his cycle of concerts in more or less the same cities as I but with far less spectacular success: he did not have the crowd of supporters following him nor the leading musical figures whose attachment to me so greatly enhanced my prestige. Nevertheless, Medtner has his aficionados among the elderly theoreticians and professors at the Conservatoire, who went so far as to present him with an address printed in old orthography, as if to emphasise their adherence to the old ways.

The concert was in the Great Hall of the Conservatoire. Medtner played well, as ever, but boringly. The concert was not improved by a singer with a gammy leg whose squeaky voice and uncertain intonation sent the whole audience to sleep in a song-cycle of relentless monotony.

In the interval we escaped to Tseitlin, who has installed himself near by, right opposite the stage door. So deep in conversation were we that we stayed talking to him for the rest of the concert. The general opinion is that I had done well to show up at the concert at all, since Medtner and his clique are aflame with ill-concealed enmity towards me.

Back at the hotel I found a telegram from Diaghilev and yet another anonymous letter from a female, well larded with familiarities and quotations from Wilde, and with a proposition. If my answer is 'yes' I am to play the Scherzo from *Oranges* as an encore, upon which I shall be met by my correspondent after the concert.

26 February

I have no detailed notes of what happened on this day. We were at Aunt Katya's and in the evening went to *The Inspector-General* at Meyerhold's theatre. There is a great hullabaloo in Moscow and all over Russia about this production: some think it marvellous, others are shocked at the sacrilege and disrespect visited upon Gogol. Whatever the case the production is still running with several performances a week, all of them sold out.

We were taken straight up to Meyerhold, with whom we chatted briefly while the entire theatre waited on the signal to start the performance. At last Meyerhold said, 'Begin!' and the moment the house lights dimmed conducted us to seats in the front row.

I enjoyed the performance although it seemed to me overstocked with business and too long. Meyerhold gets so absorbed in creating details that he does not notice how much time they take up. My main interest in Meyerhold, however, is as a future producer of *The Gambler*, and in opera this is not too terrible a threat because an opera is exactly as long as the music which has been written for it, meaning that I, not Meyerhold, am the keeper of the gate as far as time is concerned.

In Meyerhold's theatre *The Government Inspector* was presented without scenery as such; each individual scene was played on its own fairly cramped platform. Changes of scene were effected by near black-outs during which the platform was trucked into the darkness upstage, or into the wings, while a successor took its place complete with new furniture and actors, while by the light of a candle one could dimly see the silhouettes of the departing characters. These entrances and exits were very effective, imparting a mysterious kind of theatricality.

In the interval Meyerhold plied us with tea and refreshments and was extremely gracious, although demanding of compliments.

27 February

Today is Svyatoslav's third birthday, but we have had no news of him for ten days now. Grogy suffers badly from unpunctuality.

In the afternoon we had the orchestral concert with Saradzhev. It began with *Dreams*,[1] from which Derzhanovsky had dusted off the sediment of ages. I had not wanted it to be played, but Derzhanovsky persuaded me, saying that *Dreams* was my first composition for orchestra to have been played in Moscow, conducted moreover by none other than Saradzhev. If I had now moved forward from it, so much the better: people would be able to see what I had been then and what I had become now.

I listened to *Dreams* from the Green Room. It didn't sound so bad, really quite nice and tender, mildly soporific. Saradzhev conducted the *Classical* Symphony quite well, but a little short on refinement and precision. But then in the Suite from *Three Oranges* he suddenly came to life and played the 'Infernal Scene',[2] which usually does not come off very well in a concert performance, in such blazing style that the audience demanded a repeat.

I played the Third Piano Concerto and scored the usual success with it. I played an encore, but not the Scherzo from *Oranges*, although as I went back on stage I caught myself thinking, 'Well, she'll be waiting for it now, and how disappointed she will be that I play something else.' Saradzhev had really geared himself up for the *Classical* Symphony and led the orchestra much better than he had done at rehearsal. I thanked him and promised to present him with the tie I had worn earlier in the day as a memento of the Moscow premiere of the *Classical* Symphony.

---

1 *Sni* (*Dreams*), Op. 6, symphonic tableau for orchestra, 1910. It was first performed by Konstantin Saradzhev in his open-air summer season in Sokolniki Park, Moscow, in 1911.
2 Suite from *The Love for Three Oranges*, Op. 33bis No. 2.

In the evening we went to visit Morolyov, who had been very vocal in his insistence that we must pay a call on him. He lives on Marxist Street, but as it had been recently renamed, not a solitary soul could tell us where it was. We engaged a car and driver, spending a considerable amount of money before we finally found the address.

He lives with all his family, that is to say his wife and grown-up children, in a cramped, but cosy flat. Among the bound scores I found some of my manuscripts, including the first version of the March from Op. 12, some fragments of the First Sonata and other things I had sent him before I had a publisher for any of my work. In accordance with tradition we played chess and I won two games, while Morolyov managed to force a draw in a third. Altogether I had a most enjoyable evening, although Ptashka became terribly bored in the company of the daughters and fled to the Derzhanovskys, where there was a gathering discussing the afternoon's concert and where naturally there were some young composers, who are all in love with her.

At long last, late in the evening, we made our way across the whole city to Derzhanovsky's, where in fact there were not too many people, and the hero of the evening was Saradzhev.

28 February

I sent money to Eleonora and to Katya Schmidthof. The afternoon was spent in the Bolshoy Theatre at the official unveiling of Rabinovich's set models for *Three Oranges*. I had been invited to be present, but had difficulty in entering the building because no one was allowed in without the permission of the stage-door superintendent and he was for some reason not there at the time. Even so, once inside I had plenty of time to wait for the unveiling, because inevitably it took place half an hour late.

On the stairs I ran into Ekskuzovich, just in from Leningrad, but he wanted to have a preliminary look at some alterations that had been made to the theatre's stage. If I am not mistaken his initial training was as an architect.

At length everyone was gathered together and we trooped in to view the sets, which I had already seen. The room in which they were displayed was quite narrow, so that we all had to jostle and get in everybody else's way. Rabinovich had laid out his costume sketches on the floor of a larger room. The whole business was a formality, since it had already been agreed that Rabinovich's work would be accepted.

Ekskuzovich took me by the arm and led me into a corner. 'About the Leningrad production of *Oranges*,' he said, 'I have had a wonderful idea: we should commission the sets for Paris from Golovin. What do you think of that?'

'But, Ivan Vasilievich,' I gulped, 'Golovin designed the sets for *The Firebird* twenty years ago when Diaghilev presented it, so Paris would not see him as a novelty but as a warmed-up leftover from the past. Not only that, recently Ida Rubinstein presented something designed by him and it made no impression at all.' Ekskuzovich, deflated, went off. He obviously has no idea what in the scenic design department might interest Paris.

Old Suk[1] came up to me, introduced himself and told me that he had intended to conduct *Oranges*, but that Golovanov had got his hands on it while he, Suk, was away. 'Very cunning fellow, that Golovanov,' he concluded in his Czech accent.

We dined with Tsukker at Prechistenki. It had been announced that Trotsky was to give a lecture that evening in the Hall of Columns, and we very much wanted to hear him – Trotsky is a first-class orator. Tsukker, however, prevaricated, evidently not wanting to go to the trouble of getting tickets for us, Trotsky being at odds with the government at this point in time.[2] In the end he did telephone one of his colleagues who was supposed in his turn to approach someone else again to get us tickets. But the final answer was that there was not a ticket to be had for the lecture, so we could not go to it. Instead we attended a Persimfans concert devoted to Beethoven, at which Tseitlin was soloist in the Violin Concerto. This was not, of course, wildly entertaining, nor is Tseitlin a first-class violinist, but in view of all he had done for us we could not not go.

On the way to the concert I began cautiously to press Tsukker on the subject of getting Shurik released, letting him know I was not impressed that after several weeks there was still no movement. And this is the truth: either Tsukker is essentially a coward, or he is simply reluctant to get involved in anything that smacks of 'counter-revolutionary' business. To some extent this became clear in his lengthy and evasive answers. I asked him to speak more plainly, because if it was genuinely distasteful to him to engage himself in the case, then I wanted to try other approaches while there was still time. For instance, I had heard of the Political Red Cross, which supports 'politically ill' people, or I could speak to Meyerhold as an Honoured Red Army veteran. I am sure he has many supporters among the Communist elite.

1   Not the Czech composer Josef Suk but the violinist and conductor Václav (Vyacheslav) Suk (1861–1933), who had been living and working in Russia since 1880, from 1906 at the Bolshoy Theatre. In 1927 he was appointed Musical Director of the Stanislavsky Opera Theatre, a post he held concurrently with the Bolshoy position.
2   This was about the time when the 'United Opposition' of Trotsky, Kamenev and Zinoviev was visibly beginning to lose the power struggle with Stalin over International Communism vs Communism in One Country. Between July and October 1926 the Opposition was defeated and Kamenev lost his Politburo seat. Trotsky and Zinoviev were expelled from the Party in November 1927, Kamenev at the Fifteenth Party Congress a month later. Tsukker could see which way the wind was blowing.

Tsukker responded irritably to both suggestions, saying that the Political Red Cross is a toothless organisation, and Meyerhold's reputation in Communist circles is by no means high enough to influence the release of someone convicted of political unreliability. In sum, what he was saying was that whichever way one looked at it, nothing could be done. This annoyed me very much and opened up a crack in our relationship.

Tseitlin was most appreciative that we had come to his concert. On the way back afterwards we passed the Hall of Columns, where a large crowd was milling about outside. The atmosphere surrounding Trotstky's lecture seemed to be charged with electricity, and we were happy that we had not, in fact, got in to it, for fear of finding ourselves embroiled in a political imbroglio. That would be a most unwelcome development: there are enough problems trying to extricate Shurik from his predicament without adding to them.

1 March

Derzhanovsky informed us that the head of the Political Red Cross is Peshkova, Gorky's former wife.[1] He knows her and had tentatively broached with her the subject of my concern. It is all right to speak to her openly, since the whole point of her role is to rescue people who have got themselves into political difficulties. Hers had been an illegal organisation in Tsarist times when its mission was, naturally, the opposite of what it is today, that is to say in those days it was Socialists and Communists whom she helped. In recognition of such services rendered she obtained legal status from the Soviet Government; the Bolsheviks tolerate her though it goes against the grain and act on her applications as seldom as they can. Even so, some of her actions do bear fruit.

Derzhanovsky and I decided it would be worth going to see her, especially as her office is on Kuznetsky Most, not far from the International Book Store (Mezhdunarodnaya Kniga) which is where Derzhanovsky works. Climbing the stairs I felt a little uneasy, as though I were engaging in a conspiratorial activity with an anti-government organisation.

Peshkova welcomed us very kindly and vaguely searched her memory for the name Rayevsky, although she said she did not believe she had made any applications on his behalf. To pursue her enquiries she summoned from the

---

1   Yekaterina Peshkova, née Volzhina (1887–1965), humanitarian activist, married to Maxim Gorky (real name Alexey Maximovich Peshkov) from 1896 to 1903 and the mother of his son Maxim, born in 1897. This remarkable woman seems to have been entirely incorruptible, as dedicated to the task of helping via her organisation, a branch of the Red Cross popularly known as Pompolit (from Pomoshch Politicheskim, Help to Politicals), Socialist and Revolutionary victims of political repression in Tsarist times as she had formerly been helping their fellow victims from the other side of the tracks after the Revolution.

next room her assistant, a Jew who spoke the most terrible Russian. On looking through his records he found that the organisation had indeed interceded on behalf of Rayevsky among others, and had succeeded in getting his term reduced by a third. I knew this had happened, but I did not know until that moment that it had been the result of efforts by the Political Red Cross. Peshkova then with exemplary simplicity and directness advised me as follows: 'You see, if you were to go yourself to the GPU[1] and plead for Rayevsky, it is not impossible that they would agree to your request, but they would remember that you had done so and it could be used against you in the future. For this reason I do not recommend that you approach them personally. But it so happens that I have to go to the GPU myself soon on other matters, and I will speak to one of Menzhikov's close associates (I think the name she mentioned was Comrade Yagoda). I shall try to bring the conversation round to you, and when, as I would expect it to do, the banal enquiry follows as to whether Prokofiev is happy with his stay in Moscow, I can reply: "He is very happy, except that he is distressed by his cousin's prison sentence." In this way I might be able to achieve some amelioration of Rayevsky's situation without the request coming directly from you.'

I thanked her for this masterly plan. Peshkova promised to ring Derzhanovsky tomorrow and inform him in a roundabout way about progress, so that even over the telephone I would not be compromised. The delicacy of her stratagem was in itself an indication of how careful one has to be in such questions.

Ptashka went in the afternoon with Tsukker to Gostorg to look at furs. He used his influence to engineer a special arrangement for her, whereby she was to be shown furs earmarked for export, that to say the best quality, but at discounted prices. Ptashka also called on Aunt Katya and went out with her in a sledge. One of the sledge runners got caught in a tram track and overturned, throwing Ptashka out onto the roadway. Happily the snow was quite soft and she was not injured. In the evening we were invited to the Kamerny Theatre,[2] but I was feeling out of sorts so Ptashka went on her own.

2 March

This afternoon I was supposed to play for the Moscow Conservatoire. The procedure here is different from the Leningrad Conservatoire in that

---

1 Gosudarstvennoe Politicheskoe Upravlenie, the State Political Directorate or Secret Police, later the OGPU (Joint Political Directorate), the head of which was Vyacheslav Menzhinsky from 1926 to 1934. Menzhinsky was replaced in 1934 by the legendary trio of assassins Genrikh Yagoda, Nikolay Yezhov and Lavrenty Beria, who presided successively over its regime of terror and murder until Stalin's death in 1953.
2 'Chamber Theatre', the name of Alexander Taïrov's theatre company.

the audience has to pay for tickets and the takings go to the performers. Someone rang me up in the morning and enquired if I was going to play this afternoon. I replied that I thought I was, but the discussions had taken place quite a long time ago, since when nobody had been in touch with me even to tell me when I was supposed to be there or whether, indeed, the event would take place at all.

Evidently this conversation was reported back to the Conservatoire because within a couple of hours the Director Igumnov appeared in person with a student representative. After greeting me they thanked me for agreeing to play for them and told me that a car would be sent for me at three o'clock. I felt a little embarrassed, because good manners dictated that I, as a visitor, should really have called on the Director rather than waiting for him to come to me. He soon departed, and I privately resolved to call on him tomorrow.

Promptly at three o'clock the car came for us and we set off for the Great Hall of the Conservatoire, which was full. As I walked on stage I was greeted with a speech of welcome and presented with a blotting pad and a basket of flowers. I then played approximately the same programme as I had given for the students of the Leningrad Conservatoire, although with less emotional agitation in this 'foreign' institution than I had experienced in my own.

Tea was served in the foyer at the end of the programme, with about twenty people present including Igumnov, Yavorsky, Gnesina[1] and Borisova.[2] When a crowd of students came down the main staircase on their way out of the building they spotted me and gave me an ovation, which pleased me very much.

In the evening we were invited to Lamm,[3] my acquaintance with whom went back to the first appearances of both Myaskovsky and myself as

1 Yelena Gnesina (1874–1967), pianist and teacher, co-founder in 1985 with her brother the composer Mikhail Gnesin of the world-class music institute that still today bears their name: Rossiiskaya Akademiya Muzyki imeni Gnesina, The Russian Musical Academy named after Gnesin. Yelena Gnesina herself directed the music-teaching programme and taught classes for a total of seventy-two years.
2 Unidentified.
3 During the 1920s, 1930s and 1940s Lamm hosted innumerable gatherings of musicians in his Moscow apartment to listen to and discuss new music, the orchestral scores usually transcribed by himself for two pianos eight hands, in which form all Myaskovsky's twenty-seven symphonies were first heard, many works by Prokofiev and Shostakovich (including the Fourth Symphony, twenty years before it received its formal premiere under the baton of Kondrashin), Rachmaninoff's Third Symphony, many works by Shebalin, Popov and others. The 'Lamm Circle' was an indispensable crucible of new music in Moscow mandatory for anyone wishing to become acquainted with the latest works. At one of these Wednesdays, for example, Svyatoslav Richter turned pages for Prokofiev when he played for the first time the Sixth Piano Sonata. See *Diaries*, vol. 1, p. 589.

composers in Moscow, the former with 'Silence' and me with *Dreams*. Lamm is of German origin, a fact that everyone had forgotten about until 1914 when war broke out and it was discovered that he had a German passport. He was interned, spending the whole war somewhere near the Urals, and from having nothing better to do with his time transcribed symphonies for piano eight hands. In this way he completed versions of all known Russian symphonies, and by the end of the war, when he came back to Moscow, he was so completely addicted to the vice that he continued making similar versions of all new symphonies as they appeared. Myaskovsky's are all in this form, as are a whole series of works by young composers.

After the Revolution, through the efforts of Myaskovsky and others, Lamm was appointed head of Muzsektor, but as a result of dirty tricks in some quarters there were scandals, investigations and arrests, and he was removed from his post. These days he is purely a professor at the Conservatoire and occupies two large rooms in the Conservatoire building, one of which contains two grand pianos. This last circumstance prompted some of his friends to organise 'Wednesdays', at which musicians would gather to make music, stumping up a collection for refreshments. It was to one of these Wednesday meetings that I had been invited by Myaskovsky. As well as the host and Myaskovsky there were present Feinberg, Alexandrov, Shenshin,[1] Shebalin,[2] Goedike,[3] Melkikh,[4] Saradzhev, Viktor Belyayev, and one or two others. When I incautiously began to say some rather uncomplimentary things about Medtner, I received a nudge because Goedike is a friend of his and does not take kindly to criticism of him.

---

1 Alexander Shenshin (1890–1944), composer. Study with Yavorsky, Glière and Grechaninov had imbued him with powerful analytical tools which he used not only in his own compositions but to ally himself with Kandinsky's theories of the union of painting with music. Kandinsky was impressed by Shenshin's theoretical work, in particular an analysis of two parts of Liszt's *Années de pèlerinage*: the 'Sposalizio', inspired by Raphael's painting *The Marriage of the Virgin*, and the 'Penseroso', inspired by Michelangelo's statue on the tomb of Lorenzo de Medici. By adding up the notes and bars in the music and translating them into graphic form, Shenshin was able to demonstrate the mathematical formula linking the pieces of music with the paintings that had inspired them.
2 Vissarion Shebalin (1902–1963), composer and teacher. He studied with Glière and Myaskovsky and was a close friend of Shostakovich, graduating from the Moscow Conservatoire in 1928. After a spell heading the composition department of the Gnesin Institute he returned to the Conservatoire as its Director in 1942, only to be removed after Zhdanov's Central Committee Resolution in 1948.
3 Alexander Goedike (1877–1957), pianist, organist, composer and teacher. He studied piano with Vasily Safonov and Pabst, and composition with Arensky. He wrote prolifically, but little of any of it has stayed in the repertoire. Goedike was a cousin of Medtner and an admirer of his music; his inclinations were generally conservative.
4 Dmitry Melkikh (1885–1943), composer. A student of Yavorsky, he produced an opera *The Arsonist*, four symphonies, a violin concerto, and string quartets.

After tea and refreshments the music started. Myaskovsky's Seventh Symphony was played in its eight-hand version and I followed it from the score. However, I liked it considerably less than the Eighth. Then Myaskovsky craved my indulgence to hear a symphony by Shebalin, which he described as on the long side but very interesting. The symphony did indeed last forty-five minutes, and I did not find it especially striking, although not devoid of interest. When the composer afterwards approached me I did not know quite what to say, because there is a special art in commenting on works that have just been played to you for the first time. I evaded the issue by enquiring about the situation with the score and parts, should I be able to interest any conductors abroad in performing it. But the score is not finished, and the parts have not yet been copied.

Tea followed by two symphonies occupies quite a lot of time and it was two o'clock in the morning by the time we went our separate ways home.

3 March

At half past ten Protopopov called to collect Ptashka to take her to St Basil's Cathedral.[1] He is an expert on such matters and gave her very interesting information.

I went to a rehearsal of the Quintet at the Conservatoire, which was to form part of an evening of chamber music devised by Derzhanovsky. The performers were trying very hard; they were all excellent musicians, too much so to be flummoxed by the language of the Quintet, but the rehearsal did not go well. Professorial circles in the Conservatoire were interested, however, and quite a few of them came to listen.

Goldenweiser sat next to me with the score. He made no comment on the work, merely asking me when we were finally going to play chess. But my head was full of other things and I had no wish to lose to Goldenweiser, so I declined the challenge.

Another who came in was Brandukov,[2] who is notorious for his uncompromising attitude to the Bolsheviks. 'Well, now,' he asked as an opening gambit, 'how do you like our present regime?' I was quite relieved when he went away. Not long ago five musicians including Myaskovsky and Brandukov were nominated to be awarded the title of Honoured Artist.

---

1 The Cathedral of the Blessed Saint Basil on Red Square.
2 Anatoly Brandukov, cellist, a student of Wilhelm Fitzenhagen (begetter of the usually played version of Tchaikovsky's *Rococo Variations*) at the Moscow Conservatoire, from which he graduated with the Gold Medal. One of Rachmaninoff's two closest friends (the other was Chaliapin), he was best man at Rachmaninoff's wedding and the dedicatee of the Cello Sonata and the *Trio Elégiaque*, as he was of Tchaikovsky's *Pezzo Capriccioso*. A man of great generosity, integrity, cultivation and independence of spirit.

When the citation came up for confirmation before the government, four were accepted but not Brandukov.

Igumnov caught up with me to tell me that because of some meeting or other he would not be at home today at two o'clock (I had proposed paying my return call on him at that time). Perhaps I could come at four? But I would probably still be busy with Meyerhold then, while Igumnov had engagements all day tomorrow. In short, my courtesy call to the Director of the Conservatoire was becoming farcical, and in the end I did not manage to see him.

Meyerhold came to me at three o'clock to talk about *The Gambler*, the old lithographed vocal score of which had arrived from Akopera. I invited Meyerhold to give me some tips as to how I could improve the dramatic and scenographic aspects of the libretto when I set about revising the opera, but got nothing out of him. I was asking him in particular what I could do to change the very end of the opera when Polina and Aleksey embrace, which from a dramatic point of view I find distasteful. Meyerhold replied that, yes, of course it did need something done to improve it, but just what he could not see, probably the best thing would be to talk to Andrey Bely about it, he would try to winkle him out of the suburbs of the city, where he lives. Before Meyerhold left I managed unobtrusively to work the conversation round to Shurik. Meyerhold's reaction was immediate. 'Wait!' he cried. 'Wait, I have a friend in the GPU, I'll have a word with him. But you must give me all the particulars of exactly when he was convicted and of what offence.' On that note we parted, having agreed that soon we must come to dinner at his house. Meyerhold's readiness to do something about Shurik was in sharp contrast to Tsukker's pained expression and discouraging attitude.

Ptashka was not at home when Meyerhold came, as she had gone to see Litvinov's wife. Eva Valterovna Litvinova,[1] born in England, was so pleased to find in Ptashka someone who not only spoke perfect English but whose upbringing was close to her own Anglo-Saxon culture, that she insisted Ptashka visit her. Litvinova herself was not an especially interesting woman, but graciousness extended by the powerful must be responded to with grace, so today Ptashka had gone to call on her at the Litvinovs' house on the Sofia Embankment. They live in the magnificent mansion that formerly belonged to the fabulously wealthy Kharitonenko family.[2] If I am not mistaken it was there that I had lunched one day in 1918 a few days before leaving Russia at the

---

1 'Eva Valterovna' would be the nearest a polite Russian could get in referring to Ivy, the daughter of Walter. Maxim Litvinov's English wife Ivy, whose father was Walter Lowe, was known in Soviet Russia as Eva Valterovna Litvinova.
2 The architects of the Kharitonenko Palace, built for the nineteenth-century sugar magnate Pavel Kharitonenko, on the bank of the Moscow river directly opposite the Kremlin, were D. Chichagov and Fyodor Shekhtel, the latter responsible for the superb Russian Mannerist interior design. The Litvinovs did not occupy the whole of the house but had a spacious

invitation of Prince Gorchakov, a relative of the Kharitonenko family who lived with them. Ptashka described the house as enormous and beautiful, but almost uninhabitable because of the shambles in which the house was being kept up.

Ptashka had tea with Ivy Valterovna, an occasion for which her children also came in. They presented a somewhat unkempt appearance and were quite badly behaved, although in their way endearing. Observing their manners with a disapproving eye, Litvinova said she hoped in the future to have them educated in England. It is amusing to think of this ambition coinciding with the venomous diplomatic notes her husband was despatching to England at the time.[1]

In the evening we attended a play at the Maly Theatre: *Lyubov Yarovaya*.[2] It is a stirringly produced play set at the time of the Revolution, and is currently much discussed; the title is the name of the heroine. It has one very effective dramatic device: whenever the action leads up to tragic or pathetic moments – disaster, betrayal, violence – the author immediately defuses it by introducing a comic episode which clears the air and allows the plot to move smoothly forward. Unfortunately the last act turns into pure agitprop, which does violence to its overall style. Probably the author had to make concessions to get it on to the stage. The physical appearance of the heroine, a dedicated

---

apartment within it. From 1929 until 2000, to the profound irritation of successive Kremlin leaderships, the Kharitonenko Palace on the Sofia Embankment housed the British Embassy to the USSR, and it is to this day the residence of the British Ambassador. As Margaret Thatcher is reported to have argued when successfully resisting yet another attempt to evict the unwelcome British occupants, 'prestige has no price'. The first-floor balcony looking straight across the river to the Kremlin has long been an excellent place for guests to drink Pimms and reflect on the oddities of history. Great Britain having been the first country to recognise the Soviet Union and establish a full mission there, the diplomatic plates on its official cars still bear the numbers 001.

1 Diplomatic and trade relations between Great Britain and the Soviet Union were under great strain at this time, mainly on account of the continuing fall-out from the 'Zinoviev Letter', implicitly inciting revolution among the British working class and alleged to have been sent by Zinoviev on behalf of the Comintern to the Executive of the Communist Party of Great Britain. Zinoviev explicitly denied any connection with the letter or its contents; although to this day the true authorship cannot be confirmed it is generally regarded as a forgery, probably from White émigré sources. Forgery or not, it contributed to the fall of Ramsay MacDonald's Labour Government at the end of 1924 and the election of Stanley Baldwin's Conservative Government, which accurately perceived medium-term electoral advantage in Bolshevik-bashing. The Comintern philosophy still having a measure of influence in the Kremlin, Litvinov as Foreign Minister reacted violently to the newly aggressive British stance. The culmination of the stand-off came in May 1927 when the offices of the Soviet Trade Delegation to Britain were raided by Special Branch, incriminating documents were found, and the Foreign Secretary Austen Chamberlain immediately broke off all diplomatic and trade relations with the Soviet Union. They were not restored for two years.

2 Civil War drama published in 1927 by Konstantin Trenyov (1875–1945) about a dedicated Communist schoolteacher secretly helping an underground Revolutionary group and unexpectedly encountering her husband, believed killed in the First World War. The play's irreproachable ideological stance made it immensely popular; it spawned two equally successful films, the first directed in 1953 by Yan Fried and the second in 1970 directed by Vladimir Fetin.

Revolutionary, is distinctly unappealing, which it occurred to me might reflect an obliquely counter-revolutionary insinuation on the part of the producers.

4 March

In the morning I was visited by the violinist Tsyganov[1] to rehearse the *Songs Without Words*[2] for the chamber-music concert. Tsyganov is a good player, but I had comprehensively forgotten the piano part and made a complete mess of it. Tsyganov has two concerts in the immediate future: one with me and one with Medtner, and this morning he had come to me straight from the latter. With a twinkle in his eye he told me that Medtner's wife, on hearing whom he was about to see, escorted him to the door with a very sour grimace.

Ptashka went with Tsukker to Gostorg and chose a beautiful blue fox fur. Not only that, but they promised tomorrow to bring out from the cold store some squirrel. Squirrel used to be looked down on in Russia, but it is much prized abroad and this has been noticed in Russia, with the result that the price has gone up.

The Samoilenkos had asked me most particularly to go to see what had become of their old flat, so today we went to reconnoitre. Inevitably we found that it was now occupied by a large number of different families, but the Samoilenkos' former servant is still in charge of the main apartments. At first she would not hear of letting us in, but eventually relented and proved to be friendly. She even showed us a pile of photographs of Boris Nikolaevich because he had asked me to try to get hold of some them to bring them back. There was also a portrait of him in oils, wearing full-dress guards uniform with impressive side-whiskers, but we did not take it for fear of getting into trouble with the Customs inspection.

We visited Aunt Katya again, taking fresh caviar because of Shrovetide, for which she provided the *bliny*. Then I went to see Kucheryavy while Ptashka went with Cousin Katya and Nadya to the Art Theatre to see *Tsar Fyodor Ioannovich*.[3] Kucheryavy lives in a rather deserted part of Moscow, in

---

1 Dmitry Tsyganov (1903–1992), violinist who in 1923 with the brothers Vasily and Sergey Shirinsky (respectively second violin and cello) and Vadim Borisovsky had founded the Moscow Conservatory Quartet, which in 1930 became the Beethoven Quartet. One of the most durable of Soviet chamber music ensembles, the quartet became Shostakovich's most trusted partners, premiering thirteen of his fifteen string quartets (many of which were dedicated to quartet members), the Piano Quintet and the Second Piano Trio.
2 In the version for violin and piano made in 1925 with the assistance of Kokhánski. See above, pp. 191–2.
3 Play by A. K. Tolstoy (1817–1875), the second in a trilogy clearly showing the influence of Shakespeare's historical tragedies. Tsar Fyodor Ioannovich (Ivanovich) is the son of Ivan the Terrible. The trilogy begins with the death of Ivan and ends with Tsar Boris (Godunov). Konstantin Stanislavsky chose *Tsar Fyodor* for the inaugural production of the Moscow Art Theatre on 14 October 1898, with Ivan Moskvin as Fyodor and Vsevolod Meyerhold as Prince Shuisky.

Tverskaya-Yamskaya, but the building is new, with mainly working-class people living in it. He has a small, but clean and tidy and surprisingly sequestered flat, which is an extremely rare thing in today's Moscow. The tune he now sings is very different, and much less buoyant, from the letters he wrote to me when he first came back to the USSR. Then he was saying that everyone should return to the USSR whatever their sympathies in order to put their hands to the task of rebuilding the economy. Now he was full of complaints about the impossibility of working productively, everything and everybody prevents it, and the bureaucratic red tape saps the will to live. Grandiose schemes exist, but only on paper. He should have stayed in America, but his wife dragged them back because she missed Moscow so much, although now she is here she would do anything to go back. Liza, whom I remember as a nine-year-old little girl in America pummelling me furiously with her fists, has turned into a devotee of my music. She has a friend who is so thrilled with my concerts that Liza asked me to sign a photograph for her. When I said goodbye, Kucheryavy, lowering his voice, asked me if when I got back to Europe I would contact the director of a major glue-manufacturing concern in Germany with whom Kucheryavy has done business in the past and would like to maintain some relationship, to see if there could be a way for him to get out of the country again.

I walked back all the way along Tverskaya Street and bought warm *baranki*[1] from a stall on the street. Ptashka had enjoyed the play, but had been disconcerted by the indiscreet conversation of Katechka and Nadya, who had been saying in the theatre things like: 'Oh, how wonderful everything was in those days (the time of Tsar Fyodor Ioannovich)!' 'Oh, how I love those costumes!' 'The programme's got yet another notice about buying bonds to benefit the Red Army! I'm so fed up with them!'[2] Even though Katya was only whispering, her remarks came out quite loudly because of her deafness. Ptashka kept digging her in the ribs, but Katya could not understand why she was doing it.

5 March

In the morning I went to another rehearsal of the Quintet, while Ptashka went again to look at furs. There are no other notes of what happened during that half of the day. At five o'clock we went to dine with Meyerhold, who lives on Novinsky Boulevard in an old, crooked, leaning house in a courtyard. Inside, however, it was very comfortable. Bely had not been prised out of his suburb as he is too occupied with his work to go out anywhere. I had

---

1 A doughnut-shaped roll, rather like a bagel.
2 See below, p. 884, n. 1.

in any case no very high hopes of his advice over *The Gambler*, but was sorry that he had not come because it would have been pleasant to meet and talk with him. Meyerhold showed me a painting by Dmitriev, the artist who had designed the scenery for *Three Oranges* in Leningrad. The painting was a rather outlandish representation of the roulette tables in a casino and seemed a blatant hint that the designs for *The Gambler* should be entrusted to him. I do not consider this appropriate behaviour for a serious artist, and said I had not much cared for the *Oranges* designs. 'No more did I,' said Meyerhold. 'In that sense I'm not impressed by his hint.'

'Whom do you have in mind as a designer?' I asked.

'I still have to think about it. When I directed *The Government Inspector* I decided in effect to do without scenery at all.'

His wife then appeared. She was formerly married to Yesenin,[1] and their two children now live with the Meyerholds.

We sat down to dinner, which concluded with some superb melon, a real *coup de théâtre* in Moscow in March, with snow still on the ground. In the last act of *The Government Inspector* melon is served on stage, and most people salivating in the audience assumed that they were props made of papier-mâché. But Meyerhold was proud of the fact that the melon was 100-per-cent real; he believes that such scenic-gustatory devices create a genuine effect in the theatre. He buys the melons from the former Yeliseyev shop,[2] and when he went there today before dinner to get one they asked him if they should charge it to the theatre's account.

Since I could see the vocal score of *The Gambler* sitting there on the desk of Meyerhold's piano, I played him some of it, mainly from Babulenka's part. I believe her part will require the fewest changes when I carry out the

---

1 Sergey Yesenin (1895–1925), one of the best-known and -loved Russian poets of the twentieth century. Zinaïda Raikh was the second of his five wives, the third (a brief union) being Isadora Duncan. The marriage to Raïkh lasted longest, from 1917 until 1921, and produced a son, Konstantin, and a daughter Tatyana; these were the children now living with the Meyerholds. The remainder of Yesenin's short life was a gradual tragic decline into alcoholism, uncontrollable rages, mental instability, and despair. He committed suicide in 1925.
2 'Yeliseyev's Shop and Cellars of Russian and Foreign Wines' opened in Tverskaya Street in 1901. Muscovites were stunned by the magnificent decoration and the range of exotic foodstuffs on display. 'There were coconuts stacked like cannon-balls, each the size of a toddler's head; there were bananas hanging down in heavy garlands; there were unfamiliar seafoods, variously shaped and mysteriously coloured; and there were, of course, bottles of wine ranked in countless batteries reflecting the bright light of high-power electric bulbs. The townsfolk dubbed the store the Moscow Temple of Bacchus. A temple indeed, with cut-glass chandeliers, huge mirrors, gilded reliefs, carved stalls and marble-topped counters creating a shopping space unparalleled anywhere in Europe and reminiscent of an opulently decorated place of worship.' (*Moscow Times*, 31 August 2010.) In the Soviet era the shop was called Gastronom No. 1, but it was still a far cry from the usual gastronom and most people continued to refer to it as 'The Yeliseyev Shop'.

revision I plan for the future. It is a long time since I have seen the *Gambler* music, and I enjoyed playing it now.

After dinner Ptashka went to *The Snow-Maiden*[1] at the Bolshoy Theatre, where she had been offered a seat in the box reserved for the Artistic Committee. She is learning the part of the Snow-Maiden, and could not possibly pass up the chance to see a production on the Moscow stage. I went with the Meyerholds to see *The Magnificent Cuckold*[2] in his theatre, a play translated from the French that Meyerhold nevertheless wanted me to see because he had produced it according to entirely different principles from *The Government Inspector*. As we were going to it in a taxi, Meyerhold's wife remarked how much she loved travelling in train sleeping-cars. Meyerhold pensively echoed the thought: 'Yes, I love it too . . .'

So the decorated Red Army soldier has allowed himself to become infected by bourgeois tendencies.

The production of *The Magnificent Cuckold* contained much that was theatrical in the contemporary sense of that term: an array of conventionally Constructivist scenery and conventionally introduced gymnastics which so entranced Meyerhold that the pace of the drama, or so it seemed, was continually being held up. This was irritating because the playwright, having developed his plot very ingeniously, was denied the opportunity to produce an intensive enough denouement, so that towards the end interest slackened.

In the intervals Meyerhold showed off to me his accordion players, remarkable virtuosos on their instruments, who supply the music for his production of Ostrovsky's *The Forest*. I was most interested to hear them, particularly as they have invented quite a few orchestral effects. When I was asked which of my works I might recommend to them, I suggested after a little thought the Deshevov Scherzo from Op. 12,[3] which I thought could be highly effective on the accordion.

There has been an attack on me in *Life of Art*,[4] asking why I hide my true colours by not stating openly my attitude to the Soviet regime. The

---

1 Rimsky-Korsakov's fairy-tale opera *Snegurochka*, first performed in 1882, revised in 1898.
2 *Le Cocu magnifique*, a play by the Belgian playwright Fernand Crommelynck, was first produced by Meyerhold in 1922. Meyerhold was fascinated by Belgian theatre because of its close ties to Symbolism and Surrealism, which accorded with his own concept of theatre. He also staged plays by Maeterlinck and Verhaeren, and often expressed his admiration for the baroque grotesqueries of Ghelderode. See A. Piette, 'Crommelynck and Meyerhold: Two Geniuses Meet on the Stage', in *Modern Drama*, 39, No. 3 (Autumn 1996), pp. 436–47, for details on the 1922 Meyerhold production of *The Magnificent Cuckold*, a revival of which Prokofiev saw. *The Magnificent Cuckold* was the title under which Antonio Pietrangeli's 1964 film starring Claudia Cardinale and Ugo Tognazzi was released in Britain and America.
3 Scherzo, Op. 12 No. 10, dedicated to Vladimir Deshevov.
4 The literary and cultural paper *Life of Art* (*Zhizn' isskustva*) began life in Petrograd in 1918 as an erudite journal dedicated to Formalism (at that time a respectable branch of literary theory with

impression given is that the magazine was reluctant to give space to this attack but could not go so far as to refuse altogether to print it. It therefore appeared sandwiched between an exceptionally laudatory article about me and another about Medtner, comparing the two of us in my favour. To Meyerhold I said, 'Look, I shall have to respond to this attack!' Meyerhold winced. 'I wouldn't get involved in such trivialities. Better to maintain an Olympian silence. I myself publish a little theatre magazine expressly so as to have a way of replying to attacks on me and those artists who are sympathetic to my ideas. I can use it to rebut what they say about you.'

I therefore did not react to the *Life of Art* article. The most interesting thing was that the émigré press in Europe made no mention at all of the many laudatory articles published about me in the USSR; the only one they reprinted was this one. 'See,' they say, 'Prokofiev went back to Russia and that's what he got for his pains.'

6 March

In the afternoon, the concert of my chamber music for the Association of Contemporary Music. I was glad that it was taking place in the Hall of Columns and not in the Conservatoire. I was slightly late and did not hear how Feinberg and Shirinsky[1] played my *Ballade*. The second item was the five pieces of Op. 35bis played by Tsyganov and myself. Tsyganov played well, better than my accompaniment, but the success was only moderate. Why is this? After the violin pieces the Moscow players rose to the heights and played the Quintet with a brilliance and intensity I had not expected. It sounded wonderful. Of course, in time they will play it even better; even so the performance was incomparably better than the Boston one, when Koussevitzky's comment had been: 'My dear, this piece doesn't sound at all.'

I was terribly pleased, hugging myself throughout the performance: I did not know how it could happen that a piece long buried could have risen from

---

its attendant concepts of defamiliarisation and the central importance of the text as distinct from biographical or social or historical context). It featured writing and criticism from such as Mikhail Kuzmin, Viktor Shklovsky, Roman Jakobson, Boris Eikhenbaum and Yury Annenkov. Trotsky sat on the fence: 'The methods of formal analysis are necessary, but insufficient ... The form of art is, to a certain and very large degree, independent, but the artist who creates this form, and the spectator who is enjoying it, are not empty machines, one for creating form and the other for appreciating it. They are living people, with a crystallised psychology representing a certain unity, even if not entirely harmonious. This psychology is the result of social conditions.' (L. Trotsky, *Literature and Revolution*, trans. Rose Strunsky, Russell & Russell, New York, 1924, pp. 171, 180.) By 1923 *Life of Art* had become a more conventional, less independent literary-theatrical magazine, and in 1929 it ceased publication to be amalgamated the following year with the overtly proletarian *Rabochy i teatr* (*Worker and Theatre*).

1 Sergey Shirinsky, Tsyganov's cellist colleague in the Beethoven Quartet.

the dead and come back to life. The audience greeted it warmly, of course not to be compared with the effect my more popular works create, but they were clearly listening with great interest to something they liked. The players congratulated me and shook my hand. Myaskovsky was ecstatic: 'Absolutely incredible! Not a bar when the interest flagged, not even for a second.'

During the interval following the Quintet the Green Room filled up with people, among whom were Rabinovich and Dikiy, who chided me in mildly aggrieved tones for the letter I had written to Ekskuzovich praising the Leningrad production of *Oranges*. Ekskuzovich had lost no time in circulating it to the newspapers. Rabinovich and Dikiy saw that the letter could be used by the Mariinsky Theatre as a weapon in their fight to have their production chosen for the foreign tour rather than the Moscow one now in preparation. I did my best to reassure them.

The interval was followed by the Fifth Sonata. As it was the first Moscow performance I took great care over it and played it cleanly, but the reaction was still short of enthusiastic. It is not a crowd-pleaser. Then there were some of the Op. 12 set, and *Suggestion diabolique*. This the audience greeted with an enormous ovation, treating it as my farewell appearance. The afternoon concert finished quite early, as later in the day we were leaving for the Ukraine and were pressed for time since we had a full programme of things to do before evening.

We first went to have dinner with Derzhanovsky, where conversation revolved around the Quintet, drawing more praise from Myaskovsky. Then a quick visit to Aunt Katya, and back to the hotel to pack the suitcases.

As we left Aunt Katya and were summoning a cab, Meckler jumped out of nowhere and hailed us. It was as though he had been shadowing our movements. He was greatly agitated over my concerts; if I have turned him down for this season I must certainly work with him in the autumn. As we were in such a hurry I invited him to come with us in the car, and en route he unveiled his plans for future concerts, proposing fees of 1,000 roubles for provincial dates, more for appearances in the capitals. According to him there could be up to twenty concerts with fees amounting to 20,000 roubles. As we were getting out of the taxi and going up the stairs he thrust a packet of notes into my hand saying, 'Here's a thousand roubles, and I'll bring another four thousand tomorrow.'

These five thousand clearly were to be regarded as an advance for the autumn concerts. It was a substantial amount of bread to be casting freely upon the waters; nevertheless I could not see Meckler as a serious impresario – in fact he was more like a clown. In addition, when everything is so problematical and erratic I really did not think this was the time to be tying myself up in obligations to Russia for next season. I gave the money back to him and asked him to postpone any further discussions until my return from the Ukraine.

In the intervals of packing our cases there were interruptions from Razumovsky, involving complicated discussions about authors' rights, from Tseitlin, and from Tsukker. Tsukker read me a professorial lecture about how much better it would be for me to relocate permanently to the USSR, the sooner the better, if for no other reason that I would be able to work with fewer distractions. He was sure this would be the case. Tsukker has begun seriously to irritate me.

Piling into a car we were taken to the Kursk Station, so familiar to me from childhood journeys from Sontsovka to Moscow. But there was no time to lose: pausing only to buy a few things to eat from the buffet we settled ourselves in our sleeping car. The compartment was roomy, but the carriage was old and squeaky. Altogether it was not a prestige train: our carriage was the only first-class one, the others were all third class and there was no restaurant car. We left at eleven o'clock on our way to six concerts in the Ukraine: two in Kharkov, two in Kiev and two in Odessa.

7 March

We were all day travelling to Kharkov. I have known this line well since childhood – how many memories are linked to the times I passed through these stations! At Kursk we had coffee and bought slices of greasy goose. We flashed through Sontsevo but did not stop there; I stood and watched through the window. Here was Belgorod, where we got out to stretch our legs. The air was beginning to smell of the south, but there was a cold wind blowing. How many times passing through Belgorod had we eaten a bowl of the famous cabbage soup, the pride of the Belgorod station buffet.

Arriving in Kharkov at half past five in the evening, we were met on the platform by Tutelman, Vorobyov and Dzbanovsky.[1] Vorobyov was that same Ukrainian government official who had sent a telegram to Persimfans threatening to have my concerts in Kharkov banned if I dared appear under any auspices other than the Ukrainian State Theatres. At the time both Tseitlin and I were most incensed and felt like taking up the gauntlet and fighting, but now that I was finally in Kharkov to appear (by agreement with Ukrainian State Theatres), here was Vorobyov coming to welcome me at the station, the epitome of a charming and modest man. We were put into rather a nice open-topped car and taken across town to the 'Red' Hotel, which in Ukrainian is 'Chervonny'. Kharkov (Kharkiv) is large, dirty and unattractive. Not far from the centre are a number of rather good German-style buildings. Germans, it seems, have played a significant role in Ukrainian architecture.

---

1   Alexander Dzbanovsky (1870–1938), composer and critic.

By the terms of my contract our hotels are paid for by the State Theatre organisation. We were allocated a ridiculously vast suite consisting of two rooms with a bathroom in which, for instance, there was only hot water. To take a bath one had to fill it and then wait half an hour for the water to cool down enough to get into it. The telephone in the room allowed one to ring someone in the town, but not for room service. I had to hunt through the telephone directory for the number of the hotel we were in in order to get through to it on the outside line. No piano has been sent in to our room, but I was taken into the adjoining one belonging to the manager of the hotel, where I was able to practise for a while.

It was soon time for the concert. The hall was full, and the piano quite good. My programme included the Second and Third Sonatas, *Visions fugitives*, some smaller pieces and the Toccata. It went down very well with shouts of bravo and demands for encores.

Shteiman[1] appeared during the interval. He has put on weight and seems dissatisfied with his lot. It is true that he has not fulfilled Tcherepnin's brilliant prophecies for his future, but still and all he is the Chief Conductor of the Ukrainian Opera. After him came Lapitsky,[2] whose manners are not the most polished but I know him to be an interesting man. In his time he has done much to enliven the dramatic side of opera productions, and that is a subject close to my heart.

Vera Reberg,[3] from whom I had already had a letter, came at the end of the concert. She was looking well, despite her health problems as a child. Promising to call on her tomorrow we hurried back to the hotel, as I was tired after a day and a night on the train. As a matter of fact I have been tired ever since we arrived in the USSR.

---

1 Mikhail Shteiman (1889–1949), pianist and conductor, fellow student of Prokofiev in Tcherepnin's conducting class at the St Petersburg Conservatoire. He came to the attention of Diaghilev, who employed him as a staff conductor. In this capacity Prokofiev had come across him again in London in June 1913 and had enjoyed spending time with him. Shteiman continued to be dissatisfied with the opportunities afforded by his position with the National Opera of the Ukraine and emigrated to Paris later in the year. Here he had a moderately distinguished career, and was invited to conduct the jubilee concert for Glazunov's fifty years of musical activity in the Salle Gaveau in 1932. Prokofiev was present, but does not mention meeting Shteiman again, or on any other occasion in Paris even given that one presumes they must have run across one another occasionally, although on the whole Prokofiev steered clear of émigré musical manifestations. See below, pp. 1000–1.

2 Iosif Lapitsky (1876–1944), opera producer. After working at the Bolshoy Theatre in the early years of the twentieth century he founded and directed the Musical Drama Theatre in St Petersburg, where Prokofiev had seen productions when a student at the Conservatoire.

3 Vera, Zinaïda and Nina Reberg were the three daughters of Dr Alfred Reberg, the Prokofievs' family doctor in Sontsovka. The family had later moved to Kharkov. Prokofiev had last seen Vera when on holiday with Max Schmidthof in February 1913, Nina and Zina later the same year. See *Diaries*, vol. 1, pp. 7, 88, 304, 366, 484, 637.

I wanted to take a bath, but the enamel had peeled off in several places and this gave the tub something of a leprous appearance. We tried for a long time to summon someone from the hotel staff, but this was not a simple matter because some sort of elections were being held today and the staff was out voting. Eventually it was explained to us that the pockmarked appearance of the bath was not because it was dirty but because it was clean: after each guest it is scrubbed with acid, which eats the enamel. Even so, we decided to postpone the pleasure of bathing until we get to Kiev.

8 March

In theory today was a free day and I could rest. But there was a constant stream of visitors, of whom the most stimulating was Lapitsky. He turned up with the vocal score of *Oranges* and outlined to me an intelligent and well-thought-out project to produce it in Kharkov. I had to play the score through to him and give an account of how various scenes had been done in other productions. Lapitsky got very excited and said that I was the only true opera composer; he would very much like to collaborate with me on something new. I agreed with alacrity, without actually committing myself, because I sense that Lapitsky, with his love for the theatre, could supply me with an interesting subject and treat it in an illuminating way. His taste is by no means perfect, but this does not mean he is without hidden depths of potential originality.

I went out for a walk in the afternoon and came across a shop called 'Proletarian', in which I saw my works displayed – not, however, in their original editions but counterfeit ones reprinted by a Ukrainian publisher. I did not hesitate to go in to demand an explanation. I explained my connection to the editions they were displaying in their window, and asked what they thought they were doing selling them. 'Our suppliers are a music organisation in Kiev,' was the reply from the shop manager. 'But this organisation has illegally printed my works and your shop is therefore handling stolen goods.'

The manager looked round and, lowering his voice, said, 'Please do not speak so loudly. What you are saying could make a poor impression on our customers.'

'It is to be regretted that your business is such that one can discuss it only in whispers.'

It was a fairly unproductive conversation because the fact is that the villains are not the shop but the publishers. The manager undertook in future to source the proper editions from Moscow, but griped that orders took a lot longer to arrive from Moscow than they did from Kiev.

In the evening Ptashka came with me to the Rebergs, going there on foot through largely deserted side streets deep in snow. As we walked we recalled that in the south there are many homeless orphan children who roam the streets in gangs. The technique is for one of their number to jump on the feet of passers-by, knocking them over while the others grab their bags and purses, stabbing with their knives and biting to infect the victims with syphilis. But the streets we went along were quiet and somnolent.

Vera Reberg has followed the medical calling of her father. Her mother, Maria Iosifovna, lives with her. She is now an old lady, extraordinarily kind and gentle; old age has made her more beautiful. She recalled the days in Sontsovka and Golitsinovka with great ardour. Nina is married, with two children, and lives some hours away from Kharkov. To my enquiries about her Vera replied with some coolness, evidently there is some sort of a rift between the sisters. Zina died some years ago; she always suffered from a weak heart. We spent a very pleasant evening, mother and daughter both touched by our visit.

9 March

I continued my discussions with Lapitsky and played him more of *Three Oranges*. Rosenstein came by to take us to the Conservatoire. He is a cellist and former student of the St Petersburg Conservatoire whom I have known for a very long time. He was one of the very first people to play my *Ballade*; I performed it with him at some concert or other in my Conservatoire years.[1] Now he is Director of the Kharkov Conservatoire and yesterday burst in on me requesting, in the name of our old friendship (although in fact we were not friends at all) to play for the students at his Conservatoire. I never refuse to play for music students; in fact I love doing so. Consequently today I found myself playing in front of an engagingly cheerful crowd of young people a succession of Gavottes, Tales, Marches, and other short pieces. When I finished, the hall exploded in an orgy of sound. A student made a speech of thanks in Ukrainian: I kept hearing the word 'pershy',[2] which is Ukrainian for 'first' (first composer, First Prize, first acquaintance, and so on).

We left the Conservatoire in the fine weather with Rosenstein and some of the other professors to go back to the Chervonny Hotel. Some girl students were following us all the way, sometimes behind us and sometimes in front. At first I paid no attention, then found it amusing and finally annoying, until finally right in front of the hotel they suddenly formed a group round us, pushing and shoving each other and saying, 'No, go on, you do it,' and eventually coming up to me one by one to present me with white flowers which

---

1 Yakov Rosenstein (1887–?) cellist and conductor. In Kharkov he had established the Conservatoire's orchestra which two years later was to become the Orchestra of Ukrainian Radio and later the Kharkov Philharmonic. See *Diaries*, vol. 1, pp. 593, 596–8.
2 Cf. Russian 'pervy', 'first'.

were being sold at the crossroads, it being the beginning of spring. This was a very nice touch.

The second of my two concerts took place in the evening. It included the Fourth and Fifth Sonatas, which was not a particularly good idea since nobody understands the Fifth while the Fourth is too slow to generate much enthusiasm. But I had nothing else prepared and so had to throw in the sonatas to fill the hole. When I was talking about this to Tutelman in Moscow, he said, 'Doesn't matter. But keep the Fourth and Fifth Sonatas for the second half, then they won't affect the ticket sales, and afterwards you'll be leaving the city anyhow.'

All the same, the gavottes, excerpts from *Oranges* and *Suggestion diabolique* with which I concluded the programme roused the audience to wild enthusiasm and generated the usual tremendous success. Afterwards the organisers wanted to arrange a supper, but I begged to be excused.

The artist Khvostov[1] showed me sketches of the costumes for the projected Kharkov production of *Oranges* – a mixture of Modernism and fantasy. It was hard to judge, but my first impression was that I did not like the costumes much.

10 March

In the morning the Leontovich Quartet[2] came to play me compositions by modern Ukrainian composers. My enquiries on the subject of Leontovich elicited the information that he was Mykola Leontovich, regarded as a national treasure of the Ukraine, a composer who had perished in the Revolutionary struggles. Apparently he was shot by the Bolsheviks, who subsequently caused a quartet to be formed bearing his name. The musicians played me works by Lyatoshinsky,[3] Lisovsky,[4] Novosatsky[5] and

---

1 Alexander (Oleksandr) Khvostenko-Khvostok (1895–1967), Ukrainian artist and designer influenced by Constructivism and by the work of the Suprematists Konstantin Malevich and Alexandra Exter (in whose workshop in Kiev he trained).
2 Mykola (Nikolay) Leontovich (1877–1921) was a Ukrainian composer, choral conductor and Orthodox priest who gave his name to the Kiev Philharmonia after being assassinated by a Soviet agent in 1921. As part of the Philharmonia a string quartet was formed in 1926, which grew to have international resonance and made recordings, some of which are still available on historic recording labels.
3 Boris Lyatoshinsky (1895–1968), composer, conductor and teacher, a student of Yavorsky and Glière in Kiev. Initially attracted to Modernism, Lyatoshinsky was one of the composers accused of decadent Formalism in the Zhdanov Decree of 1948, and subsequently lost his teaching positions in both the Kiev and Moscow Conservatoires.
4 Leonid Lisovsky (1866–1934), composer who studied with Solovyov at the St Petersburg Conservatoire.
5 Unidentified.

Kozitsky,[1] any of which could have been written fifty years ago and then would have been perfectly pleasant music, but today are totally superfluous provincial efforts.

In the afternoon I went to see Turkeltaub, the representative of the Ukrainian Society of Authors, which rejoices in the euphonious acronym of Utodik (Ukrainskoye Tovarishchestvo Dramaturgov i Kompozitorov – Ukrainian Association of Playwrights and Composers). Since this organisation works in tandem with its Moscow counterpart, I wanted to raise with him the question of the illegal Kievan reprints of my scores and also to find out what would be an appropriate fee to ask the Kharkov State Opera if they do in fact stage *Oranges*. It appears that what the State Opera has so far offered in negotiations with Weber[2] is so minuscule than even doubling it would be only half what they are able to pay. It is true that the discussions have so far come to nothing, but it is good to know for the future.

In the evening we left Kharkov for Kiev. Tutelman was travelling with us and Vorobyov, the important Communist, also came to wave us goodbye at the station. Although we were all ready with our luggage in good time, Tutelman was in no hurry and waited patiently for the car which was supposed to come to collect us. At the last moment it was discovered that the car was not in fact coming, and there ensued an unholy panic. We procured two racing drivers manqués in two cabs, one for Ptashka and me with our bags and the other for Tutelman and Vorobyov, and set off on a crazy dash right across the town. The mud was terrible, as were the snow, the puddles and the potholes. We got spattered with mud from head to foot, and even when we got back to Paris we were still finding traces of the Kharkov mud on the suitcases.

We made the station in time, only to discover that despite Vorobyov's leverage it had proved impossible to secure a separate compartment for Ptashka and me. This was upsetting, because I was going to have to play a concert tomorrow in Kiev, and really needed my sleep. Tutelman, worried, ran all over the station and summoned the stationmaster, with the result that only as the train was about to depart did we cram into the corridor of our carriage. It looked as though we were going to have sleep there, but in the end things turned out reasonably well. We didn't get our separate compartment, nor pillows nor bed linen, but Ptashka was found space in a small compartment with a woman delegate to some meeting or other, while Tutelman and I were put into a larger four-berth compartment with two other passengers. Tutelman did his best to look after me, insisting that I take the lower berth and offering me an inflatable cushion that he had with him

---

1   Filip Kozitsky (1893–1960), composer, teacher and senior Communist Party cultural figure in the Ukraine, a student of Yavorsky and Glière in Kiev.
2   The Russian Musical Editions Berlin director.

in his case. He regaled me with accounts of his drinking exploits and stories about the violinist Kubelík,[1] who had arrived in Kharkov with a Negro valet. In America he would probably not have been allowed into a decent hotel, but in Kharkov he made a great impression.

Ptashka's sleeping companion proved to be an important Ukrainian delegate connected to the Ukrainian Government. She was a very ordinary woman, more than ready to talk about her village and her five children.

11 March

There being no restaurant car, when I awoke the next morning I got out at a main station to have coffee. In spite of the crush at the counter I managed not only to obtain and drink coffee myself, but to get some to take back to Ptashka in the carriage. I had to pay for the glass and the spoon; Ptashka later presented them to her ministerial companion, who accepted them with every sign of pleasure. We did not arrive in Kiev until one o'clock; on this line the trains drag themselves along at a glacial pace that has to be experienced to be believed. Before getting into Kiev we crawled across the Dnieper, still partially ice-bound. The ice was being dynamited in order to prevent flooding, and presented a very beautiful spectacle.

We were met at the station and conveyed in a shabby car to the Continental Hotel. In contrast to the ugliness of Kharkov, Kiev is very beautiful. I had not properly appreciated it when I came here for concerts with Glière in 1916. Tree-lined streets, magnificent buildings, but how much destruction has been wrought, the result of the city having changed hands so many times from White to Red and back again! Still today there were many abandoned houses with gaping windows and shattered frames.

In the afternoon I gave a press interview and then spent the time quietly in order to be in form for the evening.

The concert took place in the Opera House. Backstage were threescore or so people hanging about, but nobody seemed to be in charge. The beautiful hall was full. I played the same programme as I had at the first concert in Kharkov. While I was playing, a light suddenly came on in the prompter's box, right under my feet. Then the light went out but a face appeared, listening intently to my performance. The face disappeared, but the light came back on. This annoyed me intensely, so much so that I had to struggle hard against the temptation to apply my boot to the middle of the face. During the interval I went round everywhere to try to find someone in

---

1 Jan Kubelík (1880–1940), Czech violinist and composer. The conductor Rafael Kubelík was one of his eight children. Among the many honours heaped on this great musician, violinist and composer of six violin concertos was the Gold Medal of the Royal Philharmonic Society, awarded in 1902.

authority, but despite the mass of people, obviously members of the theatre company, chatting, goggling at me, flirting with each other and generally having a lovely time, no one could conceive where such a person might be.

As in Kharkov, the concert was a huge success. A certain Mme Goldenberg, a teacher at the Conservatoire, pestered me with unusual persistence in the Green Room to come tomorrow to listen to her students, some of whom would be playing my works. But tomorrow I was desperately in need of a break from music, and hardly knew how to get rid of her. When we returned to the hotel, Ptashka scolded me for my rudeness, but how else could I combat such importunate demands?

12 March

It was snowing heavily so we stayed in all day. Malko and his wife came to lunch; he is here to conduct a concert in which my *Classical* Symphony has been programmed, but the performance clashes with my concert. There's intelligent planning for you! At lunch he talked, as usual, without stopping, skating so expertly from one inconsequential anecdote to the next that afterwards it was impossible to determine anything he had actually said. All the same, his stories about Yesenin and Isadora Duncan, whom he had met several times in Russia, were very colourful. He described Isadora as a truly amazing woman, and quoted one of her sayings: 'Liszt was forever reaching for the sky, but to Schubert it came down of its own accord.' That is, one must admit, quite wonderfully put.

After they went, a young composer, Shipovich, was brought in to see me. He is twenty, a phlegmatic young Jewish boy of no great intellectual pretensions. His phlegmatism was in sharp contrast to his egregiously bumptious papasha. Shipovich played several of his compositions, driving me to despair with his two-bar phrases and the primitive construction of his melodies, but in the March from his ballet *The Little Hump-backed Horse* I detected some not bad moments.[1]

Goldenberg had persisted yesterday with her telephone calls and now even sent someone to fetch me, so finally I gave in and went to hear her students'

---

1 The original ballet *The Little Hump-backed Horse or The Tsar-Maiden* (*Konyok-gorbunyok ili Tsaritsa*) was a setting of the fairy-tale choreographed by Arthur Saint-Léon to music by the court composer Cesare Pugni in 1864. Over the decades it underwent numerous revisions and restagings by Petipa and Gorsky among others, with additional numbers contributed by composers such as Drigo, Tchaikovsky, Glazunov, Asafyev, etc. As a result it was fair game for any choreographer or composer, and Shipovich was by no means the only one to try his hand. In 1960 Alexander Radunsky commissioned from Rodion Shchedrin a completely new score for his staging, which was a success at the Bolshoy Theatre and subsequently at the Kirov as well, staged by Alexander Ratmansky.

examination. At the Conservatoire a surprise awaited me: the exam was actually very interesting. They were all very young and green, from ten to sixteen years old, including a pair of chubby little chaps playing duet versions of numbers from *Chout*. Three girls read a lecturette on the form of my Gavotte, illustrated by coloured diagrams (based on Yavorsky's analytical theories) on the blackboard, but either it was too complicated for their little brains or they were tongue-tied in the presence of the composer. One of the little girls got completely confused, and had to be helped out by her more self-assured friend. It ended with another girl addressing a speech of welcome to me and so I had to play them three pieces myself. But this also was very enjoyable, the children crowding round the piano whooping with delight.

It is so good that there are establishments where young people's interest can be stimulated and developed in this way. If the Revolution, which brought in its train the destruction of the intelligentsia, has also caused a dearth of audiences for concerts of good music, the losses can quickly be restored by such an approach to education. We parted good friends with Mme Goldenberg, and her showcase was one of the most striking memories of my visit to the Soviet Union.

13 March

Several suppliants this morning, it being a more common practice in the south to appear at the door of visiting celebrities than it is in Moscow or Leningrad. I was sorry for them all, and doled out five roubles here, a *chervonets*[1] there. Some were genuinely grateful, others went away grumbling. Ptashka was indignant, complaining that decent people would never come to the door begging, anyone who did was either a chancer or a professional. I asked one of them to show me evidence that he was who he said he was, and he immediately pulled out a document to show that two years ago he had served in the GPU. 'Well then,' I said, 'you had better apply to them. I confine my assistance to colleagues in the arts.' Such a document would, however, probably have an effect on vulnerable visitors such as NEPmen,[2] who would hasten to pay up to get rid of their unwanted petitioner.

In the afternoon I gave my second concert in Kiev, this time not in the Opera but in another, smaller hall. It coincided with Malko's orchestral concert which on top of everything else contained my *Classical* Symphony. It

1 A ten-rouble banknote.
2 NEPmen were those who had taken advantage of Lenin's reluctant relaxation (the 'New Economic Policy') of the forcible nationalisation of *all* aspects of production and distribution during the years of War Communism, which had resulted in widespread famine and near-total economic collapse, the only growth being in the black market. NEPmen were small traders, entrepreneurs and businessmen, harassed and at best grudgingly tolerated by the authorities and regarded with envy and suspicion by their materially poorer but ideologically purer compatriots.

was a stupid situation – for ages there is nothing, then two at once. The result was that my concert was delayed for an hour and a quarter because it was reported that the audience for Malko was very small indeed and the performance was likely to be cancelled. The start of mine was therefore postponed, to give the audience from the cancelled concert the chance to come over to the one that was going to take place. In the meantime a tragic situation was developing with the young students I had seen yesterday. I had given them all cards with passes to be admitted, but they were not being allowed in. One of them did manage to get in, found me and told me what was happening. I promptly insisted to one of the organisers that they *should* be admitted, and was promised that this would be done, but a little while later another emissary got through to me and informed me that they were still not being let in. But eventually they were, and the concert started.

Except for the Fifth Sonata everything on the programme was a colossal success. My new student friends were particularly zealous in their enthusiasm, hurling themselves actually on to the stage, which was not very high above the floor, so that I even had difficulty elbowing my way through them to leave the stage. The noise was deafening. Afterwards we dashed back to pack and leave for Odessa. Just before we left, Goldenberg's pupils came in to make me a present, bound in a hand-illustrated folder, of their analysis of my March from *Three Oranges*. The analysis had been done by tracing out the harmonic progressions according to the precepts of Yavorsky, in consequence of which I could understand nothing about it whatsoever.

We had a compartment reserved for us in the International Company sleeping-car. Apart from ourselves hardly anyone appeared to be travelling in it.

14 March

In the morning, Odessa, where we were met on the platform by a dozen or so people none of whom I knew, representatives of the Philharmonia and the Opera. It was not clear to me which of these institutions was presenting my concerts, and it was only later that I learnt that, having been invited by Tutelman, that meant I was under the auspices of the opera company. But the Philharmonia was adamant that *they* must be the responsible organisation, so the Opera sold me on, for twice what they were paying me according to what I was told by Philharmonia directors. That said, the Opera was paying my fee in dollars, whereas the Philharmonia was paying the Opera in roubles.

We had rooms in the Bristol Hotel, now renamed the Red Hotel although people still use the old name. Sadly, our rooms do not look out over the sea. We have two gigantic rooms which, however, are separated from the corridor only by flimsy doors, so we can hear everything else going on all over the hotel. Also the telephone is directly opposite our door, and the noise from that prevents us getting even a minute's rest.

We walked round Odessa. For Ptashka to be here was more momentous than it was for me. It was my first time here but Ptashka had lived in the city when she was very young with her grandfather, who was a State Councillor and President of the Court. She instantly recognised the Opera House. We walked down to the sea. The port was deserted and the sea itself grey. Spring has not yet come to Odessa.

The concert in the evening was in the Opera. The house was full and there were even fifteen rows or so of seats on the stage, which always lends a sense of occasion. I looked with interest at the auditorium, of whose beauty the Odessans are very proud. The audience responded reticently at first to my performance, but warmed up little by little although not reaching the heights of yesterday in Kiev. Pavlusha Sebryakov[1] came into the Green Room at the end, and we went back together to the hotel.

15 March

I have no notes of what happened on this day. My second concert was in the evening, in the same hall, similar circumstances, and with approximately the same level of success. There was a supper afterwards, after which the local tenor sang *The Ugly Duckling* in a quite superb performance, spoiled only by his accompanist. But his singing was so excellent and free that I wanted to play for him myself, and we went through several of my songs.[2]

---

1 Pavel (Pavlusha) Sebryakov was the son of Dr Tatyana Sebryakova née Zhitkova, the daughter of Prokofiev's maternal great-grandfather Pavel Zhitkov, and her army doctor husband. Pavel was the brother of Sergey Sebryakov. Pavel and Sergey were Prokofiev's first cousins once removed.
2 'Many years later, when I knew Sergey Sergeyevich well, for some reason I reminded him of the occasion [when Prokofiev had severely criticised the eighteen-year old David Oistrakh's performance of the scherzo from the First Violin Concerto] and of the concerts he had given in Odessa at the time. To my astonishment he remembered everything down to the smallest detail: the exact programmes he had played, the number of encores, and Chishko, with whom he had performed *The Ugly Duckling* at a banquet, also the "unfortunate young man" who, as he put it, "had had the rough edge of his tongue". "Do you know who the young man was?" I asked. On learning that it was I, Sergey Sergeyevich was visibly embarrassed. "You can't mean it!"'
(D. Oistrakh, 'On the Unforgettable and Beloved Prokofiev', March 1954, in S. Shlifshteyn, op. cit. Prokofiev was later to express again his appreciation of the artistry of Oles (Alexander) Chishko (1895–1976), a fine tenor, composer and musician, for his admirable portrayal of Pierre Bezukhov in the production by the Maly Theatre of Part One of *War and Peace* conducted by Samuil Samosud. Chishko had studied composition at the Leningrad Conservatoire with Tyulin and Kushnaryov.

16 March

In the morning we had a visit from Gorchakov's sister. Revolution and the incursions of the Bolsheviks to the south had separated her from her family. At one time she had tried to escape to Romania by swimming across the river, but the attempt had ended in failure. She is now studying in one of the medical schools, lives a half-starved existence, and generally gives an impression of almost feral mistrustfulness, needing to be addressed in the most sympathetic, loving tones to get any human response at all. When she did speak, it became clear that her greatest fear is of being sent off somewhere into the countryside when she has finished her training. I said that I would put in a word for her with the doctors who are on the board of the Philharmonia.

As it happened, one of the doctors came just then, to take us in his car to Arcadia, a little place on the coast a few kilometres outside Odessa. Hitherto, compared to Kiev, we had not seen much destruction in Odessa, the most damage seemed to have been suffered by the trees lining the streets, many of which had been cut down for firewood. But now, going out to Arcadia, the route lay along a boulevard (Franzussky [French] Boulevard, I think it was) which had been the scene of an attack by the Bolsheviks and both sides had pounded the street with artillery. A great number of houses and villas, many of them magnificent, were in ruins. Dr Goldman pointed out some houses on the outskirts of the city that were now holiday hotels and hostels for workers, but they were a drop in the ocean of the surrounding devastation.

Arcadia has an exceptionally nice beach, sheltered from the winds by low hills and warmed by the sun from the south. All of a sudden we found ourselves in a completely different climate. Dr Goldman told us most interesting travellers' tales about his journeys last year to Transcaucasia, and beyond the Caspian Sea to Bukhara and Khiva, to which the only access is by aeroplane. It was all the more interesting to us because, living in Paris, we have no idea of these half-wild regions on the remote fringes of Russia. But Soviet citizens go there for rest and relaxation.

Returning to Odessa we said goodbye to Goldman and took ourselves to the London Hotel for lunch, which has windows looking out over the sea. There we were joined by Presnyakov,[1] who used to teach the plastic arts, movement and eurhythmics, at the St Petersburg Conservatoire. He was not much liked personally, but people were interested in his classes because the prettiest girl students naturally vied to get into it. Now his manner was

---

1 Valentin Presnyakov (1877–1956), a former Mariinsky Ballet character dancer, director of movement and opera producer at the St Petersburg Conservatoire. From 1933 until 1938 he was Balletmaster and Choreographer at the Yerevan Opera and then moved to Voronezh to become Artistic Director of the newly established Ballet School in the Voronezh Academy of Music. Prokofiev had not been impressed by his choreographic skills. See *Diaries*, vol. 1, pp. 279, 560.

primarily supplicatory: his main topic of conversation was how he could go abroad, since he was utterly disenchanted with life in Russia.

When we went back to the hotel, Stolyarov[1] called for us to drive us to the Conservatoire, of which he is now the Director. I had promised to play today for the students, of whom there had gathered a huge multitude, made to seem especially huge by the comparatively constricted dimensions of the Conservatoire.

I remember Stolyarov from the time when he was a violin student in St Petersburg. Later he had taken up conducting and was now the Director of the whole institution, although his appearance seemed to me insufficiently substantial and directorial for the position, as I jokingly observed to him. 'Surely they don't take any notice of what you tell them? You might at least grow a beard!'

I did not play a great deal, but the packed hall erupted in a fearsome explosion of sound: the southern Odessan temperament was really outdoing itself. When Stolyarov and I emerged on to the street and got into an open-topped car to go back to the hotel, the entire Conservatoire complement, several hundred souls, poured out on to the street and sent us off with ear-splitting cries. As we moved away I bowed in acknowledgement. It was in the nature of a national riot, but a very pleasing one.

Home again, we packed our things and set off for the station. There was an amusing incident just as we were leaving. For two days some individual had been eating and drinking his fill, ordering the most expensive dishes in the restaurant downstairs and claiming to be with Prokofiev's party more or less in the capacity of his secretary. At the same time he was telling elaborate stories about life abroad and various episodes in the life of Prokofiev. The restaurant manager and the waiter made a careful note of what he ate and drank, and put it all down on my bill. When, as I was leaving the hotel, it was discovered that this gentleman was nothing whatsoever to do with me, there was panic in the management. The maître d'hôtel screamed, 'Just wait till I get my hands on him! He won't get away with this!' No obstacles were put in our way, however, and we were escorted to the door with much bowing and scraping. The leaving party at the station was much the same as the welcoming party had been, consisting for the most part of doctors – the medical profession seems to have a governing role in the Odessa Philharmonic Society. Gorchakova was also there with a bouquet of violets; I recommended her to the care of Dr Sigal, an influential member of the medical

---

1   Grigory Stolyarov (1892–1963), violinist, conductor and teacher. In 1929 he was invited to become Musical Director of the Stainslavsky–Nemirovich-Danchenko Opera Company, from which he moved to become Rector of the Moscow Conservatoire during the war years. Subsequently he divided his time between the Operetta Theatre and national radio, with the orchestra of which he made a good many recordings for Melodiya.

establishment. Needless to say, he professed himself ready to do anything in his power for me, but as I later found out, did precisely nothing for her.

Our sleeping car was through to Moscow, but was not an International Company one. Nevertheless, we had a comfortable half-compartment.

17 March

We reached Kiev at eleven o'clock the next morning. Here our carriage was coupled to the Moscow train, which meant we had an hour and forty minutes to wait, and we decided to take advantage of it to take a tour round the city. We hired a cab and went to the monument to Vladimir.[1] He stands on his hill with a cross in his hands – revolutions and civil strife have not dared to harm him. It was a warm, sunny day, the snow melting and forming rivulets that gurgled down the hillsides. Far away in the distance we could see the twists and turns of the Dnieper, but it looked wintry and uninviting.

After a rather bad lunch in the station we returned to our carriage where we found in the next compartment Segovia,[2] who has been giving concerts in Kiev and was also on his way to Moscow. Segovia is a charming young Spaniard wearing horn-rimmed spectacles. He is said to be a remarkable guitarist, although I have never heard him. A representative of Rosphil was travelling with him, Kulisher, a gloomy-looking Jew. Segovia was delighted with our company and chatted away in Spanish the whole time to Ptashka, complaining about the fact that he never got a word out of Kulisher, who does nothing but sit and chain-smoke, poisoning the whole compartment with the fumes. At the next main station we ran out with Segovia to the buffet and bought a chicken. Then, leaving him to go on talking to Ptashka, I went to bed as I had a headache.

18 March

We arrived in Moscow at 11.40 the next morning. Tsukker met us and took us to the Metropole, where we were given our old room. Tsukker took us straight away to the Kremlin, where we joined a group touring the Armoury Museum with a guide. I showed Ptashka the Crown of Monomakh,[3] truly an

---

1 The five-metre high bronze monument, standing on a twenty-metre tower on top of a hill overlooking the Dnieper, dedicated to Prince Vladimir Svyatoslavich (958–1015) – St Vladimir, who brought Christianity to Kievan Rus in 988 and thus Christianised Russia.
2 Andrés Segovia (1893–1987), one of the best-known and most influential Spanish guitarists of the twentieth century, dedicatee of innumerable additions to the repertoire.
3 The famous fourteenth-century gold, jewel-encrusted crown of the Grand Prince of Kiev. It was used in Coronation ceremonies of Muscovite Grand Princes and Tsars until Peter the Great assumed the title of Emperor in 1921 and replaced the Monomakh cap with the Imperial Crown. Both are now in the Armoury Museum of the Kremlin in Moscow.

extraordinarily magnificent object. Then we were taken round by one N. N. Pomerantsev, who is in charge of picture restoration in the Kremlin cathedrals. He is a most interesting man, fanatically devoted to his profession, a cultured and refined professional who works for a pittance in extremely unpropitious circumstances. He showed us with passionate reverence paintings by Rublyov which have been cleaned of the layers of paint laid over them when the cathedrals underwent restoration 'in uncultivated Tsarist times'. I felt awkward entering a church wearing a hat, and made to remove mine. Seeing my movement to do so, Pomerantsev said, 'We regard these churches as museums. There are no religious services here now. It's impossible to work here without head-covering: see how cold it is.' He was right, the temperature was 15° below zero. In accordance with the museum status Ptashka was taken right up to the high altar to see the Rublyov icons.

Our tour of inspection was very interesting, but seemed endless. We were hungry, it was extremely cold and my feet had turned into shoe-trees with rigid toes. Eventually I protested, and at four o'clock, expiring from hunger, we repaired with Tsukker to the Bolshaya Moskovskaya Hotel where we were served a meal in a private room.

In the evening we went to Meyerhold's theatre to see Ostrovsky's play *The Forest* in a fascinating and admirably crafted production, as is everything Meyerhold does. Its defects were slowness of pace, which comes from his passion for saturating the production with detail. One gets an impression of the richness of his invention, but this invention is not infinite: it is quite often repeated from other Meyerhold presentations.

19 March

Rehearsed with Persimfans for my final concert, although there are no new works in the programme. I had lunch without Ptashka, and then dropped in to Aunt Katya.

In the evening we went to a production by the Art Theatre Opera Studio of *Yevgeny Onegin*, which gave me exceptional pleasure. The peasant scene in Act One was omitted as liable to give offence to the Government of Workers and Peasants. The ball at the Larins was very well staged, the modest dimensions of the stage in this theatre actually contributing to the atmosphere. This was no extravagant occasion in a magnificent ballroom as one usually sees it in great theatres, where it is difficult to single out either Lensky or Onegin, but a hop in a rural landowner's home, with a dining room and a large table spread for tea and refreshments in the foreground. The dancing was going on behind in the hall, seen upstage, while the quarrel between Lensky and Onegin took place downstage beside the tea table, which brought it into sharp relief. In the duel scene the size of the stage precluded both participants being on the stage: only Lensky was in view while Onegin was out of sight in the wings. Thanks to this the whole duel was presented, so to say, as experienced by Lensky. The last act ball was courtly and refined but restrained, as if to underline the aloof formality of high society. I was fascinated to watch the artists in this theatre who were, as is proper for Soviet artists, mostly young, impersonating the burnished sheen of pre-Revolutionary manners at the court of Nicholas I, which were of course completely outside their own experience. Several of the aristocratic young ladies were conspicuously Jewish in appearance,[1] as incidentally was Lunacharsky's brother, to whom we were introduced in the backstage cafeteria where we were invited for tea in the interval.

20 March

We had a visit in the morning from Shura Sezhenskaya, my second cousin, who had so displeased Ptashka on their first acquaintance. But today she appeared in a more favourable light. Her son is a member of the Komsomol.[2] As if in response to our surprise at this information, she said, 'Well, what of it? When children in the old days used to be crammed with the catechism at school, it didn't necessarily mean that they became very religious. It's just the same now: when they have atheism stuffed down their throats they don't necessarily become anti-religious. Political education in schools today is just as boring a slog as the catechism was in the schools of Tsarist times. On the other hand, by joining the Komsomol my son will have a better chance in life.'

In the afternoon I gave my final concert in Moscow, with the Persimfans Orchestra in the Hall of Columns. The hall was full and the atmosphere one of a gala. In the programme was the *Classical* Symphony, which Persimfans performed more note-perfectly than Saradzhev had managed, although rhythmically slightly unsteady, followed by the Second Piano Concerto, and to end with the *Scythian Suite*. Aware that this was my last appearance, the audience bade me farewell with a mighty triumphant roar.

Rykov, the head of the Government, was at the concert. He heard the first half of the programme, and when he was leaving through the artists' entrance, Tsukker introduced us. Rykov is a small man with an intellectual's little goatee beard and rotting teeth. 'How have you liked being here with us?' he enquired. 'My visit here has been one of the most powerful experiences of my life,' I replied. In responding thus I avoided categorical praise

---

1 And hence obviously anachronistic, as Jews were barred from aristocratic society in Tsarist times.
2 The Communist Youth Union (Kommunisticheskii Soyuz Molodyezhi).

of Bolshevism while employing flattering terminology to convey an impression of great approval. Rykov smiled and hurried on with a pleased expression.

Meyerhold's red fez was easily distinguishable among the audience. 'You see,' he explained, 'in the spring I get nervous and so have my hair cut very short. But as it is still quite cold, I have to wear a fez.'

The Green Room was full of people: Mme Litvinova with her children, Myaskovsky, Asafyev, Belyayev, Yavorsky, Protopopov (who brought flowers for Ptashka but was immediately hurried out by Yavorsky so that he shouldn't chat too much to the ladies), Saradzhev, Oborin, who bears a striking resemblance to Dukelsky, and others. Blumenfeld[1] also put in an appearance: fifteen years ago he was said to be dying of paralysis[2] but although he walks with a limp and his tongue has difficulty articulating the words, he is as vital as ever and his eyes lit up when I introduced him to Ptashka. I stressed to Saradzhev that the premiere of the *Classical* Symphony belonged to him, and presented him with the tie I had been wearing on that occasion. I made sure Nadya Rayevskaya met Meyerhold and entrusted to him the responsibility for pursuing Shurik's release from prison.

The concert over, we called in briefly at the hotel and then went with Tse-Tse to dine at the Prechistenki restaurant. It was cold, and I was tired after the Concerto. Several taxis were waiting on the square, but none of them wanted to take us. Tsukker, an ultra-orthodox Revolutionary Guardsman, got very angry and only with difficulty succeeded in persuading one of them. When we arrived at the restaurant and I wanted to pay, he screeched, 'No, no, today this is on me. You go on, don't wait for me.' It was obvious that he had been forced to accept a non-metered tariff but did not want to admit it.

I had planned to go with Ptashka to *Turandot*[3] at the theatre, but I was exhausted after so many people and so many spectacles, and so sent Ptashka off with Nadya while I went to see Myaskovsky. Asafyev, who had come back

---

1   Felix Blumenfeld (1863–1931), legendary pianist, conductor and composer, uncle of Heinrich Neuhaus and Karol Szymanowski. As a conductor at the Mariinsky Theatre he had undertaken the premieres of Rimsky-Korsakov's *Invisible City of Kitezh* and the Russian premiere of Wagner's *Tristan und Isolde*, as well as the Paris production of *Boris Godunov* with which Diaghilev had ignited Paris's passion for Russian music. In 1905 he had joined forces with Rimsky, Glazunov, Lyadov and the student body protesting against the Tsarist government's Directorate of the Conservatoire, leading to the strike and temporary closure by the authorities of the institution. Pianists who passed through his hands include Vladimir Horowitz, Heinrich Neuhaus, Maria Yudina, Simon Barere and Maria Grinberg. See *Diaries*, vol. 1, pp. 368, and *passim*; vol. 2, p. 109.
2   His long periods of ill-health are said to be the result of syphilis, contracted in his youth.
3   Not Puccini's unfinished opera but a production of Carlo Gozzi's 1762 *commedia dell'arte* play at the Vakhtangov Theatre Studio.

to Moscow for a short stay, joined us and it was so pleasant to be able to sit and talk, free from any pressure. I took from Myaskovsky two bulky packages containing my old diaries, which I had decided to risk taking out of the country with me. Asafyev also handed over, at his own request, a voluminous bound notebook with piano pieces from my earliest years. Then all three of us walked through the quiet side streets to Derzhanovsky's, where by custom people gather on Sunday evenings.

Among the guests was the Austrian pianist Wührer,[1] who is shortly due to play several concerts in Moscow, including in his programmes quite a number of new sonatas by Russian composers. On Derzhanovsky's terrible old piano he gave a really rather good account of Myaskovky's Fourth Sonata, although playing from the score.

It was not too late when I got back, carrying my heavy packages through the deserted, icy streets because as bad luck would have it there were no cabs. Ptashka returned, delighted with *Turandot*. Budyonny[2] had been at the performance and was the cynosure of all eyes.

21 March

With the end of my concerts a pre-departure feeling descended. Someone arrived from Persimfans with our foreign passports. They had been ready for some time, so it was a good thing I had applied for them almost as soon as I arrived in the USSR. I also got my German visa and had to wend my weary way across town to what seemed like the ends of the earth to the Polish Consulate to get a transit visa. Tsukker had been vehemently opposed to my going through Poland, which was a hostile country. In any case, he averred, the Poles would not give me a visa, and he recommended going through Riga. But if I could go through Poland I would save a day, so heedless of his hysterical jeremiad I went anyhow. They were in fact perfectly civil at the

---

1 Friedrich Wührer (1900–1975), Austrian pianist who left a large recorded legacy, mainly of the core Austrian/German Romantic literature, notably Schubert. He was, however, a committed advocate of new music, associated with Pfitzner, Reger and Schoenberg, and founded the Viennese branch of the ISCM (International Society for Contemporary Music).
2 Marshal of the Soviet Union Semyon Budyonny (1883–1973), a close ally of Stalin and implacable opponent of the innovative ideas of Mikhail Tukhachevsky, branding him a 'wrecker' for advocating the creation of an independent tank corps at Tukhachevsky's show trial in 1936. In July–September 1941, Budyonny was Commander-in-Chief of the Soviet armed forces facing the German invasion of Ukraine. Operating under strict orders from Stalin not to retreat under any circumstances, Budyonny's forces were encircled, a disaster that cost the Soviet Union 1.5 million men killed or taken prisoner. It was one of the greatest routs in military history; Stalin placed the blame on Budyonny and demoted him in favour of the more capable Semyon Timoshenko, but otherwise did not punish him, allowing him to retire after the war as a Hero of the Soviet Union.

Polish Consulate, took our passports and asked me to come back the following day.

While I was on this mission Ptashka went with Tsukker to Gostorg where through some special dispensation he had managed to extract from the cold store a good squirrel fur coat at a 10 per cent discount. The best furs are earmarked for export abroad, the inferior ones for the home market, and Tsukker's special arrangement consisted in being allowed to select from the foreign export stock.

The Chinese revolutionaries have taken Shanghai. Tsukker was beside himself with excitement and was shouting about it in the street, which embarrassed Ptashka no little.[1]

Ptashka and I had lunch on our own together, and then went to Gostorg to pay for the chosen squirrel fur.

Asafyev called in during the afternoon. He was in low spirits, because he was being sent on business to Vienna but with so little money he would barely be able to survive. At first he had not wanted to go at all, but then changed his mind, being ready to pay some of the expenses from his own pocket, but then there were difficulties over his passport, so the whole thing is turning into a mess.

At half past six a car was sent for me to go to the Art Theatre as I had promised to play for them. They had invited me yesterday, and even asked how much I would like to be paid, but I replied that it would be a pleasure for me to play for the Art Theatre and I would take no fee. We were welcomed most cordially by Stanislavsky, Knipper-Chekhova[2] and Luzhsky.[3] Stanislavsky was especially outgoing: learning that Ptashka was a singer and had loved his opera studio, he immediately invited her to join the company, saying, 'That's splendid. Come to Moscow and appear with us.'

After I had played and acknowledged the applause I was presented with a wonderful bouquet of white lilacs. Clutching them to my bosom we went to Aunt Katya's, to whom I gave part of the bouquet, and then on to the Derzhanovskys, where had gathered Asafyev, Myaskovsky and Saradzhev. As we were leaving, I wanted to take at least some of the flowers, but this upset Lyolya, who exclaimed, 'How selfish he is! He gets a thousand roubles a concert, yet doesn't want to leave us his flowers!'

---

1 On 21 March 1927 the Chinese General Labour Union put into operation carefully laid plans for a combined general strike and insurrection, led by a trained and armed militia of 5,000. Chiang Kai-shek's Nationalist forces of the Kuomintang were standing by, but were not needed as by the evening the workers were in control of the city.
2 Moscow Art Theatre actress and widow of Anton Chekhov.
3 Vasily Luzhsky (1869–1931), actor and director, one of the founder members of the Moscow Art Theatre.

22 March

The pre-departure scramble continued, with another journey across the city to the Polish Consulate, where I was handed my visa with no hindrances. On my way back I bought the train tickets. No sooner had I returned when Tsukker was on the telephone. Somewhat crudely I teased him with my account of how easy and pleasant it had been to obtain my visa about which he, Tsukker, had made such a drama. Tsukker is a vain man and took offence, but let him, I thought, these aggressive heroes of the revolution really annoy me and the shifty way he prevaricated over ameliorating Shurik's position finally damned him in my eyes.

While we were packing during the afternoon Asafyev came in to say goodbye on his way to the Nikolayevsky Station to go back to Leningrad. As I had two overcoats I palmed one off on him. Then Lyolya came to help Ptashka sew the squirrel furs together so that they would look like a fur wrap and not just pieces of fur. She stayed doing this until nine o'clock. We smoked a great number of Russian cigarettes, which after the ones one gets in Europe I very much like, although Russian connoisseurs are scornful about the tobacco used today. I had in my pocket the notebook of my visit to Italy in 1915, which I had got back from Myaskovsky, and laughed as I read the passages describing my arguments with Diaghilev when he was commissioning *Chout* from me.

The telephone rang. A call from the Comintern. As a matter of fact I was not certain exactly who was calling me, but the lengthy title with which he announced himself included the word Comintern, and any communication from that organisation must be treated with caution. The gist of the matter was, would I please appear this very evening in a concert hastily arranged to celebrate the capture of Shanghai? The very last thing I wanted to do was to appear at such an event, but I would have to be extremely careful how I phrased my refusal. I decided on a counterattack.

'Excuse me, I should like to know who is organising this event for you? Do you really think to invite an artist to appear in public is an appropriate course of action a few minutes before the concert begins? My performance would not be properly prepared; I simply cannot participate in such an important event without notice. Please excuse me on this occasion, and inform your organisers that future such events should be arranged on a more serious level, in which case I shall be at your service.' Quite safe, since tomorrow we leave for Paris.

At ten o'clock Ptashka and I went to have dinner at the Europa Hotel. It was the first time we had dined there in the evening although we had several times had lunches there, and we discovered that at dinner times they have a stage on which are performed entertainments (not very interesting ones).

We seated ourselves as far away as possible. As we were finishing the meal Tseitlin joined us to go through the accounts for my performances with the Persimfans Orchestra. The outcome was quite a disappointment; there is considerably less money than I expected to be transferred abroad, but I have been drawing quite a lot of expenses for living, the hotel, travel and so on – it dribbles away imperceptibly.

23 March

This was the day of our departure, and it coincided with Borovsky's arrival from abroad to begin his tour. He also was staying at the Metropole, further along our corridor. When I went to his room Tsukker was putting together the programme for his first recital, which was to include some of my works. Because of yesterday Tsukker was cool towards me. What an idiot. Borovsky looked slightly stunned; arriving back in Russia had had a powerful effect on him and he was obviously worried about whether he was about to face success or failure, not to mention what the Bolsheviks' attitude to him would be: might they arrest him? Although it was difficult to imagine how they could: he had taken the precaution of becoming a Latvian citizen.

Tseitlin called in and we went together to the Central Customs Office, the reason being that it is illegal to take manuscripts out of Russia without specific authorisation. This is in fact a perfectly good regulation that protects Russian libraries from being ransacked. But I knew that I had my old diaries, a stack of letters I had received during my stay, as well as music manuscripts, the vocal score of *The Gambler* stamped with 'Property of the Imperial Theatres', and other things. It was a question I had raised some time ago with Tsukker and Tseitlin, but in the good old Russian way they had put off doing anything about it until the last possible moment.

We were received courteously in the Customs Office and directed to the railway station, where my manuscripts were to be sealed by order of the Customs authorities. The packages were so heavy we could hardly carry them. In the Customs department of the station a female official riffled two fingers through the briefcases containing the letters, and then directed everything to be sealed, a very satisfactory outcome to the whole business. Just as well she did not read any of the diaries, because just at that point I remembered certain expressions in them that would definitely have been regarded as counter-revolutionary.

When all this was done Tseitlin and I went back again with our sealed packages, while he regaled me with the history of Persimfans, an institution several Communists have told him is the only truly Communist organisation to be found anywhere in the USSR. Tseitlin himself is not a fit man and his wife is also unwell. Elections are due to the board of directors of the orchestra, and there is considerable confusion in the ranks. He suffers from curvature of the spine and the doctors have put him into a plaster corset, but after two days trying to wear it Tseitlin threw it away and continues his activities without it.

While we were out doing this Nina Koshetz's mother had come to our room and persuaded Ptashka to take with her a bracelet and brooch for her daughter. Ptashka said nothing to me about this, but later I found out that she was trembling with fright all the time until we crossed the border.

We had lunch with Borovsky in the Prechistenki restaurant, where he consumed the Russian dishes with evident relish. Afterwards we went to bid farewell to Aunt Katya and then rushed back to finish the packing. Ptashka found time to buy herself a brocade dressing-gown and a brooch. Back in the hotel there was still the final commotion to go through. Katya and Nadya came to help, but were more of a hindrance. Try as we might Katya could not be persuaded away from packing the things we were leaving behind for her as presents. To make matters worse, men arrived to take away the piano. In short we barely made it in time to get to the station, accompanied by Tseitlin. Tsukker had given up by then and did not come. I gave Tseitlin my remaining ten-rouble notes and asked him if he could to transfer them to my account abroad.

The train was due to leave a few minutes after five o'clock. Besides Katya and Nadya, staggering under the load of presents they had received, there were Myaskovsky, the three Derzhanovskys, Tseitlin and the singer Derzhinskaya. Our train, in contrast to the one in which we had arrived, was extremely smart with several International Company sleeping-cars, a restaurant-car – the full complement for an international journey. All our well-wishers cast envious eyes on us, knowing that in two or three days' time we would be in Paris. Myaskovsky brought some boxes of sweets. That morning I had presented him with several ties, shirts and other elegant articles of toilet, knowing his weakness for such things.

The train moved off. It was a marvellous, clear March day, the rays of the setting sun slanting low in the sky.

24 March

Next morning, first Russian and then Polish Customs. Once my sealed packages had been passed I could break the seals and transfer the contents into my trunk. The Customs official knew who I was, and slapping the trunk with his hand, asked jovially: 'What have you got in here, then? Oranges?' He explained that when he was on leave he had gone to Leningrad where he had hoped to see a performance of *Three Oranges*, but for some reason had not managed to do so.

At the Polish border we changed to an International carriage through to Paris, as bright and clean as a new pin. One could have been forgiven for thinking that the foreigners were flaunting their style on purpose to show up the relative shabbiness of the Russian carriages.

Warsaw in the evening and quite a long time to wait there, during which we went to dinner with Mme Grossman. Warsaw has smartened itself up greatly in the past few years, and from being a distinctly provincial city is beginning to look like a European capital.

25 March

Next morning we were in Berlin, where whether we wanted to or not we had to spend time obtaining a Belgian transit visa as there is no Belgian Consulate in Russia. We saw Weber again, also Tanya Rayevskaya and Sasha, who frankly does not shine. In the Hotel Fürstenhof we ran into Sasha Tcherepnin and his wife. The sight of this young boy and his rich, elderly woman made me gnash my teeth with rage. Sashenka has been playing concerts with a cellist including, as he was quick to inform me, my *Ballade*. 'Well, I expect you played it as badly as you did in Paris,' I said, leaving Sasha rather stunned. I urged Ptashka to hurry up and finish her conversation with Louisita, reminding her ostentatiously that we were in a hurry to have dinner and had no time to stop and chat. We soon parted, Ptashka remonstrating with me for my behaviour, but I simply said that I could not bear to see them together. After dinner with Tanya, Sasha and Weber in a large but, as it proved, somewhat seedy café, we left in the evening for Paris on the ruinously expensive Nord-Express.

26 March

At nine o'clock our Nord-Express drew into Liège, where there was a lengthy hiatus (how stupid to be immobilised for such a long time after hurtling along at breakneck speed). Andryusha and Germaine[1] came to meet us and took us to their house for coffee. They have rather a nice Renault which Andryusha drives himself. The Brichants have moved to a splendid new house; things are evidently going well for them. Paris at half past three, met by Paichadze and Grogy,[2] who had somewhat unimpressively not bothered

---

1 André (Andryusha) Brichant, the son of Prokofiev's second cousin Sonya, who had married a Belgian, and his wife Germaine. See *Diaries*, vol. 2, pp. 488, 494–5, 506–9, 513, 532, 538.
2 Popa-Gorchakov.

to shave. Also he had failed to reserve hotel rooms for us although I had both written and cabled to him about this. I lost my temper and gave him a real row. What sort of secretary is he? Paichadze agreed that he needed taking in hand. Nevertheless, we got a nice room in the Victoria Palace. We were very tired. Ptashka would have liked to go to see Svyatoslav straight away, but then decided to wait until tomorrow. We talked to him on the telephone, and he babbled away enchantingly.

Diaghilev rang at seven o'clock, having learnt from Paichadze of my arrival and found out my phone number. He knew of my success in Russia, congratulated me and wanted to see me straight away to talk over things as he was going to Monte Carlo in a few days. I said that we were going to our friends the Samoilenkos that evening and the easiest thing would be if he came there. Although he does not know them, it would be in no way beneath his dignity to come to their house them since Stravinsky, Dukelsky and Larionov are all frequent visitors. Diaghilev wanted to know if there was a quiet corner in which we could talk, and being assured that there was, said he would come. News of my Russian successes must have made a great impact on him for him to ring me up and agree to come to the house of someone he does not know in order to talk to me. It was very nice at the Samoilenkos. Needless to say they inundated me with questions and were fascinated by the Moscow chocolates I had brought them. Diaghilev, however, did not show up: Nouvel telephoned to say that he had developed a boil on his chest.

27 March–3 April

The most urgent tasks on returning to Paris were to find a furnished flat in which to live until the summer, and to buy a car. I did experience some feelings of unease at buying a car: I was proposing to spend the money I had earned from starving, poverty-stricken Russia on a car, just like that. But there was at least a half-decent explanation: I had begun haggling over the potential purchase of a car even before going to Russia, and not with Russian money either, but with American dollars. And if I was now in an easier position financially to buy one, it was because the Russian money I had earned made it more possible to spend American dollars on a car without too much soul-searching. Not, perhaps, completely convincing, but still.

For both of these enterprises all roads led to, and intersected at, Benois. He had been telling us that in April he would be going back to Russia (so why couldn't we have his apartment?), and his son-in-law Braslavsky was an expert in the automobile business and therefore would be a source of good advice.

After visiting the Villa d'Avray to see Svyatoslav, who was blooming and had evidently had a wonderful time surviving our absence staying with a Scientist family, I made my way to Benois. Alexander Nikolayevich was as charming as ever, with a thousand questions about Russia, but he is not after all going there and so the question of his apartment does not arise. He had not seen Braslavsky for several weeks and did not know his telephone number.

Dined in the evening with Diaghilev and talked about my ballet, about the imminent arrival of Yakulov and about my going to Monte Carlo for discussions with Massine,[1] to whom Diaghilev has assigned the production of *Ursignol*. I am pleased about this, as Balanchivadze had struck me as over-erotic and therefore effete. My new ballet is, in short, now firmly set up on all four legs. I took along with me to the dinner the notebook I had brought back with me from Moscow, in the suitcase Myaskovsky had carefully preserved for me, containing my diary of the trip to Italy in 1915 when I went to see Diaghilev about *Ala and Lolli*[2] and *Chout*. Now, in between two dishes, I read out some choice passages with descriptions of Diaghilev and our conversations. Nouvel and Kokhno found these very funny, I giggled more than anyone, but Diaghilev looked cross and said, 'Quite right, I'm glad I said what I did, it was fully justified and I would say the same today.'

We soon tracked down Braslavsky and drove round the main automobile dealers with him: Renault, Peugeot, Donné, Fiat. There was a very nice 10-horse-power Fiat tourer, expensive even though the price of Fiats has

---

1   Léonide Massine [Leonid Myasin] (1896–1979). Hand-picked by the jilted Diaghilev to replace the 'traitor' Nijinsky, he became the premier danseur and choreographer of the Ballets Russes, remaining so – except for a three-year interregnum from 1921 occasioned by Diaghilev's fury at his marriage to Vera Savina – until the impresario's death in 1929, and thereafter in the company's reincarnation as the Ballet Russe de Monte Carlo. Important creations of Massine for the Ballets Russes both as dancer and choreographer besides *Le Pas d'acier* include Falla's *The Three-Cornered Hat*, Rossini–Respighi's *La Boutique fantasque*, Offenbach's *Gâité Parisienne* and Rimsky-Korsakov's *Capriccio espagnol*. Had it not been for his three-year banishment he would also no doubt have staged *Chout* in 1921. See *Diaries*, vol. 1, pp. 705, 757; vol. 2, pp. 21, 25–8, 506, 509, 517, 527, 541, 590, 595, 597.
2   The ballet originally commissioned by Diaghilev and rejected on this Italian visit of 1915, to be replaced by the Russian folk-inspired tale of the Buffoon, *Chout*. Diaghilev's criticisms were that the music lacked authentic Russian flavour and was a provincial attempt at amorphously international Modernism. 'Your Petrograd has no concept of valuing anything truly Russian: it is a swamp from which you must extricate yourself, otherwise it will simply swallow you up.' Prokofiev, while ready to accept the ballet's shortcomings, nevertheless extracted and reworked the music of four of its scenes to make the *Scythian Suite*. See *Diaries*, vol. 2, pp. 22–4, 52.

fallen considerably due to the fall in the value of the franc. Observing that we were interested in Fiats but were put off by the price, Braslavsky suggested we look at some second-hand models which he knew of and could recommend.

We put off doing this until the following day, and in the meantime I went to see Bashkirov, who has been bombarding me with letters, waiting for me at my hotel and generally making every effort to see me. I found him, needless to say, in bed because he drives his taxi all night and sleeps during the day. He was most alarmed at my intention to purchase a car, saying that under no circumstances should I do this through Braslavsky, of whom he had heard several stories, none of them particularly flattering. My guide should be none but Rudnev,[1] the owner of the taxi he, Bashkirov, drives at nights. Rudnev is a former instructor at the Imperial Flying Academy and formerly a very famous airman. Emigrating after the Revolution to Paris, he spent his last remaining money on a taxi which he uses during the day and hires out to Bashkirov for 50 francs at night. Because this vehicle represents basically his entire worldly goods, he takes care of it as the apple of his eye, polishes and repairs it himself, alert to the slightest noise or knocking from the engine. There is no greater expert on automobile construction than he. In addition, he is personally the most honest and serious person one can hope to meet.

These arguments seemed convincing to me, and the following day Rudnev – who indeed is a considerable person as well as being charming – and I went to inspect the second-hand Fiats Braslavsky had recommended. They proved to be junk, and when Lyolya[2] rang up Ptashka to enquire the result, Ptashka told her that 'Serge said they were more like washbasins than cars'. Lyolya, in amazement, asked her to repeat what she had just said, after which Braslavsky disappeared over the horizon in a cloud of dust.

Next, I saw in an advertisement a Delage for sale. It looked good – and what a make of car that is! Some time ago, at a time when the German currency had lost almost all its value, I was on a train travelling from Ettal to Paris when beside me in the compartment was an impeccably turned-out Viennese on his way to Paris to buy a Delage on behalf of his employer. In Austrian money at the time such a car would cost several millions, but his obdurate boss would have nothing but a Delage. 'You

---

1 Yevgeny Rudnev (1886–1945), famous Russian pioneer aviator, test pilot, war combatant and instructor, author of a well-known and convincingly entitled flying manual *Praktika polyotov na aeroplane* (*How to Fly an Aeroplane*) published in Moscow in 1915.
2 Alexander Benois's daughter Yelena, Braslavsky's wife.

know what I mean by a Delage, I suppose?' said this man to me in an offhand way. Although I had never heard of it, his tone of voice was such that I hastened to reply, 'Oh yes, of course. . .' From that time on I have venerated the marque, and now all of a sudden here was a chance for me actually to become the owner of a Delage![1] I dragged Ptashka and Rudnev along to look at it, but Rudnev judged that although not quite a wreck it was still not up to the mark, and when we went back to have a second look the car had been sold.

In the meantime B. N. had been spending all day scouring garages, and soon found an extremely elegant Panhard,[2] also a fine make, which had the additional attraction of the letters SLP emblazoned on its radiator, being my and Ptashka's combined initials. We tried it out in the Bois de Boulogne. The engine sang sweetly and the car drove very well, but the interior was somehow not very comfortable, rather hard and upright. We decided not to rush into anything but to go on looking for something better.

During these days Bashkirov and Rudnev had a good many lunches and dinners with us at our hotel, discussing all the while various makes of car, their respective qualities, and the chances of picking one up second-hand.

4 April

In the morning I went to the publishers to go through and correct with Conius the violin parts of the Second Symphony. Returning home I found Bashkirov there: he had come across a superb Ballot car, one of the best French makes, for 27,000 francs. New they cost, I am told, 85,000. I went to look at it with Rudnev

---

1 The Delage was certainly the epitome of fast, luxuriously built limousines and touring cars. Early 1928 might not have been the best time to look for a bargain, however, since the previous year the Delage Straight Eight racing car, driven by the celebrated Robert Benoist, having won outright all four European Grand Prix races, became Champion du Monde des Constructeurs to enormous publicity.

2 The Panhard, a fine and imaginative example of French automotive engineering, was properly named the Panhard et Levassor, after its two original designers. From 1925 onwards the engines were made with sleeve valves, a far more elegant and quieter (but unfortunately less efficient) solution to the all-important problem of controlling incoming fuel mixture and outgoing exhaust gases than the conventional poppet valve which bangs noisily up and down on to its seat in the cylinder head thousands of times a minute. Panhard ingeniously, if slightly inaccurately, promoted this system as 'valveless', and from then on proudly added two S's (standing for Sans Soupapes), one on either side, to the linked letters PL (Panhard Levassor) on the circular brass medallion all its cars carried in the middle of the radiator.

and took it for a test drive. It runs splendidly: 90 versts an hour without even thinking about it.[1] Rudnev (the expert) approves. It is comfortable to sit in. It looks marvellous from the outside. We decided to buy it, and put down a deposit of 3,000 francs. I can scarcely believe that I am now the owner of such a huge machine![2] But the fact is I have earned quite a lot of money recently. That evening Bashkirov, Rudnev and the Paichadzes dined with us at the hotel, and we celebrated the new acquisition with two bottles of champagne.

5 April

Finished the corrections to the transition section and announced to Paichadze that the Symphony was now ready for printing. But once again he is prevaricating: it will be an expensive job and will not bring in much income. I boiled over: this is simply intolerable. When are they going to publish my music without all these arguments! I said that the Symphony must immediately be sent for engraving, and that was my final word.

Went with Bashkirov to look at the car, which is being cleaned and polished and serviced. We dined with Koshetz; Marochka, aged fifteen but already looking like an eighteen-year-old, has learnt my Op. 32 Gavotte, and played it very well. Maria Viktorovna told me that Borovsky has summoned her to Moscow and she has agreed to go. Before we (Ptashka and I) had gone to Moscow she said she could not understand why we would even think of going to You-Ess-Ess-Are-ia, and that if Borovsky were to go she would wash her hands of it. But now she is all agog to go herself. I taxed her with this, to her no little embarrassment.

6 April

Ptashka is in a bad mood because she does not like B.N. and is annoyed that on account of the car business he has swum so vigorously back into our

---

1 As one verst is very slightly more than one kilometre – 1,0668 km, to be precise – the Ballot's maiden drive must therefore have touched 60 mph.
2 The Ballot was a relative newcomer to the French automotive world: Edouard Ballot began manufacturing cars only after the First World War. The marque was also quite short-lived, being taken over in 1931 by Hispano-Suiza, which allowed the firm to collapse a year later. As can be seen from photographs Prokofiev's car was a Ballot 2LTS, a four-cylinder two-litre model production model derived from Ballot's successful 2LS racing car, with single overhead camshaft and valves set at forty-five degrees, giving it a more lively performance than the more usual vertically aligned valves. None of this will have meant much to Sergey

world. But after all, he did find us an excellent car. After I had paid the rest of the money and completed all the formalities we (Bashkirov at the wheel) went to the publishers. There we collected Ptashka and Paichadze and went for a spin into the Bois. We found Grechaninov sitting on a bench, and took him for a drive with us. 'What's this,' he asked, 'the fruits of your trip to Russia?' 'No,' I replied, 'it was all sorted out before I went.'

After that Bashkirov and I went, just the two of us, to St Germain. The car drives superbly, but Bashkirov drove cautiously as he is not yet familiar with it, besides, I have not yet insured it. When I get back from Monte Carlo I shall have a few more supplementary driving lessons (as I have forgotten much of what I learnt) and shall then start driving independently. We put the car away in a Russian garage, one recommended by Rudnev. They were mightily impressed with it, valuing it at not a centime less than 40,000.

In the evening Ptashka and I went to a Wednesday Meeting at the Christian Science Church, the first time I had attended one. It was interesting and moving to hear the testimony of people who had been cured of their illnesses. I saw Miss Crain, who said she hoped I would visit her again soon.

7 April

Moved out of the hotel and into the apartment at 5, avenue Frémiet. This necessitated the packing up of all our things, occasioning much groaning from Ptashka. That done, we went to Sèvres to collect Svyatoslav. His hostess cried to see him go, but he was thrilled. The flat is very nice, the windows in two of the rooms overlook a garden on the far side of which is the Seine. I hastily packed my things and, commissioning Bashkirov to get the car painted, at half past seven in the evening left for Monte Carlo. I was going at Diaghilev's invitation to advise Massine on the tempi, and also to clarify the general line of the production, since he takes a very specific view of the subject. Diaghilev is paying my fare for a first-class couchette. I had expected the train, which was an extremely fast one, to be empty, since at this time there are more people leaving Monte Carlo than going to it, but it turned out to be packed. B.N. accompanied me to the station and gazed with envy at the train, consisting only of first-class carriages and bound for Monte Carlo, the kingdom of roulette and, in his eyes, a place of limitless possibilities.

Sergeyevich – although it will have to Rudnev – but he certainly relished the 'sweet song' of the engine. The Ballot might not have had quite the cachet of a Delage, but it was still a class conveyance.

8 April

My neighbours in the couchette were astir early in the morning and stopped me sleeping. I read the *Tales of Belkin*[1] in the 1830 edition, a copy of which Nouvel had asked me to take to Kokhno. I read them with great enjoyment, having completely forgotten them. Even so, Pushkin's world, especially in such things as 'The Shot', is now very far away from me.

At 12.30 Monte Carlo, and Kokhno to meet me at the station. I was installed in a modest hotel, the Ravel, with a view of the sea. Lunched with Diaghilev, but there was not much talk of *Ursignol*, it was almost as though it was not the reason for my having come. We then went to the rehearsal of *The Firebird*, which is being revived for the twentieth anniversary of the Diaghilev Ballet – and indeed of *The Firebird*, with new settings by Goncharova. They were not very interesting in the first scene, but very beautiful at the end. Stravinsky put in an appearance, having come over from Nice. The orchestra applauded him as he arrived, and he acknowledged their greeting with a wave of his hand. Me he congratulated on my successful visit to Russia, but in a rather insincere, bombastic manner.

After the rehearsal we went together to Menton in Stravinsky's car. He owns two, one of them a small, elderly Renault which has been newly repainted, the other a new and enormous Hotchkiss. The one we were travelling in was the first of these, but six people squashed into it: Stravinsky's elder son[2] drove with Stravinsky and Kokhno sitting beside him in the front, Rieti, Rieti's wife and me in the back. Going round a corner the son struck one of the car's wings on a wall and we could have overturned, which would have simultaneously put out of action quite a tally of composers. Stravinsky spent the remainder of the journey in a state of great anxiety, shouting: 'Watch out, Fedya, be careful – have you seen that goat?' In Menton we had tea (I paid), and then returned home. In the evening we were at the Diaghilev performance, where Stravinsky introduced me to his second son, Svyatoslav.

---

1 *The Tales of the Late Ivan Petrovich Belkin* is a collection of five short prose stories by Pushkin ('The Shot', 'The Snowstorm', 'The Undertaker', 'The Station Master', 'The Squire's Daughter') written in the autumn of 1830 when Pushkin was quarantined in his country estate at Boldino by a cholera epidemic. Pushkin contributes a fictitious preface explaining that all the stories were told to Belkin, a landowner who has recently died leaving the manuscript that forms the content of the book, by various acquaintances. 'The Shot' concerns an expert marksman who nevertheless cannot be provoked to engage in a duel even when insults he has received would appear to demand satisfaction. A dramatic revelation in the final paragraph reveals the reason. The stories are all little masterpieces of simple, unpretentious writing that nevertheless infuses the dexterous story-telling with great suggestive power.

2 Stravinsky and his first wife, Yekaterina (Katya) Nosenko, had four children: Fyodor (Theodore), born in 1907, Lyudmila born in 1908, Svyatoslav (Soulima) born in 1910, and Milena born in 1914.

I said, 'How sad that both our sons should include an ass in their names. The Stravinskys did not get the joke until I spelled it out letter by letter: o-s-l-a.¹ Stravinsky laughed wryly and left.

9 April

Met up with Massine in the morning, and sitting in front of the casino in the sunshine we discussed the staging of the ballet. The starting point was that Massine has ccompletely rejected the scenario Yakulov and I proposed. I did not raise any particular objections, because it was more important to settle a direction with Massine and stop any of his ideas actively conflicting with my music. He had with him a book of Rovinsky's² researches into Russian engravings (an astonishing number of which, by the way, seem to be indecent) from which he is proposing to quarry subjects for his choreography. I lunched with Diaghilev, but without Massine – relations between them are still strained.³ Then Diaghilev, Massine and I got together with Kopeikin, the future accompanist for the ballet, and I played the score through to them. Massine made suggestions, Diaghilev and I reacted with our comments. Generally, we planned quite a lot of the work. At the end Diaghilev and I had tea together and he tried to persuade me to add to the *Ursignol* music the overture I had written for Romanov's ballet. I declined to do this, and seeing that further discussion on this point was useless, Diaghilev changed the subject and asked me all about Russia, which he is very anxious to visit himself. I said that the main thing they would worry about in Russia, if he were to go there, was that he would siphon off their dancers. Accordingly, before going, he should declare with all due ceremony, perhaps even in writing, that he had no intention of doing so but was coming purely to look; if he would do that they would welcome him.

There was a performance in the evening, but it was all old repertoire, and dull.

10 April

Spent the morning again with Massine, talking about the ballet. At first it was hard to get much of a dialogue going, since for example my conception of the opening number had been an elemental wave of popular movement, while

---

1 A grammatical pun: the Russian for an ass or donkey is 'osel' – pronounced 'osyól' – but as Russian nouns including proper names decline, the accusative form is 'osla', the four letters of which appear in Svyat-osla-v.
2 Dmitry Rovinsky (1824–1895), collector and historian of lithographs, engravings, etchings and prints of all genres, whose collection numbering over 40,000 examples is now in the National Library of Russia in St Petersburg.
3 Because of the 'betrayal' of marriage to Vera Savina.

Massine's was of Baba-Yaga's fight with a crocodile (based on Rovinsky).¹ But then he said that of course there would be no actual Baba-Yaga, nor any crocodile, on stage; it was more a route to expressing the kind of elemental forces he wanted to represent. In the afternoon Diaghilev was busy with the next performance, and went away in the evening to Nice to discuss something or other with Stravinsky, which was a great pity since we could well have done with more time to talk over my ballet. But Diaghilev evidently trusts Massine and allows his creative instincts free reign. Massine suggested a new title: *Pas d'acier*, which I immediately translated (into Russian) as *The Steel Gallop*.² I liked the new name, but Diaghilev did not approve: '*Pas d'acier* sounds too much like *Puce d'acier*' (referring to Leskov's story 'The Flea').³

11 April

Diaghilev has been telling me about *Oedipus*, which he heard for the first time yesterday at Stravinsky's. The composer played, assisted by his two sons, one on his right and one on his left, and all three sang. Diaghilev is

---

1 Baba-Yaga is one of the best-known and most alarming characters in the cast list of Russian folk legends. A hag-like witch, she flies on a broomstick or a pestle, steals and cruelly enslaves naughty children, and lives in a hut supported on chicken-legs (cf. the fourteenth number in Musorgsky's *Pictures from an Exhibition*). Satisfyingly complex, even if always frightening she is not necessarily pure evil: in an alternative incarnation she is the Earth Mother, the awe-inspiring source of natural wisdom, obeyed by all the elements and animals. She can reveal the secrets of life and death, but only to those brave enough to ask. One of her encounters, with the crocodile – the guardian of the underworld – is the subject of a famous eighteenth-century *lubok*, the genre to which Rovinsky devoted his most extensive researches. The *lubok* was the popular folk-art woodcut sold at bazaars and market places, usually illustrating religious, historical and social themes but often satirising political and military events, Peter the Great and Ivan the Terrible being popular targets. According to Rovinsky, 'Baba-Yaga Rides Off to Fight the Crocodile' is an Old Believer satire on Peter the Great's religious reforms. The Old Believers' nickname for Peter was 'The Crocodile', and Baba-Yaga wears Estonian costume – Peter's wife Catherine being of Estonian extraction. The *lubok* has a little verse underneath that reads: 'Yaga-Baba rides to fight the Crocodile, with a pestle, on a swine/Under a bush they have a glass of wine.'
2 This ballet has not been lucky with its name. *Ursignol* was probably too clever an in-joke, but Massine's suggestion suffers from obscurity as well as being virtually untranslatable. Prokofiev's instantly conceived Russian version, which indeed became the ballet's title in Soviet Russia, is *Stal'noy Skok*, but there is a specific indication of velocity in 'skok' – the word for a horse's gallop – which the usual English title, *The Steel Step*, fails to convey. But at least the English is a fair approximation of Massine's French, whatever that is supposed to mean. A 'pas' does, of course, carry more of a balletic overtone than a 'step', because of the primacy of the French language in ballet terminology.
3 Leskov's story is actually called 'Levsha' ('The Left-hander') and concerns a craftsman of exceptional virtuosity from the city of Tula, famous for the quality of its metalworking, in particular the manufacture of ordnance. The left-handed craftsman is commissioned by Tsar Nicholas I to outdo the fabulous workmanship of an English-made metal flea brought back to Russia from his travels in Europe by his assassinated brother Alexander I. The metal flea is so tiny it can be seen only through a magnifying glass, but it contains a clockwork mechanism by which it can be made to dance. 'Puce' is French for 'flea'.

wildly enthusiastic, but evidently did not like everything about it – it is very long and not at all scenic. Diaghilev suggests producing it initially in concert format, not in a staged version.¹

Then he informed me that since I was so opposed to giving him the overture I had written for Romanov's ballet, if I would change my mind he would in return let me have the Russian rights for *Le Pas d'acier* as from January 1928, should Lunacharsky show interest in making an offer for it. I agreed. Today '*Pas d'acier*' today struck me as sounding like '*Pas d'argent*',² but it is still better than Diaghilev's notion of *The Dragon-fly and The Ant*.

At three o'clock I left Monte Carlo to return to Paris.

12 April

Return to Paris.

This evening saw the first performance in France of my Quintet. They did not play as well as in Moscow; it was tentative and lacking fire. But among musicians it was a success: Marnold, Poulenc, Prunières and others considered the Quintet one of my best pieces.

12 April–5 May

The flat at No. 5, avenue Frémiet is very attractive and comfortable. Grogy, as Svyatoslav calls Gorchakov,³ is also installed in it. I worked until lunchtime, in the space of four days orchestrated an additional number for Diaghilev and then buckled down to finishing off Act Five. By the 5th May it had made real progress and I could see the end in sight. In general I was plunging wholesale into *Fiery Angel*.

---

1 According to Boris Kokhno, Diaghilev was anything but enthusiastic. Stravinsky had needed some persuading to write a new theatre piece for Diaghilev's jubilee, and had refused all entreaties to divulge what it was he was working on, saying only that it was to be a 'surprise'. 'For months Diaghilev waited impatiently for Stravinsky to finish his work, and then, one day in Monte Carlo, he received a message inviting him to come to Nice, where Stravinsky was living at the time, to hear the new score. I saw Diaghilev leave Monte Carlo one morning, radiant and smiling, and return from Nice in the evening troubled and perplexed. Stravinsky's surprise was *Oedipus Rex*, an opera oratorio in two acts, written in Latin; scenically it was a static work, having no relation whatever to the dance.' (B. Kokhno, *Diaghilev and the Ballets Russes*, trans. Adrienne Foulke, Harper & Row, New York, 1970). Cocteau's original libretto was written in French and then translated into Latin. Stravinsky had first considered setting the text in Ancient Greek, but decided instead on a medium 'not dead but turned to stone', with the important part of the narrator (Cocteau himself in the premiere production in Paris on 30 May 1927) directed to be spoken in the language of the country in which the performance was taking place.
2 A French pun: 'pas' can mean either a 'step', or 'negative', while 'argent' is 'silver' or more commonly, by extension 'money'. 'Pas d'argent' therefore means 'no money'.
3 Gorchakov's first name was Gyorgy.

My time after midday I generally consecrated to the car. B.N. undertook to be my teacher. I was sure I would have forgotten everything I had learnt at Christmastime, but as soon as I started driving again it was not too bad and on the second day, under the guidance of B.N., I already drove out of the city. Soon we began to make excursions into the surrounding country, taking friends and acquaintances with us in turn: Maria Viktorovna, Paichadze, Samoilenko, etc. On the 23rd April, my birthday, we made a major trip with Samoilenko to Orléans and even further to the château de Chambord, whence the last Bourbon had missed his chance to claim the throne.[1] We spent the night in a hotel in the grounds of the château, and the next day visited Blois before returning to Paris in the evening. B.N. and I took it in turns to drive, and while I was at the wheel I touched 75 kilometres an hour. The Samoilenkos were enchanting companions. The only shadow over these expeditions was that Ptashka cannot bear Bashkirov, and this was the cause of several family rows.

At the end of April I ventured out on my own, which caused a series of minor accidents: I crumpled one of the mudguards coming out of the garage, and crashed into the back of a car belonging to the Turkish Embassy, which had slowed down too quickly in front of me. Some teeth also got torn out of the gears in the back axle as a result of a bump sustained when I started jerkily. This last resulted in four days of repairs at a cost of 1,500 francs, not to mention a certain demoralisation and timidity when I took to the wheel again. But generally the car enabled me to keep in contact with the spring, as almost every day I got out into the fields and woods, and this was a source of great joy to me.

6 May

Had to go to Magdeburg to play a concert. I was reluctant to go, but it was too awkward to refuse. I had been hoping there would be a problem with visas, but they came through and I left at 8.20 this morning. In Aachen there was a wait of four hours from four o'clock until eight o'clock until my next

---

1 Henri Charles Ferdinand Marie Dieudonné, comte de Chambord, was the last surviving Bourbon claimant to the French throne, and after the failure of the Second Empire and the renunciation in 1873 by the rival Orléans branch of the family of their claims he actually seemed to have some prospect of success. Chambord's obduracy in insisting on the Bourbon *fleur-de-lys* in preference to the tricolour, however, lost him so much popularity that the National Assembly preferred to establish a temporary Third Republic until Chambord died, at which point the field would be clear for the more pliant Philippe d'Orléans, comte de Paris. But Chambord did not die until 1883, and by that time the French had decided they no longer wanted anything to do with a monarchy.

train, so I bought a map and walked out of the town to the surrounding parks. It was a wonderful spring day and I walked the whole time, thinking out some details of the libretto.

At eight o'clock I was allocated a sleeper berth and continued my journey.

7 May

Arrived in Magdeburg at seven in the morning. Since the rehearsal was not due to start until twelve, as soon as I had washed and changed I again went off to stroll in the parks. When it is wonderful spring weather and all the trees are blossoming, such walks are pure delight.

At twelve I presented myself at the rehearsal. Beck, the conductor, is my age. I had met him when I was in Berlin for the production of *Oranges* there. He is an active campaigner for new music here, in opposition to the routine provincialism of Magdeburg.[1] When the rehearsal was over I remembered that before leaving Paris I had had a letter from Weber telling me about a forthcoming premiere at the Berlin Staatsoper of a ballet based on the *Scythian Suite*. I asked Beck to telephone Weber – was it, perhaps, today? Indeed it was. I therefore made haste to get to Berlin, which is two hours away by express. Weber had two stalls seats, so no one in the theatre administration knew I was there. *Scythian Suite* (the score not altered in any way) was on after two boring numbers. For the *Scythians* the choreographer Terpis had elected to dredge up some scenes from Dante complete with demonic forces, tormented souls and an angel sent to relieve them from their sufferings. The result was neither good nor bad, but less awful than I had been expecting. Fusing Dante together with the Scythians did, however, strike me as an exercise in dubious taste. The piece was moderately well received; as it was the last item on the programme the public made a dash for the cloakroom. I did not put in an appearance backstage, and went to have supper with Weber in a café.

8 May

Having stayed overnight in the Fürstenhof, I got up at seven to go back to Magdeburg. There a public rehearsal had been scheduled, but not many people were present; the hall was less than half full. The reason was that it was the end of the season, a fine Sunday, and people preferred to go out of town.

---

1 Walter Beck (1890–1960) was appointed Kapellmeister in Magdeburg in 1924 as a radical new broom in succession to the previous incumbent Dr Walter Rabl, whose near-obsession with Wagner, Bruckner and Mahler had for example presented the Magdeburgers with no fewer than twenty-one performances of *Parsifal* between April 1920 and June 1921.

It went well, however, and was a success – four calls back to the stage. In the afternoon Beck and I also felt we would like to go out of town, and went for a long walk of fifteen kilometres, coming back on the Elbe by steamer. It was a splendid walk, but rather stuffy on the boat. We spent the evening with friends of Beck, an artist and his wife, kind, unpretentious and cultivated people.

Yesterday I had asked Weber why I was receiving from the Berlin Staatsoper only 1.5 per cent of the take. Weber explained that the Staatsoper paid 3 per cent but Terpis had taken half of that. This was a large slice to have grabbed for himself, but those were the only terms on which he was prepared to put the ballet on. Not bad. All the same, Weber was right to act as he did and to meet the extortioner halfway, because it is no bad thing either for me or for the publishers to have a piece of mine in the Staatsoper repertoire, even if they pay so little that it makes hardly any difference how large or small a percentage they give me.

9 May

Wrote postcards, bought my return train ticket, caught up on my diary and, so as not to lose time, had my tooth attended to. Concerts here start at 7.30 in the evening. I played better than I had the day before, although Beck's conducting was sometimes late. There was quite a lively response from the audience, and Beck and I had to come out to take a bow several times. I was presented with a bunch of tulips from the ladies yesterday: 'Better red flowers than blue hands.' From the concert hall I went back to my hotel, changed, packed, had something to eat and then at ten o'clock left for Paris, seen off by Beck and the two ladies, the artist's wife and her sister. It was terribly stuffy in the sleeping-car and I had great difficulty getting off to sleep.

10 May

Changed trains in Frankfurt in the morning, and arrived in Paris in the evening. In my absence B.N. had been to see Ptashka several times, buttering her up, having lunch and finally asking for 200 francs but only on condition Ptashka would not tell me. Her response was: 'It's no good you asking me not to say anything – the money is Seryozha's, so whyever should I take it without telling him?' And, indeed, it was a rather low trick to play.

14 May

We set off in the car to look for a dacha: Ptashka, Grogy and I. We took Grogy along just in case, although in fact he did nothing during the whole trip except bowl along with us and acquire a nice tan. It was a splendid journey. By evening we had reached Loches, an ancient castle and town where we stopped for the night. I slept like the dead, despite having at times reached 75 k.p.h. and frequently gone for long stretches at between 60 and 70, so that our average speed, even allowing for stops, was about 43 k.p.h.

15 May

Continued our journey as far as St André-de-Cubzac, where we stayed the night.

16 May

Passed through Bordeaux, a noisy, crowded town and very awkward for motorists, and carried on along a marvellous, smooth road to Arcachon. Pine forests lined the road on either side. Here we set about finding a dacha to rent, not in Arcachon itself, a rackety, expensive and decadent sort of place, but in the country round about. We failed to find anything appealing, however, and headed north, skirting the bay.[1] We stopped for the night at Andernos, a quiet and attractive little town on the other side of the bay.

19 May

Eventually we found a dacha at St Palais-sur-mer, near Royan, that had everything we wanted: spacious, no neighbours and right on the sea. It had already been let to somebody, but the prospective tenant had reneged and we succeeded in reaching both him and the owner of the property, at different ends of the country, by telephone, and signed the agreement there and then. At five o'clock we set off back on the return journey to Paris, getting to Poitiers at eleven o'clock at night to get a bed for the night. This leg of the journey had not been without its difficulties: the road was dreadful and we had to use our not very bright headlamps to see where we were going.

20 May

We travelled at great speed, up to 88 k.p.h. The only hold-up was between Versailles and Paris, where the whole road was choked with cars. We got

---

1 The Bay of Arcachon, known simply as 'le bassin', is a geomorphological oddity: a large lagoon almost enclosed on the ocean side by the largest sand dune in Europe, the dune du Pilat, and whose waters derive from a mixture not only of sea but a great number of inland fresh waterways. Among other benefits are the ideal conditions for oysters, harvested in great numbers and renowned for their texture and flavour. Andernos-les-bains is on the north-east shore of the bassin.

home at seven o'clock in the evening, sunburnt, dusty and tired. The final tally for the trip: 1,688 kilometres in seven days. Baby boy was fine. There was a mass of letters and telegrams. The Moscow premiere of *Oranges* took place yesterday. The Princess de Bassiano sent me a cheque for 2,000 francs for my recital at their house last year. My first thought was to return it, because all I had done was play for them semi-officially after lunch one day, but then I decided to use the money to pay for an official invitation to Asafyev to come from Russia, and the cost of his fare.

21 May

A stack of cables from Moscow congratulating me on the latest success of *Oranges*.

Went to the theatre where Diaghilev was supervising the fit-up of the scenery. Yakulov had returned to Paris but Diaghilev had seen very little of him because Yakulov was apparently in a permanent drunken stupor, although his explanation for his state was that he was in the throes of a bout of malaria. Even so, it was through Yakulov's efforts that a lunch had been arranged for Diaghilev and Lunacharsky, which was attended also by Yakulov, Lunacharsky's wife and Larionov. Not without a hint of satisfaction Diaghilev's account of this lunch went as follows: 'At first I listened politely to what he had to say, but his discourse never departed from the style of a pre-Revolutionary member of the liberal intelligentsia.' Lunacharsky had launched an attack on the decadent West, but Diaghilev retorted that this was such old hat: a Soviet *Narkompros*[1] really should be seeking out talents as one hunts for mushrooms in the forest – one day there will be saffron milk-caps under one tree, tomorrow white mushrooms[2] under another. So the West is not necessarily to be written off as decadent, talents can spring up here as there, and can take different forms.

Lunacharsky was positively obsequious to Diaghilev, and at the end of the discussion his wife summed it up by saying that had she been a blind person listening to it, she would certainly have concluded that Diaghilev was the Soviet minister and Lunacharsky the representative of bourgeois culture. But there was one thing Lunacharsky said that utterly reduced Diaghilev to silence, and this was when he announced, 'You know, we recently scored an enormous triumph for Russian art in Vienna. I took an exhibition there of

---

1 Lunacharsky's portfolio in Lenin's first Bolshevik Government, which he was to continue to hold until 1929, was that of 'Narodny Kommissar Prosveshcheniya' – 'People's Commissar for Enlightenment'.
2 To a Russian the 'white mushroom' is not just any old white mushroom but an especially prized example.

old icons, and this exhibition created the most tremendous impact.' 'When I heard this statement from the lips of a Soviet minister and official atheist,' said Diaghilev, 'I truly did not know where to put myself!'

In the afternoon I attended the first concert of Koussevitzky's season. The programme included a really beautiful Suite in F major by Roussel, of whose music I can hardly say I am generally overfond. But this time the first movement was extremely good, the second and third movements less so. It was followed by a perfectly appalling new piece by Milhaud,[1] in which the composer took part, playing the trivial solo piano part. His wife was sitting with us and on this occasion, uncharacteristically, was not too disagreeable since she was genuinely nervous for her husband. In the evening we dined at the Fairbanks, charming Americans who are Christian Scientists.

22 May

Attended the Christian Science Church in the morning. When I got home the Bassianos' car was already waiting for us. A most pleasant (and delicious) lunch, Suvchinsky there, and the hostess seated me beside her. In the course of thanking her for the cheque she had sent me, I explained my intention of putting it to use for Asafyev's visit. 'But only on condition that you bring him to us.' I promised. The *Principessa* is a charming woman.

After lunch everyone goes into the drawing room to drink Turkish coffee (which is very delicious). Here there took place the following hilarious conversation:

Countess Wolpe, addressing her enquiry to Ptashka: 'Is it your husband who has written an opera about a parrot?'

Ptashka's embarrassment is noticed by Bassiano, who with a sheepish smile corrects the Countess: 'Perhaps you are referring to Stravinsky's opera *Le rossignol*?'

The Countess: 'No, no, it wasn't a nightingale, it was another kind of bird . . .'

It turned out she meant Rimsky's *The Golden Cockerel*.

On the way back from Bassiano I called in at the Koussevitzkys, where I found Stravinsky. We had tea together and talked cars. He could not wait to tell me that Andrey Rimsky-Korsakov, who had previously always reviled his music, was now writing that he, Stravinsky, was the leading and nonpareil

---

1 *Le Carnaval d'Aix*, a twelve-number fantasy for piano and orchestra consisting of a series of dances and characteristic genre pieces. The eleventh number is an attractive tango entitled 'Souvenir de Rio'. Milhaud himself was a native of Aix-en-Provence so this offering was by way of a salute to his home town.

composer in the world when he writes Russian music, but when he turns to the international style he, Andrey, does not understand him. How is it, I ask myself, that Stravinsky feels he has the right to speak this way in my presence? Nevertheless, we kissed very tenderly as we parted, although Stravinsky outstayed his welcome shamelessly and thus prevented me from going through my Overture with Koussevitzky in anticipation of its forthcoming performance.

23 May

Played through *The Queen of Spades*. I do not like this work much. If you except individual passages of great brilliance (but surely that can be no basis for a proper evaluation?) the remainder is written too hastily and indifferently, as if dashed off, and too much of it lacks any real point.

24 May

Yakulov lunched with us. Lunacharsky is still in Paris; he and Rakovsky are very interested in *Le Pas d'acier*. Yakulov thinks it would be a good idea for me to ring Lunacharsky, but my inclination is to stay out of sight, although to be sure, if I am to make any further visits to Russia I probably should telephone him. On the subject of Dranishnikov Yakulov had put in a word to Lunarcharsky, who said he did not believe it would be appropriate to ask Ekskuzovich since evidently *Oranges* (in the Mariinsky production) will be touring several countries and it would be awkward to anticipate the decision about Dranishnikov. But presumably these countries do not include France?

Gave the score of the Second Symphony to be engraved. At last, after so many trials and tribulations!

25 May

Massine rehearsal. The ballet company has arrived from Barcelona, bringing with them enormous scenery structures created by Yakulov half as high again as a man standing. The dancers eye them cautiously with sidelong glances. Massine has devised some interesting machine-like movements.

I still managed to do some work on *Fiery Angel* in the afternoon, squeezing the last drops out of Act Five.

Had a meeting at five o'clock with the man who does the tracing for the engraving, and explained some details of what is required.

In the evening, another Massine rehearsal, which by coincidence was taking place in the same hall where Romanov rehearsed his ballet some time ago.

26 May

Rehearsals with Massine and then with Koussevitzky for the *Overture*. A terrible symphony by Tansman, aptly characterised by Suvchinsky as 'a shop full of stolen goods'. In the afternoon, the general rehearsal for the opening performance of Diaghilev's season.

Sauguet's ballet: faux simplicity, very boring. Oh for some real liveliness![1] Berners's *Neptune* was more interesting, but once again stylised; these people simply know nothing about how to compose music! Stravinsky conducted *Firebird* himself and did it very well. The whole set-up for the rehearsal was in itself interesting, Diaghilev such a personality, and a mass of celebrities: Picasso (very nice), Cocteau, Les Six, etc.

In the evening I went to Orlov's[2] concert – my Sonata No. 3, a bit too fast and lightweight, but technically more assured than I am.

27 May

Koussevitsky rehearsal. I am not entirely happy with the way the Overture is going, but it is better than it was in Moscow. In the afternoon, worked on *Fiery Angel* and really got the fifth act by the throat. Diaghilev first night in the evening, a great crush of people, we barely got in – and it was not worth the effort. *Neptune* was all right, but Sauguet's piece was awful, although the Constructivist sets – depicting an operating theatre[3] were not bad. *Firebird* very nice indeed, as Stravinsky always is after the kind of trash Diaghilev seems to like serving up these days. There are never any really strong numbers; that is why it is all so amorphous and flabby. Spessivtseva has broken her leg, and Danilova danced the role unrehearsed.

28 May

The Koussevitzky concert. The Overture was the first item, but to my amazement it scored a success and provoked calls for the composer, to which at first I paid no heed, believing them to be merely a claque of my friends, so it

---

1 *La Chatte*, to a libretto by Kokhno (using the pseudonym Sobeka) based on the Aesop fable, *The Cat-maiden*, with ingeniously feline choreography by Balanchine and a consciously simplistic score, tailored to Diaghilev's demand for a 'pretext for dancing' to showcase Spessivtseva (who was injured and as Prokofiev notes did not in fact dance the first performance) and Lifar.
2 Nikolay Orlov (1892–1964), pianist. A pupil of Konstantin Igumnov, he left the USSR in 1922 and had a successful career in the West as a specialist in Chopin. See *Diaries*, vol. 1, p. 325; vol. 2, p. 236.
3 By Naum Gabo and Antoine Pevsner. The scenery was built of transparent materials that reflected a brilliant kaleidoscope of light.

was some time before I took a bow. Dreadful symphony by Tansman. Then Tailleferre's concertino, quite pleasant but with two bars lifted note for note from Rachmaninoff with the same melodic coutour. So that's the fruit of ten years' work by Les Six. I told her about it; she was covered in confusion and said she would make changes to it. Had a talk to Milhaud; he said many nice things which somewhat embarrassed me: 'Very nice of you to say so ...' Milhaud: 'Let's be honest with one another, we're neither of us particularly nice people,' so all the more flattering. Much praise for the Overture from the French musicians.

After the Spessivtseva débacle there is yet another catastrophe for Diaghilev: the truck with the *Romeo and Juliet* settings has gone missing en route from Barcelona.[1]

29 May

Managed to do a little more orchestration. Christian Science Church, then to Bassiano in Falla's car along with Mompou.[2] Ehrhardt[3] was there also, and we talked about the possibility of *Fiery Angel* or *The Gambler* for Dresden.

At Koussevitzky's, Tailleferre also there. Koussevitzky asked guardedly my views on Tansman, and proposed that I make a version of the Overture for full orchestra. He and Natalya Konstantinovna were both very loving. In the evening to Polignac's, a colossal gathering with a lot of people outside on the street. The hostess guided us to seats in the front row for *Oedipus*, Ptashka next to Zéro,[4] a most appropriate name in all respects. I assisted Stravinsky. The chorus sometimes lost its way. As I was thus quite occupied, I found it hard to judge, but there is no doubt it is a strong and solid piece of work. It would have been all the better without the excessively deliberate attributes plucked out of ye olde antique shoppe. I should like to see what happens with his next work, and the one after that, in which no doubt there will be even more rigorous purifications. Poulenc was completely nonplussed. Rouché about an opera based on Rostand.

30 May

In the morning I went to the general rehearsal of *Oedipe*. This time it seemed tediously long, apart from which the orchestration is glum to the point of

---

1 The ballet by Constant Lambert. See above pp. 312–13, n. 3.
2 Federico Mompou (1893–1987), Catalan composer, mainly of miniatures, who studied in Paris. Prokofiev had met him during his concert tour of Spain in February 1923. See *Diaries*, vol. 2, p. 708.
3 Otto Ehrhardt (1888–1963), a leading stage director at the Dresden Opera.
4 Unidentified.

ludicrousness. Désormière came to see me in the afternoon and I played him *Le Pas d'acier*. Mme Cuin rang to pursue yesterday's conversation with Rouché. 'We are all' – meaning herself, her husband, Rostand's widow and presumably Rouché – 'tremendous admirers of you'. I begged to delay consideration until after the 7th.

31 May

No rehearsals today. I wanted to go out for a drive, but the car is still being painted. I asked the painter to come and see me, as he has twice failed to keep his word, but then I felt sorry for him, he is no doubt a former officer now spattered all over with paint while there I was in my smart pale yellow gloves. But his calamitous situation is no excuse for not keeping his promise!

Ploughed on with orchestrating *Fiery Angel* and almost finished Act Five: all that remains is the final six bars, about which I am not sure.

Savich called to go through the Suite from *Oranges* which, unfortunately, he is due to perform at the same time as the premiere of *Le Pas d'acier*. In the evening a recital by Koshetz, rather uninspiring.

1 June

In the morning a piano rehearsal and in the afternoon the first read-through with orchestra. It took three hours to get through twenty minutes of music. Everything sounded good but there was much cursing and muttering. I got very tired and my head ached.

2 June

Koussevitzky rehearsal in the morning – the *Classical* Symphony, followed by Myaskovsky. After lunch I went to the general rehearsal of Satie's *Mercure*.[1] The circumstances of such rehearsals are always interesting: the lighting, the orchestra, the dancers, nothing ready, lots of shrieking and running about. Only Picasso, responsible for the designs, preserved what can only be described as an Olympian detachment, as he does generally in life and amid the infighting that distinguishes current artistic trends.The music is worthless, but there is something appealing in the settings, the men's costumes particularly nice as they are presented with breasts.

---

1   This ballet was not originally a Ballets Russes commission; its first production was by Etienne de Beaumont's Soirées de Paris company in 1924. Diaghilev's production had designs by Picasso, choreography by Massine and starred Massine and Vera Petrova.

Dukelsky came to dine and asserted that Stravinsky is finished; all that remains is mass hypnosis. He believes the time has come to explode the myth by publishing an article proposing the mummification of Stravinsky.

In the evening a great gathering at Prunières': Ravel, Falla, Honegger, Koussevitzky, Rubinstein. Koussevitzky and Rubinstein, foaming at the mouth, tore into both *Oedipe* and Stravinsky's abominable conducting.

3 June

Spent the morning at Koussevitzky's rehearsal of the *Classical* Symphony, then on to Massine's rehearsal. He has the whole troupe assembled now and is visibly nervous because it has not yet all come together. This was followed at two o'clock by a second orchestral rehearsal. Stravinsky came, sat where he could look at the score and praised the ninth number, which was what was being rehearsed. The orchestra is exhausted, hardly has the strength to play. Désormière was angry with them. After the break, the rehearsal continued as a stage-orchestra rehearsal. Inevitably it was a shambles and a madhouse, Diaghilev, Massine, Désormière, everyone shouting at the tops of their voices. I tried to keep calm, taking a leaf from Picasso's book. Dukelsky dined with us again this evening and came with us to *Oedipe*, complaining about it all the time. True, it is boring, although there are splendid passages in it.

4 June

Another piano rehearsal, but in the theatre and on a bare stage. There are some things I don't agree with: generally Massine has quite unnecessarily departed from the scenario we originally agreed. In the afternoon Koussevitzky gave his concert, beginning with the *Classical*. It was well played, but the first two movements were too fast. I like the first movement to have a certain gravitas, while the second movement ought to be Larghetto[1] rather than Andantino or Allegretto. The performance was a great success and I took two bows. Stravinsky came, evidently on my account as he did not stay to listen to Tchaikovsky's Sixth Symphony or the other works on the programme.

After the concert I finally managed to have a drive in the car (after a two-week hiatus) but the paint job has not been well done. We drove out of the city accompanied by Dukelsky and the Paichadzes, and had dinner at the 'Hermitage' in the Forest of Meudon. It was my first time driving in Paris at night.

---

1   As marked.

5 June

Took the car to go to rehearsal, but it was cancelled as the company had been given a day off.

Dukelsky and the Englishman. I am disconcerted by the rudeness and do not want to go in the car, but Ptashka finds this awkward, this makes me angry. We get rid of the Englishman and drive to Poissy, but I am in a bad mood. In the evening, a gala dinner at the Koussevitzkys in honour of a lady from Boston: three composers and three beautiful women. Afterwards the young people danced and Koussevitzky as well.

6 June

A holiday, and so a good day for practising driving around Paris. At nine to the rehearsal with Savich; he is accustomed to inferior orchestras and does not know what a good one is capable of giving him. At ten, Diaghilev's rehearsal, the last one to piano accompaniment. Yakulov's sets have visibly made progress and are beginning to look very interesting. Diaghilev is especially pleased and never stops praising Yakulov. I spoke to Diaghilev about writing an article for the press, especially aimed at *Vozrozhdenie (Renaissance)*.[1] Diaghilev said that if such an article were to be written it would have to be done with the utmost delicacy, otherwise everyone would simply say that 'Diaghilev has been putting pressure on the editors' and so on.

Otherwise it was a free day, so Ptashka and I went to L'Isle-Adam, a charming and beautiful spot with a bathing beach on the river, but the Sunday crowds were unbearable.

7 June

Lighting rehearsal at eight o'clock in the morning. Diaghilev had been working until after three a.m. and Yakulov until seven, but Diaghilev was back by half past eight. I lunched at home and was back for the orchestra rehearsal at half past one followed by the stage-orchestra rehearsal at three. The orchestra played feebly: they had rehearsed with Koussevitzky all morning and had our performance to face in the evening. Désormière assured me that they would play well in the evening. How glad I am not to be conducting. The rehearsal went on until five, but then there will be two more

---

1 Conservative émigré newspaper published in Paris during the 1920s and 1930s.

hours of synchronising the scene changes and lighting cues to the music. I went home to dine and was back in the theatre for nine o'clock. Diaghilev missed dinner and did not have time either to change or to shave. Ptashka took pity on him and requested permission to kiss him, which was granted with every sign of pleasure. In our box were Koussevitzky, Suvchinsky, Paichadze and Dukelsky, a sustaining presence in the event of a flop. My amazement at the programme. Massine's choreography is strong and inventive at times, but at others worrying in its lack of sensitivity towards the score: its contrasting *forte* and *piano*, the ballet's counterpoint is there, but always in four or eight whereas I have moved away from four-square inflexibility. I was in effect seeing the first act for the first time. The orchestra played not badly, without especial flair. The conclusion of the first act represents a distinct raising of the emotional temperature, due in part to Massine, in part to Yakulov and in part to me, and this generated a success. I went out to bow, without hurrying in case there was any politically inspired booing, but there was none.[1] Four curtain calls, a real success. During the interval, a mass of congratulations: Prunières, Rubinstein[2] ('I am your devoted slave'), Tansman, Koussevitzky – but no Stravinsky. Towards the end of the interval Fatma Hanum produced champagne, gratefully consumed by Ptashka, Mme Paichadze and me. We returned to our seats as the second act began. Kokhno and Dukelsky related the argument they had got into with Cocteau ('We've seen all this before in music-hall.' 'No, on the contrary, it has nothing to do with music-hall and your attempt to drag that in has failed because the public obviously accepts it.') Dukelsky almost happy; I am embarrassed. I go up to Diaghilev, Cocteau appears again, the expression on his face as if asking for me to slap it, which I am almost tempted to do. Diaghilev drags him away. Paichadze and Suvchinsky protect us. Applause for Grigoriev,[3] appearance of Stravinsky, preparations for me to acknowledge applause from the stage. Afterwards, supper with Diaghilev, we drink to *Bruderschaft*[4] (for the third time).

1 Stephen D. Press reports that in anticipation, or perhaps hopes, of scandalous scenes, Diaghilev armed himself with a pistol and sat in the orchestra pit next to the first flute, ready to fire into the air at the first sign of protest. No doubt the sedate response of the audience was a disappointment. (S. Press, *Prokofiev's Ballets for Diaghilev*, Ashgate, Aldershot, 2006.)
2 Arthur.
3 Sergey (Serge) Grigoriev (1883–1968), the Ballets Russes's indispensable, indefatigable and omniscient Balletmaster, famous for his encyclopaedic knowledge of the entire Ballets Russes repertoire, which enabled him to continue rehearsing and reviving all the company's productions after Diaghilev's death for Col. De Basil's subsequent Ballet Russe de Monte Carlo and well into the 1950s for the Royal Ballet in London. See *Diaries*, vol. 2, p. 58.
4 See above, p. 3 n. 3.

8 June

Went to the rehearsal of Dukelsky's Sonata,[1] underlining passages diligently. It is an attractive piece, although with rough edges, as is common on a first reading. Dukelsky a little ill at ease. Took the car for a drive out of town in the afternoon. Second performance [of *Le Pas d'acier*] in the evening, less good than the first but a great success with the audience. I did not appear for a bow. We left straight after the show as we were very tired.

9 June

Reaction has set in, fatigue and a bad head.

The right-wing papers (Russian) are hostile, but not targeting me specifically. This is very good news. The Borovskys have returned from Moscow, Maria Viktorovna full of complaints. Borovsky played thirty-two concerts. Third performance in the evening. By tacit agreement neither I nor Désormière showed ourselves in the theatre, in order to avoid exposure to any kind of incident: I was in the wings until the start, thereafter in the box, and again at the end of the performance in the wings until the public left the theatre. There was a smaller audience today, but still a great success. Conversation with Massine about the Société des auteurs.[2] Mme Sert about the production.

Finished orchestrating Act Five [of *Fiery Angel*].

10 June

Koussevitzky rehearsal: *Sacre* in shreds, Dukelsky a bit better. In the afternoon the Schubert Waltzes with Romanov; he still intends to revive *Trapèze*.[3]

---

1 'In the early spring of 1927 I was again asked by Koussevitzky to play my concerto with him at one of the four Paris concerts he was planning that season. Having lost my faith in that work and knowing it to be too difficult for me, I suggested writing a short piece for piano and orchestra instead. The idea appealed to Koussevitzky and I began work, helping myself to some odds and ends, such as discarded *Zéphyr* material . . . My hastily contrived sonata for piano and orchestra (I didn't dare call it concertino) was announced by Koussevitzky and rehearsals were about to start . . . My so-called sonata was well enough liked by musicians . . . but it was, in reality, distinctly small beer. Koussevitzky thought the sonata meritorious, the critics were kind and I was told to complete the symphony, for which I stored away some rather promising thematic material.' (V. Duke, *Passport to Paris*, Little, Brown & Co., Boston and Toronto, 1955, pp. 193, 197, 199.)
2 Société des auteurs et compositeurs dramatiques (SACD, founded in 1777 by Beaumarchais (from entirely justifiable disgust at the pittance he was getting from the Comédie française for *The Barber of Seville*) to protect writers and composer of stage works.
3 See above, p. 220.

Another conversation with Massine in the Société des auteurs. This is all a mere matter of principle, since essentially we are talking about copecks. Samoilenko is ill. We have a free evening.

11 June

Koussevitzky concert. Roussel anaemic on second hearing. The Dukelsky piece is nice enough, but sounded better on the piano. Dukelsky's attire – the music almost invisible in the shade of the spectacular trousers. *Sacre* I listened to with great pleasure. Then a dreadful piece, Florent Schmitt's *Psalm*.[1] Tea with Paichadze, Borovsky, Volkovyssky.[2] Dukelsky's probing questions as to how he can extricate himself from his present position, in particular his relationship with Diaghilev. In the evening, the final performance of *Le Pas d'acier*, a better one this time and a very great success. I did not come out for a bow. Backstage I thanked Diaghilev, *Bruderschaft*, my dedication of the ballet to him ('Let this be the first expression of our "thou" relationship'). Encounter with Tcherepnin: 'Apparently you saw Sashenka[3] in Berlin? Well, au revoir, au revoir . . .' Dukelsky related the denouement of the spat with Cocteau.[4] Romanov: the Waltzes were wooden and the tempi terrible. Only moderate success. Awful arrangement of the March from *Oranges*.

---

1 *Psalm 47*, Op. 38 (1906) by Florent Schmitt, a gigantic post-Wagnerian cantata for soprano, organ, chorus and orchestra. The grandiose histrionics of its idiom would certainly have been as far from Prokofiev's taste as is possible to imagine.
2 Brother-in-law of Vera Janacopulos.
3 Nikolay Tcherepnin's son Alexander. See above, p. 571.
4 According to the account in *Passport in Paris* Cocteau continued to make an 'inflammatory, anti-Russian speech' in the theatre foyer. Dukelsky, having persuaded two émigré ex-officers from General Wrangel's White Army to act as his seconds, went round to Cocteau's house the following morning. When Cocteau appeared, Dukelsky slapped his face and said, '"Now will you accept my challenge?" The effect of my action was most unexpected: Cocteau grabbed me in his arms, embraced me and sang out: "Embrassons-nous, Dima, embrassons nous!" I disengaged myself with some difficulty and left, utterly nonplussed. A day later Diaghilev received a letter from Cocteau explaining his reasons for declining a duel with me and describing my "cowardly" visit to him. We haven't spoken since.' (V. Duke, op. cit., pp. 196–7.) In his letter, which was actually sent to Kokhno for transmission to Diaghilev, Cocteau writes: 'I very much regret having caused a disturbance on Serge's stage, but in view of Dima's ugly mug, his rose, his top hat and Louis XV cane, his denunciation of Parisian frivolity was hard to take . . . he shielded himself at the stage door by offering his arm to a lady [Mme Paichadze] . . . Do tell Serge how much I regret this incident . . . My views were of an aesthetic as well as of a moral order. I do reproach Massine for having turned something as great as the Russian Revolution into a cotillion-like spectacle within the intellectual grasp of ladies who pay six thousand francs for a box. I was not attacking the composer or the stage designer.'

12 June

Touched up Act Five. Grand reception at Koussevitzky's, with an array of delicious food and dancing. Dukelsky played foxtrots and made eyes at Mme Lazar,[1] then left to go for a drive round Paris with us.

13 June

Dinner with the insane Maxwell.[2] Titles, the Turkish Ambassador. Monte Carlo, lots of money, a Prokofiev Festival with *The Gambler*. The two names most on everyone's lips at the moment are Prokofiev and Lindbergh.[3] As Lindbergh will no doubt soon be forgotten, what does he matter? I am plotting to organise four boxes for Horowitz's concert filled entirely by people in full evening-dress and ball gowns. Very good, but still a disappointment; it could have been more profound and expansive.

Checking up on Bashkirov's cheque. Where did he get the money from? A bad end.

14 June

A mechanical instrument concert. Introduction lauds Stravinsky as the leading composer of the present, and possibly of all, time. Heart and soul in mechanical instruments. Stravinsky pumping his way through *The Firebird*, terribly dry, no pedal, and tempi quite different from when he conducted it.[4]

15 June

Horowitz evening at Polignac's. Rather boring.

---

1 The wife of the Romanian composer Filip Lazar (1894–1936).
2 George Maxwell, the American representative of Russian Musical Editions.
3 Charles Lindbergh (1902–1974), the American Air Mail pilot who less than a month earlier had flown his single-engined monoplane *Spirit of St Louis* from Long Island to Le Bourget airfield in Paris to become the first person to fly non-stop in either direction between New York and Paris (although this was not the first non-stop *transatlantic* flight, which had been achieved eight years earlier by Alcock and Brown in a Vickers Vimy flying from Newfoundland to Ireland, just over half the distance of Lindbergh's feat).
4 The performance will have been on the Pleyela player-piano. 'Normal practice at Pleyel seems to have been to fix everything to do with tempo and rhythm on the roll, leaving only dynamic nuance to the operator. And while, as Rex Lawson has pointed out, this will have fitted in with Stravinsky's increasingly severe view on interpretation in general, it may well have ruled out any idea of synchronising one or more Pleyelas with other instruments and voices, or indeed with each other.' S. Walsh, op. cit., p. 324. See also Lawson, 'Stravinsky and the Pianola', in J. Pasler (ed.), *Confronting Stravinsky*, University of California Press, Berkeley, 1986, pp. 284–301.

16 June

Carried on transcribing Act Five. Evening chez Mme Dubost, a million people there. *L'Éventail de Jeanne*.¹ Abominable, except for Ravel's contribution. The hostess: 'What did you think? I: 'There are some not bad moments.' My impression is that she was not terribly pleased by my response.

17 June

Took the Koussevitzkys for a drive. Lunch at Dampierre.² Koussevitzky delighted, child-like with everything, spluttering with enthusiasm over the car, nature, me, my music, and disparaging Stravinsky. He will not perform *Oedipus* in America. Called me the leading composer and recommended his tailor. 'I see, I see, if you turn the wheel to the right, the car goes to the right. It's quite simple.'

18 June

Rehearsal of the Quintet for Bassiano, much of it going with greater precision than formerly. The work is beginning to arouse interest; becoming, as I always intended, something for the discerning musician.

To Marnold's for the afternoon, where I played the Overture, Op. 42, and *Le Pas d'acier*. He and his friends were ecstatic. Marnold and Blois plan to start a new magazine, with a pro-Prokofiev agenda.

Telephoned Cain,³ high time I did so as the idea is of course interesting, although I know in advance that it will not lead anywhere as it is not really suitable.

19 June

To Bassiano's, driving in our own car. The Quintet was performed, decently except for a few gaffes although without much in the way of Russian elan.

---

1 See above, p. 42, n. 1.
2 Dampierre-en-Yvelines is a small village in the Île de France, dominated by a magnificent seventeenth-century château set in parklands laid out by Le Nôtre.
3 Henri Cain (1859–1937), dramatist, opera and ballet librettist. Late in life Cain succeeded in his dogged ambition to create operas from the plays of Edmond Rostand: in 1935 Ibert and Honegger collaborated in a version of *L'Aiglon* with Ibert responsible for Acts 1 and 5 and Honegger the middle three acts. It was produced in Monte Carlo in 1937. The year before, Franco Alfano (the same who selflessly completed Puccini's *Turandot*) wrote an opera to Cain's libretto drawn from *Cyrano de Bergerac*, produced in Rome and later in Paris in 1936. It was revived to unexpected success ('back from undeserved obscurity') by the Metropolitan Opera New York in 2005, with Plácido Domingo in the title role.

Praise came from Ravel (the instrumentation), Poulenc and others. We brought Auric and Poulenc back with us in the car.

To Samoilenko's – he is better, but his eyesight is suffering.

To Cain. A charming elderly man of the old school, his apartment a veritable museum. Very complimentary about me. He spoke of the legacy of Rostand. We arranged a read-through for tomorrow.

Ptashka and I are in a sulk because she is not ready to leave, while I am desperate to get to the dacha, which is ours from tomorrow.

20 June

Finished transcribing Act Five.

Visited Cain. Not inclined to proceed; I explain my reasons, pointing out several places where the libretto is not dramatically convincing. He is a very nice old man, and we part friends. The Collected Works [of Rostand] are now finished.

25 June

Ptashka took her driving exam, and came back weeping: she succeeded in upsetting the examiner over something or other and he immediately began criticising her, at which Ptashka got confused and drove badly, so failed to get the all-important *carte rose*. I therefore went alone to Versailles to the Bassianos for lunch (I like their company) and afterwards took Suvchinsky to Clamart.

Dined in the evening at the Koussevitzkys, who were exceptionally loving, as they have been throughout their stay this time. Sadly they are not going to Royan for the summer, as we thought we had convinced them to do, but to the mountains. Needless to say, the Lazars and the Tansmans are tagging along too. Natalya Konstantinovna is already in despair.

Stravinsky is in London in a great state of nerves, depressed by the failure of *Oedipus* in Paris. Someone asked him what he was going to compose next, to which he replied: 'At least there won't be any hammers in it' – a dig at *Le Pas*. But the hammers were not really my fault. My idea was that the sound of hammering should be heard coming from the wings, the precise timbre to be worked out during rehearsals. I even sent Diaghilev quite a detailed score to be performed by a selection of large and small hammers. But then everything turned to ashes: inevitably, having been forgotten about, it was remembered only during the very last rehearsals, when Diaghilev ordered the rhythm simply to be drummed into the dancers on stage – a crude and clumsy solution. So there had been a concept that could have been effective – but it was never realised.

26 June

A day of tidying up and packing. In the morning attended the Christian Science Church.

27 June

Leaving Gorchakov to finish up various minor matters and Gabrielle to clean and tidy the flat, we (that is, Ptashka, Svyatoslav and I) drove away at half past eleven en route for St Palais-sur-mer, near Royan. Besides ourselves, the car was weighed down with an enormous quantity of my music and papers, and Miss Olmsted was also with us for the ride. The weather was showery and at one point we ran straight into a flood, but we carried on, albeit not as fast as before. In addition to this I had begun a bad headache. Still, that day we got beyond Orléans as far as Amboise, where I went on strike because not only was my head aching, my left eye was watering so much I could hardly see to drive. Amboise is a delightful place on the banks of the Loire, with an old castle. Leonardo da Vinci is buried here. Miss Olmsted gave me a treatment and by evening I was feeling better.

We covered 224 kilometres that day, at an average speed (not counting stops) of 34.4 k.p.h.

28 June

My headache and my eye were both better. Miss Olmsted said, 'Once and for all, if God acts in a certain way, it should not be undone.' We set off again at 9.15 in the morning. At Tours Miss Olmsted left us to return to Paris by train. She is soon going to California and says that getting to know us was one of the best memories of her entire three-year stay in Europe. The car was going well and the weather stayed beautiful. We stopped for lunch at Poitiers. Svyatoslav behaved himself like a real grown-up. Towards evening the countryside began to assume a more southerly aspect, and at eight minutes past six we were in Royan, having covered 307 kilometres that day at an average speed of 48 k.p.h. At 6.17 the train from Paris arrived, bearing Gorchakov, Gabrielle and all our things. However, it emerged that he had not taken to Pleyel for safe-keeping the trunks we had left behind, and one trunk that he was supposed to have brought with him to Royan he had forgotten and left in the flat. I lost my temper and told him he must return immediately, at his own expense, to Paris to deal with the trunks. Grogy said he would do so, but then going to Ptashka to explain what had happened, burst into tears. Ptashka appealed to me at least not to send him back today; I yielded, and we set off for St Palais and our dacha, eight kilometres further on from Royan railway station. The dacha proved to be delectable, much better than we thought. It is very large, simply but attractively furnished, and spotlessly clean. The garden is also big and well tended. The sea is right in front of us. We retired to bed, without pillow-cases because they were in the trunk Grogy had forgotten. Decided not to send him back to Paris.

29 June

A beautiful morning with the scent of flowers mingling with the salty smell of the sea. This dacha is heavenly. One side of the house gives on to the garden, the other has a long balcony directly below which are the waves. Walking along it is like being on the deck of a ship.

In the morning we unpacked our belongings, after which Grogy settled down to washing the car and I to *Fiery Angel*. What remains to be done on *Fiery Angel* is the final scene of the first act and all of the second act, libretto and music. Today I transcribed from Bryusov the material I need for the scene with the fortune-teller with which Act One ends. In the afternoon I took the car into Royan and visited the Zakharovs. After a long time spent trying to ring them up I eventually discovered them in a tent on the beach. Chatted happily for a while, and decided that we would come over to them for dinner tomorrow.

In the evening I played through some of the chess games from the New York tournament.

30 June

Worked all morning on the libretto for the scene with the fortune-teller. In this connection I dug out the correspondence I had had with Demchinsky the previous summer and his proposal for the libretto. Mentally got angry with him for having taken so long over it and let me down by producing such a small and inadequate result. It could have been so much better, I think. And although when I wrote back to him I told him that I had adopted many valuable suggestions from him, this was because I was still hoping for more to come, because the fact is that all I derived from him were a few trifling things, at the most a spur towards more independent work on my own.

At one o'clock we were intending to go to the Zakharovs, but something had happened to the clutch in our car, and we had to walk in the heat into St Palais and there rent a car. The Zakharovs fed us a delicious Russian dinner and afterwards we sat on the sandy beach by the sea while the children splashed in and out of the water. However, a cold breeze was coming off the sea; the real summer is not yet upon us. Svyatoslav paddled enthusiastically barefoot, but then sat down in the water and soaked his trousers. We had to put another pair on him, but he did exactly the same thing with them. Having removed the second pair, we had no more to hand so had to wind one of Zakharov's handkerchiefs round him.

In the evening I again played through games from the New York tournament. I have let chess lapse recently, and returning to it is very enjoyable now.

1 July

Worked intensively on the libretto for Act Two, almost all day with breaks, and on the whole enjoyed it. I now feel distant from *Fiery Angel* and the effort to continue working on it is purely to have it over and done with. Even so, I succeeded in sketching out almost the whole of the first scene of the second act. I do not yet know if it is good, or whether it will need changes.

The car has been mended, and Ptashka and I toured the enchanting surrounding countryside. Not too far, however, as about every hour it came on to rain. It's July, and summer has still not seriously started. The sea also changes all the time, a very beautiful effect.

2 July

Again settled down to the libretto in the morning. Until the piano comes from Paris it is important to use the time to get on with the libretto for Act Two Scene Two. Selected a few extracts from Bryusov's scene with Agrippa with a view to fashioning a new scene (departing from Bryusov) between Rupprecht and Agrippa. By eleven o'clock I was tired, stopped work and took Grogy out for a drive into the forest. I have had a letter with bad news: the insurance company with whom the car is insured has gone out of business, so I am currently not insured. I must be extremely careful when I drive not to crash into anyone else – as if this is something I would not mind doing if I was insured!

Went into Royan in the afternoon and drank coffee with Boris.[1]

This is how I spend the evenings: reading articles from the Christian Science Journal and playing through New York tournament games.

3 July

Hoorah, glorious weather, beautiful, warm and aromatic. This is a heavenly place!

---

1   Zakharov.

Worked intensively and completed the libretto of Scene Two. In the afternoon took the car into Royan and brought back the whole Zakharov family: Boris and Celia and their daughter, and Frieda[1] with her five-year-old son. Frieda has separated from her husband and now lives with the Zakharovs. We walked along the beach, had dinner and drank fizzy drinks. At ten o'clock I took them home. It was a lovely, merry time. Zakharov is dazzled by our dacha. 'Something like this I'd buy like a shot,' he said.

Our Gabrielle took him for Celia's father and the children's grandfather. He does, it is true, look somewhat mangy and green about the gills (although dressed in style), but a grandfather – that is a bit much!

4 July

Looked through and ironed out the Act Two libretto. I think now it may do. Also the piano arrived – good timing, tomorrow I shall be able to get on with the music.

A letter from Myaskovsky. Evidently there has been no let-up in the envious mud-slinging from my success there.

Some good news: the currency conference has agreed to transfer $1,000 to me in payment for the publication of my works. I was afraid that one result of the friction that has recently arisen with Soviet Russia would be increased difficulties over transferring money abroad.

Memory is one of the most important attributes of immortality. If one imagines a man totally devoid of memory, he will not be able to understand immortality. And if we are doubtful about the truth of immortality, it is only because our former lives have been cut off from us through a failure of memory. And further, memory has the amazing capacity of being better able to preserve the good than the bad. For example, our childhood or youth seem so seductive to us because their unhappy aspects fade into oblivion while the happy ones remain (at the time we thought differently and looked to the future). Or another example: when we have quarrelled, after a time we are ready to make up because the hurt of the quarrel subsides while the blessings of the former friendship rise up again in the memory. Conclusion: memory is an attribute of the Divine, created for the purpose of gradually dissolving evil (unreality), on a similar principle to the divine creation of the world.

---

1 Elfrieda Hansen, Cecilia Hansen's pianist sister. Prokofiev had been seriously attracted to her when they were fellow students at the St Petersburg Conservatoire. See *Diaries*, vol. 1 *passim*.

5 July

Made a start on composing the music for the end of Act One. Got as far as the fortune-teller – a passage of no great significance. The composition, however, went without difficulty, although I shall have to go through again very thoroughly what I have composed. I played through the whole of the first act, and it pleased me. All the same, it really is time I finished with this work.

In the afternoon we went into Royan on various errands. Had coffee with the Zakharovs. He, being an incorrigible card-player, dragged me into the casino. He sat down at a chemin-de-fer table and promptly won 200 francs, but then lost 400. I found myself attracted, but chary of devoting so much time to the activity.

The middle of the table has several openings into which the croupier deposits the cards the house has won back and the percentage of winnings due to the government. The deftness with which the cards and chips were secreted into the inner pocket of the table was for me the most engaging part of the activity.

6 July

Worked for two hours in the morning. The music is well under way, but I am still not sure whether it is good or only all right.

It rained again today, which spoilt our intention to begin bathing.

7 July

Continued composing Act One, the fortune-teller.

8 July

Worked a lot. The rain poured down all day, but eased off towards evening and we took the car into Royan. Dined with the Zakharovs (Boris, inevitably, was 'at work' in the Casino when we arrived), returning home in the dark and in another downpour, which meant we had to drive the whole way at walking pace. During the night there was such a storm it shook the house.

A long, detailed and affectionate letter from Tseitlin, saying that discussions are already under way for my return visit next year.

9 July

Worked energetically; finished the first act and made a start on the second. It then transpired that the opening is pitched too low for the voice, and so I assigned to Gorchakov the task of transposing it. Outside the rain and storms continue; there is as yet no hint of summer. As a matter of fact the rain seems to be widespread all over the world: in England it has rained without stopping for three weeks and one lady in despair committed suicide by poisoning.

Good news: *Le Pas d'acier* was performed in London on 4th July with enormous, 'clamorous' success. The curtain rose and fell twelve times. All the newspapers are signalling the success, although the verdict of many of them is hostile, *The Steel Step* being called 'a noisy piece of nonsense'. But I had not expected it to have any success at all: my music is not liked in England and as if that were not enough the recent rift with the Bolshevik regime in Russia could, one would have thought, have led to protests against the choice of a Bolshevik subject. Indeed, before Diaghilev left for London I advised him not to present the ballet there. But look what happened . . .![1]

A very interesting interview[2] given by Diaghilev: he names this ballet as the most important he has ever presented, with the exception of *Les Noces*. So what about *Petrushka*? Or *Le Sacre*? If, despite all his love for Stravinsky, Diaghilev makes a statement like this, he must be aiming a bullet straight at Stravinsky for his renunciation of the genre of ballet, and for the opera he wrote for Diaghilev's twentieth jubilee.[3]

---

1   As Lynn Garafola has pointed out (L. Garafola, *Diaghilev's Ballets Russes*, OUP, New York, 1989) with the previous year's General Strike still fresh in the ruling class's minds it was hardly to be expected that the mainstream press would approve, especially taking into consideration the confusion generated by the incomprehensible narrative of the first act, largely the result of the amendments – to which the music had necessarily been tailored – made unilaterally by Massine to Prokofiev's and Yakulov's original scenario (see S. D. Press, op. cit., pp. 74–9 and 210–16, for a detailed account of the difference between original conception and the production as realised). 'Since we could not make out what it was driving at we are unable to judge the music' (*The Times*, 5 July 1927). But after the interval it was a different matter: 'Many will dislike it, it will be overpraised, but no one will be bored by it and, judging by the tempestuous reception it received last night, it will become a regular feature of the Russian Ballet programme,' wrote the *Daily Express* on the same day, while the conservative Cyril Beaumont, writing from the hindsight vantage point of 1940 (C. Beaumont, *The Diaghilev Ballet in London*, Putnam, London, 1940) is positively enthusiastic: 'So the rhythmic force ceaselessly grew in intensity until there appeared on a central platform two figures bearing giant hammers, which they swung and wielded more and more strongly until, at the height of the tumult, the climax was reached with the Constructivist elements adding their quota – signal discs snapping on and off, and wheels spinning faster and faster. At this point the curtain fell to the accompaniment of a frenzied burst of applause. The second part of this ballet made a considerable impression on me and renewed my admiration for Massine's rare ability to contrive movements appropriate both to the theme of the piece and to the rhythm of the music, and then to combine the component parts into one vast orchestration of sound and expressive action, ever increasing in intensity until the conclusion was attained.'
2   In the *Observer*, 3 July 1927, article headed 'The New Ballet'. Diaghilev explains that Prokofiev's musical language has become much simpler: 'He is full of melodies, and one part of *Le Pas d'acier* could have been composed by Mozart, if Mozart had lived at the present day.' Comparing his two 'sons', Stravinsky is described as being 'more tied to the gods', while Prokofiev is 'friendly with the devils'.
3   *Oedipus Rex*.

10 July

The weather has brightened up, and it was really sunny in the afternoon. Grogy went for a swim and was dashed by a wave against a rock. He came back covered in blood from eighteen scratches.

I continued with Act Two. Paichadze has written that Bruno Walter's position in Berlin has become uncertain, and furthermore that the general climate of opinion in Germany is turning against foreign operas, so I must prepare myself for more uncertainty over *Fiery Angel*. His advice is to press on as fast as possible, but news like this is hardly an incentive. Nevertheless, despite everything I am driving the second act forward. *Angel* must be liquidated, and only after this has been done can I turn my attention to musical sonnets, the new form I have been pondering in fits and starts since last summer.

In the evening I played through some chess games and read articles from Christian Science journals, which I like very much and which I find give me a great deal more than formal 'instruction'.

11 July

Blue sky and warm weather, but bathing still does not tempt as the water remains cold.

In the morning I composed, getting as far as the entry of Glock.

The afternoon passed peacefully with no particular incidents.

12 July

Today is the first day I have done no composition, but even so I managed something in Glock's part. Dictated a pile of letters to Grogy and posted them in Royan. Ptashka went shopping with Frieda, while Celia and I sat out in deckchairs on the beach and the children played round about and kept us entertained. Boris was nowhere to be seen: he stayed closeted at the card tables in the casino.

I am worried that the second act is turning out to be boring. Or is it simply that I am bored, composing it?

13 July

Finished Glock, but did no more after that as my head was beginning to hurt, so spent the afternoon walking and resting. Then, engrossed to the point of intoxication, read Dostoevsky's 'The Eternal Husband'[1] until my headache,

---

1 Novella first published in 1870.

which had begun to pass off, redoubled its effect. Read through again the draft of the libretto Demchinsky had sent me and which I had rejected. And rightly so, ponderous and dramatically tedious as it is. I simply cannot understand how the same man who earlier had given me such stimulating suggestions for the roulette scene in *The Gambler*, and in the presence of the author and Meyerhold had delivered such a brilliant critique of Remizov's *Alaley and Leila*,[1] could suddenly have sent me such a clumsy attempt!

14 July

Moved on beyond Glock's exit from the stage. I have been making use of old material and it is turning out well. In any event, Act Two today made real progress. In the afternoon, it being a national holiday in France,[2] we went to the Zakharovs and, the weather being fine, went swimming with them. However, besides the Prokofiev team only Elfrieda came in, Celia looked on and Boris, unable to restrain himself for long, escaped to the casino. Although it was a sunny day the water was cold and one had to force oneself to go in. Svyatoslav, seeing his Mama enter the water, burst into tears. Encouraged to follow suit, at first he was willing but as soon as the water reached his tummy he was immediately in floods of tears again and rushed out. Eventually he was carried aloft into the sea and then splashed, provoking a mixture of laughter and tears. We dined with the Zakharovs, drank champagne and played Lotto, and later in the evening watched the fireworks. Svyatoslav squealed in terror and later told Gabrielle how he had seen the sun explode in pieces.

15 July

Slept badly after the swimming. My composing was not such as to make me think it good, and I made use of material from other acts of the opera. Generally out of sorts and not much use for anything. Was annoyed by a letter from the insurance agent who seems incapable of arranging insurance for the car. Altogether I felt I was coming apart at the seams, which is shameful for a Christian Scientist.

---

1 In 1916 in St Petersburg Prokofiev had considered a libretto originally conceived as a ballet by Remizov as a possible subject for an opera, but had been talked out of it by Demchinsky backed up by Asafyev and Suvchinsky. See *Diaries*, vol. 2, pp. 144–5, 185, 197, 648.
2 La Fête Nationale, Bastille Day, *Le Quatorze juillet*, the anniversary of the storming of the Bastille fortress-prison on 14 July 1789.

16 July

Had good long sleep and feel better today. Did not compose for very long, but the time I spent was fruitful. The second act is progressing, not exactly slowly, but not as fast as I had insouciantly calculated.

The day was hot. We took the car into Royan for various errands and then bathed at home in St Palais, but the water was icy. Svyatoslav cried tearfully, 'That's enough!' when he was tugged into the water.

17 July

Composed, getting as far as the spiritualist séance. I must hurry up, it is really time to finish. Before lunch went out in the car and drove through the lovely fields and woods. In a wood I stopped the car and sat for a while lost in contemplation. In the afternoon Ptashka and I went to the lighthouse at Coubre. There is a restaurant there, surrounded by cars and holidaying people, but not far away along a side road we came to a heavenly stretch of open sea with a deserted sandy beach. We dreamed of coming back there to swim.

Read *Virgin Soil*, a libretto fashioned from Turgenev's novel by the writer Krasheninnikov[1] and given to me by him in Moscow as a proposed subject for an opera. After reading three scenes I still had not encountered any dramatic action. What a way to compose a scenario! But I'm told Krasheninnikov is an experienced writer.

My old diaries.

18 July

The world of God's creation is made as it is, and there is no other possible way of making it. What is evil? Let us see whether it is possible for the world to be constructed otherwise than as it is: for love of another one substitute love for oneself; for infinity finitude, and so on. The result is a new world, a finite one that harbours within its very finiteness its own dissolution. Why should this second world have been permitted to arise? Precisely so that through it mankind comes to understand that God's world has alone been

---

1 Nikolay Krasheninnikov (1878–1941), novelist, essayist and author of librettos based, besides Turgenev's novel, on Pushkin's *The Captain's Daughter* and Tolstoy's *War and Peace*. *Virgin Soil* was Turgenev's last and in most commentators' opinion most prophetic novel, published in 1877. It deals sympathetically with the attempts by idealistic students and intellectuals, the often derided *Narodniki*, to 'go to the people' with educational propaganda and plans to politicise the peasantry for action against the Tsarist regime.

created exactly as it has been and that in no particular could it have been created differently. Passing through evil to re-enter this first world, man is enabled more profoundly to understand the wisdom underlying the creation of the world of good. Of course the attempt to construct this other world, the world of evil and mortality, appears in the world of immortality as no more than a fleeting illusion, instantly to be forgotten. This is probably one reason why Christian Science considers evil to be illusory.

19 July

Yesterday I composed none of the spiritualist séance, but thought about how to tackle it. Not merely the character of the scene, the movement, the orchestration, but also the bar-by-bar dispositions, in a word everything except the music itself. Today I began to compose the music. I worked a great deal, in the morning and the afternoon, and in the early evening. While I was working out movements and harmonies, Ptashka said, 'That sounds a bit like Feinberg,' but of course at a slow tempo it is one thing, while at speed, and especially in the orchestral colours I have in mind, it will be quite another.

In we afternoon we bathed, but the water is still cold and going in is grisly at first. Svyatoslav sets up a howl as soon as there is any suggestion that he goes near the water.

Finished reading *Virgin Soil* in Krasheninnikov's version. Not interesting either as a libretto or as a play.

20 July

Sat all morning going over yesterday's work. It is an awful nuisance to do this, but I think the spiritualist séance is going to turn out a marvellous scene, and it is one I have always been nervous of.

Some letters from America. Haensel, as usual, has not managed to come up with a single decent engagement. Gottlieb, on the other hand, has surfaced with a guaranteed offer of a concert in Chicago. Ah! He will underwrite it with his own money! And then will trade on it for the rest of his life, as a platform to establish his credentials and experience in his professional world of insurance.

In the afternoon I drove into Royan to do various things. Dropped in to the Zakharovs to consult with Celia about the violin glissandos in the spiritualist séance, but they had gone out for a bicycle ride. When I got home, I found they had come to see us.

In the evening, I caught up on my diary and played through the Lasker–Capablanca match. Capablanca had presented me with the book of the match some years ago, with a dedication in Spanish 'to my friend Prokofiev'.

In Ettal B.N. and I had read through the moves, in awe of their magisterial economy.

21 July

Toiled further at the second segment and finished it. From the German publishers came the translation of the Act Five libretto with a request to check the translation immediately and return it, which I settled down to in the afternoon. Then for a change of scene drove round the vicinity with Ptashka. What a delectable, beautiful and welcoming corner of France this is! Incidentally, the car is now fully reinsured. 'Now you can write it off completely if you like,' writes Paichadze.

In the evening read the *Christian Science Monitor*, caught up on my diary, and played through some chess games. Ptashka, sitting opposite, was also engaged in her activities. I love our evenings together very much.

'The overcoming of the carnal mentality is a warfare that brings much satisfaction' (Christian Science).[1]

22 July

Completed the spiritualist séance, because I had stopped just before the end, and then finished the whole first scene. Hoorah! Scene Two and the transition thereto will be material from the original version and therefore I expect to be able to deal with it quickly. Composed more after lunch, and then played through Act Three from the lithographed copy sent to me by the publishers. I was pleased with it. It contains a great deal of music and is well done. Then went with Ptashka and Svyatoslav to drive round a bit. It is such lovely countryside!

23 July

No composing, but much thought about the entr'acte and the second scene. There will be virtually no new music here, so today I fitted the old material to the text which had been deliberately written to take account of the existing music. After lunch, drove into Royan and brought back the Zakharovs, four grown-ups and two children, to our dacha. We walked, drank coffee and played Lotto for five francs a card (so addicted are the Zakharovs to games of chance that they brought Lotto with them in order not to miss a day). We had dinner, drank two bottles of fizz, and then I drove them home.

---

1 In English in the text.

24 July

Worked a great deal; almost completed the entr'acte and the second scene in one breath. But then my brain became so fogged that I stopped work and did very little for the rest of the day. We would have liked to go for a drive, but one of the tyres was flat. The baby today said the word 'slyapa'. I tried to teach him to say 'shlyapa' but all he would say back was 'shlapa'.[1] Ptashka is frenetically pasting my reviews into the book. She is a long way behind in this task (about eighteen months) and has stockpiled a huge quantity of folders. First she has to sort them, then those that do not concern me have to be weeded out, and the remainder 'artistically' arranged on the page and glued in.

25 July

Thank God, the composition of *Angel* is at last finished.

After lunch we went into St Palais from where we telephoned to Bordeaux to the Compagnie Transatlantique to find out when the liner bringing Ptashka's parents from New York tomorrow is due to arrive. It transpired that the boat should dock at five o'clock in the morning, and the passengers will disembark at seven. Accordingly Ptashka and I were already on the road to Bordeaux at 4.40 p.m. to meet them. We covered the 130 versts most enjoyably at an average speed of 44.5 k.p.h. with stops of no more than five minutes altogether (we had a minor disagreement over the map, but this did not hold us up for long) and at 7.50 arrived in Bordeaux. When we had come through it in May, I had an impression of narrow streets thronged with cars and bicycles so that it was barely possible to squeeze through them, but now on a summer's evening the town was empty. Leaving our things (coats and toothbrushes) at the hotel we repaired to 'Le Chapon fin'[2] for dinner. Bordeaux has two famous restaurants: 'Le Chapon fin' and 'Le Chapeau rouge'. One of them is so excellent that Stravinsky made a special trip by car from Paris to savour the divine cuisine, but en route he developed a stomach ache and was unable to eat anything. The cooking at 'Le Chapon fin', in fact, turned out to be good but not earth-shattering, although when I asked for a good wine (Château Climent, Haut-Barzac, 1915, 25 francs a half-bottle) it proved so incredible we had never in our lives drunk anything like it. We did not drink much – half a bottle between two – but were more intoxicated

---

1 The word is 'shlyápa', meaning 'hat'.
2 'Le Chapon fin' at 5, rue Montesquieu, was established in 1825 and by the turn of the century had become something of a mecca for the refined gourmet, patronised by such as Toulouse-Lautrec and Sacha Guitry. In 1933 it was one of the first restaurants to receive a Michelin award and at the height of its fame it had three stars. It is still there, but a glance at internet reviews eighty-five years or so after Prokofiev's visit suggest it may have lost much of its former lustre.

that we had been for a long time. We went for a short stroll afterwards and then collapsed into bed, after all we had to be up early in the morning.

26 July

In St Palais we have so grown used to the quiet that here in Bordeaux our sleep was continually disturbed by one noisy interruption or another. We were called at six. It was a heavenly morning, we got up in good spirits and were on the jetty with the car by seven o'clock. It was not long before we spotted Mémé and Avi on the upper deck, but it took more than an hour and a half for them to disembark and come through Customs. Avi has aged, having been seriously unwell throughout the winter. Olga Vladislavovna is interested in Christian Science but has not fully accepted its teachings and still resorts to medication, albeit with some circumspection. We went off to drink coffee and then did some shopping until setting off at 11.18 for St Palais. It was very warm, but the car went well and the roads were good, if twisty. We travelled fast and achieved an average speed of 54.1 k.p.h. not counting stops. Pretty good – the best I have ever done! One stop, however, was a long one, on account of the pinion jamming in the starter motor. Adding to this a couple of short stops, we thus did not arrive at St Palais until three o'clock, hungry. I slept soundly during the afternoon, and then we went swimming in the still cold sea. In the evening Avi had a seizure, but it soon passed off.

27 July

Got down to orchestrating the music I had composed while I have been at St Palais. I worked hard and completed about twenty-five pages of score. Grogy is now transcribing my shorthand notes into full score, but so far he has done only six pages.

Generally I spend the evenings fully occupied with reading Christian Science journals, bringing my diary up to date and going through chess games: the Lasker–Capablanca match, and mine against B.N. in Ettal. What a pity there is no such ferociously partisan chess partner for me here as B.N. was; on the other hand perhaps it is just as well, because after the intoxicating evenings we experienced in Ettal I often woke the next day with a bad head, and at the moment I have to concentrate all my efforts on keeping going with *Angel*, and after that *Gambler*.

28 July

Following yesterday's intensive work I have a heavy head today, and it is raining to boot, which means I cannot go out to take the air. All the same, I completed thirteen pages of score. If I carry on working at this rate, tomorrow I shall finish the first act. In the afternoon a letter came from my bank in New York, saying that a further $770 has been transferred to my account from Moscow. This is payment from the Bolsheviks (Gosizdat),[1] but I had calculated that they owe me $1,000. Perhaps the balance is being set aside.

In the evening, read Christian Science journals. One of the articles says, with typical American decisiveness: 'We must make Christian Science business of our lives.'[2]

29 July

Again sat down with a will to orchestrating, finished Act One and made a start on Act Two. This amounts to forty-six pages in three days, i.e. an average of more than fifteen pages a day. Played through Act Two, and was pleased with it. A letter from Paichadze: he and Vera Vasilievna are coming in a week's time to stay with us for a week. I am very happy that they should do this; they are nice people, even though he is even slower getting my works into print than Oeberg was.

30 July

Got on well with the orchestration, but achieved only eleven pages as in the afternoon we went into Royan for a minor repair to the car and to do a bit of shopping. Called on the Zakharovs: Boris as usual was at the Casino in the middle of a losing streak.

In the afternoon, going for a stroll in a break between two pages, I reflected that mathematics is undoubtedly the highest form of human understanding, and that the [Christian] Scientist mathematician would be capable of discovering new laws in the field. How excellent it would be to discover a mathematical formula demonstrating the superiority of spiritual over material power! 'If I give you a dollar and you give me a dollar, each us will have one dollar. But if I give you an idea and you give me an idea, each of us will have two ideas.'

31 July

A successful orchestration session, but did not achieve as many pages as they were more complex. At half past four we went to the Zakharovs to

---

1 The USSR's State Publishing House.
2 *Sic*; in English in the text.

bathe but they, on the pretext that we were late (which was not the case at all) had already gone down to the beach and finished their swim. When I jokingly suggested that we should go back and have our swim at home, Boris and Cecilia donned their wet swimming costumes once more (Celia by no means averse to showing off her maidenly figure) and we all plunged with a beach ball into the waves, which for the first time were reasonably warm. I asked Celia how Boris's affairs stood, to which she replied: 'He won today', and then added, 'by not going to the Casino at all.' Over dinner Boris gave an account of their life in St Petersburg under the Bolsheviks and their flight, which was in many ways like Bashkirov's in that it consisted of going by boat to Finland and circumnavigating Kronstadt. Bashkirov's way of telling his story, however, had been far more portentous and laid much more stress on the various hazards he encountered. Once the Zakharovs had paid a visit to Glazunov, when his mother was full of complaints about the Bolsheviks, one of them being 'now we even have to wash the child's underclothes at home!' – the child in question being Glazunov, then sixty years of age.

We had some adventures on the road home: the headlights went out while we were going along, with the result that anyone could have bumped into us as it was a dark night. The lights then came on again, but we ran out of petrol and had to go and fetch some from somewhere, fortunately only a verst or so. By eleven o'clock, when we finally made it home, Mémé and Grogy were waiting by the door.

1 August

Twelve pages today, up to Glock leaving the stage. Nothing else to report. Gorgy lubricated the car, and we took photographs of him doing it, or rather his feet sticking out from underneath the car.

2 August

Eleven pages, although my head was far from clear and towards the end I was not making much sense. Went swimming, I in a 'triton' – an inflatable bathing costume that allows you to float in the water. The advertising material shows a gentleman floating with a cigar in one hand and a book in the other. The device does genuinely keep one afloat, but I was nervous about getting water into my ears.[1]

---

1   Prokofiev had never learnt to swim.

3 August

Another eleven pages, again to the point of stupefaction.

Went out in the car for a while. Weather, air and countryside are all ravishing.

Svyatoslav went right into the water for the first time. Yesterday he had set up such a howl that an unknown Russian woman came rushing up and started to berate me, saying he was likely to have a nervous breakdown. I said, 'He doesn't have any nerves,' at which the woman went away, obviously taking me for a cretin. Today he started up again with the screeching, but Ptashka said, 'Do a pee-pee in the water.' 'Can I really?' he asked. 'Yes, you can.' After that he calmed down and bathed with enjoyment.

Diary.

4 August

Only eight pages, as after lunch we went into Royan to have the car repaired and dawdled about all day. Found Celia on the beach sunning herself in a pink bathing costume. They leave in four days' time, and must start getting ready, as she has concerts in Holland. How about that, our summer has hardly begun and already people are rushing back to town. The car is not completely mended, but it is possible to drive it. Another thing is that petrol has spilled on the brakes, which now squeal, and on the return journey I squashed a chicken. At home we bathed, and I floated in my 'triton'.

Read some of my old diary and got absorbed in it.

5 August

A good jump forward, about fifteen pages.

We were expecting Paichadze tomorrow, but today there was a telegram that they have to put off their departure. A pity; our life has been rather isolated and we have been looking forward to the Paichadzes' arrival.

6 August

Am now orchestrating the spiritualist séance. This is to all intents and purposes a purely mechanical exercise; in any case there is no creative work at all in the orchestration of this section. The imaginative process all took place during the composition of the music; now all that remains is the writing out of a million notes, with which activity I busied myself until my head was ready to fall off my shoulders. Were at the Zakharovs in the afternoon, got stuck there and stayed to dinner. The evening before I had written to the

Borovskys telling them that the Zakharovs' dacha was about to come free, and today while we were sitting with the Zakharovs a telegram arrived from Borovsky enquiring whether they could rent it. The Zakharovs havered: what would be involved, how could it be done, perhaps the Borovskys would not like it? But it would be no bad thing if they were to take the place of the departing Zakharovs. Olga Vladislavovna, who came with us today, very much took to Cecilia and Frieda, less so to Boris, no doubt because of his insincere manner.

7 August

Continued orchestrating the spiritualist séance. The sheer number of notes is quite appalling! And what torment it will be to the orchestra, the conductor and the singer to have to learn them – worst of all to the répétiteur. Of course, I really should not have begotten such an indigestible monster, but despite everything I remain convinced that one day, once learnt, it will be seen to be splendid music.

We were expecting the whole Zakharov tribe (five persons) but Boris appeared in the morning to say that Celia had a stomach upset and they would not be able to come to us. Either Celia is having an attack of nerves before the Dutch concerts, or this is a fabrication so that they can spend their final days gambling in the Casino.

In the afternoon we went to Ronce-les-Bains, not a particularly attractive place but the road there was delightful.

8 August

Have almost finished the séance scene. The proof of the Second Symphony is lying here, the printing of which had so surprised me, but I want to devote all my efforts to completing the orchestration of *Fiery Angel*.

9 August

The spiritualist séance is finally disposed of, and I am approaching the end of the first scene. It is a large corpus of stunningly good music on a subject with which I would not now engage for anything you might care to mention. Nor would I embark on *The Gambler*. A few days ago Ptashka was reading *The Gambler*, which she did not know, and I leafed through its pages. The year it was written[1] coincided with the birth of Christian Science; to think that at the

---

1 1867: Dostoevsky's novella, not Prokofiev's opera.

very moment when in America this great doctrine was in process of being created our Russian genius was lurching between a mad woman and the gaming table, and then dashed off at white heat his autobiographical novella about both of them! Whatever the case, *The Gambler* and *Fiery Angel* both belong to that period of my life from which I have moved away.

My plan is to bring both works to state of completion and then to finish with this dark world. First I will fashion a light-hearted comedy as a new point of departure, then move on to some sonnets, then a luminous symphony, and after that, perhaps, to more substantial conceptions.

10 August

Completed the first scene. Understandably work on the entr'acte proceeded more slowly, as this is a purely orchestral number and the texture is more complex, not to mention the fact that my sketches were fairly superficial and require quite a lot of work.

A letter from Maria Viktorovna saying they would be thrilled to come and stay with us for a week. The question of the Zakharov dacha has faded from view, as Boris, good businessman that he is, wanted 2,000 francs for three weeks. Went into Royan to send M.V. a telegram with details of trains, how we would meet them, and so on.

Went swimming again after a gap of a few days. It was rather cold. My greatest pleasure is to stop up my ears and my nose with my fingers (nose with the thumb, ears with the third finger) and disappear below the water. But because the water tends to push one out again, Ptashka would take up a position by my shoulders to hold me under.

11 August

The entr'acte is moving along, but not very fast, as I have to add in all the polyphony and these are in any case hard pages.

I read a newspaper review of a biography of Mechnikov, the brilliant atheist.[1] I should dearly love to have a conversation with a real atheist. How

---

1 Ilya Ilyich Mechnikov (1845–1916), renowned biologist and pioneer of immunology through his discovery of phagocytes (mobile cells carried around the body in the blood supply). In 1888, although by this time Director of his own Institute in Odessa, Mechnikov left Russia because of hostility to his radical notions of physiology and the workings of the immune system, and joined Pasteur in Paris, where he remained for the rest of his life. Together with Paul Ehrlich he was awarded the Nobel Prize for Medicine in 1908, mainly in recognition of his work on the pathology of inflammation and his 1901 treatise *L'Immunité dans les maladies infectieuses*. Mechnikov is also recognised as the first Russian biologist to spell out the historical roots of Darwinism both in Russia and in Europe. From his extensive reading he constructed a

is it possible to be an atheist? It seems to me an atheist must be either a person who has not thought matters through to the end, or who does not care either way (which is equivalent to not thinking things through to the end), or has been disappointed in his faith, i.e. a man whom religion has failed to convince that God exists and who, content to accept this position, nevertheless cannot attain proof of the contrary – that God certainly does not exist – and thus similarly has not succeeded in thinking things through to the end. An atheist who does make the attempt to think things through to the end will inevitably lose his way in the web of contradictions. Either he must accept that nothing exists except mould, chemical reactions and random events – but then to hell with science, for what conceivable difference can it make for one lump of mould (man) by means of another lump of mould (the chemical reactions of his brain) to contemplate yet another lump of mould? – wine, women and cards, and a bullet to the forehead. Or else, God forbid, he must admit the merest hint of some order to the world, of Will in Nature (like Schopenhauer), or worse, from his point of view, of creation in Nature. At this point, of course, he is no longer an atheist, for he cannot reasonably be sure what this creation is. Is it purely mechanical (in which case how can it result from a creative act?!) or has it come about from some conscious origin, that is to say from God?

12 August

Continued with the entr'acte.

A telegram from M.V. to say that she and Natasha[1] will come tomorrow.

Read my old diaries, Max, much to repel me there, harmful emotions, and yet I remember him with love.

13 August

On to Scene Two, but I worked only in the morning.

In the afternoon went into Royan to get something fixed in the car and to meet M.V. She arrived in wonderful spirits and is full of admiration for our dacha, especially its balcony overlooking the sea.

Spent the evening sitting around and talking: this is the first evening I have not read any Christian Science, written anything in my diary or played through a couple of chess games.

---

convincing and coherent demonstration of the way in which the basic ideas of Darwin's theories grew out of the irresistible march of modern secular scientific thought from the eighteenth century French Enlightenment of Diderot, d'Alembert and the Encyclopédistes onward.

1   Her daughter.

14 August

Rained all day and I did a lot of work.
Read my diary. The death of Max evoked the strongest emotions.

15 August

Had a headache, but not a very severe one. Worked on it, by dinner-time it had begun to pass off and by evening it had gone altogether. Nevertheless the day was lost for any work.

Grogy is overstraining himself with the spiritual séance: these pages are dense with microscopically small and complex figures, and there will be more than twenty-five pages.

16 August

After yesterday's day off I buckled down to work with unprecedented energy. Hoorah, the end is in sight. It might even be finished altogether the day after tomorrow. Hard to believe that I shall finally be able to despatch my *Fiery Angel*. True, even then a lot of work will still remain to be done: the piano score, proof corrections to the full score, checking Grogy's transcription, but all of this is supplementary to the main job. I am longing to compose a luminous symphony – indeed, I have a mass of plans. A letter from Myaskovsky venomously critiquing *Oedipus Rex*, the score of which I had sent him.[1]

In the splendid weather of the afternoon went with M.V., Ptashka and the children to Royan and then went swimming. There were big waves and although it was not particularly hot the water seemed to have warmed up.

---

1   Myaskovsky's letter of 10 August sent from Moscow includes the following rancorous put-down, no doubt prompted in part by the perceived arrogance of Stravinsky's reported recent statements from the safe distance of Paris: 'His interview with Sabaneyev has recently appeared here; in it Stravinsky says that it is too early for him to come to Russia, which is not yet prepared to appreciate his music. He is right, of course: there are still too many musicians here who know literature, we have not yet become such barbarians as the European public who have no interest in knowing anything, least of all anything Russian, and are incapable of appreciating the sources of his inspiration; unfortunately so far they are all too ludicrously apparent, all the Glinka-isms and above everything the archaisms, old friends distorted beyond recognition – Musorgsky, Tchaikovsky, and, alas, Rachmaninoff. Jocasta, Oedipus – Rangoni (*Boris Godunov*); The Speaker – *Khovanshchina, Mazeppa*, the Pretender – while all around circles Korsakov (*From Homer*), and the chorus comes straight from Rachmaninoff's "Fate". But, taken all in all, as we say, once one has got past the tedium of the first act, it is a strong and even good piece.'

References are to Rimsky-Korsakov's little-known secular cantata *From Homer*, Op. 60, actually the orchestral introduction and opening chorus of a projected opera on the legend of Odysseus and Nausicaa, and to Rachmaninoff's song 'Fate' ('*Sud'ba*', Op. 21 No. 1), based on the opening bars of Beethoven's Fifth Symphony. This is the song that the composer and Chaliapin went

17 August

Worked. In the afternoon we went to the Courbe lighthouse. The sandy beach there is deserted and the sea unbounded nature with hardly any people. We had intended to bathe and had even gone there wearing bathing costumes, but it came on to rain and we returned home through a downpour, with fountains of water erupting from under.

Took up *The Gambler* and thought of a few changes to the first act.

In the evening one of my teeth started to hurt, the same one I had worked on in the train in America, which I thought I had cured for ever. It was not very painful today, however, and soon completely stopped hurting.

18 August

When I sat down to work in the morning I discovered that there were no pens, and no ink either – Ptashka had pinched the lot. I flew at her, and then regretted it. She is not in a good state at the moment: her father has been having angina attacks, yesterday evening and the day before. Olga Vladislavovna, who at one time seemed to be sympathetic towards Christian Science, will not now hear a word about it. The afternoon was stormy, downpours alternating with sunshine. The waves come right up to the garden, and the wind howls. I worked a good deal and read my old diary. This is undoubtedly the main activity of the summer.

The arrival of M.V. has to some extent disturbed our evenings. Nevertheless, every evening I manage to read articles from the *Christian Science Sentinel*, write up my diary (for the day and catching up on previous days) and before going to sleep play through a couple of chess games.

19 August

Worked all morning and after lunch, and finished Act Two at 2.15, thus completing the entire opera. It is hard to believe, the more so because getting to the end of the second act of a five-act opera hardly gives the illusion of completing the whole work. Of course, I still have to make the vocal score of the second act, nevertheless the opera is finished, finished, finished!

---

especially to Yasnaya Polyana in 1900 to perform to the aged Tolstoy, whose response was to enquire why anyone needed music like this, going on to remark that Beethoven was rubbish too, as were Pushkin and Lermontov. As his guests were taking their leave, Tolstoy kindly said he hoped his comments had not caused offence, to which Rachmaninoff returned that if he had not taken offence on behalf of Beethoven, he would hardly be likely to have done so on his own account.

Went to Royan in the afternoon, and had a slight collision with another car on the way. The other car's mudguard was damaged, ours had not a scratch. We stopped. But as soon as there was general agreement from the assembled crowd that it was the other driver's fault, he suddenly stepped on the accelerator and sped away.

Read my diary from autumn 1914, which despite the war was a very lively time.

20 August

Hah! The burden of orchestrating *Fiery Angel* is finally lifted – a nightmare that has been hanging over me for two years! However, it will not dissipate altogether overnight. Today I wrote out the instructions to the copyist to ensure accurate preparation of the orchestral parts, and then turned to the task of making a vocal score of the end of the first act, and to checking Grogy's work.

We went swimming in fairly cold water.

Read my diary from autumn 1914. Very absorbing, a shame there is no more, as I have only half the notebooks here, the rest are in Paris.

21 August

A telegram from Borovsky: he will arrive this evening. And then another: he missed the train, so will be here tomorrow morning. A closer look at this second telegram revealed that it was sent at 10.30, while the train was due to leave at 10.40. How is it possible to miss a train ten minutes before its departure?! Probably he simply overslept, woke up at ten o'clock only to realise with a start that he would not have time to pack a suitcase and get to the station, and sent the cable immediately, before the train left.

Had a headache in the afternoon, but it passed off in the evening. Worked on the vocal score and finished Act One.

22 August

M.V. and I went early in the morning to meet Borovsky, who arrived at 8.40, the same disorganised baby bear as ever, wildly glad to see his daughter. Talked to him for a while, and then settled to work. But Borovsky had left his beautiful cane at the station, and so before lunch we went back to Royan to fetch it. We discussed a possible motor trip to Biarritz; the Borovskys are very keen on this plan. As *Fiery Angel* is finally out of the way, I am not against it either. We went swimming, M.V. as well, while Borovsky walked along the shore.

24 August

Leaving the children in the care of Olga Vladislavovna, we set out with the Borovskys on our motor trip. The first point on our itinerary was Montagne, on the banks of the Gironde, where there was a ferry across to the opposite side of the river. We had hoped to be able to take the car over in order to avoid going round by Bordeaux, but the mysterious ferry, about which it had proved impossible to get any information in Royan, was nowhere to be seen: it sails when it feels inclined, and had in fact gone over the night before. We therefore continued on our way and had lunch in Bordeaux, at 'Le Chapeau rouge', a celebrated restaurant even better than 'Le Chapon fin' where we had eaten before when going to meet Mémé. They did indeed give us a lunch of great artistry, and the vintage Haut-Sauternes we drank was truly outstanding, going straight to our heads so that before I could take the wheel again we had to get some air by strolling round Bordeaux. On our way once more we proceeded towards Biarritz through an extensive forest – Les Landes.[1] Tormented at first by a road composed of stones and bricks, we then emerged onto a superb carriageway and pressed on with exemplary speed, doing 70, 80 and even up to 90 k.p.h. By evening we were at Capbreton, where we decided to stop for the night as we knew that was where Balmont was living. It did not take long to track him down: we had not even had time to find a hotel when we espied him sitting in a café with Anna Nikolayevna. After embracing I said that we would find ourselves a bed for the night and would then come back to dine together with all four Balmonts (besides the two who were there Elena Konstantinovna[2] and Mirra[3] were also in Capbreton). While we were looking for a hotel, my companions insisted that Balmont was drunk, but I retorted waspishly that that was merely their imagination. We failed to find any rooms in the three hotels we tried, so had to retrace our steps past the café where we had seen Balmont in search of another hotel somewhere in the neighbouring forest. Balmont was waiting for us, but as soon as I stopped to speak to him up rushed Anna Nikolayevna and whispered to me that we could not possibly have dinner with Balmont today – he was completely drunk. I had to try to invent a plausible excuse, but this was not so easy: Balmont was already bordering on irrationality and

---

1 Les Landes is today an area of almost 10,000 square kilometres of flat, sandy, pine forest, but until the sophisticated drainage techniques of the nineteenth century it was a huge, barren swamp because millennia of glacial movements had laid down an impermeable strata of grit on which the coastal sand dunes could not be prevented from encroaching.
2 Tsvetkovskaya, third and most faithful of Balmont's wives, who stayed with him until his death in penury in 1942. Anna Ivanova was an equally devoted relative of his late *second* wife.
3 Balmont's eccentric and wayward daughter. See *Diaries*, vol. 2, pp. 219–21.

demanded that we ignore the hotel problem and dine with him, or we could stay in the pub he was sitting in. He made me drink port and would not let me go, rudely abusing me when I tried to leave, then called me a genius and burst out laughing at the notion that a genius to whom all doors should be open was unable to find a hotel that would let him in. Then he wanted to know if I truly appreciated his, Balmont's qualities, and when I launched into protestations that the main reason I had come was to tell him about the success of 'our' *Seven, They Are Seven* in America, he suddenly began thanking me profusely for being kind to his daughter in Moscow, when as a matter of fact this amounted to no more than her single visit to me and the provision of a complimentary ticket to my concert. Seeing that this encounter was destined to drag on and on, and it was getting dark, I said I must go back to the car as something in it needed fixing, hoping thereby to make myself scarce, but Balmont evidently suspected what I was up to and insisted on accompanying me. There was no help for it but to return with him. Eventually I managed to persuade him that I would merely go and reserve rooms at the hotel in the wood (by great good fortune there was no room in the pub) and would then come back to spend the rest of the evening at his house, so in the meantime he should take himself home. The hotel proved to be some distance away, and we also discovered that one of the tyres was losing air, so I took the car to a garage. We had dinner, M.V. complaining of a stiff neck. Needless to say, we decided we could not face going back to Balmont.

25 August

I got up early and went to see about mending the tyre. Yesterday we had covered 311 kilometres at an average speed of 50.5 k.p.h. This is very quick, especially considering that before we got to Bordeaux we had to make a detour along little roads to Montagne, where we could not travel at speed, averaging no more than 36 k.p.h.

We set off directly for Biarritz, bypassing Balmont: let the genius sleep off and repent his 'riotousness'. Skirting Bayonne, a pretty town, we came to Biarritz, rendezvous of the fashionable: bankers, expensive cocottes and all manner of international riff-raff. This is where Lunacharsky was headed when *Le Pas d'acier* was being presented in Paris. What struck me most of all was the extraordinary number of magnificent automobiles, split-new and shiny-clean. Our Ballot is by no means a discreditable marque, but it was mud-spattered from top to bottom from having been driven through the rain, and people cast sidelong glances at it – but is there not a certain *chic* in so obviously having travelled a long way? All would have been well if, just as we were getting into a real traffic-jam (and the traffic here is as bad as in the centre of Paris) something had not broken in the foot-brake. Worse still was when after some proddings backwards and forwards it brought the car to a complete standstill and then, freeing itself, stopped working altogether leaving the car at the mercy of the handbrake. With enormous difficulty, accompanied by the imprecations of the police, we managed eventually to get to a garage and left the car to be repaired while we went on foot to have lunch. To add insult to injury it came on to rain hard, and we had dressed up to the nines for Biarritz.

The Grand Hotel, where we went in to eat, was full to bursting and we had to wait a long time for a table, but we were excellently fed and the wine was good. Sitting at the next table was a cocotte with silver-painted fingernails. After lunch we strolled along the sea front, and thought how beautiful it would be if all those people could be removed. We took tea in the Casino, where it was time for dancing (le fifoclock); Ptashka danced with Borovsky who, tubby little porker that he is, somehow manages to be lithe in his movements, which I can never be.

The car was repaired and we proceeded on our way to St Jean-de-Luz. At one point, when we had stopped at a level-crossing, a frantic hen burst into the car (probably in an effort to get away from it) and got herself wedged between Borovsky's back and the window. To this day he cannot work out how she managed to get free and fly out past my head.

In St Jean-de-Luz we stopped at the Hôtel de Postes. We wanted to be by the sea, but there were no rooms available. Borovsky is such a feeble fellow that when I was making a turn and called out to him to put his arm out as a signal so that the car behind would not run into us, he was daydreaming. 'Hand!' I shrieked, Borovsky was embarrassed, and so was I. Happily the car behind did not run into us, and I later apologised for shouting at him. We dined at a Basque restaurant. Borovsky got tipsy and we all laughed at him. In the evening I was so tired I barely made it into bed. The Borovskys went to the Casino to see if they could find some friends there. Ptashka thought she would like to go with them, but soon came back.

26 August

In the morning I sought out the Kokhánskis who were, as ever, exceptionally friendly. At eleven o'clock, along with some English women, friends of M.V., we went swimming (not the Borovskys, though). The beach was fairly populated with elegant bathers, the sea a deep blue and quite warm. Ptashka had a wonderful time swimming and diving beneath the waves. I on the other hand modestly trod water near the beach, because the bottom drops down steeply here compared to our St Palais.

After that we drank aperitifs in the Casino, which is where people go to drink and dance after bathing, to warm up. Ravel came to sit with us, and we were also joined by Leika Lyuboshitz, who is now very full of herself as she has secured a good position in America.[1] She put up meekly with my caustic remarks on this subject.

After a quick lunch we set off again, as I had formulated a plan to get at least a glimpse of the Pyrenees. The weather was wonderful and the views superb. The car was in fine fettle after yesterday's repair (apparently they had to tighten up some sort of cone), but suddenly began to play tricks in the mountains, as if the brake was permanently stuck on so that it was very slow going up hill and very sluggish coming down. This spoilt our journey as far as St Jean-Pied-de-Port, where the car was repaired again. This place, near the Spanish border – its name translates not as Saint John Pig's Trotter but Port as in port[2] – is the gateway to Spain. We turned north again, skirting the Pyrenees making for Dax. To tell the truth we did not see the real Pyrenees, they are further off, only the lovely foothills could be seen from where we were. The car was once again running sweetly, and we flew from summit to summit at 80 kilometres an hour. Even so we did not make Dax by nightfall, and stopped for the night at Peyrehorade, a little town that turned out to be a delightful spot. We drank the local red-white wine, known as 'vin gris' because it is neither white nor red. At first we were taken aback by the cost – for a local product – but the host assured us it was an excellent wine, and so it proved, as well as being exceedingly intoxicating.

27 August

Soon after Dax we plunged back into the forest. Not, however, wishing to take the same road back and wanting in any case to avoid the section with the stony surface, we took another route, to Mimizan, where we arrived safely although not without running over a white cockerel en route. This was not my fault: the road was clear, the hens were all on the left and the cock on the right, but realising at the last moment that he was alone, without warning he launched himself at the hens straight under the car and all I saw was his severed wing beside the wheel. At Facture we came on to the road from Arcachon to Bordeaux, smooth as a table top but dangerous for high speeds, and arrived in Bordeaux around three o'clock to lunch at 'Le Chapon fin'. The sun and the long drive had somewhat exhausted me, but I rested over lunchtime and afterwards we continued

---

1 At the Curtis Institute in Philadelphia. See above, p. 219.
2 *Sic*. Prokofiev seems here to be confusing the French *porc* with *port*. 'Pied-de-port' in the Basque language means 'foot of the pass'. It was the last stop for pilgrims making their way to the Cathedral of Santiago de Compostela in Galicia, north-west Spain.

on our way. Driving fast, we ran into a cart that was on the wrong side of the road. It was not much of a bump, however, and the only damage was to a mudguard while the other idiot escaped unscathed.

We were home for dinner. Mémé (whom Borovsky omitted to greet notwithstanding that she had spent four days looking after his daughter) presented both children in perfect order. Svyatoslav was three and a half years old today. There were a few letters, among them from Dukelsky with the information that he had completed his Symphony, and a piquant little verse. In all we had covered 738 kilometres. Borovsky sat beside me in the front the whole way exclaiming delightedly all the time. M.V. sat beside Ptashka, often aggravating her with her reflections on life, such as: 'Manicure? I never do my nails myself, I always go to a manicurist,' etc.

28 August

It was pleasant to be home! I immediately got down to work, and enjoyed reading more Christian Science. Did more work on the vocal score. So absorbed was I that Ptashka had to drag me out to be with the Borovskys, who are leaving tomorrow, otherwise it would have been impolite.

Borovsky feasted his eyes on the sea, the stars and the searchlights on the cruisers coming into Royan. M.V. drank liqueurs and talked nonsense. They leave tomorrow, as he has students waiting for him. I told him what he was doing was making a living from other people's fingers.

29 August

Got up early to take the departing Borovskys to the station. What a glorious morning! They nearly did not get away at all so much luggage did they have; there was barely enough room in the carriage.

In the afternoon I checked the work Gorchakov had done, worked on the vocal score for Act Two and had a look at passages from *The Gambler*. A proposal has come in from Zagreb to stage *Oranges*, but all they are offering is 500 marks for the whole season. Pennies!

30 August

Checked Gorchakov and carried on with the vocal score. Worked on *The Gambler*, making quite a few changes in the first act, and was pleased with the result.

Took the automobile into the garage in Royan to have the mudguard straightened out and to strengthen the springs. A telegram from Paichadze: he is coming tomorrow.

The orchestral parts of the first movement of the symphony have come for proofing. I have been waiting and waiting for them, but now they are here I am in a fright – whenever shall I find the time to read them?

31 August

Gambler in the morning. After lunch got through ten pages of proof corrections because after all Paichadze is coming and I want him to see that I am reading the proofs.

Ptashka and I went to meet Paichadze, whom we were very pleased to welcome. He has many interesting things to tell us. Belyayev's heirs have instituted a lawsuit against the Belyayev publishing company because it is not fulfilling his testamentary instructions. They are not publishing anything; all that happens is that Artsybushev draws an enormous salary.[1] The firm may come up for sale, in which case Koussevitzky will try to buy it. It would be a very good thing if our publishing house were to be augmented in this way.[2] Incidentally, a new composer has joined us – Lopatnikoff.[3] A year or two ago he came to see me in the summer and played for me a rather vulgar concerto and an interesting sonatina – they seemed almost to have been written by different composers. It is this sonatina that has now been accepted for publication.

We talked all evening, so I wrote nothing in my diary this today, read no Christian Science and played no chess games.

1 September

In view of the presence of a stranger I did not feel like working at the piano on *The Gambler*, and therefore concentrated on proof-reading the Symphony. I got through fifteen pages of score.

We bathed twice. Paichadze is an excellent swimmer and in his youth even worked as an instructor. He vowed that he would teach me to swim. The thing I am most frightened of is putting my face into the water. Today I

---

1 See above, p. 130.
2 No such merger took place; M. P. Belaieff is still in business now based in Hamburg, publishing and organising a concert series. There is, however, a close connection with another publisher, Schotts Music in Mainz. See www.belaieff-music.com.
3 Nikolay Lopatnikoff (1903–1976), Estonian-born composer who after a brief period of study at the St Petersburg Conservatoire left Russia for Finland and then Germany until the outbreak of the Second World War, when he emigrated to the United States. He remained there for the rest of his life, teaching in the music faculty of Carnegie-Mellon University in Pittsburgh. His output includes two piano concertos, the opera *Danton*, four symphonies and a quantity of chamber and instrumental music, among the most striking of which is for mechanical piano.

screwed up my courage and forced myself, i.e. I understood that the water would support me (after all, it easily supports the 'triton').

Paichadze says that this season the Boston Symphony has committed itself to paying enormous sums for the hire of orchestral material, as Koussevitzky has programmed a mass of new music. Most of this trade has fallen to our publishers. Alarmed guarantors of the orchestra have sent letters imploring Koussevitzky to moderate his ardour, but he replies that it is thanks to the first performances he programmes that the Boston Symphony is attracting so much attention, and therefore he does not find it possible to take their advice. Splendid! Clearly he feels his position to be impregnable.

In the evening I made Grogy and Paichadze play chess together. Both of them made a host of mistakes and at the end Paichadze unexpectedly won.

2 September

Settled down to *The Gambler* and made good progress. In the afternoon, dictated letters and proofed ten pages of the score of the Symphony.

Bathed. Under Paichadze's supervision I swam: managed four strokes, not much but I could more or less feel the water supporting me. Ptashka and Grogy were given more advanced teaching by Paichadze.

In the evening I played chess blindfold against Paichadze. I won without making mistakes or without losing on exchanges.

3 September

I expected that after yesterday's proof-reading and blindfold chess I would have a leaden head, but no, therefore I plunged into *Gambler* and after lunch continued with the *Fiery Angel* piano score – those pages in the second act that Grogy had transcribed.

Paichadze told me the sad story of the *Scythian Suite* at the publishers: Nijinska[1] wanted to make a ballet from it for Buenos Aires. She was sent the music, but Conius (the old man is really past it) had a brainstorm and sent instead copies of the Suite from *Chout*. The music took three weeks to get there, and then there was an anguished telegram. A new package was sent out, but it will take another three weeks and Paichadze is afraid it will be too late for the season. When Conius realised what he had done, he suffered a severe stomach upset.

---

1 Bronislava Nijinska, the sister of Vaclav Nijinsky, who having left the Ballets Russes in 1925 was working as a freelance choreographer until in 1932 she founded her own company, the Ballets Nijinska Théâtre de la Danse.

Paichadze and I went to Royan to meet Vera Vasilievna,[1] but she did not come; we found a telegram from her on our return home.

In the evening we had another chess session in which I played blindfolded, but neither of us played as well this time. I gained a piece (a win, not an exchange) and a little later on a rook. Paichadze resigned.

4 September

Gambler in the morning, vocal score and symphony proofing in the afternoon.

We did not bathe yesterday because of the rain, and today we all went bathing together. I swam a little, in an ordinary swimsuit no less, rather than the 'triton'. Even Svyatoslav scrambled into the water: Paichadze has so far won his heart as to overcome his fear of the water.

According to Paichadze, Stravinsky is now at work on another work for the stage.[2] So much for the rules so oracularly voiced by Stravinsky: first he spends all his life writing theatre works, then 'renounces' them for ever, announcing that the only worthwhile music is 'pure' music, and now via *Oedipus* he has returned to the bosom of the stage.

In the evening, more chess *à l'aveugle*. Paichadze played badly and lost again.

5 September

Gambler in the morning, but with less success as I felt exhausted and my head was beginning to ache. In the afternoon we went to the 'wild coast' of the lighthouse at Courbe. Once more we revelled in the fantastic beach and

---

1 Paichadze's wife.
2 *Apollon musagète*. This work, it emerged, was a commission from the Library of Congress in Washington for its Music Room, endowed by Elizabeth Sprague Coolidge, and the ballet would thus effectively be paid for by her. The size and nature of the room dictated the chamber-like scale of the stage performance and its scoring. The choreography was to be by, and to feature the dancing of, Adolph Bolm. At this stage, neither Diaghilev nor Lifar seems to have known about the American commission, but as time went on the Ballets Russes production choreographed by Balanchine with Lifar as Apollo would be seen as the real premiere rather than the Washington performance. See S. Walsh, op. cit., pp. 451–5. To secure the work's future prospects Stravinsky had reserved the European rights to Diaghilev's company, and when the composer first played the music to the impresario in Nice, the reaction was ecstatic: 'After lunch he played me the first half of the new ballet. It is, of course, an amazing work, extraordinarily calm, and with a greater clarity than anything he has done so far; a filigree counterpoint round transparent, clear-cut themes, all in the major key; somehow music not of this world, but from somewhere above.' (Diaghilev writing to Lifar, quoted in S. Lifar, *Diaghilev*, Putnam, London, 1940; see R. Buckle, op. cit., p. 494.)

the illimitable ocean, but swimming was difficult because of the waves, so we stayed close to the shore and let the approaching rollers break over us. The water was warm. In the evening my headache returned and I retired to bed at nine. But I brought to mind a saying I had recently read: that one must not present oneself to God ill; man is created in God's image and likeness, therefore illness is as little attributable to man as it is to God. Around ten o'clock my head was better, I got up and persuaded Paichadze not to leave tomorrow. He decided to stay another day.

6 September

The last day of Paichadze's visit was distinguished by heavenly weather. In the morning I did good work on the first act of *Gambler*, and in the afternoon we went bathing. I managed to swim, successfully on my front and less so on my back. But the water was dirty, and there were jellyfish all around, some whole ones and some in pieces. In the evening I won an interesting blindfold game against Paichadze, introducing my knights right in the heart of his defence and deploying them from there. We talked about Dukelsky, because I was writing a letter to him. Paichadze does not believe that Dukelsky will grow into a great composer because he lacks conviction, the resolute faith that would allow him to suffer for his art and yet hold the line against all odds. Dukelsky is too ready to sacrifice the line and to compose musicals purely for the sake of material well-being. His meteoric rise in the Diaghilev pantheon Paichadze ascribes to personal reasons: Nouvel had taken a great fancy to him and pushed him forward in every way he could, but when Nouvel and Diaghilev became convinced that Dukelsky was after all not on their level, at the first hint of failure they tipped him out of the window.

7 September

Got up at seven as I was nervous that the car might have a flat tyre. Took Paichadze to the station to catch his train. He departed thanking us for the holiday he had had with us. On my return got on with proof-reading and with the *Fiery Angel* vocal score, and spent the evening in my accustomed pursuits of reading Christian Science, my diary, and playing through chess games.

8 September

Morning on *Gambler*, completed drafting the revision of Act One. Next I shall turn to revising the orchestration and generally bringing the act to a finished state. In the afternoon I was proof-reading the Symphony, when there was a sudden call from the garden: Vera Alexandrovna, the wife of Suvchinsky, and her father Alexander Guchkov. From a letter she had sent we were expecting her to call the day after tomorrow, while Suvchinsky himself was unsure whether he would be coming or not. I was delighted with the opportunity to become better acquainted with her father, a romantic figure if one not universally admired, mainly because of the notorious 'Order No. 1'. In his time he had been in Africa fighting with the Boers against the English, had fought a number of duels, had been President of the State Duma, and as the first Minister of War in the Revolutionary Government had authored 'Order No. 1', which proclaimed that 'soldiers should not carry out the commands of their officers' – a curious document that precipitated his fall from power.[1] 'And now he's just a little old man,' as someone said of him. But Guchkov was full of energy, lively and articulate, with a polished command of words. As Ptashka was out, they said they must hurry to get home, probably out of delicacy so as not to interrupt my work, and I said I would accompany them. Guchkov has rented a modest cottage in the forest, not far away from us. He lives alone and had invited his daughter to stay, and with her Marina Tsvetaeva and her husband, Efron.[2] When I conducted them back to their cottage, Vera Alexandrovna announced that she would in turn come back with me, and on the way revealed that her father and husband could not stand the sight of one another, neither of them making the slightest effort to conceal the fact. It had therefore been decided that Petya[3] would come down as soon as her father went away. He was supposed to be leaving in four days' time, but had unexpectedly delayed his departure for a week, and it is now not certain when Suvchinsky might put in an appearance. It occurred to me that I could ask Suvchinsky to stay with us, but I did not want to do that without asking Ptashka, and any case it would be an odd situation

---

1 See p. 126 above.
2 Marina Tsvetaeva (1892–1941), one of the greatest, and most tragic, Russian poets of the first half of the twentieth century. She met the writer and journalist Sergey Efron (1893–1941) at Maximilian Voloshin's literary haven at Koktebel in the Crimea and they married in 1912. Despite Tsvetaeva's many intense love affairs, including that conducted by correspondence with Boris Pasternak, and the precariousness of her own position both abroad and in Russia due to the increasing riskiness of Efron's attempts to exonerate his White Army past by spying for the NKVD, the bond between them endured until Efron was shot in 1941. In 1925, soon after the birth of their third child Gyorgy ('Mur'), Tsvetaeva, her husband and their two remaining children (the younger daughter having died of starvation in the orphanage into which her grief- and remorse-stricken mother had placed her during the years of post-Revolutionary Moscow famine) had left Prague, where Tsvetaeva and her elder daughter had joined the already exiled Efron, to settle in Paris. Here they lived in great poverty, largely because both husband and wife were regarded with great suspicion by the émigré community.
3 Suvchinsky. Petya is a diminutive of his Christian name Pyotr, although in France he is in any case better known as Pierre Souvtchinsky.

to have the husband in one dacha and his wife and father-in-law in another. Just like the plot of an operetta.

9 September

Began re-orchestrating *The Gambler* from scratch. Although in the original version the opening had been done with considerable care, I shall now make it more sumptuous. After a morning's work I had done only two pages, despite being completely absorbed. Generally it is becoming clear that the revision of *The Gambler* will be a substantial job, and I dare not even think when it will be finished. Once again I give thanks to God for my working system, whereby I write a short score and Grogy takes on the job of sorting out the details.

In the afternoon I proof-read the Symphony, and then another package of letters arrived. When on earth shall I be able to finish with it all? I see no end to it.

Read my old diary, my travels through Switzerland. It was also the period of my romantic letter to Zakharov.[1] What a *petit-maître*[2] he showed himself to be then, and now how he has gone to seed, with his pale, stony face reminiscent of a statue.

10 September

Carried on with the orchestral Introduction to *The Gambler*, but did not finish it. It is obviously set to gobble up three days of my life. What has happened to the speed with which I used to swallow twenty pages a day? Probably it will pick up later on. In the afternoon we were in the village of St Palais where we saw the Guchkovs, father and daughter. The daughter and I played out a little scene we had concocted for the benefit of the former Minister in which she and I discussed my pressing need for Petya to come urgently so that he could help me with the libretto. The result was that I sent him a telegram, not, however, before having imposed on the surprised

---

1 See *Diaries*, vol. 1, pp. 387–9, 446, 529, 559, 691. In 1913 Prokofiev and Zakharov, who had been close friends at the Conservatoire, had quarrelled mainly on account of the acute mutual hostility between Zakharov and Prokofiev's even more intimate friend, the charismatic but as it turned out less than reputable Max Schmidthof, who committed suicide. Prokofiev here refers to his unconcealed desire after the tragedy to re-establish good relations with Zakharov, in which, after some understandable reservations from the latter, he succeeded. A little later the same year, to cement the new bond, Prokofiev sent a 'Musical Letter' to Zakharov, who had gone to study in Vienna. This charming work appears in the catalogue as *A Musical Letter to B. S. Zakharov in Vienna from S. S. Prokofiev in St Petersburg*, sans op.
2 Pompous, smug.

father-in-law a condition that Suvchinsky should stay with me, a condition to which he raised no objection. Ptashka and Svyatoslav then came up, and we all went off to eat ice-cream. Guchkov was gallant, brought flowers to Ptashka and generally charmed her. Ptashka did not let slip the opportunity of letting me know that Vera Alexandrovna was flirting openly with me, and would likely have to explain herself to Suvchinsky. I said I would be glad to, as it had struck me that her reaction to the plan for the arrival of Suvchinsky had betrayed a certain lack of enthusiasm.

11 September

Ptashka and I were both upset to read in the newspaper of the death of N. P. Ruzsky. My memories of him are inextricably bound up with my early musical career in St Petersburg. He was always extraordinarily kind to me, and he was very good to Ptashka also when she was living alone in Paris before we were married. The last time I met him on the street in Paris was just before I went to Russia. 'Nikolay Pavlovich,' I said, 'it looks as though I shall soon be going to Moscow . . .', to which he replied, 'Why on earth would you do that . . .?' His son had come to one of the Koussevitzky concerts and asked us to go down to see his father at Le Vésinet just outside Paris. We were always going to make an expedition there by car, but in all the excitements of the *grande saison* we never did so. A great pity.[1]

In the afternoon we took the Guchkovs out for a drive along the beautiful country roads. But the errant cone was playing up again and several times made the car stop. I mended it, getting myself covered with oil, but at least the car got under way again. Then we took tea at our house, while Guchkov talked about the Old Believers, he himself having come from an Old Believer family.[2] He talked us into going to the cinema, but it was not a successful

---

1 See above, p. 117, and *Diaries*, vol. 1 *passim*; vol. 2, pp. 44, 61, 535. Ruzsky, an amateur cellist, was the dedicatee of Prokofiev's *Ballade* for cello, Op. 15.
2 The Old Believers were on the 'wrong' (i.e. heretical) side of the Great Schism that occurred in the Russian Orthodox Church in the middle of the seventeenth century. Old Believers refused to accept the arbitrarily determined changes introduced by Patriarch Nikon into Orthodox ritual and liturgy, for which they were anathematised, persecuted and suppressed, all of which had the predictable effect of prolonging the strength of their beliefs. The main points of dissension were, and are, centred on textual and ritual details, such as the spelling of Jesus's name and the configuration of the fingers when making the sign of the cross (mainstream Orthodox practice brings the thumb, index and middle finger to a point, symbolising the Trinity, with the fourth and fifth fingers bent down to the palm of the hand, while Old Believers point the index and middle fingers upright, symbolising the dual human and divine nature of Christ, with the thumb, fourth and fifth fingers combining to a point). Devout Old Believers also consider the shaving of the male beard to be a sin. To the modern secular mind such distinctions may appear ludicrously trivial, but for many believers (not merely Old Believers)

visit, the only good thing about it being the two-kilometre walk home in a bright, cool moonlit night. Ptashka was most impressed by Guchkov, but in the car he gave her and Svyatoslav chocolates from which they suffered stomach pains at night.

12 September

Yesterday I completed the difficult Introduction to *The Gambler* and today embarked briskly on the smoother road ahead. Grogy and I made a calculation of the total number of pages of full score needed for *Fiery Angel*; it amounted to more than 800, as against 450 for *Oranges*. Quite an opera!

A telegram from Suvchinsky saying that he would come in five days' time. Also a long telegram from Koussevitzky: they are in Paris. They will celebrate their wedding anniversary on the 15th rather than the 8th and are pressing us to come back for it. We would be able to talk about America as well. At first I thought that to go all that way would be merely an exercise in boot-licking, but after all America is business, and if it can be combined with a celebration, so much the better. We could come back together with Suvchinsky.

13 September

Worked a lot on *Gambler*. It goes more easily now, and the work is enjoyable. Drove into Royan with Gorchakov, he at the wheel, I giving directions. Although he has his *carte rose*, he has not been behind the wheel for three months, also after my departure he will have to bring the car back from the station, so it is important for him to get some practice.

14 September

In the morning I took Ptashka to the railway station to catch the train, then worked all day on the vocal score of *Fiery Angel* and checked Gorchakov's transcription, which has now reached the end of Act Two. Once this had been done the pencilled notation was inked in, and the last 100 pages of *Fiery Angel* were ready for despatch.

---

rituals and doctrinal minutiae give external expression to the inner essence of their faith. Old Believers argue for the living continuation of an inclusive 'microclimate' enabling the salvation of one's soul, brought about not only by living according to the commandments of Christ, but also by maintaining traditions that contain the inner spiritual power and knowledge of past centuries manifested in external forms. The seventeenth-century anathemas were not formally revoked by the Moscow Patriarchate until 1971, but it is still the case that most Old Believer communities eschew Communion with the main Russian Orthodox Church.

Read my old diary, savouring it. It puts me in a good temper.

In the evening read some Christian Science. Hitherto I have not been very attracted by accounts of cures. I know that Christian Science has the power of healing and that is enough for me. Anecdotal press reports of new examples in the papers strike me as superfluous and therefore uninteresting.

After I have finished reading and before turning in I love to go out on to our long balcony over the sea and walk up and down it for fifteen or twenty minutes or so, looking at the sea and at the stars, and turning my thoughts to abstract subjects.

15 September

I asked Grogy to wake me at seven o'clock, and he in turn asked the girl to rouse him at half past six, but she made such a racket doing so that I leapt out of bed like a man possessed. At nine I was sitting in the train on my way to Paris. Buying a newspaper at one of the places we stopped, to find out whether the Alyokhin–Capablanca match had begun, I read of the death of Isadora Duncan, the widow of the late Yesenin.[1] She was sitting in a car with a long scarf thrown over her shoulder. As the car accelerated the scarf got caught in one of the wheels. She was thrown out of the car, suffocated and met her end underneath the vehicle.

There were a lot of Russians on the train. When I went to have lunch in the restaurant-car and sat down at one of the tables, the maître-d'hôtel seated two Russian girls with me. They evidently knew who I was and were so stunned at finding themselves in my company that I had to bite my lip to stop myself from laughing out loud. I felt a compulsion to speak to them to distract myself from the urge to laugh. But the paroxysm passed, I forbore to speak, and they did not dare enter into conversation themselves.

As the Koussevitzky residence was completely full up, Ptashka – who met me at the station – and I went to our own apartment on the avenue Frémiet. The people we had sub-let it to for the summer had left it extremely dirty. After changing we made our way to the Koussevitzkys. As usual on such

---

1   Isadora Duncan (1877–1927), the American dancer and choreographer, who discarded the 'ugly and unnatural' formations of classical ballet in favour of a barefoot, improvisatory style, clothed in flowing garments and long scarves inspired by Greek mythology, had moved to Moscow in 1922 in sympathy with what she perceived as the ideals of the Revolution, and married the poet Sergey Yesenin. The marriage was short-lived; Yesenin suffered a mental breakdown and committed suicide. The manner of Isadora Duncan's death has passed into legend: she was being driven in an open-topped car wearing, inevitably, a silk scarf hand-painted by Roman Chatov, when it unravelled and became trapped in one of the road-wheels. The sudden pull seems to have jerked her out of the car and under the wheels, and may indeed have caused her death by strangulation. 'Affectations', noted Gertrude Stein sardonically, 'can be dangerous.'

occasions they had laid on a wonderful dinner with fresh caviar, lobster, *cruchons* of wine and some unfamiliar little birds, but the company was less interesting than the year before. Afterwards Koussevitzky played the double-bass with Casadesus[1] on viola d'amore. This produced most interesting sonorities, and the melody being played on the two instruments two octaves apart produced a striking effect. The Koussevitzkys were very affectionate; serious talks were postponed until the morrow.

When Mrs Newman[2] asked Paichadze to send her husband my Quintet and Second Symphony, I shouted across from the other end of the room, 'Just send the covers!' She was offended.

16 September

We overslept, having gone late to bed the night before, but were awakened early by the noise of crates being unloaded. Paris does not enjoy the quietness of blessed St Palais. Had a row with Ptashka, because she had left her day shoes at the Koussevitzkys and now wanted me to go back to fetch them. I thought it was embarrassing to turn up in the morning in search of a pair of shoes. Of such things are domestic disagreements born.

Spent all day at the publishers discussing various small matters and correcting mistakes in the lithograph of the *Fiery Angel* vocal score. I had another look at Lopatnikoff's Sonatina and still liked it, but once again did not think much of Fédorov's pieces.[3]

Gorchakov had asked me to ask Paichadze if the publishers would consider publishing his piano pieces under their imprint but at his expense. Paichadze replied that the firm would not publish any work paid for by a third party; if Gorchakov's music was interesting they would take it under their normal conditions. For the time being I can offer only provisional endorsement of it, to the extent that it is better than Fédorov's, which I would not myself publish.

Evening at Koussevitzky's. We talked of America: he undertook to find me another manager, and I promised to pay Haensel $1,000 towards what I owe him as soon as I have another manager to move to. Koussevitzky assured

---

1 Henri Casadesus (1879–1947), uncle of the more famous pianist Robert Casadesus. See p. 177 n. 1 above.
2 Wife of Ernest Newman (1868–1959), music critic for almost forty years of *The Sunday Times*, biographer of Wagner, Strauss and Elgar among other composers.
3 Vladimir Fédorov (1901–1979), French musicologist, librarian and composer, born in Chernigov in the Ukraine. In turn librarian of the Music Department of the Sorbonne University, the Bibliothèque Nationale and the Paris Conservatoire, he wrote extensively on Russian music and would later contribute the chapter on Prokofiev to the second volume of Roland-Manuel's *Histoire de la musique*, published in Paris in 1963 (pp. 1023–35).

me that I shall have a mass of engagements and recommended appearing together with Ptashka when the engagement is not an orchestral one, a suggestion that filled her with joy. In general both Koussevitzkys were again heart-warmingly kind, and said that if in the autumn we still had difficulties finding an apartment, we were to move into their house and stay as long as we like. He plans to perform *Le Pas d'acier* in one of his first concerts and will then take it on tour, if Paichadze can get the parts copied in time.

17 September

After dropping in briefly to the Borovskys and making phone call after phone call all morning to Paichadze about the parts for *Le Pas d'acier*, at 10.40 we boarded the train in company with Suvchinsky and left for St Palais. Suvchinsky was in high spirits and relayed all sorts of fascinating information. Stravinsky has become deeply involved in the life of the church and is a committed supporter of one side (even to the extent of giving it money) in the dispute now dividing the Orthodox Church.[1] I said that for me Stravinsky's religious zeal was an enigma: his autocratic arrogance on the one hand contrastingly sharply with his exaggerated piety on the other – but a piety of a somehow formal, pharisaical cast. Surely this is religiosity rather than true religion, but then if it is merely a vagary, a caprice, then to what end? Suvchinsky insisted that it is a wholly serious persuasion, Stravinsky is deeply concerned with such matters, some of which, indeed, he approaches with such fervour that he will brook no discussion whatsoever on them. But not

---

1   In the summer of 1927 matters had come to a head between the beleaguered Moscow Patriarchate and the émigré Russian Orthodox Church Outside Russia (Russkaya Pravoslavnaya Tserkov' Zagranitsey), established in 1920 under the ambiguous blessing of the then Patriarch Tikhon in response to the declared hostility of the Bolshevik regime to the Orthodox Church. Since then the two branches of the Church had existed in uneasy communion. In July 1927 Patriarch Sergius I, recently freed from prison (in fact Sergius was officially *Acting* Patriarchal Locum Tenens because Metropolitan Peter of Krutitsy, the titular successor to Patriarch Tikhon, was still incarcerated and was to remain so until his execution ten years later), signed an *ukase* pledging the Church's loyalty to the Soviet Union and the interests of its government. This provoked the declared alienation of ROCOR from the Moscow Patriarchate, a split that remained unhealed until canonical communion was formally restored in 2007. Even since this reconciliation, however, deep divisions remain, involving ownership of Church property outside Russia (for example the Cathedral Church of the Dormition and All Saints in Ennismore Gardens, Kensington), as well as doctrinal and liturgical differences. These differences have been only exacerbated by the recent post-Soviet influx of 'New Russians' into Western Europe and America with a very different outlook from the first wave of 1920s emigrants and their descendants, whose religious practices and culture had until the fall of Communism held sway over the Russian Orthodox Church Outside Russia. Stravinsky, after a brief flirtation with Roman Catholicism, naturally took the side of ROCOR. 'The Slavonic language of the Russian liturgy has always been the language of prayer for me' – I. Stravinsky and R. Craft, *Expositions and Developments*, Faber and Faber, London, 1962, p. 76.

everyone comes to religion from a moral perspective; some people's attitude is extremely formal.

I could not, of course, regard this response as satisfactory. Suvchinsky suggests that the sheer process of creating does not come at all easily to Stravinsky, and this impels him towards a mystical path. Stravinsky is at the moment composing a ballet for Diaghilev.[1] At this, Ptashka laughed and said a strange idea had occurred to her: here is Suvchinsky talking to me about Stravinsky, and perhaps on another occasion he would be discussing me with him. Suvchinsky assured us that this was not so, that he does not discuss me with Stravinsky, because Stravinsky always comes out with the same opinion: 'Prokofiev is talented, but a barbarian.'

We arrived in Royan at 6.22 and were met by Grogy, who had managed to drive the car in successfully, and by Vera Alexandrovna meeting Suvchinsky. Immediately a disagreement broke out between the spouses: Suvchinsky did not want to go to Guchkov's house at all (the 'White Terrorist'), but V.A. insisted on the grounds that her father would be leaving tomorrow and it would be discourteous not to see him at all, and furthermore 'the old man was even heating up the water for his bath'. Quite right on her part. And although Pyotr Petrovich still wanted to come to us, we persuaded him: 'Pyotr Petrovich, better not come straight to us, please go and see your father-in-law,' and eventually he agreed.

18 September

Settled down very happily to *The Gambler* – Alexey's aria. But I did not work for long as the Suvchinskys came for lunch. Guchkov had now gone away, so all was well. Afterwards I took them for a drive in the car, and then did more work on *The Gambler*. On the subject of Guchkov, P.P.[2] said, 'You remember how he was explaining to you how Orthodox Christians cross themselves using three fingers, while Old Believers use two, and the reasons why two fingers is right? Well, if you ask him how he crosses himself, you will find that he never does it at all. That absolutely sums him up.'

19 September

Morning and afternoon on *Gambler*, and then I took Grogy's mother out in the car. This was an obligation, as tomorrow she goes back to Kishinyov.

---

1 *Apollon musagète*, but see above, p. 629, n. 2.
2 Pyotr Petrovich [Suvchinsky].

Suvchinskys came to dine. P.P. loves walking in the woods and tormented his wife today by making her walk with him for six hours on end. There was more talk of Stravinsky. Suvchinsky finds in him a quality of, as he put it, 'secondarity'. By this he means that it is a habit of Stravinsky to start with already existing material and to transform into something new, so that the resulting work bears his, Stravinsky's, own features. This trait runs through all his work: the material of *Petrushka* is drawn from street songs; the stuff of *Le Sacre* almost verbatim from Rimsky-Korsakov and Musorgsky; *Pulcinella* from Pergolesi; then on to 'Bachism' and so on.

Suvchinsky mentioned in passing that not long ago, in a Russian restaurant in Paris, he had met 'a friend of yours' who was running it. It took Suvchinsky a long time to summon up her name, but eventually he did: Meshcherskaya, her married name now Krivoshein.[1] Ptashka asked the name of the restaurant. Suvchinsky replied: ' "Astrakhan" or "Samarkand", something like that.'[2]

20 September

Worked a lot on *The Gambler*. Dictated letters. Got very tired. Sensational news: Alekhine won the first game of his match against Capablanca. I am stunned. Alekhine is clearly on exceptional form, as Capablanca is so strong,

---

1 Following an unhappy but brief first marriage, Nina Meshcherskaya's second husband was Ivan Alexandrovich Krivoshein, the son of Alexander Krivoshein (1858–1921), who served as a much respected Minister of Agriculture from 1908 until 1915 and played an important role in the implementation of Stolypin's agrarian reforms. Already out of favour in the inner circles of the Imperial Court for his unavailing attempts to steer the Tsar towards taking more account of the Duma, he eventually lost his job altogether for opposing Nicholas II's decision to take personal command of the Russian Army. After the October Revolution Krivoshein threw in his lot with Denikin's White Volunteer Army, served as the head of General Wrangel's government in Crimea, and with his sons went into exile in France on Wrangel's ultimate defeat by the Red Army. Alexander Krivoshein died in Paris in 1921. For Prokofiev's intense youthful relationship with Nina see *Diaries*, vol. 1, pp. 279ff. *passim*; vol. 2, pp. 3–73 *passim*, 235–6, 240, 246, 265, 331, 445, 508, 511, 604, 614, 682, 689–90.
2 It was the 'Samarkand'. In her memoir *Four Thirds of Our Life*, written in Paris but published in Moscow in 1999, Nina Meshcherskaya, with whom Prokofiev had made an unsuccessful attempt to elope in St Petersburg in 1915, describes the restaurant in Paris she started in 1925 in an effort to alleviate the grinding poverty in which she and her family were then living: 'We took over a stinking room above a former café, brightened it up with colourful hangings and put lamps with orange shades on the tables. An upright piano appeared, someone recommended two pleasant young waitresses who had some experience of restaurants, and the "Samarkand" was launched on its new path. I ran it and served behind the bar. The "Samarkand" was somewhere between a cheap eating house and a self-consciously expensive restaurant . . . On Sunday afternoons we used to put on inexpensive meals for our particular clientele, who mainly came in after morning service at the church in the rue Daru, which was near by. Some came with the whole family, some – those who had nowhere else to go – on their own.'

standing head and shoulders above all the rest, that for him to be defeated especially in the opening game is something quite extraordinary. It had not been in vain that I took out a subscription to the London *Times* so that I could immediately get hold of the results and the details of the games.

21 September

Perfect sunny weather, it is even hot on the beach. Should we renew our bathing? We decided to wait one more day, to let the water warm up.

Again worked hard on *The Gambler*. Proof-reading the Symphony has been put to one side for the time being. But the work is going smoothly and enjoyably. By five o'clock my brain had completely given up and I decided to go out in the car. Ptashka came with me and took the wheel, while I gave her instructions. The Suvchinskys dined with us, and drank a bottle of fizz. After dinner I quizzed him about what had impelled him to publish the *Musical Contemporary*.[1] Suvchinsky enjoyed recalling those days and let himself go talking about the inauguration of the magazine, about his quarrel with A. Rimsky-Korsakov, Weisberg's sardonic suggestion that the new journal would have to be called '*Prkfv*',[2] and other remininscences.

22 September

Today again the weather was neither one thing nor the other, and there was no bathing. *Gambler* to the point of stupefaction again, and then a run in the car with Ptashka driving. In the evening, Christian Science and my diary.

23 September

In the morning I worked on *The Gambler*, but broke off in the afternoon as my head was beginning to ache, although not severely. The Suvchinskys

---

1 The journal was founded in St Petersburg by Suvchinsky and Andrey Rimsky-Korsakov, son of the composer, in 1914. See *Diaries*, vol. 1, p. 773.
2 The editorial board of *Musical Contemporary* consisted of Suvchinsky (who had put up the money), Boris Asafyev under his pen-name of Igor Glebov, and Andrey Rimsky-Korsakov, whose wife was the conservatively inclined composer Yulia Weisberg. It was not long before the progressive instincts of Suvchinsky and Asafyev and their promotion of cutting-edge composers such as Prokofiev and Stravinsky were at odds with the traditionalist approach of Rimsky-Korsakov, backed up by his wife and his brother-in-law, Maximilian Steinberg, and an unbridgeable gulf opened between the two sides. Suvchinsky and Asafyev, joined by the like-minded critic Viktor Belyayev, decided to cut their losses and found a new journal, which Weisberg caustically suggested should be entitled '*Prkfv*'. In fact it was called *Melos*, but launching in September 1917 it managed only two issues before succumbing to the chaos of the October Revolution. See above, p. 494, n. 4.

called. I took advantage of his presence to discuss with him the titles of the individual numbers in *Le Pas d'acier* as so far they have had only rough working titles. Suvchinsky offered several good ideas which would be appropriate both for Soviet Russia and for abroad; after all, one must have an eye to both contexts. Once the Suvchinskys had left my headache got worse. I lay down and gave myself a Christian Science treatment. The more confident one is in healing, the more effective the process. But how can I be confident when I know how little progress I have made? Then a wonderful thought struck me: all right, I am not confident of now being able to cure the pain in my head. But this being so, am I confident that in time I shall be able permanently to become free of headaches, even if it should take a year, or three years, or five? Yes, of this I am profoundly certain. And if this is so, then the proposition may be formulated differently: the ultimate fate of my condition is a settled matter, but in order for the complete cure to take effect a certain number of years must elapse. And to put it yet another way: my headache condition is cured, but the manifestation of this state will occur only after some time. And finally, this being the case, I can be sure that the work I do now on healing myself will bring a result, and it matters not if the result should come immediately, because it certainly will eventually. Apparently these reflections were on the right lines, because the headache soon abated, and by evening it was completely gone.

During the night a great storm with lashing rain blew up. The worst of it was that the rain found its way through all the gaps in the windows and doors, and the shutters were so rusty that they could not be lowered. We had to mop the floor with cloths because the water was already seeping down and damaging the ceiling in the kitchen. 'Call the dog and let her drink from the floor.' The rain never ceased all night and kept us awake.

24 September

I was in the middle of *Gambler* when I was interrupted by the caretaker of the property and his wife coming to repair the shutters, all the hinges of which Grogy had wrenched off the previous night when trying to lower them. In the afternoon the skies cleared and the sun came out. Suvchinsky came with us in the car to La Rochelle, a distance of about 75 kilometres, as Suvchinsky needed to see his acquaintance Prince Svyatopolk-Mirsky.[1] I was glad to take

---

1 Prince Dmitry Svyatopolk-Mirsky (1890–1939) is better known in English-speaking circles as D. S. Mirsky, the name under which he produced, while lecturing on Russian Literature at London University during the 1920s, a series of masterly studies of Russian history and literature, the best known of which is the two-volume *History of Russian Literature from Its Beginnings to 1900*. Mirsky (he renounced the princely title at an early age) had served in Denikin's White Army before emigrating to Great Britain in 1921, where he took a leading role

him, as it seemed an interesting journey. Indeed, the first part of the route lay through attractive fields until, just before Rochefort, we crossed the river on a raft and then from Rochefort to La Rochelle sped along a magnificent road at 80 k.p.h., sometimes touching 90. From the sea came a breeze that, coming across the meadows, was tinged with the scent of grass. Our headlong speed across the wide open space brought Suvchinsky to a paroxysm of delight.

In La Rochelle we met the Prince, whom I had encountered before at Bassiano's. He is a singular personality: having started his career as a Guards officer serving under Denikin he took part in the capture of Oryol;[1] he later became disillusioned with the White movement. In recognition of distinguished labours in the field of Russian literature he was honoured by a professorial appointment at London University. Communication between him and Suvchinsky had opened up on the soil of Eurasianism. The three of us walked round the town, which contains several ancient and beautiful buildings, then Suvchinsky entertained us to an appetising lunch during which the Prince undertook the selection of the cognac with quasi-religious solemnity.

Conversation with Suvchinsky turned yet again, as it had done several times in the preceding days, to Stravinsky, to the direction he was taking and in particular to his religion. Suvchinsky insists that the strength of his religious feeling is wholly genuine and stems from the hardness of the creative process, and from an ever-present terror induced partly by uncertainty about the path chosen and partly by concerns for his ultimate fate and the state of his health (he invariably carries a cross in each of his pockets).

I said, 'This kind of fear is not a Christian feeling!'

Prince: 'On the contrary, it is precisely Christian; the Bible constantly refers to the fear of God.'

---

in the Eurasianist movement, hence his connection with Suvchinsky. However, his developing parallel enthusiasm for Marxism eventually caused him to join the Communist Party of Great Britain, and he appealed to Gorky for help in gaining absolution from the Soviet authorities for his past transgressions. Satisfied (foolishly, according to Virginia Woolf, who prophetically confided to her diary 'soon they will put a bullet in his head') that this would afford the necessary protection, he returned to Russia in 1932, to survive only five years before being disastrously accosted on a Leningrad street by his old friend and colleague, the left-leaning historian E. H. Carr, who with glad cries and – given that this was high season for Yezhovshchina paranoia – remarkable insensitivity ignored Mirsky's desperate attempts to disavow the relationship and dragged him off to lunch. Carr should have known better. Soon afterwards Mirsky was arrested as a British spy and sent to the camps, where he died in 1939.

1   The struggle for control of Oryol, on the Oka river 220 miles south-west of Moscow, was a critical moment in the Civil War: the combined Red Army of Trotsky and the Black Army of the Ukrainian anarchist Nestor Makhno routed Denikin's White Army after it captured and held the fortress for one week in October 1919. This was the battle that finally put paid to Denikin's attempts to reach Moscow and was the beginning of the end of the military threat to the Bolshevik regime.

I: 'But that fear is of quite a different kind. It is the fear not of the consequences of events that may occur, but of not measuring up to the image and likeness of God.'

Prince: 'Not at all. It is the purest kind of funk in the face of eternal punishment.'

At this point Suvchinsky, in explanation of Stravinsky's fears, added something quite incredible: 'Yes, yes, the fear of being a divinely chosen instrument, the fear engendered by feeling one's skin to be a drumhead being beaten by a drummer from above.'

I: 'Your conception of God owes more to Beethoven than to the New Testament.'

And suddenly I was overcome by a feeling of shame that we should be arguing about God while polishing off our second bottle of wine, so I tried not to prolong the conversation, which soon turned to other themes.

25 September

Slept badly, having drunk a lot of coffee yesterday, although for a Scientist it is shameful to submit to such an effect. Also, St Palais is so quiet that here the slightest extraneous noise is disturbing. We got up early and by a quarter to nine were on the road back to St Palais, Suvchinsky having persuaded Mirsky to come with us. It had rained during the night, however, and although the sun was now shining the road was wet and slippery and we could travel at only half yesterday's speed. After Rochefort we took a different route, nearer to the coast, and by an extremely twisty road came to Marennes where we had to take a ferry across a tributary of the river to Tremblade (exciting for the motorist). In Tremblade we ate oysters and were home by noon. Suvchinsky, sitting in the back seat, suddenly let out a screech: he had been thrown about by a pothole in the road and banged his head on the roof the car. It raised an enormous bump, and even made a hole in the roof-lining. At home all was well, and I immediately sat down to *The Gambler*, working until five o'clock. At seven the Suvchinskys and Mirsky came to dine; I had brought from Tremblade a box of oysters (ten dozen) most of which we consumed. It was a very happy evening. I played the Fifth Sonata, to which Suvchinsky listened absorbed.

26 September

Heavy-headed. Is this not happening rather too often? I did not work on *The Gambler*, instead went for a long walk and dictated three letters. My headache did not develop into a really bad one, and passed off altogether by the evening. I caught up on my diary and read Christian Science.

27 September

For the last three days work on *The Gambler* has been proceeding very slowly. Today I spent nearly all day on it and moved it forward significantly. The Suvchinskys called in unexpectedly. Last night someone had been walking round their cottage and tried the lock on the door. Also it is growing dark and cold, so today they are moving out to Royan and the next day will go back to Paris. Suvchinsky was critical of the title *Le Pas d'acier*,[1] and suggested naming the ballet *The Year 1920*. I like this name, but isn't it too late? When they left I again sat down to *The Gambler*. Ptashka walked home with them, but Suvchinsky then came back once more with her and talked volubly, being very complimentary about Ptashka, saying how my character had improved, and generally being eloquent and charming.

More money has come in from Moscow: $513, presumably from Muzsektor. Full marks to them, for paying in advance of schedule.

28 September

Worked very productively on *The Gambler*; it is a long while since my work has proceeded so smoothly and easily. In the afternoon, despite their leave-taking yesterday, the Suvchinskys appeared yet again. They are bored in Royan, and had come over on foot. I took them back in the car and went as far as Saujon to show them round. That evening Olga Vladislavovna said, 'I don't know why you don't stay yourselves for a month or two in Royan, if you don't have any special need to be in Paris. You could rent a flat very cheaply in Royan.' Since we do not know how long our apartment in rue Frémiet is going to remain available to us, possibly for no more than another month, I was incautious enough to support this idea. Ptashka burst into floods of tears, protesting that never could she have imagined her life ending in a little provincial town, and more nonsense along similar lines. In short the evening was ruined, and even though Ptashka has become interested in chess I read through the Alekhine–Capablanca match, the one won by Alekhine, in solitary state. It was a most interesting game, distinguished by admirable clarity.

I started reading through *The Gambler* with a view to writing notes on the characters.[2] It might also give me some ideas for the revision I am engaged in.

---

1 Or rather the Russian version *Stal'noy Skok*, literally *The Steel Gallop*.
2 See *Diaries*, vol. 2, Appendix 1, pp. 715–17.

29 September

Worked almost all day on *The Gambler*. Went splendidly, I almost finished orchestrating Act One. I stopped because I was beginning to have some heart pains. Reasoned with myself.

Studied the third game of the match. Alekhine got into trouble on his ninth move, and then endured an agony lasting five hours. It is very unpleasant to be forced into sustaining such a game.

30 September

Finished orchestrating the first act of *The Gambler*. It has taken a month. It will be good if the other acts can be done as quickly. Alas, Act One is the shortest.

1 October

Began looking through Act Two and making plans for its revision. Worked all morning on that, and then in the afternoon after doing some of the piano score of Act One transported Ptashka's parents to Royan where they are going to base themselves for the winter. The climate is better there than in Paris for Avi, who is not well, and they will not have to struggle with the train journey. At the request of Ptashka, who was putting together the diary of our visit to Russia, I was getting her some details from my notebook when I happened upon the letter from Natasha.[1] Ptashka began asking all sorts of questions about who she was, what I had to do with her, how did we meet. I told her something but kept it rather vague. Next, Ptashka began asking me about the Meshcherskaya whom Suvchinsky had mentioned. I told her the story of our unsuccessful elopement in which Bashkirov had played a role, waiting round the corner in his car. Towards the end of the evening the conversation reverted once more to the question of an apartment in Royan and Ptashka again became angry, so much so that we decided to spend the night in separate rooms 'so as not to upset one another'. But at two o'clock

---

1 The only reference to a Natasha in the detailed account of the winter 1927 visit to the Soviet Union is the one to Natasha (Natalya) Goncharova, a former student friend from Conservatoire days whom he met at the second of the *Three Oranges* performances at the Mariinsky Theatre he attended, on 20 February. At the Conservatoire there had been considerable mutual attraction, and he had received several affectionate letters from her. Presumably the attachment, at least from her side and at least on paper, had continued during the visit. See *Diaries*, vol. 1, pp. 248–502 *passim*.

Ptashka woke me up saying that she could hear someone walking about below the window, and there was even the muffled sound of a bicycle bell. Although I did not believe there was any real danger, for safety's sake Ptashka returned to the marital couch and I even went so far as to turn the key in the door of our bedroom.

2 October

Next morning, as the day before, I continued revising Act Two, adding and correcting material, and in the afternoon worked on the vocal score of the first act, spending more or less the whole day. Ptashka thinks I am a slave to my work.

In the evening Christian Science and my diary.

3 October

In view of the imminent departure of Ptashka's parents, we brought Svyatoslav in to sleep with us, but he wheezed and moaned all night, tossing from side to side just like an old man, and disturbed our sleep. Either because of this or because it had been such a painfully demanding day's work yesterday, *The Gambler* did not go so well, rather limped along.

Alekhine lost a second game to Capablanca after keeping step by step with him for the first six games. I am devastated and even Ptashka feels the same.

4 October

Gambler all morning. I was recomposing the second act, the scene between Astley and Alexey, trying out some things to liven it up because in the original it certainly has its longueurs. Continued work on this in the afternoon, and then turned to the vocal score.

The weather is still marvellous and today I called on the agent to enquire if we could extend our stay in the house until the 15th instead of having to leave on the 10th. In the evening Ptashka and I watched as the sun, without a cloud in the sky, buried itself in the ocean in a ball of fire, so quickly you could almost see it moving.

5 October

Much the same as yesterday: recomposing the second act of *The Gambler*, followed by work on the vocal score in the afternoon.

The weather has turned noticeably cooler, although it is still sunny and very nice. Olga Vladislavovna came over from Royan in the afternoon and we took her back in the car. The car refused to start, so Olga Vladislavovna had in fact boarded the little local train, but then we ran the car down a little slope and the engine started itself, so we caught the train up and collected Olga Vladislavovna from the next station. Suvchinsky sent Vernadsky's 'Russian History' published by the Eurasianists, most interesting.[1]

6–12 October

I did not make any diary entries during this week as the days passed exceptionally uneventfully in a similar manner to their predecessors. But in this unvariedness there was no hint of boredom; on the contrary, the work was going extremely well and the weather stayed amazingly good throughout.

The recasting of the arrival of Babulenka proceeded very quickly; in fact there was hardly any recasting to be done, merely a little light retouching. After this I got on with writing the score of Act Two, at the same time finishing the vocal score of Act One.

Little happened to speak of. The 8th was my name-day, but we all forgot it. That day, however, I did less work as I had a headache, not a bad one; severe attacks have been rare events recently. Grogy was cheeky to Ptashka, she took offence and treated him coldly for a few days. Finally, Paichadze informed me in a rather offhand way that Bruno Walter, disgruntled at my delay, had rejected *Fiery Angel* for production. It is true that I had held matters up, but not fatally, and there was no real reason why the opera could not be produced at any time during the season. What seems to be behind the rejection is that of late there have been too many foreign operas produced in Germany, and this has caused something of a patriotic backlash in favour of home-grown work. It is said that Bruno Walter fought against this, but felt that I was not helping him by failing to come up with the finished work, and so he 'took offence'. At first when I read Paichadze's communication I was upset and even angry, but with the help of Christian Science soon calmed down and my anger dissipated. It is simply the case that *Fiery Angel*, laden as it is with devilry, is not smiled on by fortune. First to derail it was Demchinsky,

---

[1] The monumental magnum opus of the historian G. V. Vernadsky (1888–1973) is entitled *Russian History* (*Russkaya Istoria*), but this was the fruit of his later years as a distinguished professor at Yale University, well away from the fevered disputes characteristic of the Parisian Eurasianophile movement. The first of the five volumes (*Ancient Rus*) appeared in 1943 and the fifth (*The Muscovite Kingdom*) in 1968. What Suvchinsky had sent was either a shorter book entitled *Outline of Russian History* (*Nachertanie Russkoy Istorii*) published earlier in the year in Prague, or perhaps more likely a long article published in Paris the same year in the Eurasianist journal *Yevraziistii Sovremennik* entitled 'The Mongol Yoke in Russian History', dealing with the effects of the Tartar–Mongol invasions of Russia. Both essays are sympathetic to the Eurasian historical thesis, of which Vernadsky was one of the leading intellectual protagonists.

then I had to summon up all my strength to drag it to the top of the mountain, and now Berlin has delivered the *coup de grâce*. But how much music has been squandered!

13 October

The move back to Paris is everywhere in the air: the piano has been taken, the carpenter has been to measure up the books for crating, Ptashka is packing the trunks; only I stubbornly keep scribbling away at the score.

Alekhine has won a second game against Capablanca. I am flabbergasted. This is a real achievement for Alexander Alexandrovich! At the start of the match I really did not know on which side my sympathies lay, as I am friends with both men. But now they are unhesitatingly with Alekhine. In the evening I went through the game with Ptashka.

15 October

Departure. Sixteen pieces of luggage went with Grogy and Madeleine on a lorry to the station while Ptashka, Svyatoslav and I and a whole pile of other luggage (but lighter stuff, as the car's springs are not too strong) left at the same time in the Ballot. It was very pleasant driving, but by 5.30 it was already getting dark and we stopped for the night at Châtellerault.

16 October

At 9.18 we were on our way again. In Dangé we turned off the main road on to a smaller one to take a shortcut to Blois. This was, however, a miscalculation as the road had so many twists and forks in it that I twice lost the way, and of course on small roads, even very good ones like these, one cannot keep up as fast an average speed as on a major road. The views of the countryside in its autumn colours were beautiful and revealed unexpected vistas of castles, one called Montpoupon, but we were in much too much of a hurry to get to Paris by nightfall. I am not very keen on driving with headlights.

We had lunch in Blois and from there on raced on along the excellent high road to Paris. Most of the way we were doing 70 k.p.h., occasionally 80, rarely as little as 60.

The old girl purred along splendidly, singing sweetly all the way. The Ballot really does have a superb engine, melodious rather than noisy. We could have been in Paris just at the onset of darkness, but twenty kilometres or so from the city we got caught up in the most incredible tailback of cars returning from the races, and this stretch of the journey was covered at walking pace. We finally arrived at our avenue Frémiet at seven o'clock in the evening. Grogy and Madeleine were already there and waiting for us. We are able to resume our occupation of this flat for another two months, after which apparently the owner is due to return. Ptashka travelled the whole way like a real trouper despite battling a vicious sore throat. But she managed to conquer it.

Later in the evening she was reading a Russian newspaper and happened on an advertisement for the 'Samarkand' restaurant. 'That's the restaurant where your fiancée is waiting at table,' she laughed, and then by way of an afterthought added, 'Not much of an address.'

18 October

Made a very energetic start on orchestrating Act Two. In the afternoon I visited the publishers. Paichadze has still not lost the tan he acquired while with us in St Palais. All the main composers published by our house are in Paris: Stravinsky, Rachmaninoff, Medtner, Grechaninov, myself. All, that is, except Dukelsky, who has disappeared somewhere or other – true, his affairs in London are not prospering. Paichadze gave me Medtner's latest opus (Op. 48),[1] but this is not so much a decline as a collapse.

In the evening the Shcherbachovs came to us to dine, husband and wife; it turns out they have already been in Paris for two weeks. Needless to say I lost no time in plying them with questions, how is Asafyev and why is it that he has not written for three months? Apparently there has been a wave of repressions connected with the rift with England and a series of manifestations of ant-Soviet feeling within Russia, as a result of which a number of remaining members of the intelligentsia have ended up in prison and exile. Among others Tyulin was locked up for about five weeks, after which he was released. Asafyev was not himself touched, but as the authorities take a lively interest in anyone who corresponds with people abroad, he was in a panic, and therein lies the explanation for his silence. Now the period of most acute danger has passed and calm has returned. Dranishnikov asked the Shcherbachovs to hurry me up with sending him *The Gambler*. We did our best to entertain them in style: champagne, lobster, Havana cigars, etc.

19 October

The Gambler went well, I spent almost all day on it. I am relieved that the move back to Paris has not slowed the pace of my work.

---

1 *Two Fairy Tales*: No. 1 in C ('Dance Tale'); No. 2 in G minor ('Dance of the Elves').

Paichadze rang up to tell me that Moscow has sent 6,000 marks for *Oranges* – a gigantic sum on a scale I had only dimly expected. A letter from Bashkirov in which he expresses a great desire to see me; for four months now he has been 'with the noose around his neck' (translation: he has been losing) and similar desperate phrases to describe his utter powerlessness to help himself. But the memory of the Rudnev cheque, from which he siphoned off some of the money, is still too strong and I have no desire to see him.

In the evening we invited the Paichadzes, whom it is always a pleasure to see. It seems *Oranges* played in Moscow for two months (half of May, half of June and all September), with no fewer than eleven performances, taking a total of 45,000 roubles. Paichadze is due to play vint[1] with Rachmaninoff tomorrow; they are friends and Paichadze is obviously very proud of the relationship. Rachmaninoff's wealth is estimated today at one and a half million dollars and his concert fee is $3,000 a time. Nevertheless, he is as bored as the devil. The Suite from *Chout* (four numbers) was performed for the first time in Leipzig, only its second performance in Germany, and seems to have been no more than moderately well received, getting mixed reviews. Some know-it-all figures are of the opinion that they have heard it all before, in *Petrushka*. How do you like that? But if one thinks of it, all Japanese look alike the first time you are in Japan. In the same way the good Germans plunging headlong into new Russian music are so shocked by the difference from anything else they are exposed to they are not yet capable of detecting anything beyond this difference. Hence the similarity of the dissimilar.

20 October

The Paichadzes stayed until half past twelve last night. In the country we had got used to going to bed at eleven, so we did not have enough sleep and today, to make matters worse, I ran up against a particularly difficult passage in *The Gambler*. So work was slow and painful. But at least I got through the most tricky part.

Evening with the Samoilenkos. He is recovered now and gets about without a stick, but you can feel the most enormous scar on his leg, almost a ravine. They seem to have taken away almost a quarter of his thigh! They talked of the Stahls, who live a lavish style and throw expensively refined

---

1 A popular card game, mixing elements of whist, bridge and preference, involving the classic elements of bidding, trumps, the winning of tricks and the attempt to achieve (or frustrate) a contract by the end of the hand. The name 'vint' ('screw' in Russian) derives from the clockwise bidding procedure and the skill of persuading one's opponents to 'screw up' their bids beyond the point at which they could reasonably expect to meet their contract. Prokofiev had been very fond of vint in his St Petersburg years. See *Diaries*, vol. 1 *passim*.

dinner parties, while they themselves are permanently on a diet and spend their time being treated by doctors recommended by Stravinsky. One in particular, based outside Paris, charges 200 francs a visit and will not see more than one patient a day, but he did cure Stravinsky of a very painful affliction: the skin between the toes continually cracking open (Fatma Hanum mistakenly said between the legs[1]). Now Stravinsky recommends him to everybody.

21 October

The Gambler made good progress today. We've said goodbye to Astley, and the Marquis has come.

In the afternoon I went into the publishers and had a mild argument with Paichadze about the firm's deducting 15 per cent of the money from Moscow, which he insists is agreed in one of the points of the contract, but I do not think it is. It was decided this must be looked into. I took home with me the second folder of my old diaries. Very interesting. Spent the evening at home.

22 October

Worked on *Gambler* morning and afternoon.

At five o'clock Suvchinsky came round and today he was very nice. I played him some passages from Medtner's Violin Sonata No. 2, the score of which was on the piano desk, and we were both appalled by some examples of unfathomable ugliness. Later on Shcherbachov came; he had meant to play me his Sinfonietta, the one I did not hear when I was being entertained by him in St Petersburg, but had not managed to get home to collect it as he had spent all day rushing about the town. He had much to say about musical life in St Petersburg. Standards at the Conservatoire have greatly improved, in his opinion, as the entrance requirements have been strengthened. This year there were forty-eight applicants for the composition class, of which only eight were selected. He told a touching story of a homeless boy who had walked three hundred versts for his attempt to enter the Conservatoire, and during the exams had slept on a bench on Nevsky Prospect, but unfortunately proved not be talented. When he was turned down, he said, 'Yes, if I had had better conditions in which to work, I would not have presented the things I did.' Eventually he was found a place in some residential institution or other, and next autumn he will be able to submit himself for examination.

---

[1] In Russian the same word, *nogá*, does duty for both 'leg' and 'foot', as incidentally does *pálets* for 'finger' and 'toe'.

The Shcherbachovs are leaving for Russia tomorrow. I sent with them a fountain pen and some music, and presented Shcherbachov with my Quintet.

23 October

Worked a great deal. In the afternoon Rudnev and I looked at the car, which is being painted. I told him about the damage the car had suffered during the summer, and Rudnev gave his verdict. Generally he found the car to be in good condition. It emerged that Rudnev, Bashkirov and some other people had gone in Rudnev's taxi to the seaside and stayed for two weeks in, of all places, St Palais, a kilometre and a half from where we were. Small world! And we never once ran across one another. When B.N. gets to hear of this, he will tear his hair out.

On the 21st Ptashka turned thirty. In the evening we went to a concert performance of *The Snow Maiden*:[1] Ptashka is studying the part of the heroine just now, and I love this opera very much indeed despite its many failings, dramatically speaking. The performance was average, the best being, naturally, Koshetz's. During the interval Ptashka remarked, in the presence of other people, that I understood nothing about singing. I was angry and did not speak to her for the rest of the evening. This was stupid, but neither was it very intelligent to make such an observation about me in public.

24 October

Work went smoothly and well. Was reconciled with Ptashka. Under the influence of C.S., if we do have quarrels, they are soon over. Had lunch with Diaghilev. Yesterday I telephoned Nouvel to say that although I did not have any special matters to discuss with Diaghilev, if he happened to be free I should very much like to see him. The result of this was an invitation to lunch today. It was the first time we had met using the intimate form of address. I was slightly flustered, but Diaghilev carried it off with aplomb. Altogether he was most affable, although he could not resist telling me about the new ballet Stravinsky is writing for him.[2] 'Full of tunes, and all in C major' – i.e. precisely what I have been doing all the time, in the Third Piano Concerto, *Le Pas d'acier*, and so on. He was obviously doing this to tease me. He is leaving soon for a tour of Germany, Czechoslovakia, Austria

---

1 *Snegurochka* (1881), opera by Rimsky-Korsakov.
2 *Apollon musagète*. In fact Stravinsky was not writing it for Diaghilev but in response to a commission by the Library of Congress in Washington, paid for by Elizabeth Sprague Coolidge (see above, p. 629 n. 2) It would seem that in late October Diaghilev still did not know that the ballet was not being written for the Ballets Russes, or perhaps was not yet ready to admit the fact.

and Hungary. *Le Pas d'acier* had been requested but he is not taking it because of the difficulty of transporting the Constructivist set. Bad luck for the ballet, and bad luck for me, saddled for eternity with massive scenery.

Lunacharsky is in Paris. Diaghilev is not averse to the idea of meeting him for lunch, although he refers to him as 'a Russian fool from a wealthy background'. But he does not want the initiative to come from him; if I were to invite them both together he would gladly accept. But neither am I very keen to take the initiative, especially at a time when Soviet diplomats are in the process of being expelled from here.

Back at home I read my diaries of the Conservatoire years, when I was eighteen–nineteen years of age. Very interesting.

25 October

Went to see Miss Crain. I am having a good spell with my heart, but I need to cure it finally, once and for all. I also still get headaches from time to time. Miss Crain said I must remember that there is but a single head, a single reason, and that is God. This head cannot therefore be sick. This is what must be kept in mind all the time, rather than depending solely on one's own brains. When one's mind is enfolded in that of God, one's head in that of God, any pain is bound naturally to disappear. I drew her attention to the disappearance from my hands of the rashes from which I suffered for more than ten years but for six months now have completely vanished. The main reason I came to see her, however, was the toothache which I successfully vanquished while on the train coming away from San Francisco.[1] Now the filling has dropped out. If I go to the dentist he will drill it out, dig around in the root, inject it with disinfectant and other drugs, and I cannot help regretting that this tooth, which responded so well to C.S., must now be subjected to medical intervention. Miss Crain said I should not be afraid of this, but should now concentrate my attention on ensuring that no infections or inflammation develop around the affected area. Then the dentist would not have to drill or inject drugs, but would merely have to carry out the mechanical side of the treatment. Miss Crain asked me if I regularly attended the Christian Science Church. I said that I had done so in the spring but was not doing so now because I was driven to despair by the out-of-tune singing of bad music, while the chorales that are sung there remind me of being in a German church. Nevertheless, she recommended me to attend and try not to pay attention to the quality of the singing, which is quite beside the point. As always I left her with my spirits greatly elevated.

---

1   See above, pp. 255–6.

Worked on *The Gambler* and got as far as Babulenka. There is not much to revise in this part, and I raced ahead.

In the evening the Zakharovs, recently back from Finland, should have come to dinner, but they were bidden by Rachmaninoff, with whom Medtner is staying – Celia is studying his Sonata – and accordingly are required to commingle with the effluvium of this desiccated spring. Our dinner is therefore off, I branded Boris an apostate, and he retaliated by inviting us next Saturday.

26 October

Morning and afternoon on *Gambler*.

In the evening Ptashka and I went with the Samoilenkos to the cinema to see *Ben-Hur*, a film set in the time of Jesus Christ and the dominion of the Roman Empire. I found the content of the film almost in complete accordance with Christian Science. I do not much enjoy going to the cinema as I do not see well enough and the light keeps flashing in my eyes. My eyes are not yet completely cured. Also, today I am feeling quite tired: when we left the cinema it was as though fatigue was sitting on top of my head like a hat. But there were many episodes in the production, like the sea battle and the chariot race, which left an indelible impression on us.

27 October

After yesterday I expected to have a headache, but I did not, and worked hard and well.

Spent the evening at home. Massine telephoned, but I asked Grogy to take the call and say that I was busy. Why should I talk him after the rude letters he sent?

28 October

Almost finished Act Two.

Ptashka being out, I read my old diaries. Nothing else happened today.

29 October

Finished Act Two. This is truly excellent, and consistent progress: one act per month, Act One in September and Act Two in October, and the move back from the country has in no way interrupted the flow, as I had feared it might. The second act is longer than the first, but it does contain long passages with Babulenka which hardly needed any rewriting, only some sprucing up of the orchestration. There is more to be done in the third act, but it is a shorter one.

Dined with the Zakharovs. Now that I have been reading my old diaries with all their romantic ups and downs in our relationship, it was particularly interesting to see him again. He and Celia and Frieda were uncommonly warm and friendly today, and Zakharov was like his old self, most amusingly imitating Medtner who, going through his Second Sonata with Celia, was nervous and kept jumping up to take his jacket off. It was extremely funny, at least as impersonated by Zakharov. The concert of works by Medtner is next week, put on by the organist Dupré,[1] in a private hall. The most amusing thing is that Grogy received an invitation but I did not. Needless to say, I would not have gone anyway, not wishing to frighten Medtner.

30 October

Checked Grogy's transcription of the first act of *The Gambler* and continued with making the vocal score of the second.

Was at the Christian Science Church, following the advice of Miss Crain. The chorales today were quite pleasant and did not evoke so strongly the atmosphere of a Protestant church: one of them was a version of Mendelssohn and another of a Spanish song. The solo singing was disastrous, but I kept myself firmly in check and did not lose my temper. As for the sermon, I get more out of it when I read it at home on my own and can reflect. Perhaps if I knew English better I would find it easier to understand the sermon in church.

31 October

A mild headache which, however, did not get worse. All the same, I did not do much work, producing only a few pages of the vocal score.

---

1 Marcel Dupré (1886–1971), organist, pianist, composer and teacher. In 1920 Dupré, a pre-eminent organ virtuoso many of whose compositions are still regarded as among the most testing ever written (even Widor, with whom he studied composition and whom he succeeded as organist of the great Cavaillé-Coll instrument in Saint-Sulpice, considered some of them unplayable), gave a series of ten recitals in the Paris Conservatoire of the complete organ works of Bach entirely from memory. He was a superb improviser and wrote many books on harmony, counterpoint, acoustics and organ-building, perhaps reflecting the fact that Cavaillé-Coll, a family friend, had built a large organ in the Dupré home when Marcel was fourteen. The list of the organists he taught includes Jehain and Marie-Claire Alain, Jeanne Demessieux, Jean Guillou and Olivier Messiaen, to name only a few. As a composer he by no means restricted himself to the organ, producing piano, choral, orchestra and chamber-music works.

Went to see Kostritsky,[1] the former dentist of the Tsar. He told me that the filling of the tooth had fallen out and the root was exposed. He filled it temporarily, and if in four days' time all seems to be well, will make it a permanent repair. This is a splendid test for Christian Science: a fight against the corruption that could infiltrate the root.

Kostritsky said, 'You are very young to have the popularity you currently enjoy.'

'I am thirty-six.'

Kostritsky: 'Good heavens! I would not have thought you were more than twenty-eight. But your teeth are hardly your best assets.'

1 November

Before embarking on the revision of Act Three I read through the corresponding passage in Dostoevsky and got so absorbed that when I straightened my back I found I had lost that inner freshness so necessary for composition. Accordingly I did not compose, but completed a substantial portion of the Act Two vocal score.

Read my old diary in the afternoon. Despite all the idling about with girl students in the Conservatoire and the huge amount of work I had to do for the conducting class, I doggedly kept up my intense, impassioned labour on the Second Piano Concerto! I would work without stopping for several hours every day. I also noticed that sometimes when I did have to stop for an interruption, the composing would be even better as a result. And there was something else: throughout the period of my separation and then break from Nina Meshcherskaya, when I was unable to work or even concentrate properly at all, there were still those odd moments when marvellous inspirations would come upon me for *Chout*!

Today I worked on my tooth with Christian Science in order to appear in good shape before Kostritsky and allow him just to fill the tooth without having to carry out any other treatment. Soon, without difficulty, I became aware that my tooth was now free of disease.

2 November

Reading my old diary yesterday, I saw that on one occasion I had worked on the Second Piano Concerto all morning right through to three o'clock completely forgetting about lunch. That pierced me: nowadays I compose for two hours and that is enough. It is true that when I am orchestrating I sometimes work

---

1   Sergey Kostritsky, dentist to the Imperial Family. He is frequently mentioned in the diaries of Nicholas II and the Empress Alexandra Fyodorovna.

through the day, with breaks, but when I am composing it is rare that I can go for more than two hours at a stretch. I sat down to revise Act Three, but the work would not flow. I gave up work for a while and then went back to it. By the end of the day, unexpectedly, I found I had done a sizeable amount.

As I was out for a stroll in the afternoon a curious thing happened. I had been told by Shcherbachov that Alexander Benois was living somewhere in our area. He was someone we very much wanted to see, but were unable to find out his precise address. As I was walking along the rue de Passy today, the thought came to me with crystal clarity that I would meet A.N., and would say to him, as a joke, 'Alexander Nikolayevich, because despite our efforts we have not been able to discover your address, I am walking round the neighbourhood on purpose to meet you on the street.' Hardly had I gone ten paces when Benois himself appeared, walking towards me, as it seemed to me perfectly natural he should. I went up to him and repeated the phrase that had been in my mind. C.S. says that a person in the highest stage of development will possess the gift of foreseeing the future in the same way as being able to read the thoughts of others. Probably this is the form in which it will reveal itself.

As for the encounter itself, A.N. was as enchanting as ever, insisting that I go home with him and being reluctant to let me depart. Koka[1] had left the day before in his new car for Rome, taking Marusya with him. The trip will take about five days – who would have thought it, Marusya! Koka has secured an excellent commission from the Costanzi Theatre in Rome.

Returning home, I found a Miss Johnson there, an American pianist and Christian Scientist, with her mama. She played the piano for me, not badly but not at all remarkably either. In person she is quiet and modest. I did not know what to say to her. Well, what *is* there to say in such circumstances?

We dined with the Samoilenkos, Paichadze also there. It was a very pleasant evening, but I was tired after the day and had little to say, preferring to listen passively to the conversation. Paichadze said that *Chout* is to be given in two cities in Germany, and there is also a possibility that Romanov wants it for La Scala. But, there are not enough copies of the orchestral material. Thanks, dear publishers, for eternally sticking in my throat!

3 November

Tinkered with Act Three, achieving something but not much. Went through Grogy's transcriptions and read my old diaries. Made a start on dictating to

---

1 Alexander Benois's son Nikolay. His wife was the singer Maria (Marusya) Pavlova. See above, p. 74. The Costanzi Theatre, originally built in 1880, is Rome's Opera House. In 1926 it was acquired by Rome City Council. At the time of Nikolay Benois's appointment the theatre was undergoing major reconstruction to reopen in February 1928 under its new name of the 'Teatro Reale dell'Opera'. With the end of the monarchy and the departure into exile of King Victor Emmanuel III and Crown Prince Umberto in June 1946 the 'Reale' was dropped from the name.

Grogy the journal of my visit to the USSR, using the abbreviated notes I had made at the time. It is time I did so, as I am likely soon to find myself back in Russia and old impressions will be hard to disentangle from the new ones. That first visit is probably one of the most important of my whole life, so it should be recorded in detail.

To begin with it felt awkward dictating my diary, but I soon got used to it, as I have got used to dictating letters to Grogy. If more intimate passages crop up, I shall leave them out and insert them myself later on.

4 November

I could not work in the morning as I had an appointment with Kostritsky, who lives on the other side of town. My tooth turns out to be neither infected nor completely free of infection, so Kostritsky put in another temporary filling and asked me to come back in five days. A strange man, this former doctor of the Tsar. He always seems to want to get rid of his patients as quickly as possible, even if this means taking less money from them. Someone read in the recently published diaries of Nicholas II: 'Went to see Kostritsky,' and then the following day another entry: 'Spent an hour and a half with Kostritsky.' When Kostritsky was asked if the Tsar often suffered from toothache, he replied proudly, 'The Tsar did not come to see me to attend to his teeth, but just for conversation.'

In the afternoon I worked and read my old diaries. Again there is much about Zakharov, which made it all the more interesting when he, Celia and Frieda came to dinner. We had a lovely time, except that Borusya was withdrawn and came to life only when we started talking about roulette, but this is little enough when you consider what promise he held out in his youth! He blossomed even more when after dinner Ptashka sang some Rimsky-Korsakov. She had never sung for them before, and they were obviously impressed, especially by my songs. They found it amazing, indeed incomprehensible, how things of such complexity could be sung with such effortless freedom. Boris and Celia leave for Holland the day after tomorrow.

5 November

Gambler in the morning; in the afternoon the car came back with Gartman, a former Russian pilot now an automobile mechanic.[1] Everything had been

---

1 Maximilian Gartman (1890–1960) had been one of the most successful and decorated First World War fighter pilots of the Russian Air Force, rising to the rank of Lieutenant-Colonel. During the Civil War he served in the Volunteer Army and became a high-ranking staff officer in General Wrangel's Russian Army in the Crimea, from which he was evacuated with the remainder of Wrangel's forces and civilian dependents on 14 November 1920.

gone through, checked and rechecked in the repair shop, and the car had been resprayed, but it was still an absolute nightmare to start the engine. One possible cause, which will have to be checked yet again, is the magneto. I enjoyed driving round Paris again, though I kept away from the centre.

At last a postcard from Asafyev. For fear of political repercussions he has kept mum since July.

6 November

We were planning to go out of town in the car with the Samoilenkos now the car has been fully serviced and lubricated after the summer, but just at the wrong moment the dry, sunny weather broke and we had to cancel the trip. Another reason was that I had a headache which persisted all day.

I attended the C.S. Church and worked all day on my headache. Many good thoughts came to me. How important it is to understand clearly God's love towards to his creation, mankind. A clear perception of this refreshes and warms the human being like a ray of sunshine, and what development can take place in a man! I also had thoughts about the Third Symphony (C.S.), and even conceived a theme, but I do not yet know whether or not it is the right theme.

In the evening I undertook a long walk of about ten kilometres, ending up at Paichadze's; Ptashka and Fatma Hanum were already there. The latter observed that I am looking more and more like a solid citizen, and teasingly addressed as me 'General'. To frighten me she proposed a walk to Versailles, a distance of twenty kilometres. I accepted the challenge with alacrity.

7 November

Today I worked well, although I got bogged down revising Act Three. It's time to get down to the score.

In the afternoon I took the car to the automobile electrician to have the magneto repaired, as I simply don't have the strength to start the engine. He cranked the handle so hard that the end flew off and smacked him in the teeth. I was upset by the accident, but I managed to drive back through Paris all right and felt quite at home doing so. There is progress: the magneto has been repaired, even though it took a whole afternoon's messing about to achieve it.

8 November

I looked through the whole of Babulenka's part in Act Three and changed a few things, but leaving most of it as it was. It will have a tender, moving feeling to it. Generally I feel Babulenka is the most successfully realised of any character in any of my three operas.

The newspapers are carrying a report of a successful production of *Oranges* in Serbia (where they pay composers two copecks). So far nobody has sent me a thing about it, neither a printed programme, nor photographs, nor reviews.

Spent the afternoon again shuttling the car from one workshop to another adjusting the electrics and the engine-starting mechanisms. They tell me it will now start easily.

Evening at home reading C.S., writing up my diary and working on the vocal score.

9 November

More good work on the General (the final scene of Act Three). I even encroached on Ptashka's time; normally my working time is until twelve, after which I leave it free for her to sing from twelve until one, but even so I did not quite finish the scene. No composition in the afternoon, but more work on the vocal score. Ptashka and I went in the Ballot right across town to Kostritsky, I negotiating the daunting Paris traffic quite painlessly.

10 November

Worked on the General: quite fruitfully, but less so than yesterday, and again I did not finish the scene. Again a discussion about how to proceed: *Chout* is being requested in a number of German cities, but there is no orchestra material available. Very nice, thank you. The manuscript scores of *Three Oranges* and *Chout* have been lying in a cupboard for a year now gathering dust. This is not very clever of Paichadze.

In the evening, went to a lecture on C.S., but the lady lecturer spoke very slowly and not clearly enough.

11 November

Finished the General, but there is still the middle scene to do, Alexey's solo. Worked on it but did not finish it. Got tired.

In the afternoon went out of the city in the car with Paichadze and Frieda and had tea in St Cyr, a pleasant airing. As we were going along Frieda confided to Ptashka 'in extreme secrecy' how impossible Boris Zakharov has become. Sometimes he is in a bad temper for days on end, and stays in bed doing nothing but smoke cigarettes from morning till night. Celia is in torment because of it and dissolves in tears because the 'silly fool' imagines that without him she would be quite lost. I did not expect this of Boris; quite the opposite, I thought he was a great family man. But on reflection it is quite possible, I have known his character since the time about which I have just been reading in my old diary, and the fact that in the end he has not had a successful career is unlikely to have improved his nature.

Played bridge in the evening with the Paichadzes. God only knows how long it is since I engaged in this activity, and now I prefer to play with less expert players so as not to disgrace myself too much.

12 November

In the morning I finished off Alexey and at noon met Fatma Hanum below the Eiffel Tower to walk to Versailles as planned last week. The weather was marvellous and we were in high spirits. Fatma Hanum is an invigorating companion and we completed the walk in dashing style, pausing for a snack in a little restaurant in Sèvres.

'Have you any symptoms?' enquired Fatma Hanum as we approached Versailles. 'My right cheek is beginning to hurt when I make a stride with my left leg.'

At three o'clock we were already at Versailles railway station, having walked 17 kilometres in 2 hours 40 minutes (stopping 20 minutes for lunch). There was a train at 3.10 and at 3.35 we were back in Paris, very happy with our walk. Ptashka, however, was most annoyed, which very much surprised me.

Once home again, I felt so exhilarated that I finally despatched the third act revision and tomorrow shall get on with orchestrating it. Worked on the piano score and read my old diary. The rash on my hands that I thought had gone for good has started to itch again although not yet seriously. Could this be because I am just getting to that time in the old diary when the problem first surfaced? Seen from the perspective of everyday life this would seem paradoxical, but from a C.S. viewpoint there could be many connections.

13 November

Went to C.S. Church with Ptashka.

Settled down to orchestrating Act Three. With the first two acts I began orchestrating on the ninth of the month, but with the third act I am four days later. I shall have to get a move on. At first, indeed, it did not go very well, but because I spent nearly all day on it and concentrated on a few passages in Act Three, by the end I had done around nineteen pages of score, a good slice.

Schubert, Koshetz's husband, paid us a call; we both like him.

14 November

Act Three orchestration. I had an afternoon appointment with Kostritsky, who filled the tooth. Koussevitzky has given a concert in Boston in aid of poor Russian students in Paris and raised 20,000 francs for them. Bravo! Read my old diary, the account of the competition exam in the Conservatoire. This day still arouses the strongest agitation in me.[1] In the evening I carried on orchestrating, provoking from Ptashka the observation that I spend all my time either working or engaged on other matters, while devoting no attention to her. And I thought she was simply angry at my having gone for the walk with Fatma. Very silly of her.

15 November

Worked very hard. At first the orchestration refused to take wing, but later progress improved. Act Three is shorter than Act Two, but it contains a mass of new material, which is why progress on orchestration is sluggish.

Went in the Ballot to buy a radiator muff to protect against frost, and some anti-freeze liquid you add to the water in the radiator which prevents it freezing right down to minus 18° Centigrade.

Dictated to Grogy some of Moscow diary.

19 November

Today and for the past three days I have mostly been engaged on orchestrating Act Three, work that has provided me with great enjoyment, sometimes total absorption. Nothing else happened of great moment.

We received at last a telegram confirming Ptashka's and my recital for the radio in London. Needless to say, Ptashka is already starting to become nervous about it. It irritates me that for two weeks before the concert the atmosphere at home is already charged with electricity. Nevertheless, we attended a concert performance of *Prince Igor*, in which the singers, orchestra and conductor were all bad, only the baritone, Andronov-Elsky,[2] was good.

---

1 See *Diaries*, vol. 1, pp. 647–64, and *passim*, for a detailed account of Prokofiev's triumph in the Rubinstein Competition, which was also his graduation performance as a pianist from the St Petersburg Conservatoire, playing his own First Piano Concerto.
2 Yury Andronov-Elsky was a well-known singer and choral conductor in Parisian émigré circles, where he formed his own vocal quartet.

This was the first time I had been to the new Salle Pleyel (for some reason I was not invited to the opening ceremony).[1] It is quite nice, a large, unfussy space. Paris has long been in need of such a hall. We sat to one side and the orchestra did not blend particularly well. But then, I think *Igor* is only averagely well orchestrated. There were a good number of slip-ups in the playing.

20 November

Orchestrated, followed by C.S. Church, then more orchestration and dictation to Grogy of the Moscow diary.

In evening I went to the opening of a new chess club named for Znosko-Borovsky,[2] for an exhibition session with Bernstein.[3] I enjoyed it very much. As is the general rule with Russians, the session began 40 minutes late. Since there were more players than there were boards, the players were doubled up with the suggestion that the pairs play against the master in consultation. I invited Znosko-Borovsky's wife to play with me, on the grounds that she is barely capable of moving a chess piece correctly, and therefore I would effectively be able to play independently. However, I played the fool with her, and with Znosko-Borovsky and with Bernstein, setting out an extra pawn, and as a result the game was not a serious one. Early on I exchanged a knight for three pawns but could not sustain them and after an hour and a half Bernstein won, after two beautiful moves. I left soon afterwards, and all the remaining games except one fell to him.

21 November

Orchestrated. I am now getting on fast and although I started orchestrating Act Three four days late it looks as though I shall finish it before my self-imposed deadline.

---

1 The splendid new Salle Pleyel opened with a grandiose concert on 17 October 1927 involving the Orchestre de la Société des Concerts du Conservatoire, Robert Casadesus as soloist, conducted by Stravinsky, Ravel and Philippe Gaubert. The programme included music by Stravinsky, Falla, Ravel, Franck, Dukas and Wagner. One can understand Prokofiev's feeling of having been snubbed, especially given his relationship with Pierre Blois, who worked in a senior position at Pleyel.
2 Yevgeny Znosko-Borovsky 1884–1954), journalist, literary and theatre critic and chess-player. He had been a leading light in the St Petersburg Chess Club that had been played such an important part in Prokofiev's pre-emigration years and had hosted the 1914 International Chess Tournament described in detail in vol. 1 of the *Diaries*. A naval officer decorated for gallantry in the First World War, Znosko-Borovsky left Russia for Paris in 1920 and became well known partly as a distinguished championship player but more as the author of books on chess such as *The Middle Game in Chess* and *How Not to Play Chess*, the latter containing such valuable maxims as 'Avoid Mistakes'. See *Diaries*, vol. 1, pp. 155–6, 176, 583–4, 654, 672–5.
3 Osip Bernstein (1882–1962), chess master, a leading contender in the 1914 St Petersburg International Chess Tournament. See *Diaries*, vol. 1, pp. 640–41, 644, 646–7, 652–4, 657.

To have a break from my labours in the afternoon I took Schubert out for a drive, and he brought Marina[1] along. She must have been playing truant from school to do so. Despite her fifteen years she is already a grown-up young lady and has absorbed much from her mother, although Koshetz was probably more beautiful. We drove about, had tea at the Hermitage in the Forest of Meudon, and at half past five I came back to continue orchestrating.

Fatma asked me what had caused yesterday's disgrace when I capitulated to Bernstein. I explained that when he had put me in an impossible position I turned over my king and sidled out of the hall along the wall, at which Znosko-Borovsky announced to the assembled company that 'Board No. 9 has resigned'. Fatma laughed, and from then on whenever someone loses at bridge, she says, 'Board No. 9 has resigned.'

24 November

Today I glimpsed the end of Act Three because I have finished orchestrating the Babulenka and the General has made the appearance that culminates with his descent into madness. I am extremely pleased with the new version of Act Three. Before there was not much musical material and one could say it depended largely on effect rather than music, but this act has really taken off now. In my old diary I have been reading about the period in 1916 when I was composing the third act of *The Gambler*.

At home I had a telephone conversation with Stravinsky, who came from Nice today. I was asking him about the new biographical-explanatory rolls Duo-Art is suggesting I make for them, similar to those Stravinsky has recently done.[2] Stravinsky was nice, and explained the process in great detail. The result is a most interesting way of working.

---

1   The daughter of Nina Koshetz and the artist Alexander von Schubert.
2   Prokofiev refers to the Aeolian Company's imaginative project of 'AudioGraphic' piano rolls. Since the early 1920s Stravinsky, who had in any case long been interested in the possibility of mechanical musical instruments, had had the use of a studio provided for him by Pleyel in its rue Rochechouart headquarters, where among other activities the Pleyela music rolls were edited and manufactured. The following account of Stravinsky's collaboration with Pleyel and later with Duo-Art in New York is reproduced from an article on the website of the Pianola Institute, whose generous permission is gratefully acknowledged.

    'Stravinsky was able to use his studio as an office, a congenial location for composition, a workshop for creating new piano roll versions of most of his early works, and as a pied-à-terre for entertaining guests, not least his future wife, Vera Soudeikina. In close co-operation with Jacques Larmanjat, Pleyel's head of music rolls, he made new arrangements of *Firebird, Petrushka*, the *Rite of Spring*, the *Song of the Nightingale, Pulcinella, Les Noces*, and a host of smaller works. Pleyel cannot have made much money from the sale of Stravinsky's rolls, for they paid the composer on five counts for each and every roll of his that they manufactured, whether or not it was subsequently sold. These payments were for the mechanical copyright, for exclusivity (since the rolls represented the very first "recordings" of the works concerned), for the arrangement of the work for music roll, for the performance of the work (even though Stravinsky did not actually record any of the rolls at a

25 November

Orchestrated the final scene of Act Three. In the afternoon I visited the publishers to collect my money. Down in the basement has been languishing for three years my black, elephant-skin-covered trunk containing my diaries, letters, etc. Today I took from it several notebooks from my Russian period, the ones that ended up with me in Kislovodsk in 1917 and which happily eventually came with Mama to Paris via Constantinople. Over the three years I had forgotten exactly which notebooks these were, but now realised to my delight that they were the very ones that were not among those I had recently brought back from Moscow. It means that not one of my diaries has been lost. The only things that have disappeared are my letters from the beginning of 1917 and perhaps from 1916, the letters to my father I wrote between the ages of fifteen to seventeen, and some chess games.

Hitherto the Apocalypse has seemed to me an absurd agglomeration of incomprehensible images. Now it is beginning to assume for me a more figurative, and therefore more interesting, cast. Plans to compose a large-scale work on the Apocalypse. But first, a major-key symphony.

26 November

More orchestration, bringing me almost to the end of Act Three. In the afternoon I went to the Salon d'Automne,[1] smothered in naked bodies. Adriana

---

keyboard), and for the musical copyright of the original work. In 1924, Stravinsky's contract with Pleyel was acquired by the Aeolian Company in New York, and in January 1925 the composer travelled to America for a concert tour, and to record some piano rolls for the Duo-Art system. The Sonata for Piano was actually published on roll before the sheet music appeared, and the first movement of the Concerto for Piano was also issued. The Aeolian Company was keen to publish many of Stravinsky's works in its new "AudioGraphic" series of rolls, on which copious programme notes and illustrations could be printed, so in addition to his actual keyboard recordings, Stravinsky worked on preparing *Firebird, Petrushka, Apollon musagète, Baiser de le fée* and other works for the new system. Unfortunately, the Depression of the late 1920s caused the abandonment of this project, and much of the work was destroyed. However, a series of six rolls of the *Firebird* was published (*Stravinsky, My Life and Music, First Series: To The Firebird, in Six Rolls*). Although Aeolian became Stravinsky's main music-roll publisher, Pleyel retained the rights to sell its own rolls of his music in France and one or two other European countries, and so he remained quite close to the company throughout the 1920s, appearing as conductor at the opening of the new Salle Pleyel in Paris in 1927. Pleyel in the first half of the twentieth century was a most remarkable enterprise, thanks in large measure to Gustave Lyon, its imaginative and resourceful managing director for over forty years. For further information about Stravinsky's pianola works, you can read Rex Lawson's article, "Stravinsky and the Pianola", spread over issues 1 and 2 of the *Pianola Journal*. See our *Pianola Journal* pages for more details.' (www.pianola.org/history/history_stravinsky.cfm)

1. The Salon d'Automne had begun in 1903 as an initiative by artists such as Rouault, Derain and Matisse to organise an annual showcase in opposition to the conservativism of the official Paris Salon. By the late 1920s it was itself part of the establishment, home to the most eminent of the Montparnasse circle.

Janacopulos's[1] sculptures are not bad. But when she modelled my head three years ago, the result was only moderately successful.

27 November

C.S. Church in the morning, and then we went with Ptashka's friend Franciz to look at the villa she has built forty kilometres or so outside Paris. It was an enjoyable trip, but the villa itself is too small for the price she is asking. If we ever do set about buying something, it could only be a building that is already there – that is the way to get better value.

We went to dine at the Salon d'Automne, where they now have a culinary exhibition as well. We were served a phenomenal dinner: by the third dish we were already stuffed to the gills, so that afterwards we could hardly move. Thanks to all today's excursions I did not manage to finish Act Three, as I had anticipated doing.

28 November

Hoorah, finished Act Three, a day less than Act Two and two days less than Act One.

In the afternoon I had to chase about on passport matters in view of our forthcoming visit to London. Received a postcard from Zakharov in Oslo congratulating me on a very successful performance of the Suite from *Oranges* in the presence of the King. I signed the contract for two concert appearances in London (BBC) and one in Freiburg, also one in Paris for the Princesse de Polignac. This winter I have turned my back on concert engagements, but they turn up all on their own, and with higher fees as well.

Conius: Rachmaninoff composed his best things whilst under hypnosis from Dahl.[2]

I: Then it is infernal music, as it comes from the devil.

Conius: Well, we don't know whether Dahl was a practitioner of black magic or white magic.

I: Where hypnosis is concerned, it can only be black.

---

1   Adriana Volkovysskaya, the sculptress sister of the singer Vera Janacopulos, wife of Prokofiev's estranged friend Alexey Stahl. See above, pp. 33, 42.
2   Depressed by the failure of his First Symphony, allegedly ruined at its premiere by the conducting of an inebriated Glazunov, Rachmaninoff yielded to the entreaties of his cousins the Satin family and underwent a course of treatment by the hypnotist Dr Nikolay Dahl. According to the account in the composer's own autobiography, this was extremely effective and the muse returned in a spate of inspiration, producing in quick succession some of Rachmaninoff's most enduring masterpieces, including the Second Piano Concerto, the Cello Sonata and the Second Suite for Two Pianos.

30 November

When I went out in the morning to post a letter I ran into Boris Nikolayevich Bashkirov round the corner. I was surprised, and he was surprised at my surprise. It seems he had given the concierge a note for me to the effect that he would be waiting for me on the embankment, and if he had not entirely ceased to exist for me, would I please come out and see him. The concierge had not yet given me the letter, but it so happened that I came out anyway. Bashkirov has lost one of his front teeth, had not shaved, and looked generally down at heel. I could not forget the cheque he had illicitly got hold of and the money he had tried to get out of Lina Ivanovna behind my back when I was away. How could I rein in my anger? I did not even try. He started, naturally, to tell me about the difficult situation in which he found himself, about his despicable brother Vladimir who was refusing to send him any money, and about how he was now under threat of deportation from France. Finally, waving his bandaged right hand about, he said that he needed to leave Paris for somewhere warmer. 'But if they do deport you,' I said, 'might they not send you to Algeria?' Despite his pathetic appearance I somehow could not take him seriously, in fact the attempt was hopeless. Doubtless to an onlooker observing the scene at that moment the sight of our two figures would have brought to mind an image of Pontius Pilate and Christ – myself, plump and reasonably well dressed, clearly in the role of Pilate. B.N. accompanied me to the postbox and back. As we approached our entrance, I was expecting him to ask me for money, and therefore started talking something inconsequential in order to deflect the moment. But he said nothing about it, merely: 'When they give you my letter, please tear it up without reading it.'

In the afternoon I intended to do more on the vocal score, but I had a headache and instead walked along the embankment to try to clear it. We dined with the Samoilenkos, where another guest was a Monsignor Yevreinov, a Russian who had become a Catholic and was intent on planting the seed of Catholicism among the Russians. I had tried everything I could to avoid having dinner with him and even yelled into the telephone receiver, 'I shall spit in the Monsignor's coffee,' quoting Dostoevsky,[1] but the Samoilenkos were frightfully offended and Boris Samoilenko went so far as addressing me, instead of the usual 'Sergusya', as 'Sergey Sergeyevich'. So we had to give in and accept. In fact the Monsignor, as one might have expected,

---

[1] 'In the most insolent tone, as if glad that he could insult me, he looked me up and down and cried: "Whatever makes you think that Monsignor would interrupt his coffee for you?" Then I too cried, but even louder than he: "Understand that I spit in the Monsignor's coffee! If you do not complete preparing my passport this instant I shall go to him myself."' (Dostoyevsky, 'The Gambler', 1866.)

turned out to be a very worldly gentleman, with a gratifyingly elegant St Petersburg turn of phrase and huge buckles on his shoes, with which he played continuously. Tamara Hanum[1] was mentioned in conversation, and Fatma said that this evening she was dining with friends at the 'Samarkand'. Ptashka glanced over at me and giggled.

2 December

Today and yesterday evaporated on getting things together for England. I practised the piano, changed money, collected music from the publishers, bought the tickets. Although it would have been cheaper to buy return tickets, we decided to have them only for one way as we have a plan to return by air. When Miss Crain called on us she said, 'You must fly, it is such a wonderful feeling when you leave the ground and soar above it; then you see how tiny all the people are crawling down below you, and how inconsequential their terrestrial interests.'

Ptashka has been singing rather well of late, her voice has become noticeably stronger and her understanding has grown, but she feels as though she is suffocating with all the strangled vowels and crepitating consonants of the English language. Paichadze recommends staying at the Albermarle Court, where Stravinsky and Diaghilev put up: Stravinsky was there for several weeks and was enamoured of it.

Over the past few days I have still managed to make good progress with the vocal score of Act Two.

3 December

In the morning we did our final packing and at eleven o'clock left for the station. The train was at twelve, the 'Golden Arrow', a magnificent de luxe train consisting of new Pullman carriages in which we were served a delicious, although rather expensive, lunch. We crossed the Channel in a flat calm, but it was cold and our feet were frozen until one of the sailors gave us his mackintosh, a gesture that earned him a fine tip. On the boat with us was the Spanish composer Nin,[2] a stylish man, bare-headed, with a light

---

1 Fatma Hanum's sister.
2 Joaquin Nin y Castellanos (1879–1949), Spanish-Cuban pianist and composer. Nin's daughter was the writer, feminist and diarist Anaïs Nin. Her unexpurgated diary, *Incest: From a Journal of Love*, contains an account of the incestuous relationship she claims to have had with her father. Confusingly, the earlier novel *House of Incest*, her first work of fiction, is not about incest at all, or even much about sex, 'incest' being used metaphorically to explore self-love or obsession with traits and characteristics identical with those one recognises in oneself. In this novel actual incestuous experiences, even if obliquely susceptible to interpretation in the light of the later diary's claims, can only be inferred from some of the surreal, dream-like images.

overcoat. I have heard a few of his pieces, which seemed to me to be inferior Falla. He did not greet us; Ptashka is sure that this was because at some time or other I had snubbed him, but I do not recall the occasion. In short it was a ridiculous situation, but while we were having our passports checked we found ourselves face to face. Ptashka nodded to him, and we had a very pleasant conversation. He was also going to play for the radio (BBC). Then there was a shout of 'Mr Nin!' and we parted. Next for us was another Pullman, in which we had tea and I dozed as it was already getting dark outside the window.

In London we went to the Albemarle Court and were given the very same room as Stravinsky had had. But there is no piano, even though I had written to the BBC to ask them to have one sent in. This is a pity as Ptashka needs to vocalise otherwise she gets hoarse. On her mood depends the entire outlook for our stay in London.

We strolled about London with great enjoyment.

4 December

Terrible fog, electric light on all day. Went twice to the BBC. Awful muddle with the piano: Steinway say they do not know me and would not provide a piano. We were enraged, although tried with the help of C.S. not to lose our tempers. They promised to send one tomorrow.

Proofed *The Gambler* second act.

Ptashka is hoarse; if it's like this tomorrow we shall not be able to work then either. Mood is therefore leaden.

5 December

Mood not of the best owing to Ptashka's hoarseness. No piano; they have made yet another muddle, and this time I shouted down the telephone that I cannot practise on a table. At Duo-Art I was received by an assistant, they are overburdened with work, rolls of Debussy were playing, I said that no doubt Debussy himself would be interested to hear them. They are overworked. I dropped a hint about orchestrating the Overture; this seemed to go down well. Will be decided after Reed's visit to America.

Dukelsky rang up: matters have improved with the operetta, he wants to play me *Dushenka*[1] and his Symphony. He will try to come round today, but not before ten as he is busy until then. The piano arrived about six. Ptashka

---

1 *Dushenka*, aka *La Mignonne*, is a concert aria for soprano, contralto and chamber orchestra to a Russian text by Hyppolite Bogdanovich. There is also an English version: 'What is the use of lovin' a girl (if the girl don't love you)?'

sang a bit but is still hoarse; I practised the Second Sonata. Ptashka seems a bit better, but there is no chance of its being good, the best we could hope for would be Acceptable, the worst failure. My advice is not to risk it. Ptashka agrees, but all the same, while I am dressing, I hear her mournfully singing 'I remember us together', as if still hoping against hope. But this time we are both so strongly under the influence of C.S. that Ptashka's attitude[1] is much better. At the BBC Clark[2] expressed his regret but without going so far as to make extravagant protests. I suggested the Second Sonata, he preferred some *Visions fugitives*; the original programme was long and he was not averse to shortening it. I sat in the adjoining room, not for long, and then went out to play. In the large studio with padded walls were sitting about thirty people, but they were some distance away. I did not look at anyone, but sat straight down to play with an air of getting down to business. For some reason I played well, persuasively and with expression, without rushing. It is very helpful to have a piano with a heavy touch to play on at home. Sonata No. 3 followed after a short interval. After that a Hungarian quartet came on, and I went out to practise *Visions fugitives*. To finish I played four of the *Visions* and the Scherzo.[3] At the end, once we were off air, I was applauded, politely but not excessively. Calvocoressi gave me his address and sent his regards to Tcherepnin. He wanted me to go into the hall and meet his wife. Clark was circling around but did not introduce me to anybody, although a number of people were looking at me with interest. I said goodbye and left.

At home Ptashka was waiting impatiently for me to get back. She was upset, but behaved heroically.

6 December

Proof-read.

Dukelsky took us to lunch. He speaks like an Englishman, having almost forgotten his Russian. He was depressed when I told him Diaghilev had taken against him, but did his best not to show his dismay. He came back with us. *Dushenka*. An excellent theme, one I've heard before, the rest in parts somewhat reminiscent of 'Did you hear?',[4] at other times hard to

---

1   The word is in English in the text.
2   Edward Clark (1888–1962), conductor and composition pupil of Schoenberg who had introduced the latter's Chamber Concerto to London in 1921. He became the extremely influential Musical Adviser to the BBC in 1923. In 1942 he married the composer Elisabeth Lutyens, with whom he had long been associated; he is credited with having been the first to interest her in serial techniques.
3   The tenth of *Ten Pieces for Piano*, Op. 12 (1912–14).
4   The first line of a famous early lyric by Pushkin, 'The Singer', set by many composers including Medtner and Anton Rubinstein.

understand as he was pounding the piano even though the orchestra would have to be *piano* otherwise the voice would not be heard. The Symphony is very interesting, but the Andante is a very old friend. Running through my head was an idea from the fifth of my *Sarcasms*, and the second subject from *Le Sacre*. If it is well orchestrated it will be a good work. I advised him to take it slowly at the beginning. He plans to come to Paris in February – my advice on this subject. The article about Glinka – he wants me to sign it. For now I made some suggestions about changes in it.

7 December

Spent most of the 7th and 8th shopping. Dukelsky drove us around, showing us the best places for value and style in men's clothes. Dukelsky is reading an article commissioned by Suvchinsky about Diaghilev. Much well-aimed good sense in it. The ancient mummies to whom Diaghilev pays obeisance. Went to a revue which had one number by Dukelsky in it; it was boring. Ptashka and I bewailed Dukelsky being at home in such an atmosphere.

In the midst of all the running about I still do some work reading the proofs of the second act. On the 8th, the first rehearsal with Ansermet;[1] he was all but sight-reading as only in the interval – just before the read-through – did I manage to go through with him some of the tempi and the subterranean traps. Given the circumstances they got through it not too badly. I cannot get hold of the money I need to pay for my purchases, despite having warned Clark about this. There is a deduction of 25 guineas. I am greatly surprised; we go to the administration and are referred to another, higher-up, official. But this one agrees immediately to have a word and hopes to get the matter settled. Clark, profiting from the occasion, asks me to add the Schubert Waltzes, and feeling that I have no choice, I agree.

9 December

Around twelve I got to the rehearsal. Ansermet was making a great effort and had grasped the ideas well, but time was short and the result was crude.

Dukelsky came as well and made some pertinent observations, among them that the third movement is superfluous although, on the other hand, it would be a pity to lose it altogether. I took him to task for yesterday, describing his work as theatrical dregs, but lo and behold he is being offered a commission for a new operetta with an advance of £200. In the afternoon

---

1 For a radio concert with the BBC Symphony Orchestra in which Prokofiev played the Second Piano Concerto. According to David Nice the tape cannot be found in the BBC Archives. (D. Nice, op. cit., p. 251.)

I practised the Concerto which I can play all right but with a certain lack of polish, and the Schubert Waltzes.

We booked tickets on Imperial Airways. Ptashka has for a long time dreamed of flying in an aeroplane. In Paris, before we left, we had decided that we might fly. Now, when we had actually taken the decision, many people were saying, 'Well, yes, flying is all very well, but I wouldn't do it myself.' At first I experienced a slight twinge of unease, but quickly conquered it with the help of C.S. and today collected the tickets with a confident, interested air. Just at that moment a bus arrived bearing passengers from the flight that had just arrived from Paris. One stout, elderly woman, looking more like the wife of a Russian landowner from the Urals, emerged triumphantly from the bus but another lady had evidently suffered airsickness; she had to be helped to a chair.

11 December

Carried on with the vocal score of Act Two. Attended C.S. Church.

Schubert called in the afternoon with tickets for tonight's jubilee concert by Koshetz celebrating fifteen years of concert activity, with a programme consisting entirely of songs dedicated to her, accompanied by the composers. Schubert tried all he knew to get me to participate, but I declined to join this parade of the monkeys. I sent her a basket of flowers, and in the evening the Suvchinskys called for us and we went together to the concert. Quite a number of composers have dedicated rather good songs to Koshetz, among them five by me,[1] seven by Rachmaninoff and a quantity by Tcherepnin, but of mine she sang only one, two by Rachmaninoff and the remainder were all incredible rubbish, each song feebler and more vulgar than its predecessor, so much so that in such company even a romance by Labunsky appeared respectable. Of course there were tributes, congratulatory speeches, flowers and an emotional response by Koshetz. During the second half there appeared in our box Zoya Lodi,[2] recently arrived from Russia, who related to me the exceptional success she had had with *The Ugly Duckling* when touring the south of the country all the way from Astrakhan to Odessa.

In the final section of the programme the vulgarity level of Koshetz's songs rose to extraordinary heights, but the obsequious pomp with which they and their pseudo-esteemed composers fawned on Koshetz reduced Zoya Lodi to despair. Suvchinsky whispered, 'Surely you can't go to see her after this?!' (Koshetz had invited us to supper afterwards.) Initially I had

---

1 The *Five Songs Without Words*, Op. 35, and although there is no dedication on the score, the *Five Poems of Anna Akhmatova*, Op. 27.
2 See above, p. 366.

thought it would be amusing to observe the maudlin hullabaloo that would inevitably envelop the Koshetz household after her anniversary triumph, but 'Estrellita'[1] and some other idiotic Mexican pieces, evoking wild applause from the audience, brought me to a state of incandescent fury, and screaming at Koshetz's sister, who was unlucky enough to be present, 'I refuse to set foot in such obscenity,' I rushed out of the box. Ptashka was appalled at my behaviour, but Suvchinsky was at one with my opinion. The upshot was that instead of going to Koshetz we went to a café and there tried to slough off the debris of this jubilee.

12 December

Next morning a lingering aftertaste from yesterday's concert, the result partly of Koshetz's fall from grace and partly of my own choleric rudeness. But worst of all is that I am quite ready to repeat word for word what I said yesterday.

In the afternoon I finished the piano score of the second act. Visited the Princesse de Polignac about my appearance at her house on the 16th December. She was thrilled with my suggestion that one item on the programme should be my two-piano version of the Schubert Waltzes with her at the other keyboard. Old girl Singer[2] can still bash the keys pretty usefully. This evening she had guests: the Samoilenkos, Paichadze, Zoya Lodi, the Suvchinskys and Professor Karsavin, the last-named making his first visit. V.A.[3] has had her hair cut and looks like a young girl. She had called on Koshetz today ('What!' I exclaimed. 'Did Pyotr Petrovich allow this?') and needless to say Koshetz's sister had given her an account of my behaviour which it seems did not surprise her as it is not the first time I have flown at her for vulgarity (although it is the first time I have done so with such harshness). This evening we had a very pleasant time, despite Pyotr Petrovich breaking a crystal vase.

13 December

Made a start on revising Act Four. But either London had distracted me or the three acts I have done have tired me out because I did not have much energy to work. All the same I managed to do something.

---

1 'Estrellita', 'Little Star', is probably the most popular melody by the Mexican composer Manuel Ponce (1882–1948). It exists in innumerable versions for voice, piano, guitar, orchestra, violin, etc., and has been recorded by Flagstad, Heifetz, Domingo, Deanna Durbin and Koshetz herself, among many others.
2 The Princesse de Polignac was the former Winnaretta Singer, heiress to the Singer sewing-machine fortune.
3 Vera Alexandrovna Suvchinskaya née Guchkova, Pyotr Suvchinsky's wife.

Today is the third anniversary of Mama's death.

The Russian newspapers are carrying descriptions of the lives of three commanding figures: Sologub,[1] who died recently, Proust and Nekrasov.[2] All great men, but what impenetrable darkness of spirit in them all! The terror of life in Sologub, Proust's 'lost time', Nekrasov's failure of faith and loveless jealousy ... What a beacon of light is offered by C.S., but to what black abysses does that human soul descend which is outside its rays!

14 December

Worked on Act Four. Nikita Magalov came and played me his new composition, *Allegro*, which in fact proceeds at a moderato tempo. But he has genuinely come on since his last visit in the spring. At that time it was all insipid Chopiniana and first-period Scriabinisms, but now there are hints of independence – not, true, of any notable originality but at least he has got over the sickly-sweet overtones of his previous efforts. If he makes a comparable leap forward over the next six months his music stands a chance of becoming interesting. I spoke encouragingly to him and advised him not to practise the piano as much as five hours a day (people who do five or eight hours a day never turn into anything much) but to apply himself more to composition. There are a million pianists, but far fewer composers.

15 December

Continued work on Act Four. In the afternoon went with Ptashka and Svyatoslav to Mama's grave. As we were approaching Bellevue, another car came out of some gates on the left side of the road, and although by rights he should have looked to his right and let us through, having failed to do so he almost drove straight into us. Just in time he almost came to a halt, so that all we did was rip

---

1   Fyodor Sologub (pen-name of Fyodor Teternikov) (1863–1927), poet and novelist, one of the founders of the Symbolist movement. His best-known novel, *The Petty Demon*, is a relentlessly harrowing study of how horrible life could be in rural Russia, personified by the appalling Peredonov, a sadistic, perverted and paranoid local teacher in the local school (Sologub himself taught for many years at schools both in the provinces and in Petrograd). Sologub's poetry was admired by his peers including Blok, Akhmatova and Mandelshtam. Prokofiev had come across the writer in the months leading up to the October Revolution, notably during his brief and signally unengaged membership of a delegation from the Society of Workers in the Arts, headed by Sologub, to the Soviet of Workers and Deputies in Petrograd. See *Diaries*, vol. 2, pp. 122, 148–9, 189.
2   Nikolay Nekrasov (1821–1878), poet, editor and publisher, indelibly associated with the radical literary movement epitomised by Belinsky, Chernyshevsky and Dobrolyubov but also shrewd enough to have been the first publisher of Dostoevsky. He himself described the main subject of his poetry as 'the sufferings of the people'; his masterpiece is the long satirical poem 'Who is Happy in Russia?' in which seven peasants walk the length and breadth of Russia to pose the question to representatives of the various classes but fail to get a convincing answer.

off his bumper and put a dent in our rear mudguard. The result was that a policeman turned up, an official report had to be made and an hour wasted. In fact both of our cars were insured so the only people to suffer would be the insurance companies, and that not very much. Mama's grave was overgrown with grass; we asked the one of the female cemetery gardeners to tidy it up.

Miss Crain told us about a Christian Scientist she knew of who was about to go to America and wanted to sell his Hispano Suiza for thirty or thirty-five thousand francs. I was excited by this, because the one car I would think of exchanging my Ballot for would be a Hispano.[1] I made a telephone call and the American will bring it round to show it to us.

In the evening I started the transcription of Act Three. Zakharov telephoned: they are just back from Holland and will leave for America the day after tomorrow. They invited us to come to them tomorrow. Grogy played me his new Sonata. In among the jumble of maladroit meanderings there were glimpses of a rather good theme. It was true that the piece was not without signs of my influence, but then all composers like having their ideas pinched!

16 December

Finished the first scene. I lunched with an Englishman, Trefusis,[2] whom I met yesterday at Polignac's when I was rehearsing the Schubert Waltzes. He

---

1 The Hispano-Suiza (the Suiza reflecting its gifted Swiss engineer Marc Birgikt), was in its day (the middle of the 1920s) the ne plus ultra of the luxury automobile, the most expensive marque ever made. The company began life in Barcelona building cars for King Alfonso XIII in a patriotic bid to challenge the Rolls-Royce hegemony. The car Prokofiev was salivating over would have been its most widely produced model, the H6, with six cylinders in line, overhead camshaft and (to reduce weight) an aluminium block into which thin steel sleeves were inserted to accommodate the pistons. Lord Emsworth's car in P. G. Wodehouse's *Blandings Castle* stories is a Hispano H6 (although Bertie Wooster, being a young blade-about-town rather than a peer of the realm, had an open Bentley Red Label, driven naturally by Jeeves). Just before the Second World War the firm stopped producing cars to make aircraft engines, and has never again entered the automobile market, despite a flurry of excitement at the 2010 Geneva Motor Show about a rumoured new model which proved to be smoke without fire.
2 Denys Trefusis (1890–1929), a decorated war-hero who had unwittingly found himself in a *mariage blanc* with Violet (née Keppel) Trefusis, herself a partner in one of the most intense and scandalous lesbian relationships of the 1920s, with Vita Sackville-West. Vita, hardly a disinterested observer, wrote later of Denys that she 'could compare him to many things, to a racehorse, to a Crusader, to a greyhound, to an ascetic in search of the Holy Grail . . . a tragic person'. The Trefusises had married in 1919 at the insistence of Violet's mother, Alice Keppel, the former mistress of King Edward VII, Denys having reportedly agreed never to have sexual relations with his wife (a very different arrangement from that obtaining between Vita and her husband, Harold Nicolson). This agreement did not, however, stop Denys destroying in a fit of jealousy all Vita's letters to Violet. By 1921 Vita's relationship with Violet had ended in any active sense, and although Violet's passion remained undimmed until the end of her life in 1972, in 1923 she (Violet) began a long-term but socially more discreet affair with the Princesse de Polignac. The fact that Prokofiev met Denys at a Polignac soirée indicates that at this time he and his wife were at least on speaking terms, but by the time of his early death from tuberculosis in 1929 the couple were completely estranged.

is nice, speaks Russian and was recently in Moscow, where he had seen a performance of the *Oranges* production at the Bolshoy Theatre.

I then went back to the Princesse's to rehearse the Waltzes with the pianist Février,[1] who is an exceptional sight-reader, after which I returned home to await with increasing excitement the Hispano-Suiza, standing by the window as if to catch the first sight of my beloved. She duly appeared, enormous and green, but we were soon disappointed because the coachwork was inconvenient and unattractive. We took it out for a trial drive in the Bois de Boulogne. The car pulls excellently, but we decided to think about it.

Went to the Zakharovs, where it was very nice. I kissed Celia and Boris kissed Ptashka. In the evening I played at the Princesse de Polignac's, where there was less of a crowd but among the guests were Rothschild and Paléologue[2] (with whom I reminisced about Petersburg and the French Embassy), and the Princesse's brother Singer, a sewing-machine manufacturer. His daughter had today bought my compositions from the publishers for 400 francs, Paichadze will have been rubbing his hands with glee. I played quite well: the Second Sonata, a few trifles and the Waltzes with Février. The last-named had the greatest success.

17 December

All day was spent on the Hispano. Rudnev was summoned, we went to the Hispano showroom to compare, then the owner arrived and we went to inspect the car. Rudnev immediately found that the car was so elderly that its market value would be zero, that is to say, it could still be serviceable but would be difficult to sell when the time came. And since the bodywork was trash, especially compared with the elegance of our Ballot, we decided to wash our hands of it. And so ended my brief affair with the Suiza. But I did no work today. Received a nice letter from Stravinsky.

18 December

Gave some thought to the entr'acte, but as nothing seemed to come of it. I practised the Third Piano Concerto in preparation for my concert in Freiburg in January. At five o'clock we headed over to Mme Dubost for a reception in honour of Schoenberg, who is currently visiting Paris. I missed the first of his

---

1 Jacques Février (1900–1979), pianist and teacher noted for his performances of French piano literature, especially Ravel, who in 1930 specifically requested that he give the French premiere of his Concerto for the Left Hand.
2 Maurice Paléologue (1855–1944) was French Ambassador to the Russian Imperial Court between 1914 until the October Revolution. Prokofiev had been his guest at the French Embassy on several occasions. See *Diaries*, vol. 2, pp. 92, 97, 131.

concerts through being in London, and was too idle to go to the second.¹ Today I was introduced to him: he is ordinary-looking, small and extremely bald. We exchanged a few muttered commonplaces in German, neither of us having much idea what to say to each another. I said I had never been to Vienna and he replied that yes, it was a rather out of the way place. After Count San-Martino came rushing up I moved on to other people.² The German pianist Steuermann³ performed a piano transcription of his Chamber Symphony⁴ but I did not like it: there was nothing to cling on to, and it was mind-numbingly long. The arrangement of Johann Strauss Waltzes⁵ for flute, clarinet, piano and string quartet, which he conducted himself in rather an entertaining way, struck me initially as silly and I was even casting my eyes around for someone on whom I could unburden my disparaging comments, but then started to notice some intriguing aural combinations. When all was said and done, nevertheless, Schoenberg succeeded in turning the old salon maestro's famously jaunty waltzes into a dreary tedium. Jostling through the countless throng of guests, I several times narrowly avoided bumping into Janacopulos, who was looking very beautiful but who, so I heard, had failed to draw much of a crowd to her concert yesterday. After receiving pleasing intimations from two young conductors – Golschmann⁶ on the success of the Suite from *Oranges* in Scotland; Désormière on a forthcoming Diaghilev gala performance of *Le Pas d'acier* in ten days' time at the Grand Opéra – we left and made our way home.

1 The concert on 8 December with the composer conducting the Colonne Orchestra had included *Pelleas und Melisande*, excerpts from *Gurrelieder*, two Bach arrangements and *Pierrot Lunaire* with Marya Freund. On 15 December *Pierrot Lunaire* was repeated, along with the *Suite*, Op. 29, the *Eight Songs*, Op. 6, for soprano and a group of solo piano pieces played by Steuermann.
2 Prokofiev does not seem to have mentioned that he had been the first person to play a work of Schoenberg's in Russia: the *Drei Klavierstücke*, at an Evening of Contemporary Music recital in St Petersburg in June 1911. See *Diaries*, vol. 1, pp. 214–15.
3 Eduard Steuermann (1892–1964) was in fact Austrian, not German, and was born in that part of the Ukraine near the border with Poland that was within the territory of the Austro-Hungarian Empire until the end of First World War and the subsequent war between Ukraine and Poland saw it formally become part of Poland. (It is now in Ukraine.) Steuermann, having studied with the composer, was the pianist in the first performance of *Pierrot Lunaire*. He emigrated to the United States in 1938 and became a leading performer there, premiering Schoenberg's Piano Concerto with Stokowski and the NBC Orchestra, also teaching at the Juilliard School of Music, where he continued to mentor a distinguished roster of pianists, among them Moura Lympany and Alfred Brendel.
4 *Kammersymphonie*, Op. 9 (1906). Schoenberg himself transcribed the work for piano four hands, but the two-hand version was made by Alban Berg.
5 *Kaiserwalzer* (1925).
6 Vladimir Golschmann (1893–1972), Paris-born violinist and conductor. He had been running his own series in Paris, the Concerts Golschmann, since 1919, served as Director of Music at the Sorbonne, and was also one of Diaghilev's stable of conductors. Before emigrating in 1931 to America (where he became the longest-serving Music Director in the history of the St Louis Symphony) he was to enjoy a brief spell from 1928 to 1930 as Principal Conductor of the Scottish

20 December

In spite of a quite sharp frost we decided to take up the Trefusises' invitation to visit them today. The Ballot was almost impossible to start in such cold weather, but once running conveyed us in great style, and by lunchtime we were at their house in St Loup-de-Naud, seventy kilometres away. They live in a marvellous small castle they have recently bought[1] and the interior of which they have done out with all modern comforts, although the furniture is all antique. We did not stay long, and accompanied by the host, were back in Paris for dinner. Ptashka was in time to get to hear Zoya Lodi, who was singing today at a semi-private concert; while acknowledging the artistry of her interpretations, she was disappointed in the smallness of her voice.

21 December

Finished the entr'acte but am not sure how good it is. Altogether the fourth act is proceeding with less elan than its predecessors. But I must press on to the end, otherwise it will stretch out to all eternity.

A letter from Tseitlin raising a tremendous fuss about my declining a concert tour this season and offering an increased fee, so much so that I even hesitated, but the better part is to hold firm and not play: they will value me all the more, and on this visit I absolutely must not turn myself into an organ-grinder.

22 December

Thought about the roulette scene and composed some snatches and interjections from the gamblers, in place of the less successful material I had before.

National Orchestra (now Royal Scottish National Orchestra) in Glasgow. Presumably the Suite from *The Love for Three Oranges* was one of the try-out showpieces that secured him the position.

1 The ancient Tower of St Loup-de-Naud was the Princesse de Polignac's present to her lover Violet Trefusis. Like the Sackville-West house at Sissinghurst (which also has a Tower) it had started life as a military barracks and surely had romantic associations for Violet. After her death the Tower was acquired by the writer and high-ranking official in the Mitterrand government (Mitterrand was a friend of Violet and had been a frequent visitor to the Tower) Thierry de Beaucé, who wrote evocatively of his first impressions: 'There was nothing particularly enticing about it; rather the opposite, because everything looked terribly bare in the cold light of February . . . There was the tower rising out of the mist, with the clock tower near by . . . two starkly vertical structures in the middle of a vast romantic plain stretching all the way to Poland. And all this in an area regularly visited by many species of migratory birds . . . The last thing I wanted to do was unsettle the shades of all those vanished people who had left traces of themselves in it.' De Beaucé sold the Tower in 1999, after which he lived in Marrakesh.

23 December

The recomposing and revising of the roulette scene went well to begin with, then ground to a halt, then picked up momentum again, but overall was not successful. I was tired and not in a very good mood, a shameful admission for a Christian Scientist. But the evening brought a most loving letter from Natalya Konstantinovna[1] containing the good news that Brennan, the manager of the Boston Symphony, has agreed to act as my manager for the forthcoming season. This means that next season I shall have a good tour in the United States. It also means farewell to my amiable, though somnolent, Haensel!

24 December

Worked well on the roulette scene both in the morning and in the afternoon. Sent Persimfans a telegram rejecting their proposed booking of the hall, which means a final veto on the concert. Before doing so I did experience some qualms: is it not hasty to turn down good engagements ($500 plus any residual profits – never in my life have I been offered such good conditions) but when I considered that agreeing would mean having to interrupt my peaceful composing life to prepare (and very seriously) for these performances, once again I wanted nothing more than to wave goodbye to all those dollars, especially given that a review of my finances revealed that I had enough money for more than a year, so why should I break a lance simply to accumulate a bit more wealth?

25 December

Peace on earth and goodwill to all men. In pursuance of this aim the company in the flat upstairs played music, stamped and screamed until five in the morning and stopped us getting any sleep. Attendance at the Christian Science Church next morning revived me, and I met a lot of friends there: the Wacks, Miss Crain, the man who wants to sell his Suiza (who was not over-friendly), Mrs Getty, whom I did not recognise but who very nicely came over to me. I fully accepted the service today and was not too irritated by its musical aspects.

In the afternoon we brought Svyatoslav into the sitting room, where stood the Christmas tree we had decorated yesterday. He was quite stunned both by it and by his presents. The composing did not go well today, so I finished quite a good section of the third-act piano score.

---

1 Koussevitzky.

26 December

Worked. In the afternoon went to Diaghilev's rehearsal of a double-bill at the Opéra. *Le Pas d'acier*. We all went in the Ballot: I, Ptashka, Grogy and Paichadze, who wanted to catch Diaghilev at the rehearsal as he owes money to the publishers. They had already learnt *Le Pas* last season, so now were going through it quickly, leaving out passages and doing it all anyhow, in a mere twenty minutes. I was upset, particularly as Désormière fussed around for a long time on the trivial *La Chatte* by 'his' composer.[1] Diaghilev was happy (no more than that), friendly but distracted, no doubt by the lack of success in Germany[2] and financial worries. Once again I got flustered over the 'you'/'thou' difficulty. Drew me aside to talk about Massine (the three authors and the lawyer).[3] I graciously agree.

Simultaneously with the orchestral rehearsal there was another rehearsal with piano going on somewhere way up above. I clambered up with Diaghilev who cursed the Grand Opéra for having refused (on grounds of conserving the authentic style of Napoleon III) to put in a lift. Appalling Frenchmen, who don't know how to play anything but *de la belle musique* (*Samson et Dalila*).[4] I played. The new version is completely incomprehensible. Danilova and Lifar were going through their *Firebird* steps to the same music. At the end of the rehearsal Massine accosted me. Paichadze and Ptashka came to my assistance, but not very forcefully. We went away with the distinct impression that the Diaghilev ballet is in danger of disintegrating.

27 December

Worked a little in the morning, and then took the Ballot in so that I could hear the stage rehearsal, but I had to play for half of it as the French musicians are not even trying. Massine has revised the choreography, but God only knows what he is aiming at. The Recruiters are good, though. Massine – more discussion on the details of the agreement. I agree to write a

---

1 Sauguet.
2 The tour, arranged by Nouvel, had been a long one, not just Germany but also Budapest, Warsaw and Vienna. The 'lack of success' was probably financial, not artistic. The financial worries Prokofiev refers to were largely over whether Lord Rothermere would continue to underwrite the Ballets Russes' London seasons.
3 Attribution, and therefore royalties, of authorship of the libretto was contentious as between choreographer (Massine), designer (Yakulov) and the composer, mainly due to the changes imposed by Massine, specifically objected to by Yakulov and eventually by Prokofiev. See D. Press, *Prokofiev's Ballets for Diaghilev*, Ashgate, Aldershot, 2006, for a detailed discussion of this disagreement and the many modifications the scenario underwent in its complicated gestation.
4 Opera (1877) by Saint-Saëns.

letter to Yakulov, and he agrees to release my fee. I go to have lunch with Larionov, and then drive across town to Kostritsky.

Performance that evening. In our box: Paichadze, Samoilenko, Vera Alexandrovna. The playing is disgraceful, and so is the acoustic.[1] I am beside myself. Ptashka is also on tenterhooks, and for some reason this inflames me even more. She has a stomach ache. All the same, it is a success. The Ballot is out in the courtyard, we took our guests home.

28 December

In the morning worked on the roulette scene, then went to the Opéra to the rehearsal to talk further with Massine. His small-mindedness. B.N. came in the afternoon. I feared tedious explanations, but our conversation turned out to be a pleasant one. He has broken with his family and feels lonely, obviously he just wanted to talk. After an hour and half I decided on a plausible excuse to take him out: the car was freezing up and needed to be driven. But he insisted on coming back with me, suggesting a chess match under the same conditions as Alekhine–Capablanca. This aroused my interest: he knows only too well the bait to put me on the hook. Ptashka was thoroughly put out.

29 December

A bad head started in the morning, so I decided to use the day for getting visas and tickets. I also went to Kostritsky, who cleaned my teeth wonderfully well. I really am ashamed of smoking; perhaps it is time I tried to give up? Obtained my French re-entry visa, the visa for Germany, bought train tickets and got money from the publishers. My head ached all day, but not severely, and towards evening passed off. Generally speaking, my headaches now are not so much less frequent as less severe. I know from Christian Science that eventually they will cease altogether, and I find it interesting to discover the route they are taking to this end.

In the evening the second of the Diaghilev evenings at the Opéra: sold out, ticket touts, a well-dressed audience. We were in Diaghilev's box along with Larionov, Nabokov,[2] Monteux and many others; himself in full

---

1 In the Grand Opéra.
2 Nicolas Nabokov (1903–1978), composer, writer and high-profile artistic administrator, notably as Secretary-General from 1951 until 1963 of the Congress for Cultural Freedom, a lavishly funded CIA-inspired offensive aimed from Western Europe to challenge the perceived superiority of Soviet cultural life, institutions and products over their American and Western counterparts. Nabokov, as did Stephen Spender and Irving Kristol with the similarly funded *Encounter* magazine, always denied any knowledge of this hinterland and this may well be the case, but the gaff appeared to be blown when Thomas W. Braden, Head of CIA International

evening-dress but soon disappeared backstage and I hardly spoke to him. Nabokov, on the other hand, so I am told, sucks up to one and all. He has already, alas, sold his Diaghilev commission, *Ode*, to our publishers. He said he would like to come to see me, to which I said, 'With pleasure.' During the performance of *Firebird* we swapped caustic observations on the Bird's provenance: Sadko, Scriabin. I said jokingly, 'What a great romantic composer Stravinsky would have become had he not strayed from the path.' Kokhno was apoplectic. Stravinsky can do no wrong.

30 December

Revised the roulette scene and worked without stopping, because if I do stop the drumming from upstairs drives me to distraction. I am not smoking (at least while thinking or resting). I have long been thinking I should give up. However, I have not yet decided whether to give up completely or just cut down. The comfort factor.

In the afternoon Svyatoslav's Christmas-tree party, with children (some quite grown up): the small Rieti, Tanya Zakharova and Lyalka. Tsvetaeva's children are ill.[1] Grown-ups: Vera Alexandrovna, Schubert, Benois, Larionov. We got very tired. Massine telephoned.

31 December

Finished the revision of the roulette scene, practised the Concerto and began orchestrating Act Four.

Miss Crain. Her account of the cure. I did not smoke, and did not seem to crave it unbearably, although from time to time it would have been nice. But the sensation of 'see, I've broken the habit' is even better.

Operations Division at the time, revealed in the *Saturday Evening Post* in 1967 that funding for *Encounter* 'came from CIA and few outside the CIA knew about it. We had also placed one agent in a Europe-based organisation of intellectuals called the Congress for Cultural Freedom.' Some years later, in a *World in Action* programme for Granada Television in 1975, Braden went further: 'There was simply no limit to the money it [CIA] could spend and no limit to the people it could hire and no limit to the activities it could decide were necessary to conduct the war – the secret war . . . It was a multinational.' Cosmopolitan, highly cultivated and well schooled in his chosen discipline of composition, having studied in Stuttgart with Busoni, Nabokov (first cousin to the writer Vladimir Nabokov) moved in elevated circles both socially and politically, and wielded considerable influence. Diaghilev commissioned his oratorio-ballet *Ode* in 1928, and this was followed by a *Lyrical Symphony* and several operas and ballets, mostly composed after his emigration to the United States in 1933. Nicolas Nabokov produced two entertaining and attractively written books of memoirs, *Old Friends and New Music* (Boston, 1951) and *Bagazh: Memoirs of a Russian Cosmopolitan* (New York, 1975).

1   The elder daughter, Ariadna, and the two-year-old son Gyorgy ('Mur'). Marina Tsvetaeva's second daughter Irina had died in an orphanage in Moscow in 1920.

1928

1 January

Travelled to Freiburg. Got up at seven, full of energy, and by eight was at the station with half an hour to spare before the train left. At eight in the evening I was in Freiburg, a nice little town I had visited twice before, with Ptashka. The hotel is good, and not too expensive.

Strolled around and found the town, well laid out as all German towns. The theatre is splendid and there was a performance of *Rosenkavalier*, but it was late and the performance had only half an hour left to run, so I went back to the hotel, read C.S. and went to bed.

2 January

Went to rehearsal. Nobody seemed very interested in my arrival. Lindemann[1] is a young man. The posters describe me as 'Professor', etc., and Lindemann addresses me as Herr Professor. I find this very strange and long to tell them I am no sort of professor. The orchestra rehearses well, no comparison with the rush one has in London. And I played the Third Concerto well.

Spend the afternoon wandering about, bought a few things, read C.S., grappled with thoughts of various kinds. The concert was at eight, starting with a little Suite by Stravinsky, the first time I have heard it.[2] Naturally there was a good deal of wit in it, but it was noisy and crude in its striving to appear chic. The naive Freiburgers found it appropriate to be shocked and to boo. I played well, not suffering from nerves but nonetheless having to reason with myself. I have a new approach: I *cannot* make a mistake. Why didn't I think of this before? I took three curtain calls.

---

1   Ewald Lindemann, described as 'the model of an intellectual conductor with a pronounced leaning towards Stravinsky', was appointed Music Director of the Augsburg Philharmonic in 1931 and remained until 1933. Perhaps his tastes did not accord well enough with those of the town's music lovers. His conducting career seems to have evaporated thereafter as the only other trace of him is as a music teacher in Berlin in the 1950s.
2   Either Suite No. 1, consisting of arrangements for small orchestra of four of the *Five Easy Pieces* for piano duet (1917), or Suite No. 2, a similar arrangement of the remaining Galop from the *Five Easy Pieces* plus the earlier (1914) *Three Easy Pieces*, also duets. Both Suites had recently been published by Chester.

1 February

Wrote out the five final bars of the roulette scene, and lo, the scene is finished, hoorah! Now I settled down to compose a new orchestral entr'acte, covering Alexey's headlong flight home from the casino. Some time ago, strolling along the banks of the Seine, it had suddenly come to me that it would be a marvellous idea to have this entr'acte accompanied by cries of 'He's won two hundred thousand!', 'Les jeux sont faits!', etc., in other words the exclamations ringing in Alexey's ears as he rushed through the darkened gardens of the casino. Now I decided to put this plan into effect. In the afternoon I prepared the vocal score of the roulette scene; I must not allow the difficulties of this section to hold me up if the commitment to starting work on producing *The Gambler* at the Mariinsky is genuine. In the afternoon I called at the publishers to discuss with Paichadze the Duo-Art proposal. At the very least they are ready to pay me for making an orchestral version of the Overture, Op. 42.

In pursuance of my ambition to correct various of my vices (a recurrent theme with me) I decided to conquer my tendency to lose my temper. For this it is essential to understand clearly that losing one's temper is the worst thing one can do. If x plays a dirty trick on you or acts stupidly that is quite bad enough, but it is even worse to get angry about it. I resolved to make this a fixed rule and to abide by it. During the day I had several occasions for anger, for instance with Ptashka, but I repeated to myself: 'What she has done is stupid, but to get angry about it is even more so.'

The outcome of the day was very good in two ways: first, unpleasant scenes were avoided, and second, I felt I had won a victory over myself and was a better person for it.

2 February

Got up with what threatened to be a headache and even went for a walk instead of working in the morning, but then settled down to composing, and conceived the whole of the entr'acte. This is excellent, even taking into consideration that there is almost no new music in it: all the material is drawn from the preceding scene.

Bashkirov telephoned: he is having trouble with his carte d'identité. But I declined to meet him; I do not wish to give him any more money, and it is really better not to see him than to listen to him whining and still not give him anything. I did, however, pass on the news that I had persuaded his brother to pay for his dental treatment.

After lunch I spent the whole afternoon on the vocal score. Then I read some of my old diary, the year before graduating from the Conservatoire, which was very interesting. Last summer and autumn I read so much of the diary I got rather tired of it, but now I have taken it up again with renewed pleasure.

Conius's riddle: what do you call someone who has eaten his father and his mother? Answer: a spherical orphan.[1] In the evening we attended a concert by Straram, which was very dull. Both ancient Rameau and young Delannoy[2] were equally soporific. I was sitting next to Marnold, and to annoy him castigated Delannoy, because Marnold had just poured scorn on Myaskovsky's Sonata No. 4, which I had given him. Delannoy, of course, deserved to be chastised even without the urge to annoy Marnold. I listened with interest to the Berg Concerto, but it is somehow a flabby piece, without bones. The audience was scandalised, just as if this were not Paris but some provincial hole: booing, clapping, whistling; they succeeded in stopping the performance twice, at which Straram rose to the occasion and loudly declared that whatever they thought or did the work was going to be played to the very last note, and anyone who did not want to hear it was welcome to leave the hall. For this I went round to shake his hand after the performance.

My Quintet was performed in the French section of the international musical celebrations in Siena, as Prunières portentously informed me.

3 February

Worked all day on the vocal score and all but complete the roulette scene. When I have finally finished, I will no longer need to fear holding up the Mariinsky Theatre.

In the evening I was looking forward to playing bridge, but Fatma Hanum had not managed to get a four together.

I have not lost my temper for three days. What a clever fellow!

4 February

Worked on the vocal score and checked Grogy's transcribing of it, as I am preparing the score with all kinds of abbreviations which he later fills out, so it is always essential to verify what he has done.

Paichadze rang up to tell me that Straram has programmed my Second Symphony for the 16th February, which is very pleasant news. Obviously it had not been a wasted effort to go and shake his hand the day before yesterday. Or perhaps it is to annoy Stravinsky, who is conducting two

---

1 Like most puns this does not really work in translation. A *krúgly sirotá* is an orphan who has lost both parents, as distinct from only one, but the literal meaning of *krúgly* is 'round', 'spherical'.
2 Marcel Delannoy (1898–1962), composer and critic, largely self-taught but favourably viewed by Honegger and Ravel. Delannoy was one of the ten composers contributing to the collaborative children's ballet commissioned by Jeanne Dubost, *L'Éventail de Jeanne* (see above, p. 42).

concerts of his music, one before and one after the 16th. Since Straram is no admirer of Stravinsky and my Second Symphony is by way of being one of his hobby-horses,[1] he must have thought, well, let's do it again, and lo and behold there it is, programmed.

A headache came on in the afternoon. I lay down and 'treated' it. But I had to send the roulette scene (the first half of it) off to the copyist, and to check Grogy's work, and to read and sign several urgent letters, and as my head was getting worse and worse I had to put off the major bridge session Fatma Hanum had arranged. Better news was a wonderful postcard from Asafyev: apparently the production of *The Gambler* has been agreed, and Ekskuzovich is now requesting dates by which the orchestral material can be supplied, following which the contract can be signed.

5 February

My headache passed off yesterday evening, and this morning I feel on top form, the result of yesterday's communication from Asafyev. There is no doubt that *Gambler* and my visit to Russia have brought about my supremely happy mood. Ptashka is also very happy at the prospect of another trip to Russia.

Went to the C.S. Church and filled the rest of the day with work, finishing the vocal score of the roulette scene and starting the same thing for the first scene of the act. The only thing I did for relaxation was to go to the Samoilenkos for an hour in the evening.

6 February

Yesterday's good mood was still there when I got up next morning, and I got on straight away with revising the final scene. However, I was soon distracted by more correspondence. One letter was a more pessimistic communication from Asafyev (the theatre administration is worried that the material will not be ready in time; a good thing I had sent off a telegram about this yesterday). Another was from Tseitlin, still hoping that I would eventually agree to appear with them and informing me that Tsukker has left the Persimfans organisation. Yet another was from Tarumov about concerts in the Caucasus and even in Turkestan (we looked up the map to see where Samarkand is). Finally, there was one from Kolechka Myaskovsky warning me that this year problems have arisen with permission to take foreign currency out of the country, and Persimfans has lost many of its most prominent protectors. This last is extremely important, because before setting out on this trip I

---

1 Prokofiev's Second Symphony was performed in a Straram Concert in May 1926. See above, pp. 288–9, 301–3.

wanted through Tseitlin to test the waters about the sort of treatment I could expect this time in terms of entering and leaving the country. The point is that last time, admittedly with the unofficial permission of Litvinov,[1] I used a Nansen passport, something that is potentially an offence punishable with prison. Beforehand, therefore, it would be rather timely to establish whether on this occasion they would be likewise disposed to turn a blind eye. All this information, all these dilemmas about what might or might not be possible, were deeply troubling and drained time and energy while at the same time I was desperate to get on with work. Despite these worries the revision of the third scene turned out quite well, and in the afternoon I succeeded in completing the piano score of the first.

Another cause for inner disquiet is that the engine of the Ballot is being stripped down, and this is like a close friend undergoing an abdominal operation. Grogy inconveniently chose this moment to become depressed, and went to consult a healer. It helped him; he came back reinvigorated and at once threw himself into his work, but did not achieve much today, the very time when it is essential he presses on full speed ahead. To sum up, I spent the whole day at boiling point and could keep calm only with the help of C.S. Just imagine: at the end of April we could be in Turkestan!

10 February

For the last four days I have worked almost without stopping on *The Gambler* and almost finished the revision of the final scene. In any event I have come through the passage of greatest danger: the embrace of Alexey and Polina. In the old version I had inflated this to a torrid illustration of the sexual act, which is just about the least arresting event one can put on to a stage! The producer must rack his brains how to portray it without overstepping the borders of delicacy while making clear what is going on, meanwhile the audience feels uncomfortable and does not know where to look. One way and another it is a moment on stage that never succeeds in evoking any pleasure in the audience, only curiosity or, worse, embarrassment. For this reason in the new version I toned it down considerably, cutting off abruptly on the high note, which is actually more effective musically. The dramatic impact is quite different from what it was formerly: it can now be interpreted either as a kiss or as an onrush of tender feeling. As usual during the mornings I concentrated on the revision, and in the afternoons got on with the vocal score, corrected Grogy's copy and involved myself with the copyists of the parts, who now constitute the biggest

---

1 See above, p. 414.

source of delay and are a much greater source of concern to me than my own work.

Ptashka obviously does not want to understand how stressful my work is at the moment, and constantly pesters me about her singing, complaining that I do not pay her enough attention, to such an extent that I shouted at her to leave me in peace, thus breaking my vow not to lose my temper. This is bad, but clearly it is not a vice that can be instantly sloughed off.

Stravinsky is back in Paris to conduct his two gala concerts. I met him twice at the publishers, where he sat for hours with Conius working out bowings for his *Apollon*. On this occasion Stravinsky was amiable and even invited me to go and have coffee with him, but somehow it still fell to me to settle the bill. He told me that *Apollon* had turned out very well, but had cost him enormous effort. He was complaining of painful temples, the result of the Paris wind. Most of our conversation, in fact, revolved round automobiles.

Straram started rehearsals of the Symphony today, beginning with strings alone. I listened to it with feelings of slight hostility: it is music I have largely moved away from. No, now I have to compose a Third Symphony!

21 February

The Borovskys came to dinner. He is just back from London, but before that he was in Russia and therefore I plied him avidly with questions, aware that he of all people would give me the most reliable information about the situation there: concerts, attitudes to visiting artists, passports, all such matters. The conversation had a decisive effect on my projected visit. Since in all my political negotiations I had opted to work mainly through Tseitlin, I was most anxious to find out whether he could absolutely be relied on, and whether he was still in good standing with the authorities. Borovsky gave reasonably satisfactory answers to these questions, although he reported a hint of dissatisfaction from Tseitlin that Prokofiev, while having in advance of his last visit declared his willingness to accept whatever conditions would be offered, once there did his utmost to screw as much possible out of them. Tsukker, apparently, belonged to the opposition,[1] so for the present his departure does not present a political loss to Persimfans.

---

1 The Unified Opposition in which the leading figures were Trotsky, Zinoviev and Kamenev. In addition, Persimfans was inevitably embroiled in the ideological wars that disfigured much of the Soviet musical world through the 1920s, despite the peace-making efforts of such enlightened arbitrators as Lunacharsky. Representing one side, with which were associated such internationally minded musicians as Myaskovsky, Derzhanovsky, Sabaneyev, Lamm, Tseitlin and Persimfans, in Leningrad Asafyev and Shcherbachov, stood the Association for Contemporary Music (ASM), while on the other was the 'simplistic musical primitivism' – as

Borovsky, reading Dukelsky's article about the Diaghilev Ballet, was greatly impressed with it and professed astonishment that such a flirtatious popinjay should command such an acute intelligence.

22 February

Orchestrated in the afternoon and in the evening ate *bliny* in a Russian restaurant with Borovsky. Met by chance there Vladimir Bashkirov, who was drunk but exquisitely courteous. I could not pass up the chance to tease him about the first time we met, when he went out to dine without wearing a tie, a sartorial deficiency that is for all eternity associated with him.

After dinner we went to one of Prunières' evenings where there was a chaotic crush of celebrities. 'Oh, how stout you have grown,' said someone to me. 'It's because he is so inflated with acclaim,'[1] rejoined his companion.

23 February

Nabokov has rung me up five or six times, and today he came to play me his *Ode*, which he not only played but sang at deafeningly loud volume. It made a mixed impression on me: there were interesting moments but there were also less successful parts, some lacking in colour and some exhibiting a calculated vulgarity – the evil influence of the Paris style of the past few years. This will no doubt soon fizzle out of its own accord. One passage struck me as especially tedious and derivative, obviously from Korsakov's *Kashchey*.[2] I said as much. 'But that is precisely the part that Stravinsky liked best,' exclaimed Nabokov.

I: 'Stravinsky praised it because he is a mischievous man.'

Nabokov: 'I personally am not going to write any more music of that sort in any of my new works.'

---

the Asmovskys derided it – of the Russian Association of Proletarian Musicians (RAPM). At the beginning of 1928 the Modernist, progressive ASM line was still influential, hence the departure of the Rapmovsky-inclined Tsukker. By the early 1930s, however, RAPM's dogmatic insistence on mass song as practically the only acceptable musical form was to assure its short-lived supremacy until April 1932. At that point the Party Central Committee, fed up with a near-decade of sterile bickering and influenced by the recently repatriated Maxim Gorky, declared a plague on both houses by abolishing at a stroke *all* proletarian organisations (the ASM had already disbanded anyway) in literature and the arts with its Resolution 'On the Reconstruction of Literary and Artistic Organisations', ushering in the new and relentlessly conformist era of the artistic unions, including the Union of Soviet Composers.

1 'C'est parce qu'il est gonflé de gloire.'
2 *Kashchey The Immortal*, one-act opera (1902) by Rimsky-Korsakov. Kashchey, the subject of several folk tales collected by Afanasyev, is also the evil genius of the Stravinsky–Fokine–Benois ballet *The Firebird*.

Nabokov brought his wife, Natalya, along, a pretty little thing. I thought she was nice, but Ptashka found her repellent.

24 February

My head was aching, so I did not work but went for a long walk. I thought back to Schopenhauer and my admiration for him. But this mainly derived from his practical recommendations on how to live, and the way he translated me from the world of everyday life to the world of abstract ideas, which at the time was quite new to me.[1] But I never caught on to his fundamental philosophical system. Indeed, according to this system Schopenhauer himself illustrates with extraordinary brilliance the cul-de-sac into which he has entered.

My headache passed off in the evening. Went to Borovsky's concert in which he did not play everything well. But I love his performances of my music. I heard *Sarcasms* as if they were the work of another composer, so far away from them have I grown. Closer to me is the Scherzo of the Op. 12 pieces, and Borovsky plays it wonderfully. After the concert we had supper in a neighbouring café and then Borovsky wanted us to go on to some *boîte* or other, but I was dropping with fatigue and wanted to go to bed, so we cried off.

25 February

I could not do as much work as I should have liked as I went to the Pasdeloup rehearsal which included excerpts from *Chout*. I had expected Rhené-Bâton to be conducting and therefore did not plan to go, but the orchestra secretary telephoned to tell me that instead it would be Wolff, my friend from the days of the famous Metropolitan Opera fiasco.[2] Wolff told me that he had rehearsed the score intensively with the orchestra, and it did indeed sound very good. I came home feeling very pleased with the orchestral effect of *Chout*.

---

1 'My sense of inner peace and happiness had come from Schopenhauer and the truth of his insight: do not pursue happiness but strive to be free of pain. What a wealth of possibilities is contained in this truth! And for the person who accepts it and incarnates it in his own being, what rapture-inducing revelations does it have to offer!' See *Diaries*, vol. 2, p. 230 (September 1917).
2 Albert Wolff, as the then head of French repertoire at the Metropolitan Opera, had been present when Prokofiev played excerpts from *The Love for Three Oranges* and *Fiery Angel* to the General Director of the Met, the ferocious Giulio Gatti-Casazza, with resounding lack of success. Afterwards the only voice speaking up for Prokofiev's music had been Wolff's, apparently prompting Gatti-Casazza to call him 'an anarchist'. See *Diaries*, vol. 2, pp. 492–3.

In the afternoon I dictated a letter to Tseitlin, a very diplomatic one. My aim was to test the waters with Litvinov, to establish whether I would be able to enter and leave the country as easily as I had done the previous year. This is a subject requiring much tact and delicacy so as to avoid stupid mistakes, saying not too much and not too little.

In the evening I played through the whole of the third act of *Fiery Angel* and was genuinely pleased, even moved, by it. When I had finished, Ptashka came into the room and said, 'Well, thank God you've finished.' I felt as if I had been doused with a bucket of cold water, but seeing how offended I was Ptashka hastened to explain that she had herself been listening in a state of unprecedented emotional tension, and her nerves had been so strongly affected that she was glad when it had ended.

26 February

Again a headache, but not a terribly bad one. All the same, I am getting them too often. C.S. Church did not succeed in dispelling it. In the afternoon I did my best to cure it by walking in the Bois de Boulogne, which was lovely except for the Sunday crowds by which it was inundated in the sunshine. My car has finally been repaired; I tried it out today and it pulls very well, as though several more horsepower have been added to it. Around five o'clock the headache began to subside and I went with Ptashka to the Pasdeloup Orchestra's Festival of Russian Music, in which Wolff conducted five pieces from the *Chout* Suite. He performed them not at all badly and, unusually for Pasdeloup, from memory. The success after each number was very great. In the other, rival, afternoon concert Pierné[1] played the *Classical* Symphony but I am sure it was bad; I did not attend. In the evening I accompanied Ptashka. Her singing has made great strides; there is no comparison with the recent past.

27 February

Orchestrated, but only in the morning because in the afternoon, it being Svyatoslav's fourth birthday, guests had been invited. As a matter of fact, a number of grown-ups also joined the party and there was a large gathering speaking in tongues – Russian, French, English and Italian. Tsvetaeva, the Nabokovs, Maria Viktorovna, Vera Suvchinskaya, the Samoilenkos, Rieti's

---

1 Gabriel Pierné (1863–1937), composer, conductor and organist, Chief Conductor of the Concerts Colonne. Pierné also conducted for the Ballets Russes, and was on the podium for the first performance of *The Firebird* in 1910.

wife, Frieda, Schubert, and so on. Tsvetaeva's three-year-old son,[1] a monstrous infant built like a wrestler, calls Svyatoslav Svyatotat. We had tea, then we fed those who stayed cold meats and they stayed until eleven. It was a convivial, happy day. Vera Suvchinskaya had to leave early, as Petya was waiting for her somewhere; he could not come himself owing to pressure of work.

28 February

Morning brought an infuriating letter from Millet (copyist), who as is now apparent has been handsomely leading me up the garden path and instead of completing copying the score of Act Three has in truth only just started on it. *The Gambler* seems fated not to be produced this spring. I worked on myself, read C.S. and successfully suppressed my rage.

Continued orchestrating, did some of the vocal score, corrected Grogy's work. One more leap and the *Gambler* orchestration will be finished.

29 February

The orchestration of *The Gambler* is finished, accordingly so is the entire opera. I do not count the completion of the vocal score: in my book the opera is complete when the score is finished. A good day to finish a major work: the twenty-ninth day of February occurs only once every four years! Waiting for the copyist to come I made every effort of which I was capable to stop myself screaming at him or unleashing the stream of sarcastic insults I so desperately wanted to. But the worm proved to be not only a cheat but a coward: he left the music with the concierge and did not venture upstairs at all.

In the evening I read my old diary, the time of the Conservatoire competition. My feelings are now very far from what they were in those days. Any contest is an intense manifestation of egoism, a desire to prevail over the corpses of others, thus a form of baseness that must be resisted. Nevertheless, I cannot read these passages in my diary without strong emotions: they were written at white heat and described in such detail that they draw me inexorably into the atmosphere of that time!

1–9 March

Once I had finished the *Gambler* score I proceeded to finish off the vocal score and to correct Grogy's full score. Both tasks were accomplished on the

---

1 Gyorgy, always known as Mur.

5th March and thus finally removed from my shoulders the burden of *The Gambler*. Now the problem is the copyists, of whom I now have a rabble of an army: some turn down the work, others are late, a third group simply promise one thing and then do not deliver, and all the while I have to run around to ferret out new ones, go back to the old ones – it's a complete Ministry of Copyists. And still I do not know whether it may be a complete waste of time, whether this rush to have it done is necessary, because I do not know whether *The Gambler* is going to be produced this spring or only in the autumn. On the 2nd March I decided I must send Asafyev a peremptory telegram: 'No contract received, astonished by duplicity of theatre', with the aim of providing Asafyev with something he could show to anyone he might judge it useful to influence. On the 5th, the day I finished the vocal score, the answer came, signed by Shkafer, the Chief Producer:[1] 'Question of *Gambler* resolved, formalities will be quickly implemented.' The initial reaction was a renewed excitement because it now looked as though was going to be produced and we would be going, although on closer inspection the woolly phrasing of the telegram said precisely nothing. Simultaneously there was a letter from Tarumov about concerts in the Caucasus, which would cover my expenses while in the USSR without making too many demands on me.

On the 2nd March Nabokov came to see me and suggested a joint visit to Remizov, which he had mentioned the last time we had met. I was delighted to go with him and found Remizov just the same lovable scarecrow as ever, in fact more lovable since this time there was less talk of devilry and more of humanity. Remizov reminisced, among other people, of Demchinsky, who had at the time been so fiercely critical of the unstageability of his *Alaley and Leila*,[2] and this led me to give an account of the whole 'Demchinsky saga' over *Fiery Angel*. Remizov commented, 'Yes, I know people like that, they lack the ability to grasp the whole but are at the same time a storehouse of valuable things. I have myself more than once had to humble myself in my efforts to prise out of them the things I needed.' Before we left they gave me an autograph album and asked me to write something in it. 'I'd like to get Stravinsky's signature to go alongside yours,' said Remizov. Nabokov commented, 'Oh yes, of course, like Schiller and Goethe! And whom would you like beside mine? Dima Dukelsky's?'

---

[1] Vasily Shkafer (1867–1937), tenor and opera producer who sang principal roles in Kiev, St Petersburg and Moscow before the Revolution. With a senior position in the Bolshoy Theatre at the time of the Revolution, he became President of the Bolshoy Theatre Soviet (Council) and moved to Leningrad to become Opera Director at the Mariinsky Theatre, or rather as its official title was between 1920 and 1935 the State Academic Theatre of Opera and Ballet (Akopera). Shkafer published his autobiography, *Forty Years on the Russian Opera Stage*, in 1936. (V. P. Shkafer, *Sorok let na stsene russkoy opery 1890–1930*, Kirov Opera and Ballet Theatre, Leningrad, 1936).

[2] See above, pp. 24, 607.

Nabokov brought me his Sonata No. 1, which is already in print. On the frontispiece is inscribed: 'To my Natashenka' (his wife), and a funeral cross. What could this cross possibly signify – an end to all their previously accustomed relations? The Sonata has an attractive first subject and a deliberately vulgar-sounding (Cocteauesque) tune for the Andante but with a sophisticated development in the major-minor, followed by a technically very assured Finale, albeit with a derivative theme unpleasantly reminiscent of Bach.

On Sunday 4th accompanied by the Nabokov couple we took the car out of the town into the country. After its stay in the repair shop the car is running very well. 'Natashenka' is employed during the week as a model in a grand *maison de couture*, and the moment I dropped a hint about this Sunday excursion, Nabokov leapt at it. It was indeed a very pleasant excursion despite the fact that Ptashka and I had had no sleep at all the night before owing to the twenty-year-old son of the woman upstairs celebrating his hundred days (before his high-school graduation), which was the occasion for all-night-long whooping, shouting, music, female shrilling, window- and door-slamming, in short a magnificent display of Russian youth letting its hair down. And these émigrés see themselves as the future builders of the Russia of the future! God forbid. The disapproving French were so exasperated by the nocturnal din that the next evening there was a police patrol outside the house, and a good thing too as they were trying to continue the party.

On the 7th March Cooper conducted an orchestral concert of Russian music which concluded with three numbers from the *Three Oranges* Suite. Ticket sales were not spectacular, but a lot of complimentaries had been handed out, causing a terrible crush at the entrance. I ran into Diaghilev, just back in Paris from Monte Carlo and turning up at the concert with a huge entourage in tow, including Nabokov, Rieti and Sauguet and their wives (a bespectacled young man doing duty for Sauguet's consort). As neither they nor we had anything remotely resembling an invitation we went *en masse* to find the organisers of the concert, and having eventually secured two boxes stormed into the hall, Diaghilev creating such a commotion that everyone turned to look at us. Diaghilev was in an excellent mood and took pains to assure me: 'Serge, don't imagine for a moment that I have come to hear *Oranges*, but I do desperately, desperately want to hear Borodin's Symphony.' *Oranges* was a success, and the March, the last item in the programme, had to be encored. The Nabokovs, Paichadze and ourselves went to drink coffee afterwards. Nabokov gave an account of the new ballet enterprise Ida Rubinstein is in process of starting up, her way of giving a home to all the offerings incautiously rejected by Diaghilev. The resultant slate is proving to be so strong that Diaghilev is seriously worried, all the more so as Idka, of course, has greatly more money than he has.

Among the more minor events of these nine days: we went with the Suvchinskys to see a Soviet film, which was interesting, and the Suvchinskys were particularly nice that evening. Ptashka and I went to see the play *Le Rabatteur*,¹ but it was fairly thin stuff. It never ceases to amaze me how few people know how to write a comedy. If I had not been a composer, what marvellous comedies I could have cooked up, and how successful they would have been! I played bridge at Samoilenko's, and met there Tamara,² who had been hearing on all sides Prokofiev's complaints to all and sundry that she, Tamara Hanum, had lost 150 francs to him at bridge but had not paid her debt. 'Well, what about settling for fifty?' enquired Tamara. 'No, but you could discharge your obligations by giving me your bridge table.' After considerable resistance Tamara eventually consented, and the following day Grogy was despatched for the green baize table, bearing a bouquet of tulips in exchange.

10 March

A telegram from ITHMA,³ the Viennese concert agency with whom I have been in correspondence latterly and which has now swung into action, proposing a concert in Zurich on 26th March. This gave me an idea: to use the Zurich engagement as an excuse to drive to Switzerland by car. If Russia collapses in a heap until autumn a Swiss excursion could be a pleasant consolation prize. So taken was I by this notion that I immediately bought a motoring map of Switzerland and began to plan a route. In the evening we were at the Samoilenkos and suggested they come with us. However, Russians encounter enormous difficulties obtaining visas for Switzerland, and that for me is precisely the advantage of this engagement, as I would get the visa automatically.

Began looking through the piano transcription of *Le Pas d'acier* I made somewhat hastily in the autumn of 1925, and only five numbers. I must now set about completing and getting it published.

11 March

Today we did not attend the C.S. Church but instead went out to Le Vésinet, twenty kilometres or so outside Paris, where there was a requiem service for the soul of the late N. P. Ruzsky, who departed this life six

---

1 *The Pander*. Comedy by Henri Falk. It was later, under the title *Aventure à Paris* (1936), a successful film, directed by Marc Allégret and starring, among others, Arletty.
2 Tamara Hanum, Boris Samoilenko's sister-in-law.
3 International Theater und Musik Agentur.

months ago. When I had learned of his death last autumn I sent the family a telegram, but it was returned as not having reached the right address, since when I have heard nothing of them. Today it was necessary to discharge the obligation.

The *panikhida*[1] took place in a small Russian church converted from an orangery by the deceased man himself. I found the whole family assembled, mourning and faded. I was especially shocked by Tanya, who after all is six months younger than me and who has stayed in my memory as a girl in the fresh bloom of youth.[2] In the twelve years since I last saw her she has lost her looks, grown sallow and even wrinkled. I, no doubt, have also changed. Olga Petrovna[3] did not recognise me at first but when she did she was touching and affectionate and we promised to come and see them next Sunday. Life is clearly very difficult for them after the magnificent home they left behind in Petersburg.

12 March

The publishers gave me their accounts for 1927. Sales increased, earning me 1,450 marks as against 1,300 marks in 1926. Not such a great sum, but where there was a substantial upward leap was in the hires of material, which rose to 4,150 marks from 2,150 last year. A significant role in this increase had been played by Koussevitzky's concerts in America. Altogether, including the opera and ballet bonuses (but not those for France or Russia), the publishers will be paying me 8,726 marks for the year 1927, that is $2,100, a big rise from 1926 when the sum was 4,845 marks ($1,150). I now have at my disposal capital amounting to $10,000, which is not bad at all bearing in mind that I did not play any concerts this year. Stravinsky's income from the publishers, although it greatly exceeds mine, was down this year, and Paichadze's explanation for this is that he had so many performances in 1926 that it was inevitable there would be something of a reaction.

In the evening I was playing through some Medtner, and on the last page of his E minor *Fairy Tale*, Op. 34, I discovered a tune lifted bodily from my

---

1   The *panikhida* is a special memorial service for the dead in the Eastern Orthodox and Greek-Catholic liturgies. The *First Panikhida* is equivalent to the Western funeral service, and subsequent *panikhidy*, like a Western memorial service, can be requested by the family of the deceased, usually at particular intervals after the death: the third day, ninth day, fortieth day, first anniversary, third anniversary, and so on. *Panikhida* services generally take place after the ordinary service of Vespers, Matins or Divine Liturgy.
2   Prokofiev had had a somewhat spiky relationship with the two Ruzsky daughters when he was an intimate of the household in St Petersburg but it had subsequently become more cordial. See *Diaries*, vol. 1 *passim* and vol. 2, pp. 61, 71, 82, 120.
3   Nikolay Ruzsky's widow.

piano piece 'Despair', written ten years or so before.[1] I am thrilled! Medtner has spent his whole life denigrating me, and here he is unconsciously (I am sure it was unconscious) turning to me for inspiration.

13 March

I decided a long time ago that I must compose in a quite different style, and that I would set about it as soon as I had extricated myself from the revisions of *Fiery Angel* and *The Gambler*. If God is the unique source of creation and of reason, and man is his reflection, it is abundantly clear that the works of man will be better the more closely they reflect the works of the Creator (in other words the nearer they come to him). I must unflaggingly hold on to this thought all the time I am working. One should not work unless one feels oneself to be sufficiently pure.

Today, thinking about this, I managed to compose something: material for some piano pieces I want to write as an interlude before settling to the Third Symphony. I might perhaps call them 'Things in Themselves'.[2]

A telegram informing me that the Zurich engagement has fallen through. Buying the map of Switzerland was a waste of money.

14 March

Had a go at composing some of the piano pieces in which I want to encapsulate yesterday's testamentary inspiration. I also worked on a piano transcription of *Le Pas d'acier*. At Asafyev's request I bought copies of Debussy's articles and his correspondence with Durand.[3] The mimosa-like elusiveness of Debussy's style in his letters is not unlike Myaskovsky's. The letters are more patriotic than interesting, but I came across one phrase very much to the point: 'We in France love so many good things that there is no room left for music.' And indeed the Frenchman will spend his money first of all on fine food and women, next on antique furniture, and only then will he consider paying for a ticket to go to a concert.

1 'Despair' ('Otchayaniye'), *Four Pieces for Piano*, Op. 4 No. 3 (revised for publication in 1911 but originally composed two years earlier).
2 Prokofiev here thinks back to his intensive readings of Kant and Schopenhauer, in particular Schopenhauer's critique of the Kantian proposition of the 'Ding an sich', the 'Thing in Itself', the relationship (if any) between the object as perceived (the phenomenon) and the object as it independently is (the noumenal). Prokofiev's two piano pieces, Op. 45, were eventually published in 1928 as *Veshchi v sebe*, usually known by their French title *Choses en soi*.
3 Durand & Cie, the leading French music publisher, which since 1970 had been issuing a steady stream of virtually the entire canon of Saint-Saëns, Fauré, Dukas, Debussy, Ravel, Satie, Milhaud, Messiaen, etc., etc. The company had been founded by Marie-Auguste Durand, who had started life as a composer. He died in 1909.

15 March

I felt too exhausted to much incline for work. I composed a little and transcribed some of *Le Pas d'acier*, and dictated to Grogy my diary of my USSR visit. It is high time for this: a year has gone by since the events it describes.

In the evening, a Straram concert. It started with Bach's Brandenburg Concerto, the one for strings alone, then Stravinsky's *Symphonies of Wind Instruments*. The audience at Straram's concerts have been so rowdy of late we worried that during the Stravinsky the booing and catcalling might start up again, and the anxiety prevented us concentrating on listening to the music. But today the audience was restrained, perhaps in response to sharp press criticism of its uncivilised behaviour. The *Symphonies* do have some interesting moments and there is an overall convergence of mood, but there can be no doubt that they also have a disheartening lack of flow. In Sashenka Tcherepnin's cello work there was much that had been lifted from other people – a failing common both to the son and the father – first from Musorgsky, later on not so much actually from me as after me. The end was imaginative, however.

Strauss's *Bourgeois Gentilhomme* is from start to finish an obscene, provincial joke: the composer takes off his trousers and thereby thinks himself a great wit. But it is brilliantly orchestrated, and this I do not understand: the sheer process of orchestrating like that must be a delight to the composer so how is it that Strauss, while smacking his lips, cannot see that he is slavering over such repulsive material? But the orchestral clothing is, in fact, astonishing. Stravinsky, for example, laying down the law about everything as usual, declared that piano and strings (the strings being respectively hit with a hammer and stroked with a bow) do not go together, and therefore composed his Concerto without any string instruments. But here the piano brought into the middle of scurrying strings sounds wonderful.

After the concert we took Marnold and Paichadze home in the Ballot. Marnold was delighted with the ride, but hit the window so sharply with his stick when I took a wrong turning that I was afraid he would break it!

16 March

Once again a cloudy-feeling head. Probably it is longing to have a good ache but doesn't quite dare to. I concentrated on it, but could not get down to composition. Instead transcribed *Le Pas*. Took the Ballot to Zenith, where they tuned the carburettor. The car goes splendidly now. Grogy played me excerpts from his Second Concerto, which he has been scribbling in spare moments snatched from his work on *The Gambler*. Some of it is not bad, and this to all appearances goes even for some of the orchestration. He has evidently absorbed something from writing out more than a thousand pages of my scores.

24 May

In the morning, the general rehearsal of the first of Koussevitzky's concerts. Lopatnikoff's Scherzo is pleasant but muddy; the orchestration misconceived. In person he is awkward, with extraordinarily broad shoulders. His wife Eleonora, toothy and Jewish, is very forward with her opinions. Toch's[1] Concerto is thin on material, but inventively worked if one ignores the tedious middle movement. Toch, Suvchinsky, Paichadze, Dukelsky, Byutsov[2] (to whom I had given a letter of recommendation to Koussevitzky), Tansman and his wife – Natalya Konstantinovna is very well disposed to this couple. A pointless piece, *Phaedra*,[3] by Honegger.

In the afternoon I proof-read the Symphony. The concert took place in the evening, we sat in Natalya Konstantinovna's box with the Tochs, but there was only a small audience and she was upset. Lopatnikoff leapt up immediately to take his bows.

Afterwards we went to drink coffee with the Borovskys, Paichadzes and Lopatnikoffs. I took them home in the car. Mme Lopatnikoff produced an appalling impression on Ptashka and Maria Viktorovna.

25 May

Because of the quandary I am in over *Fiery Angel* I worked on my piano pieces, and composed well all morning. Schubert came, very happy that Koshetz will sing in *Fiery Angel*, although there is not much for her in it.

---

1 Ernst Toch (1887–1964), pianist and prolific composer, born in Vienna but living in Germany until he emigrated to America in 1933, his music having been proscribed by the Nazi regime. His oeuvre encompasses four operas, seven symphonies, choral works and a large quantity of chamber music and solo piano works. The first of his two piano concertos was composed in 1926. In America he continued to compose although his concert music was not widely performed, and produced many Hollywood film scores including *The Private Life of Don Juan*, starring Douglas Fairbanks senior, in his last role as the ageing Lothario, and Merle Oberon.
2 Vladimir de Bützow, as he was known in emigration in France, was the son of a prominent Tsarist diplomat, Yevgeny Byutsov. With a penchant for vaguely spiritualist compositions such as a ballet, *The Black Swan and the Lily*, he hovered around the fringes of Paris musical life and at one stage provided the talent for the aspirational cultural programme of Nina Meshcherskaya's 'Samarkand' restaurant. Her memoirs describe him as having 'the most unbearable character but impeccable musical taste'.
3 Incidental music to Ida Rubinstein's production of d'Annunzio's play *Fedra*, a reworking of the classical tragedy (Euripides' *Hippolytus* not Racine's *Phèdre*) she produced in 1923, casting herself in the title role.

Lopatnikoff came at five o'clock, by invitation, for me to look through his Scherzo. His score is full of elementary errors, hardly literate: flute, piccolo and horn too low; bassoons and clarinets too high. I worked with him for an hour and a half, for which he thanked me as he left.

Bridge in the evening with Zakharov, Celia and Fatma Hanum. Celia and Boris play with scrupulous finesse and great attachment to the game, but still were down 250 points. I was up 115.

26 May

An interesting letter from Elena. Did good work on *Choses en soi*. To the publishers in the afternoon, where Dukelsky gave a very amusing account of an encounter between Stravinsky and Rachmaninoff, at which he was present. Paichadze was irritated by Dukelsky's hyperboles and said it had been nothing like that at all, merely an exchange of pleasantries. I proof-read the Symphony.

Dukelsky and Zakharov came in the evening. They played the four-hand version of Balakirev's First Symphony (very interesting indeed) and Myaskovsky's Third, which both of them agreed was no good. Zakharov is a superlative sight-reader, as indeed he always was at the Conservatoire.

27 May

Took Svyatoslav to Sunday School. In the afternoon the Borovskys brought Natasha round to see Svyatoslav. The parents were dressed in their best today, their daughter like a little *matryoshka* doll. We drove out into the Bois and then went to the Koussevitzkys, who are At Home on Sundays. Their place was jammed right up to the windowsills, so Dukelsky, the Borovskys and ourselves could hardly get in at all. Had a discussion with Koussevitzky about Lopatnikoff. I said Lopatnikoff should be made to rewrite his score.

28 May

Slightly heavy head, and so did not work. Grogy announced that he was suffering bleeding in his throat and would have to leave. I asked him if he would be going back to Kishinyov, and he said no, but how is he going to survive? He said he would consult Miss Crain, and I said that when everything was sorted out he should come back.

We went out into the forest in the afternoon; the warm weather has arrived and it was even hot. A telegram from Moscow, indicating that *The Gambler* will go ahead.

29 May

Composed, and in the afternoon proof-read the Symphony. Went to see Mme Schmitz[1] about America in 1929–30 – getting organised well in advance. In the evening Ptashka and Dukelsky went to the Gershwin concert while Zakharov and I played bridge with the Samoilenkos. Zakharov enjoyed himself hugely, but when he went down 420 points doubled, lost his temper and threw a tantrum when bridge was interrupted by the return of Ptashka, Dukelsky and the Borovskys from the concert. I was even quite pleased by this; it reminded me how I would have been until recently. Everyone thought Dukelsky was Ptashka's brother. For some reason Dukelsky is an admirer of Gershwin and says that even though Diaghilev does not like his music he will not be able to resist having Gershwin, the novelty, thrust upon him when he goes to America.

30 May

Composed, and read proofs. Of Gorchakov there is no sign, meanwhile the work we were engaged upon continues to mount up and I do not know whether he has finally left us or not, I do not even know his address. Ptashka says his mother had wanted him to marry a well-off girl but her father would not give his consent. Grogy had been pinning his hopes on having something published in order to raise his stock with the father, but there was nothing I could recommend in its present state. Therein lay the cause of his disaffection. The day he left he had received a letter from his mother that had upset him.

Koshetz came at five o'clock. There had been a preliminary telephone call in which she asked me to call on her, but I did not want to, vulgar thing that she is, and made her come to me. She is unhappy about only having a small part in the opera.[2] However, she behaved civilly. I spent the evening at home. It was stuffy and hot.

31 May

Morning rehearsal for the second of Koussevitzky's concerts. Met Suvchinsky on the street, and a little later Lourié. Suvchinsky walked between us, talking now to me, now to Lourié. I stalked on ahead, disgruntled.

Hindemith was playing his Viola Concerto, Op. 34 No. 4. This is the first time I have seen him. Splendid, vigorous stuff; at one time I had contemplated something similar for a piano concerto. The second movement is not

---

1 Wife of Robert Schmitz. See above, p. 243.
2 *The Fiery Angel*. Koshetz was singing the part of Renata, the principal female role, but the concert included only an edited version of the second act.

as good, boring and too long, with an insufficiently arresting theme. The third movement and the finale are very good although they make a strange impression, as though their themes could equally well be laid out horizontally from right to left or from left to right and nothing would thereby be changed!

Sofronitsky[1] gave a concert in the afternoon: a good pianist, but an idiotic programme.

A dispute with Dukelsky over Scriabin: I was somewhat apologetically defending him (even so, nevertheless ... etc.) but Dukelsky dismissed him with a shrug of the shoulders, which annoyed me so much that I told him he was merely influenced by the opinions of others without having any himself. For the first time Dukelsky was seriously offended, and I said, 'There was a time when the one really good thing about you was your good character, but now even that has left you.' Dukelsky walked out. I had tea with Sofronitsky, who appears to set great store by simply being in my company. But there is something awkward and uncouth about him, allied to the typical Muscovite chip on the shoulder, a sense of his own superiority and a hidden bewilderment at my being so Parisian.

The Koussevitzky concert in the evening. Terrible piece by Ferroud.[2] Hindemith's Concerto was a success. Dukelsky ecstatic over Brahms, which sent me to sleep. Stravinsky came to hear the Hindemith and then stayed to listen attentively to Brahms. Can this be yet another new direction?

1   Vladimir Sofronitsky (1901–1961), less well known in the West than he deserves as he made only one major tour (this one) and never recorded for a Western label, but in Russia his profoundly poetic interpretations of the Romantic repertoire, in particular of Chopin and Scriabin, caused not only audiences but his peers such as Svyatoslav Richter, Emil Gilels and Maria Yudina (alongside whom he studied in Leonid Nikolayev's class at the Leningrad Conservatoire) to regard him with undisguised admiration. ('A giant who played Schumann and Debussy magnificently and Scriabin like no one else' – Richter in B. Monsaingeon, op. cit., p. 78.) Another reason why his Western renown is less than in Russia is that although he made many recordings for Melodiya he seems to have been one of those artists whose particular magic of colour and phrasing was somehow resistant to the barriers of the microphone and the production process.
2   Pierre-Octave Ferroud (1900–1936), composer and critic, a former student of Guy Ropartz and much influenced by Florent Schmitt. He was one of the founders of the chamber-music organisation Triton. In a letter to Asafyev in 1932, Prokofiev grudgingly relaxed his strictures on Ferroud: 'Ferroud is a capable representative of the younger generation in France, and his Symphony is certainly better than his strange undertaking on a story by Chekhov [the 1928 opera *Chirurgie*, based on a Chekhov short story]. I read him your reviews of his symphony, leaving out the parts where you snap at him. He listened with great interest, almost greedily, and asked if you might be able to have his Symphony performed in Leningrad. Actually, if you don't find it too awful, maybe you could show it to one of the conductors.' (*Selected Letters of Sergei Prokofiev*, ed. and trans. Harlow Robison, Northeaster University Press, Boston, 1998.) Ferroud was killed in a car crash in Hungary in 1936.

1 June

Composed in the morning. Fiedler has been trying to persuade us to buy a flat in a house now being built in the Bois de Boulogne. It's very tempting, but costs a great deal of money and the building will be ready only after the winter.

To the Koussevitzkys, who were charming. A meeting with the manager whom they wanted me to meet. Koussevitzky envisages my 1929–30 tour having thirty to forty concerts with fees amounting to $20,000, from which I would clear $10,000.

This manager took Ravel to America this year, and will take Honegger next year. Ravel is a hopeless conductor and could barely play the piano, but people were interested in him (to see him, but once they had taken one look they were no longer interested; there will be no future engagements for him). He has returned now with money in his pocket and has gone on the booze, something I did not expect!

On returning home found a postcard from Savich telling me that he had conducted the premiere of Le Pas d'acier in Moscow.[1] This upsets me: Derzhanovsky is a fool. Savich is a provincial amateur.

2 June

In the morning, an orchestra rehearsal of Le Pas d'acier, with which Diaghilev's season is to open. There is only the one rehearsal, but it lasted over two hours. It came across quite well; this orchestra is good and even the horns could be heard in the *forte* passages (horn-players in France only know how to play *piano*). At the end they rehearsed Ode, for which Nabokov put in an appearance, cursing life in Monte Carlo and endless arguments with the ballet company. My appearance there had been a ray of sunshine, he emphasised. Ode was rehearsed in segments and sounded good; Nabokov has a better sense of the orchestra than Dukelsky. I hear that he has recently become very bad-tempered and at the publishers yesterday went so far as to bang the table with his fist and scream that Koussevitzky had ignored him when making up his programmes. Because of this I was rather curt with him today.

Dukelsky is now staying with some dandified baron or other and it is a contact that is ruining him. When he came to see me today about the Sonata I was still asleep, and after waiting a while he went away again. Then Koussevitzky's manager came and we had a talk about America. He is clearly

---

1 The four-movement Suite, Op. 41a, which Prokofiev had drawn from the ballet in 1926. It was performed in an ASM concert in Moscow on 27 May.

serious about working with me and addresses me very respectfully. The tour will not take place until 1929–30, but it is the early bird that catches the worm.

3 June

C.S. Church. I asked Miss Crain if Gorchakov had been to see her, but he has not, although he had said he would within a couple of days.

I had a headache in the afternoon and felt terribly sleepy; I slept right through a visit from the Nabokovs and did not go to the Koussevitzkys in the afternoon, which annoyed Ptashka.

In the evening my headache passed off and we went to hear a choir from Antwerp perform Mozart's Requiem and Milhaud's *Oresteia*. Janacopoulos was singing: she has sadly gone off, the voice suffering from strain and the timbre unpleasant. The Milhaud is a fraud. The only good bits are those with declamation, shouting and percussion, that is to say where there is no actual music. But those parts are excellent and made me think of my own project for combining speech with music.[1] Dukelsky wants to clear things up over the money. Quite sharply, I answered, 'There is no need for any explanations. If you want to repay the money, do so, but there is no hurry. If you need more, I will let you have it with pleasure.'

Spotting me greeting Stravinsky, Nabokov exclaimed, 'How fascinating to witness the very essence of Russian music saluting itself.'

---

1   Soon after his return to Paris from Brazil Milhaud composed incidental music to his friend and former employer Paul Claudel's translation into French of the *Oresteia* trilogy of Aeschylus. (When Claudel, who combined his work as a poet and dramatist with a high-level diplomatic career, was posted to Rio de Janeiro as *ministre plénipotentiaire* – the diplomatic rank immediately below that of ambassador – from 1916 to 1918 he had taken Milhaud with him as his cultural affairs secretary, providing an introduction to Latin American music that left its mark on the composer's aesthetic for the rest of his long and productive life.) Malcolm Macdonald's review for *Gramophone* of May 1958 of a recording by Igor Markevich with the Lamoureux Orchestra and soloists of *Les Choéphores (The Libation Bearers)*, the title by which the second play of the trilogy is known in France, explains the work's unusual configuration as follows: 'Milhaud, at the time, had strong views on the proper nature of theatrical incidental music, holding that the spoken word and the sound of music were on sufficiently different planes to be incompatible (the history of opera has largely been the history of attempts to resolve this conflict, instinctively felt by most audiences). As far as the *Oresteia* were concerned, Milhaud's solution was to write substantial pieces, without speech, for solo singers, chorus, and orchestra, inserting these into the dramatic action. A rare accompaniment to the spoken word, by contrast, was allotted to spoken chorus and seventeen instruments of percussion only (one classic performance of 1919 was a triumphant success: on that occasion, which must have been an enjoyable one, the percussion players included Cocteau, Auric, Poulenc, and Honegger). Another theory on which Milhaud was consciously working at the time was that of polytonality, and a great deal of the *Oresteia* music does disclose a shifting polytonal chordal accompaniment, richly scored, to a fundamentally diatonic vocal line.'

Afterwards we went with the Nabokovs to Dubost (Dukelsky had not been invited, so went home), but it was rather silly and boring there. We went off to a café with Nabokov, who was very good company and told stories about the nonsense that has become endemic to the Diaghilev ballet.

4 June

A very nice letter from Myaskovsky containing incredible praise for *Fiery Angel*.[1] But *Fiery Angel* has met with little success.

Composed, but not very much. Gorchakov appeared after a week's absence. Thank God I did not fly at him but politely enquired after his health and proposed that we work out an arrangement to our mutual convenience (payment in advance for six weeks' work transcribing the Russian diary). We agreed that he would work half the day for half the previous salary.

---

1   Moscow, 30 May 1928: 'In my last letter to you I launched into hysterical ecstasy over Act 5, which stunned me with its overall power and the amazing vividness of certain moments, such as Renata's final cry of anguish at the appearance of the sun. But at the time I had only an intuitive foreshadowing of the rest of it, the result of a feeling rather than a thoroughgoing absorption. Now, going through this music a second time, I have been overwhelmed by how appropriate and convincing it is. Do you know what particularly impresses me? It is the incredible, if I may put it this way, humanity of your music, and the images it conjures up. The characters of Rupprecht and Renata are no longer from the theatre, still less opera – they are absolutely living people, so profound and true are the intonations with which you have delineated them. Their first conversation in the room, Renata's telling of her story: these are so full of character in content as well as being so perfectly realised as to pure musical structure and subtlety of texture, the vocal line so expressive, so supple and withal so *practical*. I was equally enthralled, if not more so, by the whole of the third act, so powerful in its inner conviction . . . I believe I am not mistaken in regarding *Fiery Angel* as the composition in which you have achieved your full stature as a musician and as an artist, for the creation of characters such as Rupprecht and Renata in all their depth and unimaginable human complexity could only have come from a genius who has plumbed the full reach of his powers.

'But now I have to tell you something that will upset you. Excerpts from *Le Pas d'acier* have nevertheless been performed by the capable American Vladimir Savich – some people here describe him as a genius. Unfortunately I could not attend the rehearsals as I was away from Moscow, so am unable to comment fully on the quality of the performance. The success was only moderate. To a man commentators are critical, indeed hostile. Your only defenders are a few old friends: I, Derzhanovsky, V. V. Yakovlev [Vasily Yakovlev, Myaskovsky's musicologist brother-in-law] and some of my students and their friends in the greenness of youth (this last was an especial and pleasant surprise to me). The antagonists bellow with one voice that there is nothing new here; we have seen it all before; it is too loud; there is too much "white-key music"; too much dissonance; and so on. But my impression is that in fact the disappointment stems from something else: that you have actually presented too much that is truly new rather than the friendly, lively but unthreatening – because familiar – idiom they were hoping for, almost as though expecting the Third Piano Concerto or the March from *Oranges*, or similar. So when you put before them cyclopean blocks of sound, alarming polyphonic and harmonic strata, when you start pile-driving in these strange edifices, terrifying in their massive scale and potency, everyone loses their head and when, despite everything, they hear a familiar snatch of something they are used to, they stop up their ears to everything else and write it all off as old hat and boring.'
(*S. S. Prokofiev and N. Ya. Myaskovsky: Correspondence*, Sovetskii Kompozitor, Moscow, 1977.)

5 June

Pre-general rehearsal of *Ode*. Nabokov very kindly seated me with his wife. Diaghilev appeared in jovial mood: how dare you (sit with another man's wife)? *Ode* has some nice moments – specifically 'nice', I am not yet sure whether they are really any good – but there are also boring or at least unsuccessful passages. But the production, which some genius had dressed up with cinema footage and all kinds of special lighting, caused a scandal. A licensing committee had forbidden the use of the chemical retort on stage. Diaghilev hurried off to telephone the Minister of Internal Affairs. I asked Stravinsky if he thought the musical material of *Ode* was good. His answer was expressed with childlike fresh-faced innocence. I took the Nabokovs home after the rehearsal.

In the evening I went to Horowitz's concert. He has an excellent technique but is not a profound pianist. The audience went wild.

Glazunov and his mother are coming to Paris in a fortnight's time.[1]

6 June

Ode general rehearsal. Diaghilev worked through the night until seven in the morning, but was back at nine. And it still is not together. The retort is irrevocably banned, the Minister having ruled that although he sincerely sympathised with the dilemma, he could not lift the ban: were it to explode the whole place could blow up. My opinion of the music stayed much as it had been. I still believe Nabokov is talented but has not yet found the means to express himself, although I am less certain of this than I am with Dukelsky. Dukelsky was not present.

In the afternoon I proof-read the piano score of *Le Pas d'acier*, which has been engraved with a million mistakes. For a break I took Ptashka into the town and dropped into the publishing house to get some money. Paichadze was not there but I found Rachmaninoff in conversation with Conius.

---

1 Prokofiev had obviously been unable to work out exactly what relationship the two ladies he had met in Glazunov's apartment when he called on him in February 1927 had to the composer. The elder was Olga Gavrilova and the younger her daughter Elena. Olga had assumed the maternal role in the affairs of a man who was by all accounts incapable of looking after himself in any normal domestic sense. Both women joined Glazunov in Paris soon after in June 1928 the Soviet authorities gave him an exit visa to serve as a jury member of the Schubert centenary festival in Vienna, with permission to reside abroad for up to a year. Glazunov subsequently married Olga and adopted Elena, and never returned to the USSR, although nominally retaining his post as Director of the Leningrad Conservatoire until 1930. He gave ill health as the justification for his annual applications to extend the foreign residence permit, an arrangement to which the regime tacitly gave its blessing until Glazunov's death in 1936.

Rachmaninoff was very friendly but did not rise from his chair to greet me (he is fifty-five, I am thirty-seven). He was looking rather sprightly, his thousands of wrinkles somehow smoothed out. Conversation turned to my embonpoint, in which connection I mentioned my father, who suffered from consumption yet still at the age of thirty weighed nearly seven poods.[1] I was also on my best behaviour and we chatted amiably about my son, about American copyright, and so on.

I: 'Where's the boss?'

Rachmaninoff (wishing to flatter Conius): 'Well, what do you need him for? Here's his number two.'

I: 'Yes, but I won't get any money out of him.'

Rachmaninoff (brightening up at the mention of money and laughing): 'No, that you won't, that you won't!'

The opening of the Diaghilev season took place that evening with *Le Pas d'acier*. Consistent with Diaghilev's bountiful style I was not even given a proper seat but a *strapontin*[2] which squeaked. The music was played too fast, which was horrible: Désormière had forgotten what we had agreed. Not everything worked perfectly on stage. But it had a great success. Nouvel summoned me to take a bow; I resisted, after all it was not a premiere. Then I changed my mind and started off to do so, but it was too far to the stage and I was late. Diaghilev said: 'Twelve minutes of applause and you couldn't stir your stumps to come and take a bow . . .' Once again *Le Pas* drew many compliments. But in Russia it has been a failure.

Ode went far better than at rehearsal, but it does have boring places where the composer had 'padded' it at Diaghilev's request, indeed at one point booing was heard. Nevertheless, all in all it was a success. Nabokov came on stage, shyly bowed to acknowledge the applause, and obviously embarrassed kissed his niece's hand. After an interminable interval we had Stravinsky's *Les Noces*. It is such a strong piece, but everyone was tired and it went rather blandly.

7 June

General rehearsal of Koussevitzky's concert. A feeble piano concerto by Roussel, with a theme I had used in *The Giant*.[3] Bravo Borovsky, who learnt

---

1 One pood (a measure officially abolished in 1924 but still in common use up until the Second World War) was equivalent to 16.38 kilograms, so according to Prokofiev his father weighed around 17 stone.
2 A folding chair, used for extra seating in a theatre or concert hall.
3 Prokofiev's childhood opera, written when he was nine.

it in six days. Florent Schmitt's piece was disgusting. Much of *Skyscrapers*[1] was interesting, but vulgar.

Lunched with Borovsky. Hertz,[2] the incorrigible conservative, has suddenly got interested in modern music, and pulling his thick beard, flirted with Ptashka.

The Koussevitzky concert in the evening was just dull. It is really impossible to keep cramming in so many boring novelties.

8 June

Proof-read the piano transcription of *The Steel Step* and dictated some letters.

The Nabokovs called. He delivered himself of a stream of affectionate remarks and offered some advice about publication. They dined with us and we went together to the cinema.

9 June

Borovsky's recital. He played well, with an occasional tendency to dryness. As an encore he played the fifth *Sarcasm*. Nabokov sat with us in our box. Dukelsky pressed me to come clean about why I had cooled towards him. I assured him he was mistaken.

10 June

C.S. Church. Ptashka and I have been on bad terms the last few days, but today she made the first move towards reconciliation. She is sometimes unbearable when we are at odds, but her great quality is that she is always the first to call a truce. We made a trip into town with Camb, from Denver – nice, bland Americans. Went to the Koussevitzkys' At Home in the afternoon, and in the evening to the Ghirshmans.[3]

11 June

First rehearsal,[4] for strings alone, a few places sound peculiar – 'my poor mother' even funny, enough to make Dukelsky and me laugh. A sour taste,

---

1 Jazz-influenced ballet by John Alden Carpenter. See above, pp. 250, 270–1.
2 The conductor Alfred Hertz. See above, p. 255.
3 Roman Ghirshman (1895–1979), wealthy Ukrainian-born archaeologist whose special interest was in excavating the sites of ancient Iran and Afghanistan.
4 Of a programme consisting of Dukelsky's Symphony, a Suite from Rimsky-Korsakov's *The Fair Maid of Pskov* and a preview of some of the *Fiery Angel* music (basically Act 2, with some excisions).

Dukelsky said, like putting his teeth on edge. I inveigh against the 30s. After the rehearsal I went with Conius, who has been correcting Dukelsky's orchestral parts, to the publishers, where I was greeted affectionately by Rachmaninoff: 'Look, here is Sergey Sergeyevich!' He asked me to tell him about Nabokov, someone having told him he was a flower blooming between two abysses.

Lunched with Hertz and played to him, Dukelsky observing that 'here goes Prokofiev again, foisting his music on people', which earned him a sharp rebuke from Ptashka. He certainly is a cheeky young fellow. Spaak[1] in the afternoon. He came to see me about *Fiery Angel*, but I successfully steered him towards *The Gambler*. Took him to meet Paichadze.

In the evening Ptashka went to *The Magic Flute* conducted by Walter, but I stayed at home.

12 June

Second rehearsal, winds and strings. Dukelsky's Symphony is uneven, much of it does not come off but Dukelsky is enraptured by all of it. After the second movement he remarked, 'And now for the third, in which nobody has messed up the orchestration,' but in fact the first page of it, which I orchestrated, is the best. Despite this, I believe the Symphony is a step forward. *Fiery Angel* went well from the start because it is written in broad lines in contrast to Dukelsky's short-breathed phrases. It sounded good, as I expected it to. The rehearsal over, I drove an exhausted Koussevitzky home.

In the afternoon I thought I would go to the general rehearsal of *Apollon*,[2] but it turned out that this had taken place the previous day. At half past five there was a run-through for the singers at Koussevitzky's. They had all conned their parts admirably.

We had dinner at Koussevitzky's and then accompanied him to Diaghilev's premiere of *Apollon*. Diaghilev was in a bad temper. *Apollon* makes me angry, although I try my best to persuade myself not to be a prey to naked contrariness. This is the nature of my dual relationship with myself and with others: on the one hand, were I to encounter a work like this without knowing who its author was, I would simply write it off as a mediocre ballet. But Stravinsky is my 'colleague' and my rival, hence there is an obligation to act nobly. So what must I do? Must I pronounce a bad ballet good? The applause was quite prolonged, but hardly warm. Stravinsky runs out on stage. He does not walk off again; the curtain just rises and falls. During the interval no one mentions

---

1 Paul Spaak, Intendant of the Théâtre de la Monnaie in Brussels.
2 Stravinsky's ballet *Apollon musagète*, with choreography by Balanchine.

Apollon (or is this only to me?). My gaffe with Rothschild (that he fell asleep during *Apollon*).

13 June

Third rehearsal. Dukelsky's Symphony gains in clarity, although much of it is still obscure. Some people approve the second movement, others think it is mere playing with beautiful effects. About the second subject of the finale: 'It's from me, with a nod towards Glière . . .' This made Suvchinsky chortle, but he praised the Symphony to Dukelsky's face as the work of a mature composer. I held my tongue. The present situation is a reversal of its former self: in the past I always used to express my admiration of the Symphony but now, seeing its defects, am critical of them. Others began by being sceptical but now see its merits and shower it with praise. Dukelsky sticks his nose in the air and cleaves to his new admirers.

According to Nabokov, Stravinsky, putting on airs in front of a young composer, asked him what he thought of *Apollon*. Nabokov found something or other in it to be complimentary about. Stravinsky: 'Yes, that was very successful. I don't know how God contrived to make me compose it.'

Then *Fiery Angel*, the first time with the singers. They were hard to hear, even though in the second scene they were singing at the top of their voices. The problem is down to the acoustic of the hall, all the same it is upsetting. Borovsky and Prunières are greatly impressed, as of course was Koussevitzky. Suvchinsky and Nabokov left without saying a word. Altogether *Apollon* and *Fiery Angel* have aroused in musical circles very strong partisan feelings, mute responses, bewilderment and the like. But *Apollon* is Stravinsky's latest creation whereas *Fiery Angel* is not new, at least in conception, and the appearance I am now making is with a work from which in many ways I have moved on.

14 June

Koussevitzky had the brilliant notion of taking the second scene *pianissimo* (playing the preceding orchestral entr'acte *forte* throughout). The singers now projected excellently, until just before the end a slow crescendo in the orchestra naturally covered them all. Roussel and Poulenc extolled its virtues.

The concert in the evening drew quite a large audience. In the box were Natalya Konstantinovna, ourselves, and the Zakharovs. Many conductors were present: Stokowski, Hertz, Beecham and others. A very enjoyable Suite from *The Fair Maid of Pskov*. Dukelsky's Symphony went well and was warmly received. *Fiery Angel* went well too and was greeted with very enthusiastic applause. I had asked Koussevitzky not to bring me out straight away; he complied, nevertheless, I had to come back three times, which for the composer of a symphonic work is quite a lot. During the interval there was a frightful crush in the box, everyone congratulating me with genuine warmth. Altogether, the occasion was a real success.

Sabaneyev (in response to my disbelief): 'No, truly, I liked it very much indeed.'

I: 'But how hard you will find it to convince yourself of that!'

In the second half *Pictures from an Exhibition* sounded marvellous, earning Koussevitzky a thunderous ovation. He was radiant, and so was I. Afterwards we gathered at the Zakharovs, as had been planned some time ago; their original idea was a small party, but eventually everyone came: Koussevitzkys, Stokowski, Hertz, Dukelsky, Borovsky, Paichadze, the Samoilenkos, Larionov and Goncharova, the Obukhovs, the Kedrov Quartet,[1] Ghirshman. There was barely enough food, but they were flattered to have so many famous lions. At one point, when I was for some reasons exchanging kisses with Zakharov, I explained to Fatma Hanum that we had been friends for twenty-two years, at which Zakharov swiftly interposed, 'Except for two dreadful years.'[2] So he remembers it to this day! 'It was all because of the circulation of the blood,' I countered. All of a sudden Fatma took me aside and started asking me about Meshcherskaya, without naming her or perhaps not knowing her name. Was it true that I had tried to seduce and abduct her because the 'someone's' parents were opposed to the match? I laughed and said that not only that, but Bashkirov had been waiting round the corner with his car.[3]

Fatma (after a pause): 'In America I was always under the impression that you were a man without a past.'

I (to erase any such impression): 'But when I went back to Russia, how many from my "past" appeared!'

Fatma: 'And what about her? Did she ever appear in your life again?'

---

1 See above, p. 112.
2 In 1912, when they were both students at the St Petersburg Conservatoire, a serious rift had occurred in their previous close relationship on account of Prokofiev's (as Zakharov saw it) unhealthy infatuation with another student, Maximilian Schmidthof, to whom the Second Piano Concerto, and the Second and Fourth Piano Sonatas were posthumously dedicated. After Schmidthof committed suicide in April 1913, Prokofiev instigated a rapprochement with Zakharov that slowly regained its former intimacy. See *Diaries*, vol. 1, pp. 267–9, 387–9, 490–91, and *passim*.
3 See *Diaries*, vol. 2, pp. 39–43, for an account of the farcically bungled elopement.

(Oh and how! considering that a portrait of her father-in-law[1] hangs on the Samoilenkos' own wall.) But to deflect any further questions: 'No, in my eyes she damned herself for ever with her indecisiveness about running away with me.'

15 June

Haensel visited me and we had delicate talks about my leaving him. Haensel conducted himself like a gentleman, gave his consent and did not even ask me about the money I owe him ($1,000). His comment about Koussevitzky's manager was that he was an honest man, but not influential. He recommended me to seek guarantees from my new manager.

16 June

I bought all the newspapers because it would be interesting to see how *Fiery Angel* had been reviewed following its successful performance. But there was nothing in any of them. At three o'clock Dukelsky and Marnold came: Marnold wanted to hear the former's Symphony and look at the score. Afterwards I put the chessboard in front of Dukelsky and Marnold, but Marnold took two games off him. I then beat Marnold three times.

We went out to dinner, Ptashka, Dukelsky and I, then on to the Samoilenkos, where other guests included Somov,[2] Borovsky and Shukhaev.[3] It was a very pleasant evening, although I was rather passive and listened more than I talked. Fatma, also on her own, tried to engage me in conversation, but we kept being interrupted.

---

1 The man whose portrait was on the Samoilenkos' wall was Alexander Krivoshein (1858–1921). (See above, p. 639, n. 1.) Like many émigré Russians the Samoilenkos regarded Alexander Krivoshein as a particularly heroic figure in the struggle to move towards constitutional democracy in Russia. Kirill Krivoshein, the younger brother of Nina Meshcherskaya's husband Igor, wrote a memoir of his father: *Alexander Vasilievich Krivoshein, The Fate of a Russian Reformer*, published in Moscow in 1993.
2 Konstantin Somov (1869–1939), painter, drawn early into Diaghilev's *Mir Isskustva* circle by his friend Benois. Emigrating after the Revolution first to America and then to Paris, two of his best-known portraits are the *Woman in Blue* (of his childhood friend the poet Elizaveta Martynova), and of Rachmaninoff.
3 Vasily Shukhaev (1887–1973), painter, graphic and theatre artist, also a member of the *Mir Isskustva* circle. Like Somov he moved to Paris after the Revolution but returned to Leningrad in 1935. Two years later he was arrested and spent ten years in the harshest camps of Kolyma in north-eastern Siberia. Rehabilitated in 1947, he moved to Tbilisi where he remained for the remainder of his life.

17 June

C.S. Church. Versailles, to Bassiano. What splendid people they are: artistic, thoroughbred to the core. Horowitz wanted to assure me that he is not merely a salon pianist, he has already learnt my Op. 32,[1] and during the summer will study my Concerto. But which one? I recommended No. 3; I need to keep No. 2 for myself for America. Navarra,[2] straightforward little pieces, Ptashka conversed with him in Spanish. A great crowd at the Koussevitzkys; they with their present affectionate feelings towards us. It seems that we have a plan to go together by car to Haute Savoie, we to look for a dacha and they to go to the one they have already taken. A reading by Marina Tsvetaeva in the evening, for which the tickets cost 400 francs, which is rather expensive: others have cost 100 or 50. Very good verses, although sometimes hard to understand. But how detached I feel now from poetry. Suvchinsky is somewhat shamefaced: he stupidly sold our tickets for *Fiery Angel* having 'not understood' the music when he came to the rehearsal. I said: 'That is extraordinary; after all it's not a new piece . . . Suvchinsky: 'There is no one writing sensibly about music at the moment. Come the autumn I shall set the ball rolling with an article about you.' I: 'That won't worry anyone: you write in such a convoluted way that no one will understand anything you say.'

18 June

In the morning came back via the town of Versailles in order to deal with my tax affairs, which have been hanging over me for a year and a half. The assessment is 3,000 francs, of which I have to pay 2,200 but they let me off 870 francs. Taking into consideration the high taxes one has to pay in France I have got off quite lightly, and also have been allowed to postpone payment until I have the money to pay.

After lunch I dictated some of the mounting pile of accumulated letters to 'half-pay' Gorchakov. To Dubost at five o'clock for three 'opéra-minutes'.

---

1 *Four Pieces for Piano*, composed soon after Prokofiev arrived in America in 1918, a conscious attempt to write for his new market. 'Because Fischer had indicated that to ensure wider distribution of my music (and more profits for his firm) they would like to publish a few more pieces in addition to *Tales of an Old Grandmother*, perhaps more accessible, like for example the Gavotte, today, I jotted down some ideas for a set of dances to keep the rogues quiet.' (*Diaries*, vol. 2, p. 343.)
2 André Navarra (1911–1988), French cellist of exceptional gifts that manifested themselves at a very early age when he graduated from the Paris Conservatoire at the age of fifteen with the top prize. From then on, unusually, he abandoned further formal study, preferring to work out his own pedagogical method to perfect his skills, a method that he passed on to a great number of students, notably at the Musik Hochschule in Detmold, alongside a long and distinguished performing career.

Question: how many minutes should an 'opéra-minute' last? Milhaud 'good', which when I said this to him pleased him very much, since we understood the word differently: he thinks he is a good composer whereas I consider him a bad one (this needs developing). Stokowski came up to me and asked if I would be at the lunch tomorrow; he was generally very nice to me. I was polite, but immediately withdrew into the background. Sofronitsky recital in the evening: good moments but uneven and in many places not absolutely secure. He has not really prepared himself for performing abroad, where you cannot allow yourself to make mistakes. But his playing does have *Flüss*.[1]

Finished proofing the piano reduction of *Le Pas*, a horrible piece of engraving.

12 July

We have arrived at Vétraz.[2] I came down with Astrov,[3] not the most interesting companion but the journey was fine. Ptashka was in the train with Svyatoslav and the English nanny, who turns out to be hopeless.

I settled down to revising the Op. 42 Overture for full orchestra.[4] This was at first not an easy task, but went more smoothly once I had developed a new concept. I corrected proofs of the orchestral parts of the Second Symphony.

I like our château. Ptashka is irritated by the owners, and calls the wife a 'dairy maid'.

8 August

In the afternoon, I took Ptashka and Svyatoslav over in the car to the Koussevitzkys. My plan was for a walking expedition and for Ptashka and Svyatoslav to stay there with Natalya Konstantinovna as she loves them very much. As the car drew up out ran Stravinsky's two sons; himself was within apparently having tea. He was very charming, full of praise for the car when he inspected it. Everyone in high spirits. Talk about Beethoven, an adversary

---

1 Flow.
2 The house Prokofiev rented for the summer of 1928 was the Château de Vétraz, near Annemasse in Haute Savoie.
3 Mikhail Astrov, Prokofiev's new secretary whom he had met at the offices of Edition Russe de Musique, his publishers, owned by the Koussevitzkys, and who remained with the composer for the rest of his time in Paris.
4 This was being done at the request of Herman Schaad of the Aeolian Company, now owners of Duo-Art, for whom Prokofiev had composed the *Overture for Seventeen Instruments* to inaugurate their new 250-seat concert hall in New York in 1926. Schaad was willing to pay for a symphonic version, and Koussevitzky was interested in performing it in America.

in principle but a worthy one. Not for that is Beethoven loved. Criticism of Rimsky-Korsakov; I said Rimsky's main defect is that he is so four-square, his inheritance from Liszt. Stravinsky agreed, but said that quadrangularity is not always bad, citing passages from Weber and the coda of Tchaikovsky's Fourth Symphony. He asked me what I was engaged on – nothing? Resting from the exertions of the winter season? I starting telling him about the piano pieces (could not possibly mention the *Fiery Angel* Symphony), but our conversation was interrupted by the summons to dinner. Paichadze had cooked a wonderful *shashlyk* out of doors, accompanied by superb wine. Stravinsky's sons had a little too much to drink and imitated Englishmen. Conversation then turned to what Stravinsky was engaged upon in his separate hut at Annecy:[1] he works for four hours in the morning, then breaks for lunch, and then another three or four hours before dinner. He is doing a ballet for Ida.[2] Tchaikovsky. I am stunned. The difficulties of composing his own themes has propelled him towards using those of others. It's an easy way to go, reflected success, with his brilliant technique ... and yet, Andersen, the situation in Switzerland, Tchaikovsky's music – what a hodge-podge! He loved Svyatoslav. Wouldn't it be good to have him as a godfather! We all stayed the night.

9 August

All night someone was being violently sick, and Natalya Konstantinovna was worried for Ptashka, who is pregnant. But it proved to have been Stravinsky, who had overindulged on the *shashlyk*. We men gathered round him as he lay on his bed fully dressed except for his unbuttoned trousers, leading me to think he must be suffering from dysentery. By lunchtime he was better, and left with his son to go to Thonon for a reunion with friends living at the other end of Lake Geneva in Switzerland.[3]

Apparently Svyatoslav had been asking, for no particular reason, 'Mama, what does Stravinsky mean?' Ptashka relayed this to the maestro, who was delighted and immediately began to explain to Svyatoslav, 'Stravinsky – well, you see, this is me, this is Stravinsky, look here ... ' and so on.

We set out at a quarter to four in the evening, touchingly waved off on our walk. The start of the climb was lovely, a path through the woods. We walked

---

1 It was actually a room in the neighbouring cottage of a stonemason and his family. The arrangement was not a success. See S. Walsh, op. cit, pp. 473–4.
2 This was *Le Baiser de la fée*, a commission from Ida Rubinstein, suggested by Benois, to put together and orchestrate a ballet based on Hans Andersen's fairy-tale 'The Ice Maiden', culled and transformed from non-ballet songs and piano pieces by Tchaikovsky.
3 The friends were, or should have been, the collaborators from Lausanne on *The Soldier's Tale*, Ramuz, Ansermet and Auberjonois, but in the end only the last-named made it. See S. Walsh, op. cit.

for a long time, and at nine o'clock, very tired, we arrived at a chalet at the foot of Mount Joly, finding which brought us great joy. Dinner and bubbly. Thinking of Port Arthur and scurvy, I wondered if they would have survived better had they drunk wine.[1] While checking in we described ourselves as musicians, as a result of which we were brought an accordion. We did not think much of it. Our sleeping quarters were in the attic, Paichadze and I lay on straw covered by a blanket. I dropped off to sleep, but Koussevitzky did not sleep at all. At three o'clock we were disturbed by the arrival of a noisy party shouting and making a terrible racket, but they were not let in.

We left again at six, Koussevitzky not feeling very well. We walked slowly, which suited me fine. We decided to change our route. Koussevitzky went back with the serving boy, while Paichadze and I continued to the summit. I found a better, but steeper, way up. At first the way lay through green meadows, but higher up there was bare rock and grey scree. Why did we choose Mount Joly, which is not very beautiful? There was not much room at the summit, but the views all round were marvellous. Koussevitzky hardly made it back to the chalet, and I was not in the best of shape either. We rested for a while, by four o'clock everyone was feeling better and we set off to walk down to St Nicolas, which boasts a single hotel. There was a magnificent view of green and smiling country from the terrace where we had dinner. Koussevitzky, Paichadze and I went out for another walk, and Paichadze recounted his experiences in 1921, the sleeping-car and the incident with coins in a flower vase. Koussevitzky also reminisced about the sleeping car. I listened, but did not tell any stories.

11 August

We got up at 5.30, having slept the sleep of the dead. The Great Second Republic of Poland (four representatives of) waved us goodbye. It was an easy and pleasant ascent to the Col de Voza. A slight tiff with Koussevitzky over the coffee, as a result of which I returned alone down the rocky road to the isolated hotel at nine o'clock. The sun was hot, but the air was cool coming off the glacier. I greedily drank down three cups of coffee.

The rest of the company soon came back, Koussevitzky scolding me for walking off, which he said spoilt the mood. We rested at the hotel and then at three o'clock commenced our descent. Last year Koussevitzky and Paichadze had lost their way and ended up in a bog. Now it was a dry summer but we still managed to lose ourselves in a thicket of bushes and trees. Koussevitzky

---

1 During the winter of 1904–5 in the disastrous (for Russia) Russo-Japanese War, when the Japanese were besieging Port Arthur, the Russian naval base in Manchuria, the garrison was severely afflicted by scurvy and dysentery owing to the lack of fresh produce.

was annoyed, and dropped his spectacles; Paichadze bruised his hand, but nothing could dampen my spirits. When we finally found the way down, we entered the valley of Chamonix, which is wonderfully beautiful.

By evening, dog-tired, we reached Chamonix itself. It was Saturday and there were a million people there; we wanted to find a better hotel but they were all full and we were lucky to find an attic. Paichadze was glum today.

12 August

This morning we did not rush away so as to get a decent rest. Chamonix is full of people, like a more cramped version of Kislovodsk, but the air is not to be compared with that of Kislovodsk, which is far better. After lunch we climbed up through the forest to reach the bare slopes of the mountain, with marvellous views over Chamonix to Mont Blanc.

Pretty tired we arrived at the Chalet de Planpraz in a charming, wide-open space among the mountains. The little rooms were delightful with bare boards reminding one of dachas in Finland and Russia. The landlady's very nice young daughter. Koussevitzky and I shared a bottle of champagne. I slept in the same room as Paichadze, who talked to me about anthroposophy, whose proponents do not attract me: religio-philosophical speculations.[1] There was a thunderstorm.

13 August

We walked somewhat lazily up to the Col du Brévent, but the crossing over the saddle and its far side are truly wonderful. Everywhere you look are mountains of varying formations, some rocky, some smooth, some green. It was a very interesting walk. Breakfast by the side of a mountain stream, consisting of sandwiches and water from stinking horn cups. We then continued our ascent up to the Chalet d'Anterne, where we had lunch. Unpleasant landlord with whom, as the expedition's treasurer, I haggled over the bill. Then down to Servoz, a long descent along a cobbled road, at the end of which we lost our way and found ourselves on a much better road that, however, did not take us in the right direction. Darkness came on. The car. We finally got home at ten o'clock, where they had given up expecting us so were surprised but overjoyed to see us.

1 Anthroposophy is a religious philosophy developed by Rudolf Steiner in a movement progressively breaking away from the theosophy of Annie Besant and Madame Blavatsky. Although he loved the poetry of Andrey Bely, Prokofiev had been dismayed by what he considered the poet's irrational adherence to the tenets of anthroposophy despite having been cruelly rebuffed by the community at Dornach in which Bely had spent five years as a dedicated disciple of Steiner. See *Diaries*, vol. 2, p. 681.

8 September

Asafyev arrived today, by car from Geneva, after I had gone four times to the station to meet him. He looks in excellent form. He talked all day, telling me how Rimsky-Korsakov had failed to convince Musorgsky of the unacceptable coarseness of his writing, and resorted to stratagems that, however psychologically wrong they might have been, nevertheless had their effect. Among young composers he approves of Shostakovich (a bad character though) and Popov.

9 September

Marvellous expedition to Evian and along the lake on board a yacht-like steamer. Asafyev sat beside me in the car. He loves the French countryside but talks so much he sometimes forgets to look at it. He does not like *Apollon*. He is critical of Nabokov, especially *Ode*, but has somewhat condescending praise for Dukelsky (his songs).

10 September

Started orchestrating the second movement of the Symphony.[1] Played Asafyev the two *Choses en soi*. He prefers the longer one to the shorter, which made sense to him only on a second hearing. This surprised me. He is uncertain about the title, but did not rule it out completely. I was nervous playing the work to him. He agrees that it represents a new side to me. We recalled our parallel development at the Conservatoire, and after. It was in Moscow, through Derzhanovsky, that the three of us, he, I and Myaskovsky, first bonded.

11 September

A trip to the very beautiful Lake Annecy, Talloires[2] is lovely but Stravinsky had already left for Holland.[3] Asafyev is in ecstasy. We returned at dusk along the slopes of Mount Salève. Asafyev is writing an article about *Le Pas d'acier* (I have the proofs here at the moment). He likes it very much, although he had not been impressed by the beginning of the piano score I had taken with me to Russia. Propaganda about Russia.

---

1 Symphony No. 3, based on material from *Fiery Angel*.
2 The Stravinsky family had spent the summer in the small village of Talloires on Lake Annecy.
3 To perform his Piano Concerto at the Scheveningen Festival.

12 September

Got down to work orchestrating and polishing the second movement of the Symphony. In the afternoon went on foot with Asafyev into Annemasse on various small errands. He is a stout walker.

13 September

Ever since he arrived here I have been wanting to have a talk to Asafyev about C.S., but did not know how to broach the subject. When a conversation started about European views on religion I asked Asafyev if he had ever heard of C.S. He had not. I began to expound it, somewhat nervous until I remembered that speech is a gift from on high. Asafyev immediately showed interest and told me the story of how he had been cured in the Catacombs of Rome. He had a bad heart, the doctors sent him to Paris for a change of air but matters got worse there. He then went with his wife to Italy and suffered a heart attack in Pisa after a funeral, regaining consciousness at the sound of a bell but unable to move. Despite this they continued to Rome, where they met a remarkable monk who showed them the Catacombs. He told Asafyev, 'You are well, and still have much to accomplish.' Asafyev believes this to have been hypnotism, as all his illness cleared up. In the evening I gave him *Science and Health* to read.

14 September

An excursion to Onnion, where I have been once before. Very beautiful. Asafyev's first 'real contact with these enchanting mountains'. The caves.[1] They are at quite a high altitude and Ptashka should not really have come up. The caves are not deep, and there are no steps down, but the way in and the main hall are 200 metres. Electric light would be no bad thing!

We did not speak about C.S.

15 September

Worked on the Andante. I played the first movement to Asafyev and it made a strong impression on him. An idiotic letter from the Swiss Consul: they need a deposit. Went for a walk. Asafyev is reading *Science and Health*, but slowly: it is not easy, containing as it does many new thoughts. I think this is all for the best; there is no point in pressing him. Conversation about the Mighty Handful, about the malevolence of Rimsky-Korsakov's character,

---

1 The caves at Onnions contain traces of occupation by Neanderthal hunters from 50,000 BCE.

and about some secret or other in Balakirev's life, also the aristocratically epicurean dissipation of Glinka and Borodin, along with the extremely attractive nature of both individuals. The death of Glinka. Asafyev warmly defended the proposition that Tchaikovsky, so far from being, as I had said, hidebound by polite conventions, was in fact the most sensitive personality and greatly underestimated in many respects. Often he would match a letter precisely to the level of the recipient. For instance his letters to the young Glazunov are truly wonderful. 'But I did not appreciate them at the time,' Glazunov apparently told Asafyev recently.

16 September

Asafyev and I went into Annemasse to meet Lamm, arriving from Geneva. He was much more animated than he had seemed to be in Moscow. We had a most enjoyable day. I played the first two movements of the Third Symphony and the two *Choses en soi*. The greatest impression was produced by the first movement of the Symphony, less by the second. Lamm and Asafyev argued good-naturedly about Moscow–Leningrad but were very friendly towards each other and orchestrated some of *Khovanshchina*, which Asafyev had brought with him in its original form. In the evening Asafyev had a surprise for me: he told me of the proposal by students at the Conservatoire, following my visit there in 1927, to elect me as Director. They had had a confidential meeting with Asafyev to find out how I would react. But Asafyev said there could be no possibility of it while Glazunov was still there. Only a handful of the professors were aware of the approach, and Glazunov knew nothing of it. I was absolutely stunned by the idea, as I love the Conservatoire very much, and the idea had in fact occurred to me even though until this minute there had been nothing to base it on. At half past ten we took Lamm back.

17 September

I completed the music for the second movement and Asafyev finished his article on Stravinsky, very profound and insightful, setting out the true position of *Apollon* in a serious and scholarly way. Asafyev was thrilled with the Overture to the Romanov ballet. It was such happy music, he said, just what was wanted. He thought it not a good idea to incorporate it into the Quintet.

18 September

Finished orchestrating the second movement. We walked into Annemasse. Asafyev, to whom I had given a printed lecture on C.S., an excellent overview of a subject that is hard to assimilate, suddenly said, 'It is necessary to believe that evil is an illusion, but this a difficult proposition, at least at first.' It follows that he is reading and thinking about C.S. In the evening we compared *Cherevichki* and *The Night Before Christmas*,[1] giving all due credit to the latter but reserving more affection for the former. Asafyev played it on the piano, and I was staggered by the overture's second theme, which I had forgotten since the production at the Conservatoire and which now came back to me as if emerging from a mist along with all the rest of the performance in the Conservatoire. What breadth and beauty this tune possesses!

19 September

Did (that is, orchestrated) the middle section of the finale. At two o'clock went to Annemasse to collect Lamm and then went with him, Ptashka and Asafyev to Chamonix. There we took the funicular railway to Planpraz, which I had enjoyed when I went there with Koussevitzky. Going up had a powerful effect on me, my ears became completely blocked, but thanks to C.S. I was not frightened by the phenomonen. Asafyev and Lamm, however, were. When we got to the top we had to go a little higher up to reach the hotel. Ptashka is now very heavy, and could hardly make it. There were good views of Mont Blanc, and down to the valley full of swirling mist. Next morning at seven, Lamm, Asafyev and I walked up to Col du Brévent, as I had done before with Koussevitzky and Paichadze, and once again enjoyed tremendous views. After this we descended to Chamonix and on the way to Vétraz made a detour to Servoz to see the Gorges de la Diosaz.[2] These seem at first to be nothing special, but the further one gets into them the more wonderful they are, even after the splendid vistas of the Col du Brévent – a recommended destination for loving couples. We returned to Vétraz delighted with our expedition, Asafyev naturally having experienced the greatest pleasure from it while I was the 'host'. Lamm then went back to Geneva.

---

1 Two operas, the first by Tchaikovsky and the second by Rimsky-Korsakov, based on the same short story by Gogol, 'Christmas Eve'. The first version of Tchaikovsky's opera was entitled 'Vakula the Smith', Vakula being the village blacksmith who finds himself the reluctant hero of Gogol's comic tale of supernatural derring-do in the Ukrainian village of Dikanka, in the course of which, to win the affections of his sweetheart Oxana, he must somehow contrive to bring back to her the slippers of the Empress (Catherine the Great, no less). Tchaikovsky called his revised *second* version, premiered in 1887, *Cherevichki*, usually translated as *The Tsarina's Slippers*. Rimsky's opera, to his own libretto, was first performed in 1895, and employs more overtly Ukrainian folk idioms, whereas Tchaikovsky's score relies more on character depiction and a generally lyrical tone.
2 A spectacular gorge cut through the rocky mountainside by the river Diasoz, with cascading waterfalls.

21 September

Asafyev and I talked that evening of C.S., a conversation that had a profound effect on both of us. We touched on various matters in which he needed clarification. Since he is finding it hard to take in everything at once I gave him a summary of one particular lecture on C.S. that encapsulates the whole teaching in an exceptionally clear and simple manner. It pleases me that Asafyev is less attracted by its healing than by its moral and cognitive aspects.

24 September

Finished orchestrating the fourth movement. All that remains is half of the scherzo.

25 September

At last we have received (very late) our Swiss visa and decided to go there for a four-day visit. At 7.30 in the morning, although it was raining, we went on foot with Asafyev to see him off as the car battery was being charged up. Lamm's nephew had been commissioned to get him across the border without a visa. Asafyev forgot to give me back my umbrella; an illegal immigrant crossing the border on the pillion of a motor-cycle sporting an umbrella must have been a rare sight!

26 September

Ptashka and I left for Switzerland. We have been waiting two months for a visa, but at the border no one asked to see it.

The outskirts of Geneva are clean and prosperous-looking. There we found Lamm, his brother and family, and Asafyev who had arrived unscathed yesterday. The four of us went out of the city past the Palace of the League of Nations. The roads are excellent and it is generally a highly civilised place, but one cannot go very fast because of the innumerable exhortations not to. Along the valley of the Rhone, going deep into the mountains through Diablerets and Ansermos, the car went splendidly and we savoured the views. By evening Lamm, sitting beside me, announced that we were 8 kilometres from Spietz, but we seemed to be carrying on for ever in the dark. Ptashka was very quiet, I began to worry about her and at length remonstrated with Lamm as it turned out Spietz was not 8 but 23 kilometres distant, and the hotel we ended up in was quite expensive (I paid the bill for everyone).

27 September

Ptashka groaned with pain when she got up, which made me anxiously ask myself whether she ought to have come with us. Also, we were late getting under way, while I like to set out early. Our quarrel spoilt our appreciation of Lake Thun and Lake Brienz. But then our route took a most interesting climb up to the Grimsel Pass.[1] The colours as we climbed higher were of such a wild beauty we might have been on another planet. Further on it was cold and there was snow. In the middle of the pass we had lunch at a little restaurant. Coming out of it, it felt like March in St Petersburg, which brought on for me pleasant memories of the past. We descended to Gletsch only to climb up higher still to another pass: the Furka Pass, which runs between two glaciers. We visited a cave underneath one of the glaciers, where the daylight – in effect submarine – was the most amazing blue. We then descended to Andermatt and to the Devil's Bridge (at a height of 1,500 metres). I thought of Yurevskaya,[2] and of Suvorov's crossing of the gorge, about which I had just been reading a book.[3] What a devilishly dark and gloomy abyss it is, especially at nightfall.

We spent the night in Andermatt.

28 September

Rain was falling as sleet as we went up to the St Gotthard Pass, the clouds pressing in on us all around, above and below. The impression was of a savage grandeur as the car struggled slowly up the incline. At the highest point of the pass the mist suddenly dispersed and we could see a hotel by the side of the deserted lake. Down we went again, through mist as thick as milk, negotiating the difficult hairpin bends. From a comparison of the vegetation with that in Russia Asafyev was able to establish the latitude in both countries. All of a sudden a green valley appeared out of the mist – Airolo. We had lunch and drank some excellent Italian wine, which I love. Ptashka made herself understood in Italian. By evening we were ensconced in a hotel in Lugano with a balcony directly overlooking the lake. Asafyev was particularly happy, because he remembered having been there fifteen years ago, although he recognised very little, Lugano having grown so much in the meantime.

---

1 The high mountain pass between the valleys of the Rhône and Aar rivers.
2 See above, pp. 233–4.
3 Prokofiev had visited the Teufelbrücke once before, during his tour of Switzerland in the summer of 1913. It had made a great impression on him then. See *Diaries*, vol. 1, pp. 458–9.

29 September

Sunshine. We thought we might return home via the Simplon Pass, but this involved going through a small part of Italy, which we could not do without a visa, and a visit to the Italian Consulate proved abortive. We drove along the shores of the lake, one side of which is in Italy and the other in Switzerland. After lunch we headed back in the direction of the St Gotthard.

Lugano is a charming and beautiful place but I would not want to live there. We suffered a flat tyre, a puncture caused by a nail. Spending the night in Airolo, I worried about the climb tomorrow with a damaged tyre.

30 September

Going up the St Gotthard is more testing from the south than from the north. Another puncture – these things always come in series. This time Lamm showed his mettle and helped.

Today the fog was less when we got to the top. The pass is impressive, all the same. Two St Bernards appeared, and Ptashka had her photograph taken with them. At Andermatt we stopped for lunch, and then made the ascent up to the Furka, where the weather was murky and clammy. The old girl was really labouring; even with a good run at it we still had to go down to bottom gear. Before we got to the top I asked Lamm and Asafyev to get out and walk for a while, and even so we barely made it. In a rage I said it was time to sell the old thing, but in fact it transpired that one of the sparking plugs was faulty so she was running on only three cylinders, like a horse on three legs. When we came from the Furka Pass we took the Rhône valley and arrived in darkness at Fische, where we spent the night. The villages in these parts are really backwoods, dirty places, the streets unlighted and with terrible surfaces. So much for civilised Swizerland. But the hotel in Fische was comfortable.

1 October

As we were getting ready to leave next morning, another disaster: the tyre had gone flat again during the night. Two nails were discovered in it. There was no garage, the nearest 20 kilometres away. At first we were in total despair, but then decided to pump up the tyre and set off, pumping it up again as necessary by the roadside. In this manner we succeeded in getting as far as Brig. The road was awful to begin with, but got better. Ptashka was feeling unwell as a result of the sausage she had at lunch, but this too passed off. Towards evening we reached the border with France at the point where the Rhône flows into Lake Geneva. Once again no one asked to see our passports. We were home by eight. Asafyev was concerned that he had received no letters; he was worrying about his wife and about the fate of the long article he had despatched to Russia.

2–5 October

On the 2nd Asafyev left for Paris, where he wanted to burrow around in libraries.[1] Also, he hoped to find there the letters he was expecting. We had grown very fond of him over the time he spent with me; he had blossomed. After his departure I got on with putting together and proof-reading the Second Symphony. On the afternoon of the 5th we left to return to Paris after a mild contretemps with the landlord, mainly over the well and because of Ptashka's attitude. She, I, Svyatoslav and the English nanny travelled by car, Astrov and the luggage went by train.

6–7 October

The journey back to Paris. The Jura was very interesting, beautiful and leafy with the golden tints of autumn, a softer beauty than that of Switzerland. The incident with the typewriters at Customs. Ptashka groaned with pain whenever we were jolting over bumpy surfaces, but on good roads she was fine. We arrived in Paris at four o'clock on the 7th and made for the Koussevitzkys' empty house, but Ksyusha would not let us in, to our astonishment, anger and embarrassment. We had great trouble finding a hotel as everywhere was full. Eventually we got rooms at the Hôtel Poussin, a small establishment at the Porte d'Auteuil.

8–28 October

Just as two years ago, the search for an apartment. Olga Vladislavovna took charge of Svyatoslav. We were delighted to see Asafyev again; he has had a royal welcome from Prunières, Honegger and Ansermet and so is beaming. He spends all day in the libraries on his historical researches (studying form with Fiedler – the father of the chess master – five- and seven-bar phrases, but when they are eight-bar then 5 + 3), in order to pay his dues on the official reason for his trip, which is the social context of music in France in the so-and-so century. His discussions with Ansermet, whom he concluded had been well primed by Stravinsky. Ansermet approves of Nabokov but refuses

---

1   Asafyev was on the look-out for material, mainly songs of the French Revolution, that he could use for his ballet *The Flames of Paris*.

to hear a word of Dukelsky, which is unfortunate as I had hoped via Asafyev to influence Ansermet to take Dukelsky's First Symphony to Russia. Asafyev and I looked through Dukelsky's orchestration of his *Dushenka* and Sonata,[1] but our conclusion was that the Sonata is uneven in this respect and *Dushenka* simply not good. I must write to Dukelsky to urge him to work more seriously.

Suvchinsky had made no effort to seek out Asafyev, but one day when Ptashka and I had taken the Ballot to fetch Asafyev, just at the entrance to the building where he was staying we bumped into Suvchinsky, who happened to be passing by. Their meeting was like that of two long-lost lovers, even though Suvchinsky was upset that Asafyev had apparently been quite prepared to leave Paris without seeing him. They both sat in the car and I suggested that I drive them to the Bois de Boulogne, like a chauffeur escorting a pair of lovebirds.

I heard *Le Baiser de la fée*, but found it dry and unengaging. It was performed after *Cherevichki*. How intoxicating are the two broad themes, the one in the Overture and the 'Apple Tree'![2] But Stravinsky manages to make even Tchaikovsky sound dry.

A dinner with Asafyev, Suvchinsky, Ptashka and me. Suvchinsky took us to a restaurant in the Halle des Vins that from the outside looked most uninspiring, but the food was delicious. Suvchinsky on Stravinsky: 'I now know him better than anyone. This is a man whose ambition was to carry out a superb master-plan but lacked the strength to achieve it. The strategy was excellently formulated, but there were not enough troops on the ground.' Was Suvchinsky finding it necessary to come out in my presence with this criticism of Stravinsky because Asafyev had already been talking to him, promoting me at Stravinsky's expense?

When Dukelsky came back from London he was upset by my letter. 'Someone here wants to poison me. Who is it?'

I: 'The same person as earlier poisoned me, and whose name contains the root of the verb you used.'[3]

Dukelsky was introduced to Asafyev and then played his new Second Symphony to him and to Suvchinsky. We all had the same strange impression: we had expected a step forward from the First Symphony, but there was little sign of this; it seemed lacking in clarity and colour. *Five Pushkin Songs*

---

1   The Sonata for Piano and Orchestra, see above, p. 595–6.
2   In the same way as Gogol seldom resorts directly to Ukrainian patois in his stories but relies on more or less classical Russian for his effects, Tchaikovsky's ethnic colouring is for the most part achieved by subtle nuancing of basically Russian melos. Oxana's lyrical aria 'The Apple Tree has come into flower' is, however, an exception in making use of an actual Ukrainian folk song. It still sounds like Tchaikovsky, though.
3   The word Dukelsky used was 'TRAVit', which in Russian means to poison.

were nice. I then played the two *Choses en soi*. Dukelsky admired the longer one; Suvchinsky was silent at first but then praised both of them, though in a somewhat inarticulate manner. After this we all had a very jolly dinner together. Suvchinsky inveighed against Stravinsky for being such a materialist and obsessively concerned with extorting money from all and sundry. Why does he do this? In order to surround himself on all sides with Hotchkisses.[1]

The search for a flat continues to take up much of my time although I long to be able simply to sit and work. Four possibilities all fell through. Dukelsky is going away again, but not before consulting me on his orchestration of *Dushenka*, which advice, however, he immediately rejected. Asafyev finds him a nice lad, his personality typical of the music he writes.

Diaghilev arrived back on the 22nd October and opened discussions about (1) commissioning a ballet from me; (2) ditto from a Soviet composer to be recommended by me. My recommendations coincided with that of Hindemith (not surprising, since the latter had derived it from Asafyev, a circumstance of which Diaghilev was not, of course, aware). I brought Asafyev into this discussion; we dined once and lunched once together. I played the two *Choses en soi* to Diaghilev; he liked them but found them on the dry side. I also played him Shostakovich's Sonata No. 1 and Popov's *Vocalise*. Asafyev commented that both works demonstrated that their composers were making headway. On reflection Diaghilev settled on Popov and commissioned Asafyev to arrange that he visit Paris for a month, travelling third class. He plied Asafyev with questions about various antiquarian editions, which he has taken to collecting – an enthusiasm of his later years, even to the detriment of the ballet company. Asafyev is delighted that his officially sanctioned visit has concluded with a ballet commission to a Soviet composer: he will get a big pat on the back for this.

In the course of a third meeting Diaghilev and Kokhno set out for me a subject of the desired ballet: the parable of the Prodigal Son, to be recast on to Russian soil. The eloquence of both men was very persuasive. Asafyev was jubilant, sensing that Diaghilev had divined exactly what I needed at the present time. I too like it. And although I have never wanted to work with Kokhno, I believe I will accept the scenario. Diaghilev attributed the version to Kokhno, but I am sure that three-quarters of it comes from Diaghilev.

---

1 Stravinsky possessed a Hotchkiss (see above, p. 578). Hotchkiss et Cie made motor cars in its Paris factory from 1903 until 1954. Never one of the big-volume manufacturers, they made products that were well engineered, expensive and prized by connoisseurs, largely on account of the marque's success with its racing cars, which regularly won the Monte Carlo Rally during the 1930s.

Asafyev left on the 29th October, seen off by me and by Milhaud with his wife. It will not be long before we see one another again, as I am due to visit the USSR in December. I finally found a furnished apartment on the 26th, not spotlessly clean but quiet and spacious and with a view from the windows of the avenue du Bois. Not before time, because both I and Ptashka (especially given her condition) were becoming quite distraught. We moved there on the 28th and I immediately set to work on the scherzo of the Third Symphony.

2 November

Pressed on with orchestrating the scherzo of the Third Symphony so as to leave my hands free for the new ballet. But at six o'clock I met Diaghilev in the Grand Hotel for a tensely overwrought bargaining session over the fee, which threatened to spiral out of control. Diaghilev sat there, slumped and morose, repeating in a pained voice: 'I have no money, I cannot give you any more . . .' I was asking for 25,000 francs, which is little enough; Idka would pay 75,000. But he would not agree to this. Further discussion was postponed, and I went to play bridge at the Samoilenkos. It was my first excursion after the summer, and it cost me 340 francs as my opponents were club players, and pretty strong.

3 November

Finished the Third Symphony. I went to the publishers in the afternoon and gave Paichadze the bad news: in a word, 50,000 francs for the engraving. There I met Sabaneyev. He has performed a complete volte face: his article on *Fiery Angel* appeared recently in an English newspaper and is very flattering. He has discovered in me unsuspected profundity and warmth, which apparently I have been concealing hitherto out of false modesty. He informed me that he has written another article for America, and expressed a desire to come to visit me. I declined on the pretext of having just moved house. When he had gone, Paichadze said, 'Don't let him into your house, everything that comes out of his mouth stinks and he will poison the whole apartment.' I replied, 'That is because he has spent all his life heaping dirt all over everybody.'

In the evening we went to hear Gieseking.[1] He is a first-rate pianist, one of the very best: Rachmaninoff, Horowitz and he. After the concert I went back

---

1 Walter Gieseking (1895–1956), German pianist who lived the first sixteen years of his life in France, where his father was a distinguished doctor and lepidopterist (an interest his son also maintained throughout his life). After the family moved back to Hanover in 1911, Germany was Gieseking's main base, and although his huge repertoire embraced the masterworks of German – and Russian – composers, it is for his interpretations of French composers, especially Debussy and Ravel, that he is still revered.

to see him. At first he did not recognise me, but then said, 'I was told that you were in the hall.' Going out, I came face to face with the Stahls. We did not greet one another, but made off as quickly as possible in opposite directions. It was not a fracas, more of an amusing vaudeville.

4 November

As the Psalmist says, 'This is the day which the Lord hath made; we will rejoice and be glad in it.'[1] If each of us begins the day with this song on his lips and in his hearts, he will be blessed and will bless others. I copied this out from the *C.S. Sentinel*.

This afternoon Ptashka was visited by her friend and her husband, who is an obstetrician. He examined Ptashka and told her that the baby would be born in a month's time.

'Boy or girl?' we asked.

'Which would you like?'

'A girl.'

'Then I am sure a girl is what it will be. But at the same time I'm taking out my little book and writing down in today's date: boy. That way, if it turns out to be a girl, I can say I told you so. But if it's a boy, then all I have to do is bring out my notebook and show you that as far back as today I wrote in it that it will be a boy.'

5 November

The Symphony is finished, but I still have no agreement with Diaghilev. I therefore got on with proof-reading the score of *The Steel Step*. Out of stinginess Paichadze had given it not to a real engraver but to one who works from tracing paper. The result was not only a mass of mistakes but something hideous to look upon. I did the proofing with curses on my lips directed both at the engravers and the publishers.

In the evening I attended a concert of music by the Tcherepnins, father and son. Not much good: neither of them has any great originality of thought. In addition, the son lacks a strong technique. Sasha is in America with his adorable wife.[2]

Nikolay Nikolayevich greeted me affectionately. This is because in Monte Carlo in the spring I walked arm in arm with Sasha for two minutes, and thus have been forgiven for my lapse in Berlin. *Fiery Angel* (in the

---

1 Psalm 118:24.
2 Heavy irony. See above, pp. 149, 571.

performance by Koussevitzky) was extravagantly praised, and I was invited to call on Tcherepnin for him to play me his new opera.

6 November

Continued proofing the score of *Le Pas d'acier*. A trillion mistakes.

This afternoon I had another conversation with Diaghilev about the fee. He said twenty thousand, I said twenty-five. The justification I advanced for my stance was that otherwise I would not survive. To this Diaghilev responded that he was paying Hindemith even less.

I: 'But Hindemith really needs Paris, where he is practically unknown, so in fact you are paying quite dear for him. Whereas me you want to keep at near-starvation level.'

'Just take a look at your face,' said Diaghilev, indicating the mirror from which looked out a pink, plump visage.

Again we could not agree. Diaghilev asked me to think it over and talk again. In the evening I went to a concert by Saint-Rome, a very gifted pianist and protégé of the Koussevitzkys. He played quite well, but there were thirty-five people in the audience.

7 November

Proof-read the corrections that had been made to the piano score of *Le Pas d'acier*. Needless to say, many of them had not found their way into the new version.

Called on N. N. Tcherepnin, after a long interruption. He played me the new opera he is in the process of completing, *Vanka the Steward*.[1] Of course, Tcherepnin is and always will be Tcherepnin, and will never be able to transcend the limitations of what is in his head, but this looks like being his best piece. There is dramatic invention in plenty, and I felt myself being drawn back to the stage. It's time, at last, to get down to my chess libretto!

Over tea we competed in tearing Lermontov to pieces. *A Hero of Our Time*, which I recently re-read after a twenty-year interval, is nothing more than a provincial high-school novel! But Pushkin never grows stale.

---

1 Tcherepnin in fact took until 1932 to finish this comic opera, a rustic farce based on Sologub's strange Symbolist drama *Vanka the Steward and the Page Jehan*. The play itself was first produced at the Kommissarzhevskaya Theatre in St Petersburg in 1908.

8 November

On reflection, and after having discussed it with Paichadze, I decided that it was not sensible to fall out with Diaghilev over 5,000 francs. I therefore telephoned him and signalled my agreement. Diaghilev was delighted, and at six o'clock I came to him at the Grand Hôtel, having put on a dinner-jacket as afterwards I was going to have dinner with some Americans.

'Look at you, on parade for a meeting with the board of directors,' commented Diaghilev.

But the pleasant atmosphere was soon dispelled when I informed Kokhno that his share of author's rights from the Society of Authors should be not one-third, as he wanted, but one-fifth. Kokhno dug in his heels, and so did I.

'Then you will have to find another scenario,' said Kokhno.

'Well certainly,' said I.

'But how can we do that when we are leaving tomorrow for England?' objected Diaghilev.

So once again there was a dispute, and one that upset me greatly in that Diaghilev was not willing to support me against Kokhno. I said to Diaghilev, 'I have made very substantial concessions to you that you evidently do not appreciate. And so, even though we are talking about halfpennies in this matter of the percentages, on principle I will not give an inch.'

And that was how the matter rested.

I was furious. It was impossible for me to give in. In a way it was even a good thing that it had come to this. If I am so little valued that the whole enterprise can go to the devil because of Kokhno, then perhaps it is all for the best for us to part company without further delay.

9 November

In the morning I began to consider my position: since the ballet seems to have flown out of the window, to what should I now devote my energies? I decided to compose two more *Choses en soi*, and to complete a suite for orchestra by adding two more numbers to the Overture and the *Matelote* I had written some time ago for Romanov.[1] But then Diaghilev rang up and said that what had happened yesterday had been so unexpected that he had not known how to react. But since my argument with Kokhno boiled down to a difference of 2,000 francs, he proposed an increase in my fee by that amount in return for which I should accept Kokhno's demand for one-third of the royalties, since for him to accept less would be an undesirable precedent, as he had previously always received such a share. I gave my consent to

---

1 See above, pp. 195, 201, 207, 210, 213.

this, and the contract was signed in that evening. Diaghilev even made a little speech, directed at Kokhno and at me: 'Clearly, gentlemen, there has been some friction hitherto, but now we must all work together as friends on the ballet, and so . . . and so, generally speaking . . . well, that is more or less what I wanted to say to you!'

10 November

I at once set to work on the ballet. I had some themes ready, that I had composed in the spring and summer. I also found, when looking through my sketchbook, some I had written earlier that were ideally suited for the purpose. New ideas also came easily to me.

In short, I was fully armed for combat. After a few days I even began to feel that I had stockpiled so much music that was printed but not performed that perhaps it was time to pause a little and review where I stood? Yes, but only once the ballet was done. And this was a project I thought I would be able to achieve quickly and easily.

I received two important letters, one from Koussevitzky's manager and one from Derzhanovsky, about two tours: in America next autumn, and in Russia very soon, at Christmas.

At Pierné's afternoon concert he was due to perform the Suite from *Three Oranges* but I did not attend. I was afraid to: the old man is losing his powers now, and when he accompanied my Violin Concerto everything fell apart.

11 November

Instead of the C.S. Church we went to the Russian Church because Tchaikovsky's service for the Divine Liturgy[1] was to be given on the thirty-fifth anniversary of the composer's death. A prayerful atmosphere was noticeable by its absence: the public stood jammed up close, pushing and jostling, a deacon read something unintelligible eliciting responses of a garbled 'lordamercyus',[2] the bishop stood on the dais magnificently swinging the censor left and right. But none of this had anything whatsoever to do with God, or Man created in his image and likeness. I did not much like Tchaikovsky's music either: it lacked profundity and if there was any emotion in it, it was the wrong sort. The effect was of music composed by a worldly gentleman wishing to play at being in church.

1 Tchaikovsky composed his *Liturgy of St John Chrystosom*, Op. 41, in 1878. It is an unaccompanied choral setting consisting of fifteen numbers drawn from the Church Slavonic text of the Russian Orthodox Church for the principal daily service, known as 'obednya'.
2 'Pomílui Góspodi': literally 'Have mercy on me, Lord', which Prokofiev renders as a gabbled 'Pomelóspodi'.

I did not compose in the afternoon as I get on better doing so in the morning. Nevertheless, a theme for the first number (the sisters) came to me during the evening.

12–18 November

I worked intensively on the ballet all week, mainly in the mornings, but also some in the afternoons and evenings. The composition itself proceeded with exceptionally little effort, helped by the fact that I had decided to compose *The Prodigal Son* in a simple style eschewing sophisticated elaborations. Diaghilev's parting words to me had been: 'Your piano pieces are a shade arid. I want the ballet you are writing for me to be more straightforward.'

And that is what I was doing. By the end of the week it was clear that I had already cleared the halfway mark and that if I were able to maintain such a pace I would be able to roll up the whole thing in two weeks. This would be a tremendous feat, but it must be remembered that I had a clutch of themes derived from what I had jotted down in my notebook in the spring, and not only that but a whole number (the slaves) taken from the *Matelote* I had written for Romanov in 1925 (for which, incidentally, he has never paid me), as well as one theme for the second number from my sketchbooks of the same year. That said, the composition process was generally extremely trouble-free. It drove out all other activities, which perforce were compressed into the evenings.

Meyerhold appeared and was very nice. He is returning to Russia in ten days' time to stage *The Gambler*, which he will then take on to Berlin where he has been engaged to direct. Less welcome was a letter from the Bolshoy Theatre stating that they would no longer be able to pay bonuses for *Oranges* in dollars. But what use are roubles to me? Paichadze had to send a negative response to the theatre.

The Borovskys, who have relocated to Berlin for this season, paid a visit. Borovsky has been playing my works to acclaim in a whole series of concerts round Europe, and is now greatly enamoured of my two *Choses en soi*.

I played bridge once and won back 300 francs.

B.N.B.[1] rang up a few times, but his calls provoked such irritation in Ptashka that I tried not to speak to him. Recently Ptashka's increasing weight has made her very nervous, so she needs a great deal of looking after. The expected event is now only two weeks away.

---

1 Boris Nikolayevich Bashkirov.

18 November

Went to the C.S. Church, then composed, and then went to the Lamoureux concert at which Albert Wolff was conducting the Suite from *Chout*. Although it was very warmly received, he did not conduct it as well as he had done the previous year, setting an insanely fast tempo for the final dance, whirling his arms about like a windmill the while. However, I said nothing, as I wanted to ask him to grant an interview to Dukelsky, with a view to programming one or other of his symphonies.

19 November

I seem to be experiencing mild fatigue from all the composing, but I do not want to slacken the tempo, so as to finish the ballet inside two weeks.

In the evening I went to the theatre with the Meyerholds to see a modern Broadway play. It included music-hall acts, prohibition liquor smuggling, detectives, and gunfights. The action took place in the wings of a theatre, which allowed for the dramatic high points to be interrupted by the irruption of scantily clad chorus-girls all singing and dancing. We were thus treated to the tried-and-tested theatrical principle of interspersing comedy and tragedy.

20 November

Composed a great deal. No slackening of the tempo.

They have been bringing all kinds of baby dresses for the soon-to-be-born daughter. I find it amusing that a creature who is still deep in someone's belly, and breathing by who knows what means, is having bespoke clothes made, and very fancy ones to boot!

22 November

Kokhno has at last worked out and sent from England a more detailed libretto for *Prodigal Son*. But all the major lineaments of the ballet have already been composed. This is fine: the music having been written before the arrival of the libretto means that I have no connection with the libretto, especially as far as the future is concerned. Kokhno has dreamed up some new details, some of them rather silly.

Today I composed less well. Is the powder losing its charge? This thought made my mood less propitious, but there was nothing else I wanted to do.

Today sees the opening of Idka's ballet season, but Ptashka and I went to the operetta to see *Rose Marie*,¹ which has already been playing every day for several years in all the main cities. But my God, what a horror – and the main thing, what an incredible bore! And dramatically speaking how inept and unimaginative! I do not speak of the music, borrowed wholesale from the Modernists of yesteryear. But that is the taste of the mob. I yawned vigorously through the whole performance.

23 November

As Diaghilev is back from England, I telephoned him at the Grand Hotel and told him I had almost finished the ballet. Diaghilev was so taken aback he could scarcely believe his ears. 'So, then, it can't be ... much good?' he asked, adding that he would come this very day to listen to it. I composed a bit more during the afternoon, tidied it all up, and went through the ballet on the piano so that I would be able to play it. At five o'clock there appeared at the door Diaghilev, the Meyerholds and the Borovskys. I introduced Meyerhold to Diaghilev and reacquainted M. V. Borovskaya with Meyerhold.² Today Diaghilev was at his most engaging, youthful and alive.

'When?' he enquired immediately of Ptashka.

'Du jour au lendemain,'³ she replied. 'But what eagle eyes you have, Sergey Pavlovich!'

'You're telling me,' he said. 'After all, I have thirty women on my hands, and have done for twenty years on end!'

He then proceeded to give an unusually venomous account of Idka's premiere yesterday, after which I bundled the Meyerholds and Borovskys into the dining room for tea while I shut the door and played Diaghilev the excerpts from the ballet I had composed. He was tremendously taken with the first and second numbers, the robbing and the awakening of the Prodigal, and the music for his return. But he was a lot less keen on the Siren and her pas-de-deux with the Prodigal, and he suggested dispensing altogether with the Romanov *Matelote*. 'You obviously haven't noticed that this is in an altogether different style. You write with such tenderness these days, but then you were so given to hammering in nails.'

---

1   Operetta by Rudolf Friml and Herbert Stothart, book by Otto Harbach and Oscar Hammerstein II. Its hit song, the 'Indian Love Song', became one of Duke Ellington's most popular numbers (and most frequently parodied, unforgettably by the Comedian Harmonists).
2   Maria Borovskaya, née Baranovskaya, had in her youth studied with Meyerhold. See *Diaries*, vol. 2, pp. 565, 571, 577.
3   Literally 'From one day to the next': 'Any day now.'

I had not yet conceived the end of the ballet. I said, 'In this libretto the end is envisaged as a kind of apotheosis, but this is inappropriate: we need something more nuanced.'

I suggested borrowing a theme from the second *Chose en soi*, which I love very much, but Diaghilev was reluctant to accept this. 'It should be simpler,' he said. 'Softer and more tender.' And indeed I felt myself that the theme I had suggested was not quite right. We parted on good terms, Diaghilev happy with what he had heard of the ballet. Later that night, falling asleep, I was still searching for a new theme, limpid and unclouded. I thought that a melody illustrating a parable from the Gospels should seem to be coming from on high. About one o'clock at night I got up and jotted down two bars.

24 November

Straight away in the morning I worked on the idea that had come to me last night, the concluding scene of the ballet when the father embraces his son. My aim as I worked was to preserve the essence of the previous night's afflatus. The result was an absolutely superb theme, and all day I was walking on air as if it was my name-day.

At half past twelve I went to the publishing house and met Paichadze and Stravinsky, with whom I went out to lunch. Stravinsky was most affable, and for the first time in his life paid everybody's bill. We then went to the orchestral rehearsal of *Le Baiser de la fée*. Stravinsky conducted, I sat with Sudeikina[1] and we discussed cars. Idka appeared and sat in the front row. When in the break she stood up and looked round at us, Sudeikina and I slipped stealthily out into the corridor so as to avoid an encounter with her. Quite a lot of people were present at the rehearsal, including Ansermet, who has still not programmed a single work of mine in his concerts with the Orchestre de Paris. Now, however, he suddenly flew to my side with a charming smile and questioned me about the Third Symphony. Suvchinsky also came up; since Asafyev's departure he had vanished from sight, but today was publication day for the first issue of the weekly *Eurasia* newspaper, on which Suvchinsky has been working like a slave, so this is why he has not been seen.

'Will things get easier now?' I asked.

---

1 Vera Sudeikina (1888–1982), born Vera de Bosset in St Petersburg, daughter of an extremely wealthy electrical-goods manufacturer. A gifted but essentially dilettante actress, dancer, painter and designer, she and Stravinsky met in Paris in 1921; they soon became lovers but the respective spouses took very different views of the resultant liaison. Yekaterina Stravinsky was evidently reconciled to a *ménage à trois* while the bisexual Sergey Sudeikin threatened to kill his wife before departing permanently for America. Stravinsky and Vera Sudeikina married in 1940 on Yekaterina Stravinsky's death. See *Diaries*, vol. 2, p. 89 n. 3.

'Far from it,' replied Suvchinsky. 'Now I have to get on with the second issue . . .'

During this period a decisive shift has occurred in Suvchinsky's musical outlook, and evidently by no means the least significant role in this was played by Asafyev. By this I mean that Asafyev undermined some foundations, and a part of the edifice collapsed. The nub of the matter is Stravinsky, whom Suvchinsky has taken to criticising in the most vicious terms, calling him a political and religious dinosaur and attacking *Le Baiser de la fée*. He said, 'You may think this is a dreadful thing to say, but this ballet is just plain badly orchestrated: there are whole passages which simply do not come off at all. As for the music, it is parched and boring. People suffer from a variety of phobias: persecution mania, dread of crossing the street, to name but two. Stravinsky's phobia is a terror of the blank page: when he sits down to compose he is in dread of not being able to fill it up. What if today he really cannot do so? His instinct therefore is to rush to inscribe on to the blank page some ready-made formulae, and then proceeds to embroider them.'

Le Baiser de la fée certainly was a tedious, colourless thing. At one point there was a glimpse, repeated several times, of a phrase from Rachmaninoff's Second Piano Concerto. Not willing to believe that Stravinsky had been riffling through Rachmaninoff's pockets, I concluded that Rachmaninoff had himself lifted the phrase from Tchaikovsky, and Stravinsky, who was composing a ballet based on themes of Tchaikovsky, had quite legitimately gleaned it from its original source. But Suvchinsky said that he had already innocently asked Stravinsky whether this passage was originally from Tchaikovsky, to which Stravinsky had replied: 'No, it is my own.' Ay – ay – ay!

Stravinsky is a golden idol with feet of clay. And these feet are cracking under him. The crack is already opening to the air, but nobody yet has noticed it. Suvchinsky is the first rat to leave the sinking ship. When the idol topples, all will be clear to everyone, but for now any talk of feet of clay will elicit merely a compassionate arm round the deluded one's shoulder. When the time comes, God grant me grace to remain a noble and sympathetic witness, and not be singed by a flare from the fire of triumph.

Home again, I savoured playing over my new theme which, as I walked along, I had not been able to remember in its entirety. It made it all the more enjoyable to renew the acquaintance!

25 November

Attended C.S. Church. Although in the course of the service some good thoughts came to me about music and artistic creation as they relate to C.S., as soon as I got home I caught myself grumbling to Ptashka about her capriciousness yesterday. I worked for quite a long time, but not to any great effect. In the evening Dukelsky arrived from London, full of the tunes he is coming up with for *Mistress Into Maid*,[1] which he is currently composing. But I do not like them much. Since he had not dined and we had nothing in the house, I went off with him to eat in a Russian restaurant where gypsy singers, tipsy retired generals singing along to the gypsy songs and wallowing in memories of the past combined to produce an atmosphere horribly alien but at the same time partly because of this somehow fascinating to observe, if only our table had not been quite so close to the music. The fascination was intensified by the knowledge that in four weeks' time I would find myself in Moscow.

As we emerged on to the street, Dukelsky fished around in his pockets and produced the address of a certain establishment, whither he invited me to accompany him. Wishing him joy, I bent my steps homeward.

26 November

I worked better today and moved the final number forward.

Suvchinsky dropped in, as he just happened to be passing. The visit was, however, symptomatic of his volte-face. Lunch with Meyerhold, Diaghilev and Kokhno. To the latter I returned his libretto with an elegant bow, saying that it had arrived after the music had been composed and was therefore probably more useful to him than to me. Kokhno hesitated, but accepted it. Meyerhold and Diaghilev spent the whole of lunch discussing possibilities for working together, in particular ways in which Meyerhold's theatre company could be brought to Paris. There is a chance that next spring their performances could run in repertoire with the Diaghilev company, that is to say performances by each company on successive evening turn and turn about, with combined publicity. Saying goodbye, Kokhno enquired when I might be able to 'receive him' (with a slight ironic underlining of the word 'receive') in order to play him the music. Politely laughing off this approach, I said that I would prefer, if he would not mind, to delay this until I had completed the whole score of the ballet.

In the evening, went to Borovsky's concert in the hall of the Conservatoire. Diaghilev and I were given seats in the 'royal box' – the President's box. Diaghilev relished the Musorgsky, grumbled about the Rachmaninoff and

---

1 This, Dukelsky's only opera, was based on Pushkin's short story 'Baryshnya-Krest'yanka' ('The Aristocratic Peasant-Girl'), one of the *Tales of Belkin*. Dukelsky wrote his own libretto. The creation of an opera clearly presented the composer with many problems as he worked away at it for over thirty years. It was finally produced in Santa Barbara in 1958, by which time Vladimir Dukelsky had irrevocably become the American citizen Vernon Duke, and after that one production it vanished into obscurity.

the Scriabin, and was rude about the Medtner. Regarding my pieces on the programme, I said that the Third Sonata was an old work, I nowadays reject the fifth *Sarcasm*, and only the *Tales*, Op. 31, and the Gavotte from Op. 32[1] were worthy of serious consideration. Diaghilev said, 'Don't apologise,' and said he liked the Gavotte very much.

I did not much care for the way Borovsky played my pieces. Ptashka was annoyed with me today for my grumbling at her yesterday and did not come to the concert.

27 November

Stitched together the last number, all but a few details that still need finishing off. Made peace with Ptashka. Dukelsky came at four o'clock and played his Second Symphony, which this time I liked better despite too much of the material of the last movement being uninteresting. *Mistress Into Maid*, of which he played almost all the first act, contains much entertaining dialogue, but only about a quarter of it is music. Ansermet was supposed to be there as well, to listen to Dukelsky's Symphony and my Symphony No. 3, but his rehearsal overran and he failed to turn up. Dukelsky and I played two games of chess because he was boasting of how much he had improved, but he lost both games, and quite quickly as well.

In the evening I wrote my diary and played the piano. Silent practice is extremely helpful for learning repertoire.

28 November

Finished off the last number and composed the final *envoi*. Suvchinsky came to call, heard the ballet and was tremendously impressed, even by the Siren, the music for which had failed to earn the commendation of either Diaghilev or Dukelsky. In general, NEP – Suvchinsky's New Esthetic Policy[2] – is continuing and Stravinsky came in for vituperative abuse. But it is also a fact that my other recent works – the Second Symphony, *Le Pas d'acier, Fiery Angel* – were all met with complete silence from Suvchinsky.

Dinner with the Meyerholds: Suvchinsky, Dukelsky, Ptashka and me. Dukelsky obviously fancies Meyerhold's wife,[3] and suggested he could help her make her lips more shapely when applying lipstick. In between he told a

---

1 *Tales of an Old Grandmother*, four pieces for piano, Op. 31 (1918), and *Four Pieces for Piano*, No. 3 (1918). Both works were written in America.
2 A pun on Lenin's New Economic Policy, which brought to an end the almost total paralysis of production, including food, of the War Communism years.
3 The actress Zinaïda Raikh.

number of risqué jokes. It is extraordinary how fashionable it has become among the émigré community to tell indecent stories; this is something that people coming from Russia never do.

29 November

Once again we put our apartment at the disposal of Dukelsky and Ansermet. This time the latter did come, but much later than arranged, for which he apologised profusely and was generally very nice. He listened to both of Dukelsky's symphonies and my No. 3, and was full of praise for everything. It was thus impossible to tell whether he really liked any of it and whether he might include it in his programmes. A clever technique?

In the evening I went to the station to see Meyerhold off and handed him the manuscript of half of the Third Symphony to have the parts copied in Moscow, there being a dearth of copyists in Paris. Meyerhold and I parted on the friendliest of terms. He promised to write and let me know how things were going with *The Gambler*, how I was personally regarded by the ruling Establishment, and what the reasons are why I am having difficulty being paid in currency – whether this is a result of hard times generally or a conspiracy against me in particular. The train on which he was travelling had five carriages marked 'Paris–Negoreloe'.[1] Clearly, however doubtful relations with the Bolsheviks may be, an entire train-load still goes there each evening.

30 November

Finished the tenth number, in which I combined three themes. Normally I am against this practice because it hardly ever sounds as it should do, but in the present case after so much homophonic music more complexity is essential to increase the tension in the lead-up to the Prodigal falling into the embrace of his father, and to highlight the introduction of my lyrical theme.

Called at the publishing house and met there Stravinsky who, aware that I have not yet attended a performance of his ballet, promised to get me a ticket. I also saw Bechert,[2] who told me that the proposed arrangement with the Moscow manager (by which he would receive roubles but I would be paid in hard currency) would not work, and therefore the concerts in Vienna and Budapest could not take place. There were also some strange telegrams from Koussevitzky advising me after all to fulfil my forthcoming American season under Haensel's management, that is with the very person he had

---

1 The border station between Poland and the USSR.
2 Either an employee of Edition Russe de Musique or an impresario in Vienna or Budapest.

been volubly criticising for the past three years. In short it looks as though the concerts are cracking up on every front, but for some reason I am not upset by this: all will eventually turn out all right. In any case, I must go to Russia regardless of the amount of currency I shall earn.

Spent the evening at the Samoilenkos, where Mayakovsky was also present for the first time. I was glad to see him, having had hardly any contact with him since his battle with Diaghilev in Berlin[1] (I had no more than a fleeting glimpse in Russia). Mayakovsky was the same giant of a fellow as ever, except that the lines on his face are deeper now than they were when he was a 'handsome twenty-two-year-old'.[2]

He has fallen in love with Sasha-Yasha's niece, a beautiful girl and free spirit, and she it was who had brought him to the Samoilenkos.[3] Dukelsky, needless to say, wasted no time in trying to captivate her himself, playing ragtime to her on the piano, to which she listened with an appearance of benevolent interest.

Towards the end of the evening I asked Mayakovsky to read some of his poetry, which he did incomparably and at full volume. But his new lyrical poems, dedicated to this same Tatyana, were weaker, although 'The Bath' and the older 'The Sun' were wonderful. Dukelsky cried out that the latter was divine, and that he felt inspired to write an oratorio on 'The Sun'.

I: 'What are you thinking of, Dementy? You'd do better to leave writing about the sun to me, and you concentrate on the samovar.' (The samovar is

---

1   See *Diaries*, vol. 2, pp. 679–81.
2   'In my soul there's not a single grey hair/Nor any hint of senile tenderness!/The huge power of my voice pulverising the world/I go on my way – handsome, twenty-two-years old.' (Vladimir Mayakovsky, Prologue to 'A Cloud in Trousers', 1915.)
3   The twenty-two-year-old, strikingly tall, long-legged, blonde and beautiful Tatyana Yakovleva had not been in Paris for long, having quickly found work as a model in Coco Chanel's salon, when in October 1928 she met Mayakovsky. For the poet, despite his continuing attachment to Lilya Brik at home in Russia, it was love at first sight, and he pursued Tatyana relentlessly for the six more weeks or so he spent in Paris before returning to Moscow. Prokofiev's 'free spirit' tag was exactly right: she was deeply attracted to Mayakovsky but in the end declined his insistent urging to accompany him back to Soviet Russia as his wife. In the midst of the passionate but short-lived affair she found time to disappear to Barcelona on the spur of the moment with Chaliapin, as Mayakovsky obliquely mentions in his love poems to her. While still in Paris Mayakovsky wrote the extraordinarily powerful and direct poem 'Letter to Tatyana Yakovleva' and, reportedly somewhat to her embarrassment, declaimed it and other verses dedicated to her to the Russian community in Paris on several occasions. After his return to Moscow correspondence between Mayakovsky and Tatyana continued for another year, but by that time Mayakovsky had undergone another *coup de foudre* with the artist Veronika Polonskaya, and Tatyana had married her French admirer the Vicomte Bertrand du Plessis, who was to be killed as a fighter pilot with the Free French in July 1941. Nevertheless, a place for Tatyana Yakovleva remained in the poet's heart: there is a well-founded legend that three hours before he committed suicide on 14 April 1930 he went to the post office and sent a telegram to her in Paris: 'Mayakovsky has shot himself.'

mentioned in the poem.¹) But Dukelsky would not give up. 'Sometimes the samovar shines more brilliantly than the sun.'

I: 'Yes, when it reflects the sun.'

Everyone laughed.

As we were leaving I kissed Mayakovsky goodbye. He made a great impression on everyone, but there is something severe and strained about him. Nobody liked Tatyana much, except Dukelsky.

1 December

Diaghilev telephoned in the morning and asked if he could come back today and listen to the ballet again. I said he would be most welcome. 'Then Boris and I will come at five o'clock,' he said. There was nothing to be done: I was obliged to welcome Kokhno (Boris) as well, and having earlier promised myself that he would not hear a note of the ballet music until I was able to hand over the completed piano score.

I spent all day putting my manuscript paper in order that I would be able to play a decent rendition. This was all to the good: at least it impelled me to finish off some passages and stitch together some fragments that were still floating.

Diaghilev listened with great concentration and I could overhear him from time to time whispering to Kokhno: 'Very beautiful . . . splendid . . .' But we had a real disagreement over the third number, the Temptress. My conception had been of a shadowy, mysterious being, seen through the eyes of an innocent youth, seductive but as yet unknown. Diaghilev, however, wanted a sensual creature, whom he proceeded to describe in a string of graphically obscene expressions. However, although I not the least bit inclined to involve myself with creating sensuous music I did not say as much to Diaghilev, contenting myself with observing that I had conceived

---

1   The 1920 poem 'The Strange Adventure that Befell Vladimir Mayakovsky One Summer at the Dacha' describes how the poet impulsively invites the Sun in to take tea, an invitation that is unexpectedly and alarmingly accepted:

> 'You asked me in?
> Get kettle on,
> And, poet, get some jam in!'
> The tears were running down my face,
> The heat was something dreadful,
> But I showed him
> The samovar:
> 'Welcome, sit down,
> Your Radiance!'

the ballet in distinctly more aquarelle terms than those he was now suggesting, from which it followed that voluptuous excesses of this sort would be out of place. Diaghilev grew heated: 'Then what sort of prodigal son is this? The whole strength of the story lies in the fact that he goes astray,[1] then repents, and the father forgives. If all he had done was run away from home and got himself robbed blind by thieves, then his return would have been marked not by the outstretched arms of his parent but by a good thrashing.' In the end this question was left unresolved, and I informed Diaghilev that I had completed the final number.

Diaghilev: 'What? Completely finished? Foo, how alarming...'

The implication was that Diaghilev was staking everything on the final number, and if I had fallen flat with it then the whole ballet would be written off as an unmitigated disaster. But I knew the ending was good, and was able to play it reasonably calmly. Diaghilev was pleased, and even suggested I play it more slowly so that the melody would sing out more beautifully. He also made me play the triple counterpoint combination slowly and judged it successful. Overall, Diaghilev departed highly satisfied, and going down the stairs announced that his dream was to have a spring season without including a note of Stravinsky. Incredible! Hitherto Stravinsky has been a god for Diaghilev, who never made any secret of his preference for him over me. Is this yet another sign of the god's fall from grace?

2 December

Was at C.S. Church. No composition in the afternoon as mood somewhat apathetic. A theme appeared, but of no more than average distinction: if after being left to ripen it cannot be transformed into something more interesting I shall discard it. Played bridge in the afternoon and went down 110 points.

In the evening Rachmaninoff gave the first Paris concert of his life. Until now Paris has displayed little appetite for Rachmaninoff's music, and Rachmaninoff has avoided it. Today's audience was a glittering assembly of the fashionable public. I went with the Samoilenkos. Diaghilev and Glazunov were both in the hall. I went up to the latter murmuring a few polite phrases. It was a pity there was no Beethoven in the programme: this composer brings out the best in Rachmaninoff's playing. He played Bach very well, Chopin unevenly, technically astounding but with a mannered approach to lyrical

---

1 The Russian verb 'bludit', which Prokofiev here puts into Diaghilev's mouth, with its derivatives has two meanings: one is to wander or roam, the other is specifically to fornicate.

passages, as if hammering in nails. His own music he played badly, destroying his own poetry which in his later years he seems to have forgotten, replacing it with virtuosity. In spite of all this the effect was very strong; there is no doubt that his is a formidably interesting personality. The way he walks on to the stage is incredible: a sort of sidelong, hesitating shuffle that makes you wonder if he is even going to make it to the piano. This makes even stronger the impression he creates when he begins to play. The audience erupted in a frenzy of delight. In the crush on the stairs at the end of the concert, just as Rachmaninoff's daughters were also going down, I slightly lost my balance and said sotto voce, 'Just like Rachmaninoff', at which Fatma Hanum shied away from me. 'Please don't go spoiling my relationship with my clientele,' she said later. In a bid to improve finances Fatma has gone into the hat business, very successfully too, and the Rachmaninoff family are among her customers.

3 December

It was a struggle to compose today, nevertheless the opening of the new version of the third number (the Siren) suddenly came right, also the start of the ninth number. After all!

Practised on the dummy keyboard and caught up on my diary.

We are expecting Ptashka to give birth any minute.[1] Today was the day predicted by the doctor as long as ago as when we were in America. We would like it to be a daughter, but have not yet settled on a name. The choice is between four names, two Russian and two international: Svetlana and Lyudmila; Lydia and Natalya. If it turns out to be a boy I should like him to be Askold,[2] but Ptashka does not like this idea (from the point of view of English).

Although Ptashka is so enormous that she is quite ready to go straight away to the clinic, we decided on a visit to the cinema today, and went out to the boulevards in search of a film. But we could not find a programme we liked (as it is the tenth anniversary of the ending of the war everywhere is showing films with a war theme) and came home instead.

4 December

Did not compose much, but managed something to get a little juice flowing. Work is not progressing with great vigour, but from time to time some not bad moments arise.

---

1 'Any minute' written in English.
2 See above, p. 26.

The post brought a cheque from Diaghilev for 5,000 francs, also from Stravinsky a ticket for *Le Baiser de la fée* in his box. *Le Baiser de la fée* was preceded by the premiere of Sauguet's *David*, but this was a zero, and sloppily performed. For the *Fairy's Kiss* Sudeikina was very kind and seated me in the front row so that I could have a better view. The most powerful impression of the *Fairy* is of boredom. Of course there are many singular things in it, and I would be very glad to hear it again, gladder than for example *Apollon*, because this score at least lacks the latter's actively offensive material. The programme ended with a ballet based on music from *Tsar Saltan*[1] – sumptuously staged, but what awful music! Four-square, replete with picturesque but content-free material, and with a nasty tendency to veer now towards Wagnerisms, now to pure vulgarity. I shared my thoughts with Nouvel, sitting next to me. When the curtain fell Sauguet, in the adjacent box and in a bad temper because of the failure of his *David*, began in a loud voice, presumably in an attempt to annoy us: 'Well, that's Russian music for you! I of course, as a Frenchman, cannot understand how anyone can find anything to like in it!' Nouvel embarked on a lengthy explanation about how we did not much like it either, and in fact did not consider it particularly Russian.

Meeting Diaghilev as we left the theatre, I informed him that I would probably soon be presenting him with a new woman.[2] Diaghilev was delighted with this news, and patted me on the cheek, right there on the street.

5 December

Composed a little more of the Siren, and played the piano for a long time.

The dentist extracted the root of one of my teeth, which came out in pieces, with the aid of cocaine. When the anaesthetic wore off my gums hurt and my enjoyment of life was spoilt.

Ida Rubinstein's season of performances has come to an end. On the surface it was spectacular, costing a huge amount of money and with the same composers and choreographers as Diaghilev's but without the Diaghilev genius presiding over it. So what was the outcome? The choreographers' productions were inferior, the composers produced duller music, and there was no sign of the sense of occasion that characterises a Diaghilev production!

---

1 *The Tale of Tsar Saltan, of his Son the Renowned and Mighty Bogatyr Prince Gvidon Saltanovich and of the Beautiful Swan-Princess*, opera by Rimsky Korsakov, 1900.
2 New music for the Temptress or Siren in *Prodigal Son*.

6 December

Made a start on the full score of *Prodigal Son*. It progressed easily, but it is amazing how necessary it is to get into training: after six or seven pages today my brain was too tired to do any more. But when I was orchestrating *Fiery Angel* I could get up to twenty pages a day.

Ptashka is waiting every minute of the day for the contractions to begin, heralding the appearance into the world of our daughter. Her doctor had predicted that they would start even before Rachmaninoff's concert, that is to say a week ago. I went to an orchestral concert in Mme Dubost's box. She is one of the committee members of the orchestra and when she met me at the *Baiser de la fée* performance, in answer to her enquiry how I liked her orchestra, I told her I did not know as I had never been invited to hear it. So she had invited me to her box.

8 December

I have returned to a thought that has come to me several times in the past. Many people either have no understanding at all of love for one's neighbour or for God, or apprehend this only indifferently, seeing it as something dreary, stale, unappetising. Routine has taken the edge off it. I believe, however, that it can be reinvigorated if instead of 'love' one substitutes the idea of 'interest'. God did not simply create the world and mankind and leave it at that, he maintains in his creation the sort of interest that the engineer takes in the bridge he is building, or the composer in the sonata he has composed. This is a critical aspect of a relationship: that it either has, or lacks, an element of interest. The most acute form of interest is love. If God had no interest in the world it would not have been worth creating; only where there is interest in the world is there any point in its creation. Directing man to rise to the pinnacle of his potential, God requires also that he be interested in the engineer and in his neighbour, that is to other versions of himself. The command to 'love our neighbour' often sounds like forced labour, but being interested in other, near versions of ourselves is anything but boring! If we are truly interested, we have laid the foundations of love.

9 December

Morning at C.S. Church, then a little composing. It turned out that the separate fragments I had composed over the past few days when combined would go well together for the third number. I wrote the whole thing out at a sitting. But then my head started to ache, and my jaw from the tooth that had been pulled the day before yesterday and the wound had reopened. The second half of the day was spoilt in consequence.

10 December

Two letters from Russia, the first from Asafyev on his return from abroad, writing that my music was being warmly received in Leningrad. The other was from Derzhanovsky, who tells me they are still hoping to obtain for me a respectable amount of hard currency but so far have not been able to clinch this.

I consulted Paichadze as to whether or not I should go. The conclusion was that as a bargaining tactic I should threaten not to, but even if they fail to come up with enough, I should nevertheless in the end go . . .

Played the piano and orchestrated *Prodigal Son* and laid out patience (the hankering for patience always seems to come over me when I am waiting for Ptashka to make me a father).

Had a visit from Nikita Magalov, who played for me the compositions he had written since coming to see me last season. Although his music sparkles from time to time, on the whole it is not vivid enough to be distinctive. I advised him to start the practice of having a notebook in which to jot down melodic ideas as they come to him, which he could then work on to develop into genuine individuality. Once he has gathered enough striking ideas he should set himself the task of writing a sonata based on them.

11 December

Completed the orchestration of the first number. I thought I would be able to polish it off in a day, but it took four: I got stuck over the Father, and in any case did not devote very much time to orchestration work as I spent quite a lot of time at the piano. Now that I have decided I am going I have to be in form so as not to be a bundle of nerves when I walk out on stage.

Ptashka is in a placid frame of mind, but – when will this baby be born?

13 December

In the morning Ptashka said that her pains seemed to have started, meaning that the birth process was under way. They had started during the night, but she did not want to wake me up. I did not mention that today was the fourth anniversary of my mother's death. At eleven o'clock we went to the clinic, the same one where she had given birth to Svyatoslav and where we had already booked a room, but we came home for lunch as it was clear that the business was not going to be accomplished so quickly. In the evening we went back again, this time for good. I telephoned Mrs Getty,[1] whom Ptashka has been consulting every three days, and asked her to support Ptashka with her work.

Dr Fabre also came to the clinic, a Russian doctor married to a Frenchman, the brother of the tenor who had been the first interpreter of *Seven, They Are Seven*. At first the lady doctor and I played patience, and then at one o'clock in the morning she advised me to go home and sleep. Ptashka, however, obviously wanted me to stay in the clinic, so I went to doze in another room, which happened to be exactly underneath the one occupied by Ptashka. I dropped off for about an hour and a half, but then was awakened by the two-day-old boy who was sleeping in the corner in his cradle and who started to cry. I could hear people running about upstairs, also at regular intervals Ptashka's groans, which by now had grown quite loud. I began working at Christian Science healing on her behalf. At about five o'clock Dr Fabre sent a message to me, as we had agreed, that the birth was beginning.

14 December

I went upstairs but did not try to enter the room, as I recalled that when Svaytoslav was born I had not been allowed in. Behind the door I could hear fitful ejaculations from Dr Fabre: 'Breathe deeply and calmly! Push! Don't push now! Push again! A boy!'[2] It was one minute past five in the morning. Well, and we had been expecting a little girl. But as a matter of fact I am not too disappointed. The actual birth had proceeded in an exemplary fashion, the baby was a strong little boy weighing 3 kilos and 620 grams. Ptashka also was in fine shape. I went out to telephone the news to the baby's granny.

Ptashka gradually came back to herself. The baby was hideous and looked like Mischa Elman (could anything be worse?!). At seven o'clock the doctor and I went to our respective homes. It was still dark outside. I went into an all-night café to have some coffee, and looked with curiosity at the clientele. What sort of people could they be at this time of day? Three postmen came in, and a man who was obviously chilled to the marrow. After this I walked home in a wonderful mood, watching the streetlights go out one by one as day dawned. At home I had another cup of coffee, enlightened Mémé[3] with all the details and told her that I was not the slightest bit sleepy. The moment I had said this I fell sound asleep for two hours, after which I got up and went back to the clinic.

---

1   A Christian Science healer. See above, pp. 66–9.
2   The instructions were given in French.
3   Family name for Lina Codina's mother, Olga Vladislavovna Codina.

15 December

The infant is already a little less unattractive to look at. My feelings for him are much more loving than they were to the new-born Svyatoslav. At that time I was more inclined to look at things outwards from the family than into it. But the most remarkable reaction of all was when I brought Svyatoslav to see his new little brother (when we had bought Svyatoslav a 'little brother' for Christmas, a clockwork doll, he said he would rather have a little sister, but we told him that would be too expensive). Despite this preference Svyatoslav was utterly fascinated, excited even, by his brother. When he saw him he squealed and then said, 'Dear tiny one, my own little brother.'

Ptashka feels well and looks well, and is overjoyed every time I come to see her. I come twice a day for two or two and a half hours at a time, but she does not think this is enough.

I want to make a suite for piano from some of the *Prodigal Son* numbers, as I have already turned some of them into quite free piano pieces.

16 December

Went to church, and then took Svyatoslav to see his brother again, which again provoked exclamations. Last night Ptashka had not slept so well, and had a slight temperature.

We debated the baby's name, as tomorrow is the last day we can register him at the town hall. I still want Askold, but Ptashka is adamant that this sounds terrible in English. All right, but when earlier we had been thinking about a girl and I suggested Galina, it emerged that this sounds terrible in Italian. By the end I even got quite annoyed, but concealed this from Ptashka as she has to be cosseted at the moment. We decided to leave the matter until tomorrow, but tomorrow really is the last possible day.

In the evening I played bridge at the Samoilenkos. Boris Nikolayevich said that when he was in Shanghai and the Russian cruiser *Askold*[1] came there all

---

1 The *Askold* had an interesting, chequered, history. She was one of Admiral Vitgeft's Russian Imperial Fleet blockaded for six months by the Japanese in Port Arthur after the disastrous Battle of Port Arthur (see *Diaries*, vol. 2, p. 284n). When by command of the Tsar and against the advice of Admiral Vitgeft the fleet broke out and attempted to rendezvous with Admiral Rozhdestvensky's Baltic Fleet, they were intercepted by the Japanese Admiral Togo and although the resulting Battle of the Yellow Sea was inconclusive only half the Port Arthur ships succeeded in turning tail back to the relative safety of their effective prison, while the other half made it to various other ports where they were interned by the Chinese, British and French authorities. *Askold* was one of the vessels that made it to Shanghai. Returned to the Imperial Navy at the cessation of Russo-Japanese hostilities, *Askold* joined the Allied forces in the Mediterranean during the First World War and participated in the Dardanelles operation. Seized by the Royal Navy and recommissioned as HMS *Glory IV* after the Soviets withdrew from the Allies following

the English found it highly amusing that a ship should be called the 'Cold Arse'!¹

Dr Alexinsky,² who knows his theology, said, 'Askold? No such name,' by which he meant not a canonical one.

I burst out: 'Excuse me! What about Oleg, then? He was nothing but a heathen and a thug!'³

'Perhaps,' countered Alexinsky, 'but there was another Oleg, and he was a saint.'⁴

17 December

I decided I would have to yield on Askold, and the baby was registered today in the town hall with the name of Oleg-Sergey, that is to say not Oleg Sergeyevich, nor Oleg *and* Sergey: in France it is quite common to give a child several names. To Ptashka 'Oleg' means nothing; she wanted to name her son Seryozhka, but to have two Sergey Sergeyeviches in the family would lead to impossible complications later on, so the upshot is Oleg, although Ptashka still harbours hopes that one day he will be Sergey.

There is still no telegram from Derzhanovsky. I have already sent him two enquiries, as simply for the passports I have to apply to seven different offices. And there is little incentive to work, either on the proof-reading or

---

  the Treaty of Brest-Litovsk, she was returned again to the Russian – now the Soviet – Navy at the end of the Civil War, only to be scrapped in Germany two years later.
1 The *Askold* had five thin funnels, as a result of which during her brief time as a Royal Navy ship she was nicknamed the *Packet of Woodbines* after the cheap cigarettes enjoyed by generations of tommies, sailors and RAF personnel, because the makers, W. D. & H. O. Wills, marketed them with considerably less tobacco than more luxurious smokes and only put five in a packet. They, and the rival Player's Weights, were the perfect size for the mandatory fifteen-minute smoke-break for which one was fallen out.
2 Grigory Alexinsky (1879–1967) had been a member of the original Bolshevik Party but had split from Lenin in 1909 and formed his own Left-Marxist Group, serving in the Second Duma. When the Duma was dissolved he emigrated and was associated with Plekhanov's Edinstvo group in Paris. Moving to the far right of émigré circles, he involved himself in the so-called High Monarchist Union (*Vysshy Monarkhichesky Soviet*) and became President of the Russian Council in Paris. A writer and translator, in 1937, as Grégoire Alexinsk, he produced a rather feeble attempt at a scandalous bestseller, *Les Amours secrètes de Lénine*, purporting to be Lenin's amorous letters to a certain Mlle Lise de K.
3 According to the *Primary Chronicle* of Nestor, the Kievan monk-historian writing at the start of the twelfth century, Oleg, who may have been a brother of Rurik, on the death of Rurik in 882 marched south to Kiev and by means of a trick took the ruling Varangian princes Askold and Dir prisoner and murdered them, establishing Kiev as his capital and becoming himself ruler of Rus' from his capital Kiev.
4 The Blessed Oleg of Bryansk, patron saint of all Olegs, who as grandson of the famous martyr Prince Michael of Chernigov, put to death with extreme torture by the Mongol Horde when on a mission to try to negotiate the survival of Kievan Rus', himself took monastic vows in the thirteenth century and devoted himself to a life of uniquely rigorous asceticism.

the ballet when at the back of one's mind is the knowledge that one is on the point of leaving. On the other hand, slaving away at practising the piano and then not going is also stupid. One way or another, I must go.

19 December

Still awaiting a cable from Derzhanovsky. I rang up Paichadze about something or other, and he said innocently, 'By the way, there's a telegram for you that has been here a couple of days.' This proved to be the very telegram from Derzhanovsky: he has not managed to get any currency, and so my visit must be put off until February or March. Everything is thus completely changed. I am very upset: although going to Russia involves a mass of difficulties and problems, only now that the answer is negative do I realise how strongly I am drawn to go there and how much I had set my heart on it! Now I must concentrate seriously on the ballet and try to finish it by the end of January. Postponing the trip meant having to write a heap of letters. I went to see Ptashka, but today she was in an anxious state, as I was, and the result was a slight tiff.

In the evening I went to Glazunov's concert, from which I derived some pleasure.[1] I recalled that in my youth I used to play a four-hand version of his

---

1   Prokofiev is uncharacteristically restrained in his criticisms of Glazunov's debut appearance in Paris – uncharacteristic, that is, both in his customary response to music and performances that failed to please him, but also in the absence of the personal antipathy to the man and his music so pervasive on the many occasions he is referred to in vol. 1 and the early part of vol. 2 of the *Diaries*. The concert, taking place as it did in the hothouse atmosphere of the Russian émigré elite in Paris, provoked a satisfying war of words between its culturally progressive and reactionary wings. The opinion of the progressives, in contrast to the unctuous ballyhoo generated by the reactionaries clustered round the Russian Conservatoire of Music, can be judged by the long and vitriolic review by Boris de Schloezer that appeared in the Milyukov-edited newspaper *Poslednye Novosti* (*Latest News*) on 30 December 1928. It was precisely the great eminence of Glazunov and his presumed importance to the perception of Russian music internationally that prompted a doubtless hypocritically reluctant de Schloezer to insert a fly into the ointment. For him, Glazunov was worse than an irrelevant dinosaur, because 'one cannot say that his is a star whose lustre age has dimmed; new and young it never was . . . All he did was construct endless autonomous aural systems that moved under their own motive power in accordance with their own purely private specific musical laws, bereft of psychological influences or the slightest admixture of alien poetical or visual stimuli . . . The prolific composer of eight symphonies, two piano concertos, six overtures, four quartets, etc., etc., amounts to little more than an academic whose passionless obsession with craftsmanship, superficially appropriate for all times and places but in reality good for neither, consists of nothing but formulaic classroom routines.' The savagery of the critique provoked outrage among the diehards, embodied in a letter to the editor published on 13 January in support of 'one of the greatest artists of the world of music today' signed by many leading musical figures including Medtner, Tcherepnin, all three Coniuses, Tarnovsky, Prince Sergey Volkonsky and Fyodor Akimenko, Stravinsky's first teacher. On the same page Milyukov felt obliged to publish an apology on behalf of the 'highly esteemed' Glazunov, 'a figure of such stature whose achievements in the history of Russian music are so incontrovertible that no criticism of him can possibly diminish his significance'. As far as *Latest News* was concerned, de Schloezer, the paper's senior writer on music as he was for the *Nouvelle Revue Française*, was squashed and he never in that organ again returned to the subject of Glazunov.

Symphony. Not many people were there, mainly Russians, almost no French at all; not to be compared with the great occasion of Rachmaninoff's concert. The concert began with his *Festive Overture*, which has much enjoyable music in it, probably due to sentimental memories, even that which was stolen from others. But *Stenka Razin* was pretty hard to listen to, the only point of interest being that Stravinsky purloined a motif from it for *Le Sacre*. The Second Concerto, which I was hearing for the first time, is, however, quite unbearable: I cannot understand how a composer who, after all, has in some respects a fairly glorious past, can allow himself to do such a thing! It was played by Gavrilova, the same who had received us in Leningrad in the role of Glazunov's wife.[1] She is now married to Tarnovsky. The second half consisted of the Seventh Symphony: in this work there is much that gives pleasure: the second subject of the first movement is positively splendid! During the interval I felt ill at ease after the telegram from Derzhanovsky and the contretemps with Ptashka, and therefore was excessively polite to some and rude to others. Catching a distant glimpse of Sashka's[2] wife – that vulgar old woman who grabbed herself a nice young boy, I simply cannot bear it – I nodded to her rather negligently, not being quite certain was it indeed she or not. Then all three Tcherepnins, father, son and the woman, were suddenly at my side, Sashenka lisping in a childish voice, 'Papochka, papochka,' in imitation of what the imaginary Oleg would be saying to me. At this point the wife suddenly asked, 'Did you not recognise me? You think it is polite?'[3] I replied that I had not been sure who she was. 'You think it is polite?'

1 See above, pp. 486–7, 708. Elena Gavrilova, cruelly described in the de Schloezer review as 'exceptionally mediocre', was the daughter of Olga Gavrilova, the elder of the two women Prokofiev had been understandably somewhat bemused to encounter in the Glazunov apartment in Leningrad. When Glazunov eventually married Olga, the mother rather than the daughter, in Paris in 1929 he formally adopted Elena, who thus became both his adopted daughter and his step-daughter and assumed the professional name Elena Glazunova. She had, however, by this time married the pianist and teacher Sergey Tarnovsky (1882–1976), who had studied with Anna Yesipova in the St Petersburg Conservatoire (several years before Prokofiev joined her class). Tarnovsky's main claim to fame was that as professor of piano at the Kiev Conservatoire he had for five years been the young Vladimir Horowitz's teacher before Horowitz moved to St Petersburg to work with Felix Blumenfald. In Paris Tarnovsky looked after his stepfather-in-law's business and professional affairs, and later moved to California with his wife, where his reputation as a teacher and chamber musician continued to grow. Elena's second husband was Herbert Gunther, following which her stage name changed yet again to Elena Gunther Glazunova. She died in 1999, and in accordance with the will she had drawn up twenty years previously bequeathed all the effects and archival material of her adopted father, including his Bechstein concert grand piano, to a Glazunov museum to be established in St Petersburg. This duly took place in 2003 and the collection is now housed within the Musical Museum of the Sheremetev Palace, a branch of the St Petersburg State Museum of Theatre and Music.
2 Alexander Tcherepnin.
3 The last phrase in English.

Madame repeated her question. This made me angry, so I added for good measure: 'And then I wanted to avoid your remarks,'[1] turned on my heel and began talking to some other people. I did not go into the Green Room after the concert so as not to have to encounter the Tcherepnins, but I will go to the reception tomorrow honouring Glazunov.

Going home I thought of Russia and realised how strongly I am drawn to her. The fact is, what on earth am I doing here when I could be there, where I am wanted and where I find everything much more interesting? My restless mood was calmed by C.S.: happiness does not depend on where one is or one's surroundings; the kingdom of heaven is to be found within us.

20 December

Went to see Ptashka in the morning in order to liquidate yesterday's 'bone of contention' (Mayakovsky's phrase).[2] She was gentle and affectionate. Since I am not going to Russia, I must get on with orchestrating the ballet, where I have ground to a halt on the second number. I dictated some letters.

Lunched with Mme Dubost, Klemperer on one side of our hostess and I on the other. Klemperer was gracious, but I doubt that he is much interested in my music; he prefers Stravinsky, but even he, so I hear, was not immune to sarcastic comments at the morning rehearsal: 'It's not the composer conducting now, it's a conductor!', as if to say, what sort of a conductor is this composer? Cortot, on the other hand, started talking about a Prokofiev Evening at which I might conduct the *Scythian Suite*. And in truth my heart has definitely got stronger this year: perhaps I should return to conducting? But I should have to do a lot of work over the summer.

Went to the afternoon reception for Glazunov sponsored by the firm of Pleyel. It was a modest, intimate affair, and very crowded. Glazunov discoursed to a group of respectable old gentlemen on the respective merits of this or that collection of Russian folk songs. I went to up to congratulate him most sincerely on the Seventh Symphony. N. Tcherepnin said not a word about yesterday's bickering, evidently having decided to pay no attention to any ill-will between me and Sashenka's wife. Someone told me that when the *Scythian Suite* was performed in Milan, Toscanini went to the rehearsal and was most disconcerted, but afterwards admitted that, all the same, there were moments where 'il y a de la race'.[3]

---

1 In English.
2 Mayakovsky's colourful coining ('mezhdusoboichik') actually means something like 'a you-and-me-having-a-go-at-each-other'.
3 'One can sense the breed.'

Diaghilev is presenting four performances at the Opéra, none of *Le Pas d'acier* (the sacred building must not be profaned with a Bolshevik item) but amounting to a complete Stravinsky festival.¹ So what was he talking about that time on the staircase when he told me he would be doing without a single work of Stravinsky in the spring? It's all musical – or is it anti-musical? – politics. Today was the first night, and I went to it. A pleasant ballet, cooked up from Handel.² I went backstage to talk to Diaghilev about his concept for the fourth number, for which he had asked me not to stick in the old *Matelote* I had written for Romanov but to compose something different. But Diaghilev was distracted and in a disagreeable mood today and I could get nothing out of him. I appealed to Kokhno, who replied, 'A simple pas-de-deux in which the two dancers' legs intertwine.'

21 December

Tried to compose the 'servants' dance' that I had failed yesterday to talk to Diaghilev about, but could get nowhere with it. Dictated letters to send to Asafyev. Orchestrated the second number. In the evening went to listen to Hindemith's *Konzertstück*, Op. 40: a good first movement, less good second and bad third (weak material unimaginatively developed). Klemperer also conducted *Pulcinella* wonderfully well; I listened to it with extreme pleasure, marvelling at Stravinsky's mastery. During the interval Suvchinsky bore down heavily on Kokhno, excoriating *Le Baiser de la fée* and saying, 'What is this nonsense? Kindly tell me please, just what is this nonsense?' Kokhno at first looked sideways at me, not daring to criticise Stravinsky openly in my presence, but finally confessed that both he and Diaghilev were in despair over the piece. I stood silently by, until eventually I put in: 'But in what way is *The Fairy* inferior to *Apollon*?' Suvchinsky and Kokhno began a wobbly defence of *Apollon*, along the lines of: 'Yes, well, I accept that *Apollon* is not quite the thing, but . . . ' As for myself, I find *Apollon* inferior to *The Fairy*, on the grounds that at least the latter has the advantage of Tchaikovsky's material, granted in a desiccated form, whereas *Apollon* has nothing at all. But my interlocutors, deeming it risky to dismiss *Apollon* altogether and yet being unable to mount an adequate defence of *The Fairy*, were reduced to the expedient of finding some way to support *Apollon*.

There is sad news from the Nabokovs: at the end of the summer their daughter was born, a very sickly child, and she has died after three months of

---

1   The programme included *Apollon musagète*.
2   *The Two Beggars*, music by Handel arranged by Thomas Beecham, choreography by Balanchine, settings and costumes by Juan Gris.

life. They also have financial difficulties: the manager of their estate in Poland has effectively stolen it from them, and as he is a Pole there is nothing they can do about it. Idka did not present his ballet; she was right not to do so, as it is not a good piece and would have damaged his reputation.

Supper with Szigeti. He is performing my Concerto in a week's time. I said I would go to the rehearsal. He: 'I beg you not to. I have played the work thirty-five times and almost feel that I myself composed it . . . and then all of a sudden up comes someone else with a claim to be the author, one who is entitled to suggest to me how it should be played. This is very unpleasant. Please just come to the concert.' I promised.

22 December

Did no work, as I had to rush about on various errands, and to visit Ptashka. If only they will let her come home soon!

To signal a reconciliation with the Tcherepnins I went to listen to Sashenka playing his First Concerto with the Pasdeloup Orchestra. It has some good things in it (some long-held notes near the beginning) but a lot of it is unoriginal rubbish. Were it to be pruned of all the dross and the remaining pearls collected together, the result would be about three minutes of decent music.

Suvchinsky and Vera Alexandrovna came, and I played them excerpts from *Prodigal Son*. Suvchinsky seemed to like it, but not extravagantly so, whereas I had been expecting him to be ecstatic. We had dinner together and went to the theatre to see *Jazz Hilton*. There is much that is interesting in this jazz music, and of course ragtime could play the same role in a symphony as once upon a time the minuet used to. For instance: what if it were all to be played *piano* and discreetly, without any uncontrolled outbursts?

Eurasia magazine has around sixty to eighty subscribers from the Kremlin, while at the same time Suvchinsky is getting threatening letters from right-wing émigrés. He is beaming.[1]

23 December

C.S. Church, following which I took Svyatoslav to visit his little brother. Then home to continue orchestrating the ballet. Fourestier came to listen to the Third Piano Concerto, which some female pianist is to play with them

---

[1] Prematurely, as he – unlike many of his more naive colleagues – would eventually be shrewd enough to realise (see above, p. 62 n. 3).

soon. The Orchestre de Paris[1] has begun tentatively to twitch in my direction. The Tcherepnins, father and son, came in the evening to listen to *The Gambler*, which elicited a continuous stream of approbatory exclamations. 'That's the genuine article from the Great Man,' said Sasha in an aside while I was playing Babulenka's music from Act Three. The Great Man is how Sasha has referred to me since he was fourteen. Not a word was said about his wife. So enthusiastic was my singing of *Gambler* that afterwards my voice was reduced to a whisper.

24–26 December

These three days passed quietly and peacefully between home and visiting Ptashka at the clinic. I orchestrated the second number and completed the composition of the ninth – a parodic treatment of various items of borrowed material. Kokhno had wanted me to come up with something harsh and insolent, but I rejected this and produced instead a more roguish piece of frivolity.

Read my American diary for 1919 and 1920 and found them interesting, absorbing even in places, but there are some unpleasant memories as well. I have changed greatly since those times.

27 December

Finished orchestrating the second number and completed all the orchestration for No. 7. There was in fact almost nothing to orchestrate in the latter, nevertheless, I feel that a third of the ballet is done. This is a good feeling. Not only that, but I composed themes for the new servants' dance, having at Diaghilev's request put to one side the original idea of using the music I composed for Romanov's ballet. This, plus two visits to Ptashka and half-a-dozen hands of patience, took up the whole day.

---

1   Louis Fourestier (1892–1976), French cellist, conductor and composer, winner of the Prix de Rome in 1925 for his cantata *La Mort d'Adonis*. Already Chief Conductor of the Opéra-Comique, he was, with Ansermet and Cortot, the third member of the triumvirate at the artistic helm of the new Orchestre Symphonique de Paris formed earlier in the year. Ansermet in fact was not to last long in this position, jockeyed out (probably for being Swiss rather than French) in favour of Monteux the following year. The laudable intention behind the new orchestra was to elevate orchestral standards in Paris by contracting players full-time and paying decent salaries, forbidding the curse of deputies. Prokofiev, in referring to the Orchestre de Paris, is technically jumping the gun as this was to be the title of the later orchestra formed at the behest of André Malraux in 1967 to replace the lapsed Orchestre de la Société des Concerts du Conservatoire, and led initially by Charles Munch. Fourestier himself had a distinguished career in the French repertoire, heading the conducting class at the Paris Conservatoire in succession to Munch from 1945 to 1962, leaving an extensive discography and spending two seasons as head of French repertoire at the Metropolitan Opera, New York, from 1946 to 1948.

28 December

Did a great deal of work and orchestrated the whole of No. 8. Good going: a number a day. In the afternoon brought Ptashka and Oleg home from the clinic in a Red Cross ambulance in order to avoid her having to get out of bed too early and walk up and down stairs. They carried her on the stairs lying prone on a stretcher, head first, so that going down her head had to be down. There was much fussing about in the afternoon as the baby had to be weighed on the scales both before and after feeding so that we could tell how much he had guzzled. Svyatoslav buzzed about the whole time in ecstasy at the arrival of his little brother. Mémé muddled everything up in her anxiety.

At nine o'clock I went out to go and hear Szigeti play my Violin Concerto. This was the first time I had heard his interpretation, and I must say that it was the best performance of the work I have heard so far – clear, logical and all as if laid out on a plate.

Ansermet's accompaniment was less than first-class: he had not thoroughly drilled the orchestra and also was too reticent, too often suppressing the orchestra to favour the soloist. I agreed with all the tempi except one place in the middle of the third movement, where the first violins have a rhythmic figure over which the soloist enters with scales and trills. This figure should be played like clockwork, slowing down very gradually, even prolonging the rallentando into the coda, which I have marked *meno mosso* as far as figure 50. Ansermet and Szigeti altered the tempo and thereby caused 'the machine to break down'. The Concerto had a great success, there were cries of 'bis', 'encore', after the scherzo in which Paichadze joined from his seat next to mine. I stopped him, saying people might think it was me, to which Paichadze replied, 'Nothing wrong with that, if the composer feels like calling "encore"; it is quite understandable that he would like to hear his music again. It would be less appropriate if he were to start calling for the composer to take a bow!'

Paichadze received a letter from Derzhanovsky today asking him to pass on to Prokofiev that there is nothing for it but to postpone my visit as he has not managed to obtain any hard currency at all. He begs me to be assured that this is in no way a result of negligence as my presence is eagerly awaited both as man and musician; the problem is entirely due to the generally catastrophic situation. I was dismayed by this as the earlier telegram had held out the hope of acquiring some money at least in a month or two, but this letter made no mention of it at all. The meaning is quite clear: I shall be coming for *The Gambler* in any case for which I shall need to have some roubles, and presumably I shall give some concerts as well, and that being so where is the need to spend any hard currency on me? But there and then I decided to dig my heels in: yes, I would come for *The Gambler*; yes, I would need some roubles; but in return I would give concerts in the Caucasus (it would be pleasant to go there in the spring) where I was not being offered hard currency in any case, and in the capitals I would restrict my appearances to gratis performances for workers' organisations whereby I would shut the mouths of any authorities that might feel inclined to put pressure on me.

30 December

C.S. Church, then some work on sorting out various pieces of the ballet because Diaghilev was to come in the afternoon to listen to it. He duly appeared with Kokhno and Lifar. The New Woman and the plundered plumage of the final number were rapturously approved of. Of the men's dance, which for some reason Diaghilev insists on calling the dance of the clowns, and of the drinking scene, I played only fragments because they are not finished yet, and Diaghilev made some very pertinent suggestions which I shall adopt. He also suggested a sensible cut in the final number just before the concluding theme. Both he and I were euphoric over the meeting; Diaghilev gave it as his opinion that this ballet was one of my finest achievements.

Ptashka was in low spirits, but when Diaghilev feasted his eyes on Oleg, played with him and sang the praises of both children, Svyatoslav and Oleg, she cheered up and the evening passed happily.

Seven years ago today the premiere of *Three Oranges* took place.[1]

31 December

Orchestrated No. 10, but not much. We had no plans to celebrate the New Year with anyone, so I went to bed at eleven o'clock.

---

1   In Chicago. See *Diaries*, vol. 2, pp. 654–6.

1929

1 January

Finished orchestrating the tenth number of *Prodigal Son*, making five of the numbers fully orchestrated. Played a few hands of patience. In the evening went to an extremely amusing Italian marionette show. I laughed and applauded.

3 January

Most gratifying telephone call from Diaghilev, initially hesitant and seemingly unwilling to broach the main reason for the call. It proved to be about a revival of *Chout*. A new production, however, would have to be based on the orchestral suite and we would have to create a new scenario as up till now foreigners are totally baffled by it, hence its lack of success for example in England. If *Chout* can be revived and renewed in this way, a full evening consisting of three of my ballets would be feasible. I am thrilled, although taking care to conceal my delight from Diaghilev. This afternoon I went to the publishers to collect the scores of both the ballet and the suite, and took them round to the Grand Hotel and gave them to Kokhno to pass on to Diaghilev, also incidentally to get a ticket for this evening's performance in his season. Kokhno displayed interest in talking about *Chout* – is he contemplating another role as librettist? – and took the opportunity of thrusting into my hand a form for signature and submission to the Society of Authors confirming the authorship of *Prodigal Son*. Probably he was nervous that I would refuse to grant him the one-third percentage of royalties he has claimed. I signed without demur but requested the insertion of a note stating that Kokhno had taken the subject from the Gospels. He ventured a protest, but eventually agreed: what if I were to refuse to sign or simply walk off?

Kokhno: 'Why do you want to drag in the Gospels? I have a feeling there is an ulterior motive, but cannot work out what it might be.'

I: 'Simple justice. After all, you didn't create the parable of the Prodigal Son, did you? I just want this noted in the citation.'

Of course there is an ulterior motive: I had already composed three-quarters of the music when Kokhno sent me his libretto, and most of the narrative impulses that inspired me flowed not from him but directly from the Bible. I assume that Kokhno will have some influence on Diaghilev's production, but I want to eliminate this so as to be left with the biblical story and my music.

Went to a C.S. lecture in the evening, but it proved uninteresting. After it I went to the performance in Diaghilev's box, which was full of people I did not know and who talked all the way through. Diaghilev introduced me to Markevich, a new sixteen-year-old composer.[1] He will come to play me his compositions in the near future. According to Diaghilev it was he who characterised Sauguet's brand of vulgarity as 'naked' and Dukelsky's as 'overdressed'. Met A. Rubinstein, with needless to say a beautiful woman on his arm. He told me a story about one woman whose dream was to meet the great Ravel. When the dream came true, she looked with astonishment at the diminutive maître and exclaimed, 'Comment, c'est ça Ravel?'[2]

4 January

Diaghilev announced yesterday that he would come today with Balanchivadze, so I waited expectantly for them. However, Balanchivadze arrived with Kokhno and Lifar. I played the *Son* for them. Kokhno's response was the most enthusiastic of the three: the entry of the Beautiful Woman aroused in him a feeling 'akin to actual physical pleasure'. Balanchivadze's comments at this stage displayed little evidence of his having understood what the ballet is about. As far as they went, they seemed to indicate an intention to approach it in a manner at variance from what I want – is this Kokhno's influence?

---

1 Igor Markevich (1912–1983), composer and conductor who was born in Kiev but grew up and studied in Paris. Diaghilev's ardent championing of his youthful 'second Igor' protégé, immediate commission of a piano concerto and plans for a ballet (inevitably to a libretto by Kokhno) pitched the young composer straight into the centre of progressive music-making in Paris. As the impresario's letter published in *The Times* of 13 July 1929 boldly states, he was 'the man who will put an end to the scandalous period of music of cynical-sentimental simplicity [. . .] my young countryman, in whose music I sense the very birth of that generation which can protest against the Paris orgies.' Diaghilev's untimely death, however, condemned the steady stream of compositions to relative obscurity, the early promise faded. By 1931 and the failure of Markevich's ballet *Rébus* Stravinsky was ready to put the boot in: 'Once again Prokofiev is the model – I really think it is time to put an end to this habitual borrowing from Prokofiev, and [Markevich's] technique is too accomplished to attribute the principal shortcoming of the work to that. The piece is just boring. [. . .] In my opinion, Markevich is not a *Wunderkind* but an *Altklug* [precocious] which is perhaps even more dangerous to the future of his art than if he were a veritable *Wunderkind*.' (Letter to Willy Strecker of B. Schotts Söhne, 29 December 1931.) Markevich turned more to conducting, in which his exceptional gifts had already been recognised. The combination of the war and a serious illness caused him to abandon composition altogether in 1941 and to put his works away in the bottom drawer, but in the 1970s he unearthed and began conducting them again, in so doing reviving an interest that has since been sustained and has recently led to a substantial recorded presence.
2 'Good heavens, you mean this is really Ravel?'

Larionov is extremely excited at the idea of reviving *Chout*. He will again be responsible for the scenery and costumes, but completely redone.

5 January

Much occupied with orchestrating the third number of *Prodigal Son*, which is making slow progress. However, I think it will be good.

6 January

C.S. Church in the morning, and quite a good amount of No. 3 after lunch.

Dukelsky has returned from London; he and I went to eat *bliny* at a Russian restaurant. He is agitated because they are ready to perform his Symphony in London but Koussevitzky has taken the material to America, where he has not so far made any move to perform it. The result is no performance in either country, because our 'funeral parlour' of a publisher declines to produce another set of parts.

7 January

Finished orchestrating No. 3. Markevich came and played me the Overture he has composed. His claims to talent are difficult to endorse, but it is dangerous to say that he has none. The Overture, messy and incoherent, certainly lacks melodic charm; despite this there might be something in it. I suggested that he orchestrate at least some of it and then send me the score. When he went away he forgot to take with him a folder containing his songs.

In the evening we entertained the Samoilenkos, Schubert, Dukelsky, Larionov and Goncharova. We told her that had the baby been a daughter she would probably have been Natalya Sergeyevna, in other words the same as her, Goncharova. Dukelsky announced that he had discovered a new talent in himself, that of sketching, and proceeded to draw everyone's portrait – quite accomplished, but not particularly good likenesses.

I had toothache during the night, but worked on abating the pain. Fell asleep at three a.m.

8 January

A concert given by a singer, a relation of Dukelsky, who accompanied her in the second half, which was devoted to his songs. As a singer she was not outstanding, but I enjoyed the songs. Sitting behind us was a French critic, I don't know who, but he fell asleep during their performance. Literally, not metaphorically. Needless to say, we never stopped teased Dukelsky about this afterwards.

9 January

A blazing row with Ptashka, who was angry that I had yet again gone off to eat *bliny* with Dukelsky. This put me beside myself with rage and I stormed out banging the door behind me. I soon calmed down, however, and was full of remorse. It was a lesson to me: such behaviour achieves nothing whatsoever. I was so angry with her because she was in the wrong, but the only way I can impress this on her is by ensuring my own conduct is above reproach.

10 January

Pegged away little by little orchestrating the ballet and creating a two-hand piano version. I cannot finish the composition of the last three numbers; my touch seems to have deserted me.

11 January

Attended Sofronitsky's recital, at which he played unevenly. Dukelsky and I were with him afterwards; I brought along a bottle of champagne which we demolished instantly. I found myself sitting between two of Scriabin's daughters, the plain Krysa by his first wife and the attractive if dissolute Ariadna, by his second. Unable to restrain myself I referred to Schloezer as a bicycle salesman. Ariadna reacted with equanimity to this abuse of her grandfather.[1]

---

1 Scriabin's first wife was the pianist and teacher Anna Isakovich (1875–1920), from whom he had separated acrimoniously while engaged on the composition of the *Divine Poem* (Symphony No. 3) in Switzerland in 1904. This union produced four children, the eldest and the youngest of whom, Rimma and Lev, both died young; the survivors were two daughters, Maria and Yelena. Yelena, a fellow-student of Sofronitsky in Leonid Nikolayev's class along with Shostakovich and Maria Yudina, had married Sofronitsky in 1920). The marriage of Sofronitsky and Yelena Scriabina broke up not long after the pianist's return to the USSR in 1930. He was too independent a spirit to be favoured by the regime and this tour to Warsaw and Paris was to be the only time he was allowed to go abroad. 'Krysa' (it means 'rat') seems to be a not very flattering nickname, but it is not clear whether it refers to Yelena or Maria, although the context suggests the former. Scriabin's second wife, Ariadna Scriabina's mother, was Tatiana Schloezer (1883–1922), who was Boris de Schloezer's sister. Prokofiev seems here to have made a rare slip of the pen, as Boris was therefore Ariadna's uncle, not her grandfather. Ariadna, born in 1905, was active in the French Resistance during the Second World War and having defiantly converted to Judaism in 1940 in order to marry her lover and fellow poet Dovid Knut, was murdered by the Gestapo two weeks before the liberation of Toulouse in 1944. Their son, Yosi Knut was born in 1943, Dovid having escaped the Gestapo to Switzerland a few months before. See above, p. 322, n. 3.

Dukelsky was in a contrary mood, angry at Sofronitsky for not having included his Suite in the programme; he sat at the keyboard and played ragtime throughout the evening. 'Put another nickel in, in the nickelodeon,' we said, 'and it'll go on playing!'

13 January

C.S. Church. Afterwards the reconciliation with Ptashka somehow came about of its own accord and was followed by an atmosphere of great tenderness. We talked about how to avoid such quarrels in the future. We went out for a walk together for the first time since the baby was born.

14 January

I had just embarked on composing a mildly Mozartian theme for the fourth number when there was a telephone call from Diaghilev. I said, 'I would not have come to the phone for anyone else but you, because I am just in the middle of composing a new theme for you.' Diaghilev wanted to stop the conversation there and then, but I said it did not matter, I would remember it. He had just come back from Bordeaux and wanted to know what was news in Paris. I was flattered: it was an honour that had never before been vouchsafed me. However, I had been sitting at home almost all the time and so had little to communicate to him.

It was in fact not just one theme I was composing but two, and I think they are both good. I decided to construct the piece in the form of a compressed sonata-allegro. The two successful melodic inspirations combined with the harmonious relationship with Ptashka to put me in an excellent mood.

15 January

Did not compose much, but the exposition (except for the final theme) is ready now. Peace reigns at home, but Ptashka is not sleeping well at nights and is therefore enervated and jumpy.

16 January

Composed a closing theme, quite slight but one to end with all the same. Then an idea came to me, one-two-three, just like that! I could put together a symphony out of the music for the ballet! I already have the sonata-allegro, and what a beautiful Andante I could make from the theme with which the whole ballet now ends! But is there a danger in pursuing this idea? All very well to try it once with *Fiery Angel*, but every time I come up with a piece for the stage . . . ? In any case, I cannot think more about it until I have finished the ballet.

In the evening I visited Celia,[1] just back from Java and leaving the day after tomorrow for London and other European cities. Boris has stayed behind in Shanghai to give some lessons at extremely lucrative rates. What can this mean? Divorce? A brief separation from one another? It did not seem appropriate to ask searching questions, and Cecilia replied evasively to my enquiries as to when Boris might be returning. She was looking blooming and attractive; perhaps Boris's only guarantee resides in her innate coolness.

17 January

Tried to compose the development, but once again the muse deserted me. In the evening I went to a lecture by Marina Tsvetaeva on Bryusov. A lot of what she said was interesting, but two years ago Ostroumova-Lebedeva had drawn a livelier and more macabre picture of him.

So as not to let the time go to waste I worked on a piano transcription of the ballet score. Relations with Ptashka are perfect. Oleg, who was born with a full head of hair and a hint of side-whiskers, is now going bald, moreover like his papa he is losing his hair from the forehead back. At home he is not, by the way, called Oleg, as Ptashka does not really like the name despite the fact that it draws compliments on all sides from the Russians. He is called 'bratik'[2] because that is what Svyatoslav calls him. Svyatoslav's affection for his 'bratik' has not lessened at all; the other day, as a treat, he offered him his grimy finger to suck.

18 January

Carried on with the development, but not very far (how I should like to polish it off in one go!).

Finished orchestrating the ninth number, thus completing all of this task except for the three numbers that I have not yet finished composing.

Spent the evening quietly at home playing rummy with Ptashka.

---

1   Hansen, violinist wife of Boris Zakharov.
2   'Little brother' – 'brat' is the Russian for 'brother'.

19 January

I simply cannot make the development work, most frustrating. But I must be patient. Transcribed No. 9 for piano two hands. A day without incident.

20 January

C.S. Church. Afterwards I had the urge to compose, but again nothing came of it. Washed my hands of it and decided to devote a few days to proof-reading the score of *Le Pas d'acier*.

21 January

Did not attempt composition but read the proofs, cursing Paichadze for having given my score to such a wretchedly bad engraver.

Lunched with Ptashka in a Russian restaurant where we had *bliny*, and then in the afternoon went to Dubost to listen to Sofronitsky. While I was greeting Milhaud, an unknown man standing beside him introduced himself to me: Arens, a councillor from the Soviet Embassy in Paris.[1] Hitherto I have kept my distance from the Soviet Embassy, fearing that they might invite me to play at a reception there and that this would be reported in all the papers. But since my Soviet passport has been extended and I am planning to go to Russia, I thought I ought to be polite. At first Arens said nothing to me; I did likewise. But later he came over to the group in which I was standing and mentioned that in the Embassy they had a large collection of music by Soviet composers that they were unable to make head or tail of. I said I would be delighted to come and help them identify which works would be most likely

---

1   Ivan Arens (1889–1938), Second Councillor of the Embassy of the USSR in Paris. In 1923 Arens had been a member of the Soviet delegation to the Lausanne Conference on the Middle East headed by the Soviet diplomat Vatslav Vorovsky, Old Bolshevik and close associate of Lenin. Vorovsky, Arens and one other man were at dinner in a Lausanne hotel when without warning a young émigré from Petrograd of Swiss origins, Maurice Conradi, pulled out a gun and shot them. Vorovsky was killed outright, Arens and his companion severely wounded but survived. Conradi's father, aunt, uncle and elder brother, all partners in the family's well-known chocolate factory and shop on Nevsky Prospect, had all been liquidated, accused of being agents of the international bourgeoisie and the business nationalised without compensation in the first wave of terror. At his trial Conradi's somewhat unlikely defence was justifiable homicide, on the grounds that 'any killing of a Bolshevik was a step forward for humanity'. Such was the sympathy for his ordeal allied to horror at what was widely perceived as the regime-caused famine in Russia, that his argument prevailed in the Swiss courts and Conradi was freed. The incident, coming at a time when the USSR was struggling to establish trade and diplomatic relations with most European countries, resonated throughout Europe and caused the complete severance of Soviet–Swiss relations until well after the end of the Second World War.

to be well received in Paris (I consider this my duty towards Moscow composers). Arens was thrilled by my offer and wrote down my address. I then introduced him to Ptashka, at which he bowed and scraped and kissed her hand. Altogether he makes a good impression, is well dressed, but speaks with a strong Jewish accent.

22 January

'No good is, but the good God bestows' (*Science and Health*).[1] This is very importance guidance in being able to discard false desires and pleasures and to value the genuine article. It is a dictum by which one should live one's life.

23 January

Read proofs. Resolved not to curse and swear but meticulously to mark up all the engraver's errors and shortcomings. This will be the worse for him, as he will have to make all the corrections himself. Got on with this quite well. I still do not feel inclined to compose: I have been overdoing this aspect of my work and must husband my strength for a few days.

25 January

Great harmony with Ptashka.

26 January

A bad headache all day. Had a few ideas for the development section of the ballet's fourth number.

Played through Rachmaninoff's Fourth Piano Concerto, Medtner's Second and Stravinsky's *Le Baiser de la fée*. Rachmaninoff's second subject is good, but the remainder is rather lifeless. Extraordinary how all three composers begin to dry as they enter their fifth decade. To the list can be added Glazunov, making four great composers who should, like Scriabin, have died at the age of forty-three. Stravinsky, however, is too bright a spark to be a dear departed: it will be quite some time before we bury him.

27 January

I have finally finished the development of the fourth number even though I'm not certain it is of top quality. Then, the reprise section as far as the coda

---

1 Noted by the author in English.

came to me of its own accord, with several very happy inspirations. With breaks, I worked all day, and then put the coda aside until tomorrow. I am very pleased that this number is done, even with my reservations about the coda.

28 January

Finished the fourth number in a surge of activity, breaking all my fingernails in the process. I am extremely happy, because this section of the ballet has cost me not a little trouble and grief. Inertia carried me on into the succeeding number, in which I even managed to produce a little, or perhaps more accurately to get an idea of what I might do with it.

In the evening I went to hear my Quintet at Pro-Musica, but, good God, what a wretched performance. They plodded along not together, played in the wrong keys, sometimes got out by as much as a bar and stayed out for the whole movement; in short it was a disgrace. I was told they had had only one rehearsal, on top of which the first violin, Darrieux, was suffering from bronchitis. But imagine, one rehearsal for that Quintet!

Catching sight at the far side of the hall of Marnold, whom I have not seen for seven months, the old man might have died for all I knew, I went over to talk to him. On my way back, there in an otherwise empty row along which I had to pass to return to my seat, sat Stahl. I am sure he sat there on purpose so that I would have to step over his knees. But fortunately I saw him in time and was able to take another route, so the encounter did not take place.

29 January

Woke up in the night fretting over the performance of the Quintet. I decided I would send a letter of complaint to the Pro-Musica management. I was still so angry in the morning I could not even make myself read C.S., something I do every morning before settling down to work. Eventually I did succeed in sitting down to read a short and very interesting article that presented an image of a moth flitting up and down on a sunny day and casting a shadow on a white-painted wall. In runs a puppy, barking at and trying to catch the shadow without realising that the moth itself is right beside him, so fixated is he on the shadow rather than the real thing. The moral is that the more clearly a man understands his true essence as a reflection of God, the less he will fear other men barking at him since their growls are directed only at his material 'I', which is no more than a pale reflection of the real man, the image of God.

The article had an effect on me. I decided not to write my letter of complaint. On the other hand, to remain silent would be to endorse a slovenly performance. The solution was to compose a letter sticking to a strict recitation of the facts and asking how many rehearsals there had been. Was it true there had been only one? And why had I not been invited to attend it?

I did not compose today but read the proofs of the *Pas* score. Called in at the publishers, where Gorchakov was playing his new compositions. They are better in the sense that they have fewer actual mistakes, but there is not much sign of talent.

30 January

A slight headache, therefore I went for a long walk in the Bois de Boulogne with Svyatoslav. He went along pretending to be a chuff-chuff, splashing happily through the mud and singing 'chizhik-pizhik' at the top of his voice.[1] At one point, when I found myself on one path and he on another, he observed philosophically, 'You go that way, I go this, we each have our own way.'

My headache cleared up in the afternoon. Marnold called and we played two games of chess. True, I let him revoke moves, but he won the first game and looked all set to win the second. At this I decided that was enough revoking, so waited for his first lapse of attention and won the second game. He listened to *Choses en soi* and liked them very much.

31 January

Read proofs and worked out some of the pas-de-deux. In the evening went to Straram's concert, fairly boring. Schumann's Third Symphony sounded so dull even that failed to grab the attention. Strauss's *Zarathustra* has a stunningly arresting opening (no music, but how splendid it sounds!) but that is all, thereafter nothing. In the Green Room Straram rushed up to me and asked which of my works he could perform. I told him, whatever he liked. He will come to talk about it in a day or two. I will also talk to him about Dukelsky's Symphony.

1 February

Read proofs and composed some of the pas-de-deux, the outline of which I have sketched out. I fear it is not quite what Diaghilev wanted; it's not

---

1 A (very) Russian nursery rhyme. A 'chizhik' is a little bird like a siskin, so an approximate translation could be:

Siskin, piskin, where've you been?
On Fontanka, drinking gin.
Drank a glass, put one more down,
Now my head goes round and round.

Vodka would be more accurate, but harder to rhyme.

passionate enough. He now wants the exact opposite of what he was advocating to me in Rome in 1915. A trait he shares with Stravinsky is to insist with unassailable conviction that only such-and-such music is worth composing, and then a year later to maintain the opposite.

2 February

'When we think only of good, of God and his Infinite ideas, harmonious conditions are externalised' (Christian Science).[1] Absolutely true. A reflection of God is invariably harmonious, but we, thinking in material terms and constructing around ourselves a material atmosphere, cannot see this. As soon as we switch to the cycle of good and ideas of the divine, harmony is restored.

It disturbs me very much that since giving birth Ptashka has become so involved in a medical atmosphere. For the actual birth a midwife was necessary – this is accepted by the most advanced Scientists – but once it is over one should dispense with doctors as quickly as possible. Ptashka seems in some ways to have grown away from Science without entirely embracing the world of doctors: she is between two stools, and this is not good at all.

5 February

Yesterday I seem to have, unexpectedly, finished the fifth number. This the one I had been most afraid, either that it would not be successful, or that if it was Diaghilev would not approve of it. As it happened he rang up and said that he would like to come to listen to the new numbers. I asked him to do this tomorrow, hoping that by then I would have finished No. 6.

In the afternoon I went to the garage and was in the process of explaining to the mechanic certain matters that needed attention in the car. This mechanic always assumes a very imperious manner, and I have been much exercised as to whether I should tip him, and if so how much. At this moment another motorist appeared, evidently an important figure, and you should have seen how my mechanic, excusing himself, rushed over to the new arrival to demonstrate something on his car. I waited patiently for twenty minutes, but when the mechanic came to the end of his explanation and started washing the windscreen of the other car I lost patience, went over to them and said, 'I'm waiting for you, it's not your job to wash headlights just now.' 'Yes, yes, of course, right away,' said he, but still lingered. I marched

---

1 Written in English.

out of the garage in a rage. There was I wondering whether I should give the great man a tip, while all the time he was being another man's slave. At home I soon forgot the incident, but woke up in the middle of the night still fuming, and could not get back to sleep. Eventually I made myself think it through with the aid of C.S., calmed down and slept deeply.

6 February

A bad headache, most untimely as I wanted very much to finish the sixth number before the arrival of Diaghilev, and practise playing through what I had already written without splitting too many notes. But instead I had to go for a long walk to make sure my headache did not get worse. At five o'clock Diaghilev came, accompanied by Kokhno, Lifar and Nouvel. Diaghilev was in the sunniest of moods and showered Ptashka with compliments. He asked me from whom he might commission a new ballet if Hindemith did not produce one in time. What could I tell him of Martinů? Or Villa-Lobos? I tried to give him some information about the latter, recommending him but with some reservations. Mention of Dukelsky would not have been appropriate, now was not yet the time. I played Nos. 4, 5 and 6, none of which Diaghilev had yet heard, and to my amazement he approved of all three. I was pleasantly surprised as I had feared the pas-de-deux[1] would be judged too *amoroso*, also I was expecting to be told that a sonata-allegro (No. 4)[2] had no place in a ballet. Diaghilev did have some pertinent observations on the pas-de-deux, namely that it should have a slower tempo and therefore its material would need to be shortened, which I said I could do. Kokhno then proceeded to think up aloud a scenario for the fourth number which had so unexpectedly come into existence. In this endeavour he had several 'genius ideas' which, however, he as precipitately retracted. Light was clearly dawning gradually that the genesis of a subject was not after all such a simple matter, and there ensued in consequence voluble protestations about there being something, somehow, not quite right about the music, that in short it was not really danceable. The problem seemed to be the distinctly feminine cast of the second subject, but the Siren, who at that time was already on stage, could not be introduced into it because the whole idea of the number was to separate her two dances. And to bring in another woman would be to divert attention from the first, which would also not be desirable. Luckily attention shifted to the other numbers and the question was shelved. Obviously Diaghilev and Kokhno

1 'The Prodigal Son and the Siren'.
2 'The Men's Dance'.

wanted to think it over. They left at nine o'clock. On his way out Diaghilev invited us to his box for *The Snow Maiden*,[1] told me that he was free to come back any day, and asked me to get hold of Villa-Lobos but as from me not from him (Diaghilev) in order to avoid any entanglement on the latter's part.

After three hours of playing and impassioned discussion my head was threatening to split into a thousand pieces, and I called off going to the Samoilenkos to play bridge. But by midnight my headache had gone.

7 February

My head felt wonderfully clear this morning, and not only did I fulfil all the suggestions Diaghilev had made (including expanding the conclusion of the ballet), I also finished the sixth number, completing in other words the composition of the work. All that is left is to orchestrate three of the numbers, and of course to stitch together the fourth number in consultation with Diaghilev. I took a look at this number: its components are as if screwed together, and it can be taken apart and reassembled at will. In its present form it can serve as a sonata-allegro for my Fourth Symphony, but for the ballet it can be however Diaghilev wants it.

My mood was good and my spirits high.

8 February

I should have telephoned Diaghilev to arrange our next rendezvous, but did not do so as I have not heard back from Villa-Lobos. Diaghilev rang twice demanding to know what sort of orang-utang he was dealing with. Lobos himself did not pick up the telephone until evening, but was terribly pleased with the invitation and grateful for my good offices; he would be at our disposal whenever convenient. In this way I have become his benefactor. It was decided we should all meet at my house the day after tomorrow.

After working hard all day I decided on impulse in the evening to go to an orchestral concert to hear Rubinstein. Ptashka was in bed and took offence that I should be leaving her alone. I lost my temper: what, was I never to take a step without asking her? I listened to Beethoven's Fourth Symphony with enjoyment, also the Second Piano Concerto of Saint-Saëns, every note of which I still know from my Conservatoire days. Saint-Saëns is such an excellent orchestrator of his piano concertos – how strange it is that I have never

---

1 Pantheistic opera (1881) by Rimsky-Korsakov.

had the chance to listen to a performance of any of my own! Falla and Florent Schmitt provoked acute boredom.

9 February

To a rehearsal by Poulet who is performing the Suite from *Oranges*. The orchestra's personnel is youthful,[1] and the chicken himself[2] has made great efforts. He has come in for a good deal of criticism, but the results are not bad, much better than I was expecting. I asked the manager for a box, as Diaghilev had said he wanted to come. The manager's eyes glistened at the mention of Diaghilev, but then I could see a flicker of doubt pass across his face: perhaps I was just name-dropping so as to get the tickets. But just then Diaghilev telephoned announcing his intention of coming.

In the evening there took place the premiere of *The Snow Maiden* at the Russian Opera (Kuznetsova–Massenet).[3] The production was sumptuous and we were in Diaghilev's box. But Cooper's tempi drag and the voices, except two of the men, Popov and Piotrovsky,[4] were generally so-so. In the interval Diaghilev, referring to me, said to Volkonsky,[5] 'Now he's written a chef d'oeuvre, and what a chef d'oeuvre . . . !'

1 Gaston Poulet (1892–1974), outstanding French violinist and conductor. As a young violinist (at the age of eighteen he won the First Prize and Gold Medal at the Paris Conservatoire in front of a jury consisting of Joachim, Thibaud, Boucherit, Enesco, Casals, Auer and Weingartner) he had given the premiere of Debussy's Violin Sonata with the composer at the piano, and his string quartet (formed at the suggestion of Fauré) caused Debussy to say that, although their performance was not how he had imagined the piece, henceforth it should always be played like that. Encouraged by Toscanini to take up conducting, he formed his own orchestra, the Concerts Poulet, which appeared regularly under his baton at the Salle Pleyel and the Théâtre Sarah Bernhardt from 1926 until 1932, as well as being appointed a Principal Conductor of the Concerts Colonne Orchestra.
2 'Poulet' is the French word for a chicken.
3 Maria Kuznetsova (1880–1966), famous lyrical soprano and star of the Mariinsky Opera until the October Revolution, when she emigrated to Paris to continue a high-profile international career taking leading roles in Sweden, at Covent Garden and Drury Lane. While at the Mariinsky she had created several major roles including Fevronia in Rimsky-Korsakov's *Invisible City of Kitezh*, Woglinde in the first Russian production of *Das Rheingold*, Fausta in Massenet's *Roma*, the title role in the same composer's *Cléopâtre* (she was later to marry Massenet's nephew, the banker and industrialist Alfred Massenet, who bankrolled the private Paris Opéra Russe company giving the performance) and Yaroslavna in the Rimsky–Glazunov realisation of Borodin's *Prince Igor*. A talented actress who had initially trained as a ballerina, Kuznetsova also took the stage as Potiphar's wife in the Ballets Russes production of Strauss's *The Legend of Joseph* in 1914. Her first husband was Nikolay Benois, son of Alexander Benois's watercolourist brother Albert and thus the nephew of A. N. Benois and the brother-in-law of Nikolay Tcherepnin.
4 Prokofiev had last seen and talked to Piotrovsky on a train travelling to Vilnius on his way to the Soviet Union in January 1927. See above, pp. 407–8.
5 See above, p. 304, n. 1.

Catching sight of Sonya Avanova,[1] I went over to greet her. 'Ah,' she said, 'at last you've recognised me! Now let me introduce you to my husband.' And who should her husband be but ... Kirill Zaitsev![2] Here was a really unexpected connection! I had recently been reading articles by him in the newspapers and knew from it that he was now attached to an émigré Monarchist group. His beard was now flecked with grey and he was broader across the shoulders than he had been. 'Such a long time since we saw each other,' he said. 'It's awful to contemplate.' 'Fifteen years,' I replied.

They have been married just two weeks. Not long ago he was in Belgrade, where he had seen the Meshcherskys. When Ptashka came up I introduced her to the couple. We went together into the foyer, I with Sonya, he with Ptashka. Sonya and I talked, needless to say, about Koshetz, whom I called once or twice 'Nina'. Noticing Zaitsev's ears flapping, I hastened to refer to her more formally as 'Nina Pavlovna'. As we were saying goodbye I complimented Zaitsev on his talents as a bridge-player and said we must arrange to play. Zaitsev replied that he had not played since St Petersburg times. We exchanged addresses and parted. It was a very strange feeling to think that characters from two different dramas had married one another, Zaitsev from one part of my life and Avanova from a completely different one! And although a beautiful woman she is a crude personality and I don't believe that Zaitsev will stay with her. But it was an interesting encounter with a strong whiff of the past which still, evidently, holds some sway over me. Why is this? Is it because the Revolution has erected such a barrier between me and the past? Or is it that life abroad, far away from Russia, has provoked such a strong desire to recall all that is Russian? Or did it just come from re-reading my diaries? I don't believe it is simply a matter of age.

The performance went on interminably. Diaghilev's box is a centre of attention. Our host, Massenet, came in to ask him if he thought the costumes were good.

10 February

Schubert telephoned. I told him I had met Sonya Avanova and that she had married an acquaintance of mine. Schubert: 'Yes, yes, from Socialist to Monarchist.'

---

1 Close friend and admirer of Nina Koshetz; Prokofiev had come across Avanova in Koshetz's company when they were together in Yessentuki in 1917. See *Diaries*, vol. 2, pp. 216, 217, 275.
2 Kirill Zaitsev had been, for a time, Prokofiev's rival for the affections of Nina Meshcherskaya. Seeming to bear his temporarily victorious opponent no ill will, after the failed elopement Zaitsev had become an admirer of Prokofiev's music and they had struck up a guarded friendship over the bridge table. See *Diaries*, vol. 1, pp. 407–780 *passim*; vol. 2, pp. 3, 55, 57.

I: 'From Socialist?'

Schubert: 'Well, of course. What do you think she was doing sharing a flat with Kerensky?'

The plot thickens!

At three o'clock there appeared Diaghilev, Nouvel, Kokhno and Lifar. As the parts of my fourth number can all be unscrewed and reassembled in any order to suit the demands of the ballet, I had drawn out on a notepad an easily readable diagram of the piece so that Diaghilev could find out where he was at any point. I entitled the diagram 'General Educational Aid'. Diaghilev tore out the page from the pad and swiftly secreted it in his pocket. But we did not get to discuss this number at all. In this way my General Educational Aid served no purpose except to be added to Diaghilev's collection of manuscripts. Neither did we discuss the changes I had made to No. 5 or the new ending of No. 6. All Diaghilev had time to say was that he was pleased with the ending of the ballet (which now has five and a half bars instead of the former four) before Villa-Lobos made his entrance accompanied by a Spanish pianist and a Frenchman. Lobos, evidently, was nervous and endeavoured to boost his sang-froid by sucking on a cigar, the fumes from which penetrated every room in the house. The playing went on for two hours, the Spaniard mangling his way through the elaborate and difficult Lobosian fabrications. There were expansive perspectives, interminable modulations, and just occasionally simple, straightforward melodies with here and there attractive tinges grafted on to them.

Evidently Lobos, not knowing what would appeal to Diaghilev, had decided to set out all his wares, but had not devoted nearly enough attention to his idiosyncratically contoured melodies, which were in fact the only things that stood any chance.

Eventually, at five o'clock, I announced that Poulet's concert, in which my *Oranges* Suite was the second item on the programme, had started, and we had to decide whether we were going to it or not. Lobos, full of apologies, departed with his companions, and we – Diaghilev, Ptashka, Nouvel and I – jumped into a taxi and went to the concert. Diaghilev, muffled up in his beaverskin coat, said, 'He is talented, but has not an ounce of taste. There are some people who lack taste but are redeemed by the size of their talent, just as there are some unintelligent people who are saved by their tact. We have, in fact, one very great composer who lacks taste.'

I: 'You must mean Tchaikovsky.'

Diaghilev: 'No, I am not speaking of Tchaikovsky. Tchaikovsky does not so much lack taste as stand outside any manifestation of taste. I am speaking of Stravinsky. Stravinsky has no taste at all, beginning with the ties and socks he chooses to wear, but he has the gifts of a genius and great intelligence, and that is what saves him.'

Diaghilev is in a phase of disagreement with Stravinsky, otherwise he would never have spoken of him in such terms. Reverting to the subject of Villa-Lobos, I said that in playing such a quantity of music he had not succeeded in discerning what might have been of interest to Diaghilev.

Diaghilev: 'He reminds me of a lady composer who once played me her compositions, *terriblement modernes* as she informed me in her English accent, and when I said to her that they were a bit too modern for me, she was very proud, much prouder than she would have been if I had accepted them. She went about boasting everywhere that her style of music was too *moderne* even for Diaghilev.'[1]

The key to understanding this conversation is this: the term 'modern' in music used to be attached to the search for new harmonies, then moved to the search for beauty in all kinds of insincere contrivances and complexities. More perceptive composers soon tired of this and went back to seeking simplicity – not, however, the old simplicity, but a new one. Diaghilev of course was with this new wave, but composers who were slower on the uptake were still thirled to their constructions and mistaken views of the blind alleys into which they were heading as new horizons of hitherto unsuspected promise. To some extent Lobos belongs to this group: he has several paths out of his predicament but does not know which to take.

We were on time for the concert. I put Diaghilev in the front row of the box with Ptashka, so that the manager could see he was present. Poulet conducted quite well and with spirit, the only section that dragged was the Prince and the Princess. I am not over-fond of this Suite and warned Diaghilev in advance that it is no more than passable, but he was delighted with it and said that he would play it in London during his season there. The work was very warmly received. Backstage afterwards Blois advised me to leave Pleyel and move to Gaveau, who would offer me substantial financial underwriting for concerts. I said, 'But the Gaveau is such an awful piano!' Blois: 'I assure you, they are not much worse than Pleyels, if at all.'

11 February

In the morning I orchestrated some of the sixth number, but not much. Lunch at Dubost's, delicious food but I do not really like lunches while I am working because they cut the day in two and it is hard to do any work

---

1   This anecdote sounds suspiciously as though the lady composer might have been Ethel Smyth, whom Diaghilev was likely to have encountered at the house of the Princesse de Polignac, a generous supporter and promoter of Dame Ethel's music.

in the second half. Arthur Rubinstein had everyone in stitches. One lady said to him, 'You are so ugly, it's incredible!' 'Am I to take that as a declaration of love?' he enquired. 'No,' she replied, 'I mean it in all seriousness.'

The Nabokovs visited us in the afternoon and we were very glad to see them although worried about introducing them to Oleg, knowing that they had recently lost their daughter. But we managed it. They dined with us and we went together to Borovsky's concert, where they gave us seats in the royal box (*loge d'honneur*). Borovsky was not on particularly good form today. We all went to a café afterwards: we, Nabokovs, Borovskys, Lazar and his beautiful wife, and Robert Lyon.[1] The last-named annoyed me and I was brusque with him.

12 February

Orchestrated. Diaghilev phoned and asked to postpone our meeting as there was a powerful frost and he was unwilling to risk coming out on to the street.

Was visited by Blois, who interviewed me for an article, and then Le Flem,[2] who wanted to get to know *Seven, They Are Seven* which the Orchestre Symphonique de Paris is interested in performing. Borovsky also came and I played him excerpts from *Prodigal Son*, which he liked very much, although saying just before the end that he detected in it 'the lucidity of maturity'. This would be a good description of the apotheosis from *Apollo*, but I hope without its tedium. After that we went to have dinner at Prunier. So delicious!

13 February

It was freezing again today, and again the Diaghilev meeting was postponed. It is certainly a very hard frost, and although our apartment has a good heating system it is cold and uncomfortable at the moment. Sofronitsky

---

1 Robert Lyon was the son of Gustave Lyon, legendary Managing Director of Pleyel and the man who had provided Stravinsky with his all-important studio (and private living) space in the Pleyel establishment in the rue Rochechouart, as well as collaborating enthusiastically in his schemes to compose and transcribe works for the Pleyela player-piano. Robert had already begun to play an important part in Stravinsky's career, particularly in America where among other services he had been instrumental in securing the commission for *Apollon musagète* from Mrs Coolidge and the Library of Congress. He was also a key figure in the administration of the Salle Pleyel's and the Orchestre Symphonique de Paris, which had been set up largely under Pleyel's auspices.
2 Paul Le Flem (1881–1984), French (Breton) composer, choral conductor, teacher and critic. Most of his works were written before the First World War, after which there was a long gap before an Indian summer just before the outbreak of the Second World War.

came in the evening and announced with a completely straight face that a chauffeur had frozen to death while at the wheel. The car, apparently, continued on its way, upon which two bystanders chased after it until they managed to dislodge the driver and bring his car to a halt. Amazing! Things are not going well for Sofronitsky, not helped by the fact that he is terminally incompetent at managing his affairs. He borrowed 100 francs from me. He asked whether I had telephoned Arens. I replied, 'Why don't you ring him up, and if he asks about me, tell him I shall be glad to come and look through the Moscow composers' works he has there.'

'I don't have his number.'

I: 'Here it is, on the visiting card he gave me.'

Svyatoslav was looking today at some pictures from Russia of a children's beauty contest, and said, 'Look at all those funny bare ladies!'

14 February

Oleg is two months old today. It is the occasion for our first party of the season, since there has not previously been an opportunity, what with childbirth, its prelude and aftermath. The occasion was exploited to spring-clean the flat, which meant I was prevented from doing any work. Nevertheless, I composed something very valuable *in abstracto* – an Introduction to the Fourth Symphony. I had been trawling through material in the ballet for the purpose, but had not found anything suitable, so created something new, and gained much thereby.

The first guests to arrive were Rubinstein and the Nabokovs; I played them *Choses en soi* and some of the ballet, to the noisy acclaim of all although Rubinstein did not fully grasp the middle section of the first *Chose*. Later came Valechka Bolm, the Sofronitskys, the Samoilenkos and Mme Dubost. Valechka, whose romance with him Dukelsky had blathered on about so much, has grown very pretty but very smarmy. She is an actress and is married to an Englishman. The Nabokovs stayed to dinner and afterwards we went together to the cinema to see a silly film.

15 February

Finished composing the Introduction to the Symphony and orchestrated the fourth number of the ballet. Diaghilev rang up and again asked for our meeting to be postponed until tomorrow. While speaking to him I took the opportunity of telling him how good I thought Nabokov's Overture, which he had played to me the day before. The Overture genuinely has its attractions. Nabokov himself called in again, coming from the rehearsal of his *Ode* which the Orchestre Symphonique de Paris has programmed for this evening. He was complaining that Ansermet had wasted all the rehearsal time on *Le Baiser de la fée*, leaving only enough to skim through *Ode*.

At the concert in the evening *Ode* sounded only mediocre: to blame were the way the composer has orchestrated it, the acoustics of the hall, an inadequate singer, and not enough singers in the chorus. Some parts of the piece are nice, but a lot of it is boring; there should be cuts in performance. It was followed by *Le Baiser de la fée*, during which I sat next to Diaghilev. He set himself to identifying the Tchaikovsky works from which various themes had been taken. Diaghilev: 'The instrumentation sounds like Glazunov.'

I: 'No, if it had been done by Glazunov it would sound fine in any hall, but this would sound better in a room that isn't the kind of barn we are in now.'

Diaghilev: 'What's the use of orchestrating music in such a way that it needs a special hall built for it?'[1]

Nabokov came up and criticised the dreariness of *Le Baiser*, but Diaghilev clearly had found *Ode* no less dreary. Chuckling, he said, 'D'Indy used to go on about *Kitezh* being boring until someone retorted, "Well, D'Indy should know plenty about being boring!"' As much as to remind Nabokov that rather than criticise others for being boring he would do better to make sure his own works do not suffer from this defect!

The last item was *Les Noces*; Nabokov with his wife, I and Ptashka sat at the back of the hall. As always *Les Noces* produced a strong impression on me but Nabokov had chapter and verse about the melodic material having been taken from *Znamenny* chant.[2] Borrowed sources yet again!

16 February

Got up late. It transpires that today Brodsky[3] is playing my Violin Concerto, so this time it was I who telephoned Diaghilev to request a postponement of

---

1 'Tiresome, lachrymose, ill-chosen Tchaikovsky, supposedly orchestrated by Igor in masterly fashion. I say "supposedly", because it sounded drab, and the whole arrangement lacked vitality.' (Diaghilev writing to Lifar on 28 November 1928, trans. Stephen Walsh and quoted in S. Walsh, op. cit., p. 476.)
2 *Znamenny* chant is the melismatic unison singing of liturgical texts used throughout the Russian Orthodox Church until the seventeenth-century reforms of Patriarch Nikon, after which the Church gradually adopted a more Western polyphonic style, *Znamenny* continuing, however, among the Old Believers. Notation is not by means of notes on a stave but by so-called *kryuki* (literally 'hooks') consisting of several components that, in combination, can contain not merely one pitched sound but a series, i.e. a melody, and even beyond that indications of phrasing, mood, spiritual significance and so on.
3 This was not Adolph Brodsky, dedicatee of Tchaikovsky's Violin Concerto following Leopold Auer's dismissal of it as unplayable – he had died in Manchester three weeks earlier. His namesake Jascha Brodsky (1907–1997) had also been born in the Ukraine but had emigrated to Paris in 1926

our meeting; he agreed. Composed the opening of the Andante to the Fourth Symphony (four bars preceding tune) and orchestrated the fifth and sixth numbers of the ballet, but only partially because Diaghilev has still not confirmed his acceptance of the complete music. Brodsky played warmly and with technical assurance, but the orchestral accompaniment was poor. I had the programme open on my knees, in which were printed the names of all the orchestral musicians. Whenever an instrument failed to come in correctly I marked 'cretin' against his name, with Blois sitting alongside watching what I was doing.[1] The tuba blared particularly loudly.

The Samoilenkos invited me to play bridge in the evening, but the other players did not seem very exciting so I stayed at home.

17 February

C.S. Church in the morning, followed by more orchestration. Diaghilev came at five o'clock, this time on his own. He has finally decided to rent an apartment for himself in order to have somewhere to put his collection of antiquarian books, and is also installing Kokhno and Lifar in it. He is trying to secure Matisse to do the settings for *Prodigal Son*, but this is proving difficult as you cannot get access to him: Matisse is the most expensive painter these days, he is painting pictures and putting them in the bank because after his death their prices will immediately jump to ten times their present level. Putting together the two facts that Diaghilev has taken to visiting the circus[2] and that he enquired whether I happened to have a copy of the piano score of *Renard*, I deduce that he is planning to present it. So much for the vaunted prohibition of Stravinsky. And what about *Chout*?

I then played him the pas-de-deux in which he again identified the need for a cut, which I was glad to accept since now I can incorporate the excised passage into the Symphony.[3] As for No. 4, it elicited the expected groans about the music not being good to dance to, that the scenario called for a bellicose kind of number whereas this music did not lend itself to anything

---

to study with Lucien Capet, and a little later with Ysaÿe in Belgium. Eventually he went to America where, like his namesake, he founded a celebrated string quartet – the Curtis Quartet – as well as directing a long-lasting and much respected violin class at the Curtis Institute in Philadelphia.

1 Presumably another Orchestre Symphonique de Paris performance, since Blois worked for Pleyel, the underwriters of the orchestra.
2 Doubtless the Cirque Médrano on the rue Rochechouart, whose stars were the famous Fratellini Brothers, clowns and inspirations for such creations as the Satie–Cocteau *Parade* and Milhaud's *Le Boeuf sur le toit*.
3 Prokofiev's plan for the Fourth Symphony was for its thematic material to consist solely of music that was conceived for but not used in the ballet score for *Prodigal Son*.

particularly distinctive ('of course, any music can have something or other staged to it'). I said, 'On the contrary, I have always considered that in this number there is much eminently danceable music, and if anything really isn't suitable I can take it out for you.'

Diaghilev: 'Not everything that is fast and rhythmically accented is danceable.'

This made me angry. 'I notice that no one pointed this out at the beginning; only when Kokhno could not invent a scenario was it discovered that the music is not good for dancing.'

Diaghilev: 'There's no need for a scenario at this point. All we need is some strong, vivid music because what I want is for it to be danced by the two best dancers. But if there is no brilliant framework for them they will not dance it. I know what will happen: I will give my orders and they will obey, but half an hour before the performance they will suddenly discover they have pulled a tendon and cannot perform.'

At this point the Nabokovs and Suvchinsky appeared as we had arranged to have dinner with them. Diaghilev, leaving, advised me not to think about it for the time being but to finish orchestrating the other sections of the ballet. Then, in a week or so, the new piece would magically compose itself. Irritated, as soon as he had gone I played Nabokov and Suvchinsky the sonata-allegro. They found it both good music and eminently danceable. We went off to eat *bliny* at Aga's, then sat in a Turkish coffee-house where we met an inebriated Schubert. Suvchinsky, upset by the schism in the Eurasian movement,[1] was out of sorts.

18 February

Polished up and orchestrated the pas-de-deux. Went into the publishers, where Paichadze quizzed me about Nabokov, who is moving from another publishing company to ours. The piano score of *Le Pas d'acier* has been published, in a rather disgusting red cover chosen by Paichadze. From the description he had given me of it I was expecting it to be a darker shade. We went to dine at the club where afterwards I played bridge with hardened club gamblers, in a room so frigid that I began shivering from a combination of fright and cold.

---

1 Between the left and right wings of the movement: the former being those who were inclined to be persuaded by the blandishments of emissaries from the Soviet Union offering a popularly based accommodation with the regime (who proved eventually to be OGPU-inspired agents provocateurs from TREST), and those (like Suvchinsky) who were not.

19 February

Got up late (at eleven) and went to collect the car, which is today coming out of the repair shop. It cost me 2,200 francs. Is the insurance company really not going to reimburse me for this?

Lunched at Dubost's, the Nabokovs were there as well. Afterwards we drove out of the city with them. In the evening I caught up on my diary and read. I did no composition or orchestration today.

20 February

Sofronitsky telephoned while I was in the middle of orchestrating this morning. He was at the Embassy where he and Sabaneyev were sorting through music – would I not like to join them? I went in the Ballot – a good thing to turn up at the Soviet Embassy in one's own car. Ran into Sabaneyev at the entrance, and he led me through a maze of staircases and corridors to Arens's office, not forgetting to ask me as we went whether I had read his highly flattering article about me (I had not).

As he had been at Dubost's, Arens was very courteous, speaking Russian with a detectable accent. Piles of publications by Muzsektor[1] were strewn all over the sofas, armchairs and the floor. There was music by new composers, old composers and composers in between. Goedike, Weisberg, Feinberg, Zhitomirsky[2] – none of these could sustain exposure in Paris. I picked out Myaskovsky (not everything by him, however), Shostakovich, Mosolov, Shebalin and Deshevov, and expressed my regret that there was nothing by Popov. I took a few of the scores to show to conductors. Arens was very pleased, but lost no time in telling me that the Embassy wanted to impose on me to play at a reception they were holding on the 5th March. This was precisely what I had been dreading, or at least had been hoping against hope they would not pounce immediately. It was impossible to refuse: my Soviet passport was already out of date and in theory I was existing as an anti-Soviet. I therefore assented, smiling graciously, although I did mention that I detest playing during receptions. Soon after this I went home, giving a ride through the Bois de Boulogne to Sofronitsky and Sabaneyev. At home I

---

1 See above, p. 423, n. 1.
2 Not the critic and musicologist Daniil Zhitomirsky but the composer and teacher Alexandre Zhitomirsky (1881–1937). He had been a student of Lyadov at the St Petersburg Conservatoire, where he later himself taught composition. In the mid-1920s Zhitomirsky was an enthusiastic member of the recently established Leningrad Association of Contemporary Music, intended under the auspices of Leningrad heavyweights such as Asafyev, Andrey Rimsky-Korsakov, Ossovsky, Karatygin, Steinberg and others to be a counterpart to the main Association of Contemporary Music in Moscow and affiliated to the ISCM.

found the Nabokovs and a quite pleasant but insignificant man, a composer called Bazilevsky who had brought the Nabokovs.

In the evening I played bridge at Frieda's[1] with Meyerovich[2] and his wife, a pretty little Irish girl who Ptashka thought was probably Jewish. We reminisced about Japan.

The obligation to perform at the Embassy nagged away at me, and I woke up in the middle of the night thinking about it. It would be most disagreeable if the émigré press prints a story about it and I come in for a lot of abuse. But it is clear that the time is approaching when I shall have to choose: either Russia, or emigration. Faced with this choice, it is clear that it must be Russia.

21 February

Orchestrated and completed No. 5.

The Nabokovs lunched with us; they are leaving for Belgium later today. After lunch we went for a drive into the country. Nabokov was happy that today he has transferred his compositional activities to our publishing house. I read him a small cautionary lecture to the effect that he possesses a real gift for melody but needs to work harder at it: he employs too many formulaically contrived figures. Too many of his ideas also stem from Tchaikovsky. To love Tchaikovsky is an honourable trait, but it is important not to let it degenerate into the sugary-sweet, otherwise he will turn into a neo-Grechaninov. Nabokov heard me out patiently, but said he doubted whether he would be able completely to eliminate all these habits. I said, 'If you work at them continually you will leave them behind, but if you don't you will end up drowning in Grechaninov lemonade.'

In the evening Ptashka was gloomy and complained that I was not paying enough attention to her (I was reading an English detective novel).

22 February

The saga with the Embassy continues to unsettle me. The émigré world will cast their stones, but then I have so little contact with them anyhow.

Finished orchestrating No. 6; the whole work is now orchestrated except the disputed No. 4. But I intend to orchestrate this as well, if not for the ballet then for the Symphony.

---

1 Elfrieda Hansen, sister of the violinist Cecilia Hansen.
2 Alfred Meyerovich (1884–1959), pianist. Prokofiev had met and become friendly with him and his violin-and-piano duo partner Mikhail Piastro, in Japan in 1918. See *Diaries*, vol. 2, pp. 287–97 *passim*.

Was visited by the composer Gradstein,[1] a Polish Jew, who played me some scherzo-like compositions, not devoid of talent. I gave him some pointers.

23 February

Paichadze gave me my publications account for the year 1928. It shows an increase over the previous year: 9,620 marks as against 8,726 for 1927. But closer inspection reveals that sales have fallen (1,398 marks against 1,449 marks) and hires similarly (2,930 marks against 4,153 marks). The overall increase is accounted for by adding in some opera receipts from Russia. For the details I shall have to consult Paichadze. The works whose sales increased rather than decreased were the Violin Concerto, *Tales of an Old Grandmother*, the March from *Three Oranges*, the Sonata No. 5(!), Sonata No. 4 and *Visions fugitives*.

28 February

Svyatoslav had his fifth birthday yesterday but we celebrated it today because the little boys don't go to school on Thursdays. There were ten guests from five to ten years old, of all nationalities. We got the electric train going, and the gramophone, put on colourful paper hats and organised a lottery with silly prizes. Along with chocolate to drink there was a birthday cake with five candles. The younger ones concentrated seriously on eating, the older ones (like Tanya Zakharova) were on their best behaviour and were slightly embarrassed to be wearing the same kind of hats on their heads as the small fry.

3 March

Nothing much happened over the past few days. I worked on the Andante of the Fourth Symphony and orchestrated the Allegro. I proof-read (grinding my teeth the while) the score of *Le Pas d'acier*. Read Tolstoy's *The Cossacks*[2] and enjoyed it very much.

Was at the C.S. Church today, and did not go anywhere this afternoon. Did a little more work on the Andante of the Symphony and read proofs. It still grates on me that I have to play at the Embassy.

---

1 Alfred Gradstein (1904–1954).
2 Novella by Tolstoy, published in 1863.

5 March

My appearance at the Embassy reception continues to throw me off balance, even waking me up at night. I kept imagining frenzied assaults by Monarchists that would cause a scandal in our apartment building. But this morning I took myself in hand and commenced reading C.S., the one sure way of following the path of truth. As always in such circumstances I alighted on a wonderful article which I read through twice and put me in a much more balanced frame of mind.

Sofronitsky called me at half past four in a huge Embassy automobile which, nevertheless, once we were inside it rattled and squeaked like a sleeping car on a Russian train. Sofronitsky, with whom it is never possible to tell whether he is being serious or playing the fool, exclaimed, 'Suppose people think His Excellency is in the car and throw a bomb at it?'

I: 'But there is no ambassadorial flag on the car.'

Sofronitsky: 'Even so, wouldn't it be a good idea to draw the curtains?'

Arriving at the Embassy we passed a few policemen then drove into the courtyard and went inside. I wanted to take my overcoat off in the cloakroom, but Sofronitsky said it would be better to leave them in the Artists' Room. This entailed passing a table where we were asked for our invitations, and as we did not have any were invited to sign our names. Ascending the grand staircase we were met by a gentleman with very black whiskers, who seemed to have some trouble speaking Russian. We introduced ourselves to him and he suggested that we go down again and leave our coats there. We did so, I taking the opportunity to complain at Sofronitsky. At the bottom the throng was already gathering, the aroma of perfume rising from the ladies and the footmen murmuring, 'Oui, monsieur.' Well, that's the Soviet Embassy for you! Up we went once more and this time found the Artists' Room, in fact a drawing room just behind a large hall in which armchairs had been set out in rows and there were two grand pianos. Arens came out to greet us, conducting himself like an old friend. He presented to me various Secretaries of the legation and then took me into another room where the invited guests were gathered. There I met Roussel and Sauguet, Ehrenburg, and also Samoilovich, the man who with Chukhnovsky had rescued Nobile's polar expedition.[1] As his first words were that tomorrow he would be giving

---

1   The ill-fated expedition led by the Italian airship designer and pilot General Umberto Nobile to fly over the North Pole took place in 1928, two years after the semi-rigid airship the *Norge*, designed and piloted by Nobile, had been the vehicle for Roald Amundsen's successful bid for this hitherto unachieved goal (the claim by the American Richard E. Byrd to have done this a few weeks earlier has never been finally verified or dismissed but seems unlikely on the basis of the demonstrably altered log of sextant readings coupled with the known maximum airspeed capabilities of his Fokker F-VII aeroplane). There is no question that the *Norge* did fly over the

his two hundredth talk about his polar exploits, I took care to avoid any mention of what clearly bored him to distraction and veered into music, in which he displayed a commendable knowledge of my compositions. Beside him stood his wife, a lady of deeply provincial aspect.

Arens asked me to begin playing, saying that two chords would be enough to quieten the public down. Sofronitsky and I went over to the two pianos, but as we were doing so I was buttonholed by Sikar, the dictator who presides over the issuing of French visas. He launched into a string of compliments, which gladdened my heart because now I shall be able to arrange French visas for all and sundry. We played the Schubert Waltzes on two pianos; the audience in the hall listened quite well, but noise came through from the adjacent room where guests were still arriving. Later, however, when Brodsky was playing and Kubatskaya[1] was singing, it was very noisy. Kubatskaya told me that Stalin had been present at my concert in Moscow and afterwards had referred, not without pride, to 'our Prokofiev'. This is splendid: now I can go to Russia with nothing to fear. I then played solo some of my pieces, to which a score or so listened attentively while the buzz of conversation continued from the next room. Nevertheless, I decided to pay my dues to

---

Pole, in which case it would have been the first to do so, but the subsequent row over whether the triumph should be attributed primarily to Norway (Amundsen) or to Italy (Nobile) became so rancorous that at Mussolini's urging Nobile was pressured into designing and leading a second, indisputably all-Italian, airship (unsurprisingly named the *Italia*) and expedition. On the way back from the Pole on 25 May 1929 the *Italia* ran into a storm and crashed onto a drifting ice floe, leaving thereon the wreckage of its gondola with ten men (one of whom was killed on impact) and, miraculously, some supplies and radio equipment. The main body of the ship, with nothing to hold it down or steer it, disappeared into the air with six men trapped on board. No trace of the six or the envelope was ever found but a huge international mission was mounted to find and rescue the nine on the ice, not least by Amundsen who at the cost of his own life (the flying boat on which he was travelling was also lost without trace) put aside his rivalry to rescue his opponent and his men. These included besides Nobile the Swedish meteorologist Professor Malmgren. Both of them were injured with broken limbs, but Malmgren and two others set off on foot. Realising that his weakness and injuries were diminishing any chance of his companions' survival, Malmgren in an echo of Captain Oates insisted that they carry on without him, which they did and were rescued almost a month later by the famous First World War air ace Boris Chukhnovsky (1898–1975) who spotted them on a reconnaissance flight in a Junkers from the Soviet icebreaker *Krasin*. Chukhnovsky himself crashed on the return flight to the *Krasin* and was alone on the ice without food or shelter for five days, but was able to direct the icebreaker to the stranded men by radio, insisting that they be rescued before him or his aircraft. Professor Rudolf Samoilovich (1881–1939), eminent geologist and Arctic explorer, Director of the Institute for Far Northern Studies, was on board the *Krasin* in overall charge of the Soviet mission to rescue Nobile and his colleagues. A somewhat highly coloured account of the disaster and the rescue was the subject of the joint Italo-Soviet 1969 movie *The Red Tent*, directed by Mikhail Kalatozov, starring Peter Finch as Nobile, Sean Connery as Amundsen, Nikita Mikhalkov as Chukhnovsky, Grigory Gai as Samoilovich, not forgetting Claudia Cardinale providing the love interest as the beautiful nurse Valeria.

1 Siranush Kubatskaya (1890–1952), soprano, the sister of Levon Atovmyan.

those who were listening, and played four small pieces decently enough. At the end the audience surged up and shouted 'encore!'

Heading for the buffet I encountered Mayakovsky, just in from Moscow, and Lukyanov (a former 'Sokol'[1] acquaintance who had escaped from Russia on the same boat[2] as Boris Bashkirov but later executed a volte-face and was now employed in the Soviet telegraphic agency in Paris). I asked him if making a run for it on the boat had been as terrifying as Bashkirov's description made it seem? He replied that yes, it had been a searing experience, but Bashkirov had been the most frightened of all of them. Arens then introduced me to a very stylish gentleman in his fifties wearing the rosette of the Légion d'honneur, who at once gushingly eulogised my music, saying that he played all of it on the piano. Afterwards I asked Arens who he was. Arens told me he was Adjutant-General Count Ignatiev and, seeing the dumbfounded expression on my face added, 'He's one of us now.' Also present at the reception were the German Ambassador and several French government ministers. Arens regretted that I had come without my wife and expressed the hope that at some time I would be able to play for him personally, as on this occasion he had been too busy receiving his guests to hear anything of my performance.

I returned home stocked with impressions aplenty and even with a smile on my face. This reception with its French and German grandees, Count Ignatiev, the impressive vistas of the Russian Embassy's splendid apartments still retaining the gold crowns on the walls, displayed every appearance of high style. Ptashka listened to my account with interest and was sorry she had not accompanied me.

In the evening we attended a concert of music by Stravinsky. This being, apparently, the fifth such evening of his works this season, the audience to hear the Octet, the Serenade, the Sonata and *L'Histoire du soldat* was not numerous. I derived pleasure, more or less, from the first movement of the Sonata, a few things in the Octet and one or two moments, not many, in the *Soldier's Tale*. At the end of the programme we went back to see him, and after some conversation about our children and Stravinsky's wish to come to see them, he asked, 'Well, Seryozha, did you like what you heard today?' Hesitating slightly, I said, 'Much of it.' 'But not all?' enquired Stravinsky, a little hesitantly in turn. 'Best of all for me was the Allegro of the Sonata,' I managed, and then went on about how difficult it is both to play and conduct in the same concert, and how much I had appreciated the economy of his

---

1 International sporting and gymnastic organisation of which Prokofiev had been a committed member in St Petersburg; he even composed a march for the movement. See *Diaries*, vol. 1, p. 187, and *passim*.
2 Crossing the Gulf to Finland.

gestures when conducting the Octet. We parted with the promise that he would come to see my sons. Secretly I was pleased at having with total decorum landed a blow on Stravinsky.

6 March

Occasionally, from driving the car and working the heavy pedals, I get a stomach-ache. Apparently this is known as 'automobile sickness'. I worked hard on myself today to deal with it.

7 March

A new theme came to me for the fourth number of the ballet, the section of the work most in contention. I do not yet know whether the theme is good, but in any case it is not an everyday sort of tune.

8 March

The émigré press is carrying reports of the Embassy reception mentioning my part in it. *Latest News* is unexceptionable, but the right-wing *Vozrozhdenie* (*Renaissance*) is malicious, calling me a rubber doll, which is an unpleasant image to be featured in a newspaper. Another page of the same edition has an announcement that Professor Alexinsky's[1] Monarchist Group has decided to recognise Prince Oldenburg[2] as Emperor; this they do in all seriousness, evidently failing to appreciate the operetta-like nature of such a pretentious declaration.

What can have been the émigré press's source for the details of the reception? For naturally they cannot possibly have had a correspondent there. Subsequently it emerged that the smear had originally been written by a French hack, writing under the name Candide, whose girlfriend had been present, and the Russian papers seized on it to reprint. *Latest News* delicately omitted the rubber doll, but *Renaissance* had everything in full. It was not long before Schubert was on the phone telling me he had laughed like a

---

1 See above, p. 752.
2 Prince Alexander Oldenburg (1844–1932), surviving son of Prince Peter of Oldenburg, who among other accomplishments had been a competent composer (Clara Schumann, no less, had his Second Piano Concerto in her repertoire); a ballet score he wrote for Petipa contained a pas-de-deux which the choreographer recycled for *Le Corsaire*, in which form it is still heard today. Alexander's son, the homosexual Prince Peter (grandson of his namesake), contracted a *mariage blanc* with the Grand Duchess Olga Alexandrovna Romanova, youngest daughter of Tsar Alexander III and sister of Nicholas II, thus although the marriage was eventually dissolved on grounds of non-consummation his elderly father's link to the Imperial family could be considered decisive for the purpose.

drain, followed by the Samoilenkos, who were more diplomatic. They circled round the subject, without actually referring to the reception, and invited us to dinner. Altogether the incident did upset me, although I had brought it on myself. Those three days of silence from the papers and the impressive effect of the reception itself had lulled me into a false sense of security.

Ptashka was also upset. I read C.S. to calm myself, but took the precaution of secreting *Prodigal Son* away in an inaccessible corner in case the Monarchists should come round to make a scene and tear up the manuscript. At dinner with the Samoilenkos no questions were asked, the conversation was confined to other more pleasant and interesting matters and the sore point was kept away from – nobody mentioned it.

9 March

Finished No. 4 of the ballet, but am still not convinced it is successful.

Met Stravinsky at the publishers. 'I hear wonderful things about your ballet,' he opened, and went on to say that he would like to come to my house to listen to it. I replied that I would much rather play him *Choses en soi*. Stravinsky then surprised me by praising the Violin Concerto (why that, of all things, I cannot understand) and asked me to inscribe a copy of *Le Pas d'acier*, even though I know he particularly dislikes it. In short, he did everything the opposite of what one would expect. He had recently read an interview with Richard Strauss, who declared that nowadays the only composers are to be found not in France but in Germany and Russia. Stravinsky: 'To which I would propose an amendment: only in Russia, and even there only Stravinsky and Prokofiev.' I laughed and turning to Paichadze added, 'In other words only those who are at this moment in your office, so take care the ceiling doesn't collapse.'

When Stravinsky had left Paichadze shared with me his impressions of the effect my appearance at the Embassy had had on the Russian colony. In the intervals of continual phone calls, Paichadze said, 'I stick up for you, of course, and tell everyone that Prokofiev was asked five times to do this, and simply could not go on refusing, as he has plans to visit Russia.'

When I got home there was a telephone call from Diaghilev. Negotiations have completely broken down with Matisse and the settings will be commissioned from Rouault.[1] I have not heard of Rouault, but Diaghilev

---

1 Georges Rouault (1871–1958), painter and lithographer associated with Fauvism and Expressionism. The characteristic black outlines and luminous colouring of Rouault's painting may have stemmed from his early apprenticeship in stained glass, and are certainly appropriate to the predominantly Christian subject-matter of his mature work. From today's perspective, the choice of Rouault to provide the visual setting for *The Prodigal Son* seems inspired, even predestined.

says that he is top-drawer. As, however, he tends to say of whomever he settles upon.

10 March

C.S. Church. I had a headache, so went for a walk in the Bois de Boulogne. It was heavenly spring weather, so the idea of a long motor trip was very attractive. Because of my headache and the walk I did not manage to put the finishing touches to the fourth number, nor to practise playing it through on the piano in preparation for Diaghilev's visit. Celia called in; she is in Paris for a few days between two concert tours. Boris is still in Shanghai. Celia let slip that she enjoys travelling alone.

Around five o'clock Diaghilev appeared, accompanied by Kokhno and Lifar. I played No. 4, stumbling and making mistakes as it was written out on manuscript paper that already had multiple crossings-out. Personally I did not like it very much, but Diaghilev and company were pleased with it, asked for one passage to be cut, and overall judged it excellent, ready to be orchestrated. At this point Rouault was announced, a red-faced gentleman in his mid-fifties, somewhat toad-like in appearance. I played the entire ballet including the new number – its first complete, integrated performance. While I was playing Diaghilev explained various details of the drama in a loud voice; the chattering did not particularly bother me since Diaghilev had warned me that Rouault has no understanding of music and the play-through was merely for form's sake. During the final number I noticed that Rouault had fallen very quiet and was breathing heavily, as if asleep. When the performance was over he began to speak of a rose-coloured minaret that he was thinking of for the decor, then about Matisse and about Moreau,[1] while Diaghilev told a story about having invited Renoir to his box for a performance of the Ballets Russes, to which Renoir had come attired in a black frock-coat, red knitted gloves and a cap with an inordinately long peak. Ptashka noticed that Rouault was wearing new patent-leather shoes, but his socks were falling down and wrinkled, and in one place his flesh could be seen through a hole. As we were saying goodbye it emerged that in ten days' time Diaghilev wanted to take Rouault to Monte Carlo, as in Paris people will not leave him in peace to work. 'Splendid,' I cried. 'I'll take you there in my car.' At this the company dispersed, and Diaghilev invited Ptashka and me to lunch tomorrow so that afterwards we could go to look at Rouault's paintings.

---

1 Rouault had been Gustave Moreau's student at the Ecole des Beaux-Arts, and on his mentor's death had been appointed Curator of the Musée Moreau in Paris.

11 March

The age-old question: does God exist or not? takes on a different meaning if it is posed in a different way: is there or is there not a consciousness behind the creation of the natural world? The atheist, obviously, is convinced there is no such consciousness. But if it is accepted that creation is a conscious act, it follows this must be the work of God! There are some inconsistencies in the theories of atheists: how can it be that the consciousness-free creation of the natural world finds it possible to include within itself the elements that combine to make the conscious human being? And when conscious man becomes aware of this, it transpires that he is not as intelligent as unconscious nature, before which he continually stands in astonishment and awe and learns from it. This is a shameful and stupid conclusion. And yet, how elegant and well-proportioned the universe becomes, the moment the notion of intelligent creation is accepted.

In the morning, while I was working on the orchestration of the new fourth number, I received a pneumatic post letter,[1] a most inefficient and complicated system, from Rouault. He would like to come in the car to Monte Carlo, and not only himself but his trunks and his daughter. At lunch with Diaghilev I tried to persuade him to come with us, as I was not sure that without his presence I would be able to endure the great artist's toad-like company! Diaghilev, however, cannot stand travelling by car and point-blank refused. After lunch we looked at pictures by Rouault, gloomy and unappealing. But some of the lineaments and colours made me think that he might be able to produce severe, yet colourful scenery and costumes to go with a biblical subject.

12 March

Telephoned Stravinsky (he had rung me yesterday when I was not at home) to ask when he might be free to come and listen to my ballet. Yesterday at lunch Diaghilev had told me, 'Yes, yes, Stravinsky was telling me you have been pleading with him to come and listen to *Prodigal Son*,' so now I decided no, not on your life – I would play it to him but not right away. Therefore on the phone today I told him I was working on the conclusion of the ballet (quite true) and would be happy to play it for him but as late

---

1 Pneumatic postal systems, invented and developed in the nineteenth century, were still in use in some cities – Paris, Berlin, Prague, New York, even London for strictly limited and private use in the City – until after the end of the Second World War. Cylinders containing letters, bills, receipts, cheques, etc., were propelled along underground tubes from point to point. Paris, for example, had a total of 467 kilometres of pneumatic postal tubing and La Poste produced special stationery to fit inside the cylinders.

as possible before he goes away: when would that be? Friday, apparently. 'Well, what about Friday afternoon?' I asked. Stravinsky agreed, and added in a fatherly post-scriptum, 'You do your work, Seryozha, that's the best thing. I will ring you again on Friday morning and keep all après-midi free for you.'

So, obviously he is very anxious to hear the ballet. It would be ideal if I can have already sent it to Diaghilev by Friday afternoon!

During the afternoon I received another missive from Rouault, once more on the subject of the car journey. Diaghilev commented, 'All his life he has been slaving away in a cellar, et maintenant il a découvert le luxe!'[1] (cars, sunshine and so on).

Dined at de Noyelle's, an exclusive affair, full evening-dress, high-ranking officials from the French Foreign Ministry. The most elevated knowledge of art and music mixed with bourgeois narrow-mindedness and tedium.

13 March

This morning, when I was orchestrating No. 4, Fatma Hanum telephoned to ask me to dinner, unexpectedly they are entertaining today Stravinsky and Paichadze. My initial reaction was of reluctance to spend time with Stravinsky, but I fought with myself and conquered my negative feelings. And indeed it turned out to be a very jolly meal, the 'pocket Sabaoth' himself unassuming and charming. From the outset he was full of praise for the dill vodka because of the delicious burps it gives rise to, then went on to rhapsodise over the wine of precisely such-and-such a year, and the cheese, all of which was indeed most mouth-wateringly presented by Mme Samoilenko with onion juice and cognac on the side.

Our relations were friendly and completely free from strain, and this was a source of great pleasure to me, but even if you were to cut me with a knife I still cannot entirely trust Stravinsky's sincerity!

In the afternoon we took the Ballot out into the country, the last few days have been so sunny and the spring air so entrancing, but the countryside is still brown, there is so little green it is more like autumn than spring.

14 March

Finished the orchestration of No. 4 and also the piano score. The ballet is thus completely finished, this time for good. Thanks be to God.

---

1 'and now he has discovered luxury!'

15 March

Did a little work on the Andante of the Fourth Symphony. Played the piano in preparation for Brussels. Went shopping for a car trunk. Hurrying home, I found Stravinsky and Sudeikina already there, being entertained by Ptashka. I played the two *Choses en soi*; Stravinsky approved of the first ('interesting technique') but found the second one more conventionally Prokofievan. Suvchinsky then arrived and I played *Prodigal Son* from start to finish. Stravinsky sat with his nose buried in the other copy of the score.

Previously, everyone to whom I played *Prodigal Son* had responded enthusiastically to it, so I was very surprised that Stravinsky confined himself to polite but meaningless compliments. Suvchinsky said nothing except a quiet 'wonderful piece'.

Afterwards we went to eat *bliny* in the Russian restaurant but Stravinsky, although amiable, was more subdued than he had been at the Samoilenkos. As we parted he again thanked me for playing, and invited me, when I am in Monte Carlo, to visit him in Nice, whither he is off tomorrow. Altogether this encounter with Stravinsky left me with a sour taste in my mouth, and even more so for Ptashka, who commented, 'It was a bad idea to play the ballet to him; his desire to hear it was merely to give him the wherewithal to criticise it.'

16 March

At noon I called on Diaghilev to give him the completed piano score of the *Son*, and to collect my cheque for 5,000 francs. Diaghilev was radiant: he had just come off the telephone to Stravinsky discussing the latter's impressions of yesterday. In Stravinsky's opinion the new ballet showed no sign of my having taken any steps forward; the music was no different from what I had been writing before. He, Stravinsky, had no wish to criticise or reproach me, there was no question that alone among contemporary composers I composed music he could listen to and respect, nevertheless his opinion having been sought he felt it his duty to express it honestly.

Diaghilev asked, 'Do you really find the technique in this work no different from that of previous ones?'

Stravinsky replied that this might possibly be so in certain respects, but all the same it was not better than *Chout*, and one of the best things Prokofiev had ever done was – the Violin Concerto.

I exploded: 'But when it was premiered in 1923 there was no more devastating criticism of it than that from Stravinsky and his group!' (the group at the time including Diaghilev).

Diaghilev proceeded with his rehearsal of the Stravinsky critique. 'Prokofiev has no sense of the contemporary ethos; his melodies still have that baroque cast to them whereas today's melodic style aims at a classical purity of line.'

'How dare Stravinsky criticise my melodies,' I shrieked, 'when he is incapable of composing two bars of a tune himself?! Does he really think the tune that ends *Prodigal Son* is baroque? Or does he believe the one that concludes *Apollo*, which is taken straight from Schumann and Wagner, an example of a true melodic gift?'

'A classical melody', put in Kokhno waspishly, 'can only be one that bears the imprint of an irreproachably prescribed model' – thereby insinuating the charge of derivation at all the themes in *Apollo*.

Diaghilev: 'But at least he was kinder about one of the piano pieces you played him yesterday (*Chose en soi* No. 1). Which was that?'

I: 'The one I played to you in the autumn, and you said it was dry.'

Diaghilev smiled: 'There you are, then, that is why Stravinsky liked it.'

This whole conversation had given him enormous pleasure. Diaghilev had had a bone to pick with Stravinsky ever since *Behzeh*,[1] written not for him but for Idka, so was delighted not only that my ballet had occasioned such a venomous response from Stravinsky but that to justify his spite he had had to resort to such incredible sophisms. He asked me to sign the copy of the piano score I had presented to him; I did so and wrote that the ballet was dedicated to Diaghilev. He was clearly flattered by this, more so than by the two other ballets I had dedicated to him, and said that he was especially pleased since *Prodigal Son* was his favourite among my works. He kissed me and we parted until Monte Carlo.

In the afternoon I went to see Paichadze to collect money and began relating to him the exchange I had had earlier in the day with Diaghilev. I had only just got a few words out when who should appear in his office but Stravinsky. Biting my tongue in mid-sentence, I asked Stravinsky, 'How have you been after the *bliny* yesterday?'

Stravinsky: 'Excellent. I really overate at lunch.' Then, turning to Paichadze, 'All we ever seem to do is eat and eat, drink and drink! Thank God, Lent is coming up.'

'When exactly is Lent?' I enquired.

Stravinsky: 'Oh, you Russian atheist! It starts the day after tomorrow, for heaven's sake!'

(Nice, isn't it? We all stuff ourselves, but I'm the atheist!)

---

1   *Le Baiser de la fée* – *The Fairy's Kiss*.

Stravinsky prepared to take his leave, as his train leaves in a few hours for Nice. 'Well, Seryozha, you must definitely come to visit when you go to Monte Carlo.'

I: 'Certainly, and I hope you will play me some of the Second Concerto.'

Stravinsky stuttered, 'Maybe yes, maybe no, it will depend on how I feel,' and then added, 'but you must definitely come, ring up and come over.'

I replied, in a similar tone of voice, 'Maybe yes, maybe no, depends how I feel.'

Stravinsky hurled himself at me and playfully grasped me by the throat. 'Well, all right then, I will play one movement for you, but it is still in a very raw state, and you must promise not to tell anyone about it.'

On this we said goodbye and Stravinsky departed.

18 March

At eleven o'clock in the morning I left for Brussels on the non-stop express, which consists exclusively of Pullman coaches. I was in second class, but in Pullman that is also very comfortable. On the way I consulted an automobile road map to see the route the train was taking. It was a wonderful, sunny day, but the vegetation was still sere and dead-looking.

In Brussels I was met by Putzeys, the impresario. The best he could say of the ticket sales was that they were moderate: enough to cover my fee but my other expenses will represent a loss. He is handing out complimentary tickets to make the hall look respectable.

I have not performed in public since last May, and before that the preceding January, but over the past weeks I have been practising conscientiously, so my playing was up to standard and I did not suffer too much from nerves. The only place that really worried me was the chromatic section of the second *Chose en soi*, but that too passed without incident. The *Choses en soi* – their first performance – were not badly received, but there was applause in places where they should not have been any, during the Prelude from Op. 12 and the March from *Oranges*, which I played as an encore. This provoked much noisy shouting, and demands for it to be played again. At the end of the concert, with which I was generally satisfied, half-a-dozen assorted well-wishers came back to see me, after which I went to have dinner in a small German-style pub.

19 March

Did not sleep as long as I should have liked, because at six o'clock a bell went off just opposite my door.

Did a number of small errands: went to see Putzeys (mentioned Ptashka and Sofronitsky and collected my cheque), then to Le Boeuf,[1] with whom I discussed an orchestral appearance next season. Called on Napravnik, son of the conductor, who has a music shop and a daughter with an extraordinary resemblance to her celebrated grandfather.

At four o'clock I made my way to the Monnaie, as previously agreed with Spaak.[2] I had imagined that they would have something to show me or at least something to discuss, but the opposite was the case: they simply exploited my visit to make me play through the whole opera while De Thoran[3] followed from the score. From time to time I asked Spaak to translate what was being said: an assistant conductor, or he may have been a répétiteur, who had obviously gone through the score with a fine-tooth comb, sat beside me and kept saying things like, 'You are playing this passage faster than it is written . . .' On top of this, heaven knows when I last played *The Gambler*, and I kept getting completely muddled with the French text, so all in all it was a most harrowing experience.

When I had played through the first two acts we broke for a meal, during which I equipped myself with the score so that I could look through it, and in the evening I played the rest of the opera. The premiere is scheduled for the 29th April, obviously designed to beat the Leningrad production to the post. I immediately sent off an open letter to Asafyev alerting him, and via him the management, to this threat, taking the opportunity to castigate the latter as a bunch of dilatory idlers for letting slip the chance of the world premiere. I wanted to write this on a postcard of the Monnaie, but the building does not look particularly impressive outside so I judged it might attenuate its effect.

20 March

I had hoped they would let me hear some singers today, but they had not yet sufficiently conned their parts. Thus, having no further business in Brussels, I left at nine o'clock and was home in time for lunch. Had a most joyful reunion with Ptashka.

21 March

Began orchestrating the slow beginning of the Fourth Symphony. Read proofs of the Quintet.

---

1 See above, p. 3.
2 Paul Spaak (1876–1936), writer, member of the Académie royale de langue et de la littérature françaises de Belgique, Intendant of the Théâtre de la Monnaie.
3 Corneil de Thoran (1881–1953), Belgian conductor, Music Director of the Monnaie.

Svyatoslav has had his hair cut, which does not suit him at all. Oleg is trying to articulate a few words. He is a lovely little boy, who laughs amazingly often.

Dukelsky arrived from London in the evening. The tour of his operetta in the English provinces has brought him in some money, which he proposes to spend on travelling to America, partly to see his mother but mainly to try to get a commission for another operetta. Strangely, his turn towards the world of operetta and his lack of success in serious music has made him less interesting. All the same we chatted until midnight and I went out with him to have supper, which made Ptashka cross.

22 March

Played Dukelsky the first movement of the Fourth Symphony. He approved: 'Written in the best of your styles.' But when I told him of the Symphony's provenance, from the music of *Prodigal Son*, his disapproval grew heated: 'A ballet is a ballet and a symphony is a symphony. To combine dance music with purely symphonic music is the height of ignorance!'

I: 'In principle I agree with you. On this occasion it was only because there was quite a lot of undeveloped material left over from the finished ballet, and some ideas that it had not been possible to include, and I was reluctant to waste them. But my main justification would be that when I played the Symphony to you, you found it good, and it did not occur to you that it was half-brother to a ballet; and when I played the ballet to Diaghilev, who does not know the Symphony, he considered it the best of my ballets, and you must grant that Diaghilev knows quite a bit about ballet! The point is that everything depends on the composer's skill in using his material, and it may be that it was in demonstrating this I particularly wished to shine.'

I played Dukelsky only the first movement, but the second is to all intents and purposes nearly finished as well.

25 March–7 April

(rough notes)

Ptashka and I, just the two of us, set out at eleven o'clock in the morning, and went round to join up with the Chalons.[1] Their car with all the dogs. Ready to leave only by two o'clock. Bad headache. Lunched at Fontainebleau, though my bad head meant I did not feel up to much. After lunch the

---

1 Jean Chalon was a friend of Alexander Borovsky.

Chalons had a puncture. At their recommendation we went ahead, agreeing to meet up at Bligny. The elderly secretary. Could not get as far as Bligny owing to my headache. Stopped for the night near Avallon in a picturesque village. Although it is spring the weather is still cold: we had a fire which stayed in almost all night, lighting up the room, and got going again in the morning while we had coffee. Very nice. Reached Bligny where we waited for the Chalons, but they telephoned to say they had had a second breakdown, so we decided we had to press on without them. Stayed the night in Lyons in a good hotel. On the 27th continued our journey south along the banks of the Rhône, quite fast, in fact set a new record of 110 k.p.h. Ptashka and I are getting on very well except for one small disagreement: she does not like getting up early in the morning so we do not leave before ten, and I do not like driving at dusk. We stopped soon after 6 p.m. but she would have liked to go on further. Spent the night in Aix-en-Provence (Milhaud's town, all the trappings of a spa resort). A lovely place. On the 28th we arrived on the shores of the Mediterranean and had lunch by the sea at Saint-Raphaël. The sea is blue and the sun beginning to warm up. Beyond this the drive was tiring, the road very twisty. Arrived in Monte Carlo at four o'clock. We were afraid that in Easter week everywhere would be full, but we found a good room with bath and a view of the sea at the Albion, where the year before I had stayed with Dukelsky. Expensive, however. After a wash and brush-up we strolled to the post office, and then to the Salle de jeux of the Casino. Neither Ptashka nor I had the slightest desire to gamble. It was boring and enervating in the Salle de jeux, although the faces of some of the gamblers were twitching with the strain. In the evening went to the Hôtel de Paris and left a note for Diaghilev. Met Rouault who was delighted to see me and spoke incomprehensibly but at length; he walked us back to our hotel.

I had planned to stay three days in Monte Carlo but Ptashka liked it very much and Diaghilev wanted us to stay as well, so we stayed there a week. The weather was marvellous all the time. As for *Prodigal Son*, all I did was coach the pianist in the right tempi for the forthcoming rehearsals because at present the company was rehearsing a ballet by Rieti[1] and Stravinsky's *Renard* – alas for *Chout*, *Baika*[2] had been chosen instead. The pianist was very busy and Kokhno had not seen fit to give him my piano score in advance, so he could only pick away at it pretty feebly. Diaghilev was alternately charming and impenetrable. Our group also included Rouault, a somewhat

---

1 *Le Bal*, to a libretto by Kokhno based on a story by Sologub, choreographed by Balanchine, sets and costumes by de Chirico.
2 The Russian title, taken from Afanasiev, is *Baika pro lisu, petukha, kota da barana* (*The Tale of the Fox, the Cock, the Tomcat and the Ram*).

primitive individual although by no means as repellent as he had first appeared, Lifar, Kokhno and Pavka, a delightful old man, Diaghilev's cousin (known as '*l'aieul*').[1] All of them became very fond of Ptashka and towards the end of our stay even kissed her hand (they were Diaghilev's boys, after all!). We lunched and dined several times with Diaghilev. On one occasion he was forty-five minutes late; we settled ourselves at another table and when he turned up resisted all his persuasions to join him, having our lunch on our own. But when I went to pay the bill I found Diaghilev had already paid it. At that we did go over to his table. 'Very kind,' I said, 'now you are entertaining me at a separate table, as if I were in the kitchen.'

Diaghilev: 'Because of your capricious behaviour.'

Other acquaintances who were in Monte Carlo were Shteiman[2] and his wife. Also Celia, who was playing a concert there: rumour has it she and Zakharov are divorcing. In the end I got bored being idle in Monte Carlo, although I did orchestrate some of the first movement of the Fourth Symphony and also planned out the finale, although I am not sure it will survive in that form; I shall have to put it to one side and look at it again in a fortnight or so.

As Stravinsky had asked me to telephone him, I did so but did not catch him in. He rang back later, but they were suffering a bout of belated 'flu and I should phone again in two days. But since it was clear from the telephone conversation that he was not going to play me any of the Second Concerto, I did not do so.

---

1 'Grandpa'. Pavel Koribut-Kubitovich was in fact Diaghilev's first cousin, the son of his mother's sister-in-law Maria (Marisha), and despite his venerable appearance a mere six years his senior. When Diaghilev's mother died after giving birth to him in 1872, Marisha, along with the much loved nurse Dunya (immortalised in Bakst's 1906 portrait of Diaghilev with his Nanny), took charge of the baby until his father remarried two years later and the infant Sergey acquired a stepmother, Yelena. Cousin Pavel, and until she died (not long after the Bakst painting) the Nanny, remained throughout his life Diaghilev's closest companions from his childhood. Tamara Karsavina, in the Epilogue she added in 1947 in the revised edition of her memoir *Theatre Street*, writes of Pavka as follows: 'No doubt it was not his faculty alone for utilising human material that made Diaghilev's association with his cousin close and permanent . . . He loved goodness of heart and simplicity. He was genuinely fond of those with whom he surrounded himself. It occurs to me from some of his casual remarks that in his self-imposed expatriation Pavka supplied for him that bit of home atmosphere which made a link with his original background.' (T. Karsavina, *Theatre Street*, Dance Books, London, 1981.) According to the writer Pyotr Pertsov (1868–1947), Dunya (Avdotya Alexandrovna Zuyeva), 'with her brown clothes and unhurried movements brought to Diaghilev's metropolitan and "decadent" apartment the style and cosiness of an old-world country landowner's estate. This feeling was enhanced when the master of the house himself sometimes dropped his "Napoleonic" persona and appeared at the tea-table in just a dressing-gown like Oblomov's – an elegant, flowered one, to be sure.' (P. Pertsov, *Literaturniye Vospominaniya 1890–1902* (*Literary Reminiscences*), Academia, Moscow, 1934). See above, p. 202.

2 See above, p. 550.

On the 4th April Ptashka and I set out on the return journey by car. We called at the Stravinsky house in Nice, but he was not at home – apparently he was just then on his way to Monte Carlo. He lives in a large house with a garden on the outskirts of Nice, with a view of the sea.[1]

From Nice we took the road to Grasse, a most beautiful place in the mountains but with a view through them to the sea. Grasse is a centre for the manufacture of perfumes, so we bought some. From Grasse the road climbed higher to the pass, where the wind was so cold it cut you like a knife. Nearing Digne we joined the road I had been on the previous year (with Dukelsky) but we did not go as far as the town, turning left and stopping for the night at Forcalquier. Here we found a small, old-fashioned hotel with massive walls. Our room had a bedroom opening off it with no windows. But we were happy about this, because in the intense cold it was warmer like that.

Pressing on next morning we reached Avignon and turned north along the Rhône, then to make a change in our route turning left to Vichy. Climbing to 1,200 metres we ran into snow. Surrounded by white, we took photographs of each other. Spent the night at Saint-Galmier where Ptashka drank the waters. Tiny place though it is, it boasts a new and luxurious hotel. Next morning, the 6th, we pressed on and lunched in Vichy, after passing the excavations on a narrow little road through Glozel.[2] The weather was just like March in Russia: thawing snow, streams, mud, beautiful and cold. Everything is still closed in Vichy, but to reward ourselves after a difficult

---

1 The Villa des Roses in the rue Carnot, which Stravinsky had bought in August 1924, but 'at what a price!!! I do not even dare to type it,' as he wrote to Ramuz. (See S. Walsh, op. cit., p. 393.)
2 In 1924 a seventeen-year-old boy called Emile Fradin while ploughing on his grandfather's farm accidentally stumbled on an underground chamber containing human bones and ceramic fragments. A local doctor and amateur archaeologist, Antonin Morlet, identified the artefacts as of Neolithic and medieval origin, published a paper co-authored with Emile, and provoked a furore in professional archaeological circles. In December 1927 René Dussaud, Curator of Antiquities at the Louvre, supported by Félix Regnaud, President of the French Prehistoric Society, declared the whole site and its contents a fake and accused Emile Fradin of fraud. In January 1928 Fradin counter-sued for defamation. The controversy became known as the Dreyfus Affair of archaeology. At the time when the Prokofievs were at Glozel the case was about to come to trial: Fradin was found guilty in June 1929 but two years later the verdict was reversed on appeal and the following year Dussaud was found guilty of defamation. The most controversial finds on the site are the so-called 'Glozel tablets': around a hundred ceramic tablets bearing inscriptions in something like the Phoenician alphabet. If they genuinely are Neolithic, Glozel would be evidence that Neolithic man had a script, and his intellectual development would be entirely re-evaluated. The jury is still out, but most experts now believe that although Emile Fradin was neither a fraud nor a forger, the site is probably Gallo-Roman with some later, medieval enrichment. Emile Fradin died in February 2010 at the age of 103. See *Carnets Secrets*, 2007, http://www.philipcoppens.com/glozel.html.

journey we treated ourselves to an expensive restaurant meal before continuing on our way to Bourges (a famous cathedral, which we visited cursorily, because of the cold). Ptashka was determined come what may to get as far as Orléans; her insistence got on my nerves because it meant my having to drive in the dark.

Next morning we were only 115 kilometres from Paris on a superb road, but it was Sunday and there was a mass of traffic coming in the opposite direction. The accident. Arrived home at half past twelve.

The children are well and Mémé seems even to have blossomed from the experience. The flat is clean and tidy; there is a pile of post on the table but I still have the noise of the engine in my ears because of the high speed at which we were travelling.

8 April

Paichadze handed me the proof of *Prodigal Son*. It is a long time since my works have been so slow getting into print. Even more unpleasant news from Moscow: Derzhanovsky has been kicked out of *Kniga*[1] as a result of which I have no one with a personal commitment to protecting my works in the USSR. Myaskovsky wrote, 'It seems you are planning to come here in April? Why? There won't be anything interesting at that time from the musical point of view, and our "ideologues" have decreed that your music is harmful, or at least alien, to the workers . . .'[2] My view is just the opposite: I should go precisely in order to make people believe once again in my music, which envious people have been taking advantage of my absence to spit on.

11 April

In the evening was at Samoilenkos for a Mayakovsky Evening, at which he read excerpts from *The Bedbug*, his play for which Meyerhold has suggested I write music.[3] There are good moments in the play, but also some quite

---

1 The *Mezhdunarodnaya Kniga* organisation was established in the USSR in 1923 to handle the importing of foreign books and music and the exporting of Soviet publications. It operated alongside VOKS (Vsesoyusnoe obshchestvo kul'turnykh svyazyei) which was responsible for the exchange of cultural manifestations such as exhibitions, concert and theatre tours, etc. See above, p. 415.
2 Letter of 30 March 1929 in *S. S. Prokofiev and N. Ya Myaskovsky*, op. cit., p. 303. Myaskovsky had heard from Siranush Kubatskaya of Prokofiev's intention to revisit the USSR.
3 Prokofiev having declined, despite his admiration for both Meyerhold (at whose instigation the play had been written) and Mayakovsky, the director turned to the young Shostakovich who produced in his first score for the stage a biting, raucous counterpart to the dystopian Soviet-Brave-New-World satire on the end of NEP and the already glimpsed horrors of

intolerable farcical clowning, which only goes to show what a gulf exists between Russia and the rest of the world! Mayakovsky's play depicts a new and incredible world that is utterly foreign to me. But one must be calm in one's attitude to such things, after all the previous world was that of Ostrovsky, which was equally strange and equally enclosed for its inhabitants, who longed only to get out into the fresh air. No doubt it is the same for the world of *The Bedbug*, whose characters want to get away, anywhere at all so long as they can be free!

Through the veneer of his roughness Mayakovsky was gentle, although it is not in his nature not to show off. He wanted us all to play give-away draughts, not for money but for forfeits. I am hopeless at draughts, but I won one of the four games we played, although not for forfeits. Mayakovsky explained how to measure a person's stupidity: you put a reel of cotton in your pocket and thread the other end of it out through the button hole in your jacket. Then you get your friend to pay out the thread, very carefully, and he continues scrupulously pulling it out until he cottons on to the fact that something is up. The length of the resulting thread is the measure of your friend's stupidity.

12 April

Monteux's first appearance as the new Conductor of the Orchestre Symphonique de Paris. He has replaced Ansermet, who was sacked for not drawing big enough audiences. (Ansermet conducted fifty concerts and included only one work of mine, the Violin Concerto!) A home must be found somewhere for my Third Symphony, and Monteux looks the most promising as Koussevitzky is temporarily silenced – I hear he is not giving any concerts at all in Paris this season. I therefore decided to sit through an entire programme of the most tedious music so that I could go to see Monteux afterwards: Fauré, d'Indy and the Second Symphony of Brahms, enough to send anyone to sleep. Brahms can be listened to only at times of desperate hunger for music. His Second Symphony is not without its merits – many of them! – but even though the themes are often stolen from others (Beethoven, Haydn), nevertheless it is still a deeply dull work. Monteux was friendly and said he would like to perform something of mine, if possible a new piece. I replied that, as it happened, I did have such a thing, and Monteux asked me to get in touch by telephone. I decided it would be best if I were to ring not Monteux

---

Stalinist orthodoxy. Mayakovsky reportedly asked Shostakovich to make the music as vulgar as possible, an invitation Shostakovich accepted with enthusiasm.

but Paichadze, and ask the latter to write to Monteux about my Symphony No. 3.

14 April

Suvchinsky came in the afternoon, as I had asked him to advise me about titles for the various numbers in *Prodigal Son*. I do not want Kokhno's titles to be left as they are in the forthcoming published score. Learning that I am definitely not going to Russia this spring, Suvchinsky advised me not to sever relations completely: at the moment they have no hard currency and times are desperately hard, but within a few months if only the harvest does not fail their natural timber and oil resources will enable them to climb out of the crisis. Suvchinsky had very interesting things to say about Rouault: he is an artist whose star is rising and who is destined to be in the front rank.

In the evening Diaghilev invited us to his box for *Prince Igor*. It was not a very exciting production: vocally poor, and the orchestra did not sound very good from our box. Diaghilev appeared with Markevich in high good spirits, obviously taking advantage of Lifar's absence in Monte Carlo to have a fling. Markevich is sixteen and looks like a baby mouse. Ptashka gave Diaghilev a packet of photographs we had taken in Monte Carlo; seeing Lifar arm-in-arm with Ptashka, he passed the snapshot to Pruna saying: 'M. et Mme Lifar.' It was indeed the case that Stravinsky had gone over to Monte Carlo on the day we left, that is to say when we called on him in Nice. The performance that night was *Apollo*, which Shteiman had been rehearsing, but Stravinsky unexpectedly announced that at his mother's request he would like to conduct the performance in the evening, and took the baton from a surprised Shteiman.

15 April

Orchestrated the development of the first movement of the Fourth Symphony . . . dictated letters, went to the publishers. Suddenly I felt myself clapped on the shoulders and turned round to see – Diaghilev. He had come to buy a copy of the piano score of *Ruslan* – evidently for the education of Markevich. I showed him the full score of *Prodigal Son*, which had just come from the copyist. Diaghilev opened the first page, and said, 'I thought it was to begin with winds alone.'

I: 'No, I thought it would have more go about it with strings.'

Ansermet came in; in a few days he will go to Russia to conduct, but he says that the number of his concerts has been reduced for lack of money (interesting how all the foreign artists are going, not those in the front rank of stardom, but they cannot invite me). He will conduct a lot of Stravinsky, but also my *Chout*. Ansermet asked me to play *Prodigal Son* (he is going to conduct it in Berlin in June), and I obliged while Diaghilev stood back and fretted about which numbers I should be showing Ansermet. I asked Diaghilev, 'Suppose I were really to conduct the ballet' (Diaghilev had spoken about this a few times), 'would it be for money, or gratis?'

Diaghilev: 'Well, of course I wouldn't charge you anything.'

I (joking): 'In that case, it doesn't strike me as a very attractive proposition.'

Diaghilev: 'Well, let's say a bottle of champagne after the show. You know, Igor conducted for me in Monte Carlo for nothing.'

I: 'He got paid by his mamasha.'

Diaghilev: 'And your wife will pay you. Your beautiful wife.'

I: 'Whom you embarrass with your kisses.' (Yesterday, as we parted, Diaghilev suddenly kissed Ptashka.)

Diaghilev laughed and turned to go. Thus ended our conversation about my fee!

16 April

Orchestrated the first movement of the Fourth Symphony, finished the development and started the recapitulation.

At last, after a long interval, a postcard from Asafyev. But it is the most pessimistic communication I have ever received from him: he is suffering from headaches, his nerves are bad, he is losing work and influence. Of the cheerfulness and vigour from his trip abroad, and of C.S., not a trace. Not only that, but there is little to rejoice over in the musical life of the capital:[1] the young composers now have a 'different orientation'; in Moscow only Myaskovsky 'stays firmly adherent to your music'; Dranishnikov and Radlov are on their way out of Akopera[2] ... The upshot is that it is high time for me to go the USSR and fight for my renown there, but at the same time it is also important to consolidate my position abroad (Gaveau? Columbia?[3]

---

1 The context seems to indicate Leningrad, where Asafyev lived, but Moscow had become the capital of the Russian Soviet Federation of Socialist Republics in March 1918, and of the Soviet Union in 1923.
2 Leningrad State Academic Theatre of Opera and Ballet, as the former Mariinsky Theatre was officially known between 1924 and 1935, before it was renamed in memory of the assassinated Sergey Kirov in 1935.
3 The Columbia Gramophone Company had been making gramophone records with the new electrical process since February 1925.

America?). My Third and Fourth Symphonies will make my name. But most important of all is my new approach to music!

18 April

Had my photograph taken by Wassermann. At the Straram evening concert Cooper was conducting three numbers from the *Oranges* Suite. I did not attend: what a suburban idea, to play just three numbers. Olga Vladislavovna listened on the radio and said that the March was encored.

20 April

Consulted a lawyer as there is an attempt to evict us from our flat, owing to the machinations of the concierge.

Suvchinsky and Rouault came to dinner, the latter with his wife, a very presentable lady who had clearly at one time been a beauty but is now getting on in years and provincial. Our 'primitive' really let himself go and talked without ceasing from eight o'clock until midnight, often interesting but also inclined to start on one topic and then to swerve to a completely unrelated one, losing himself in all manner of artistic professional niceties and names of which only he himself had any idea who they were.

Blois was also present; it is two years since he left Pleyel and revived his relationship with Gaveau. During the last month he has twice engaged me in discussions about my transferring my allegiance to Gaveau. Pleyel has recently inveigled the fashionable pianist Iturbi[1] away from Gaveau, so Gaveau would be happy to return the favour by poaching me. Gaveau would pay well, in the region of 100,000 francs (last time Blois talked about it, it was 150,000) and would make every effort to promote me, not like Pleyel, where they take me more or less for granted. I said the proposition interested me (hardly the word, at 100,000 francs!) and Blois will have a serious talk with Gaveau the day after tomorrow.

---

1   José Iturbi (1895–1980), Spanish pianist, harpsichordist and conductor. Pleyel will have been particularly pleased with the catch as they needed another famous artist to perform on the massive, deeply inauthentic cast-iron-framed pedal harpsichord favoured by Wanda Landowska, with whom Iturbi had studied. Iturbi's penchant for exhibitionism eventually led him to Hollywood, to some extent at the cost of his deserved reputation as a serious artist particularly in the French and Spanish repertoire. In Hollywood he starred as himself in 1940s MGM musicals such as *Thousands Cheer* and *Anchors Aweigh*, with Gene Kelly and Frank Sinatra, and provided the soundtrack for the Chopin biopic, *A Song to Remember*, starring Cornel Wilde.

23 April

Rose at seven, at eight kissed a sleepy Ptashka goodbye, and set off for Brussels. As it was my birthday there was a cake, a piece of which I sampled with my coffee. Arrived in Brussels at 12.40 and went straight from the station to the theatre since the rehearsal was due to start in twenty minutes. Spaak and De Thoran were elegant as ever, polite and friendly. De Thoran handed me a piece of paper and asked me to make notes and discuss them afterwards rather than interrupt the rehearsal. I sat in the stalls with Spaak at a desk on which a score was laid out ready, the original, that is to say the one written out by Gorchakov.

My impression of the first act was decidedly mixed: the orchestra lacked sonority, the singers were hard to hear, and in places the music simply sounded wrong. There were several reasons for this: the empty theatre was boomy; the singers were nervous; from over-acquaintance with the vocal score I had myself forgotten what I had intended with the orchestration. Act Two was better. Then came the roulette scene, which was also all right. The overall impression created was one of untidiness and clutter: I must write another opera, much simpler, with fewer scrappy fragments and disjointed lines!

The rehearsal over, I went in search of a room (everywhere was taken) and ended up in a noisy and expensive room in the very same Grand Hôtel I had vowed never to stay in again. But Brussels is full up and I was tired, so I went to sleep.

24 April

The ringing of bells combined with the staff mess-hall directly opposite prevented me from sleeping after six o'clock, so I struggled out of bed and went for a walk. At one o'clock Acts Three and Four were rehearsed, and they went better than the first two yesterday. There had been two reasons for the disappointment of yesterday: (1) the singers' nervousness in the presence of the composer; (2) their not being used to the orchestra. Today both one and the other were more familiar. But there is another and more important reason: the third and fourth acts actually work better than the first two; Act One is the least successful in terms of the drama, the music and the orchestration. I went so far as to ask De Thoran, 'Ne pensez-vous pas, que le premier acte n'est qu'une cochonnerie?'[1] De Thoran conceded that it is weaker than the others, but added that it is redeemed by the introduction of so many new characters to the audience, who working hard to assimilate them will not have time to pay much attention to the narrative of the act.

---

1 'Don't you find the first act a bit of a pig's breakfast?'

As a result of this conversation, as I walked round Brussels that evening I cogitated what should be done to improve the first act. First, some passages are musically ineffectual. Second, the long declaration between Alexey and Polina would benefit from being broken up by the interpolation of a short scene between the General and the Marquis. The General stuffs money into his wallet and thanks the Marquis for his services. He then hands Alexey a 1000-franc note and asks him to change it at the hotel desk. The pair then exit, while Alexey and Polina resume their exposition. This insertion would have the double virtue of illuminating the relationship between the dramatis personae, and relieving the monotony of the long exposition. Rimsky-Korsakov used to say that some cuts make a work longer. In the same spirit it could be said that there are some additions that, by introducing variety, can make it shorter. Later that evening I made some changes in the score and also found two possible cuts in the first act.

25 April

In the morning I discovered a third cut I could make in the first act, touched up a few things in the orchestration, and continued to think out the scene I was now planning to insert. The librarian worked from 6 a.m. to transfer my changes to the orchestral parts. An interviewer from *Le Soir* came, very affable and eager. At one o'clock the whole opera was run right through, but alas still missing Babulenka, who is ill; also Polina is ailing. The scenery has been fitted up, but looks ludicrously undistinguished. I am used to working with Diaghilev and with Russian theatres where the settings are works of art in themselves, so was taken aback to see such a drab, commonplace example of conventional design. De Thoran had a bad headache and I felt guilty raising queries with him about modifications to some of the tempi. Sitting in the stalls with Spaak and the score I made notes as they came up of inappropriate tempi or nuances, as well as things I wanted to change in or add to the orchestration. Diaghilev cabled asking for a pair of seats for the premiere to be reserved for him. This is most inopportune: I mean I am pleased he is interested, but not just now when the opera is not coming together and when the first act needs rewriting. After the rehearsal I went to bed and slept.

In the evening I had intended to go to the opera by Pizzetti,[1] but it was cancelled owing to an epidemic of illness among the singers. Instead I spent the evening going through the French text and noting down what I wanted to change, in the cause of which I intended to invoke Spaak's assistance.

---

1 *Fra Gherardo*, premiered by Toscanini at La Scala, Milan, the previous year. The opera deals with a humble, pious yet fiery rebel, in thrall equally to reforming zeal and the lusts of the body, between which he veers, as *Time Magazine* described the plot, 'like a medieval Elmer Gantry'. Or, as it might be, a Rasputin.

26 April

In the morning I finished the text of the scene I had invented to insert in the first act, and then went through the French version of the *Gambler* libretto, covering six pages with notes but getting no further than the end of the second act. Rehearsal at one o'clock, to piano accompaniment, which I thought would be less interesting but in fact proved more productive for the singers in refining their acting. Not only that, but it was the first time they had been in their costumes, which (the costumes) are far more interesting than the scenery and immediately greatly enhanced the impact of the production. I had taken Spaak to be a gentle soul, but today he dug in his heels over a series of trifles and drove the producer to such a rage that eventually he blew up and left the stage. When he returned it seemed to be my job to act as go-between so that peace could be restored for the rest of the rehearsal. The women principals are still indisposed, but are expected to recover in time for the performance. Today I sat close up, at the edge of the stage, and could see the expressions on the singers' faces, could hear all the words, and when I saw them decked out in make-up and costume I completely lost that feeling of pointlessness that had so depressed me on the first day, when I was too far away to see any of the detail, could not hear the words, and the orchestra was playing badly and too loud.

This is a mainly young company. The singers behave very well towards me, and there is no hint of the tragicomedy that occurred in Berlin when I was told I should go round and thank them.

In the evening I studied Spaak's translation of the libretto and then sat with him in his office while he willingly made the changes I wanted. As a translator he is very resourceful and inventive, always ready to go the extra mile to meet the author halfway.

At eleven o'clock in the evening I welcomed Ptashka; we were overjoyed to see one another and talked until past one in the morning. She brought with her an irritatingly crass letter from Derzhanovsky.

27 April

Woke early with a heavy head. Much annoyed by the Derzhanovsky letter. To avoid giving way to anger I set to work, not least on my headache. While Ptashka slept I went for a walk round Brussels and watched fish being transported from one pool to another in the park opposite the royal palace.

An interview with an old fogey from the Paris newspaper *Le Figaro*, who was obviously more interested in telling me about himself than seeking information.

'I interviewed Leoncavallo, in this very hall.'

'When was that?' I asked in astonishment.

'Oh, now you're asking! How do you expect me to remember?'

He then ticked off my compositions: '*Symphonie classique, Chout, Le suicide* . . .'

I: 'Do you mean *Suite Scythe*?'

'Oui, oui, précisément.'

At one o'clock the general dress rehearsal, to which Paichadze came. Polina, however, had no voice at all: she was reduced to miming while De Thoran sang her part, which ruined the impression and generally dampened the spirits of the other singers. Still, we had the first appearance by Babulenka who, to my surprise, sings really rather well. Of course there can be no question of refinements or tempo nuances or any such finessing; everything has to be accepted as is, provided it does not actively fly in the face of the overall conception. The best singer is the Alexey: he is young and dashing and has a good voice. The roulette scene went on the whole pretty well, although lacking sparkle. Even though the chorus is at full strength I urge the choristers to sing at the top of their voice, in the final entr'acte they are hard to hear. I emerged from the rehearsal exhausted and not in the best of spirits. Nevertheless, *The Gambler* has this one great advantage, that the interest level grows continually and the action increases in intensity from the first act through to the last. This is, axiomatically, no compliment to the first act, but perhaps the couple of cuts and the extra scene will liven it up.

After a rest in the hotel we went in the evening to Honegger's *Judith*: De Thoran let us have his box. There is not much music in *Judith*, but the fight scenes are splendidly done. First-class! Even they do not have much music, but to have the fights *with* music – that really would be something! On the other hand, just before the fights he has filched a tune wholesale from the *Scythian Suite* (at the opening of 'Night'). During the interval I pestered Paichadze, asking him what would happen were I to start an action against Honegger for stealing my thing. If I did and won, given Honegger's position at the summit of fashion, what publicity! Falla's *La vida breve*, which came after, is tedious and inconsequential.

28 April

Woken again at crack of dawn by a variety of noises, and again I have anything but a clear head.

Paichadze, Ptashka and I went for a walk to look round the town. By evening I had walked my bad head off and sat down to look again at the French text, getting this time as far as the end of Act Three. I then took it to Spaak and worked with him until well after ten o'clock while he with great generosity and skill produced new versions for all the changes I wanted. Even so, my headache returned afterwards.

29 April

Was woken at nine o'clock by a telephone call from Princess Shakhovskaya, Natasha Nabokov's mother, to whom I had sent a note yesterday at Nabokov's request. Then came a long press interview. Ptashka went out with the Princess to buy lace, while Paichadze and I strolled about and had lunch. Nouvel rang up: he has come especially for the premiere, Diaghilev also, with Markevich (a honeymoon trip?). The premiere of the opera took place at eight o'clock, accompanied by torrential rain. Ptashka, the Princess and Nouvel shared one taxi, Paichadze and I went in another. I felt in good spirits.

Except for a few boxes the theatre was well filled with a fashionably dressed public. Ptashka, Paichadze and I were in one of the dress-circle boxes, while the Princess and Nouvel were in the adjacent one. Diaghilev and Markevich sat in the third row of the stalls. Polina had almost fully recovered. Her voice is not particularly melodious, it tends from time to time to hoarseness, and her intonation is not always reliable. But even this was a pleasant change from the total silence of the dress rehearsal. With a full house the orchestra sounds completely different. In short, all was reasonably well. I was afraid the first act would be boring, but the scene with the Baroness Würmerhelm did make its effect. During the interval Spaak rushed up and reminded me that I still had the vocal score of the third and fourth acts, which would be needed by the prompter. I went back myself to the Grand Hotel to fetch it. The rain was still falling in sheets but it was good to be in the fresh air. The first act was not greeted by much applause, but it is the least interesting and therefore the success can only grow, so much is clear, and I was in no way downcast. And so it proved. Diaghilev came up to me with Markevich after Act Three and complimented me on it. I asked Diaghilev, 'What possessed you to bring Markevich? Was it to show him how to write music, or how not to write it?' Diaghilev laughed. 'Look, that is if I may say so rather too delicate a question. Permit me not to answer it.'

And that, apparently, was all there was to be said on the subject of *The Gambler*. Diaghilev was fussing about which was the best restaurant in which to dine late at night. I suggested we all went to the one opposite La Monnaie, but the suggestion went in one ear and out of the other, Diaghilev evidently preferring a *tête-à-tête* dinner with Markevich. The last act went not badly, but Polina was not feminine enough towards the end. During the embrace the lights were dimmed but then brought back up again too quickly, which threw the singer out. De Thoran was adroit in rescuing her, however.

The end of the performance drew several curtain calls. Many in the audience already knew where I was sitting and turned in my direction, and then Alexey directly motioned towards me from the stage, upon which the entire audience turned towards our box. I went to the front rail and bowed. I then retired to the back of the box, but the audience continued applauding and I had nowhere to hide: the box was not a deep one and had no ante-room. I bowed once more and applauded the singers. Once the applause died down we went backstage, where I embraced De Thoran and congratulated Alexey and Polina. Paichadze on behalf of the publishers issued a general invitation to dinner, but some people had prior engagements, others simply dispersed and still others said they had an early start on the morrow. Our little group dined together and we drank champagne. I noticed that De Thoran and some of the singers were at a nearby table. Strange! Had they been less friendly to me I might have taken offence, but as it was I did not want to do so.

30 April

We packed our things in the morning and at 1.25 took the train back to Paris. Diaghilev and Markevich were supposed to be on the same train, but Nouvel explained that they had slept badly and would be taking the next train. Evidently the seclusion of the honeymoon trip is destined to continue. Arrived in Paris at five o'clock. All was well at home, except that Oleg burst into tears as soon as he saw me. The Symphony has arrived from Moscow, so while I still hope that Monteux will give the premiere on the 17th, so much of the orchestra material still remains to be copied! (Derzhanovsky managed only seven of the parts, in a dreadful hand.) I went to Paichadze's office to telephone (our telephone is not working at the moment) and also to see the lawyer: today at 1.30 our case is due to be heard, to establish whether our not the landlord is entitled to evict us. The lawyer had gone to Marseilles, but had left word that, as we wanted, we could stay until the end of June. At home there was much rejoicing on this account, but in reality what cheek to imagine that punctilious payers such as we had always been could be chucked out on a whim.

Muzsektor in Moscow sent me a registered package containing Tchaikovsky's *Cherevichki*. I played it through with great enjoyment. Who can have sent it to me – Asafyev?

1 May

In the morning I took the Symphony to Paichadze, who had already summoned the copyists (one of them, Astrov, does his scribbling at home). There is a chance that everything will be finished by the 10th; if only Monteux does not cancel, seeing that he still does not have the material. Paichadze phoned him and a meeting is set up for next Sunday. The *Gambler* premiere took place the day before yesterday, the Third Symphony should be on the 17th, and *Prodigal Son* on the 21st, moreover rehearsals for the two latter events will be meshing concurrently. It is a long time since I had such a concatenation of premieres.

At home I read the second proofs of the piano score of *Prodigal Son* and practised conducting it. Although there is no confirmed agreement with Diaghilev about a conductor's fee, he has announced my participation in his brochure, so I think I can take it he does intend to pay me something. And, indeed, in the afternoon a pneumopost arrived from Nouvel asking me to call in tomorrow for a discussion about 'the forthcoming season'.

2 May

Stayed put and worked on conducting: after a seven-year lacuna I have to get myself back in form, although I must beware of being too energetic, as I cannot be sure how much my heart will put up with. Lately it has been behaving itself; I have been quite unaware of it.

Finished the second *Prodigal Son* proof.

Saw Diaghilev, who offered me 2,000 francs, which is a pittance. But I declined to haggle, saying merely that I was sure we would come to an agreement if he could see his way to increasing his offer. We eventually agreed on 3,000, even though he kept insisting he would not give a penny more than two and a half, and that I had tricked him into agreement ('Vakula the Smith').[1] He praised the fourth act of *The Gambler* and much of the roulette scene: 'Quite unlike anything else, as Markevich says . . .' So now it seems the *maîtres* are to be subject to assessment by Markevich. I even asked what had been Markevich's overall impression of the opera. 'To begin with he was wincing,' Diaghilev replied, 'but at the end his verdict was "c'est formidable".' Wincing indeed – the little wretch.

3 May

From Meyerhold comes a copy of a new Moscow rag with a most malicious article about me. True, I am not the only one selected for censure – others include the Communist Roslavets – but still: 'Time was when Prokofiev was regarded as a genius, but every one of his new works brings fresh

---

1 The hero of Gogol's story 'Christmas Eve', basis for Tchaikovsky's opera *Vakula the Smith* (in its later revision *Cherevichki – The Tsarina's Slippers*) and Rimsky-Korsakov's opera *Christmas Eve*. Vakula fulfils the impossible task, imposed on him by his village inamorata Oxana, of obtaining the Empress's slippers.

disappointment ... atmosphere of sterility ... culture takes revenge on falseness ...' etc., etc. Of course taking into consideration the recent letters from Asafyev and Myaskovsky it is clear that the past two years have seen a distinct cooling towards me in Russia. This is regrettable, but it is not terribly alarming: the Third and Fourth Symphonies are still unknown there, nor has anyone any idea of *The Gambler*, or *The Prodigal Son*, or *Choses en soi*. All these works will come to my aid.

I started conducting – and immediately could feel my heart protesting. This is very worrying. I immediately began working to counteract it; I am confident that I shall overcome the problem.

In the evening I attended the first performance of Poulenc's Concerto for harpsichord.[1] He has developed a great facility for his little march-like tunes, as a result of which you can find some rather nice ones among them, but in the end they do become oppressive. I would say this: the harpsichord's part is more attractive than the orchestra's, while the tuttis are occasionally enjoyable but more often than not misconceived. Diaghilev was present with Markevich, and was very critical of the Concerto. Next we went into the next-door hall, where the young violinist Brodsky was performing my two *Songs Without Words*, for which the audience unexpectedly favoured me with an ovation. I went backstage to see Monteux, who repeated his desire to perform the Third Symphony, talked about rehearsals, and arranged to come to see me tomorrow to listen to it. It looks as though he has decided to pay serious attention to me. I had been afraid that he would be reluctant to take on the Symphony, or not take it seriously.

4 May

Yesterday Marnold unexpectedly delivered himself of the opinion that I had taken to composing too hastily, that I should step back a little and reflect, and that there was a lot of music with which I ought to become better acquainted (for example I do not know Berlioz well enough). Since he was clearly basing this pronouncement on *Prodigal Son* and the Fourth Symphony, I answered as follows: 'Yes, it is true that I composed these two works within the space of five months, and that is a fairly short time; but what is a better example of haste is that you, after five minutes listening to them, feel entitled to spout your opinion.' Marnold was rather taken aback and said that, of course, he would have to listen to them again, but he still thought it would be a good idea for me to visit him to get acquainted with the compositions of Berlioz.

1 *Concert champêtre*, composed for Wanda Landowska, who was playing the work for the first time in the Salle Pleyel with the Orchestre Symphonique de Paris conducted by Pierre Monteux.

Conducted again, but cautiously because of my heart. I have been working on it, and felt better today.

5 May

C.S. Church. Today is Easter Day in the Orthodox Church. We – Ptashka, I, Svyatoslav, Oleg and the Danish nanny – went after lunch in solemn procession to the Paichadzes, who had made a *kulich* and a *paskha*.[1]

We were home again by five, as Monteux was due to come to hear me play through the Third Symphony. I had prepared for this by working out a version for piano that I hoped would create the best impression, and I also timed it: thirty-four and a half minutes; thank God the Fourth is shorter. Monteux paid no compliments but listened attentively and then alarmed me by saying that it would be impossible to perform it without extra rehearsals. However, he clearly did not want to let it slip through his fingers, and therefore promised to devote all his efforts to procuring two additional rehearsals. Learning that in all this season hardly any of my works had been programmed by the Orchestre Symphonique, he enquired, 'Vous n'êtes pas bien avec Stravinsky?'[2] I replied that, on the contrary, whenever we meet we embrace, but whenever I appear to be on the point of achieving a measure of success in any field, some hidden forces in the circle close to Stravinsky contrive to throw up obstacles in my path. Thus, whenever I am embraced by him, I invariable find myself wondering if the kiss is genuine or one of Judas's? Monteux commented, 'Oui, il doit avoir peur de vous.'[3]

He stayed for three hours getting to know every detail of the Symphony, but offered no opinion as to its merits. His American wife, doubtless an intelligent woman, sat with Ptashka and regaled her with the details of Monteux's courtship.

6 May

Lunch at Mme Dubost's, with Monteux and Milhaud as well as ourselves. I listened while the failings of the management of their concerts were

---

1 *Kulich* is a round, pannetone-like cake, topped with icing and decorated with flowers, and with the Russian letters X and B, standing for Khristos Voskres (Christ is Risen). The *paskha* (the word is the same as the Russian for Easter, from the same root *Pascha*, the Latinised version of the Hebrew word *Pesach*, meaning Passover) is a tall, pyramid-shaped creation consisting of a cholesterol-fatal mixture of as many as possible rich foods that have been forbidden during Lent, the basis being a light white (for purity) cottage cheese, with butter, eggs, sour cream, almonds, vanilla, dried and crystallised fruits, etc.
2 'Are you not on good terms with Stravinsky?'
3 'Yes, he is right to be afraid of you.'

mercilessly dissected. Monteux got his two extra rehearsals for my Symphony, making five in all.

Then I went to the publishers to chivvy them up with the copying of the orchestra parts, and was at home by five to receive Désormière, to whom I played *Prodigal Son* and imparted a few observations on the way I thought it should be conducted. He will conduct the first rehearsal and I will take over the rest. That is excellent, as it means I shall hear it before having to conduct.

7 May

A very nice letter from Spaak: the second performance of *The Gambler* had had more energy than the first and had been very warmly received.

Conducted the *Son* and sorted out the parts. Today was less busy, so Ptashka and I went to buy some ties for me. While we were out Blois called, probably about Gaveau, although this idea has suddenly gone very quiet. This is a pity as it would have been a serious proposition.

In the evening I went to a concert by Monteux, a Russian programme. Tchaikovsky's Fourth Symphony, which in Paris they drive so relentlessly, I listened to with French ears. And indeed, alongside passages of marvellous creative inspiration there are so many lapses into bad taste, or simply into bad technique. Horowitz played Rachmaninoff's Third Concerto. I do not believe I have heard this work since that memorable spring of 1915, when in the grip of melancholy I played it repeatedly on the piano. There are many very fine passages in it, but as a whole it is inextricably embroiled in the pit of sterile music.[1]

Ariadna Nikolskaya[2] came rushing up to me, I don't know to whom she is currently married. She still wants to compose and has come to Paris for a couple of months to study the theory of composition, but to whom should she go? I introduced her to Ptashka, who found her beautiful, but not as beautiful as Maria Viktorovna has always claimed. Our former male Conservatoire fellow students – Shteiman, Tarnovsky – glowed with pleasure

---

1 Made miserable by the vacillations of his first love, Nina Meshcherskaya, compounded by her family's wholly understandable refusal to sanction a hasty marriage followed by a perilous journey through war-torn Europe and an uncertain future, Prokofiev wrote in his diary in April 1915: 'Altogether the whole business was seriously affecting my life: I could think of nothing else; I lost the ability to work at anything; I did nothing except play Rachmaninoff's Third Concerto, for which I had suddenly developed a great liking, and the late sonatas of Scriabin, in memory of that wonderful composer's untimely end.' See *Diaries*, vol. 2, p. 41.
2 Ariadna Nikolskaya, when a piano student at the St Petersburg Conservatoire, had been a celebrated beauty and an object of fascination not only to Prokofiev but to a large swathe of her male peers. Prokofiev had later encountered her sharing a house, and it seems a *ménage à trois*, in Los Angeles with Maria Baranovskaya, with whom Prokofiev developed a close but probably platonic relationship, and who eventually married the pianist Alexander Borovsky. Ariadna had ambitions as a composer and Prokofiev had given her some coaching. See *Diaries*, vol. 1, pp. 251–717 *passim*; vol. 2, pp. 291–2, 306, 559–67, 571–81, 586.

on seeing her, with happy memories of their student days. Of course, as a fifteen-year-old girl she was even lovelier than she is now.

8 May

Had a bad headache from early morning. Could this be from the beer I drank last night? Worked on it, and by dinner-time it had gone.

In the morning Ptashka telephoned the Koussevitzkys, who had arrived back yesterday evening. We went to dine with them and embraced cordially. The winter incident was all forgotten. Virtually the only one of my works Koussevitzky had performed was the *Classical* Symphony, but at least he played it fourteen times. He did not perform the Second Symphony, I was told, because of Stokowski: they had agreed between themselves to perform it at the same time so that both could claim the American premiere, but Stokowski started ducking and diving and meanwhile the season slipped away. This may not have been such a bad thing: the Second Symphony would quite likely have upset a lot of people, which in view of my impending tour would have been most unhelpful. Koussevitzky's advice to me was to compose a Fourth Piano Concerto without delay, so that I would have something new for America. He said, 'You people are extraordinary. Stravinsky writes a Second Concerto that nobody wants; they would be far more interested in a symphony but no, he composes a concerto. You, on the other hand, really should write a concerto, but you persist in turning out symphonies.' When I started to explain that the Fourth Symphony had been built out of material derived from *Prodigal Son*, he exclaimed, 'But that's fine! After all, Beethoven used material from *Prometheus* for his Third Symphony.'[1] I was thrilled by this magnificent precedent: no one is going to argue that Beethoven was a bad symphonist!!!

9 May

As soon as I woke up I started thinking about the Fourth Concerto. Not only does it need to be composed, but I need to learn to play it. To achieve this before I go to America means that it must be short and simple. But perhaps that is just what I should do in any case. I have enough mastodons like the Second Concerto! Lying in bed I composed a theme.

Jasmin brought round the transcribed material from *Prodigal Son*, and Astrov and I made corrections to it. In the afternoon I visited Monteux and played him the Third Symphony.

---

1 The finale of the *Eroica* Symphony (and the *Eroica* Variations for piano, Op. 35) are based on the last movement of the music Beethoven wrote in 1800 for the ballet *Die Geschöpfe des Prometheus*.

10 May

First orchestral rehearsal for *Prodigal Son*. Désormière took it while I sat with the score. Everything sounds clear and secure; no changes are needed. Désormière took it all at a slow tempo and Diaghilev, who had come in to listen, joked to Larionov, 'What sort of a ballet is this supposed to be, all Adagio! Doom and gloom!' When tunes came that I had given to the violins or cellos, he exclaimed, 'What's all this? Cellos singing? Violins too? What *would* Igor say?' Diaghilev was relishing the fact that the cellos had melodies to sing, savouring in anticipation the disgruntled criticism of the dry and dogmatic Stravinsky.

When I requested a box, as Koussevitzky had asked me to invite him, Diaghilev replied that I could have two seats in the stalls, which angered me very much. I countered: 'Respectable establishments usually allocate a box to the composer.' But Diaghilev is being stingy; tickets cost 200 francs and sales are going through the roof. *Prodigal Son* has had an unprecedented seven advertisements. *Le Pas d'acier* had four.

11 May

Conducted a little in the morning and slightly overdid it; I became breathless. Afternoon saw the first rehearsal of the Third Symphony: strings alone. Monteux has studied the score with great care. Despite the absence of wind instruments today, much in the first movement sounded very interesting. Bypassing the second movement he went straight to the third, which proved to be easier than I expected for the orchestra. But the first third of it, lacking variety as presently does, will not do. It needs to be shortened and revised, so that there is less monotony. Walking home, I racked my brains to think of a solution.

Felt tired in the evening, and my heart was not good, which caused me much concern. I worked on it and made an effort not to succumb.

Blois telephoned, asked how Brussels had gone, and added that everything was now agreed with Gaveau. We would have to have a meeting to settle the details and finalise the agreement. To maintain the urbane tone that had characterised the negotiations hitherto, I suggested that we meet tomorrow at Yakovlev's exhibition.

In a word, bravo! This is a major step forward, in something on which I had almost given up.

12 May

Went to C.S. Church, worked on my heart condition, and when I got home, although not feeling particularly well, settled to revising the Symphony's scherzo. I worked quite intensively and had no trouble trimming and adding, although I am not yet certain all the alterations work.

In the afternoon we were at the Koussevitzkys, who have revived their Sundays At Home. He played me discs of the *Classical* Symphony which the Boston Symphony has just recorded. They were extremely interesting and very well played; it was a pity that Koussevitzky hurried the tempi too much, turning the Larghetto into something more like an Allegretto! I asked his opinion about Gaveau; his opinion was that of course I should accept the proposal.

13 May

Today is a free day, and very timely since I am feeling lethargic and my heart is still not in the best form, even though I have continued to work hard on it.

Went to Serebryakova's exhibition;[1] she is at the moment painting Svyatoslav's portrait. It was a lovely exhibition, full of sun and colour, and there was one seascape we would have bought straight away, had we an apartment to put it in, and the Gaveau agreement signed and sealed! The model for a series of nudes was her own daughter. A woman in a bathing costume (a very beautiful picture) was, we found out later, Marusya Pavlova.

From that we went on to Yakovlev's exhibition, in his new genre of painting as distinct from the drawings on which he used mainly to concentrate. What I had not expected from Sasha-Yasha was the joyless, grey impression they conveyed. We had arranged to meet Blois there but he did not show up. We grumbled at him, but it later turned out that we had mistaken the time. At seven o'clock in the evening he came to our house. Gaveau is offering 100,000 francs, but in the form of a guarantee for a prescribed number of concerts, thus he is not simply offering this sum as a fee but tying it to a number of engagements that must be fulfilled. I said if the number were to be ten concerts it would be acceptable, but were it to be twenty I would not be interested. In addition he proposed to arrange two festivals[2] of my works a year in the Grand Opéra accompanied by a fanfare of publicity. Blois will speak again to him about my demand for 10,000 francs a

1   Zinaida Serebryakova (1884–1967), niece of Alexandre Benois, daughter of the sculptor Yevgeny Lanceray and the brother of the architect Nikolay Lanceray. She joined the *Mir isskustva* movement in 1911 but the relatively conservative style of her landscapes, portraits and genre paintings of rural life made her an uneasy member of the group. After the Revolution she endured hardship and poverty, and in 1924 stayed behind in Paris after completing a commission for a large mural. Although her two younger children were eventually allowed to join her, the two elder ones were not, and she did not see either of them again until 1960.
2   This term is to be understood not as a festival in the present-day sense of the term but as a concert dedicated to the works of a single composer.

concert and then arrange a meeting. I told Blois that friendship was one thing, but for his services in arranging this matter I thought I should pay him a percentage. Blois boiled over at once and cried, 'Not for the world!'

We dined with Prud'homme, my conveyancing lawyer, La Bergerie (a Député)[1] and his wife, Krasin's daughter. It was a very pleasant, lively, French company.

14 May

In the morning I took myself to the *Prodigal Son* orchestral rehearsal. My heart is better; I have been working a great deal on it, even so I stayed away from conducting practice during these three days. For the first half of the rehearsal Désormière was taking them through Auric's *Les Fâcheux*,[2] and I was even glad of only fifty minutes left for me; this was quite enough after my seven-year break from conducting. Désormière presented me to the orchestra, adding that the introduction was of course quite unnecessary, the orchestra applauded indifferently, I responded with some equally facile pleasantries, and the rehearsal commenced. The orchestra behaved well and it did not take me long to feel in control. It was important that I had put in some practice over the preceding two weeks, but had I done more of it the results would have been better still. A slight disaster occurred in the fourth movement, when we could not get the 5/4 rhythm together. After trying for a while we moved on, and afterwards I asked Désormière if it had been my fault. He said it was – I had been waiting for the orchestra instead of continuing my beat without paying any attention to them, and the result was that in addition to the five-in-a-bar shape the rhythm sounded uneven and the orchestra completely lost its compass. When Nouvel came into the hall I told him it was my debut on the podium after seven years. He said, 'I suppose you feel just like a schoolboy?' 'Exactly,' I replied.

My heart held up well and now that the schoolboy had passed his exam his mood immediately lightened. All the time I kept in mind that the reflection of God in man, at the same time as it reunites him with God, distances him from illness and fear.

15 May

Today there were two full orchestra rehearsals of the Symphony, one in the morning and one in the afternoon. As they began the development of the first movement I experienced a rush of anxiety. Ptashka came to the

---

1 Elected member of the Assemblée nationale, i.e. the equivalent of a Member of Parliament.
2 See above, p. 65.

afternoon rehearsal, and Monteux gallantly played through the entire Symphony for her, but the Symphony has not yet coalesced at all. The cuts and additions I made to the scherzo have helped, but not enough; I need to do more thinking.

Schefner, the writer of the programme notes, is embroiled in some sort of conspiracy against me. For the performance of the Violin Concerto in December he wrote some quite snide comments, and now, suddenly recalling this, I demanded to be shown the notes before they were printed. Schefner sent me a proof, and I saw that he had indeed included some stupid and unflattering things. I was expecting him to turn up at the morning rehearsal to collect the proof from me, but for all the sight I had of him he might have drowned in the sea. I told Monteux, who exclaimed, 'Ce sont des intrigues de Stravinsky?'

I: 'Je ne crois pas; plutôt de la part de ses amis.'[1]

Schefner was summoned to the afternoon rehearsal and appeared, looking unhealthy and dishevelled. Ptashka begged me not to make a scene, so I was gentle with him, supplicatory even, apologising for being troublesome. Schefner said that it was probably too late ('so why did you send me the proof?') but he would go to the typesetter and see what could be done.

16 May

Fourth rehearsal. Yesterday the errors in the score of the Symphony were all corrected and Astrov made the necessary changes in the parts. My heart is behaving better, but is still not completely right. I am working intensively on it. Perhaps it is all to the good that because of it I feel in permanent contact with God, but what is bad is that as soon as I feel better I begin moving away from him. I caught myself doing this, and felt ashamed.

Monteux has been working most diligently on the Symphony. He is musical and conscientious, but one cannot expect flights of inspiration from this short, stocky bourgeois. The scherzo still needs some changes: the over-weighty texture of the strings in the trio must be lightened (I also considered compressing it but could not make this work) and the tension created by the percussive knocks in the reprise must be heightened. At the end of the rehearsal I repeated my complaint to Monteux that Schefner had not given me a firm undertaking to amend the programme notes. I said, 'It is a matter for regret that you on the one hand are making such tremendous efforts to prepare the performance, and on the other there is someone aiming to spoil

---

1 'Is Stravinsky plotting against you?' 'I doubt it; more likely it is his friends.'

the success and influence the public against the Symphony by introducing negative comments in the programme notes.'

At this Monteux seriously lost his temper and sent for all the whole management of the orchestra. 'Cela m'embête de voir partout la main de Stravinsky!'[1] he shouted, insisting that either the printed programme be changed or, if it was too late for this, that it be scrapped and not distributed.

It would have been better not to bring Stravinsky's name into it, but evidently it is not the first time he has run up against this tendency. I left without waiting to hear the end of this noisy altercation, and decided I would not revert to the subject of the programme.

At home I busied myself with the revisions, mainly to the scherzo, but alas realised I would not have enough time to complete them. I therefore started a fresh page on which I roughed out the changes I plan to make after the performance.

We dined at the Koussevitzkys and went together to the Grand Opéra for the opening night of Ida Rubinstein's season. My Violin Concerto was performed at the Straram concert today, but it was with Darrieux[2] and he is not interesting. Idka's evening started with Bach orchestrated by Honegger,[3] quite nice but too long. Then Sauguet's *David*, boring rubbish I had heard before, in the autumn. Finally, Ravel's *Boléro*:[4] the setting is a Spanish taverna with a huge table on which the dancers dance, while the orchestra plays a motif that is repeated a thousand times in increasingly rich instrumentation. Ravel himself conducted in a most entertaining style, holding the baton like a surgeon's lancet and pointing it with great precision, impassively maintaining the slow tempo.[5] At the end of the ballet they forgot to press the button to lower the curtain: the music stopped but the curtain stayed resolutely up!

1 'I am outraged to see everywhere the hand of Stravinsky!'
2 Marcel Darrieux, Concertmaster of the Paris Opéra Orchestra, had been the stop-gap soloist at the first performance of the Violin Concerto conducted by Koussevitzky in October 1923. See *Diaries*, vol. 2, pp. 536, 712.
3 *Les Noces d'Amour et Psyché*, choreographed by Bronislava Nijinska, to music drawn from movements of Bach's French and English Keyboard Suites.
4 Another Rubinstein commission, staged by Nijinska and designed by Benois.
5 The tempo of *Boléro* was the occasion of a famous war of words. When Toscanini brought the New York Philharmonic to Paris in 1930 and performed the piece considerably faster than the composer was used to taking it, whipping up a predictable ovation from the excited audience, Ravel, who was present, refused to take a bow. Backstage he remonstrated with Toscanini who, it is said, retorted that 'it was the only way to save the piece'. Ravel's recording lasts 15 minutes 50 seconds, Toscanini's 13 minutes 25 seconds (Stokowski's is faster still). In a July 1931 interview for the *Daily Telegraph*, Ravel stated, 'Before its first performance, I issued a warning to the effect that what I had written was a piece lasting seventeen minutes and consisting wholly of "orchestral tissue without music" – one very long, gradual crescendo. There are no contrasts, and practically no invention except the plan and the manner of execution.'

The French composers vied with one another in mutual criticism: Honegger of Sauguet, Milhaud of Ravel. With me Milhaud was friendly and praised *Prodigal Son*; Désormière had shown him the score. I was angry that I had wasted time attending such a pointless performance; I would have done better to go to bed and sleep, as there is a rehearsal tomorrow. We got home at midnight; Astrov was still pasting corrections into the parts.

17 May

General rehearsal of the Symphony, to which no one was admitted except Ptashka and, towards the end, a belated Suvchinsky who got there in time to hear the finale. The Symphony went well, Ptashka was especially pleased, saying that there was no comparison with the day before yesterday. The scherzo has a more slimmed-down aspect. Even though I would still like to make a few more changes, I shall not do anything about them until after the performance. The Symphony was the first work to be rehearsed, and I left to return home as soon as it was over, without enquiring about the fate of the programme note.

At three o'clock I went to a stage rehearsal of *Prodigal Son*, not before time since until this point I had not seen a single dance step. Not only that, but I must co-ordinate the tempi, which they could well have altered since I was in Monte Carlo. Some tempi can be adjusted slightly in order to accommodate the dancers, but with others it is the dancers who must be pulled into line with the music. This was not, however, a very helpful rehearsal: they were just working with small fragments that had thrown up problems, so all that happened was an apparently endless repetition of the same place. After the rehearsal I called on Koussevitzky, from whom I had begged some coaching in conducting. Koussevitzky, incidentally, had expressed an interest in getting to know *Prodigal Son*, so I played it for him on the piano while he followed it with the score. Most of the technical discussion centred around the fourth number, the one in 5/4 time. Koussevitzky recommended conducting it using short, precise gestures, but his main advice was to know it thoroughly, preferably by heart. As for the rest, he said that conducting is easy if you just want to get successfully through the piece, but very difficult to achieve refinement. Further advice was not to wave the arms around too much, but to confine oneself to a precise, clear beat. As for the music, he was exceptionally enthusiastic, stating his opinion that it is one of my best works and represents a huge advance in technique.

The orchestral concert took place in the evening. The hall was not full – to blame were the organisers, who had placed almost no announcements in the Russian newspapers. I sat in a box where the sound was not nearly as good as what I had heard in the morning from the back of the hall. From here the strings dominated everything else.

There was little applause between the movements, either because they were not liked, or because of obedience to instructions printed in the programmes not to applaud between movements (the programme notes were, however, quite acceptable and the changes I wanted had been made). The applause at the end of the work was quite warm, the few boos being answered by loud cries of 'bravo'. A battle between the two factions ensued, culminating in an ovation. I rose to my feet to acknowledge the applause three times. Koussevitzky, sitting beside me, told me he considered it the greatest symphony since Tchaikovsky's Sixth. Among those coming to congratulate me were Prud'homme, Blois (who whispered in my ear that negotiations with Gaveau were going splendidly), Suvchinsky ('I must talk to you about this Symphony') and many others. Diaghilev was there but said nothing. Schefner hoped I was content with the programme note, and I apologised again for the trouble I had caused. I went to thank Monteux, who had conducted decently, but without a grand line.

18 May

Early in the morning I was already at the rehearsal of *Le Pas d'acier* and *Prodigal Son*. The ballet company was also on call, but were not ready by the time the rehearsal was due to start, so Désormière suggested using the time to work through problematical passages in *Prodigal Son*. I agreed, and he immediately found himself just as caught out by the 5/4 number as I had been at the previous session. But Désormière is more experienced than I am: he took the music apart, went back to the beginning playing it slowly, and after twenty minutes the piece began to flow properly. During *Le Pas* I made a series of comments about keeping the tempo slow, as it had been very hurried at last year's performances.

Diaghilev arrived brimming over with compliments about the scherzo of the Symphony and also the conclusion of the first movement, 'and much else in it besides'. Nevertheless I had the feeling that there was a good deal in the Symphony he had not liked. I asked him straight out, 'What would you say is your principal criticism of this Symphony?'

Diaghilev: 'The strings dominate too much, it is really suffocating.'

I: 'Well, that is a triviality! The problem was the acoustic of the hall. Downstairs at the back it sounded quite different.'

After the break I took my place on the podium for *Prodigal Son* with the dancers on stage. It was premature, as the orchestra is still playing very roughly. For me the potential stumbling block was still the 5/4 number, and this I conducted using short gestures, *à la* Koussevitzky, knowing it almost by heart. It went better. By the end of the rehearsal I was tired but my heart was behaving itself. When I got home I felt I had earned a holiday, and did little further work. I did not watch what was happening on stage, but Ptashka reported that the women's dances contained more than a little indecency, which certainly does not conform to the biblical account. This is the result of Diaghilev spending his time swanning about Paris with Markevich, while Kokhno and Balanchivadze were unable between them to devise any movements other than suggestive ones. This is completely at odds with my music and with Rouault's scenery, which is very powerful and biblical in feeling.

In the evening we went to Rossini's *L'Italiana in Algeri* and afterwards to a reception honouring Monteux at Mazel's. In neither case was it a worthwhile expenditure of time.

19 May

C.S. Church in the morning. Yesterday we were visited by Fabersha,[1] who tried to insist that we had both ourselves and the children inoculated against smallpox. We refused.

In the afternoon I went to the *Prodigal Son* choreography rehearsal. Because rehearsals have been taking place in various places I had to go to four halls in four different parts of the city before I found it. I went mainly on my own account, in order by conducting it to establish definitive tempi, but as it turned out the production itself has a mass of lacunae: the sisters in the final number do not enter on time; the penultimate number, the music for which is all leaps and syncopations, has been constructed with flowing movements; in the second number there is no correlation between the entrance of a character and the emergence of a new theme, and so on. I made my thoughts known to Balanchivadze and to Kokhno, and when he arrived to Diaghilev. Some adjustments were easy and could be put into effect, but it was too late for more complex ones as the general rehearsal is tomorrow. I said it would be desirable to moderate the lasciviousness of the Siren's dance: a loose woman in biblical times would not have behaved in the same way as a modern prostitute, the representation must be refracted through the prism of the intervening centuries. I fear, however, that my words will have fallen on deaf ears and therefore came back from the rehearsal depressed. Accompanied Ptashka to the Koussevitzkys, who receive guests on Sundays, but today was not a very engrossing occasion.

20 May

General rehearsal of *Prodigal Son* in the morning. I arrived at a quarter to nine, but Désormière announced that he would start with Rieti's *Le Bal*. I was

---

[1] Dr Fabre, who had attended Lina at the birth of her second son Oleg.

just about to take myself off to the café when it transpired that Rieti was late bringing his score, so Désormière proposed a closer look at some passages from *Prodigal Son*. Although Rieti chose that moment to appear, to punish him for being late Désormière worried away at *Prodigal Son* for forty minutes, which was extremely valuable, and only then turned to *Le Bal*. Meanwhile Diaghilev stood on stage supervising the hanging of the scenery, checking the costumes and lighting, and so on. Once again I approached Diaghilev and Kokhno with a view to getting the lubricious elements toned down, but all I got in response was a muttered 'Yes, yes, we'll have to think about that . . .' I badgered Rouault about it, told him of my concerns, and he was most willing to support me: 'I myself do not approve of the sisters, they are almost showing their naked behinds,' he said. 'Do say something to Diaghilev.' I urged. 'They will listen to you more than me, because it is your domain.'

The actual general rehearsal began after the break. Again I did not see much of the activity on the stage. Diaghilev sat behind me, not far away, and from to time came up to ask for a number to be repeated or for the tempo to be slightly altered. I conducted quite well and did not feel tired at the end. My heart was fine – this is a victory! The 5/4 number was acceptable, no more, and was done three times, once because of a mistake I made. Five in a bar is not in itself so difficult but what complicates this music is that in the middle there are two bars with two beats, as a result of which the conductor has to cue now to the right, now to the left, and this in turn risks unsettling the musicians because they are not quite certain when precisely to come in.

The rehearsal over, I went up to Koussevitzky, who was sitting in a little group with Paichadze and Stravinsky, the latter appearing only right at the end. Koussevitzky had praise both for the work and for my conducting, but was dissatisfied with the orchestra. Full of admiration for my *Son* were Mme Dubost, Mme Sert, Sauguet(!) and Blois. Marnold was restrained and Suvchinsky did not come. Rouault reported that he had tackled Diaghilev about the bare behinds but his representations had made no impression at all. We joined forces to try one last time.

'I keep hearing about this,' said Diaghilev, 'and I must tell you that I very much like this bare bottom. The choreographer does not presume to interfere with your music, and you should not interfere with his dances.'

I: 'My music is not composed for Balanchivadze; Balanchivadze's job is to create dances for my music. He has not remotely understood its spirit, and I shall publicly state this loud and clear. The ballet, which was staged while you were away, has shit on the music, and you must know that in principle you are defending the indefensible.'

Diaghilev: 'There is no question of principle here. The simple fact is that, thank God, I have been the Director of this ballet company for twenty-three years, and can see with perfect clarity that the ballet has been well staged. Therefore no changes will be made.'

After such a categorical statement there was no point in continuing the conversation. I went to sit next to Stravinsky and opened my heart to him.

'I fully sympathise with you, Seryozha,' said Stravinsky. 'Everyone is tiring of these indecencies and they are quite inappropriate here. But, as a general observation, I would not have gone near a Gospel subject for this theatre.'

A little later, when Ptashka, Rouault and I were having an animated discussion about the production, Diaghilev suddenly appeared from I don't know where, and exclaimed in some agitation, 'This is sheer dilettantism on your part!' (How can it be dilettantism to discuss a production that cuts right across the direction of the music?)

'In that case we have nothing further to say to one another,' I replied, and rushed out in a fury, slamming the door.

Rouault and Ptashka stayed with Diaghilev for a little while longer. Rouault spewed forth a lot of nonsense but Ptashka said, 'What is bad is not just that they show their bottoms, but they do so at the wrong time.' Afterwards she remembered with some surprise that during the conversation she had sometimes said 'si'.[1]

Returning home I was in a very bad frame of mind. It was horrible to have made a scene. But it is also horrible that two shits should have vandalised the ballet and that Diaghilev saw fit to defend them. This evening there was a performance of Stravinsky's *Renard* at Polignac's, but we did not go; I was not in the mood and had no desire to be in company.

21 May

Next morning my sour mood continued. Mentally I pursued the conversation with Diaghilev: 'Yes, indeed you have been the Director for twenty-three years and you have had some achievements of genius; this gives you the right to speak with authority. But you have also had some failures and the choreography of *Prodigal Son* is one of them. It is unworthy of you to use your authority to prop up an obvious failure from stubbornness, from commercial calculations, and apparently from a compulsion to reinforce that same authority!' and so on and so forth.

---

1 Spanish, one of the many languages in which Lina was fluent.

Eventually my anger burnt itself out and I made a great effort to conquer my bad mood. What, after all, is it that has so angered me? I am fighting in a good cause: that of protecting a Gospel parable from indecency. But where I am wrong is in enlisting anger in my struggle to defend the truth of the Gospel; this is inadmissible. Moreover, it is essential to get over my bad mood before the premiere today, otherwise all the work I have done on it over the past days will go for nothing!

Went to the publishing company offices to see whether the piano score of *Prodigal Son* is published yet. Stravinsky was sitting with Paichadze, and I asked, 'Is this business or just a kind of gentleman's club?' The answer was, they were just chatting. Stravinsky was friendly and sympathetic over my clash with Diaghilev – he also was 'en froid' with him over *Renard* – and talked about his Second Piano Concerto, which he hopes to finish in the summer. 'The style is elegant and virtuosic, in the best sense of the word; it owes something, if you will, to Weber; the themes are very simple, so much so that some phrases might even seem hackneyed, but I have put my personal stamp on them to such an extent that I am quite easy about them.'

All this was extremely interesting except the last: Stravinsky, being unable to invent his own thematic material, takes that of others and 'clothes it in his own imprimatur'! But I held my tongue, not wishing to dispel the pleasant atmosphere. When I returned home I took a nap, and by evening my spirits had greatly improved. The nervousness I had suffered during the afternoon about conducting also lessened.

By the time I arrived at the theatre the show had started; in fact the first item, Auric's *Les Fâcheux*, was already coming to an end. Stravinsky presented me with a copy of *Renard* before going on to conduct it. Hearing its complex rhythmical patterns I completely lost my fear of my 5/4 number. It was the first time I had listened to *Renard*, but it made little impression on me, partly because it was difficult to hear in the wings of the theatre and partly because I was not paying close attention. It was quite a success: Stravinsky came out a few times to acknowledge the applause, but Larionov did not appear.[1]

Next, the stagehands began putting up the scenery for *Prodigal Son*. I went up to Désormière's room to look through the score and concentrate on my performance. Stravinsky came in, made the sign of the cross over me and kissed me, adding, 'Although you are not a believer.'

'What makes you think that I am not a believer?' I said. 'You are very much mistaken.'

---

1 The revival of *Le Renard* had Larionov's original designs but new choreography by Lifar.

'Wait a moment, Seryozha, don't go out just yet, give me time to get to my box. I want to see you make your entrance.'

I did as he requested and then went on. I was greeted with quite noisy acclamation. In the front row, two seats along from the podium, was Rachmaninoff; several times while I was conducting I remembered his presence. It went pretty well; the orchestra had pulled itself together and played better than at the rehearsal. The 5/4 number I conducted with immaculate precision, which did not, however, prevent the orchestra making a few slips. As soon as the performance ended there was a storm of applause. I made my way from the pit into the wings, not hurrying, so that the ballet troupe could take their bows before me. Balanchivadze was one of the first out, probably afraid that I would not want to appear alongside him and therefore making sure that he could take his bow before I did. But I had no intention of spoiling his triumph and we all went on stage together, I holding Rouault's hand. Kokhno was reasonably tactful and hung back – probably Diaghilev had told him to do so. There were a good number of curtain calls, I do not recall how many.

First to appear backstage were Stravinsky and Paichadze, who congratulated me, embraced me and took their leave, after which I immediately went to change my shirt, which was wet through. Ptashka and the Koussevitzkys came to my room, and we went down together to the theatre foyer, where the Samoilenkos, Rubinstein, Mme Ghirshman, Blois and others were waiting. Boris Samoilenko had been overwhelmed particularly by the ending of the ballet. Koussevitzky said, 'This is a work of genius; you have two hits, the Symphony and now this!' The Samoilenkos took us off to the buffet to drink champagne. A little later Diaghilev looked in for a moment, kissed Ptashka, offered me his congratulations and said, 'We must sit and talk, but not now, another time, now we are all tired.' On the stairs I met Rachmaninoff, went up and took him by the hand, and asked him how he had liked the ballet. His affectionate reply was: 'A lot of it very much, especially the opening of the second scene' (did he mean the end of the first or the start of the second?) 'and the very end.'

After this Ptashka and I went to the Koussevitzkys, where supper was speedily prepared. Koussevitzky kept on repeating, 'A thing of genius', and, 'Your conducting was excellent, what a pity you are doing just the one performance.'

22 May

Were it not for a bad headache I would have been in holiday mood today. Walked in the Bois de Boulogne in the warmth of the sun, and then slept. My headache cleared up and I went to the publishers, where the *Prodigal Son* piano score has been issued. Paichadze, however, had little joy for me: I wanted them to make an immediate start on engraving the Third Symphony, but it appears that Ravel's orchestration of *Pictures from an Exhibition* is ahead of me in the queue. Then there are the new parts for *Le Sacre*, then the score and parts for *Le Baiser de la féé*, and as if that were not enough, the piano score of *The Gambler*. In short, having reached the age of forty and achieved an honourable measure of renown, I still have to beg for the publication of each and every work. No better is the situation with Myaskovsky's songs, which he has asked to be published. Paichadze hums and haws: nobody is rooting for it, but I should feel very awkward giving a negative answer to Myaskovsky.

In the evening, a performance of *Le Pas d'acier*. If all the tickets for last night had long been sold out, today the house was very empty. The tempi in *Le Pas* were better, but the orchestra played very sloppily. The production still leaves much to be desired, but it rises to a big climax at the end, and was a palpable success. I received many congratulations on yesterday's premiere, along with critical comments about Mr Fox. Natalya Koussevitzky was present; unexpectedly she introduced me to Lourié, whom I have steadfastly ignored since his return from Soviet Russia. Most of this time he has been pursuing an apparently indissoluble friendship with Stravinsky and has therefore adopted a hostile attitude to my music, but in the last few months he has produced some cool reviews of Stravinsky's latest works and *pari passu* has taken to praising mine.[1] We bowed ceremoniously to one another and smiled.

23 May

Lunched at the Koussevitzkys. Stravinsky was also there and Diaghilev was expected but failed to appear. The lunch was magnificently served. Stravinsky talked almost non-stop and much of what he said was interesting although he spoke almost exclusively about himself in self-approbatory terms. Relations between him and Diaghilev continue to be frigid, so it was not a surprise that Diaghilev stayed away.

In the evening, the second performance of *Prodigal Son*. The audience was larger than yesterday's, but there were still quite a number of empty seats. Nouvel gave us his box and we invited the Samoilenkos, Shalonov and Mrs Newman. *Prodigal Son* was listless: Désormière's tempi were not right

---

1   See S. Walsh, op. cit., pp. 456–62 for a characteristically clear and insightful account of Lourié's intimate relationship with Stravinsky and with Vera Sudeikina, and the fluctuating trajectory of this relationship.

and his conducting was short on magnetism, allowing the orchestra to lose focus. Many people told me that it had been better when I was conducting. I do not claim to be a great conductor; the musicians were simply on high alert because of the premiere. The response was more than averagely successful, but it is disappointing all the same that *Prodigal Son*, in which so many high expectations had been invested, should, as a result of a series of factors exclusively concerned with the production, have been reduced to a routine event.

24 May

Today I looked closely at the first two movements of the Third Symphony in the light of the notes I had made during Monteux's rehearsals. I made a few changes: to be specific, I identified some variances in the tempi and made three small cuts. These movements are now ready for the engraver, as soon as Paichadze manages to dig up the necessary funds. Blois came in the afternoon to announce that Gaveau has agreed to ten concerts a year at a fee of 10,000 francs apiece, and in addition two Prokofiev festivals at the Grand Opéra. He offers a three-year contract. In a few days the firm will invite me to attend for final negotiations.

We were at the Koussevitzkys for the evening: he played four gramophone recordings of the *Classical* Symphony, from which one must be chosen. This was difficult: they were all so good I did not know which to choose.

Lourié had visited them in the afternoon. His comment on *Apollo* was that it is a wonderful work in which not a single note has not been taken from somewhere or other.

25 May

Felt lazy (because of the heat?) and did very little. Read the proofs of the piano score of the Quintet and sorted out the press reviews of *The Gambler* to send to Asafyev and Meyerhold. Called in to the publishers' office where they told me Rachmaninoff had bought a copy of *Prodigal Son*.

In the evening I was invited to the house of a certain M. Orcel, a rich Frenchman, where Sofronitsky was taking part in a whole evening of chamber music devoted to my compositions: the 'Jewish Overture',[1] pieces for violin and piano, the cello *Ballade*,[2] some songs, the Third Piano Sonata, *Visions fugitives* and other pieces. The performances were not good, but the general attitude to me was.

---

1 *Overture on Hebrew Themes*, Op. 34, composed in 1919.
2 *Ballade* for cello and piano, Op. 15, composed in 1915.

26 May

C.S. Church. Afterwards, at home I found a long letter from Derzhanovsky. Gusman,[1] who is head of repertoire at the Bolshoy Theatre, wants not only to do a production of *Le Pas d'acier*, but to invite me on to the repertoire committee of the theatre. So that I do not lose all contact with abroad he proposes that I should spend each year three months in the autumn and another three months in the spring. The letter excited me. Six months, of course, is ridiculous, far too long, especially now that I am just beginning to make headway abroad. But a month in the autumn and a month in the spring, say, would be very interesting. The most important thing is to have a guarantee at the highest level that I would have absolute freedom of movement in and out of the country.

In the afternoon I attended a C.S. lecture but I am ashamed to say that I was so sleepy that I had a real struggle to make myself pay attention.

Dinner was at Paichadze's, a very grand affair.

27 May

Made the changes in the scherzo of the Third Symphony that I had conceived during the rehearsals.

In the afternoon I had intended to listen to the dress rehearsal of Rieti's *Le Bal*, but was late and got there only when it was about to end. I did not speak to Diaghilev as I was still sulking over the *Prodigal Son* choreography ('the Captain deserting the bridge of his ship at the critical moment'). After *Le Bal* they rehearsed Auric's *La Pastorale*, which has been revived with new choreography and some cuts. Auric has always hankered after operetta, and after *Pastorale* has finally switched to it. *Pastorale* has one tune, in C major, with such a circus feeling that Diaghilev leapt from his seat and said, 'Play that as fast you possibly can!' Désormière objected that the orchestra could not play it any faster, at which Diaghilev himself started conducting, standing

---

[1] Boris Gusman (1892–1944), musical and literary critic, screenwriter, Soviet cultural official, currently Head of Repertoire at the Bolshoy Theatre. Later he would become Head of the Arts Division of the All-Union Committee of Radio and Film Affairs, in which capacity he was particular help to Prokofiev. He was an early and committed supporter, and remained so until he was repressed in the wave of purges towards the end of the 1930s. It was Gusman's commission on behalf of the Committee in 1934 that was responsible for the making of one of the most immediately and enduringly popular works in the entire Prokofiev canon, the Suite from Faintsimmer's satirical film *Lieutenant Kijé*, for which two years earlier the composer had provided somewhat randomly conceived packets of incidental music. Gusman also organised a series of conspicuously promotional broadcast concerts during the visit Prokofiev was to make to the Soviet Union in 1934, including the First Piano Concerto, the *Symphonic Song*, Op. 57 (which went down as badly with the Moscow press as it had with the Paris critics), and the *Egyptian Nights* Suite, Op. 61.

behind Désormière and urging on the tempo. Someone told me that during the piano rehearsals he wanted only the accompaniment to be played so that he would not have to listen to the theme.

28 May

Haensel has come over from America with his wife. We treated them to a delicious lunch at Prunier today. Haensel was uncommonly nice, relishing the food. Then they came home with us, and I presented them with road maps of France and guidebooks with lists of hotels and restaurants as they are going off tomorrow to motor round France. There is little news about concerts in America. Koussevitzky, needless to say, is getting carried away, saying that I ought to go for five months and, as I did in 1926, for two and a half months around Christmas.

Not having succeeded in reaching agreement with Paichadze about the publication of my Third Symphony or about Myaskovsky's songs, and with Koussevitzky leaving tomorrow for Berlin, I requested an audience with him. At seven o'clock Paichadze and I were at his house. We had a pleasant conversation. Myaskovsky's songs were accepted, but since according to Paichadze no one is buying songs at the moment, it was decided to ask Myaskovsky to suggest some other works besides. As for my Third Symphony, I succeeded, not without a struggle, in pushing through my request to have the score and perhaps the string parts engraved. Paichadze tried to insist that our Paris engraver is so overloaded with work that he would not be able to undertake it in the foreseeable future, but I reminded him that there is a good engraver in Bordeaux, and he capitulated.

Evening at the Diaghilev performance. First on the bill was *The Steel Step*, which as before was greeted enthusiastically, and then the premiere of Rieti's *Le Bal*. The music is pleasant enough, but it is the music of a man who has lost his way and is reduced to clutching at straws. Chirico's[1] sets are mediocre but his costumes are excellent. The production was a success from the very first moment, eliciting loud applause after every number. I caught myself resenting it. What could this be? Jealousy? Unwillingness to tolerate the success of others in my presence? But this is shameful. Far better for me to be angry that meretricious and derivative music, however superficially pleasing (attractive dross) should evoke such enthusiasm. But this is just it: the moment something of this ilk is juxtaposed with my ballet I am forced subconsciously to measure one against the other, and this 'noble

---

1 Giorgio de Chirico (1888–1978), Italian Surrealist painter, best known for the brooding 'metaphysical' cityscapes he produced in the first two decades of the century, and for his acknowledged influence on other Surrealists such as Max Ernst, Salvador Dalí and René Magritte.

anger'¹ must be stamped on at once. What does it matter if the public lacks the cultivated understanding to tell the difference? Let it enjoy itself. The conclusion of the ballet was greeted with an ovation. Rieti took several curtain calls, but the pit was yelling for 'Chirico' who, however, appeared only at the end. I went up to Rieti in the interval and congratulated him. To him I was friendliness itself, and I was pleased to see that my congratulations touched him.

29 May

Evening brought a fairly depressing letter from Spaak. The further *Gambler* performances have been postponed until the autumn because of the illness of Polina. Do they really not have an understudy? I did not want to think that there could be other reasons for the cancellation after so much effort, the great success it had enjoyed, the excellent press notices... The day was spent in discussions with Ptashka about where to go for the summer. We were so late in finding a dacha that it was going to be very difficult to find one suitable. We concentrated on Yonne,² a picturesque *département* in the middle of France, and not too near Paris, so that dachas are not as sought after as other places, yet not so far away that it would not be feasible to search by car. We sent off letters of enquiry to various places.

30 May

Nabokov's wife called yesterday and we went together to *Prodigal Son*. But once again it was a disappointment, partly because of the staging but also because of the orchestra, which was full of deputies and therefore came seriously to grief in the 5/4 number and the clarinet solo in the robbery scene. Goodness knows what the three clarinets were playing, their entries were all wrong, and when they finished one could hear Désormière cursing. When I went in to see him during the interval he was beside himself with rage, and asked me to write him a letter of complaint for him to present to the musicians' union. A more undisciplined musician than the French player does not exist!

I wrote my letter to Désormière, and also a long one to Myaskovsky about his songs and my premieres.³

---

1 '... fool me not so much
   To bear it tamely; touch me with noble anger' (Shakespeare, *King Lear*, Act 2 scene 4).
2 A *département* of Burgundy in eastern France, whose principal town is Auxerre.
3 'I am a dreadful swine not to have written to you before, but between three of my works' premieres I have been as if lost between three pine-trees. But there was another reason as well: I thought I would wait until the owner of our publishing company arrived so that I could talk to him about publishing your songs. The issue is that the publishers would like to have a closer connection with you, and for it not to be limited to songs, which they regard as commercially the least attractive: songs do not sell in the West.' (Prokofiev to Myaskovsky, 30 May 1929.)

In the course of bringing order into my Third Symphony I dug out the notes I had made during the *Gambler* rehearsals.[1] No joke, this – there were seven pages of them! I composed the scene I now planned to insert into the first act.

Following our journey to Monte Carlo, that is to say after a gap of two months, I finally took the car to a garage on the outskirts of the city to be lubricated.

31 May

A number of letters, including one from Meyerhold from which I deduced that things in Russia are not very good (if I go there I shall be pressed to write politically acceptable music). There was also one from the Philharmonic Society in Brussels offering three concerts of my music for a fee of $750; I think I should probably be able to get $1,000. Blois called while I was out, which was a pity. It's time the Gaveau business was settled. The Borovskys also visited, in gloomy mood. They are having money problems. In the evening we all went to the cinema to see a Russian film: *Women of Ryazan*.[2] It contained many images pulling me back to my native land, particularly the fields of waving rye. To go, or not to go?

Completed the interpolated scene.

1 June

Lunch at Bassiano's in Versailles. Delightful people, delicious food, a wonderful garden. A long conversation with Honegger about motor cars: he was going straight after lunch to put down a deposit on a new one. I drove him to the Bugatti showrooms.

In the afternoon another long conversation, this time with Mémé, who is constantly at odds with Ptashka. Mémé is a wonderful person, but what a difficult character! So stubborn and quick to take offence.

Evening at Benois'.

2 June

C.S. Church. Thought about a C.S. hymn book. Some time I must look through the one they have and add to it. Too many of the hymns are at best incidental, and how many more splendid ones could be included!

Caught up on my diary.

---

1 In Brussels.
2 A silent film (1927) by Olga Preobrazhenskaya about the downtrodden situation of women in rural Russia before the Revolution. One of the most enduring productions of early Soviet cinema, due to its psychological insights and superb acting.

3 June

Just as I was emerging from the hairdresser's on the Champs-Elysées but hesitating to poke my nose into the street because of the rain, I heard a voice say, 'Greetings.' It was Glazunov, walking slowly along in the rain, with no umbrella. 'I'm on my way to Godowsky,' he explained. I was embarrassed that he had been the first to salute me, and hastened to express my pleasure at our meeting.

Later, at the publishers, I saw Stravinsky and told him of the encounter. Stravinsky related in turn how at the concert conducted by Glazunov that had taken place a few days ago (I did not attend) he, Stravinsky, went to see Glazunov afterwards in the Artists' Room, but Glazunov, apparently deliberately, did not recognise him. 'Alexander Konstantinovich, look, it's me, Stravinsky!' he cried, at which Glazunov coldly shook his hand and turned away. In a most uncharacteristic manner, Stravinsky added resentfully that it was a long time since he had felt so discomfited as after this incident.[1]

Blois called and set out the proposed agreement with Gaveau. Gaveau, it seems, is the hidden principal as the contract itself would be with de Valmalète,[2] an impresario who is close to Gaveau. The agreement is not precisely the one I have been expecting, but the figure of 100,000 francs for ten concerts is guaranteed, and he will also sponsor two orchestral concerts to the tune of 50,000 francs. What I hear is that this is not enough to pay for anything really good. I studied the agreement and made some notes.

4–10 June

On the 4th and the 6th of the month I was at performances of *Prodigal Son*, once with the Borovkys. The clarinettist, following Désormière's intervention – my letter in his hands – had been dismissed, and this had had an effect on the other members of the orchestra which was now playing better although still badly by most standards. In contrast to the first night the hall was far from full, and Diaghilev was not present. Kokhno flitted past from time to time and greeted me civilly, but I was cool in return. Suvchinsky sat with Lourié and when the performance ended said to me, rubbing his hands, that 'an article will be written'. By this he meant that Lourié would write a review in *Eurasia* magazine, something he had been reluctant to

---

1 Glazunov had conducted the Orchestre Symphonique de Paris in the music to his ballet *The Seasons*. Writing to Steinberg a few days later, Glazunov tells a completely different story, according to which the two composers greeted one another cordially and Stravinsky, after the usual Green Room congratulations, politely asked to be lent the score so that he could study it.
2 Marcel de Valmalète, who founded the music agency that bears his name in 1924. He was the brother of the distinguished pianist and teacher Madeleine de Valmalète.

commission Lourié to do before being certain that the latter liked the work. It was clear that Lourié was impressed, and made as if to wish to speak to me, but I briskly greeted him and as briskly shook his hand before departing. Better for now to let his favourable opinion mature inside him.

On Saturday the 8th I was served with a summons to appear in court. At first I thought this was a recurrence of the business over the apartment, but it proved to be Kokhno taking out an injunction against the publication of the piano score of *Prodigal Son* on the grounds that it was on sale with no mention of his name as author of the libretto. The cheek of it! What a scoundrel! When the cover of the score was being printed, I had asked Paichadze, 'We're not going to credit Kokhno with the scenario, are we? What kind of a librettist is he anyhow?', to which Paichadze replied, 'Of course we're not.' And that was how it was printed, but the problem is that Kokhno is listed by the French Society of Authors as the librettist, and this is the basis for his suit.

The next day was Sunday the 9th, and as usual Koussevitzky was receiving guests for tea. Paichadze, who had received a similar summons, and I agreed to stay and talk about the situation afterwards. When I came into the room Stravinsky was already there. The incident had disturbed him deeply.

'I came specially because of it,' he said. 'This is less Kokhno's doing than Diaghilev's. Without Diaghilev he would never dare do such a thing. The only time a Greek breathes easy is when he's hurting someone – it's an internal itch that demands to be scratched.'

I realise that Stravinsky is at loggerheads with Diaghilev over the cuts made to *Apollo*,[1] all the same I am touched that he is moved to take my part in such a way.

On the 10th Paichadze, Stravinsky and I went to see a lawyer specialising in literary cases. He was elegant and pessimistic: once authors of a work have been linked in the submission to the Society of Authors one cannot be cited without the other. Stravinsky did most of the talking, getting very heated, producing a string of arguments and vilifying Kokhno. I know Stravinsky to be an Honorary Member of the Society of Authors because he likes nothing better than to be able to drop this fact into conversation, so I was waiting expectantly for it to be brought up. But only at the very end of the discussion was it mentioned, just as we were leaving. The lawyer explained that Kokhno's most imminent demand was that the piano score be removed immediately from sale, whereas settlement of the dispute could be expected to take many

---

[1] It seems Diaghilev considered Terpsichore's variation musically too similar to Calliope's and decided to cut it altogether, not in Paris or at least in the London premiere because the composer conducted these performances himself, but during the autumn 1928 tour. See Richard Buckle, *Diaghilev*, Hamish Hamilton, London, 1984, and Walsh, op. cit., pp. 469, 478, 482.

months. What we must try to establish is that the publishing company was issuing the music, not the text, therefore the only relevant author is the composer of the music. It might be that the court would agree with this argument. In the meantime Paichadze, for safety's sake, would send 900 of the 1,000 copies printed to Berlin, where they could not be so speedily impounded.

Going our separate ways at the crossroads, I thanked Stravinsky for his comradely feelings. 'Believe me, Seryozha,' he said, 'I am very interested in this matter and not merely out of love for you but from detestation of Kokhno. However, we are not just dealing with Kokhno in this instance, we are also dealing with Diaghilev, and there is more besides: his line of fire is aimed not just at you but at our publishers.[1] Paichadze and I will increase the costs of the material he hires. You will see, he will end up paying for our lawyer!'

11 June

Woke at six still smarting over the Kokhno story. Tried to conquer my anger by reading C.S. A person develops in proportion to his success in overcoming obstacles. The Kokhno business must be seen as nothing more than a hurdle to be negotiated. Treat it as an exercise, an exercise in building up immunity to all earthly passions and defilement. Such is the only correct attitude to this conflict and the only way any benefit can be extracted from it.

Went to my first meeting with Gaveau. Blois was waiting for me downstairs. He repeated his protestations about not wanting to hear one word about taking a percentage for his efforts to bring about an agreement with Gaveau: when he, Blois, had lost his position with Pleyel I had been the only one to maintain cordial relations with him (something I do not actually recall), everyone else turned their backs on him. Gaveau is an elderly gentleman with a long nose and glittering eyes; he speaks quietly and with great courtesy. After exchanging the conventional pleasantries he asked de Valmalète to come in and began to go through the contract, a process that took over an hour. They then asked for forty-eight hours to consider. We parted with elaborately studied politeness on both sides, but I was unhappy with the outcome and asked Blois, 'What was all that play-acting about? Are they going to agree or are they not? After all, it is perfectly obvious that in offering guarantees of this sort they are going to lose something, and that something will fall to be paid by Gaveau.' Blois explained that Gaveau wants de Valmalète to contribute to the costs and this is causing the latter to haggle.

---

1   At the height of the row about the cuts to *Apollo* Paichadze had threatened to ban further performances by the Ballets Russes.

Horowitz came in the afternoon; I demonstrated some of my compositions to him as he is planning to play them next season.

In the evening I played bridge with the Samoilenkos. Professor Alexinsky, with an air of fatherly indulgence, forgave me for my appearance at the Soviet Embassy and partnered me at the bridge table. But I have already been invited to another reception on the 18th. Should I accept or decline?

12 June

We accompanied the Koussevitzkys to the station to see them off on their way to America for a three-day stay – he is receiving a second honorary doctorate somewhere amid the ritual pomp of a medieval ceremony. Then Fiedler, who is urging us to buy a flat, took us off to view a building under construction. But it was expensive, too far away from the centre, and cramped.

In the afternoon I made some changes to the third act of *The Gambler*. Suddenly there was a telephone call from Diaghilev to ask if I would conduct the first performance [of *Prodigal Son*] in London. I replied that I had no particular desire to do so, but before discussing the proposal it would be helpful to receive payment for the performance I had conducted in Paris. He then asked if I would be coming to the closing performance of the season that evening. I said I was not sure. 'Yes, well,' returned Diaghilev, 'it is completely sold out so I cannot be sure there would be a ticket for you.'

I remained silent while Diaghilev continued to talk, saying that if my decision about London was final, of course he would not dream of insisting because the opening in London would in any case be a sell-out; it was not an occasion for which any great efforts had to be made to bring in an audience. If, however, I were to change my mind, we could settle the details tomorrow but not later, because he would be leaving tomorrow for Berlin.

I said, 'No, my decision is unlikely to change.'

The whole exchange took place in a lively, almost bantering tone, with Diaghilev doing most of the talking and me saying very little. Afterwards Ptashka was indignant and said she was very surprised at my tone of voice. I should have said straight out to Diaghilev, not concealing my voice, that I was not at home. I think quite the contrary: it would have been wrong to let Diaghilev know that I am in any way upset by Kokhno's aggressive move, but right at the same time show him that I am not much interested in what he has to say and am gently but firmly disengaging from him. It is a clear signal to him that I have taken note of his role in the affair.

While visiting one of her friends Ptashka met Pruna, who on learning of Kokhno's legal action exclaimed in a fury that the man is universally detested. Hitherto everyone has kept their feelings to themselves, but now all of a sudden they are giving vent to them. If Kokhno had done any such thing to him, Pruna, all that would now be left of Kokhno would be a damp smear on the ground.

13 June

A very sage review of the choreography of *Prodigal Son* has appeared in one of the French newspapers: 'Nous avons l'impression que les nouveautés de M. Diaghilev sont réglées désormais par quelque professeur de culture physique qui serait devenu subitement fou en parcourant une galerie de tableaux modernes.'[1]

Called at the publishers. Paichadze's outlook is pessimistic: Kokhno is sure to win his case tomorrow and will be empowered to sequester all copies of the *Prodigal Son* score.

Ptashka and I went on to Mme Dubost's, where a crowd of people had come to hear a children's choir from Czechoslovakia sing. I received many congratulations on the success of *Prodigal Son* yesterday: the Diaghilev season had ended with a full house and at the end of *Prodigal Son* the curtain had been raised and lowered seven times.

I caught a fleeting glimpse of Stahl, looking fresh as a cucumber.

In the evening we went to a concert by Koshetz, who has recently come back from America. The only piece of my music she sang was Fata Morgana's curse. Taken out of its context in the opera it sounded to me rather ludicrous. For that reason I long resisted taking a bow when there were calls for me to do so. Afterwards there was supper at Koshetz's, and among the guests was Stokowski, very friendly, but why does he not engage me next season when he knows perfectly well from Koussevitzky that I am coming to America?

14 June

Preliminary judgment had been given yesterday afternoon in the matter of the seizure of the printed scores of *Prodigal Son*, but because of visiting Dubost and then the Koshetz concert I had not learned the result at the time. Today, with some hesitation, I telephoned Paichadze to be informed that we had won: the court refused Kokhno's application and awarded costs against him. Kokhno now has the right to institute actual legal proceedings, but this is a lengthy undertaking that would take a year or two and cost a great deal

---

1 'We have the impression that the new productions of M. Diaghilev are henceforth determined by some professor of physical culture or other who has suddenly gone mad while inspecting an exhibition of modern pictures.'

of money. Needless to say I was thrilled by this outcome, Ptashka even more so. But I immediately made an effort to take myself in hand, not to glory in my triumph at the expense of another's misfortune. If I had earlier succeeded in regarding Kokhno's aggression as an experience to be undergone, now I must make myself regard victory over him as an experience in personal decency.

Dukelsky came to lunch. He had come from London yesterday and already knew from Paichadze about the case. Today I could tell him the result, but purposely did so *en passant*. Dukelsky was astonished: he had been sure Kokhno would not miss the target. He played me the end of *The Aristocratic Peasant Girl*,[1] but it was note for note out of *Apollo*. I launched such a furious onslaught on him that, abashed, he promised to revise it.

Gorchakov also came by. He has been acting as a Scout leader in Nice and is as brown as an Indian. He showed me his new compositions. Among the usual collection of drivel as before were glimmerings of two really rather good ideas. I suggested that he gather together all those passages I had at one time or another marked out from his writings and make from them a set of piano pieces. If he did that it might be possible to look at publishing them.

15 June

As has been my practice during the past few days I worked on revising *The Gambler* by incorporating the changes I had noted down in Brussels during the rehearsals, also checking the French and German translations. This represents a tremendous amount of work that has to be done before the piano score can be given to the engraver. Along the way I have been thinking about an orchestral fantasia I could make from the music to *The Gambler*.[2]

A Larghetto movement for the Divertimento[3] is turning into something very lovely. I have been composing the themes for it gradually for a while.

---

1 *Mistress Into Maid (Baryshnya-Krest'yanka)*, Dukelsky's only opera, based on one of Pushkin's *Tales of Belkin*. See above pp. 740–1.
2 This conception seems not to have been realised, but in 1931 Prokofiev created a five-movement orchestral suite from *The Gambler*, entitled *Four Portraits and Dénouement from The Gambler*, Op. 49.
3 The *Divertimento* for orchestra, Op. 43, has a balletic provenance. The first and third movements had their origins in re-orchestrated versions of the later-added Overture and *Matelote* for the Romanov ballet *Trapèze* of 1925–6, while the finale, entitled 'Epilogue', makes use of material that was conceived for *Prodigal Son* but was eventually discarded. As Prokofiev wrote to Asafyev in October 1929, the 'still, limpid' (David Nice, op. cit.) Larghetto is 'a continuation of the atmosphere and lyricism of *Prodigal Son*'. Nine years later, after his final return to Russia, Prokofiev made a slightly altered piano version of the four-movement orchestral work, the *Divertissement* for piano, Op. 43a.

Yesterday Gorchakov told me that he had been to see Stravinsky in Nice to show him his compositions. Stravinsky, in the course of a homily of moral admonitions, had this to say: 'I insist(!) that young composers compose at the piano, so that in the process of so doing the flesh of the fingers can copulate with the flesh of the instrument.'

16 June

Worked on *The Gambler*.

Evening at the Samoilenkos. Present also was Taïrov,[1] fresh in from Moscow.

17 June

A female friend of Ptashka's has suggested a dacha in Brittany on the Atlantic coast, about 100 kilometres north of Rochelets, where we had stayed in 1921. Her description of it was tempting, so we decided to have a look at it.

As it happened, tomorrow there is a big tea at the Embassy to which I had been invited and which I had promised to attend, so it was actually very convenient on that day to be a long way away from Paris.

No sooner had we decided to make the trip and begun to look at the map than I was fired with a desire to get going immediately. I rang Taïrov and asked if he would like to come along with us. He was on the point of agreeing, but at that very moment received a telegram from Barcelona and had to go there without delay. B. N. Samoilenko and Schubert said they could come, however.

We dined with Koshetz and then went with her to *Tsar Saltan*, not an opera I am especially fond of, although it has its good moments.

---

1   See above, pp. 278–9. In 1923 Taïrov had taken his Kamerny Teatr on a tour of France and Germany which was supposed to last five weeks but actually continued for seven months. This was because of the sensational success his productions achieved, particularly in Germany (he was less admired in Paris, which is why Diaghilev had been ambivalent about asking him to produce *Le Pas d'acier*) where he was regarded as the leader of the international revolutionary movement in theatre; a bust of Taïrov was commissioned by the University of Cologne. Financially, however, the tour was a disaster and the theatre faced bankruptcy on its return to the Soviet Union, where faint rumblings of official disapproval for the company's Western, cosmopolitan inclinations were also already beginning to be heard. Indeed a repertoire that included O'Neill (*Desire Under the Elms, The Hairy Ape*), Shaw (*Saint Joan*), Wilde (*Salome*) and Brecht-Weill (*Threepenny Opera*) was by the end of the 1920s not calculated to win the political backing the company needed. In 1929 Taïrov was setting out again to re-establish the European contacts that had made his reputation earlier in the decade.

18 June

The four of us set off by car to look at the dacha: Ptashka, Schubert, Samoilenko and I. The weather was perfect, the company agreeable and the roads good. We spent the night at a little place on the Loire.

19 June

Passed through Nantes and then cut north to the little town of Trinité-sur-mer. The landscape changed abruptly to one of sand, low hills and bushes. Not so attractive, but the ocean is wonderful.

By lunchtime we were in Trinité and in the considerable heat went to inspect the dacha. Round it was a fairly good garden, but the house itself was not up to much, pretty much a ruin. Ptashka's friend had obviously not suspected this in sending us here.

Having decided it was not for us we sat on the beach, had lunch and then made a move to start the return journey. We were not too disappointed: we had not found a dacha, but we had had an enjoyable excursion. Coming home we took a more northerly route via Rennes, where we were forced to spend the night as one of the wheels had started to smoke.

20 June

All morning was wasted in the garage fussing about with wheel bearings, and as a result it was late in the evening by the time we got back to Paris. I dislike driving in the dark, but B. N. Samoilenko sat beside me and enlivened me with his presence.

21 June

Blois has made unremitting efforts with Gaveau, with de Valmalète and with me, to get each of us to make concessions so that we can end up reaching agreement. Paichadze and Koussevitzky are also advising me to be flexible and not to let this opportunity slip through my fingers. I had an appointment today with de Valmalète and this time he made a much better impression. He told me quite candidly that he very much wanted to have me on his list, but his resources are not unlimited and he cannot take such a big risk. Gaveau is extremely mercenary and tries with every trick in the book to minimise his own exposure.

A recital by Celia in the evening. She played a lot of meretricious stuff, which was tedious. The hall was full of people I know.

22 June

As I had not been at the Embassy reception and am anxious not to fall out with them because of our need to renew our passports, I decided today to call on Arens and explain the situation.

He received me in a very friendly manner, and I began by showing him press notices of *Le Pas d'acier*, selected expressly to lay stress on the factory workers and general Bolshevistic aspects of the ballet. All this had been carefully typed out together with translations into Russian and notes of the source newspapers and dates. It was an impressive document and produced the most favourable effect on Arens. On top of this I presented him, great music-lover that he is, with a score of *Le Pas d'acier*, inscribed personally to him. After this the tone of the conversation became exceptionally friendly and I simply told him that although my Soviet passport had been renewed for eighteen months I was still continuing to use my Nansen passport, on the grounds that since the Ministry of Foreign Affairs had issued me with a Soviet document without taking possession of my Nansen papers I was within my rights to do so. But I added that I believed it was now time to put an end to this situation. Arens had this to say in reply: 'I think so too: it is not, of course, that we would make difficulties for you over this, but you could get into trouble with foreign police authorities if they get to know that you have two passports.' With this he took our Soviet passports and said I should report back to the Consulate in two days or so, when they would extend the passports' validity for me. 'Naturally, you will have to pay for this,' he added. 'I am quite ready to do so,' I said.

The conversation then turned to the possibility of a visit by Myaskovsky, and Arens promised his co-operation: he would write to Moscow expressing the Embassy's view that this would be a desirable eventuality. Wishing to make myself agreeable to him, I said that that my publishers and I had agreed the switch from dollars to roubles in the matter of the fees due to me for performances of my operas. 'But what am I going to do with these roubles?' I asked, half jokingly.

Arens: 'Build yourself an apartment in Moscow. And then, why not engage engravers in Moscow to engrave your works, even if they are destined for the foreign market?'

Both these ideas struck me as interesting. I had already been thinking about an apartment there.

23 June

The Chalons, who have a small estate near the Lac du Bourget, have sought out for us a 'stunningly beautiful' castle which is not too expensive, about 7,000 for the summer. So today we took a train and went to look at it, a journey of some eight hours. As evening drew on we alighted at Culoz, a big railway junction through which trains pass on their way to Geneva, Milan, Aix and Evian. Last year Dukelsky and I had gone through it in the Ballot on the way from Monte Carlo to Paris, but although on that occasion we did not stop the place itself remained imprinted on my memory. After dinner we went to look at the exterior of the castle, which stands on the top of a small hill about a kilometre from the station. It is without a doubt impressive, and quite forbidding in aspect, with towers and wall slits for firing your arquebus through. Tomorrow morning we have an appointment with the owners, and since according to the Chalons they are somewhat autocratic chatelaines, we decided not to disturb them today and instead made our way back to the little hotel by the station to sleep.

24 June

Next morning we climbed up to the castle, which is an incredibly imposing pile. We were overcome with the desire to live in it. We met the owner, Mme de la Fléchère, dressed in a fashion long out of date but with the courteous manners of the aristocrat, even if she did talk rather too volubly, presumably out of anxiety to let her castle. To quote the immortal formulation of Bashkirov, we had 'mixed impressions': on the one hand the medieval building dating back to the fourteenth century (rebuilt in the sixteenth) was really most attractive and the view on all four sides divine – hills, mountains, meadows, the river Rhône, part of a lake. On the other hand we do not really need such a monstrous edifice with its hidden corners smelling of mould and others thick with dust. How on earth are we going to get the place in some sort of order? The bathroom was appalling and the kitchen like something from a set for an opera, but how, if you please, were we ever to cook anything on an oven like that? I stated my view that despite this we should take the château, particularly in view of the time pressure – in five days we were going to be evicted from our flat – and of not actually having anywhere else in mind to look. Nevertheless, knowing all too well Ptashka's disposition, which is never to be satisfied with anything, I said that I would leave the decision up to her. Her response was to agonise for half an hour and then decide, but without any great conviction, that yes, probably we should take it. When we got down to discussing the agreement with the owner she acted in true blue-blood style: everything was done verbally, nothing in writing. That done we boarded the train once more and after another eight hours of heat and soot were back in Paris.

25 June

Ptashka is appalled at what we have done agreeing to rent the castle. Her bad mood began yesterday while we were still on the return journey in the train. It now seems I had forced her into renting this dreadful barracks. I protested that, on the contrary, I had prudently ceded the decision to her.

'Yes, but you wanted to, didn't you?'

'Yes, I did want to, but God only knows why. I have not the slightest desire for it now.'

Worked in the afternoon.

26 June

Saw Arens again. Our passports have been renewed and are ready. The charge for this was 900 francs, not an inconsiderable sum but I am glad to have it settled. We spoke of my returning to Russia in the autumn and I raised the question of there being no obstacles put in my way to leaving the country at the end of the visit. Arens said that Soviet citizens who have current business abroad and who are visiting the USSR are sometimes granted permission to leave the country immediately. Because of *Le Pas d'acier*(!) this provision could be seen as covering my situation; the Embassy had already requested this privilege on my behalf. Arens repeated his willingness to support Myaskovsky's travel abroad. In a week's time he would himself be going to Moscow and would press the appropriate buttons.

Blois came rushing round in the morning with the news that after putting up a fight Gaveau had finally agreed to cover de Valmalète with a second guarantee and therefore at that stage everything was settled. However, just yesterday the whole matter seemed to be heading for disaster, because whereas initially Gaveau had very much wanted me, someone had subsequently been whispering in his ear. 'Who, for example?' I enquired.

Blois: 'Perhaps he has been consulting one of our adorable French composers.'

In the afternoon I went into the publishers. Kleiber has taken my Second Symphony for Berlin, and Klemperer for South America. The latter, however, has made only a provisional commitment, and personally I feel the proviso to be a large one: on the way he will get cold feet and will not perform it. Matters are less good with *Fiery Angel*: four major German theatres have turned it down on grounds of the difficulty of the music and the undramatic nature of the libretto. I know that there are parts of it that dramatically speaking are problematical, but there are also parts that are exceptionally dramatic. It is inevitable that the first time the opera is produced some passages will be subjected to cuts and chops and changes. I am less upset than I was that *Fiery Angel* is not going to be produced, as the music has already been heard in the Third Symphony.

Stravinsky has returned from Berlin and already left to go home to Nice. His concert in Berlin coincided with the presence in the city of Diaghilev and his company, but Diaghilev did not go to Stravinsky's concert and Stravinsky did not attend the Diaghilev performances.

Yesterday we went to meet the Koussevitzkys, already back from their second, brief, trip to America. He went to be fêted with the award of a doctorate *honoris causa* from Harvard University, and thus is a double doctor (Agrippa[1] was thrice so honoured). Koussya was beaming all over his face and gave us a detailed account of the ceremony. He is an ambitious man, and such formalities are very much to his taste.

28 June

Blois and I spent all morning with de Valmalète discussing various minor points in the contract, and by lunchtime we had reached agreement on all of them. Tomorrow Blois will type it out on embossed paper and I will attend for a signing session.

29 June

Signed the contract with de Valmalète ('Valdemalète').

'The sum total of evil belief Jesus designated a lie; and a lie is a negation – nothing. Therefore, thinking about evil is thinking about nothing.'[2]

July

July began under the banner of packing and departure. Because we are giving up the apartment the procedure was even more onerous than usual. In view of the accumulation of possessions, books and children the number of cases, boxes and trunks has steadily increased geometrically. Of course the main burden of the removal fell on Ptashka, but instead of tackling it with courage and good humour she spent the preceding two weeks in a depression that affected everyone around her. Five of the heaviest boxes were despatched to Gaveau's store room and two taxi-loads of assorted impedimenta to Ptashka's singing teacher, while

---

1 Agrippa of Nettesheim, the sixteenth-century magician and writer on occult practices who is a character in *Fiery Angel*.
2 Noted in English; presumably a quotation from a Christian Science publication.

Astrov[1] took fifteen or so suitcases with him on the train to our dacha. On top of this I had a full load in the Ballot.

Among other events preceding our departure were: a visit to the circus with the Koussevitzkys where we saw lion-tamers and a man being shot from a cannon; a row with Paichadze over *The Gambler* arising from the Germans having shown interest in the latter but Paichadze unwilling to do anything about it because there is no money to produce new material; I wrote forceful letters to Myaskovsky inviting him to come for the summer; Robert Lyon, famous for his rudeness, suddenly responded to my letter about leaving Pleyel with unexpected graciousness; Blois refused yet again any percentage for his efforts in arranging the contract but asked, if Koussevitzky comes next season with the Boston Symphony Orchestra, to be appointed manager of the tour, as he had been for the New York orchestra on a previous occasion. For this reason I took Blois to meet Koussevitzky, but Blois havered and mumbled and Koussevitzky likewise so neither thought much of the other.

At long last, on the 5th, the time came to depart. In the morning we did the inventory and then went to look at yet another flat that had been suggested for us to buy. After some hesitation we turned it down, and it was not until after two that we were finally able to get under way in the Ballot. We made up a cot for Little Brother on the back seat, Elsa (a very splendid Danish girl rejoicing in the surname Bach, whom I introduced to everyone as the composer's granddaughter) beside him, Svyatoslav in her lap. Every inch of remaining space was crammed to the roof with our belongings. Ptashka and I sat in front.

As a result of leaving so late we managed only 250 kilometres on the first day, but even that was good going. We stopped for the night at Avalon, a delightful little town. The children were as good as gold during the journey and the following day towards evening we drove in triumph through the gates of our castle, to find Astrov had already arrived with our things, having mislaid the cook and the Danish nanny who were late for the train.

The château is colossally impressive with its feudal turrets. Inside, it is a daunting, but spacious prospect. There are many rooms and all of them are far away from one another, so at first we could not work out the best way of allocating them. The owners told us that they had spent five days cleaning the house, but the dust of centuries still lay everywhere and we had to engage a cleaning woman who gave it another three, going through the cupboards, under the beds, and especially the canopies hanging over each four-poster

---

1   Mikhail Astrov, whom Prokofiev had come across at the Edition Russe de Musique publishing house and engaged as secretary in succession to Gyorgy Gorchakov.

bed. The owners turned out to be genuine titled gentry: the Comte de la Fléchère de Beauregard, as attested by a leaflet conveniently 'forgotten' on one of the side tables, containing the address spoken by the Abbot on the couple's wedding day. They are actually very nice people, although the Countess talks too much and if you do not yourself bring the conversation to an end there is no hope of her ever drying up. The Count is awkward and evidently ran his business affairs in a chaotic manner (or perhaps did not run them at all) which eventually collapsed in ruin with the destruction of the vineyards of which no one had been around to take care during the war. The castle boasts a good deal of ancient furniture, some of it valuable, some of it just crazy. Some of the armchairs are embroidered with the Count's coronets, which have nine bells. There is a stone spiral staircase in one of the towers, in which one step is for some reason (why?) always wet. Although electricity has been installed everywhere, I came across a bronze candlestick on the main staircase, nailed into the stone wall. I showed it to Chalon, and he said, 'That's not old, it's off a piano.'

The musical tasks I have set myself for the summer are as follows: revise the *Sinfonietta*; finish the *Divertimento*, the material for which is almost ready; finish the Fourth Symphony; if there is time compose an orchestral fantasy on themes from *The Gambler*; get my piano-playing into fighting trim in view of the large number of concerts during the coming winter; practise conducting in private; go through and correct the proofs of the orchestral parts of *Le Pas d'acier*, which will soon have been lying for a year, ditto the piano score of *The Gambler*. Both are due to be engraved soon. Shall I really manage to get all that done?

Work began with a problem to be overcome: Gaveau sent no piano until the 20th of the month. Swine. True, without the piano I looked through the *Sinfonietta* and made a note of what I wanted to change, but the real work could not begin until the piano arrived. As always with revisions the work initially seemed trifling, just a few strokes of the pen, but in fact it proved to need a complete rewrite, just as *The Gambler* had done, and was obviously going to take a month to accomplish. By the 1st August I had completed only the first movement.

In the meantime the lost and found cook lost little time in leaving us for good for Aix-les-Bains (a more amusing location). We embarked on a series of misfortunes finding a replacement, a thing hard to come by in these parts, and those we did find speedily departed as a result of the utterly impossible nobiliary stove. Another plague was the extraordinary proliferation of cockroaches, huge, black ones that soon began to leave the sanctuary of the kitchen to penetrate into the upstairs rooms. On the walls appeared scuttling, watery centipedes. Ptashka took all these manifestations very badly, could not sleep at night, regarded our servant as a good-for-nothing cheat, in short completely failed to keep in perspective these minor inconveniences of life, blowing them up instead into tragedies.

Klein[1] paid us a visit for a few hours. He has recently married and is spending his honeymoon motoring round Europe. As ever we were very glad to see him. I told him of the influence Christian Science has had on the music I have composed in recent years. Some remarks about C.S. he casually let fall have great relevance to questions I have been thinking about.

The Chalons' small estate is 12 kilometres from where we are now. They are friends of Borovsky and are the people who found our castle for us. Chalon is a nice man, a great lover of music and by way of being professionally involved in it although to no great effect despite his undoubted capabilities. He is French, but with some Anglo-Saxon characteristics. His wife, of Spanish extraction, is very charming. They are most hospitable, have excellent 1830 vintage wine, are also Ballot owners and have a whole tribe of dogs. I immediately put him to work on the French text of *The Gambler*, those passages I did not manage to go through with Spaak.

I was thrown into a flurry by a telegram offering an engagement in Chicago, to conduct and play in three concerts for a fee of $1,000 – not much for such demanding work, but on the other hand a sizeable sum of money. But they do not want to pay the publishers for the hire of the material. I had to weigh up the situation from every point of view, send cables to Paris and New York, and it still is not certain whether or not the engagement will be confirmed.

Somewhat unexpectedly we have developed a quite wide circle of acquaintances in the vicinity of Culoz, where my fame appears to have spread largely from the fact of my works having been programmed several times in Lyons during the winter. In addition, the Countess turns out to be a passionate music-lover, and as she knows without exception every château in the district they all got to know instantly that she had a maître staying with her, and became interested.

I discovered that in his business Chalon is a supplier of Maison Pleyel, and as he had recently bought a second-hand Pleyel grand piano lost no time in boasting to Robert Lyon that Prokofiev had played on this piano (it was not bad, in fact). Old man Lyon, who was visiting them, had formerly professed the greatest love and admiration for me and also flirted with Ptashka, once tweaking her nose in a grandfatherly gesture. Now he suddenly exploded and burst out, 'I don't want to hear a word about this person! In the days when he was starting out on his musical career we did everything for him, but as soon as he makes his way in the world he thumbs his nose at us!' (Wonderful,

---

1 See above, pp. 244, 247–8, 269–70, 354–5.

is it not, considering Pleyel never actually did anything for me except smile sweetly.) But Robert stoutly countered his father's attack: 'Que veux-tu?[1] We never supported him with any guarantees, while Gaveau offers him very attractive guarantees against loss via his agent de Valmalète; it's quite obvious that Prokofiev would take them. In his place I would do exactly the same.' Thus Robert, whom everyone thinks a thoroughgoing boor, has for the second time displayed the manners of a gentleman while the old man, who used to make such a show of loving me, slings mud at me!

August

Revising the second movement of the *Sinfonietta* threw up many more difficulties than the first. At the time when I composed this Andante at the age of eighteen, it created an effect by its inventiveness, but now the inventions have lost their lustre and in their place has grown up something I do not like at all. Such, for example, is the opening theme, and it is proving very resistant to modification. The middle section likewise has many passages that now strike one as dull, and stubbornly refuse to change. I regretted not having to hand the black notebook with piano pieces I had written at the time, from which I could have looked out replacement material to work with. Eventually I did manage to compose some fresh material, altered other passages, some I left as they were, and after a considerable amount of work ended up with a good Andante, much better than I expected. I then pounced gladly on the third movement, the Intermezzo, expecting it to be the work of a moment, but got well stuck with that as well, although the problems were different from the Andante: here there was less that needed to be recomposed, but the retouching was for some reason very awkward.

In parallel with the recomposition of the *Sinfonietta* I read the proofs of the orchestral parts for *Le Pas d'acier*. My thoughts kept turning back to the sets and the production, to the Diaghilev season as a whole, and to his role in the Kokhno affair. I found the whole experience left a disagreeable taste in my mouth, and this feeling – because of the Kokhno saga – extended even to *Le Pas* itself.

In between working there were pleasant expeditions with the Chalons. The area is full of little taverns where one can dine gloriously. Chalon proved quite expert in correcting the slips in Spaak's translation of the *Gambler* libretto which I was continually ferreting out. At a distance of 23 kilometres was Aix-les-Bains, a big and fairly unattractive spa town, and near by was staying Koshetz. She laid on a big Russian lunch party for us; among the

---

1 'What do you mean?'

guests the Kokhánskis and La Argentina,[1] whom Chalon had long been avid to meet. Without warning Koshetz's sister brought out the news that apparently Stahl was dying, having suddenly developed cancer of the throat. Janacopoulos was on tour in Java; Stahl had asked the doctors if he would live until she returned but they could not guarantee this. He first wanted to summon her by telegram, but then changed his mind and submitted to a surgical operation. The news saddened me greatly. Our quarrel, of course, had been a farrago straight out of an operetta and recalling Stahl always brought feelings of pleasure. Indeed, the news was all the more of a shock because Stahl seemed to be getting younger every year that passed and the last time I saw him (at Mme Dubost's) he was as fresh as a cucumber.

Another neighbour, somewhat farther away, was Stravinsky. He was staying at Talloires, on the shore of Lake Annecy, 60 kilometres distant. I wrote to him asking if I could pay him a visit, something I was not only quite ready to do but savoured the prospect. In recent years I have tended to avoid him, but now quite the reverse: I wanted very much to see him. There were several reasons for this change of heart. In the first place, of course, the success and adulation heaped on Stravinsky in the West, so far exceeding my own, had always seemed disproportionate in relation to my just deserts. But all the work I had done with Christian Science on countering egocentricity, the desire to compete, and envy had borne fruit, and I by now felt I had succeeded in eradicating these flaws. Needless to say, my recent successes and the good number of concerts I had in prospect contributed significantly to my achieving this state of mind. Another spur was that each time we had met recently Stravinsky had been so warmly affectionate and even-tempered, and on the latest occasions even touching (making the sign of the cross over me as I went out to the conductor's podium) that my ingrained suspicion had yielded to the conjecture that Stravinsky, who had always paraded his religiosity, was likewise working on his moral compass, and it was thus incumbent on me to meet him halfway. And lastly, over the Kokhno business he had leapt so energetically to my defence, and his support will be so material a factor in any future conflict, that I was very reluctant to let my present feelings towards him evaporate.

In short I was waiting anxiously for his answer as to whether I should go or not, when quite unexpectedly he drove in through the gates of our castle, accompanied by both his sons. A lovely gesture: I ask permission to go to see

---

1 Antonia Mercé y Luque (1890–1936), whose stage name was La Argentina, was born in Buenos Aires to Spanish parents and trained initially as a ballet dancer. Soon abandoning it for native Spanish dance, however, her choreographed and stylised versions of flamenco became extremely popular in Paris before and after the First World War, and she is widely credited with having introduced flamenco as a theatrical art form.

him, whereupon he jumps into his car and immediately drives over to me. Stravinsky was in high spirits and full of interesting things to say, talking animatedly and all the time, although mostly about himself, or abusing Milhaud, Diaghilev and Casella – who, according to Stravinsky, is not really Casella at all but Kassel, a Jew. Of course we showed him proudly all over our magnificent castle. Entering my room and seeing the proof-sheets on which I was working strewn about everywhere, he observed with a touch of malice: 'Aha, bohemian disorder!' The room did indeed resemble that hackneyed image of Beethoven composing. Stung, I hastened to explain that I was working at top speed on the proof-reading and making corrections in thick red ink, which meant the pages had to be spread out all around so that they could dry.

Stravinsky wanted to know all kinds of financial details: how much were we paying for the castle, how much would I earn in America? Composition of his piano concerto was making progress. Two movements were complete; he would probably not give the work the title of concerto, perhaps Divertissement. This, apparently, was designed to neutralise objections levelled at the First Piano Concerto that it was insufficiently virtuosic. 'Divertimenti seem to be all the rage,' I exclaimed. 'I'm also making sketches for one, and Myaskovsky is just finishing his!' Stravinsky replied that in that case he would do better to find another title, such as Capriccio.[1] He knew all about Stahl's illness from a letter from Sudeykina, who had even visited him in hospital. The operation had been risky, but he survived, and had even recovered enough to go to meet his returning wife at the station. But in excising the tumour the surgeons had also had to remove his vocal cords, so that he had lost the power of speech permanently and was forced to whisper at the first meeting with his wife, pretending that he had a cold in order to spare her too much of an initial shock. At the present time they are planning a holiday in the Haute Savoie, not far from here (last year we also saw them in Evian). This account yet again moved and disturbed me. I felt a strong desire to see Stahl again, recalling his sharp, mischievous conversation and the twinkle in his eyes. But he is no longer the man he was and no longer has a voice in which to carry on the conversation. And I cannot imagine anything that would be more remote from his thoughts than Christian Science!

As we were without a cook we decided to take Stravinsky to dinner in Arlemarle, 8 kilometres away, where Chalon had introduced us to a first-class restaurant concealed behind a simple exterior. I rolled out my Ballot,

---

[1] The Capriccio for piano and orchestra was first performed on 6 December 1929 in the Salle Pleyel, the composer at the keyboard with the Orchestre Symphonique de Paris conducted by Ansermet.

which looked very elegant alongside Stravinsky's Mathis,[1] except that the Mathis is new and my Ballot is distinctly elderly. I was in front with Stravinsky beside me, and the two boys and Ptashka in the back. Fedya asked me not to drive too fast because the bad road had made their light car bounce about more than my heavier one. The dinner in Arlemarle was first-rate, but Stravinsky declined the fish (laveret, a local speciality) on the grounds that he does not have strong enough bacteria to digest fish, even the freshest, before it begins to putrefy in the stomach. (A dubious proposition.) I would not allow Stravinsky to pay the bill, and afterwards accompanied him several kilometres so that he would not take a wrong turning at the crossroads.

Suvchinsky came the following day (the 21st). I rushed out to welcome him in great good humour, but his first words were to tell me of the death of Diaghilev. 'No?!' I exclaimed, and for a time was quite unable to take in the fact, so alive and vital was the very image of Diaghilev. As Suvchinsky elaborated: 'The day before yesterday . . . of a boil . . . in Venice,' I began gradually to absorb the truth of what had occurred. From a boil – he had always been afraid of boils. When I returned from Russia and we arranged to meet, he cancelled the meeting because he was suffering from a boil, at which I had been very much astonished.

It so happened that Diaghilev's death coincided with a period during which, as a result of our disagreement over the staging of *Prodigal Son*, I was to some extent estranged from him. His having sided against me in the Kokhno affair only served to accentuate the distance between us. I had begun to think that with these ballets the cycle of my relationship with him had come to an end. From a professional point of view his death, so it appeared to me, would not impact on me as it undoubtedly would on other, younger composers: Rieti, Nabokov, Dukelsky. For them, of course, many of their hopes now lay in ruins. But it is of Diaghilev as a leader of genius, Diaghilev as a fascinating personality, Diaghilev as a 'thing' (I remember Suvchinsky once saying about Chaliapin, 'I love him as a "thing"!') that I have the keenest sense of loss.

Ptashka was also very upset and could not get over the fact that yesterday, when Diaghilev was lying on his bier, we were sitting here with Stravinsky taking it out of him wholesale. In slight justification I can say that the attacks all came from Stravinsky, but this is scant justification because we were thoroughly enjoying listening to it. Stravinsky was relating for the third time their falling-out over the cuts in *Apollo*. Diaghilev, in Stravinsky's opinion, did not in the final analysis understand very much about music:

---

1 At the time Mathis was the fourth-largest automobile constructor in France and was bidding fair to rival Citroën for the medium-range saloon market. An association with Ford took chief designer Charles Mathis to the United States during the Second World War, but his attempts to restart his own marque in France after the war with innovative engineering and futuristically streamlined bodywork were not successful and it ceased production in 1946.

understanding was replaced by custom and experience. In my heart of hearts I did not agree because I had a high opinion of Diaghilev's musicianship, which he had demonstrated with his observations about the composition of *Prodigal Son*. Stravinsky then went on to relate how in the hurly-burly of the Gare du Nord someone had touched him on the shoulder: it was Diaghilev saying to him in a strained voice, 'So you're off to London? I'm going to London too. Let's have a talk on the journey.' But neither on the way nor in London did they see one another again although they were staying in the same hotel (in Albemarle Court, where Ptashka and I had stayed). Both sides, evidently, had wanted to avoid one another.[1]

All evening was spent in the shadow of the event. Who would inherit the rights and the sets and costumes? Surely not Kokhno? Would he try to carry on? Of course he would if he could get his hands on the right to do so; it would be his last chance to make a public reputation. But this he would not be able to do. Possibly he could try to fight on with the season since there were contracts with Spain, Holland and one or two other places, and there might even be a new production in the shape of the ballet composed by Hindemith. But it would not last long: the whole enterprise had always been sustained by Diaghilev personally, his intellect and his authority.

Next day I had a bad headache. I did no work, but walked in the mountains for three hours. Suvchinsky talked for a long time to Ptashka about singing; he has a strong tenor voice himself and is going through a phase of absorption in the art. He discovered that Ptashka has a good understanding of the craft and, what is more, an ability to explain technical matters clearly.

Suvchinsky had had an encounter with Glazunov at Kedrov's daughter's wedding in the Russian Church. Glazunov had come up to him while the happy pair were being congratulated and began accusing Asafyev of masterminding plots in the Conservatoire. Taken aback, Suvchinsky told him that according to his information the situation was precisely the opposite: Asafyev had lost virtually all connection with the Conservatoire and was sitting in Detskoe[2] hardly ever leaving the place, absorbed in his scholarly studies. Glazunov seized on this: 'Yes, yes, holed up there, plotting his dirty tricks from the bunker ...' Suvchinsky added that at this moment Medtner appeared from another quarter, and from yet a third Tcherepnin, and at the sight of so many antiques he simply took to his heels.

The Eurasian movement, according to Suvchinsky, has entered a new phase. A Soviet officer, Langovoy, whom I had once met at a Eurasian

---

1 Stravinsky had been engaged to conduct *Apollon musagète* and *Baiser de la fée* with the BBC Symphony Orchestra in the Kingsway Hall.
2 The former Tsarskoe Selo, where Asafyev lived, had been renamed Detskoe (Children's) Village. See above p. 478, n. 3, 491–3.

congress in Berlin and with whom I had had a conversation about Myaskovsky, has now risen high in the ranks of counter-espionage, and through him Arapov,[1] a Evraziist, has received official permission to travel legally to Moscow for talks.

In Suvchinsky's opinion Marx's exegesis of how capital will be overthrown is masterly, but there is much missing from all the prescriptions for what should follow, both in Marx's own projected programmes and in the new concepts developed by the Soviet government. It is in precisely this area that the Evraziisti could be useful. First, they could serve as a channel of communication for foreign relations, a channel that would be less immediately odious to foreigners than the Bolsheviks themselves. In any case, Arapov is now in Moscow and it will be interesting to see what may come of all this.

In the evening a letter arrived from Stravinsky. He had come home from seeing me to find a telegram announcing the death of Diaghilev. Evidently he was feeling, as I did, regret at the hard things we had been saying about him. It was similar to what had happened when we were together in Milan in 1915, when he had spent the whole time excoriating Scriabin, and Scriabin died within the month. On my return to Russia I received a letter from Stravinsky expressing sorrow at Scriabin's death.

The following day, the 23rd, as previously arranged with Stravinsky we – that is Ptashka, Suvchinsky and I – set off in the car to visit him. The weather was wonderful and we drove through beautiful scenery, stopping for lunch on the shores of Annecy in the restaurant we had visited the year before with Asafyev. Stravinsky is staying on the opposite shore of the lake, in a marvellous little place where he and his family have almost taken over the local *pension*. Two hundred paces, a 'piano shot' away, is the small portable cabin[2] where he works. The conversation, naturally, was about Diaghilev. Stravinsky

---

1   Pyotr Arapov (1897–1937?) was a nephew of General Baron Wrangel, Commander-in-Chief of the White Army, and had served with him in the Crimea until Wrangel, the remains of his army and a large number of refugees were evacuated by ship across the Black Sea to Constantinople. Arapov probably began as a genuine sympathiser of the Evraziists' political, historical and cultural ambitions but was at some point 'turned' by the OGPU chief Alexander Yakushev who was presented as the head of the fake anti-Bolshevik underground organisation the Monarchist Union of Central Russia, a counter-intelligence decoy set up by OGPU as part of 'Operation Trust' expressly to flush out potentially dangerous leaders of Royalist and other opposition movements in Western émigré communities. By 1929 Arapov, who had already made two illegal visits to the USSR, was certainly a double agent. John Costello, the historian who was allowed limited access to the TREST files by the FSB, reported that they comprised thirty-seven volumes and were such a bewildering welter of double-agents, changed code names, and interlocking deception operations 'with the complexity of a symphonic score' that even FSB historians had difficulty separating fact from fantasy. In the purges of the 1930s Arapov was arrested and died in Solovki Camp in the remote Solevetsky Islands, the place described by Solzhenitsyn in *The Gulag Archipelago* as 'the Mother of the Gulag'.
2   Stephen Walsh describes it as a 'prefabricated summer house' (S. Walsh, op. cit., p. 485).

played the second and third movements of the Concerto (the first movement is not yet finished). It was interesting, and better than I had been led to expect from our conversations. But it was hard to judge from a first hearing and in a poor performance. I begin to understand his conception of 'good manners': here and there the march-like accompaniment of second-inversion dominant-seventh chords emphasised by brass orchestration verges on what one might think of as vulgar. But it is wonderfully done and full of felicitous juxtapositions.

After this Fyodor sketched a quick and accomplished portrait of me, and then we sat down to dinner. At table Stravinsky and Ansermet embarked on a philosophical discussion, in which Ansermet displayed a high level of education, Suvchinsky injected a stream of technical terminology and Stravinsky took part relatively inconsequentially. I remained silent: since I have become involved with Christian Science I regard it as an expression of the divine, while philosophy is an expression of the flesh. All epistemological questions are but approximations with no hope of an approach to the essence, symbolised by ever-decreasing fractions.

The conversation then changed tack to a resumption of our discussion on the subject of fish. As a joke, but with a straight face, I asked, 'Which do you think is worse for you, grouse which is slightly off (because it tastes better like that) or perfectly fresh fish?'

Stravinsky, without pausing for thought: 'Fish, of course! Saliva slows up the decomposition of the grouse, and the grouse in any case decomposes more slowly in the stomach. Whereas fish, when it is quite fresh, bypasses the saliva, therefore decomposes very quickly in the stomach and is thus much worse for you.'

After this remarkable interlude we reverted to philosophical themes, and then to Diaghilev. The telegram Stravinsky received said, 'Décédé sans souffrances.'[1] Kokhno will not of course be the heir. 'And of course the suit against you will lapse of its own accord now,' added Stravinsky, although it was not clear to me why this should be so.

We left at ten o'clock in the evening promising to come back to play Beethoven quartets in four-hand arrangements. Saying goodbye the sons kissed me. The elder daughter was not present, but the younger one was, a splendid girl aged sixteen already speaking not perfect Russian. Nowadays I am quite happy to drive at night with headlamps. At midnight we dropped in on Koshetz, whom we woke up. She came out with no make-up, which actually suits her better. We continued on our way and Suvchinsky, sitting next to me, said, 'Apparently Diaghilev was very religious. Stravinsky just told me. I did not know that. Did you?' I said I did know. I remember that

---

1 'Died without suffering.'

whenever there was occasion to inform Diaghilev of some misfortune that happened to someone he would say, 'Lord, thy will be done,' and make as if to cross himself. But this is not real piety, it is relative piety, piety that that sits alongside the foul language and scabrous expressions with which Diaghilev's everyday discourse was liberally embellished. It is that kind of piety according to which people declare that if they do not sin they have no need to repent, but then sin and afterwards forget to abase themselves.

The presence of Suvchinsky did not prevent me working. He spent hours walking in the mountains, whence his high singing notes sometimes carried to us. Ptashka was in a bad mood because she was not singing well, and the reason she was not singing well was that she was tired, and what was making her tired was all the housework because we do not have a decent cook. I said it would be better if we just ate omelettes and drank milk and felt happy about it rather than constantly creating dramas over culinary inadequacies. One evening I played Suvchinsky the three complete movements of the *Sinfonietta* and the sketches I had made for the fourth movement. He liked them very much, but what produced the strongest impression on him was the first movement of the Fourth Symphony: 'This is entirely new music from you, new melodic territory.' This was curious because I had played him the opening Allegro movement before, during the winter soon after composing it. True, I had not played him the Introduction then, but Suvchinsky seemed rather vague about it and could not now remember that this was not the first time I had played it. On the other hand the Larghetto of the *Divertimento*, which I was now playing him for the first time, made little impact, and I so love this Larghetto! What does this mean? Is it that my music gets through to him only after some time has elapsed?

Once or twice we talked about religion. Suvchinsky's talk, as always in such circumstances, was peppered with technical expressions and references to various writers. He commands outstanding erudition and a retentive memory. But this does not faze me now, and I was able to joust successfully with him, privately relying on Christian Science. We differed on several points: on questions of the sacraments, on the doctrines of the Orthodox Church, on Suvchinsky's conviction that life beyond the grave is the mirror image of this life in that the greater the suffering here and now, the greater the bliss of the afterlife. We differed when I asserted that man, as the Son of God, has a right to be happy ('He has no such right! He must suffer!' cried Suvchinsky). Where we agreed was that essentially there is no such thing as a genuine atheist, that to say an atheist who has truly thought the question out to its ultimate. Suvchinsky was at one with me in saying that atheism had developed in a decadent period of philosophy, and atheists keep on constructing one theory out of another while simply ignoring God. To my astonishment we also concurred on the unreality of evil. This I did not expect from Suvchinsky! One of these conversations I suddenly realised we were carrying on over dinner with wine, which Suvchinsky likes to drink, and judging this to be shameful tried to bring it to a close. A similar thing had happened two years ago.

September

Suvchinsky came for a few days but actually stayed for two weeks, which I welcomed.

On the 7th I finished the *Sinfonietta*. Nevertheless, autumn has already begun! All I have managed to do during the summer is revise one old piece! With this sense of tardiness at my back I embarked the very next day on the *Divertimento*. I spent a few days finishing the composition of the second movement and recomposing the third. The work went pleasantly so that by the 15th I was already in a position to settle down to the orchestration, during which all manner of details and questionable passages get resolved. I had orchestrated the first movement two years ago for Diaghilev,[1] but when I had heard it I was not happy: it sounded coarse and turgid, while the character of this movement calls for a drier, sharper sonority. I also decided to use a smaller orchestra. This would make it more attractive to perform, and in any case what is the point of extra instruments if one can do without them? By the 22nd the first two movements were fully scored, and by the 26th the third movement as well. It was all going quickly and easily, much more so than the revising of the *Sinfonietta*. Simultaneously with this I was correcting the proofs of *Le Pas d'acier*, grinding my teeth at the stupidity of the engravers.

Soon after Suvchinsky left, Ptashka's singing teacher, Telly, arrived for several days, and on the 15th Maria Viktorovna. Borovsky himself is in South America but so far has not sent any money. Fortunately, their rich old lady friends in America make presents of money (in dollars) to Natasha. Maria Viktorovna is living on this money.

Ptashka's bad mood gradually softened by the middle of the month and after that our relations became very loving. She began to make real progress with her singing, and this had a beneficial effect on her character. By the end of her stay she sang several times in front of guests. On the 30th we hosted a big reception for all the neighbouring landowners as we owed them some return on the hospitality they had offered to us. The de la Flécheres came as well, as they are going away for six weeks. It seems they are not only Counts but Marquises as well, but they use only the Count title, because although a

---

[1] The piece that began life as the Overture composed for Romanov's ballet *Trapèze* and was orchestrated at Diaghilev's request for *Le Pas d'acier* but not used. See above pp. 194–5, 200–1, 579, 581, 843, n. 3.

Count is lower in the hierarchy than a Marquis, the title is the more ancient. I played and Ptashka sang.

Another interesting gathering was a great picnic at Pierre Châtel, a most impressive fort on a hill overlooking the Rhône, now abandoned and even up for sale.[1] We descended into an immense grotto spiralling downwards like the shell of a snail. At the bottom it was cold and dark but we searched for and found an opening low down through which one could crawl on one's stomach into a whole system of other caves extending for half a kilometre.

Chalon and I worked on cleaning up Spaak's translation. Chalon is not a fast thinker and we spent an unconscionable time, but in the end achieved excellent solutions to the passages Spaak had given up on. A few times Chalon caught out Spaak in Belgian turns of phrase, and when he did he pounced on them like a hawk. Once Chalon failed to turn for a meeting we had arranged, leaving me waiting impatiently; this made me very angry and we almost fell out over it, but it was all smoothed over at our next meeting.

I dreamed often of Diaghilev and Stahl. In my dream I felt shy of asking Diaghilev how I could converse with him, seeing that he had died? Stahl spoke to me in a cheerful, sonorous voice and I dared not ask him how it was that he was able to talk without any vocal cords?

3 October

All these days I had been working at top speed on orchestrating the finale of the *Divertimento*, and to my surprise today found myself racing towards the finishing line – and crossing it. A wonderful feeling: I had scarcely hoped to finish it before leaving! To the same extent as I had found myself getting stuck in the *Sinfonietta*, so did the *Divertimento* forge smoothly ahead. Of course, had the summer been longer, and had I been quicker over the *Sinfonietta*, and had the proofs of the orchestral parts of *Le Pas d'acier* not been such a mess, I might have been able to complete my entire 'shipbuilding' programme, that is finish the Fourth Symphony and create an orchestral Fantasy from *The Gambler*. Koussevitzky put a moral brake on the Fourth Symphony by persuading me it would better to save it up for next season, a jubilee year for the Boston Symphony.[2] In fact the Symphony is very well

---

1 Owing to its commanding position the Chartreuse (Charterhouse) de Pierre Châtel was originally a military fort before becoming a Carthusian monastery at the close of the fourteenth century. This it remained until the French Revolution, after which it fell into disrepair for 150 years. Shortly after Prokofiev's visit it was bought by the wealthy Mme Zappa, who devoted her energies and considerable resources to restoring the buildings. It is now occupied by the Institut Gandhi, which runs spiritual retreats in it.
2 The Boston Symphony Orchestra was founded in 1881, so during the 1930–31 season would celebrate its half-century.

advanced: the first movement is fully orchestrated, the second composed, the third is taken entire from *Prodigal Son* (the only question on which I am havering is the tonality) so the only real work remaining to be done is in the finale and even that I largely sketched out in April in Monte Carlo. Seen in this light, therefore, there is not so much still needing to be composed. The *Gambler* Fantasy will require more work: I have not yet thought it out in detail although substantial sections are clear in my mind. Nevertheless I shall evidently have to shut up shop on the composing front for the current season, as it is so crowded with travelling and concerts.

4 October

After sustained work throughout the summer it seemed strange this morning not to have to sit down to the score! Instead I settled down to reading proofs, and finished *Le Pas d'acier* – no small achievement with 231 pages of score and 471 pages of orchestral parts, including masses of errors and alterations!

In the last few days my heart has not been very good. What can be the cause of this? It is time to finish with it for good and all. My chest hurts. I have to remember that every experience constitutes a task that must be despatched, and leads to the way forward.

The newspapers are full of the scandal at the Paris Embassy: a Councillor Besedovsky, seeing off the premises some visitors from Moscow, ran through the outer fence and through the police demanded that his wife and son, detained within the Embassy, be allowed to come out to him. Thank God Arens is not involved.[1] He is the first person I must see as soon as I get back

---

1 In a way he was involved. At the time of his meeting with Prokofiev, Arens was actively engaged in denouncing to Moscow his colleague, First Councillor and Acting Ambassador Grigory Besedovsky (1896–1951), for opposition to Stalin's recently promulgated decree abolishing the New Economic Policy, an indiscretion exacerbated by Besedovsky's clandestine and unauthorised approach to the British in search of capital investment for industrialisation projects in the USSR. Feeling the net closing in, on 3 October 1929 Besedovsky made a dramatic bid for freedom by climbing over the wall of the Embassy compound and asking for political asylum. This was by no means the end of Besedovsky's secret activities, however, as following no doubt genuine active service in the wartime French Resistance he was later unmasked as the author on behalf of OGPU of several forged early Cold War disinformation memoirs and diaries purportedly by senior Soviet politicians, notably the former Foreign Affairs Commissar Maxim Litvinov. The fakes were good enough to deceive even such a well-informed Soviet historian as E. H. Carr, who in 1955 wrote a laudatory introduction to Litvinov's supposed memoirs *Notes for a Journal*. Besedovsky's own unreliable memoirs, published in Russian in Paris in 1931 as *Na putyakh k Termidoru* ('The Path to Thermidor', after the July 1794 move against Robespierre that marked the effective end of the Reign of Terror) was also published in English the same year under the more prosaic title *Recollections of a Soviet Diplomat*. Ivan Arens, having survived the Lausanne assassination attempt, was later to fall victim to Stalin's purges, arrested and executed in 1938.

to Paris, to find out what has happened with my obtaining an exit visa to allow me to leave the country when I go to Russia.

5 October

In the past few days Ptashka has sung several times for neighbours, not badly, and has already attracted some admirers and friends. This has put her into the sunniest of moods. But yesterday she also had a problem with her heart, and a more severe one than mine. It is a great pity she has moved so far away from C.S. To be precise, it is not so much that she has moved away in the full sense of the word as that she is not as closely involved as she was. But if one is convinced that the world is essentially created as a spiritual entity and that everything in it is regulated spiritually, what sense does it make to circle round this truth and stay on the periphery! I write this also for myself: remember it, remember, remember!

6 October

I found a good system for overcoming antipathetic feelings towards doctors: try mentally to enter into their lives, what interests them, even the smallest details; try to linger on their more attractive features, because even doctors have some of them; in short, get under their skin, as an experienced playwright does with his characters, depicting them not as monsters but as people. Then a way of communicating with them will be found.

A whole day free from scoring and proof-reading. I therefore caught up on my diary.

10–26 October[1]

Left Culoz on the 10th October. On the 11th, at half past four, an accident[2] in the car. Lost consciousness, first memory is of the car on its wheels right way up; lost consciousness again, feverishly drifting in and out of sleep. We had to stay longer in the hotel, I was in bed for five days. Conversations with M.V.[3] about her husband, tragic but restrained; the cause her relationship with Boris, another time only about Vladimir, a third time about his

---

1 The Diary entries from 10 October until 21 November are rough notes in the form of an aide-memoire, which the author did not subsequently amplify. Some references are therefore tantalisingly obscure.
2 Written in English in the text.
3 Viktorovna (Borovskaya).

madness.¹ My back – at first all right, bruises appeared ten days later. My hand.²

Visit to Arens – decision to go, despite their not giving me anything in writing they do guarantee permission to leave the country on the basis of discussions to take place while I am there. Ptashka at first seemed not to be interested in this (she did not fully understand the implications) but was then remorseful; a very tender week.

Our flat – rue Bassano.

On the 24th news of the death of Aunt Katya. Her last letter to me arrived on the day she died.³

Last week has been entirely taken up with preparations for the trip: money, passport, purchases, presents.

27 October

Left at 12.10. Seeing me off were Ptashka, Svyatoslav, Ptashka very loving. This departure less joyous than two years ago, because I have grown unused to travelling alone. But the journey was pleasant.

28 October

Berlin in the morning. Saw Weber and had lunch with him. I bought a toy (about the first time I have paid any attention to my children). Left again at six in the evening (I got my Polish visa straight away although I had been afraid I might be held up for twenty-four hours). Weber came to the station with me. Slight nervousness at the Polish border anticipating complications over having two passports; the conductor took my passport away. Warsaw next morning: cable to Myaskovsky and a letter from Ptashka. Dozed. Negoreloe in the evening. Customs officials relaxed and polite. They looked at Ptashka's letter.

---

1   At some later point Maria Viktorovna Baranovskaya and Alexander Borovsky separated. We find the couple still together in Berlin in May and again in November 1930 (see below pp. 948, 953, 972–3, 977) but eventually she went to America, Borovsky himself remaining based in Europe until 1941, when he also emigrated to America. Their daughter Natasha went to America with her mother, attended Sarah Lawrence College and became a poet and novelist living in San Francisco. She has published two novels, drawn on her own experiences and the history of her mother's Polish family: *Daughter of the Nobility* (Holt, Rinehart and Wilson, 1985), and *Lost Heritage* (Sila-Nova Press, 1995) and collections of poetry.
2   As Prokofiev explained in a letter to Myaskovsky on 23 October, 'In general the only mementos this misadventure has left me with are a smashed tooth and bruises all over my body. But one other consequence may be awkward, because when I fell I pulled some muscles in my left wrist, with the result that for the time being I can play everything on the piano except octaves in the left hand.' (S. S. Prokofiev/N. Ya. Myaskovsky, op. cit., p. 323.)
3   Prokofiev's much loved aunt Yekaterina Rayevskaya died on 22 October 1929.

30 October

Slept well, alone in my 'Vladivostok' compartment.[1] Moscow at eleven o'clock in the morning: Myaskovsky (beard has grown, he has aged, starting to look like his father); three Derzhanovskys (Lyolya showing signs of a moustache), Meyerhold, Oborin, Lamm. The talk, of course, was of the catastrophe: at one point the news here was that I had been killed. 'Ran into a tramcar – how humiliating!'[2] Only available hotel is right in the centre, the Stoleshnikov. Meyerhold had invited me to stay with him, but this would be inconvenient. We went in Derzhanovsky's car to the hotel. The room is fine, quiet and the bed is clean. The window overlooks a square where a church has recently been demolished.

Derzhanovsky's temperament has lost much of its vitality. Flowers from Lyolya and Yekaterina Vasilievna.[3] Lyolya free and at my service. Derzhanovsky and I walked round Moscow. It is dry, warm and sunny, and there was I thinking it would be snow and mud. The crowds on the streets are grey. Comparison with a big Japanese city: they have built pedestrian crossings over the traffic. Meyerhold is installed in a new apartment of his own, a wonderful place. His mood though the reverse of wonderful – 15 per cent have recently been purged.[4] He is now a consultant to the Bolshoy Theatre and has a powerful influence. He says it is essential that I have a similar position there, even though I reside abroad. He telephoned Gusman who immediately arranged an advance of money for me, because everything is very expensive. I changed some dollars and collected the things that had been confiscated by Customs.

Had lunch, after which I went to the theatre. Alexandrovsky[5] (thick neck, leg over the arm of his chair) and Gusman. A bulky package: 500 [roubles].

---

1   A long-distance sleeping-car, as found on the Trans-Siberian Railway.
2   On 23 October, the day after Prokofiev received Aunt Katya's last letter and the day before getting the telegram announcing her death in Moscow, Prokofiev wrote to her: 'We lost a wheel at high speed, as a result of which the car turned over. Happily we came out of it with minor injuries and the children were completely unharmed. This is a miracle, because the car was going at about 80 kilometres an hour and was completely smashed up. We all had to lie up for about a week. Up to now, Ptashka had bruises around her eyes and I've lost a tooth, not to mention all the bruises on both our bodies.' (Quoted in D. Nice, op. cit.; translation by David Nice, who also adds the information that the shaken family was eventually driven back to Paris by some Americans who were among the many kind onlookers who assisted at the scene. No doubt Prokofiev made good use of this unforeseen early opportunity to put into practice his recently developed technique for interpersonal relations with the medical profession.)
3   Vladimir Derzhanovsky's wife, the singer Yekaterina Koposova-Derzhanovskaya. Lyolya (Yelena) was her half-sister. See *Diaries*, vol. 1, pp. 587–90, and above, pp. 415, 432.
4   Presumably valued members of his theatre company who had been dismissed for 'counter-revolutionary' tendencies.
5   Sergey Alexandrovsky (1864–1937), by profession a lawyer, Director of the Bolshoy Theatre.

I hurried back to the hotel, where Myaskovsky was waiting for me. In my haste I almost ran straight past; Myaskovsky, Lyolya and Yekaterina Vasilievna were standing at the entrance to the hotel laughing at me. Lyolya and Yekaterina Vasilievna had brought bread with them as they do not serve it with coffee. They left, leaving Myaskovsky with me. Spoke about Aunt Katya, and worse: Nadya.[1] I asked him to find out whether it would be possible for me to see her. Then back to Meyerhold to talk about the Bolshoy Theatre. Mayakovsky arrived. His clothes – a silk shirt? At least it was very clean. We went to the printers where he was to read *The Bathhouse*.[2] A new Renault, which apparently he had brought back with him from Paris. We were on the stage. Mayakovsky, as ever, read magnificently, bawling it out. The play is better than *The Bedbug*, full of wit and lighter in texture, especially the end. Meyerhold, however, thinks it not as good. Audience of workers and semi-skilled. Their opinions were mixed, which was interesting. One of them began quietly but soon wound up to berate the author for being incomprehensible. Another, somewhat embarrassed, defended him and expressed his gratitude. We then went to Lamm (I was driven there). A scene reminiscent of two years ago: Myaskovsky, Shebalin, Saradzhev and a dozen or so others whose identities I never worked out. Three Myaskovsky pieces transcribed for eight hands, I followed the score with Saradzhev. They were simple, almost provincial, in four-bar phrases, but had some marvellous moments. The *Sinfonietta*[3] was, however, rather disappointing. I left at midnight and walked back, with mixed feelings. I have been longing for some vigour, but this was just tired old blancmange.

31 October

In the morning I walked about Moscow, looking at the crowds and feeling out of touch. Returned to the hotel. Lyolya and Derzhanovsky came, Lyolya wanted to come out with me but Derzhanovsky tagged along, evidently to her annoyance but not to mine. Derzhanovsky already has plans for me to perform on the radio.

Went to Persimfans: Tseitlin, Mostras and Yurovsky, who had most opportunely dropped in. An affectionate reunion, memories of how last

---

1 Nadya Rayevskaya was the wife of Prokofiev's imprisoned cousin Shurik (Alexander). See above, pp. 428–9, and *passim*. Before long Nadya herself would be arrested and sent to the Belomor Canal labour concentration camp where she spent four years until her release in 1933, two years after Shurik himself was finally released.
2 Mayakovsky's last play is a satire on Soviet utopianism and as such was not well received by the authorities, who banned Meyerhold's production of it.
3 *Sinfonietta* in B minor for string orchestra, Op. 32 No. 2 (1929).

time all matters got settled here, which I made use of to pursue my question of how I might get my passport back. A flurry of telephone calls, including to Litvinov, on whom I should like to call, he was very nice last time. Returned home and ate in the fairly noisome (smells from the kitchen) dining room of my hotel. Having read the notice in the morning – 'Do not treat the waiter as a lackey' – I did not tip him. Seeing the look on his face I enquired, and got the reply, 'We get a salary.' I gave him a tip.

I presented Derzhanovsky with my hat. We went to Myaskovsky's where I played him *Choses en soi* (my finger is better, it works even though it still hurts a little). Myaskovsky made me play each piece through twice. He preferred the second to the first, even though there is more genuinely new in the first. He liked the middle section less. I left him the *Sinfonietta*. He has made enquiries as to whether it is all right for me to visit the Rayevskys, and the answer was yes, so when I left him I went there. Anna Petrovna,[1] Alyonushka,[2] midway between a young girl and a young lady.

To Meyerhold's for dinner. He is all fired up about Shurik and Nadya, although this is not the first time he has reacted so. Nevertheless, he does have connections. After dinner Gusman, Meyerhold and a pianist. We played through *Le Pas d'acier*, and I outlined its possibilities (playing four-hands). It produced a different effect.[3] Plans – if it can be produced. Also there was Oborin, a gentle, friendly young man who reminded me of a less brash Dukelsky. At half past one at night the Meyerholds accompanied me home. Meyerhold on the subject of the purges, the implications on the Resolution of some party conference or other. Gusman was among those listed to be purged, but at a meeting of the whole theatre company the list was gone through, beginning with others, and when they got to Gusman's name they had shouted, 'Gusman, we want Gusman.' I asked if I could attend one of these purging meetings.[4]

---

1   Anna Petrovna Uvarova, a family friend, sister of Katya Uvarova. See above, p. 429.
2   Shurik's and Nadya Rayevsky's middle daughter, Alyona.
3   Presumably the effect of hearing the music rather than reading the score.
4   Until the end of the decade of the 1920s in the Soviet Union the term 'purge' ('chistka' meaning 'cleaning') was used as shorthand for the political expression 'purge of the Party ranks', in other words the theoretically desirable objective of keeping party membership free from any taint of counter-revolution, anti-Soviet tendencies, slackness, corruption, incompetence – anything that detracted from the professedly high ideals of the Communist Party. Clearly in November 1929, at least on the surface and at least in the circle of Prokofiev's friends and associates, the term had not yet acquired the fatal connotations that it would in the 1930s, when the NKVD was headed by Yagoda and then Yezhov, culminating in the Great Purge of 1936 to 1938 – the era of 'Yezhovshchina'. In 1929 it was still just about possible to suffer no more than professional disqualifications and financial hardship by being purged (expelled) from the Party, whereas later it was understood that to be purged meant at the least to be imprisoned and, more likely than not, executed or done to death in a labour camp.

1 November

Went with Malyshev, a young, clever lawyer recommended by Meyerhold, to arrange my passport. Through high-ups? Or more lowly functionaries? Self-criticism. The main thing is to find out what needs to be done and to be able to do it. In Frenkel's office. His type: outwardly a shabby Jew, but a great command of language with emphases, quick timing, all impressively skilful. Formerly an officer in OGPU.[1] At first it appeared nothing could be done, but then Frenkel made a phone call and offered some suggestions. We left. Malyshev – the business with the hat. He explained. We went to the same office as two years ago to go through the formalities, but now much of it has been renewed and is better. While we were waiting, a café, stylish and attractive. It was rather good, a few tarts around. A new building under construction. Malyshev: it's being constructed by OGPU.

Myaskovsky came to see me. He regrets the loss of the old *Sinfonietta*, but considers the revision masterly. The working day stops at five o'clock. We dined at four(!) at Meyerhold's. Talked to Eva Valterovna Litvinova in English, which gave her great pleasure. At my hotel I found Olesha,[2] a colourless, withdrawn individual.

---

1   Naftali (Natan) Frenkel (1883–1960), Odessa-born of Turkish extraction, an OGPU officer best kept as far as possible away from. He first learnt his trade gun-running through Gallipoli in the First World War, then as an undercover OGPU agent in the NEP era buying up gold and precious stones, followed by a stint as a member of the Odessa criminal organisation run by the gangster Mishka Yaponchik ('Mishka the Jap', nickname for Moishe-Jakov Volfovich Vinnitsky), specialising in murder, torture, extortion, smuggling, denunciations and blackmail. Eventually he formed his own gang, which was broken up by OGPU in 1924. Frenkel and his associates were all condemned to death, but the sentence of Frenkel (the only one not to be executed) was commuted to ten years' imprisonment, and through the intervention of the head of the Solovetsky Labour Camps Directorate (USLON), Fyodor Eikhmans, was released early and in 1927 went to work for the 'production department' (i.e. forced labour by convicts) of USLON, charged with extracting the maximum of labour for the minimum of expenditure. In 1929 he had a desk job in Moscow as the Moscow representative of USLON, and the following year began his rise through the administrative ranks of the Soviet Union's Gulag system, heading the White Sea Canal and the Baikal–Amur Railway forced-labour construction projects. By 1941 Frenkel was head of the entire NKVD Directorate of Railway Construction Labour Camps (GLAVKA) and Deputy Director of the GULAG system as a whole. Three times awarded the Order of Lenin, he retired with the rank of Lieutenant-General.
2   Yury Olesha (1889–1960), novelist and short-story writer, was like his friends and colleagues Ilf and Petrov, Isaac Babel and Sigismond Krzizhanovsky, raised in Odessa and shares with them penetrating psychological insights, an imagination bordering on fantasy and a brand of satire that contrives an ambiguity able to undermine both bourgeois philistinism and Socialist ideals. His masterpiece is *Envy* (*Zavist'*), published in 1927. During the 1930s the increasing rigidity of Socialist Realism condemned Olesha to silence and he wrote little for the remainder of his life except diaries, which were published posthumously.

2 November

Leningrad. Someone took my trousers, cannot find out much about where they might have gone to. Asafyev: suffering from neuralgia, but insisted that I go out to him straight away. But I am reluctant to bury myself in Detskoe immediately. Went to the Europa (Europa Hotel). Enormous room just like last time, but they did not have a smaller one. Paced up and down realising that there is no one I particularly have to see. But that is how I myself arranged things. Called Dranishnikov, cries of joy, he is busy in the theatre all morning but will be at home from half past three. I agreed to go then. Went out for a walk: Nevsky, Morskaya, the Conservatoire, Mariinsky Theatre, Sadovaya, an hour in all. Warm, foggy, and muddy. Back home; rang Lidusya,[1] somewhat apprehensive since she had not replied to my letters. She answered the telephone herself in a flat voice, but as soon as she realised who was speaking exclaimed delightedly. I said I would visit her this evening. Called Demchinsky (which I had not done the last time I was in the city). At first he could not understand who I was, then said, 'Greetings to you.' I asked if I could come to see him, and immediately set off to do so. He could not restrain himself from sarcastic comments about my staying at the Europa: 'High-ups wouldn't think of staying anywhere else.' I said, 'It's really time to leave off that sort of thing, Boris Nikolayevich.'

He has hardly changed at all, a little thinner and a little older, whereas V.F.[2] is if anything even younger-looking, having dyed her hair. He retains the calm delivery and beautiful cadences of his speech. I tried to be discreet and to keep my ego in the background so as to provoke his irony as little as possible. He is living reasonably well, although his second son has died he seems reconciled to the tragedy.

Leningrad is even more beautiful when shrouded in mist.

We reminisced a little about Boris Nikolayevich,[3] Eleonora,[4] but only fleetingly. I promised to drop in again to play chess, but now it was time to go to Dranishnikov's. V.F., usually waspish, was today as friendly as could be. I went past Pervaya Rota Street[5] but did not recognise our house, it has been painted a different colour.

Dranishnikov was bubbling over with energy: he is now the premier conductor in Leningrad, perhaps even the Soviet Union. Outwardly he has

---

1 Lidia, one of the two Karneyeva sisters with whom Prokofiev had been friendly in his Petersburg years, now married to Barkov, an army officer. See *Diaries*, vol. 1 *passim*; vol. 2, pp. 46–6 *passim*, 92, 137, 159, 268, and above, p. 481.
2 Varvara Demchinskaya was Boris Demchinsky's wife.
3 Bashkirov.
4 Damskaya.
5 The street in which Prokofiev and his mother had lived. See *Diaries*, vol. 1 *passim*.

coarsened; he complained about the amount of work he has to do, the theatre director Lyubimsky, self-criticism, everyone going in fear of everyone else. The Philharmonia is in a state of total collapse, he does not conduct there, Malko is abroad. They gave me dinner with delicious grouse but at a ridiculous time, half past four. Back to the hotel, then to Lidusya. The trams are working well, there are plenty of them and because there is so little traffic on the streets they are quick. Lidusya has aged and lost her figure: she has changed more in the past two years than in the ten before that. Masses of stories about her sisters and about Lev,[1] reminiscences of Max[2] and our joint letters and telegrams. Her husband is correct and taciturn, putting in an appearance only from time to time. He came in for tea and sat gloomily in the corner while I tried to make conversation with him.

3 November

To Detskoe and Asafyev's, who in fact is physically quite well but frightened to go out. At first he was simply groaning and panic-stricken, but gradually it emerged that the position he now finds himself in is genuinely impossible. Music cheered him up. I had a bad headache and went out for a walk on my own for an hour. Popov came and played his Symphony and a Suite, but I did not much like either of them. Shades of Scriabin, but I felt the need for more clarity and lucidity of structure. If Diaghilev had lived and had commissioned a work from Popov, as we were urging him to, he would not have been at all satisfied. Of my Largo Popov's opinion was that there was something not proletarian enough about the music, though it was melodic and simple (he may have been being slightly ironical in saying this).

Returned to Leningrad, and the same evening back to Moscow for a rehearsal of *Oranges* the next afternoon at two o'clock. My visit to Leningrad had turned out to be virtually incognito, and I went so far as to enquire cautiously of Asafyev whether it might be a good idea to put a notice in the newspapers, or to arrange a performance of my *Sinfonietta* in the Philharmonia, but he does not write for the newspapers any longer and the Philharmonia is in chaos.

4 November

Arrived in Moscow next morning, dropped my things off at Meyerhold's and went straight to the Bolshoy Theatre. First was an orchestra rehearsal.

---

1   Lev (Lyova) Karneyev, younger brother of Lidia and Zoya Karneyeva. See *Diaries*, vol. 1, 170–71, 409, 414–15, 494, 504, 519–21, 712, 755; vol. 2, pp. 46, 49, 137, and above p. 481.
2   Maximilian Schmidthof, Prokofiev's most intimate friend in his Conservatoire years, who committed suicide in April 1913. See *Diaries*, vol. 1 *passim*.

They played decently, but Nebolsin[1] was mediocre, with an unclear beat. I have not heard *Oranges* for a long time and it was pleasant, with a lot of invention but also a lot dashed off rather hastily. From that we went straight to a chorus rehearsal, and then a stage piano rehearsal with chorus and extras. The huge stage filled up and assumed a festive atmosphere. Dikiy, Gusman, Meyerhold – whose orders are obeyed. The staging did not go at all well, Dikiy in despair. With some difficulty Meyerhold succeeded in getting him two additional rehearsals. After the rehearsal I went to call on Kucheryavy but he was out. Back at Meyerhold's we had *bliny*, as there had been an issue of white flour on account of the holidays, all of which had been sacrificed to the *bliny*. Oborin, whom Meyerhold likes very much. His Sonata No. 1 is average, but excerpts from No. 2 were very nice, so there is progress there. It is more interesting than Popov, and more contemporary. Malyshev informs me that my passport will be ready on the 9th. Bravo, how did it happen so easily? Or has it not really happened at all?

In the evening, after the second act of *Carmen* which I saw from the Director's box, I went with Meyerhold to a company meeting in their hall; table set up on the stage, but who was sitting behind it? It began with speeches of high-flown vulgarity, but it was interesting to witness someone being inducted as a new Party member. Meyerhold encouraged me to play, and when I showed him my damaged hand reassured me that nobody would understand anything but it was important that I play something, even if only eight bars. He introduced me to Agranov,[2] who was reserved, but civil. Quite a handsome face. When my presence was announced the hall burst into loud applause. I played, somehow managing to produce something although I had not touched a piano for three weeks and could play only very softly with my left hand.

Spent the night at Meyerhold's between sheets of princely luxury, and sank into blissful oblivion.

5 November

Bliny all day long. At eleven stage and orchestra rehearsal, not in costume. Met Rabinovich, most affectionate greeting, promised to present me with his sketches and spoke of American plans. Again the rehearsal had a festival atmosphere, the orchestra was fine except that Nebolsin made some blunders, the entry of the March being one example. Outside on the streets the crowds

---

1   Vasili Nebolsin (1898–1959), conductor. Having been initially appointed in 1920 to the post of Chorusmaster at the Bolshoy, by 1922 he was regularly conducting opera and ballet productions and continued to do so for the rest of his life.
2   An OGPU officer.

looked grey, but inside the theatre and in its precincts there were good-looking faces to be seen, and people seeing friends off on the sleeper train.

Back to Meyerhold's, for mushrooms with sour cream. To Litvinov's at five o'clock, we didn't know what to expect, but it was dinner Moscow-style. The Litvinovs have bought a new flat, somewhat cramped but contemporary in style. E.V.[1] very lively, talking English to me, asked about Ptashka. Meyerhold also animated, slightly artificially so in the presence of the Minister. Nice children, the daughter is a real beauty. Conversation about the purges, the logic behind them, he fears them.[2] We left together, Litvinov at the wheel. A reception planned for me on the 7th, but I am away then and even if I decided to stay my evening-dress is in the trunk in Leningrad. A new uniform is being introduced for Narkomat[3] personnel, rather military in appearance. Left for Leningrad at 9.30 p.m.

6 November

Letting up the blind in the morning saw the sun shining on the white snow that had fallen during the night, already, alas, melting. Hôtel d'Europe,[4] room nothing special this time. As arranged (and as I had written to Ptashka beforehand) went into the Philharmonia across the street and summoned Asafyev. First of all he and I went to drink coffee (which was disgusting, although the dirty-brown-coloured pastries were good), then walked through the city to the Conservatoire. Wolf,[5] out of place, greeted me affectionately, also Nikolayev and Tyulin. Walked through the Conservatoire; hordes of students rushing about, we peeped into the Director's office. Who is Director now?[6] At the main entrance Ossovsky, looking older. Went out again walking with Asafyev, Embankment, the Palace green but discoloured, Peterburgskaya Storona.[7] Asafyev went back to work while I continued my stroll over to Kamenny Ostrov[8] from where I took a cab back to Dranishnikov's.

---

1 Eva Valterovna – Ivy Litvinov.
2 It is not clear from this shorthand note who is afraid of the purges, but the context suggests that it must be Meyerhold or Litvinov.
3 In 1925 the Narodny (People's) Commissariats (Narkomat) for Home and Foreign Trade had been merged into one gigantic monolith responsible for all retailing and distribution of products of all kinds, headed first by Kamenev and then by Anastas Mikoyan.
4 The Europa Hotel.
5 Yevgeny Wolf-Israel, principal cellist of the Mariinsky Orchestra and professor at the Leningrad Conservatoire. See above, pp. 489–90.
6 Glazunov. See above, p. 708, n. 1.
7 Peterburgskaya Storona (Petersburg Side) is a district of the city consisting of several islands on the north bank of the Neva, the largest of which is the Petrogradsky Island.
8 'Stone Island', a large island to the north of Peterburgskaya Storona, connected to the central area by the long Kamennyostrov Prospect.

Dinner. Conversation about *Cherevichki*, heavily revised, should be good. Looked at *Vakula*[1] out of interest because of the revisions I have been making in my works, but mine are more substantial. Tyulin. Conversation about Shostakovich's *The Nose*.[2] Short on material. 'But you should hear it with the orchestra.' Impression: a general groan.

7 November

Wrote letters and worked out programmes for New York, so did not leave the hotel until half past ten. Holiday. Nevsky overflowing with people demonstrating. Impressive. They walked slowly, a lot of red banners to be seen. Illuminated tramcars so elaborately decorated you are asked not to touch them. Radios with heavy percussion blaring through loudspeakers on the street.

Called on Nouvel's brother. Walked along Kirochnaya Street – where the Meshchersky family used to live. Building is well preserved, still looks impressive, inside the courtyard curtains and greenery. Nouvel's brother is an elderly man, a singing teacher.

To Detskoe. The cab driver refused – cannot cross the Neva. I said to take me to the Oktyabrsky Station. Got there two minutes before the train, queue of fifty people. On the train without a ticket I was fined eight times the cost. Good, clean air in Detskoe, but muddy. I photographed Asafyev. Talked about his moving to Moscow. He attempted to stick up for Popov's Symphony. Not much mention of C.S., although he did say, referring to my accident, that he immediately understood what it meant. About Myaskovsky and his religious views, Asafyev said Myaskovsky never discusses them with anyone and it is impossible to bring up the subject, but evidently he is a sceptic and there is a large and painful empty place in his life. Opinions on my Second Symphony.

Left to go to the Mariinsky Theatre. How I love it, all the same, and how much closer I feel to it than to the Bolshoy. I could not make out the audience, what sort of people it consisted of and what they thought of the performance. The intelligentsia dress like the workers. Radlov – conversation about the new broadcast of *Boris Godunov*, skilfully done but a bit

---

1 The later version of Tchaikovsky's opera originally called *Vakula the Smith*. See above, pp. 723, n. 1, 815.
2 Surreally satirical opera (1927–8) by Shostakovich, based on the story by Gogol, written in an advanced montage-style idiom ranging from popular song to serial techniques and extreme vocalisation but subjected to strict formal compositional devices. In 1929 it had received an unstaged concert performance, which caused general bewilderment (as the composer predicted it would). Two months after the discussion noted in this diary entry it would be produced at the Maly Theatre, but after its initial run it would not be seen again until it was revived by the conductor Gennady Rozhdestvensky and the producer Boris Pokrovsky forty-four years later in 1974.

far-fetched, the people made more prominent. The new edition,[1] first time I have heard it. Badly orchestrated. The only scenes that sound well are the massed crowd scenes because of his ability to handle the chorus. Pimen has a new section added, good music but inordinately long. In the interval I walked about studying the audience. The stalls looked terrible, but apparently the whole performance had been block-booked. Went to see Dranishnikov in his room.

Talked to Lyubimsky after the performance, young, Jewish, hard to understand, not to be compared with Ekskuzovich. Conversation emollient. They are ready to revive *Oranges* immediately for roubles, and to produce *The Gambler* next year, also for roubles. Walked over with Mme Radlov and Dmitriev to Palace Square to see a rehearsal of a mass event produced by Radlov. We could not get in as we did not have a pass. Floodlights. A huge white sheet over the arch. Quite interesting as a setting, but not as a rehearsal. Got back to my hotel after one o'clock.

8 November

Called on Katya Schmidthof having earlier forgotten her married name and her address. Met her unprepossessing husband and son, who were there. Then to Demchinsky's: presents, gloves for him (I took a photograph of him wearing them), perfume for her, at which she immediately blushed like a young girl. We chatted some more, then played chess, but in both of them the lust to win has dimmed. The result was a draw. I was in a rush, as Radlov's wife was calling for me. Got a ticket for the evening performance. In the hotel I was immediately cornered by Lidusya with her husband and by Katya Schmidthof. Lidusya has done something to restore her good looks. Katya's features have somehow fallen in and she complains of weakness in her lungs.

Went to the mass event. Benches for the government high-ups to sit on, the people behind, cold. Motor cars from the factories, a schoolgirl, working people *à la* Mayakovsky, smokescreen, alarms and excursions, declaration of the pledge, fireworks. I hurry back to the hotel, Demchinsky, a few minor requests.

Departure, Katya Schmidthof at the station to see me off.

---

1   Early in 1928 Pavel Lamm and Boris Asafyev had produced scholarly restorations of the vocal and full scores of both Musorgsky's own versions of *Boris Godunov*, the 'original redaction' of 1869 and the 'revised redaction' of 1874, drawn from the composer's manuscripts without the amendments carried out by Rimsky-Korsakov. The production of Musorgsky's 1869 version in the Lamm–Asafyev edition was premiered in the Mariinsky Theatre (Akopera) on 16 February 1928, produced by Sergey Radlov with designs by Vladimir Dmitriev (1900–1948) and conducted by Vladimir Dranishnikov.

9 November

The crack express, but still an hour late, and I have to be at the rehearsal. I have a room at the Bolshaya Moskovskaya, now the Grand Hotel, the one Derzhanovsky had not managed to procure for me before.

The rehearsal: stage and orchestra, without costumes. Dikiy near breaking point from the strain: a very badly run and disorganised theatre. Scenery seems have got mislaid somewhere.

Dinner at Gusman's. The Meyerholds desperate to get into the Taïrov premiere but no tickets have been sent round. We rang up, pleading for tickets in Meyerhold's name, then Gusman's, then mine, but to no avail. Went to the cinema to see *Wreckage of an Empire*,[1] a provincial offering which one hopes to God will not be shown abroad.

10 November

Decided at long last to do some piano practice, seems not too bad, the left hand has graduated from being able to play only *piano* to *mezzo-forte*. Wrote letters and postcards and looked at *Three Oranges* in preparation for my forthcoming conducting engagement on the radio on the 17th. At Anna Petrovna's[2] were Nadya and little Sonya. They face eviction from their flat. Dinner at the Derzhanovskys': Myaskovsky, Saradzhev. I played them *Choses en soi*; it took some time for it to get through to them and I played the pieces four times. We were joined by Polovinkin, Yavorsky, Protopopov and some other people I did not know. I told Polovinkin of Dukelsky's latest doings. Myaskovsky and I played his Third Symphony in a four-hand arrangement: the first and second movements were good, the third has not yet been transcribed (Shebalin has taken it to work on it) and the finale is mediocre. I went back to my hotel at two, but it was very noisy in the hotel at half past seven and I did not get enough sleep.

11 November

General rehearsal. But the chorus hardly acts at all and according to Dikiy there is no power on earth that can move them, so that some of them idly flap their hands like cheap dolls. The Prince tries too hard to be clever, but what his character needs is simplicity, ardour, good humour, on occasion a watercolour lyricism. Meyerhold is exasperated by the sloppy stage

---

1 *Oblomki Imperii*, 1929 movie by Friedrich Ermler about a shell-shocked Red Army soldier who has lost his memory after being left for dead during the Civil War.
2 Uvarova, family friend.

management and by Rabinovich's complicated scenery – the intervals for scene-changes are too long.

From the rehearsal I went to see Morolyov; I could barely get out of the tram, such was the crush. His elder daughter is married to a commissar from the Caucasus, by no means a stupid man. When conversation flagged we played chess – a draw. Morolyov did not understand anything whatsoever of *Choses en soi*.

To the Bolshoy Theatre, to give a talk to about fifty people in the former foyer of the Tsar's box. I did not know what subjects I should touch on: mostly about Diaghilev, something about America, Belgium, England. A mass of questions that went on for an hour and a half. On the subject of *Le Pas d'acier*: why Soviet and English machines and suchlike, from a group of proletarian musicians. Could I compose an opera on the subject of the Civil War? No. Could not understand my reason for declining. On another day: 'Prokofiev should be purged' (today's fashionable expression). Alexandrovsky thanking me said he was surprised by my patience.

12 November

Katya, Alyona (Rayevskaya) and Katya Ignatieva came to see me. They are facing eviction; documentation about the children's father and mother.[1] A proposal to perform in Kharkov, but no hard currency. On the stage of the theatre they are being given instruction on how to run around the stage. Ptashka has asked me to buy her a fur coat. I practise the piano and dine at Meyerhold's. I am rung up there and invited out for the evening on Friday. *The Army Commander*.[2] I sat with Radlov. The poetry itself by Selvinsky was not bad, but the dramatic action was totally incomprehensible. Declamation with music, the very thing I am interested in developing myself. Pathos of the concluding scene. How I want to write an opera or declamatory work with

---

1   Prokofiev's cousin Alexander (Shurik) Rayevsky, now in gaol, and his wife Nadezhda (Nadya) had three daughters: Katya, Alyona and Sonya. Katya Ignatieva née Rayevskaya was Shurik's sister, the children's aunt and the composer's cousin. She had married Pavel Ignatiev, an army captain, in 1908 but the marriage was unhappy and ended in divorce three years later. See *Diaries*, vol. 1, pp. 37, 277–8, and *passim*; vol. 2, pp. 141, 155, 215, 699, and above, pp. 365, 429.
2   *Komandarm 2* (*Army Commander Two*), a play in verse by Ilya Selvinsky (1899–1968), a leading figure in the Literary Constructivist movement that emerged in the early 1920s and whose manifesto called for art 'to reflect as closely as possible the organisational pressure of the working class in the construction of Socialist culture'. This was to be exemplified by the so-called *gruzovikatsia* of the text, a near-untranslatable concept referring to the mechanical-engineering principle of the power-to-weight ratio, whereby each word would be freighted with more and more meaning condensed into it in order to do more work. Selvinsky himself led a colourful life as, among other professions, an artist's model, a lorry driver, a wrestler in a circus and a welder in a power station. During the Second World War he served as a battalion commissar and was severely wounded in action.

emotional power, but where to find the right subject? Must develop this thought. Radlov's three boxes. In the Green Room during the interval the Norwegian Ambassador, a splendid gentleman, and his wife, with Kollantai.[1] Kollontai is not old, but already not young; at one time she was probably very pretty. With me she was quietly friendly.

13 November

First rehearsal. Broadcast concert of my music (arranged through Derzahnovsky; I conducted three numbers from *Oranges* for 500 roubles). First performance of the *Sinfonietta*.[2] Saradzhev, excited by how the revision has been done, took all the time rehearsing it. A hall with terrible acoustics. Not many strings, but still managed to cover the wind, while over the radio it was the other way round, so either it was the ether or the hall that was no good, or more likely both. Eventually some sort of balance was achieved, but there was still no pleasure to be had from the orchestral sonorities – no overtones, castrated. Saradzhev was on the podium all through the rehearsal so I did not rehearse today. After, I went to Muzsektor to talk to Yurovsky. The three-year agreement expires in a month and a half. We will renew it automatically. Yurovsky was nice, spoke of Myaskovsky and the bad odour he is in because of ideological conflicts; it is time for him to leave Russia, otherwise he will not have any work. I said that I have no connections in Germany and they would not like Myaskovsky in France. The idea of America.

---

[1] Alexandra Kollontai (1872–1952), an early Revolutionary associate of Lenin in Russia and in exile. After the October Revolution she was awarded a ministerial post, that of People's Commissar for Social Welfare, which she used to great effect to champion women's equality and the eradication of illiteracy. It was not long, however, before Lenin found her independence and single-mindedness inconvenient and sidelined her in a succession of diplomatic posts, including that of Soviet Ambassador to Norway, thus becoming the world's first female ambassador. Perhaps unfairly she is most famous for her advocacy of free love, which was misinterpreted, often wilfully, as pure licence. Her views were in fact more rooted in the political conviction that true Socialism could not be achieved without a step change in attitudes to sexual morality. It is a widespread calumny that she advocated 'the satisfaction of sexual desires as simply as getting a glass of water'. The relevant passages in her *Theses on the Communist Morality in the Sphere of Marital Relations*, first published in the newspaper *Kommunistka* in 1921, are in fact far subtler and more perceptive: 'Communist morality demands that people are educated in sensitivity and understanding and are psychologically demanding both to themselves and to their partners. [. . .] The greater the intellectual and emotional development of the individual, the less place will there be in his or her relationship for the bare physiological side of love and the brighter will be the love experience. [. . .] The sexual act must be seen not as something shameful and sinful but as something which is as natural as the other needs of the healthy organism such as hunger and thirst. Such phenomena cannot be judged as moral or immoral.' Her opinions on the stifling effect of conventional family bonds were, however, genuinely radical.

[2] In its revised version, given the new opus number of 48.

Hunt for furs with Lyolya. Lyolya understands what is required, but with some difficulty, and conversation often has to be in whispers. Met Meyerhold at seven o'clock, a full box: the pair of them, I, Myaskovsky, Radlov, Oborin and Petrov-Vodkin. Procession. Act One all right but a bit dull; Act Two very beautiful with the stage full of people, but the Prince's laughter was irritatingly artificial. Gusman came to the box at the end of the act and took me backstage for a celebratory ceremony behind the curtain with a wreath, presentation scroll, all the artists applauding. Acts Three and Four not bad but the final chase, of course, did not work. Shebalin visited the box in the interval. Supper in a club off Tverskaya Street.

14 November

Short on sleep because of last night's supper and an early start to the rehearsal, which I began today. There was very little work to do: these particular numbers are easy and the musicians all knew them. Many of them were from Persimfans, and also they were trying their best in the presence of the composer. Then Saradzhev rehearsed the *Sinfonietta* and the Violin Concerto. The first was very long drawn out, and the second plain bad: Saradzhev and the soloist did not agree and Saradzhev seemed not to be listening. Then *Visions fugitives* in an arrangement for a quartet of wind-players by the oboist. Very enjoyable and if I make one or two corrections it could be published. Talk of commissioning an opera. I quoted what Radlov had said. It would not necessarily have to be agit-opera, so long as it was not obviously against the grain of the times, and it would be good to have a powerful emotional content. Mention of Eurasianism, which surprised me very much. They would obtain some hard currency. Compared to the discussion with Radlov, all this put a very different complexion on the matter. These interesting conversations almost made me late to get back in time for Myaskovsky, who was coming to see me. We had something quick to eat together and then went off to see Zhilyayev.[1] I sounded him out on the possibility of

---

1 Nikolay Zhilyayev (1869–1938), composer, pianist, teacher and critic. Zhilyayev, a man of enormous erudition and culture – he had learnt Norwegian in order to cultivate a friendship with the idol of his youth, Grieg, and signed his early journalistic writings 'Peer Gynt' – had a significant influence on a wide circle of prominent musicians including Scriabin, Khachaturian and Shostakovich. Among his students at the Moscow Conservatoire were the conductor Kirill Kondrashin and the musicologist Daniil Zhitomirsky. Zhilyayev's perceptive encouragement of the young Shostakovich had tragic consequences because it brought him into even closer contact with Shostakovich's great admirer Marshal Tukhachevsky (Tukhachevsky, who had been another of Zhilyayev's students, was arrested and executed as an enemy of the people in 1937, not long after having written personally to Stalin to make representations on Shostakovich's behalf after the catastrophic 'Muddle Instead of Music' article in *Pravda* of January 1936). With horrible inevitability the same fate befell Zhilyayev a year later.

teaching in America, but Myaskovsky showed little enthusiasm for the idea. Is this because he does not see the writing on the wall or because Yurovsky has only an imperfect grasp of the situation? Why was Myaskovsky dragging me off to see Zhilyayev? Whatever the reason, I tagged obediently along. Zhilyayev is a strange man. First I played him *Choses en soi*, but then for almost an hour he made me play my earliest opuses, most of which I am now ready to repudiate. He did not seem so interested in my later compositions.

Returned home and lay down to rest. At five o'clock to the Meyerholds, where Myaskovsky had also been invited to dine, but he did not come. Originally I had been going to dine at Myaskovsky's, but he hummed and hawed and stopped short of inviting me. Malyshev says that Myaskovsky had asked for an advance of money from the Society of Authors but had been turned down, so he has no money to ask anyone to dinner. Went to a performance of *The Bedbug*, excerpts from which I had already heard from Mayakovsky's lips in Paris, and at that time I had not found it much to my liking. Now I was confirmed in my opinion that the play is really crude, and not particularly inventive as a piece of stagecraft.

Misha appeared and introduced me to his rather attractive girlfriend, and together we looked at the theatre museum containing all Meyerhold's productions. We could not stay until the end of *The Bedbug* as I was due at the Bolshoy to play through *Le Pas d'acier* at ten o'clock, in the same room as I had given the talk. Partnered by the same répétiteur as before I gave an energetic if slightly messy four-hand account of *Le Pas*. I had been asked beforehand to give an account of the ballet's plot, but instead of this I explained something of the ideas that underpinned Diaghilev's, Yakulov's and my conception of the work. The underlying physical movements had been drawn originally from sport, but later from machines. The costumes and characters were all intended to be a novelty to Western audiences. Nevertheless, not only had much in the Paris production turned out otherwise than originally desired, it was obvious that for a production in the USSR many aspects would have to be interpreted quite differently than they had been for a Western presentation.

After the play-through I answered questions put to me. About sixty people were sitting in the hall, I was behind a table on the platform. With me on the platform were Meyerhold, a secretary taking notes, and a boilerman or fitter who was acting as presiding officer and who was in fact quite competent in the role. The questions, of which there were thirty or forty, ranged from the practical to the provocative. The former were easy to deal with and I enjoyed replying to them when, as was often the case, they concerned interesting aspects remembered from the previous production or stimulating possibilities. As for the barbed ones (why was there no melodic material stemming from the Revolution whereas some of it had religious overtones; what factories had Massine visited, were they controlled by the proletariat or by capitalist bosses?), after the experience of the day before yesterday I knew better what to expect and gave them considered and detailed responses, although I began to show my irritation when some of the questions made me lose patience.[1] One question came from a young lady who announced her failure to understand: were the bracelets given to the commissar supposed to be a joke? How could such an attitude on the part of the composer to the realities of our life here be justified? I replied that she had phrased the first part of her question correctly: she clearly did not understand anything. The only ironically treated characters were the cigarette-sellers and the anti-Soviet orator. Belyayev[2] made a rather unsuccessful speech (the others all left but he came back). Gusman twice came to my defence, but was attacked for his pains. The last word was Meyerhold's, who specifically countered any suggestion that there could be objections to the ballet. What difference did it make if it had been produced in the West? What we should be interested in is how we are going to do it here. As for the way the factory had been conceived, it was obviously the view of an enquiring but politically illiterate comrade. On this note the meeting came to an end. The word 'illiterate' caused a howl of rage. A second purge of Prokofiev!

15 November

Third and final rehearsal. The Prince and Princess were recorded on to a gramophone disc by the radio station for educational purposes. After the rehearsal there was a discussion with Lopashev[3] and Derzhanovsky. I, it seems, am a pistol ready to be fired at the West. More about the opera project. Lopashev confirms that they are ready with a contract and an advance payment. I replied that I could not sign a contract without having settled on a subject. Went with Lyolya to buy a fur coat and to the other Society of Authors. I had a bad head and went to lie down as this evening there is to be a big party at the Meyerholds'; by evening my headache had gone. Myaskovsky, Oborin, Pasternak,[4] Mayakovsky, Petrov-Vodkin,

---

[1] 'That is the realm of politics, not music, and therefore I shall not reply.' Such, according to the report of the meeting in *Proletarsky Muzykant*, was the only answer Prokofiev would vouchsafe to this question. (Quoted in D. Nice, op. cit., p. 272.)
[2] Viktor Belyayev (1888–1968), musicologist and critic.
[3] S. A. Lopashev was a director of Moscow Radio.
[4] It is not known whether this was the painter Leonid Pasternak or his son, the poet and novelist Boris.

Olesha, Pshibyshevsky,[1] Kerzhentsev,[2] Litvinova, Agranov, a sprinkling of Generals. Got to know Pshibyshevsky a little, an interesting man. I played some pieces and a singer sang some songs by Brahms. Pshibyshevsky commented on the inappropriateness of Romantic music. When I asked if my compositions (those that had not already been commandeered by Meyerhold) would be welcome at the Conservatoire he replied that certainly they would, and that he would invite me in the summer (I hope not in the same way as Leningrad). Talk with Agronov, skilfully introduced by Meyerhold. Agranov was business-like, asked practical questions and wrote everything down, promising to make enquiries. I emphasised the nobility of Shurik's character: true, he had committed a crime against the state, but (half jokingly) I hoped that five years' imprisonment would have taught him to keep any further noble impulses firmly under control. It looks as though the wheels have begun to turn in this matter. A long conversation with Litvinova, which eventually became boring. Mayakovsky was showing off, so I twitted him with being a tenor, and he was quite rude to me. I said, 'I played and behaved normally, not showing off, but when it's your turn you go putting on airs just like a tenor.' Mayakovsky: 'But you asked me to recite, and I never asked you to play.' But then he did read, 'To You' ('Foo, how stupidly this has turned out, it's impossible to read'). 'To You' was very cleverly done.[3] Then *The Bathhouse*, but it was not very interesting. I went into another room and sat on a sofa with Petrov-Vodkin talking about America, and I recalled that we had met at Bellevue at an Easter Day service. I mentioned Christian Science and he was extraordinarily interested, saying he did not expect there to be such evidence of spiritual life in America. How incredible that people, millions of them, should be in such total ignorance of this. As I walked home I was very happy at the thought that Shurik and Nadya should soon be released.

---

1   Boleslav Pshibyshevsky (1892–1937), musicologist, recently appointed Director of the Moscow Conservatoire, where he remained until 1931. Son of a renowned Polish writer, in the mid-1930s Pshibyshevsky was convicted of homosexual acts and condemned to three years' hard labour constructing the White Sea–Baltic canal. Worse was to follow: in 1937 he was arrested for spying and executed the same day immediately after his trial.
2   Platon Kerzhentsev (1881–1940), journalist, diplomat (ambassadorial posts included Sweden and Italy), politician and leading figure in Proletkult. With a succession of senior posts Kerzhentsev was at this time rapidly climbing to the top of the *nomenklatura*, and at the end of 1930 would become Executive Director of the Council of People's Commissars (Sovnarkom). In 1936 as head of Sovnarkom's Committee on Cultural Affairs he would unleash a savage propaganda campaign against artists and intellectuals now perceived, following the Stalin-sanctioned *Pravda* editorial of 28 January that year vilifying Shostakovich, as bourgeois Western-influenced Enemies of the People.
3   'Vam' ('To You'), explosive 1915 poem excoriating stay-at-home indifference to the sufferings of Russian troops at the front.

16 November

Kucheryavy came in the morning, obese, overweight and short of breath. I gave him some medicine. We talked of America and of Christian Science, but he was not interested. Went with Lyolya in search of a collection of astrakhan skins[1] she had heard of, but they did not show them to us, saying – in a whisper – come back tomorrow. I even took Malyshev along and asked him if it was legal. It was the kind of situation where you expect *Ogpushniki* to pop out at any second. Malyshev explained that I was legally entitled to buy, but this Jew was breaking the law in speculating and selling on goods belonging to another. At four o'clock I was expecting Lopashev, but he failed to appear. Departure the day after tomorrow is already in the air, causing a precipitate rush to accomplish a whole series of tasks such as ticket, visas; Malyshev was a great help. When I saw Meyerhold I asked him how much money I should give Malyshev. Dined at Meyerhold's, Asafyev also there. *Bruderschaft*[2] with Meyerhold. Meyerhold on Mayakovsky: he is in the final analysis a provincial; his showing off yesterday was nothing but a profound provincialism.

The second performance of *Oranges*. At seven o'clock there was quite a gathering in my box: the Kucheryavy couple, Anna Petrovna and two of the young Rayevskys, Mostras, Lyolya, Derzhanovsky and Yekaterina Vasilievna. Asafyev and I sat on extra chairs in the stalls, as did Gusman, Kerzhentsev and Rabinovich, as all the tickets had been sold, Gusman rubbing his hands with satisfaction. Many places in the production fell short in the staging, but it also contained many beautiful moments. The intervals are a disaster, each one lasting thirty to forty minutes, although Gusman proudly informed me that they had managed to shave five minutes off each. The Prince's laughter continues to irritate me: instead of being youthful and infectious it is more like a senile reflex. But Kozlovsky[3] is the darling of Moscow, why I do not know as the voice is quite ordinary although he has considerable intelligence, and at the end of the performance there were many more calls for 'Kozlovsky' than there were for 'composer'. It is some kind of holiday in the world of

---

1   Astrakhan fur is the skin of the karakul lamb from Uzbekistan. Those who object to the wearing of animal skins for fashion understandably feel especial revulsion for the manner in which the two main kinds of 'Persian lamb' furs are obtained: either they are from newborn lambs less than ten days old and preferably a few hours, or (known as broadtail and even more prized) they are from foetuses taken from the pregnant ewe, who is inevitably also slaughtered in the process.
2   See p. 3 n. 3.
3   Ivan Kozlovsky (1900–1993), celebrated lyric tenor whose reign at the Bolshoy Theatre lasted until well into the 1950s, singing principal roles in more than fifty operas. Stalin had a well-known penchant for Kozlovsky and frequently summoned him to perform at parties and even on occasion simply to sing in private.

higher education at the moment, hence the preponderance of young people in the audience.

Was told something about the possibility of joining the Bolshoy's housing co-operative on very favourable terms. Five hundred roubles – an 'industrialisation bond'![1]

Conversation about the rescue of my piano.

17 November

Maria Viktorovna's brother came to see me in the morning, a handsome young man not without a certain *chic*. As it was nine o'clock in the morning I was still in my pyjamas to receive him, before completing my morning toilet. Then there were several telephone calls, followed by the arrival of Lyolya to come with me to look at the furs which by now had been procured and which my companion pronounced good. After putting down a deposit we left them to be made up into a coat. I went away in a light, European-style coat.

Went to Yavorsky, miles away in Zamoskvorechie. His flat was cramped: two rooms three-quarters filled with two enormous grand pianos. Also there were the immensely grand Kubatsky[2] and his ballerina wife. Dinner was

---

1 The 'industrialisation bond' ('zayom industrialisatsii') system was the Soviet solution to the problem of how to generate in a non-capitalist society with virtually no foreign investment the huge capitalisation needed to move from the limited market economy of the New Economic Policy to the Stalin-inspired planned economy of full State industrialisation. In the 1930s this would be addressed by compulsory five-year plans, a massive drive to enforce collectivisation of agriculture and destroy the independent peasant farmer (the 'kulak') – not to mention the increase in the supply of forced labour through the Gulag system – but in the second half of the 1920s the approach was still a voluntary programme of government bonds ('obligatsii') issued initially in units worth five or ten roubles. As well as military, industrial and infrastructure objectives, the principle extended to a large house-building programme. Two such issues of 'Bonds for Industrialisation' were announced in 1927 (for 200 million roubles) and again in 1929 (for 550 million roubles). Increasingly strident propaganda campaigns were launched to overcome the ingrained resistance of the peasant to anyone who wants his money, in support of which Gorky, recently returned to the fold, was wheeled out to add his voice. Newspapers and posters featured hortatory *chastushki* such as this one from Yaroslavl: 'Wipe the sweat from off your brow, You don't need to break your back, So sign up for your bond right now – Help the farmer get his tractor.' (*Yaroslavl Week*, 11 October 1928. See above, p. 544.)

2 Viktor Kubatsky (1891–1970), cellist and conductor, was first cellist of the Bolshoy Orchestra, which he also regularly conducted in concert performances, and founder member of the Stradivarius Quartet. Well connected politically and an excellent administrator, Kubatsky succeeded in securing immediately after the Revolution, from no less an authority than an impromptu committee consisting of Lenin, Chicherin, Dzerzhinsky and Lunacharsky, a mandate to scour Russia and impound or rescue important musical instruments either still in the possession of their aristocratic owners or detected by Customs in the luggage of departing citizens crossing the frontier, or abandoned in the mass exodus of the intelligentsia after the Revolution. Kubatsky was provided with a special train, an armoured lorry and a warrant to travel unimpeded to any region of the country he had reason to believe harboured valuable

excellent, although Yavorsky is no longer in as high favour as he was. Yavorsky's views on Suvchinsky, when I raised the question of his coming to Russia, and on Mayakovsky. Kubatsky took me back in a taxi. It is possible that he is to be made head of Sovphil,[1] in which case he would like to arrange a serious concert of my works. I said this would be better next autumn as my visit planned for April would not be long enough.

After a rest I went to the radio station at eight o'clock. The hall, not too large, was full. Lopashev, who had had to endure Derzhanovsky shrieking down the phone at him for not treating me correctly, apologised and asked if I could come to see him tomorrow. Although tomorrow is the day I am due to leave the business with him might turn out to be serious, and I therefore told him I could come at ten o'clock in the morning. There was a panic just before the start of the concert: Saradzhev had forgotten his pince-nez. A flurry of telephone calls: he is getting old and forgetful. Derzhanovsky then said a few words and Meyerhold made a speech about me which had been written by Derzhanovsky and embellished by Meyerhold. There was no printed programme, Derzhanovsky announced each work with its movements, the last of which in the *Sinfonietta* came out rather stupidly as he sometimes added redundant explanations such as: 'The Finale, with which the *Sinfonietta* comes to an end.' This raised a titter in the hall. Saradzhev's tempi for the *Sinfonietta* were not quite right, he was probably flustered by the pince-nez incident even though they managed to get them to him in time. I listened from the wings, from where the piece sounded even worse than it did in the hall. It was followed by the Violin Concerto, then the *Overture on Hebrew Themes* and a second performance of the *Sinfonietta*. This time I heard it on the radio monitors in another room. The sound was clear, but raucous and dry.

After this I went on to conduct three numbers from *Oranges*: the Eccentrics, the Prince and Princess, and the March. Up to this point the audience, consisting largely of musicians, had been fairly restrained, but my appearance was greeted by a prolonged ovation, during which I three times

---

instruments. The results formed the nucleus of the unrivalled State Collection of Rare and Valuable String Instruments, whose President was Kubatsky himself and whose master luthier, to ensure conservation and optimum playing condition, was the great Jindřich Vitáček. Shostakovich later dedicated his Cello Sonata of 1934 to Kubatsky, who gave the first performance with the composer at the piano and was on tour with him in Archangelsk on the fateful day of the *Pravda* editorial condemning Shostakovich's opera *Lady Macbeth of Mtsensk*: 28 January 1936.

1 'Philharmonia' is the generic term in Russia for a regionally based music and concert-management organisation rather than a specific group of musicians. The main such organisation for Moscow was called Rosphil (Rossiiskaya Filarmonia) from 1920 until 1928, when its title changed to Sovphil (Sovetskaya Filarmonia), until 1931 when it changed again to Mosphil (Moskovskaya Filarmonia) which it still is.

turned to open the score on the desk but had to turn back again and bow. My beat was clear, but I did not feel at all at home on the rostrum. The orchestra, however, knew the pieces by heart and saved me. Despite this Myaskovsky thought that I had directed the Prince and Princess with great feeling. After the March the audience refused to disperse and demanded an encore. I came out to bow four times but the clamour for it to be encored could not be stilled. Although I had declared from the outset that I did not want to maintain the 'tradition of repeating the March', in the end tradition insisted on being upheld and after the fifth curtain call I did play it again.

Polovinkin on his *Children's Pieces* in relation to *Oranges*: 'Only now have I understood that this is a work we must all approach in order to learn how to compose music.' Was this sincere, or merely amiable small talk in the light of *Children's Pieces*?

Supper at Derzhanovsky's: Asafyev, Myaskovsky, Polovinkin, Saradzhev, the Meyerholds. Myaskovsky had several interesting observations on the revisions to the *Sinfonietta*. Walked home after two o'clock accompanied by Meyerhold and Asafyev.[1] Warm, windy and damp – just like March. We said goodbye on Tverskaya Street but at three o'clock Meyerhold rang me to tell me that two letters had arrived from Ptashka and there was also an express letter from Berlin.

18 November

Slept in all four and a half hours. People started arriving in the morning: Maria Viktorovna's brother (gave him 150 roubles from M.V. and stunned him with the news that she had a husband[2]); Anna Petrovna for the things for Shurik and Katya; people after my photograph and sent by Pshibyshevsky for the music (all the same, how badly the Leningrad Conservatoire has behaved!). At ten Lopashev, and then Derzhanovsky. I delicately proposed a fee of $6,000 and said I would be able to start from the 1st July. The job would be for a year; however I would not sign a contract until there was a definite project. He replied that he thought such a sum might be possible; the radio was headed by an old Party man who was in favour of my participation. If necessary an application for hard currency funds could be made to the Politburo. He asked me if I could send him books about the Eurasia movement: in his case this would be permitted. He would like Asafyev as an assistant. Our talk lasted two hours, after which I went to call on

---

1 'Asafyev and I brought up the rear, with Meyerhold and his wife forging ahead in front and Saradzhev beside him, whispering something very confidential, obviously smarming up to him.' (Subsequent note by author.)
2 Borovsky.

S. Gorodetsky, whom I had seen at the Dramsoyuz[1] the day before yesterday. I hear bad reports of him: he became an industrious boot-licker of the Communists and went so far as to poison the reputation of his writer colleagues but then himself disappeared from the scene as a writer. I called on him for old times' sake (the Scythian Ballet[2]) and because he happens to live just opposite. A particularly interesting flat right on Red Square, where secret doings with Godunov took place. One felt one might find unfortunate victims still immured in the walls. Vaulted ceilings, an antique setting altogether, but somehow not very comfortable. He spoke of possible librettos which he was keen for me to consider, and I asked him to send them to me. I don't want any agitprop or attacks on religion and reserve the right to do any alterations or adaptations I feel necessary.

I hurried to Meyerhold for the letters and then went with Lyolya to see about the furs. The coat has been splendidly made, a really good piece of work. But it weighed a ton! Malyshev was there as well. Paying the bill was accomplished smoothly and in a civilised manner: 1,240 roubles; all the same Lyolya says the furs are good-quality furs. Went to see Alexandrov and Frenkel, the latter on this occasion not very impressive, standing unshaven in the middle of the room with a pimple on his nose. Safely behind his desk, however, he looked a real grandee. Back at home I found Asafyev and Myaskovsky; we exchanged presents. Malyshev brought my ticket. I could not get through to Tseitlin on the telephone, but gave Malyshev a tie to present to him. Myaskovsky said (quoting Mayakovsky), 'It's the same as saying "good morning" to a dog.' Myaskovsky authorised me to sign on his behalf a contract for his *Sinfonietta*. We left together, I to dine with Meyerhold. Wooden toy. Malyshev came by with the car to take me to the station and my sleeping-car. I was seen off by the two Meyerholds, two Gusmans, Asafyev, Myaskovsky, Anna Petrovna with Alyona, Saradzhev, Lyolya and Yekaterina Vasilievna (Derzhanovsky has keeled over); flowers and chocolates.

The train left at 6.40. Slush and rain outside. Goodbye until April.

19 November

At first I was on my own in the compartment. We arrived at Negoreloe in the morning. They were very nice in Customs. I was sorry to be leaving the

---

1 The main Dramsoyuz (Obshchestvo Dramaticheskikh i Muzykal'nykh Pisatelyei – Society of Dramatic and Musical Authors) was established in Leningrad in 1925.
2 See *Diaries*, vol. 1, pp. 707–87 *passim*; vol. 2, pp. 5, 81, for the uneasy relationship between Prokofiev and the poet Sergey Gorodetsky in 1914 over a the creation of a satisfactory libretto for *Ala and Lolli*, the Scythian ballet rejected by Diaghilev but the music for which became the four-movement *Scythian Suite*.

USSR, but my visit had achieved what I had set out to do: clearly and incontrovertibly strengthen my position. The Poles were unhappy about the caviar which I was taking as a present for Weber and insisted that I put it in a transit case. The journey across Poland took all day. I had seen no snow in Russia, and there was none here either. Once again I was alone in the compartment and caught up on my diary. In the evening I walked around Warsaw, which has now begun to assume the air of a capital city, the architecture reminiscent of Leningrad, which is, however, conceived on a much more elegant scale.

20 November

Berlin, clean in the sunshine. I thought I had a lot to do, but it turned out otherwise. All the shops were shut by reason of a remembrance holiday for the deceased, and the entire population of the town seemed to be wearing hired top hats in order to visit the graves of their parents. I had wanted to buy a briefcase, as requested by Derzhanovsky. Weber was ill and Kleiber, with whom I had made an appointment to discuss *The Gambler*, was busy (the swine). I had lunch with Tanya Rayevskaya and then strolled about Berlin, not too easy in a heavy fur coat, and wrote up my diary sitting in a café.

At ten o'clock in the evening I took the Nord Express thanks to the through ticket to Paris I had bought for roubles, and had a lovely small compartment to myself. What luck, to go from Moscow to Paris all the way in solitary state.

21 November

I had been apprehensive about French Customs because of the Zeiss camera and the fur coat, but nobody looked at anything. In the next compartment, however, they found something with some Germans.

21 November–12 December

Ptashka met me at the station, in the most loving way. Little brother is eleven months old now. They have fixed up a little swing for him in a doorway, and he rocks backward and forward without stopping, pushing himself off on his little legs. I wonder he doesn't get seasick!

My immediate tasks and plans are as follows: on the 24th December we leave for America. Before that, on the 29th November there is a recital in Turin. I had done some rough preparatory work on the whole programme during the summer, but because of my hand started playing the piano again only at the very end of my stay in Moscow. On the 12th December I have the Second Piano Concerto in Amsterdam, which I have to practise, and on the 22nd December my own concerts in Paris, for which I need to practise the Third Concerto. I also have to refresh my memory of the First Concerto, which I am due to play on the Sunday after we arrive in America. All in all I am going to have to spend most of my time at the keyboard. Even so I cannot do more than two hours a day, and usually less, an hour and a half. In addition all sorts of passport and other chores have been piling up. In my spare time I have to proof-read the vocal score of The Gambler, pegging away and getting through a few lines a day.

On the 28th, just as I was getting finally ready for Turin, there were unexpected cables and telephone calls cancelling the engagement. Annoying, but financially this is now de Valmalète's business, not mine. On the other hand, seeing that I had made arrangements to be away, instead of Turin decided to go to Brussels to see The Gambler again, now incorporating the added scene. This time I was a little disappointed by the production. Audience response was muted, staging details either did not come off or were not attempted at all, and it did not sound particularly good owing to the acoustic of the theatre. The producer was, of course, not first-class. Some of the principals were good but others were mutton-heads. The new scene came off very successfully.

It is high time I wrote another opera. I have been devoting a great deal of thought to the principles of opera composition. Every scene must have its own form, that is to say it must be justified not merely dramatically but in purely musical terms as well. The voices must sing, and not only sing but the rhythmical origins of the text must often be reflected in the music. Jewelled – over-refined – surface texture can be lost or blurred, but it is more important to convey the truth and invention of the over-arching lines.

On the following day I spent four hours with Spaak correcting the French translation. I went to a concert at which I heard for the first time Nabokov's Symphony (quite pleasant) and Markevich's *Sinfonietta*. The latter began with all the freshness of youth, but as it went on its lack of variety and quasi-*Rite of Spring* imitation became very wearing.

Back in Paris, on the 1st December I attended an OSP concert. It was the first time I had been to a concert this season, and also my first incursion into the Pleyel empire since defecting from it. The effect was to say the least unexpected: the management, in the shape of the Lyons *père et fils*, was terribly obsequious. The occasion was the premiere of Poulenc's *Aubade*, with the composer playing the solo piano part. I had not previously heard him perform: for a composer he is pretty good, better than Stravinsky, Dukelsky or Milhaud. The music was not egregiously bad, or perhaps it is just that I am getting used to it. Here and there it was actually quite nice.

A mass of people and greetings in the interval. Stravinsky was wearing something dark, a knitted shirt, under his jacket (is this a new style?). He was very friendly and asked sympathetic questions about the car accident. I went backstage to congratulate Poulenc and complimented him on his playing. He returned the compliment by telling me he had been playing *Prodigal Son* all summer, and generally could not have been more affectionate.

The first item after the interval was the Suite from *Oranges*. As I entered the hall I saw the Stahls leaving: a protest against my behaviour. As a performance it made little sense: Ansermet began with the March (which one should never do) and the only other numbers were the Scherzo and the final Flight. They were not particularly well played, the rhythm shaky. At first the response was no more than moderate, but when the applause began to die down Florent Schmitt called out in a loud voice, 'Bravo, that's real music!' At this the applause redoubled and people began standing up to see who had been responsible for this intervention. Schmitt left the hall, arguing furiously with someone or other. After the concert I went round to see Ansermet, who informed me with an air of innocence that *Apollo* would be included in my concert in Brussels. 'Vous comprenez, cela sera un festival Prokofieff, dans la première partie duquel on va introduire *Apollon*.'[1] Not bad, is it? Of course, such a thing should never have been allowed.

The same evening there was a concert by Rachmaninoff, very much a gala occasion, we had to pay 300 francs for a pair of tickets. I had seen him at the publishers a few days earlier. He came in with his younger daughter,[2] stooping because he had hurt his back. He looked old and worn out. I tried to be gentle and affectionate. He seemed very ready to talk, and his daughter (a young lady of twenty-three or thereabouts) also did her best to keep the conversation going, correcting her father when, meaning to say Sabaneyev, he actually said Prokofiev. He was not in form for his recital, playing less well than last year. Still, I was going to go backstage to shake his hand until as his last item he played his new paraphrase of some appalling piece of vulgarity by Kreisler,[3] (and the paraphrase was mediocre as well). This drove me into such a frenzy of disgust that I did not go. How dare he affect such an imposing figure with the public and then inflict such rubbish on them!

The next event was the premiere of Stravinsky's *Capriccio* on the 6th December. Dining with me the previous evening, Nabokov showed me the article he had written on Diaghilev, in which he said among other things

---

1 'You understand, it will be a concert devoted to your works, but it will also have *Apollo* in the first half.'
2 Tatyana, who three years later married Boris Conius, son of the violinist Julius Conius.
3 *Liebesfreud*. It was preceded by Mozart's Sonata in D, K. 576, Chopin's Sonata in B flat minor, Ballade No. 1 and one of the A flat Waltzes, Liszt's *Sonetto 104 del Petrarca*, and of Rachmaninoff's own music a *Moment musical* from Op. 16 and a Prelude from Op. 32.

that Diaghilev had been the fount of ideas for many composers, including the suggestion to Stravinsky that he transform his projected piano concerto into *Petrushka*, and also that he compose a liturgical ballet, which became *Les Noces*. These are facts that are widely known, but when Stravinsky read the article he became apoplectic: no one would dare to give him ideas. Nabokov, embarrassed, wrote a letter of apology to Stravinsky, but he declined to answer and turned his back on Nabokov whenever they met. Nabokov found this all very petty, but since Stravinsky wields such power at Pleyel (where Nabokov is currently employed) it was essential to effect a reconciliation. At his request, taking advantage of the maestro's sunny mood and friendly feelings towards me at the rehearsal for *Capriccio*, I essayed to bring the conversation round to the subject, but Stravinsky immediately exploded, saying that Nabokov was not a bad composer but that he was an intriguer and we can confidently expect more dirty tricks from him. 'You and I, Seryozha,' added Stravinsky, 'confine our activities to music, and so never have any cause to quarrel.' Oh really? And he was looking me straight in the eye as he said it.

The hall was full of musicians for *Capriccio* and it was the most exceptional success. I happened to be in a box with Suvchinsky and Lourié. The latter was terribly effusive with me, spluttering with compliments exactly like a young girl. I liked the first movement of *Capriccio* better than the other movements because it contains the best material. The finale, on the other hand, is brilliantly effective but the content is of doubtful value. Stravinsky was upset that when he met Ravel afterwards; Ravel had not a word to say about the work. As for me, I believe that it is certainly Stravinsky's most successful work of the past six or seven years.

A couple of stories: (1) les truffes du père Igor[1] (Nouvel about Stravinsky's children); (2) Svyatoslav Stravinsky to Markevich: 'Isn't it rather unpleasant also to have the name Igor?' Markevich: 'I think it would be even worse to be named Stravinsky'; (3) Schmuller[2] giving a lecture on music: 'Stravinsky has contributed much to the history of music. It does not necessarily follow that he has contributed much to music itself.'

Rehearsed the Second Piano Concerto with Poulenc. He was deeply impressed and played the accompaniment rather well, accentuating the thematic material. This was very useful: the Second Concerto has hitherto always been a bogeyman for me, but this time, when I went to Amsterdam on the 12th I played it with confidence and the slight nervousness I did experience did not affect the result. The trip to Amsterdam was successful.

---

1 'Father Igor's truffles'.
2 Alexander Schmuller (1880–1933), violinist and conductor, Principal Conductor of the Rotterdam Philharmonic Orchestra from 1928 to 1930.

Monteux, suffering an excess of hostility towards Stravinsky, put his heart and soul into the *Classical* Symphony. It had a huge success and I was invited back for next season. Audience and orchestra stood to applaud me.

On the 8th December Ptashka performed at the American Club, her first appearance since Riga. She rehearsed diligently for her performance, and worried equally diligently, so much so that in the days leading up to the concert she completely lost her voice and we thought she would not be able to sing. But sing she did, and rather well, having quite a success. She has an attractive voice. There were a good many American Christian Scientists in the audience, whose presence undoubtedly helped. I sat with Maria Viktorovna, who listened with the greatest possible interest, it being the first time she had heard Ptashka perform. Another figure from the past was, for some reason, Zaitsev. When I returned from Holland it was time to get down to preparing for my concerts with the Lamoureux Orchestra on the 22nd, and our departure for America two days later. Unexpectedly, through the Ghirshmans, the chance cropped up of a flat on the rue Valentin Haüy. It was not particularly spacious but it was not expensive and we took it. Ptashka was also offered an engagement to appear in my concert but because of the throes of packing this had to be declined: it would have been a choice between either singing but not singing well, or not getting the packing done. I practised the Third Piano Concerto and studied the score of the *Divertimento*, which had only just been returned to me by the copyist, in order to be able to conduct it.

This was quite an event. It was the first occasion on which this venerable French institution, the Lamoureux Orchestra, was devoting a whole programme to a contemporary composer – the first fruits of the collaboration with Gaveau. There were three rehearsals for two programmes, mine on the Sunday but a completely different programme on the Saturday. Although they had already played the *Classical* Symphony and the *Chout* Suite, it was still desperately little rehearsal time. On the day of the concert the hall was almost full. Conversation on the street outside with Svyatoslav Stravinsky about complimentary tickets – was he offended? But his family was not with him: they were at some dull concert in the Salle Pleyel. Despite some gaps among the expensive seats there were a good many people standing, which made the hall look full. The audience consisted mainly of French; there were not many Russians present. By the end of the first item, the *Classical* Symphony, it was clear that the evening was going to be a success. After I played the Third Piano Concerto it was a positive smash hit, approaching the 1927 Moscow and Leningrad performances. Gaveau and de Valmalète were rubbing their hands. After five numbers from the *Chout* Suite (also greeted with enthusiasm) I conducted the first performance of the *Divertissement*, but the response to this was significantly cooler and more restrained. I had not expected this! Did they not understand the piece? Had they had too much by then? Or was it, as someone said to me, that I did not conduct it particularly well? (But at the rehearsal Lourié had specifically complimented me on my conducting.) The final work was the March from *Oranges*, which had to be repeated and was once again a success. Altogether a very successful concert and an excellent parting shot before America.

24–31 December
Paris–New York

We set out on our journey at 11.45 in the morning. On the steamer along with us were Rachmaninoff, Elman, Levitsky (a pleasant young man rather in the Dukelsky mould),[1] and Brailowsky.[2] A real *boîte à musique*. Many well-wishers at the station, and photographers. Some people were there to see off both me and Rachmaninoff, and had to run from carriage to carriage to say their farewells and godspeeds. Nabokov, for some reason, had dragged along Markevich. Nabokov passed on the news that, as an expression of Christmas goodwill, Stravinsky had sent word that he forgave him. We reached Cherbourg that evening to board the *Berengaria*,[3] 52,000 tonnes, an unbelievable colossus of a ship with seven decks, all illuminated. The first day out we rolled a lot, the second day we got used to it, and by the third day the sea was calm. Dekosov[4] was good company; we went to the cinema together. Rachmaninoff had the most luxurious suite imaginable. He did not show himself much, walking round the empty decks on his own, looking bored. Seeing that I was disposed to be friendly, he invited me to his state-room in the evenings, and I went there almost every night to play patience – a touching idyll. I was invited to sing(!) in a charity concert. My response was to express my thanks for the honour, but I feared I would be unlikely to afford the honoured ladies and gentlemen of the audience much pleasure.

---

1 A pianist acquaintance.
2 Alexander Brailowsky (1896–1976), Kiev-born pianist who gained a reputation for special affinity with Chopin's music, performing cycles of the complete piano works on several occasions. He eventually settled in Paris and became a French citizen.
3 The *Berengaria*, Elbe-built in Hamburg, her 52,000 tonnes symbolising the might of Imperial Germany, was originally launched as the *Imperator*. When seized by the Allies after the First World War, however, and handed over to the British she was taken over and renamed by Cunard. Until the launch of the *Queen Mary* in 1936 she was the pride of the Cunard fleet, rivalled only by the *Mauretania*. In 1938 a wiring malfunction caused a fire after the ship docked in New York, and the cost of the necessary remedial work was so prohibitive that she was towed back to Southampton and thence to the Tyne to be scrapped.
4 Unidentified.

After suggesting a duet with the great 'violinist' Rachmaninoff, I more seriously recommended Brodsky,[1] who was in second class.

In the end the concert took place without the participation of any celebrities and was a something of a fiasco. Our state-room was splendidly spacious and the food was top class, caviar and so on. We docked in New York twenty-four hours late, on the afternoon of the 31st December. How beautiful New York is as the liner makes its way into the harbour, and how much it changes on each new arrival. Haensel is away in Florida and Parmelee has gone to the country for New Year; the only person to meet us was a representative from Steinway, a Russian called Greiner.

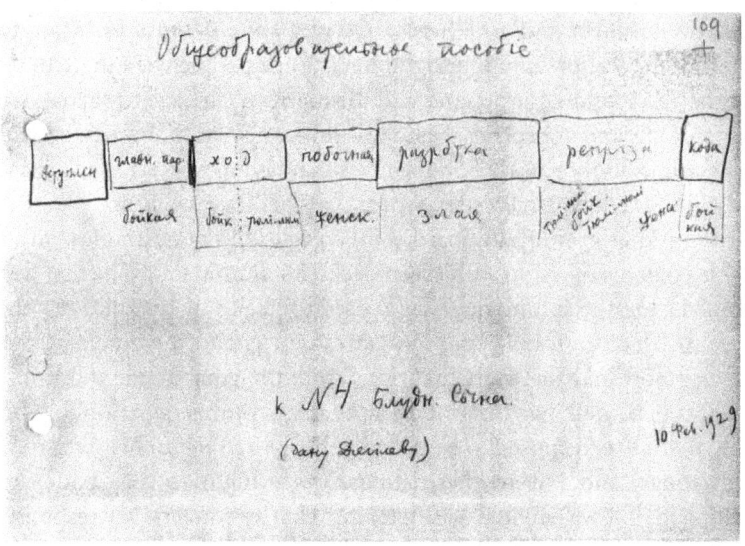

The 'General Educational Aid' by which Prokofiev demonstrated to Diaghilev the modular construction of the fourth number ('The Dancers') of *Prodigal Son*.
© The Serge Prokofiev Estate

---

1 See above, p. 782.

1930

1 January

Disembarking in New York yesterday, after completing all the formalities (which took quite a long time) we went to the Great Northern Hotel where Parmelee had reserved two rooms for us. This was the same hotel as we had come to four years ago, in New York quite long enough for the place to begin showing its age. In Europe it would certainly have lasted a good twenty years, but here it is probably soon due for demolition. A Steinway was already in position, a nice instrument but in need of tuning. We had no plans to celebrate the coming of the New Year anywhere in particular, but between eleven and twelve o'clock at night ventured into Broadway, which was a surging sea of revellers whistling raucously on penny whistles, blowing into squeakers, letting off crackers and generally making an unbelievable racket. It was pandemonium, but in its way very impressive.

2–4 January

Little happened of any consequence. I did not make much effort to see people, wishing to minimise any distraction from my concert preparations. Ptashka was moody, mainly on account of my appearing in New York with Koshetz rather than with her, feeling that I was not doing enough to promote her as a singer. But it was not my choice to be 'singing' with Koshetz; Haensel put it all together without consulting me. And as for creating a reputation for Ptashka's vocal artistry, nothing is more ill advised than attempting to generate publicity in a void. What she ought to do is get her voice in trim and sing right, left and centre, anywhere she can. The reputation will follow of its own accord.

We did go out now and again, however – to Vladimir Bashkirov, for instance, who telephoned us. With a salary of 50,000 a year he has come up in the world: a beautiful wife and an apartment on Fifth Avenue, no less. He was very affectionate to me. Greiner, the Russian new Manager at Steinway,[1] invited us home for a real Russian dinner.

---

1 Alexander Greiner (1888–1958) was actually Latvian, not Russian, but had studied at the Moscow Conservatoire. Immediately after the Revolution he acted as Secretary to the American YMCA Mission to Moscow, and afterwards emigrated to the USA. From 1926, in succession to Ernest Urchs, he was until his death Steinway's Concert Artist Manager and as such a key figure to generations of pianists. One of his last actions was to persuade Van Cliburn to participate in the first Tchaikovsky International Piano Competition, which had been openly designed to

Aslanov appeared, visibly aged, ill and rather touching. He had known Dukelsky's father, an engineer, and was in a position to state categorically that these Dukelskys were not Jewish. So there is hope yet that Dima will develop into a real composer.

I went twice to see Koshetz to rehearse the songs. She is the same as ever, making it a *point d'honneur* to sing with all her composers in turn: Prokofiev, Glazunov, Medtner. Ariadna[1] was with her, keeping discreetly in the background; she has been touring with Koshetz as her accompanist. She showed me a new work she had composed, not very individual but at least more correct than those I had seen in California.

Walking around New York produced a huge impression. The rate of construction is incredible. Altogether it is an incredible city.

5 January

We attended a great social evening at Mme Wiborg's.[2] Kokhánski played, accompanied by Iturbi,[3] a Spanish pianist who has made a huge career for himself in America. Massine danced a solo; he is currently choreographing some great New York production, for good money no doubt.[4] Not long ago he married a Soviet ballerina, who plied me eagerly with questions about Moscow news.[5] Boring but influential ladies flitted past: Mrs Vanderbilt, Mrs Otto Kahn, also a good-looking old man. I was surprised to see someone assisting him with his coat, but it turned out he was a Russian Grand Duke. We got back at 2 a.m., a waste of time as my concert is tomorrow.

The cut of my tail-suit waistcoat is no longer fashionable and looks very out of date: nowadays they are worn much more open. I must buy another immediately as these things are noticed in New York.

---

demonstrate to the world the superiority of Soviet instrumental training. Cliburn won convincingly, became an overnight sensation in both the Soviet Union and America, and received a national hero's welcome home with a tickertape parade on Broadway that was no doubt just as jubilant and noisy as the Prokofievs' New Year's Eve stroll.

1   Ariadna Nikolskaya. See above, p. 818, n.2.
2   See *Diaries*, vol. 2, pp. 513–14, 517. Prokofiev had met this wealthy New York music-loving socialite in the company of the Carpenters in Paris in 1920.
3   See above, p. 808
4   Massine had accepted a three-year engagement to choreograph live shows for the magnificent new 6,000-seat Roxy movie palace on West 50th Street just off Times Square. He also had a few sidelines, however, including a musical by Edward Pola called *Woof, Woof*, which opened at the Royale Theatre on Christmas Day 1929 and closed, unlamented, a month later.
5   Eugenia Delarova (1911–1990). Soon after leaving the USSR for Paris in 1926, where she got a job dancing at the Folies Bergères, she met Massine at the studio they both frequented for dance classes during the Paris run of *Le Pas d'acier* in June 1927. She became his second wife and came with him to America in 1928 to join the dance company at the Roxy Theatre.

6 January

In the morning Greiner collected me to Steinway's to have my photograph taken. I nearly boiled under the fiercely bright lights. Greiner told me stories about how Rachmaninoff sat there patiently but Horowitz jigged about like a flea.

In the afternoon Ptashka went to work with Luboschutz, the accompanist of choice for absolutely everyone in New York.[1] He praised Ptashka, with the result that all traces of her sour mood vanished. Strange to relate, his opinion carries some weight, because he puts himself about everywhere and talks with authority.

The evening concert with Koshetz was at Town Hall. Some were of the opinion that this was a mistake; it was too modest a venue, and it would have been better for me to wait to appear with the Boston orchestra. Others, however, took a different view, and said it was of no importance. The hall is not up to much (the now semi-ruined Aeolian Hall was a nicer place to be),[2] and the hall was three-quarters full, as I was told although it looked no more than half full to me. I played in a state of mild fury at New York's indifference to me, and therefore was not nervous. At first my feeling was of completely cold detachment, but then when I got to *Suggestion diabolique*, the March from *Three Oranges* (which was encored) and harmonisations of Russian songs I had done at some point that Koshetz had dug up from somewhere or other, and about which I had totally forgotten, the audience began to wake up.[3] Horowitz has been making a sensation playing *Suggestion diabolique* in America this season, so I exerted myself trying to play it not worse than him,

---

1 Pierre Luboschutz (Pyotr Lyuboshitz) (1891–1971), Odessa-born pianist, brother of the violinist Leya Lyuboshitz (see above, p. 219, n. 2) and of the cellist Anna Lyuboshitz (the Luboschutz Trio became a well-known piano trio in the United States), had been a pupil of Igumnov at the Moscow Conservatoire before coming to America to accompany Zimbalist, Piatigorsky and other luminaries. In 1931 he married another Russian-born pianist from Paris, Zhenya (Génia) Nemenoff, and the Luboschutz–Nemenoff piano duo had considerable success, eventually jointly heading the piano department of Michigan State University.
2 Town Hall, on West 43rd Street near Times Square, has had a chequered history since it was built by the League for Political Education in 1921 as a meeting place open to all, initially to promote the universal suffrage implications of the Nineteenth Amendment to the US Constitution. Its exceptional acoustic properties may have been a by-product, but are sufficiently impressive to have attracted over the decades a steady stream of front-rank performers. As a concert hall it is still under the shadow of Carnegie Hall and Lincoln Center, but many people would argue that this is a result of its proximity to the relative sleaze of the Times Square district rather than the intrinsic properties of Town Hall itself. The slightly smaller Aeolian Hall on 42nd Street, belonging to the Aeolian Piano Company, was where Prokofiev made his Manhattan recital debut in November 1918, but the building was sold to a cigar retail chain in the mid-1920s and ceased to be a music venue. See *Diaries*, vol. 2, pp. 348–9, 470.
3 In March 1920 the ethnomusicologist Alfred Swan had given Prokofiev two Russian folk songs, 'The White Snow' and 'The Snowball Tree on the Hill', from an 1886 collection of folk songs

and it went well. *Choses en soi*, needless to say, went so completely over the audience's heads they seemed hardly worth playing, but then on the other hand how could I not play my latest and most substantial composition? In the Green Room afterwards were Ziloti[1] (with whom relations seem to have cooled over the past few years but who was cordial today), Klein, Sudeikin, Saminsky and an apparition from the past, Serge Bazavov.[2]

After the concert I took my suitcases straight to the station and at a quarter to twelve, still in my tails, took the train to Cleveland. Even though Ptashka and I had been constantly quarrelling, she was still sorry to see me go.

Before the concert, in my anxiety not to forget to take with me everything I needed for Cleveland, I forgot some of the music I needed to accompany Koshetz today. As a result, Ptashka and Parmelee had to make a dash back to the hotel to get them. Haensel stepped on the fringe of her dress and tore part of it off.

7–11 January
Cleveland

Arrived in Cleveland at one o'clock in the afternoon on the 7th and checked in to the excellent Cleveland Hotel, unfortunately rather too far away from the concert hall. A rehearsal was due to start an hour and a half after my arrival. The orchestra is large and of very good quality; inevitably among the musicians are a number of Russian Jews who knew me from St Petersburg Conservatoire days. The Principal Conductor, Sokoloff,[3] another Russian who has been living in America for twenty years, was away and his place was filled by the mediocre but conscientious and willing Ringwall.[4] The Concerto (I was playing the First Concerto after an interval of many years) went well from the start. When I followed it by conducting four numbers from *Le Pas*

---

from Arkhangelsky and Olonetsky provinces, collected by Fyodor Mikhailovich Istomin and Gyorgy Ottonovich Dyutch and published as *Pesni Russkogo Naroda* by the Imperial Russian Geographical Society. Swan suggested he harmonise them in a modern idiom. (The historical Olonetskaya Gubernaya, centred around Petrozavodsk, ceased to exist in 1922.) 'The Russian songs harmonised by Prokofiev are insignificant pieces of shit. But if I do, nevertheless, have them published I'll send them to you.' (Letter to Myaskovsky of 4 May 1930.)

1 See above, pp. 126–7 n. 2.
2 Serge Bazavov was a cousin of Prokofiev's first love, Nina Meshcherskaya, and during the two years of the relationship the two young men had seen a good deal of one another often over the bridge table. See *Diaries*, vol. 1, pp. 473–730 *passim*.
3 Nikolay Sokoloff (1886–1965), Kiev-born violinist and conductor. He was the founding conductor of the Cleveland Orchestra in 1918 and served as its Principal Conductor until 1933.
4 Rudolph Ringwall (1891–1978), violinist and conductor. He had played second violin to Sokoloff in the latter's string quartet, and became his assistant in Cleveland in 1926. Later he was second violin to Joseph Fuchs in the Cleveland String Quartet, and became known as a witty and articulate host on radio stations broadcasting classical music.

d'acier at first I found it difficult to hear clearly, but gradually got used to the sound in the hall. We had three rehearsals for the two performances, the first with a well-filled hall and press in attendance, the second half empty and with no press. The orchestra management apologised for the unmusicality of their citizens, whom it had proved impossible to educate into attending concerts despite the low cost of tickets. Applause for my Concerto No. 1 seemed genuine enough, but that for *Le Pas d'acier* was merely polite although the orchestra clearly liked it. I was informed that one of the critics was an excellent musician but the others were not very knowledgeable. The result, however, was exactly the other way about: the unmusical one had praise for *Le Pas* while his musical colleague found it mere noise, much inferior to the *Classical* Symphony, which Koussevitzky had conducted here not long ago. But I remember that when, twelve years ago, Koussevitzky performed the *Classical* Symphony for the first time in America, similarly authoritative critical opinion was that it was complete rubbish.

In Cleveland, as it happened, I received a packet of hot-off-the-press New York reviews of my concert there on the 6th. They were an unrelieved disgrace, the confections of semi-intelligent cretins sitting grandly in their chairs in the offices of important newspapers in a great city and solemnly pronouncing verdicts on music of which they understand precisely nothing. Will they understand something in the future, and if so, how long will it take them? Of course they will not. Even so, in one or two of them there were faint signs here and there of an element of doubt creeping in: are we perhaps making fools of ourselves, might it not be time for a smidgeon of praise?

I spent four and half days in Cleveland, but the time passed almost imperceptibly. Between the concerts and rehearsals I proof-read *The Gambler* (a very time-consuming occupation) and wrote letters. I had a telephone call from Miss Crain, who now lives in Cleveland, and went at her invitation to a Christian Science lecture and to one of their Wednesday meetings. Huge churches and a mass of people. Miss Crain introduced me to a number of Christian Scientists, who were very kind, came to the concerts, and drove me about in their cars.

12 January

In the morning I returned from Cleveland to New York to find Ptashka despondent and in a very bad mood. But it was not long before I had a call from Sudeikin, who has been designing for some years now at the Metropolitan Opera. He asked me if I could come to a meeting with Serafin,[1]

---

[1] Tullio Serafin (1878–1978) had been Assistant Conductor to Toscanini at La Scala until Toscanini left to go to New York, and took over as Musical Director until the First World War and briefly

the Met's Principal Conductor, and with Dr Lert,[1] a producer, to discuss *Fiery Angel*. It appears that all three are admirers of my music, and even Gatti has vouchsafed the occasional strangled expression of interest in my music. In short, there are signs of a change of heart at the Metropolitan. I still have uncomfortable memories of the awful atmosphere in which ten years ago my three operas had been auditioned.[2] Yes, they were all in existence even then, although not in their final finished forms.

At six o'clock in the evening, therefore, I was at Sudeikin's where we were joined by Serafin. I outlined the subject. Serafin was delighted by it, until Sudeikin suddenly began to complain that it was not dramatically convincing. This was rich coming from Sudeikin, who had cooked up the whole idea – or had it all been a clever chess ploy? The vocal score is in Paris, and I accordingly cabled Paichadze asking him to send it quickly, since the Met is at present busy with a production of *Sadko* and today's discussions are preliminary in nature. After Serafin left I repeated the entire synopsis of the opera to Sudeikin, and this time it appeared to him more theatrically credible. Dr Lert came in the evening, announcing that it had been his dream to produce *Three Oranges* in Frankfurt when he was stage director there. A genuine change of heart! Indeed! Better late than never.

Next morning I attended the Christian Science Church and then went to lunch with the Kleins in their superb apartment. Dukelsky visited me in the afternoon: he has not made a breakthrough in America but still has hopes.

13 January

Dined with the Koussevitzkys, who are resting after four concerts in forty-eight hours. They are in a glorious suite at the new Savoy Plaza Hotel, with a fantastic view over New York.

---

  afterwards. He was Principal Conductor at the New York Met for a decade from 1924 until 1934, furthering a reputation that lasted throughout his long career for nurturing outstanding singers, including Rosa Ponselle, Joan Sutherland, and Maria Callas, with whom he made at least a dozen complete opera recordings for EMI. By no means a reactionary exclusively wedded to the nineteenth-century bel-canto repertoire, Tullio Serafin was commendably open-minded not only about German opera but operas by contemporary composers, being responsible for the Italian premieres of Berg's *Wozzeck* and Britten's *Peter Grimes*.
1 Ernst Lert (1883–1995), Austrian stage director, librettist and theatre historian. He had recently arrived at the Met from La Scala, preceded by a spell at the Opern- und Schauspielhaus in Frankfurt. As a writer, his best-known book is *Mozart auf dem Theater*, a study based on his own experience of producing Mozart's operas in Leipzig, where he was director of productions for seven years before the First World War.
2 See above, pp. 10–11 n. 5, 277 n. 1, for references to Prokofiev's previous experiences of the Metropolitan's General Director Giulio Gatti-Casazza's indifference, if not outright hostility, to his music.

It was all very relaxed and affectionate, but they are not in general paying the attention to me I had expected from them. It seems doubtful whether he will perform the *Sinfonietta*, which Ptashka had given to him – very long and difficult, and is it really so very interesting? – and although he has been thinking of a programme exclusively of my works it seems that there may not be enough time to rehearse it. I said that it was extremely important to me to have a whole programme in New York 'pour me poser bien'[1] in this most satiated of cities. Koussevitzky replied that he would think about it, and would try, but the uncertainty remains.

At eleven o'clock we repaired (all of us in evening-dress) to Mme Loomis, who is mad about Russians and had organised a soirée for Russian New Year. Grand Dukes were in evidence, and a Cossack Choir, and there were noisy proclamations of death and damnation to the 'diabolical Bolshevik usurpers'. After my time in Moscow, I could not avoid the feeling that mentally ill people were playing at theatre. When Grand Duke Alexander Mikhailovich (the same elderly thoroughbred whom I had seen at Wiborg's) stood up, everyone else got to their feet as well. I whispered to Dukelsky, 'Is it all right to sit down now?', but he said no, it was not safe yet. Orlov[2] told me that Alexander Mikhailovich, on hearing him play, had said, 'Marvellous. What lightness! Just as if you were playing a balalaika.' Fate spared me intercourse with the Grand Duke, but I was introduced to the son of the Grand Duke Konstantin Konstantinovich, a very good-looking young man.[3] 'You're Prokofiev?' he asked me. 'You are the toast of the town in London.' 'But I thought London had less time for me than anywhere . . .' The Grand Duke: 'I heard you being very highly spoken of at Lady Cunard's.'

The Cossacks danced a Lezginka, and altogether it was rather embarrassing. We went home at two, and the Koussevitzkys went back to Boston.

---

1 'to present me in the best light.'
2 Nikolay Orlov (1892–1964), pianist and Chopin specialist, a former student of Igumnov in Moscow. Prokofiev had seen him as a concert platform rival, especially in Moscow. See *Diaries*, vol. 1, p. 325; vol. 2, p. 236.
3 The Grand Duke Konstantin Konstantinovich (1858–1915), grandson of Tsar Nicholas I, was a very different and greatly more cultivated person. A poet and playwright who published under the pen-name K. R. (Konstantin Romanov), he was also a capable musician and served as Chairman of the Russian Musical Society. A homosexual, he nevertheless from a sense of duty fathered nine children, several of whom were murdered within twenty-four hours of the murder of the Tsar and his family in 1918. The young man Prokofiev met at the party was a fortunate survivor. See *Diaries*, vol. 1, p. 441; vol. 2, p. 48.

14 January

Dukelsky rang up to persuade us to go to a party being given by a millionaire in honour of Gershwin after the premiere of a new musical by him.[1] Gershwin is America's God of operetta, and also tries his hand at serious music in which he sometimes achieves a spiky wit, not always successfully. Dukelsky said that as Gershwin had been at my house in Paris he hoped we would put in an appearance today.[2] 'All the stars of the operetta and musicals world will be there; it will be the most spectacular party of the season,' spluttered Dukelsky. At midnight he came round for us so we dressed and went with him even though our real desire was go to bed. It proved to be rather a strange evening. A cabaret diva sang in a bass voice, a beautiful woman who is said to earn $4,000 a week. Gershwin himself played. His papa, a diminutive semi-intelligent Jew who has forgotten nearly all his Russian, stood beside me (I was sitting in a chair) and delivered himself of various ludicrous malapropisms: 'Now he's playing his panto concert . . . this tune's played by the violence.' 'In Russian we say "fiddles",' I said. 'Yes, yes – middles.'

A large amount of champagne was dispensed; one gentleman, swaying on his feet and smiling vaguely, was delicately steered to the recesses of the apartment, there to reflect on 'dry' America. At two o'clock, finding it hard to keep our eyes open, we left, chuckling over Dukelsky and his 'most spectacular party of the season'.

15 January

A violinist called Rabinovich who had played my Violin Concerto with Koussevitzky on the 10th came rushing up to me in the hotel lobby: 'You know, Koussevitzky told me I played it more beautifully than anyone else so far, better than Szigeti, better than Kokhánski . . .' I: 'Yes, I saw Koussevitzky and he told me you played not at all badly.' Exit an embarrassed Rabinovich.

16 January

The Kokhánski salon is now unquestionably the place for everyone to be. The Spanish pianist Iturbi, who has recently come to America, was there today. He came up to me and said he wanted to play my works. 'You are such

---

1   It was not in fact the premiere of a new show but the first night of the revival of *Strike Up The Band*.
2   Gershwin had spent some months in Paris in the spring of 1928, during which he met on several occasions Nadia Boulanger, Ravel, Stravinsky, Prokofiev, Poulenc and Milhaud. The musical result of this sojourn was *An American in Paris*, which was premiered by Walter Damrosch in December 1928.

a famous man,' I said, 'I hardly know whether I dare believe in my good fortune.' He (swallowing my sarcasm): 'No, seriously, I really want to play your Third Concerto,' and then immediately started talking to Ptashka in Spanish, wanting her to telephone him the moment we return to Paris. He leaves for there tomorrow.

We were invited to dinner with the Bazavovs. He is a terribly nice, boring and homely man – Tanya and Nina Meshcherskaya used to call him 'the hippopotamus' – but with perfect manners. I was genuinely pleased to see him, and his natural courtesy, of course, avoided any questions I might not have wished to answer. His wife is the sister of Bakhmetiev,[1] a passionate admirer of my music. Bakhmetiev was also present, a good-looking man, very full of himself, who never stopped talking. Also of the party was Olin Downes, the *New York Times* critic.[2] Seven years ago he fell out of an aeroplane and landed on his head, a circumstance that prompted the largest American newspaper to offer him the job of music critic. Around that time he came to see me in Paris and promised to take an interest in my compositions (even though it was clear he understood little of them), but from then whenever he happened to hear any of them he felt able to declare that I was a worthless composer. To fall on one's head is not of itself a sufficient condition to begin to understand music. Today he was bowing and scraping with alarmingly exaggerated politeness, while I expatiated on the activities of Asafyev, whom Downes has for some time wanted to enlist as USSR *Times* correspondent.

Downes: 'We must meet again soon.'

I: 'Yes, as a matter of fact I have been wanting to show you one or two things . . .'

Downes (flattered, thinking that I was interested in his opinions of my music): 'Oh certainly, of course, with pleasure!'

I: '. . . by younger composers: here for instance are some reviews of pieces by one of them whom you will not yet know but soon will: Nabokov.'

Downes (visibly cooling): 'Oh, that is most interesting.'

Conversation with the Bazavovs was about music and about Bakhmetiev's match factory, in which Bazavov has a job as a manager.

---

1 Boris Bakhmetiev, former Russian (not Soviet) Ambassador to Washington. See *Diaries*, vol. 2, pp. 339–41, 344, 421.
2 Olin Downes (1886–1955) was Chief Music Critic for the *Boston Post* from 1906 until 1924 and for the *New York Times* from 1924 until his death in 1955. Of conservative inclinations, musically speaking, and harbouring a particular enmity to the Second Viennese School, he was nevertheless prepared to champion at least some works by composers such as Shostakovich, Prokofiev, Stravinsky and Ives. No contemporary composer, however, could inspire the adoration he felt for Sibelius.

17 January

Lunch with Mrs Reis, representative of the League of Composers. At lunch were Smallens, Greenberg and other members of the League.[1] Mrs Reis, in collaboration with Stokowski, is now undertaking large-scale productions, hiring for the purpose no less a venue than the Metropolitan Opera. Here they staged *Les Noces* and *The Rite of Spring*, and next year they want to put on *Le Pas d'acier* and *Prodigal Son*. Plans were discussed over lunch. Back at home Ptashka sang some Falla songs to Arbos,[2] who is currently touring America with great success and is staying at our hotel. Ptashka had invited him ostensibly to consult him on matters of correct Spanish style and pronunciation, but in reality because she wanted him, as chef of the Madrid Philharmonic, to hear her and bear her in mind for engagements. But Arbos took his pedagogic role seriously and instead of listening constantly interrupted with explanations, in the course of which his enthusiastic demonstrations involved him in showering my bald patch with spit as I was at the piano to accompany her while he stood behind me.

We dined with the Bashkirovs and afterwards went with them to a Gershwin musical, the same one whose premiere was being celebrated three days ago.[3] The staging was terribly static and unimaginative, bearing as much

---

[1] The League of Composers is America's oldest organisation devoted to the promotion of contemporary music. In 1954 it became the US chapter of the International Society of Contemporary Music, after which it has been known as the League of Composers/ISCM.

[2] Enrique Arbos (1863–1939), Spanish violinist, composer and conductor. As a violinist he had an impeccable pedigree, having studied with Vieuxtemps and Joachim, and led both the Boston Symphony and Berlin Philharmonic Orchestras as well as holding down a violin professorship at the Royal College of Music for over twenty years. In 1904 he became Principal Conductor of the Madrid Symphony Orchestra, a position he held until the year of his death. He conducted the first performance in Spain of *The Rite of Spring*. As a composer he is probably best known for his orchestration of Albéniz's collection of virtuosic piano pieces *Iberia*.

[3] *Strike Up The Band*, based on the political satire by George S. Kaufman, had had its first Broadway run in 1927. It was George and Ira Gershwin's first full-length integrated score for a book musical. The 1930 revival seen by Prokofiev opened on 14 January at the Times Square Theatre, an important change from the original production being the removal of 'The Man I Love', which had in the meantime become a standard. Prokofiev might have liked the score better if this irresistible number, the showstopper of the original production, had been included. Nevertheless, the production did feature the Red Nichols Orchestra in the pit with Nichols himself, Benny Goodman, Glenn Miller, Gene Krupa, Jack Jenney, Babe Russin and Jack Teagarden, so even for Prokofiev there must have been some incidental pleasures. Not the least of these could have occurred during 'I Got A Crush On You', when Krupa introduced his recently invented 'freeze beat': at certain pre-arranged points everyone – band, dancers, singers and actors – froze for a couple of bars. Gershwin was entranced. According to trumpeter Max Kaminsky, 'Gershwin was crazy about Gene's playing, and no wonder, because Gene was the first white drummer in a Broadway pit band who could swing the beat so that chorus girls could kick in time.' The show ran for 191 performances, and the Gershwins' next musical, *Girl Crazy* – Krupa at Gershwin's insistence still in the pit – for 272. See Burt Korall, *Drummin' Men*, Schirmer Books, New York, 1990.

relationship to true operetta as oratorio does to opera. All the humour depended on linguistic witticisms of a strictly local character. But that isn't theatre! Theatre is movement! The music was pleasant, trivial for the most part, occasionally witty. There is one very good, even ingenious ensemble, but Gershwin either does not understand where his best qualities lie, or else is not willing to risk outstaying his welcome with the audience. He probably thinks extending such moments would be too expensive a gamble for him.

18 January

We were at Mrs Steinway's, the owner of the firm, a very nice old lady. We talked of the New York critics. What a dog's life – two, three, even four concerts a day, and an article about them has to be produced that very evening! Moreover the critics are often not free agents, and are subject to directives of various kinds. For example, a critic attacks the Metropolitan with every justification for so doing. Otto Kahn picks up the telephone and speaks to his banker friend, who owns the newspaper. 'It's rather awkward, you know, for your organ to be criticising our theatre . . .' and the result is an order to the poor critic: either praise, or go to the devil.

In the afternoon Dukelsky played me some excerpts from his new Double-bass Concerto, assuring me the while that in no way at all was it a way of buttering up Koussevitzky. The music is feeble; nor does he understand the instrument. The songs were better, but heaven knows what he thinks he is playing at. Dukelsky seems to be withering on the vine. I had been afraid that flirting with operetta would damage him, and he evidently thought the same as he has gone in quite the opposite direction, towards aridness. In exactly the same way, Rachmaninoff got infected by dryness as soon as people started teasing him about the lyrics he was using being too accessible.

In the evening I saw Sudeikin, who has already done some pencil sketches for three of the settings for *Fiery Angel*. They were very expressive. We talked long, developing staging possibilities for *Angel*. Sudeikin then told me how he had it out with Stravinsky when, on returning from America, he began to suspect that there was something between Stravinsky and his, Sudeikin's, wife.[1] During lunch Sudeikin smashed a glass and poured wine over Stravinsky, and then 'gave him a little shaking'. After that they went together for a long walk around the streets, talking wildly and incoherently and, when finally parting, kissed. They never saw one another again. 'Pure Dostoevsky,' explained Sudeikin, who I believe remains to this day not indifferent to his departed wife.

---

1   Stravinsky and Vera Sudeikina began their love affair in Paris in 1921. However, they did not marry until 1940, on the death of Stravinsky's first wife Yekaterina (Catherine).

19 January

While we were at Mrs Steinway's Olin Downes had rung up and asked me to come to help him sort out a bulky parcel of music by Russian composers he had received from Moscow. Today I complied, and spent three hours with him. The music was almost all by people known to me: Myaskovsky, Feinberg, Polovinkin, Shostakovich, etc. There was also a collection, new to me, of the work of proletarian musicians, the likes of Davidenko[1] and others, the very people who had asked me awkward questions in Moscow and were plotting to sabotage *Le Pas d'acier*. One or two of them were quite entertaining as exemplars of the style: a chorus speaking rhythmically to the accompaniment of a small drum and a solo voice emerging from this background. Downes then interviewed me and I enlarged on how melody and substance are now the chief concerns of my compositional work; however I observed that melody, provided it is true melody, that is to say a genuinely new melodic invention, is the hardest thing of all to penetrate people's understanding. I did not let Downes off the hook, pointing out that in his writings he had said he failed to find any content in my music. He drank in attentively what I had to say, and when he said goodbye, thanked me for an enjoyable talk 'with a real musician'. And adding, 'Violinists, pianists – after all, they don't really interest me.'

21 January

I am practising the programme for my recital and also the Second Concerto for Boston. Ptashka is also preparing for her first appearance, consequently her nerves are in a bad state and she feels unwell, and the atmosphere at home is not the best.

A letter Koussevitzky has sent me has driven me to distraction. When we met he told me that although he would like to arrange a programme consisting of my works he was not sure whether there would be enough time to rehearse it. In my innocence I rather stupidly wrote to him that I hoped he would try, and in reply have received this slap in the face. Koussevitzky, who has a tendency to forget today what he said yesterday, now writes that the time has not yet come when an all-Prokofiev concert would be viable. He has thus put me in the position of a supplicant making a petition papa in his

---

1 Alexander Davidenko (1899–1934), an ideologically committed member of the Russian Association of Proletarian Musicians. In 1925, while still studying at the Moscow Conservatoire (under Kastalsky and Glière) he formed the forbiddingly named 'Production Collective of Student Composers of the Moscow Conservatoire', or Prokoll, which produced a large body of massed choral works to Revolutionary texts.

wisdom declines, and not simply so but puffed up with self-importance like a turkey cock. My first reaction was that under no circumstances would I stay with Koussevitzky in Boston but would put up at a hotel. But then I thought better of it, especially after I had been to see Klein who, in answer to my question about how best to control one's irascible impulses, said, 'Remember that no matter how unjust something may seem to you in the hot flush of anger, God still disposes of everything in the best possible way. And if we mortals make mistakes, why should we let this make us angry?'

22 January

Without giving up our hotel room, which still had the piano in it and all our things unpacked, we travelled to Boston. I decided not to be hard on Koussevitzky, merely to observe gently, should a suitable occasion arise, that he had adopted an inappropriate tone in his letter. As it happened it was even easier: Natalya Konstantinovna came herself in the car to meet us at the station, a rare and unexpected courtesy on her part, especially as the telegram announcing our arrival had been signed by Ptashka and there could have been some uncertainty whether or not she and I were coming together. Koussevitzky himself was in bed with a temperature, and I tried my best to feel sorry for him in order to rid myself of any residual hard feelings. Our conversation was amicable, Koussevitzky racking his brains non-stop to put a programme together. He had come up with a good idea, namely to start with Mozart and end with Bach, with the *Scythian Suite* and the Second Concerto in between, but the necessary Bach score could not be obtained and now he could not think what to replace it with.

23 January

The Koussevitzkys live outside Boston, right in the country surrounded by snow and forest. The house is enormous, a country mansion. It was rather cold in our room, so a gas fire blazed all night, shooting out gleams of flickering light, which was very pleasant. In the morning the sun shone brightly on the snow. My concerts with Koussevitzky are in a week's time; but we had come for these two nights because Ptashka has a concert with a big women's university near Boston. Ptashka is fretful and nervous, but we are not quarrelling. I banged my finger on a trunk yesterday, and it is painful.

Koussevitzky paced from room to room agonising about the programme. I teased him, saying, 'There, you see, you didn't want an all-Prokofiev programme, and now God is punishing you.' He has already announced a provisional programme with Albéniz in place of Bach, and it appeared in the evening papers, along with a report to the effect that Prokofiev had arrived, but regrettably none of his new compositions were to be played. The voice of the people has made its mark on Koussevitzky: now he would like to include the *Sinfonietta*, but it transpires that Paichadze did not after all send the material. Devil take him and his brilliant new technique for publishers to support their authors. We paced up and down our rooms (Koussevitzky in one, I in another) and finally came up with a classic formulation of the Paichadze problem: working with Paichadze is like sharing a room with a madman and waiting for the moment when he will strike you on the back of the head.

At seven o'clock a car was sent from Wellesley College to take us to the concert. Wellesley is an hour and half away from Boston, with two thousand young female students, and they have an annual concert series of eight serious concerts. And indeed the hall was full of girls, although a few dinner-jackets were also to be seen. But we were not in good form: the middle finger on my right hand was still sore, so I was unable to make the glissandos in the Prelude and *Suggestion diabolique*, and Ptashka had only half a voice. On top of that the programme was rather beyond the maidenly intellectual reach. Our success was only moderate, each of us getting one encore. We got $750, had five minutes' chat with a group of young ladies, quite pretty, and were then taken back to find Koussevitzky still racking his brains over the programme.

24 January

Got up at 7.30, Ptashka moaning and groaning, for the train at nine o'clock direct to Philadelphia where we arrived at half past five, I in quite good shape but Ptashka very tired. During the journey I caught up on my diary and corrected the translation of a booklet about Christian Science which had recently been published in Russian but with a mass of mistakes and unidiomatic turns of phrase in the Russian.

In Philadelphia we were in the same hotel as Smallens, noisy and tousled as ever but a *bon garçon*. Ptashka has completely lost her voice. We decided it would be better for her not to sing, but for me to play ten of the *Visions fugitives* instead. The hall was not a large one, but it had a good atmosphere, with columns, and it was full. The first half consisted of a boring quartet by Honegger, and I was to begin the second half. The concert had been organised by the Contemporary Music Society, and the response was completely different from that of yesterday's beauties. Here the performance was greeted with loud applause, and I had to bow several times after the Andante of the Fourth Sonata. In short, the evening was a great success. I also played better than the evening before; my finger had almost healed. Altogether instead of a selection of gavottes I could have played a more serious programme, for instance *Choses en soi*.

Getting up on to the stage was something of an obstacle course, because there was a short flight of four steps which had been wheeled into position.

These wobbled as I mounted them, obliging me to regain my equilibrium at each one, subject to the fascinated gaze of the audience. Ptashka stayed behind at the hotel and sobbed, but afterwards we all sat together in Smallens's room.

25 January

Next morning we journeyed back from Philadelphia to New York. I read the reviews that had already appeared of the previous night's concert: they were good. The first thing that happened in New York was a phone call from Sudeikin: in the Met this afternoon would be the premiere of *Sadko*, and there was a seat for me in the front row, next to Mrs Kahn(!).[1] I barely made it for the start of the performance, worried that I would not recognise my hostess. But it turned out she was in a box with Sorin.[2] The opera went strongly, although the Italian Serafin overheated some of the tempi. But be careful! Not a word, I must bite my tongue to prevent any critical comments escaping. Sudeikin's designs were good in the Russian style and sometimes very successful: particularly effective was the ship disappearing in the mist after Sadko sinks beneath the waves. Sorin sticks to Mrs Kahn like a leech. He took me in to be introduced to her. She chattered away in French, was complimentary about Sudeikin's settings and reminded me that she expected me tomorrow at five.

In the evening we entertained the Kleins. Ptashka was upset that Mrs Kahn had invited me without her, but I explained that it was a purely business matter. Klein was diplomatic about expressing an opinion, but took my part.

26 January

Taken by Kleins to a concert by the singer Onégin.[3] The voice is superb, but the programme was so unbearably vulgar and the singer so horribly

---

1 Mrs Kahn (née Wolff) was the wife of Otto Kahn, Chairman of the Metropolitan Opera Board. In 1920 in New York Prokofiev had met her socially a few times and had hopes of her exerting some influence on her husband's willingness to support Prokofiev's bid to have his operas performed at the Met, but without result. See *Diaries*, vol. 2, pp. 496, 588.
2 Savely Sorin (1873–1953), society portrait painter. He had learnt his craft first in Odessa and then in Repin's workshop at the Imperial Academy. Fast gaining a reputation as a portraitist, he painted many notable Russian Silver Age arts figures, including Akhmatova, Karsavina and Chaliapin. Diaghilev included him in his first *Mir Isskustva* exhibition in 1916. Emigrating in 1920 he went first to Paris and then to New York, where his expressively imagined, highly polished likenesses of the rich and famous kept him in constant demand.
3 Sigrid Onégin (1889–1943), Swedish mezzo-soprano of Franco-German origin, who had made her Metropolitan Opera debut as Amneris in 1926 having earlier had the distinction of singing the small role of Dryad in the premiere production of the revised version of Strauss's *Ariadne*

coquettish with the audience that I fled, much to the embarrassment of the Kleins, who know her and had invited us to the concert. From five to seven I was with Mrs Kahn. After preliminary courtesies I outlined the plot of *Fiery Angel*. She made some comments as to the need for a chorus. 'We have such a large theatre that the audience sitting in the boxes opposite the stage are on 7th Avenue while the action on stage is on Broadway. So you see, operas that are delicate and intimate are a failure; the only successful ones are those conceived on a broad-brush scale.' The upshot was that she would like to stage *Fiery Angel*, but would have to discuss it with Serafin and Gatti.

Serafin I know to be on my side, but Gatti is a sphinx. We decided to postpone future discussion until the beginning of February: I shall be back from Boston and the vocal score should by then have arrived from Paris.

In the evening I went to Sudeikin to report on the interview. He thought the Empress's comments were interesting: might it not be a good idea to introduce a chorus to enliven the uniform tenor of the second act? In his opinion Gatti would be interested, but for the season after next, not the next one. The main obstacle to fear was the clique lobbying to commission a Gershwin opera. Gershwin may be known for operetta or musicals, but no matter, he is an American.

27 January

Learnt the Second Concerto and rehearsed with Ptashka for her next concert.

In the evening, a concert by Milstein,[1] a violinist who is making a tremendous career here. Afterwards there was a reception at Greiner's, mostly full of Russians only half of whom could I identify. Marina[2] gives a good impersonation of a grown-up young lady, alternately charming and insolent. Koshetz slobbered over both my cheeks; she grows more stout with every passing year. Aslanov is now an endearing greybeard. His proudest

---

auf Naxos in Vienna. Born Elisaveta Elfrieda Emilie Sigrid Hoffmann she initially sang under the name Lilly Hoffmann, but after marriage to the Russian pianist Yevgeni Onegin (not surprisingly another pseudonym, real name Lvov) she became Sigrid Onégin and enjoyed a distinguished career on the operatic stage and in recital in Europe and America, her rich but mobile contralto voice being compared with that of Ernestine Schumann-Heink.

1 Nathan Milstein (1904–1992), violinist with one of the longest and most distinguished careers of the twentieth century. One of a quartet of great Russian violinists born in Odessa (Heifetz, Elman, Milstein and Oistrakh, the first three also studying under the same teacher, Leopold Auer at the St Petersburg Conservatoire), he formed a lifelong personal and musical bond with Vladimir Horowitz (another Ukrainian Jewish musician) and together they had given the first performance in Russia of Prokofiev's First Violin Concerto in a violin and piano arrangement, in Moscow on 21 October 1923, three days after the Paris premiere.

2 The daughter of Nina Koshetz and Alexander Schubert.

memories are of how he launched Prokofiev and Myaskovsky, and the carnage that attended the first performance of my Second Concerto.

28 January

Ptashka felt sick after the fruit cup that was served yesterday: God knows what goes into what they drink in dry America. Dukelsky has a sensational tale to tell of Sławinski, the dancer who once upon a time staged *Chout*.[1] He was appearing as a member of Pavlova's company in India, where he amused himself with the native women. Returning to London he felt unwell and went to the doctor. The doctor examined him and said, 'Wait here a minute.' A quarter of an hour later in came some policemen in gloves and masks, clapped him in handcuffs and transported him in a hermetically sealed van to hospital, whence he was sent to a leper island as he was showing symptoms of leprosy.

Digesting this revelation we barely had time to pack and get to the train. We arrived in Boston at half past ten in the evening and stayed again with the Koussevitzkys. Once more our rustic room with the gas fire, snow outside a metre deep and wonderful winter air.

Koussevitzky and I did a little work on my Second Concerto. Lying on his desk was a Schoenberg score, which I noticed was all written in C, just as mine are, and with an entire introductory preface devoted to the principle. What can this mean: has he come to the same conclusion twenty years after me, or did he see a score of mine and simply take a leaf out of it?

29 January–1 February

Two rehearsals and two concerts with the Boston Symphony – *Scythian Suite* and the Second Piano Concerto. I have finally succeeded in learning the latter, although in performance there are still one or two lapses, especially in the cadenza. My Fourth Concerto will be easier to play! Koussevitzky's direction of the *Scythian Suite* is quite brilliant. At the first (afternoon) concert its success was quite big, but at the second (evening) hearing it was very big indeed. Koussevitzky is full of praise for my pianism and declares that I am now one of Boston's own. Dukelsky came, and is overwhelmed by the sound of the *Scythians* (he was hearing it for the first time) but considers that I was not on the right track when I composed it and the material is no more than

---

1 Tadeusz Sławinski (1901–1945), Polish dancer in Diaghilev's Ballets Russes, appointed as a last resort by Diaghilev to choreograph *Chout* in collaboration with the designer Larionov. See *Diaries*, vol. 2, pp. 597–8.

average. The best and most serious of the Boston critics, Philip Hale[1] and Parker,[2] were very complimentary and came to both performances to deepen their understanding. Both were bashful and shy when I met them.

At the Koussevitzkys there is a ban (a perfectly reasonable one) on playing the piano, so between the rehearsals and the performances we were given the use of a car to go to Symphony Hall, which I also made use of to visit the Christian Science Publishing Society. I had two reasons for this: (1) I wanted to obtain for Asafyev the job of correspondent for the *Christian Science Monitor*, as this would be an ideal position for him both in terms of his inclinations and his erudition; (2) I needed to bring the brochure consisting of thirteen articles translated into Russian which I had entirely checked and corrected (it was full of unidiomatic phrases, non-existent Russian words, wrong punctuation, etc.) to the attention of the appropriate person. I first called on Heitman, to whom Klein had introduced me in New York. He was extremely gracious but busy, and referred me to one Harrison, in charge of publishing. But when I got to his office it was already late, and he had gone home. I called again the following day but he was at a meeting and I was received by his secretary. In fact it was quite useful that matters turned out this way, because although I came with every appearance of humility, I was not without a certain pride in the importance of the work I had done. The competent, down-to-earth secretary proved to be a specialist in translation matters. In the first of my corrections I had myself evidently made an error. She suggested passing it to a third party for independent scrutiny, and then took me to see the head of the music department, who knows me and said he would take note of my brief for Asafyev. It is hoped that he will be commissioned for a series of articles.

2 February

When the two orchestral concerts were over there was a chamber concert, which had been proposed by Burgin, at the Chamber Music Club. The fee was a mere $300, but I accepted it because of Ptashka. She sang pretty successfully, although it could have been better still. She was well received, and presented with a bouquet. Dukelsky was full of praise, Koussevitzky as well but more moderately. That evening we packed our things.

1　Philip Hale (1854–1934) was chief music critic of the *Boston Post* from 1903 until his death, and also wrote programme notes for the Boston Symphony's programmes.
2　Henry Taylor Parker (1867–1934), the critic of the *Boston Evening Transcript*, signed all his reviews with his initial H.T.P., which according to *Time Magazine* usually stood for 'Hard-To-Please or Hell-To-Pay. But he was seldom vitriolic. His reviews were famed chiefly for their length, their ornate, old-fashioned sentences, their freshness and independence of viewpoint.'

It is still the case that Koussevitzky has pickled my Third Symphony in aspic (yet again the material has got held up somewhere, or so they say). Now he will not be able to perform it until April, but I must take it back to Europe in March for it to be performed in Brussels. So much for the present prospects for 'the best symphony since Tchaikovsky's Sixth', as Koussevitzky described it when he heard it in Paris.

3 February

Return from Boston to New York in the afternoon, accompanied by Dukelsky, who spent the journey making up verses about Stravinsky (his problems composing a tune of his own) and embellishing them with rather good drawings of the composer.

In New York we returned to the same hotel room. When I telephoned Sudeikin, his feeling was that *Angel* would get a production, although perhaps not until the season after next. The vocal score has arrived – for once Paichadze has not let me down. Sudeikin wanted to know if I had thought more about revising the opera and including a chorus, but in the excitement of the Boston concerts I had completely forgotten about this suggestion.

I tortured myself all evening thinking about how I might brighten up the second act. Ptashka urged me to stop thinking and go to sleep; I would have a clearer head in the morning.

4 February

During the night an idea came to me for a crowd scene: peasants clustering round a dead horse and accusing Renata of witchcraft. Renata then appears on a horse led by Rupprecht, hidden up to her waist behind bushes.

Went over to Sudeikin, uncertain how he would take to having a horse on stage. But he liked the idea, and it gave him the thought that the entire middle section of the opera might be captioned 'The Journey of Rupprecht and Renata', consisting of a series of miniature scenes. He immediately came up with concepts for the other scenes: Renata shows Rupprecht a fresco of the Fiery Angel ('if the plot needs words to be understood then the libretto is a bad one; the action ought to make everything clear without the need for words, and therefore it is a good plan for Renata to show the Fiery Angel'); then Rupprecht would buy secret folios from the black magic practitioner; a victim accompanied by the chorus would be led to be burnt at the stake; manifestations from the spirit world would occur in the soothsayer's house. All these ideas fitted so well to the music that with the exception of the episode with the horse I would hardly need to compose any more music. After five hours' work we had sketched out reconstructions of the second and third acts: in Sudeikin's conception this would be one continuous act of seven scenes. Even if *Fiery Angel* does not in the event suit the Metropolitan's plans, it will still have been worth while to have had all these discussions in order to achieve the kind of revision I had so earnestly sought from Demchinsky.

5 February

Went back to Sudeikin to refine the alterations we had worked on yesterday. Suddenly Sudeikin asked me, 'Do you consider yourself to be a genius?' As I hesitated, he said, 'I, for instance, do consider myself to be one.' Not wishing to see my own distinctions crumble to dust, I replied that probably I did too, while being uncomfortably aware that another answer would have been possible. Then together we went back to my hotel, where I played him passages from *Fiery Angel*. The music made a tremendous impression on him, although he made the comment that alongside magnificent set pieces there were unbearably long recitatives. I explained diffidently that I had begun composition of the opera ten years ago, at which time my views on the way to compose operas had not yet crystallised, whereas now I am steadily developing my operatic style.

In the evening we met with Mrs Kahn, who had unfortunately not been able to get hold of Serafin as she had hoped. I nevertheless played; she listened attentively and expressed her pleasure although I do not think she understood the music as Sudeikin had done, even selecting the passages he thought I ought to demonstrate to her. We decided that the best course of action would be to give a shortened libretto to Gatti and the vocal score to Serafin, and to arrange a meeting for when I should return from California. We then went with Mrs Kahn to the Kokhánskis, who were holding a reception today for Orlov. Ptashka and Dukelsky had in the meantime been to Orlov's concert and came on to the reception from it. Among the guests were Glazunov, Grechaninov, Ziloti – all the old guard. Ziloti is a character straight out of Gogol. Glazunov got a little drunk and talked happily to me, wanting to know if he would be welcomed back at the Leningrad Conservatoire or whether they had already washed their hands of him. My private opinion is that on the whole they are not holding their breath for his return, so I found it difficult to reply and stammered inconsequentially.

6 February

Lunch with Engel,[1] who proposed a commission from the Library in Washington for a chamber piece, with a fee of $1,000. I enquired

---

1 Carl Engel (1883–1944), French-born pianist, writer on music and publisher. A regular contributor to the *Musical Quarterly*, he headed the Music Division of the Library of Congress.

whether a quartet would be acceptable? And could it be not very long in duration?

In the evening my concert in Brooklyn with the Boston Orchestra. Koussevitzky and I were transported thither in a splendid automobile. Before my appearance Koussevitzky conducted the Sixth Symphony of Tchaikovsky and I followed with interest the technique and gestures of his conducting style. My performance went well and had a good success. Koussevitzky's opinion is that the quartet commission was an important one and it was right for me to have accepted it. Their performances are arranged with great style and prestige. Stravinsky's *Apollon* had come about and was first performed under the same auspices.[1]

7 February

So it goes: in the morning I have to put together an abridged libretto with Sudeikin, in the evening my most vital concert engagement – and I have a bad headache. I went, nevertheless, to Sudeikin, but we did not get down to work. He told me some interesting things about Diaghilev, who had in his youth visited a special German sanatorium with the object of ridding himself of his unhealthy tendencies (there followed a description of the said sanatorium), but it was of no help. Sudeikin then quizzed me on my biography, and I became so absorbed in stories about my finishing at the Conservatoire, my first meeting with Diaghilev, then my summer sojourns in Sablino[2] and my journey to America, that I failed to notice my headache had disappeared.'That gave your blood a good cleaning-out,' said Sudeikin.

I was afraid of tonight's concert, or rather I was afraid of being afraid. But remembering what Klein had said, 'God's love envelops and preserves you,' I visualised a wall around me, keeping me from harm. And also: 'He who recognises God's presence and puts his trust in God is freed from deceitful feelings of personal responsibility, and all those troubling strivings of the human will are stilled.'

I played almost calmly and for the first time made no mistakes in the cadenza. My success was great, and the orchestra rose to signify their appreciation. At the end of the *Scythian Suite* Koussevitzky had brought me on to the platform, now after the Concerto it was my turn to lead him on, it was a question of papa loving mama and mama loving papa, a real parade of devotion. After the concert the Knopfs[3] took us and the Koussevitzkys to a noisy night-club at the top of a skyscraper, but it was not very interesting there.

---

1 See above, p. 629 n. 2.
2 See *Diaries*, vol. 2, pp. 53–8, 193–230 *passim*.
3 See above, p. 267.

8 February

This afternoon will be a repeat of yesterday evening's concert, but I have already endured my New York baptism of fire and am able to face it with equanimity. I went round to Sudeikin's to compose the abridged libretto, but he was still asleep. I apologised for being late, since our appointment had in fact been for earlier. In the end I wrote it myself, and he approved it when I read it to him. Sudeikin attempted to start up another conversation about interesting matters and reminiscences, but today I had come to work. Having completed more than half I left to dress for the concert, promising to send the ending from the train. At the hotel Ptashka was hurriedly packing, as that evening we were due to leave for Los Angeles. This afternoon's programme does not include the *Scythian Suite* (Koussevitzky, having decided not to tax the patience of New Yorkers any further, inserted in its place a tedious Symphony by Bax) and the audience greeted me with more restrained enthusiasm. Generally this audience was less demonstrative than yesterday's.

In the Artists' Room Rosing, now Director of the American Opera Company, proposed staging *Fiery Angel* should plans with the Metropolitan Opera fail to come to fruition.[1] I suggested *The Gambler* or *Three Oranges*

---

1 A 1930s production of *Fiery Angel* directed by Vladimir Rosing (1890–1963) is a tantalising unrealised prospect. If ever there was a man ready to fall in with and help realise Prokofiev's ideas of operatic composition and presentation, it must have been Rosing. This extraordinary man, born into an aristocratic St Petersburg family with high political and cultural connections, ceaselessly poured his protean enthusiasms into singing (tenor), opera direction and management in Europe, Britain and America (with notions of acting, staging and movement, and use of the vernacular that were extremely innovative for the time), writing novels and plays, undertaking effective political activity on behalf of the doomed Provisional Government and its leaders, giving recitals and making recordings. In 1923 he met George Eastman, philanthropist and inventor of Kodak film, and was invited to head the Opera Department Eastman was projecting for his School of Music in Rochester. The Rochester American Opera Company came into being a year later. It was to sing in English and be non-hierarchical, having no stars, although Mary Garden did join them to sing Carmen and the conductors included Goossens and Coates. By early 1928 the company had dropped Rochester from its title, and the American Opera Company gave a seven-week New York season in the Gallo Theater on Broadway, followed by two national tours. Despite President Hoover's personal plea to Congress for the company to be underwritten for establishment as a national institution, six months or so after this meeting the beginnings of the Wall Street Crash put paid to its future existence.

A short list of Rosing's associates across the spectrum of his activities gives some idea of the range and all-inclusiveness of the doors open to him: Adrian Boult, Harry S. Truman, Dwight D. Eisenhower, George Eastman, Fyodor Kommisarzhevsky, Albert Coates, Martha Graham, Nicolas Slonimsky (as accompanist!), Ezra Pound, George Bernard Shaw, Fred Gaisberg, Mary Garden, Augustus John, Felix Yusupov, Alexander Kerensky, Herbert Hoover, Leslie Heward, Eugene Goossens, Paul Horgan, Reuben Mamoulian, William C. Bullitt, Thomas Mann, Douglas Fairbanks junior, Lionel Barrymore, Birgit Nilsson, Boris Christoff, Rudolf Nureyev. A vivid description of his unusual personality as man and artist is to be found in Ivor Newton's wonderful autobiography, *At The Piano, The World of an Accompanist* (Hamish Hamilton, London, 1966): 'Rosing had one of the vividest and most magnetic personalities I had ever

instead of *Fiery Angel*.¹ He will continue negotiations when I return from California. Another proposal has come in from Paris, via Nouvel, for a ballet that Lifar would like to stage at the Opéra. Rouché has given the plan his blessing. Suddenly I seem to be in great demand. I dashed back to the hotel, finished the packing and, accompanied to the station by Dukelsky, we left for California at 8.40 p.m.

9 February

In order to have some chance of rest after three days of concerts I had reserved a separate compartment, so that we travelled in exceptional comfort. The train was wonderful, with a drawing room and an observation balcony. I had chosen a warm, southern route, so we were heading south to New Orleans. I dealt with correspondence. I would have to decline the ballet commission: I simply do not have the time for everything, and in any case since the departure of Diaghilev from the scene I am less inclined towards the ballet! But might there be a chance of persuading them to take one of my old ones?

10 February

In the morning we changed trains at New Orleans, with a two-hour wait in between. We had a look round the town. In the old quarter there are interesting houses with lacy wrought-iron balconies. Beyond New Orleans the

---

    come across; rarely have I known anyone who could hold an audience in such a sheer ecstasy of enchantment through a whole recital. A Rosing audience was unlike any other. There was electricity in the air and people crouched forward in their seats as though they were watching some fierce and terrifying melodrama. With Rosing, nearly every song was a melodrama – sometimes a grand-guignol melodrama. He acted every song; often he overacted it, sometimes he all but clowned it. The purists were scandalised. The man could do everything but sing, they said. He was a mountebank, a buffoon. He had no right in a concert hall; he ought to be on a fairground. It was outrageous, unparalleled. So it was. Perhaps they were right, but it came off, because, despite all his eccentricities, Rosing was never cheap; in everything he did there was such an overpowering impression of stern, unflinching sincerity. The man simply threw himself into his music and its poem. He sang – eyes closed and feet wide apart, like a blind goalkeeper – not only with his voice but with his heart, brain, body, hands and feet. If he tore a passion to tatters, you felt that that particular passion was much more effective in tatters than intact. If he made a mess of a song, well, it was a glorious mess.'

1 Rosing did eventually get to direct a production of *The Love for Three Oranges*, for New York City Opera at City Center in 1949. This time, unlike its previous New York airing in February 1921 in the original Chicago Opera production ('I felt as though I was being savaged by wild animals' was Prokofiev's reaction to the press reviews), it was a smash hit, awarded a three-page colour feature in *Life Magazine* entitled 'A Slaphappy Fairy Tale Makes a Smash-Hit Opera', revived by popular demand for the next two seasons and, in a typically Rosingesque piece of chutzpah, taken on tour to Chicago to show them how it ought to be done.

train has to cross the high-water Mississippi river by means of a pontoon raft; it is not possible to build a bridge at this point because the sand of the river bed is so unstable.[1] Thereafter we moved gradually into desert. It was warm and I could sit out on the rear platform without an overcoat. I finished the libretto and sent it off to Sudeikin. Wrote letters. In the evening I was handed a telegram from the Gloria Swanson Studio in Hollywood asking for confirmation that I was actually on the train. Another commission? Or merely wanting to photograph me alighting from the train in Los Angeles? Ptashka teased me for being a 'celebrity'. I said that probably the star they would really like to engage is the highly photogenic Svyatoslav.

11 February

The heat and the desert continued. I carried on with my correspondence and to relax sat out on the rear platform, although sometimes the dust drove me back in. Our American neighbours engaged us in conversation. One said, 'What a boring country'; the other said, 'What a wonderful country.' A third asked, 'Would you happen to know why all the cows round here have white faces? The cows' bodies are all kinds of colours but the faces are always white.'

12 February

Next morning when we got to a station there were Indian women in brightly coloured shawls selling beads, little boxes, postcards. Ptashka wanted to buy something, but on examination it was all desperate rubbish. I got out of the train with my camera, but the moment they saw it they turned away and covered their faces with their kerchiefs.

It was now very warm, and the carriages became red hot. I was told that in summer all the passengers can do is lie motionless and rub ice over their foreheads, while the guards hang wet sheets across the compartments.

We arrived in Los Angeles at five o'clock in the afternoon. Nobody was there to meet us. We are staying at the Biltmore, a very luxurious hotel. Among the post that was awaiting our arrival was a letter from Nelson,[2]

---

1 Until the construction of the Huey P. Long Bridge in 1935 this was the only way to get across the river. The problem of the shifting sands (actually silt deposits brought downriver), and the fact that the bedrock is 1,000 feet below the surface of the water, was solved by laying down a layer of fine sand fifty metres thick and relying on the extra-massive weight and girth of the huge piers to hold them in place. So far it has worked.
2 Paul Nelson (1895–1979), cosmopolitan architect with a passionate belief both in the ability of technology to improve the lot of modern man and that there was no reason why an architecture based on modern technology should be less beautiful than the architecture of the past.

Gloria Swanson's architect. She has invited us to lunch tomorrow and wants to talk about a film project she is planning. This is good news. It smells of money.

Rodzinski[1] called, young and energetic, to go through the Third Piano Concerto. It is not, apparently, to be an all-Prokofiev programme as had been mooted earlier: Rodzinski has programmed so much new music here that he has been prevailed upon temporarily to moderate his enthusiasms. The *Scythian Suite* will therefore be played in one of the later concerts. Despite the disappointment of there not being a concert devoted to my music, I liked Rodzinski: an attractive Don Quixote tilting against the windmills of the wealthy local *grande-dame* rich sponsors.

13 February

In the morning, a rehearsal with Rodzinski, and then at noon Nelson's wife called for us in Gloria Swanson's magnificent Rolls and took us to lunch with the star. Nelson is a delightful man with light blue eyes, an American architect working in Paris and with a French wife. He had by chance been in Los Angeles when Gloria came across a project he was working on there (I saw it, very witty and ingenious), a private house on top of a skyscraper. As this was exactly the kind of thing she was in search of for her next picture, she immediately fastened on to him.[2] Nelson is an artist, and strongly disapproves of

---

According to the *New York Times*, reviewing an exhibition devoted to him at the Columbia University School of Architecture in 1990, 'Nelson was everywhere and knew everyone: he was a friend to Hemingway, Fitzgerald and Pound; he painted with Braque, made architecture that earned the praise of Le Corbusier, and had Léger choose colours for his buildings' interiors. He served as an aviator in World War I, designed a screening room for Joseph P. Kennedy senior and sets for a film for Gloria Swanson, and had a long association with R. Buckminster Fuller. This man was not just an architect: he was more like the Zelig of twentieth-century modernism.' (Article by Paul Goldberger, *New York Times*, 6 April 1990.)

1 Artur Rodzinski (1892–1958), Polish conductor, was spotted by Stokowski conducting *Die Meistersinger* at the Warsaw Opera and immediately invited to become his assistant at Philadelphia. Shortly before meeting Prokofiev in Los Angeles he had been appointed Music Director of the Los Angeles Philharmonic where he had already made a reputation for innovative programming, and this high-profile appointment was followed by similar positions with the Cleveland, New York Philharmonic and Chicago Symphony Orchestras.

2 The movie was *What a Widow*, produced and bankrolled by Swanson's lover at the time, Joseph P. Kennedy, father of John F. Kennedy. Kennedy also had a part in the film. Paul Nelson spent nine months of his life on the art direction; although the film itself is lost the designs still exist and are among the very first examples of movie sets designed in the International Style. With its star, the lavish production, the designs and songs by Vincent Youmans, it ought to have been a hit. But it was not, and among other casualties was the romance between Swanson and Kennedy, partly because when the latter was searching for a title, screenwriter Sidney Howard's fortuitous invention so pleased him that he promised him a Cadillac. Only later did Swanson discover that the car had been charged to her garage account.

the inferior calibre of the music for the picture, which is why he has been recommending me. The production is being financed by a banker from Boston, Kennedy, a charming, soft-spoken man, still young, who admires my music, and thus had come about the lunch invitation. We drove for quite a long way: Gloria lives in the movie enclave where is the studio in which she makes her films. As a woman she is so beautiful and famous that it seems quite impossible to touch her. As for me, I stepped into the background the moment I had introduced Ptashka, and left her to make conversation. After lunch I was taken into a special screening room,[1] because I am so inexperienced as never to have seen a film incorporating dialogue or a music soundtrack, although I know that this cinematic form has been in existence for a year or two now.

The difficulty is that the score would be needed by the 1st April, which means that I would have to compose it here in America between my concert engagements. This obligation would represent terrible pressure, and I kept thinking, would it not be better to transfer the idea to the next picture? I left soon afterwards in order to rest before my concert, but instead of sleeping kept turning over in my mind whether I could in fact produce simple music which would be attractive to the masses and still bear the imprint of my personal handwriting in it?

I did not play the concerto as well as I should have done: after all the last time I had played it was six weeks ago in Paris and I had hardly looked at it since. But unexpectedly it was a great success and I took seven curtain calls. Afterwards we sat in a café with Nelson and Kal,[2] who was good company and rather touching. He had been on holiday to New Zealand and Fiji, of all places!

14 February

In the morning I pulled myself together and practised those passages in the Third Concerto that had not been satisfactory yesterday. I read the synopsis of the film, but it contained so many technical expressions that I could not understand anything, so I gave it to Ptashka to read and she explained it to me as far as she was able. The screenplay is rubbish, but Nelson's architectural designs are very attractive. I thought some more about the kind of

---

1 Another of Paul Nelson's Los Angeles commissions was to design a viewing room for Joseph P. Kennedy. Because of the client's abrupt departure from Hollywood it was never built, so this one must have been in Gloria Swanson's own house.
2 Prokofiev had known the musicologist and critic Professor Alexey Kal since St Petersburg days, and had encountered him again in 1920 during Prokofiev's concert tour of California. See *Diaries*, vol. 2, pp. 79, 559–87 *passim*.

music I might be able to compose, and a very good theme suggested itself to me. If I don't get the commission I will still have the theme.

The concert was in the afternoon, a repeat of yesterday's programme. I played better but there was less applause from the audience: the day-time audience, consisting mainly of women, is always less demonstrative. Glimpses of some old acquaintances afterwards: a somewhat decrepit Altschuler,[1] and Misha Rumanov.[2] I rang Nelson, who said that my music could be limited to a minute and a half during the showing of the cast list. I asked him to find out what fee would be paid. Half an hour later he rang back and said that Kennedy himself did not know what to suggest, and asked for my proposal. I told him $5,000, reasoning that for $1,000 it would not be worth my while, I would do better to concentrate on my concert engagements, but if he were willing to go to $2,000 or $3,000 he would make a counter-offer. After another half-hour Nelson rang again and, somewhat embarrassed, said that the price was so high there could be no question of a bargaining counter-offer. Kennedy explained: 'Prokofiev is a first-class musician, but his is not a name sufficiently popular with the American mass public to justify such expenditure.' But what about the artistic desiderata? Gloria is a superb actress, the designs are not bad, but so far the music is just street stuff, and this is something they do not seem to notice. All very well for Kennedy to be wearing a beautifully tailored suit, but his cuffs were dirty. When it was suggested to him that he should get them washed, he pulled them back under the sleeves of his jacket and said, 'Never mind, the plebs don't notice things like that.' All in all I had been right in the morning: I did not get a contract, but I do have a nice theme.

15 February

Because the heat in LA makes it impossible to wear my winter overcoat, I bought myself a beautiful lightweight coat, as a reward for my excellent, albeit non-existent, new contract.

I managed to get out of the rehearsal in San Francisco, to which we were supposed to be dashing, by means of telegraphing my inability to get there, and we went instead to see Mrs Garvin in Santa Barbara. She is a friend of Ptashka's, and at one time had arranged and paid for a nanny for Svyatoslav.[3]

---

1 Modest Altschuler (1873–1963), founder and conductor of the Russian Symphony Orchestra of New York, with whom in December 1918 Prokofiev had made his American orchestral debut. See *Diaries*, vol. 2, pp. 322, 335–6, 364–6.
2 Husband of Ariadna Nikolskaya, in whose *ménage à trois* with Maria Baranovskaya Prokofiev had spent a quite lurid time on his first visit to California in 1920. See *Diaries*, vol. 2, pp. 563–97 *passim*.
3 A rich friend of Lina Prokovieva. See above, pp. 35, 45, 73.

Now she said that, should anything happen to us, she would adopt our children. It was a three-hour train journey to Santa Barbara, part of the way along the Pacific Coast, which Ptashka was seeing for the first time and which I much enjoyed seeing again. Mrs Garvin drove us round in her splendid car, the weather was marvellous, the views spectacular, and I was very happy to be having a day off. She has a large house, very comfortable in the American style, with a lushly green garden and views over the ocean and to the mountains. Santa Barbara is home to eighty or so super-millionaires – that is to say, with more than five million – and Mrs Garvin showed us her neighbours' gardens, far grander than hers, with fabulous clearings, manicured to the last blade, urns with artfully trickling water, and mossy glades into which one's feet sink as into the most expensive carpet. A paradisal place, but not for us – too far away from everything we need.

16 February

We slept wonderfully well in the quietness of our rustic surroundings. Although our hostess had promised to spare us any social obligations, it transpired that there would be a small lunch in a country club, followed by no more than a glimpse of a polo match, and then a few people would come by on the strength of it being Sunday. When, after all this, we learned that we were bidden to go somewhere to dine, I point-blank rebelled. Polo proved to be a game played on horseback, with the players careering about the field, rather lovely to watch. At eleven o'clock, having taken the precaution of a little piano practice and some work with Ptashka, I boarded the train and left for San Francisco, ending up on an upper berth and in consequence not getting much sleep.

17 February

Arrived in San Francisco in the morning. Hertz said that as there was no rehearsal today he would be going out of the city into the country, and suggested I accompany him. On the way we could take a look at the Third Concerto. I was delighted to accept, and Hertz called for me in his car. The car was then loaded on to a ferry and sailed across the bay, right past Angel Island of blessed memory, on which I recognised the hospital to which I had been banished.[1] On the other side of the bay we disembarked at a little place called Sausalito and then along a rough country road up a mountain where, on the hillside, Hertz has a tiny wooden cottage with mimosas in flower and a wonderful view over the mountains and the bay. I was in ecstasy. We played

---

1 On first arriving in the United States in August 1918. See *Diaries*, vol. 2, pp. 317–21.

four games of chess (I won all of them) and lunched on the provisions Hertz had brought out with him in a hamper. Before it got too late in the evening we returned to San Francisco and went to his home for dinner. His house there is also in a superb position, with enormous windows looking out on to the Golden Gate, the narrow strait that separates the San Francisco Bay from the ocean. All Mrs Hertz has to do to bathe in the Bay is go down the stairs. Hertz himself has a bad leg and so does not do this. We played two more games, winning one each. Once when Mischa Elman was asked what the result of a similar encounter had been, he replied, 'I won one, and made a mistake with the other.'

In the evening we went to hear Hofmann play. I thought Hofmann was *vieux jeu*, and in the last analysis I suppose he is, but from time to time in his playing there are glimpses of an impish boyishness which is deeply attractive.

18 February

Rehearsal, and a meeting with Misha Piastro, whom I knew when we were both thirteen years old at the Conservatoire, and then again in Japan.[1] He is now Concertmaster of the San Francisco Orchestra and has three children by that same beautiful girl he had a fight with in Japan.[2]

Hertz rehearsed the Concerto very decently, chuckling benevolently into his beard at those passages he considers dissonant. Then I spent half an hour rehearsing three numbers from *Oranges*. Lunched with the Daniels, friends of Ptashka: he is nice, and reminds me slightly of Demchinsky in appearance.

The concert took place in the evening in an enormous hall seating 10,000, almost full. I played the Concerto better than I had done in LA, and conducted the *Oranges* numbers with freedom. It was a good success. In the Green Room there were Miss Olmsted and Miss Cobbe, who had been Svyatoslav's nanny in 1925, an elderly Russian and some young people wanting autographs. Returning to my hotel I packed my suitcase, as I am off again at crack of dawn tomorrow.

19 February

Got up at half past six, and at 7.45 boarded the train to take me back to Los Angeles. The journey was pleasant, but not outstandingly beautiful, although it is always a pleasure to look at the Pacific Ocean.

---

1 See *Diaries*, vol. 1, pp. 8, 17, 20, 23, 55–6, 95, 148, 162; vol. 2, pp. 287–94.
2 See *Diaries*, vol. 2, pp. 294–7.

I got back to the Biltmore at nine o'clock in the evening, fifty minutes before the start of the concert. I had to change hurriedly and run through a few things with Ptashka (I had practised my own pieces yesterday). Ptashka came back today from Santa Barbara by car and was in a subdued mood because, as is invariably and fatally the case before every concert, her voice was not in good order. The concert was right there in the lobby of the hotel. There was not a great crowd, but only members of the Pro Musica organisation were admitted, in addition to a few invited guests. My playing was fairly detached. Ptashka's interpretation was fine, but the voice would not project.

After the concert there was supper, also in the Biltmore. Rodzinski flirted with Ptashka. I showed everyone the article from the San Francisco newspaper calling for me to be appointed to deputise for Hertz, who is leaving the job. A piquant thought: to be music director and chief conductor of a great American orchestra, with a salary of $24,000 or $30,000 a year!

20 February

Reviews of yesterday's concert were mixed. The predominant note was one of deferential disapprobation. Just as in Cleveland the critic I had thought most highly of wrote a load of rubbish. Ptashka was in tears because they were unkind about her.

We packed up again – a recurrent feature of our gypsy life. After lunch Mrs Garvin took Ptashka away to stay with her in Santa Barbara for five days, and at six o'clock I entrained for Chicago. I was starting a headache, the result of three days rushing about, but as I was falling asleep succeeded in conceiving a main subject for the quartet. I switched on the light again and noted it down.

21 February

Felt tired, with a heavy head, so did little all day except let the train carry me onwards. Developed yesterday's thematic material a little. I shall look at the second subject, which I composed earlier, when I get to New York.

22 February

After El Paso, on the border with Mexico, the line turns north-east towards Kansas City, and therefore the temperature drops even though one can still step on to the platform at stations without an overcoat. The train forges on over featureless plains, reminding me of the steppe near Sontsovka.

I was more active today, catching up on my diary and writing letters.

23 February–1 March

Arriving in Chicago on the 23rd I installed myself in the Congress Hotel, where a piano was already in place, very necessary as I needed to practise the First Piano Concerto. Almost immediately Gottlieb appeared bearing flowers – he had expected Ptashka to be coming with me. Since my last visit to America I had been keeping my distance from him, but here he was, as devoted and anxious to serve as ever, and with the same exquisite tactlessness.

On the 25th I played the First Concerto and conducted the *Divertimento* – its American premiere. On the 28th and the 1st I played the Second Concerto and conducted three numbers from *Le Pas d'acier*. Stock[1] has a cold and has left the city to recuperate. The conductor was De Lamarter, as it had been in 1918.[2] He is musical, but waves his arms about while conducting like a fly being boiled alive. Furthermore, he had not really studied the score, so did not know what to ask of the orchestra. As a result I had in effect to coach them in the accompaniment to the Concerto, standing behind De Lamarter. But this had the effect of making me feel myself a proper conductor when I stepped up to the podium myself for the *Divertimento* and *Le Pas*. I knew exactly what I wanted from the orchestra, and the result was that I conducted the pieces far better than I had done in Paris and in Cleveland. For the first time *Le Pas* scored a real success with the public, who responded with loud applause after the train.[3] The *Divertimento* was also not at all bad, despite only having one rehearsal, but the response was muted. Who would have thought that this piece could be so hard to like after the first hearing! Needless to say, the greatest success was reserved for the two Concertos, especially the Second. The reviews were mixed for the composer but universally laudatory for the pianist and conductor. All in all I seem to be gaining a reputation as a conductor. The orchestra is excellent and behaves well towards me, but with 180 concerts a year it never has enough rehearsal time.

---

1   Frederick Stock (1872–1942), Music Director of the Chicago Symphony from 1911 until his death. Prokofiev had been the soloist at the world premiere of the Third Piano Concerto with the Chicago Symphony under Stock on 16 December 1921, shortly before the premiere of *The Love for Three Oranges* at the Chicago Opera. See *Diaries*, vol. 2, pp. 336, 583–646 *passim*.
2   Eric De Lamarter (1888–1953), Associate Conductor of the Chicago Symphony. Prokofiev had worked with him in December 1918, and had not been overly impressed. Ibid., pp. 360–63.
3   The second number of the ballet (not the four-movement Suite Prokofiev drew from the ballet music) is 'Poyezd s meshochnikami' – 'The Train with the Bagmen'. 'Meshochniki' ('meshok' is a bag) were enterprising peasants and small traders who rode the trains to bring their bags of foodstuffs and other scarce wares to the cities for unofficial trading during the famine years of War Communism – the practice that drove Lenin to abandon the unsustainable rigour of complete state control of production and distribution and ushered in the short-lived era of the New Economic Policy, to be swept away by Stalin's collectivisation programme and the demonisation of the 'kulak' ('fist') peasant farmer.

From my old acquaintances I saw the Bolms, the Anisfelds, the Carpenters, and Dr Schmidt.[1] The latter threw a great dinner for me, which Ptashka also attended, having made the journey from California. After her less than successful performance in Los Angeles she had sung well at a private concert in Santa Barbara, and this had raised her spirits. She was also pleased with herself for managing the journey from Santa Barbara to Chicago on her own. On the 1st March I sent her on to Detroit ahead of me, so that she could have a proper night's sleep before her concert.

The Chicago Opera was away on tour, but in general it is now in such dubious hands that its future looks bleak. They have built a new theatre, with good acoustics but vulgarly decorated. The old theatre is widely missed. The *Oranges* sets were lost in a small fire. I said to Carpenter, as a joke, 'I suppose it was Johnson who set fire to them?'[2]

Carpenter: 'I think so too, because my ballet's sets were lost at the same time, and he didn't like me much either.'

2–3 March

By morning I was in Detroit, where Ptashka had arrived the day before and installed herself on the twenty-fourth floor, from which there was a view across the river as far as Canada. The day passed in various rehearsals as the concert was of chamber music: the *Overture on Hebrew Themes*, the Violin Pieces,[3] and then I had to rehearse her songs with Ptashka as well as my own solo pieces. The members of the Detroit Pro Musica are pleasant people with a genuine interest in new music, and helped in as many ways as they could. The evening concert proceeded in a very lively and responsive fashion, much more so than Los Angeles or New York. Ptashka had a good success, and the *Jewish Overture* had to be repeated. Afterwards they fed and watered us with sandwiches and coffee, and shook our hands. Next day we wrote letters and looked at the reviews, which were less enthusiastic than the audience's reaction, and early in the evening left for New York.

Detroit is a big city and boasts a number of impressive skyscrapers. But apart from them it is not an attractive place, being afflicted with the ugliness characteristic of most towns in the Midwest of the United States.

1   Dr Schmidt, a friend of the faithful Gottlieb, had entertained Prokofiev when he was staying in Chicago for the rehearsal period of the premiere of *Three Oranges* in 1921.
2   Herbert Johnson, former Business Comptroller and later Executive Director of the Chicago Opera, who had borne the brunt of Prokofiev's animosity at the time of the cancellation of the original contract to stage *The Love for Three Oranges* following the death of the Opera's Artistic Director Cleofonte Campanini in 1919. See *Diaries*, vol. 2, pp. 444, 451–549 *passim*.
3   The version for violin and piano, Op. 35 bis, made in 1925 of *Five Songs Without Words*, Op. 35.

4–7 March
New York

Our almost month-long trip to California finally came to an end on the 4th March. We stayed three and a half days in New York before setting off again for Havana. I had intended to use this period to work on *Fiery Angel*, but Sudeikin, I discovered, was busy with designs for *The Flying Dutchman* and had put thoughts of *Fiery Angel* to one side. It was clear that *Flying Dutchman* was in the plan for next season, and *Fiery Angel* probably for the season after next. The (abridged) libretto that Sudeikin had undertaken to have translated into French and passed to Gatti had been completed only yesterday and not yet typed out. It was rather amateurish: the original Russian had first been converted into bad English, the bad English then turned into better English, and thence eventually into French. The resulting version had nothing whatsoever remaining of my text: not only was any hint of clarity or vivacity conspicuous by its absence, a good quarter of it was plain wrong. There was nothing for it but for me to sit down and correct it myself, pecking away at the typewriter for two whole mornings and giving myself a bad headache into the bargain. I did this work at Sudeikin's house, cursing continually at both him and the translator, and sorely trying his patience. The situation with Serafin was little better: he had just left the city for a week, although he had at least taken the vocal score with him. After consulting Mrs Kahn it was decided that the best way forward would be to give the revised libretto to Ziegler, head of the theatre's finance department, asking him to pass it on to Gatti in anticipation of further discussions on my return from Havana.

There was no word from Rosing either, but I did not feel like telephoning him, in any case I succeeded in finding out his telephone number only fifteen minutes before our departure. This matter was therefore also postponed until my return.

The Koussevitzkys came to New York for one of the orchestra's regular subscription concerts there. He played a Haydn Symphony with four horns which I had suggested to him, and a brainless Suite by the American composer Greenberg. A strange person, Koussevitzky: he does not play my music, and keeps postponing Dukelsky's Second Symphony, but can apparently always find room for the rubbish of a Greenberg or a Lazar.

Also in New York at this time was the current idol, Toscanini, the ubiquitous worship of whom robs Koussevitzky of his nightly repose. Last spring Toscanini had played my *Classical* Symphony (the first Russian work he had ever performed) so I decided I would go and shake his hand. I signalled my intention to his friend and devoted admirer Max

Smith,[1] with the result that I received an invitation to attend his rehearsal. It proved to be an extraordinarily interesting occasion. Toscanini grew very heated, lost his baton, screamed '*Vergogna!*'[2] at the orchestra – but this was not the most interesting aspect. What was, was his obvious total disregard for anything except the music he was conducting. Even his gestures are much less fluent than Koussevitzky's. Our dear Koussya is always striking an attitude and thinking about the effect he is making on the audience, but Toscanini forgets about everything; there is not a single thought in his head except the music he is interpreting at the time. And how he knows the score! Altogether it was a most useful occasion for me, that is to say from the perspective of my conducting: (1) know the score better; (2) immerse myself more deeply in the music and the musicians.

Our meeting took place during the break. Toscanini was pleasant and straightforward and pronounced my name correctly, but when he said he was pleased to make my acquaintance he had evidently forgotten that we had met four years ago at a lunch hosted by Steinway's.[3] He asked what I was currently composing, at which I deliberately mentioned the *Sinfonietta*, even though it was already completed. 'Excellent,' he replied. 'We will perform it next year.' Had it not been for Paichadze falling down on the job, he would probably have been able to include it this year.

At 6.50 in the evening, accompanied as is now tradition to the station by Dukelsky, we boarded the Havana Special and departed for the South.

7–15 March
Havana

All day on the 8th was spent in travel vertically from north to south. It was interesting seeing the vegetation gradually changing to sub-tropical as the temperature rose. Evening brought glimpses of palm trees as we entered Florida. The air was warm and scented; even so, when we got out of the train at stations it was advisable to wear a coat. Disappointingly it was night for almost all of our traversal of Florida, but I got up at six o'clock to observe our approach to Key West. The railway line crosses a long chain of small, low-lying islands connected by bridges across the shallow sounds. Key West itself is not particularly interesting. We disembarked from the train and boarded

---

1 Thomas Max Smith (1874–1935), music critic, at this time foreign music correspondent for the *New York Herald Tribune*. Toscanini sought his guidance on his decision to conduct the New York Philharmonic in 1926–7, and Smith also had a hand in the arrangements for the Philharmonic's European tour in 1930.
2 'Shameful!'
3 See above, p. 263.

a medium-sized steamer. All along the pier stood people in bathing costumes, both blacks and whites, who called to the passengers to throw coins into the water: as soon as someone did they would dive in and retrieve them.

Going out into open sea was at first very enjoyable: the turquoise blue of the sea turning suddenly to deep aquamarine. But then the wind got up and the ship began to pitch and toss, so that Ptashka and I took to our cabin and tried to control our rising gorges. Just before Havana (the whole voyage took six hours) the sea calmed and we emerged to summer sunshine on deck near the bow. From the sea Havana is not beautiful, although the old port is attractive and we took a photograph of it. Examination of our passports provoked a scene: why was Ptashka's passport in the name of Lina Prokofieva when the authorities had been informed that Lina Llubera had been engaged to sing?[1] Eventually she was allowed to go ashore, but her passport was confiscated without a receipt for it being given. We of course were reluctant to surrender the passport without a receipt, and there ensued long and acrimonious negotiations in English and Spanish which eventually, thanks to the intervention of the Pro Arte representative (Pro Arte being the organisation that had engaged us), ended in a receipt being given. Once this was settled we were driven into Havana, in a state of high dudgeon.

Orlov had recommended a French *hotel-pension* in a residential quarter of the city with many delightful, often magnificent, houses. The President of Pro Arte, Mme de Gibarga, and her husband called with their car to drive us round the outskirts of the city, which were beautifully presented but not yet finished. The entire wealth of Cuba comes from sugar: during the war the price of sugar had risen sky-high and an avalanche of money poured in, causing a construction boom for the beautification of Havana. But the war ended, the price of sugar sank, and much of the construction remains unfinished. We drank coconut milk produced in front of our eyes (nothing to do with milk, by the way!) and listened to somewhat monotonous local Negro music accompanied by quite complicated but unobtrusive drumming on a variety of drums.

There were two concerts, which took place in a very good, newly built hall seating 2,800. I played solo in the first concert, joined by Ptashka in the second. There was a good audience for the first concert, politely welcoming to begin with and then a distinct success. Nevertheless, a complete concert of my music is strong medicine for a tyro audience such as that of Havana, and this was especially noticeable in the performance of *Choses en soi*. For this reason the second concert was much less full, about a quarter of the house, although the programme was an easier one and the presence of Ptashka

---

[1] Lina Prokofieva's professional name was Lina Llubera, derived from the full name of her father, the Spanish tenor Juan Codina y Llubera.

provided some distraction. She sang better than she had done in her previous concerts, being rewarded with a good success and a bouquet of red flowers, but even so she could have sung still better. The most interesting development was the appearance of a representative from the contemporary music circle. Such a thing apparently exists in Havana, taking a lively interest in new music and publishing its own journal, and – O unexpected gratification – evidently much appreciating *Choses en soi*. I agreed to contribute an article about Myaskovsky to the journal.[1]

Between the two concerts the organisation which had engaged us, Pro Arte, arranged a reception. It was a gala occasion, and very dull. A great many beautiful women were present, dressed in Paris modes, but too heavily made up. We were taken to the world's most famous cigar factory, Partagás. Machine methodology is unknown here; all cigars are made by hand just as they were fifty years ago, with wondrous dexterity.[2] These cigars are smoked by the Kings of England and Spain, and 'all the monarchs that are left'. Ordinary 'Havanas' are nothing by comparison. I sniffed them, the aroma was divine, but I had no desire to light up.[3] The process begins with the tobacco leaves being dampened with water, and then left for a year or two to ferment. During this time they give off such a powerful smell of ammonia that when I entered that part of the factory where they were I could hardly stop the tears flowing. Other people, I was told, are convulsed by ungovernable fits of sneezing.

In the evenings Ptashka and I wandered round without either coats or hats in the warm, close air. Between the palm trees gleamed the moon, high in the sky, almost at the zenith. These strolls were a delight, but every day by the time evening came I was utterly exhausted; the northerner is not used to a warm, humid climate. During the day, however, I was able to work as a breeze refreshed our room.

My Cuban friend, Capablanca, was in Europe.

On the 14th we returned to New York. The sea was rough, and we spent most of the voyage to Key West lying in our bunks. We did not actually throw up, but kept experiencing that sickening rising to the throat. I wanted to close my eyes, but a spider was crawling across the cabin ceiling, now getting dangerously near the bunk and now disappearing again. Near Key

---

1 He was as good as his word. See below, p. 955. The article duly appeared in the July–August 1930 issue of *Musicalia*, Havana, in Spanish, so it might have been translated by Lina and sent in that language. A translation into Russian is included in V. Varunts, op. cit., pp. 91–3.
2 This is still the case for quality Cuban Habanos.
3 'A million surplus Maggies are willing to bear the yoke,
 A woman is only a woman, but a good Cigar is a Smoke.'
 Rudyard Kipling, 'The Betrothed'
 Or perhaps: 'If there are no cigars in Heaven, I shall not go' – Mark Twain

West the sea stilled and we went out on deck. Ptashka scanned the waves for sharks, which are said to be no rarity in these parts. Useful information for fishermen: the best bait to catch a shark is a dead dog.

After American Customs in Key West (we were searched for alcohol; had fruit confiscated lest they carry bacteria; allowed to bring in 100 cigars for presents) we boarded the train for the journey of two nights and the intervening day to New York. All day on the 15th we watched the countryside gradually changing as we travelled north, enjoying the northern landscape and the signs of burgeoning spring.

In a newspaper I saw a picture of Amter, the copyist who in 1919 had copied *Oranges* for me, and had talked to me of Communism, foaming at the mouth with ecstasy. He had shown me his compositions: complicated scores which I tried to get Coates to perform, without success. Recently there had been Communist demonstrations in New York (presumably financed by Russian money) and Amter along with a few other ringleaders had been arrested. That was why their pictures were in the papers.[1]

16 March
New York

On our return to New York I found the correspondence had been piling up. It seems that both in Moscow and Kadnikov they had again run out of money.[2] Gusman, on retiring from his position,[3] had forgotten to make the

---

1 Israel Amter (1881–1954) was born in America but studied music at Leipzig University before the First World War, where he completed an opera *Winona* on the subject of a romance between a US Army officer and a Native American woman. Back in the United States he became active in the left wing of the Socialist Party that developed into the Unified Communist Party and its later incarnation the Communist Party of America. Amter served as CPA representative to the Comintern in 1923–4 and as a leading organiser of the Party's Unemployed Councils movement was along with William Z. Foster and Robert Minor arrested in March 1930 at its New York demonstration, charged with inciting a riot, and gaoled for six months. No shrinking violet where his beliefs were concerned, Amter stood for office under the Communist Party of America banner for Senator of Ohio and Governor of New York State in 1932, 1934 and 1942, and Senator for New York in 1940. Under the Smith Act of 1940, in effect equating membership of any leftwing political group with conspiracy to overthrow the US Government, a large number of Socialist, Communist and labour union leaders were indicted. In 1951 Amter was no exception, although by that time his frail state of health meant that he was not actually put on trial.
2 Cousin Katya Rayevskaya, on her return to Penza after visiting Moscow, had been arrested and gaoled and was now exiled to the north-west Russian town of Kadnikov near Vologda. Katya and Shurik were eventually both released from their separate ordeals in 1932.
3 Boris Gusman had not survived the purging at the Bolshoy Theatre but found another one at the Belorussian State Cinema (Belgoskino, based, oddly, in Leningrad) where, as he continued to be in any position in which he found himself, he could be helpful to Prokofiev. At Belgoskino he would be instrumental in securing for Prokofiev the commission to write the score for the satirical film directed by Alexander Faintsimmer to a screenplay by Yury Tynyanov, *Lieutenant Kijé*.

arrangements I had asked him to. This necessitated a hasty letter to be sent off to the Bolshoy Theatre. I rang up Sudeikin, who told me that Serafin had returned, and that he had perused the vocal score of *Fiery Angel* which, with the exception of a few places where he had reservations, had much impressed him. Gatti, apparently, has also read through the libretto. Gatti, Serafin and Sudeikin are due to meet tomorrow, after which Gatti's decision will be made known.

In the evening we were invited to a quartet evening at which my *Jewish Overture* was on the programme. I was to be an honoured guest along with Grechaninov, who had also been dignified with this status. Ptashka and I arrived after the start of the concert and sat discreetly at the back of the hall. However, I was recognised and invited to seat myself in a more visible position in one of the boxes, a suggestion I declined saying that I was perfectly fine where I was.

The performance of the *Overture* was rather feeble and its reception lukewarm. There were a few attempts to call me to the stage, which soon died down. But then all of a sudden the lady president of the society came on to the platform and said, 'If I am not mistaken, Prokofiev is in the hall. Perhaps he would like to stand up and be recognised by those present.' General movement and shuffling of feet in the hall. I sat with my nose buried in the programme. Nobody responded to the invitation to stand up, and a tittering began to spread. The lady president, discomfited, made her exit from the stage. When the next item on the programme began, Ptashka and I stealthily made our escape, having declined to attend the post-concert supper.

17 March

Because of our impending departure for Europe there were a lot of things to do: steamer tickets, visas, discussions with Haensel who, it emerges, wants to take 20 per cent from me while I hold out for the 15 it has been hitherto.

The most satisfying development has been the meeting with Engel in order to settle finally the quartet commission for the library in Washington: $1,000 to be paid by the 1st January 1931, all agreed verbally. Since Engel is now head of Schirmer, I asked him if he would consider taking on the representation of our publishers as our current representative, Maxwell, has succeeded in alienating all the American orchestras through his insufferably aggressive manner. To my amazement Engel replied, 'With pleasure', so I immediately sat down to write a long letter to Koussevitzky.

Unwelcome news from Sudeikin: Gatti's opinion of the libretto of *Fiery Angel* is that it is 'unacceptable', thus blackballing me for the second time, ten years after the first. On the other hand, *The Gambler* had been put forward at the same time, and Gatti's response was that such a subject might be more suitable.

18 March

Mme Stokowski has invited us to her box for the performance of *Le Sacre* which her husband is to conduct in April. However, as we sail for Europe in ten days' time, the Stokowskis invited us instead to lunch today so that we could inspect their brand-new, highly contemporary apartment. My relations with Stokowski have developed oddly: on the one hand he almost burst a blood vessel with excitement over my Second Symphony, while on the other he did not invite me to play with his orchestra while I have been here in America. But since Koussya is not playing my Third Symphony and obstinately continues to ignore the *Sinfonietta*, I must do my best to use Stokowski's gesture to effect a rapprochement. As bad luck would have it that morning I began to develop a bad headache, but it would have been very awkward to decline the lunch invitation. I rang up Klein asking for help. In the event lunch was a pleasant occasion: my headache did not completely disappear but did not trouble me too much. Stokowski talked very interestingly about India, which had made a great impression on him, and generally showed himself to be a more widely cultivated individual than our dear Koussya. Stokowski will conduct my Overture, Op. 42, in three weeks' time. This will be its first hearing in the version for full orchestra.

I also went to see Rosing, who was indisposed and therefore asked me to call on him to discuss a production of *Fiery Angel*. People are very much in two minds about his company: some say they have attracted the necessary sponsorship for next season, others that they have not two cents to rub together. Their productions are also criticised, but on the other hand they tour to every city in America. Rosing likes the subject of *Fiery Angel*, but with an orchestra of thirty-six, which is all they have, how are they going to put it on?

19 March

Rosing has come up with a suggestion that one of my 'students' should, under my direction but at their expense, create an alternative version of *Fiery Angel* for a thirty-six-piece orchestra. My response was that they would do better to raise some money and commission a new opera from me, which I would write in the first instance for a small orchestra.

Visited Serafin, whose wife is Russian, and played him excerpts from *The Gambler*. I messed up the roulette scene incredibly, but he was very pleased with it and promised to give Gatti the libretto tomorrow. We shall see what comes of it. My joy at the Metropolitan's change of heart has proved premature: any change is, for the present at least, only partial.

In the evening I left for Montreal, where I have a concert tomorrow.

20 March

An icy wind was blowing in Montreal and the snow lay deep underfoot. I stayed with the Fortiers, extremely nice people who welcomed me back in the friendliest manner.[1] Medtner had been their guest for six weeks.

The concert was in the Music University, in a small hall barely half full. My playing was somewhat detached, as was at first the audience, although towards the end they warmed up and demanded two encores.

After the concert there was supper with guests at the Fortiers'. Fortier complained about the unmusicality of Montreal.

I slept in Medtner's bed, but had no dreams at all.

21 March

Saying farewell to the Fortier family – a short *séjour* but a very pleasant one – I left for Chicago at noon. As I emerged on to the street with a suitcase in either hand, my hat blew off. I ran after it, feeling the cold terribly in my head. A taxi-driver with difficulty retrieved it at the end of the street.

The snow seen at first through the windows of the carriage gradually gave way to a grey landscape: no sign yet of the green grass of spring. How beautiful it would be then, however, with the forests, fields, lakes and rocks.

Caught up on my diary.

The newspaper review of yesterday's concert I read says that the programme was not serious enough. Who would have thought it!

22 March

In the morning, Chicago. Gottlieb, Congress Hotel.

Ptashka arrived from New York at half past three. With two concerts in front of her, she is nervous.

---

1 See *Diaries*, vol. 2, pp. 466–9.

23 March

The first concert is today, in the small hall of a rather aristocratic club. An audience of about 120 included the Carpenters and Mrs Rockefeller-McCormick,[1] and then a little later Volkov the former Russian Consul[2] and Mme Bolm made an appearance. We reminisced about my earliest days in America ten years ago.

My playing was relaxed; Ptashka's singing mediocre.

24 March

Lunched with the Rachmaninoffs: he and his wife, I and Ptashka. The previous day I had been astonished that he rang me up to wish us well. During the meal Rachmaninoff was in a wonderful mood and was even poking fun at Medtner, telling anecdotes about his travels in America. Evidently Medtner cannot bear American sleeping-cars: either the noise wakes him up, or the curtains flap, or something. One morning, infuriated and exhausted by his night in the sleeper he got out of the train intending to change to the next train, and fell asleep on a sofa in the station waiting room. Up came an official to inform him that sofas were for sitting on, not lying on. His wife, wishing to protect her husband's slumbers, tried everything to explain to the official who Medtner was. But the guard was adamant, and poor Medtner was forced to sit up.

Rachmaninoff announced his intention of coming to the concert especially to hear Ptashka. Ptashka begged him not to, it would embarrass her, but Rachmaninoff protested that he had bought his ticket with money earned by the sweat of his brow and could not contemplate not getting his money's worth. He teased Ptashka by extracting the ticket from his pocket and showing it to her.

There was an audience of about a thousand people in Orchestra Hall, but it still looked empty in such a large space. Nevertheless, surprisingly, the programme was uniformly warmly received. Ptashka sang not at all badly and had a success. The concert went with a swing. Ptashka could see

---

1 Edith McCormick née Rockefeller was the first wife of Harold McCormick, the principal benefactor of the Chicago Opera at the time of the premiere production of *The Love for Three Oranges* in December 1921. He had left her for the ambitious Polish *chansonnière* Ganna Walska, much to the prurient delight of the Chicago press at the time. See *Diaries*, vol. 2, p. 582.
2 Volkov was the Russian (not Soviet) Consul in Chicago during the period of Prokofiev's protracted dispute with the Chicago Opera over *The Love for Three Oranges*, and its eventual premiere production. See *Diaries*, vol. 2, pp. 360–657 *passim*. Beatrice (Beate) Bolm was the wife of the dancer and choreographer Adolph Bolm. When first in New York Prokofiev had been close to the Bolms and benefited from their experience and hospitality. See *Diaries*, vol. 2, pp. 330–591 *passim*.

Rachmaninoff sitting in the stalls, keeping his gaze fixed attentively on her. He left at the interval, however, as he had a train to catch at ten o'clock to go to Detroit.

After the concert we went on to two places, despite a fierce storm. With us were the Bolms, the Anisfelds, the Volkovs, and Gottlieb. The Brewsters have a marvellous home, filled with contemporary art by the best artists. A remarkable collection!

Volkov has fallen on hard times, but today had shaved and put on a dinner-jacket. He drank champagne with enjoyment as it is some years since he had any.

25 March

Last night's storm developed into a snowstorm which in turn precipitated a general catastrophe. It was impossible even to poke one's nose out of doors. We began to wonder whether we would ever get a car to take us to the station. But eventually one did turn up. In our compartment it was warm and snug, and within an hour or two we were out of the blizzard.

We read the press reviews of yesterday's concert. At first Ptashka did not want to see them, and indeed the first impression was that they were not very good, but on subsequent perusal they seemed better. Rosenfeld[1] tried his best. Yesterday, for old times' sake, I had presented him with some of the cigars I had brought back from Havana. I think the cigars helped.

The evening before Rachmaninoff had been telling us how not long ago, at a concert by Hofmann, he heard him play as an encore a spiky, biting march. After the concert Rachmaninoff, assuming that Hofmann had played something of his own, said to him, 'Fancy you writing something like that these days,' to which Hofmann replied, 'But it was a March by Prokofiev' (from Op. 12). This was relayed in the guise of a compliment, but in fact it conceals a dig at me when you consider what a feeble composer is the man whose work Rachmaninoff had claimed he believed my March to be.

26–28 March

Returned from Chicago to New York to face all the chores associated with our departure to Europe.

Serafin told me on the telephone, 'Gatti has read through the libretto of *The Gambler* and cannot understand how an opera can be made of it. But he is interested.' Since there is no chance of its being staged earlier than the

---

1 Maurice Rosenfeld, the much feared music critic of the *Chicago Daily News*.

season after next, Serafin advised me to send Gatti the vocal score as soon as it is in print.

With Rosing it was a different story. It will be a month before he knows whether or not they will have money to carry on next season. To save time he and I sketched out a preliminary understanding: an agreement can be finalised by telegraph if need be, but at least we will have a starting point as a basis. As to whether they will be in funds or not, there are various rumours in circulation. Mrs Borden, for instance, whom I had seen in Chicago, told me she had succeeded in getting sponsorship – to be precise a promise of sponsorship – in the amount of $25,000 for a tour to Chicago, but only on condition that a similar sum could be found in New York.

Sudeikin, now that my operatic enterprises are poised to take a leap forward, has nevertheless busied himself with the *Flying Dutchman* production (after all, the sea he contrived for *Sadko* was a triumph!). It is of course understandable that he must devote his energies to an imminent Metropolitan commission; all the same I cannot entirely rid myself of a certain feeling of betrayal – he tried, and did not at once succeed, so on to the next thing – and therefore when I met him I behaved, not exactly truculently, but with a touch of militaristic brusqueness. As he parted, he observed languidly, 'You astonish me with your excessive cheerfulness. Do you not think it is a trifle too Rupprechtesque?'[1]

28 March–3 April
Voyage from New York to France

We sailed at five o'clock in the afternoon on the 28th, aboard the *Île de France*. She is the pride of the French fleet, but it would have been more interesting to be on the *Europa*, the new German high-speed liner, which although we had a twelve-hour start on her still caught us up halfway across.[2]

---

1 The Knight Rupprecht is the Candide-like hero of *The Fiery Angel*, exposed to all kinds of disastrous natural and supernatural predicaments by the dangerously unbalanced Renata, by whom he is obsessed.
2 The SS *Île de France* entered service in 1927 with the reputation of being, not the fastest transatlantic liner or the largest, but the most luxuriously and stylishly decorated. Instead of imitating a French château or an English castle, the decoration was strictly contemporary, modelled on the 1925 Paris *Exposition des Arts Décoratifs et Industriels Modernes*, the genesis of the Art Deco style. In keeping with French ambition to continue leading the world in gastronomy, her dining room was the largest afloat, rising through three decks and boasting a grand entrance staircase. In his strictures about their accommodation Prokofiev does not mention it, but the *Île de France* was for its time unique in equipping cabins with beds rather than bunks. The SS *Europa* had just made her maiden voyage to New York on 19 March 1930, seizing the westbound Blue Riband from her sister ship the *Bremen*. The new steam turbine engines gave her an average speed of 27.91 knots and a crossing time of 4 days, 17 hours and 6 minutes.

Our efforts to keep pace produced an appalling quantity of smoke, which completely obliterated the *Europa* from view, but when suddenly the smoke-screen lifted the passengers who had all flooded out on deck were able to see her steaming away ahead of us.

We were seen off in New York by Dukelsky and Koko Shtember,[1] who thrust a watch into my hands saying, 'When you get to Russia give this to my sister Nadya – Nadya, you understand, not Sonya. Nadya, mind, not Sonya.' So insistent was he that in the end I was totally confused as to whom I should give it to. Aslanov also came to the ship but he has now grown so enormous and there was such an incredible scrum that he could not find us and left a note.

We had heard so much about the fantastic luxury of the *Île de France* that, as is inevitable in such cases, we were disappointed. We had actually had a better state-room in the *Berengaria*. Nevertheless, we were allocated a bath, no doubt the company's way of recognising my talents. The passenger list was also less distinguished than on the *Berengaria*. Among our fellow passengers was Grechaninov, in whose case the company was generous enough to amend his second-class ticket so that he could feed and associate in first class, and only had to go down to second class to sleep. Grechaninov is essentially a nice man, and very youthful for his sixty-seven years. His wife, by contrast, is fairly unbearable, a pretentious, vainglorious woman who, nevertheless, made valiant efforts to be pleasant.

The captain[2] invited groups of guests to his table by rote: one evening diplomats, another engineers, and so on. When it was the turn of musicians we were his guests along with Grechaninov.

---

1 Nikolay Shtember, like Prokofiev, had been a piano student of Anna Yesipova at the St Petersburg Conservatoire, and they had become close friends, Prokofiev often visiting the Shtember household headed by Nikolay's father, the artist Viktor Karlovich Shtember who was first cousin to Medtner, another frequent visitor. Shtember painted a large and superb portrait of Medtner in 1908, and there is a touching memoir of 'Uncle Kolya' by Irina Shtember, Nikolay's sister, in Z. A. Apetyan (ed.), *N. K. Medtner, Articles, Materials, Reminiscences*, Sovietsky Kompozitor, Moscow, 1981, pp. 82–93. Nadya and Sonya were Nikolay's sisters. Prokofiev admired Nikolay as a musician and liked him as a person, heeding his advice on several occasions. The Toccata, Op. 11, is dedicated to Nikolay Shtember. See *Diaries*, vol. 1 passim.
2 Captain Joseph Blancart was in his own right quite a celebrity, mainly owing to the feat of seamanship by which he had averted disaster as the newly completed *Île de France* attempted to leave the docks basin at St Nazaire on her very first sea trials. Something went wrong with the engine controls and it was impossible to stop the 43,500-tonne ship, 92 feet across the beam, steaming at an inexorable 10 knots towards the bascule bridge closing the basin from the sea. A quick-witted bridge operator realised what was happening and managed to open the bridge in time, but with an opening of 100 feet there was no more 4 feet of clearance on either side – a manoeuvre that would normally never be attempted under power but only with the help of a fleet of tugs. Blancart took the helm himself and steered her precisely through without a scratch.

The boat rolled and pitched quite strongly, but this no longer affects me and I did a lot of work on the proof-reading of the *Gambler* vocal score. Having texts in three languages to proof makes this a particularly painstaking process.

4 April

All the same, we should have gone on the *Europa*, not the *Île de France*. We were promised to dock at Le Havre in the afternoon of the 3rd, but did so only at one o'clock in the morning of the 4th. I was in a hurry to get to the concert of my works in Brussels, and had asked Cuvelier to cable me on board when the rehearsal would be. But the only telegram that came for me was from Mémé, letting us know the children were all right, so I did not know just how much of a rush I was in. But that there was some urgency was without doubt, especially as the formalities took until 2 a.m. to complete. We were woken at 6 a.m. and by half past seven were on the train to Paris, where we finally arrived at a quarter to eleven. Despite my longing to sleep, I decided to leave at six for Brussels.

A searching conversation with Ptashka about the flat. She would like to go straight to Le Cannet to the children, as she is very tired. I said that, seeing that we had rented the apartment, we should first of all inspect it to see what needs doing to it. Once the necessary renovations were under way, that would be the time to go to Le Cannet. Ptashka might be tired, but if so it was due to the concert appearances she had undertaken for her own pleasure, not to mention that there were only six in a period of three months. The flat proved to be in a shabby condition: it needed cleaning and painting, the wallpaper needed changing and the rugs shampooing.

Paichadze and his wife came to meet us, and Mlle Artner from the Valmalète office. By the time I had looked over the apartment, squabbled with Ptashka, discussed with Paichadze and the lady from Valmalète the mountain of business that had accrued, it was six o'clock and time I was on the train bound for Brussels. On the way I read a bizarre letter from an unknown woman in Leningrad, certainly deranged, who poured out all her troubles, declared her undying love for me, and summoned me to come and take her away. The address she had written to was incredible and I could not understand how such a letter could have ended up in my hands via the Valmalète office. The thought flashed through my mind that it might be from Natasha,[1] but closer inspection revealed that it was not, it was merely some crazy female for some reason haunted by my image.

---

1 Natalya Goncharova, with whom Prokofiev had carried on a flirtatious relationship (one of many) when she was a voice student at the St Petersburg Conservatoire in 1913. See *Diaries*, vol. 1, pp. 248–502 *passim*, and above, pp. 515, 645.

Arriving in Brussels I still could not raise anybody on the telephone, and dropping on my feet with exhaustion went to bed still having no idea about the fate of my concert tomorrow. In the middle of the night I was woken by a telephone call from Ansermet, who had evidently been dining somewhere well but not wisely, and on getting back to his hotel had seen a note that I had called him. The concert is tomorrow, all is as it should be, rehearsals have been going well, and he will come round to my hotel at eight o'clock in the morning to settle the tempi.

5 April

Ansermet appeared at eight o'clock and we rapidly went through the tempi of the Symphony and the *Divertimento*. I twitted him, declaring that I would tell everyone how a drunken Ansermet had rung me up at three o'clock in the morning and ruined my night's sleep. The rehearsal was at nine; it was good to hear the Third symphony, and a few little adjustments came into my mind. The *Divertimento* I was hearing properly for the first time, by which I mean sitting quietly and listening in the hall. When I had conducted it in Paris and in Chicago I had had no time to listen.

The concert was in the afternoon. The piano was positioned some way from Ansermet, so there were some roughnesses and minor discrepancies in ensemble, exacerbated by the fact that we had not talked the performance through in enough detail. Ansermet conducted the rest of the programme well. The Symphony was well received, and he was called back to take a bow four or five times. The Third Concerto was a great success, but the same cannot be said of the *Divertimento*. Hard to imagine! Evidently time is needed for people to familiarise themselves with it. I must make a two-hand piano version and have it printed immediately. The programme ended with four numbers from *Chout*, which were very warmly received and I stood to take a bow from my seat in the hall.

Took tea with the Le Boeufs. Le Boeuf is a charming and interesting man, but his sole topic of conversation was his new hall, which is indeed quite a triumph. In the evening Ansermet and I went to the cinema. Ansermet told me that Stravinsky is writing a choral symphony for Boston 'which, as a matter of fact, is not a symphony at all'.[1] I was interested in the details, but

---

1 Koussevitzky's initial commission of a symphony for the Boston Symphony's fiftieth-anniversary season had envisaged a purely orchestral work, and that is what Stravinsky originally agreed. But early in 1930, on the Russian Christmas Eve (6 January), he had made a note of the Latin text of Psalm 39, and according to Stephen Walsh 'from that point on, the Symphony [of Psalms] had become, not merely choral, but severely, ritualistically sacred . . . Even the unavoidable dedication to the Boston Symphony is, somewhat incongruously, overridden by the assertion that the Symphony is "*composée à la gloire de DIEU*".' (S. Walsh, op. cit., p. 493.)

Ansermet only mumbled. 'If you have been entrusted with a secret,' I said, 'of course I don't want to wring it out of you.' Ansermet: 'No, there's no secret, but Stravinsky himself doesn't like talking about it, probably because he is not sure he will be able to fulfil the task he has set himself.'[1]

6 April

Repeat of yesterday's programme. I listened to the Symphony from Le Boeuf's box. The Paris performance had been a better one, but had not sounded so good in that hall. Le Boeuf was sitting beside me; he is a good musician and quite capable of understanding form, drawing attention to the canon in the development section of the first movement. At the opening of his hall he had conducted – from memory – the Overture to *Meistersinger*.

The audience response was much the same as yesterday's.

7 April

A day off, which enabled me to practise the programme for tomorrow's recital. Carried on proofing *The Gambler*.

8 April

My recital. I was embarrassed that it was in the same enormous auditorium and fearful that it would resemble the Arabian desert, but it was not bad at all, about half full. A warm reception from the audience. Met Lyolya Brichant,[2] and had tea with him after the concert.

9 April

Return to Paris, which I managed in one day. Ptashka greeted me frigidly at first, but became more loving later on. We still bickered about the flat, where everything is still all over the place, and Ptashka is already tired.

---

1 Although the assumption had, naturally, been that the premiere would be given by Koussevitzky, who had paid through the nose for the work, with his orchestra, Stravinsky had imposed a contractual condition that the first performance must take place by the end of November 1930. As scheduling complications precluded Boston from complying until the 19 December it was to be none other than Ansermet to whom fate made a gift of the world premiere, in the Palais des Beaux-Arts in Brussels, six days earlier.
2 Husband of Prokofiev's cousin Sonya Brichant, who had offered practical and moral support to Prokofiev at the time of his mother's escape from Russia and eventual arrival in France in 1920. Lyolya is usually a girl's name (short for Yelena) but clearly not in this case.

10 April

I had intended to call on Arens at the Soviet Embassy to have a talk with him and clarify the situation about my going to Moscow in May. But Paris is experiencing a wave of anti-Soviet sentiment at the moment: the abduction of Kutepov[1] has aroused great anger and there is also indignation about anti-religious persecution within Russia. Normally I would not pay much attention to the mood among the émigré community, but a letter from Myaskovsky, in which he flatly advises me not to come because of a change in the musical landscape whereby power has passed to my adversaries the proletarian musicians, did make an impression. It seems it would be a bad idea to go at the moment, and in any case I am tired from all the dashing about from place to place I have already been doing, not to mention that I

1 General Alexander Kutepov (1882–1930), a First World War Russian Army hero and the last Commander of the historic Preobrazhensky Regiment, a prominent White Army commander with a reputation for ruthless insistence on discipline during the Civil War, had been appointed Governor of the Black Sea Region by General Wrangel. On the ultimate defeat of the White Army in November 1920 Kutepov took the traditional route into exile of evacuation to Gallipoli, thence to Bulgaria and eventually to Paris, where following Baron Wrangel's death in 1928 he found himself leader of the émigré Russian Combined Military Union (Rossiisky Obshchii Voinskii Soyuz, or ROVS) which, despite its impressive-sounding name, belligerent ambitions and apparent capacity to rattle the Soviets, was memorably and disparagingly characterised by Vladimir Nabokov, in his first published short story in English, 'The Assistant Producer', as 'W.W., a bunch of White Warriors, a sunset behind a cemetery'. ROVS had certainly been infiltrated by OGPU agents impersonating the entirely bogus 'TREST' counter-revolutionary underground movement within Russia, whose stories the naive Kutepov was all too ready to swallow. On the morning of 26 January 1930 he was inveigled out of his flat by one of them, his own former Chief of Staff General Steifon, whom he had himself sent twice to Russia on 'secret' missions to contact the imaginary conspirators and report back. Kutepov was promptly abducted in broad daylight and never seen again. It was clear to most people who knew anything about it that this was an OGPU operation, but the connection was vehemently denied and the details remained opaque despite the suspiciously (to Parisians) lethargic attempts by the Commissioner of Police, the magnificently named Charles Adolphe Faux-Pas Bidet, to bring anyone to justice. According to Stéphane Courtois and Jean-Louis Panné in their compilation of Soviet atrocities *Le Livre noir du Communisme, crimes, terreurs, répression*, published in Paris in 1997, the plan had been to get Kutepov to Moscow where he would after torture recant in a spectacular show trial and thus further discredit ROVS. However, either he was knifed in the struggle, or perhaps overdosed with chloroform from which he died. He may well have ended up under several feet of concrete in the suburban garage of the driver of the taxi into which he was unceremoniously bundled. OGPU responsibility, denied for so long, was casually revealed four decades later in the *Red Star* obituary of the man who had actually organised it on Stalin's express orders, Sergey Vasilievich Puzitsky, 'an ardent Bolshevist-Leninist and pupil of F. E. Dzerzhinsky. Not only did he participate in the capture of the bandit Savinkov and in the destruction of the "TREST" but he carried out a brilliant operation in the arrest of Kutepov and a number of White Guard organisers and inspirers of foreign military intervention in the Civil War.' (*Krasnaya Zvezda*, 22 September 1965.) See C. Andrew and O. Gordievsky, *KGB: The Inside Story*, Harper Collins, London, 1990, also C. Andrew and V. Mitrokhin, *The Sword and the Shield: The Mitrokhin Archive and the Secret History of the KGB*, Basic Books, New York, 1999.

shall have more of the same facing me all over Europe throughout the month of April.

In the evening I left for Turin.

11 April

Arrived in Turin at midday, with a recital to play this evening. The hall was pretty empty and the audience on the cool side. The director, Gatti, however, is an admirer of my music and was generous in his praise, saying that for a first exposure it could be counted a success. He smiled as he paid me my fee of $400, which cannot but have represented a loss to him.

Not every Gatti is a swine, apparently.

12 April

The press notices echoed Gatti, and were favourable. The journey from Turin to Cannes was very interesting, through the mountains. Arrived at Le Cannet at eleven o'clock at night. The dacha is not terribly comfortable, but there is a pleasant garden full of flowers. Svyatoslav has hardly grown at all, he has caught the sun but is otherwise little changed. Bébin is a sturdy little fellow, but shy and capricious. Ptashka came from Paris this morning and instantly overdid the caresses, so much so that she frightened him. I tried to be more cautious with Bébin and not force my attentions on him.

14 April

On the surface relations are harmonious among the dacha residents, but in reality there were all sorts of undercurrents. Mémé, as is her wont, let fly at Avi, often very sharply, added to which were the barbs she directed at Ptashka. Elsa was homesick for Denmark, and I found occasion to be irritable with Ptashka.

I busied myself with the proof-reading, and on the 14th left for Monte Carlo, ready for the first rehearsal on the 15th.

15 April

Monte Carlo was not its usual elegant self. Most of the people seemed to be German tourists, in whom elegance is not the distinguishing characteristic. But the dominant impression for me was the void created by the absence of Diaghilev. Monte Carlo was so inextricably associated with him that I, not seeing his form, not sensing the constant presence of the Russian Ballet, roamed round the town as if it were an empty shell. I went to dine in the restaurant Sergey Pavlovich had frequented and spoke of him with the maître d'hôtel.

The rehearsal was conducted by Paul Paray,[1] who not so very long ago had left the room when Borovsky played some of my works in recital. Now he conducted correctly but without affection, and even found words to praise the Concerto for its clarity, rather than for its music. I then took the baton to rehearse the orchestra in three numbers from *Oranges*, remembering the impression I had gained from Toscanini's rehearsal, namely the overriding importance of keeping one's mind firmly fixed on the piece and on the orchestra: therein is found the gauge of success. The orchestra is not so much bad, in fact not at all bad as there are good musicians in it, as entirely impervious to the music and to the performance. This is a very typical trait of French orchestral players.

16 April

The second rehearsal took place in the morning, but I had a bad headache which, however, began to wear off around three o'clock, the time of the concert. Despite its being in the middle of the afternoon, full evening-dress was *de rigueur* for the concert: such is the convention hereabouts, it being considered more befitting a gala occasion.

I played the Third Piano Concerto, not without a sprinkling of wrong notes, and did my conducting stint quite well. During the performance I spotted sitting in the fourth row Svyatoslav, the first time Ptashka had brought him to any of my concerts. Both of us were worried that he would shriek 'Papa!' as I came on to the stage, but he is a big boy now and behaved himself impeccably.

In the Artists' Room were Grigoriev and Pavka, echoes from Ballets Russes times. I was terribly pleased to see Pavel Yegorevich;[2] we went to dine in Diaghilev's restaurant and sat at the very table where he always used to eat. But we scarcely touched on S.P.;[3] somehow neither of us wanted to cloud the pleasure of the evening although, needless to say, all our conversation circled round the subject.

Ptashka and Svyatoslav stayed the night and we had a good time together.

1 Paul Paray (1886–1979), French composer, organist and conductor excelling in French music as well as having an encyclopaedic command of the complete orchestral repertoire. Having relinquished the directorship of the Orchestre Lamoureux to Albert Wolff in 1928, he was Music Director of the Monte Carlo Opéra from 1928 until 1934, of the Concerts Colonne from 1932, and conducted at the Paris Opéra. Leaving Paris in 1940 he accepted again his old post in Monte Carlo for the duration. A favoured guest conductor of American orchestras after the war, in 1951 he was appointed to the Detroit Symphony, which under his direction became one of the best orchestras in the States, and made a series of still much prized recordings for Mercury Living Presence.
2 Koribut-Kubitovich (Pavka), Diaghilev's cousin.
3 Sergey Pavlovich [Diaghilev].

17 April

Spent all morning chasing around after the visa for Italy, which eventually I succeeded in obtaining, and at 1.40 left for Milan. Ptashka and Svyatoslav went back to Le Cannet.

It was a splendid train and the journey was beautiful. But there was shattering news: the suicide of Mayakovsky! Apparently because of a woman – can it have been Tatyana? Surely not! Doubtless there was a combination of burdens weighing on his soul – artistic worries, political conflicts, and perhaps a woman as well if the newspapers are to be believed.[1]

Towards evening I was in Milan, and checked in to the Hotel Regina, which was fairly horrible.

18–21 April

I had to spend four days in Milan. I transferred from the Regina to the Continental, where Diaghilev and I had stayed in 1915.[2] I was afraid it was going to be dreadfully expensive, but in fact there were rooms at quite reasonable prices.

The concert was taking place in the middle of an art exhibition, in a specially built hall, and as it was to be broadcast on the radio there was all the same sort of fuss and ado as there had been in Moscow with the *Sinfonietta*: there seems no way of regulating the sound; either it sounds good in the hall and not good on the radio, or vice versa. The orchestra was reseated, microphones moved, the lid of the piano opened and closed and eventually removed altogether. In short a tremendous amount of time was spent on activity that had no bearing whatsoever on preparing the performance musically. Gaveau had sent a piano from Monte Carlo as there is no concert instrument in Milan, but it did not arrive in time for the concert, so although the programme stated that the piano was by Gaveau in fact on the stage stood some kind of locally made instrument.

By the second rehearsal they managed to get the sound more or less balanced, but in this temporary pavilion the Concerto somehow lost its seriousness. The conductor was Pedrollo,[3] an elderly, bald Italian who, I learned later, was the composer of an opera based on Dostoevsky, so there was he, an Italian, with an opera on a Russian subject while I, a Russian, had written on the Italian subject of the *Love for Three Oranges*. I conducted the Suite from

---

1 But see above, p. 743, n. 3.
2 See *Diaries*, vol. 2, pp. 27–9.
3 Arrigo Pedrollo (1878–1964), Italian composer and conductor. Pedrollo composed in all eight operas, one of which was *Delitto e castigo* to a libretto by G. Forzano based on Dostoevsky's *Crime and Punishment*. Its first performance was at La Scala on 16 November 1926.

Oranges, doing my best to explain myself to the orchestra in bad Italian and French. The orchestra was friendly but inattentive. The audience at the concert was peculiar, although the critics were out in force as were many local musicians, who were complimentary about the Piano Concerto and its execution. The applause was less than ecstatic, but a lot better for the Concerto and the Suite from *Oranges* than for the other works in the programme. The March had to be encored, the loudest calls of all coming from the Director.

Between the rehearsals I continued proofing *The Gambler* and bought all the Russian papers to read about Mayakovsky. How typical of him were the letters he left! And at the same time what incredible composure!

22 April

Once more in Paris, but not in the apartment, at the Victoria Palace. Relations with Ptashka are ideal; having seen how odious was the atmosphere in the home of her quarrelsome mother, she has resolved to avoid it in her own.

A lot of letters, the most important being from Borovsky who has just returned from Russia and Berlin. He had seen Asafyev, who categorically advises me not to come. Essentially all he does is add a final point to what Myaskovsky had already written to me, except that Asafyev decided not to commit his thoughts to paper but to transmit them verbally via Borovsky. Myaskovsky is the more courageous of the two and wrote in plain language: that is the difference in their characters.

In sum, therefore, the proletarian musicians have forced me out of Russia. But my own belief is that their ascendancy will not last long. How have they got where they are? Through politics. They lack high-grade specialist qualifications, and that will be the measure of their short-lived influence. I must put off my visit to Russia; that is the sum of it. For six months? A year?

End of April–20 May

Even closer relations with the Nabokovs. He is affectionate, most entertaining company, mimicking Diaghilev and Larionov with devastating accuracy, and impersonating a haemorrhoidal old general trying to get comfortable in an armchair. He is working on a long article about me for *The Number* (*Chislo*), the new Russian-language journal in Paris.[1]

---

1 *Chislo* was a quarterly, modelled on the traditional Russian 'thick' journal containing belles-lettres, poetry, essays on philosophy and culture, and novellas, established and jointly edited by Irma de Manziarly, a Russian-born close confidante and adherent of Jiddu Krishnamurti, married to a wealthy Frenchman, and the poet and translator Nikolay Otsup. It lasted from 1930 until 1934 and provided a serious platform for many young Russian émigré writers.

When I mentioned that a theme from *Le Pas d'acier* had been described in Moscow as 'religious', Nabokov replied, 'More than that: one of the songs Plevitskaya sings has the same tune.'[1]

An article by Burtsev in *Latest News* fulminates about the abduction of General Kutepov by the Bolsheviks. One of the kidnappers is said to be

---

1   Nadezhda Plevitskaya (1884–1940) possessed that rare thing, a genuinely natural talent that retained its authentic purity and individuality through fortune and international celebrity, even if it appears that a similar transparency was lacking in its owner's life. Born the ninth child of a semi-literate peasant family in a village near Kursk, Plevitskaya sang in the local church choir, ran away to join the circus, moved to Moscow where she sang in a restaurant, finally to be spotted at the 1909 Nizhny Novgorod Fair by the tenor Leonid Sobinov who championed his discovery everywhere, even at the Imperial Court. There, so legend has it, the Tsar came up with the sobriquet by which she became known, the 'Kursk Nightingale'. During the Civil War, by this time a committed Bolshevik sympathiser, Plevitskaya was singing for the Red Army troops when she was captured by a White detachment commanded by General Nikolay Skoblin, known for his summary brutality to enemy prisoners. Plevitskaya, however, retaliated with the capture of his affections, and they eventually fled together to Turkey, where they married. In exile, throughout France, Germany, Central Europe, America – everywhere there were Russian émigré communities longing to be moved by the true spirit of the old songs of their lost homeland's folk music – she became immensely popular. Chaliapin, who had heard her sing in Russia and told her, 'May God preserve you, dearest Nadyusha. Sing me your songs that have come from the earth, songs that I as a townsman and not from a village do not have myself,' brought her to a party in the Rachmaninoffs' apartment whereupon Sergey Vasilievich, like everyone else, instantly fell under her spell, improvised an accompaniment and insisted that they go together to the Victor studios and make the recording of the song 'Powder and Paint' that can still be heard in their performance. Skoblin, to all appearances the archetypal White General in exile, rose high in the ranks of the ROVS; as a couple they epitomised everything the émigré community held dear from their lost paradise. Plevitskaya – in Nabokov's story 'La Slavska' – had in reality by no means lost her Bolshevik leanings, while her husband had begun actively working for the NKVD, a classic double agent, even, *pace* Eric Rohmer's film *Triple Agent* about the affair that was to bring their life to an end six years later, a *triple* agent working simultaneously with the Soviets, the émigré community and the Germans. The affair in question was the abduction in 1936 of General Miller, successor to General Kutepov as head of ROVS, whose deputy Skoblin had by this time become. It was a carbon copy of the Kutepov plan but with very different outcomes: first Miller had secretly left a note to be opened if he did not return from an assignation with Skoblin of which he was evidently suspicious; secondly the NKVD's consignment this time survived the kidnapping and the drugging, arriving alive in Moscow still in the trunk in which he had been hidden, to be interrogated and tortured for nineteen months before being executed; thirdly Skoblin, the prime mover of the plot, unaware of Miller's prior fingering of him, was immediately picked up by the ROVS team but escaped and somehow got himself to Spain, where he was quickly found by his NKVD masters and is presumed to have been liquidated. The French police, motivated at last (Commissaire Faux-Pas Bidet having been replaced) to do something about their foreign guests' unwelcome habit of kidnapping and murdering each other on the streets of their capital, arrested and charged Plevitskaya with complicity in the outrage; she was found guilty and sentenced to twenty years' hard labour (an unsually harsh penalty). She died in 1940, still in the women's prison at Rennes. In Russia Plevitskaya is still revered; a museum in her memory was opened in her home village in 2009. See C. Andrew and O. Gordievsky, op. cit., pp. 163–4; also Mary-Kay Wilmers, *The Eitingons: A Twentieth Century Story*, Faber and Faber, London, 2009, pp. 243–60, for an account of the Miller affair, Plevitskaya, Skoblin and their relationship to the author's own shadowy forebears.

Arens. Apparently he is no longer in the Embassy, having been recalled to Moscow. Has he been sacked?[1]

An evening of readings from Remizov, to an audience consisting almost exclusively of Russians. As always when I find myself in such a gathering a peculiar sensation comes over me: half the people look on me as a celebrity, the other half as a Bolshevik. Rachmaninoff was friendly. I tried to be polite to Medtner, but the moment I hinted that I preferred Dostoevsky to Turgenev, he flew at me.

On the 10th May I had a telegram from Vladimir Bashkirov in New York: Boris has typhoid and is in hospital. Could I please find out the details and let him know? I went, feeling strange, as it is eighteen months since I had any contact with him. Perhaps he is delirious with fever? But he was not at home; he had just gone out. The next day I rang up, and again he had gone out. The usual bluff. What should I do, cable Vladimir with the truth? If I did, it would be the finish for Boris. In the end Boris rang me himself, spluttering and stammering: he was ill, typhoid of course, he is being ejected from the hotel, has nothing to eat, etc., etc. I decided to soft-pedal my reply to Vladimir: he is recovering, details to follow by letter.

Met Stravinsky on the street; we embraced. He is composing a symphony with chorus, to Latin texts from the Psalms. It is a very interesting idea, except for the Latin, the effect of which will be that the Psalms will be taken as something dry, clerical, rather than as incandescent poetry. I related to Stravinsky how our American fate is being torpedoed by Maxwell falling out serially with all organisations showing interest in playing our music. Stravinsky agreed, although with reservations. In general I was very glad to see him, and felt a rush of tenderness towards him. Nevertheless, when Nabokov unleashed a stream of sarcastic comments aimed at him, what a happy feeling it gave me!

Koussevitzky arrived back from America on the 13th May. We found a plausible excuse not to go to the station: Koussevitzky, having promised to perform the *Sinfonietta* in one of his Boston concerts, failed to do so. In the meantime Monteux asked if I had anything new for an OSP concert in May. I said that I must keep all my new powder dry for the concert of my works de Valmalète had promised to arrange for me. Monteux telephoned de Valmalète and agreed with him that in the autumn there would be a concert devoted to me including the premiere of my Fourth Symphony. On learning this I consented to let him have the *Sinfonietta* for the end of May. Applying to the publishers for the material I discovered that Koussevitzky had not only

---

1   Possibly, but he was later appointed Soviet Ambassador to Canada, and thence to the post of General Consul in New York, which was his position at the time of recall to Moscow in 1937, subsequent arrest and execution on 11 January 1938.

not performed the *Sinfonietta* in America, but had forgotten to bring the material back with him. When I heard this, I practically expired with rage. Telegrams flying back and forth to Boston. Hasty production of a new copy of the material. Postponement of the Warsaw performance of the *Sinfonietta* (scheduled for the 22nd May). I had no direct contact with Koussevitzky; everything was done through the publishing house – which, by the way, has no director at present, Paichadze being away on Koussevitzky's personal business. Meanwhile Monteux had a fainting fit in his bath, as a result of which the last concert of the season, the one with the *Sinfonietta*, was cancelled. A right royal mess, in short, except for Warsaw which was the least of my worries, but the behaviour of Koussevitzky, who did not even see fit to telephone me and apologise, fell some way short of admirable.

In terms of music, I mainly worked on the finale of the Fourth Symphony, which is proving obstinately difficult. The second and third movements, by contrast, fell into place almost imperceptibly. The second movement, in fact, had been done in rough last year, and needed only polishing and orchestrating, and there was not much work in the third movement either.

Why did I leave it in B minor? For a C major symphony it would have been more natural to transpose it to A minor or C minor. But I left it as it was not from laziness, but because it sounds much fresher in B minor after the Andante than it would do in the other keys. Those who do not believe me can try it for themselves.

I completed the score of the second movement on the 4th May, and of the third on the 18th. Besides this I transcribed the *Divertimento* for piano two hands. For some unknown reason it is proving difficult for people to assimilate. I hope that with a piano transcription it will more quickly become palatable, and attract some champions.

For some time now Suvchinsky has been out of sight and out of mind. I found him in a certain perturbation of spirit: he is secretly planning to visit the USSR. In this connection he has his contacts in Moscow, but more importantly with Gorky.[1] *Eurasia*[2] has ceased publication for lack of money, and the Yevraziisti are riven by many differences of opinion. While waiting, Suvchinsky has taken up singing; he has a strong tenor voice.

---

1   In 1930 Gorky was still living in Italy, although the previous year he had returned to Russia on a visit, during which he inspected the already widely ill-reputed Solovki Islands penal labour camp in the White Sea, manifestly spruced up for the occasion, and wrote a favourable essay on its 're-educatory' effects, which provoked at the time, and still does, heated views as to its objectivity. The essay was subtitled 'The Stormy Petrel of the Revolution becomes the Nightingale of SLON' (the acronym for the camp) and appeared in Gorky's collection of travel pieces called 'Around the Unions of the Soviets'. It was not until 1932 that after several more visits he yielded to Stalin's relentless cajoling and returned permanently to the Soviet Union.
2   The newspaper: see above, pp. 738–9.

There has been a falling out between him and Stravinsky, mainly on account of Markevich. Stravinsky said, 'I loved Seryozha Diaghilev dearly, and perhaps I ought not to say this, but it may be better that he died, otherwise he would no doubt have put up this boy against me.'

Suvchinsky: 'What are you saying, Igor Fyodorovich? You are just like Boris Godunov, seeing in every young man a pretender to your throne.'

This conversation produced a coolness. To me Suvchinsky elaborated his theory, that those composers are important who bring something new to music, to its language and its content. If you go down the list of composers, you do not find many who match these criteria. Beethoven, for example, must be seen as an exception. In the most recent times the only candidates are Debussy and Prokofiev. All his life Suvchinsky has oscillated like the beam from a lighthouse between Stravinsky and me, and is currently veering to my side.

On the 17th May Mémé brought the children. Since at Le Cannet Ptashka and Mémé had been at one another's throats, I went to meet them at the station. But Mémé was in a sunny mood, the children also were ruddy with health and brown as berries. The repainting of the flat is not yet finished, but two rooms are ready so Mémé and Elsa with the children went there straight away while we stayed on at the Victoria Palace, where we dined in the restaurant. When a wandering violinist began to scrape on his fiddle, Svyatoslav said pensively, 'What rotten music.' Ptashka and I both tried to ingratiate ourselves with little brother, but he is shy and won't respond. Ptashka is being lovely to me all the time, but she has taken the rearrangement of the flat very much to heart and is nervous about its successful realisation. On the 20th I left for Warsaw.

20–26 May
Visit to Warsaw

In Warsaw there was a concert entirely of my music on the 23rd. The orchestra should have been performing the *Sinfonietta*, but owing to Koussya's carelessness the *Divertimento* and the Overture, Op. 42, had to be substituted for it, and after trying out the Overture that too had to be abandoned: it was too difficult with only two rehearsals.

Warsaw's response to me was splendid; my least popular piece was the ill-fated *Divertimento*. Fitelberg was kind, and took me to see the new mansion he is building next to Paderewski Park. After the concert we were besieged by a group of five retired Russian lieutenants asking for help. Fitelberg angrily shouted abuse at them when they surrounded our car after the concert. I felt some sympathy for them, but all the same, how disgraceful to assault us like that! The same thing, I was told, happened after Orlov's concert.

The music shops were displaying reprints of my works in their windows. Someone is making a fortune out of it, but at least it shows that there is interest and a demand – to put it another way, 'disinterested glory'. In other windows there were Gaveau posters advertising the fact that I play their instruments, with pictures of their piano accompanied by my portrait, but such a hideous one that it was painful to look at it.

Maria Viktorovna, who has now settled in Berlin, suggested that I spend at least the day there from morning until evening on my way back, promising to line up some bigwigs who would help to strengthen my musical connections in Berlin. I complied, the more readily as such a stay fitted in well with my train timetable. In the end she did not produce any bigwigs, but she did introduce me to a very nice lady, Frau Lucie Mankiewitz, on whom Erich Kleiber was supposed to make a social call, but he did not come. Then we were driven out of town to drink tea in a noisy riverside restaurant. All in all it was not a particularly productive time, but very pleasant. In the evening, seen off by Mar-Vik, I got the train to Paris. On the journey was visited by a rather good theme for the scherzo of the string quartet.

26–31 May

On the 26th I returned to Paris and the restoration of a loving relationship with Ptashka, who has not been feeling at all well all the time I was away: it seems to have been some kind of heart spasm.

A letter from Moscow with good news: *Oranges* is still in the repertoire and has been given eleven times since November. Another letter was from B. Bashkirov, starting simply 'Sergey Sergeyevich' without any prefatory 'Dear'. He is still ill and in difficult circumstances, and since I 'had taken it upon myself to inform Vladimir of the situation', he now wants me to send Vladimir a telegram requesting money. A day or two later Boris lay in wait for me at the entrance to our building; I took him for coffee to the café on the corner. Tatyana[1] has thrown her son Kolya Sidorov, aged fifteen, out of her house, and he has been sleeping rough in the park. Not only that but he shoplifted a book about tennis from a bookseller's stand and now has been arrested. It is essential that he be rescued and a lawyer found for him, all of which will cost money. Boris himself is being evicted from his hotel for not paying the bill, and has no money for anything to eat. In short, Vladimir must be cabled at once. Finally, Boris ended up his tale of woe by asking me for money. I said I would write to Vladimir but not send a telegram as it

---

1 Tatyana, née Bashkirova, younger sister of Vladimir and Boris Bashkirov and of the Princess Magalova. Kolya must be the son of a previous marriage as in 1919 Tatyana was married to a man called Yakhontov (see *Diaries*, vol. 2, pp. 414, 428).

would be impossible to explain this complicated story in a cable, and (sensibly!) refused to give him any money. There followed a truly theatrical scene: Boris ran round the square demanding money, and when I tried to make my escape, screamed, 'But where am I to get any from?' I quickened my pace and spread my arms out in a typically French gesture of helplessness.

Two more letters followed, this time addressed to 'Dear Sergey Sergeyevich'. In them Boris complained of abscesses and insisted that he needed an operation. Can it be that he has been taking drugs, and the abscesses are a result of that? I wrote to Vladimir.

1 June

Working on the finale of the Fourth Symphony, and also doing something on the Quartet. Otherwise I am trying to deal with the furnishing of the flat. There are so many villains among painters, decorators, furniture-dealers and the like. Ptashka takes each instance of their cheating as a personal affront and expends a tremendous amount of nervous energy on the whole business. In my opinion when doing up an apartment it would be better to assume from the start that a certain percentage of the total cost, say 10 per cent, will disappear in pilfering. That way one need be angry only once and thereafter stay calm about it.

3 June

In the evening we entertained at home Meyerhold, the Suvchinskys and the Nabokovs. Meyerhold has been having technical problems with the theatre,[1] and that is why no one has seen them, but now 'clear blue sky begins at last to be seen'. Suvchinsky has seen Chaliapin and together they wandered round the streets of Paris. This time Suvchinsky was not pleased by Chaliapin: he has taken to pronouncing solemn words of wisdom, but the oracular statements that emerge are distinctly peculiar. For example: 'There, they say that there are various Karl Marxes and various Jesus Christs. But I say to you, that what a man needs is to be comfortable, to be comfortable!' Suvchinsky reproduced this phrase in a passable imitation of Chaliapin's voice.

---

1 After the political attacks on the Meyerhold Theatre's production of Mayakovsky's *The Bathhouse* (*Banya*) (with music by Shebalin) and the banning of further performances, Meyerhold took his company abroad to Berlin and then to Paris. In Berlin the performances were wildly successful but he and Zinaïda Raikh had a furious argument with Michael Chekhov, who had already left the Soviet Union, and who desperately tried to persuade Meyerhold and Raikh not to return ('They will kill you!'). In Paris the company was less successful largely because of the hostile attitude of the large émigré Russian population.

4 June

Two extremely long telegrams from Vladimir in New York, asking me as a mark of personal friendship to find out exactly what was the position with Kolya Sidorov and, if I could, to help. Whatever money it costs would be repaid, but not a penny must be given to Tatyana, and not a word about Boris. Soon after I received the telegrams Tatyana appeared, and inevitably pleaded passionately with me to give her money. The boy has indeed been arrested; he will need a lawyer, and there will be all kinds of costs to defray.

In the evening there was a performance of Markevich's *Ode*, well scored for a small orchestra, words by Cocteau.[1] Markevich has succeeded in attracting support and money from snobbish circles in Paris and is thus enabled to put on concerts of his music. Some people are happy for him, others are irritated by it. In any event I recognised among the audience many faces familiar from Diaghilev performances. *Ode* itself is not bad, but at the same time not very interesting. It has a lot of formulae borrowed from Hindemith. At the conclusion of the programme Désormière came out to announce that by request of numerous audience members *Ode* would be repeated – and so it was. But it had already been decided at the morning rehearsal that it would be played twice. Markevich approached everyone asking how they had liked it. I replied, 'Why don't you dedicate it to Beckmesser?'

Markevich: 'Who is Beckmesser?'

I: 'A poet.'

He had no idea what I was talking about. He also asked Nouvel, 'And how did you like it?'

Nouvel replied, 'Not as much as you do,' and then boasted of his witticism to all and sundry.

Nouvel clearly did not approve. Suvchinsky, however, was enraptured. Nabokov equivocated.

5 June

Dictated an article about young Russian composers for Havana. They have a very good Contemporary Music Society there and when I was there I had promised to write an article for them.

---

1 This seems to be the work known as *Cantate*, the music for which had been conceived originally as a ballet for Diaghilev's Ballets Russes to a libretto by Kokhno, but which was abandoned on the death of the impresario. Cocteau later provided a text to fit the music, which is scored for soprano, male chorus and orchestra.

6 June

A Horowitz concert, with a great gathering of the *beau monde* in the audience. Horowitz's talent is exceptional, not so his brains. For this reason there was a danger that his huge success in America would stifle his growth as an artist. But no: the Liszt Sonata was played with a stunning tenderness. The programme included a whole group of my pieces, including *Suggestion diabolique*, which when I heard it in America had really set my ears abuzz: no pedal, with incredible elasticity. Now he played it well, but using the pedal, without that elastic springiness, and the final glissando lacked brilliance: he had hurt his fingernail, as he explained to me afterwards.

7 June

First meeting with Koussevitzky: we shook hands politely but spoke only just before he was leaving. I asked him how he had liked Nabokov's Symphony, which the latter had recently played to him. His answer immediately elicited a slight conflict of views. I said I thought the first movement was the best, to which Koussevitzky rejoined, 'That's because it most resembles your music. I preferred the second and third movements.'

9 June

Tea with Stokowski at Hammond's.[1] To spite Koussevitzky I was particularly cordial to Stokowski, who has over the past few years begun to wake up to my music: he has performed the Second Symphony, and just recently, in April, the Overture, Op. 42 (albeit with a dreadful cut, about which I learned only later). He is now talking of mounting a staged production in New York of *Le Pas d'acier*.

---

1   John Hays Hammond junior (1885–1965), known as 'the father of radio control systems', was the son of an American mining engineer who had made a fortune in the mines of South Africa. As a very young man Hammond junior impressed both Thomas Edison and Alexander Graham Bell with his combination of mechanical and electronic inventive genius and his entrepreneurial instincts, and before long had established his own Hammond Radio Research Laboratory in Gloucester, Massachusetts. With over 800 international patents on over 400 inventions in the fields of radio control and naval weaponry, he amassed an even greater fortune and eventually built his own replica castle, complete with drawbridge, on the Atlantic coast of Massachusetts to house his collection of Roman, Medieval, and Renaissance art. Hammond Castle is now the Hammond Museum. Surprisingly in view of his electronic inventions, the Hammond Organ was nothing to do with him: this was the brainchild of his namesake, the almost equally gifted electronics engineer Laurens Hammond.

11 June

Paichadze spends all the time away travelling on the Lord Koussevitzky's private affairs, and the business of the publishing house is being neglected. Although he is here at the moment I decided to register a protest by keeping away from the place. I did, however, write a businesslike letter to Paichadze on the subject of printing my works. He responded by telephone and asked me to come in for a personal discussion. I did so, and the result was a decision to engrave the piano score of the *Divertimento* and the string parts of the Third Symphony. The full score is already engraved, and it would cost too much to do the wind parts: they can be produced by the lithographic process. When I objected that Stravinsky's things are published immediately whereas mine are subjected to chronic and hopeless delays, Paichadze showed me an excerpt from the expenditure accounts of the past few years, which demonstrated that they regularly spend twice as much on me as they do on Stravinsky, and even then could not manage to publish everything. We parted reasonably peaceably.

12–15 June
A motor trip

Chancellor Bethmann-Hollweg, one of the diplomatic heroes of the war, settled down on his estate near Berlin following the Revolution and his retirement, to play Bach.[1] He had a son, a tall, courteous, silent man. This

---

[1] 'Heroic' as a description of Bethmann-Hollweg's record in the preliminaries to, and course of, the First World War would probably today be regarded with raised eyebrows. He might have been temperamentally unsympathetic both to the belligerence of Tirpitz, Ludendorff, Hindenburg and the military leaders, and to the atrocities carried out in German and Axis-occupied territories, damningly detailed in Isabel V. Hull's *Absolute Destruction: Military Culture and The Practices of War in Imperial Germany* (Cornell University Press, 2005), but he did nothing to counteract them, nor to mitigate the genocide of Armenians by the Turks from 1915 onwards. Responding to the direct appeal of Special Ambassador to Turkey Wolff-Metternich to rein in the murderous Talaat Bey ('Our newspapers must give voice to concerns about the persecution of Armenians and stop showering praise on the Turks. What they are doing is made possible by our work, our officers, our artillery, our money. Without our help the bloated frog will collapse in on itself'), Bethmann-Hollweg had merely this to say: 'Our only goal is to keep Turkey by our side until the end of the war, regardless of whether Armenians perish in the process or not. If the war continues for much longer we will yet have great need of the Turks. I do not comprehend how Metternich can make such a proposal.' Not perhaps his fault, but the fact that Adolf Hitler was later to base his own genocidal programme for Jews and other minorities on the presumed international acceptance of Bethmann-Hollweg's cynical pragmatism in relation to Armenians hardly makes one warm to him.

son has an enormous open-topped Mercedes, in which he drove to Paris. As the Nabokovs are very friendly with the son, a motor tour of France in the Mercedes was arranged: Bethmann-Hollweg, the two Nabokovs, Ptashka and I.

We drove through Rouen, Deauville (still deserted) and St Michel, then from north to south right through Brittany, intimate and charming but empty of people, finally via Nantes reaching the castles of the Loire. Here the countryside is miraculous, and the castles romantic. The last place we stopped for the night was Chambord (as we had done in our first tour in the Ballot with the Samoilenkos and Bashkirov), and on the evening of the 15th we were back home in Paris.

Bethmann is an excellent driver and it is a powerful car; in the open air, the wind and the sun turned our faces into copper frying-pans. But it was a trip of rare pleasure: the silence of Bethmann redeemed by the Nabokovs' boisterous gaiety. Perhaps a little too much coarse language: once they burst into our room and insisted on taking pictures of us *en deshabille*.

18 June

A proposal from the one-armed pianist Paul Wittgenstein to write him a concerto for the left hand.[1] At first this seemed a ridiculous notion, but ... if the fee is decent, it should not take me too long.[2]

Lunch *chez* Koshetz, with Stokowski. Marina is now a grown-up seventeen-year-old, her demeanour oscillating between the charming and the revolting. After lunch Stokowski came back with me to listen to the Third Symphony, which he promised to perform in the winter. Nabokov went to see him in the evening and played him his Symphony, which Stokowski also said he would take.

Vladimir Bashkirov and his wife have come to Paris where he has a flourishing bakery business. He asked me not to reveal his presence to Boris or

1 Paul Wittgenstein (1887–1961), older brother of the philosopher Ludwig Wittgenstein, had studied with Theodor Leschetitsky and had embarked on a promising career as a pianist before having his right arm amputated as a result of a war wound while serving with the Austrian army in the First World War. With the considerable resources of the Wittgenstein family fortune (deriving from his industrial magnate father Karl) behind him, Wittgenstein commissioned a number of composers to write left-hand concertos for him, including Prokofiev, Ravel, Strauss, Korngold, Britten and Franz Schmidt.
2 Because when he received them Wittgenstein did not like or play most of them, Prokofiev probably did not know that several Wittgenstein-commissioned left-hand concertos were already in existence, including those by Hindemith and Korngold (both 1923), and Strauss (*Parergon on Sinfonia Domestica* and the Symphonic Studies *Panathenäenzug*, 1927). (The Hindemith work came to light only in 2001 on the death of the composer's wife Hilde.) The works that have entered the repertoire mostly came later: Ravel, who was still in the process of writing at this time, Prokofiev and Britten (*Diversions*, 1940).

Tatyana. I gave him a detailed account of the situation with Kolya Sidorov, which is just now being resolved. Vladimir fished out a package of 1,000-franc notes to reimburse me for my expenses, and thanked me extravagantly for my trouble.

20 June

Vladimir Nikolayevich[1] took us to dinner at Les Ambassadeurs, the most exclusive restaurant in Paris. He danced superbly with both ladies (who would have thought it back in Petersburg and Samara days!);[2] I have forgotten everything I ever knew about it. Seeing how insouciantly he settled the colossal bill, I forced myself to pester him about at least paying Boris's hotel bill and to get his teeth fixed. V.N. promised he would. There is a picture of him in today's paper and an interview with him about the market in bread.

After Stokowski had shown interest in Nabokov's Symphony, Nabokov went to Koussevitzky and asked if he was planning to perform it, or if it should be given to Stokowski. Koussevitzky said he definitely intended to play it, and not just in Boston but also in New York. When Nabokov mentioned in passing the disarray at the publishers, Koussevitzky screamed at him, 'I know all about the Prokofiev Fronde! Don't tell me you are party to it too!' The conversation degenerated into an out-and-out war of words, as Nabokov eventually lost patience and started objecting strenuously to this misinterpretation (or at least, that is what he told me).

21 June

Taking advantage of Vladimir's agreement, I went to pay Boris's hotel bill. It turned out to be a colourful mission. I presented myself to the hotel proprietor in the morning, judging that there would be little risk of running into Boris then as he would still be asleep, and on behalf of his brother proposed to pay what was owing on production of the outstanding account, which by the way extended back to 1928. The hotel was small, as was the proprietor. He became flustered, rooting around in the past years' books, then suddenly drew himself up and declared importantly that he would not put up with the situation any longer. Eventually the total owing amounted to 1,908 francs, which I paid by cheque, giving instructions that not a word about my visit should be said to Boris, on the grounds that 'if you let him know anything about it you will not get anything more out of him for months'.

---

1 Bashkirov.
2 See *Diaries*, vol. 1, pp. 671, 752; vol. 2, pp. 131–2, 155–6.

23 June

Finished the Fourth Symphony.

End of June

Several more lunches and dinners with Vladimir, who laughed till he cried at Boris remaining in ignorance that his bill had been paid. From Kugel,[1] Wittgenstein's representative, I received the somewhat unexpected response that $5,000 for a concerto for the left hand was acceptable. However, Kugel is demanding 10 per cent as a negotiating fee. This made me angry, but Vladimir counselled accepting, in order not to lose the commission altogether.

We have tarried too long in Paris, but have no dacha to go to. As is her wont, Ptashka does not know what she wants, and taxes me with not being energetic enough about it. Without a car it is difficult to search for a dacha. We took the train to Dieppe, to have a look at the Channel coast. Dieppe seems to be a main centre and port, but a few kilometres outside it there is no gas or electricity. Not having found anything, we returned.

July

Worked on the Quartet. Looked over Gorchakov's Symphony, which has been long awaiting my attention.

Continuing the search for a dacha, went to Entretat on the Channel coast, to the left of Dieppe.[2] Entretat is a pretty place, but there are no dachas to rent there. This year we have left it too late, waiting in the city. Everybody has gone away: the Nabokovs to Germany, Samoilenkos to Corsica, the Meyerholds to the Pyrenees. Still in town are Vladimir Bashkirov and his wife, with whom we had a number of dinners and visited various elegant places. A tragicomic letter arrived on the 10th from Boris: he has discovered that Vladimir was in Paris and left[3] without seeing him, for which he blames me, of course, and for that I shall answer before God.

On the 14th I was called on by a stonemason, a young German, whom Boris had known when living with us in Ettal. Coming to work in Paris, he had met Boris and was shocked by his poverty-stricken situation. As far as I could understand from what he told me, Boris pitched him a yarn and managed to extract 200 francs from him. He now came to see me in the capacity of an envoy, modest and respectful in bearing, but giving me to

---

1 Konzertdirektion Georg Kugel in Vienna were Paul Wittgenstein's managers.
2 That is, west, or rather south-west.
3 As he assumed.

understand that Boris considers I have never fully repaid to Vladimir what I owed him[1] (which he was happy for me to pass on to Boris), and therein lies all Boris's misfortune. I told the stonemason to come back tomorrow for my answer, but inside I was seething with anger. I had no way of proving either to him or even to myself what I owed or did not owe, because ever since 1920[2] I had been giving him money without any receipts or keeping an account; besides, he had lived for two years at my expense in Ettal, and how is one supposed to keep an account of that? Time was when Boris had written to Vladimir that I had fully discharged my debt; now, apparently, it was all my fault that he had no money. I decided to have it out with Vladimir and let him go and confront his brother. It would be all the more effective since Boris had already mentally despatched him back to America and condemned me to judgement before the throne of God for having allowed this to happen.

In the evening, it being the *quatorze juillet* and the populace celebrating on the streets of Paris, we invited Vladimir Nikolayevich and his wife to dinner in a restaurant whose windows overlook the Place de Rennes, opposite the Gare de Montparnasse, so that while having our dinner we could watch the dancing in the streets. Larionov and Goncharova were with us, as Vladimir is at my recommendation contemplating buying some of their pictures for his New York apartment. After dinner we went to the Place de la Bastille, but nothing very exciting was going on there, and Larionov dragged us to a series of somewhat dubious night-clubs. In one of them men were dancing with other men, at another our womenfolk were not allowed in as the management were kindly providing their own – attired in bathing costumes. Finally we ended up in a thoroughly disreputable place where there was a clutch of completely nude women, so that the cramped space was white with naked flesh. Embarrassed, we tried hastily to beat a retreat, but we were too late: they had already seated us at a table and the naked bodies were pressing closely round. Thrusting 20 francs into expectant palms for the disturbance, we nevertheless succeeded in extricating ourselves and emerged as from a bathroom. Larionov then led us through narrow lanes and courtyards: at night by moonlight it was very picturesque, as if from another century. The whole escapade made a profound impression on Vladimir's wife, a pretty young American, who will doubtless regale her girlfriends in America with the details for years to come.

1   In 1918 and 1919 in New York, when Prokofiev was chronically short of money, Vladimir had lent him money, had him to stay with him in his apartment and found another place for him to live rent-free. He had also been helpful finding a conduit for funds to transfer to Prokofiev's mother who was still marooned in the Caucasus. See *Diaries*, vol. 2, pp. 344, 399, 421–6.
2   Boris Bashkirov had made his escape from Russia to Finland in 1920, from which time Prokofiev was in touch with him and among other offers of support provided him with funds to get to France in 1921.

Next morning Vladimir and I met by arrangement outside Boris's hotel and together entered to confront him. As soon as he saw us – the man who had paid him his money and the brother on whose behalf he had done so – he rushed up the stairs in front of us and ceremoniously flung the door to Boris's room.

Our entrée was as theatrically managed as can be imagined. Boris was asleep, and to his half-wakened state our appearance must have seemed even more like a mirage. After greeting him, Vladimir said slowly, 'Well, so you're still in bed?'

'I'm not well, Volodya, look, see these abscesses on my hands . . .'

'It's probably syphilis, don't you think?'

'Good heavens, Volodya, what nonsense you talk . . .'

Vladimir took up a position near the stove, I sat on the only chair, and Boris sat on the bed.

'What were you thinking of, sending a stonemason to do your panhandling for you?' asked Vladimir, and embarked on a long speech in which he mercilessly eviscerated Boris: 'Forty years old, living on your own, and you haven't even learnt how to beg properly. But here's Sergey Sergeyevich, he works, he's made a life for himself, look what marvellous children he has!'

Boris sat quietly taking it on the chin, then suddenly went on the attack: 'I'm really surprised at Sergey Sergeyevich going to see Dovglevsky . . .'[1]

Vladimir: 'In the position Sergey Sergeyevich occupies he is perfectly entitled to go and see Dovglevsky if he wants to.'

Boris: 'But it's precisely because of his position that he ought to keep away.'

Vladimir: 'I would with pleasure call on Dovglevsky myself if he would see me, because there is no point whatever in breaking off relations with Russia if there is any possibility of maintaining them. Now get up, get dressed, and we'll go and redeem your chauffeur's licence.'

We went out, and about five minutes later Boris came out as well, and we went to the café where he had pawned his licence. Boris walked a little in front, Vladimir furtively catching my eye from time to time and having difficult not bursting out laughing. The café proprietress was summoned and Boris held a lengthy whispered conversation with her: pawning this sort of official document was strictly illegal and she did not want to produce the licence in front of strangers. But eventually the licence book was produced, and Vladimir paid out 350 francs.

Sitting at the table, Vladimir asked, 'Would you like some coffee?'

'Yes, Volodya, I've not had any today yet.'

Coffee was ordered, and Vladimir took out a thick packet of banknotes.

---

1 An official at the Soviet Embassy in Paris.

'I'll give you another 500 francs,' he said, and began slowly peeling off 100-franc notes, moistening his thumb like a street trader, smoothing each one out on the table before taking the next one, and so on. At length, having handed him all the money and delivered himself of yet another hortatory lecture, Vladimir stood up and we left. The following day he went back to America.

This all took place on the 16th July, and we still have not even a sniff of a dacha to go to. I decided on desperate measures: I wrote down from Indicateur Bertrand[1] the addresses of all the agencies for country-house lets in the country surrounding Paris, composed a general letter, had Astrov make twenty-four copies of it, and sent it out to all of them, enclosing a stamp for reply.

Ida Rubinstein telephoned: she is planning to mount a ballet season the year after next and asked if I would compose a new ballet for her. I still bear a grudge over Demasy's *Juditha*[2] (although thank God I never wrote the piece), but seeing that she rang me herself and behaved with tact, I decided to be correct and go to see her for a talk about it. I said I was prepared to do it and that I would prefer a biblical subject, and on the 28th wrote requesting $5,000 for a 25–30-minute ballet. The basis for my demand was that I knew Stravinsky had got $6,000 for a 45-minute piece,[3] which he considered an excellent fee. A couple of days later Ida telephoned her agreement and said we must meet to discuss the artistic side. Thus in a short space of time two worthwhile commissions had fallen into my lap. The dacha situation was also sorting itself out, near Rambouillet, next door to Rachmaninoff, which could certainly make life interesting. In view of the commissions we decided we could afford to buy another car, so set about looking at second-hand models, although nothing more than a year old. The one we were most attracted to was a four-seater 11-horsepower Talbot, a convertible, but in the end it was too expensive. It was raining every day, so perhaps it was just as well we were still in town.

At one of the Russian Opera performances (not Soviet, émigré companies) I ran into Coates, with whom I have not been in touch for about eight years.[4] He came straight up to me and was very friendly, promising to telephone, and a few days later turned up at my house, where he sat beaming and drinking port. I decided dutifully to return the compliment and called on him the following day.

1   A high-class estate and lettings agency, still in business for *maisons à louer* and desirable *résidences secondaires*.
2   See above, pp. 77, 188–9, 197, 200.
3   *The Fairy's Kiss*, in 1928.
4   Not quite true: Coates had been at the premiere of Prokofiev's Second Symphony in Paris, conducted by Koussevitzky, in June 1925.

August

Nothing came of the dacha in Rambouillet: the place is beautiful, the house itself not new but somehow not comfortable; there was not a single armchair in it. We are beginning to feel that it is impossible to find anywhere: we went to Bois-le-Roi, to Chantilly, and even looked at a run-down castle in Avallon, but nothing was even halfway attractive. At last we found a good house in Naze near L'Isle-Adam, an hour from Paris. We planned to move out there on the 10th of the month. At the same time, suddenly all my plans fell into place: the rain stopped, we bought a car, the one-armed pianist confirmed the commission of a left-hand Piano Concerto. The car is a Chevrolet, quite small but with an 18-horsepower 6-cylinder engine, and absolutely new in appearance. Someone had bought it on an instalment payment plan and then had to withdraw for lack of funds, therefore we were offered it for 20,000 francs instead of 36,000. In America the Chevrolet is not a particularly covetable marque, but in Paris, which imposes high import duty on American cars, it is much admired. To sum up, the Ballot was an elderly aristocrat, while the Chevrolet is a youthful democrat. Driving around town and up hills is a thousand times easier; it is so nippy and powerful. But on the open road, old lady Ballot was nonpareil.

Lifar came to see me. He is now Chief Choreographer of the Grand Opéra and is very anxious that I should write a ballet for him. He is even prepared to pay thirty to forty thousand francs from his own pocket. But I showed him the amputee's letter, mentioned Ida, and said I could not do it for less than a hundred thousand, besides which rather than a commission for a new ballet I should greatly prefer it if the Opéra would mount a production of *Three Oranges*. So the ballet project had to be abandoned. But for some reason I played Lifar the Andante from the String Quartet, which I had just finished, and Lifar was overwhelmed by it. 'Fabulous! Pure Mozart!' Just at this moment Ida's secretary came to ask if our appointment could be postponed for two days. Lifar lost his head completely, and in a split second came to a decision: 'Put it on paper! I agree to a hundred thousand.' We exchanged written agreements and said we would meet two days later for lunch at the restaurant where Sergey Pavlovich[1] always lunched, prior to going to see Rouché. This was on the 11th.

On the 12th we moved out to the country, and our lunch took place the next day: Ptashka, I, Lifar and Larionov. Larionov has managed to stay close to Lifar, and it seems he will design the sets while Goncharova does the costumes. After lunch we went to Rouché, for the meeting that Lifar had already set up. Not much happened: we exchanged brief letters of agreement

1 Diaghilev.

according to which he commissioned a ballet from me and undertook to produce *Oranges* in a year's time. The upshot is that the ballet is to be an Opéra commission, and about Lifar's hundred thousand not a word was said. On my way out, I said to Rouché that I considered it a great honour. Not to be outdone in the courtesy stakes, he replied, 'Not at all, the pleasure and the honour is ours.' Lifar rubbed his hands with glee: 'You see, everything is settled now, and you may tell the world you are a composer of the Opéra.'

I went back to Ida and gently declined her proposal, saying that my discussions with the Opéra had begun before she had approached me. This was true, since Lifar had been working on Rouché for a whole month, and Ida knew from Rouché that a proposal to commission a Prokofiev ballet was in the wind. She asked me not to close the door on her finally, but to consider writing a ballet not for next autumn but for spring the following year. We agreed to return to the table later, and in the meantime she would think of a biblical subject.

Our dacha belonged to one Stevens, a relation of the painter.[1] It had plenty of room and was handsomely fitted out, with a garden, flowers, fruit trees, a stream running through it, and even a little swamp. One of our most successful finds.

I got down to the ballet immediately, dredging up a deal of material from my notebooks, and thus being able immediately to come up with an outline of several numbers. Lifar and I touched only very approximately on the subject, but we established the general context as soft and lyrical, and were able to rough out the various numbers in musical and choreographic terms. A firm skeleton thus exists for the ballet, and how we tangle and untangle the details of the plot – that is to say, who loves whom and who leaves whom – is not ultimately so very important.

The 15th to the 18th was a holiday period, and Paichadze came to stay. Our relationship is at last once again on its former friendly footing.

On the 18th I finally signed my agreement with Wittgenstein to compose a left-hand Concerto (although I do intend eventually to revise it for two hands). It is not due until next summer, so I shall have time to do the Lifar ballet first. Not long afterwards a cheque arrived for half of the Concerto fee – minus the 10 per cent.

On the 19th Lifar performed the opening ceremony for a memorial at

---

1 Alfred Stevens (1823–1906), Belgian-born but active in Paris, where he became well known, initially for following the lead of Courbet in genre paintings of the daily life of humble people, but later for equally realist depictions of gorgeously apparelled society ladies in their elegant drawing rooms.

Diaghilev's grave. I sent a telegram, as did Paichadze. Lifar deserves a medal for arranging this.

Svyatoslav, who is now six, will be going to school in the autumn, but no school will accept him unless he has been inoculated against chickenpox, so we were obliged to do this. Christian Science teaches that you should not go against the law, but if you submit to inoculation you should look on it as compliance with a formality and not as a medical procedure.

Towards the end of August I was in correspondence with the Meyerholds, who had first been in the Pyrenees and then in Vichy. But Ptashka had lost their address, so I had not been able to contact them until they eventually returned to Paris. On the 31st August I took the Chevrolet into Paris and brought them back with me to the dacha. I had had the Chevrolet's roof altered so that it can be opened, which is very pleasant in the summer.

Another person who returned to Paris was Gorchakov. He was supposed to have been at sea in the tropics, having signed on as a seaman on a small vessel. But on the eve of sailing one of the ship's officers made an indecent proposal to him and Gorchakov punched him in the face, for which he was arrested. During the night, however, he was freed by his comrades and made haste to return to Paris. There he did not know where to find any sort of a job, but on impulse went into our publishers where without thinking twice about it accepted the only vacancy they had, which was the errand-boy who does the sweeping up, delivers the orchestral material, and so on. Well done him. I asked him, 'Now you're the errand-boy, are you going to continue composing?' Gorchakov: 'I'll try. It would be a shame if a biography such as mine were to go to waste.'

1 September

Meyerhold told me that the 'proletarian musicians', not content with agitating against Le Pas d'acier, have singled me out for official persecution in the Moscow Conservatoire. The wall newspaper there has put up several attacks on me. And what is Pshibyshevsky, who, when I was in Moscow, had gone out of his way to be friendly, doing about it?[1]

We have acquired a small ciné camera, and decided today to shoot our first film. Zinaïda Nikolayevna[2] thought up the scenario: a bandit (Meyerhold) kidnaps Ptashka's child and conceals him in a dungeon (we found a picturesque setting for this in the way down to a well in the garden). A chase ensues. But then Ptashka suddenly wakes up – it had all been just a dream. We spent all day setting up and shooting the film and were totally absorbed in it, our

---

1 See above, p. 882.
2 Zinaïda Raikh, Meyerhold's actress wife.

anxiety to succeed giving rise to all kinds of arguments. When, at the conclusion of the film, the children were being bathed, Meyerhold attached a rope to a branch of the tree and in the foreground, right in front of the camera, swung it backwards and forwards to create the poetic effect of wind in the trees.

2 September

Went into Paris in the car, as both we and the Meyerholds had errands to run there, besides which I wanted to take the film in to be developed. Wittgenstein had come to Paris and I wanted to meet him. He proved to be quite a young man, insignificant-looking but very animated. I persuaded him to come back to the country with us, and he willingly agreed although pulling a rather long face when he realised Meyerhold would be coming with us: he 'cannot bear Bolsheviks'. I explained to him that, first and foremost, Meyerhold was a superlative artist, and his acceptance of the accolade of 'Honoured Soldier of the Red Army' was mainly due to his desire to keep his theatrical activities free from unnecessary interference.[1] In the end we all travelled amicably together, getting to La Naze in time for dinner, during which we were able to admire Wittgenstein's skill in managing with one arm. Astrov, who had been amazed to learn that there existed in the world people able to pay 125,000 francs for a concerto, was disappointed at Wittgenstein's unimpressive appearance. Ptashka took him to task for this: 'What did you expect, that he would appear in evening-dress with medals?'

During the evening I played Wittgenstein two themes which I thought could go into his concerto, but realising that they were not simple melodies, warned him that he should listen to them several times before passing judgement on them. After the first hearing Wittgenstein screeched, 'You could play them to me solidly for two months and they would still not mean anything to me.' After this he demonstrated his technical prowess, or to be precise gave examples of the physical possibilities employed in repertoire that has been written for the left hand; they included versions of Chopin studies,[2] of Mozart and even Puccini. I asked him, 'What prompted you to

---

1   In April 1926, recognising many years of close co-operation with Red Army regiments and in particular the creation and direction of theatrical troupes within the Army, Meyerhold was 'by unanimous decision of the leadership and membership of the Moscow Rifle Regiment' awarded the title of Honoured Red Army Soldier, a distinction confirmed by the USSR Revolutionary Military Council in the person of its Deputy Chairman Iosif Unschlicht. Meyerhold was proud of this honour. The document in question is preserved in the Russian State Military Archive where it recently came to the attention of researchers. In the same Archive is the Order dated 8 February 1938 signed by Major Nemudrov, on headed paper of the People's Defence Commissariat of the USSR, directing that by reason of the Report from the Chief of Staff of the Moscow Military District, Meyerhold's name be removed from the list of Honoured Red Army Soldiers.
2   Presumably the versions for left-hand alone by Leopold Godowsky.

commission a concerto from me when this is the kind of music you like?' He replied that he liked my way of writing for the piano and he hoped that I would be able to come up with technically interesting challenges. I began probing more specifically into his wishes, into the form of the concerto he envisaged, how long it should be, but he had little to say, evidently preferring to leave me a completely free hand. Zinaïda Nikolayevna and Ptashka, who were sitting in the corner and listening to the obvious passion with which he played with one hand, felt wholehearted sympathy for such a man having suffered the loss of the other hand as a result of the war. But I demurred: 'I do not see any extraordinary brilliance in his left hand; it may even be that his misfortune has unexpectedly been transformed into a blessing because as he is he is unique, but with the usual two hands he could well not stand out from the crowd of averagely gifted pianists.'

4 September

We drove the car into the city as we both had matters to attend to. I saw Lifar, who handed me a bulky package containing 30,000 francs, the first tranche of money for my ballet. What an excellent fellow! Then I had to collect our film, which has been developed. As soon as I got it I had a quick look: the images seemed to have come out clearly, although I had been warned that the first attempt is invariably a lemon. Impatiently I hurried back to La Naze, only to discover that Zinaïda Nikolayevna, despite Ptashka asking her not to, had already tried to operate the projector, which she had seen done in Moscow. But when she switched it on there was a shower of sparks and everything stopped. I rushed to examine the projector and realised that it was calibrated for Paris voltage, whereas in La Naze the voltage was double, and the projector could be used only with a transformer, so it had completely burnt out. While I was desperately trying to see what could be done with it, Zinka cautiously pushed the door open and said, 'Can I come in?' 'Not at the moment,' I said. 'No, you can't!' Zinka took offence, went upstairs and did not come down for dinner, and I angrily complained to Meyerhold that one should not meddle with equipment with which one was not familiar, the result being that now the machine was useless and we would not be able to see the film. Ptashka reported that upstairs Zinaïda Nikolayevna was in tears and calling me all kinds of names.

5 September

The departure of the Meyerholds had long been fixed for today, but after yesterday's contretemps it was a very uncomfortable moment. Zinka went out on to the station platform without saying goodbye. Meyerhold came up to me to do so, although Ptashka said that he too would have liked to go without a farewell. However, colliding in the rush with his wife he thought better of it and turned to me. We kissed, I followed them on to the platform and coldly kissed Zinka's hand. As the train pulled out Meyerhold and I waved to each other. After they had gone we were left with an unpleasant taste in the mouth.

7 September

'The sum total of evil belief Jesus designated a lie; and a lie is a negation – nothing. Therefore, thinking about evil is thinking about nothing.'[1]

9 September

Went to Paris and brought back Lifar, Nouvel and Koribut[2] in the car. It was pleasant to breathe the atmosphere of Diaghilev for a while. While we were having tea we filmed some more, but it was rather silly, no one knew what to do so people waved their arms about, took off their hats, and Lifar coltishly embraced Ptashka.

I played some passages from the ballet and the Quartet, which were appreciated. All the guests left in the evening, although I did my best to persuade them to stay the night.

10 September

Worked on the ballet, and in between orchestrated the Suite from *The Prodigal Son* consisting of those parts that had not found their way into the Fourth Symphony. It all came together quite easily, except for the very end, which will have to be composed anew, since it does not work as it is.

13 September

After an exchange of telegrams with the Nabokovs on the subject of was it not time to think about carving the duck, we set off in the Chevrolet to pay them a visit. Our route started through the Forêt de Compiègne and continued to Rheims and Verdun. Here there were many cemeteries of war graves, the remains of trenches and war-blasted buildings that had not been repaired but left as an attractive reminder of the delights of war. The Chevrolet went very well, although on level roads it is not as smooth as the Ballot, and therefore I kept to 60–70 kilometres an hour, occasionally going

---

1 In English (*sic*) in the text; also quoted on p. 849 above.
2 Diaghilev's cousin Pavel Koribut-Kubitovich (Pavka).

up to 80. We stayed the night in Verdun, where everywhere there were postcards for sale, and busts of the commanders, and souvenirs of all kinds: in short the heroic town is trading briskly on its glory. It was horrible to think that all around every square metre of ground had been soaked in blood.

14 September

We passed through the Vosges, but not the most elevated part, smiling, gently rolling countryside. The Chevrolet is tremendous on hills, incomparably better than the Ballot. Towards evening we arrived at the Nabokovs in Kolbsheim, not far from Strasbourg, where their rich friends have a château with a small guest house and garden to one side. It is very nice, Ptashka and I had each a room to ourselves, she downstairs and I upstairs.

Lighting is by candles and my window looked out on fields. Marvellous. Nabokovs were in good spirits and gave us a hearty welcome, although a little too prone to indecent language.

18 September

After four days of extremely pleasant country life at the Nabokovs we returned on the 18th, taking with us Nicky,[1] who needed to go to Paris. The Chevrolet zoomed us through the Vosges Pass, where we stopped for lunch. Then, going off the road to near the edge of a precipice, we decided to do a quick bit of filming to a script we thought up there and then.

The conceptual problem we had to resolve was this: we had three characters, but only two could be in shot at the same time since the third (which we took in turn) had to shoot the sequence. This, then, was our scenario: Ptashka sits dreamily on the edge of the cliff; Nabokov, who is walking by, begins to pester her with unwelcome addresses; Ptashka tears herself away and runs to me to complain; I pick up a stick and approach Nabokov, threatening him with upraised arm; but ... who should he be but my dear old friend, so we sit down together side by side, clap each other on the knee and embrace. As we were filming, faces appeared in the windows of the nearby hostelry observing us with interest, taking us for a real film crew. After this we continued on our way, staying overnight in Joan of Arc's homeland.

19 September

In the morning we found it for some reason practically impossible to get away and wasted God knows how much time. I completely lost my

---

1 Nicolas Nabokov.

temper, and we set off in silence. After we had been on the road half an hour, Nabokov said, 'Sergey Sergeyevich, if my presence is disagreeable to you, I can get out at the next town we come to and take a train to Paris.' 'Nikolay Dmitrievich,' I replied, 'do we need to have recourse to such formalities?'

This broke the ice and the rest of the way to Paris was fine. We dropped Nabokov and I went into the publishers, where I discovered that Meyerhold had bought copies of all my latest compositions. I thought I would see him at his hotel and put a full stop to our stupid quarrel, but he had already left for Moscow. We went on to La Naze in the evening; the children were in good form and the garden wonderful.

20 September

Got down to the ballet and also played the piano, as the concerts begin in October.

21 September

'Unhappiness is a phase of selfishness. An unselfish person cannot be unhappy, because unselfed love brings thought in direct at-one-ment with divine power.'[1]

Went into Paris, and rang up the Paichadzes. They said, 'Come round, we are having a farewell cocktail party for Koussevitzky.' So we went. Relations with Koussevitzky after our contretemps in the spring had not gone beyond telegraphic exchanges. We congratulated them on their twenty-fifth wedding anniversary and they invited us to call on them. The cocktail party was enjoyable, although not without a certain frisson of awkwardness. As we said goodbye, Koussevitzky said he would perform the Fourth Symphony in one of his first concerts.

28 September

Paichadze and the Samoilenkos came to visit. We went in search of mushrooms, but fruitlessly.

We devised an enormous cinema session, a complete drama involving an Indian in a turban (Paichadze), a criminal (Samoilenko) and a detective (me), plus their women. We worked with a will, breaking off at intervals to go hunting for the plentiful fruit in the garden.

---

1 In English (*sic*) in the text.

October

The dacha is in low-lying ground by the river and was beginning to get damp, so on the 9th we decamped to Paris. Before this, the Nabokovs came to stay (Nabokov approved of the Quartet's Andante), and they were followed by Gorchakov. His compositions are not bad; to be precise there are successful moments drowning in a sea of intellectualised contrivances. On the 3rd there came news that we will not get any compensation for the wrecked Ballot, as the expert assessment was that the cause of the accident had been *manque d'entretien*.[1] So that's what you get from your insurance!

On the 12th I travelled to Berlin for a radio concert of my works – not a big programme, an hour's music with an invited audience, not open to the public, so a less significant occasion than it might seem. There was a rather average, scrappy performance of the Overture, Op. 42 (its first performance in Germany); the *Divertimento* (also receiving its German premiere performance) was a little better but not first-class. In the Larghetto the double-bass melody was out of tune, which therefore clashed alternately with the bassoons and the cor anglais. I played the Second Piano Concerto, a little nervously but not badly. Among the invited audience (Maria Viktorovna, Lopatnikoff[2]) was a pianist called Dmitriescu, who had played the work in concerts, and this rather put me off.

I was in Berlin for four days. Went with Maria Viktorovna to a Bruno Walter concert where I was bored to extinction by a Mahler Symphony. 'I cannot stand any more of this, I have to leave,' I said to Maria Viktorovna.

'Out of the question. They sent us the tickets, and we would be seen leaving . . .'

'Well, do you want me to crawl out on hands and knees?'

Mahler is full of noble impulses, couched in derivative and third-rate music. In the interval I caught a glimpse of Meri Bran, who evidently still exists. Weber invited me to tea and to meet Vinogradova, a young female composer. I had in fact met her before, in Paris about eight years ago, when Zakharov had asked me to listen to her compositions.[3] These had proved to be extremely provincial and feebly Glazunovesque, as I pointed out, causing her to burst into tears. Now she said that it had been a hard lesson, but one that had been of benefit. So she thinks, but I did not find much to support this notion. There are indeed flashes of originality in the music, but only to a modest extent. She has been accepted by Koussevitzky and our publishers, I believe mistakenly. The composers in our publishers' catalogue fall into two groups: Koussevitzky's legitimate children, and his illegitimate ones.

---

1 Lack of maintenance.
2 See above, pp. 627, 636, 701–2.
3 Not quite so long ago, in fact, May 1926. See above, p. 319.

Those in the first group are sanctioned by Stravinsky and myself, for example Dukelsky and Nabokov. The others Koussevitzky has invited through personal inspiration, without reference to us. Such individuals generally turn out to be second-rate and wither on the vine after a few years. Examples: Vogel,[1] Fédorov,[2] and now Vinogradova. Personally she is a very nice woman, and her husband, Bik, talked very interestingly about how he had been climbing high in the mountains well above the snow line.

On the 16th, before I left, Maria Viktorovna laid on a big reception in my honour. There were many attractive women present, and emerging talents who regarded me with reverential awe.

The next day I returned to Paris, and the remainder of the month passed without particular incident. Suvchinsky listened to the Quartet and pronounced it 'musique à rêver'.[3]

A gathering took place on the 29th of Lifar, Nouvel, Larionov and Goncharova. I played through the whole ballet, except for the three numbers that are not yet finished. But the libretto has not yet assumed a satisfactory form. It seemed like a good idea, to knock up a ballet taking its choreographic and musical outline as the starting point, but to clothe the skeleton with a convincing libretto is not so simple.

The Nabokovs paid us a visit. His Symphony is to be played in Strasbourg in March – it is having a lot of success everywhere – and I am to play my Third Piano Concerto in the same concert. There is a plan to organise a chamber-music concert the evening before, in which works by both of us would be played. He suggests that Ptashka sing a group of songs by him and a group by me. I like this idea, because a black cat has come between Ptashka and Natasha.[4] Ptashka finds Natasha's demands rather trying.

2 November

Nikita Magalov visited. He and Vladimir are the two serious members of the otherwise feckless Bashkirov tribe. Nikita is gradually developing some promise as a composer, although he does not work hard enough. From Kolya Sidorov, on the other hand, not a word after all the trouble that was

---

1 Wladimir Vogel (1896–1964), Moscow-born Swiss composer of German extraction. He had studied first with Scriabin in Moscow and later with Busoni in Berlin. Drawn to Expressionism, he was, along with composers such as Max Butting, Hanns Eisler, Stefan Wolpe, Kurt Weill, George Antheil and the critic H. H. Stuckenschmidt, a member of the radical left-wing group of Weimar Republic artists the November Group.
2 Vladimir Fédorov. See above, p. 636.
3 'Music of which one can only dream.'
4 Nabokova, Nikolay Nabokov's wife.

taken on his behalf, to get him into the school in Chambéry and safely out of sight. Typical.

5 November

To the Opéra, to see Beethoven's *Prometheus*, the production that secured Lifar's position in the theatre. In the box were the two of us, the two Picassos and Nouvel. Kokhno forced his way in during the interval. Ptashka ignored him and so, apparently did I by turning round just as he was on the point of greeting me. However, he talked for quite a long time to Nouvel and Picasso. I sulked.

I cannot honestly say that Lifar's production is particularly good. I love the Overture to this ballet, especially the principal theme on the strings. As the work progresses, however, the music deteriorates even though there is a glimpse of the tune Beethoven takes into his Third Symphony. An important precedent to quote in anticipation of attacks on my Third and Fourth Symphonies.

7 November

There is a big reception at the Embassy, and I have been invited. I am hesitating whether to accept or decline. On the one hand it is important to maintain good relations in view of my visit to Russia; on the other there is widespread disquiet at the moment over the Kutepov affair and also various persecutions that are going on inside Russia. I decide not to go, but to send regrets from Liège, since if I do attend all the newspapers will write about it and snigger revoltingly.

A long letter from Dukelsky, who has come back to life after silence for half a year. It was good to hear from him, even though he is still paddling about with his musicals.

8 November

'Are we still clamorous for success built upon a material basis? Are we conspiring to displace another and expecting to benefit thereby? Are we envious of someone else's position, prestige, power? None of these false snares of mortal desire will get us into the kingdom. Each idea of mind is already in his right place, and cannot displace, misplace or replace another.'[1]

This is an important truth to know, when thoughts assail me that people are not sufficiently interested in my music, and I question why it is that Stravinsky's music interests them more.

---

1 In English (*sic*) in the text.

In the evening Lifar, Nouvel, Goncharova, Larionov. Played much of the ballet music, discussed it, and had dinner.

9 November

A Poulet concert, including the premiere of Tansman's Concerto for Two Pianos. Well, they do say every stitch can help to cover a naked man, but these stitches are so familiar they look pretty threadbare. Post-concert tea at Schmitz's, where was also Podolsky, a manager working in the Far East with whom I had a stimulating conversation about the possibility of my touring there in two years' time. He is shortly going to China, Australia and Java, will make enquiries there, and we will continue our discussions in the spring. Afterwards I realised how very much I want to go: how alluring a prospect it is to go skimming over the surface of the globe!

10 November

To old Mme Meindorf's,[1] where I met a Dutchman recently back from Russia, where he had come across Shurik. Also present was Bada,[2] whom I had last seen eighteen years ago, and then only rarely. He had forgotten that we never progressed to the intimate form of address and attempted to 'tutoyer' me. I affected not to hear and responded in the second-person plural, and that is where we remained.

The Dutchman had been living in Russia before the Revolution and had amassed a valuable collection of pictures, as a result of which he was reluctant to leave the country when the Bolsheviks took power. Staying there did him no good as they confiscated the collection anyhow, but he was permitted to live somewhere in the country working as a peasant (he speaks reasonably good Russian). When his relations abroad sent him $200, however, he was arrested and sent to the Butyrka prison.[3] It was the time when all the kulaks were being arrested and the gaols were full to bursting: for two days he was forced to stand up as every cell was packed shoulder to shoulder with prisoners. Someone then advised him to try to get work in the prison workshops,

---

1 The mother of Nadya (née Meindorf), wife of Prokofiev's gaoled cousin Alexander (Shurik) Rayevsky.
2 Nadya's brother.
3 The notoriously brutal Butyrka prison was the main Moscow transit gaol for prisoners awaiting transfer to the Gulag. It was on one of the many occasions when she was waiting outside the Butyrka in an attempt to deliver a food parcel to her imprisoned son, Lev Gumilyov (who eventually died in the Gulag in 1953) that Anna Akhmatova was asked by another woman in the despairing queue 'if she could describe this. And I said: "I can."' The result was *Requiem*, the 'tortured mouth through which one hundred million voices shout'.

as there was more space there, and he found a place in the cobbler's shop. His neighbour on the bench there, learning that he was Dutch, said, 'I've been to Amsterdam myself.' Knowing that it was safer not to get drawn into conversation, the Dutchman stayed silent. His neighbour continued, 'Before the war I worked in the Ministry of Foreign Affairs and one of my jobs was to take discharged Letters of Credit back to Amsterdam banks.' The Dutchman did not respond to this either. But afterwards they did start talking, when the neighbour offered him a clean pair of long johns, which in the indescribably filthy surroundings appeared to the Dutchman like a gift from heaven. This neighbour was none other than Shurik Rayevsky, and they became friends. His hair had turned grey and his body was bent, but he was keeping his spirits up and surviving his captivity. Some months later the Dutchman was released and left the country – how this was achieved, he did not reveal; no doubt his foreign relatives paid a handsome ransom. He could not believe it when he finally crossed the border out of Russia. There he had lost every penny he possessed, but in the meantime his family had become wealthy, they had clubbed together and were now paying him an allowance. He is content with his good fortune and enjoying the chance to relax. His story produced a profound impression on me.

At home I found Hammond, Stokowski's friend. He leaves for America tomorrow and had with him the piano score of *Le Pas d'acier*. He asked me to explain every necessary detail of the plot, to serve as material for a projected American production.

12 November

Ptashka and I went to the cinema, where the accompaniment to one of Chaplin's films was the March from *Oranges*.

13 November

Left for Liège, where I am to perform the Second Piano Concerto, and then go on to Warsaw.

14 November

Rehearsed with a somewhat provincial conductor and orchestra. In the intervals proof-read the orchestral parts of the *Sinfonietta*, which is going to be played in Warsaw. But our dear publishers have perpetrated such abominable, hastily produced parts that one's hair stands on end.

Brichants in Liège; I spent the evening with them.

15 November

The concert went well and was a success, without any occurrences of note.

I feel I am almost suffocated by the parts I am having to proof, but the very idea of playing from them uncorrected is unthinkable.

16 November

Left for Berlin.

17 November

Arrived early in the morning and immediately got down to more correcting of the *Sinfonietta* proofs.

Lunched with the Borovskys, who were in a sour mood. In the evening, went to a Bruno Walter concert, just as I had done on my last visit. There has for several years been a mutual grumble between me and Bruno Walter, on account of his failure to produce *Fiery Angel* as he had promised to do (although he regarded that it was I who had let him down by not providing the material quickly enough). Not long ago someone told me he was interested in Christian Science, and I therefore decided to go backstage to see him afterwards and shake hands. 'Only don't start criticising Mahler,' I was advised – he had again programmed Mahler. Walter was affable and we talked about Musorgsky's *Pictures from an Exhibition* in the Ravel orchestration, which he had also performed today.

Saw Coates at the concert, good-humoured and affectionate as ever. He and I and the Borovskys went to have supper at an enormous café with a floor-show. Coates flirted with Maria Viktorovna and told her suggestive stories. An inebriated female customer suddenly appeared on the stage and began dancing, tripped over and fell flat on her face. She was escorted from the premises.

18 November

Travelled on from Berlin to Warsaw, sitting in the compartment until late at night proofing the *Sinfonietta* orchestra parts. My companion, a German engineer, is returning to Russia where he was working for a year before taking a holiday. He told me that despite the prevailing chaos and disorder, some wonderful factories are being built. I asked him what was his view of the trials now taking place of Russian engineers.[1] His answer was that he could not say whether the engineers were guilty or not, quite possibly not, but one thing he did know, and that was that all too often the government was encountering, if not passive resistance, at least indifference to Soviet planning among the engineering fraternity.

19 November

Early morning in Warsaw: more proof-reading. Fitelberg called for me on his way and we went together to the rehearsal – still with not all the parts ready. The programme was wholly devoted to my works: the *Sinfonietta*, the Second Piano Concerto, and *Chout*. Bravo Warsaw: the second all-Prokofiev concert in a single year, 1930!

Szymanowski appeared, charming as ever. His health is not good, therefore he lives in the country. The University of Krakow has made him an Honorary Doctor.

After the rehearsal Fitelberg treated me to *krupnik*.[2] This extremely strong drink made from honey is a Polish speciality, and very heady indeed. One drinks it hot, and it produces a real kick in the nose. I liked it very much.

20 November

Rehearsals continued. Fitelberg likes the *Sinfonietta*. I am enjoying my time in Warsaw. We had lunch with some old friends of Fitelberg. We looked in at the Conservatoire, but the building is unimpressive.

---

1 The 'Prompartia Trials', or 'Industrial Party Trials' held in November and December 1930 constituted one of the earliest of the Moscow show trials, a precursor of the elaborately scripted and choreographed Great Terror trials of 1936, 1937 and 1938 (the Chief Prosecutor in the Prompartia Trials was Vyshinsky, prefiguring the starring role he was to have in the later productions). Eight senior engineers and economists responsible for the great engineering projects of the late 1920s and early 1930s were accused of having secretly conspired with the Western Powers, especially France (President Poincaré was forced to publish a denial, triumphantly reproduced in *Pravda* as proof of the plot) to wreck the industrialisation ambitions of the Soviet Union. Confessions were insisted on and obtained through torture, but although the defendants were sentenced to be executed, the sentences were commuted to long terms of imprisonment, in contrast to later victims who were shot within twenty-four hours of being sentenced. Some of the Prompartia 'ringleaders', particularly the thermal engineer Leonid Ramzin, who in 1943 was to receive a Stalin Prize for the invention of the flow-through boiler, were eventually amnestied and allowed to continue working. All were officially rehabilitated in the Khrushchev era.
2 A kind of sweet liqueur made of grain spirit, clover honey and a variety of herbs to add spice.

21 November

Fitelberg had not had enough sleep last night: yesterday when we went for a walk in Paderewsky Park, his bulldog ran on to the ice of the frozen lake, and fell in. Although we turned back and made for home straight away, and wrapped the dog in a blanket, she was coughing all night and the anxiety she caused in the family was almost enough to cancel the concert.

Even so, the concert went splendidly: just as last year, it was a bona fide great success, the *Sinfonietta*, however, drawing less applause than the other works. Afterwards there was a brief appearance from Frieda Hansen;[1] she has gone back to her husband and is living somewhere near Warsaw. Boris[2] writes to her occasionally from Shanghai. After this we went to supper with Tatyana Yakovleva, the same for whom Mayakovsky had fallen so heavily at the Samoilenkos' party.[3] She is married now to a French vicomte who is a Secretary at the French Embassy in Warsaw, and enthusiastically producing children. Prone to gaffes, she is gradually being schooled in the niceties of life in diplomatic circles, and on the whole is much loved. She perpetrated one such gaffe this evening, having originally intended to invite all of our group, but then having left some out. This upset me and I went in a bad temper, but found myself in a truly cultured and musical international environment, and generally much enjoyed myself for the rest of the evening.

22 November

At noon I was on my way once more, in a superb carriage of the Nord Express. Next to me was the French Ambassador, with whom Tatyana tried hard to get me acquainted. In the next compartment was Chamiec,[4] the Chairman of Polish Radio, with whom I had a long talk.

Arrived in Berlin in the evening, and there on the platform was Mar-Vik, and behind her Weber. The train did not wait long, and as we were pulling out again, de Chamiec slyly enquired who was the attractive woman with whom I was strolling arm in arm up and down the platform.

---

1 Elfrieda Hansen, pianist sister of the violinist Cecilia Hansen. She and Prokofiev had been friends when fellow students at the St Petersburg Conservatoire. See *Diaries*, vol. 1 *passim*.
2 Zakharov, Cecilia Hansen's estranged husband.
3 See above, p. 743.
4 Zygmunt Chamiec (1882–1948) had developed his knowledge of radio as an army officer during the First World War. After the war he, like many of his former colleagues, established a private broadcasting company and in 1925 his station, Polskie Radio S.A., was awarded the government's charter to organise a national radio network and began broadcasting in April 1926. Chamiec remained Director of Polish Radio until 1935.

23 November

By lunchtime I was in Paris for a tender reunion with Ptashka. I was very tired, but we went to an afternoon concert of the OSP, in which Borovsky, who had in the meantime got to Paris himself, was playing Weber's *Konzertstück*.

That evening Ptashka related to me her experiences when trying to buy a wardrobe of which we were in need. The dealer, who had been recommended by the chess-player Bernstein,[1] suggested one second-hand, and Ptashka went to see it in the owner's apartment but in the end they could not agree on the price. As she was leaving, Ptashka caught sight of a portrait on the table that seemed to her familiar, and asked who was the subject. 'That is my father-in-law, Krivoshein,' replied the proprietress, not without a touch of pride. 'Why do you ask?'[2] Ptashka remembered where she had seen a similar picture: at the Samoilenkos. 'Oh, I must have just seen one like it somewhere,' she said hastily.

I explained that Krivosheina was Nina Meshcherskaya. I was no less stunned: for heaven's sake, how many wardrobes must there be in Paris? And of all places to happen on one belonging to Nina Mescherskaya! Ptashka had long been interested in her, and learning from Suvchinsky that she was serving in a Russian restaurant, had secretly been hoping to come across her in one or other such establishment. I wanted to know some details. Ptashka thought she was very nice, her coiffure slightly old-fashioned, and wearing no make-up – an unheard-of state of affairs in Paris. The apartment had two rooms and was far from lavish but immaculately tidy, and in a very good street albeit in a poor building, bearing the same number, 22, as the old Meshcherskaya apartment in St Petersburg. The most interesting aspect of it was that while Nina would naturally have known from the dealer who Ptashka was, Ptashka had no notion of Nina's identity. The wardrobe, as well as being too expensive, was narrow, and Ptashka said, 'My husband has rather broad shoulders, and I don't think there would be enough room for his suits to hang in it. But', she added naively, 'I will discuss it with him.' A fantastic encounter!

24 November

When I woke up in the morning and went into the bathroom to shave, I suddenly felt ill and collapsed face downwards into a chair. When I recovered consciousness I got up, but the next thing I knew I was lying on the floor in a different position in the same room. Coming to once more, I decided to

---

1 Osip Bernstein (1882–1962), chess master. Prokofiev had met him at the St Petersburg International Chess Tournament in 1914. See *Diaries*, vol. 1, pp. 640–57 *passim*.
2 See above, pp. 639 n. 1, 714.

get as far as the armchair in the sitting room, but fell again halfway there and regained consciousness for the third time when Elsa gave me a glass of water to drink. I then managed as far as the chair before fainting a fourth time. Elsa went to rouse Ptashka. I felt quite happy in the chair and tried to reassure Ptashka, who had rushed in still half asleep and in a state of some excitement. I spent most of the remainder of the day lying down and working intensively on my ailment. But it produced no improvement: I had a high temperature and was prey to all manner of disagreeable sensations. I felt as though I had succeeded in doing some preliminary work, but lacked sufficient strength to pursue it. I needed the help of a practitioner. Ptashka telephoned Miss Colvy, who came over, the first time she had visited us. We conversed almost gaily, and she worked. At night I was plagued incessantly by the music I had heard in yesterday's concert, to such an extent I felt I was suffocating and wanted to cry out. The music assumed geometric forms, turning into something like waves of clay that surged round and round inside my head.

Salvation from them was achieved by recalling Christian Science hymns. Hitherto I had not paid them any attention, but now an extraordinary thing happened: little by little the clayey billows were replaced by softer, calmer music, and I slept.

25 November

Considerably better. I feel as though the course of a serious illness has been arrested. But I am very weak and stayed in bed all day: the root of the disease has been cut out, but I need to recover my strength.

26 November

Felt not bad, but still did not get up. I sorted out correspondence, which has accumulated during my trip to Warsaw.

27 November

Got up. Dictated letters to Astrov in reply. Ptashka, however, is now not well herself. Thank God our concert in Brussels has been postponed from the 4th to the 11th December.

28 November

A letter from Olga Naumova, Koussevitzky's niece and secretary. The Fourth Symphony was played in Boston on the 14th November. After the coolness which had grown up between us I really did not know whether or not in the end he would perform it, or whether he would pay the fee for the commission – $1,000, but it was only a verbal agreement. The critics were muted, and evidently the public reaction was no more than average. As with the *Divertimento* and the *Sinfonietta* I had been counting on an immediate success but, surprising as it may be, none of my latest works has scored straight away. Why is this?

Ptashka and I had a few laughs remembering the story of the wardrobe, but as time went on forgot that we had ever contemplated buying it.

1–5 December

At the beginning of the month I was still feeling in less than perfect health, and now Astrov took to his bed.

I made a version for piano two hands of the *Classical* Symphony, something I should have done a long time ago but was afraid too much would be lost in a transcription for piano. In fact such is the case in only a few passages: the finale, for instance, comes across as slightly trivial.

I finished off the Quartet. I had made such detailed sketches in the summer that the final touches were quite easy.

6 December

I attended a meeting of a sub-committee assembled to choose works for the international festival to be held this summer in Oxford.[1] Each country has its own committee, but since so many foreign composers live in France a special sub-committee was set up for them, and the members appointed to serve on it were myself, Nin,[2] Harsányi,[3] Honegger and Sasha Tcherepnin. The two last-named were away, and so there gathered in Nin's apartment he, I and Harsányi, an insignificant Hungarian composer. I proposed Dukelsky's Second Symphony and struck out something by Tansman. From my compositions Harsányi proposed the Quintet. Committee members are allowed to

---

1 The International Society for Contemporary Music annual festivals of new music, nowadays known as World New Music Days, are held each year in a different location. The 1931 festival took place in Oxford between 21 and 28 July, the first time the festival had been held in Great Britain and designed in part to showcase the recently formed BBC Symphony Orchestra and its conductor Adrian Boult. Two concerts of British music were followed by six more including twenty-nine recently composed works from thirteen different countries.
2 See above, pp. 668–9.
3 Tibor Harsányi (1898–1954), Hungarian pianist and composer who had studied with Kodály at the Budapest Conservatoire. Moving to Paris in 1923, he became involved with the group of composers in L'École de Paris, which included émigré composers such as Tansman, Martinů, Alexander Tcherepnin and Marcel Mihalovici.

propose their own compositions, since if membership were to preclude consideration of one's own work, nobody would agree to serve.

10 December

Ptashka and I left for Brussels.

11 December

Since the main hall was occupied by an orchestral rehearsal, we rehearsed in the adjacent small hall. What was happening in the main hall was Ansermet's first reading of Stravinsky's *Symphony of Psalms*, in preparation for what was to be the work's premiere. Today was the first rehearsal at which orchestra and chorus were brought together.

While Ptashka was doing her vocal exercises I went to listen to the Symphony and found myself quite alone in the auditorium. In this way I became the first person to hear the work, even before Stravinsky, who came only later that evening, to appear unexpectedly in the Artists' Room in the interval of our concert. He was in his friendliest mood and complimented Ptashka: 'How pretty you are looking! Confess, now – you're wearing make-up?' His presence, however, did throw Ptashka off-balance. She was in any case not in her best form, and knowing that Stravinsky was in the audience made her sing even worse. I also was put off by the trivial character of the second half of the programme, which happened to consist of my most popular *morceaux*. But I have performed so often in Brussels it is a problem now to put a programme together.

12 December

Went again to the Stravinsky rehearsal and sat next to him, looking at the score. The falling sequence of chords at the beginning of the opening movement sound splendidly; also good are the trombones accompanying the chorus deep down and *staccato*, although the effect is hardly one of striving to fix one's gaze on God – it is as though a sort of infernal muffled roaring creeps all the time into the accompaniment to the singing of the psalms. The fugue becomes drowned in a sea of intertwining voices and dissolves into haziness. The middle section of the finale is very strange, but the concluding bars are very fine, as is the end of the first movement.

We had lunch together after the rehearsal. Stravinsky never ceases to abuse Jews, the chief object of his ire being Milhaud. Einstein is 'a veritable synagogue yid'. He praised my piano-playing. Rachmaninoff is a pianist of the older generation.

The conversation turned to Chopin. I voiced my opinion that there should be a ban on performing his music for fifty years, as it is impossible today to listen to the sentimentality of his emotions. We should wait until they have entirely cooled, and then, in half a century's time, Chopin will be perceived as Mozart is today. Stravinsky readily agreed.

After this Ptashka and I went back to Paris. Stravinsky has just completed a big tour of Germany, which he said had afforded him 'great satisfaction'.

13 December

Once back from Brussels, my preoccupations and concerns were pre-concert ones for the concert of my works due to take place on the 18th, including the first performance of the Fourth Symphony. I checked carefully all the orchestra parts of the Symphony and polished up the Second Piano Concerto, which in Paris must be played impeccably. In parallel with this I practised the programme for Antwerp, where I go the day after the Paris concert. In between I continued with the piano transcription of the *Classical* Symphony.

14 December

Completed the Quartet.

15 December

First rehearsal for the concert of my music. Monteux began with the Overture, Op. 42, with which he has taken great pains. The orchestra reads well, and the Overture got quickly onto its feet, better than in Berlin. But I, of course, am mainly interested in the Symphony. It seems to sound good, but all will become clear in the finale. In the Andante the contra-bassoon and the tuba sounded as they are meant to, and I do not understand why the Boston papers were so taken aback. Probably Koussevitzky brought them out clumsily.

18 December

The fourth rehearsal. Nabokov and Suvchinsky came to listen and were enraptured by the Fourth Symphony, especially the second movement and the second subject of the first. Monteux has coached his players in the score with great care, but even with four rehearsals did not manage to nail down the fourth movement.

At the evening concert the enormous Salle Pleyel was less than half full, perhaps not more than a third. At the last moment Monteux wanted to change the order of the programme, putting the Second Piano Concerto before the Symphony. I was happy to agree, since once I had despatched the Concerto I would be in a calmer state to devote my full attention to the Symphony. However, later people told me that the pianistic success of the Concerto overwhelmed the Symphony, to which the reaction was no more than polite. Despite this Monteux brought me out to take a bow. I am generally inclining, nevertheless, to the view that the Symphony is destined to be only moderately successful. Or at least that is what I think now, even if before the performance I had been expecting more of an instant impact.

Quite a lot of people came to the Artists' Room afterwards. My heart lifted when some people designated the Symphony my best work, but only a handful did so. Then we went to the Chalons. Chalon had originally suggested a modest glass of wine but when the party grew to around thirty people a more lavish entertainment was organised with champagne, and we split the cost between us.

19 December

Travelled from Paris to Antwerp for my concert that same evening, a piano recital at the invitation of the Nouveaux Concerts organisation. Afterwards there was a splendid supper at Fester's house, where I met again some old acquaintances from my previous visit in 1923.[1] I was a little disgruntled that none of my music had been performed in Antwerp since 1923, but this was not in fact the case: in the last two or three seasons at least one orchestral piece had been programmed. Last year it had been *Three Oranges*, and this year the *Classical* Symphony.

20 December

Back to Paris – and straight to an all-Stravinsky concert, one of a new series by Siohan[2] in a new, small hall, which was full.

The programme contained no new works. Siohan conducted *Pulcinella* quite badly and then Stravinsky himself was the soloist in his First Concerto, which I have ultimately come to the conclusion I do not like. But Stravinsky does play it with great fire.

---

1 Georges Fester, nephew of the founder, was one of the co-owners of Mund & Fester, a prominent marine-insurance company based in Hamburg but with a large branch office in Antwerp. See *Diaries*, vol. 2, pp. 709–10 for an account of Prokofiev's enjoyable 1923 visit to Antwerp, which had included a revelatory visit to the Plantin House Museum, a seminal inspiration for the setting of *The Fiery Angel*.
2 Robert Siohan (1894–1985), composer and conductor. The Concerts Siohan premiered a number of works by French composers.

Afterwards there were wine and canapés at Sudeikina's. Present were Lifar, Suvchinsky, Larionov, Arthur Rubinstein, Lourié, Paichadze and others. Stravinsky was in the best of spirits, telling a string of risqué and Jewish jokes.

21 December

Lunch at Arthur Rubinstein's. Besides Ptashka and me, Stravinsky was there with Sudeikina, and a beautiful Chilean woman.[1] Rubinstein has rented a little house with a garden at the top of Montmartre, a delightful place. Lunch was delicious and served on silver plates. Rubinstein declared that he was proud to receive us in his house. We had to rush away before the end, however, to go to a lecture on Christian Science. This proved much less interesting than the last one I had heard, or perhaps we were to blame for not having given ourselves enough time to switch into such a different environment from the Rubinstein lunch. We then went home to meet Lifar, Larionov and Nouvel, to whom I played through the ballet, which met with great approval. We made accurate timings of several individual numbers, even though the ballet's scenario has not yet been worked out.

22 December

Sent a mountain of Christmas cards, most of them to America to people who had entertained us and otherwise showed courtesy to us during our recent stay there.

23 December

An unexpected telephone call from Capablanca, who had got our number from someone or other. I invited him to dinner, and afterwards we went to the English Chess Circle, where he was holding a simultaneous session. I also was given a board, but the lustre of my former glory days in simultaneous

---

1 'My Chilean friend, a relation of Juanita, wanted to visit Andalusia. My tales about the feria at Seville and about Granada excited her imagination. "But I will not go if you are not my guide ..." All I remember of this little tour is the night in Seville when I was lucky enough, thanks to my friend Juan Lafita, to gather the best flamenco singers and guitarists to play for us. My lovely Chilean lady showed a great dislike for this sort of entertainment; she made me leave in a hurry and later, out in the street, burst into a violent attack on these players. "How can you stand this dreadful yelling, Arthur, you, such a refined musician! I call them barbarians and nothing else." A great part of my friendship for this lady was considerably weakened that night. I was happy when I had delivered her safely back to her home in Paris.' A. Rubinstein, *My Many Years*, Jonathan Cape, London, 1980, p. 295.

matches has irretrievably dimmed: I had to concede the whole match in order to avoid defeat. All the other boards lost as well, so the result was: of eighteen matches Capablanca won eighteen. He and I then strolled along the Champs-Elysées, chatting amicably about this and that. About Alyokhin, naturally, not a word. A cold wind was blowing, and I said I would like to go home. Capablanca was amused at the idea that he, a native of the tropics, was less fearful of the cold than I.

24 December

We had a Christmas tree for the children, and presents: Mama for little brother, Svyatoslav for Elsa, Elsa for Astrov – in short, everyone for everyone else and that is fine except I hate having to think up what to give people.

25 December

Nothing particular.

26 December

Left for Ghent early in the morning and arrived at two, just in time to go straight to the rehearsal. Defauw, the conductor,[1] turned out to be an admirer of mine and had performed the *Scythian Suite* in Milan, Rome and Brussels. I passed a peaceful evening, strolling round a quiet Ghent, and at ten o'clock went to bed to sleep the sleep of the dead. Only one incident ruffled the otherwise tranquil surface: in a side street I happened on a bar from which came sounds of music and laughter, while bright lights could be seen behind the closed shutters. At one of the windows, craning their necks to see, stood two old women peering through a chink in the shutters. Were they recalling their youth? Or searching for their errant sons?

27 December

Rehearsal in the morning, concert in the evening. The hall was full and all three of my pieces (the Second Piano Concerto, the Suite from *Oranges* and the *Classical* Symphony) were greeted with ringing applause. Sleepy Ghent, indeed! After the concert Defauw, the orchestra management and I sat in a restaurant and drank champagne.

---

1 Désiré Defauw (1885–1960), violinist and conductor. He was later to become the first conductor of the Orchestre National de Belgique, and emigrated to North America in 1940, where he held the music directorships of the Montreal Symphony and the Chicago Symphony Orchestras.

28 December

Went back to Paris and carried on with the transcribing of the *Classical Symphony*.

29 December

A Christmas party, for the children and for the grown-ups. Among the latter were old Mme Meindorf, whom I collected and returned in the car. She is a wonderful old lady, bright as a button, and found something to talk about to everyone. I showed the films we had made in the summer, which were a greater success than the commercial ones we had rented for the occasion.

30 December

Put together a fat package of material for Podolsky, just in case the Pacific tour should materialise.

31 December

Four married couples celebrated New Year at the Samoilenkos: our hosts, the Paichadzes, the Testenoires and ourselves, all making a contribution. We brought champagne, caviar and pineapple, the Paichadzes a turkey, the Testenoires a pie with trimmings. It was a lovely evening.

1932

Prokofiev wrote nothing in his diary, or at least nothing that has survived, between the 'lovely evening' with friends on New Year's Eve 1930 and the spring day drive into the country on 2 May 1932. The reason is not known. Although the projected third visit to the Soviet Union was prudently postponed sine die *because of the depressing reports on the cultural and political situation, coming in oblique but unmistakable language from confidants such as Asafyev, Myaskovsky and Derzhanovsky, and there was no visit to the United States, the eighteen months marked a period full of achievement and incident. Prokofiev and Lina undertook a concert tour in early spring 1931 to Bucharest, Budapest and Vienna. The major commissions already under way – the left-hand Piano Concerto for Paul Wittgenstein, the String Quartet for the Library of Congress in Washington, and the ballet – as yet untitled and unscripted – for Lifar and the Paris Grand Opéra were all completed, although only the Quartet was performed, in Washington by the Brosa Quartet and in Moscow by the Roth Quartet. The two Sonatinas, Op. 54, were composed, in their deceptive simplicity, spareness and understatement a continuation of the direction begun in the* Choses en soi *to which the composer attached such importance. Six new solo piano pieces, Op. 52, were versions of other material: three from* Prodigal Son, *one apiece from the* Five Songs Without Words, *Op. 35, the String Quartet and the Sinfonietta. Prokofiev finally got down to the suite he had been promising himself to make from* The Gambler, *except that it turned out not to be a suite but* Four Portraits and a Denouement. *It received its premiere in Paris at an all-Prokofiev concert in the Concerts Colonne series in March 1932. Once the left-hand Concerto for Wittgenstein was finished it was not long before he followed Koussevitzky's shrewd advice and made a start on a new Concerto (No. 5) for himself to play, revelling in virtuosic octave passages and massive two-handed chords. The only problem was the bidding war that would develop between Furtwängler in Berlin and Koussevitzky in Boston for the world premiere. The family spent a happy summer vacation away from Paris in St Jean de Luz, near Biarritz, and Prokofiev sustained two more car accidents, neither of them fortunately as serious as the one that had seen the end of the line for the aristocratic old lady Ballot.*

2 May

A spring day – I went for a drive in the afternoon to the Forest of Meudon. The rain came on from time to time, but it only made the forest the more aromatic. I sat in the car with the window open and read: (1) Christian Science, (2) Marx's *Das Kapital* in an abridged version in French.

I finished incorporating the subtle details I wanted to add to the Sonatinas[1] and sent them off to be engraved.

We dined with the Chalons, the Samoilenkos also there, and in honour of their oenological erudition rare wines were produced: a German wine from 1875, and similar treasures. Singular, without a doubt, but on the whole they leave me cold.

3 May

Almost finished Op. 55,[2] that is to say the composition, there is still much to be done in realising it. I cannot get the coda right, it will not hang together, it's very difficult. And this is the very part I want to be good.

In the evening we went to Zederbaum's to listen to the Third Symphony on the radio, broadcast from Berlin. About a quarter of it could be heard but for the rest there was too much interference, so the only result was frustration. Not a note of the scherzo came through.

4 May

Horowitz's concert. What an astonishing pianist he is: with Rachmaninoff's decline into dryness he has a good claim to be number one. What fabulous gradations of tenderness, especially when he plays Liszt!

Saw Nabokov; I am somewhat estranged from him. He pressed Ptashka's hand and asked her why I have this attitude to him.

Bridge at our house: Kepin, Alland and Staroselsky, whom Kepin had brought along. We had planned to go on until two, but in the end it was four

---

1   Two Sonatinas, in E minor and G major, Op. 54.
2   The Piano Concerto No. 5 in G, Op. 55.

before we finished, although I desperately wanted to go to bed. I have a chess-player's attitude to bridge, that is to say I am not interested in the way the cards fall, only in the way the game can be developed. Today my attention was concentrated on the endgame: the average player approaches the final cards of a hand as fate or God will determine, whereas the real player can often manipulate the play to a successful outcome.

6 May

Ida Rubinstein, whom I have not seen for almost two years, all of a sudden invited me to come to her house and reinstate discussions about commissioning a ballet. This is pleasant news, seeing that because of the 'world financial crisis' nobody is commissioning anything. But I have cooled towards the notion of a biblical theme I proposed to her two years ago. I now believe a ballet should be exclusively a dance production, emanating exclusively from the music and music, moreover, specifically written for the dance. But Ida still hankers after a biblical subject.

On my way home I was in such a good mood I hardly noticed the crowds of people standing on the streets. When I got home I learned that while I had been talking to Ida someone had assassinated President Doumer. Apparently the person who shot him was a Russian. This is horrible.

7 May

The President, wounded yesterday, has died of his injuries. What a pointless act, to do in the old man. No one knows what prompted the Russian idiot to barge in like this, and now the Russians will suffer for it.[1]

8 May

No, the ballet needs to be light and danceable. A beautiful melody for it has come to me.

---

1 President Paul Doumer was shot and killed at the opening of the Paris Book Fair by a deranged young Russian émigré, Pavel Gorgulov. Gorgulov claimed at his trial that he was in the grip of a mysterious compulsion to kill a president, and there is some evidence that he had planned attempts on the lives of Hindenburg, Lenin and Masaryk, but the plea of insanity failed and he was guillotined on 14 September 1932. The pointless crime had little effect except on the already edgy Russian émigré community in Paris, who understandably feared hostility if not actual reprisals.

11 May

At tea chez Dubost I got to know Afinogenov,[1] the young author of *Fear*, the play which is currently in production in ninety of Soviet Russia's theatres. He has recently come from Moscow, but the fall of the proletarian musicians occurred after his departure.[2] Even so he is in a position to confirm the big changes in musical and literary life that are taking place. Afinogenov was an attractive character, straightforward, with a clear, direct gaze.

12 May

A letter from Demchinsky – after an interval of several years. It was an interesting letter, refined and very 'Demchinsky'. Nevertheless, how Christian Science develops a higher perspective and applies it to everything! And how much that formerly seemed splendid to me now seems redundant in Demchinsky; the solution to everything that before seemed insoluble is now obvious.

Saw Koussevitzky, just in from America, at Steinert's.[3] Our meeting was civilised and friendly. Our relations are now on the footing that I always, I now realise, desired: good without being over-intimate.

Have been turning over in my mind a Fantasy for cello and orchestra. I have some new material with which some old themes I have never used would go admirably.

---

1   Alexander Afinogenov (1904–1941), playwright, had an early play successfully produced by Proletkult and subsequently became a leading figure in RAPP, the aggressively anti-intellectual Russian Association of Proletarian Writers, the literary equivalent of RAPM for musicians. *Fear* (*Strakh*), however, the play he wrote in 1931 about an ageing scientist unable to accommodate himself to the changed world he now lives in, is far more interesting in its exploration of philosophical and psychological problems in a Soviet society beginning to come to terms with Stalin's mercilessly authoritarian rule. For the old scientist, political solutions cannot provide an answer because mankind is driven by fear and self-interest: 'There are 200 million people in Russia, and all of them are frightened.' When both RAPP and RAPM fell victim to the in-fighting that resulted in the creation of the Unions of Writers and Composers, Afinogenov became a powerful figure in the Writers' Union, only to fall from grace in the Great Purges, accused of Trotskyism along with most of his former radical colleagues, but miraculously avoided arrest and execution. Given a top post in the Soviet Information Bureau after the Nazi invasion, he was killed not long afterwards by a Luftwaffe bomb that hit the Central Committee building in Moscow.
2   The Decree on the Reformation of Literary and Artistic Organisations was not in fact promulgated until 23 April 1932, but rumblings of growing official disfavour had been in evidence since the autumn of the previous year, with a serious of articles in the newspaper *Govorit Moskva* (*Moscow Speaks*). RAPM responded with a vigorously defended Letter to the Editor on 10 September, but the cracks were appearing and the damage had been done. Prokofiev already had a rough, if obliquely expressed, idea from Myaskovsky's letters of what was going on.
3   A bridge-playing acquaintance.

17 May

First rehearsal with orchestra of *The Duckling* – a new version for small orchestra.[1] It sounds nice, if a little harsh. The bass trombone's low B, however, which I had been worried about, came out very well. But the main thing was that it was Ptashka's first try-out with orchestra. She was nervous, but did make all her entries on cue.

Rieti and Mme Casa Fuerte,[2] both of whom thus demonstrated their affection for Ptashka, came to listen.

18 May

Drove out of town with Graham. He lives in such a dreary suburb that I have long cherished a desire to take him and his children out into the green of the country in the spring weather. Only he and his three-year-old were able to come on this occasion, and I took Svyatoslav along as well. My choice fell on the Forest of Chantilly, which was marvellous.

Graham talked long and volubly about Christian Science. Topics touched on included Ptashka and her anxieties, which have such an effect on her performances. Graham told of a singer who had lost his voice and went to church and to consult a practitioner in an effort to confront the phenomenon. He did not realise that the net result of so doing was to acknowledge the reality of evil and to set up for himself an idol of which he was afraid. Art is not a personal matter: art is a manifestation of God. Generally speaking it is extremely important to understand that man is created as an individual but not a distinct personality, and to be able to distinguish between the two. To rid oneself of the 'person', with all his baggage of cares, does not necessarily entail losing one's individuality; on the contrary it cleanses one and enables one better to reflect God.

I was astonished to learn that Graham sleeps no more than four hours a night; he needs no more than that. He considers that the mind does not tire, and does not require sleep for inspiration.

I also discussed with Graham a subject for Ida's ballet, explaining that whereas I no longer felt drawn to the notion of a biblical theme her own

---

1   Prokofiev made two orchestral versions of the Hans Andersen fairy-tale 'The Ugly Duckling' based on a text by his first love Nina Meshcherskaya, the 1914 original having been scored for voice and piano. In 1925 he had made a string orchestra version for Nina Koshetz; this one, made for Lina, better known and generally accounted more successful, added wind instruments to the strings for extra pungency.

2   Yvonne Giraud, Marquise de Casa Fuerte, was a violinist and Parisian socialite who gathered around herself a devoted coterie of musicians including Rieti, Sauguet, the members of Les Six especially Poulenc, and inaugurated a concert series for new music called Sérénade, also patronised by Mme de Noailles. See below, p. 1002.

enthusiasm for it had increased. Furthermore, it was important for me not to start on a project that might provoke a quarrel with Russia. He said, 'Why not focus on the building of the Temple of Solomon? For Russia that would be appropriate, as it could be seen as the construction of an idea.'

19 May

This was Ptashka's day. It began with the general rehearsal, at which she sang *Duckling*, the voice sounding not bad although it could have been better. They also played Markevich's *Partita* for piano and orchestra and Rieti's *Sinfonietta*. The *Partita* conveyed an impression of energy but at the same time it is strange that this nineteen-year-old youth is showing no signs of evolving. I heard the same Hindemithery and Beckmesseristics as I had two years ago. Rieti's *Sinfonietta* was pleasant enough, although not all the melodies were free of triteness and were too often reminiscent of other music.

The concert took place in the evening. Ptashka was very nervous and as a result lost her voice. A lot of people we knew were in the hall: there were many interesting people in the audience and also a high proportion of snobs. To the latter I have an aversion: they are often cultivated and possess both taste and understanding, but they always try to make a fashion out of art, as if it were couture. They decree, for example, that today Monsieur x is the outstanding talent, so Monsieur x is launched with a fanfare, ascends to the heights, and two years later everyone has forgotten about him because he is no longer fashionable. Diaghilev sometimes took account of the snobs. But what is truly remarkable is that whenever he yielded to snobbish pressure what he produced soon faded, whereas what he produced for the sake of art still lives.

On stage Ptashka looked wonderful, especially at the end when she was presented with a bouquet of white lilies to go with her white gown. At the beginning her voice lacked projection and nerves even caused the occasional touch of hoarseness, but by the second half the voice had settled down and she got a very good response. Even so, she could have done better. Afterwards, through the good offices of Poulenc and Rieti, we were invited to the Noailles.[1] This is a snob citadel of the highest aspirations, but one with a

---

1   Marie-Laure, Vicomtesse de Noailles (1902–1970) was, with her husband the homosexual Vicomte de Noailles, one of the wealthiest and most adventurous (in both her aesthetic predilections and her private life) of the great Paris patronesses of the arts before the Second World War. Among the objects of her enlightened bounty were the films of Buñuel, Dalí, Man Ray and Cocteau, as well as the compositions of Poulenc and Rieti. Among her lovers were, when young, Cocteau and Markevich, and later the Surrealist painter Oscar Dominguez. The environment in which this après-concert party will have taken place was the minimalist interior created by the designer Jean-Michel Frank (another beneficiary of the Vicomtesse's unlimited purse) of the Noailles' *hôtel particulier* at No. 11, Place des États-Unis, which today houses the Galerie-Musée Baccarat of the crystal and glassware manufacturers.

serious cultivation of music. I did not want to go at all, but everyone else was going so we went along as well.

The Nabokovs, apparently, had spent the whole time during the performance of *The Duckling* tittering into their sleeves, and when at the Noailles they made a bee-line for Ptashka she snubbed them. The Noailles have a magnificent house, and gave us supper, but it was not long before all I wanted was to go home and sleep.

20 May

In the morning, as I was lighting the water heater in order to shave, there was an explosion which singed my hair, eyebrows and eyelashes. My eyes could have been in danger too, but I managed to close them in time. For half the day I had to lie down with my eyes closed, as the eyelids had been slightly burned and were swollen. I had a headache too, but was better by the evening.

21 May

I am seized with the idea of cutting down on my hours of sleep. The moment one realises that sleep is not necessary for true repose, it becomes necessary to reduce it.

Lunched with Afinogenov and then drove out of town with him, to Rambouillet. Afinogenov is an attractive person, natural, a merry soul, all of which is a particularly welcome antidote to all the accretions of yesterday's encounter with the snobs. That was the genuine 'rotten West'.[1]

22 May

Pyatigorsky, a good cellist, came to see me. Koussevitzky cannot praise him highly enough. Pyatigorsky is very keen that I should compose a cello concerto for him, which he promises to play everywhere. I already have, as it happens, an idea for a Fantasy for cello and orchestra. If Pyatigorsky could come up with the money I would do it. But where is he to get it, however much he boasts of his admirers? He came with his cello and played my *Ballade*[2] with me, very well.

---

1 The phrase 'the rotten West' ('*gniloy zapad*') was not, as it might seem, a common Soviet term of abuse, but one coined by the more rabid Slavophils, Slavonic Nationalists, of the nineteenth century. As such it was taken up ironically and thus given even wider currency by pro-Westerners such as Belinsky, and it figures, similarly ironically, in the novels of the cosmopolitan Turgenev.
2 *Ballade* in C minor for cello, Op. 15, composed in 1912 for Prokofiev's amateur cellist friend Nikolay Ruzsky. See *Diaries*, vol. 1, pp. 241–2, 606–7, 641–3, 543, 588–9.

26 May

Ida Rubinstein invited me for further discussions about the ballet. How was I getting on with my biblical subject? I said, well, look, what about the building of the Temple of Solomon? Rubinstein got very excited, and said it was both a new and a seductive idea. She said she would think about it and take advice on how it might be realised in practice.

28 May

Poulenc, who is notorious for miserliness, invited a whole company of people for the weekend to his place in the country, near Amboise on the Loire, 250 kilometres from Paris. We set off today in our car: besides Ptashka and myself we took Février,[1] and Rieti with the Marchesa. Février was highly entertaining, and never drew breath the whole way. Other guests who arrived were a couple called Laporte (charming) and Sauguet.

Poulenc has a pleasant house with wine cellars in the basement, and good views over the green and welcoming Touraine countryside.

29 May

The weekend party is very gay. We went into Amboise whence we brought back for lunch an extremely aged lady, in her youth a famous cocotte, who had amassed millions and spent them all. This was an unexpected divertissement for the weekend, but Poulenc had a plan to introduce her to Laporte, who is a publisher, with a view to his publishing her memoirs. Once the ex-cocotte had departed we settled down to bridge, to the displeasure of the ladies who went to tour the Touraine in my Chevrolet, Ptashka at the wheel. In her inexperience she crumpled one of the mudguards, which upset me.

30 May

Return journey.

To Honegger's in the evening for a business meeting of the new chamber-music organisation into which I have been dragged.[2]

---

1 Jacques Février (1900–1979) pianist, later in the year to partner the composer in the premiere of Poulenc's Concerto for Two Pianos. He was also chosen by Ravel to be the first French pianist to play the Concerto for the Left Hand after Paul Wittgenstein had give the work its premiere.
2 This was Triton, a chamber music society established by Pierre-Octave Ferroud, Poulenc and Florent Schmitt to present new music. Programmes would be chosen by a panel consisting of, among others, Prokofiev, Georges Antheil, Honegger, Milhaud and Poulenc. The first concert took place on 16 December at the École normale de musique, clashing with the opening of *Sur*

31 May

Began orchestrating the 'Music for Piano and Orchestra'.[1]

Afinogenov came to dinner with us, and afterwards we went to the cinema together. He is making use of his foreign travels to research émigré life, elements of which he wants to incorporate into his forthcoming play. For this reason he frequents all manner of émigré gatherings, and had attended a lecture by Tsvetayeva, responded to by Balmont. As transmitted by Afinogenov and in light of the volte-face presently taking place in Russia, I can see that such speeches do present a shabby face to the world.

1 June

I worry about how to reconcile the building of Solomon's Temple with the Soviet Union. In fact, no such attempt should be made, as inherent within it would be the seeds of hypocrisy. Only when I have a perfectly transparent perspective with all hints of special pleading rigorously expunged can I write. I went to Graham to talk the problem through.

But for him the answer was quite clear: the builders of the Temple, even though they were using material means of expression, were building in the name of an ideal. The more spiritually I convey the ideal of the construction, the more valuable will be my work.

2 June

The opening of a big exhibition of the work of Russian artists – émigré artists, but I still went, especially as it included a portrait of me by Shukhaev.[2] There

---

    le Borysthène (*Na Dnepre, On the Dnieper*), the title Prokofiev and Lifar eventually came up with for the abstractly conceived ballet, at the Grand Opéra. The first programme, organised by Honegger, Poulenc and Prokofiev, included the European premiere of the four-movement Sonata for Two Violins, Op. 56, played by Robert Soetens and Samuel Dushkin, although by agreement with Triton the world first performance had already taken place in Moscow at one of the all-Prokofiev chamber concerts during the composer's late November visit (see below, pp. 1022 n. 3, 1026), when it was played by the two violinists of the Beethoven Quartet, Dmitry Tsyganov and Vasily Shirinsky.
1 Prokofiev's original title for the Fifth Piano Concerto.
2 Vasily Shukhaev (1887–1973), a close friend of Alexander Yakovlev (Sasha-Yasha), after training at the Academy of Fine Arts in St Petersburg spent several years in Italy. He left Russia in the early 1920s and settled in Paris, making, however, extended visits to Spain and Morocco. He returned to the USSR in 1935 and two years later was arrested and sentenced to nine years' hard labour in the Gulag on the usual charge facing artists (and others) returning to their changed homeland after a period in the West. Shukhaev was to survive the ordeal and, following the instincts that had drawn him to the south of Europe, spent the remainder of his life in Georgia.

were a million people at the exhibition, almost all of them Russians, standing about on the street outside, just like the Orthodox Easter Prime service. My portrait effectively dominated the show, first because of its size and secondly because of the extremely rosy colour of the cheeks – 'charcuterie' as someone described them, suggesting a resemblance to a sucking-pig. I knew a lot of people there. Benois introduced me to Korovin[1] and Bilibin,[2] whom I do not much care for. I talked for ten minutes or so with Zaitsev and his wife. 'When can we play bridge?' I asked him. Zaitsev told me he had recently, after a long interval, met Meshchersky.[3] 'Is he still alive?' I asked. Zaitsev: 'Yes, and very little changed.'

Someone asked why my portrait was so much larger than life. I said, 'Shukhaev proposes to hang it in a tower in Casablanca.' (It was true that Shukhaev had gone to Casablanca to decorate some grand palace there.)

1 Konstantin Korovin (1861–1939) encompassed in his life as a painter and theatre designer almost the gamut of Russian artistic styles. Starting with a classical training both at the Moscow School of Painting, Sculpture and Architecture, where his closest colleagues were Valentin Serov and Isaac Levitan, and at the Imperial Academy of Arts in St Petersburg, he was overwhelmed by the French Impressionists on his first visit to Paris in 1885. In Russia he joined Savva Mamantov's Abramtsevo Circle and designed for Mamontov's Private Opera Company. He was a member of the *Peredvizhniki* (*Wanderers*) Group and later of Diaghilev's *Mir Isskustva*, influenced by both Impressionist and Art Nouveau styles. After the First World War, during which he worked as a camouflage consultant at the front, and the October Revolution, Korovin continued to produce designs for large-scale opera and ballet productions until in 1923, in a gesture of rare enlightenment by Enlightenment Commissar Lunacharsky, he was persuaded to go to Paris for the sake of his health and that of his severely crippled son Alexey, also a gifted painter. There tragedy struck: his entire collection of paintings was stolen on the eve of what was to be a major retrospective exhibition of his work and he was left penniless, reduced to turning out potboilers of 'Russian Winter Scenes' and the like for the equally hard-up émigré community. His international reputation, however, secured him work in opera and ballet productions in Europe and America until his sight failed, after which he turned to literature, producing an exemplary book of memoirs and the life story of his close friend Chaliapin.
2 Ivan Bilibin (1876–1942), illustrator and designer, a product of Princess Tenisheva's Talashkino community, is best known for the series of Russian Fairy-Tales, notably those by Pushkin, he illustrated with an instantly recognisable blend of Old Russian imagery, Japanese woodblocks and Art Nouveau. A member of Diaghilev's *Mir Isskustva* and a designer for Ballets Russes productions, including under Golovin's overall supervision the costumes for the legendary 1908 *Boris Godunov* production, Bilibin left Russia after the Revolution and went first to Cairo and Alexandria and thence in 1925 to Paris, where he made a further career as a decorator of grand mansions. In 1936, after accepting a commission to decorate the Soviet Embassy, he decided to return to the USSR, and died of starvation in the blockade of Leningrad in 1941.
3 Alexey Meshchersky, prominent industrialist in Tsarist times, known as the 'Russian Ford', father of Prokofiev's early love Nina Meshcherskaya. According to his daughter's memoirs he had been imprisoned in the Butyrka in 1918 but released, and had then used the escape route via Finland to end up in Paris. See *Diaries*, vol. 1, pp. 375–766 *passim*; vol. 2, pp. 39–43, 265, 508.

4 June

Orchestrating 'Music'.

A bridge party in the evening with Kepin and Tikhomirov, both of whom are excellent players. I have also begun playing properly. But the play dragged on, and we met the dawn . . .

5 June

A jubilee concert celebrating fifty years of Glazunov's musical activity. I remember his twenty-fifth jubilee (yes, such a span has occurred in my own life!). On that occasion the tall figure of Rimsky-Korsakov, with his striking features yet still somehow awkwardly put together, came out to conduct Glazunov's First Symphony but before that could be seen standing in the hall next to one of the columns beside the platform. Why would he be out in full view of the audience, I remember thinking, rather than come straight on from the Artists' Room? That jubilee was an occasion of great pomp and magnificence accompanied by an avalanche of delegations and garlands from the length and breadth of Russia. Today's manifestation in the Salle Gaveau was much more modest, with far fewer people, about a thousand, practically all of them Russians (although in one speech someone who had obviously composed his address in advance referred to being 'here, in the presence of the finest musicians of France' – except that none of them were actually present). Glazunov's legs are giving him trouble; he moves with difficulty and during the addresses a chair was brought on to the stage for him to sit on. Among those who spoke were Volkonsky, who has now become Director of the Russian Conservatoire in Paris, and Pirtsev, who is Director of the 'Russian National Conservatoire' in Paris.[1] The celebration

---

1 The internecine rivalry, impenetrable nomenclature and political intrigues in the education world of the émigré Russian musical community in Paris in the 1920s and 1930s reminds one of the confusing situation with present-day symphony orchestras in Moscow. Soon after the setting-up in late 1923 of the artistically and pedagogically distinguished Russian Conservatoire (largely through the efforts of Nikolay Tcherepnin, who had since its inception served without fee as President, and Volkonsky, a music department was also instituted within the *Russky Narodny Universitet*, the Russian National (or People's, the word has both meanings in Russian) University. On 14 February 1931 its Head, Yury Pomerantsev, the same who had brought the nine-year-old Prokofiev to the attention of Taneyev in Moscow all those years ago, wrote a letter to Rachmaninoff explaining that the Department now wished to leave the University's aegis and spread its wings independently as the 'Russian National Conservatoire': would the maestro agree to lend his name to it? Rachmaninoff agreed, but a month later received a telegram from Princess Saxe-Altenberg and the leading figures of the rival Russian Conservatoire – Julius Conius, the composer-barrister Yevgeny Gunst and the singer Kedrov – requesting that since Tcherepnin was soon to retire would Rachmaninoff accept *that* institution's Honorary Presidency and give his name to it. He had no choice but to agree. On

was a blatantly émigré occasion, making it perfectly obvious that Glazunov has burnt his boats and has no intention of returning to Leningrad. Next came a group of St Petersburg Conservatoire students; I was sitting next to Cecilia[1] and we spent the whole time reminiscing about Conservatoire days (probably those audience members observing us will have concluded that we were conducting a romance). We were both surprised: here were we, who could reasonably be counted the most eminent alumni present, so how could they put on a show without asking us? Of course we would not have appeared, but at least they could have asked. As a joke I suggested to Cecilia that we could form a separate delegation consisting of just the two of us, and appear as 'Prizewinners of the Conservatoire'! We said as much to Glazunov when we went backstage to the Artists' Room after the ceremony to shake his hand. I asked Cecilia, 'Suppose I were to go on to the stage and salute Glazunov as the current Director of the Leningrad Conservatoire. What do you think would happen?'

Cecilia: 'You'd be booed.'

I: 'No, they wouldn't dare, out of respect to Glazunov, whether or not he is in fact Director of the Leningrad Conservatoire.'

Cecilia: 'In that case they would beat you up the moment you left the stage.'

6 June

Did a lot of work on the orchestration of the second movement.

Ptashka was singing on the radio this evening but I had to go to the second meeting of the new chamber-music organisation and could only listen at the Samoilenkos later on. The broadcast quality was not very good and it was impossible to tell from the timbre of the voice who was singing, only from the style. Ptashka sang flat in the first three of her songs, but after that was

---

the same day A. I. Konovalov, the President of the Russian Musical Society (*Russkoe Muzykal'noe Obshchestvo*) wrote to Rachmaninoff explaining that the management of the Society had been taken over by the Russian Conservatoire. But things were in a bad way, Konovalov wrote in a confidential addendum to his letter, because the Conservatoire's new Director, Kedrov, had immediately left for a concert tour lasting several months, leaving the organisation rudderless. More than that, Konovalov confided, Gunst had secretly contrived to sabotage a substantial part of the Conservatoire's funding, from a wealthy industrialist called Gromov, in order to divert it to a new, *third*, Conservatoire to be established under his, Gunst's directorship. Rachmaninoff was appalled, and on his return to Paris from New York in March 1932 did what he could, became as promised the institution's first Honorary President and allowed it to be renamed the Conservatoire Russe de Paris Serge Rachmaninoff, the name it still bears today.

1 Hansen.

not bad. The programme was a Russian one, but included a number of my things, including the *Ballade* for cello and some solo piano pieces.

At Honegger's, among other matters for discussion, we were trying to think up a name for the organisation. I suggested something along the lines of 'F sharp', but the suggestion was not taken up, as they wanted more of a composite name. Next I suggested 'Nousomcontem' (a play on words 'nous sommes contents' and 'nouvelle société de musique contemporaine')[1] but this was judged too flippant. Eventually someone came up with 'Triton' and although this was not particularly successful we were all tired and so accepted it.

12 June

Felt out of sorts. But how greatly my mood depends on Christian Science!

13 June

A 'Sérénade' concert, consisting of pieces commissioned by the Noailles for a festive occasion at their country estate, receiving their first Paris performances. Most of the pieces were semi-humorous, some pure music-hall (like Poulenc's on the vulgarest possible tunes, not bad). Sauguet's was less good, Auric's very bad indeed. Markevich contributed a *galop*, pretty trivial although one of the sections could pass muster. Nabokov's had some quite good parts, but was spoilt at the end by an inappropriate 'Slavonic' effusion. All in all the snobs' club had got together some eminent musicians to have a laugh, but the result was not funny even though everyone laughed heartily to keep up appearances.

Ferroud[2] said to me, 'If you're not too demanding, you can find some good moments here and there.'

I: 'Provided you agree that we're not talking about music, you can find nice things to say about all of it.'

---

1 'We are content'; 'New Society for Contemporary Music'.
2 Pierre-Octave Ferroud (1900–1936), composer and critic, one of the founders of Triton. Ferroud had studied with Guy Ropartz and was much influenced by his fellow Tritonian Florent Schmitt. 'Ferroud is a capable representative of the younger generation in France and his Symphony [Symphony in A] is certainly better than his strange undertaking on a story by Chekhov [the comic opera *Chirurgie*]. I read him your reviews of his Symphony, leaving out the parts where you snap at him. He listened with great interest, almost greedily, and he asked if you might be able to have his Symphony performed in Leningrad. Actually, if you don't find it too awful, maybe you could show it to one of the conductors.' (Letter to Asafyev of 9 April 1932, in H. Robinson (ed.), *Selected Letters of Sergei Prokofiev*, Northeaster University Press, Boston, 1998. Ferroud was killed in an accident while motoring in Hungary in 1936.

Suvchinsky came running up to me. The fellow had simply vanished all winter long; even though he lives very near he did not attend a single one of my first premieres, and now he turns up, beaming all over his face. 'I'll come to see you one of these days very soon,' he said. 'Pyotr Petrovich,' I replied, 'I am so unused to you now I think you had better not come.'

Chastened, Suvchinsky turned to Ptashka: 'Really, Sergey Sergeyevich is such a bad psychologist!'

15 June

Afinogenov's wife, an American, has come to join him from the USSR. We had been speculating what the wife of such a dear man would be like, and an American, no less. She proved to be all right, by no means a disaster but not as nice as he is. Her conversion to Communism is of a more recent vintage than his, and her views are therefore inclined to be more uncompromising.

We decided to go on an expedition to Le Havre, the main attraction being that part of our round trip would be by steamer up the Seine. I gave Afinogenov the map so that he could follow the road, advising him that correct interpretation was a test of intelligence. Afinogenov studied it intensively and gave the right indications, but even so at one point we ended up taking not the shortest route.

On top of this Ptashka caused us to leave an hour later than intended, and owing to my mistake we went to the wrong railway station in Rouen. In short, although we made rapid progress on the road we missed the train at Rouen and had to take the next one, arriving in Le Havre only at one in the morning. Then we found all the hotels full and it was two o'clock before we were in bed.

16 June

Got up at six, having slept no more than four hours at most, more like three in reality. The steamer from Le Havre to Rouen left at seven. The Seine estuary at Le Havre turns into what is in effect a bay which in the grey morning light was not terribly attractive. But before long the sun came out from behind the clouds and warmed us, and the boat entered the Seine river proper, yielding wonderful views of the banks, sometimes quite high and dotted about with small towns and settlements on their heights, sometimes low and flat with lush meadows marked off by trees. Afinogenov began to enjoy himself and the excursion took on a pleasant atmosphere. In Rouen we bought a variety of things to eat and set off in the car for Paris, stopping for a picnic lunch on the grass.

Afinogenov proposed a collaboration with me on an opera. The idea accords with my own wishes: it is time I created something genuinely Soviet.

In addition, I sense that Afinogenov has a good knowledge of the stage. I said, 'But it must be constructive in character, not destructive.' I began thinking, not so much of an opera, as of a play with rhythmic declamation, an idea that has been in mind since as long ago as 1924.

17 June

Saw an exhibition of paintings by Lundström.[1] He is a Christian Scientist and Graham has spoken to me of him. His pictures depict music as he feels it: lines, colours, broken by flashes of lightning. The music is either the most modern – Debussy, Ravel, Stravinsky – or the opposite – Mozart. One of his subjects was the Scherzo from *Oranges*. I looked at them and tried to understand how such and such a piece of music heard in his head could give birth to these particular colours and lines. Honesty compels me to admit that I remained stubbornly unmoved. Yet the very fact that Lundström is a Scientist testifies to his not being a charlatan: this must genuinely be how he feels it.

18 June

Today a remarkable event occurred in the annals of music: the critics of Paris gathered for lunch in a restaurant and on this occasion invited me as their guest. Such a thing is hardly commonplace: it is usually composers who invite critics in the hope of winning their indulgence. How did it come about? In the first place, they are all very well disposed towards me. In the second, all through the winter season and especially on Saturdays you would find them hurtling in a body from one concert to the next so as not to miss any of the programmes, and as there are seven of them they would cry: 'Seven! We are Seven!' and as my spirit thus accords with them, they invited me to lunch. The restaurant was unpretentious but they were very kind to me. I felt genuinely flattered, and at the end of the meal presented each of them with copies of my Sonatinas, which have just come out but are not yet on sale.

One of them, Dumesnil,[2] took me home with him afterwards and described the Normandy Islands in the Channel,[3] which he insists absolutely must be seen and visited. The islands are under the protection of England

---

1 Vilhelm Lundström (1893–1950), Danish painter, best known for geometric, hard-edged still-lifes and Cubist-influenced nudes.
2 René Dumesnil (1879–1967) wrote both on literature, notably on Flaubert, Maupassant, the Realist school, and on music (he was music critic of *Le Monde*). In 1930 he produced an influential two-volume survey of contemporary music in France, *La musique contemporaine en France*, published by Armand Colin.
3 The Channel Islands.

but have independent governments; one of them even has its own local queen, whom they had seen travelling round the island on a donkey.

Today is Stravinsky's fiftieth birthday. He is away in the country, near Grenoble. I sent him a congratulatory telegram, but got around to it only in the evening, so he will not receive it until tomorrow.

In the evening I went to the ballet, a production by the Monte Carlo company organised by De Basil, whose artistic director is Kokhno.[1] We had heard that it was fresh and lively, continuing the tradition of Diaghilev, and so today we decided to see it for ourselves. The ballerinas are young and ardent,[2] the chosen designers and composers contemporary, and so the tradition does after a fashion continue although without the creative flair of Diaghilev, rather clipping a few vouchers from his last seasons. We saw Auric's ballet *La Concurrence*, the music of which is negligible although Nabokov for some reason tried to find good things to say about it.[3]

19 June

Dined with Bour.[4] Also present was, first, Gaubert, who has recently been promoted to the musical directorship of the Opéra. He was very surprised to hear of the fiasco over *Oranges*, said that no doubt some external pressure

---

1 Following the death of Diaghilev in 1929 the self-styled Col. W. De Basil (born Vasily Voskresensky in Kaunas, Lithuania, 1888–1951) formed the company he called the Ballets Russes de Monte Carlo in partnership with René Blum, Director of the Monte Carlo Opera Ballet, shrewdly engaging Massine and Balanchine as choreographers and Diaghilev's faithful and omniscient *régisseur* Sergey Grigoriev as balletmaster. Balanchine's new works were not popular and he soon left to form his own company, Les Ballets 1933 (it was because this enterprise was not financially successful in Europe that Balanchine later that year accepted Lincoln Kirstein's invitation to start a ballet school in New York: the School of American Ballet, which became the New York City Ballet, for whom Balanchine was to create work for the next forty years). The Ballets Russes de Monte Carlo with De Basil, Massine and Blum lasted until 1938, when there was a terminal falling-out between De Basil and his
partners, leading to the creation of two rival companies, the former calling his the 'Original Ballet Russe' and the latter calling theirs the 'Ballet Russe de Monte Carlo' (both opting for the singular).
2 The three 'Baby Ballerinas': Tamara Toumanova, then aged thirteen; Irina Baronova, and Tatyana Ryabushinskaya.
3 The one-act ballet *La Concurrence* (*The Competition*) was choreographed by Balanchine for the inaugural season of Col. De Basil's Ballets Russes de Monte Carlo in 1932, the only production for which a new score was commissioned. The rivalry in question is between two tailors' shops facing each other on the town square, and is mirrored balletically by a fouetté contest between three young girls – the Baby Ballerinas.
4 Ernest Bour (1913–2001), French conductor specialising in contemporary and avant-garde scores. He was later to undertake the French premieres of Hindemith's *Mathis der Maler* and Stravinsky's *The Rake's Progress*, and it is his recording of Ligeti's *Atmosphères* that is heard on the soundtrack of Stanley Kubrick's film *2001: A Space Odyssey*.

had been brought to bear, and promised to look into it.[1] And secondly, Valéry.[2] [Ida] Rubinstein had talked to him about the construction of the temple, but after some thought he had concluded that it was not a subject that was suitable for a ballet. He would therefore have to come up with another concept. I was pleased that such a man as Valéry would involve himself thus: he is musical and, despite his enormous fame, a gentle man. I tried discreetly to bring him into the orbit of my own thoughts: the subject of the ballet should be positive, not negative, not decadent and not erotic.

20 June

A concert by Arthur Rubinstein, who played the Rondo I dedicated to him.[3] The programme stated that it was a first performance but this is not the case: Borovsky had already played it. Rubinstein's performance was better, but still not free enough. It had a moderate success, and I was called out only after the March from *Oranges*, which followed the Rondo. In the Artists' Room Rubinstein apologised profusely to me: in truth he does play the Rondo much better than he had just done so, but seeing me in the audience had put him off and tied his fingers in knots.

21 June

Poulenc came to dinner with us, and we also invited Fatma, to whom Poulenc is very partial. After dinner, at Poulenc's request I played him excerpts from the 'Music for Piano and Orchestra'. He was staggered by the complexity of the piano part: he himself is also writing a Concerto, but much lighter and easier in style.[4] I recalled how on the journey back from the weekend we had

---

[1] After the enthusiasm of Lifar, Prokofiev had been extremely disappointed that Jacques Rouché declared the *Love for Three Oranges* to be 'outdated'. 'Sleeping in a corner of the box, I dreamt sweetly that at last M. Rouché could have a lively opera which would bring a bit of life to the poor subscribers.' (Letter to Rouché of 29 July 1932, quoted by D. Nice, op. cit., p. 300.)

[2] Paul Valéry (1871–1945), Symbolist poet, essayist, philosopher and cultural leader, the very model of a Public Intellectual. As a young man Valéry had suffered a profound existential crisis, caused in part by the death of his mentor Stéphane Mallarmé, and had not written anything at all for nearly twenty years. The silence was broken in 1917 by one of his most celebrated long poems, 'La Jeune Parque', an allegory of the effect of fate (the *Parcae* are minor Roman deities also known as the Fates) on human affairs, implicitly influenced by the ungraspable horrors of the First World War. By the 1930s Valéry had been elected to the Académie Française and was internationally acknowledged as a pre-eminent representative of French culture at its most admirable, the country's spokesman at the League of Nations.

[3] No. 2 of the *Six Pieces for Piano*, Op. 52. Like Nos. 1 and 3 of the set it is a version for piano of a number from the ballet *The Prodigal Son*: this one is 'The Siren'. See above pp. 737, 744–7, 774–5, for an account of the musical genesis of this section of the ballet.

[4] The Concerto for Two Pianos in D minor, composed to a commission from the Princesse de Polignac and premiered later in the year by the composer and Jacques Février conducted by Désiré Defauw. The solo Piano Concerto was a much later piece, from 1949.

spent at his country house all the French people in the party had spent the time criticising their composers for lack of intelligence: Debussy was limited, Ravel plain stupid, Stravinsky clever but 'sale caractère'.[1] Later in the evening we played bridge: Poulenc with Steinert and Fatma for fun, and I with my serious bridge companions at another table.

22 June

The Afinogenovs dined with us. We talked intensively about the proposed opera (or non-opera). He said he would give me his play *Fear* to read, which he considered his best work. 'But', he added, 'its qualities derive from the subject.' Well, of course: form and content must be created in parallel.

23 June

Went to see Idka. She and Valéry have arrived at Semiramide as a subject for the ballet. The idea appals me.[2] But Sert was there also, expounding in detail his ideas for the production. The play would end with Ida ascending to the top of a tower and reading Valéry's verses from there. Needless to say, so enticing a prospect was this for her that no reservations could possibly be entertained. Nevertheless, I privately decided I would call on Valéry to explain my feelings. I had no desire whatsoever to compose a ballet about Semiramide.

24 June

Finished orchestrating the Concerto. For recreation afterwards, I went to play bridge with Kepin, and did not finish until three.

25 June

Had a talk with Valéry. He is not much drawn to the Semiramide project either, but it will be easier for him to comply than to come up with a completely new conception, since he had been thinking about it earlier and now had quite a store of developed ideas. When he heard me say that I

---

1 Bad character.
2 Prokofiev will doubtless have known Rossini's opera with its story of murder, concealed identity, incestuous lust and high tragedy, but whether or not there ever was a real Semiramis, warlady and Queen of Babylon, alleged to have practised mass castration of her defeated enemy troops, she had been for centuries a figure of legend for Herodotus, Dante, Voltaire and many others.

classify the Semiramide subject as negative, he immediately proposed another idea: a soul is born into the world and comes into contact with other individuals, but each individual reveals himself as a double – one side the outward appearance, the other the soul. This is the point of departure, from which any number of collisions and conflicts could be elaborated. I said at once that the idea appealed to me ten thousand times more than Semiramide. Valéry promised to give it more thought, and on that we parted.[1]

26 June

At ten o'clock in the morning there was a private screening of a Soviet film, *Golden Mountains*,[2] at the Théâtre Pigalle, invitation only, and the theatre was full. Three rows in front of us sat Nabokov with Suvchinsky. I buried my nose in the programme. Nabokov, by contrast, made a great show of loudly discoursing on the Communist subject-matter of the film. The film has excellent photography and astoundingly beautiful voices; such velvet tones I have never heard in the cinema, and not very often in life. But the pace is very slow, and the pauses between the words are too long. The music was by Shostakovich, consisting mostly of songs from street and factory. They were ingeniously orchestrated but not developed at all, presumably following socially inspired directives to make the music readily intelligible to an uneducated public. Nevertheless, here and there at moments of dramatic tension the music would become positively Meyerbeerian, and that was not good.

In the afternoon I left for London to make a recording of the Third Piano Concerto, a project that had been under discussion for some time.[3]

---

1 *Sémiramis*, a melodrama to a text by Paul Valéry with choreography by Fokine, music by Honegger and designs by Alexander Yakovlev, formed part of Ida Rubinstein's farewell season of ballet at the Paris Opéra in 1934, along with the Gide–Stravinsky *Perséphone*, Ibert's *Diane de Poitiers*, and Ravel's *La Valse*.
2 *Golden Mountains* (*Zlatye Gory*), an improving tale of a young peasant turned factory worker at the giant Krutilov (i.e. Putilov) works in Petrograd who turns the tide for the striking workers against the machinations of the boss and his son, was directed in 1931 by Sergey Yutkevich and had a score by Shostakovich.
3 The conductor was Piero Coppola (1881–1971) and the orchestra the London Symphony Orchestra. Italian born and trained, but living in Paris, Coppola was from 1923 until 1934 the Musical Director of *La Voix de son maître*, the French branch of The Gramophone Company (the English branch being His Master's Voice, which made this recording in its Abbey Road Studio 1 and issued it as HMV DB1725–27). In April 2009 a copy of the original recording was transferred and restored by Dr John Duffy, remastered by Andrew Rose, and reissued on Mr Rose's Pristine Classical website, whence it can be downloaded and enjoyed in near-original clarity and projection, along with similar treatment accorded the composer's conducting of seven numbers from *Romeo and Juliet* with the Moscow Philharmonic Symphony Orchestra recorded by Melodiya in 1938. Piero Coppola was mainly active as a conductor in France, where he enjoyed the support of Debussy and Ravel, making the first recordings of *La Mer* and *Boléro*.

27 June

I am making a gramophone record for the first time in my life, and not solo but with an orchestra to boot, so have spent the last two weeks practising the Third Piano Concerto very diligently. The sequence of events today was as follows: first we rehearsed for an hour or an hour and a half with the orchestra and then attempted to record an experimental disc. Wrong notes at this stage did not matter as the objective was to check the balance of the sound as between the piano and the orchestra and the internal balance of the orchestral instruments. They then played the sample disc and found places where the piano sound did not come through prominently enough, ditto the second violins, bassoons and oboes. The latter two desks were shifted a metre or so, and the some of the second violins incorporated with the firsts, after which a second trial disc was recorded.

This version sounded so good it was a pity that it had to be discarded (playing it through on a wax disc spoils it irretrievably). My playing comes out vigorously and well in places, but elsewhere it can be mannered, especially where I am slightly hesitant or artificial. Generally, even the slightest hint of mannerism in the playing, which would be imperceptible in an ordinary performance, will be picked up and accentuated in a gramophone recording.

Then we set about making a final, finished recording of the first side. This naturally heightened the emotional tension and I could not be completely relaxed. Nevertheless, the first side was good except that the clarinet played some wrong notes in the second subject. We repeated it, and this time the clarinet played correctly but my own playing was less good. This pattern continued for three hours. I found it very interesting but was glad when the session came to an end, as I was tired from all the concentration.

28 June

The second three-hour session. It is hard to perform a complete side of a record, that is to say four minutes of music, without making a single mistake. But the moment you begin to play more carefully your performance instantly becomes artificial and loses spontaneity. At the end of the session we received a visit from Prince George, the King's fourth son.[1] He had expressed interest in learning about the recording process; his visit had begun with a jazz recording in the company's jazz department and was followed by a peep into

---

1 The future King George VI (1895–1952), whose Coronation took place on 12 May 1937, the day fixed originally for the Coronation of his elder brother King Edward VIII, who had abdicated in order to marry the American divorcée Wallis Simpson.

a studio in which an actress was being recorded in a recitation. Here the Prince had lingered on account of the physical charms of the actress, so I and the whole orchestra had to sit and wait since we could not begin recording a new side until the Prince had come in. The weather was hot, and I had removed my jacket and waistcoat, and also unhooked my braces in order to allow me more freedom of movement. Collingwood,[1] who was in charge of the recording and who had studied at the St Petersburg Conservatoire, said to me in Russian, 'Might be better to take them off altogether.' When the Prince entered and we were taken to be presented to him I did undo the buttons but did not replace my jacket.

The Prince is an obviously thoroughbred young man, an attractive but frail-looking figure. He shook hands with us all but did not seem, at first, to know what to say. He then picked me out for more conversation and asked me when I had composed the Concerto, had I played it before in England, and where I normally resided. I answered his questions good-humouredly and when he asked me where I lived it was on the tip of my tongue to say, 'In Paris, but I often go to the Soviet Union.' However, this would have been tactless, since here he is the host and I the guest, so I felt I had to confine my reply to Paris. In the Prince's presence we recorded one phrase and then immediately played it back. After he left we continued our work.

Each section was recorded two or three times. The next stage is for them to make negative images of the recorded discs by the galvanic process; these are then sent to Paris for the final selection to be made.

29 June

Nikitina,[2] a former dancer with Diaghilev's company, managed to get a rich lord to fall in love with her and with the help of his money decided to recall her

---

1 Lawrence Collingwood (1887–1982). He had studied conducting (with Tcherepnin) and composition (with Steinberg) at the St Petersburg Conservatoire from 1912 until 1917, thus overlapping with Prokofiev himself, and had also assisted Albert Coates at the Mariinsky Theatre. After the Revolution, when Trotsky's Treaty of Brest-Litovsk had brought Russia out of the war, Collingwood returned to Russia to act as liaison officer for Churchill's military adventure in support of the White Army forces in Northern Russia. An outstanding conductor, especially of opera, he was appointed by Lilian Baylis as the first Music Director of her new Sadler's Wells Opera Company, a post that he combined with acting as The Gramophone Company's Chief Recording Supervisor, continuing (as Musical Adviser to what was then EMI) until 1972. In this capacity he earned the unstinting respect not only of his own mentor Coates but such luminaries as Elgar, Beecham, Barbirolli, Gui, Boult, Cantelli, Furtwängler and Sargent.
2 Alice Nikitina (1904–1978) joined the Ballets Russes in 1923 and created principal roles in *La Chatte* (at extremely short notice, replacing an indisposed Olga Spessivtseva), Massine's *Zéphyr et Flore* (Flore, 1925), Balanchine's *Apollon musagète* (Terpsichore, 1928) and *Le Bal* (The Lady, 1929). After Diaghilev's death she appeared with various companies including the Cochran

dancing days by organising a complete evening at the Théâtre des Champs-Elysées. Stravinsky, Poulenc and Sauguet all figured in the programme; of my works there was the Gavotte from Op. 32[1] orchestrated by Rieti, and the first movement of the *Divertimento* played as an orchestral entr'acte. The show was well produced and there were a good many interesting people in the audience, but the dancing of Nikitina herself never caught fire.

Stravinsky thanked me for my telegram and apologised for not replying, but he had left for Frankfurt before it arrived and it had had to be sent on to him. I asked him how his pieces for violin and piano were progressing,[2] and Stravinsky replied, 'I am going through it note by note, under a microscope.' But in the summer he proposes to work less and have a rest, as he is suffering from colitis brought on by an excess of work the previous summer (as if composition could have any effect on the intestines!). I asked him if he thought I should accept Nikitina's invitation to supper after the performance, to which he replied, 'Of course you should go.'

Backstage there was an amusing incident when some bewhiskered Russian was reading to Nikitina an inordinately long poem of congratulation, but Nikitina could not stop to hear the end of it as there were other, more important, people waiting to shake her hand. Something else happened, in its way equally comic: Ptashka and I went up to Stravinsky to ask him if he thought it was time to go to the restaurant or if we should wait for Nikitina to get there, when Stravinsky suddenly called out over our shoulders, 'Ah, Boris Kokhno.' Kokhno pushed himself in front of us and offered his hand to

---

Revues, Ballets Serge Lifar and De Basil's Ballets Russes de Monte Carlo, before retiring from dancing and launching a new career as a coloratura soprano. Her somewhat breathless autobiography, *Nikitina by Herself*, was published in London in 1959 in a translation by Moura Budberg, a.k.a. Countess Benckendorff, a.k.a. Baroness Budberg, the larger-than-life former lover of H. G. Wells, Bruce Lockhart and Gorky. It contains an account of the Diaghilev years and of this Théâtre des Champs-Elysées self-promotion.

1 No. 3 of *Four Pieces for Piano*, 1918.
2 The Suite from *Pulcinella*, recomposed from the 1925 Suite prepared for Kokhánski and now to be known as *Suite Italienne*; and the *Duo Concertant*. Both the new works were being written for Samuel Dushkin, the young violinist for whom and with whose guidance on violin technique Stravinsky had composed the Violin Concerto, premiered in Berlin on 23 October 1931. Stravinsky's remark about the microscope is borne out by Dushkin's own account of the laborious compositional process, as quoted by Stephen Walsh (op. cit.). Whenever Dushkin had even the most minor suggestion for an adjustment in the solo part, Stravinsky 'behaved like an architect who if asked to change a room on the third floor had to go down to the foundations to keep the proportions of his whole structure'. And if the suggestion were rejected, Stravinsky would say, 'You remind me of a salesman at the Galeries Lafayette. You say, "Isn't this brilliant, isn't this exquisite, look at the beautiful colours, everybody's wearing it." I say, "Yes, it is brilliant, it is beautiful, everyone is wearing it – but I don't like it."' And finally, 'First ideas are very important. They come from God. And if after working and working and working, I return to them, then I know they're good.' (S. Dushkin, 'Working With Stravinsky', in E. Corle (ed.), *Igor Stravinsky*, Duell, Sloan and Pearce, New York, 1949, pp. 507–8.) The two works were premiered by composer and violinist in a German Radio broadcast from Berlin on 28 October 1932.

Stravinsky, who then engaged him in amiable and animated conversation. I considered this a grossly overdone demonstration and Ptashka and I withdrew.

Supper was in an extremely expensive restaurant, but was a grotesque occasion. Kokhno had annoyed me, and Stravinsky's behaviour even more so. Stravinsky, seated between Ptashka and Nikitina, completely ignored Ptashka while flirting outrageously with Nikitina and being obsequiously attentive to Kokhno, to the point of indecency. Supper ended at two o'clock, and although people were still drinking champagne Ptashka and I decided it was time for us to go home. Saying goodbye to Stravinsky I turned my back on him as a mark of protest at his conduct. I walked off about fifteen paces and waited for Ptashka, who was still making her round of good nights (there were twelve to fifteen people still at the table). Stravinsky suddenly got up and came towards me, addressing me by name. Since I was half turned away from him I could legitimately not notice him, and therefore continued on my way out. But Stravinsky caught up with me and at that point I had no choice but to hear what he was saying. I stopped and turned to face him as Stravinsky, slightly drunk and in a sheepish tone of voice said, 'Seryozha, why are you going so early?'

'Igor Fyodorovich,' I said, 'it's time to go home, it's already two o'clock.'

He repeated his question and I repeated my answer.

Stravinsky: 'Why are you in a bad mood?'

I: 'Igor Fyodorovich, you are sufficiently intelligent not to ask me such questions.'

Just then Ptashka came up, I said good night to Stravinsky and we left. (Now, writing these words, I am a little ashamed that I did not maintain my position on the moral high ground: if Stravinsky finds it appropriate to flatter Kokhno, good luck to both of them. Kokhno is an insignificant nobody and I do not need to take any notice of him. But I should do so without any hatred or malice.)

30 June

I was invited to join the prize-giving jury of the Paris Conservatoire examinations. I cannot deny that I found this very flattering. Eleven pianists played and it all finished about eleven o'clock at night. Rabaud,[1] a weak composer but, as it proved, an uncommonly kindly Director, seated me next

---

1 Henri Rabaud (1873–1949), composer of profoundly conservative inclinations, and conductor both at the Paris Opéra and of the Lamoureux Orchestra, succeeded Fauré as Director of the Paris Conservatoire in 1920 and remained in the post until 1941.

to him. We were altogether a jury of ten or eleven people, among us Nin and three stout gentlemen wearing rosettes. The system of awarding marks was explained to me and I tried, as conscientiously and seriously as I could, to apply myself to the task in hand, noting down my impressions of each student.

The competition test piece was Chopin's F minor Fantasy, Op. 49, and to hear it played eleven times was wearisome. After two hours an interval was announced after which there was a public test of sight-reading, for which a work had been composed especially by Paray, with copies distributed to us examiners to check for accuracy. I must say, they sight-read extremely well, although despite a perfectly decent standard of execution none was particularly distinguished in the Fantasy. During the sight-reading I amused myself by unearthing mistakes in the manuscript before me, and while none was very terrible I found eleven examples. I pointed them all out to Rabaud and said, laughing, that if the students were now to be told of it they would mutiny and protest that this was the cause of them making mistakes while reading! Rabaud laughed as well, but in truth it was quite irrelevant because although they were good readers, the students had all made at least a hundred mistakes in the text, whereas no more than two or three of those identified by me could conceivably have affected their performances.

The sight-reading over we began voting, basing of course our assessments on the Fantasy, as the point of the sight-reading was to give a general indication of intelligence. When it came to translating the votes into decisions, there were some variations in the results of the votes we had cast. At one point I found myself cogitating the question of whether we should award two or three first prizes? Personally I would have given only one. I heard someone say, 'It's your turn to vote.' But Rabaud corrected him at once: 'Don't hurry, we have plenty of time.'

Had I been asked to write the test piece for sight-reading I would write in two parts and with no dissonances, but such as to rack their brains.

In the evening there was a Triton meeting at my house, to which Cortot came at my invitation, as he organises chamber-orchestra concerts and could be useful to us.

1 July

Having been invited to many different houses during the winter we thought it was time to arrange a tea party of our own in response. Ptashka drew up a list and it soon rose to about sixty, even though a lot of people were not included.

The party took place today: the hospitality was pretty decent and about fifty people came, among them Arthur Rubinstein with his fiancée,[1] Poulenc, Sauguet, Ferroud, Nikitina, Sasha-Yasha, Shukhaev, Mme Valéry,[2] Mme de Felz, and so on. In the evening, after most of the guests had left, there remained our close friends the Samoilenkos, Paichadze, Shukhaev, Goncharova and Larionov.

Paichadze said that Stravinsky had been in the publishing house the day before and said, 'Seryozha is angry with me, but I don't know why ... perhaps it was because I was not more attentive to his wife, or perhaps because I and not he was sitting next to Nikitina ...' Paichadze had replied, 'I doubt that. Prokofiev would hardly be worried where he was sitting, especially as you are his senior in years.'

I said, 'It's true, Stravinsky was fairly revolting in the way he was making up to Nikitina, but what really upset me was the demonstrative nature of his friendship with Kokhno.'

Paichadze: 'Kokhno does surprise me, but Nikitina not at all. That very day at lunchtime Nouvel had told him that Nikitina has 20 million francs sitting in her bank account, and the information produced an incontestable effect. It could mean a commission.'

2 July

If yesterday's reception had been organised by Ptashka, today it was my turn to make all the preparations for tomorrow's bridge tournament. There would be eight people in all, the best of those with whom I had been playing through the winter. In this sense the tournament was to be the deciding event of the season. I collected up to fifty packs of cards. As play would be carried on with ordinary cards on two tables, Astrov today prepared the duplicate deals in advance, so that there should be no delay in the tournament itself. He did so by simply dealing the cards, not contriving any specific problem hands, although built into some of the games were tricky situations from last year's tournament, and also six problems derived from newspaper articles. This added some venom to the contest, as every time an awkward situation developed in the course of play everyone immediately suspected one of the set problems.

---

1 'It is said of me that when I was young I divided my time impartially among wine, women and song. I deny this categorically. Ninety per cent of my interests were women.' (Rubinstein interviewed after his Carnegie Hall appearance in 1937.) The fiancée was Nela Młynarska, ballerina daughter of the Polish conductor Emil Młynarsky. The marriage took place later the same year, produced five children, one of them being John Rubinstein the actor, and although Rubinstein continued to have love affairs into his nineties the couple never divorced.
2 Mme Valéry was Jeannie Gobillard, a friend of Stéphane Mallarmé's family and also a niece of the painter Berthe Morisot, who made a fine portrait of her as a young woman.

In the afternoon I went to see Idka, where I found Valéry and Sert. Valéry again set out his position and said he was ready to undertake *Semiramide*. To me he confided, 'Don't imagine that this is going to be the exotic Semiramide of the ancient Orient, who repulses everyone who comes near her. What interests me is the psychological and spiritual side.' I did not demur. I need the commission, and am content to let Valéry take responsibility for the subject.

I have material gathered for a Sixth Sonata, which I currently have no plans to compose. I shall use this material for *Semiramide*, but in such a way as to keep the Sonata at the back of my mind as well. In truth I shall be concentrating more on the Sonata than on *Semiramide*.

In the evening we had the Afinogenovs to dinner, as we had been dubious about inviting them to yesterday's concourse of the bourgeoisie. He presented me with a copy of *Fear*, and I gave him my photograph, both with touching inscriptions.

3 July

The tournament commenced in an atmosphere of high excitement. By three o'clock everyone was present, and I introduced the principles according to which it had been devised. The main points were the fairness of the timetable and the fact that the result would in no way depend on whether any given hand consisted of good or poor cards. There were also a few minor procedural rules that it was important to obey. Last year the scores were calculated after every hand according to a specially devised (by me) table. This year the ranking would be achieved by conventional bridge scoring after every six hands, at which point the existing partnerships would change. In the first round I partnered Meindorf and immediately ran up against one of the problem hands Astrov had devised. We played very cautiously but were unable to prevail against the stronger pair of Tikhomirov–Kepin.

In the next round Kepin and I played as soulmates, with unusual success, and won convincingly. In the third, I was with Février, not a particularly comfortable partnership but we were still victorious. At the end of this it emerged that Février was in first place and I in second. To my astonishment Altman was bringing up the rear, having lost heavily in the first round owing to mistakes by his partner, who having arrived after a good lunch in a mildly inebriated condition had not been giving the play his full attention. In round two Altman was flustered and himself made mistakes. Finding myself elevated to the number two position in such strong company, by exercising extreme caution I made strenuous efforts not to fall back. I did in fact lose, but not seriously, and the others, zigzagging between themselves, were not able to overtake me. And this was how it finished: 1st Février, 2nd myself, 3rd Tikhomirov, 4th Kepin. Of course the first two did not really deserve to be so high, but today Février played extraordinarily well and I benefited from the cautiousness of my tactics. Kepin was disappointed, but today he was playing nervously. Especially dismayed was Meindorf, who was third from bottom.

The tournament finished at nine o'clock in the evening. I was dreadfully tired. It was a pity Alyokhin could be present, but he was away travelling.

4 July

I decided to go away for a few days to the Channel Islands Dumesnil had told me about, to see a way of life unchanged since the Middle Ages, to walk, to have some time to myself and to read Christian Science. Paichadze had given me the proofs of the Suite from *The Gambler*,[1] so I would have something to occupy myself with while travelling. It was a convenient time to go: the orchestration of the Op. 55 'Music'[2] was finished and without a contract it was too soon to make a start on Idka's project – Valéry had promised to provide some provisional sketches for a libretto within a week.

The day was spent on visas, finding out steamer timetables and the clearing of accumulated correspondence.

5 July

Left at noon. It was hot at first in the train, but then it came on to rain and was cooler. I read Afinogenov's *Fear*. In view of our projected collaboration I subjected it to especially keen analysis. The play deals with contemporary life, the conflict between the old intelligentsia (at least those who are ready to collaborate with Soviet power) and the emergent newcomers, less cultivated but more vigorous.

For my libretto I should like Afinogenov to produce something less Chekhovian, springier and more concise, where the key to the drama depends more on the action and less on the words.

At six o'clock I arrived at St Malo. The rain stopped and it was a lovely evening. A cutter ferried us out to the steamer, which docked on the island of Jersey as darkness began to fall. This group of islands has its own government which, although it is a dependency of England, does not levy taxes as the English do. They say also that if a bankrupt banker ends up here they will not give him up for extradition. As we entered the harbour in twilight I imagined myself such a fugitive banker, finding sanctuary from all

---

1 Published as *Four Portraits and Denouement from The Gambler* for orchestra, Op. 49. The four portraits are Alexey, Babulenka, the General and Polina. The denouement is, of course, the roulette scene in the casino.
2 Piano Concerto No. 5.

tribulations and anxieties at last in these welcoming islands, where he would be doomed to stay until the end of his days.

It is a beautiful island and there are a number of hotels along the shore, in one of which, the old-fashioned Grand Hotel, I stayed.

6 July

Went round the island in a charabanc which left at eleven and wandered about until six, not hurrying, stopping often for various inducements to pass the time agreeably. We visited a twelfth-century church, a lighthouse, a ravine, had lunch at one small hotel by the sea and afternoon tea at another.

7 July

Next morning I went over to Guernsey in quite a large ship which was on its way to England. Then another coach trip round Guernsey, again with stops and excursions. Guernsey is smaller than Jersey, more like a very large garden. I am enjoying my trip very much. I started on the proofs, but they have been engraved by a new process and are so bad they will all have to be done again from scratch.

Read a lot of Christian Science and thought a little about such matters. Composed a few new themes.

8 July

Today is the day for the Island of Sark, or Sercq as it is known in French. Sark is the smallest of the islands but also the most interesting to me because it is ruled by its own Queen, whose title is the Dame of Sark and who lives in a palace (more of a villa in fact) called La Seigneurie. This miniature kingdom has been in existence since the sixteenth century. Since time immemorial the island has been parcelled up between forty families who administer it under the sceptre of the Dame but subject to the ultimate authority of England. Sark is an hour's sailing in a small boat, coming into a tiny bay where there are no buildings but a tunnel cut into the cliff which leads to a road that climbs up the hill. Beyond that is a smiling British landscape devoid of towns, but dotted here and there cottages with smallholdings. There are a few hotels, also of the rustic type. I stayed in one of them and was fed marvellously. In the twenty-four hours I was there I walked all over the island (cars are not allowed anywhere). There are many splendid views of the rocky and indented shoreline, but one cannot say that the island is especially scenic: it is attractive and intimate, its charm residing mainly in its remoteness, its medieval aspect and its disconnection from the world at large. The inhabitants are polite and bow when they encounter you; there are many tourists. The medieval feeling of Sark is quite different from that of Nuremberg, which works on the imagination by virtue of its architecture. Here the effect is produced not by architecture but by the way of life.

After the little holiday in the Channel Islands the family by various routes gathered in a rented dacha at Ste-Maxime, on the Riviera between Toulon and Cannes, for an idyllic summer. Prokofiev's summer tasks were to practise the new Fifth Piano Concerto in preparation for its premiere, which took place in Berlin with Furtwängler and the Berlin Philharmonic on 31 October, successfully despite having only one rehearsal, and work on the Sonata for Two Violins for the launch of Triton. In the third week of November 1932 Prokofiev set out alone for his third visit to the Soviet Union, to a musical landscape significantly changed by the abolition of the warring (pro-Western) Association for Contemporary Music and the (xenophobically anti-intellectual) Russian Association of Proletarian Musicians and the establishment of its centralised replacement, the as yet unknown quantity of the Union of Composers.

20 November

Departure from Warsaw was at seven in the morning so I got up at half past five. Ptashka still has to sing on the radio and is then going on to Prague; she doesn't know how she will manage it without me. All day I was travelling through Poland, studying the score of *Le Pas d'acier* and dozing.

Reached Negoreloe[1] at four o'clock. With the sun setting the sky was golden behind me as I stood on the rear platform. A brief stop at the frontier, with its arch. An official in a Red Army uniform: 'May I see your passport, please? Are you alone?' Negoreloe. My dozen parcels. I wait ages for the inspection and ask, 'Have they not come out to the train yet?' Then the inspection, quite friendly, but they did find and confiscate some women's things. Derzhanovsky, Shebalin, bringing money, also from Lenfilm. Soft-class train. I treat them in the restaurant-car. Derzhanovsky complaining that he is getting old, but on the whole he looks much the same to me. Music will get on the right track once Prokofiev, Myaskovsky and Shebalin all join the Party and take charge. No linen, or rather blankets, for the bunks.

21 November

Into Moscow at a quarter to ten. Afinogenov in a leather coat, especially for my arrival. His car is in for repair so we are in Golovanov's. Shurik,[2] Nadya

---

1　The border station between Poland and the USSR.
2　Prokofiev's cousin Alexander Rayevsky (Shurik) and his wife Nadya had finally been released from prison and exile, as had Shurik's sister Katya (Ignatieva) from exile in Kadnikov earlier in the year.

and Lamm also there. Shurik in good spirits. Superb room in the National Hotel. I sorted out the music and telephoned Golovanov. People dispersed. I had two hours free so went for a walk and sent a telegram to Ptashka. Not many vehicles on the street but crowds of pedestrians. The people look unprepossessing; worst of all is the lack of short fashions for the women, and the ubiquitous thick stockings or felt boots. A phone call from abroad. I booked a call to Ptashka, went out for another walk and returned but the call was late so I cancelled it and sent another telegram. I ate in the restaurant, starchy and pretentious, two menus, one in dollars, the other in Soviet money. One dollar equals 20 roubles. The inevitable cold sturgeon. Golovanov and Kubatsky, no longer director, a conductor now. We went through the Concerto[1] and the *Gambler Portraits*. Arthur Rubinstein came bursting in; I do like him. I began to relax a little. Myaskovsky: his beard even more spade-like, but he is the same as ever. Flowers from Zinka,[2] I telephoned her, Meyerhold is in Leningrad. Derzhanovsky.

Shurik dropped in: simply amazing cheerfulness and a fine attitude to the world.

A performance of *Pskovityanka*,[3] I was given a seat in the Director's box. It was preceded by *Vera Sheloga*,[4] at first seeming rather pointless but ultimately gripping. The bells. Malinovskaya[5] – pleasant woman, no longer young. Arkanov.[6] They showed interest in the new ballet.[7] I explained my principles of ballet composition, and outlined the subject. Rabinovich.[8]

22 November

Rose at eight, still dark outside, the first rehearsal is at nine o'clock in the Bolshoy Theatre. Some old friends in the orchestra. I was on the stage where

---

1 Piano Concerto No. 5.
2 Zinaïda Raikh, the wife of Vsevolod Meyerhold.
3 Rimsky-Korsakov's opera *The Maid of Pskov*, completed and first performed in 1873 but finally revised in 1892, the version made famous by Chaliapin in the role of Ivan the Terrible.
4 One-act opera (1898) by Rimsky-Korsakov, often performed as a prologue to *Pskovityanka*, consisting of material composed for but omitted from the longer work. Vera Sheloga, who does not actually appear in *Pskovityanka*, is revealed in the denouement as the mother of Olga, the Maid of Pskov, the father being none other than Tsar Ivan. Lina had seen the Mariinsky Theatre (Akopera) production on the first Soviet visit. See above, p. 525.
5 Yelena Malinovskaya (1875–1942), theatre administrator, Director of the Bolshoy Theatre 1920–24 and again from 1930 until 1935. In the earlier period she had played an active role, with her Bolshoy colleague Viktor Kubatsky, in the acquisition and establishment of the State String Instrument Collection.
6 Boris Arkanov was the Deputy Director of the Bolshoy Theatre.
7 *On the Dnieper*.
8 Isaak Rabinovich, theatre designer. See above, pp. 198, 437, 454, 468, 507, 534.

it is difficult to hear;[1] we rehearsed the Concerto for two hours. Rehearsal fairly dull, everything gradually coming together. *Portraits* was rehearsed at the end. We telephoned Rubinin,[2] and went directly to see him in his office, near where I had been the last time, very grand but he personally is unpretentious and straightforward, a cultivated man. I told him about Paris, all sorts of anecdotes. He had received the letter and was prepared to do whatever he could, but was unsure of the precise procedure. After he made a phone call he told me I would have to begin by seeing Arkadiev,[3] and if necessary he, Rubinin, would give him a nudge.

I tore myself away to go back to the hotel for a rest. Tomorrow I shall see Derzhanovsky and through Atovmyan[4] arrange a meeting with Arkadiev on

1 Presumably the orchestra was in the pit; the stage would be set with scenery, stage cloth, etc., for the opera or ballet performance later in the day but as there would not be room for an additional concert grand piano in the pit the soloist for the rehearsal would be alone on the stage.
2 Yevgeny Rubinin (1894–1981), Soviet diplomat and high-ranking official in the Ministry of Foreign Affairs. In 1935 he would be appointed Soviet Ambassador to Belgium. One may infer that Prokofiev is seeking his advice about his status in the event of his taking up more permanent residence in the USSR.
3 Mikhail Arkadiev (1896–1937), official in the Ministry of Culture, later to be appointed Director of the Moscow Arts Theatre. In July 1937 he would be arrested and charged with counter-revolutionary activities, sentenced to death by a Stalin Fast-Track Military Tribunal on 20 September 1937 and shot the same day.
4 Levon Atovmyan (1901–1973), composer, arranger, editor and administrator. A vocal defender in the 1920s of the composers he admired against the attacks of RAPM, he was quickly identified as a knowledgeable and valued supporter by Prokofiev, Myaskovsky, Shostakovich and like-minded genuinely creative spirits. In at the start of the Composers' Union he became Director of its Moscow City Committee, with the responsibility of organising performances and allocating funds and commissions. After being 'repressed', exiled to Turkmenistan in 1936 and then sentenced to ten years in the Gulag, he was unexpectedly reprieved and rehabilitated at the beginning of the war and became Director of Muzfond, the financial, commissioning and grant-dispensing arm of the Union. He kept this vital position until the Zhdanov purges of 1948, and among many other benefactions arranged the loan that enabled Prokofiev to buy the dacha at Nikolina Gora outside Moscow on which his failing health increasingly depended. Liked and trusted – rare qualifications – both professionally and personally he provided innumerable mainly unsung services – financial, musical, editorial, moral – particularly to Prokofiev and Shostakovich. The extensive correspondence between Prokofiev and Atovmyan from 1933 to 1952 is documented by the musicologist Nelly Kravetz in S. Morrison (ed.), *Prokofiev and His World*, Princeton University Press, 2008; from it can be seen just how much Prokofiev continually relied on Atovmyan to go-between and channel money to Lina and the children during the war years of evacuation from Moscow, as well as acting as Prokofiev's representative to publishers, concert and broadcasting organisations, etc., and making arrangements of his works for various combinations. Not the least of these was his complete oratorio drawn from the film score of *Ivan the Terrible*, which has only recently come to light and received its world premiere with the London Philharmonic Orchestra and Chorus under Vladimir Jurowski in London in January 2012. The writer and translator Valentina Chemberdzhi, daughter of the composer Nikolay Chemberdzhi (see below, pp. 1027, 1046 n. 1) and from a family having close connections with the leading musical figures of the day, had this to say about Levon Atovmyan: 'The one person who could do anything in the world was Levon Tadevosovich. He was simply a guardian angel sent to help all composers. The love and respect

Chistie Prudy Boulevard.[1] His is a less lavish office, in which we talked for half an hour or so, but little was said about the teaching.[2] But in general it became clear that there is no obstacle to my promotion.[3] Arkadiev on ballet and on *Three Oranges*. Afinogenov came into the room, and willingly agreed to write a reference for a passport for me.

Went to visit Shurik, frightful crush on the tram, but all very good-humoured. Shurik met me at the entrance door to his building and took me in: an unbelievable entrance hallway but down in the basement it was warm and dry and cosy. The girls[4] are quite big now. Cousin Katya came, looking very decorous, but now is not the time to get involved. We all left, but Shurik did not want to go out with Katya. Went to a Torgsin,[5] disagreeable impression.

Quartet Rehearsal. Derzhanovsky says that it is now quite a different matter from when it was played by the Roth Quartet.[6] We did not manage to get there in time for the Sonata.[7] Then to Afinogenov, where we were half an

---

he felt to anyone who wrote music defies description. And he had a clear understanding of everything: who was Prokofiev, who was Shostakovich, who was Chemberdzhi, who was Khachaturian . . . You should not think that his involvement in their fate had anything whatsoever to do with the size of their renown. He would help absolutely anyone . . .'

1 Chistie Prudy ('Clean Ponds') is the name of a lake set within a park, and by extension an area of the city as well as a main thoroughfare also (since 1990) a Metro station. (In the seventeenth century it was known as the Dirty Pond because of the revolting inflow of blood and animal remains from the nearby slaughterhouses, but when the area became part of the Menshikov family's Moscow estate the lake was cleaned up and acquired its more salubrious name.)
2 The proposal that Prokofiev should teach a composition course at the Moscow Conservatoire.
3 That is, within the Soviet cultural establishment.
4 Alexander and Nadezhda Rayevsky had three daughters: Katya, Alyona and Sonya.
5 Torgsin, an acronym for the Russian for Trade with Foreigners, were hard-currency retail shops which existed in the USSR between 1931 and 1935. In some ways they were the precursors of the 'Beryozka' outlets selling gramophone records and matryoshka dolls familiar to generations of tourists to the Soviet Union, but Torgsin shops were open to Soviet citizens as well as foreigners provided they had either hard currency or valuables with which to barter. As such they were a barely concealed way of expropriating for hard currency at a time of general hardship as much as possible of any wealth remaining anywhere in private hands.
6 The performance had been announced for 10 October 1931 by the Brosa Quartet, who had given the first, much admired, performance of the Quartet in Washington on 25 April 1931 and then toured it in Europe, but in fact it took place on the 9th and was given by the Roth Quartet. This ensemble had been formed originally in Budapest by Feri Roth, former leader of the Berlin Volksoper, and had an extraordinary pedigree: the three upper strings had studied with Hubay and the cellist with Schiffer, assistant to David Popper. It was one of the first Western ensembles to be invited to perform in Soviet Russia, giving two concerts in Moscow in 1931, one of which included the new Quartet. But Prokofiev had been upset with Myaskovsky's account, in his letter of 20 October, of the perfomance, in which he describes what he calls the 'monotonous pulse' of the second movement: 'You write the basic figure in quavers, while the first movement has the same basis (in the sense of the predominant shape and duration of the figuration). The Roths played all the quavers of both movements at the same speed, which produced an annoyingly monotonous effect.' In a letter to Feri Roth on 8 November, Prokofiev sharply criticised the interpretation as obviously having been too slow.
7 Sonata in C for Two Violins, Op. 56.

hour late. In a courtyard (a garden), two rooms, access through the kitchen, a decent study because of the books. Champagne, caviar, a Russian-American dinner, not as tasty as in 1927 but very filling. We talked about the play,[1] but it was disappointing. (1) Parisian; (2) Dneprostroy,[2] but long (three acts); (3) excerpted material. Reasons why it is not suitable; I will try to make adjustments and corrections: I have not much experience of writing music for satire, whereas I have plenty for emotion, dreams, hopes, crowd scenes. He promised to think about it; tomorrow he goes to Sochi to work, evidently he has had enough of the Americans here. Walked home thinking about a subject.

23 November

Got up at eight again for the rehearsal at nine: *Portraits*, the *Classical Symphony* and *Pas d'acier*. Orchestra very attentive, responsive to gestures and applauded me. Golovanov complimentary about *Pas*. A proposal to have a repeat performance of the Concerto on the 5th; they undertake to deal with the passport, visas, etc., which made me inclined to agree: it is a much easier job to play a concerto than it is to have to deal with visas and such-like.

At home I slept, I had a headache and was tired. Walked back so as to get some air. First visited Myaskovsky, talked about everything but not for long, only half an hour. He was proof-reading the Eleventh Symphony. My first experience of a Red funeral: but mourning is still evidently black.

Then the second rehearsal for the chamber-music performance: the two violins, very interesting how the sonata will be. Would they be able to hold their concentration, or was it me? They have not yet learnt it thoroughly.[3] Accompanied home by Yekaterina Vasilievna,[4] who talked to me about Gorky, the Union of Composers and other conflicts and affairs.[5] To get some rest I decided to spend the evening at home in the hotel and go to bed early,

1 Perhaps Afinogenov's *Fear* or another potential (Soviet) opera subject.
2 A vast construction enterprise created in 1926 to create a series of hydro-electric generating stations on the Dnieper.
3 The first performance of the Sonata for Two Violins was given by Dmitry Tsyganov and Vasili Shirinsky, the first and second violins of the Beethoven Quartet.
4 Koposova-Derzhanovskaya, Derzhanovsky's soprano wife. See above, p. 429.
5 On 23 April 1932 matters had come to a head in the long-running war between the internationally inclined writers, composers and visual artists and their hardline proletarian opponents. In music the two wings were represented by the pro-Western and Modernist-oriented ACM (Association for Contemporary Music) and the RAPM (Russian Association of Proletarian Musicians), which proclaimed that mass song should be the exclusive basis of Soviet music. On that date the Central Committee of the Communist Party published its Resolution 'On the Reconstruction of Literary and Artistic Organisations'. This was to be followed by the liquidation of both ACM and RAPM and the creation of a single, centrally

but Meyerhold telephoned, then Zinka, then Meyerhold again, and finally Mirsky.[1]

24 November

Up at half past seven. Shurik with Nadya.

Today's rehearsal was attended by a group of composers, about fifty of them. Golovanov was reluctant to have them there at first, but I pleaded for them. It made Golovanov nervous and he hurried the *Classical* Symphony. At the end the orchestra applauded me, especially after the middle movement. I played the Concerto today on a good Bechstein, but it was still too far away. I then conducted *Le Pas d'acier* and felt that it sounded splendid. Myaskovsky is rehabilitated, at least among musicians. Shurik was in ecstasy.

At home Myaskovsky and Derzhanovsky were with me, the former about Saradzhev, the latter for an interview, because 'the high-ups want you to speak out'. At first I could not find the words in the interview, but later on inspiration descended and I could say what I wanted to.

We had lunch in my room, Derzhanovsky tucking in with a will, Myaskovsky with more decorum. After they left I had from half past two until half past six on my own, during which time I read, rested, practised the Concerto and my recital programme. Called for Saradzhev, and then a preliminary meeting at Rubinin's with Goldenweiser, very friendly, conversation mostly about chess, touching only tangentially on the Conservatoire. At Derzhanovsky's there were Myaskovsky, Lamm, Polovinkin and Mosolov. I was obliged to play one of the Sonatinas. Polovinkin also played: whenever he goes a little mad it is interesting, but where he is more orthodox you can see the poverty of the music. I asked for some Soviet songs to take back to Ptashka, but this is not such a simple matter: Derzhanovsky kept pushing Polovinkin's songs but they are very old-fashioned, full of ninths and augmented triads, and what kind of an example of Soviet creativity can that be! Derzhanovsky and I went through and edited my interview, which he has succeeded in turning into something so complicated it is almost unintelligible. In between we solemnly chomped our way through a pretty decent supper, sitting around

---

controlled Union, the imposition of the doctrine of Socialist Realism, which demands of the artist, according to the following definition said to have originated from Gorky's writings, 'the truthful, historically concrete representation of reality in its revolutionary development. Moreover, the truthfulness and historical correctness of the artistic representation of reality must be linked with the task of ideological transformation and education of workers in the spirit of Socialism.' Once established, the Union of Composers became an all-powerful organisation controlling music publishing, performing organisations, concert halls, radio and television, performing and publishing rights, and music teaching establishments such as conservatoires.

1 Prince D. S. Mirsky. See above, pp. 641–3.

until 2 a.m., which put me in a bad mood because I have a concert tomorrow. Out on the street there was a snowstorm.

25 November

Rehearsal today started at eleven and there were about 150 people – composers – present. Platform, and suddenly Goldenweiser was beside me and we seemed to be getting on well. But the acoustic! We decided to repeat the programme on the 5th, as many musicians were unable to get tickets. Someone from Intourist rang up on behalf of Chalon enquiring where I was staying. In the afternoon he came bustling in, full of bonhomie, and fascinated to know about Moscow. I explained who would be in the box in the theatre for the concert starting at eight. I arrived with Chalon and took him in to the Director's box, where there was Malinovskaya. A disagreeably supercilious tone in our conversation about Lifar, but I tried to be accommodating. 'Well, let him come with you in April and we will see.' Semyonova.[1] Golovanov conducted *Portraits* quite well as to tempi, but forced the pace in the Concerto. As for musicality I cannot say, as I could hear only approximately. The performance was a success, but not wildly so. When I went out to play I was calm and was greeted with an excellent response, but not as demonstrative it had been in 1927. The Concerto went very respectably, but I am not sure that everything could be heard. Encores were called for. In the interval I saw Miss Kucheryavaya: her father[2] had died in March. I was told that the concert was attended by Bubnov[3] and Voroshilov,[4] and the Stalin

---

1   Marina Semyonova (1908–2010), the first, and in many people's opinion, still the most consummate of all Soviet ballerinas. Graduating from the Vaganova School in Leningrad she first joined the Kirov Ballet but in 1930 was brought to the Bolshoy Ballet in Moscow apparently on the express orders of Stalin. Here she was prima ballerina assoluta until 1960 when she retired at the age of fifty-two, with another near half-century of inspirational teaching still to come. She died on 9 June 2010, a few days short of her hundred and second birthday. Prokofiev's diary entry is no more than a note of the name, but he cannot fail to have been impressed.
2   See *Diaries*, vol. 2, pp. 315–87 *passim*; and above, pp. 461, 543–4.
3   Andrey Bubnov (1883–1938), Old Bolshevik and member of the Politburo. On the dismissal of Lunacharsky Bubnov was appointed People's Commissar of Education (Narkompros), a post he held until October 1937 when he was arrested in the Great Purges, convicted of counter-revolutionary and anti-Soviet activities on 1 August 1938 and shot the same day. As Narkompros Bubnov's policy had been in sharp contrast to Lunacharsky's liberal, broad-based cultural aspirations, putting much greater emphasis on vocational, primarily industrial training.
4   Kliment Voroshilov (1881–1969), Soviet military commander and one of Stalin's most assiduously sycophantic supporters, in which role he was generally more successful than in his military commands. At this time, having replaced Mikhail Frunze after the latter's suspicious death from an overdose of chloroform during a surgical operation in 1925, Voroshilov was Chairman of the Revolutionary Military Council, and two years later would be appointed Marshal of the Soviet Union and People's Defence Commissar. However, his handling of the 1939–40 Winter War against Finland was so manifestly incompetent that even Stalin saw he had to be replaced, following which he was made Deputy Premier responsible for, of all things, culture.

moustache was even glimpsed at one point in the Government box. In the *Classical* Symphony the Gavotte was encored. I conducted *Le Pas d'acier*, and it went well, with plenty of fire. After countless curtain calls it was necessary to play something myself, so I did the second 'Grandmother', the third Gavotte[1] and the March from Op. 12. At this the hall erupted, as it had done in 1927.

The auditorium lights were dimmed, and we went to a supper celebrating the fifteenth anniversary of the orchestra. Myaskovsky, Golovanov and I were at the top table. There were speeches about abroad and at home. A number of generalisations were voiced about abroad, true enough in their way but some of them exaggerated. I escaped early, as there is another concert tomorrow.

26 November

Mirsky. Somehow he did not tell me anything. I mentioned my Afinogenov project and he promised he would think about a subject. The concert was at one o'clock. In the box I bumped into Meyerhold, a veritable eruption of a meeting. Zinka was nice. Golovanov has corrected some of the tempi. The order of the programme was the same as the day before and with a similar crescendo except that my encores were *Visions fugitives*, the Gavotte and *Suggestion diabolique*. Myaskovsky detects some correspondences between the denouement of *The Gambler* and *The Battle of Kerzhenets*.[2] Atovmyan about two telephone calls from Leningrad and invitations to banquets, which I detest, so asked him to telegraph my regrets. Meyerhold took me to his place in his Ford for coffee and refreshments. Rescue from the Leningrad ordeal: a phone call[3] to say I will not be able to attend, I am working. I rang up Ivy Valterovna.[4] Rested in my hotel. Kucheryava: how her father had perished after having been accused of being an Enemy of the People, reasons unclear; her unhappy marriage and present attitude to life. I tried to console her and gave her money, afterwards regretting that it was not enough: she has no bread, only potatoes. Shurik: I suggested dining together with Chalon, but Shurik was in a hurry. Talked of Katya's erratic moods, while all Shurik

---

1 The Gavotte from the *Four Pieces for Piano*, Op. 32, of 1918, the first being the Gavotte from the Op. 12 set of 1913, and the second that from the *Classical* Symphony of 1917.
2 Symphonic interlude from Rimsky-Korsakov's opera *The Legend of the Invisible City of Kitezh and the Maiden Fevronia*. When Prokofiev was courting Nina Meshcherskaya in 1913 and a frequent visitor to her family home in St Petersburg her father, the industrialist Alexey Meshchersky, always asked Prokofiev to play it for him, as it was a particular favourite of his. See *Diaries*, vol. 1, p. 639.
3 No doubt made by Atovmyan.
4 Litvinova. See above, pp. 436–7 n. 1, 541–2.

wants is peace and clarity. Chalon liked the concert, sent a telegram, my good offices. He liked the people who were in the box at the concert. I entertained him to dinner: cold sturgeon, vodka, champagne, pears. Car took me to Shebalin for a gathering of composers. Present in addition to those who were there on the 24th[1] were Feinberg, Shenshin, Oborin, Meyerhold, and Shebalin himself. I played the *Divertimento* and the Second Sonata and then asked for reactions, which were that people found it generally interesting and worthy of respect but without any particular enthusiasm. There was then a performance of Myaskovsky's Symphony No. 11 arranged for two pianos eight hands. Beautiful harmonies but as always he cannot completely rid himself of a tendency towards provincialism. I managed to get away before it got too late and walked home in the white of winter.

27 November

A hot bath; what I had to eat; what your money buys you in the restaurant and my impression thereof. I have accumulated a little over 6,000 in royalties. Went with Chalon to a rehearsal of the *Overture on Jewish Themes* and the *Sonatina*. We walked through the snow-covered Moscow streets and took photographs. At Tsyganov's place the *Overture* was done well, Chalon thrilled and took photographs. I showed a fashion magazine to Tsyganov's wife. Lunch invitation from the French Ambassador courtesy of Chalon. Had a better sleep, although not ideal. Practised the *Sonatina* and other pieces. Excellent lunch at Meyerhold's: chicken in aspic, fruit compôte, first-rate. Ionov:[2] unexpected success with the music scores; the breadth of his interests. To Ivy Valterovna's in Meyerhold's car. Charming and very animated, she assumed I was a foreign national. Then after a long rest I practised the *Sonatina*, because I was worried about it. The Conservatoire, remembering Persimfans. A spirited performance of the Quartet, although the ensemble faltered at one point. I played a few small pieces to great applause. Goldenweiser, Shatsky.[3] The Sonata for Two Violins received a good performance and was well received. I got through the *Sonatina* with no mishaps, hoorah! Perhaps not the greatest success ever, but still. Calls for encores, although not the *Sonatina*. To cheer myself up I played the Gavotte from Op. 2 and to my shame the March from *Oranges*. The *Jewish Overture*,

---

1 At Derzhanovky's.
2 Unidentified music administrator in Moscow.
3 Stanislav Shatsky (1878–1934), who had replaced Boleslav Pshybyshevsky as Director of the Moscow Conservatoire earlier in the year. He was not in fact a musician but an educator with radical theories about the *mens sana in corpore sano* development of children in extra-school environments such as summer camps, playgroups, clubs, and so on. He served as Director of the Conservatoire until his death in 1934.

however, was a real success and had to be encored after insistent demands. Then it was time to go to the train; I took my last bow already in my leather coat with my briefcase under my arm.

Quick packing at the hotel. Atovmyan had seen Chemberdzhi[1] applauding vigorously; acquaintances of his had heard a good broadcast of Ptashka singing *The Ugly Duckling* in Prague. In Golovanov's car to the station; I could not get a place in an International Company Wagons-Lits carriage but I did get a separate compartment. Tried to tempt Derzhanovsky into coming along – the 'Red Arrow'.[2] He hesitated but in the end did not go. I did not press it too hard: he had made rather a mess of the interview, which appeared today in a shortened and garbled version. It is important, none the less.

28 November

I slept well. Arrived in Leningrad at half past ten. Asafyev at the station (yesterday was the premiere of *Flames of Paris*[3]); Shcherbachov and someone from the Philharmonia. Taken in a splendid car to the Yevropeiskaya Hotel. Rotten weather after the Moscow snow. The room is a double, with bath, but less lavish than in Moscow and not as sparkling clean. Asafyev talked: he is seeing more people now and is being invited to become a member of the Party. I tell him he should stop moaning and act with more courage. Dranishnikov has not changed, at the rehearsal it was clear he had barely learnt the score. There are some changes in the hall: fleas in the red divans. The rehearsal began with *Portraits*, then the Concerto. Tyulin, Deshevov and especially Asafyev expressed their admiration for the Concerto.

Returned to the hotel. Lidusya telephoned,[4] she came to see me. Looking older and complaining about her heart, but they live quite well as her husband is a naval specialist. I rang up Demchinsky and went to see him. Measured but elegant speech. Their situation is clearly not easy; they have

---

1 Nikolay Chemberdzhi (1903–1948), composer and former active member of 'Prokoll', the proletarian-inclined students' collective of the Moscow Conservatoire (see p. 908 n. 1 above). His daughter Valentina became well known as a translator, biographer and musical memoirist, notably of the pianist Svyatoslav Richter and Prokofievs' first wife Lina.
2 The 'Red Arrow' sleeping-car service between Moscow and Leningrad was inaugurated in 1931 and has run nightly ever since, except during the blockade of Leningrad during the Second World War.
3 The ballet by Boris Asafyev, choreographed by Vasily Vainonen with Natalya Dudinskaya and her husband Konstantin Sergeyev in the leading virtuoso roles, that caused a rift between Asafyev and Prokofiev when Prokofiev realised on seeing the score that he had plagiarised wholesale many of the tunes from French Revolutionary times Prokofiev had collected for him in Paris as starting points for his own compositions. See below pp. 1070–2. The subject, the French Revolution, was designed to underline the continuity of true Revolutionary ardour and progress as exemplified by both late eighteenth-century France and twentieth-century Russia.
4 Karneyeva. See above, pp. 481, 511.

had to draw in their horns. Their son. I need to breathe a different air now. Walked back to the hotel at midnight. No snow in Leningrad, it has turned to dirty slush.

I compare my experiences with those of 1927. I feel more remote now, my affection for the city itself, its streets, has vanished. Or is it simply that I am generally less attached to things, places, physical objects?

29 November

Second rehearsal, from ten o'clock until one, a working session with no listeners present. Then a meeting in the management offices until two. I asked Dranishnikov about *Oranges*, to be told that it cannot be produced because of the deposit. I was upset by this as the deposit was rescinded three years ago. Went upstairs to the restaurant and caught up on my diary. Then I walked over to Dranishnikov's.

Impossibility of finding a copy of the evening *Red Gazette* newspaper, which carries the interview. The Radlovs. Director Buchstein.[1] Dranishnikov has already had a word with him about *Oranges*. The matter was instantly resolved; and there could also be a ballet triple-bill evening. Excellent dinner, the Director took me and the Radlovs by car. Insists on my appearance tomorrow at the Congress of Arts Workers, who want to see me. I shall have to give a speech.

30 November

No rehearsal today, so I got up in a leisurely fashion, thought about the speech I have to make, and having done so tried to remember what I was going to say. Took a photograph of Suvchinsky's old house, the paint all peeling; it is now a school. Buchstein took me to the Congress. The actual session had finished and people were assembling for photographs. My entrance was greeted with applause, thank goodness I may be spared making a speech. My photograph was taken and a pencil sketch made of me. We went into the Mikhailovsky Theatre,[2] where the composers and musicians

---

1 Even in the annals of the Leningrad/St Petersburg Philharmonia little information can be found about V. S. Buchstein, who occupied the Director's chair of the Philharmonia for a brief period in 1932. But that he was not universally beloved can be seen from a letter Shostakovich wrote to the critic P. Markov on 25 June 1932. After complaining about the dual burdens of toothache and poverty, Shostakovich continues: 'But life has its own dialectic laws. Not everything is bad. Buchstein, whom I cordially dislike, has fallen ill. It is possible he will die. This news has afforded me quiet joy and assuages my soul, hardened as it is to misfortune.'
2 The Mikhailovsky Theatre has had a good many changes of name. In Soviet times it was known as the Leningrad Maly Opera and Ballet Theatre ('Malegot'), towards the end of the Soviet Union briefly the St Petersburg Malegot. After the Soviet Union's collapse it became the Musorgsky Opera and Ballet Theatre, but from 2001 it has reverted to its original name of the Mikhailovsky Theatre.

had arranged a reception for me in the foyer (a telegram from Atovmyan in Moscow had alerted them to the fact that Prokofiev hates formal addresses of welcome and the like). Even so there were about seventy people. A speech from Iokhelson, a former Chairman – as I learnt only afterwards – of the Leningrad branch of the Association of Proletarian Musicians.[1] He said approximately what I had planned to say had I made my speech at the Congress: the growth of interest in music, the desirability of my joining in this work, the use of Soviet themes, links with the Western world of music, all of it couched in the most flattering terms with repeated references to Sergey Sergeyevich this and Sergey Sergeyevich that.

It was obviously necessary for me to reply. I spoke briefly and not very eloquently, laying stress on what he had said and stopping short of the practical details of any exchange. My announcement that I do in fact intend to spend as much time in the USSR as possible was greeted with prolonged applause. A private aside to Asafyev reassured me that he would have said much the same. After this we adjourned to the next room where there was tea and quite lavish hospitality. I agreed to take questions and answered thirty or forty, but they were factual and on the whole well disposed, less treacherous than they had been in 1929. Many of the questions came from Steinberg, Andrey Rimsky-Korsakov and Weisberg, who were sitting just opposite me.

Out on the street I met Dobychina: what I heard about her, my behaviour, about Benois and her wish to invite him, a commission I undertook to pass on. At the hotel I rested for a little while, when Struve[2] telephoned. At first I was surprised, taken aback even, but then very pleased. I promised to get her a ticket. Buchstein called for me in the evening and took me to the party to mark the closing of the Congress. Would I consider a teaching position in Leningrad? I answered somewhat evasively but did not rule it out altogether. There was supper, followed by a series of staged excerpts from productions, which were very interesting. One of them featured a brilliant coloratura soprano, Barsova.[3] I got away at one o'clock.

1 Vladimir Iokhelson (1904–1941), Chairman of the Leningrad Branch of RAPM, later Literary Director of the Leningrad Maly Theatre and a senior official of the Leningrad Composers' Union. In February 1936 infamous for his biased chairmanship of Composers' Union meetings convened specifically to criticise Shostakovich's opera *Lady Macbeth of Mtsensk* in the wake of the savage *Pravda* editorial of 28 January 1936, and for the part he played in suppressing performances of Shostakovich's Fourth Symphony when it was already in rehearsal.
2 Lidia Struve, a fellow student at the St Petersburg Conservatoire to whom Prokofiev had been for a time seriously attracted. See *Diaries*, vol. 1, pp. 593–743 *passim*.
3 Valeria Barsova (1892–1967), one of the most celebrated lyric-coloratura sopranos of the Bolshoy Theatre. She had cut her teeth as a very young singer opposite Chaliapin in the Zimin Private Opera Company in Moscow, and by 1920 was already a star of the Bolshoy, from which she retired in 1948 loaded with State honours and having had a crater on Venus named after her.

1 December

Third rehearsal, not that three is enough! Progress is slow and Dranishnikov seems to be treating the work rather superficially. The management extended the rehearsal by an hour. A violinist asked me which I thought the better orchestra, Leningrad's or Moscow's? I told him, 'Moscow's.' He said, 'I realise you are an authority, but allow me to disagree with you.' 'That is your privilege,' I said. The orchestra, after three breaks, was on the point of dispersing. I said, 'You would do better first to learn the music and then have your break.' In general I was not at all satisfied. A lot of people came to the rehearsal, including Vera Alpers, whose younger brother has died.[1]

The rehearsal went on until after two o'clock, after which there was time off until the concert, which I spent quietly at the hotel except for a short walk. In the evening the hall was full, with people standing as in 1927 except that then they were everywhere including the gangways between the seats, but today only behind the columns. The Director told me that there was a festival atmosphere. Sollertinsky,[2] a polyglot with a command of twenty-six languages, spoke the opening address in a most expressive tenor voice. After my strictures on superficiality, Dranishnikov had evidently worked all day and was as nervous as a child. He conducted everything much better, with more or less correct tempi. I was not nervous, and the Concerto went well, but the applause as I entered and left the platform was less than it had been in 1927. In the interval I took a bow while the applause was still continuing. Struve sitting next to Chalon: he had brought her in with him as nobody had been given the necessary instructions to admit her. She has survived the eighteen years since I had last seen her remarkably well and is still a very attractive woman. But she is as shy and timid as ever, and almost immediately began to say she must go. I asked her to telephone me tomorrow. Tanya Granat was the very opposite, her eyes, teeth and figure as strikingly assertive as before.[3] Also there were

---

1 Sergey Alpers, who had been a member of Felix Blumenfeld's piano class at the Conservatoire and who, in Prokofiev's estimation, had the makings of a good pianist. See *Diaries*, vol. 1, pp. 81, 270, 274, 314, 465, 510, 608–9.
2 Ivan Sollertinsky (1902–1944), one of the most cultivated, articulate and erudite men in all Russia, among other things a philologist especially of Romance languages, an expert on the history of theatre, but best known for his extraordinary knowledge and appreciation of music. In that capacity he was both a professor at the Leningrad Conservatoire and Artistic Director of the Philharmonia. For Shostakovich he was an indispensable confidant, colleague and soulmate, and the composer was deeply affected by his early death in Novosibirsk, where the Philharmonia had been evacuated during the war. Shostakovich's Second Piano Trio, completed later the same year, is dedicated to his memory.
3 Tatyana (Tanyusha) Granat, a young friend of the Karneyeva sisters, with whom Prokofiev had had a stimulating summer dalliance while on holiday at Terijoki in 1915 and 1916. Her gleaming teeth and eyes were commented on at that time and clearly had not lost their appeal. See *Diaries*, vol. 2, pp. 46, 49, 53, 132, 137, 209.

Alexey Tolstoy and Gavriil Popov. There was a letter from Petrov-Vodkin, who is very ill.

Second half: *Classical* Symphony and *Le Pas d'acier*, conducted not badly by Dranishnikov, many curtain calls at the end, one could hope for an encore. In the Green Room, Demchinsky; Eleonora:[1] 'You know I have a little boy now, two months old.' Whom can she have got as a husband? A Latvian, apparently. Lidusya,[2] Khaikin.[3] A lot of people were not admitted to the Artists' Room. After the concert, hardly had I got to my room when Chalon burst in, congratulating me on the success. We drank 'Narzan' water[4] and beer and ate some cake he had brought.

2 December

Got up later, rested and went for a walk. Struve phoned, I stammered a bit but asked her to come over and promised her some perfume. She was embarrassed, but willingly agreed. Gusman has come up with a film project: Tynyanov,[5] whom I know in connection with Griboedov. The plot of the film is most attractive and would be welcome in foreign markets as well, where it could do very well. A meeting has therefore been fixed for tomorrow with Tynyanov and the director of the film.

Asafyev, his bad headaches: talking of his fears; and of death, the true nature of which can only be imagined by those who are left behind; of his success and the pressure being put on him to join the Party. Tyulin brought in a request for scores from the Director of the Conservatoire (I outlined my

1 Damskaya.
2 Karneyeva.
3 Boris Khaikin (1904–1978), conductor, a student of Malko and Saradzhev at the Moscow Conservatoire. From 1936 until 1943 he would be Music Director of the Maly Opera and then from 1944 until 1953 Principal Conductor of the Kirov Opera, in which capacity he was responsible not only for the successful production of Prokofiev's opera *Betrothal in a Monastery* based on Sheridan's *The Duenna*, but tragically for the disastrous, ill-prepared, closed but official play-through of Prokofiev's last opera *Story of a Real Man* in December 1948, one consequence of which was to ensure that there would never in the composer's lifetime be a production of both parts of *War and Peace*.
4 A pungent mineral water from the spa town of Kislovodsk (meaning 'bitter waters') in the Caucasus.
5 Yury Tynyanov (1894–1943), outstandingly gifted linguist, translator, literary historian, theorist and critic, novelist, screenwriter. His 1927 novella *Lieutenant Kijé* (*Podporuchik Kizhe*) was the basis for the film by Alexander Faintsimmer for which Prokofiev composed some of his most successful and best-loved music. Tynyanov was also the screenwriter for the film. Author of a number of studies of Pushkin and his circle, notably the Decembrist Küchelbecker, Tynyanov was also deeply interested in Griboedov, whom he included as a character in several of his literary historical novels and about whom he published many articles in literary journals. He was still working on a detailed analysis of *Woe from Wit* when he died of the multiple sclerosis he had suffered from since youth; it was published posthumously.

resentment about the treatment I had had from them in 1929). We went together to a rehearsal of the Sonata for Two Violins and the *Jewish Overture*. The latter went well, but there were a few hiccups in the former; nevertheless, both Tyulin and Asafyev liked it very much, Asafyev laying stress on its continual flow of melody. Back to the hotel for Struve to come at half past five; presented her with perfume and chocolates. At first I was glad to see her, it was a pleasant change that she had not allowed herself to collapse like most of the others, but her conversation soon proved to be fairly obtuse with but a single theme: to leave the country and go abroad. To do so she would be ready to abandon her children and her husband, with whom her obsession has caused a rift. She has relatives abroad and believes that there would be opportunities.

People were continually knocking at the door and bursting in, although their appointments were for tomorrow. Another interruption was Chalon, but typical of a Frenchman he disappeared immediately without coming in. After Struve left, Chalon and I went in the magnificent Intourist car he has at his disposal to Dranishnikov's to look at his furniture. The furniture made a tremendous impact; Chalon feasted his eyes on every piece. We were offered champagne, but I was in a hurry. Nikolay Radlov[1] took me to an exhibition of fifteen years of Russian painters, a huge and extremely colourful show. The contemporary subjects were interesting, but what most attracted me were Petrov-Vodkins's *nature-mortes* and Filonov's textile and mosaic fantasies.[2] After an hour and a half there I was very tired, and went to rest for a while in the House of Scholars, now located in the

---

1 Brother of the theatre and opera producer Sergey Radlov, Nikolay Radlov (1889–1942) became one of the Soviet Union's best-known illustrators and cartoonists, a career he combined with designing for theatre productions. A frequent contributor to magazines that brightened Prokofiev's student years such as *Apollon* and *Satyricon*, after the Revolution his cartoons, particularly of literary and artistic figures, were a staple of the satirical magazine *Krokodil*. As an illustrator his penchant was for children's books and *skaski*, and from various accounts he seems to have been an exceptionally lovable personality.
2 Pavel Filonov (1883–1941), 'artist and explorer' – his own description of himself – from an uneducated peasant family, was a prominent figure in avant-garde artistic circles in Petrograd in the early years of the century and the immediate aftermath of the Revolution. A strong theoretical basis underpinned his aesthetic which consisted, unusually, in rejecting both the abstraction of Malevich and Tatlin and the representational direction that led eventually to Socialist Realism, but instead aimed to develop a version of the natural world based not on reproduction but on analysis transfigured by the artist's imagination into a parallel representation. Filonov called this technique 'analytic art' and its products 'made pictures' (*sdelanye kartiny*). In this his ideas corresponded to the invented language of the Futurist poet Velimir Khlebnikov, and the two formed a close bond. Filonov's uncompromising ideas, however, failed to engender much practical or ideological support from either of the more established wings of the artistic community and he existed in great poverty until eventually dying of starvation in the Leningrad blockade.

former palace of the Grand Duke Vladimir Alexandrovich on the Neva Embankment.[1] Not an especially fine building, but of good, solid quality, able to survive the cavalry squadron that was quartered there and similar depradations. Chess tournament: Botvinnik[2] is losing. Rokhlin[3] expressed pleasure at my presence, describing me as a chess veteran. Nikolay Radlov reappeared and drew me off to his apartment on Millionaya Street, not far away; it was half past eleven by the time we got there. We talked, and he asked me about the Meshchersky family. I said that some of them were in Serbia and some in Paris, but I had had no occasion to meet any of them there. This led on to how one can prosecute a love affair these days: it is too cold in the Summer Garden, and in the museums there are too many people about, while nobody has living accommodation suitable for the successful deepening of a relationship. I walked back at one o'clock through the snow, which was very slippery.

3 December

Sebryakov[4] came in for coffee. His opinion on the construction industry, and despite everything the many successes. Since he is a pessimist this is convincing, the more so as he is a specialist in such matters and occupies a professional position.

---

1 The House of Scholars (*Dom Uchonykh*) had been instituted in 1920 as a meeting place and resource centre for scholars in all disciplines. It had space for concerts, debates and lectures and functioned as a sort of public face of the Academy of Sciences. In 1932 it had been named the Gorky House of Scholars.
2 Mikhail Botvinnik (1911–1995), international chess Grandmaster and three times World Champion, the first world-class player to develop within the Soviet Union and thus a focus for the ever present Soviet drive to establish intellectual superiority over the West. At this time Botvinnik had won several internal national championships but had been prevented from competing with credible foreign or émigré contenders such as Alyokhin or Capablanca or Flohr. However, with the support of Nikolay Krylenko, who was about to be supplanted by Vyshinsky as Chief Prosecutor of the Great Purges show trials and who from his membership of the Party Central Control Commission was Head of the Soviet Chess Association, a match was arranged between Botvinnik and Flohr in Moscow in 1933, which ended in a draw. (Krylenko, who had earlier distinguished himself in the show trial of the Roman Catholic hierarchy in 1923 by shouting, 'Your religion, I spit on it, as I do on all religions, on Orthodox, Jewish, Mohammedan, and the rest. There is no law here but Soviet Law, and by that law you must die,' had argued that 'We have to know our real strength... We must finish once and for all with the neutrality of chess. We must condemn once and for all the formula "chess for the sake of chess", like the formula "art for art's sake". We must organise shock brigades of chess-players, and begin the immediate realisation of a Five-Year Plan for chess.'
3 Yakov Rokhlin (1903–1995), chess master and author of numerous books, a senior figure in the Leningrad chess hierarchy.
4 Sergey Sebryakov.

At half past twelve a meeting about the film: Gusman, Tynyanov and two producers, everyone very refined and respectful. The leitmotif was outlined, and it looks as though it will not entail a great deal of work. All sorts of other people came in to discuss various details. Then on to lunch with Demchinsky. He weighed in with an attack on cheerfulness and joy: music should convey the widespread general sense of alarm in a situation from which neither science nor society can offer a way out. I said, 'When the sea rages in a storm, how essential is the firm rock among the waves.' He said, 'But no one will grasp the rock; and suppose they did, on what could its peace and security be based? On health, on reliance on oneself, on one's own individual self?' I: 'On trust in God.' He (with an immediate change of tone): 'Ah, but that is an entirely different question.' And thus his assault was beaten off. I gave him a suit of clothes and some other things, and would have offered money but could not bring myself to do so.

At the hotel I packed my things. Lidusya darted in for a brief visit. The concert started at a quarter to nine, once again full with people standing in the aisles. I asked for more to be admitted during the interval. The Quartet received a not very good performance: the Scherzo was muffed and the Andante finale dragged. I played some short pieces well; they were a great success and provoked cries of 'encore'. The Sonata for Two Violins was not very well played either, but they got away with it. The cello *Ballade* got a good reception despite a feeble cellist, the Second Piano Sonata rather a cool one (I was relaxed and played it decently but perhaps not atmospherically enough). The *Jewish Overture* had to be repeated. I started to look at my watch in view of the train I was due to catch. I was taken to the station still in my tails, having packed my things before the concert. Tyulin and Iokhelson came to see me off along with some younger ones, very touching, and a few others. Asafyev had left for Moscow yesterday to attend a conference. I was in an International Company sleeper, together with a quiet, stolid army officer. I was sorry to be leaving Leningrad.

4 December

Atovmyan and Shurik met me on arrival in Moscow at half past ten, and I immediately plunged into an avalanche of discussions and meetings. Asafyev came for me in the National Hotel and we went together to Ionov to put together a recommendation that Leningrad should be provided with the performing material for *Oranges*. My passport and ticket have been procured. At last a letter from Ptashka, the first I have had: she had been so clever as to send it to Moscow on the day I left for Leningrad. At five I went with Meyerhold to dine with Golovanov where there were three People's Artists:

Yurev,[1] Nezhdanova[2] and Meyerhold[3] himself. Other guests were the wife of Bubnov (a noisy Vampistaya[4]) Myaskovsky and Asafyev. The table was groaning with food and drink, elaborately served. It was all delicious and convivial, although I had suggested (and would have preferred) a working session about my future productions at the Bolshoy Theatre. It went on until eight o'clock, and at the end we had photographs taken and I went with Meyerhold and Myaskovsky to the National Hotel for a Union of Composers reception held in my honour. Here there was more food, a gathering of between fifty and seventy people with me in the place of honour. I replied to a short speech of welcome with an equally short speech in response, trying to lend an unofficial tone to the proceedings, but this did not stop a flood of other addresses, among others from Ippolitov-Ivanov,[5] now an old man, and Bely,[6] a leading VAPMan[7] who also saluted me. There was a queue to speak to me as if it were a dentist's waiting room: Goldenweiser about the Conservatoire; the Philharmonia about future appearances with them; VOKS[8] about contacts with foreign countries (I recommended Stock, Désormière and Robert Schmitz, the last-named because of his ability to have Soviet music played in Pro Musica concerts). Some of the Proletarian composers came up to me and I was very amicable, asking about their music

1 The actor Yury Yurev (1872–1948), the star and for a time Director of the Alexandrinsky Theatre in Petrograd/Leningrad, although since 1929 he had been a member of the Maly Theatre in Moscow and was shortly to join Meyerhold's company before returning finally to Leningrad in 1935. In 1932 he was a People's Artist of the RSFSR but in 1939 gained the top accolade of People's Artist of the USSR.
2 Antonina Nezhdanova (1873–1950), outstanding lyric coloratura soprano who had sung principal roles at the Bolshoy Theatre since soon after her graduation in 1903. She also at the time was a People's Artist of the RSFSR and would later achieve USSR status. The Moscow Tchaikovsky Conservatoire is in Nezhdanova Street, named in her honour. She was the wife of the conductor Nikolay Golovanov.
3 The only one of the trio never to make People's Artist of the USSR: his reward was to be arrested and shot.
4 A pun. Bubnova was a member of VAPM, Vserossiiskaya Assotsiatsiya Proletarskoi Muzyki, 'All-Russian Association for Proletarian Music', an earlier name for what eventually settled into the familiar Russian Association of Proletarian Musicians or RAPM. Prokofiev calls her, instead of a VAPMistaya a VAMPistaya, to suggest a relationship to a vampire.
5 Mikhail Ippolitov-Ivanov (1859–1935), much-respected composer, conductor and teacher. Invited originally by Tchaikovsky to come to teach composition at the Moscow Conservatoire, he became its Director in 1906 and retained the post until 1922.
6 Viktor Bely (1904–1983), alumnus of the Conservatoire 'Prokoll' group and a prominent member of the now defunct Association of Proletarian Musicians (he edited its organ For Proletarian Music (Za proletarskuyu musyku)).
7 That is, member of VAPM.
8 Vsesoyuznoe Obshchestveo Kulturnoi Svyazi s zagranitsei: the Society for Cultural Relations with Foreign Countries, official Soviet government organisation responsible for international cultural relations. It existed from 1925 until 1958 and was the precursor of the multiplicity of 'Friendship Societies' to be found in virtually all Western countries until the end of the Soviet Union and, rightly or wrongly, widely suspected of being little more than propaganda fronts.

with interest and telling them it should certainly be heard abroad as having been born of Revolution. Meyerhold delivered himself of a sharp-tongued speech in which he upbraided Malinovskaya (who was not present) for not performing Prokofiev in the Bolshoy Theatre. General applause for this. At midnight I went home to sleep but many people stayed until three in the morning. After the dinner at Golovanov's I had not been able to make many inroads into the lavish hospitality on offer.

5 December

The final day of my stay in the USSR began with the news that Golovanov has a temperature and will not be able to conduct the concert today. The programme will have to be changed and I shall have to play a half-hour solo set as well as conduct the *Classical* Symphony and *Le Pas d'acier* in the second half. There has been a fire in the Bolshoy Theatre library. Rehearsal at eleven and the concert at one, to a half-full hall, which spoilt the overall impression of my visit. But today is a working day and these days to ask for time off from work can simply lead to dismissal. A stupid time to schedule a concert. But Shurik told me that yesterday at the box office there were many people wanting to buy tickets who were not able to. What could this mean? At all events the concert went well and I was complimented on my conducting. Afterwards, while I was amicably and half-banteringly conversing with Malinovskaya, in came Myaskovsky and Shebalin. Malinovskaya said, 'I appreciate I am not the person you came to see, but I would still like a word with you if you please. You are all smiles now, but yesterday when I was being attacked, not only did you not utter a word in my defence, I am told you applauded.' Myaskovsky was embarrassed and I did not know whether I should stay or leave the room. At this point Meyerhold himself entered, and inevitably this was the signal to start a fight with him as well. When Meyerhold and I were safely out on the street again we could not stop laughing.

At the hotel I packed all the scores I had collected and sorted out a whole suitcase full of things for Shurik, Nadya and Katya, and another one for the Derzhanovskys. Atovmyan sent off a cable to Gusman and helped me pack the scores, paper is scarce and we had not been able to get hold of any decent string. Eventually we left at half past nine in Golovanov's car. An extraordinary Dutchman. The farewell party seeing me off consisted of Shurik, Nadya, two of their daughters, A.P.,[1] Katya, Derzhanovskys, Lyolya, Shebalin and Atovmyan. In my International Company sleeping-car I drank tea and fell into bed half dead.

---

1 Anna Petrovna Uvarova, a family friend who helped look after the children during their father's imprisonment.

6 December

Did not get to the border until 12.40. Thanks to the Narkompros[1] permit the music was not touched. The items that had been confiscated when I came into the country were returned in good order. I felt sorry to be leaving. In Poland I had a compartment to myself and slept soundly. Reached Warsaw in the evening; Fitelberg and his wife and sister – and my passport.

7 December

All day in Berlin.

8–17 December
Paris

I had a week in Paris between the USSR and America. I arrived at 11.25 in the morning to be met at the station by Ptashka and Astrov. Very loving relations with Ptashka, apart from a slight shadow cast right at the beginning when she complained about the people surrounding her and also things that had gone wrong during her visit to Prague. In the evening I attended a rehearsal of *On the Dnieper*[2] at the Opéra, on stage with orchestra and scenery and some of the costumes.

There are a good many instances of mismatches and inappropriate treatment: (1) Lifar's choreography with the music, at several points but particularly in the first number where he has choreographed massive groups of dancers to light, delicate music; (2) Larionov's settings, which in relation to the music lack poetry. The musical performance also leaves much to be desired: although Gaubert is obviously trying his best the 'senators' (as Stravinsky refers to the musicians in the Grand Opéra Orchestra with their venerable and patrician air) play out of tune and pay little attention to nuances. Rouché screamed incessantly at Lifar, of whose customary bumptiousness not a trace was left, the old man had completely squashed him. Near the end I had my own contretemps with Lifar, when for some reason

---

1 People's Commissariat for Education.
2 The very first, provisional, title of Lifar's ballet, once a scenario of sorts had been worked out, was 'Un dimanche soir', but as the story-line gradually became more linked to Lifar's own background (the hero is called Sergey and he hails from the Dnieper, the river that flows through Kiev) it became 'On the Dnieper'. Since the river is invariably referred to as the Borysthenes by classical Greek and Roman sources, many of whom cite with approval the cynical aphorisms of the local sage, the third-century BC philosopher Bion of Borysthenes, the title decided on for the ballet in Paris rather than the Slavonic Dnieper was the more Romance-derived *Sur le Borysthène*.

during the introduction he suddenly decided to raise the curtain on a totally empty stage.

From the rehearsal I went on to a Stravinsky concert including the premiere of the new duets, to which he had sent me an invitation, but by the time I got there the concert was nearly over. In the Green Room everyone wanted to hear what I had to tell them about Russia. Stravinsky asked me to dinner, but I declined as tomorrow there is an early rehearsal.

Suvchinsky: 'When are you going to give me a full report?' 'When I return from America,' I replied (irritated by his having ignored me for the whole of the past year). Markevich was unduly friendly and French; I exchanged two words with him and then continued my conversation with Suvchinsky, but the latter rushed in pursuit of Markevich so I walked away.

On the 9th there was a Lamoureux Orchestra rehearsal for a concert of my music conducted by Wolff, who having diverted extra rehearsal time from other concerts had made a very good job of preparing the *Sinfonietta*. The score of the Fifth Piano Concerto had been mislaid. Nevertheless, on the 10th the general rehearsal and the afternoon concert took place: the *Sinfonietta*, the Violin Concerto, six numbers from *Chout*, the Fifth Piano Concerto (Paris premiere) and the March from *Oranges* (rather stupid, but Wolff wanted to end with it). There was a large audience and an exceptionally warm response, especially for the Fifth Concerto, the most enthusiastic the work has so far received. Stravinsky came, full of praise for the Fifth Concerto, as well as the *Sinfonietta* and the Violin Concerto: the God Mercury has been transmogrified into a little angel. As Ptashka was leaving she caught sight of Boris Bashkirov, who glared at her with a malign expression. He was looking well, and presentably dressed (where did he get the money?). Ptashka was worried that he might create a scandal – after all I was just back from Russia – but Samoilenko told her he would crush him with his little finger if he were to try anything. The Samoilenkos came to dinner with us after the concert, with the Shukhaevs. Paichadze joined us later.

Now we had to get ready for America: passports, visas, boat tickets and dealing with a pile of letters that had accumulated over three weeks. The 16th, the eve of our departure, was the date fixed for the premiere of *On the Dnieper*; bad timing meant that it clashed with the first Triton concert, which included the first performance in Paris of my Sonata for Two Violins as well as a very nice Sonatina for violin and cello by Honegger. Dushkin and Soetens[1] gave my Sonata a quite splendid performance, better than in the

---

1 Robert Soetens (1887–1997), French violinist of Belgian extraction. As a gifted young boy he had had lessons with Ysaÿe but the family then moved to Paris where he studied at the Conservatoire. In 1925 Ravel chose him as his partner for the premiere of the violin-and-piano version of *Tzigane*. His performance in the Sonata for Two Violins so pleased Prokofiev that, Stravinsky having rewarded *his* violinist (Samuel Dushkin, the other violinist in the Sonata) with

USSR, and the work enjoyed a signal success. We then made a dash straight for the Opéra, where *On the Dnieper* was the final item on the programme. Stravinsky also achieved the double, calling the Sonata 'un bijou'. In the box at the Opéra were Ptashka and I, the two Samoilenkos, Mesdames Szigeti and Chalon. The orchestra was better than it had been at yesterday's dress rehearsal and the scenery also looked better because the lighting had been improved, although Goncharova's costumes still failed to shine. The end of the first scene elicited significant applause, for the dancing of Lifar. The end of the ballet, however, produced little in the way of response and although there were calls for me to appear I did not come on to the stage. At the end of an extremely long performance what the audience really wants is to go home. There was the usual post-first-performance announcement from the stage mentioning that the music was by Prokofiev, choreography by Lifar. Larionov was in a fury that there was no mention at all of his name. Ptashka and I went backstage to shake hands with Rouché, Lifar and the two ballerinas.

We left Paris at ten o'clock in the morning on the 17th, arriving in Cherbourg before nightfall. The *Europa* is not a large liner but it is a nice one, and our cabin was on the upper deck. Bruno Walter and his wife were also aboard. I look on the ship and the voyage as a rest-home.

On the 22nd we reached New York.

---

a new concerto, motivation to accept a commission to do likewise for Soetens followed swiftly, with the result that the violinist premiered the Second Violin Concerto in Madrid in 1935 and, rather like Szigeti with the First Concerto, played it so often it grew to be associated with him. For this Soetens happily had plenty of time: he died a few weeks after his hundredth birthday and was still performing until the age of ninety-five.

1933

Between the third week of December 1932 and April 1933, Prokofiev (without Lina) was in the United States for six weeks, appearing as soloist in the Third Piano Concerto with Bruno Walter, who also conducted the new Gambler *compilation, and launching the Fifth Piano Concerto in concert series with the Boston Symphony under Koussevitzky and the Chicago Symphony under Frederick Stock. It was, on the whole, a satisfyingly reputation-enhancing tour, and made some money as well. He also composed the* Symphonic Song, *Op. 57, which with the benefit of hindsight may be seen as a step along the road to the grand nobility of the Fifth Symphony, first full symphonic expression of the composer's Soviet period but at this point over a decade in the future. Having left Paris the day after the premiere of* Sur le Borysthène *at the Opéra he will have had the Atlantic between him and the dismal reviews of the new ballet to take the edge off the disappointment, although the diary entries recording his reaction to the rehearsals and the first night probably would not have led him to anticipate a critical triumph. At the end of the American tour in mid-February he took a relaxed southerly route home on an Italian liner, the* Conte di Savoia, *round Gibraltar to the south of France rather than straight across the North Atlantic.*

April–June
Visit to the USSR

I left Paris at 5.46 on the 8th April, accompanied to the station by Ptashka, Svyatoslav and Weber, who by chance was in Paris. His tales of what is happening in Germany were horrible to hear. Stravinsky is on a blacklist for being Jewish; this has put him in a frenzy that is almost comical.[1] But I slept the whole way through Germany.

Arrived in Prague on the 9th, a mass of stories here too. The following day there was a rehearsal of the Third Piano Concerto for Prague Radio; the orchestra was good but the conductor was of the Glazunov persuasion, invariably late. The performance was on the 11th, to an invited audience, closed to the public.

Next day I went on to Moscow, arming myself with provisions for distribution to friends and relations. Warsaw at six o'clock in the morning, and at half past four in the afternoon the border at Negoreloe on a beautiful sunny, but cold day. I ran into Glinsky, the manager of the National Hotel in Moscow. The Customs officials were unusually polite, making only the most cursory inspection. I drew out some money from my savings bank account. Sleeping-car. Low spirits, but I did my best to remove from them all egotistical elements.

14 April

Moscow at a quarter to ten: Afinogenov, Myaskovsky, Derzhanovsky, Atovmyan, Shebalin. A bright, clear day and warm although snow could still be seen under bushes that had not thawed. Afinogenov's car is actually a Ford but the car in which I went was a superb Lincoln. A comfortable, quiet two-room suite had been reserved for me at the National Hotel, as last time,

---

1 Two months after Hitler was appointed Chancellor by Hindenburg at the end of January 1933, a Kultur Kampfbund ('Fighting Front for Culture') was already in existence with the aim of boosting German culture and ridding Germany of Jewish and Bolshevik art. Lists of undesirable artists circulated, Stravinsky's name among them as a Jew, which of course he was not. In any case his racial origins were at this early point less important than the suspicion that he was promoting a poisonous Untermensch Slav, probably Bolshevik, aesthetic which must be rigorously purged. See S. Walsh, op. cit., pp. 518–19.

but garishly decorated and overstuffed with too much furniture. The whole party came in to have coffee with me, to go over plans for how I was to spend my time and to look through the music I had brought with me. Gradually they all dispersed, and I went with Atovmyan to the Union of Composers to collect some spending money.

On the way there and back I greedily took in Moscow, on my return had a meal in the unpleasantly pretentious hotel restaurant, then rested for half an hour and set off to meet Myaskovsky. He is trying to make some improvements in his flat, but still has not managed to develop the skills to do so. He is not composing anything at present. He has already looked at the proofs of the first movement of the Fifth Concerto and succeeded in adding another one to the mistakes I had found. At least this time it was only one. I played him the *Chant symphonique*, the first time anyone has heard it. He approved, except for some cadences that were to his taste unacceptably straight. We discussed foursquareness in form and the need for renewal in compositional techniques.

From there I went on to the Rayevskys near by, not quite knowing whom I would find because of the problems with internal passports encountered by people returning from exile. But there were Alyonya, her sister Katya and the two Uvarovas, Katya and Anna Petrovna. Shurik was already in the Urals.[1] I was very impressed with Alyona who has grown up, has become responsible and talks very intelligently.

In the evening I went to see the play *The Introduction*[2] at the Meyerhold Theatre – Meyerhold himself is in Leningrad. The play is a piece of naive propaganda that dramatically speaking does no more than stumble along. Meyerhold has conceived some interesting moments, such as a drunk engineer embracing an enormous bust of Goethe and addressing it (him) in the formal second-person plural, but it is far too long. I had taken off my overcoat and laid it across my knees, but during the interval was accosted and told to take it to the cloakroom. I said I would, but instead disappeared back into the auditorium and took care not to show my face during the second interval. I read Shurik's letters from the Urals which Alyona had lent me.

---

1 Alexander Rayevsky, despite his period of exile having ended, was not having any luck obtaining a residence permit for Moscow and the family was going to have to move to the Urals.
2 Based on the first novel by the impeccably proletarian Yury German (1910–1967) who collaborated with Meyerhold on the production, dealing with an American scientist enthralled by the possibilities of the Five Year Plan. German's novel, which appeared in 1931, had drawn high praise from Gorky, which had ensured its critical success as well as the support of the political hierarchy. Later, German produced a string of what are in effect thrillers in which the dedicated detectives of Dzerzhinsky's Cheka unmask the crimes of dastardly economic and social enemies of the state.

The Introduction ends with a group of German professors setting out for the USSR, where there is nothing to distract one from getting on with real work, a land free from oppression, jazz or inebriated bourgeoisie. I went back to the hotel and had supper in the National Hotel's restaurant, to the accompaniment of jazz and dancing.

15 April

A stream of people all morning, and crucially discussions with Atovmyan on the subject of the tour to the Caucasus, *Lieutenant Kijé*, and accounts. There is a proposal that I should teach a Conservatoire course for composers who have already graduated. At one o'clock Derzhanovsky and Saradzhev for lunch and to go through the Third Symphony. I presented Saradzhev with a suit of tails. Myaskovsky had praise for the major new work I had left for him to look at. He suggests the Russian title should be not be *Symphonic Song* but either *Symphony-Song* or *Song-Symphony*.[1] When they left I rested, as I could feel a headache coming on. Alyona came to pick up a women's fashion magazine; I gave her some money and a few little trinkets, and we talked for an hour. 'I have no desire to go abroad, as the others seem to want to, except perhaps for a visit.' Bravo! We went out together, and then I went to the Bolshoy Theatre for *Dionysus*,[2] a ballet by Shenshin. It was quite well and attractively staged, but the music is second-rate. In the interval I looked into the Director's box: Arkanov, Gorodinsky,[3] Kubatsky. I left early and went back to the hotel as I was tired. There was a sudden fall of wet snow on the streets.

16 April

Managed a bit of piano playing in the morning. Then read through two interviews I had given to journalists yesterday, and had a discussion with the

1 *Symphonic Song*, Op. 57. After Prokofiev had ended his visit and returned to Paris, Myaskovsky on more considered reflection and in the context of what would be likely to lead to success in Soviet Russia, was to be more equivocal: '*Chanson symphonique* [sic] is not altogether what is needed here; there is a certain meagreness in the form (too much striving after refinement), and it lacks that element we perceive as the monumental – that manifest simplicity and expansiveness in contour of which you are so exceptionally capable but for the present seem to be concerned scrupulously to avoid. Don't be angry with me, please.' (Letter of 17 June 1933, *Prokofiev/Myaskovsky Correspondence*, op. cit., pp. 399–400.)
2 Also known as *Ancient Dances*.
3 Viktor Gorodinsky (1902–1959), musicologist and critic, as Director of Rossiiskaya Filarmonia (Rosphil) a high-ranking member of the musical *nomenklatura*, and later to be an enthusiastic henchman of Zhdanov and Shepilov in the preparation of the Central Committee's 1948 Resolution condemning the 'Formalist' tendencies of Prokofiev, Shostakovich, Khachaturian, Myaskovsky, Shebalin, Popov and others. According to some reports Gorodinsky may have been the author of the *Pravda* article attacking Shostakovich's *Lady Macbeth of Mtsensk*.

producers of a possible second film commission, *The Revolt of the Fishermen*,[1] but I very much doubt if I shall have time to compose the music.

I then went to see Pshybyshevsky, who is temporarily standing in for Arkadiev. He greeted me with great friendliness and I gave him a report on exchanges and recommendations for conductors, for which he thanked me warmly. Although the concert plan for next season has already been discussed there is to be another conference on the subject, which I will be invited to attend. Among the names I mentioned were Malko and Gorchakov, the former arousing some interest but the latter a more ironic response.

In the evening I was due to attend a performance of Afinogenov's *Fear*, but another play had been substituted and so I stayed at home and did my packing. Shostakovich, just back from Sverdlovsk, called in. I assumed that I was receiving a visit *en hommage* but was speedily disabused: he wanted me to take a score of his to Lenfilm. I told him about the performances of his works in the West I had attended. We went together to the Central Telegraph;[2] his wife,[3] charming woman. Lourié's mother also came to see me: she has not had a letter from him for some time. She wanted me to let him know that she is in good health and life treats her reasonably well although there are difficulties. If possible, he could transfer money to her via Torgsin.

Left at half past twelve on the 'Red Arrow' sleeper in new, Soviet, livery and with the radio blaring out until two o'clock in the morning. Luckily the loudspeaker in my compartment was broken. Atovmyan came to see me off.

17 April

Leningrad at 1.20 next morning, sunny but chilly. No one to meet me except a secretary from the Philharmonia, and a shabby little car – to get a Lincoln you need hard currency. The first room I was offered in the Yevropeiskaya

---

1 Based on the 1928 novella by the German-Jewish Marxist writer Anna Seghers (pen-name of Netty Reiling Radványi), *Der Aufstand der Fischer von St Barbara*, which tells of the spontaneous uprising of Breton fishermen against a monopoly. The German theatre director Erwin Piscator, a committed Marxist and Communist fellow-traveller, who had left Germany in 1931 and lived in Moscow until 1934, was commissioned by the International Film Workers Studio in Moscow to make a film of the book. He did so (the only time he directed a movie) but despite lavish facilities and huge crowd scenes in Murmansk and Odessa it was not a success. The music for the film was eventually provided by three composers, the Hungarian Ferenc Szabó, Nikolay Chemberdzhi and Vladimir Fere, a former student of Myaskovsky.
2 The very large Central Telegraph Office on Gorky (now again Tverskaya) Street, a few blocks from the National Hotel.
3 Shostakovich's first wife, whom he had married in 1932, was the astro-physicist Nina Varzar, mother of the two Shostakovich children Galina and Maxim.

Hotel was not much good, but the next was fine and an upright piano was brought in. No copy of Op. 35 bis[1] could be found anywhere in Leningrad and a telegram was sent to Moscow.

At noon there was a rehearsal of the Quintet in the Philharmonia; they have already rehearsed it five times and it is beginning to come together, but so far without sparkle.

Lidusya came in the afternoon, delightful but bird-brained.

Spoke on the phone to Dranishnikov, arranging to meet tomorrow to go through the Third Symphony. Asked him to give Asafyev a good cuff round the ear for hiding, and make him come to the meeting. Evening at Demchinsky's, who as usual was full of edifying prescriptions delivered with calm gravitas. I told him of my time in America and showed him photographs, but we did not get into any philosophical discussions. Played chess, a match that went on until one in the morning.

When I got back, the hotel restaurant was full of the local dandies dancing to a jazz band. I ate hurriedly and went to bed.

18 April

Rehearsed the chamber-music programme. In the afternoon went to Dranishnikov's to fix the tempi for the Symphony. According to Dranishnikov, Asafyev, whom I had mildly twitted on the telephone yesterday for ignoring me, is in such distress that he has taken to his bed. Sheer 'Freudism' of course, says Dranishnikov.

At seven I received a deputation from Belgoskino[2] accompanied by Gusman and Faintsimmer. Needless to say they would not hear of my accepting any work for a Moscow studio. We discussed some details. At half past eight the violinist came (Op. 35 bis having been with some difficulty procured) and at half past nine an interview with a correspondent from the *Red Gazette* (*Krasnaya Gazeta*). The throughput was like a dentist's waiting room. When he left, at around eleven, I went for a walk and then to bed.

---

1 The arrangement for violin and piano of *Five Songs Without Words*, Op. 35.
2 Abbreviation of Gosudarstvennoe Upravlenie po delam Kinematografii Belorussii – the Belorussian State Directorate of Kinematographic Affairs. Despite its title and ostensible remit, almost as soon as this organisation, officially a department of the Belorussian government, was formed in 1925 it removed itself from its native soil and set up shop in Leningrad on the reasonable grounds that there would probably be people there who actually knew something about making movies. Indeed the studio proved to be one of the most productive in the Soviet Union, providing facilities for a host of peripatetic directors (like Alexander Faintsimmer) and creative teams but almost nothing to establish a Belorussian national cinema.

19 April

Two orchestra rehearsals today, at ten and again at one. It was a pleasure to hear the Third Symphony again after so long, but the playing was mediocre and Dranishnikov is not yet secure in his tempi.

The chamber-music concert was in the evening. Not a full hall, a little over half. The reason is the general lack of money in the population: in order to increase the value of money and lower the price of goods the government is restricting the supply of banknotes.[1] The Philharmonia is suffering a run of dreadful box-office receipts: Ansermet's gross receipts were half today's and Barsova's concert was cancelled when bookings levelled off at a total of 60 roubles. Even so it is depressing. The Quintet received a decent if uninspired performance. My performance of the Second Sonata went well, while the smaller pieces were a little uneven: I have played almost no recitals this season and am out of practice at performing solo. They were a great success, however, with much shouting and many curtain calls.

To see me in the Artists' Room came a recovered Asafyev, Meyerhold, Lidusya and Vera Alpers.

20 April

Orchestral rehearsal in the morning: *Scythian Suite* and the Concerto. No better than average standard of playing.

Asafyev called in the afternoon, after which I called on Lidusya and then Meyerhold. Demchinsky dined with me, reverting to his customary attacking mode: I travel too much, yesterday's concert lacked a real sense of occasion; I am producing a lot of compositions but would it not be better to stop for a while and take stock? Then, I am running away from life and this is something life will not forgive; even my relaxations, like bridge and chess, are essentially escapes from life. I objected that the purpose of my visit to the Soviet Union had not been undertaken to accumulate more laurels but in the interests of gradually acquainting audiences with my work. In recent years, I went on, I had worked unremittingly and devoted much thought to the direction my creativity was taking, precisely in that plane so dear to Demchinsky, that is to say the spiritual plane. I conceded that his strictures on bridge and chess were accurately aimed. To my regret the conversation then took another turn, and although there was much I could have said to justify my lapses in this direction, I lost my chance.

---

1 It was also part of the drive towards state capitalisation exemplified by the Industrial Bonds programme.

Gusman had mentioned earlier in the day a subject for an opera he thought might interest me: Lavrenyov's 'Story of a Simple Thing'.[1] Demchinsky warned that as a subject for an opera it might hold only a temporary interest. I objected that this depends on the angle from which it is approached.

21 April

General rehearsal. The Third Symphony was unspeakably bad. I tackled the orchestra's manager: 'Exactly like a herd of cows hauling a load of dung up a mountainside.'

The manager: 'Our orchestra is Number One in the USSR.'

I: 'Being Number One in the USSR does not give you the right to play worse than an orchestra abroad.'

In the afternoon Meyerhold appeared, having brought his Ford up to Leningrad by loading it on to the 'Red Arrow'. There were still ice floes on the Neva; it was a lovely sunny day, but not warm. A ferry sank on the river and the passengers were saved only by using lifebelts to get to the shore. Zinaida's comment on the train was: 'The Arrow smells of the cemetery' (meaning it is stuck in the past and has not found the way to relate to our new life).

The director of the *Revolt of the Fishermen* film came to discuss the project with me.[2] It is a relationship I should like to maintain for the future, but for the present it simply represents hack work for me.

The concert was in the evening. The hall was full, but not overflowing, as it had been last time. Dranishnikov's tempi are still unsteady, but the Symphony had an unexpected success – not huge, but perfectly acceptable. The Third Piano Concerto really caught fire and I played the Toccata as an encore. I took many curtain calls after the Concerto and the *Scythian Suite*. The Director of the Philharmonia talks about my coming back next year, although after the hard words this morning it was looking as though this would be the last time.

Afterwards walked to Nikolay Radlov's with his wife who is all lipstick and looks as though she has stepped out of the pages of a fashion journal. Shaporin was there, also Sergey Radlov, with whom I played chess until four in the morning (won one, lost one, which is pretty good seeing that he is category one). He suggested that I write a *Till Eulenspiegel* ballet from a

---

1   Civil War novella written in 1924 by Boris Lavrenyov (1891–1959). Lavrenyov himself had fought on both sides, having started with the White Army and then crossed over to the Reds.
2   Presumably Piscator.

Revolutionary perspective for the Mariinsky Theatre, a proposal I deflected. He wants to revive *Oranges* in the autumn, in a revised production.

22 April

One free day before I leave. I did not sleep well.

Was at Belgoskino, the first time I had been in the studio. It was very interesting. We discussed the production and the music, and I was shown some sample footage of costumes and the treatment of dialogue. I criticised the conventions of Russian theatrical style, the way dialogue is handled there: the Americans are so much more natural. The only good part was that the 'Finis' was followed by a party. I was then filmed playing the Gavotte and the Toccata for the news. The lights were so blinding as to make one extremely hot, and the session dragged on. I did not play the Toccata excerpts well but there was no time to repeat them. I went back to the hotel and slept.

In the evening Demchinsky and then Vera Alpers, who accompanied me to the station. 'You might at least kiss my hand.' Gusman also came. Asafyev was on the train with me and we talked until half past one.

23–27 April

Returned to Moscow for two weeks. No Atovmyan to meet me at the station, and no car either, the streets awash with slush, my room at the hotel has been taken so I have been given the one Rubinin occupied in December. It is a large corner suite with a minute bedroom. Derzhanovsky came to fetch me in a tiny rented car with paraffin lamps. Today is my forty-second birthday and it is also exactly a year since the demise of RAPM. An event commemorating the latter had originally been planned, on a more celebratory scale than what in fact took place, which was an orchestral concert consisting of Myaskovsky's Twelfth Symphony (average: Glazunovian, four-square, simple in the sense of the old simplicity, not the new). It formed the prelude to Shebalin's big new symphony, also not much good, with two unnecessary fugatos;[1] then a Suite from Shostakovich's *Bolt*: brilliantly assimilated vulgarity, more a caricature of vulgarity, in other words precisely what ten years ago in Paris had so upset me in scores such as Milhaud's *Train bleu* and similar offerings from Poulenc, Sauguet and Auric. Ansermet said it could have all been made into a Parisian 'Sérénade'.

On the 24th I heard a chamber concert in which Shostakovich played his *Twenty-Four Preludes*, similarly a pastiche of all different styles with not a

---

1 Prokofiev had heard a piano reduction of an earlier version of this work at one of Lamm's Wednesdays on his first visit in 1927: see above, p. 540.

single idea of his own. Generally they are attractive pieces and well put together, but for that reason all the more disappointing in the futility at their heart. How sad that the foremost Soviet composer should be writing typically decadent music of the 'rotten West'.

Rehearsals proceeded for my symphonic and chamber-music programmes, except that there was no oboist so the Quintet was replaced by the Quartet. Saradzhev is a good musician but not a leader: he veers between ingratiating himself with the orchestra and screaming at them, and the orchestra cares not a rap for him. The quality of the orchestra is no better than in Leningrad but the musicians try harder, despite their contempt for Saradzhev. Quite a lot of musicians came to listen to the rehearsal: Myaskovsky, Glière, Lamm, Alexandrov.[1] The performances, the chamber music on the 26th, and the orchestral concert the following day took place in front of audiences and their response similar to Leningrad. After hearing the Symphony Asafyev said that he had for the first time detected a genuine spirituality in it, and had been moved by it.

On the day I arrived back in Moscow, the 23rd, I heard the general rehearsal of *Yevgeny Onegin* in the Bolshoy Theatre with sets by Rabinovich, very good except for Tatyana's bedroom. As for the music, it retains its freshness astonishingly well. Rabinovich's wife, beside whom I was sitting, is a charming woman. The auditorium was full of Moscow's artistic elite, many of them good-looking people. The general impression when one first comes to the Soviet Union is of drabness, but as one looks below the surface the outlines of attractive and lively features often begin to appear. I met the management of the theatre in a body in the Director's box and had a very cordial reception from them without, however, touching on any specific topics of conversation.

On the 25th I was again in the Bolshoy for *Swan Lake* to see Semyonova, whose virtuosity, precision and lightness make her truly an outstanding dancer. I took Alyona, we got tickets in the front row and it was a pleasure for me to have my young niece as a companion, especially one as attractive to look at as she. Our outing was a secret, as Katya had now arrived from Kadnikov but I did not want to see her until my concerts were over.

28–30 April

Did the things I had put off until the concerts were over. Visited Rubinin just to keep up the relationship, also Ionov, to whom I put a proposal to provide the USSR with my scores in return for Soviet money.

---

1 Not Alexander Alexandrov, founder of the Alexandrov Ensemble – better known as the Red Army Choir – and composer of the Soviet National Anthem, but the rather more retiring Anatoly Alexandrov (1888–1982), a product of and later professor at the Moscow Conservatoire and composer of impeccably orthodox symphonies, a piano concerto, piano sonatas and chamber music. See above, p. 430 n. 1.

I was visited by the head of the composition faculty at the Conservatoire, who invited me to do some work with students there, but the invitation has come late in the day since the Union of Composers has already identified a group of composers who have just completed their training to send to me. The business with the Conservatoire was postponed until the autumn.[1] Another visit was from a representative of the Moscow Philharmonia, who told me it had been decided to extend invitations to all those conductors whose names I had put forward. This is splendid news. They would even like to invite Smallens to head the Philharmonia for a two-year period, but this proposal made me nervous and I asked to be allowed to check all the letters before they are sent.

Starting on the 29th the young composers came to make my acquaintance: Sokolov[2] on the 29th and Vitachek[3] on the 30th. The work they submitted was technically sound; at first glance I could see nothing that called for comment and I began to wonder if, having been taken on to instruct, I would in fact not find anything to instruct about. But gradually various questionable practices did emerge: ninth chords, passages cribbed from Tchaikovsky, parallel fifths and octaves, and so on. Each day I worked with one of them while the other three looked on, ending up after the two-hour sessions with completely addled brains.

I spent some time with Katya Ignatieva, pathetic and poignant.

1 May

Atovmyan had said he would get me a ticket for the grandstand on Red Square so that I could watch the May Day parade, but failing in the endeavour, something having gone wrong, had in shame and confusion gone into hiding for five days, a step that caused considerably more inconvenience than

---

1 Prokofiev's appointment described him as a 'consultant professor'. He held the position until the spring of 1937, although once he had become a full-time Moscow resident he may not have been as conscientious as he was to begin with: his Conservatoire file alludes to 'dismissal on grounds of absence of pedagogical load'. (S. Morrison, *The People's Artist – Prokofiev's Soviet Years*, OUP, 2009, p. 23.)
2 Probably Vladislav Sokolov (1908–1993) who had recently graduated from Dmitry Kabalevsky's class at the Moscow Conservatoire School (not the Conservatoire itself). If it was he, his main professional interest and skill lay in choral conducting, in which field he rose to some prominence as conductor and teacher.
3 Favii Vitachek (1910–1983), composer and teacher, son of the distinguished Czech-born luthier Jindřich Vitáček who, having moved with his family to Moscow in the early years of the century, was appointed curator of the State String Instrument Collection (see above, pp. 884–5 n. 2). His son had graduated from Myaskovsky's composition class at the Moscow Conservatoire in 1931 and later pursued a mainly teaching career in musical literature, score-reading and orchestration at both the Moscow Conservatoire and the Gnesin Institute.

remaining in view. I observed the scene from the window of my corner room. The tanks arrived at five in the morning. At nine I tried myself to go into the square, but there were cordons everywhere, it was hard to move and I had difficulty even in getting back the hotel. The aeroplane fly-past was very effective; I counted 250 but the reports said 600. The tanks also rattled the windows as they ground past, but I was later told that one had come to a halt immediately opposite the grandstand and could not be moved either backwards or forwards. The most interesting part of the parade was the procession of demonstrators: just below my window two ribbons, one from Gorky Street, the other from the Bolshoy Theatre, coalesced to form one enormous stream of people that entirely filled the lower end of Gorky Street from pavement to pavement. On Red Square itself, so I was told, a wall of people eighty abreast advanced without stopping from half past eleven until half past five. Seen from above the bright red banners looked very pretty, as did the red hats worn by the women, sometimes changing to white and multi-coloured ones. There was a sea of flags and placards, most of them red, and an endless succession of bands playing a variety of marches, jolly tunes, and sad ones like 'Marusya's Taken Poison'.[1]

The display came to an end at six, and I ventured out to play chess at Goldenweiser's, a strong and long-standing opponent. The contest promised extra piquancy because of the difference in our musical outlooks. The chess set was a magnificent one which had been presented to him by Chertkov,[2] on a morocco-leather board. The first match was proceeding on

1   A lachrymose song about the suicide of a village girl disappointed in love. Long believed to be a folk song, it was in fact written in 1911 by Yakov Prigozhy, the leader of the Gypsy orchestra at the legendary 'Yar' restaurant on the St Petersburg Prospect, a haunt of the literary and artistic elite including Kuprin, Chekhov, Rachmaninoff, Chaliapin, Gorky, not to mention Rasputin. In 1927 Mayakovsky wrote a very funny and bitter parody of its damp-eyed sentimentality.
2   Vladimir Chertkov (1854–1936), writer, publisher, secretary and amanuensis to Lev Tolstoy. Tolerated with barely concealed animosity by Tolstoy's wife, he nevertheless dominated the writer, his household and his growing army of quasi-religious adherents from 1883 until Tolstoy's death in 1910, to the extent of persuading Tolstoy to change his will and bequeath all rights in his writings to Chertkov instead of to his widow and family. To quote from the liner notes in a Toccata Classics CD: 'As a young man, Goldenweiser was on particularly close terms with Lev Tolstoy: he met him in January 1896 and remained on close terms with him until his death. He stayed at Yasnaya Polyana and frequently played to Tolstoy. Goldenweiser kept a record of Tolstoy's remarks and took notes about the daily life at, and visitors to, the house. Goldenweiser was not Tolstoy's official biographer, and this unusual position gave him a good deal of freedom; his report of his friendship and time spent with the writer was published as *Vblizi Tolstogo* ('Close to Tolstoy'). Goldenweiser always had a pencil and notebook with him, and he had the gift of writing things down unnoticed. He thus preserved the characteristics of Tolstoy's spoken language for posterity. He even copied letters from Tolstoy, his friends and acquaintances into his notebook. His record of the last year of Tolstoy's life – 1910 – is particularly detailed, making up almost half of Goldenweiser's book. Tolstoy's only known musical composition was a Waltz in F which Goldenweiser wrote down after the writer had played it to him in February 1906.'
(*Alexander Goldenweiser Piano Music Volume 1* (TOCC0044, 2008).)

an even keel and in accordance with logic when something suddenly happened, I made a breakthrough, succeeded in concentrating all my pieces' firepower, and Goldenweiser quickly had to capitulate. The second match dragged on interminably: Goldenweiser contrived a dangerous pawn breakout but I remained in control of all moves and counter-moves and by midnight it was clear that the result was a draw.

2–5 May

Each day from twelve until two I spent with the young composers (they cannot be called students as they have all graduated from the Conservatoire): Tsvetov, Yatsevich[1] and Lev Shvartz.[2] Of them, the second possessed the greatest technical command, although his Symphony was not well conceived orchestrally. The third submitted some treatments of Asiatic material which were not notably inventive but at least done differently from Borodin, indeed the source material itself was different. At the conclusion of our sessions they asked me if overall they had not made too depressing an impression on me. I replied that the worst aspect was the general attitude to harmony, the over-reliance on augmented ninths, and that more effort should be made to combat the dead hand of rigidity in rhythm and symmetry. We parted friends.

Shurik appeared from the Urals (I had paid for his journey), buoyant as ever and not the slightest embittered.

Faintsimmer came and professed himself very happy with the tunes for the film, which in between doing other things I had composed a few days ago. He wants me to come up with a test piece including drums, to see how the cinema soundtrack can handle them.

I left gramophone records of the *Classical* Symphony with Moscow Radio.

On the 3rd I played the Second Sonata and some smaller pieces at the Theatrical Workers' Club (in a room crammed so full one could hardly breathe and on an ear-splittingly noisy piano), prefacing my performance with some remarks about how Soviet music is perceived abroad, and a little about non-Soviet music as well. There was laughter when I talked about Rachmaninoff 'gloomily making a great deal of money' and Chaliapin, on finishing making a film, having departed for Jerusalem.

On the 5th I played a recital at the Moscow House of Scholars. The previous day I had given a report to a gathering at the Composers' Union on

---

1 Yury Yatsevich (1901–?) composer of six symphonies, two violin concertos, song-cycles, solo piano works.
2 Lev Shvartz (1898–1962), composer, pianist and teacher. Works include a piano and a violin concerto, a symphony, the opera *Dzhannat* and numerous scores for feature and animated films.

exchange visits by conductors from abroad. The VOKS representative said to me, 'I have about forty letters from foreign musicians all wanting to come here, but I don't think any of them are important and I don't propose to reply.' 'That may well be so in thirty-five of the cases,' I replied, 'but the remaining five might be interesting.' He promised to bring me the list so that I could look through it, and we fixed a date to do so, but he later telephoned to say that he had not been able to collect together all the letters. A delightful example of Russian inertia.

The work I had done with my students, seeing some of their clumsy attempts to write something in a contemporary idiom, the equally unsuccessful essays by the proletarian musicians to achieve a simplicity that will never without the necessary technical skills yield up its secrets, and finally the hints I kept hearing that my music is too complex to be appreciated by the masses, combined to persuade me that now is indeed the time to produce work that will genuinely appeal to the masses but is at the same time good music. The work I have already done on finding melodies and the search for the 'new simplicity' will stand me in good stead for this challenge. I thought about it, and in the light of my reflections composed a theme and some ways of developing it.

6 May

The radio broadcast the discs of the *Classical* Symphony, played by the Boston Orchestra, that I had given the station. There is an odd situation here: they tend to put out interesting programmes before nine o'clock in the morning and after midnight, that is to say before the working day and after the theatre. I was not able to listen because the only radio set the National Hotel possesses is in the Director's office.

Ptashka arrived at 9.45. Derzhanovsky had gone all the way to Negoreloe to meet her, where the Customs officials had been polite and not aggressive. A group of Rayevskys and Derzhanovskys were at the station to greet them on arrival in Moscow.

The evening performance in the Bolshoy Theatre was a jubilee celebration of Nezhdanova, a very glamorous occasion with a roster of celebrity appearances. It was a good time for Ptashka to arrive. The performance was followed by a series of tributes on stage, in which I took part as a representative of the Union of Composers, along with Myaskovsky, Gnesin[1] and

---

1 Mikhail Gnesin (1883–1957), composer and committed proponent of Jewish traditional music. Mikhail was the younger brother of the formidable Gnesin sisters Yevgenia, Yelena and Maria, who had founded in the new wave of the Russian Enlightenment at the end of the nineteenth century what became the Gnesin Institute of Music (today the Gnesin Russian Academy of Music). Mikhail taught composition there, and eventually became the Institute's Director.

Vasilenko.¹ After this there was a supper that lasted until 7 a.m., but we made our excuses and left after two o'clock, on the grounds that I had a rehearsal and concert the next day.

7 May

A repeat performance of the programme of my orchestral concert, in my opinion a redundant one since the general shortage of money meant that the hall was not full. On the other hand it was good for the musicians in the public to have the chance of a further hearing of my Third Symphony even in an indifferent performance.

In the afternoon I called on Arkadiev, who was welcoming, although several people have warned me that the welcome is as far as it ever goes. I gave him an account of my activities abroad and showed him a selection of my press interviews. He mentioned in passing that he had been present at one discussion in which it was noted that while I successfully resolve the most complex technical issues in my compositions, it would be desirable for me to devote more thought to music for the masses. I replied that this was precisely the direction my own thoughts were taking at the moment, and I had already made considerable progress.

8 May

The usual flurry of last-minute activity before leaving: packing, a mass of people who insist on talking to me, and a discussion with the artist Vano about animated films. This could be very interesting, if he is truly a good draughtsman.²

At 8.30 in the evening we boarded an International Company sleeping-car in the Blue Train to Tbilisi. In our carriage were several members of the Georgian Government.

9 May

We were still asleep when we passed through Kharkov. At Lozova and succeeding stations we were brought face to face with the famine in the Ukraine. People were asking for bread, and we saw pitiful and emaciated faces. But the restaurant-car in our train, with its supplies from Moscow, fed us well.

---

1 Sergey Vasilenko (1872–1956), composer, conductor and teacher. After studying with Taneyev at the Moscow Conservatoire he became a Professor there; among his students were Aram Khachaturian and Nikolai Roslavets.
2 Ivan Ivanov-Vano (1900–1987), one of the founding fathers of the Soviet animated-film genre.

The train had a 'Culture and Rest Carriage' similar to the observation-cars on American trains, with comfortable chairs and chessboards (I won two games), a platform at the rear and a section for a cinema. The film that was showing, however, was rubbish, a piece of naive propaganda.

In the evening we arrived in Rostov.

10 May

Approximately at noon we disembarked from the train at Beslan for Vladikavkaz and the Georgian Military Highway, but as we did so the Georgian government officials shouted to us that the road was closed until later in the year. We scrambled back on to the train and were lucky that our compartment had not been sold to someone else. Continuing our journey we went on to the open platform at the back of the train, but were warned that people have been known to throw stones. At stations we were subjected to sarcastic remarks along the lines of 'Of course, only proletarians travel in trains like this.' At one station a drunk in a velvet blouse, evidently a dispossessed kulak, addressing me as 'ty',[1] said, 'All right, if you want to send us into exile, well, go ahead then', swung his arms and threw a packet of money on to the ground. The Government officials sniggered at the idea that it was I who had ordered the deportation. That evening Mdivani,[2] Georgia's Commissar of Light Engineering, entertained us royally with wine from Kakheti,[3] showered us with compliments and did his best to get us drunk, in which he succeeded although we did manage to preserve some sense of decorum.

---

1 The intimate, second-person singular, considered insulting unless to a child or a close friend or relative.
2 One of the more interesting travelling companions, Polykarp 'Budu' Mdivani (1877–1937), former Old Bolshevik associate of Stalin, with Stalin and Ordzhonikidze the third member of the triumvirate that had instigated the Red Army's invasion of Georgia in 1921 to topple the anti-Moscow Menshevik regime then in power. Mdivani had quickly proved anything but a complaisant camp-follower of his tyrannical compatriot. As Chairman of the new Georgian Revolutionary Committee he fought hard, but ultimately unsuccessfully, to protect what remained of Georgia's autonomy and to frustrate Stalin's and Beria's determination to bring their former country abjectly to heel, a dispute that became known as the 'Georgian Affair'. Inevitably, as Stalin progressively consolidated his power base, his stubborn ex-colleague, given to widely reported sarcastic gibes about Stalin's mother needing round-the-clock protection from Beria's squads to ensure she did not give birth to another Stalin, was beginning to feel the net closing on him. Eventually in 1936 Stalin and Beria felt strong enough to strike: Mdivani was one of the first victims of the Great Purge, arrested and shot – along with his wife, son and daughter – for Trotskyite conspiracy, sabotage and espionage. He is said to have declared at his trial that to be shot was too mild a punishment for his real crimes, which were to have 'betrayed my people and helped these degenerates, Stalin and Beria, to enslave Georgia and bring Lenin's party to its knees'.
3 The mountainous easternmost province of Georgia, bordered by Russia to the north-east, Azerbaijan to the south-east and the Caucasus Mountains to the north.

11 May

Having passed through Baku in the night we are now heading west through Transcaucasia. I spent much time on the outside rear platform where the guard in charge of that carriage (a pianist) not only offered me a seat but said that if I would play the piano he would eject all the other passengers. Sitting outside on the platform I composed a good theme, appropriate for mass consumption.

The poet Vasili Kamensky[1] (*An Enthusiast's Path*) accosted me: 'Ah, Seryozha Prokofiev, I'm Vasya Kamensky.' At first this over-familiarity put me off, but he turned out to be a decent fellow and I was very attracted by his invitation to stay with him in his house near Perm and the Kama river for a few days next May.

At six o'clock we arrived, somewhat late, in Tbilisi. Nobody was there to meet us as we had been expected to come by the Georgian Military Highway. Clinging to our disintegrating luggage we made our way on a sort of wagonette to the Orient Hotel, where we ran into the entire team of representatives from the local Philharmonia and found the room that had been reserved for us. This had enormously high ceilings and vast, uncurtained windows. We ate *shashlik* and 'greens' – a bunch of herbs, onion, tarragon and other plants we did not recognise. Later in the evening we ascended the funicular at the top of which was wonderful air and a view over the lights of Tbilisi.

12 May

Rested for a while, and did very little Tbilisi sight-seeing. The streets were full of beautiful faces, far more so than in Moscow. It had been suggested that tomorrow I should play the two-piano version of the Schubert Waltzes, but it emerged there was no second pianist with whom to play them. In the evening we went to the Georgian theatre,[2] which was very good. The actors were so excellent we were absorbed even without being able to understand a word of the language.

---

1 Vasily Kamensky (1884–1961), Futurist poet, playwright and artist associated with his better-known colleagues David Burlyuk, Velimir Khlebnikov and Vladimir Mayakovsky. The Poet's Café in Moscow, hotbed of Futurism and Anarchism in which Prokofiev had met Kamensky in 1918, had in fact been his initiative; he had raised the money to get it going and organised (if that is the right word) its programme. Inventor of 'ferroconcrete poetry' (*zheleznobetonnye poemy*) he was also one of Russia's first aviators. See *Diaries*, vol. 2, pp. 261–2. His memoir, *The Path of an Enthusiast*, was published in 1931.
2 Presumably the Rustaveli Theatre.

13 May

Concert in the Small Hall with 600 seats, full to bursting and people turned away. Initial response moderate, but by the end very warm. At midnight we took the sleeper to Yerevan.

14 May

Travelled all morning with distant views of beautiful mountains, but the actual terrain through which we were passing was empty and depressing. The line goes near the Turkish border, a fact I neglected to take into consideration when at one of the stops I got out of the train to photograph something or other. The local GPU[1] invited me to explain myself and then removed the film saying, however, that it would be returned to me if on examination nothing compromising had been recorded on it.

By afternoon we were in Yerevan and a cloud of dust. We were met, and transported by horse-drawn cab into the town, one or two kilometres distant. Everywhere there were building materials, pitiful hovels, pot-holes in the road, and dust, dust without end. The town itself is under construction but the buildings are unlovely and the roads problematical. An imposing Party headquarters had been constructed of pink tuff, but then a decree was issued that tuff was for export only and the other buildings planned to complement it had to be abandoned.[2] Apparently Yerevan's original population of about 30,000 has swollen to 130,000 due to the surge of Turkish Armenians fleeing from Turkey, most of whom join the Communist Party. Membership of the Internationale thus has an undercurrent of Nationalism. Superhuman efforts are being made to build a new city which no doubt will in time be a fine one, but for the present the main impression is of gardens being dug up and pressed into service as dumps for construction materials. Because there was no possibility of finding a hotel in which to put us up, they had found us a private apartment, very modest but the room was clean if no more than passably comfortable. Ptashka lost heart and went to bed, while I went to the House of Culture to see the Director of the local Philharmonia, who entertained me to dinner and the wine of the region, at which we were joined by

---

1 Secret Police. See above p. 439 n. 1.
2 Tuff, or tufa, is formed by volcanic ash which has over millennia been solidified by the elements. Western Armenia in particular is full of it, and because it is relatively light and easy to work it has always, as it has in other regions where there was a lot of volcanic activity in the past, been used as a building material. Armenian tuff boasts a wide range of colours according to the specific elements contained: blacks, browns, oranges, pinks, violets are some of the most common and contribute greatly to the distinctive character of much Armenian architecture, old and new.

a group of Armenian composers, among them Kushnaryov, whom I already knew from Leningrad in 1927.¹

15 May

We did not sleep well, disturbed by the wailing of a child in the room next door. Bad timing for today's concert. The baby's mother was a fifteen-year-old girl, and the baby was crying for lack of the right kind of food. We bought a kilo of rice for her. In the morning we feasted our eyes on the twin peaks of Ararat, the Greater and the Lesser, directly opposite the balcony of our room.² Eventually, very late, a car came to collect us, obtained somehow from the local administration by Makedonsky, the Philharmonic Society Director. We went to Lake Sevan, a journey of 67 kilometres along a very decent highway. The lake is huge, 70 kilometres long, and lies at an altitude of almost two kilometres above sea level.³ We went out in a motor boat to a small island on which there used to be a monastery, which has been turned into a vacation complex, although two very beautiful ninth-century churches remain, the interiors of which are in ruins.⁴ The lake is full of trout, but all for export, and it was only with the greatest difficulty and exhaustive explanations and appeals that an exception was made for us and two enormous and extremely delicious trout cooked, which lacking any suitable implements we ate with our bare hands.

1 See above, p. 519.
2 Mount Ararat, revered by Armenians as the symbol of their national identity and irredentist aspirations, the Home of the Gods as Mount Olympus is for the Greeks, is a mere 20 miles on the wrong side (from the Armenian perspective) of the border with Turkey. It dominates the capital city of Yerevan.
3 At the time when Prokofiev visited it, Lake Sevan was still one of the four largest lakes in the world, unique in losing only 10 per cent of its water through river drainage, 90 per cent through evaporation. In a grandiose dream of adding millions of productive new hectares to the country's landmass, the Armenian Supreme Soviet had just decreed a gigantic civil-engineering project to lower the water level by 55 metres, shrinking the volume of water from 58.5 cubic kilometres to a mere 5 cubic kilometres and in the process releasing vast amounts of water for irrigation and hydroelectricity generation as well as more land. Work had begun on deepening the bed of the outflowing Hrazdan river and constructing a tunnel 40 metres below the surface. The project was interrupted by the Second World War but resumed soon thereafter, following which the water level began to fall by more than a metre a year. Only the death of Stalin brought to an end what promised to be one of the world's greatest ecological disasters, at which time the surface stabilised at 18 metres below its original level, the volume of water lost approximately 15 per cent. Efforts continue to be made to raise the water level by means of tunnels from the Arpa and Vorotan rivers, but much irreversible degradation of the ecology, plant and marine life has nevertheless occurred.
4 The island of Sevanank, now a peninsula due to the lowering of the water level. The monastery was built by King Ashot I and his daughter Mariam in AD 874, and of the foundation's original three churches the two that survive (and are now restored) are those of St Arakelots and St Asvtatsatsin.

Back in Yerevan I slept and then at nine o'clock was already sitting waiting in my tails. But they did not come for me until ten to ten; they had been searching for a cab but had not managed to find one anywhere. It was announced to the waiting audience that Prokofiev, tired after his expedition to Lake Sevan, was sleeping. I was incensed at this and wanted to protest. The concert proceeded much as it had done in Tbilisi: a small hall filled to overflowing by an audience that listened attentively and really let itself go towards the end. Because of the heat and the lack of air the windows were left open and through them could be heard clearly the clinking and clanking of the trams on the city's one and only line. Whenever the piece I was playing so permitted I stopped to let them go by. Afterwards we repaired to a cellar café where we were treated to tea, cakes and ice-cream. Some local traditional musicians had also been invited, who played the *duduk*, a kind of short oboe which, however, when played *piano* changes to a softly sonorous clarinet-like or flute-like timbre, and also the *tār*, a kind of mandolin or guitar.[1] Kushnaryov explained that there is a Persian influence in this music, and I was struck by how much Rimsky-Korsakov drew on it for *Sheherazade*, not just the melodies but the way they are treated.

16 May

Today the rice-fed child had stopped crying, but at seven o'clock in the morning workmen started repairing the balcony, bashing merrily away with their hammers. Since it had been 2 a.m. before we got to bed, we did not get enough sleep. Once again the Government car was sent for us, and with Kushnaryov as a guide we went to Echmiadzin, a monastery dating from the fourth century AD and the residence of the Armenian Catholicos,[2] whom the

---

1 *Duduk*-playing is regarded as the very root of Armenian traditional music, dating back to the first century BC. The instrument is a double-reed pipe, known in the Armenian language as an apricot pipe because it is usually made of apricot wood. The reed is uncommonly large, which gives the instrument both its characteristic melancholy timbre and its unusually sophisticated breathing requirements, necessitating 'circular breathing' – the stopping of the epiglottis while allowing the passage of air stored in the cheeks to pass through the reeds. According to the ethnomusicologist Jonathan McCollom, 'the most important quality of the *duduk* is its ability to express the language dialectic and mood of the Armenian language ... The *duduk* is meant to invoke feeling and the native emotional accumulation of historical memory' (quoted in *The Armenian Weekly*, Watertown MA, 12 February 2010). No wonder Prokofiev was interested. The *tār* is a long-necked lute-like instrument, the body shaped like a double bowl, usually made of mulberry wood. It is played with a plectrum. Originally from Persia, the Armenian version of the *tār* has additional strings, both singing and sympathetic.
2 The Catholicos of All the Armenians is the primate of the Armenian Church. The Cathedral of Echmiadzin, built in 300 by St Gregory the Illuminator, founder of the Armenian Gregorian Church, is the most ancient place of Christian worship in all the countries of the former Soviet Union, and the monastery that surrounds it is still the residence of the Armenian Catholicos.

Soviet Government, notwithstanding their basically anti-religious stance, leave in peace, judging it politic to allow the cement that binds all Armenians together to remain within the Union. Nevertheless, all his land has been requisitioned and he survives on parcels sent from abroad. About twelve monks are left in the monastery. One nun (the Mother Superior), who is ninety years old, invited us into her cell, which was quite spacious, with windows overlooking the garden. But her conversation was entirely about various mundane squabbles, and she invited us, not without a touch of *amour-propre*, to look at her portrait in the museum (she was very beautiful in it). In the museum we were also shown ancient Armenian books with wonderful illuminations, and some pictures by Aivazovsky,[1] not very good. Kushnaryov, a most charming and knowledgeable man, regaled us with a stream of legends including that of an Armenian princeling's correspondence with Jesus Christ. Then we looked round an Eastern bazaar before returning in the usual cloud of dust to Yerevan.

At nine in the evening we left to return to Tbilisi, seen off by the friendly and courteous but perpetually inefficient Makedonsky and the young Head of the Cultural Department. My camera film was not returned; they promised to send it on although obviously had no intention of so doing. The head of the Cultural Department persuaded me not to make an issue of it: 'It was just a kilometre from the border and that always makes them a little nervous.' I drew his attention to an open-air plaque inscribed with cuneiform script that looked just like a copy of one of the Aivazovsky paintings in the museum.

17–18 May

Tbilisi at one o'clock in the afternoon, and at three a rehearsal of the Third Piano Concerto with Mikeladze, a very gifted conductor.[2] The orchestra is not very accomplished, barely able to cope with the score, but it tries and that is more than one can say of Moscow. At nine o'clock the concert took

---

1 Hovhaness (Ivan) Aivazovsky (1817–1900), Armenian painter (the name by which he is known is a Russianised version of Aivazian) who lived and worked mainly in Crimea, apart from long spells as Court painter to a succession of Ottoman Sultans, whom he later repudiated after the Hamidian massacres of Armenians in 1895. He is best known for his seascapes and naval pictures.
2 Yevgeny Mikeladze (1903–1937), a student of Malko and Gauk at the Leningrad Conservatoire, had recently founded the Georgian National Symphony Orchestra, and was also shortly to become Chief Conductor of the Tbilisi Opera. He was, however, so unfortunate as to be the husband of the daughter of an Old Bolshevik former associate of Stalin, Mamia Orakhelashvili, who was an early victim of the Great Terror in 1937. In November Mikeladze himself fell into the clutches of Beria, was interrogated and tortured over a period of forty-eight days before being shot. One of the first actions of the newly independent Georgian State in 1991 was to name its National Symphony Orchestra after Yevgeny Mikeladze.

place in the Grand Opera Theatre. It was an exceptional success. Tarumov was happy both with the success and with the box-office takings. I persuaded him to cancel Baku.

The 18th was a free day. I proof-read the Fifth Piano Concerto; Ptashka went shopping with Tarumov's relatives for fabrics and precious stones. Sometimes it is hard to tell whether such things have any value or are rubbish, but since the rouble is in any event not worth anything I recommended her to buy them. A very convivial dinner with Tarumov. Yudina[1] and Rabinovich took me to the Conservatoire where the professors and quite a number of students had gathered. I played for them to noisy appreciation. They then played me some works by local composers, mostly either beginners or retrograde. At midnight we left for Batum, Tarumov coming with us.

19 May

Before reaching Batum the railway line runs along the seashore, the water blue in the sunshine. We arrived at one o'clock, the hotel right by the sea with a balcony overlooking the port, but primitive and the lavatory to say the least uninviting. After some discussion we succeeding in getting extra pillows, sheets and blankets, because it is cold at night. We walked along the boulevard past the town gardens, which are beautiful and elegantly maintained, good marks for that.

The concert was at ten o'clock in the evening in a deplorable temporary hall, which to make matters worse was not full. The piano was also terrible: if one played softly the note did not strike at all, a little more vigorously and it was too loud. The audience showed little appreciation of what I was doing. It was rather ridiculous that I should have cancelled cultivated Baku to be appearing in provincial Batum, but Batum was the more attractive option geographically.

20 May

A free morning, so I did more proof-reading. Tarumov had got hold of a car and took us to Zelyony Mys[2] and the Botanical Gardens, a large and free

1   See above, p. 519. One of Yudina's many career stumbles was the reason she was in Tbilisi at this time: after graduation from the Petrograd Conservatoire in 1921 she was appointed a professor there until 1930 when her publicly stated religious convictions and overt criticism of the Soviet leadership brought about her dismissal. Jobless and homeless for two years, she found a position teaching postgraduate courses at the Tbilisi Conservatoire from 1932 until 1936 when, her professional star briefly in the ascendancy once again, she secured thanks to Heinrich Neuhaus a post in the piano faculty of the Moscow Conservatoire.
2   Zelyony Mys ('Green Cape'), a seaside resort well provided with sanatoria, guest houses and hotels outside Batum. Its Botanical Gardens have a justly celebrated collection of tropical and sub-tropical plants.

expanse containing many interesting specimens. There are also tea plantations which produce rather good tea, but it is only sold abroad. At seven o'clock I was taken to the Music Training College, from where some students had come round to the Artists' Room yesterday and made me promise to visit them. The institution is unassuming and provincial: I chatted with the students and promised to send them my sonatas.

At ten we left to return to Tbilisi, but there had been an accident that morning and the line was badly congested. The train left at eleven; a crowd of young people from the Training College came to the station, seven girls and three young men, very nice and high-spirited. They presented me with a bouquet of flowers.

21 May

Because of the accident we were running very late; by morning we had only reached the pass we should have crossed during the night. But we enjoyed the delay, making use of it at each station to go round the sprawling, colourful Eastern bazaars alongside the track. It was five o'clock by the time we got to Tbilisi, and it was a good thing Baku had been cancelled as we would not in any case have made it in time. Ptashka set out on another shopping expedition and I got on with proof-reading. The Conservatoire had presented us with some things: a sketch by a local artist and various objets d'art. I promised to present copies of my compositions. Then we did our packing, for tomorrow we go north.

22 May

Rose at five to travel the Georgian Military Highway by car. We had been told on no account to be late, but no car appeared: a torrent of arguments, protestations and altercations ensued. Finally, at nine o'clock, a car was procured but then we spent two hours (yes, two hours!) driving round the entire town in search of petrol. Eventually, at eleven o'clock, we set off in a fine 8-cylinder open-topped Ford. The first section of the road is moderately mountainous, with the peaks near Mtskheti very fine. Then an extremely mountainous road as far as the town of Dusheti, followed by precipices and the Aragvi river. After the pass we stopped at the source of Narzan water, which is delicious, much better than Kislovodsk. The most spectacular part of the trip was the Darial Gorge, which is truly unique[1] in its grandeur, in the shape and texture of its mountains. When we passed through Ossetia Ptashka

---

1 In English in the text.

gathered in a handkerchief a little piece of native soil for Fatma Hanum. Then fog and Vladikavkaz. From sunshine we came into rain which thereafter never left us for a week. Vladikavkaz is a horrible little place, as I had found it to be in 1916.[1] At the Intourist Hotel, to whom the car in which we had travelled belongs, I complained about the disorganised arrangements that morning. The hotel manager, a German, said that he had already suggested two drivers, but they were both incorrigibly careless. Russian chauffeurs are skilful drivers, but they do not take care of their vehicles and pay no attention to the rules of the road which abroad are so strictly enforced: they don't sound their horns at corners, they cut in on the left, and so on. I was indignant.

We continued our journey by local train as far as Beslan, an hour away in a hard-class, grimy, Intourist carriage, but thank goodness for small mercies. At Beslan there was a two-hour wait in the evening; the stink inside was so awful we sat on our luggage outside on the platform. This was in fact a good thing to have done: we had plenty to look at, what with homeless people, beggars, invalids, pickpockets plying their trade, passengers getting on and off the overcrowded trains, wailing children and their mothers, people lying prone on the carriage roofs, a vision of hell. At long last our train came in and two porters manoeuvred our mountain of luggage along a narrow platform between two trains, jammed with people fighting their way to wherever they had to get to. We found our international carriage, but what were the chances of our compartment, paid for in Tbilisi, still being free? We could imagine the kind of muddle that had probably occurred, or it could simply have been given to an Important Personage. But by a miracle our compartment was intact and more than that, carefully made up and positively gleaming with cleanliness. From chaos and anguished shrieking we were suddenly transported into order and refinement. And it was truly a valuable lesson to have so vividly brought home to us: the inequality that still exists after sixteen years of Communism.

23 May

En route to Moscow. Rain and green fields through the window. The train was running through a famine area and at the stations people were begging for bread. Ptashka gave some to one man, but then saw him again at the next stop. And the next . . . and the next – evidently he was clinging on to the springs of our carriage. A little later on we came to stations where women

---

[1] But see *Diaries*, vol. 2, pp. 134–5, where Prokofiev's recollections of this town on his previous journey along the Georgian Military Highway are rather different: Vladikavkaz is 'a delightful town'.

were selling butter and eggs and cooked chicken, but still begging for bread.

24 May

Whenever the train stopped I tried to carry on proof-reading so that I would be able to give the score to Myaskovsky to check: he has an amazing eye and will undoubtedly find mistakes I have missed. It was eleven o'clock in the evening before we reached Moscow. No one was there to meet us; the telegram I had sent five days ago from Batum had not been delivered. By a stroke of luck we found a car and a good hotel room. Aware that today is the date of the gala performance celebrating Sobinov's jubilee,[1] I telephoned the Director's box at the Bolshoy Theatre, where I was told by all means to come, so we did. The performance itself was over, but the speeches in the star's honour were still proceeding on stage. Sobinov, deeply moved, was expressing his appreciation of the bestowal of the Order of the Red Banner.[2] Apparently we were also invited to sample the comestibles at this state institution! But the gala was not so glittering an affair as Nezhdanova's, for which Golovanov had really pushed the boat out; we left before the supper but even so it was two o'clock before we got away.

25 May

Got up late and had a bath, the first for two weeks. True, there had been a bath in our room in Tbilisi, but there the initial lack of hot water had soon been followed by the absence of any at all. Our passports and visas are all prepared, which lends a certain peace of mind to the remainder of our stay.

In the evening we attended a concert by winners of the All-Union Music Competition, and unexpectedly it proved to be very interesting as many of the performers were talented. In the box to the left of ours, with its curtains half drawn, were members of the Government. It was whispered in the auditorium that Stalin himself was present. Our seats were in the second row from the front and I did not want to peer too obviously, but at the end of the interval Ptashka glanced into the Government box and locked eyes with Stalin, who was just at that moment coming into it. Of such intensity was his gaze that she immediately turned away.

---

1 Leonid Sobinov (1872–1934), the leading Russian lyric tenor of his generation, an ideal and unforgettable Lensky as many CD reissues of his early pre-Revolution recordings still testify. See *Diaries*, vol. 1, pp. 26, 281.
2 Except for the Order of Lenin, established in 1930, the Order of the Red Banner was the Soviet Union's highest accolade. Primarily a military decoration, it was on rare occasions also awarded to citizens with outstanding achievements in other fields.

Sitting in the seat next to mine was Leonid Nikolayev. Exhausted, he complained, 'Seryozha, I've been listening to so many dozens, hundreds, of musicians . . . I detest music . . . cookery is the only thing I care about!'

26 May

Derzhanovsky wants to talk about my next visit. He thinks I do not pay enough attention to my connections with the elite: I've neglected for example to cement my relations with Litvinov and with Bubnov, even with Golovanov, which could be important because he is friendly with Voroshilov.

I had a discussion with Vano about animated films. I was critical, mentioning the superiority of American techniques in the representation of movement: every gesture, every facial expression, is reproduced with flair.

Went into 'Mezhdunarodnaya Kniga'.[1] It is so difficult to achieve any penetration of my compositions into the USSR market, when there is virtually no hard currency here. Nevertheless, the suggestion I made was, apparently, accepted.

In the afternoon I went to a rehearsal of *Machinal*[2] at Taïrov's theatre, very skilfully presented, and in the evening to *Krechinsky's Wedding*[3] at Meyerhold's.

1   'International Books' – the principal, tightly controlled, outlet for foreign books, periodicals, records. The Moscow store on Kuznetsky Most was the largest single shop, but the organisation itself had outlets all over the Soviet Union and was actively engaged in the import and export of published material worldwide.
2   Play written in 1928 by the American playwright and journalist Sophie Treadwell based on the murder by Ruth Snyder the previous year of her husband, abetted by her lover Judd Gray, and the couple's subsequent trial and execution. The moment of Ruth Snyder's death (she was the first woman to be put to death in the electric chair) was photographed by a Chicago *Tribune* reporter who was present, and published the following day in the New York *Daily News*. The original Broadway production of *Machinal*, from the French word meaning mechanical or automatic, starred Zita Johann as the Young Woman and Clark Gable as the Young Man, and is considered to have been one of the highlights of Expressionist theatre in America. The author described the play as about 'a young woman, ready, eager for life, for love . . . but deadened, squeezed, crushed by the machine-like quality of the life surrounding her'. In Taïrov's production his wife, Alisa Koonen, was apparently unforgettable in the Ruth Snyder role. Treadwell's original play was successfully revived by the Royal National Theatre in a production by Stephen Daldry in 1993.
3   The first play in a trilogy eventually entitled, presumably in a transparent attempt to placate the censor, *Pictures of the Past*, by Alexander Sukhovo-Kobylin (1817–1903), one of the most unusual and interesting (partly because he had no desire to be known as a writer, a profession for which he had an aristocratic disdain) playwrights of his era. He wrote the play, a grotesquely funny lampoon of the Russian justice system, to amuse himself while languishing in prison undergoing a Kafkaesque seven-year-long investigation for complicity in the murder of a Frenchwoman with whom he had fallen in love while in Paris. Eventually acquitted, suspicion (almost certainly groundless) continued to dog his life and he left Russia to live in France. The plot of *Krechinsky's Wedding* turns on a plausible card-sharp swindling large sums out of a Gobseck-like money-lender on the strength of a fake diamond, but the real pleasure lies in the characterisation and the acuteness of the language, which critics such as D. S. Mirsky compare to Gogol, Griboedov and Ostrovsky.

Half past midnight saw us once more on the 'Red Arrow' to Leningrad, seen off by the Rayevsky girls, of whom we have grown extremely fond. The train excelled itself this time by leaving an appallingly raucous radio to blare out in the corridors until half past one and waking us up at half past seven the next morning. I felt motivated to write to the Communications Commissar.

27 May

I had come to Leningrad for a meeting with Belgoskino, whose representative met us with a car and had reserved a good room at the Europa Hotel. Leningrad was looking cheerful in the sunshine. In the afternoon we went to the studio. Some parts of *Kijé* have already been filmed and are not at all bad. Tynyanov is a delightful person. At five o'clock there was a shoot involving one of my songs ('The blue-grey dove moans all night long'). But the Emperor Pavel could not get anywhere near the right notes (he has a tin ear). I explained, I demonstrated, I sang the tune, but all to no avail. As there was no time to be lost, Faintsimmer suggested I should somehow sing it for the filming while Pavel mimed. I tried, sweating all over my face from nervousness, and someone actually filmed me singing with a white handkerchief over my head to protect me from the heat of the lights.

We made arrangements for Ptashka to have a screen test. She very much wants to do it and can offer several attributes: her voice, and her accent-free knowledge of languages. We were back in the hotel by nine o'clock for dinner with Demchinsky. We played chess to complete the match we had begun in Moscow. It went on until half past three and ended with my losing. A disappointing result for the investment of a whole White Night!

28 May

I dreamt that my eyes had been scorched by the lights in the studio and somebody was anointing them with pressed caviar, saying that would help.

Another trip to Belgoskino for discussions about detailed requirements for the musical numbers. They played back some of yesterday's takes, or rather just the soundtrack as the film itself has not yet been developed. My voice has come out rather well; it's very amusing. Faintsimmer says he believes I have a new career opportunity![1]

---

1 The ploy, sadly, does not seem to have worked. In the film the song is sung by a female, the Princess Gagarina played (but quite possibly not sung; it seems not impossible the singer on the soundtrack may have been Lina Prokofieva) by Nina Shaternikova as she plucks rather unconvincingly at her harp. Tsar Pavel I (the Moscow Arts Theatre stalwart Mikhail Yanshin) paces imperially up and down the while, his hands behind his back.

A performance of *The Sleeping Beauty* in the evening. There is much good music in it, but also much that is unnecessary, just as there is in what happens on stage. Dutnikova, Demchinsky's niece, danced admirably. Buchstein was relaxed and friendly, Radlov also. A revival of *Oranges* in November appears to be a real possibility. After the performance Buchstein took us and the Radlovs for a drive in his car: the Neva glowing light blue in the radiance of the White Night, and the silhouette of the Peter and Paul Fortress framed in pink as though the sun was setting behind it – it all made a deep impression on Ptashka. We returned at one o'clock to a telephone call from Belgoskino summoning Ptashka to a screen test tomorrow morning.

29 May

It was a rush to get there by ten o'clock and I was furious that we were twenty minutes late, but as matters turned out my Western European phobias were irrelevant because the make-up artist was a whole hour late. Ptashka did a little scenario devised by Gusman which did not involve much in the way of action. Ptashka then sang and I accompanied her. Faintsimmer was conscientious although hardly giving Ptashka any direction. All this took until one o'clock. Everyone was very kind, although by the end they were in a hurry as it had all gone on so long.

In the afternoon I went for a long walk: the Summer Garden, Kamenny Ostrov, the Tuchkov Bridge.[1] In the evening I took Ptashka to visit the Demchinskys, where I gave him a suitcase full of presents and another suit to replace the one he had had to sell ('pawned for drink' he joked) at a difficult moment. Then to the Mariinsky Theatre for the second half of *Rheingold*. It is a long time since I heard it, and I had accustomed myself to thinking of it as an empty vessel, but starting this initial expectation I found quite the opposite – much that is excellent. Once again Buchstein, Radlov and a superb drive in the management's ancient car through the White Night.

30 May

Saw Gauk in the morning to discuss autumn concerts with the Philharmonia. Gusman came at noon to read some excerpts from the libretto he is drafting from Lavryenov's 'Simple Thing'. As a starting point it is not bad: the conflict between a man's duty to the Party and ordinary human decency to another person, but it lacks the elements necessary for extended development. It would need more involvement in the life of the society of the time and the

---

1   Reminiscent of the long walking expeditions Prokofiev often undertook in his youth: see *Diaries*, vol. 1 *passim* but e.g. p. 351.

surrounding events. We talked and improvised some ideas and by two o'clock had got it into a better shape. It might conceivably be made into a subject for an opera.

Spent the first part of the afternoon at Tyulin's and took away with me some American things. At four, on to Radlov's for two and a half hours of chess during which to my surprise I won both games. Then we had dinner (Ptashka arrived late) before going to *The Flames of Paris*.[1] We missed the first act by being late, but the second struck me as slavish in its treatment of the material. Act 3 was more lively and had more original ideas. The dancing was spectacular; Ulanova,[2] Chabukiani.[3] Better watch out, Lifar! They could overtake you. The fabulous dancing was a good counterbalance to the dreadfulness of yesterday's singing (particularly the women).

31 May

The other Radlovs, Nikolay and Nadezhda Konstantinovna, lunched with us, also Cecilia Mansurova. Lunch was vivacious and gay, the manner of conversation at times so robust that we almost seemed to be quarrelling. While I was talking to Mansurova and her husband[4] I could hear Nadezhda Konstantinovna asking Ptashka if she had ever come across Meshcherskaya in Paris, in reply to which Ptashka told the story of buying the wardrobe.

1   *The Flames of Paris*, subtitled *The Triumph of the Republic*, ballet set in the French Revolution by Boris Asafyev, with choreography by Vasili Vainonen. The premiere had taken place on 6 November 1932.
2   Galina Ulanova (1910–1998), after Marina Semyonova probably the greatest Soviet ballerina. Like Semyonova she was a product of the Vaganova School in Leningrad, and was similarly shipped down to Moscow by Stalin to adorn his capital city's Bolshoy Theatre, where in 1945 she was to create the role of Prokofiev's *Cinderella*. But having made her Mariinsky Ballet debut in 1928 she would still be there (by then the Kirov Ballet) in 1940 to create to dazzling effect, despite her initial reservations on the danceability in strictly balletic terms of the music, the role of Juliet in Leonid Lavrovsky's premiere production of Prokofiev's *Romeo and Juliet*.
3   Vakhtang Chabukiani (1910–1992), half Georgian half Latvian, one of the most heroic and athletic *premiers danseurs* of the early Soviet ballet, famous for injecting Georgian fire and temperament into a perfect classical line. Chabukiani also created many of the virtuoso male variations now standard in works such as *Le Corsaire* and *La Bayadère*. In this performance Ulanova and Chabukiani were dancing the roles of the actors Mireille de Poitiers and Antoine Mistral, characters invented by Vainonen and parachuted into the historical drama in order to provide a window for classical dancing in an otherwise mostly narrative ballet. In the Leningrad premiere these roles had been danced by Konstantin Sergeyev and Natalya Dudinskaya.
4   Cecilia Mansurova (née Wollerstein; she took her stage name from Mansurov Lane where the Vakhtangov Acting Studio was located) (1896–1976), leading actress of the Vahktangov Theatre in Moscow. Her husband was Count Nikolay Sheremetiev, scion of the princely family. Purely out of love for his wife he refused to follow his family into exile after the Revolution, and having studied the violin took a job as leader of the Vakhtangov Theatre pit band, also composing incidental music for their productions. Despite frequent arrests the management and leading artists of the Theatre always contrived to secure his release by pleading with their admirers in the

In the afternoon, having failed to meet Asafyev as arranged, we went to Belgoskino where we listened to the audio recording of Ptashka's screen test from yesterday. It wasn't bad but one could not say it was outstanding. Asafyev then appeared, having arrived back from Moscow, distressed at yet another postponement of *The Flames of Paris* there.[1]

Displaying uncharacteristic signs of *folie de grandeur* he appears to think that *Flames* is more important than *Pulcinella*. Even the best musicians are liable to lose their heads when it comes to their own compositions!

In the evening we caught Meyerhold's old production of *Masquerade*,[2] and at half past midnight took the 'Red Arrow' back to Moscow, the radio yet again inflicted on us.

1–6 June

The last six days of our stay before crossing the border again were spent in Moscow. Visited Konchalovsky[3] – wonderful stories about the family estate near Moscow. A scandalous chess game with Goldenweiser, in which we both revoked moves, he first and then I, ending in a draw. Viewed Vano's latest animated film, which was an improvement. We signed a preliminary agreement to make a film called *Tsar Durandai*.[4]

Dinners with Afinogenov and with Taïrov (disastrously late for the latter, which drove me into a frenzy with Ptashka). Supper with Yurev. Smolich[5]

---

ranks of the *nomenklatura*, but in 1944 the Count died in a hunting accident, in unexplained circumstances.

1 It eventually received its first performance at the Bolshoy Theatre on 6 June 1933.
2 Meyerhold's 1917 production of Lermontov's play *Masquerade* had been a turning point in the development of his ideas on theatrical presentation, which depended to a large extent on the non-realistic incorporation of the scenery (for *Masquerade* designed by Golovin) into the dramatic context itself rather than simply being a setting for it, and also the genesis of the new acting technique Meyerhold was later to call 'Biomechanics', essentially a series of exercises designed to develop and release the emotional potential of the actor through movement rather than through Stanislavskian character identification.
3 Pyotr Konchalovsky (1876–1956), painter. Son of a prominent art publisher, he grew up in the heart of the Moscow and St Petersburg art scene at the turn of the century. An extremely prolific as well as technically accomplished painter, he had no trouble accommodating himself – always with dignity, however – to the demands of Socialist Realism. On a later visit to the Soviet Union, in the summer of 1934, Prokofiev spent some time in Kanchalovsky's dacha outside Moscow, where Konchalovsky made a celebrated portrait of him sitting in the garden, now hanging in the Tretyakov Gallery in Moscow. He was father-in-law of the poet Sergey Mikhalkov (co-author of the Soviet National Anthem), and his two celebrated grandchildren are the film directors Andrey Konchalovsky and Nikita Mikhalkov.
4 The score was eventually composed by Alexander Alexandrov, founder of the Alexandrov Red Army Ensemble and composer in 1944 of the USSR National Anthem, since 2000 (with different words) restored to its status as the National Anthem of Russia.
5 Nikolay Smolich (1888–1968), opera director, Chief Producer at the Bolshoy Theatre from 1930 until 1936.

about producing *The Gambler* in the 'filial'[1] of the Bolshoy, and a talk with Kubatsky about a production of *Chout* in the Ballet School. General rehearsal of *The Flames of Paris* in the Bolshoy with Semyonova and Chabukiani. I told Asafyev it was high time he did a proper job of composing this ballet, as I had had to do with the Schubert Waltzes for two pianos after I had made a two-hand version for one piano. Asafyev, offended, did not reply. Myaskovsky secretly agrees with me.

Made up the itemised list with values of everything that we are taking with us.

Our departure was at eleven o'clock in the evening of the 6th, with only Atovmyan and the Rayevsky girls to see us finally away, everyone else attending the *Flames of Paris* premiere. When we reached the border we were not after all allowed to take our new possessions with us. Panic, and a lightning telephone to the Central Customs Bureau in Moscow. Eventually permission was granted, but only ten minutes before the train departed. We barely made it.

Poland; then Hitler's Berlin, *Ordnung* and cleanliness. I refused to give money to a Hitler youth soliciting donations. Nord Express, and on the 8th we arrived home in Paris. The children were flourishing. An enormous mountain of letters.

The following year Sergey Prokofiev made three more visits to the Soviet Union, and in the summer of 1935 brought his whole family to spend the summer in Polenovo, the Bolshoy Theatre Company's summer retreat in the country. On 15 May 1936 the Prokofievs moved out of their Paris apartment in the rue Valentin Haüy to make the permanent move to Moscow. After a few weeks in the National Hotel, Sergey, Lina, Svyatoslav and Oleg Prokofiev moved into their new home, a four-room apartment at No. 17 Zemlyanoy Val on the city's Garden Ring Road (later renamed Ulitsa Chkalova after the famous test pilot but now once again Zemlyanoy Val).

A few days after returning from the visit to the Soviet Union with which he concluded the Diaries begun in St Petersburg more than a quarter of a century before, Sergey Prokofiev opened his heart to his friend Serge Moreux in Paris:

'I owe you the truth, and I shall tell it to you today . . . I say truth, but perhaps I should say it is the truth at least for me. It is this. Foreign air does not suit my

---

1 The Bolshoy Theatre's second auditorium, housed then in what was previously and is now again the Operetta Theatre on Bolshaya Dmitrovka Street, opposite the stage door of the main Bolshoy Theatre. A new Filial was opened in 2002 on the other side of the Bolshoy in order to allow reconstruction of the main stage, which was finally completed in November 2011.

inspiration, because I'm Russian, and that is to say the least suited of men to be an exile, to remain myself in a psychological climate that isn't of my race. My compatriots and I carry our country about with us. Not all of it, to be sure, but a little bit, just enough for it to be faintly painful at first, then increasingly so, until at last it breaks us down altogether. You can't altogether understand, because you don't know my native soil, but look at those compatriots of mine who are living abroad. They are drugged with the air of my country. There's nothing to be done about it. They'll never get it out of their systems. I've got to go back, I've got to live myself back into the atmosphere of my native soil. I've got to see real winters again, and spring that bursts into being from one moment to the next. I've got to hear the Russian language echoing in my ears, I've got to talk to people who are of my own flesh and blood, so that they can give me back something I lack here – their songs – my songs. Here I'm getting enervated. I risk dying of academicism. Yes, my friend, I'm going back."[1]

---

1   *Tempo*, new series, No. 11, (spring 1949), pp. 5–9.

APPENDIX

Mark Twain's experience of Christian Science medical treatment

Mark Twain, on a walking holiday in the Tyrolean Alps, has fallen and injured himself. Helped back to the Gasthaus in which he was staying, he attempts to get medical help.

There was a village a mile away, and a horse doctor lived there, but there was no surgeon. It seemed a bad outlook; mine was distinctly a surgery case. Then it was remembered that a lady from Boston was summering in that village, and she was a Christian Science doctor and could cure anything. So she was sent for. It was night by this time, and she could not conveniently come, but sent word that it was no matter, there was no hurry, she would give me 'absent treatment' now, and come in the morning; meantime she begged me to make myself tranquil and comfortable and remember that there was nothing the matter with me. I thought there must be some mistake.

'Did you tell her I walked off a cliff seventy-five feet high?'

'Yes.'

'And struck a boulder at the bottom and bounced?'

'Yes.'

'And struck another one and bounced again?'

'Yes.'

'And struck another one and bounced yet again?'

'Yes.'

'And broke the boulders?'

'Yes.'

'That accounts for it; she is thinking of the boulders. Why didn't you tell her I got hurt, too?'

'I did. I told her what you told me to tell her: that you were now but an incoherent series of compound fractures extending from your scalp-lock to your heels, and that the comminuted projections caused you to look like a hat-rack.'

'And it was after this that she wished me to remember that there was nothing the matter with me?'

'Those were her words.'

'I do not understand it. I believe she has not diagnosed the case with sufficient care. Did she look like a person who was theorising, or did she look like one who has fallen off precipices herself and brings to the aid of abstract science the confirmations of personal experience?'

'*Bitte?*'

It was too large a contract for the Stubenmädchen's vocabulary; she couldn't call the hand. I allowed the subject to rest there, and asked for something to eat and smoke, and something hot to drink, and a basket to pile my legs in; but I could not have any of these things.

'Why?'

'She said you would need nothing at all.'

'But I am hungry and thirsty, and in desperate pain.'

'She said you would have these delusions, but must pay no attention to them. She wants you to particularly remember that there are no such things as hunger and thirst and pain.'

'She does, does she?'

'It is what she said.'

'Does she seem to be in full and functionable possession of her intellectual plant, such as it is?'

'*Bitte?*'

'Do they let her run at large, or do they tie her up?'

'Tie her up?'

'There, good night, run along, you are a good girl, but your mental *Geschirr* is not arranged for light and airy conversation. Leave me to my delusions.'

Mark Twain, *Christian Science with Notes Containing Corrections to Date*, Harper, New York, 1907.

Bibliography

Acton, E., V. I. Cherniaev, and W. G. Rosenberg (eds.), *Critical Companion to the Russian Revolution 1914–1921*, Indiana University Press, Bloomington IN, 1997
Adler, Jacob P., trans. L. Adler Rosenfeld, *A Life on the Stage: A Memoir*, Knopf, New York, 1999
Akhmatova, Anna, *Stikhotvoreniya i Poemy (Verse and Poems)*, Sovietskii Pisatel', Leningrad, 1976
Altmann, Jennifer G., *Le Pas d'acier (The Steel Step)*, http://www.princeton.edu/pr/pwb/05/0221/7a.shtml
Andrew, Christopher, and Oleg Gordievsky, *KGB: The Inside Story*, HarperCollins, New York, 1990
Andrew, Christopher, and Vasily Mitrokhin, *The Sword and the Shield: The Mitrokhin Archive and the Secret History of the KGB*, Basic Books, New York, 1999
Apetyan, Z. A. (ed.), *Vospominaniya o Rakhmaninove*, 2 vols., Izdatel'stvo 'Muzyka', Moscow, 1988
Artizov, A., and O. Naumov (eds.), *Vlast i khudozhestvennaya intelligentsia: dokumenty TsK RKP(b)-VKP(b), VChK-OGPU, NKVD o kul'turnoy politike, 1917–1953 gg*, Mezhdunarodnyi Fond Demokratia, Moscow, 1999
Aschengreen, Erik, trans. P. McAndrew and P. Avsum, *Jean Cocteau and the Dance*, Gyldendal, Denmark, 1986
Bal'mont, Konstantin, *Stikhotvoreniya (Poetry)*, Novaya Biblioteka Poeta, St Petersburg, 2003
Barber, Charles, *Lost In The Stars: The Forgotten Musical Life of Alexander Siloti*, Scarecrow Press, Lanham, 2003
Baring, Maurice, *The Puppet Show of Memory*, Cassell, London, 1987
Beaumont, Cyril W., *The Diaghilev Ballet in London*, Putnam, London, 1940
Beevor, Antony, *The Mystery of Olga Chekhova*, Penguin, London, 2004
Bely, Andrey, 'Pervoye Svidanie', Slovo, Berlin, 1922
– *Vospominaniya o Bloke*, Helikon, nos. 1–4 (April–December), Berlin, 1923
– trans. R. A. Maguire and J. E. Malmstad, *Petersburg*, Indiana University Press, Bloomington IN, 1978
Benn, Anna, and Rosamund Bartlett, *Literary Russia: A Guide*, Picador, London, 1997
Bertenson, Sergei, and Jay Leyda, *Sergei Rachmaninoff: A Lifetime in Music*, Indiana University Press, Bloomington IN, 2004
Blok, V., *Osobennosti variovaniya v instrumental'nykh proizvedeniyakh Prokof'eva* in *Musyka i Sovremennost'*, ed. T. A. Lebedeva, Muzyka, Moscow, 1965
Blok, V. (ed.), *Sergey Prokofiev: Materialy, Stat'i, Intervvyui (Materials, Articles, Interviews)*, Progress Publishers, Moscow, 1976; English trans., K. Cook, A. Markow, R. Prokofieva, K. Hammond, O. Shartse, Progress Publishers, Moscow, 1978
Bolshoy Theatre, Moscow, programme booklet for S. Prokofiev's *Fiery Angel*, GABT (Gosudarstvennyi Akademicheskii Bol'shoy Teatr Rossii), ed. T. Bielova, Moscow, 2004

Borovsky, Natasha, *A Daughter of the Nobility*, Holt, Rinehard & Winston, New York, 1985

Bowers, Capt. Hamilton, *In Unknown Thibetan Lands: Diary of a Journey Across Tibet*, Macmillan, New York, 1894

Brown, Edward J., *Russian Literature Since the Revolution*, Harvard University Press, Cambridge MA, 1982

Bryusov, Valery, *Ognenny Angel*, Lib.ru/Klassika; http://az.lib.ru/b/brjusow_w_j/text_0108.shtml

Buckle, Richard, *Diaghilev*, Weidenfeld and Nicolson, London, 1979

– *Nijinsky*, Phoenix (Orion Books), London, 1998

Bunin, Ivan, *Mitina Lyubov'*, Lib.ru http://lib.ru/BUNIN/mitina.txt

Carswell, John, *The Exile: A Life of Ivy Litvinov*, Faber and Faber, London, 1983

Chamberlain, Lesley, *The Philosophy Steamer: Lenin and the Fall of the Intelligentsia*, Atlantic Books, London, 2006

Chasins, Abram, *Speaking of Pianists*, Alfred Knopf, New York, 1957

Chasins, Abram, *Leopold Stokowski: A Profile*, Robert Hale, London, 1979

Chicherin, G. V., *Motsart, issledovatl'nyi etyud*, Muzyka, Moscow, 1970

Clark, K., and E. A. Dobrenko (eds.), trans. M. Schwarz, *Soviet Culture and Power: A History in Documents*, Yale University Press, New Haven CT, 2007

Courtois, Stéphane, and Jean-Louis Panné, *Le livre noir du Communisme, crimes, terreur, repression*, Editions Robert Laffont, Paris, 1997; trans. J. Murphy and M. Kramer, *The Black Book of Communism: Crimes, Terror, Repression*, Harvard University Press, Cambridge MA, 1999

Cropsey, Eugene H., 'Prokofiev's *Three Oranges*: A Chicago World Première', in *Opera Quarterly*, vol. 16 (2000), pp. 52–67

Davis, Ronald L., *Opera in Chicago*, Appleton-Century, New York, 1966

Doctor, Jennifer, *The BBC and Ultra-Modern Music 1922–36: Shaping a Nation's Tastes*, Cambridge University Press, Cambridge, 1999

Dostoyevskii, Fyodor, *Igrok* in *Sobranie sochinenii v 15ti tomax*, vol. 4, Nauka, Leningrad, 1989

Dowling, Lyle, and Arnold Shaw, *The Schillinger System of Musical Composition*, 2 vols., Carl Fischer, New York, 1946

Duke, Vernon, *Passport to Paris*, Little, Brown & Co., Boston MA, 1955

Eddy, Mary Baker Glover, *Science and Health with Key to the Scriptures* (last edn, 1910), Helen Wright Publishing http://www.mbeinstitute.org/SAH/SAH.htm

Ehrenburg, Ilya, *Neobychayniye pokhozhdeniya Khulio Khurenito i yego uchenikov* (*The Extraordinary Adventures of Julio Jurenito and his Disciples*), Helicon, Moscow and Berlin, 1922

Eisenstein, Sergey, trans. D. Matias, *Three Films*, ed. J. Leyda, Lorrimer Publishing, London, 1974

– trans. R. Kühn and R. Braun, *YO Ich selbst* (Memoirs, vol. 2), ed. N. Klejman and V. Korshunova, Fischer Taschenbuch Verlag, Frankfurt, 1988

Fédorov, Vladimir, 'Sergei Prokofiev', in Alexis Roland-Manuel, *Histoire de la musique*, 2 vols., Librairie Gallimard, Paris, 1963, pp. 1023–35; http://www.archive.org/stream/histoiredelamusi002536mbp#page/n1033/mode/2up

Figes, Orlando, *A People's Tragedy: The Russian Revolution 1891–1924*, Pimlico, London, 1997

– *Peasant Russia, Civil War: The Volga Countryside in Revolution 1917–1921*, Phoenix Press, London, 2001

– *The Whisperers: Private Life in Stalin's Russia*, Allen Lane, London, 2007
Filippov, Boris, *Aktyory bez grima (Actors Without Make-up)*, Sovietskaya Rossiya, Moscow, 1971
Forsh, Olga (pseud. of Olga Komarova), *Sumasshedshii Korabl'*, http://sheba.spb.ru/lit/d20/r210.htm
Fulcher, Jane F., *The Composer as Intellectual: Music and Ideology in France 1914–1940*, Oxford University Press, New York, 2005
Garafola, Lynn, *Diaghilev's Ballets Russes*, Da Capo Press, New York, 1998
Garcia-Marquez, Vicente, *Massine: A Biography*, Alfred A. Knopf, New York, 1995
Garden, Mary, *Mary Garden's Story*, Arno Press, New York, 1951
Gladkov, Alexander, trans. A. Law, *Meyerhold Speaks, Meyerhold Rehearses*, Routledge, Abingdon, 2004
Glebov, Igor (pseud. of Boris Asafyev), *Kniga o Stravinskom*, Triton, Leningrad, 1929
Godowsky, Dagmar, *First Person Plural: The Lives of Dagmar Godowsky by Herself*, Viking Press, New York, 1958
Gold, Arthur, and Robert Fizdale, *Misia: The Life of Misia Sert*, Knopf, New York, 1980
Goldenweiser, Alexander, *Vblizi Tolstogo: zapisi za pyatnadtsat' let*, Kooperativnoe Izdatel'stvo, 1922; http://www.zakharov.ru/component/option,com_books/task,book_details/id,289/Itemid,53/
Gray, Camilla, *The Russian Experiment in Art 1863–1922*, ed. M. Burleigh-Motley, rev. edn, Thames & Hudson, London, 1986
Grebenshchikov, Gyorgy, *Bylina o Mikule Buyanoviche v tryokh skazaniakh*, Alatas, Southbury CT, 1924
Gutman, David, *Prokofiev*, Omnibus Press, London, 1990
Haardt, Georges-Marie, and Louis Audouin-Dubreuil, *La Croisière noire: Expédition Citroën Centre-Afrique*, Librairie Plon, Paris, 1927
Harkins, W. E., *Dictionary of Russian Literature*, George Allen and Unwin, London, 1957
Ivanov, Gyorgii, *Peterburgskiye Zimy (Petersburg Winters)*, Rodnik, Paris, 1928
Izvolsky, Alexander, *Mémoires d'Alexandre Iswolsky*, Payot, Paris, 1923; trans. and ed. C. L. Seeger, *Memoirs of Alexander Iswolsky*, Hutchinson, London, 1920
Jacobs, Arthur, *Henry J. Wood, Maker of the Proms*, Methuen, London, 1994
Jaffe, Daniel, *Prokofiev*, Phaidon, London, 1998
Kamenskii, Vasilii, *Zhizn' s Mayakovskim*, Moscow, 1940
Karsavina, Tamara, *Theatre Street*, Dance Books, London, 1981
Kennan, George F., *Soviet-American Relations 1917–1920*: vol 1: *Russia Leaves the War*, Princeton UP, 1958; vol 2: *The Decision to Intervene*, Princeton University Press, Princeton NJ, 1989
King, David, *Red Star Over Russia: A Visual History of the Soviet Union from 1917 to the Death of Stalin*, Tate Publishing, London, 2009
Knyazeva, V. P., *Kratkaya Khronika deyatel'nosti 'Mira Isskusstva' 1897–1927*, www.roerich-museum.org/PRS/book4/20-Knjazeva.pdf
Kokhno, Boris, trans. A. Foulke, *Diaghilev and the Ballets Russes*, Harper and Row, New York, 1970
Kollontai, Alexandra, trans. A. Holt, 'Theses on Communist Morality in the Sphere of Marital Relations', in *Selected Writings*, Allison & Busby, London, 1977; www.marxists.org/archive/kollonta/1921/theses-morality.htm
Korabelnikova, Lyudmila, trans. A. Winestein, *Alexander Tcherepnin: The Saga of a Russian Emigré Composer*, Indiana University Press, Bloomington IN, 2008
Krivosheina, N. A., *Chetyre Treti Nashei Zhizni*, Russkii Put', Moscow, 1999

Lambert, Constant, *Music Ho! A Study of Music in Decline*, Penguin Books, London, 1955
Lermontov, Mikhail, *Tambovskaya Kaznacheysha* in *Polnoye Sobranie Stikhotvorenii*, 2 vols., Sovetskii Pisatel', Leningrad, 1989
Lert, Ernst, *Mozart auf dem Theater*, Schuster & Loeffler, Berlin, 1921; http://www.archive.org/details/mozartaufdemthea00lert
Levenstein-Johnston, Henry-Ralph, *Mariiskii lesopoval: vrachom za kolyuchei* in *Vospominaniya o GULAGe*, Andrey Sakharov Museum and Public Center Archive; http://www.sakharov-center.ru/asfcd/auth/?t=book&num=1334 pp 62 sqq
Lockhart, R. H. Bruce, *Memoirs of a British Agent*, Pan Books, London, 2002
Lunacharskaya-Rozenel, N. A., *Pamyat' serdtsa*, Isskustvo, Moscow, 1975
McQuere, Gordon, 'The Theories of Boleslav Yavorsky', in G. McQuere (ed.), *Russian Theoretical Thought*, Rochester University Press, Rochester NY, 2009
Magarshack, David, *Dostoevsky: A Life*, Secker & Warburg, London, 1962
Makarov, Yu. V., *Moya sluzhba v staroy gvardii 1905–1917, mirnoye vremya i voyna*, Buenos Aires, 1951
Mann, Noëlle (trans. and ed.), 'Georgii Gorchakov and the Story of an Unknown Biography', *Three Oranges*, no. 11, Serge Prokofiev Foundation, London, 2006
Marsh, Robert C., and Norman Pellegrini, *150 Years of Opera in Chicago*, Northern Illinois University Press, DeKalb IL, 2006
Martin, Bernard, 'The Life and Thought of Lev Shestov' (Introduction to Lev Shestov, trans. B. Martin, *Athens and Jerusalem*, Ohio University Press, Athens OH, 1966)
Martyn, Barrie, *Rachmaninoff, Composer, Pianist, Conductor*, Ashgate, Aldershot, 1990
– *Nicolas Medtner: His Life and Music*, Scolar Press, Aldershot, 1995
Massine, Léonide, ed. P. Hartnoll and R. Rubens, *My Life in Ballet*, Macmillan, London, 1968
Maxwell, Elsa, *How to Do It or The Lively Art of Entertaining*, Little Brown, New York, 1957
Medvedeva, Irina, ed. *Pis'ma S. S. Prokof'eva and P. A. Lammu* in *Sergey Prokof'ev: Vospominaniya, Pis'ma, Stat'i*, Gosudarstvenny Tsentral'nyi Muzyey Muzykal'noy Kul'tury imeni M. I. Glinki/Izdatel'stvo 'Deka-BC', Moscow, 2004
Merezhkovsky, Dmitry, *Tayna tryokh: Yegipet I Vavilon* Respublika, Moscow, 1999; http://royallib.ru/book/meregkovskiy_dmitriy/tayna_treh_egipet_i_vavilon.html
Minturn, Neil, *The Music of Sergei Prokofiev*, Yale University Press, New Haven CT, 1997
Mirsky, D. S., ed. F. J. Whitfield, *A History of Russian Literature from its Beginnings to 1900*, Routledge & Kegan Paul, London, 1949
Mnatsakanova, E., 'Neskol'ko zametok ob opera Prokof'eva Igrok', in T. A. Lebedeva (ed.), *Musyka i Sovremennost'*, Muzyka, Moscow, 1965
Mojica, José, *I, A Sinner (Yo, Pecador)*, Franciscan Herald Press, Chicago IL, 1963
Monsaingeon, Bruno (ed. and trans.), *Richter: Ecrits, Conversations*, Editions Van de Velde, 1998; trans. S. Spencer, *Sviatoslav Richter: Notebooks and Conversations*, Faber and Faber, London, and Princeton University Press, Princeton NJ, 2001
Morgan, C., and I. Orlova, *Saving the Tsar's Palaces*, Polperro Press, Clifton-upon-Teme, 2005
Morrison, Simon, *Russian Opera and the Symbolist Movement*, University of California Press, Berkeley CA, 2002
– *The People's Artist: Prokofiev's Soviet Years*, OUP, New York, 2009
Morrison, Simon (ed.), *Sergey Prokofiev And His World*, Princeton University Press, Princeton NJ, 2008
Nabokov, Nicolas, *Old Friends and New Music*, Little, Brown, Boston MA, 1951

– *Bagazh: Memoirs of a Russian Cosmopolitan*, Atheneum, New York, 1975
Nash, Jay Robert, *Makers and Breakers of Chicago*, Academy Press, Chicago IL, 1885
Nest'ev, Israel, trans. Rose Prokofieva, *Sergei Prokofiev: His Musical Life*, Knopf, New York, 1946
Nest'ev, I., and G. Edel'man (eds.), *Sergey Prokofiev: Stat'i i Materialy (Articles and Materials)*, Muzyka, Moscow, 1965
Nice, David, *Prokofiev from Russia to the West 1891–1935*, Yale University Press, New Haven CT and London, 2003
Nikitina, Alice, trans. M. Budberg, *Nikitina by Herself*, Allan Wingate, London, 1959
Norris, Geoffrey, *Rakhmaninov*, J. M. Dent & Sons, London, 1978
Odoyevtseva, Irina, *Na beregakh Nevy (On the Banks of the Neva)*, Khudozhestvennaya Literatura, Moscow, 1988
Olesha, Yury, *Zavist'*, Sovetskaya Literatura, Moscow, 1933
Ossendowski, Ferdinand Antoni, *Beasts, Men and Gods*, E. P. Dutton, New York, 1921
Oyler, Philip, 'Delius at Grèz', in *Musical Times*, vol. 113 no. 1551 (May 1972)
Paléologue, Maurice, trans. F. A. Holt, *An Ambassador's Memoirs*, George H. Doran, New York, 1924
Pertsov, Pyotr, ed. A. V. Lavrova, *Literaturnye Vospominaniya 1890–1902*, Novoe Literaturnoye Obozrenie, Moscow, 2002
Pipes, Richard, *The Russian Revolution 1899–1919*, Fontana Press, London, 1992
– *Russia Under the Bolshevik Regime 1919–1924*, Harvill (Harper Collins), London, 1992
Pozharskaya, M. N. (ed.), *Russkiye Sezony v Parizhe: Eskizy Dekoratsii i Kostyumov 1908–1929 (The Russian Seasons in Paris: Sketches of the Scenery and Costumes 1908–1929)*, Isskustvo, Moscow, 1988
Press, Stephen D., *Prokofiev's Ballets for Diaghilev*, Ashgate, Aldershot, 2006
Prokofiev, Sergei, trans. Guy Daniels, abridged and ed. Francis King, *Prokofiev by Prokofiev*, Macdonald General Books, London, 1979
Prokofiev, Sergei, ed. and trans. Oleg Prokofiev and Christopher Palmer, *Soviet Diary 1927 and Other Writings* (some stories also trans. David McDuff), Faber and Faber, London, 1991
Prokofiev, Sergei, ed. and trans. Harlow Robinson, *Selected Letters*, Northeastern University Press, Boston MA, 1998
Prokofiev, Sergey, ed. M. G. Kozlova, *Avtobiografiya (Autobiography)*, Sovietskii Kompozitor, Moscow, 1973; 2nd edn, Sovietskii Kompozitor, Moscow 1982
Prokofiev, Sergey, ed. Svyatoslav Prokofiev, *Dnevnik (Diary) 1907–1933*, 2 vols., SPRKFV, Paris, 2002
Prokofiev, Sergey, trans. and annotated A. Phillips, *Prodigious Youth: Diaries 1907–1914* (vol. 1 of *Diaries 1907–1933*), Faber and Faber, London, 2006
– *Behind The Mask: Diaries 1915–1923* (vol. 2 of *Diaries 1907–1933*), Faber and Faber, London, 2008
Prokofiev, S. S., ed. A. Bretanitskaya, *Rasskazy (Stories)*, Izdatel'skii Dom 'Kompozitor', Moscow, 2003
Prokofiev, S. S., and N. Ya. Myaskovsky, ed. M. G. Kozlova and M. G. Yashchenko, *S. S. Prokofiev i N. Ya. Myaskovsky: perepiska*, Sovietskii Kompozitor, Moscow, 1977
Proust, Marcel, *À la Recherche du temps perdu*, 3 vols., Bibliothèque de la Pléiade, Paris, 1954; trans. C. K. Scott Moncrieff and T. Kilmartin, *Remembrance of Things Past*, 3 vols., Random House, New York, 1981

Pushkin, A. S., *Povesti pokoynogo Ivana Petrovicha Byelkina*; http://lib.ru/LITRA/PUSHKIN/belkin.txt

Rachmaninoff, Sergey, ed. Z. A. Apetyan, *Literaturnoye Naslediye*, 3 vols., Sovetskii Kompozitor, Moscow, 1978

Rachmaninoff, Sergey, *Vospominaniya (zapisannye O. von Riesemann)*, ed. V. N. Chemberdzhi, Raduga, Moscow 1992

Radek, Karl, *Reissner's 'Hamburg at the Barricades'*, http://www.marxists.org/subject/women/authors/reissner/works/hamburg/app1.htm

Rakhmanova, M. P. (ed.), *Sergey Prokof'ev: Vospominaniya, Pis'ma, Stat'i*, Gosudarstvenny Tsentral'nyi Muzyey Muzykal'noy Kul'tury imeni M. I. Glinki/Izdatel'stvo 'Deka-BC', Moscow, 2004

Reissner, Larissa, trans. R. Chappell, *Hamburg at the Barricades and Other Writings on Weimar Germany*, Pluto Press, London, 1977

Richter, Svyatoslav, *O Muzyke: Tvorcheskie Dnevniki*, ed. I. A. Antonova, L. E. Krenkel' and Ye. A. Savostina, Pushkin Museum, Moscow, 2007

Robinson, Harlow, *Sergei Prokofiev, A Biography*, Northeastern University Press, Boston MA, 2002

Robinson, Harlow (ed. and trans.), *Selected Letters of Sergei Prokofiev*, Northeastern University Press, Boston MA, 1998

Roerich, Nikolay, *Serdtse Azii*, Alatas, New York, 1929; trans. as *Heart of Asia*, Alatas, Southbury CT, 1929

Roland-Manuel, Alexis, *Histoire de la musique*, 2 vols., Librairie Gallimard, Paris, 1960: vol. 1: *1960*; http://www.archive.org/stream/histoiredelamusi027097mbp; vol. 2: *1963*; http://www.archive.org/stream/histoiredelamusi002536mbp

Rosenthal, Harold, *Two Centuries of Opera at Covent Garden*, Putnam, London, 1958

Royal Opera House Covent Garden programme booklet for Prokofiev's *The Gambler*, Royal Opera House, London, 2010

Rubinstein, Arthur, *My Many Years*, Jonathan Cape, London, 1980

Ruffo, Titta (Ruffo Cafiera Titta), trans. A. Bushen, *Parabola moyei zhizni*, Muzyka, Leningrad, 1966

Sabaneyev, Leonid, *Skryabin*, Scorpion, Moscow, 1916

– *Vospominaniya o Srkyabinye (Reminiscences of Scriabin)*, Klassika-XX1, Moscow, 2000

Scheijen, Sjeng, trans. J. Hedley Prôle and S. J. Leinbach, *Diaghilev: A Life*, Profile Books, London, 2009

Schipperges, Thomas, trans. J. M. Q. Davies, *Prokofiev*, Haus Publishing, London, 2003

Schmidt, Paul, *The King of Time, Poems, Fictions, Visions of the Future by Velimir Khlebnikov*, ed. C. Douglas, Harvard University Press, Cambridge MA, 1985

Schonberg, Harold C., *The Great Pianists*, Simon & Schuster, New York, 1963

Schopenhauer, Arthur, trans. Yu. Aikhenwald, *Sobranie sochinenii v shesti tomakh*, Terra-Knizhni Klub, Respublica, Moscow, 2001

Schwartz, Boris, *Music and Musical Life in Soviet Russia 1917–70*, Barrie & Jenkins, London, 1972

Seroff, Victor, *Sergei Prokofiev – A Soviet Tragedy*, Leslie Frewin, London, 1969

Shaw-Miller, Simon, *Skriabin and Obukhov: Mysterium & la livre de vie, the Concept of Artistic Synthesis*, Consciousness, Literature and the Arts Archive, vol. 1 no. 3 (December 2000); (http://blackboard.lincoln.ac.uk/bbcswebdav/users/dmeyerdinkgrafe/archive/skria.html)

Shirawaka, Sam H., *The Devil's Music Master: The Controversial Life and Career of Wilhelm Furtwängler*, Oxford University Press, Oxford, 1992

Shkafer, V. P., *Sorok let na stsene russkoy opery 1890–1930*, Kirov Academic Theatre of Opera and Ballet, Leningrad, 1936
Sitsky, Larry, *Music of the Repressed Russian Avant-Garde 1920–1929*, Greenwood Press, Westport CT, 1994
Shlifshteyn, Semyon I. (ed.), *Sergey Prokof'ev: Materialy, Dokumenty, Vospomoniniya*, Gosudarstvennoye Muzykal'noye Izdatel'stvo, Moscow, 1956
Slonimsky, Nicolas, *Perfect Pitch: A Life Story*, Oxford University Press, Oxford, 1988
– *Lectionary of Music*, McGraw Hill, New York, 1989
– *Lexicon of Musical Invective*, W. W. Norton, New York, 2000
Slonimsky, Nicolas (ed.), *The Concise Baker's Dictionary of Composers and Musicians*, Simon & Schuster, London, 1988
Smith, G. S., *D. S. Mirsky: A Russian-English Life 1890–1939*, Oxford University Press, Oxford, 2000
Sokolova, Lydia, *Dancing for Diaghilev: The Memoirs of Lydia Sokolova*, ed. R. Buckle, John Murray, London, 1960
Stravinsky, Igor, *Chronicle of My Life*, Victor Gollancz, London, 1936
– *Selected Correspondence*, ed. R. Craft (3 vols.), Faber and Faber, London 1982, 1984, 1985
Stravinsky, Vera, and Robert Craft, *Stravinsky in Pictures and Documents*, Simon and Schuster, New York, 1978
Suvchinsky, Pyotr (Pierre Souvtchinsky), *Pyotr Suvchinsky i yego vremya*, ed. A. Bretanitskaya, Kompozitor, Moscow, 1999
Tansman, Alexandre, trans. C. and T. Bleefield, *Igor Stravinsky: the Man and his Music*, G. P. Putnam's Sons, New York, 1949
Taper, Bernard, *Balanchine: A Biography*, University of California Press, Berkeley CA, 1996
Tarakanov, M. E., *Sergey Prokof'ev 1891–1991: Dnevnik, Pis'ma, Besedy, Vospominaniya*, Sovetskii Kompozitor, Moscow, 1991
Taruskin, Richard, *Text and Act: Essays on Music and Performance*, Oxford University Press, Oxford, 1995
– *Stravinsky and the Russian Tradition: A Biography of the Works Through Mavra* (2 vols.), Oxford University Press, Oxford, 1996
Three Oranges, ed. Noëlle Mann and Simon Morrison, issues 1–22, Serge Prokofiev Foundation, London, 2001–11
Tolstoy, Ilya L'vovich, trans. G. Calderon, *Reminiscences of Tolstoy*, Century, New York, 1914
Trotsky, L., trans. R. Strunsky, *Literature and Revolution*, Russell & Russell, New York, 1924
Tolstoy, Lev, *Krug Chteniya (Circle of Reading)*, Kushnerev & Co., Moscow, 1909–10
Tolstoy, Lev, ed. and trans. R. F. Christian, *Tolstoy's Diaries* (2 vols.), Athlone Press, London, 1985
Tolstoy, Lev, trans. Peter Sekirin, *A Calendar of Wisdom*, Simon & Schuster, New York, 1997
Tynyanov, Yuri, *Podporuchik Kizhe*, Lib.ru/Klassika; http://az.lib.ru/t/tynjanow_j_n/text_0040.shtml
Varunts, V. P. (ed.), *Prokof'ev o Prokof'eve: Stat'i i interv'yui*, Sovetskii Kompozitor, Moscow, 1991
Vishnevskaya, Galina, trans. G. Daniels, *Galina: A Russian Story*, Hodder & Stoughton, London, 1984

Walsh, Stephen, *Igor Stravinsky: A Creative Spring, Russia and France 1882–1934*, Jonathan Cape, London, 2000
Wells, H. G., *The Outline of History, Being a Plain History of Man and Mankind*, Garden City Publishing Co., New York, 1920
White, Eric Walter, *Stravinsky: The Composer and His Works*, Faber and Faber, London, 1966
Wilmers, Mary-Kay, *The Eitingons: A Twentieth Story*, Faber and Faber, London, 2009
Woolf, Vicki, *Dancing in the Vortex: The Story of Ida Rubinstein*, Harwood Academic Publishers, Amsterdam, 2000
Wrangel, Baron Pyotr, trans. S. Goulston, *Memoirs*, Williams & Norgate, London, 1929
Yershova-Krivosheina, Ksenya, *Russkaya Ruletka*, Logos, St Petersburg, 2004
Young, Julian, *Schopenhauer*, Routledge, London and New York, 2005
Zavgorodnyaya, Galina, *Aleksey Remizov: Stil' skazochnoy prozy*, Yaroslavl, 2004
Zil'bershteyn, I. S., and V.A. Samkov (eds.), *Sergey Dyagilev i russkoye isskustvo* (2 vols.), Moscow, 1982
Zolotnitsky, David, *Sergei Radlov: The Shakespearian Fate of a Soviet Director*, Harwood Academic Publishers, Amsterdam, 1995

Index

SSP indicates Sergey Sergeyevich Prokofiev

Accademia Musicale Chigiana 289n3
Admiralty, Leningrad 479
Aeolian Company *see* Duo-Art
Afanasiev, Alexander 14n3, 185, 801, *Russian Folk Tales* 14n3
Afinogenov, Alexander, playwright 993, 996, 998, 1003, 1007, 1015, 1021–2, 1043, 1071; accompanies SSP to Le Havre 1003; frequents émigré gatherings 998; proposes opera collaboration 1003–4, 1007, 1016, 1018, 1025; *Fear* 993, 1015, 1016, 1022, 1046
Agnitsev, Nikolay 256; 'The Prophet' 129n4
Agranov, OGPU officer 872, 882
Aivazovsky, Hovhaness, artist 1062
Aix-en-Provence 587n, 801
Aix-les-Bains 847, 851, 853
Akopera *see* Mariinsky Theatre; Mariinsky Theatre, Leningrad
Albemarle Court Hotel, London 669, 857
Albéniz, Isaak 906n2, 909
Alchevsky, Ivan, tenor 226–7, 407, 481
Alekhine, Alexander *see* Alyokhin, Alexander, chess grand master
Alexander III, Tsar 463, 477, 791n2
Alexandrinsky Theatre 477n4, 478, 481, 482n3, 524n, 1035n1
Alexandrov, Anatoly, composer 430, 437, 539, 887
Alexandrov, General Alexander, composer and ensemble director 430n1
Alexandrovich, Paris Russian Conservatoire Director 104
Alexandrovsky Lycée 155n4
Alexandrovsky, Sergey, lawyer, Director of Bolshoy Theatre 866n5, 877
Alexandrovsky Station, Moscow 413
Alexinsky, Professor Grigory 752, 791, 841
Alfredo restaurant, Rome 288
All-Union Music Competition 1066
Alland, bridge partner 991
Alpers, Sergey, brother of Vera 496, 1030n1
Alpers, Vera, friend from Conservatoire 496, 511, 1031, 1048, 1050; attempts to gate-crash visit to Asafyev 493
Altschuler, Modest, conductor 923
Alyokhin, Alexander, chess grand master 237–8, 635, 639–40, 644–6, 648, 681, 987, 1016, 1033n2

Amboise, Loire Valley 600, 997
American Club, Paris 892
American Intervention Corps 88n1
Amsterdam 23, 235-6, 889, 891, 912, 976; Amstel Hotel 233–4
Amter, Israel, music copyist, American Communist activist 933
Andersen, Hans Christian; *The Fairy's Kiss* 717n2; *The Ugly Duckling* 159n2, 994n1
Andreyev, Leonid, writer 81
Andronov-Elsky, Yury, baritone 662
Angel Island, San Francisco 252n2
Anisfeld, Boris, artist and designer 144, 264, 271–2, 928, 938
Anna Nikolayevna *see* Ivanova, Anna Nikolayevna
Ansermet, Ernest, conductor 59, 741, 1050; Asafyev, meetings with in Paris 727; *Baiser de la fée*; attends rehearsal 738; Dukelsky, opinion of 728, 742; Nabokov, opinion of 727; Orchestre Symphonique de Paris, triumvirate of music directors 758n, 805; conducts *Baiser de la fée* 781; conducts Suite from *Three Oranges* 890; Philosophy discussions with Stravinsky and Suvchinsky 859; conducts in Russia 806–7, 1048; conducts Suite from *Chout* 807; SSP's WORKS CONDUCTED: *Divertimento* 942–3; Piano Concerto No.2, broadcast with BBC Symphony orchestra 671–2; Piano Concerto No.3 942–3; *Prodigal Son* in Berlin 807; Suite from *Chout* 942–3; Symphony No.3 942–3; Violin Concerto No.1 59n2, 759; reluctant to programme SSP's works 738, 805; Stravinsky premieres conducted: *Capriccio* for piano and orchestra 855n; *Symphony of Psalms* 942–3, 983; also mentioned 717n3
Anthroposophy 325n, 719
Antwerp 7, 382, 706, 984–5; Mund and Fester, Marine Insurance brokers 985n1; Nouveaux Concerts promoting organisation 985; Plantin House Museum 985n1
Apukhtin, Alexey, 'The Boat Cast Off' 83n3
Aragvi River, Georgia 1064
Arapov, Pyotr, Eurasianist 63n3, 858
Aravantinos, Panos, designer 381
Arbos, Enrique, Spanish composer, conductor and violinist 906

Arens, Ivan, Soviet diplomat 769–70, 846, 944; arranges new passports 846, 848; implicated in Besedovsky defection 863; invites SSP to perform at Soviet Embassy reception 785, 788–90; implicated in Kutepov abduction 949–50; supports invitation to Myaskovsky to come to Paris 846; SSP advises on scores of Soviet music 770, 781, 785
La Argentina *see* Mercé y Luque, Antonia
Argus legal dispute 114
Arkadiev, Mikhail, Ministry of Culture official 1020–1, 1046, 1056
Arkanov, Boris, Deputy Director of Bolshoy Theatre 1019, 1045
Arlemarle, restaurant near Culoz 855–6
Arletty 697n1
Armenia, tour to 1059–62
Armenian genocide 957n
Armoury Museum, Kremlin, Moscow 562
Arnhem, performance with Concertgebouworkest 237
Mlle Artner, employee of the Valmalète office in Paris 941
Artsybushev, Nikolay, lawyer and composer, Head of Belyayev Publishing House 130, 627
Asafyev, Boris, composer and music critic 170n2, 416; Christian Science 721, 722–3, 724; pressure to join Communist Party, 1027, 1031; Diaghilev proposes commission of new ballet from Popov 729; SSP's guarded proposal of USSR tour by Ferroud 704n2; folklore expedition to Far North 438; Glazunov's suspicion of plot to oust him as Conservatoire Director 857; heart attack in Rome cured by hypnosis 721; founder of Leningrad Association for Contemporary Music 526n3, 690; SUPPORT FOR SSP'S VISITS TO LENINGRAD 412: arranges VIP visit to Conservatoire 520–5; intervenes with Akopera 170, 184–5, 487, 504, 515, 530, 688, 695, 799; intervenes with Leningrad Philharmonia 442, 469, 494, 514; invites to home in Detskoe Selo 491–3, 497, 528–9, 870, 871; stage-manages and timetables visit 471, 477–8, 481, 870, 1035; editorial board member of *Melos* 495n3, 496n, 640n2; endorses Meyerhold as producer of *The Gambler* at Akopera 500, 505; editorial board member of *Musical Contemporary* 495n3, 496, 640n2; friendship with Myaskovsky 446, 508, 530, 874; opportunities for career in the West: Christian Science Monitor correspondent 914; New York Times correspondent 905; JUDGMENTS OF OTHER COMPOSERS AND WORKS: Dukelsky 728–9; Popov 518n1, 720, 729; Rimsky-Korsakov 723; Shcherbachov 478; Shostakovich 518, 720, 729; Stravinsky 56n1, 722, 739; Tchaikovsky 722; performing editions; *Boris Godunov* 875; *Khovanshchina* 722; survives Siege of Leningrad 170n2; SSP's attempts to find Western publisher for Asafyev's book on Russian opera 218, 230, 261, 309, 321–2, 328, 337–8; COMMENTS ON SSP'S MUSIC: *Choses en soi* 720; Piano Concerto No.1 523; Piano Concerto No.3 1027; Piano Sonata No.3 431; Sonata for Two Violins 1032; *The Steel Step* 720; Symphony No.2 874; Symphony No.3 1051; *Trapèze* Overture 722; SSP's possessions, actions to recover from ransacked family apartment 231n2; safekeeping for prize piano 231n2, 522; friendship with Suvchinsky 495n3, 728; advises SSP not to return to USSR 948; anxiety and pessimism about situation 438, 649, 659, 807, 816, 1031, 1035; new marriage code 438; theatre politics conference 502–4; visit to France and Switzerland in September 1928 586, 587, 720–7; guilt over role in 'Zhdanovshchina', 170n2; WORKS *A Book About Stravinsky* 56n1; *The Flames of Paris* 1–72, 727n1, 1027n3; premiere performances in Leningrad and Moscow 1027, 1070, 1071; search for material in Paris 390, 412, 727; SP's indignation about plagiarism 170n2, 1027n3, 1072; also mentioned 312, 417, 422, 423, 424, 430, 432, 436, 443, 444, 445, 479, 484, 490, 496, 507–8, 511, 527, 556n1, 565, 566, 567, 568, 699, 738, 749, 780, 814, 883, 887, 1002n2, 1029, 1034, 1035, 1050
Askold, Russian Navy cruiser 751–2
Aslanov, Alexander, composer 264, 271, 440, 898, 912
ASM *see* Association of Contemporary Music
Assembly of the Nobility, Leningrad 483, 494, 510
Assembly of the Nobility, Moscow 504, 531, 535–6, 547, 564
Association of Contemporary Music 413n3, 430n5, 441, 444n2, 473, 531, 547, 690n, 705n1, 785n2, 1022n5; Leningrad Association of Contemporary Music 785n2
Astrakhan 202, 639, 672, 883
Astrov, Mikhail, SSP's secretary 154n5 716, 727, 814, 819, 823, 825, 850, 963, 967, 981–2, 987, 1014–15, 1037
Astruc, Gabriel, impresario and theatre owner 46n2, 152n1
Atheism, *see also* Prokofiev, Sergey Sergeyevich, reflections on religion
Atovmyan, Levon, Head of Moscow Committee of Composers' Union, later of Muzfond 789n1, 1020, 1025, 1027, 1029, 1034, 1036, 1043, 1044, 1045, 1046, 1050, 1052, 1072
Audouin-Dubreuil, Louis *see* Citroën
Auer, Leopold, violinist and teacher 64n1, 171n2, 259n1, 263n6776n1912n1
Augusteo Orchestra, Rome 196n1, 283n2
Auric, Georges 30: 39, 66, 84, 148, 163, 178, 182–3, 185, 190, 299, 321, 328, 598, 1002, 1050; opinion of Dukelsky 116; relations with SSP162, 222; Milhaud's *Oresteia*, percussionist in 706n; starts writing operettas, 378; reviews Ravel's *L'Enfant et les Sortilèges* 148; pianist in Stravinsky's *Les Noces* 58n2, 326; Stravinsky's opinion 375; WORKS *La Concurrence* 1005; *L'Eventail de Jeanne* 42n1; *Les*

Fâcheux 65, 822, 850; *Les Matelots* 116, 157, 161, 177, 178–80, 314; *Pastorale* 186, 324, 834–5; Sonatina 151; Ealing Comedy film scores 30n2
Avanova, Sonya, friend of Nina Koshetz 777
Avenue Frémiet, SSP residence in 577, 581, 635, 644, 649
Avenue Kléber, Paris 370–1
Avi *see* Codina, Juan
Avivit, Shoshana, actress and writer 138–40, 160, 308–9
Avranek, Ulrich, Bolshoy Opera Chorusmaster 467

Baba-Yaga, Russian folk legend 580
Babel, Isaak, writer 425, 869
'Baby ballerinas' 1005
Bach, Johann Christian 177n
Bach, Johann Sebastian 40, 392, 396, 519, 696, 745, 909, 957; Brandenburg Concerto No.3 in G major 700; Schoenberg arrangements 677; influence on Shostakovich 517; influence on Stravinsky 55, 56n1, 132, 180, 636; English and French keyboard suites, orch. Honegger 4n5, 824; Organ works 341n1, 655n1; *St Matthew Passion* 524; Solo Cello Suites 129n
Bagmen 205
Bakhmetiev, Boris, former Russian ambassador to USA 905
Bakst, Léon, artist and designer 7, 60, 111n, 188, 304n
Baku 226n, 289, 426n2, 1058; SSP cancels appearance in 1063–4; Yakulov project for memorial tower 202–3
Balaev, Nikolay, former Russian language teacher 498
Balakirev, Mily, composer 722; Symphony No.1 702
Balanchine, George, dancer and choreographer; inaugural choreographer with Ballets Russes de Monte Carlo with Massine 1005n1; *La Concurrence* 1005n3; PRODUCTIONS FOR DIAGHILEV: *Apollon musagète* 629n2, 711; *Le Bal* 801n1; *Barabau*, 317n1; *Chant du Rossignol* 222n2, 317n1; *La Chatte* 321n1, 589; *L'Enfant et les sortilèges* 474n2; *Pastorale* 324; *Prodigal Son* 764, 827, 828, 831; passed over for *The Steel Step* 222, 573; *The Triumph of Neptune* 378n1; *The Two Beggars* 756n2; association with Lifar, 201n3; ballets created for Nemchinova 179n2; scores by Rieti 174n2
Balanchivadze, Gyorgy *see* Balanchine, George
Baliyev, Nikita, Paris nightclub owner and impresario 373n2
Ballets Russes de Monte Carlo; continuation after Diaghilev's death 1005n1
Ballot car 575, 576n1, 576n2, 577, 623, 646–7, 648, 660, 662, 675, 676, 680, 681, 689, 700, 728, 785, 795, 847, 850, 852, 855, 958, 964, 969, 970, 972, 989; major accident 865-6.
Balmont, Konstantin 6, 22, 29, 39, 47, 66, 94n2, 998; SSP visits at Capbreton 622–3; dacha at St Gilles 53, 160, 200; Tseitlin benefit evenings in Paris 12n1, 35; wives and lovers: Anna Ivanova 622; Princess Dagmara Shakhovskaya 6, 9, 42, 138; Shoshana Avivit 138–40, 160, 308–9; Yelena Konstantinovna (Tsvetkovskaya) 622
WORKS 'Birdsong' 123n6; 'The Butterfly' 123n6; *The Golden Hoop* 35; Heredia sonnet translations 15; 'In My Garden' 256, 261; 'An Incantation of Water and Fire' 52n3; 'Peter the Peasant' 15; 'Pillars' 322; 'Remember Me' 123n6; *Seven, They Are Seven* 42, 138, 623; 'There Are Other Planets' 83n3, 140
Balmont, Mirra (Mirka), Balmont's daughter
Bar Kazbek, Paris 373n2
baranki 544
Baranovskaya, Maria Viktorovna (M.V., Mar-Vik, Frou-frou), wife of Borovsky 3, 8, 25, 27, 29, 30, 31, 35, 36, 45, 46, 51, 60, 66, 131, 151, 153, 166, 185, 189, 218–19, 220, 238, 302, 305–6, 372, 385, 396, 406, 637, 690, 701–3, 737, 780, 864, 886, 953, 977, 979; relocates temporarily to Berlin 735; settles permanently 991; daughter Natasha born 88; Los Angeles ménage à trois 818n2, 923; marriage difficulties 865n1; money worries 837; complaints about Moscow following visit 595; motor tour of Riviera 622–6; arranges visit to Paris Observatory 158–9; stays with SSP in St Palais 617–21; considers renting Zakharov dacha at Royan 615–17
Barbara, Mrs, American divorcee in Paris 163
Barcelona 35, 261n1 588, 590, 675n1, 743n3, 844
Bardac, Emma, widow of Debussy 60–1
Barkov, Captain, husband of Lidia Karneyeva 481, 515, 870n1
Baronova, Irina, ballerina, *see also* 'Baby ballerinas'
Barsova, Valeria, lyric soprano 1029, 1048
Bartók, Béla 3n7, 59n2, 243, 519; *The Miraculous Mandarin* 60n1, 379n2
Barton, Christian Scientist friend of Warren Klein 354, 586–7, 590, 598, 715
Baryshnya-Krestyanka see Dukelsky, *Mistress Into Maid*
Bashkirov, Boris Nikolayevich 3, 162; arranges rent of dacha at Bellevue 96, 98–101, 121, 847; Bely, *First Encounter*, shares love of 322n2; car purchase, assistance with 574, 575–7, 582, 958; dentist fees paid by brother 686, 959; escape from USSR across Gulf of Finland 614, 790; stays in Ettal 1, 101, 107, 156, 311, 961; relations with family 174, 175, 244, 276, 681; ambition to buy farm 386; risks deportation from France, 667; identity card, loss of 686; gambling, attraction to 577; mysterious occupation in gambling club 100–2, 103, 106–7, 111, 220, 244, 311, 324; hotel bill unpaid 174, 950, 953, 959–60; hypochondriac malingering 154, 166, 174, 950, 954, 962; chronic indolence 17, 64, 193, 386; hostility of Lina 163, 221, 311, 582, 735, 1038; unscrupulousness with money

390, 597, 650, 667; introduces Nikita Magalov to SSP 75; role in SSP's failed elopement with Nina Meshcherskaya 645, 713; poetry 76n1, 155, 156, 156n1, 193, 365, 366; religious leanings 365; habitual scrounging 73, 80, 86, 160, 193, 237, 304–5, 310, 346, 353, 389, 574, 584, 667, 953, 960; sonnet competition 15, 156n3; chess with SSP 16, 341, 609–10, 612; critiques SSP's essay on Church, 17; cares for SSP's mother in Ettal 1, 5, 16, 18, 19, 23, 34, 67; brings to Paris 16, 17, 73, 157n2; works as taxi driver 220, 310, 386, 574; driving licence pawned 962; vehicle impounded 390; ticket from USA to Europe paid by SP 244; objects to SP's perceived acceptance of Soviet Union 343, 962; relations with Zherebtsova-Andreyeva 191 also mentioned 20, 75n1, 76, 91n1, 106, 139, 155, 162n2, 166, 338, 364, 652, 847, 870
Bashkirov, Vladimir Nikolayevich, businessman, brother of Boris 244, 248, 276, 691, 897, 906, 959; settles brother's debts 950, 953–4, 958–63
Bashkirova, A. D., mother of Boris and Vladimir Bashkirov 276
De Basil, Col. W, ballet impresario 594n3, 1005, 1010n2
Bassiano, Prince Roffredo Caetani 388
Bâton, René-Emmanuel *see* Rhené-Bâton, conductor
Batum, Georgia 1063, 1066
Bax, Sir Arnold, composer; Symphony No.3 918
Bayka see Stravinsky, *Le Renard*
Bazavov, Serge, cousin of Nina Meshcherskaya 900, 905
Bazilevsky, composer 786
BBC 124n1, 666, 669–71, 857n1; BBC Symphony Orchestra 671, 982n1
Beaucé, Thierry de, writer and government official 678n1
Bechert, employee of Russian Musical Editions 742
Beck, Walter, conductor 583–4
Bedny, Demian, poet 462
Beecham, Sir Thomas, conductor 59n2, 172n2, 480n2, 712, 756n2, 1010n1
Beethoven, Ludwig van 55, 67, 179, 260n2, 366–7, 377, 452, 515, 643, 716, 805, 855, 952; brings out the best in Rachmaninoff's pianism 745; Tolstoy's views on 619n1; *Appassionata* Sonata played to Lenin by Dobrowen 225n4; *The Creatures of Prometheus* 819, 974; Piano Concerto No.4 59; String Quartets 859; Symphony No.3 819, 874; Symphony No.4 in B flat 775; Symphony No.7 521; Violin Concerto 64, 535
Beethoven Quartet, Moscow 543n1, 547n1, 997n2, 1022n3
Beevor, Antony; *The Mystery of Olga Chekhova* 430n3, 1077
Belgorod, Ukraine 549
Belgoskino 933n3 1050, 1068–9, 1071

Bellevue, dacha residence near Paris
Beloborodov, Alexander, executioner of Imperial Royal Family 492n2; Beloborodov Street, Pushkin 492
Bely, Andrey 28, 322, 325, 338, 374, 505, 510n1, 541, 544, 719; meeting in Berlin 325n1; *First Encounter* 322; *Reminiscences of Blok* 28n2, 325
Bely, Viktor, RAPM composer, editor of *Proletarian Music* journal 1035
Belyayev Publishing Company 130n1, 627
Belyayev, Viktor, music critic 46, 444, 496n1, 539, 565, 881; *Melos* Magazine 496n1, 640n2
Ben-Hur, historical drama movie directed by William Wyler 654
Benois, Albert Nikolayevich 109, 776
Benois, Alexander Nikolayevich, artist 7n1, 74n1, 109n1, 111, 121, 129n3, 150, 151n1, 153, 154n3, 187, 191, 197, 231, 304n1, 318n2, 333, 388, 391, 497, 572, 573, 657, 682, 691n2, 714, 717, 776n3, 821n1, 837, 999; Art Director on Gance's *Napoléon* 195; designs *Boléro* 824n4; initiator of *Baiser de la fée* 717n2
Benois, Nikolay Albertovich 776
Benois, Nikolay Alexandrovich (Koka), designer son of Alexander 74, 109, 111, 143, 151, 231, 331, 337, 391, 572, 657; married to Maria Pavlova 74
Benois, Yelena Nikolayevna (Lyolya) 333, 391, 574
Berengaria liner 893, 940
Berezovskaya, Nyura, former Conservatoire student 273
Berg, Alban, composer 173, 677n4; Violin Concerto 687; *Wozzeck* 184n3, 901n1
La Bergerie, député of Assemblée Nationale 822
Berlin 23n1, 24, 29n4, 62n, 146; Deutsche Oper; *Fiery Angel* 264, 277, 351, 382, 606, 647–8; MERI BRAN TOUR: 83, 123–4, 125, 127, 132–6; Meyerhold proposal to stage *The Gambler* 735; Piano Concerto No.5 premiered by Furtwängler and the Berlin Philharmonic 1018; *Prodigal Son* Suite conducted by Ansermet 807; radio concert 972–3; home of Russian Romantic Ballet 382n2; Staatsoper; ballet proposal 178, 180; PRODUCTION OF THREE ORANGES: 187, 224, 364, 366, 376, 379–82, 383; *Scythian Suite* ballet 583–4; Symphony No.2 accepted by Kleiber 848; Symphony No.3 broadcast 991; *Three Oranges* Suite broadcast 378, 383, 583, 811; *Vossische Zeitung* 124
Berlin, A. M., former Conservatoire piano student 481
Berlin, Sir Isaiah, philosopher 436n1
Berlioz, Hector 816
Berman, Lazar, pianist 437n1
Berners, Lord 378, *The Triumph of Neptune* 589
Bernstein, Osip, chess grand master 663–4, 980
Besedovsky, Grigory, Soviet diplomat in Paris 863; *The Path to Thermidor* 863n
Beslan, Ossetia 1057, 1065

Besprizornye children *see* Homeless children
Bessarabia 31–2, 272n1, 387
Bethmann-Hollweg, Theodore von, Chancellor of Germany 957–8
Bidet, Commissionaire Adolph Faux-Pas 944n, 949n1
Bienstock, Vladimir; stage adaptation of *The Idiot* 150n2
Bik, husband of Vinogradova 973
Bilibin, Ivan, illustrator and designer 999
Bizet, Georges 147n, *Carmen* 262
Blancart, Capt Joseph, master of the *Ile de France* 940
Blavatsky, Mme, theosophist 246n3, 719n1
Blech, Leo, conductor 379, 380–1, 382
Bloch, Ernst, composer 336
Blois, Pierre, music administrator in Paris 64, 67, 101–3, 110–11, 113, 136, 139, 141–3, 178, 197, 333, 344, 376, 395, 397, 403, 582, 598, 648, 663; brokers SSP's contract with Gaveau 779–80, 783, 808, 818, 820–2, 826, 828, 831, 833, 837–8, 840, 845, 848–50
Blok, Alexander, poet 62n2, 510n1, 674n1; Bely's *Reminiscences* 28, 325; portrait by Somov 318n1; *the Fairground Showman* 92n
Blok, Vladimir, writer on music 494n
Blokha see Leskov, *The Flea*
The Bloody Baron *see* Ungern-Sternbert, Lt. General
Blumenfeld, Felix, pianist, composer and teacher 302n1, 519n2, 526n1, 565n1
B. N. *see* Bashkirov, Boris Nikolayevich
Bodanzky, Artur, conductor 51n2, 303
Le Boeuf sur le toit, nightclub in Paris 48n1
Boito, Arrigo, composer 131
Bolm, Adolph, dancer 336, 629, 937n2
Bolm, Valentina, actress 360, 781
Bolshaya Moskovskaya Hotel, Moscow 415, 417, 432, 448, 563, 876
Bolshoy Moskovsky Hotel *see* Bolshaya Moskovskaya Hotel
Bolshoy Theatre, Moscow 209, 1222; *Flames of Paris* premiere 1071n1; Golovanov as Music Director 426; Meyerhold appointed consultant 866–7; Nezhdanova jubilee concert 1055–6; nomenclature 369n1, 477; orchestral concert of SSP's works 1019; other productions seen by SSP; *Kitezh* 504; *Pskovityanka* 1019; *Sadko* 426; *Snow Maiden* 546; *Vera Sheloga* 1019; Polenovo summer retreat 1072; renovation 420; Sobinov jubilee concert 1066; SSP attends company meeting 872; SSP invited to join repertoire committee 834; *The Steel Step*, play-through and open discussion 880–1; *Three Oranges* production 359, 368–9, 437, 450, 466–7, 468, 507, 514, 534, 676, 735, 871
Bolshoy Zal *see* Moscow Conservatoire Great Hall

Boquel, manager at Maison Pleyel 142
Bordeaux: 20, 585, 611n2, 622–3, 625, 767, 835; *Le chapeau rouge* 611; *Le chapon fin* 611–12, 622, 625
Mrs Borden, opera sponsor in Chicago
Borisovsky, Vadim, violist, member of Beethoven Quartet 543n1
Borodin, Alexander 722: 1054, 'For the Shores of Your Distant Homeland' 229; *Bogatyri* 462n1; *Prince Igor* 61n1, 68, 285, 456, 467n2, 776; Symphony No.2 228, 696
Borovsky, Alexander, pianist 3, 25, 27, 35, 36; enjoys touring in Ballot 626; dances well 624; March Op.3 No.2 128; mother dies in Leningrad 385; other composers' works performed; Auric *Sonatina* 151; J. S. Bach 396; Ravel *Sonatine* 9; Roussel Piano Concerto 709–10; Scriabin Sonata No.2 10; Scriabin Sonata No.9 142; Stravinsky *Petrushka* 8–9, 52, 306; Tchaikovsky Piano Sonata No.1 52; Weber Konzertstück 980; SSP WORKS LISTENED TO: *Fiery Angel* 712; Piano Sonata No.5 36, 391; *Prodigal Son* 780; Quintet 151; SSP works performed; *Choses en soi* 735; *Fairy Tale* 103 No.1 128; Gavotte Op.32 741; learns second piano part of Piano Concerto No.2 47–9, 395; Piano Concerto No.3 66; Piano Sonata No.2 174; Piano Sonata No.3 142; Piano Sonata No.4 391; Prelude Op.12 No.7 52; Rondo Op.52 No.2 1006; *Sarcasms* 139, 692, 741; Scherzo Op.12 692; *Tales of an Old Grandmother* 741; Toccata 52, 139; together with SSP in Rome 282–3; considers visiting USSR 308, 310, 395; transmits Asafyev's advice not to visit 948; takes Latvian citizenship 569; tours 569–70, 576, 595
Borovsky, Natasha, Borovsky's daughter 88, 621, 702; *Daughter of the Nobility* 865n2; *Lost Heritage* 865n2
Borshch, Henrietta *see* Borshch, Yekaterina
Borshch, Yekaterina (Katyusha), pianist 259
Boston, Lenox Hotel 258
Boston Symphony, 50th anniversary 862, 942
Botvinnik, Mikhail, chess grandmaster 1033
Bouffe de Saint-Blaise, Gabriel, Paris doctor, *Les Auto-Intoxications de la grossesse* 20, 22
Boulogne, Bois de 102, 392–3, 575, 676, 693, 705, 728, 772, 785, 793, 831
Boulogne-Billancourt, suburb of Paris 15, 368, 369
Bour, Ernest, conductor 1005
Brahms, Johannes: SSP's opinion of 805; WORKS Songs 882; Symphony No.2 805; Symphony No.4 321; Violin Concerto 268
Brailowsky, Alexander, pianist 893n2
Bran, Meri, German impresario 95, 98, 111, 122–5, 127–8, 132–6, 162, 972
Brandukov, Anatoly, cellist 141n4, 540–1
Braque, Georges, artist 65, 163, 326, 332, 921n
Braslavsky, Alexander, poet, son-in-law of A. N. Benois 392n1, 572–4
Breitkopf und Härtel, music publishers 99

Bremer, Georg von, husband of Zinaïda Yurevskaya 234
Brender, V. A., Literary Adviser to Akopera 527n3
Brennan, W. H., Boston Symphony manager 114, 161, 184, 679
Brichant, André (Andryusha), Sonya's son 571n1
Brichant, Germaine, wife of André Brichant 571n1
Brichant, Lyolya, Sonya's husband 160, 943
Brichant, Sonya, relation of SSP in Liège 143, 160, 943n2
Brimont, Baronne de, writer 190n4
Bristol Hotel, Odessa 558
British Broadcasting Corporation *see* BBC
Brodsky, Adolph, violinist 782
Brodsky, Isaak, artist 478n2
Brodsky, Jascha, violinist 782, 789, 894; SSP's *Songs Without Words* 816; SSP's Violin Concerto No.1 782–3
Brosa String Quartet 989
Brown University, Providence 274
Bruderschaft 3, 596
Brussels 110, 113–16, 798; recital with Lina 983–4; SSP works conducted by Ansermet 890, 941–9434; Théâtre de la Monnaie, production of *The Gambler* 711, 799, 809–14, 837, 843, 889
Brussels Philharmonic Society 837
Bryusov, Valery 106, 325, 512–13, 768; *The Fiery Angel* 325n1, 337, 372, 601–2
Bubnov, Andrey, People's Commissar of Education, successor to Lunacharsky 1024, 1035, 1067
Buchstein, V. S., Director of Leningrad Philharmonia 1028, 1029, 1069
Budyonny, Field Marshal Semyon 566
Bunin, Ivan 21, 23–4, 37–8, 345; *Mitya in Love* 345
Burdukov, A. A, Director of Bolshoy Theatre 466, 468
Burgin, Diana Lewis; *Richard Burgin: A Life in Verse* 259n1
Burgin, Richard, violinist, leader of Boston Symphony 160, 259, 260, 263, 334, 914
Bushen, Alexandra, *Alexander Kamensky: His Life and Work* 526n1
Butyrka Prison, Moscow 975, 999
Bützow, Vladimir de 701
Byutsov *see* Bützow

Cain, Henri, playwright and librettist 598–9
Calvocoressi, M. D. (Michel), critic and writer on music 4, 173, 670
Camb, American from Denver 710
Candide, pseudonym of Paris journalist 791
Capablanca, José Raúl, chess grand master 237n2, 273n2, 609, 612, 635, 639, 644, 646, 648, 681, 932, 986–7, 1033
Capdeville tracing paper 99
Capek, Karel; *Rossum's Universal Robots* 39n1
Carpenter, John Alden, *Skyscrapers* 250, 270–1, 710, 928
Carr, E. H., historian 642n, 863n1
Carswell, John, *The Exile: A Life of Ivy Litvinov* 436–7
Carte rose, French driving licence 404, 599
Casa Fuerte, Marquise de *see* Giraud, Yvonne
Casadesus, Henri, composer 177, 181, 636
Casadesus, Marius, violinist 177
Casadesus, Robert, pianist 177, 663n1
Casals, Pablo, cellist 127n 129, 269n1, 372n2, 776n1
Casella, Alfredo 173-4 187, 221, 249, 269, 285, 288, 289–90; Songs 358–9, 375, 855
Catacombs of Rome 721
Catherine Palace, Pushkin 478n3, 492n1
Catholicos of All the Armenians 1061–2
Central Committee for the Improvement of Scholars' Living Conditions *see* Tsekebu
Central Customs Bureau, Moscow 569, 1072
Central Telegraph Office, Moscow 1046
Chabrier, Emmanuel, *Une Education manquée* 70
Chabukiani, Vakhtang, dancer 1070, 1072
Chaliapin, Fyodor, bass 26n1, 49n1, 56–7, 64, 94, 112, 524, 540, 619n1, 743n3, 856, 911n2, 949n1, 954, 999, 1019, 1029, 1053–4
Chalon, Jean, friend of Alexander Borovsky 800–1, 846–7, 851–5, 862, 985, 991, 1024–6, 1030–2, 1039; Lac du Bourget estate 846
Chamberlain, Lesley; *The Philosophy Steamer* 37n3, 447n2
Chambord; Château de 582; Comte de 582n1
Chamiec, Zygmunt, Director of Polish Radio 979
Channel Islands xv, 1004n3, 1016, 1018
Chastushki 188–9, 217n1, 450, 527, 884; about *Three Oranges* 309
Château de la Fléchère, Culoz 847–8, 850–2
Chausson, Ernest, composer 235, 323
Cheka *see* Secret Police
Chekhov, Anton: 24n1, 175n2, 938n3, 524, 567n2, 704n2, 1002n2, 1053n1; *The Cherry Orchard* 175n2; *Notebooks* 79
Chemberdzhi, Nikolay, composer 1020n4, 1027, 1046
Chemberdzhi, Valentina, biographer, translator, memoirist 1020n4
Chernetskaya, Inna, dancer and choreographer 122, 438, 450, 473–4, 475
Chernetsky, teacher at the Russian National Conservatoire of Music 141
Chernov, Mikhail, composer, musicologist and teacher 520, 525
Chernyshevskoe *see* Eydtkuhnen
Chertkov, Vladimir, writer, amanuensis to Lev Tolstoy 1053
Chervonets, Ukrainian ten-rouble note 557
Chervonny ('Red') Hotel, Kharkov 549, 552
Chess, *giuoco piano* opening 273
Chevillier, Mme, violinist 76

INDEX

Chiang Kai-Shek 567n1
Chicago 249–50, 299, 852, 926–8, 936–8; *Chout* proposal by Bolm 336; Piano Concerto No.5 with Stock and Chicago Symphony 1041; *Three Oranges* premiere production 97n1, 144, 264, 301, 557, 760, 928n2
Chicherin, Gyorgy, Soviet Foreign Minister 435n1, 884n2
Chigi Saracini, Count Guido 289n3
Chinese Civil War *see* Shanghai
Chirico, Giorgio de, artist 801n1, 835–6
Chishko, Oles (Alexander), composer and tenor 559n2
Chislo, Paris Russian-language journal 948
Chistye Prudy, district of Moscow 1021
'Chizhik pizhik', nursery rhyme 772
Chopin, Frédéric 893: 967, 984, 128, 138, 147, 165, 186, 251-2, 589, 704n1, 745, Fantasy in F minor, Op.49 1013; Chopin Competition 419n2; Sonata No.2 in B flat minor, Op.35 80, 890n3, 903
Christian Science 65, 66, 98, 109 *see also* Prokofiev, reflections on Christian Science; beneficial effect on anger 647, 669, 684, 774, 840; importance of overcoming carnal mentality 610; attendance at church 393–4, 396–7, 577, 590, 600, 653, 655, 679, 688, 739, 745, 748, 757, 760, 765, 767, 783, 787, 793, 820, 827, 834, 837, 902; effect on composition 659, 852; alienation from *Fiery Angel* and *Gambler* 353, 374–5, 616–17; illusory nature of death and evil, 354, 607, 849; calming effect on domestic relations 137, 225, 311, 364, 652, 767, 817; beneficial effect on egocentricity 854; immortality of man 91–2, 266; enhancement of inner peace 755, 792; TREATMENT OF MEDICAL CONDITIONS 99, 107, 113, 137, 159, 233, 281, 296, 311, 377, 481, 641, 653, 656, 659, 679, 693, 750, 820; attempts to treat Lina's childbirth pains 733, 750; stops wearing spectacles 115, 126; other people's attitudes: Asafyev 721–4, 807, 874; Bruno Walter 977; Kucheryavy 883; Olga Codina 612, 620; Petrov-Vodkin 882; Suvchinsky 124, 860; effect on performance nerves, 250, 252, 259, 260, 397, 404, 994; practitioners consulted; Cobbe 141, 155–6, 162; Crain 393; Getty 66, 69; Klein 244, 247–8, 270, 354–5, 852; Olmsted 159, 164, 167, 175, 180, 187, 233, 238, 600, 925; unreality of material world 89, 136;
Christian Science Monitor 85, 610, 914
Christian Science Sentinel 620, 731; *Science and Health* 69, 73, 78, 79, 82, 85, 86
Chudovsky, Valerian, philologist, translator and critic 490, 491
Chukhnovsky, Boris, World War 1 flying ace *see* Nobile, North Pole Expedition
Churayevka, artistic and spiritual colony in USA 94n2
Cincinnati Opera 302n3
Cirque Medrano 783n2

Citroën; *Croisière noire* and *Croisière jaune* expeditions 303n2
Clamart, suburb of Paris, house rented by Lina's parents 224, 228, 232, 238, 311, 599
Clark, Edward, BBC Music Adviser 670, 671
Claudel, Paul, poet and diplomat 41n2, 706
Cleveland, Ohio 900–1, 926, 927
Cleveland Orchestra 900, 921
Classical Symphony 901
Coates, Albert, conductor 96n1, 172, 324n2, 407n2, 918n1, 933, 963, 977, 1010n1
Cobbe, Mrs, Christian Scientist 141, 155–6, 162, 169, 170, 189, 925
Cocteau, Jean, artist poet, librettist, artistic animateur 36n, 41n2, 62n2, 81, 149n2, 320, 388n2, 589, 995n; argument with Dukelsky over *Steel Step* 594, 596n4; percussionist in Milhaud's *Oresteia* 706n; éminence grise of Les Six 320; Markevich (*Cantate*) 955; *Oedipus Rex* 580–1, 590–1, 592, 598, 599, 619; *Parade* 783n2; *Le Train Bleu* 73
Codina, Carolina (Lina) *see* Prokofieva, Lina; Prokofieva, Lina Ivanovna
Codina, Juan, SSP's father-in-law 261, 297, 444n1, 612, 645, 931n
Codina, Olga Vladislavovna, SSP's mother-in-law 25, 26, 29, 31–2, 57, 109, 218–19, 221, 224, 238, 261n, 297, 332, 339, 342, 357, 612, 614, 616, 620, 622, 626, 644, 646–7, 727, 750, 759, 804, 808, 837, 941, 945, 952, 6616, 66626
Coini, Jacques, opera producer 144n1 301, 379n2
Collingwood, Lawrence, record producer
Collini, Liana, romantic interest in 1918 in Kislovodsk 115, 136
Cologne; *Chout*, proposed production of 219, 224; *Fiery Angel*, possible production of 224, 383; THREE ORANGES PRODUCTION 60, 81, 92, 125, 143, 379–80
Columbia Gramophone Company 807n3
Combined Russian Military Union (ROVS), émigré organisation in Paris
Comintern 202n2, 417, 435n1, 542n1, 568, 933n1
Communist Party of the Soviet Union: Central Committee Decree (1932) 'On the Reformation of Literature and Art Organisations' 993n2, 1022n5; Decree 'On Muradeli's opera *The Great Friendship*' (1948 Zhdanov Decree) 437n1, 553n3
Compagnie Internationale Wagons-Lit 475, 476, 499, 558, 562, 570, 1027, 1034, 1036, 1056
Concertgebouw Orchestra, Amsterdam 23n3, 142n2, 233–7
Concerts Colonne 677n1, 693n, 778n1, 989
Congress Hotel, Chicago 927, 936
Conius, Yuly (Julius), violinist, teacher, Rachmaninoff's daughter's father-in-law 141, 143, 238, 327, 575, 666, 690, 708, 890n2, 1000n1
Connors, Barry; *The Patsy* 276n3

Conradi, Maurice, killer of Soviet diplomat Vorovsky 769n1
Conservatoire Russe de Paris Serge Rachmaninoff *see* Russian Conservatoire of Paris
Consuelo, friend of Lina Prokofieva 22, 106
Conte di Savoia, Italian transatlantic liner 1041
Continental Hotel, Kiev 555
Cooper, Emil, conductor 172, 175, 191, 357, 451n2, 696, 808
Copland, Aaron, composer 315, 367
Coppola, Piero, conductor 1008n3
Copyists 40, 76, 88, 89, 90, 157, 164, 167, 168, 220, 222, 229, 238, 253, 359, 362, 621, 688, 689–90, 694, 695, 742, 814, 892, 933
CORA *see* Orchestre des concerts Straram
Cortot, Alfred, pianist 31, 326n1 755, 758n1, 1013
Costanzi Theatre, Rome 657
Coué, Emil, doctor, originator of 'optimistic autosuggestion' 296
Crain, Miss, Christian Science healer 393–4, 404–5, 577, 702, 706, 901
Crane, Charles, American philanthropist and businessman 245–6, 473
Craven Hotel, London 11
Crommelynck, Fernand, *The Magnificent Cuckold* 546
Cuin, Mme, proposer of Rostand Opera 591
Culoz *see* Château de la Fléchère
Cunard, Nancy Lady, London hostess and arts patron 903
Cuvelier, concert promoter in Brussels 941

Dahl, Dr Nikolay, hypnotist 666
Damrosch, Walter, conductor 51, 55, 64, 67, 245, 265n3, 269, 904n2
Damskaya, Eleonora, harpist and Conservatoire friend 43n, 231–2, 496–7, 522, 525–6, 529, 534, 870, 1031
Daniels, friends of Lina Prokofieva 925
Danilova, Alexandra, ballerina 317n1 589, 680
Dargomyzhsky, Alexander, composer 358
Darrieux, Marcel, violinist 771, 824n2
Davidenko, Alexander, RAPM composer 908
Davydova, Lucy *see* Khodzhayeva sisters
De Grasse transatlantic liner 238, 243
DeLamarter, Eric, Assistant Conductor of Chicago Symphony 927
Debussy, Claude 36n, 130, 149n2, 263,2, 669, 704n1, 730n, 952, 1004, 1007, 1008n3; prose style 699; WORKS *Le Martyre de San Sebastien* 4n5; *Nocturnes* 60; *Pelléas et Mélisande* 183n1; *Printemps* 222n1; Violin Sonata 776n1
Defauw, Désiré, violinist and conductor in Ghent 987, 1006n4
Dekosov, shipboard acquaintance 893
Delage cars 574–5, 577n
Delage, Maurice, composer 173

Delannoy, Marcel, composer 687; *L'Eventail de Jeanne* 42n1
Delarova, Eugenia, ballerina, wife of Léonide Massine 898
Demasy, Paul: *Cavalière Elsa* 6, 7, 43, 60, 77, 170, 172, 188–9; *Jesus of Nazareth*43; *Juditha* 77, 188, 189
Demchinskaya, Varvara 345n3, 879
Demchinsky, Boris, philologist and writer 22, 490n2, 870, 875, 925, 993, 1027–8, 1031, 1034, 1047–8, 1050, 1068, 1069; relations with Damskaya 231–2; CONTRIBUTION TO *FIERY ANGEL* LIBRETTO 22–3, 64, 90, 154, 157, 231, 327, 334, 337–40, 343, 345–6, 348, 350–1, 350–2, 356–7, 368, 529, 601, 607, 647, 695, 916; Gogol's dictum 90; critical of Lavrenyov opera project, 1049; dissuades SSP from considering Remizov's *Alaley and Leila* as opera subject 24n3, 607n1, 695
Denezhny Lane, Moscow 422, 424
Denikin, General Anton, White Army General 387n4, 642
Denver, Colorado 251–2, 256, 257
Deryuzhinsky, Gleb, sculptor 33
Derzhanovsky, Vladimir, music journalist and promoter 151, 221, 256, 413–14, 413n3, 423, 429–30, 811, 866, 1018, 1043; Head of Association of Contemporary Music, 441, 690n1; ARRANGES SSP'S MOSCOW VISIT AND SOME ORCHESTRAL PERFORMANCES 531; chamber music evening at Conservatoire 540; organised SSP's first appearances in Moscow 456, 533; private chamber music recital 441–3; *Steel Step* Suite premiere conducted in Moscow by Savich 705; brokers meeting with Peshkova about Shurik 536–7; employment at 'Kniga' shop 415, 804; enamoured of Lina 424, 432, 444; provides wrong title for Gippius poem 28–9; intermediary with Gusman 834; intermediary for SSP's consultancy position with Moscow Radio 867, 881, 885, 886; originally responsible for bringing together SSP, Myaskovsky and Asafyev 720; proposes Christmas 1928 repeat visit but fails to raise funds for 734, 749, 752–4, 759; conducts press interview with SSP 1023; considers SSP insufficiently anxious to cultivate Soviet nomenklatura 1067; stays loyal to SSP through thick and thin 707n; copies parts for Symphony No.3 in Moscow 814; Tsekubu room in flat 431
Derzhinskaya, Ksenia, soprano 451–2, 570
Deshevov, Vladimir, composer 477, 481, 517–18, 546, 785, 1027; SSP recommends to VOKS 1035
Désormière, Roger, conductor 183, 955; conducts *Prodigal Son* 818, 821, 822, 825, 826–7, 830, 832–3, 836, 838, 934–5; conducts *Steel Step* 591–3, 595, 677, 680, 709
Detroit, Michigan 928; Detroit Symphony 265n2
Detskoe Selo *see* Tsarskoe Selo
Deutsche Oper, Berlin

Devil's Bridge, Switzerland 233, 725
d'Harcourt, translator of Akhmatova songs 42
Diaghilev, Sergey (Serge) 62, 74, 122, 149–50, 151, 181, 183n1, 188, 196n, 228, 246, 261, 304, 334, 336n1, 355, 467n2, 480, 504, 528n1, 532, 535, 550n1, 565n1, 572, 652, 668, 677, 680, 696, 707, 714, 740, 741, 745, 756, 777, 779, 780, 802, 806, 810, 861, 862, 877, 911n2, 913, 919, 947, 955, 964, 969, 1010; articles written about: by Dukelsky 691; by Nabokov 890–1; by SSP 593; by Suvchinsky 676; business dealings: Berlin counter-offer as bargaining chip 178, 180, 182; assignment of *Chout* rights 14; SSP conducting fees 807; *Prodigal Son* commission 730–3, 747; *The Steel Step* commission 186, 212, 215, 222; *Chout*, proposed revival of 763, 765; death, tributes and memorials to 856–7, 859, 965–6; Gershwin, indifference to 703; homosexual inclinations, early attempts to treat 917; inner entourage; Kokhno 46n1, 66, 167, 177, 189, 203, 221, 317, 355, 573, 853; Lifar 320, 324; Markevich 764, 813–14, 815, 955; Massine 179; Nouvel 151, 173, 218, 317, 572–3, 630, 652, 919, 955, 969; Pavka Koribut 202, 801, 946, 969; Lunacharsky, meets in Paris 586–7, 653; Mayakovsky, debates with in Berlin 28n3, 743; Monte Carlo, SSP finds incomplete without 945–6; OTHER COLLABORATORS, DEALINGS WITH: Braque 177, 320; Carpenter 250–1, 270–1; Dukelsky 102–8, 116, 147–8, 150, 162–3, 165–6, 173, 177–8, 182–3, 185–6, 190, 596, 630, 670; Larionov 24; Martinu 774; Meyerhold 323–4, 505; Nabokov 705, 708–9, 781–2, 948; commissions *Ode* 682; Popov 729, 871; Tcherepnin 11n6; Utrillo 317–18; Villa-Lobos 774–9; OTHER PREMIERES AND PERFORMANCES PRESENTED: *Le Bal* 801, 827–8, 834, 835–6, 1010n2; *Barabau* 317, 326; *Les Biches* 57–8, 67, 179; *Chant du Rossignol* 61n2, 178–9; *La Chatte* 589; *David* 747; *Une Education Manquée* 70; *Les Fâcheux* 30n2, 65; *The Firebird* 589; *Khovanshchina* 49n; *Les Matelots* 30n2, 157, 177, 178–80, 314; *Mercure* 591; *Les Noces* 58; *Ode* 682, 691, 705, 708–9; *Pastorale* 30n2, 324, 328, 834–5; *Pulcinella* 177; *Romeo and Juliet* 312–14, 590; *Le Train Bleu* 73, 183; *The Triumph of Neptune* 378, 589; *The Two Beggars* 756; *Zéphyre et Flore* 107–9, 116, 147–8, 150, 162–3, 177, 182, 189–90, 332–3; PARTIALITY TO CONTEMPORARY EUROPEAN COMPOSERS: Auric 65, 84, 116, 148, 157, 161–2, 177–80, 182–3, 186, 222, 299, 314, 324, 328, 822, 830, 834, 1050; Berners 378, 589; Lambert 312–13; Milhaud 70, 73, 84, 148, 590, 1050, 1892–3; Poulenc 57–8, 67–8, 84, 148, 179, 182–3, 222, 299, 375, 1050; Rieti 317, 801, 827–8, 835–6; Sauguet 321n1, 589, 680, 764, 1051; PERSONAL RELATIONSHIP WITH SSP: 184, 767; affection for SSP's children 54, 760; attends *The Gambler* premiere in Brussels 813–14; *Bruderschaft* 594, 596, 653; cooling 841, 856;

gallantry to Lina 150, 594, 737, 774, 806; PROFESSIONAL RELATIONSHIP WITH SSP: preference for Stravinsky's ballets 150, 745; SSP suspects of intriguing with Kokhno 839–40, 856; *Scythian Suite*, rejects as ballet score 154; religious feelings 859–60; reputation in USSR 476, 579; rivalry with Ida Rubinstein 696, 730, 737, 747, 797, 824, 992; Smyth, Dame Ethel, anecdote about 779; snobbish pressure, consequences of yielding to 995; RELATIONSHIP WITH STRAVINSKY: 150, 605; *Apollon musagète* 629, 638, 657, 711–12; cuts in 839, 856; reactions to 629, 652n2, 712, 720, 722, 727, 756; *Baiser de la fée*, reaction to 728, 738–9, 742, 747, 756, 806, 917; *Le Renard* revival 381n3, 801, 829–30; *Oedipus Rex*, reaction to 375, 580–1, 590, 599, 619n1; personal feelings, cooling of 745, 779, 820, 830, 832, 849, 857; strictures on taste 778–9; Tchaikovsky, comments on 778; THE PRODIGAL SON: Balanchine as choreographer 222n2, 826–31, 834, 842; choice of designer 783, 792–5, 801–2; dedicated to Diaghilev 797; dispute with Kokhno over author's rights and credits 763–4, 839–43; fee negotiations 732–4; genesis and composition 729, 735, 742, 747–9, 751, 763, 795–6; libretto by Kokhno 729, 736, 774–5, 806; publication 804, 806, 815, 830–2; reaction to score 737–8, 744–5, 797; rehearsals and premieres 801–2, 815, 818, 820, 822, 825, 826–31, 832–3, 835, 836, 842; SSP as conductor of premieres in Paris and London 807, 815, 841; Stravinsky's comments to Diaghilev 794, 796–7; transformation of music into Symphony No.4 301n3, 783n3, 800, 819; THE STEEL STEP: dedication to Diaghilev 596; Diaghilev's London press article 605; Ehrenburg, discussions with 198–9, 202–4, 208, 210, 211–12; fee negotiations 186; genesis of 184–5; hammers in score 599; Massine as choreographer 573, 680n, 681; premiere and subsequent performances 677, 680–1, 705, 709; sets too awkward to tour 652–3; Suvchinsky, discussions with 185–6, 189, 198–9; title of ballet 215, 389, 580–1; Yakulov as designer and co-librettist 202, 203–4, 205–6, 208, 209–10, 211–15, 218

Dianov, Anton, composer 340
Diederichs, Andrey, piano manufacturer 415
Dikiy, Alexey, actor and producer 437, 449, 450, 454, 466–8, 527, 548, 872, 876
d'Indy, Vincent, composer 183n3, 782, 805
The Diva *see* Janacopulos, Vera
Dmitriev, Vladimir, stage designer in Leningrad 297n2, 490, 545, 875
Dneprostroy, large hydro-electric project on the Dnieper 1022
Dobrowen, Issay, conductor 225–6, 228
Dobychina, Nadezhda, gallery owner and artist agent in Leningrad 318, 497, 511, 1029
Dolin, Anton, premier danseur 73n1, 74, 179, 183

Dom Uchonykh *see* House of Scholars, Moscow

Dostoyevsky, Fyodor 674n2, 907, 950; *Crime and Punishment* 947; 'The Eternal Husband' 606; *The Gambler* 96, 616, 656, 667; *The Idiot* 150

Doucet, Clément, pianist 48n1

Doumer, Paul, President of France; assassination of 992

Downes, Olin, music critic 76, 905, 908

Dramsoyuz (Society of Dramatic and Musical Authors), Leningrad 887

Dranishnikov, Vladimir, conductor 184, 479, 481, 484, 490, 511, 527, 528–9, 588, 649, 870–1, 873–4, 1032; *Boris Godunov* (Lamm version), produced by Akopera 875–6; concerts of SSP's works 483, 494, 495–6, 1027–8, 1030–1, 1047–9; *Three Oranges*, (Akopera production) 184, 230, 297, 309, 487–90, 514–15, 527; possible tour to Paris 530; revival 1028

Dresden Opera 590n3

Druskin, Mikhail, pianist, critic, musicologist and teacher 482

Du Guesclin restaurant, Paris 305, 307, 328

Dubost, Jeanne, Paris hostess; *L'éventail de Jeanne* 42, 146, 598, 676, 687n2, 707, 715, 755, 769, 781, 828, 842, 993

Duduk, Armenian traditional instrument 1061

Duke, Vernon *see* Dukelsky, Vladimir

Dukelsky, Vladimir: alter ego as Broadway composer Vernon Duke 72n1, 740n1, articles written: Diaghilev's Ballets Russes 691; Ragtime in Contemporary Music 180; argument with Cocteau over *Steel Step* 594, 596; composition studies: with Glière 428; with Schillinger 517n1; consulted by Diaghilev over Carpenter's *Skyscrapers*; relations with Diaghilev 150, 162, 166, 180, 182–3, 279, 378, 630, 670, 774, 856; dress sense 278, 332–3, 596, 671; erotic adventures 165, 192, 271, 278, 279, 332, 355, 358, 360, 740, 741, 743–4, 781; relations with Koussevitzky 163–4, 368–70, 702, 929; friendship with Lambert 312n3; meets Mayakovsky 743–4; lack of skill in orchestration 177–8, 182, 332, 705, 711, 728, 729; VIEWS ON OTHER COMPOSERS AND THEIR MUSIC: Auric 222; Brahms 703; Gershwin 733–4, 904; Honegger 165, 175; Poulenc 222; disparages Scriabin 703; Stravinsky 149, 175, 176, 592; HOW PERCEIVED BY OTHER MUSICIANS: Ansermet 727–8; Asafyev 720, 729, 742; Markevich 764; music seen as influenced by SSP 163–4; Ravel 184; SSP recommends Symphony No.2 772; Stravinsky 375; Tcherepnin 190; as pianist, 889: four-hand performances with Zakharov 702; in *Les Noces* 326; plays second piano for SSP's rehearsal of Second Piano Concerto 223; fear of heights on roller-coaster, 193; relations with Russian Musical Editions 189–90, 192, 711, 973; sketching, discovers talent for 765, 915; encounters Sofronitsky 766–7; COMMENTS ON SSP'S MUSIC 114; *Choses en soi* 729; praises Lina's singing 914; Piano Concerto No.2 671; *Scythian Suite* 913–14; *The Steel Step* 222–3; Symphony No.2 171, 172, 180; urges less complexity 169, 171; Symphony No.4 800; Violin Concerto 334; RELATIONS WITH SSP: admiration for talent 148, 708; criticism of 711; friendship 193, 334, 357–8, 360–1, 383, 572, 592–3, 594, 671, 710, 766; SSP recommends to Asafyev for performance in Russia; recommends to ISCM 982; recommends to Wolff 736; dismayed by attraction to operetta and musicals 278, 361, 630, 671, 800, 907, 974; stories recounted by 334, 702, 913; relations with Stravinsky 223; caricatures Suvchinsky 223; relations with Suvchinsky 223; tastes disapproved of by SSP; jazz and popular music 163, 597, 767; nightclubs and other dubious establishments 165, 740; WORKS: Double bass concerto 907; *Dushenka* 669, 670–1, 729; *Five Pushkin Songs* 728–9; *Mistress into Maid* 740, 741, 843; new 'serious' ballet (*Jardin Public*?) 278, 334–5, 360, 565; *Passport to Paris* (autobiography) 72n1; Piano Concerto 73; *Sonata* for piano and orchestra 595–6; Symphony No.1 626, 669, 710, 711, 712–13, 714, 728, 765, 772; Symphony No.2 728, 741, 929; *Zéphyre et Flore* 107, 116, 148, 162, 163, 165, 173, 177, 178, 182, 185, 186, 189–90, 332; also mentioned 166, 375, 649, 695, 704, 705, 707, 710, 713, 801, 803, 847, 868, 876, 893, 902, 903, 916, 919, 930, 940

Dumesnil, René, literary and music critic 1004; suggests visiting Channel Islands 1004–5

Duncan, Isadora, dancer and choreographer 122, 524, 545, 556, 635

Duo-Art 7, 12–13, 23, 40, 244, 248, 275–6, 463, 669; AudioGraphic rolls 664; Overture for 17 Instruments 339–40, 345, 377; orchestral version (*American Overture*) 686, 716; *Sheherazade* transcription 7, 245, 248

Dupré, Marcel, organist and composer 655

Durand et Cie, music publishers

Durashkin, stock comic figure 427

Dusheti, Georgia

Dushkin, Samuel, violinist 192n1, 997n2; 'Working with Stravinsky' 1011n2

Dutnikova, dancer, niece of Demchinsky 1069

Dzbanovsky, Alexander, composer and critic 549

Easter Day 817

Echmiadzin, monastery and church in Armenia 1061

Eddy, Mary Baker, founder of Christian Science 67n1, 69n3

Edition Russe de musique *see* Russian Musical Editions

Edwards, Misia *see* Sert, Misia

Efron, Ariadna (Alya) 388

Efron, Gyorgy (Mur) 388

Efron, Sergey, poet, husband of Marina Tsvetaeva 62, 388, 631
Ehrenburg, Ilya, novelist and journalist 198–9, 202–4, 208, 210, 211–12, 214, 788
Ehrhardt, Otto, opera producer 590
Ekskuzovich, Ivan, cultural administrator, Director of Akopera 210n1, 475–7, 494, 499, 502–3, 507, 534, 875; *Ala and Lolli*, proposed production 499; SSP as repertoire consultant to State Theatres 369; *The Gambler* 496, 499, 500, 530, 688; proposal to combine with *Chout* 515; *The Steel Step*, proposed production 499; *Three Oranges*: Akopera production 210, 212, 213, 215–16, 373, 490, 493, 514–16, 548; possible tour to Paris; Golovin as designer 534–5; Bolshoy Theatre production 368–9, 396
Elizabeth Palace, Pushkin see Catherine Palace, Pushkin
Elman, Mischa, violinist 171, 263, 272n4, 273–4, 750, 893, 912n1, 925
Elsa, Danish nanny 850, 945, 952, 981, 987
Enesco, Georges, composer, pianist and violinist 269, 776n1
Engel, Carl, composer, musicologist, publisher, Head of Library of Congress Music Division 190, 916–17, 934
Ermler, Friedrich, film director; *Wreckage of an Empire* 876n1
Ernst, Max, artist 313, 835
Esche, Sofia, Conservatoire friend 229
Esipova see Yesipova, Anna
Ettal, Bavaria 4n6, 15–17, 79, 101n1, 107, 111, 156–7, 311–12, 322n2, 341, 359, 363, 409, 574, 610, 612, 960–1
Eurasia journal 438, 738, 757, 838, 951
Eurasianist Movement 62, 124n4, 132–3, 175, 182, 389, 423, 641n, 642, 647, 784, 857–8, 879, 886, 951
Europa Hotel, Leningrad 478, 480, 483–4, 493, 508, 510, 519, 870, 873
Europa Hotel, Moscow 568
Europa, transatlantic liner 939–40, 1039
Evening Post, New York 272, 682
Evening Red Newspaper see Vechernyaya Krasnaya Gazeta
Eydtkuhnen, border town 407

Fabre, Lina Prokofieva's doctor in Paris 750, 827n1
Faintsimmer, Alexander, film director 933n3, 1031n5, 1047n2, 1054, 1068–9
Fairbanks, American Christian Scientists 587
Faleyeva, Nadezhda, actress, SSP's niece 443
Falk, Henri, playwright, *The Pander* (*Le Rabatteur*) 697
de Falla, Manuel, composer 149n2, 174n, 327, 592, 663n1, 669, 776, 906; *La Vida breve* 812
Famine, Ukraine, 1933
Fatou, Pierre Joseph Louis, astronomer 158

Fauré, Gabriel, composer, Director of Paris Conservatoire 60n1, 174n4, 190n4, 235n, 699n3, 776n1, 805, 1012n
Fédorov, Vladimir, composer 636, 973, 1078
Feinberg, Samuil, pianist 419, 421, 430–1, 437, 455, 457, 459, 483, 526, 539, 547, 609, 785, 908, 1026
Mme de Felz, guest of Arthur Rubinstein 1014
Ferroud, Pierre-Octave, composer 704, 997n2, 1002, 1014; *L'Eventail de Jeanne* 42n1
Fester, Georges, co-owner of Mund and Fester, Antwerp
Février, Jacques, pianist 676, 997, 1006; participates in SSP's bridge tournament 1015–16
Fiat 10hp tourer car 573
Fiedler, architect and estate agent in Paris 338, 344, 364, 367–9, 370, 705, 727, 841
Le Figaro, newspaper 811
Filonov, Pavel, artist and explorer
Filosofov, Dmitry, journalist and writer, cousin of Diaghilev 129
Finck, Henry Theophilus, music critic 272
Fitelberg, Grzegorz, conductor 123, 127–8, 131, 139, 172, 952, 978–9, 1037
Flament, Edouard, pianist 58n2
de la Fléchère de Beauregarde, Comte and Comtesse 851
Flesch, Carl, violinist; *The Art of Violin Playing* 59n2, 132
Florence, Pitti Palace 291
Fokine, Mikhail, dancer and choreographer 4n5, 275n2, 304n1, 691n2, 1008n1
Fontanka, Leningrad 481, 772n1
Forberg, Robert Max, Leipzig music publisher 460
Forsh, Olga, *Ship of Fools* 293, 1079
Fortiers, hosts in Montreal
Foss, Hubert J, music publisher 40, 41
Fourestier, Louis, conductor
Fradin, Emile, discoverer of Glozel archeological site 803
France, transatlantic liner 939
Franciz, Paris friend of Lina Prokofieva 385, 666
Franck, César, composer and organist 43, 663
Frankfurt-am-Main 279–81, 1011; Opera 281, 902
Fratellini Brothers, clowns 783n2
Freiburg 666, 676, 686
Frenkel, Naftaly (Natan), NKVD officer 869, 887, 989
Friml, Rudolf, composer; *Rose Marie*
Frou-frou see Baranovskaya, Maria Viktorovna
Fürstenhof restaurant, Berlin 124, 379, 406, 571, 583
Fürtwängler, Wilhelm, conductor 59n2, 132n1, 273–4, 276, 989, 1010, 1018

Gabel, Stanislav, opera producer 522
Gabo, Naum, artist 589n3
Gabrielle, nanny 600, 603, 607
Gabrilowitsch, Ossip, conductor 265
Gamma Leo, astronomical double object 158

Gance, Abel, film director; *Napoléon* 71n1, 195n1
Garafola, Lynn, *Diaghilev's Ballets Russes* 179n1, 605n1
Garden, Mary, soprano, former Director of Chicago Opera x 331, 337, 918n1
Garmisch 17
Gartman, Maximilian, former aviator, car mechanic 658
Garvin, Mrs, wealthy American friend 35, 45, 73, 923–4, 926
Gatti, concert organiser in Turin 945
Gatti-Casazza, Giulio, General Director of the Metropolitan Opera 9n5, 10, 692n2; considers and rejects *Fiery Angel* 277, 902, 912, 916, 929, 934–5; reconsiders *The Gambler* 277n1, 934–5, 938–9
Gaubert, Philippe, conductor 176, 219, 229, 230, 663n1, 1005, 1037
Gauk, Alexander, conductor 81, 96, 98, 1062n2, 1069
Gaveau et Cie, piano manufacturers 550, 779, 807–8, 818, 820, 821, 826, 833, 837–8, 840, 845, 848–9, 851, 853, 892, 947, 953, 1000
Gavrilova, Olga, wife of Alexander Glazunov 708n1, 754
Gavrilova, Yelena, pianist, adopted daughter of Alexander Glazunov 754n1
Geltzer, Yekaterina, ballerina 467n3
General Staff Headquarters, Leningrad 479
Genoa 290–1
George Cross, Russian pre-revolutionary military decoration 387
Georgian Military Highway 1057–8, 1064–5
German, Yury; *The Introduction* 1044n2, 1045
Gershwin, George 72n1, 245, 517n1, 703; possible Metropolitan Opera commission 912; reception at home 904; WORKS *An American in Paris* 904n1; Piano Concerto 245; *Porgy and Bess* 97n2; *Strike Up the Band* 906–7
Gessen, Iosif, newspaper editor 23n4, 112n, 123, 127, 132–5, 246n1, 380, 383
Getty, Mrs, Christian Scientist 66–9, 78, 85–6, 149, 679, 750
Ghent 987
Ghirshman, Roman, archeologist 710, 713, 831, 892
Mme de Gibarga, President of Pro Arte, Havana 931
Gibson, Violet, would-be assassin of Mussolini 285n1
Gieseking, Walter, pianist 263, 730
Gil-Marchex, Henri, pianist 298, 465
Gilgamesh, legend of 33–5, 38
Ginzburg, Grigory, pianist 437n1
Gippius, Zinaïda *see* Hippius, Zinaïda
Giraud, Yvonne, Marquise de Casa Fuerte, *see also* Sérénade
Girin, OGPU Officer 439, 440, 458
Givnin, con man 493
Gladkaya, Olga, singer, wife of Nikolay Kedrov 112

Glazunov, Alexander Konstantinovich, composer, Rector of Leningrad Conservatoire 288, 349, 495, 515, 523–4, 614, 745, 770, 782, 838, 898; Belyayev Concerts Committee member 130n1; conducts Orchestre Symphonique de Paris 838; debut concert after coming to Paris 753–4; vicious review by Schloezer 753n1; encounter with Stravinsky 838; host at SSP's visit to Conservatoire 521–2; jubilee concert in Paris 1000–1; letters from Tchaikovsky 722; marriage 708n1; *Prince Igor*, completion with Rimsky-Korsakov 61n1, 285n2; conducts premiere of Rachmaninoff's Symphony No.1 666; walks out of *Scythian Suite* premiere 3n1; SSP calls on 485–7, 493; leaves USSR but nominally remains Director of Conservatoire 708n1, 722, 857, 873, 916, 1001; helps Yurevskaya 47n2; WORKS *Festive Overture* 754; Piano Concerto No.2 754; *The Seasons* 838n; *Stenka Razin* 754; *Les Sylphides* (version) 57n2; Violin Concerto 64n1
Glebova, Tamara, Conservatoire friend, daughter of Musina-Ozarevskaya 527, 530
Glière, Reinhold 427–8, 437, 555, 1051; SSP's early teacher 44n1; ALSO TEACHER OF: Davidenko 908n; Knipper 430n3; Kozitsky 554n1; Lyatoshinsky 553n3; Mosolov 430n5; Shebalin 539n2; Shenshin 539n1; WORKS *The Red Poppy* 467–8
Glinka, Mikhail 423n1, 671, 722; *A Life for the Tsar* 26n1; *Slava!* 495; *Ruslan and Lyudmila* 806; Overture transcribed for two pianos 110
Glinsky, manager of National Hotel, Moscow 1043
Glozel, archeological site 803
Gnesin, Mikhail, composer 441n2, 1053, 1055
Gnesina, Yelena, music educator 538
Go, Oriental board game 273n2
Gobillard, Jeannie, wife of Paul Valéry 1014n2
Godowsky, Dagmar, silent cinema actress 59, 301, 1079
Godowsky, Leopold, pianist 301, 838, 967n2
Goedike, Alexander, composer, pianist and teacher 539, 785
Gogol, Nikolay 916, 1067n3; dictum 90–1; WORKS 'Christmas Eve' 723n1, 815; *Dead Souls*, burning of Part Two 374; *The Inspector-General* 320n1, 532; 'The Marriage' 13n3; 'May Night' 409n3; 'The Nose' 874n2
Golden Arrow, continental express train 668
The Golden Mountains, film 1008
Goldenberg, Mme, Kiev music teacher 556–8
Goldenweiser, Alexander, pianist and teacher 437, 540, 1023–4, 1026, 1035; chess games with 1053–4, 1071; *Close to Tolstoy* 437n1
Goldman, doctor in Odessa 560
Golovanov, Nikolay, Chief Conductor of Bolshoy Theatre 426–7, 432, 466–9, 535, 1018–19, 1022–5, 1027, 1034–6, 1066–7; ability to judge metronome speeds 454

Golovin, Alexander, theatre designer; proposed for foreign tour of *Three Oranges* 96n1, 188, 197, 324n2, 534–5, 999, 1071
Golschmann, Vladimir, violinist and conductor 677
Golubev, Viktor, archeologist 190
Goncharova, Natalya Sergeyevna, artist
Goncharova, Natasha, Conservatoire friend and former singing student
Gonich, singer 38
Goossens, Eugene, conductor 12, 13, 918
Gorchakov, Gyorgy, SSP's assistant 154, 363, 386–8, 393–4, 405, 456, 533, 571–2, 581, 584, 600–2, 604–5, 606, 614, 626, 638, 7715; becomes ill 689, 702–3, 706; chess with Paichadze 628; committed Christian Scientist 363, 387, 394, 404; mishap with shutters 641; mother 638; nicknamed Grogy 581; sister 560–2; TRANSCRIBES SSP's ORCHESTRATION SHORTHAND 386, 612, 619, 621, 628, 632, 634, 655, 657, 687–9, 694–5, 701, 809; TRANSCRIBES SSP's SOVIET DIARY 657–8, 662, 663, 700, 707; takes menial work with Russian Musical Editions 966; as composer 636, 655, 675, 772, 843, 960, 972, 1046; consults Stravinsky 844; WORKS Piano Concerto No.2 700–1; Sonata 675
Gorchakova, sister of Gorchakov
Gorgulov, Paul, assassin of President Doumer 992
Gorky, Maxim, writer 62, 81, 94n2, 217n1, 225n4 292–4, 345, 426, 536, 536n1, 642, 691n, 884n1, 951, 1011n, 1022, 1023n, 1033n1, 1044n2, 1053n1
Gorodetsky, Sergey, poet, librettist of *Ala and Lolli* 232n2, 499n1, 887
Gorodinsky, Viktor, musicologist and critic, Director of Rosphil 1045
Goryansky, Valentin, poet, 'Under the Roof' 256n1
Gosizdat, USSR State Publishing House 423n1, 613
Gostiny Dvor, Leningrad department store 478
Gostorg, export store 537, 543, 567
Gottlieb, Ephraim, friend and SSP supporter in Chicago 85, 250, 262, 264, 299, 609, 927, 928n1, 936, 938
Gounod, Charles, composer 112n2, 131
Gozzi, Carlo, playwright 31, 565n3; *Turandot* 565–6
Gradstein, Alfred, composer 787
Graham, Christian Science acquaintance 994–5, 998, 1004
Granat, Tatyana (Tanya), friend of the Karneyeva sisters 1030
Grand Hotel, Biarritz 624
Grand Hotel, Brussels 809, 813
Grand Hotel, Jersey 1017
Grand Hotel, Moscow *see* Bolshaya Moskovskaya Hotel
Grand Hotel, Paris 200–1, 730, 733, 737, 763
Grand Hotel, Siena 289
Grand Opéra, Paris *see* Paris Opéra
Great Northern Hotel, New York 243

Grebenshchikov, Gyorgy; *The Byliny of Mikula Buyanovich* 94n2, 1079
Grechaninov, Alexander, composer 172, 185, 393, 539n1, 577, 649, 786, 916, 934, 940
Greenberg, American composer 906, 929
Greiner, Alexander, Steinway New York manager 894, 897, 899, 912
Grez sur Loing 214, 218
Grigoriev, Sergey (Serge), Ballets Russes ballet-master 594n3, 946, 1005n1
Grimaldi, Royal House of Monaco 149
Gris, Juan, artist 70n1, 756n2
Grogy *see* Gorchakov, Gyorgy
Grossman, Mme, hostess in Warsaw 127–8, 130, 571
Grunau, waiter in Paris restaurant 4
Grzhimali, Ivan, violinist and teacher 219n2
Guchkov, Alexander, politician 126n1, 631–4, 638; Order No.1 126n1, 631
Guchkova, Mme 132
Guchkova, Vera Alexandrovna 126, 132–3, 182, 211, 229, 631, 633, 638, 673, 681, 682, 692–3, 757
Gusman, Boris, music and literary critic; Bolshoy Theatre Head of repertoire 834, 866, 868, 872, 876, 879, 881, 883, 887, 933–4; purged from Bolshoy Theatre position 868, 933n3; EMPLOYED BY BELGOSKINO 933, 1050; arranges screen test for Lina 1069, 1071; instigates *Lt.Kijé* project 1031, 1034, 1036, 1047; suggests Lavrenyov's 'Story of a Simple Thing' as opera subject 1049, 1069–70
Gustavus Adolphus, King of Sweden 227
Gzovskaya, Tatyana, dancer and choreographer 123n4

Haardt, Georges-Marie *see* Citroën
Haensel, Fitzhugh W., New York music agent 47, 115, 161, 221, 244, 256, 258, 275, 277, 609, 636, 679, 714, 742, 835, 894, 897, 900, 934
Hale, Philip, music critic in Boston 914
Hall of Columns, Leningrad *see* Assembly of the Nobility, Leningrad
Hall of Columns, Moscow *see* Assembly of the Nobility, Moscow
Hall of the Nobility, Leningrad *see* Assembly of the Nobility, Leningrad
Hall of the Nobility, Moscow *see* Assembly of the Nobility, Moscow
Hambourg, Boris, cellist 8n1
Hambourg, Jan(Ivan), violinist 8n1
Hambourg, Mark, pianist 8n1
Hammond, John Hays, electronics engineer and inventor 956, 976
Hamsun, Knut, *Victoria* 139, 140, 308
Handel, George Frideric 56n1, 177n; *The Two Beggars* (arr. Beecham) 756
Handschin, Jacques, organist and teacher 108
Hanon, Charles Louis, *The Virtuoso Piano in 60 Exercises* 502

Hansen, Cecilia, violinist, wife of Boris Zakharov 44, 171n2, 191n4, 433, 768n1, 979n1, 1000n1
Hansen, Elfrieda (Frieda), pianist and Conservatoire friend 273n3, 603n1, 786n1, 979
Hanum, Fatma, wife of Boris Samoilenko 3, 29, 60, 187–8, 219, 229, 279, 331, 594, 651, 664, 668, 702, 713, 1006; enquires about Nina Meshcherskaya 713–14; fashionable millinery business in Paris 3n2, 746; native Ossetian soil brought back by Lina 1065; attracted to Stravinsky's 'ugly, pockmarked face' 336; walks to Versailles with SSP 659, 661–2
Hanum, Milya 279n2
Hanum, Tamara 60n3 107, 279n2, 697; dines at 'Samarkand' restaurant 668
Harrison, Christian Science publisher 914
Harsányi, Tibor, Hungarian composer 982
Havana, Cuba 930–3; Partagás cigars 932; Pro Arte concert promoting society 932, 955
Haydn, Josef 138, 397, 805, 929
Hébertot, Jacques, playwright and theatrical manager 10–12, 46–7, 54, 65, 70, 72, 74–6, 79, 80, 97, 104, 109, 110–11, 113, 117
Heifetz, Jascha, violinist 64, 141n4, 171n2, 263n6, 268, 673n1, 912n1
Henderson, W. J., music critic 266
Hérédia, José Maria y Giraud, poet 15
Hermitage Museum, Leningrad 479, 485, 485n2
Herriot, Edouard, President of France 350
Hertz, Alfred, conductor 255, 710–13, 924–6
Hickenlooper, Lucy Mary Agnes see Samaroff, Olga
Hindemith, Paul 173n2, 519n2, 703–4, 729, 732, 756, 774, 857, 955, 995; WORKS Concerto for Orchestra 337; Concerto for Piano left hand 958n2; *Konzertstück*, Op.40 756; *Mathis der Maler* 1005n4; Viola Concerto 703–4
Hippius, Zinaïda, poet 12, 28, 37, 129n3, 256; 'Circles' 110; 'The Grey Dress' 28–9, 90, 256n1
Hispano-Suiza cars 576n2, 676
Hofmann, Josef, pianist 59
Holy, producer of *The Love for Three Oranges* at Berlin Staatsoper 379, 380, 381, 382
Homeless children 294n1, 551–2
Honegger, Arthur 33n3, 34, 39, 152, 163, 175, 181, 302, 592, 687n2, 705, 727, 825, 837; ISCM sub-committee member 982; percussionist in Milhaud's *Oresteia* 706n; 'Triton' Chamber Music Society committee member 997, 1002; WORKS *L'Aiglon* 598n3; *Icare* 598n3; *Judith* 153, 308, 812; *King David* 33, 49, 51, 283; *Napoléon*, film score 195n1; *Les noces d'Amour et de Psyché* 4n5, 824; *Pacific 231* 50–1, 288, 337; *Phaedra* 701; Piano Concerto 165; *Sémiramis* 1008n1; Sonatina for violin and cello 1038; String Quartet No.1 910
Horowitz, Vladimir, pianist 59, 264, 302–3, 392, 565n1, 597, 708, 715, 730, 754n1, 818, 841, 899, 912n1, 956, 991
Hotchkiss car 578, 729

Hôtel Beauséjour, Paris 384
Hotel Continental, Kiev 555
Hotel Continental, Milan 947
Hôtel Poussin, Paris 727
Hotel Regina, Milan 947
Hôtel Terminus, Paris 196
Hôtel Victoria Palace, Paris 198, 221, 297, 302, 309, 384, 572, 948, 952
Hôtel Vouillemont, Paris 201, 203
House of Scholars, Moscow 1032–3, 1054
Hussa, Dr Philip, New York dentist 277n3
Hypnosis 666, 721

Ice Campaign, Russian Civil War 387
Ignatiev, Lt. General Count, attached to Soviet Embassy in Paris 790
Ignatiev, Pavel, husband of Cousin Katya 365n1, 790
Ignatieva, Yekaterina (Cousin Katya) 155, 159, 365–6, 429, 531–4, 570, 877, 886, 933n2, 1018, 1021, 1025, 1036, 1044, 1051–2
Igumnov, Konstantin, pianist, Rector of Moscow Conservatoire 128n4, 418n1, 428, 430n1,5, 442, 538, 541, 589n2
Ile de France, transatlantic liner 939–40
Ile d'Yeu 93
Imperial Airways 672
Industrialisation Bonds 884, 1048n1
Ingerman, Dr Sergius and Dr Anna, physicians in New York 271
International Society for Help to Revolutionaries 498
Internationale Theater und Musik Agentur, Vienna 697
Iokhelson, Vladimir, former Chairman of Leningrad branch of RAPM 1029, 1034
Ippolitov-Ivanov, Mikhail, composer, conductor and teacher, former Director of the Moscow Conservatoire 1035
ISCM 566n1, 785n2, 906; 1931 Festival of New Music in Oxford 982–3
Iturbi, José, pianist 808, 898, 904
Ivanov, Vyacheslav, Symbolist poet 92n1, 287–9, 318n1
Ivanov-Razumnik, writer and literary critic 510n1, 511
Ivanov-Vano, Ivan, animated film director 1056n2 1067, 1071
Ivanova, Anna Nikolayevna, companion to Konstantin Balmont 622
Iversky Gates, Moscow 445
Izvestia newspaper 446

Jacob, Don Clément see Jakob, Maxime
Jacobi, astronomer 158
Jakob, Maxime, composer 321, 323
Janacopulos, Adriana see Volkovyskaya, Adriana
Janacopulos, Vera, soprano, wife of Alexey Stahl 4, 7, 21, 35, 42, 49, 137, 298, 677, 706, 854; falling-out over recital programme 44, 45–7
Jasmin, copyist in Paris 359, 819

Java 768, 854, 975
Jazeps, Vitol *see* Wihtol, Iosif
Jazz Hilton 757
Jewish Overture see Prokofiev, Sergey, *Overture on Hebrew Themes*
Johns, Miss, American pianist and Christian Scientist 657
Johnson, Herbert, former Executive Director of Chicago Opera 928
Johnson, Nicholas, secretary to Grand Duke Michael Romanov 492n2
Jurgenson, Boris Petrovich, music publ 191n1, 423, 442–3, 460–1, 505–6

Kabalevsky, Dmitry, composer 437n1, 518n, 1052n2
Kadnikov, north-west Russia, exile of Cousin Katya 933, 1018n2, 1051
Kahn, Mrs Otto 277, 898, 911–12, 916
Kahn, Otto, philanthropist, supporter of Metropolitan Opera 277n1, 907, 911n1
Kakheti, province in Eastern Georgia 1057n3
Kal, Professor Alexey, musicologist 922
Kalashnikova, Tanya, Paris acquaintance 122
'Kamarinskaya', Russian folk song 331n
Kameneva, Olga, politician, Trotsky's sister, Head of VOKS 461–2, 464
Kamenny Ostrov, district of Leningrad 873n8, 1069
Kamensky, Alexander, pianist 526, 690n1
Kamensky, Vasili, Futurist poet 1058
Kamerny Theatre, Moscow 278n2, 279, 462, 844
Kankarovich, Anatoly, conductor 427
Kansas City 256, 256–7, 926
Kant, Emmanuel, philosopher 86, 699n2
Kapustin, Nikolay, composer 437n1
Karakhan, Lev, politician and diplomat 462n2, 463–5
Karneyev, Lev (Lyova) 481, 871
Karneyeva, Lidia (Lida, Lidusya) 481, 484, 511–12, 513, 525–6, 526, 530, 870, 871, 875, 1027, 1031, 1034, 1047, 1048
Karneyeva, Zoya 481, 513, 526, 870n1, 871n1
Karnovich, composition teacher at Leningrad Conservatoire 498
Karsavin, Lev, historian, philosopher, theologian and Eurasianist 125, 132n2, 133, 388–9, 447n2, 510n1, 673
Kartashov, Anton, historian and theologian 21
Kaunas, Lithuania 86, 125n4, 1005n1
Kaverin, Venyamin, writer 294
Kedrov, Nikolay Nikolayevich (Kolya) 112, 141
Kedrov, Nikolay, singer, founder of Kedrov Quartet 112, 191, 522n1, 857, 1000n1
Kedrov Quartet 112, 315, 713
Kennedy, Senator Joseph P 920n2, 921n2, 922, 922n1, 923
Kepin, bridge partner 991
Kerensky, Alexander, Prime Minister of Provisional Government of Russia 14, 33n1, 231n1, 292n1,
387n3, 778, 918n
Kerzhentsev, Platon, cultural administrator, Head of Committee on the Arts 462n1, 882, 883
Khaikin, Boris, conductor 1031
Khais, Director of Leningrad Philharmonia 59n2, 212, 352, 359, 456–7, 512, 549–54
Kharitonenko Palace, Moscow 541n2, 542
Kharkov 59n2, 212, 352, 359, 456–7, 512, 549–54; Chervonny ('Red') Hotel 549–52; Conservatoire 552–3; 'Proletarian' music shop 551, 554; State Opera 426n2, 550–1, 552–3, 554
Kharkov State Opera
Khodzhayeva sisters, friends from Kislovodsk 264–5
Khvostov, Alexander, Ukrainian artist and designer 553
Kiev 554–7; Conservatoire 557; Opera House 555–6
Kiev Opera House
Kilshtedt, Maria Grigorievna, writer, *Undina* 398, 514–15
Kirochnaya Street, Leningrad
Kirov Theatre *see* Mariinsky Theatre
Kishinyov, Moldova 363, 386, 638, 702
Kislovodsk 115n1, 143, 246, 264n4, 265–6, 719, 1031n4, 1064
Kleiber, Erich, conductor 178n2, 381n3, 848, 888, 953
Klein, Warren, Christian Science healer 244, 247–8, 250, 252, 254, 259, 260, 264, 269, 270, 352, 354–5, 852, 900, 902, 909, 911–12, 914, 917, 935
Klemperer, Otto, conductor 263, 273, 276, 381n1, 514, 755–6, 848
Klimov, Mikhail, composer, Director of Leningrad Philharmonia 349, 354, 373, 421n1, 478, 512–13
Kniga, bookshop in Moscow 415, 517, 804, 1067
Knipper, Lev, composer 430, 494
Knipper-Chekhova, Olga 430, 567
Knopf, Alfred, publisher 72n2, 267, 917
Knut, Dovid, writer 322n3
Kokhánski, Pawel, violinist 71, 168, 184, 186, 191–3, 196, 207, 543n2, 624, 854, 898, 904, 916, 1011n2
Kokhno, Boris 46n1, 147–8, 150, 201, 202, 205–6, 221, 317, 355, 573, 578, 581n1, 682, 756, 763, 783, 797, 857, 859, 974, 1011–12, 1014; argument with Cocteau over *Steel Step* 594, 596n4; Ballets Russes de Monte Carlo Artistic Director 1005; suggests *Chastushki* for *Steel Step* 188–9; AS LIBRETTIST 203: *Pastorale* 186, 324n1; SSP succeeds in eliminating from *The Steel Step* 185–6; *Le Bal* 801n1; *La Chatte* 589n1; *Les Fâcheux* 65n1; *Les Forains* 321n1; *Les Matelots* 116n; *Mavra* 66n1, 358n1; *Ode* (proposed ballet by Markevich, recycled as concert work *Cantate* scripted by Cocteau) 764n1, 955n1; *Zéphyr et Flore* 177; PRODIGAL SON 729, 736, 740, 744, 756, 758, 760, 764, 774–5, 778, 793, 801–2, 806, 827, 828, 831, 838; dispute over authors' rights 733–4, 763–4; takes out injunction 839–40, 841–3, 853–4, 856; *Diaghilev and the Ballets Russes* 581n1

Kollontai, Alexandra 878, 1079
Komandarm 2 see Selvinsky, Ilya, *Army Commander Two*
Komarov, Anatoly, translator 76
Kommissarzhevskaya Theatre, St Petersburg 278n2, 524n, 732n
Kommissarzhevsky, Fyodor, theatre producer 54, 918n1
Komsomol, Communist youth organisation 215, 446, 470, 564
Konchalovsky, Pyotr, artist 1071
Koonen, Alisa, actress, wife of Alexander Taïrov 279n1, 1067n2
Kopeikin, ballet pianist 579
Koposova-Derzhanovskaya, Yekaterina, soprano 415n2, 429n3, 443, 867, 887, 1022, 883, 866
Koribut-Kubitovich, Pavel (Pavka), Diaghilev's cousin 202, 802, 945, 969
Korovin, Konstantin, artist and theatre designer 304n, 999
Koshetz, Nina, soprano 106, 139–41, 152, 158, 229, 362–3, 576, 591, 661, 664, 777, 842, 844, 853–4, 859, 912, 958; brother's health 363; commissions string orchestra version of *The Ugly Duckling* 159, 172, 222, 994n1; jewellery smuggled out of USSR 570; jubilee concert 672–3; Lina's jealousy of 352n1, 362–3; original Fata Morgana in *Love for Three Oranges* 97; shares New York recital with SSP 897–900; sings Marina Mnishek in *Boris Godunov* 137; sings Renata in *the Fiery Angel* 701, 703; sings Snegurochka in *The Snow Maiden* 652; SSP's *Songs Without Words* composed for 4n3, 185, 191, 207; suggests Labunsky as SSP's secretary 300, 352; writes book on spiritualism 116
Kostritsky, Sergey, dentist 656, 658, 660, 662, 681
Koussevitzky, Natalya, Serge Koussevitzky's wife 1; affection for Lina and Sviatoslav 166, 260, 716, 717; Asafyev's book, negligent attitude to publication 261, 321, 328; contributes to husband's anti-Schloezer article 43; supports Paris performance of *Fiery Angel* 158; reintroduces SSP to Lourié 832; promotes Moscow Art Theatre *Carmen Suite* 262; invites to name-day celebration, 367; snubs Scriabin 310; attitude to sycophants 599, 701; Symphony No.2 in America, ambivalent about performing 161; *Three Oranges*; conflict over performing material for Mariinsky Theatre 170, 173, 258; promotes in London 20; attempts to find US manager for SSP 157, 679; conflict with Zederbaum 9n1, 121; also mentioned 29, 55, 263, 334
Koussevitzky, Sergey (Serge), conductor; hospitality in America 259, 268; personal relations with Chaliapin 56; charity concert for poor Russian students 662; HONOURS: Brown University Honorary Doctorate 274; Harvard University Honorary Doctorate 841, 849; Légion d'Honneur 181; new music, emphasis on programming 628, 698; OTHER COMPOSERS, RELATIONS AND COLLABORATIONS WITH: Bloch 336–7; Copland 315; Dukelsky: Double Bass Concerto 907; Sonata for Piano and Orchestra 595–6; Symphony No.1 711–13, 765; Symphony No.2 929; Hindemith 337, 703–4; Honegger: *Pacific 231* 50-1; Piano Concerto 165; *Phaedra* 701; Milhaud 587; Myaskovsky 591: Symphony No.7 16, 261, 268, 309, 316; Nabokov 705; Obukhov: *The Book of Life* 328–31; Roussel 596, 709; Scriabin: *Poème d'Extase* 165–6; Symphony No.3 269; Stravinsky: *Symphony of Psalms* 942–3; OTHER CONDUCTORS, RIVALRIES WITH: Damrosch 245; Furtwängler 989; Stokowski 31, 956; Toscanini 929–30; Paris regular subscription concerts 165–6, 168, 176, 315; no 1929 season 805; pomposity, propensity for 114, 181, 189, 337–8; QUALITIES: as accompanist 225; as instrumentalist 368, 636; de Schloezer, newspaper polemic with 43; SSP, PERSONAL RELATIONS WITH: advises composition of a fourth Piano Concerto 819, 989; enjoys drives in Ballot 598; regular biennial engagements with Boston Symphony 47, 161, 270, 636–7, 835; recommends *Classical Symphony* to Toscanini 264; coaches SSP in conducting technique 825, 826, 828, 831; offers loan to subsidise orchestration of *Fiery Angel* 74–5; friendship 40–1, 114, 184, 371, 590, 593, 599, 637, 715; cools, then stabilises 956, 959, 971, 993; advises acceptance of Gaveau proposal 845; other SSP performances heard; Overture on Hebrew Themes 54–5; Piano Sonata No.5 23; hospitality in Paris 15, 368–70, 372, 376–7, 384, 597, 702, 710, 824, 827, 832, 839; provided safekeeping for SSP's private papers and manuscripts after Revolution 422; praises *Prodigal Son* 831; recommends Pyatigorsky 993, 996; warns against Salter, impresario 105n3; SSP composes spoof pianola piece for celebratory dinner 181; advises acceptance of String Quartet commission by Library of Congress, recommends inclusion of theme and variations in Symphony No. 2 69–70; compares Symphony No.3 to Tchaikovsky's Sixth 826; attends premiere of *The Steel Step* 594; attempts to find US manager for SSP 636, 705–6, 714, 734, 742–3; walking tour in Haute Savoie 715, 716, 717–19, 723; invites to wedding anniversary 634–5; SSP WORKS PERFORMED IN BOSTON: all-Prokofiev programme discarded 908–10; Piano Concerto No.2 258, 261, 270, 913; Piano Concerto No.5 989, 1041; Quintet (expanded forces version) 268, 547; *Scythian Suite* 31, 109, 113, 909, 913–14; *Seven, They Are Seven* 297, 309; *Sinfonietta* parts left behind in USA 950–1; parts not sent to USA 910; Suite from *Chout* 368; Suite from *Love for Three Oranges* 368; Suite from *The Steel Step* 637; Sym-

phony No.1 (*Classical*) 592, 819, 951; gramophone recording 821, 833; Symphony No.3 'pickled in aspic' 915; Symphony No.4 862–3, 971, 981–2, 984; analogy with Beethoven's Symphony No.3 819; Violin Concerto No.1 157, 160, 260; SSP WORKS PERFORMED IN NEW YORK: all-Prokofiev programme discarded 903; Piano Concerto No.2 263–4, 917–18; Quintet (expanded forces version) 268; *Scythian Suite* 917; SSP WORKS PERFORMED IN PARIS: *Fiery Angel* (Act II, edited version) 710–13, 731; *Overture for 17 Instruments* 588, 589–90; suggests making version for full orchestra 590; Piano Concerto No.2 12, 48, 49, 50, 52, 397; *Seven, They Are Seven* 48, 57, 58, 59, 60, 79; Suite from *Chout* 309, 316, 328, 329–30; Symphony No.1 591–2; Symphony No.2 (dedicated to Koussevitzky) 69–70, 75, 136, 157, 161, 163–4, 168, 169, 171–2, 173, 298, 301, 963n4; suggests radical revision 176; Violin Concerto No.1 1, 824n2; WEAKNESS FOR LESS TALENTED COMPOSERS: Fédorov 636, 973; Ferroud 704; Greenberg 929; Lazar 316; Lopatnikoff 701, 702; Tansman 321, 367–8, 370, 589, 590; Vinogradova 972, Yavorsky, reconciled with 310; also mentioned 72n1, 142n2, 263, 344, 413, 434, 633, 706, 732, 820, 850, 904
Kozitsky, Filip, Ukrainian composer 554
Kozlovsky, Ivan, tenor 883
KR see Romanov, Konstantin Konstantinovich, Grand Duke
Krasheninnikov, Nikolay, librettist 608
Krasin, Boris, cultural administrator, Director of Rosphil 207–9, 210, 212–13, 308, 328, 443, 465, 822
Krasin, Leonid, diplomat 207n2, 435
Krauss, Clemens, conductor 280–1
Kreisler, conducting student at St Petersburg Conservatoire 409
Kreisler, Fritz, violinist and composer: 409n4, 177n1 268, 890; *Liebesfreud* 890n1
Krivosheina, Nina see Meshcherskaya, Nina
Krupnik, Polish liqueur made from honey 978
Kryukov Canal, Leningrad 516
Kryukov, Nikolay, composer and sound engineer 430n4
Kryukov, Vladimir, composer 430n4
Kryuks, notation in early Russian hymnody 26n2
Ksyusha, Koussevitzky's Paris cook/housekeeper 372, 384–5, 727
Kuban Campaign see Ice Campaign, Russian Civil War
Kubatskaya, Siranush, soprano 789, 804n2
Kubatsky, Viktor, cellist, conductor and musical administrator 884–5, 884n2, 1019, 1045, 1072
Kubelik, Jan, violinist 555
Kubelik, Rafael, conductor 555n1
Kucheryava, Liza 1024–5
Kucheryavy, Nikolay, businessman and friend 406, 455, 460–1, 543–4, 872, 883

Kulich, traditional Russian Easter dish 817
Kulisher, representative of Rosphil 562
Kultur Kampfbund 1043n1
Kuprin, Alexander, writer 24, 37, 94, 1053
Kursk Station, Moscow 549
Kurtz, Edmund, cellist 327
Kurtz, Efrem, conductor 225, 323, 327, 332
Kushnaryov, Khristofor, composer 519, 559n2, 1060–2
Kutepov, General Alexander, leader of ROVS 944, 949, 974
Kuzmin, Mikhail, writer 92n1, 318n1, 497, 547n; *Travellers by Sea and Land* 92
Kuznetsova, former piano student at St Petersburg Conservatoire 306–7
Kuznetsova, Maria, lyric soprano 776

Labunsky, Felix, composer, SSP's assistant 300, 301, 341–9, 350–2, 355–7, 359, 361–4, 367–9, 370, 372, 376–7, 388, 399, 672
Labunsky, Viktor, composer 341n1
'Lacrimi Christi' wine 295
Lake Sevan, Armenia 1060
Laloy, Louis, music critic, writer and translator 36–7, 76, 79, 109, 137
Lambert, Constant, composer and writer on music: *Music Ho: A Study of Music in Decline* 312n3; *Romeo and Juliet* 312–14
Lamm, Pavel, pianist and musicologist 456, 866–7, 1019, 1023, 1051; ACM member 690n; *Boris Godunov* reconstruction 49n, 875n; employment at Muzsektor 539; 'LAMM CIRCLE' 538–40, 867; piano eight-hand symphonic transcriptions 539, 1051n; SSP rehearses Schubert Waltzes in Lamm's flat 455–6; SSP's later correspondence with 456n; visit to France 722–6
Lamoureux Orchestra 152n1, 706n, 946n1, 1012n, 1038; SSP's concerts with 892–3; Suite from *Chout* 736
Landowska, Wanda 808n1
Landsberg, Gyorgy 319n2
Lang, Dr, physician attending M. G. Prokofieva in Ettal 16, 18–9
Langovoy, Soviet counter-espionage officer 857
Lankow, Edward, bass 238
Lapin, owner of dacha at Bellevue 103, 197, 204, 208
Lapitsky, Iosif, opera producer in Kharkov 550–2
Laporte, publisher, friends of Poulenc 997
Larionov, Mikhail Fyodorovich, artist and designer 14n3: 24, 36, 221, 572, 586, 681–2, 713, 765, 820, 830, 913n1, 948, 961, 986, 1014; *Chout* revival proposed 765; *Le Renard*, designs 830; proposal for puppet ballet 36; *Sur le Borysthène* designs 964, 973, 975, 986, 1037, 1039
Laschilin, Lev, choreographer of *The Red Poppy* 467n3
Lasker, Edward, chess player and writer; *Go and Go-Moku: The Oriental Board Games* 273

Lasker, Emmanuel, chess grand master 273n2 610, 612
Lassalle Street *see* Mikhailovsky Street, Leningrad; Mikhailovsky Street, Leningrad 478
Laurelton Hotel, New York 258
Laurencin, Marie, artist and designer 57n2
Lavrenyov, Boris, novelist; *Story of a Simple Thing* 1049, 1069–70
Lazar, Filip, Romanian composer 316, 599, 780, 929
Lazar, Mme, 597, 599, 780
Lazarus, Daniel, pianist and composer 322
Le Boeuf, Henry, Belgian philanthropist 3, 23, 799, 942–3
Le Flem, Paul, composer and conductor 780
Le Havre 238, 277, 941, 1003
Le Vésinet, suburb of Paris 633, 697
Lecocq, Charles, composer; *Giroflé-Girofla* 279n1
LEF, journal of 'Left Front of the Arts' 425–6
Leipzig 391, 427n1, 489n1, 650, 902n1, 933n1
Lenin, Vladimir Ilyich 15n2, 37n3, 124n4, 198n2, 205n2, 207n1, 225n4, 292n, 293n1, 395, 398n3, 420, 422n, 423n1, 435n2, 447n2, 461n, 462, 462n1, 466n1, 510n, 517n2, 557n2, 586n1, 741n2, 752n2, 769n, 869n1, 878n1, 884n2, 927n3, 944n, 992n, 1057n2, 1066n2; Lenin Quartet 440n1
Leningrad Artists Club 526–8
Leningrad Conservatoire 132, 172n4, 191n1, 223n2, 231n2, 341n2, 346n1, 366, 479, 480, 481n2, 482, 494n, 498n2, 519n2, 526n1, 651, 704n1, 708n1, 785n2, 857, 870, 873, 873n1, 886, 916, 1001, 1031–2, 1031n2, 1062n2, 1063n1; proposal to elect SSP Director 722; SSP's CEREMONIAL RETURN VISIT 520–5
Leningrad Philharmonia 349, 349n1, 359, 367, 421n, 441, 478–9, 483n, 494, 509, 510, 512–14, 525, 871, 873, 1027, 1028n1, 1030, 1046–9
Lenkina, Zinka *see* Yurevskaya, Zinaïda
Léon, Hélène, pianist 58n2
Leonardo da Vinci
Leoncavallo, Ruggero, composer
Leonov, Leonid, *The Badgers* 216–17, 294
Leontovich, Mykola, Ukrainian composer 553
Leontovich Quartet 553
Lermontov, Mikhail; *A Hero of Our Time* 732; *Masquerade* 620n, 1071n2
Lert, Ernst, producer at Metropolitan Opera; *Mozart auf dem Theater* 902n
Les Six
Leskov, Nikolay 449; *Levsha (The Southpaw)* 449, 527n1 580
Lestang, Mme de, singer in Lyons 37
Levitsky, pianist, shipboard acquaintance 893
Levsha see Leskov, Nikolay, *The Flea*
Library of Congress 190, 629n2, 652n2, 780n1, 916, 934, 989
Liebmann, Mme, offered hospitality in Berlin 366
Liège 143, 157, 160, 224, 571, 974, 976

Lifar, Serge, dancer and choreographer 116n1, 157n3, 179n1, 201, 203, 313, 317n1, 320, 324, 589n1, 629n2, 680, 774, 782n1, 783, 806, 830n1, 1006n1, 1010n2, 1024, 1037–8, 1039, 1070; Diaghilev memorial 965–6; PRODIGAL SON 760, 764, 778, 793, 796, 802; *Prometheus* 974; SUR LE BORYSTHÈNE (*On the Dnieper*) 919, 964–5, 968–9, 973, 975, 986, 989, 997n2
Life of Art journal *see Zhisn isskustva*
Lindbergh, Charles, American aviator and author 597
Lindemann, Evald, conductor 685
Linette *see* Prokofieva, Lina Ivanovna
Lipnitzky, Paris photographer 71
Lisovsky, Leonid, Ukrainian composer 553
Liszt, Ferenc: *Les Préludes*; *Les Préludes* 9, 127, 131, 275, 298, 303, 388n2, 489n1, 539, 556, 717, 890n3 991; Sonata in B minor
Literature–Arts Circle, Leningrad 481–3
Litvinov, Maxim, politician, Soviet Foreign Minister 207n1, 414, 435–6, 435n2, 436n1, 437, 439, 447, 462–5, 502, 541, 542n1, 689, 693, 863n, 868, 873n2, 1067
Litvinova, Eva Valterovna *see* Litvinova, Ivy
Litvinova, Ivy 436, 447, 462–5, 470, 541–2, 565, 869, 882, 1025
Llubera, Lina *see* Prokofieva, Lina Ivanovna
Locks, hatters, London 13
Lodi, Zoya, soprano 366, 481, 526, 672–3, 678, 871n1
Lodz 128
Mrs Loomis, New York hostess and arts patron
Lopashev, S. A., Director of Moscow Radio 881, 883, 885–6
Lopatnikoff, Nikolay, composer 627, 636, 701–2, 972; WORKS Sonatina 627, 636; Scherzo 701–2
Los Angeles 181n3, 312n1, 818n2, 918, 920, 921, 921n1, 922, 925, 928; Biltmore Hotel 920, 926; Philharmonic Orchestra 921n1
Lossky, Vladimir, Chief Producer at Bolshoy Theatre 467, 510n1
Lourié, Arthur, composer and cultural administrator 29, 133n1, 231n2, 307n1430n2 703, 832–3, 838–9, 891, 893, 986, 1046
Lowe, Ivy *see* Litvinova, Ivy
Lozova, Ukraine 1056
Luboschutz, Pierre *see* Lyuboshitz, Pyotr
Lukyanov, former Sokol acquaintance 790
Lunacharsky, Anatoly, Narkompros (Commissar for Enlightenment) 29, 106n2, 210n1, 213n1, 231n1, 307n1, 422, 424–6, 450, 453, 461n1, 474–5, 501–4, 510n1, 514-6, 581, 586, 588, 623, 653, 690n1, 884n2, 999n1, 1024n3
Lundström, Vilhelm, Danish artist
Luzhsky, Vasily, actor 567
Lyapunov, Sergey, composer, conductor and pianist 108, 110
Lyatoshinsky, Boris, Ukrainian composer 553

Lyon, Gustave, Chairman of Maison Pleyel 664n2, 780n1, 852–3, 889
Lyon, Robert, Managing Director of Maison Pleyel 780, 850, 852, 889
Lyons (city) 30, 36–7, 356, 372, 801, 852
Lyubimsky, Director of Akopera, Leningrad 871, 875
Lyuboshitz, Leya, violinist 219, 625, 899n1
Lyuboshitz, Pyotr, pianist

McCormack, Count John, tenor 55
McCormick, Edith Rockefeller 937
McCormick, Harold, Chicago arts patron 178n1
Machinal see Treadwell, Sophie
Mack, Miss, nanny 73, 76–7, 82, 100, 111
Madeleine, nanny 648–9
Madrid 25, 27, 906
Magalishvili, Prince *see* Magalov, Prince
Magalov, Nikita, pianist and composer 75, 674, 749, 973
Magalov, Prince 75n, 174n2
Magalova, Princess Varvara 75, 162, 174, 389, 953n1, 973
Magdeburg 207, 582–3, 583n3
The Magnificent Cuckold see Crommelynck, Fernand
Mainz 364, 627n2
Maison Pleyel *see* Pleyel et Cie
Makedonsky, Director of Yerevan Philharmonia 1060, 1062
Malegot *see* Maly Opera and Ballet Theatre, Leningrad
Malinovskaya, Yelena, Director of Bolshoy Theatre 1019, 1024, 1036
Malko, Nikolay, conductor 59n2, 403, 478–9, 490, 494, 498, 509, 511–4, 516, 520–2, 530, 556–8, 871, 1031n3, 1046, 1062n2
Maly Opera and Ballet Theatre, Leningrad 1028n2, 1031n3
Malyshev, Misha, Moscow lawyer 869, 872, 880, 883, 887
Mangeot, associate of Hébertot 47
Mankiewicz, Lucie, friend of Maria Baranovskaya in Warsaw 953
Mann, Noelle, curator of Serge Prokofiev Archive, London 154n5, 201n1
Mansurova, Cecilia, actress at the Vakhtangov Studio 505n1 1070
Manukhin, Ivan, Paris doctor 14, 40
Mar-Vik *see* Baranovskaya, Maria Viktorovna
Marat Street, Leningrad *see* Nikolayevsky Street, Leningrad
Maria Viktorovna *see* Baranovskaya, Maria Viktorovna
Mariinsky Theatre 25, 38n2, 47–8, 74, 81, 96, 112, 172n2, 188n3, 210n1, 215n3, 226, 230, 409n2, 476n1, 481n2, 487, 499, 504, 525–6, 548, 565n1, 695, 776n1, 870, 874–5, 1019n4, 1049–50, 1069, 1070n2; nomenclature 369n1, 477n4, 807n2; *THE GAMBLER*, abandoned 1917 and proposed new productions 96n1, 172n2, 210n, 216, 226n1, 324n2, 403n1, 407n2, 481n2, 494n1, 499, 505, 530n, 686–7; *THREE ORANGES* 170, 173, 185, 297, 309, 354, 359, 475, 487–90, 588
Markevich, Igor, composer and conductor 706n1, 764–5, 806, 813–16, 827, 891, 893, 955, 995n1, 1038; Stravinsky's jealousy 952; WORKS *Galop* 1002; *Ode (Cantate)* 955; *Overture* 765; Partita for Orchestra 995; *Rébus* 764n1; *Sinfonietta* 889
Marlborough, Duchess of 184
Marlotte, dacha residence 198–9, 204, 212, 216
Marnold, Jean, music critic 76, 79, 174, 177–8, 200, 201, 224, 301, 581, 598, 687, 700, 714, 771–2, 816, 828
Marseilles 33–4, 37, 147, 814
Martinu, Bohuslav, composer 34n1, 774, 982n3
'Marusya's Taken Poison', folk song
Marx, Karl; *Das Kapital*
Massenet, Alfred, industrialist and ballet patron 776–7
Massine, Léonide, dancer and choreographer 38n1 61n2, 116n, 1573, 163n, 1784, 179, 179n2, 2222, 59n1, 654, 898, 1005n1, 1010n2; *STEEL STEP* 573, 577, 579–80, 588–9, 592, 594, 595–6, 605n1, 680–2, 881; Cocteau's attack 594, 596, 596n4
Mathis car 856
Matisse, Henri, artist 154n3, 178n4, 665n1 783, 792–3
Maxwell, George, American representative of Russian Musical Editions 597, 934, 950
May Day Parade, Red Square 1052–3
Mayakovsky, Vladimir 28, 31n1, 124n2, 743–4, 755, 790, 804–5, 867, 875, 880, 881–3, 885, 887, 954n1, 979, 1053n1, 1058; Diaghilev, debate with 743; *LEF* 425–6; suicide 947–8; Tatyana Yakovlevna, affair with 743–4, 979; WORKS *The Bathhouse* 867, 954n; *The Bed Bug* 804–5, 880; *Misteria-Bouffe* 28n3; 'The Sun' 743
Mayevsky, Yury, pianist and former fellow-student 346, 408–9
Mdivani, Polykarp (Budu), Georgian politician 1057
Mechnikov, Ilya, biologist and immunologist 617
Meckler, importunate impresario in Moscow 432–3, 465–6, 548
Medtner, Nikolay 46, 61, 68, 116, 141n4, 163–4, 211, 213, 225n4, 264, 275, 279, 353, 358n2, 431n1, 437n1, 519n2, 532, 539, 543, 547, 649, 651, 654–5, 670n4, 698–9, 740–1, 753n, 770, 857, 898, 936, 937, 940n1, 950; WORKS *Two Fairy Tales*, Op.48 649; Violin Sonata No.2 651, 654–5
Meindorf, Bada, brother of Nadezhda Rayevskaya 975; participates in SSP's bridge tournament 1–15–6
Meindorf, Mme, mother of Nadezhda Rayevskaya 361n2, 428n1 975, 988

Melkikh, Dmitry, composer 539
Melodiya, Soviet record label 561n, 704n1, 1008n3
Mémé *see* Codina, Olga; Codina, Olga Vladislavovna
Mengelberg, Willem, composer 23, 142n2, 427n1
Mercé y Luque, Antonia (La Argentina) 854
Mercure de France 76, 79
Merezhkovsky, Dmitry Sergeyevich, writer and philosopher 12, 21, 23, 24, 37, 129n3, 165n; WORKS *Babylon* 33–4, 38; *The Birth of the Gods: Tutankhamen in Crete* 24n, 28
Meshcherskaya, Nina, SSP's first love 126n1, 639, 645, 656, 701n2, 713, 714n1, 777, 818n1, 874, 900n2, 905, 980, 994n1, 999n3, 1025n2, 1033, 1070
Meshchersky, Alexey, former business tycoon 126n1, 874, 999, 1025n2, 1033
Metropole Hotel, Moscow 251, 414, 416, 420–2, 438, 446, 465, 469, 473, 500, 531, 562, 569
Metzl, Vladimir, composer 38
Meudon: forest of 155, 158–9; Hermitage restaurant 155n5, 592, 664; SSP's mother's grave 224, 403
Meyer, acquaintance in Warsaw 129, 162
Meyer, Marcelle, pianist 58n2, 326, 336
Meyerhold, Vsevolod, theatre director 31n1, 54n1, 62n2, 133n1, 188n3, 202n3, 226n1, 232n4, 278, 278n2, 319–21, 343n4, 450, 461n, 482n3, 490n3, 510–11, 543n3, 607, 736, 737, 740, 742, 815–16, 837, 866, 887, 954n, 960, 966, 971, 1019, 1023, 1025, 1026, 1034–5, 1036, 1048, 1049; CONSULTANT TO BOLSHOY THEATRE 866–7, 876–7; company meeting 872; purgings 866, 868, 873, 879, 881; European tour 954n; fez 188n3, 565; former employer of Baranovskaya 31, 737n2; mentor of Sergey Radlov 490n2; offers help with Shurik's imprisonment 535–6, 541, 565, 868; possible Paris season in repertoire with Ballets Russes 740; PROPOSED *GAMBLER* PRODUCTION AT MARIINSKY THEATRE 96n1, 324n2, 500, 505, 532–3, 541, 544–5, 735, 742, 833; speech to political theatre conference 503–4; SSP, article in *Life of Art* 546–7; SSP proposed as composer for *The Bedbug* 804–5; *Steel Step* open discussion in Bolshoy Theatre 880–1; PRODUCTIONS *The Bathhouse* 867, 882, 954n1; *The Fairground Showman* 92n; *The Forest* 563; *The Inspector-General* 532–3; *The Introduction* 1044; *Krechinsky's Wedding* 1067; *The Magnificent Cuckold* 546; *Masquerade* 1071; *Misteria Bouffe* 28n3
Meyerovich, Alfred, pianist 786
Mezhdunarodnaya Kniga 536, 804, 1067
Mezhkniga *see* Mezhdunarodnaya Kniga
La Mignonne see Dukelsky, Vladimir Alexandrovich, *Dushenka*
Mikeladze, Yevgeny, conductor in Kiev 1062
Mikhailovsky Theatre *see* Maly Opera and Ballet Theatre, Leningrad
Miklashevsky, pianist at Leningrad Conservatoire 531
Milhaud, Darius 41, 84, 116, 148, 173n2, 181n3, 182, 308, 312, 312n3, 319, 321, 324, 333, 375, 518, 590, 699n3, 716, 730, 769, 801, 817, 825, 855, 889, 904, 983; 'Le Boeuf sur le Toit' nightclub 48n1, 783n2; 'Triton' chamber music society 997; WORKS *Le Carnaval d'Aix* 587; *Une Education Manquée* 70; *L'Eventail de Jeanne* 42n1; *Oresteia* 706; *Saudades* 68; Symphonie de chambre No.6 276; *Le Train Bleu* 73, 1050
Millet, copyist 694
Milstein, Nathan, violinist 59n2, 912
Milyukov, Pavel, historian, politician, newpaper editor, founder of Russian Constitutional Democratic Party ('Kadets') 23, 37, 60, 123n2, 246, 753n1
Mir Isskustva 7n1, 109n1, 111n1, 129n3, 151n1, 264n2, 304n, 318n1, 318n2, 319, 714n3, 821n1, 911n2, 999n1, 999n2
Miro, Juan, artist 313
Mirsky, D. S. *see* Svyatopolk-Mirsky, Prince
Mlynarska, Nela, ballerina, fiancée of Arthur Rubinstein 1014
Modana, Italian border town 281
Molinari, Bernardino, conductor 283
Mompou, Federico, composer 590
Monaco, Prince of 149
Monomakh, Crown of 562
Monteux, Pierre, conductor 142, 143n, 233–4, 259n1
Montreal; Music University 936
MOPR *see* International Society for Help to Revolutionaries
Moreau, Gustave, artist 793
Moreux, Serge, Paris composer *manqué*, critic and friend 154n5, 1072
Morolyov, Vasily, veterinary surgeon and friend 390, 434, 436, 457, 534, 877
Morris, Ira Nelson, American diplomat 250
Morrison, Professor Simon, biographer of SSP 170n2, 419n2, 1020n4, 1052n1
Moscow Art Theatre 31n1, 262, 437n2, 490n3, 543n3, 567n2, 567n3; Moscow Art Theatre No.2 449, 527n1; Opera Studio 437n3, 504n3
Moscow Central Children's Theatre 430n2
Moscow Conservatoire 307, 366n1, 418–20, 426n1, 428, 430n1, 430n5, 433–8, 440n1, 440n2, 442–3, 447n2, 450, 453, 455, 458–60, 469–71, 494n, 501, 504, 526n3, 532, 537–8, 539, 540–1, 547, 553n3, 559n2, 561n, 879n, 882, 899n1, 906, 1026n3, 1031n3, 1035n2, 1035n5, 1051n, 1052n2, 1052n3, 1056n1, 1063n1; Proletarian Collective of Student Composers (Prokoll) 908n, 1027n12, 1035n6; proposal that SSP teach composition 1021n2, 1023, 1035, 1045, 1052, 1054
Mosolov, Alexander, *Zavod* 430, 431, 444, 785, 1023
Mostras, Konstantin, violinist and teacher 440, 867, 883
Mount Ararat 1060

INDEX 1105

Mozart, Wolfgang Amadeus 168: 171, 177n1, 186, 269n1, 435n1, 605n2, 767, 909, 964, 967, 984, *Die Entführung aus dem Serail* 61–2; *Don Giovanni* 63; *The Marriage of Figaro* 62; Requiem 706; Sonata in D K576 890n3

Muratov, journalist/guide in Rome 282–3, 288–9

Musical America journal 168n2 399

Musical Contemporary journal 62n2 640

Musina-Ozarovskaya, Darya, actress and movement coach 524

Musorgsky, Modest 90, 255, 639, 700, 720; WORKS *Boris Godunov* 456n1, 619n1, 875n1; edition by Pavel Lamm and Boris Asafyev 456n1, 875n1; *Khovanshchina* 49, 456n1, 619n1; *The Marriage* 13; *Pictures from an Exhibition* 580n1, 740; orch. Ravel 977

Mussolini, Benito 284

Muzfond, commissioning and grant-aiding department of Composers' Union 1020n4

Muzsektor, Music Division of the Soviet State Publishing Company 422, 423n1, 442–3, 460, 505–7, 529, 539, 644, 785, 814, 878

Muzyka *see* Muzsektor, Music Division of the Soviet State Publishing Company

Muzykal'nyi Sovremennik see Musical Contemporary journal

Myasin, Leonid *see* Massine, Léonide

Myaskovskaya, Valentina Yakovlevna 422

Myaskovskaya, Vera Yakovlevna 445

Myaskovsky, Nikolay Yakovlevich 4n7, 133, 308, 417, 423, 424, 431, 444, 470, 496, 508, 548, 565–6, 567, 570, 585, 807, 865, 866, 867, 876, 879, 881, 887, 912–13, 1018, 1019, 1022, 1025, 1035, 1043, 1051, 1055; considers Asafyev's role in 'Zhdanovshchina' a betrayal 170n2; Association for Contemporary Music 690n; Derzhanovsky, place of honour in his house 432; straitened financial circumstances 880; former students: Kryukov 430; Mosolov 430, 431, 444, 785, 1023; Polovinkin 430, 876, 886, 908, 1023; Shebalin 538n3, 539, 540, 785, 867, 876, 879, 954n, 1018, 1026, 1036, 1043, 1045n3, 1050; Vitachek 1052n3; awarded Honoured Artist title 540–1; Jurgenson, advice on reassignment of rights to earlier compositions 423, 442–3; introduces SSP to Lamm's Wednesday musical gatherings 455–6, 539, 867; 8-hand arrangements of symphonies 538–9, 1026; living conditions in Moscow 422; visit to flat 445; Malinovskaya, Bolshoy Theatre Director, contretemps with 1036; Muzgiz, employment in 423n1, 505–6, 529; devises system for calculating royalty payments to composers 506; nicknames 471, 688; JUDGMENTS OF OTHER MUSICIANS AND COMPOSERS: Asafyev; *Flames of Paris* 1072; Feinberg 419; Oborin 456; Persimfans Orchestra 456, 473; Saradzhev 531; Stravinsky 619; Paris, proposed visit to 846, 848, 850; proof-reading skills 1066;

Rayevskys, advice on propriety of seeing 867–8; relations with sisters 445–6, 874; Komsomolka niece 446; religion, sceptical views on 874; upset by Sabaneyev's criticism, 278; songs encored at Lina's recital in Florence 291; authorizes SSP to sign contracts 887; SSP, LETTERS FROM 4–5, 56n1, 62, 172n1, 180n, 249, 707, 836, 850, 865n2, 899n3; SSP, LETTERS TO 111, 149, 207, 603, 1021n6; advice not to return to USSR 804, 816, 948, 989; criticism of Stravinsky's *Oedipus Rex* 619; general situation in USSR 688, 944, 993n2; harmonisations of folksongs collected by Alfred Swan; prose style reminiscent of Debussy 699; sends score of *Autumnal* 340; SSP performs Myaskovsky's piano works in Portland and San Francisco 253–4; SSP's support and recommendations of Myaskovsky: Arens 785; article for Havana journal 932; Koussevitzky 16, 261, 268, 309, 316, 368; Monteux 232; Olin Downes 908; Russian Musical Editions 832, 835; Stokowski 248–9, 276, 393; Wolff 11; SSP'S MUSIC, MYASKOVSKY'S OPINIONS OF: *Choses en soi* 868; conducting skill 886; *Fiery Angel* 707; Piano Concerto No.3 419; Piano Concerto No.5 1044; Piano Sonata No.4 459; Piano Sonata No.5 149; Quintet 547, 548; Sinfonietta (revised version) 868–9, 886; String Quartet No.1 1021n6; Symphonic Song 1044–5; *Tales of an old Grandmother* 458; SSP's papers and manuscripts, preservation and safekeeping after Revolution 422–3; SSP recovers Diaries from 565, 568, 573; women, inexperience with 432; Yurovsky's advice that Myaskovsky should emigrate 878–9; Zhdanov Decree, Myaskovsky's inclusion in censure 170n2, 1045n3; Zhilyayev, visit to 879–80; WORKS Cello Sonata No.1 456n; *On the Border* 12n3; Piano Sonata No.4 687; performance by Wührer 566; *Premonitions* 12n3; *Prichudy* (*Caprices*) 248, 255, 306, 447; *Serenada* for small symphony orchestra 855; *Silence*, symphonic poem 538–9; Sinfonietta in B minor 867; Symphony No.3 in A minor 702; Symphony No.5 in D: 11; Stokowski's performances of 248–9, 276; Symphony No.6 60, Stokowski's performance of 393; Symphony No.7 in B minor 422, 456, 540, Koussevitzky's performance of 591; Symphony No.8 in A 471, 508, 529–30; Symphony No.11 in B flat minor 1022, 1026; Symphony No.12 in G minor (*October*) 1050; *Three Poems of Z. Gippius* 12n3; No. 3 'Circles' 110; also mentioned 232, 306n2, 390n, 423, 430, 436, 472n2, 495n3, 1020n4, 1046n1

Nabokov, Natalya (Natashenka), wife of Nicolas Nabokov 692–3, 696, 706–8, 710, 756–7, 780–2, 836, 948, 954–5, 957–8, 969–73, 996

Nabokov, Nicolas, composer and cultural administrator 681–2, 693, 695–6, 706–7, 710–12, 720, 727,

756–7, 780–2, 784, 786, 856, 948–50, 954–5, 957–8, 969–73, 984, 991, 996, 1002, 1005, 1008; *Chislo* article on SSP 948; Diaghilev, article on 890–1; Stravinsky's anger 891, 893; SSP recommends to Olin Downes 905; WORKS *Lyrical Symphony* 681n2, 889, 956, 958–9, 973; *Ode: Méditation sur la majesté de Dieu* 691, 705, 708–9, 781–2; *Overture* 781; *Piano Sonata No.1* 696; *Bagazh: Memoirs of a Russian Cosmopolitan* 681n2; *Old Friends and New Music*, memoirs 681n2;
Nabokov, Vladimir, novelist; 'The Assistant Producer' 944n1; 'La Slavska' 949n
Nansen passports 11n5, 377n2, 414, 689, 846
Naples, Society for Contemporary Music 291
Nápravník, Eduard, conductor 799
NARKOMAT *see* USSR Ministry of Home and Foreign Trade
NARKOMINDEL *see* USSR Ministry of Foreign Affairs
NARKOMPROS *see* USSR Ministry for Enlightenment
Narzan mineral water 1031, 1064
Natalya Konstantinovna *see* Koussevitzky, Natalya
National Hotel, Moscow 1019, 1034, 1035, 1043–4, 1045, 1055, 1072
Naumova, Olga, Koussevitzky's secretary and niece
Navarra, André, cellist 715
Nebolsin, Vasili, conductor 872
Negoreloe, border town between USSR and Poland 742, 865, 1018, 1043, 1055
Neighbourhood Playhouse, New York 14, 35, 80
Nekrasov, Nikolay, poet, editor and publisher 674
Nelson, Paul, architect and designer 920–3
Nemchinova, Vera, ballerina 179
Nemirovich-Danchenko, Vladimir; *Carmencita and the Soldier* 31, 198n1, 449n1, 561n1
Nemysskaya, Olga *see* Codina, Olga
NEP *see* New Economic Policy
Neva River, Leningrad 480, 873
Nevsky Prospect, Leningrad 477, 478n1, 479, 651, 769, 870, 874
New Economic Policy 205, 557, 741, 863n, 884n1, 927n3
New Orleans 919–20
New Times see Poslednye Novosti
New York: Metropolitan Opera 7n1, 10n5, 51n2, 142n2, 250n1, 255n1, 262n2, 263,4, 277n1, 302n3, 598n3, 692, 758n, 901–2, 906, 911, 911n1, 911n3, 918; *New York Times* 4n6, 76, 262n1, 905, 921n2; Philharmonic Orchestra 51n1, 59n2, 129n1, 168n2, 253n1, 265n1, 265n3, 269n, 273n, 824n5, 921n1, 930n1
Newman, Ernest, music critic 62, 636
Newman, Mrs 62, 636, 832
Nezhdanova, Antonina, soprano 426n1, 428, 454, 468, 1035, 1055
Nezlobin Theatre, Moscow 54n1
Nice, David, biographer of SSP 16n1, 297n2, 490n2, 671n1, 843n3, 866n2, 881n1, 1006n1
Nicholas II, Tsar 237n2, 329, 414n1, 463n2, 639n1, 656, 658, 791; execution of 492n2, 903; names Plevitskaya 'Kursk Nightingale' 949n1; order for Russian fleet to break out of Port Arthur 751
Nielle, copyist 108, 110, 111, 113
Nijinska, Bronislava, choreographer 65n1, 73n1, 223n, 313n, 324n1, 628n1, 824n3
Nijinsky, Vaclav, dancer and choreographer 54n2, 573n1, 628n1
Nikisch, Arthur, conductor 44n1, 225n2, 416, 427n1
Nikitina, Alice, ballerina and impresario 1010–11; *Nikitina By Herself* 1010n2
Nikitsky Gates, Moscow 471
Nikolayev, Leonid, pianist and teacher 341n2, 481n3, 519n2, 520, 522, 524, 873, 1067
Nikolayevsky Station, Leningrad 499
Nikolayevsky Station, Moscow 475
Nikolayevsky Street, Leningrad 516
Nikolskaya, Ariadna, pianist and composer, Conservatoire friend 818, 898, 923
Nikopol, Russia 390
Nikulin, Lev, novelist and journalist 294
Nin, Anaïs, writer, feminist and diarist 668n2
Nin, Joaquin, composer 668–9, 982, 1013
de Noailles, Vicomtesse Marie Laure, Paris hostess and music patron 994n2, 995–6, 1002
Nobel, Mme, hostess in Cologne 143, 225, 228
Nobile, General Umberto, North Pole Expedition 788n1, 789n
Nord Express 378, 406, 571, 888, 979, 1072
Nouvel, Walter, writer on music, close associate of Diaghilev 151, 153, 173, 201–2, 219, 223n1, 317, 572–3, 578, 630, 652, 680n2, 709, 747, 774, 778, 813–14, 815, 822, 832, 891, 919, 955, 969, 973–5, 986, 1014; brother 874
Novinsky Boulevard, Moscow 544
Novosatsky, Ukrainian composer 553
Novy LEF see LEF
de Noyelle, Paris host and arts patron 795
Nozière, Fernand, stage adaptation of *The Idiot* 150n2

Oberammergau, Bavaria 3n6, 5, 15–18, 20, 67, 73
Oborin, Lev, pianist and composer 419, 456, 565, 866, 868, 872, 879, 881, 1026; Chopin Competition 453
Obukhov Hospital, St Petersburg 526
Obukhov, Nikolay 171–2, 713; *The Book of Life* 328–31
Odessa 115, 121, 352, 549, 558, 560; Bristol Hotel 558–9, 561; Conservatoire 561; Opera House 559; Philharmonic Society 561–2
Oeberg, Ernest, Director of Russian Musical Editions 8, 14–15, 20, 22–3, 30, 44, 51, 61, 67, 75–6, 79–80, 101, 107, 109, 111, 137, 140, 189, 190, 192;

INDEX 1107

Gambler enquiries 96; mechanical rights 109–10; *Three Oranges* enquiries 105–6, 151, 170, 173, 185; unexpected death 236, 238, 259, 261, 297, 316, 613
Ognev, estate agency in Paris 37, 371–2, 376
OGPU 37, 133, 155, 430, 439, 462, 537, 784, 858n1, 863n1, 869, 872, 944n1
Oistrakh, David, violinist 419n2, 440n1, 559n2, 912n1
Okhotny Ryad, Moscow 420
Oktryabsky Station, Moscow *see* Nikolayevsky Station, Moscow
Oldenburg, Prince Alexander, claimant to the Imperial Throne 791
Olesha, Yury, writer 869, 881–2
Olga Vladislavovna *see* Codina, Olga
Olmsted, Miss, Christian Scientist 159, 164, 167, 175, 180, 187, 192, 233, 238, 600, 925
Omaha, Nebraska 251
Onégin, Sigrid, soprano 132n1, 911–12
Opéra de Paris *see* Paris Opéra
Orcel, host of chamber music evening 833
Orchestra Symphonique de Paris *see* Orchestre de Paris
Orchestre de Paris 758, 780, 781, 783, 805, 816n, 838n1, 855n1
Orchestre des concerts Straram 10n4
Order of the Red Banner, Soviet decoration 1066n2
Orlov, Nikolay, pianist 128, 589n2, 903n2, 916, 931
Oryol, civil war capture of 642
Osorgin, Mikhail, novelist and journalist 37n3, 38
Ossendowski, Antoni Ferdinand, *Beasts, Men and Gods* 88
Ossovsky, Alexander, musicologist, critic and teacher 191, 477–8, 479, 482, 495, 511, 520, 523–4, 873
Ostroumova-Lebedeva, Anna, artist 318–19, 496, 768
Ostrovsky, Alexander, playwright, *The Forest* 314, 546, 563, 805, 1067
Oxford bags 192n3
Oxford Press *see* Oxford University Press
Oxford University Press 40n1, 132n1, 419n2

Paichadze, Gavriil, Director of Russian Musical Editions 238, 259, 297, 316, 338, 344, 357, 364, 368–9, 375, 388, 389, 406, 571–2, 576, 592, 594, 596, 610, 636, 650, 651, 660, 676, 680, 686, 711, 730, 731, 733, 735, 738, 769, 787, 804, 840, 971, 1014; advice on visiting USSR without hard currency 749, 759; Ballets Russes, dispute over cuts to *Apollon musagète* 840; Boston Symphony's expenditure on new scores 628; *Fiery Angel*; Berlin Opera production doubtful and eventually cancelled 606, 647–8; possibility of Metropolitan Opera production 902, 915; friendship with Rachmaninoff 650; holidays with SSP in St Palais 626–30; and with Koussevitzky on walking tour 717–19; and with SSP at La Naze 965, 971; teaches to swim 627–8; Kokhno, agrees should not be credited on title page of *Prodigal Son* 839–43; *Sinfonietta* orchestral material sent to Boston 910, 930; advises SSP to accept Valmalète-Gaveau offer 845; SSP supports over émigré community's anger at SSP's Soviet Embassy appearance 792; Stravinsky-Rachmaninoff encounter in Paichadze's office 702
Paichadze, Vera Vasilievna, wife of Gavriil Paichadze 368, 388, 592, 596n4, 650
Paléologue, Maurice 676n2
Panhard cars 575
Paray, Paul, conductor and composer 946; composes test piece for Paris Conservatoire examination 1013
Paris: 1925 Exhibition 192–3; Observatory 158; Opéra 110n1, 176n2, 183n1, 195n, 201n3, 219n1, 337n, 451n2, 480n2, 824n2, 946n1, 1008n1, 1012n; Salon d'automne 665–6; Société des auteurs 595–6; Préfecture 439–40
Paris Conservatoire 41n2, 75n1, 141, 142n2, 235n1, 265n1, 715n2, 758n1, 776n1; Examination jury 1012–13; librarian Fédorov 636n1; Marcel Dupré Bach complete organ works cycle 655n1
Paris, transatlantic liner 277
Parker, Henry Taylor, music critic in Boston 914
Parmelee, publicity representative of Haensel and Jones 161, 894, 897, 900
Parry, Sir Charles Hubert Hastings, Bt 528n1
Pasdeloup Orchestra 178, 222n, 391, 395–6, 692–3, 757
Paskha *see* Russian Easter
Pasternak, Boris, poet and novelist 62n2, 198n2, 293n2, 631n2, 881n4
Pasternak, Leonid, artist 293n2, 881n4
Pavka *see* Koribut-Kubitovich, Pavel
Pavlova, Anna, ballerina 54n2, 225, 327
Pavlova, Maria (Marusya), Conservatoire friend, wife of Nikolay Benois 48 74, 109, 657
Pazovsky, Ari, conductor 426, 427n2
Pedrollo, Arrigo, composer and conductor 947; *Delitto e castigo* (*Crime and Punishment*) 947n3
Penza 155n3, 326, 365n1, 366, 429, 452, 531, 933n2
Persimfans, conductorless orchestra in Moscow 12n1, 253n2, 340, 366, 369, 377, 395, 412–14, 417–21, 427–8, 432–8, 440, 444, 453, 459–60, 465, 469–71, 483, 496, 512–13, 531, 535, 563, 564–5, 569–70, 679, 688–90, 867, 879, 1026; fifth anniversary gala 471, 500–2; filmed rehearsal 457–8
Pervaya Rota Street, Leningrad 318, 497, 870
Peshkova, Yekaterina, Director of Political Red Cross, former wife of Maxim Gorky 536–7
Peter and Paul Fortress, Leningrad 83n2, 480, 1069
Petit, Abbé, friend of French composers 66
Petrauskas, Kipras *see* Piotrovsky, Kipras
Petrograd *see* St Petersburg

Petrov-Vodkin, Kuzma, artist 154, 490n3, 510n1, 879, 881–2, 1031
Petrovskaya, Nina, muse of Valery Bryusov and Andrey Bely 325n1, 326n, 338n1
Pevsner, Antoine, artist 580n3
Philadelphia Orchestra 20n1, 249, 265n3, 269n1, 276
Philharmonia, meaning of in Russia 885n1
Phytic acid 14n2
Piano Concerto No.5
Pianola Institute 58n2, 664n2
Piastro, Mikhail (Misha, Michel), violinist 273n3, 786n2, 925
Piastro, Tosya, violinist 273n2
Picasso, Pablo, artist 68, 71n1, 74n1, 78n4, 179, 198n2, 320, 321n2, 324, 388n2, 581, 589, 974
Pierné, Gabriel, organist and composer 693, 734
Piotrovsky, Kipras, tenor 407–8, 776
Pirtsev, Director of Russian National Conservatoire in Paris 1000
Pisa 290, 721
Piscator, Erwin, theatre director 125n1, 1046n1, 1049
Piter *see* St Petersburg
Pius XI, Pope 55n1, 284–7
Pizzetti, Ildebrando; *Fra Gherardo* 810; Violin Sonata 8
Plantin House Museum, Antwerp 382, 985n1
Plekhanova-Bograd, Rosalia, manager of clinic in Boulogne-Billancourt 15
Plevitskaya, Nadezhda, folk singer 949
Pleyela player-piano 597n4, 664n2, 780n1
Plisetskaya, Maya, ballerina, wife of Rodion Shchedrin 262n1
Pneumatic postal system 794, 815
Podolsky, manager in Far East 975, 988
Polack, Dr, eye surgeon in Paris 76
Polignac, Prince Edmond de 48n1, 149
Polignac, Princesse de 48n, 149, 153, 171, 183, 190, 196, 323, 375, 666, 673, 675n2, 676, 678n1, 779, 1006n4
Polish Consulate, Moscow 123, 125, 566, 567–8
Political Red Cross 535–7
Polovinkin, Leonid, composer 430, 876, 886, 908, 1023; *Children's Pieces* 430n2
Polyakin, Miron, violinist 433
'Polyushko-Pole', melody by Lev Knipper 430
Pomerantsev, N. N., picture restorer in Kremlin cathedrals 563
Pomerantsev Yury, composer, SSP's first teacher 44, 1000
Pompeii 295
Ponce, Manuel, Mexican composer of 'Estrellita' 673n1
Popa-Gorchakov, Gyorgy *see* Gorchakov, Gyorgy
Popov, Gavriil 518: 538n3, 720, 785, 1031, 1045n3, Diaghilev proposes ballet commission 729; WORKS Octet 518, 518n1, 720, 729, 776, 785, 871–2, 1031, 1045; Septet 518n1, 538n3; Symphony No.1 871, 874; Symphonic Suite No.1 871; *Vocalise* 729
Port Arthur, Manchuria, starting battle of Russo-Japanese War 718, 751n1
Portland, Oregon 252–4
Poslednye Novosti 23n4, 37n2, 245n1, 753n1
Pototskaya, Mme, family friend from St Petersburg 526
La Poule d'eau, hotel in Grez sur Loing 214
Poulenc, Francis, composer 30: 39, 66, 84, 148, 162, 173, 181n3,182, 222, 299, 313, 321, 325n1, 336, 375, 581, 590, 599, 712, 904n2, 994n2, 995, 1002, 1011, 1014, 1050; bridge with 1007; country house party 997; percussionist in Milhaud's *Oresteia* 706n1; pianist in *Les Noces* 326; second piano for rehearsal of SSP's Piano Concerto No.2 891; 'Triton' chamber music society 997n2; WORKS *Aubade* 889–90; Concerto for Two Pianos 997n1, 1006; Harpsichord Concerto (*Concert champêtre*) 816; *Les Biches* 57–8, 65, 179; *Pastourelle* (*L'Eventail de Jeanne*) 42n1; Piano Concerto 1006n4
Poulet, Gaston, violinist and conductor, Concerts Poulet 776, 778–9, 975
Prechistenki Boulevard, Moscow 417, 420, 438
Preobrazhenskaya, Olga, film director; *Women of Ryazan* 837
Presnyakov, Valentin, dancer, choreographer and teacher of movement 560
Press, Stephen D., *Prokofiev's Ballets for Diaghilev* 594n1
Price, Christian Scientist 57, 65, 69
Prigozhy, Yakov, 'Maryusa's Taken Poison' 1053
Prince Albert, Duke of York, the future King George VI 1009, 1010
Princes Islands, Turkey 105, 143n1
Pro Musica, American music presenting organisation 243, 250, 252–4, 255, 258, 926, 928, 1035
Pro-Musica, Paris music promoting society 314, 771–2
Prokofiev, Oleg 759, 780–1, 800, 814, 945; birth 750–1; Diaghilev's reaction 760; naming 751–2; nickname 'bratik' 768

PROKOFIEV, SERGEY SERGEYEVICH; anonymous letter from Russian Woman 452; CHRISTIAN SCIENCE: reflections on; creation, accounting for 87; evil, illusory nature of 140, 266; God, existence and nature of 87, 269–270, 659, 794; art as manifestation of 994; love for his creation 773; Kant, analogies with 86; mankind, origin of 145–6; memory, explanation of 91; time, eternity and immortality 156, 266, 355, 394; COUSIN SHURIK, attempts to gain his release from prison 361, 428–9, 448–9, 452, 475, 507, 535–6, 568, 877, 886; information from former fellow-prisoner 975–6; Meyerhold 541, 565, 868, 882; Political Red Cross 536–7; DACHAS RENTED: Bellevue 96, 98–101, 102–169, 170, 197, 208; Culoz, Château de la Fléchère 850–64, 897–8; Marlotte 198, 199, 204–21; La Naze 72, 964; St Gilles-sur-Vie 53, 67, 76–100, 102, 105, 160, 200; St Jean-de-Luz 989; St Palais 585, 600–48, 649, 652; Samoreau 299, 600–48, 649, 652; Château de Vétraz 715, 716–27; fame and success, reflections on 12, 84, 835–6, 974; HEALTH: dental problems 255–6, 270, 584, 653, 656, 658, 662, 747–8, 765; eyesight 35–6, 115, 126, 159, 164, 281, 654; headaches 6, 67, 78, 82, 85, 89, 95, 99, 107–8, 110, 113, 116, 137, 137n2, 153, 160, 180–181, 187, 219, 221, 254–5, 260, 303, 311, 336, 349, 356, 360, 367, 376, 405, 468, 500–1, 562, 600, 606–7, 619, 621, 629–30, 641, 643, 647, 653–4, 655, 659, 667, 681, 686, 688, 692–3, 706, 770, 772, 774–5, 793, 800–1, 811–2, 819, 831, 857, 871, 881, 917, 926, 929, 935, 946, 996, 1022, 1045; heart 14, 29, 39–40, 59, 66, 69, 139, 233, 374, 376–7, 384, 386, 403–5, 645, 653, 755, 815–7, 820–3, 826, 828, 863, 864; neuralgia 66, 69, 78, 79, 82, 247, 270, 870; rheumatism 79; skin rashes 247–8, 260, 653, 661; unexplained collapse 980–2; mathematics, reflections on 140, 613; memory, reflections on 91–2, 194, 394, 603; MOTORING TRIPS: accidents 582, 626, 674–5, 997; places briefly visited or passed through: Amboise 600; Angoulin 53; Arcachon, bay of 585, 625; Avallon 850, 964; Bas-Samois 342, 360; Biarritz 621–4; Blois 582, 648; Bois-le-Roi 964; Capbreton 622; Chambéry 296–7; Chambord 582, 958; Champagne 351, 353; Chantilly 964; Châtelaillon 53; Châtellerault 648; Chaville 108, 153; Coubre 608; Dampierre-en-Yvelines 598; Dax 625; Héricy 349, 354; La Rochelle 641–2; Les Landes 622; Loches 585; Menton 578; Mimizan 625; Montagne, Gironde 622; Peyhorade 625; Poissy 593; Poitiers 585, 600; Ronce-les-Bains 616; Les Sables d'Olonne 92; St André-de-Cubzac 585; St Cloud 9, 221; St Cyr 660; St Jean Pied-de-Port 625; St Jean-de-Luz 624; St Loup-de-Naud 678; Vulaines 354, 372; new simplicity 341, 589, 720, 779, 989; RELIGION, REFLECTIONS ON: attitude to the church 17; healing, Christian Science's power of 635; philosophy as expression of the material, not the divine 86, 859–860; religion and science, essential unity of 366; truth, only to be apprehended by the spirit 366; trunk of papers recovered from Myaskovsky 422–423; *The Violin Clef and the Sardine Tin Key*, idea for a ballet 167

JUVENILIA WORKS: Symphony in E minor 472n2; *The Giant* (*Velikan*) 525n1, 709; excerpts from original score recovered 525

MATURE WORKS: *Musical Letter to Zakharov*;

Op. 3 *Four Pieces for Piano* No.1 'Fairy Tale' 128; No.3 'March' 128

Op. 4 *Four Pieces for piano* No.4 'Suggestion diabolique' 128, 548, 553, 899, 910, 956, 1025

Op. 5 *Sinfonietta* in A 341

Op. 6 *Dreams* (*Sni*) 340, 533

Op. 8 *Autumnal* 340–1

Op. 9 *Two Poems for voice and piano* 83: 'There are Other Planets' 140

Op. 10 Piano Concerto No.1 in D flat major 11, 168, 427, 460, 523, 855, 927

Op. 11 *Toccata* 300, 1049n1; performed by Borovsky 52, 139; performed by SSP 52, 232, 252, 288, 435, 442, 447, 550, 1049, 1050

Op. 12 *Ten Pieces for piano* 482n2: No. 7 *Prelude* 52; No. 10 *Scherzo* 670

Op. 12bis *Humoresque Scherzo* for four bassoons 482

Op. 14 Piano Sonata No.2 in D minor 34, 135, 236, 458, 676, 1026, 1048, 1054; played by Borovsky 174; special request of Lunacharsky 425

Op. 15 *Ballade* for cello and piano 114, 489–90, 552, 633n1, 833

Op. 16 Piano Concerto No. 2 in G minor 18, 20, 25, 34, 68n4, 130n1, 163, 196n1, 220, 223, 477n3, 484n1, 613n2, 656; reconstruction 3n5, 5, 22; piano reduction of orchestral part 20; PERFORMANCES BY SSP; Ansermet/BBC Symphony Orchestra, radio recording (lost) 671; Berlin Radio 972; Defauw, Ghent 987; DeLamarter, Chicago 927; Dobrowen, Stockholm 226–7; Fitelberg, Warsaw 978; Koussevitzky, Boston and New York 260–1, 263–4, 913; Liège 976; Malko, Leningrad 509, 512–4; Monteux, Concertgebouworkest 891; Monteux/Orchestre de Paris 984–5; Persimfans, Moscow 453, 460, 469–70, 564; Rhené-Bâton/Orchestre Pasdeloup, Paris 391, 395–7; Rossi, Rome 283–4

Op. 17 *Sarcasms*, No.5; Dukelsky uses theme similar to No.5 in his Symphony 671; music used for a ballet 122; performed by Borovsky 139, 692, 710; style now rejected by SSP 741

Op. 18 *The Ugly Duckling* 175n2, 359, 366n1, 459, 559, 672; small orchestra version for Lina 994–6, 1027; string orchestra version for Koshetz 159, 218, 222

Op. 19 Violin Concerto No. 1 in D♭ 71n2, 191, 249, 787; performances; Ansermet/Orchestre de Paris 805, 823; Brodsky/Orchestre de Paris 782–3; Burgin, Boston 31, 157, 160, 260, 334; Chevillier (play-through) 76; Darrieux/Straram 824, 824n2; Hansen 171n2, 174, 299; Kokhánski, New York 71, 168; Lyubochitz 219; Milstein (with Horowitz), piano, Moscow 59n2, 912n1; Oistrakh, Odessa 559n2; Pierné/Orchestre Colonne 734; Rabinovich/Koussevitzky 904; Saradzhev 879, 885; Saussine (play-through) 403; Schmuller/Monteux Amsterdam 234; Szigeti 65, 85, 111, 139, 207, 227, 268, 759; Wolff/Lamoureux Orchestra 1038; publication 95–6, 98, 104–6, 116; Stravinsky's assessment 792, 796, 1038

Op. 20 *Scythian Suite* 3n7, 42, 163, 489, 499, 573,

887; ballet proposals; Diaghilev, rejects 153; Ida Rubinstein 153–154; Nijinska in Buenos Aires 628; Terpis in Berlin 381, 583; Cortot proposal for Orchestre de Paris 755; Defauw performance in Ghent 987; Dranishnikov performances with Leningrad Philharmonic 494, 496, 1048–1049; Glazunov walks out of premiere 46n3; Honegger purloins theme 812; Koussevitzky performances 31, 109n1, 113, 909, 913; drops from New York programme 918; Lunacharsky's assessment 515; Monteux performances with Concertgebouworkest 234–5, 237; Persimfans performances 472, 500–2, 564; Rodzinski performance with Los Angeles Philharmonic 921; Rühlmann performance in Brussels 110; Sabaneyev mistakenly reviews aborted performance 5n, 306; Stokowski performances 20n1, 20n2, 393; Toscanini's assessment 755

Op. 21 *Chout*: ballet 29n4, 42, 122, 147, 186, 337, 440, 568, 573, 573n1, 656, 812, 913; duets from 557; international productions, proposals and productions; Bolshoy Ballet School 1072; Chicago Opera 336; Cologne 219, 224; German cities 657, 660; Magdeburg 207; Mariinsky Theatre 81, 216, 496, 499, 515; Neighbourhood Playhouse, New York 14–5, 34–5, 80; La Scala 332, 334, 657; revival, based on Suite 763, 765, 783; dropped in favour of *Le Renard* 801; Stravinsky's assessment 331, 796

Op. 21bis Suite from *Chout* 110, 113, 159; Ansermet in Brussels 942; Ansermet in Russia 807; composition 80; Dranishnikov with Leningrad Philharmonic 483, 494–5; Fitelberg in Warsaw 978; Koussevitzky in Paris 309, 316, 328–9, 331; Koussevitzky in USA 368; Leipzig 650; Monteux proposes for Russia 142, 235; Pasdeloup Orchestra 178, 692–3; Persimfans 420–421, 432, 434, 453, 471; Wolff with Lamoureux Orchestra 736, 892, 1038

Op. 22 *Visions fugitives* 130, 336, 518, 523, 787; arrangement for wind quartet 879; performed by Sofronitsky 833; performed by SSP 446, 495, 510, 550, 670, 910, 1025

Op. 23 *Five Poems for voice and piano* 256; 'The Grey Dress' 28–29, 90; 'The Wizard' 129

Op. 24 *The Gambler (Igrok)* 22n1, 25, 429, 612, 616–7, 644, 699, 700–1, 758, 816, 832, 851, 889, 901, 941, 942, 948, 1025; BRUSSELS PRODUCTION 711, 799, 809–14, 815, 818, 833, 836, 844, 889; reactions; Diaghilev 815; Markevich 815; Demchinsky's contribution to original version 22n1, 607; French translation 810–3, 852–3; MARIINSKY THEATRE; ABANDONED 1917 PRODUCTION 96n1, 172n2, 210n, 215n6, 226n, 324n2, 403n1, 407n2, 481n2; new production proposed 81, 96, 216, 496, 499, 515, 530, 649, 688, 695, 702, 742, 759–60, 799, 875; Meyerhold as producer 324, 500, 505, 532–3, 541, 544–6, 735; original score recovered 810–3, 852–3; other production possibilities; Bolshoy Theatre second auditorium 1071–1072; Dresden Opera 590; Germany; Kleiber, Berlin 888; Metropolitan Opera 277n1, 934–6, 938–9; Rosing American Opera Company 918; REVISED VERSION 620, 626–30, 632, 634, 643–7, 651–2, 654–66, 672–5, 678–82, 686–7, 689–90, 691, 693–5, 837, 83841, 841, 843

Op. 25 Symphony No.1 in D (*Classical*)51n1 157, 163, 170n2, 176, 220–1, 224, 229, 477n1; Conius's editorial suggestions 141, 143, 147; Lunacharsky hears rehearsal 422n1; performances; Antwerp 985; Defauw, Ghent 987; Dranishnikov, Leningrad 1031; Golovanov, Moscow 1022–3, 1025; indisposed, SSP conducts 1036; Koussevitzky, USA 368, 819, 901; gramophone recording 821, 833, 1054–15; Koussevitzky, Paris 591–2; Lamoureux Orchestra, Paris 892; Malko, Kiev 556–7; Malko, Leningrad 509, 521; Monteux, Concertgebouworkest 892; Persimfans 564; Pierné/Orchestre Colonne, Paris 693; Saradzhev, Moscow 473, 531, 533, 565; Tcherepnin, Riga 316, 357; piano transcription 982, 984, 988; Gavotte 435, 447, 504, 1025n1; Stravinsky gibe 180

Op. 26 Piano Concerto No. 3 in C 61, D, 80, 110, 116, 147, 163, 358, 652, 707n, 757, 892; Damrosch's assessment 67; played through by Borovsky 66; Stravinsky's assessment 375; PERFORMANCES BY SSP; Bruno Walter, USA 1041; Désormière (reduced orchestra for Princess Polignac) 183; Fitelberg, Warsaw 127; HMV recording with London Symphony Orchestra and Coppola 1008–10; Lindemann, Freiburg 685; Mikeladze, Tbilisi 1062; Orchestre Lamoureux, Paris 892; Paray, Monte Carlo 946; Persimfans 418, 428, 432, 434, 453, 456; Prague 1043; premiere, Chicago Symphony under Stock 927n1; Rodzinski, Los Angeles Philharmonic 921–3; Rühlmann, Brussels 110, 113; Savich, Syracuse 274–5; Strasbourg 973; PERFORMANCES BY OTHER PIANISTS: Feinberg, Leningrad 483; Feinberg, Persimfans 151, 419; Oborin, Persimfans 419, 453

Op. 27 *Five Poems of Anna Akhmatova* 38, 42, 95, 97n1, 146, 672n1

Op. 29 Piano Sonata No. 4 in C minor 351, 487, 787; performances; Druskin, Leningrad 482; SSP, Leningrad 526; SSP, Moscow 456, 458–9, 504; filmed at Persimfans rehearsal 457; SSP, Philadelphia Contemporary Music Society 910

Op. 30 *Seven They Are Seven (Semero ikh*) cantata for tenor: chorus and orchestra 9n4, 46, 52, 138, 250, 623; Damrosch interest 64, 67, 244–5; French translation 36–7; Paris critics' joke 1004; performances by Koussevitzky; Boston 245, 297, 301, 309, 368; Paris (premiere) 42, 48, 54, 56–7, 59–61, 171, 950; Straram interest 178

Op. 31 *Tales of an Old Grandmother* 447, 458, 715n1, 741n1, 787, 1025

Op. 33 *The Love for Three Oranges* (*Lyubov' k tryom apel'sinam*) 7n1, 10n5, 15, 31n1, 51n2, 85n1, 97n1, 97n2, 150, 246, 249n2, 250n1, 261, 264n2, 271, 301, 336n1, 476, 493, 553, 570–1, 634, 692n2, 707n, 760, 886, 902, 927n1, 928, 933, 937n2, 947, 1021; abridged libretto translated by Lina 20, 23, 27; BERLIN STAATSOPER PRODUCTION 187, 364, 366, 376, 379–384, 583; BOLSHOY THEATRE PRODUCTION 198n1, 216, 368–9, 396, 427–8, 437, 450, 454–455, 466–8, 507, 534–5, 586, 650, 675–6, 735, 871–2, 883–4, 953; COLOGNE PRODUCTION 60, 81, 92, 125, 137, 143–5, 219, 224, 383; KHARKOV PRODUCTION 551–4; MARIINSKY THEATRE PRODUCTION 170, 184–5, 210, 216, 230, 280, 297–8, 309, 312, 477, 479, 487–90, 490n2, 514–5, 516, 527, 545, 548, 645n1, 875, 1028, 1034, 1050, 1069; SSP invited to conduct 354, 359; ORCHESTRAL SUITE 80–1, 83–4, 90, 297, 299, 304–5, 357, 364, 378, 383, 389, 420, 432, 435, 453, 470–1, 473, 509, 533, 591, 666, 677, 696, 734, 776, 778–9, 808, 890, 985, 987, 1004; Koussevitzky, USA 368; March 20, 41, 312, 323, 341–2, 410, 418, 425, 447, 504, 510, 558, 596, 787, 798, 893, 899, 976, 1006, 1026, 1038; 500 copies ordered for Scotland 41; Paris Conservatoire performances 219–20, 229, 230–1, 315–6, 344, 352; Suite performances conducted by SSP 876, 878, 885–6, 925, 946, 947–8; PROPOSED PRODUCTIONS; Belgrade 660; Cincinnati 396; European tour of Soviet production 425, 476, 500, 514, 530, 534–5, 588; London 105–6; Mainz 364; Paris Opéra 9, 964–5, 1005–6, 1006n1; Rosing American Opera Company 919n1; Salter management for Europe 105n3; Vienna 151; Zagreb Opera 626

Op. 34 *Overture on Hebrew Themes* (*Jewish Overture*); performances; Association for Contemporary Music, Moscow 442; Detroit Pro Musica 928; Leningrad Conservatoire 1032, 1034; Literature-Arts Circle, Leningrad 481; Moscow Conservatoire 1026–7; Moscow Radio 885; New York 934; Paris 50; private house concert, Paris 833

Op. 35 *Five Songs Without Words* 4, 37, 97n1, 185, 352n1, 672; version for solo piano of No.4 'Scherzino' 989

Op. 35bis *Five Songs Without Words* for violin and piano 139, 191, 204, 207, 221, 543, 816, 928, 1047; collaboration with Kokhánski 191–193, 196; Hansen 191

Op. 36 *Five Poems of Konstantin Balmont* 307; 'An Incantation of Water and of Fire' 52; 'Pillars' 322

Op. 37 *The Fiery Angel* (*Ognennyi Angel*) 7, 13, 23, 106n2, 134, 147, 282, 325, 363n2, 612, 616, 634, 693, 748, 849n1; attempts to secure productions; Berlin Opera 264, 277, 382, 606, 977; Cologne Opera 224, 383; Dresden Opera 590; Metropolitan Opera 10n5, 277, 692n2, 901–2, 907, 912, 915–7, 918, 929, 934–5; Rosing American Opera Company 918–9, 929, 935; Théâtre des Champs Elysées 54, 61, 64, 65, 70–4, 79, 80, 101–2; Koussevitzky's offer of loan for performing material 75; Christian Science, at odds with 374, 602, 606, 617, 647–8, 699, 701; CONCERT PERFORMANCE OF ACT II BY KOUSSEVITZKY 158, 701, 703, 710–3; Demchinsky's contribution to libretto 22, 90, 154, 231, 327, 334, 337–8, 343, 346, 348, 356, 362, 695; MATERIAL RECAST AS SYMPHONY NO.3 301, 717, 720, 767–768; Plantin Museum, Antwerp 382, 985n1; reactions 712; German Theatres 848–9; Myaskovsky 707; Paris press 714; Sabaneyev 713, 730; Suvchinsky 712, 715, 741; Tcherepnin 731–732; RECONSTRUCTION 337, 339, 345–6, 348, 350–1, 356–60, 362, 376, 398, 506, 581, 588–9, 591, 595, 601, 611, 619, 621; roman à clef 325, 325n1, 338, 374; vocal score 628, 630, 634, 636

Op. 37bis Vocal Suite from *The Fiery Angel* 80

Op. 38 Piano Sonata No.5 in C major 3–4, 6, 15, 23, 25, 65, 76; publication 99, 104, 138; reactions; Borovsky 36, 391; Dukelsky 163; Koussevitzky 310; Myaskovsky 149; Stravinsky 45; Suvchinsky 62, 643; Yavorsky 310; Ziloti 149; premiere, Paris 30; subsequent performances; Kharkov 553; Kiev 558; Leningrad 510; Moscow 446–7, 548; Moscow (private, Derzhanovsky's) 431; Riga 410; Strasbourg 232

Op. 39 Quintet for oboe, clarinet, violin, viola, double bass (originally music for *Trapèze* ballet) 44n1, 78–80, 82, 84–5, 89, 148, 150, 151, 152, 161, 163, 187, 200, 332, 340, 343, 344, 348, 373, 417, 504, 636, 652, 799, 833; performances; ASM, Moscow 540, 544, 547–8; Koussevitzky, Boston (ten players) 268, 547; Leningrad Philharmonica 1047–8; Paris 581; Pro-Musica, Paris 771–2; proposed for ISCM Festival, Oxford 982; Siena 581; Versailles 598

Op. 40 Symphony No.2 in D minor; composition 65, 69–70, 75, 78, 84, 87, 89, 90–6, 98–100, 104–9, 111–4, 117, 121, 136–7, 142, 150, 159, 163–4; Koussevitzky's advice 69–70; revisions 219–20, 253, 278; Paris premiere 161, 163–4, 167, 963n4; publication 338, 340, 343, 575, 588, 616, 636, 716, 727; REACTIONS OF OTHER MUSICIANS: Asafyev 874; Dukelsky 173; Koussevitzky 176; Marnold 174, 200, 224; Nouvel 173; Poulenc 173; Stravinsky 172, 172n1, 180; Suvchinsky 175; SSP's feelings after premiere xiv, 173, 217–218, 301; subsequent performances; Kleiber, Berlin 848; Koussevitzky, Boston 819; Reiner 302; Saradzhev 417; Savich 302; Stokowski 935, 956; Straram 178, 278, 298–302, 687–8

Op. 41 *The Steel Step* (*Le pas d'acier*) (*Stal'noy skok*) 279, 355, 430n5, 641, 652, 846, 851, 853, 861–3, 949, 1018; choreographer options; Balanchine 222, 573; Massine 573, 577, 579–80, 588–9, 592, 594–6, 605, 680–2, 881; Cocteau's attack 594, 596, 596n4; commission and conception 184–186, 212,

215, 222; fee negotiations 186; COMPOSITION 217–8, 221, 226, 251–252, 260, 281–2, 316, 339–42; development; Ehrenburg 198-9, 202–4, 208, 210, 211–2; Suvchinsky 185–6, 189, 198–9; Yakulov 202, 203–4, 205–6, 208, 209–10, 211–5, 218; Constructivist sets too awkward to tour; Diaghilev; decision on hammers 599; dedication to 596; London press article 605; requests incorporation of *Trapèze* overture 579, 581; Kokhno eliminated as librettist 185–6; suggests *chastushki* 188–9; naming of ballet 215, 389, 580–1, 644; piano score 236, 239, 251, 356, 697, 699–700, 708, 720, 732, 769, 784, 787, 976; premiere and subsequent performances 591–3, 595–6, 605, 677, 680–1, 705, 709, 820, 825, 832; producer options: Meyerhold 278; Taïrov 278–9, 844n; proposed productions: Bolshoy Theatre 834, 846, 848, 868; opposed by proletarian musicians 877, 908, 966; Mariinsky Theatre 499, 581, 598; Metropolitan Opera 906; Stokowski 956; reactions: Asafyev 720; Bolshoy Theatre open meeting 880–1; Dukelsky 222–3; Marnold 598; Stravinsky 592, 594, 599, 638, 792; Suvchinsky 594, 741

Op. 41bis *The Steel Step*, symphonic suite 274n, 637, 705, 707, 901, 927, 1022–3, 1025, 1031, 1036

Op. 43 *Divertimento* 201n1, 843, 851, 860–2, 892, 942, 972, 1011; Fitelberg, Warsaw 952; premiere (conducted by SSP) 927

Op. 43bis *Divertissement* for piano 951, 957, 1026

Op. 44 Symphony No. 3 in C minor 835, 837, 849, 957; material recast from *The Fiery Angel* 310n3, 717, 720, 721–4, 730–1, 767–8, 832–5, 974; parts copied in Moscow 742, 814; performances: Ansermet, Brussels 738, 741, 915, 942–3; Berlin radio broadcast 991; Dranishnikov, Leningrad 1047–9; Koussevitzky 805, 915, 935; Monteux premiere in Paris 805–6, 814–6, 817–20, 822–826; dispute over programme notes 823–4, 826; Saradzhev, Moscow 1045, 1051, 1056; Stokowski 958; reactions: Asafyev, detects spirituality 1050; Diaghilev 826; Koussevitzky 826, 831

Op. 45 *Things in Themselves* (*Choses en soi*) (*Veshchi v sebe*) 699, 702, 720, 722, 729, 733, 781, 792, 816, 876, 910, 989; performances; Brussels premiere 798; Havana 931–932; New York Town Hall 900; reactions; Asafyev 720; Borovsky 735; Diaghilev 729, 735; Dukelsky 729; Marnold 772; Morolyov 877; Myaskovsky 868; Rubinstein 781; Stravinsky 796, 797; Suvchinsky 729; Zhilyayev 880

Op. 46 *The Prodigal Son* (*Le fils prodigue*) (*Bludnyi syn*); Balanchine's choreography 222n2, 826–31, 834, 842; Lina's objections 827, 829; SSP's objections 827–30; COMPOSITION 734–7, 742, 747–9, 751, 763, 795–6, 865; conception and commission 729–33, 747; Désormière as conductor 818, 821, 822, 825, 826–7, 830, 832–833, 836, 838, 934–5; Diaghilev's reaction to the music 737–8, 744–5, 797, 857; dedication 797; fee negotiations 732–4; KOKHNO LIBRETTO 729, 736, 740, 744, 756, 758, 760, 764, 774–5, 778, 793, 801–802, 806, 827–8, 831, 838; dispute over author's rights and credit 733–734, 763–764; takes out injunction 839–843, 853–4, 856; Lifar 760, 764, 778, 793, 796, 802; other mooted production: American League of Composers at the Metropolitan Opera 906; Berlin 807; piano pieces Op.52 Nos 1, 2 and 3 derived from 751, 989, 1006, 1006n3; publication 804, 806, 815, 830–82; reactions: Borovsky 780; Koussevitzky 831; Lourié 838–9; Rachmaninoff 831, 833; Samoilenko 831; Stravinsky 792, 794, 796–7, 828–31; Suvchinsky 741, 757, 784, 796; rehearsals and Paris premiere 801–2, 815, 818, 820, 822, 825, 826–31, 832–3, 835, 836, 842; Rouault designs 792-3, 794–5, 801–2, 806, 808, 827–9, 831; Matisse negotiations abandoned 783, 792; SOME MATERIAL RECAST AS SYMPHONY NO.4 301n3, 767, 775, 781, 783, 783n3, 819; SSP as conductor Paris and London premieres 807, 815, 841

Op. 46bis *The Prodigal Son*, symphonic suite 969

Op. 47 Symphony No.4 in C major; derived from material composed for but not used in *The Prodigal Son* 301n3, 767, 775, 783, 786–7, 796, 799, 802, 806–7, 816, 851, 951, 954, 960, 974; Introduction separately composed 781; Dukelsky objects in principle 800; Koussevitsky defends principle 819; performances: premiere, Boston Symphony 50th jubilee 862–3, 971, 981–2; Paris premiere with Monteux 950, 984–5; reactions: Nabokov 984; Suvchinsky 860, 984

Op. 48 *Sinfonietta* in A (revised version of Op.5); cancelled performance by Monteux with Orchestre de Paris 950–951; Myaskovsky's reaction 868–9, 886; performance by Fitelberg in Warsaw 951–2, 976–9; performance by Saradzhev 871, 878–9, 885, 947; performance by Wolff with Lamoureux Orchestra 1038; planned performance by Koussevitzky 903, 910, 935, 950–1; planned performance by Toscanini 930; recomposition 343, 851, 853, 860–2; Suvchinsky's reaction 860; version of Finale for piano as Scherzo, Op.52 No.6 989

Op. 49 *Four Portraits and Dénouement from The Gambler* 843n2, 862–3, 989, 1016, 1019, 1041

Op. 50 String Quartet No.1 in B minor; commission 916–7, 934; composition 926, 953–4, 960, 982, 984; performances 989, 1021, 1021n6, 1026, 1034, 1051; reactions; Lifar 964, 969; Nabokov 972; Suvchinsky 973

Op. 51 *Sur le Borysthène* (*On The Dnieper*); commission 919, 964–5; composition 968–9, 975, 986, 989, 997n2, 971, 973; interest from Bolshoy Theatre 1019; naming 1037n2; rehearsals and premiere 1037, 1039, 1041

Op. 52 *Six Pieces for Piano*; No.1 'Intermezzo' 1006n3; No.2 'Rondo' 1006, 1006n3; No.3 'Etude' 1006n3; No.4 'Scherzino' 989; No.6 'Scherzo' 989
Op. 53 Piano Concerto No.4 in B flat 958, 958n2, 960, 964, 965, 967–8, 989
Op. 54 Piano Concerto No.5 in G major 1–63, 998, 1018, 1038; performances; Koussevitzky/Boston Symphony 1041; premiere with Furtwängler/Berlin Philharmonic 1018; Stock/Chicago Symphony 1041; Paris premiere with Wolff/Orchestre Lamoureux 1038; Stravinsky's opinion 1038
Op. 56 Sonata for Two Violins in C major 997n2, 1018; performances; Leningrad Conservatoire 1032, 1034; Soetens/Dushkin, 'Triton' Chamber Music launch, Paris 1038–1039; Tsyganov/Shirinsky, Moscow 1021, 1022, 1026
Op. 57 *Symphonic Song* 301n3, 834n, 1041, 1045, 1045n1
Op. 63 Violin Concerto No.2 in G minor 1038n
Op. 65 *Music for Children* (*Detskaya Muzyka*) 430n2
Op. 67 *Peter and the Wolf* 430n2
Op. 100 Symphony No. 5 in B flat 1041
sans op *Ala and Lolli*, abandoned ballet 20n2, 38, 63, 573, 887
sans op *Musical Letter to Zakharov* 632n1
sans op Schubert Waltzes, suite arranged for two and four hands 194–196, 197, 595–596, 671–672, 675, 1058, 1072; with Feinberg 455–457, 459; with Février 676; with Kamensky 526; with Princess Polignac 673; with Sofronitsky 789
sans op transcription for pianola of Rimsky-Korsakov's *Sheherazade* 7, 8, 12, 245
sans op *Lieutenant Kijé*, film score 293n3, 834n1, 933n3, 1051, 1031n5, 1045, 1068
Prokofiev, Svyatoslav 26–8, 32, 40, 42, 45, 54, 57, 73, 76–7, 89, 94–6, 103, 111, 141, 162, 166, 168–70, 173, 179, 189, 210, 217, 221, 224, 238, 297, 311, 331–2, 339, 342, 345, 347, 351–5, 357–60, 362, 366, 370, 372–3, 376, 385, 391, 412, 456, 533, 572–3, 577, 600–3, 607–8, 615, 626, 646, 679, 702, 716, 727, 751, 920, 987; birth 26, 749; Christmas party 682; Diaghilev's reaction 760; fourth birthday 693–4; fifth birthday 787; attends concert in Monte Carlo 946; 'Grogy' name for Gorchakov 581; inoculation 966; music criticism 952; papa's zizik 303; philosophical reflection 772; reaction to brother 751, 757, 759, 768; calls him 'bratik' 768; Serebryakova portrait 821; Stravinsky's affection 717
Prokofieva, Carolina (Lina), (Lina Ivanovna), (Ptashka) 3, 32, 35, 39, 40, 45, 47, 60, 61, 62, 66, 71, 82, 85, 107, 113, 115, 172, 199, 243, 252, 256, 262, 269, 275, 317, 326, 353, 361, 367, 406, 408, 574–5, 609, 616, 626, 634, 644, 652; Belgoskino screen test 1068–9, 1071; meets Blumenfeld 565; Boris Bashkirov, bad relations with 163, 221, 305, 311, 363, 576–7, 582, 584, 681, 735, 1038; Borovskys, first meets 166; car driving experiences 599, 640, 997; accident, injured in 866n1; chess, develops interest in 645–6, 748; CHILDREN, BIRTH OF AND CARE FOR 10, 15, 20, 22–6, 34, 54, 89, 170, 353, 376, 412, 572, 615, 717, 723, 725, 730, 731, 735, 737, 746, 748, 749–51, 755, 759, 945, 946, 952; CHRISTIAN SCIENCE: influenced by 66, 67, 73, 85, 86, 149, 155–6, 159, 164, 180, 244, 246, 364, 393, 577, 652, 661, 710, 767, 773, 864, 981, 994; Diaghilev, relations with 150, 594, 737, 760, 774, 801, 806, 807, 831; grieves for 856; DOMESTIC STABILITY; LONGING FOR 32, 73, 106, 107, 143, 169, 224, 238, 334, 358, 367, 375–7, 376–7, 384, 386, 475, 577, 611, 648, 730, 849, 851–2, 860, 941, 954; party 1013–14; Culoz château, distressed by squalor of 847–8; Dukelsky, first meets 162; family photos, interest in 443, 497; *Fiery Angel*: advice to SSP to persist with 374–5; relief at completion of 693; flirted with by musicians in Moscow and Leningrad 424, 432, 433, 444, 459, 468, 482, 494, 534, 565; flying, attracted by 672; Garvin, Mrs, friendship with 35, 45, 923–4, 926; Gloria Swanson, meets 922; Gorchakov, intercedes for 600; Gorky, meets in Naples 292–4; Guchkov, meets 634; Havana, visits 930–2; home movies; with Meyerhold 966; with Nabokov 970; Koussevitzkys, relations with 370, 371, 637, 716, 819, 909; linguistic facility 26–7, 231, 264, 292, 715, 725, 905; Meshcherskaya, contemplates buying wardrobe from 980, 982, 1070; Monte Carlo, car trip to 801–4; Paichadze, taught swimming by 628; parents, relations with 261, 342, 350, 357, 611, 645, 837, 945, 952; passports 14, 377; Pope, audience with 285–7; portrait painted by Ostroumova 327, 329, 332–3, 337–8; *Prodigal Son*, protests about indecency of production 827, 829; Rachmaninoff, encounters 275, 937–8; Royan, rejects idea of living in 644, 645; Ruzsky, upset by death of 633; Samoilenkos, first meets 3; Segovia, meets in Russia 562; AS SINGER 83, 86, 90, 95, 98, 109, 110, 125, 157, 161, 243, 245, 287, 323, 327, 351, 406, 409, 433, 468, 546, 637, 660, 678, 690, 912, 924, 983, 1018, 1023; disappointments 227, 236–7, 258, 290, 291–2, 410, 441, 670, 860, 901, 906, 910–11, 926, 937, 1001; performance nerves 160–1, 227–8, 284, 662, 669, 892, 908, 909, 936, 937, 994–5; Prague and Warsaw, engagements in 1018, 1027, 1037; Snow Maiden, studying role of 546, 652; successes 160, 232, 233, 250, 252, 257, 288, 290, 291, 336, 658, 668, 693, 861–3, 864, 892, 899, 914, 928, 932, 995, 1027; knowledge of technique admired by Suvchinsky 857; teachers 198, 233, 298, 362, 849, 861; *Ugly Duckling*, sings with orchestra 994; SSP, RELATIONS WITH: antagonistic 15, 54, 95, 239, 295, 310, 311, 346, 455, 571, 582, 593, 599, 620, 636, 645–6, 652, 686, 690, 706, 710, 739, 741,

753, 766, 775, 786, 800, 900, 941, 943, 945; jealous 157, 633, 639, 645, 661, 668, 897; loving 16, 20, 40, 136, 236, 357, 358–9, 364, 378, 383, 455, 610, 652, 710, 741, 755, 767–8, 770, 799, 801, 811, 861, 865, 888, 948, 952–3, 980; tends to after fainting fit 981; Stalin, locks eyes with at concert 1066; Suvchinsky, first meets 63; Symphony No.3, attends Monteux's rehearsals of 822–3, 825; *The Gambler*, attends Brussels premiere of 811–14; USSR; Arens, flattered by 770; attracted to in principle 395, 688, 790; fails to understand risks of not being allowed to leave 865; buys furs in Moscow 511–13, 530, 537, 543, 544, 567, 568, 877, 879, 884, 887, 888; encounters Aunt Katya Rayevskaya 531–2; Cousin Katya Ignatieva 531–2; Ekskuzovich 476; Karneyev sisters 481; Katya Schmidthof 494, 509; Katyusha Uvarova 429; Litvinova 437, 447, 465, 541–2, 873; Moscow Art Theatre 449; Myaskovsky 444, 446; Nadya Rayevskaya 428; Olga Kameneva 462; Saradzhev 472; Stanislavsky Opera Studio 455, 567; Yavorsky 450–1; filmed for publicity 457; visits Kremlin Museums 562–3; disturbed by Soviet marriage code 438; attends Nezhdanova jubilee concert 1055; Odessa, returns to 559; sleigh accidents 499, 537; sympathy for Wittgenstein 968; Zakharov, first meets 44–5; Ziloti, meets in New York 276

Prokofieva, Maria Grigorievna 3, 5, 15, 23, 34, 34n2, 54, 67, 70, 73, 76–7, 83, 98, 99, 101, 105, 116–19, 311, 318–19, 493, 665, 674; death 117, 155, 174, 235; SSP visits grave 197, 224, 403, 674–5

Prokofieva, Vera, unrelated namesake 356

'Proletarian' Shop, Kharkov 551

Proletkult 207n1, 882n2, 993n1

Prompartia, Moscow show trials 978

Protopopov, Sergey, composer, music theorist, partner of Boleslav Yavorsky 305, 450–2, 540, 565, 876; *Gudochek* 451–2

Proust, Marcel, *A la recherche du temps perdu* 140n2 674

Providence, Rhode Island 270

Prud'homme, conveyancing lawyer in Paris 822

Pruna, Pedro, artist and designer 116n1, 179, 186, 324, 333, 806, 841–2

Prunières 23, 39, 146, 157–8, 302, 303, 322, 323, 390, 398, 581, 592, 594, 687, 691, 712, 727

Prunier's restaurant 7n1, 780, 835

Pshibyshevsky, Boleslav, musicologist, Director of Moscow Conservatoire 882, 886, 966

Ptashka *see* Prokofieva, Carolina (Lina) Ivanovna; Prokofieva, Lina

Puccini, Giacomo 131, 147n1, 967; *Turandot* 598n3

Purging in Soviet cultural institutions 484n1, 866, 868, 868n4, 873, 881, 933

Pushkin, Alexander 66, 229n2, 279n, 293, 358, 462n1, 478n3, 492n1, 578n1, 728, 732, 999n2, 1031n5; WORKS 'Did You Hear?' lyric 670n4; *Eugene Onegin* 220, 259n1, 279n, 462n1; *The Tales of Belkin* 740n1, 843n1

Pyatigorsky, Gregor, cellist 996

Pythagoras 21

Rabaud, Henri, composer, Director of Paris Conservatoire 235, 1012–13

Rabinovich, Isaak, theatre designer 198, 437, 454, 466–8, 507, 534, 548, 872, 883, 1019, 1051, 1063

Rabinovich, violinist 904

RABIS, society of workers in the arts 471

Rabochy i teatr, Soviet theatre journal 297n2, 490n2, 546n4

Rachmaninoff, Natalya *see* Satina, Natalya

Rachmaninoff, Sergey (Serge)33 126–7, 263–4, 275, 312, 437n1, 519, 590, 649, 654, 748, 754, 899, 963; Brandukov, friendship with 540; Chaliapin, friendship with 540; Churayevka colony in America, pilgrimages to 94n2; companionship with SSP on transatlantic voyage 893; charity concert 894; patience games 893; Conius, Julius, family and musical connections with 141n4; SSP's encounter at Russian Musical Editions office 708–9; SSP's reaction to Rachmaninoff's Fourth Piano Concerto 327; cotton wool bandaging of damaged fingers 50; Dr Dahl, hypnosis treatment by 666; daughters' marriages 141n4, 211; health problems 220; Medtner, affection for and support of 46, 61, 163–4, 654; teases him 211, 937; Moscow, now almost forgotten in 122; Nina Koshetz, love affair with 97n1; dedicates songs to 672; Obukhov's *Book of Life*, attends performance of 331; Paichadze, friendship with 650; Paris debut recital 745–6, 754; platform demeanour 746; Paris gala recital 890; Kreisler paraphrase, SSP's dismay at 890; PIANIST, PREEMINENT POWERS AS 38, 502n2, 730, 930; patronising attitude to audiences 890; tendency to dryness in later performances 907; overtaken by Horowitz 991; Plevitskaya, overwhelmed by talent of 949n; Remizov, attends reading by 950; Russian Conservatoire of Paris, accepts Presidency of 1000n1; Russian Musical Editions; encounters between Rachmaninoff and Stravinsky at 702, 890; SSP meets Rachmaninoff at 711; Scriabin, memorial recitals in Moscow and St Petersburg; Alchevsky's anger 227; SSP's tactlessness 226; Semyon Frank, helps to flee Nazi Germany 132n2; SSP's music, general opinion of 131; attends Lina's recital 937–8; pretends to believe March from Op.12 composed by Hofmann 938; *Prodigal Son*, attends and purchases score 831, 833; Stravinsky's borrowings from Rachmaninoff 279, 619n, 739; leaves hall to avoid hearing *Les Noces* repeated 269; USSR, resists approaches to consider returning to 213; wealth, fees earned 220, 650; WORKS Cello Sonata 540,

666n2; Moment Musical (from Op.16) 890; paraphrase on Kreisler's 'Liebesfreud' 890; Piano Concerto No.2 666n2, 739; Piano Concerto No.3 818; Piano Concerto No.4 327, 770; Prelude (from Op.22) 890; Songs 672; 'Sud'ba', performed to Tolstoy 619n; Suite No.2 for 2 Pianos 437n1, 666n2; Symphony No.3 538n3; Trio Elégiaque No.2 141n4, 540; also mentioned 127n2, 129, 225n4, 304n, 318n1, 418n, 714n2, 1053n1

Radlov, Nikolay, artist and cartoonist 1032n1, 1033

Radlov, Sergey, theatre and opera producer 297n2, 490n2, 527–8, 530, 807, 874–5, 877, 879, 1049, 1069; Akopera production of *Love for Three Oranges* 479, 481n2, 487–91; proposes *Till Eulenspiegel* ballet to SSP 1049–50

Radlova, Anna, poet and Shakespeare translator, wife of Sergey Radlov 528, 875, 1028

Radlova, Nadezhda, wife of Nikolay Radlov 1049, 1070

Raikh, Zinaïda, actress, wife of Vsevolod Meyerhold 31n1, 320, 545, 546, 736–7, 741, 876, 880, 881, 886, 887, 954n1, 960, 966, 968–9, 1019, 1023, 1025; ciné film débacle 968

Raisky, Nazary, tenor and cultural administrator, Director of Moscow Conservatoire Great Hall and of Rosphil 418, 428

Rakovsky, Khristian, Soviet diplomat 202, 588

Rameau 183n1, 326n1, 687

Ranchev, Bulgarian tenor 124

Ranvid family, housekeepers at Bellevue dacha 105

RAPM *see* Russian Association of Proletarian Musicians

Rapoport, chief producer of Akopera 499–500

Ratti, Ambrogio Daniele Achille *see* Pius XI, Pope

Ravel Hotel, Monte Carlo 578

Ravel, Maurice 3n7: 4n5, 36n1, 39, 60, 61, 68, 71n, 175n, 176n3, 148, 149n2, 171n, 173n3, 181, 183n3, 184, 243n2, 298n1, 326n1, 329-31, 592, 599, 625, 663n1, 687n2, 699n3, 705, 730n, 764, 825, 891, 904n2, 1004, 1007, 1008n3; WORKS *Alborada del gracioso* 222n1; *Boléro* 4n5, 824, 824n5, 1008n3; Concerto for the Left Hand 676n1, 958n1, 997n1; *L'Enfant et les sortilèges* 148, 474; *Fanfare* (*L'Eventail de Jeanne*) 42n1, 598; *Pictures from an Exhibition* orchestration 832, 977; *Sonatine* 9; *Le Tombeau de Couperin* 222n1; *Tzigane* 177n1, 1038n1; *La Valse* 4n5, 1008n1; *Valses nobles et sentimentales* 173

Rayeskaya, Tatyana (Tanya), widow of Andrey Rayevsky 124, 141, 159n1, 406, 571, 888

Rayevskaya, Alyona, Shurik's daughter, SSP's niece 429, 448, 868, 877, 1021, 1044, 1045, 1051, 1068

Rayevskaya, Katya, SSP's Cousin *see* Ignatieva, Yekaterina

Rayevskaya, Nadezhda (Nadya), wife of Cousin Shurik 361, 428–9, 448, 452, 470, 514–15, 531, 543–4, 565, 570, 867, 867n1, 868, 876, 877n1, 882, 975n1, 1018, 1018n2, 1023, 1036

Rayevskaya, Sonya, Shurik's daughter, SSP's niece 429, 876, 877n1, 1021, 1068

Rayevskaya, Yekaterina (Katya), Shurik's daughter, SSP's niece 429, 877, 1044, 1068

Rayevskaya, Yekaterina (SSP's Aunt Katya) 155, 159, 174, 326, 361, 365n1, 398n2, 429, 452, 526n2, 531–2, 537, 543, 548, 563, 567, 570, 865, 866n2, 867

Rayevsky, Alexander (Cousin Shurik) 155, 159, 428–9, 448, 452, 475, 507, 535–6, 541, 565, 568, 868, 882, 933n2, 1018n2, 1021, 1023, 1034, 1036, 1044, 1054; arrest and imprisonment 155n4, 361; encounter with Dutchman in Butyrka Prison 975–6; stoical attitude to misfortune 1019 1025–6

Rayevsky, Alexander (Sashka), son of Andrey and Tanya Rayevsky 159, 164, 406

Razumovsky, Serge, playwright and critic, Director of Moscow Association of Dramatic Writers and Composers 373, 474–5, 507, 549

Réamur temperature 411n1, 519n3

Reberg family 550n3, 552

Red Arrow, express night train Moscow-Leningrad 546, 1027, 1046, 1049, 1071

Reed, London manager of Duo-Art 669

Reiner, Fritz, conductor 59n2, 302, 396

Mrs Reis, Chairman of New York League of Composers 906

Remarque, Erich Maria, novelist 205n3

Remizov, Alexey, Modernist writer, *Alaley and Leila* 24, 37, 39, 69n2, 607n1, 695, 950

Renaissance émigré newspaper *see Vozrozhdenie*

Renoir, Pierre-Auguste, artist 317n3, 793

Respighi, Ottorino, composer, *The Pines of Rome* 275, 287–8, 316

Reuter, Director of Riga Opera 409

Revel *see* Tallinn

La Revue musicale 23n1, 23n2, 347

RGALI *see* Russian State Archive of Literature and Art

Rhené-Bâton, conductor

Rieti, Vittorio, composer 174, 288, 336, 578, 696, 995, 997; orchestration of SSP's Gavotte, Op.32 No.3 1011; pianist in *Les Noces* 326; WORKS *Le Bal* 801, 827–8, 834, 835–6; *Barabau* 317; *Sinfonietta* 995

Riga 15, 27, 46, 300, 316, 347, 385, 407–10, 416, 449, 480n2, 566, 892; Riga Opera 408, 409

Rimsky-Korsakov, Andrey, music critic and journalist, son of the composer 6, 62n2, 495, 510–11, 587

Rimsky-Korsakov, Nikolay Andreyevich: aphorism 'some cuts make a work longer' 810; conducts Glazunov's Symphony No.1 at Glazunov's 25th jubilee 1000; metronome speeds, ability to estimate 454; persuaded Musorgsky that his orchestration was deficient 720; quadrangularity 717; Songs orchestrated by composer 498; sung by Lina 658; sung by Yurevskaya 124; SSP's dream about 97; WORKS *Boris Godunov*, orchestration of 56, 137, 184n3, 456, 467n2, 565n1, 875n, 999n2;

Capriccio Espagnol 573n1; *Christmas Eve* 467n2, 723, 815m; *Chronicle of My Musical Life* 267; *From Homer* 619n; *The Golden Cockerel* 587; *Kashchey the Immortal* 691; *Khovanshchina*, completion of 49, 64, 231, 456n1, 619; *The Legend of the Invisible City of Kitezh and the Maiden Fevronia* 76, 451n2, 504, 565n1, 776n3; 'Battle of Kerzhenets' 1025; *May Night* 409; *Prince Igor*, completion of 61n1, 68n3, 285, 467n2, 662, 776n3, 806; *Pskovityanka* 525n3, 710, 712, 1019; *Sadko* 424, 426, 682, 902, 911, 936; *Sheherazade* 7; influence of traditional Georgian and Persian music 1061; *The Snow Maiden* 121, 546, 652, 775; *Tsar Saltan* 9, 747; *Vera Sheloga* 525, 1019; also mentioned 46n3, 62n2, 92n, 172n4, 172n5, 191n1, 375, 423n1, 495n2, 495n3, 495n4, 639

Ringwall, Rudolf, Assistant Conductor of Cleveland Orchestra 900

Roblin, Louise, SSP's childhood French governess 141

Rodchenko, Alexander, artist 452n2

Rodzinski, Artur, conductor 921, 926

Roediger, hostess in Frankfurt 280

Roerich, George 246

Roerich, Nikolay, artist and author 24, 94, 246-7, 360 *Heart of Asia* 246n3

Rokhlin, Yakov, chess master 1033

Roland-Manuel, Alexis 42n2, 183, 302; co-authorship of Stravinsky's *The Poetics of Music* 183n3; *Histoire de la musique* 636

Romanov, Alexander Mikhailovich, Grand Duke 903

Romanov, Boris, choreographer 38, 44n1, 152n3, 161, 16n2, 161n3, 187, 323, 332; appointed to La Scala, interested in *Chout* 332, 334; BALLET COMMISSION: 63, 67, 72-3, 75, 78, 107, 110-11, 113-14; Introduction (Overture) added 194-5, 200-1, 207, 210; Diaghilev requests for *The Steel Step* 579, 581; recycled into *Divertissement* 843n3; *Matelote* added 201, 213; recycled into *Divertissement* 843n3; possibility of revival 595; simultaneously conceived as chamber music (Quintet) 78, 148, 161; *Trapèze* title agreed for ballet 220; Schubert Waltzes version for two pianos commissioned as a ballet score 194-5, 197

Romanov, Konstantin Konstantinovich, Grand Duke 903

Rome Opera House *see* Costanzi Theatre, Rome

Rosenberg, Lev *see* Bakst, Léon

Rosenfeld, Maurice, music critic of *Chicago Daily News* 938

Rosenstein, Yakov, cellist 552

Rosing, Vladimir 918, 929, 935, 939; *Three Oranges* production for New York City Center 919n1

Roslavets, Nikolay, composer 133, 815, 1056

Rosphil, subsequently Sovphil, eventually Mosphil 207, 209, 212, 308, 472, 885, 1035, 1052

Rossi, Mario, conductor 283-5

Rossiiskaya Filarmonia (Russian Philharmonia) *see* Rosphil

Rossini, Gioacchino, composer: *The Barber of Seville* 573n1, 595n; *L'Italiana in Algeri* 827

Rostand, Edmond, playwright 598n3, 599

Rostov-on-Don 115, 212, 1057

Roth String Quartet 989, 1021

Rothschild, Baron Robert 184, 323, 327, 336, 676, 712

Rouault, Georges, artist 665n1, 792n; *Prodigal Son* designs 792-3, 794, 795, 801-2, 806, 808, 827-9, 831

Rouché, Jacques, Director of Paris Opéra 9, 60, 590-1, 919, 964-5, 1006n1, 1037, 1039

Roussel, Albert, composer 3n7, 39, 42, 173, 181, 183n3, 302, 587, 596, 712, 788; Suite in F 587, 596; Piano Concerto 709

Rovinsky, Dmitry, historian and collector of Russian popular art 579, 580

ROVS *see* Combined Russian Military Union, Paris

Royan 585, 599-600, 606, 608-10, 613, 615, 617-9, 621, 626, 629, 634, 638, 644-7

Rozenel, Natalya, silent cinema actress, wife of Anatoly Lunacharsky 425-6

Rubinin, Yevgeny, official in Ministry of Foreign Affairs 1020, 1023, 1050, 1051

Rubinstein, Anton, composer and pianist, founder of St Petersburg Conservatoire 303, 670n4, 764

Rubinstein, Arthur, pianist 128, 184, 592, 594, 764, 775, 780-1, 831, 986, 1019; fiancée 1014; March from *Three Oranges* 1006; *Petrushka* 8, 72; Rondo, Op.52 No.2 dedicated to him 1006

Rubinstein, Ida, actress, dancer and theatrical impresario 4n5, 5, 6, 193, 737, 747, 824; *The Idiot* 150; *Juditha* long-drawn out and inconclusive negotiations for ballet to a libretto by Demasy 6-7, 60, 77, 151, 153, 185, 188, 197, 200, 963; *Scythian Suite*: inconclusive negotiations for ballet 153-4, 158, 185, 187, 191, 231; *Semiramide*: inconclusive negotiations for ballet to libretto by Valéry 963-4, 1006-8, 1015, 1016; *Baiser de la Fée* 717, 738, 797; *Boléro* 824; *Fedra* 701n3; *Sémiramis*, ballet by Honegger 1008n1

Rudavskaya, Antonina, Conservatoire friend 496, 511, 526

Rudnev, Yevgeny, former aviator and car engineer 574-7, 650, 652, 676

Rue Charles Dickens, SSP's residence in Paris 29n3, 31

Rue Troyon, SSP's residence in Paris 386-7, 405

Rühlmann, Frans, conductor in Brussels 3n7, 110

Rumanov, Mikhail, husband of Ariadna Nikolskaya 923

Russian Association of Proletarian Musicians (RAPM) 133n1, 413n3, 430n5, 467n3, 690n1, 908n1, 993n1, 993n2, 1018, 1020n4, 1022n5, 1029n1, 1035n4, 1050

Russian Civil War 23n4, 33n4, 47n2, 88n, 205n2,

216n2, 217n1, 287n, 292n, 294n3, 322n1, 387n2, 466n1, 509, 517n2, 642n1, 658n1, 876n1, 877, 944n, 949n, 1049; Ice Campaign 387
Russian Conservatoire of Paris 136, 139, 141, 304n, 753n1, 1000
Russian Easter 817
Russian Musical Editions 39, 61, 344; Asafyev's book, problems with publication of 218, 267, 309, 321, 328, 337, 338; general direction and underwriting of 105–6, 109; G.Schirmer as US representatives of 934; 'legitimate' and 'illegitimate' composers 3, 972; M.P.Beliaieff Editions, contemplated acquisition of 627; Myaskovsky Songs, agreement to publish 835; Oeberg, Managing Director 189–90, 192; death of 236, 238; Oxford University Press, proposed merger with 40; Paichadze, appointment of as Managing Director 238, 259, 364; profits boosted by Koussevitzky's emphasis on new music 698; royalty payments compared with those of Muzsektor 506–7; SSP signs contract with 44; SSP's complaints about slowness to publish 957
Russian Orthodox Church 21n2: 172n5, 817, 860; Old Believers 633; schism in 637; SSP's attitude to 17
Ruzskaya, Irina (Ira) 117
Ruzskaya, Tatyana (Tanya) 117n, 698
Ruzsky, Nikolay Pavlovich, friend from St Petersburg, amateur cellist, dedicatee of *Ballade* 117n, 173, 633, 697–8
Ryabushinskaya, Tatyana, ballerina, *see also* 'Baby Ballerinas'
Rykov, Alexey, Soviet Head of State 293, 564–5

Sabaneyev, Leonid, music critic and biographer 5n1: 392-3, 690n1, 713, 785; article praising *Fiery Angel* 730; interviews Stravinsky 619n1; SSP meets in Paris 306–7, 309–10; WORKS *Scriabin* 5, 5n1, 278; *Three Russian Composers* 29n4, 329n1, 335n1; *Reminiscences of Scriabin* 5n1
Sablino, SSP's retreat near Petrograd 477, 508
Safonov, Vasily, conductor, Rector of Moscow Conservatoire 38n3, 129n3, 246, 539n3
St Basil's Cathedral, Moscow 540
St Paul, Minnesota 250–1
St Petersburg Conservatoire *see* Leningrad Conservatoire
St Vladimir, hilltop bronze statue in Kiev 562
Saint-Rome, pianist 732
Saint-Saëns, Camille 177n: 699n3, 775, Piano Concerto No.2 775; *Samson et Dalila* 680; *The Swan* 327n2
Salle Pleyel, Paris 663, 664n2, 776n1, 780n1, 892, 984–5
Salon d'automne, Paris, annual art exhibition 665
Salt Lake, Utah 256
Salter, Norbert, impresario in Germany 105, 123

Samarkand, possible tour to
'Samarkand' restaurant, Paris 639, 649, 668, 701n2
Samaroff, Olga, pianist, music publicist, wife of Leopold Stokowski 265n3, 272, 277
Saminsky, Lazar, conductor 263, 900
Samoilenko, Boris Nikolayevich, Paris friend 3n1; entertains Monsignor 667–8; entertains Mayakovsky 743–4, 804–5; New Year celebrations 3, 988; portrait of Alexander Krivoshein on wall 714, 980; social meetings *passim*; SSP visits their former house in Moscow 543
Samoilovich, Rudolf, geologist and Arctic explorer 788, *see also* Nobile, North Pole Expedition
San Francisco 252, 254–5, 337, 390, 653, 865n1, 923–6
San Martino, Count 196, 288, 677
Santa Barbara, California 923–4
Saradzhev, Konstantin, conductor 416–17, 442, 472–3, 501, 531, 533–4, 539, 564–5, 567, 787–9, 867, 885–7, 1023, 1045, 1051
Saradzhev, Konstantin Konstantinovich (Kotik), bell composer 472–3
Sasha-Yasha *see* Yakovlev, Alexander
Satie, Erik 62n2, 149n2, 312, 313n, 321n2, 326n1, 378n1, 699n3, 783n2, *Mercure* 591
Satina, Natalya, Rachmaninoff's wife 263n5, 275, 937; poor relations in Penza 326
Sats, Natalya, Children's Theatre director 430n2
Sauguet, Henri 321n1: 828, 994n2, 997, 1002, 1011, 1014, 1050, WORKS *La Chatte* 321n1, 589, 680; *David* 747, 824; *Les Forains* (*The Strolling Players*) 321n1
Sausalito, California 924
Saussine, Renée de, violinist 403
Savich, Vladimir, conductor 274, 301–2, 591, 593, 705, 707n1
Schaad, Hermann, Managing Director of Duo Art 244, 717n4
Schalk, Franz, conductor 61
Schefner, programme note writer for Symphony No.3 823–6
Schelling, Ernest, conductor 265
Schillinger, Joseph, composer and teacher 517
G. Schirmer, Inc, New York music publishers 190n1, 934
Schloezer, Boris de, music critic and writer 23, 25, 30, 36, 38, 39, 43, 84, 129, 138, 165n1, 298, 322, 753n1, 754n1, 766
Schmidt, Dr, host in Chicago 299, 928
Schmidthof, Maximilian, Conservatoire friend 47, 498n2, 550n3, 632n1, 713n2, 872n2
Schmidthof, Yekaterina (Katya) 484, 494, 508, 511, 513, 530, 534, 875
Schmitt, Florent 42, 60, 704n2, 710, 776, 890, 1002n2; founder-member of 'Triton' chamber music society 997n2; member of 'Les Apaches' group 173n3; WORKS *L'Eventail de Jeanne* 42n1; *Psalm 47* 596; *La Tragédie de Salomé* 38n2

Schmitz, E.Robert, pianist and new music promoter 243n2, 254, 318, 975; performs Myaskovsky *Caprices* 255, 306; SSP recommends to VOKS 1035
Schmitz, Mrs, organiser of 'Pro Music' concert society 243, 249, 703
Schmuller, Alexander, conductor 234, 891n2
Schoenberg, Arnold 7n3: 69n, 127n, 298, 489, 566n2, 670n4, 913 WORKS *Chamber Symphony* (arr. Berg) 677; *Five Orchestral Pieces* 175; *Kaiserwalzer* (arrangement of Strauss Waltzes) 677; Wind Quintet 298
Schopenhauer, Arthur, philosopher 618, 692, 699n2
Schroeder piano, Rubinstein Competition prize 522
Schubert, Alexander von, husband of Nina Koshetz 106, 137, 141, 159, 300, 362–3, 661, 664, 672, 682, 694, 701, 765, 777–8, 784, 791, 844–5, 912
Schubert, Marochka, daughter of Nina Koshetz 106, 362–3, 664, 912
Schumann, Robert 31n2, 138, 165, 346, 704n1, 797; Symphony No.3 772
Scriabin, Alexander 5, 23n2, 44n1, 127n2, 133n1, 141n4, 171n1, 225n2, 293n2, 306n2, 310, 335n1, 430n1, 431, 437n1, 452, 674, 682, 704, 704n1, 741, 766, 770, 818n1, 871, 879n1, 973n1; conflict with Koussevitzkys 310; death, Stravinsky's remorse 858; WORKS *Poème de l'extase* 165–6, 472; Sonata No.2 10; Sonata No.5 226–7; Sonata No.9 142; Symphony No.2 121; Symphony No.3 (*Divine Poem*) 260
Scriabina, Ariadna 322, 766
Scriabina, Yelena 766
Sebezh, Latvia-USSR border post 412
Sebryakov, Pavel 559
Sebryakov, Sergey (Seryozha) 433, 448, 559, 1033n4
Sebryakova, Dr Tatyana 433n2, 559
Secret Police 439n1, 492n2, 537
Seghers, Anna, novelist; *The Revolt of the Fishermen* 1046
Segovia, Andres, guitarist 41n1, 181n3, 562
Selvinsky, Ilya; *Army Commander Two* 877
Semyonovna, Marina, ballerina 462n2, 1024, 1051, 1070n2, 1072
Serafin, Tullio, conductor 901-2, 911, 912, 916, 929, 934-5, 938–9
'Serapion Brothers', bohemian group of writers in Petrograd in the early 1920s 294n
Sérénade, contemporary chamber music presenting organisation, *see also* Giraud, Yvonne
The Sermon on the Mount 92
Sert, José Maria, artist and designer 68, 184n1, 1007, 1015
Sert, Misia, Paris hostess and patron of the arts 68, 184n4
Sèvres 1, 3–4, 57, 65, 197, 527, 661
Sezhenskaya, Shura 441, 443, 564
Sezhensky, Konstantin (Kostya) 441–2, 443–4

Shakhovskaya, Princess Dagmara 6, 9, 42, 138 *see also* Balmont
Shakhovskaya, Princess, mother of Natalya Nabokov 813
Shalonov, acquaintance invited to *Prodigal Son*
Shang-hai *see* Shanghai
Shanghai 59n2, 175, 751–2; Communist Uprising 567–8; Zakharov relocates to 768, 793, 979
Shaporin, Yury 526: 1049, *The Decembrists* 526n3; *The Flea* 527n1
Shashlyk 32, 1058
Shatsky, Stanislav, Director of Moscow Conservatoire 1026
Shchedrin, Rodion 526n3: *Carmen-Suite* 262n1; *The Little Hump-backed Horse* 556n1
Shcherbachov, Vladimir 477–81, 484, 526n1, 528, 531, 649, 651, 657, 690n1, 1027; arranges composers' evening 516–19; close ally of Asafyev 478; WORKS *Procession* 477n2; *Sinfonietta* 519, 651–2
Shebalin, Vissarion, composer, Rector of Moscow Conservatoire 538n3, 539n2, 540, 785, 867, 876, 879, 954n1,1018, 1026, 1036, 1043, 1045n3; WORKS Symphony No.1 (1926) 540, 1050
Shenshin, Alexander, composer 539, 1026; *Dionysius* 1045n1
Sheremetiev, Count Nikolay 505, 1070
Shestov, Lev, philosopher 165
Shevchenko Theatre *see* Kiev Opera House
Shipovich, Ukrainian Jewish composer, *The Little Hump-backed Horse* 556
Shirinsky, Sergey, cellist, member of Beethoven Quartet 543, 547
Shirinsky, Vasily, violinist, member of Beethoven Quartet 543, 998, 1022
Shkafer, Vasili, Chief Producer of Akopera 695; *Forty Years on the Russian Stage* 695n1
Shklovsky, Viktor, literary critic 425n2, 547
Shmelyov, Ivan, novelist and short story writer 24
Shostakovich, Dmitry 46n3, 76n4, 172n4, 266n1, 472n2, 495n2, 517, 539n2, 720, 766n, 785, 879n, 905n2, 908, 1020n4, 1028n1, 1046; Beethoven Quartet, Moscow 543n1; Chopin Competition 419n2; 'Lamm Circle' 538n3; Sollertinsky, close bond with 1030n2; Tukhachevsky, association with 879n; Yavorsky, early influence of 305n3; Zhdanov Decree 1045n3; support from Shcherbachov 477n2; denunciation by Asafyev 170n2; denunciation by Goldenweiser 437n1; WORKS *The Bedbug* 804n3; Suite from *Bolt* 1050; Cello Sonata 884n2; *The Golden Mountains*, film score 1008; *Khovanshchina*, orchestration 49n1; *Lady Macbeth of Mtsensk*; *Pravda* editorial 449n, 879n, 882n2, 884n2, 1029n1, 1045n3; *The Nose* 874; Piano Concerto No.2 502n1; Piano Sonata No.1 517–18, 729; Piano Trio No.2 1030n2; Symphony No.1 403n1; Symphony No.4 1029n1; Twenty-

INDEX 1119

Four Preludes for Piano 1050n1
Shteiman, Mikhail, conductor 550, 806, 818
Shtember, Nikolay (Koko), pianist, Conservatoire friend 940
Shubert, Pavel, pianist 408–9
Shukhaev, Vasili, artist 714, 1014, 1038; portrait of SSP 998–9
Shumov, photographer in Paris 233
Shurik *see* Rayevsky, Alexander (Cousin Shurik)
Shvartz, Lev, post-graduate composition student 1054
Sidorov, Kolya, son of Tatyana Bashkirova-Yakhontova 953, 955, 959, 973
Siena 289, 290, 687
Sigal, doctor in Odessa 561
Sikar, visa official in the French Ministry of Interior
Singer, Winaretta *see* Polignac, Princesse de
Siohan, Robert, composer and conductor 985; Concerts Siohan 985n1
Sirota, Peter, Berlin artist manager 153
Slavina, Maria, mezzo soprano 25
Slawinsky, Tadeusz, dancer 14n3, 913
Slonimsky, Nicolas 260: 918n1, *Baker's Dictionary of Musicians* 260n2; *Lectionary of Music* 260n2; *Lexicon of Musical Invective* 260n2; *Perfect Pitch* 260n2
Smallens, Alexander, conductor 97, 906, 910, 1052
Smetsky family, Sukhum 442
Smirnov, Dmitry, tenor 480
Smirnov, Professor Alexander, literary critic and translator 497
Smirnova, Yelena, ballerina, wife of Boris Romanov 161
Smith, Thomas Max, foreign music correspondent of *New York Times* 929–30
Smolich, Nikolay, Chief Producer of Bolshoy Theatre 1071–2
Smyth, Dame Ethel, composer 149n2, 779
Sobinov, Leonid, tenor 481n2, 949n, 1066
Socialist Realism 31n1, 198n2, 321n1, 425n2, 430n5, 869n2, 1032n2, 1071n3, 1022n5
Société des auteurs *see* Paris, Société des auteurs
Society for Cultural Relations with Foreign Countries *see* VOKS
Soetens, Robert, violinist, dedicatee of SSP's Second Violin Concerto 997n2, 1038–9
Sofronitsky, Vladimir, pianist 704, 716, 766, 767, 769, 780–1, 785, 788–90, 799, 833
Sokol, youth gymnastics society 790
Sokoloff, Nikolay, conductor of Cleveland Orchestra 900
Sokolov, Nikolay, composer and teacher 526n3
Sokolov, Vladislav, post-graduate composition student 1052
Sokolova, Lydia, ballerina 116n1, *Dancing for Diaghilev* 317n1

Sollertinsky, Ivan, Artistic Director of the Leningrad Philharmonia 1030
Sologub, Fyodor, poet 674, 801n1; *Vanka the Steward and the Page Jehan* 732n
Somov, Konstantin, artist 318–19, 325, 714
Sontsovka, SSP's birthplace in Ukraine 252, 390n1, 427n3, 525n1, 550n3, 552, 926
Sorin, Savely, society portrait painter 911
Sosnovsky, Lev, journalist and Communist propagandist 470, 501
Souvtchinsky, Pierre *see* Suvchinsky, Pyotr
Soviet Consulate in Paris 395, 403
Sovietskii Kompozitor, publishing house of the USSR Composer's Union 405n, 423n1
Sovphil, All-Union USSR Philharmonia *see* Rosphil
Spaak, Paul, Intendant of Théâtre de la Monnaie in Brussels 711, 799, 809–13, 818, 836, 852–3, 862, 889
Spalding, editor of *Five Poems of Anna Akhmatova* 146
Spessitseva, Olga, ballerina 1010n2
Spitzer, Leona 19
Srednyaya Kiselyovka, district of Moscow 454
Städtische Oper *see* Deutsche Oper, Berlin
Stahl, Alexey, lawyer, Public Prosecutor of the Provisional Government 4, 7, 9–10, 21, 24–5, 27, 32–3, 35, 39, 41–3, 51, 137, 197–8, 298, 302–3, 306, 314, 650–1, 731, 771, 842, 890; falls ill 854–5, 862; quarrel 35, 45–7, 49
Stalin, Iosif Vissarionovich 105n2, 198n2, 205n1, 207n2, 292n, 293n1, 414n, 422n, 430n5, 435n1, 435n2, 436n1, 437n2, 439n1, 449n, 451n, 462n1, 462n2, 466n, 470n, 480n2, 492n2, 519n2, 527n1, 535n2, 566n2, 863n, 879n, 882n2, 883n3, 927n3, 944n, 951n1, 984n1, 993n1, 1024n1, 1024n4, 1057n2, 1060n3, 1062n2, 1070n2; personal near-encounters 789, 1024–5, 1066
Stanchev, Christiu *see* Rakovsky, Khristian
Stanford, Sir Charles Villiers 528n1
Stanislavsky, Konstantin, theatre director, founder of Moscow Art Theatre 138n1, 449, 455, 535, 543, 567
Stanislavsky Opera Studio, Moscow 455
Staroselsky, bridge partner 991
Steinberg, Maximilian, composer and teacher of music theory 172, 175, 191, 477n2, 495, 498n2, 520, 526n2, 640n2, 785n2, 838n1, 1010n1, 1029
Steinert, bridge partner 993, 1007
Steinway and Sons, New York 129, 226, 243, 268, 276, 277n1, 669, 894, 897
Steuermann, Eduard, pianist 677
Stock, Frederick, Music Director of Chicago Symphony 337n1, 927, 1035, 1041
Stockholm Concert Society 223–8
Stokowski, Leopold, conductor 20, 31, 168n2, 248–9, 265n3, 269, 272, 337n1, 393, 677n3, 712–13, 716, 819, 824n5, 842, 906, 921, 935, 956, 958–9, 976
Stoleshnikov Hotel Moscow 886

Stolyarov, Grigory, violinist, conductor, Director of Odessa Conservatoire 561
Stothart, Herbert, librettist; *Rose Marie* 737n1
Straram, Walter, conductor 10n4, 173, 178, 278, 298, 301–2, 343, 347, 371, 687–8, 690, 700, 772, 808, 824
Strasbourg 76, 232, 970, 973
Strauss, Johann; Waltzes, arranged Schoenberg 677
Strauss, Richard 33, 61n3, 280n1, 281, 528, 636n2, 792; WORKS *Also sprach Zarathustra* 772; *Ariadne auf Naxos* 911n3; *Le Bourgeois Gentilhomme* 700; *Elektra* 379n1; *Josephslegende* 38n2, 776n3; *Panathanäenzug* 958n2; *Parergon on Sinfonia Domestica* 958n2; *Rosenkavalier* 184n3; *Salome* 255n1; *Till Eulenspiegel* 315–16
Stravinsky, Fyodor (Theodore) (Fedya), Stravinsky's elder son 578, 578n2, 854, 856
Stravinsky, Igor 5, 45, 51, 71n2, 79, 163, 177, 185, 211, 224, 232, 238, 276, 279, 281, 312, 335, 336, 392, 406, 496, 572, 580, 598, 640n2, 649, 651, 663n1, 668–9, 687, 695, 698, 727, 756, 773, 780, 807, 832, 844, 891, 957, 984, 986, 1004, 1007, 1011; 50th birthday 1005, 1011; Annecy, summers in 717, 720, 854; SSP visits 858–9; anti-semitism 855, 984, 986; erroneously blacklisted in Germany as Jewish by Kampferbund 1043; *Les Apaches* group, member of 173n3; Asafyev, article by 722; Brahms, unexplained interest in 704; cars, interest in 578, 587, 729, 856; conductor, activity as 7, 35, 176, 589, 592, 738, 755, 790–1, 806; considers Diaghilev lacked real understanding of music 856–7; Diaghilev's death, reaction to 858–9; RELATIONS WITH DIAGHILEV: close 150, 605, 605n1; contact avoided in London 857; estranged 745, 779, 820, 830, 832, 849; relations with Dukelsky 149, 175, 223, 375, 592, 915; food, interest in 611, 717, 797, 856; Glazunov, encounter with 838; Kokhno's adulation of Stravinsky 682, 756; composers endorsed for Russian Musical Editions 973; visits Koussevitzky 716–17; relations with Lourié 832; Markevich, opinion of 764, 764n1; son's gibe about names 891; Monteux's general hostility towards Stravinsky 892; offended by Nabokov's article 890–1, 893; relations with 691, 706, 712, 950; offends SSP at Nikitina's reception 1011–12, 1014; Norton Lectures at Harvard University 183n3; opera, views on 13; orchestra parts; importance of the composer correcting 77; Paris Opéra orchestral musicians 'senators' 1037; PIANIST, ACTIVITY as 7, 45–6, 48–9, 50, 55–6, 60, 176, 321, 889, 985; SSP's sarcastic assessment of 131, 165; pianola; attraction to 597, 664, 783; SSP, attitude to as composer 66, 116, 180, 375, 587–8; OPINIONS OF: *Classical* Symphony 180; Piano Concerto No.3 375; Piano Concerto No.5 1038; *Prodigal Son* 792, 794–5, 796–7, 828–31; *Sinfonietta* 1038; *The Steel Step* 592, 594, 599, 638, 792; Symphony No.2 172; Violin Concerto 792, 797, 1038; SSP'S GENERAL OPINION OF STRAVINSKY'S MUSIC 84, 142, 682, 790: acknowledges Stravinsky's greater fame and reputation 974; critical of neo-baroque influence 56, 132, 180; PERSONAL RELATIONS WITH SSP 7, 224, 233, 310, 331, 375, 578–9, 664, 676, 690, 738, 745; affection for children 717, 790; drives over to visit at Culoz 854–6; support over Kokhno legal action 839–40; sympathy over car accident 891; teases with atheism 830; SSP suspects Stravinsky of intriguing against him with Diaghilev 182–3; Monteux concurs 817, 823–4; Stravinsky denies 891; Rachmaninoff, borrowings from 279, 619n, 739; Rachmaninoff, encounter with 702, 705, 739; religious observance 797; disparages Schloezer 129; Schmuller's gibe 891; low opinion of Scriabin 260; sorrow at his death 858; Les Six, tolerant attitude to 84, 175; Sudeikin's account of confrontation over wife's adultery with Stravinsky 907; SUVCHINSKY'S UNDERSTANDING of Stravinsky's problems with composition 638, 639, 643, 728, 739; objects to his materialism 729; conservatism of Stravinsky's politics 739; Suvchinsky's relations with 62n2, 66, 70; disillusioned 739, 741, 952; analysis of Stravinsky's religious faith 637–8, 642–3, 739; Tansman, friendship with 181n3; writes biography 181n3; Tcherepnin, influence on 108; Villa des Roses, Nice 803n1; WORKS *Apollon musagète* 629, 629n2, 652, 711–12, 722, 747, 756, 756n1, 806, 917, Diaghilev's cuts in 839, 839n1, 856; *Le Baiser de la Fée* 728, 738, 739, 742, 747, 756, 770, 963; *Capriccio* for piano and orchestra 798, 802, 819, 830, 858–9, 890–1, ignored by Ravel 891; *Le Chant du Rossignol* 38n1, 178, 223; *Chroniques de ma vie* 131n1, 223n1; Concerto for piano and wind instruments 7, 48–9, 50, 55–6, 60–1, 62, 176, 700, 720n3; *Duo Concertant* 1011, 1038; *Feu d'artifice* 331; *The Firebird* 35, 589, 597; *L'histoire du soldat* 45, 790; *Khovanshchina*, new ending for 49n; *Mavra* 66, 123n5, 358; *Les Noces* 58, 71, 269, 709; Octet 7, 790; *Oedipus Rex* 375, 580–1, 590, 599, 619n1; *Perséphone* 1008n1; *Petrushka* 35, 176; version for solo piano 8, 52, 72, 306; Piano Sonata 180n, 184, 790; *Pulcinella* 756, 985; version for violin and piano 168, 192; *Ragtime* 176; *The Rake's Progress* 1005n4; *Le renard* 381n3, 801, 829, 830; *The Rite of Spring* 24n3, 42n3, 71, 176, 754; *Le Rossignol* 38n1, 61, 215, 587; 'Rozyanka' ('Sundew') (*Two Songs to lyrics by Gorodetsky* No.2) 232; *Serenade* 279, 352–3, 358, 790; *Suite Italienne*; for cello and piano 192n1; for violin and piano 192n1, 1011, 1038; Suites Nos.1 and 2 685; Symphonies of Wind Instruments 700; *Symphony of Psalms* 942–3, 950, 983; Violin Concerto 1039; also mentioned 3n7, 5n1, 20, 28n3, 29n4, 36n1, 76n4, 124n2, 126n2, 131, 149n2, 165, 173n2, 174n1, 260n2, 306n2, 326n1, 341n1, 378n1, 388n2, 409n2, 472n2, 482,1, 495n3, 519n2, 685n1, 753n, 904n2, 905n2

Stravinsky, Lyudmila, Stravinsky's daughter 578n2
Stravinsky, Milena, Stravinsky's daughter 578n2
Stravinsky, Svyatoslav (Soulima), Stravinsky's younger son 578n2, 854, 856, 891
Stravinsky, Yekaterina (Katya), Stravinsky's wife
Strohbach, Hans, opera producer 60n1, 125, 144n2, 379
Struve, Lidia, Conservatoire friend 1029–32
Struve, Nikolay, Managing Director of Russian Musical Editions 8n4
Sudeikin, Sergey, artist and designer 46, 738, 900, 901–2, 907, 911–12, 915–18, 920, 929, 934, 939
Sudeikina, Vera, actress, dancer, artist, wife first of Sergey Sudeikin and later of Igor Stravinsky 46, 52, 738, 747, 796, 832, 907, 986
Suk, Vaclav, conductor 535
Sukharev Square, Moscow 205
Sukhovo-Kobylin, Alexander, *Krechinsky's Wedding* 1067n3
Suvchinsky, Pyotr Petrovich 62–3, 65, 71, 124n2, 151, 164, 175, 192, 229, 379, 423, 450, 651, 697, 701, 703, 986, 1038; Asafyev, former ally in editorial control of music journals in St Petersburg 495n3, 495n4, 496, 496n1; reunion in Paris 728; Bassianos, connection with 389, 587; Bellevue, resides in 107, 123, 174; Berlin, SSP meets in 123–4; Cecilia Hansen, opinion of 171–2; Chaliapin, relationship with 64, 954; Clamart, moves to 331, 599; contemplates revisiting USSR 951; correspondence to and from USSR goes astray 423; Diaghilev; brings news of death to SSP in Culoz 856; commissions article on 671; CONTRIBUTION TO URSIGNOL/STEEL STEP conception 185–6, 189, 198–9, 202–3, 211, 389, 644; introduces Ehrenburg 199; religious feelings 859–60; Dukelsky, opinion of 73, 165, 334, 712, 728–9; EURASIANISM, promotion of as historical, political and social ideal 62–3, 133, 182, 188, 388, 647, 784, 857–8; *Eurasia* journal, launches and edits 738–9, 757; Lourié article on *Prodigal Son* 838–9; prominent Eurasianists, connections with 132; TREST overtures, healthy suspicion of 784n, 857–8; European composers, opinions of; Chabrier 70; Honegger 165; Tansman 589; Glazunov, allays suspicion of conspiracy to eject him from Directorship of Conservatoire 857; *Golden Mountains* film watched together 1008; Gorky, correspondence with 951; Koshetz, disapproval of her repertoire 672–3; marriage to Guchkova 126–7, 132, 133, 182, 211, 229–30; dislike of her father 631–3, 638; marriage to Karsavina 125–6, 153; Medtner, opinion of 651; Meyerholds, dines with 741; Mirsky, takes SSP to see 641–3; Obukhov's *Book of Life*, opinion of 330; Polignac, Princesse de, visit to 673; Rabinovich, approves of 437, 454; REFLECTIONS ON ATHEISM 860; Christian Science 124; advocates idleness 64; Marx 858; theology 124, 164, 859, 860; unreality of evil 860–1; Rouault; dines with 808; opinion of 806; 'Samarkand' restaurant, reports existence of 639, 645, 980; Shestov, admirer of 165; singing; fine tenor voice 860, 951; vocal technique, interested in 857; REACTION TO SSP's MUSIC; *Choses en soi* 729; *Divertissement* 860; *Fiery Angel* 712, 715, 741; pianism 124; Piano Sonata No.3 446; Piano Sonata No.5 62, 643; *Prodigal Son* 741, 757, 784, 796; *Sinfonietta* (revised version) 860; *The Steel Step* 741; String Quartet No.1 973; Symphony No.2 171–2, 305, 741; Symphony No.3 825, 826; Symphony No.4 860, 984; Suite from *Three Oranges* 230; special relationship with SSP 166; advises not severing relations with USSR 806; attends *Steel Step* premiere 594; dissuades from Remizov opera project 24n3, 607n1; objects to participation in émigré event 334; snubbed by SSP 1003; stays with SSP in St Palais 634, 637–44; and Culoz 856–61; takes power of attorney over Mariinsky Theatre *Gambler* contract 210n, 530n; unsuccessful in rescuing belongings from St Petersburg apartment 231n2; suggests commissioning article about SSP 715; Stravinsky; analysis of his religious feelings 637–8; contributes to his Eliot Norton lectures at Harvard University 183n3; opinion of Stravinsky's music, fluctuating but ultimately disillusioned 739, 740, 741, 952; *Apollon musagète* 756; *Baiser de la fée* 739, 756; *Capriccio* for piano and orchestra 891; his phobias as a composer 638, 639, 643, 728; Stravinsky's jealousy over Markevich, 952; objects to Stravinsky's materialism 729; visits at Annecy with SSP 858–60
Suvorov, Field Marshal Alexander 233n2
Svyatopolk-Mirsky, Prince Dmitry, historian and writer 62, 641-3, 1023, 1025, 1067 *History of Russian Literature* 641n1
Swan, Alfred, ethnomusicologist 899n3
Swanson, Gloria 920–2
Syracuse, New York State 274, 301
Szenkar, Eugen, conductor 60, 61, 81, 125, 143, 224, 383
Szigeti, Joseph, violinist 59–60, 75n1, 95, 111, 139, 196, 206–8, 209, 212, 227, 249, 268, 280, 757, 759, 904
Szymanowski, Karol 68, 72n2, 139, 152, 177, 184, 186, 565n1; Honorary Doctorate from Krakow University 978; Violin Concerto No.1 71n2

Tabakov, Mikhail, trumpeter 434, 472
Tailleferre, Germaine, composer 42, 66, 263, 336, 590; 66, borrowings from Rachmaninoff 590; pianist in *Les Noces* 269; WORKS Concertino for piano and orchestra 590; Piano Concerto 168
Taïrov, Alexander, theatre director, founder of Moscow Kamerny Teatr 278–9, 462n1, 537, 844, 876, 1067, 1071
Tallinn, capital of Estonia 86n2, 319, 407

Tansman, Alexander, composer 181, 367–8, 370, 399, 590, 594, 599, 701, 982; WORKS Symphony 589; Concerto for Two Pianos 975; Piano Concerto 321

Tār, Armenian traditional instrument 1061

Tarnovsky, Sergey, pianist and teacher, husband of Yelena Gavrilova 302, 753n1, 754, 818

Tarumov, SSP's impresario for Caucasus tour, 1933

Taylor, Deems, composer 168

Tbilisi 11n6, 354, 504, 714n3; Grand Opera 1062–3; Music Training College 1064; Orient Hotel 1058, 1066; Rustaveli Theatre 1058; SSP's tour to 1056–64; Tiflis Bank Robbery 435

Tchaikovsky, Pyotr Ilyich 39, 126n2, 179–80, 219n2, 307, 320, 423n1, 556n, 619n, 722, 778, 786, 1035n5, 1052; Tchaikovsky International Competition 897n; *Baiser de la fée* (Stravinsky, themes derived from Tchaikovsky) 717, 728, 739, 757, 782; WORKS *Cherevichki* 723, 728, 814, 815, 874; 'The Little Apple-tree Has Come Into Flower' 728n2; *Liturgy of St John Chrystosom* 734; *Pezzo Capriccioso* 540n2; Piano Concerto No.1 265n3; Piano Sonata No.1 52; *The Queen of Spades* 226n1, 588; *Rococo Variations* 540n2; *Service for the Divine Liturgy*; *The Sleeping Beauty* 66n1, 1069; Symphony No.4 717, 818; Symphony No.6 226, 274, 276, 327, 592, 826, 915, 917; Violin Concerto 263n6, 440n1, 782n3; *Voevoda* 456n

Tcherepnin, Alexander Nikolayevich (Sasha), composer 109, 111, 149–50, 190, 303, 333, 424, 571, 596, 700, 731, 754–5, 758, 982; Piano Concerto No.1 757

Tcherepnin, Louisita, wife of Alexander Tcherepnin 149–50, 571, 596, 731, 754–5

Tcherepnin, Maria Benois 15, 109, 153

Tcherepnin, Nikolay Nikolayevich, composer and conductor; conducting class, St Petersburg Conservatoire 11n6, 81n1, 225n2, 263n3, 335n, 349n, 357, 427, 498, 521, 550, 1010n1; President, Paris Russian Conservatoire 136; *The Matchmaker (Svat)* 314; *The Romance of the Mummy* 108; Songs 672; *Vanka The Steward*

Telly, singing teacher 861

Terijoki, Gulf of Finland 245n1, 481n1, 513, 1030n3

Terpis, Max, choreographer 178, 381, 583–4

Testenoires, Paris friends of Samoilenkos 988

'The Aristocratic Peasant-Girl' *see* Dukelsky, Vladimir Alexandrovich, *Mistress into Maid*

The Working Man and the Theatre see Rabochy i teatr

Théâtre de la Chauve-Souris, Paris 46n1, 265n, 373n2

Théâtre des Champs-Elysées, Paris 45, 46n1, 49, 67, 74–5, 117, 152, 1010–11

Theatre Pigalle, Paris 68, 1008

Theatrical Workers Club, Moscow 1954

Thoran, Corneil, conductor 799, 809, 810, 812–14

Three Oranges, journal of the Prokofiev Foundation 154n5, 201n1, 297n1, 363n2

Tiflis *see* Tbilisi

Tiflis bank robbery 207n2, 435, 436n1

Tikhomirov, bridge partner 1000, 1015–16

Tikhomirov, Vasily, choreographer of *The Red Poppy* 467n3

Titian, Intendant of Deutsche Oper, Berlin 382

Tobolsk 6

Tobuk-Cherkass, Maria, soprano 35

Toch, Ernst, composer 701; Piano Concerto No.1 701

Tolstoy, Alexey Konstantinovich, poet and playwright, *Tsar Fyodor Ioannovich* 543–4

Tolstoy, Alexey, novelist 516, 526n3, 1030–1

Tolstoy, Ilya Lvovich 94n2

Tolstoy, Lev Lvovich 246

Tolstoy, Lev, novelist 24n1, 437, 602n, 1053n2; meeting with Rachmaninoff 619n1; 'The Cossacks' 787

Torgsin, hard currency retail outlet in Moscow 1021, 1046

Toscanini, Arturo, conductor 173n2, 262n2, 263–5, 269n1, 755, 776n1, 810n1, 824n5, 901n1, 929, 930n1, 946

Toumanova, Tamara, ballerina, *see also* 'Baby Ballerinas'

Town Hall, New York 899

Trachtenberg, Paris night-club owner 373

Treadwell, Sophie, *Machinal* 1067

Trefusis, Denys 675, 678

Trefusis, Violet 675n2, 678n2

Trenyov, Konstantin, playwright, *Lyubov Yarovaya* 542n2

TREST, Soviet spy organisation 62n3, 133n2, 784n, 944n, 8858n1

Tretyakov, Sergey, screenwriter and photographer 425n2, 1071n3

Triton, contemporary chamber music society in Paris 1–13, 724n2, 997, 1001–2, 1018, 1038–9

Triton, patent bathing maching 614–15, 628–9

Troinitsky, Sergey, Director of Hermitage Museum 484–5

Trotsky, Kamenev, Zinoviev *see* Unified Opposition

Trotsky, Leon 105n2, 202n2, 293n1, 422n, 436n1, 461, 462n2, 466n, 492n2, 547n4, 642n, 690n, 1010n1; lecture in Hall of Columns, Moscow 535–6

Trubetskoy, Prince Nikolay, linguist, philosopher and Eurasianist 62n3: lecture in Hall of Columns, Moscow 535–6; *Europe and Humankind* 132n2; *The Legacy of Tchingiz Khan* 132n2, 188

Trukhanov, Prince, estate agent in Paris 371

Tsarskoe Selo 478n3, 857n2

Tseitlin, Lev, violinist, founder of Persimfans Orchestra 253n2, 413–14, 415, 416, 418–20, 421, 422, 428, 432, 434, 438, 439, 440, 441, 443, 444–5, 457–8, 465, 469–71, 472, 501, 532, 535–6, 549, 565, 569–70, 604, 678, 688–9, 690, 690n1, 693, 867, 887

Tseitlins, Paris 2, 23, 35, 37

Tsekubu 431, 443

Tsukker, Arnold, cultural official, administrator of Persimfans Orchestra 413–15, 416–17, 418, 420, 421–2, 424, 426, 434, 438–40, 441, 443, 449–50, 453, 455, 459, 470, 475, 500–2, 507, 535, 537, 543, 549, 562–3, 564–70, 608, 690, 690n1; approached about Shurik's prison sentence 448–9, 475–6, 507, 535–6, 541; subsequent arrest and imprisonment 413n2; visit to Kameneva inside the Kremlin 461–5
Tsvetaeva, Marina, poet 388, 473n, 631n2, 693, 715, 768
Tsvetov, post-graduate composition student 1054
Tsyganov, Dmitry, leader of Beethoven Quartet 543, 547, 998, 1022n3
Tuchkov Bridge, Leningrad 1069
Tufa *see* Tuff, building material in Armenia
Tuff, building material in Armenia 1059
Tula, *chastushki* from 450
Turgenev, Ivan 950, 996; *Virgin Soil* 608
Turin 282, 283n3, 295, 323, 332, 888–9, 945
Turkeltaub, Head of Ukrainian Association of Playwrights and Composers 554
Turkestan, possible tour to 688–9
Tutelman, representative of Ukrainian State Theatres 212–13, 465–6, 469, 549, 553–4, 558
Tverskaya Street, Moscow 416, 544, 545n2, 879, 886, 1046n2
Tverskaya Yamskaya, district of Moscow 544
Twain, Mark 69n3, 265n2, 379n, 932n3
Tyanyanov, Yury, writer 293, 425n2; *Lt. Kijé* 293n3, 933n3, 1031, 1034, 1068
Tyulin, Yury, composer 494, 516, 518, 559n2, 649, 873–4, 1027, 1031–2, 1034

Ukrainian Association of Playwrights and Composers 554
Ulanova, Galina, ballerina 476n1, 1070n2
von Ungern-Sternbert, Lt.General Baron Roman Fyodorovich 88n1
Unified Opposition 202n2, 293n1, 461n, 466n, 470n, 492n2, 532n2, 690
Union of Composers *see* USSR Union of Composers
United Opposition *see* Unified Opposition
Universal Editions, Vienna, printing of Myaskovsky's Symphony No.7 39
Ursignol see Prokofiev, Sergey *The Steel Step*
USSR ministries, committees, institutions; All-Union Committee on Radio and Arts Affairs 834n; Central Executive (Ispol'nitelnyi) Committee 209; Committee on Arts Affairs 278n2, 462n1; Communist Party Central Committee 207n2, 209n1, 293n1, 414n, 448, 993; Resolution of 1932 'On the Reconstruction of Literary and Artistic Organisations' 690n1, 1022n5; Resolution of February 1948 'On Muradeli's Opera *The Great Friendship*' (Zhdanov Decree) 539, 1045n3; Composers' Union 133n1, 305n3, 423n1, 430n5, 467n3, 477n2, 1018, 1020n4, 1022, 1023, 1029n1, 1035, 1044, 1052, 1054, 1055; Enlightenment Ministry (Narkompros) 29n4, 213n, 231n2, 307, 307n1, 422n, 424, 501, 504, 586, 999n1, 1024n3, 1037; Foreign Affairs Ministry (Narkomindel) 435, 436n1, 439, 462n2, 846, 863n, 976, 1020n2; Home and Foreign Trade Ministry (Narkomat) 207n2, 873n3; Torgsin 1021, 1046; Trade Delegation to Great Britain 542n1; marriage code 438; Society for Cultural Relations with Foreign Countries (VOKS) 461n, 804n1, 1035, 1055
Utkin, Iosif, poet and journalist 424–5
Utrillo, Maurice, artist 317–18
Uvarova, Anna, friend of Rayevsky family 868n1, 876n2, 1036n1
Uvarova, Katya, friend of Rayevsky family 429 868n1

Vaisberg, Yulia *see* Weisberg, Yulia
Vakhtangov Studio 514, 515n1, 565n3, 1071n4
Vakula the Smith see Tchaikovsky, Pyotr Ilyich, *Cherevichki*
Valéry, Paul, poet, philosopher, public intellectual 1006–8, 1015–16
Valmalète, Marcel de, Paris music agent 300, 838, 840, 845, 848–9, 853, 889, 892, 941, 950
van Hoogstraten, Willem, conductor 253
Mrs Vanderbilt, New York hostess and arts patron 898
Varzar, Nina, astrophysicist, wife of Dmitry Shostakovich 1046
Vasilenko, Sergey, composer, conductor and teacher 1055–6
Vasnetsov, Viktor, artist 375
Vatican 284–7
Vechernyaya Krasnaya Gazeta 458, 1047
Verin, Boris *see* Bashkirov, Boris Nikolayevich
Vernadsky, G.V., historian 647n1; *Russian History* 647
Versailles 211, 231, 333, 386, 388–9, 585, 599, 715, 837; walk with Fatma Hanum 659, 661, 662
Versigny Driving School, Paris 392
verst, measurement of length 193, 576, 614
Vesuvius, Mount 294
Victoria Palace Hotel, Paris 197, 221, 297, 302, 309, 384, 572, 948, 952
Vienna Opera 61–3
Villa Christophorus, Ettal 1, 3n6, 101n1
Villa d'Avray, Sèvres 573
Villa-Lobos, Heitor, composer 41, 774–5, 778–9
Vilnius, Lithuania 86, 124n4, 407n2, 776n4
Vinogradova, composer from Tallinn 319, 972–3
vint, card game 650
Vitacek, Jindrich, luthier, curator of State Instrument Collection 884n2, 1052n3
Vitachek, Favii, post-graduate composition student 1052
Vitol, Jazeps, composer and teacher 341, 410, 444n2

Vladikavkaz, Ossetia 1057, 1065
Volkonsky, Prince Pyotr Grigorievich, Rachmaninoff's son-in-law 211, 304n1
Volkonsky, Prince Sergey, former Director of Imperial Theatres, Director of Russian National Conservatoire in Paris 304, 753n1, 776, 1000
Volkov, A, former Russian Consul in Chicago 937–8
Volkovysskaya, Adriana, sculptress 27, 33, 43, 596, 666
Voloshin, Maximilian, poet, critic, translator, memoirist 322, 338
Vorobyov, official in the Ukrainian Minstry of Education 456, 549, 554
Vorovsky, Vatslav, Soviet diplomat 769n1
Vozrozhdenie émigré newspaper in Paris 593, 791
Vyshnegradsky, Alexander, banker and amateur composer 83, 99, 101, 103, 121, 126n1, 486
Vyshnegradsky, Ivan, composer 121, 335, 430

Wagner, Richard; WORKS *The Flying Dutchman* 929, 939; *Die Meistersinger* 921n1, Overture 943, Beckmesser 955, 995; *Siegfried* 128; *Tristan und Isolde* 380–1, 565n1
Wagons-Lit *see* Compagnie Internationale Wagons-Lit
Wake, Mrs, Christian Scientist 65, 69
Walska, Ganna, socialite, former partner of Harold McCormick 10n4, 178, 249, 937n1
Walter, Bruno, conductor 59n2, 382, 389, 606, 647, 711, 972, 977, 1039
War Communism
Warsaw 40, 43, 123, 127–31, 139, 300, 453, 571, 680n2, 766n, 865, 888, 951, 952–3, 976–9, 981, 1018, 1037, 1043; Warsaw Opera 921n1
Watteau, Antoine, artist 318, *Le parc aux biches* 57n2
'We Fell as Victims', Revolutionary anthem 517
Weber, Carl Maria von, composer 830; *Konzertstück* 980
Weber, Fyodor, Director of Russian Musical Editions, Berlin 123, 187, 225, 264, 364, 373, 376, 379, 380, 382, 396, 406, 571, 583–4, 717, 830, 865, 888, 972, 979, 1043
Webern, Anton, composer 3n7, 173n2
Weill, Kurt, composer 72n1, 173n2, 175, 844n1, 973n1
Weisberg, Yulia, composer 495, 497, 527, 640, 640n2, 785, 1029
Weisbord, Mischa, violinist 272, 274
Weiss, Adolf *see* Weissmann, Adolf
Weissenberg, Alexis 265n3
Weissmann, Adolf, musicologist and critic 147, 301, 383
Wellesley College, Boston 910
Wells, H. G. 91, 436n1, 1010n2 *The Outline of History* 91n1
White mushrooms 586
Mrs Wiborg, New York hostess and arts patron 898, 903

Widor, Charles-Marie, organist and composer 41n2, 655n1
Wiéner, Jean, pianist 48, 66, 308
Wihtol, Iosif *see* Vitol, Jazeps
Winter Palace, Leningrad 479, 480n1, 485, 487
Wittgenstein, Paul, pianist 958, 958n2, 964, 965, 967–8, 989, 997n1
Wolf-Israel, principal cellist of the Mariinsky Theatre 489, 490, 873
Wolff, Albert, conductor 10, 11, 54, 64, 65, 70, 72, 101–2, 219, 692–3, 736, 873, 1038
Wolff, Baron, estate agent in Paris 370–1, 378
Wolff, Louise, music agent in Berlin 132
Wolpe, Countess of 587
World of Art see Mir Isskustva
Wrangel, Baron Pyotr, White Army military leader 24n2, 858n1, 944n1
Wührer, Friedrich, pianist 566

'Yablochko', folk song 217
Yagoda, Genrikh, Secret Police chief 537, 868n4
Yakhontova, Tatyana, sister of Boris and Vladimir Bashkirov 953, 955, 958–9
Yakovlev, Alexander (Sasha-Yasha), artist 303–4, 303n1, 303n2, 327, 336, 743, 820–1, 998n2, 1008n1, 1014
Yakovlev, V. V., musicologist, husband of Vera Myaskovskaya 445, 707n1
Yakovleva, Tatyana, lover of Mayakovsky 743–4, 979
Yakulov, Gyorgy, artist and designer 202–4, 205–6, 208, 210, 212, 213–15, 218, 220–1, 278, 327, 389, 437, 474, 504, 513, 573, 579, 586, 588, 593, 594, 605n1, 680–1, 880
Yampolsky, Abram, violinist and teacher 440
Yatsevich, Yury, post-graduate composition student 1054
Yavorsky, Boleslav, musicologist and theorist 305, 306–87, 310, 328, 341, 354, 369, 392, 426, 441, 444, 450–2, 459, 470, 501, 503, 538, 539n1, 539n4, 553n3, 554n1, 557, 558, 565, 876, 884–5; *The Elements of the Structure of Musical Speech* 305n3
Yekaterinburg 6, 414n, 492n2
Yeliseyev Shop, Moscow 545
Yerevan, Armenia 1059–62; Mount Ararat 1060; Opera 560n1; Philharmonia 1059; Lake Sevan 1060–1
Yershov, Ivan, tenor 481, 490, 522n1
Yesenin, Sergey, poet 320, 510n1, 545, 556, 635n1
Yesipova, Anna, pianist and teacher, SSP's teacher at St Petersburg Conservatoire 302, 306, 341n2, 347, 408, 519n2, 754n1, 940n1
Yevrasiistvo see Eurasianist Movement
Yevreinov, Mgr, friend of Samoilenkos 667
Yevropeiskaya Hotel *see* Europa Hotel, Leningrad
Ysaÿe, Eugène, violinist and composer 8n1, 12n2, 782n3, 1038n
Yudina, Maria, pianist 62n2, 519, 565n1, 704n1, 766n1

Yurevskaya, Zinaïda, soprano 47–8, 52, 123–4, 233–4
Yuriev, Yury, actor 482
Yurovsky, Alexander, Head of the State Music Publishing House 447, 505–8, 529, 878, 880

Zack, Léon, theatre designer 152
Zagorsky, Alexander, lawyer in Paris 83, 99, 101, 103, 105, 114
Zaitsev, Kirill, former suitor of Nina Meshcherskaya 777, 892, 999
Zak, B. A., pianist, teacher, Secretary of Russian Conservatoire in Paris 139, 141
Zak, Lev *see* Zack, Léon
Zakharov, Boris, pianist, husband of Cecilia Hansen 44–5, 46, 153, 155, 166, 173, 192, 218, 244, 258, 262, 263, 299, 301, 303, 316, 331, 357, 666, 675–6, 712; ambivalent attitude to SSP's pianism 258; bridge with 702, 703; career as pianist, disappointment in 661; overshadowed by wife's career 171n2; character and physique in decline 603, 632; Conservatoire days recalled in re-reading Diaries 658; estrangement over Max Schmidthof 713, 732; flight from Soviet Petrograd across Gulf of Finland 614; gambling, addiction to 604, 606, 607, 613, 616; Glazunov anecdotes 46–7, 614; holiday at Royan spent with 601–7, 609, 613–16; Borovskys consider renting holiday house 616–17; Kuznetsova, reintroduces SSP to 306–7; Maria Pavlova, affair with 74n2, 151; marriage, disintegration of 660–1, 768, 793, 802, 979; Medtner's mannerisms imitated 655; Rachmaninoff, invited by 654; Shanghai, teaching post in 768, 793, 979; sight-reading, superlative skill in 702; Dukelsky, four-hand piano with 702; SSP Piano Concerto No.2 second piano 220; urges SSP to hear compositions of Vinogradova 319, 972; SSP's *Musical Letter* to 632n1; Terijoki holidays in family dacha 245n1, 481n1
Zakharov, Vasily, brother of Boris 245
Zakharova, Tanya, daughter of Boris Zakharov and Cecilia Hansen 682, 787

Zamoskvorechie, residential quarter of Old Moscow 450, 884
Zamyatin, Yevgeny, science fiction writer and satirist 293n4, 447n2, 510n, adaptation of Leskov's *The Flea* 449, 449n1, 527n1
Zederbaum, Vladimir, personal assistant to Serge Koussevitzky 9, 36–7, 43, 51, 113–14, 121
Zeiss camera 888
Zelenogorsk *see* Terijoki, Gulf of Finland
Zelyony Mys, botanical gardens in Batum 1063–4
Zemlyanoy Val, SSP's residence in Moscow 1072
Zenith, carburettor manufacturers 700
Zéro 590
Zet *see* Sablino
Zhdanov, Andrey, Soviet politician, Central Committee Decree on Muradeli's *The Great Friendship*, 437n1, 553n3
Zherebtsova-Andreyeva, Anna Grigorievna, mezzo-soprano 175, 191, 366n1, 410
Zhilyayev, Nikolay, composer, pianist, teacher and critic 419n1, 430n1, 879, 880
Zhitomirsky, Alexander, composer 785
Zhitomirsky, Daniil, critic and musicologist 879n
Zhizn isskustva, cultural journal 297n2, 490n2, 546n4
Ziegler, Head of Metropolitan Opera finance department 929
Ziloti, Alexander, pianist, teacher and concert organiser 126, 127n, 129n1, 149, 168, 191n1, 248–9, 276, 489, 516, 916
Zimin Private Opera Company 54n1, 418n1, 426n2, 1029n3
Zimnyaya Kanavka, Leningrad 480
Zinoviev Letter 542n1
Znamenny Chant 27n, 782
Znosko-Borovsky, Yevgeny, chess player and writer on chess 663–4
Zurich 108, 697, 699
Zvyagintseva, Yelena (Lyolya), step-daughter of Vladimir Derzhanovsky 415, 424, 431, 432, 567, 568, 866, 867, 879, 881, 883–4, 887, 1036

1&2 Portraits of Prokofiev and Lina by Anna Ostroumova-Lebedeva, Paris 1927
3 Baby Svyatoslav with proud parents and grandmother Maria Grigorievna Prokofieva, Paris 1924
4 Lina's mother, Olga Nemysskaya Codina, with her young daughter
5 Lina's father, Juan Codina, with his two grandsons

6 *from left*: Lina, Svyatoslav, unidentified, Sergey Koussevitzky, Natalya Koussevitzky, Prokofiev (with dog)
7 Svyatoslav in his 'tasi'
8 Visitors to Culoz, August 1929: *from left* Lina, Fyodor Stravinsky, Prokofiev, Igor Stravinsky, Svyatoslav
9 Château de la Fléchère at Culoz
10 On the beach at St Gilles, July 1924

11 The Beloved Ballot motor car: *from left* Sofronitsky (standing), Prokofiev, Dukelsky at the wheel, Lina
12 *from left*: Koussevitzky, Paichadze (partly hidden), Stravinsky, Prokofiev
13 Lina, Boris Asafyev and Pavel Lamm in the Swiss Alps, September 1928
14 The Walking Tour: Koussevitzky, Paichadze, Prokofiev, with the coffee boy bringing up the rear
15 Vladimir Dukelsky, a.k.a. Vernon Duke

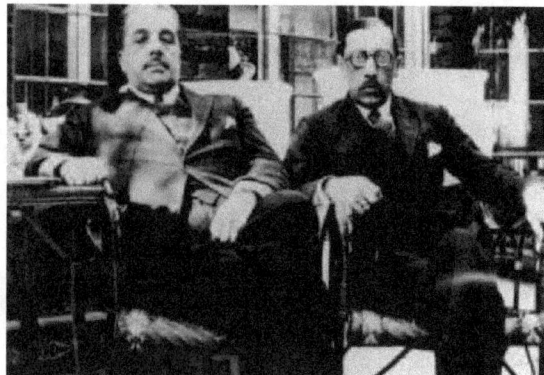

16 Group portrait of Les Six with Cocteau at the piano
17 Ida Rubinstein as Salome, portrait by Valentin Serov
18 Georges Rouault
19 Diaghilev and Stravinsky

20 Lyubov Tchernicheva and Serge Lifar wield their hammers in *Le pas d'acier*
21 Gyorgy Yakulov painted by Pyotr Konchalovsky
22 Rouault's backcloth for *The Prodigal Son*
23 Lina arm-in-arm with Lifar in Monte Carlo: 'M. et Mme. Lifar' exclaimed Diaghilev
24 *from left*: Prokofiev, Stravinsky, Ansermet, Suvchinsky

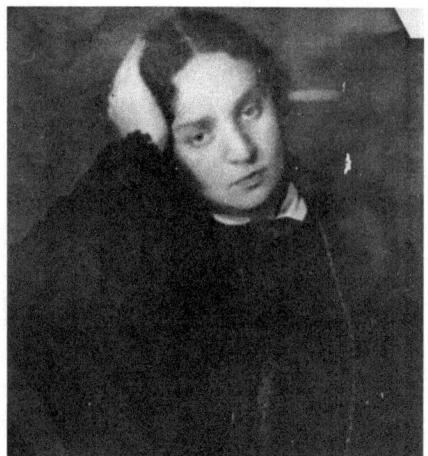

25 Maria Yudina in Tbilisi, 1931
26 Alexander Borovsky
27 The composer plays the score to the *Lieutenant Kijé* production team at the Belgoskino studios in Leningrad
28 Nikolay Golovanov, Antonina Nezhdanova and Prokofiev in Moscow, 1927
29 Yekaterina Peshkova

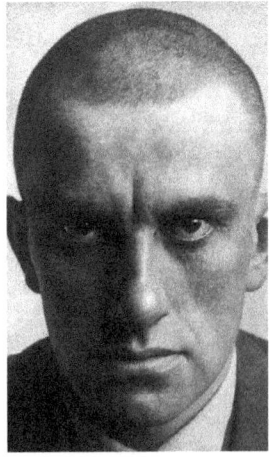

30 People's Commissar of Enlightenment Lunacharsky with his wife, silent film star Natalya Rozenel
31 Vladimir Mayakovsky
32 Olga Kameneva in her apartment in the Kremlin
33 Vsevolod Meyerhold, Prokofiev and Sergey Radlov
34 Conductor Vladimir Dranishnikov, composer, and producer Sergey Radlov surrounded by the cast of the Mariinsky Theatre ('Akopera') production of *The Love for Three Oranges* in 1927

35 Studio portrait of Prokofiev by Wasserman of Paris, 1933
36 Lina holding the year-old Svyatoslav, Paris 1925
37 Boris Asafyev with Prokofiev; behind them Myaskovsky
38 Final departure from Paris for Moscow, May 1933, snapshot by Prokofiev
39 Sergey and Lina Prokofiev in Moscow, 1933